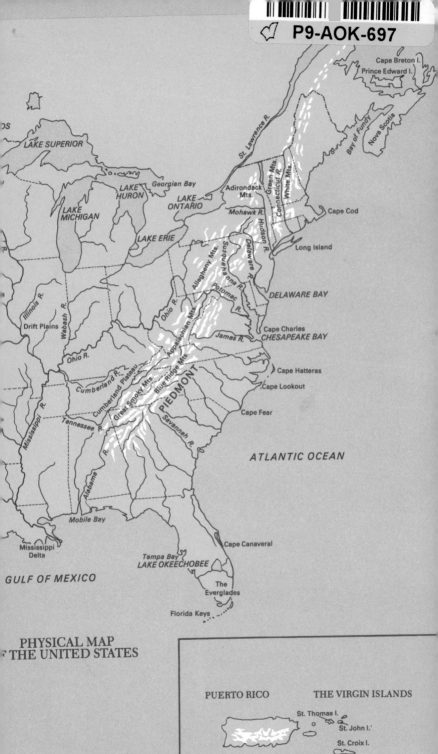

P9-AOK-697

PHYSICAL MAP OF THE UNITED STATES

AMERICA

AMERICA

A NARRATIVE HISTORY

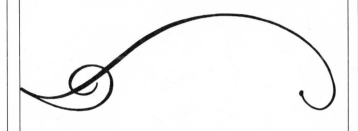

GEORGE BROWN TINDALL

W · W · NORTON & COMPANY · NEW YORK · LONDON

For Bruce and Susan
and For Blair

Time present and time past
Are both perhaps present in time future,
And time future contained in time past.

From T. S. Eliot, *Four Quartets*

*The text of this book is composed in Caledonia, with display
type set in Torino Roman. Composition by New England Ty-
pographic Service, Inc. Manufacturing by R. R. Donnelley.
Book design by Antonina Krass.*

First Edition

Library of Congress Cataloging in Publication Data

Tindall, George Brown.
America: a narrative history.

Includes bibliographies and index.
1. United States—History.   I. Title.
E178.1.T55   1984   973   83-22165
ISBN 0-393-95435-8

W. W. Norton & Company, Inc., 500 Fifth Avenue, New York, N. Y. 10110

W. W. Norton & Company Ltd., 37 Great Russell Street, London WC1B 3NU

1   2   3   4   5   6   7   8   9   0

CONTENTS

MAPS

PREFACE

This book is characterized in its subtitle as "A Narrative History." Since professional historians are currently debating the meaning of this term, I'd like to clarify, at least for students and other nonprofessionals, what the term "narrative" suggests about the approach I've taken here.

In *America: A Narrative History* I have tried to fashion the sprawling American past into a story, one brimming with vivid characters and great events. It is a story of promise and achievement, as well as the irony and tragedy of only partially fulfilled ideals. It is a story the events of which are connected in patterns of influence and consequence, not recounted in isolation from one another. By showing connections among past events, I've tried to bring out for readers their significance, their meaning.

With the narrative approach I've taken I've attempted also to put the reader in contact with the personalities and occurrences of the past. Wherever possible, the characters in this story speak with their own voice, the better to convey the flavor of American history.

Does the story I tell have a simple moral? Sir Isaiah Berlin, a distinguished Oxford don, once took as the theme for an essay on Leo Tolstoy's theory of history a fragment from the Greek poet Archilochus which said: "The fox knows many things, but the hedgehog knows one big thing." I prefer to see myself as one who runs with foxes rather than rolls up with hedgehogs. Yet if there were one single idea I should hope to implant with this text, it would be that the lessons of history are not simple lessons, that history is a complex and elusive subject, and that one should be on guard immediately against theories of single causation or pronouncements that begin "History proves. . . ."

The book in hand is designed to serve as an introduction to

American history. However much one might hope to provide a comprehensive account of all the major themes, one cannot pretend in such a limited scope to exhaust the subject. I do hope, however, that this survey will become a gateway through which readers will be drawn to explore more deeply the vast and compelling story of American history.

George B. Tindall
Chapel Hill, North Carolina

ACKNOWLEDGMENTS

A *New Yorker* cartoon of recent vintage has a publisher telling an aspiring author: "Well, it's good, but people just don't write books all by themselves any more." In truth, people don't. The single name on the title page of this book neglects the credit owed to many others. Joseph J. Ellis of Mount Holyoke College, the book's advisory editor, read successive drafts almost from the first, and supplied a judicious mixture of the criticism an author needs and the reassurance he craves. What is more, as deadlines loomed, he sped the author to completion with timely and well-formulated suggestions on the final chapters. Gary R. Freeze, graduate assistant and factotum at the University of North Carolina at Chapel Hill, helped compile the end-of-chapter bibliographies.

The influences which have contributed to this book—teachers, students, books, journals, documents I have encountered over the years, colleagues more than generous in their responses to inquiries—are more than I could acknowledge in a reasonable space, even if I had the gift of total recall. Historians who have read and commented on parts of the typescript in their areas of expertise include Herman J. Belz, Stephen Botein, Don E. Fehrenbacher, Michael F. Holt, Richard B. Latner, Richard L. McCormick, Drew R. McCoy, Michael R. McVaugh, Robert M. Miller, Charles W. Royster, Ronald E. Shaw, Michael B. Stoff, Carl Vipperman, and Peter F. Walker.

David B. Parker and Linda W. Sellars, graduate assistants and copyreaders par excellence, saved me from many grotesque constructions, and Parker further checked points of factual accuracy. Jane Lindley, administrative manager of the Department of History in Chapel Hill, routinely passes miracles at expediting administrative details. Over a period of years a number of people who served in the department's secretarial pool have typed parts of various drafts: Jamie Lewis, Pat Maynor, Rosalie I. Radcliffe, and Mary Woodall. Most of the final draft was typed by Mandy Hollowell and Ceci Long, and by Peter Hardy with the help of the Kenan Research Fund when the department was temporarily understaffed.

In the Louis Round Wilson Library at Chapel Hill, Louise McG. Hall, Mary R. Ishaq, Donna P. Cornick, Ridley Kessler, Jr., and their associates have shown the characteristic tenacity of reference librarians in tracking down elusive references.

The Department of History at Chapel Hill and the National Endowment for the Humanities aided a year's stay at the Center for Advanced Study, Stanford, California, by courtesy of Gardner Lindzey and his associates, which helped me immensely in gathering my thoughts for this book as well as other projects. Especially generous to me there were Deanna Dejan at the word processor; Margaret Amara, librarian; and Bruce Harley, on many missions in the book run to the Stanford University library.

At W. W. Norton & Company, James L. Mairs, vice-president, senior editor, and director of production, acted as impresario straordinario from the inception of the project—organizing, supervising, and coordinating, all the while patiently keeping the author's nose to the grindstone and his morale in repair. A year's leave sponsored by the company helped achieve both ends. Steve Forman performed a variety of editorial tasks with unfailing serenity. Fred Bidgood, the copy editor, proved patient and thorough in preparing the manuscript for publication. George P. Brockway, chairman, and Edwin Barber, director of the College Department, both read and marked up the typescript to the author's advantage. Nora Seton and Amy Boesky looked after essential details at crucial times. Antonina Krass designed an elegant book, and Sydney W. Cohen compiled a useful index.

My son Bruce M. Tindall helped with copyreading at this end. To him and his wife, Susan A. McGrath, to my daughter Blair A. M. Tindall, and to my wife Blossom M. Tindall, my love and gratitude, as always.

AMERICA

1

THE COLLISION OF CULTURES

The earliest Americans are lost in the mists of time, where legends abound. Like people everywhere the Indians told myths of creation, which varied from tribe to tribe: some spoke of a habitation in the sky from which humans and animals had come; still others spoke of miraculous events, such as the union of the Sky Father and Earth Mother. In the Southwest the Pueblo people had a place of worship called the kiva, a stone pit in which a deeper opening symbolized Sipapu, a place of mystery in the north where people entered the world from underground.

Some romancers have had it that the American Indians came from the mythical lost continents of Atlantis (an ancient legend) or Mu (a modern fantasy), others that they drifted across from Asia, Africa, or Europe. Their pedigree has been linked variously, but without firm proof, to the Japanese, Chinese, Hindus, Egyptians, Phoenicians, Moluccans, Polynesians, Scandinavians, black Africans, the ten "lost" tribes of Israel, or to the Welsh who followed a fabled prince Madoc in the twelfth century.

Chance contacts across the waters may have occurred. Ecuadorian pottery, dating from about 3000–2000 B.C., bears a striking resemblance to Japanese pottery of the time. The sweet potato, otherwise a peculiarly American plant, grew in Polynesia before modern times. Still, granting the odds that some cultural traits crossed the oceans, the likelihood—now almost a certainty —is that there was a real place in the north where Indian peoples entered the New World, not from underground but from Siberia to Alaska, either by island-hopping across the Bering Strait or over a broad land bridge (Beringia) from which the waters receded during the Ice Ages.

Beringia must have been the route by which the horse and camel, which apparently evolved first in America, crossed to the

Old World before they became extinct in the New, and by which the deer and the elephant (the extinct American mammoth) went the other way. There is no evidence to place the origin of *Homo sapiens* in the New World, nor in the Old World much earlier than 50,000 years ago, although the latter is more controversial. Given the advance and retreat of the ice sheets over North America, a crossing might have been possible 50,000–40,000 years ago, but the most likely time for the latest crossings would have been just after the last heavy ice coverage, 18,000–16,000 years ago, when people could still walk across and then filter southward toward warmth through passes in the melting ice.

Once the ice sheets melted and the sea rose again, these pre-Mongoloid migrants were cut off from the rest of humanity (except for the short-lived Viking settlements on Greenland and Newfoundland) until Columbus came in 1492. For those long eons about the only written records are the relatively late pictographs of Middle America, remnants of a much larger body of writing which the Spanish conquerors destroyed in order to wipe out the memory of heathen beliefs and practices. Most of these writings, mainly Aztec and Mayan, remain undeciphered. The story therefore remains in the realm of prehistory, the domain of archeologists and anthropologists who must salvage a record from the rubble of the past: stone tools and weapons, bones, pottery, figurines, ancient dwellings, burial places, scraps of textiles and basketry, and finally bits of oral tradition and the reports of

Out of the mists of time, a carved jade head of the Olmec culture, found in Chiapas, Mexico. [Museum of the American Indian, Heye Foundation].

THE FIRST MIGRATION

◄——— Principal migration routes

early explorers, all pieced together with the adhesive of informed guesswork.

Pre-Columbian Indian Civilizations

Archeological digs add yearly to the fragments of knowledge about pre-Columbian America. The richest finds have been made on either side of the Isthmus of Panama, where Indian civilization peaked in the high altitudes of Mexico and Peru. Indeed it has been possible to reconstruct a remarkable sequence of events in pre-Columbian Middle America, a story of successive peoples who built great empires and a monumental architecture, supported by large-scale agriculture and a far-flung commerce: the Olmecs, Mayas, Toltecs, Aztecs, Incas, and others.

EARLY CULTURAL STAGES On either side of these peaks of civilization, Indian life at the time of the Discovery dwindled into more primitive forms. By the best recent estimates about 100–112 million people lived in the Western Hemisphere, about 10–12 million (or 10 percent) in what is now the United States. Their cultures ranged from those of stone-age nomads to the life of settled communities which practiced agriculture. Many had passed the earlier cultural stages defined by archeologists as Lithic (Stone Age) and Archaic (hunting and gathering), and had reached the Formative stage of settled agriculture, although none of them ever achieved the heights of the cultures to the south.

The Lithic stage lasted to about 5000 B.C. Remnants of stone choppers and scrapers, similar to artifacts found in Siberia, suggest the presence of people long before the development, by about 9500 B.C., of projectile points for use on spears, and later, on arrows. With the invention of projectiles early man entered the age of the big-game hunters, who ranged across most of the Americas, chasing down mammoths, bison, deer, and antelopes.

As hunting and gathering became a way of life diet became more varied. It included a number of small creatures such as racoons and opossums, along with fish and shellfish (Archaic hooks, nets, and weirs have been found) and wild plants: nuts, greens, berries, and fruits in season. The Archaic Indians began to settle down in permanent or semipermanent villages; they invented fiber snares, basketry, and mills for grinding nuts; they domesticated the dog and the turkey or as some would have it, the dog, who knew a soft touch when he saw one, domesticated its master. In southern California, then as now relatively well-populated, tribes were able to specialize in sea animals, shellfish, and acorns. In some places in fact the Archaic stage persisted into very recent times—specifically until August 27, 1911, when a primitive man named Ishi, "the last wild Indian," left the woods and stumbled into a white settlement seventy miles north of Sacramento, California.

The Formative stage replaced the Archaic, by definition, with the introduction of farming and pottery. In these developments Middle Americans got the jump on the tribes farther north and became the center of innovation and cultural diffusion. By about 5000 B.C. Indians of the Mexican highlands were cultivating or gathering plant foods that became the staples of the New World: chiefly maize (Indian corn), beans, and squash, but also such plants as chili peppers, avocadoes, pumpkins, and many more. These were developed into the forms now familiar by crossbreeding, accidental in part, but believed to have been also the product of experiments by Indian horticulturists. Maize, for instance, began as an ancient Mexican grass which cross-bred with another grass to produce teosinte. Countless crosses of maize with teosinte over the centuries produced the types of Indian corn which the Europeans found later.

THE MAYAS, AZTECS, AND INCAS   By about 2000–1500 B.C. permanent towns dependent on farming had appeared in Mexico, and
so had pottery, which possibly diffused northward from Ecuador.
The more settled life in turn provided leisure for more complex
cultures, for the cultivation of religion, crafts, art, science, administration—and warfare. A stratified social structure began to
emerge. From about A.D. 300–900 Middle America reached the
flowering of its Classic cultures, with great centers of religion,
gigantic pyramids, temple complexes, and courts for ceremonial
games, all supported by the surrounding peasant villages. Life
centered in the cities of Teotihuacán and Monte Alban and the
Mayan culture of present-day Yucatán and Guatemala. The
Mayas had developed enough mathematics (including a symbol
for zero) and astronomy to devise a calendar more accurate than
that the Europeans were still using at the time of Columbus.
Then, about A.D. 900, for reasons unknown the Classic cultures

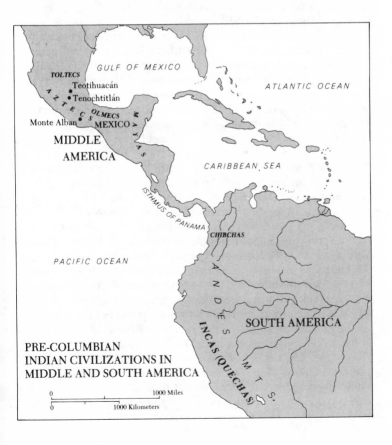

collapsed and the religious centers were abandoned. The Toltecs, a warlike people, conquered most of the region, but around A.D. 1200 they too withdrew, for reasons unknown.

During the time of troubles that followed, the Aztecs arrived from somewhere to the northwest, founded the city of Tenochtitlán (now Mexico City), traditionally in 1325, and gradually expanded their control over central Mexico. When the Spaniards arrived in 1519, the Aztec Empire under Montezuma II ruled over perhaps 5 million people—estimates range as high as 20 million. They were held in fairly loose subjugation for the sake of trade and tribute, and for the sake of captives to sacrifice on the altars of their bloodthirsty sun god, Huitzilopochtli (symbolized by the hummingbird), to feed and strengthen him for his daily journey across the sky. Because their culture was heir to the technology, arts, and religions of previous peoples in Middle America, the Aztecs are sometimes compared to the ancient Romans, in contrast to the more creative Mayas, who were the Greeks of the New World.

Farther south, in what is now Colombia, the Chibchas built a similar empire on a smaller scale; still farther south the Quechua peoples (better known by the name of their ruler, the Inca) by the fifteenth century controlled an empire that stretched a thousand miles along the Andes Mountains from Ecuador to Chile, connected by an elaborate system of roads and organized under an autocratic government which dominated life about as fully as any totalitarian state of the twentieth century.

INDIAN CULTURES OF NORTH AMERICA   The peoples of the present-day United States reached the Formative stage only in the last thousand years before Christ. There were three identifiable cultural peaks: the Adena-Hopewell culture of the Northeast (800 B.C.–A.D. 600), the Mississippian of the Southeast (A.D. 600–1500); and the Pueblo-Hohokam culture of the Southwest (400 B.C.–present). None of these ever reached the heights of the Classic stage in Middle America, although they showed strong influences from there, and they retreated for the most part back into an Archaic-Formative stage in which the English settlers found the first tribes with which they came in contact.

The halting transition from Archaic to Formative in the eastern woodland cultures is marked in the remains by such innovations as pottery, agriculture, earthen burial mounds, and tobacco and the smoking pipe. The Adena culture, centered in the Ohio Valley, was older but overlapped the similar Hopewell in the same area. The Adena-Hopewell peoples left behind enormous, and to the early settlers mysterious, earthworks and burial mounds—sometimes elaborately shaped like great snakes, birds, or animals. Evidence found in the mounds suggests a developed social structure and a specialized division of labor. There were signs too of an elaborate trade network which spanned the continent. The Hopewellians made ceremonial blades from Rocky Mountain obsidian, bowls from sea shells of the Gulf and Atlantic, ornamental silhouettes of hands, claws, and animals from Appalachian mica, breast plates, gorgets, and ornaments from copper found near Lake Superior. The Northeastern Indians at the time of colonization were distant heirs to the Hopewellian culture after its decline: the Algonquian tribes of the coastal areas and more directly, perhaps even by direct descent, the tribes making up the Iroquois League of Five Nations, a federation formed after 1600 as a result of their first contact with the French.

The Mississippian culture of the Southeast, which centered in the central Mississippi Valley, probably derived its impulse from the Hopewellians, but reached its height later and under greater influence from Middle America—in its intensive agriculture, its pottery, its temple mounds (vaguely resembling pyramids), and its death cults, which involved human torture and sacrifice. The Mississippian culture peaked in the fourteenth and fifteenth centuries, after the European discovery, and possibly collapsed fi-

A wooden carving of a mother carrying a child, found in a Hopewell burial mound in southern Ohio. [Milwaukee Public Museum]

nally as the result of diseases transmitted from European contacts.

All the peoples of the Southeast, and far into the Midwest, were touched by the Mississippian culture, and as late as the eighteenth century tribes of the Southeast still practiced their annual busk, or green corn ceremony, a ritual of renewal in which pottery was smashed, dwellings cleaned out, all fires were quenched, and a new fire kindled in the temple. The Mississippian traditions lingered among the Muskogean peoples of the Gulf area—the Choctaws, Creeks, and Chickasaws—but they also touched the Cherokees (originally Iroquoian) and the Algonquian and eastern Sioux tribes nearer the South Atlantic seaboard.

The greatest capacity for survival in their homeland was displayed by the irrigation-based cultures of the arid Southwest, elements of which persist today and heirs of which (the Hopis, Zuñis, and others) still live in the adobe pueblos of their ancestors. The Formative cultures of the Southwest, the closely related Mogollon, Hohokam, and Anasazi ("the ancient ones," in Navaho language), derived from a desert Archaic culture called Cochise and from contacts with Middle America, perhaps even from pre-Conquest Mexican outposts. The most widespread and best known of the cultures, the Anasazi, centered around the

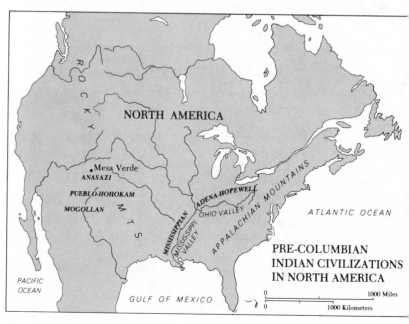

PRE-COLUMBIAN
INDIAN CIVILIZATIONS
IN NORTH AMERICA

Ruins of Anasazi cliff dwellings at Mesa Verde, in Colorado. The circular chamber to the left is a ceremonial kiva. [Denver Convention & Visitors Bureau]

"four corners" where the states of Arizona, New Mexico, Colorado, and Utah now meet.

Like other peoples of the Formative stage, they never gave up the Archaic patterns of hunting and gathering, eating small animals, rodents, reptiles, birds, and insects, along with seeds, mesquite beans, pinon nuts, yucca fruits, and berries. With the coming of agriculture they perfected techniques of "dry farming," using the traces of ground water and catching the runoff in garden terraces, or in the case of the Hohokam, extensive irrigation works. Housing evolved from the Mogollon pit houses, which suggested the later kivas where religious observances were held, and developed into the baked-mud adobe structures which grew four and five stories high and were sometimes located, as at Mesa Verde, Colorado, in canyons underneath protective cliffs.

In contrast to the Middle American and Mississippian cultures, Anasazi society lacked a rigid class structure. The religious leaders and warriors labored much as the rest of the people. In fact warfare was little pursued except in self-defense (Hopi means "the peaceful people") and there was little evidence of human sacrifice or human trophies. There is evidence, however, that a lengthy drought (1276–1299) and the pressure of new arrivals from the north about 1300 began to restrict Anasazi territory. Into their peaceful world came the aggressive Navahos and Apaches, followed two centuries later by Spaniards marching up from the South.

When the whites came, even the most developed Indian societies were ill-equipped to resist these dynamic European cultures invading their world. There were large and fatal gaps in their knowledge and technology. Mogollon Indians had invented etching, but the wheel was found in the New World only on a few toys. The Indians of Mexico had copper and bronze but no iron except a few specimens of meteorites. Messages were conveyed by patterns in beads in the Northeast and by knotted cords among the Incas, but there was no alphabet or any true writing save the hieroglyphs of Middle America. The aborigines had domesticated dogs, turkeys, and llamas, but horses were unknown until the Spaniards came astride their enormous "dogs."

Disunity everywhere—civil disorders and rebellions plagued even the Aztecs and Incas—left the peoples of the New World open to division and conquest. North of Mexico, the nearest approach to organized government on a wide scale was the Iroquois League of the Five Nations, with weaker parallels like the Creek Confederacy of the Gulf Plains and the late–sixteenth-century Powhatan Confederacy of Virginia. But as it turned out the centralized societies to the south were as vulnerable as the scattered tribes farther north. The capture or death of their rulers (one usually followed the other) left them in disarray and subjection. The scattered tribes of North America made the whites pay more dearly for their conquest, but when open conflict erupted the bow and arrow were seldom a match for guns anywhere.

EUROPEAN VISIONS OF AMERICA

Long before Columbus, America lived in the fantasies of Europeans. Seneca, the Roman philosopher, wrote in his *Medea:* "An age will come after many years when the Ocean will loose the chain of things, and a huge land lie revealed; when Tiphys will disclose new worlds and Thule no more be the ultimate." Before Seneca the vast unknown beyond Gibraltar had entered the mythology of ancient Greece. In the west, toward the sunset which marked the end of day and symbolically the end of life, was an earthly paradise, a land of plenty and felicity. There

Homer put his Elysian Fields, the blessed abode of the dead, and Hesiod, a poet of the eighth century B.C. (a contemporary of the Olmecs and the North American mound builders), located the distant Hesperides which Father Zeus provided for a "godlike race of hero-men" who lived untouched by toil or sorrow. Whether called the Isles of the Blest, Avalon, or some other name (perhaps, some thought, it was the Garden of Eden), this happy land survived in myth throughout the Middle Ages, coloring the perceptions of explorers. When Sir Thomas More envisaged an ideal society in his book *Utopia* (1516), he placed it on an island in the New World.

Peter Martyr, the earliest European historian of the New World, said in the late fifteenth century that the Indians "seem to live in that golden world of which old writers speak so much: wherein men lived simply and innocently without enforcement of laws, without quarrelings, judges and libels, content only to satisfy nature, without further vexation for knowledge of things to come." This "Noble Savage" (as John Dryden later called him) would haunt the imagination for centuries—his reputation still clings to the popular image of the Indians. And the vision of America as a place of rebirth, a New Eden freed from the historic sins of the Old World, still colors the self-image of the American people.

Fugitive myths of legendary lands and forgotten voyages gripped the medieval imagination and appeared on fanciful maps: St. Brendan's Isles, visited by Irish monks in the sixth century; Antilia, whence Christians had fled the Moors and built seven cities ruled by seven bishops; Brasil; Satanazes; and others —some of them perhaps confused reports of the Azores or Canaries, some even perhaps garbled accounts of real discoveries. Occasionally curious bits of carved wood, even corpses that looked vaguely Chinese, washed up in the Azores—vagrant reminders, like meteorites from space, of worlds unknown.

THE NORSE DISCOVERIES

Norse discoveries of the tenth and eleventh centuries are the earliest that can be verified, and even they dissolved into legend, in stories that no doubt grew in the telling before they were written down centuries later in *The Saga of Eric the Red* and the *Tale of the Greenlanders*. Like Eskimos crossing the Bering Strait to the east, the Norsemen went island-hopping across the North Atlantic to the west. Before A.D. 800 they had reached the

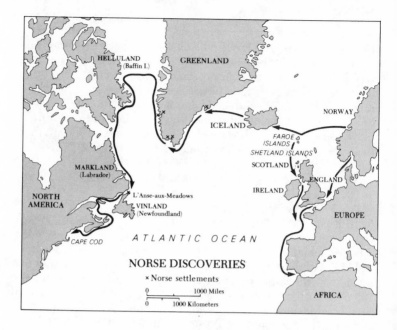

HELLULAND (Baffin I.) GREENLAND

NORWAY

ICELAND

FAROE ISLANDS

SHETLAND ISLANDS

SCOTLAND

ENGLAND

MARKLAND (Labrador)

IRELAND

L'Anse-aux-Meadows

NORTH AMERICA

VINLAND (Newfoundland)

EUROPE

CAPE COD

ATLANTIC OCEAN

NORSE DISCOVERIES

× Norse settlements

0   1000 Miles

0   1000 Kilometers

AFRICA

Faroes, and about A.D. 870 they conquered Iceland from Irish settlers while other Vikings terrorized the coasts of Europe. Around 985 an Icelander named Eric the Red colonized the west coast of an icebound island he deceptively called Greenland— Eric was the New World's first real-estate booster—and about a year later a trader named Bjarni Herjulfson missed Greenland and sighted land beyond. Knowing of this, Lief Ericsson, son of Eric the Red, sailed out from Greenland about A.D. 1001 and sighted the coasts of Helluland (Baffin Island), Markland (Labrador), and Vinland (Newfoundland), where he settled for the winter.

Three attempts to colonize the site followed: one led by Lief's brother Thorvald about 1004–1005, another by Thorfinn Karlsefni about 1009–1010—both abandoned after fierce attacks by natives they called Skraelings—and a third attempt about 1014. According to the *Tale of the Greenlanders*, this venture ended in gruesome tragedy when Lief's demonic sister Freydis baited her jealous husband Thorvald into killing two of his associates (Freydis dispatched their women) so that she could have their ships. After that the colony was abandoned and the sagas told no more of Vinland. Until the 1960s speculation had placed it as far south as Rhode Island or Chesapeake Bay. The riddle was not solved until 1963, when a Norwegian investigator uncovered the ruins of a number of Norse houses at L'Anse aux Meadows, on the northern coast of Newfoundland. This almost surely was the Vinland of the Sagas.

The Norse discoveries have an antiquarian interest, but they had no meaningful relation to later American history unless Columbus heard of them, which is doubtful. The Norsemen withdrew from North America in the face of hostile natives and the Greenland colonies vanished mysteriously in the fifteenth century. Nowhere in Europe had the forces yet developed which would impel men to colonize and subdue the New World.

THE EMERGENCE OF EUROPE

During the five centuries from Ericson to Columbus, Europe emerged slowly from the invasions, disorders, and weakness that had plagued it since the fall of Rome. In the twelfth century, a time often called the High Middle Ages, western Europe achieved comparative stability. The age of discovery, in turn, coincided with the opening of the modern period in European history. Indeed the burst of energy with which Europe spread its power and culture around the world was the epoch-making force of modern times. The expansion of Europe derived from, and in turn affected, the peculiar patterns and institutions which distinguished modern times from the medieval: the revival of learning and the rise of the inquiring spirit; the rise of trade, towns, and modern corporations; the decline of feudalism and the rise of national states; the Protestant Reformation and the Catholic Counter-Reformation; and on the darker side, some old sins— greed, conquest, exploitation, oppression, racism, and slavery— which quickly defiled the fancied innocence of the New Eden.

RENAISSANCE GEOGRAPHY For more than two centuries before Columbus the mind of Europe quickened with the fledgling Renaissance: the rediscovery of ancient classics, the rebirth of secular learning, the spirit of inquiry, all of which spread the more rapidly after Johan Gutenberg's invention of movable type around 1440. Learned men of the fifteenth century held in almost reverential awe the authority of ancient learning. The most direct though by no means the only contribution of antiquity to the age of discovery was in geography. As early as the sixth century B.C. the Pythagoreans had taught the sphericity of the earth, and in the third century B.C. Eratosthenes computed its size very nearly correctly. All this had been accepted in medieval universities on the authority of Aristotle. The story that Columbus was trying to prove this theory is one of those durable falsehoods that will not disappear in the face of the evidence. No informed man of his time thought the earth was flat.

The foremost geographer of ancient times—and of the fifteenth century—was Claudius Ptolemy of Alexandria, whose *Guide to Geography* was compiled in the second century A.D., later preserved by Byzantine scholars, and printed in many Latin editions after 1475. Columbus knew the book and also the work of a leading geographer of his own time, Cardinal Pierre d'Ailly's *Imago Mundi* (*A Picture of the World*), written about 1410 and published in 1485—a copy survives with Columbus's marginal notes. Ptolemy made the earth smaller than Eratosthenes had done and grossly overestimated the extent of Asia. Other writers favored by Columbus, especially the Florentine scholar Toscanelli, with whom he corresponded, brought the Asian coast even nearer to Portugal—to about where America actually was—and thus spurred the idea of sailing west to reach the East.

Progress in the art of navigation came with the revival of learning. The precise origin of the magnetic compass is unknown, but the principle was known by the twelfth century, and in the fifteenth century mariners took to using the astrolabe and cross-staff long used by landlocked astronomers to sight stars and find the latitude. Steering across the open sea, however, remained a matter of dead-reckoning. A ship's master set his course along a given latitude and calculated it as best he could from the angle of the North Star, or with less certainty the sun, estimating speed by the eye. Longitude remained a matter of guesswork, since accurate timepieces were needed to obtain it. Ship's clocks were too inaccurate until the chronometer was developed in the eighteenth century.

THE GROWTH OF TRADE, TOWNS, AND NATION-STATES The forces which would invade and reshape the New World found their focus in the rising towns, the centers of a growing trade which slowly broadened the narrow horizons of feudal Europe. In its farthest reaches this trade, quickened by contacts made during the Crusades, moved either overland or through the eastern Mediterranean all the way to East Asia, whence Europeans imported spices, medicine, silks, precious stones, dye-woods, perfumes, and rugs in return for the wines, glassware, wool, and silver of Europe. The trade gave rise to a merchant class and they in turn gave a boost to the idea of corporations through which the risks and profits might be shared by many stockholders.

The trade was both chancy and costly. Goods commonly

passed from hand to hand, from ships to pack trains and back to ships along the way, subject to levies by all sorts of princes and potentates, with each middleman pocketing whatever he could. The Muslim world, from Spain across North Africa into Central Asia, lay athwart all the more important routes and this added to the hazards. Little wonder, then, that Europeans should dream of an all-water route to the riches of East Asia and the Indies. Interest in the Orient had been further stirred by travelers' stories, of which the best known was the account by the Venetian Marco Polo, written in 1298–1299 and printed more than once in the fifteenth century. Christopher Columbus had a Latin version, with margins heavily annotated in his own hand.

Another spur to exploration was the rise of national states, with kings and queens who had the power and the means to sponsor the search. The growth of the merchant class went hand in hand with the growth of centralized power. Traders wanted uniform currencies, trade laws, and the elimination of trade barriers, and so became natural allies of the sovereigns who could meet their needs. In turn merchants and university-trained professionals supplied the monarchs with money, lawyers, and officials. The Crusades to capture the Holy Land (1095–1270) had also advanced the process. They had brought the West into contact with Eastern autocracy and had decimated the ranks of the feudal lords. And new means of warfare—the use of gunpowder and standing armies—further weakened the independence of the nobility. By 1492 the map of western Europe showed several united kingdoms: France, where in 1453 Louis XI had emerged from the Hundred Years' War as head of a unified state; England, where in 1485 Henry VII emerged victorious after thirty years of civil strife, the Wars of the Roses; Spain, where in 1469 Ferdinand of Aragon and Isabella of Castile united two great kingdoms in marriage; and Portugal, where even earlier, in 1384, John I had fought off the Castilians and assured national independence.

THE VOYAGES OF COLUMBUS

It was in Portugal, with the guidance of John's son, Prince Henry the Navigator, that exploration and discovery began in earnest. About 1418 Prince Henry set up an information service to collect charts and data on winds and currents. In 1422 he sent out his first expedition to map the coast of Africa. Driven partly by the hope of outflanking the Islamic world, partly by the hope of trade, the Portuguese by 1446 reached Cape Verde, by 1471 the equator, and by 1482 the Congo River. In 1488 Bartholomew Diaz rounded the Cape of Good Hope, and in 1498 Vasco da Gama went on to Calicut in India.

Christopher Columbus meanwhile was learning his trade in the school of Portuguese seamanship. Born in 1451 the son of a weaver in Genoa, Italy, Columbus took to the sea at an early age, and made up for his lack of formal education by learning geography, navigation, and Latin (still the universal language of the learned). In 1476 he reached Portugal and went on voyages to Guinea, England, and Iceland, married a girl from Madeira where he made his home for a while, and during the 1480s hatched a scheme to reach the East by sailing west. But Portugal was by then too involved with African explorations. Christopher's brother Bartholomew, a professional mapmaker, hawked the idea in the courts of England and France, but they were busy with other matters. In 1486 Columbus turned to Queen Isabella, and after years of disappointment finally enlisted the support of King Ferdinand's advisor, Luis de Santangel, keeper of the privy purse. Santangel won the support of the Spanish monarchs and himself raised much of the money needed to finance the voyage. The legend that the queen had to hock the crown jewels is as spurious as the fable that Columbus had to prove the earth was round.

Columbus chartered one ship, the *Santa Maria*, and the city of

Columbus encounters the Indians of America. This engraving illustrated the 1493 letter in which Columbus announced his discovery. [New York Public Library]

Palos supplied two smaller caravels, the *Pinta* and *Niña*, exacted in punishment for some offense against the crown. From Palos Columbus sailed to the Canary Islands and by dead-reckoning westward. Early on October 12, 1492, after thirty-three days at sea, a lookout sighted land. It was an island in the Bahamas, called Guanahani (Iguana) by the inhabitants and renamed San Salvador (Holy Savior) by Columbus—later renamed Watlings Island. According to his own reckoning he was near Japan. He therefore continued to search through the Bahamian Cays down to Cuba, a place name which suggested Cipangu (Japan), and then eastward to the island he named Española (or Hispaniola) where he traded for some gold nose-plugs and bracelets with the people he insisted upon calling Indians. The friendly islanders of what Columbus thought an outpost of Asia belonged to the Arawak-language group who, pushed out of South America, had in turn pushed the Siboney Indians into western Cuba and western Hispaniola. Columbus learned of, but did not encounter until his second voyage, the fierce Caribs of the Lesser Antilles. Because of their location the name of the Caribbean Sea was derived from their name; because of their bad habits our word "Cannibal" was derived from a Spanish version of their name (Canibal).

On the night before Christmas the *Santa Maria* ran aground off Hispaniola and Columbus decided to return home with the two caravels, leaving about forty men behind. On the way home he discovered the need to move north and out of the easterly trade winds, which had brought him westward. This course led him to the Azores and thence to Portugal. The Portuguese thus learned of the new lands first, and John II laid claim to the discoveries on the grounds that they probably lay near the Portuguese Azores.

When Columbus finally reached Palos, the news spread rapidly throughout Europe. Ferdinand and Isabella instructed him to prepare for the second voyage and immediately set about shoring up their legal claim. Pope Alexander VI, who was Spanish, issued a papal bull (after *bulla*, or seal), *Inter Caetera*, which drew an imaginary boundary line 100 leagues west of the Azores, and provided that the area beyond should be a Spanish sphere of exploration and possession. Alarmed, the Portuguese monarch dropped his claim but demanded a dividing line farther west. In the Treaty of Tordesillas (1494) Spain accepted a line 370 leagues west of the Cape Verde Islands. In 1500 Pedro Alvares Cabral, a Portuguese captain on his way around Africa, swung southwestward across the Atlantic and sighted the hump of Brazil, which lay within the Portuguese sphere.

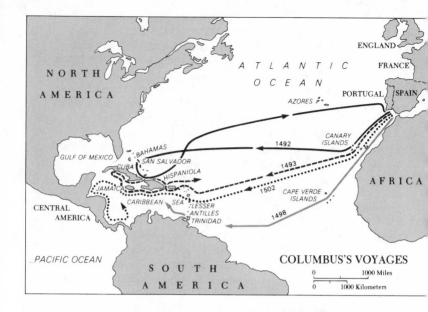

COLUMBUS'S VOYAGES

0 ___ 1000 Miles

0 ___ 1000 Kilometers

Meanwhile Columbus returned in 1493 with seventeen ships and some 1,200 men, and planted the first Spanish colony on Hispaniola, where he learned that the men left behind on the first voyage had been killed. He found the Lesser Antilles, explored the coast of Cuba, discovered Jamaica, and finally returned to Spain in 1496, leaving his brother Bartholomew in the new colony to found the city of Santo Domingo. On a third voyage in 1498 Columbus found Trinidad and explored the northern coast of South America. Back in Hispaniola he displayed a disastrous vacillation about dealing with a rebellion, and was arrested and sent back to Spain in chains. But he regained enough favor to lead a fourth voyage in 1502, during which he sailed along the coast of Central America, still looking in vain for Asia. Marooned on Jamaica more than a year, he finally returned to Spain in 1504 and in 1506 he died at Valladolid.

To the end Columbus refused to believe that he had discovered anything other than outlying parts of the Orient. Soon after the first voyage Peter Martyr, a learned Italian at the Spanish court, wrote letters in which he spoke of a New World, and noted that the size of the globe suggested something other than India, but even he did not find this New World inconsistent with the Indies. Full awareness that a great land mass lay between Europe and Asia only slowly seeped into the European consciousness, and by one of history's greatest ironies led the New World to be named not for its discoverer but for one of the first to argue with conviction that it was indeed a New World, unknown to Ptolemy. In 1507 the geographer Martin Waldseemüller published a treatise, *Cosmographiae Introductio (Introduction to Cosmography)*, in which he suggested that the New World should be called America, after Amerigo Vespucci.

Vespucci was a Florentine merchant and navigator sent to Spain as an agent of the ruling de Medici family. He knew Columbus, may have been among those who welcomed him back from the first voyage, and certainly helped outfit his ships for the second and third. Later, by his own accounts, Vespucci himself made four voyages to the New World, although there is firm evidence for only two. Vespucci did not command any of these expeditions, but his distinction as a geographer and an interpreter of what he found exceeded that of Columbus. The great popularity of his writings was important in bringing home to Europe the true nature and extent of the discoveries. This was indeed a New World.

THE GREAT BIOLOGICAL EXCHANGE

The first European contacts with this New World began a diffusion of cultures, an exchange of such magnitude and pace as humanity had never known before and will never know again short of contact with extra-terrestrial life. It was in fact more than a diffusion of cultures: it was a diffusion of distinctive biological systems. If anything, the plants and animals of the two worlds were more different than the people and their ways of life. Europeans, for instance, had never seen such creatures as the fearsome (if harmless) iguana, flying squirrels, fish with whiskers like

An iguana, drawn by John White, one of the earliest English settlers in America. [British Museum]

cats, snakes that rattled "castanets," or anything quite like several other species: bison, cougars, armadillos, opossums, sloths, tapirs, anacondas, electric eels, vampire bats, toucans, Andean condors, or hummingbirds. Among the few domesticated animals, they could recognize the dog and the duck, but turkeys, guinea pigs, llamas, vicuñas, alpacas, and guanacos were all new. Nor did the Indians know of cattle, pigs, sheep, goats, and (maybe) chickens, which soon arrived in abundance. Within a half century, for instance, whole islands of the Caribbean were overrun by pigs, whose ancestors were bred in Spain.

The exchange of plant life worked an even greater change, a revolution in the diets of both hemispheres. Before the Discovery three main staples of the modern diet were unknown in the Old World: maize, potatoes (sweet and white), and many kinds of beans (snap, kidney, lima beans, and others). The white potato, although commonly called "Irish," actually migrated from South America to Europe and only reached North America with Scotch-Irish immigrants of the 1700s. Other New World food plants were manioc (soon a staple in tropical Africa, consumed in the United States chiefly as tapioca), peanuts, squash, peppers, tomatoes, pumpkins, pineapples, sassafras, papayas, guavas, avocadoes, cacao (the source of chocolate), and chicle (for chewing gum). Europeans soon introduced rice, wheat, barley, oats, wine

John White's drawing of plantain, a plant new to the European discoverers of America. [British Museum]

grapes, melons, coffee, olives, bananas, "Kentucky" bluegrass, daisies, and that bane of the homeowner, dandelions.

The beauty of the exchange was that the food plants were more complementary than competitive. They grew in different soils and climates, or on different schedules. Indian corn, it turned out, could flourish almost anywhere—high or low, hot or cold, wet or dry. It spread quickly throughout the world. Before the end of the 1500s American maize and sweet potatoes were staple crops in China. The green revolution exported from the Americas thus helped nourish a worldwide population explosion probably greater than any since the invention of agriculture, something like a fivefold increase from 1630 to 1950, from some 500 million to almost 2.5 billion. Plants originally domesticated by American Indians now make up about a third of the world's food plants.

Europeans, moreover, adopted many Indian devices: canoes, snowshoes, moccasins, hammocks, kayaks, ponchos, dogsleds, toboggans, and parkas. The rubber ball and the game of lacrosse had Indian origins. New words entered the languages of Europeans in profusion: wigwam, teepee, papoose, succotash, hominy, tobacco, moose, skunk, opossum, woodchuck, chipmunk, tomahawk, mackinaw, hickory, pecan, raccoon, and hundreds of others—and new terms in translation: warpath, warpaint, paleface, medicine man, firewater. And the aborigines left the map dotted with place names of Indian origin long after they were gone, from Miami to Yakima, from Penobscot to Yuma.

There were still other New World contributions: tobacco and a number of drugs, including coca (for cocaine and novocaine), curare (a muscle relaxant), and cinchona bark (for quinine), and one common medical device, the enema tube. Indian healers, unlike the snake-oil merchants who traded on their reputation, were seldom quacks. But the white man presented them with exotic maladies they could not handle, for the Indians had lived in blissful ignorance of many infections that plagued Europeans. Even minor European diseases like measles turned killer in the bodies of Indians who had never encountered them and thus had built no immunity. Major diseases like smallpox and typhus killed all the more speedily. According to Thomas Harriot's account from the first colony sent by Sir Walter Raleigh to Roanoke Island, within a few days after Englishmen visited the Indian villages of the neighborhood, "people began to die very fast, and many in short space. . . . The disease also was so strange that they neither knew what it was, nor how to cure it; the like by report of the oldest man in the country never happened before, time out of mind." Now it happened time and time again. The first contacts with some of Columbus's sailors devastated whole communities, and the epidemics spread rapidly into the interior. But the Indians made some restitution. They got the worst of the bargain, but they infected Europeans with syphilis. This, rather than diarrhea, was the true "Montezuma's revenge."

PROFESSIONAL EXPLORERS

Undeterred by new diseases, professional explorers, mostly Italians, hired themselves out to the highest bidder to look for that open sesame to riches, a western passage to the Orient. One after another these men probed the shorelines of America during the early sixteenth century in the vain search for an opening, and thus increased by leaps and bounds European knowledge of the vast expanse of the new discoveries. The first to sight the North American continent was John Cabot, or Giovanni Caboto, a Venetian and possibly a native of Genoa, whom Henry VII of England sponsored after having missed a chance to sponsor Columbus. Acting on the theory that Cathay was opposite England, Cabot sailed from Bristol across the North Atlantic in 1497 and fetched up at Cape Breton or southern Newfoundland. Cabot never returned from a second voyage in 1498, but his landfall at what the king called "the newe founde lande" gave England the basis for a later claim to all of North America. For many years little was done to follow up the discovery except by fishermen who more and more exploited the teeming waters of the Grand Banks after 1500—men from England, Portugal, France, and Spain. In 1513 the Spaniard Vasco Nuñez de Balboa became the first European to sight the Pacific Ocean, but only after he had crossed the Isthmus of Panama on foot.

The Portuguese, who from their base in the Azores explored the coasts of Newfoundland and Labrador, and named the latter, meanwhile stole the march by going the other way. In 1498, while Columbus prowled the Caribbean, Vasco da Gama reached the East by sailing around Africa and soon afterward set up the trading posts of a commercial empire stretching from India to the Moluccas (or Spice Islands) of Indonesia. The Spaniards, however, reasoned that the line of demarcation established by the Treaty of Tordesillas ran around the other side of the earth as well. Hoping to show that the Moluccas lay near South America within the Spanish sphere, Ferdinand Magellan, a Portuguese seaman in the employ of Spain, set out to find a pas-

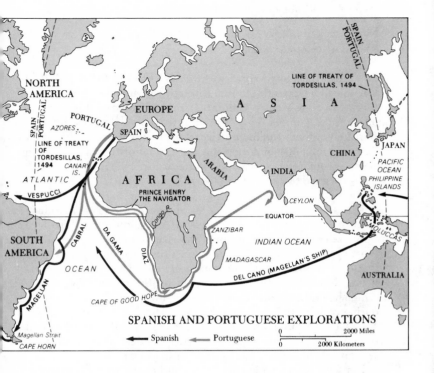

sage through or around southern South America. Departing
Spain in 1519, he found his way through the dangerous strait
which now bears his name, then moved far to the north before he
found winds to bear him westward. On a journey far longer than
he had bargained for, he touched upon Guam and eventually
made a landfall in the Philippines, where he lost his life in a fight
with the natives.

Led by Magellan's navigator, Sebastian del Cano, however,
the remaining two ships made their way to the Moluccas, picked
up a cargo of spices, and one of them, the *Victoria,* returned to
Spain in 1522. This first voyage around the globe quickened
Spanish ambitions for empire in the East, but after some abortive
attempts at establishing themselves there, the Spaniards, beset
by war with France, sold Portugal their claims to the Moluccas.
From 1565, however, Spaniards would begin to penetrate the
Philippines, discovered by Magellan and named for the Spanish
prince who became Philip II. In the seventeenth century the English and the Dutch would oust Portugal from most of its empire,
but for a century the East Indies was Portuguese.

The Spanish Empire

And the New World was Spanish, except for Brazil. The Caribbean Sea was the funnel through which Spanish power entered the New World. Columbus himself founded the first colony on Hispaniola in 1493; a few years later his brother Bartholomew started to build a castle (ruins of which still exist) at Santo Domingo, which became the capital of the Indies. From there colonization proceeded eastward to Puerto Rico (1508) and westward to Cuba (1511–1514).

CORTÉS'S CONQUEST In the islands, Spaniards found only Archaic cultures. On the mainland, however, it was different, for there they found civilizations in some ways equal to their own, but almost as vulnerable as the Archaic cultures to their power. The great adventure of mainland conquest began in 1519, when Hernando Cortés and 600 men landed on the site of Vera Cruz, which he founded, and then, far exceeding his orders, set about a daring conquest of the Aztec Empire. The 200-mile march from Vera Cruz through difficult mountain passes to the Aztec capital of Tenochtitlán (Mexico City), and the subjugation of the Aztecs, was one of the most remarkable feats in human history.

But Cortés had some advantages and made the most of them. An acute judge of character and a gifted diplomat as well as military leader, he landed in a region where the people were still fighting off the spread of Aztec power and were ready to embrace new allies. To the Aztecs and their enemies alike, Cortés seemed to fulfill legends of the Toltec god Quetzalcoatl, who was due to return in the form of a white man and conquer the Aztecs. By a combination of threats and wiles, after several battles Cortés was able to enter Tenochtitlán peacefully and to make the emperor, Montezuma, his puppet. This state of affairs lasted until the spring of 1520, when the Aztecs rebelled and stoned Montezuma to death. The Spaniards lost about a third of their men in the streets as they fought their way out. His allies remained loyal, however, and Cortés gradually regrouped. In 1521 he took the city again and with it the new emperor, Cuauhtemoc. After that the resistance collapsed, and Cortés and his officers simply replaced the former Aztec overlords as rulers over the Indian empire.

In doing so they set the style for other conquistadores to follow. Within twenty years his emulators had established a Spanish empire far larger than Rome's had ever been. Between 1522 and

A Navajo representation of Spanish conquistadors on the march, located in Canyon de Chelly, Arizona. [Shelly Grossman/Woodfin Camp & Associates]

1528 various lieutenants of Cortes, the most notable being Pedro de Alvarado, conquered the remnants of Mayan-Toltec culture in Yucatán and Guatemala. In 1531 Francisco Pizarro took a band of soldiers down the Pacific coast from Panama toward Cuzco, the seat of the Inca. Along the way he was able to play off against each other the supporters of rival claimants to the throne of the Inca, and to capture the leading claimant Atahualpa, seize his treasure, and execute him in 1533 after a trial on trumped-up charges of usurpation, idolatry, polygamy, and other crimes. From Peru, conquistadores extended Spanish authority through Chile by about 1553, and to the north, in present-day Colombia, conquered the Chibcha Empire in 1536–1538.

The Spanish were great believers in form. Before entering upon each new conquest, Spanish generals read a *Requerimiento* (Requirement) to the native people. This curious document recited Christian history from the creation to the time of Pope Alexander VI, and called upon the Indians to accept the authority of the Castilian crown, as granted by the pope. Failure to do so would result in subjugation and loss of property, and even more dire consequences. "The resultant deaths and damages shall be your fault," the paper added, not that of the Spaniards. The *Requerimiento* was repeatedly pronounced before battle, and while it may have helped to salve consciences, it required a strange naïvete. "It is not Christianity that leads them on," the great Spanish dramatist Lope de Vega had the devil say in his play *The New World*,"but rather gold and greed."

The course of empire was nevertheless marked by Spain's centuries-long crusade to expel the Islamic Moors from their foothold in the Iberian peninsula. By coincidence it was in 1492, the very year of discovery, that the Catholic monarchs captured the last Moorish stronghold, Granada, and there ordered the expulsion of all Jews (previously tolerated by the Moors) unless they converted to Christianity.

SPANISH AMERICA   The conquest of America thus seemed almost like an extension of this crusade into a new world—first conquest, then evangelization, by force if need be. The conquistadores transferred to America and there elaborated a system known as the *encomienda,* whereby Christian knights had acquired rights over land and people captured from the Moors. In America favored officers took over Indian villages or groups of villages. As *encomenderos* they were called upon to protect and care for the villages and support a missionary clergy. In turn they could levy tribute in goods and labor. Spanish America therefore developed from the start a society of extremes: conquistadores and encomenderos who sometimes found wealth beyond the dreams of avarice, if more often just a crude affluence, and subject peoples who were held in poverty.

What were left of them, that is. By the mid-1500s Indians were nearly extinct in the West Indies, reduced more by European diseases than by Spanish exploitation. To take their place the colonizers as early as 1503 began to bring in black slaves from Africa, the first in a melancholy traffic that eventually would bring over 9 million people across the Atlantic in bondage. In all of Spain's New World empire, by one informed estimate, the Indian population dropped from about 50 million at the outset to 4 million in the seventeenth century, and slowly rose again to 7.5 million. Whites, who totaled no more than 100,000 in the mid–sixteenth century, numbered over 3 million by the end of the colonial period.

The Indians did not always want for advocates, however. Catholic missionaries in many cases offered a sharp contrast to the conquistadores. Setting examples of self-denial, they went out into remote areas, often without weapons or protection, to spread the gospel—and often suffered martyrdom for their efforts. Among them rose defenders of the Indians, the most noted of whom was Bartolomeo de las Casas, a priest in Hispaniola (1502–1514) and later bishop of Chiapas, Guatemala, author of *A Brief Relation of the Destruction of the Indies* (1552). Las Casas won some limited reforms from the Spanish government, but ironically had a more lasting influence in giving rise to the so-called Black Legend of Spanish cruelty which the enemies of Spain gleefully spread abroad, often as a cover for their own abuses.

From such violently contrasting forces Spanish America gradually developed into a settled society, the independent conquistadores replaced quickly by a second generation of bureaucrats, the *encomienda* replaced by the *hacienda* (a great farm or ranch), as the claim to land became a more important source of wealth than the claim to labor. The empire was organized first into two great regions, the Viceroyalties of New Spain and Perú; eventually the Viceroyalties of New Granada and La Plata were split off from the latter. From the outset these were understood to be separate realms of the Castilian crown, united with Spain and with each other only in the person of the monarch. And from the outset, in sharp contrast to the later English experience, the crown took an interest in regulating every detail of colonial administration. After 1524 the Council of the Indies, directly under the crown, issued laws for America, served as the appellate court for civil cases arising in the colonies, and had general oversight of the bureaucracy. Trade, finances, and taxation were closely watched by the *Casa de Contratación,* or House of Trade, set up at Seville in 1503.

The culture that grew up in Spanish America would be fundamentally unlike the English-speaking world that would arise to the north. In fact a difference already existed in pre-Columbian America, with largely nomadic tribes to the north and the more settled and complex civilizations in Mesoamerica. On the latter world the Spaniards imposed an overlay of their own peculiar ways, but without uprooting the deeply planted cultures they found. Just as Spain itself harbored reminders of the one-time Arab rule, so in the New World reminders of the Aztec and Incan cultures lingered. Catholicism, which for long centuries had absorbed pagan gods and transformed pagan feasts into such holy days as Christmas and Easter, in turn adapted Indian beliefs and rituals to its own purposes. The Mexican Virgin of Guadalupe, for instance, evoked memories of feminine divinities in native cults. Thus Spanish America, in the words of Mexican writer Octavio Paz, became a land of superimposed pasts. "Mexico City was built on the ruins of Tenochtitlán, the Aztec city that was built in the likeness of Tula, the Toltec city that was built in the likeness of Teotihuacán, the first great city on the American continent. Every Mexican bears within him this continuity, which goes back two thousand years."

SPANISH EXPLORATIONS   For more than a century after Columbus no European power other than Spain had more than a brief foothold in the New World. Spain had not only the advantage of having sponsored the discovery, but of having stumbled onto those parts of America that would bring the quickest returns. While France and England remained preoccupied with domestic quarrels and religious conflict, Spain had forged an intense national unity. Under Charles V, heir to the throne of Austria and the Netherlands, and Holy Roman Emperor to boot, Spain dominated Europe as well as America. The treasures of the Aztecs and the Incas added to her power, but eventually they would prove to be a mixed blessing. The easy reliance on American gold and silver undermined the basic economy of Spain and tempted the government to live beyond its means, while American bullion contributed to price inflation throughout Europe.

To the north of Mexico the Spaniards never got a secure footing, but the "Spanish borderlands" of the southern United States from Florida to California preserve many reminders of the Spanish presence. Spanish mariners probably saw the coast of North America before 1500 (a crude outline which might have been Florida shows on a map of 1502), but the earliest known exploration of the Florida coast was made in 1513 by Juan Ponce de Leon, then governor of Puerto Rico, who later tried but failed to plant a colony on the Gulf coast in 1521. Meanwhile Spanish explorers skirted the Gulf coast from Florida to Vera Cruz, scouted the Atlantic coast from Cuba to Newfoundland, and established a short-lived colony on the Carolina coast.

Sixteenth-century knowledge of the interior came mostly from would-be conquistadores who sought but found little to plunder in the hinterlands. The first, Pánfilo de Narváez, landed in 1528 at Tampa Bay, marched northward to Appalachee, an Indian village in present-day Alabama, then back to the coast near St. Marks, where his party contrived crude vessels in hope of reaching Mexico. Wrecked on the coast of Texas, a few survivors under Nuñez Cabeza de Vaca worked their way painfully overland and after eight years stumbled into a Spanish outpost in western Mexico. Hernando de Soto followed their example in 1540–1543. With 600 men he landed on the Florida west coast, hiked up as far as western North Carolina, then westward beyond the Mississippi, and on up the Arkansas River. In the spring of 1542 de Soto died near the site of Memphis; the next year the survivors floated down the Mississippi and 311 of the original band found their way to Mexico. In 1540 Francisco Vasquez de Coronado, inspired by rumors of gold, traveled northward into New Mexico and eastward across Texas and Oklahoma

SPANISH EXPLORATIONS
OF THE MAINLAND

•••• Balboa 1513
▬▬ Ponce de León 1513
━•━ Cortéz 1519
━━ Narvaez 1528
━━ Pizarro 1531-1533
━ ━ Cabeza de Vaca 1535-1536
•••••• De Soto 1539-1542
━ ━ Coronado 1540-1542

0   1000 Miles
0   1000 Kilometers

as far as Kansas. He came back in 1542 without gold but with a
more realistic view of what lay in those arid lands.

The first Spanish base in the present United States came in response to French encroachments on Spanish claims. In 1562
French Huguenots established a short-lived colony at Port
Royal, South Carolina, and two years later another at Fort Caroline, Florida. The following year, 1565, a Spanish outpost,
named St. Augustine, became the first European town in the
present-day United States, and is now its oldest urban center except for the pueblos of New Mexico. While other outposts failed,
St. Augustine survived as a defensive outpost perched on the
edge of a continent.

In New Mexico missionary efforts began in 1581, and the first major colonization drive in 1598. Santa Fe, the capital and second-oldest European city in the United States, was founded in 1609 or 1610. An Indian uprising in 1680, the great Pueblo Revolt, temporarily chased the Spaniards out, but they returned in the 1690s. Spanish outposts on the Florida and Texas Gulf coasts and in California did not come until the eighteenth century.

THE PROTESTANT REFORMATION

While Spain built her empire, a new movement was growing elsewhere in Europe, the Protestant Reformation, which would embitter national rivalries, and by encouraging serious challenges to Catholic Spain's power, profoundly affect the course of early American history. When Columbus sailed in 1492 all of western Europe acknowledged the authority of the Catholic church and its pope in Rome. The unity of Christendom began to crack in 1517, however, when Martin Luther, a German monk and theologian, posted on the church door in Wittenberg his "Ninety-five Theses" in protest against abuses in the church and especially against the sale of indulgences for the remission of sins. Sinful men, Luther argued, could win salvation neither by good works nor through the mediation of the church, but only by faith in the redemptive power of Christ and through a direct relationship to God—the "priesthood of all believers." And the only true guide to the will of God was the Bible.

Fired with these beliefs, Luther set out to reform the church and ended by splitting it. Lutheranism spread rapidly among the people and their rulers—some of them with an eye to seizing church properties—and when the pope expelled Luther from the church in 1520, reconciliation became impossible. The German states fell into conflict over religious differences until 1555, when they finally patched up a peace whereby each prince determined the religion of his subjects. Generally, northern Germany became Lutheran, along with Scandinavia. The principle of close association between church and state thus carried over into Protestant lands, but Luther had unleashed ideas that ran beyond his personal control.

Other Protestants pursued Luther's doctrine to its logical end and preached religious liberty for all. Further divisions on doctrinal matters led to the appearance of various sects of Anabaptists, who rejected infant baptism, and other offshoots including the Mennonites, Amish, Dunkers, Familists, and Schwenkfelders. There already existed, moreover, another group, the

Martin Luther preaching. On the right, church officials—popes, cardinals, and monks—are caught in the mouth of hell. On the left are those saved through simple faith. [Bettmann Archive]

Moravians, who followed the teachings of Jan Hus, a Czech reformer martyred for his beliefs nearly a century before Luther.

CALVINISM Soon after Luther began his revolt a number of Swiss cantons, influenced by the teachings of Huldreich Zwingli in Zurich, began to throw off the authority of Rome. In Geneva the reform movement looked to John Calvin, a Frenchman who had fled to Switzerland and who brought his adopted city under the sway of his beliefs. In his great theological work, *The Institutes of the Christian Religion* (1536), Calvin set forth a stern doctrine. All men, he taught, were damned by the original sin of Adam, but the sacrifice of Christ made possible their redemption by faith. The experience of faith, however, was open only to those who had been elected by God and thus predestined to salvation from the beginning of time. It was a hard doctrine, but the infinite wisdom of God was beyond human understanding.

Calvinism required a stern moral code, for the outward sign of true faith was correct behavior. If this did not of itself prove that one was of the elect, an immoral life clearly proved the opposite. Calvin therefore insisted upon strict morality and hard work, a teaching which especially suited the rising middle class. Moreover, he taught that men serve God through any legitimate calling, and permitted laymen a share in the governance of the church through a body of elders and ministers called the consistory or presbytery. The doctrines of Calvin became the basis for the beliefs of the German Reformed and Dutch Reformed churches, the Presbyterians in Scotland, some of the Puritans in England, and the Huguenots (or Confederates) in France. Through these and other groups Calvin later exerted more effect upon religious belief and practice in the English colonies than any other single leader of the Reformation.

THE REFORMATION IN ENGLAND   In England the Reformation, like so many other things, followed a unique course. The Church of England, or Anglican church, took form through a gradual process of Calvinizing English Catholicism. Rejection of papal authority came about at first, however, for purely political reasons. Henry VIII (1509–1547), the second of the Tudor dynasty, had in fact won from the pope the title of Defender of the Faith, for his *Defense of the Seven Sacraments* (1521), a refutation of Luther's ideas. But Henry's marriage to Catherine of Aragon had produced no male heir, and for that reason he required an annulment. In the past popes had found ways to accommodate such requests, but Catherine was the aunt of Charles V, king of Spain and emperor of the Holy Roman Empire, whose support was vital to the church's cause on the continent, so the pope refused. Unwilling to accept the rebuff, Henry severed the connection with Rome, named a new archbishop of Canterbury who granted the annulment, and married the lively Anne Boleyn. And she, in one of history's great ironies, presented him not with the male heir he sought, but a daughter, who as Elizabeth I would reign from 1558 to 1603 over one of England's greatest eras.

Elizabeth could not be a Catholic, for in the Catholic view she was illegitimate. During her reign, therefore, the Church of England became Protestant, but in its own way. The structure of organization, the bishops and archbishops, remained much the same, but the doctrine and practice changed: the Latin liturgy became, with some changes, the English *Book of Common Prayer*, the cult of saints was dropped, and the clergy were permitted to marry. The thirty-nine Articles of Faith, prepared by a committee of bishops and announced in 1571, defined the Anglican creed in Protestant terms, though sometimes evasively. For the sake of unity the "Elizabethan Settlement" allowed some latitude in theology and other matters, but this did not satisfy all. The episcopate, on the one hand, tried to enforce the letter of the law, stressing traditional practice. Many others, however, especially those under Calvinist influence from the continent, wished to "purify" the church so that it more nearly fit their

Elizabeth I, who ruled England during the springtime of its power. She is portrayed here standing on a map of England. [National Portrait Gallery, London]

views of biblical authority. Some of these Puritans would later despair of the effort to reform the Anglican church and would leave England to build their own churches in America.

CHALLENGES TO SPANISH EMPIRE

The Spanish monopoly of New World colonies remained intact throughout the sixteenth century, but not without challenge from national rivals spurred now by the emotion unleashed by the Protestant Reformation. The French were the first to pose a serious challenge, and Huguenot (Protestant) seamen from the great ports of France promised to build France into a major seapower. Spanish treasure ships from the New World held out a tempting lure to French corsairs, and at least as early as 1524 one of them was plundered off the Azores by a French privateer. In 1524 Francis I sent an Italian named Giovanni da Verrazzano in search of a passage to Asia. Sighting land (probably at Cape Fear, North Carolina), Verrazzano ranged along the coast as far north as Maine. On the way he viewed Pamlico Sound across the North Carolina Outer Banks, and beguiled by hope, mistook it for the Pacific Ocean. On a second voyage in 1538, his career came to an abrupt end in the West Indies at the hands of the fierce Caribs.

Unlike the Verrazzano voyages, those of Jacques Cartier about a decade later led to the first French effort at colonization. On three voyages (1534, 1535–1536, and 1541–1542) Cartier explored the Gulf of St. Lawrence and up the St. Lawrence River looking for the Kingdom of Saguenay, another fantasy compounded of European greed and Indian tall tales. Twice he got as far as present Montréal, and twice wintered at or near the site of Québec, near which a short-lived French colony appeared in 1542–1543. From that time forward, however, French kings lost interest in Canada, France after mid-century plunged into religious civil wars, and the colonization of Canada had to await the coming of Samuel de Champlain, the "Father of New France," after 1600.

From the mid-1500s forward, greater threats to Spanish power arose from the growing strength of the Dutch and English. The provinces of the Netherlands, which had passed by inheritance to the Spanish king, and which had become largely Protestant, rebelled against Spanish rule in 1567. A protracted and bloody struggle for independence was interrupted by a twelve-year truce which ended the war in 1609 for a time, but Spain did not accept the independence of the Dutch Republic until 1648.

Almost from the beginning of the revolt the Dutch "Sea Beggars," privateers working out of both English and Dutch ports, plundered Spanish ships in the Atlantic and carried on illegal trade with the Spanish colonies. The Dutch "Sea Beggars" soon had their counterpart in the Elizabethan "Sea Dogges": John Hawkins, Francis Drake, and others. While Elizabeth steered a tortuous course to avoid open war with Catholic Spain, she encouraged both Dutch and English captains in smuggling and piracy. Sir John Hawkins, first of the great Sea Dogs, got his start as a smuggler in 1562 when he picked up some 300 black slaves in Sierra Leone and traded them at a profit in Hispaniola. Two years later he took a cargo to the Spanish Main (in Venezuela and Panamá). A third voyage, in 1567–1568, however, ended in disaster when a Spanish fleet surprised him at Vera Cruz. Only two of his five ships escaped, commanded respectively by Hawkins and his cousin, Francis Drake, whose exploits soon overshadowed his own.

Drake now abandoned the pretense of legal trade and set out to loot Spanish treasure. In 1577 he embarked in the *Golden*

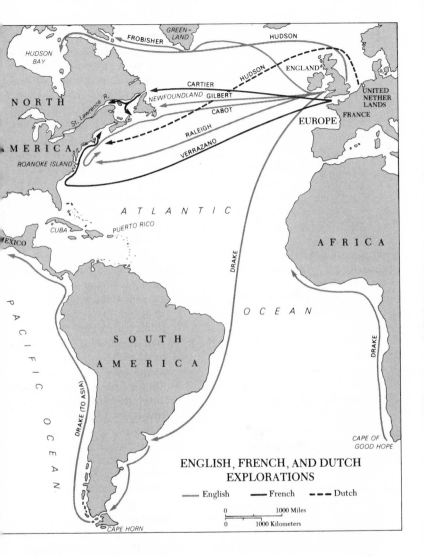

ENGLISH, FRENCH, AND DUTCH
EXPLORATIONS

——— English ——— French ‐‐‐ Dutch

0   1000 Miles
0   1000 Kilometers

Hind on his famous adventure around South America to raid
Spanish towns along the Pacific and surprise a treasure ship from
Perú. Continuing in a vain search for a passage back to the Atlantic, he was driven out to sea. He closed with the American coast
at about 43° north and spent seven weeks at Drake's Bay in
"New Albion," as he called California. Eventually he found his
way westward around the world and back home in 1580. Elizabeth, who had secretly backed the voyage, shared a profit of
4,600 percent, and knighted Sir Francis upon his return.

THE ARMADA'S DEFEAT   Such depredations continued for some twenty years before circumstances finally provoked open war. In 1568 Elizabeth's cousin Mary, "Queen of Scots," ousted by Scottish Presbyterians in favor of her infant son, fled to refuge in England. Mary, who was Catholic, had a claim to the English throne by descent from Henry VII, and soon became the focus for Spanish-Catholic intrigues to overthrow Elizabeth. Finally, after an abortive plot to kill Elizabeth and elevate Mary to the throne, the queen yielded to the demands of her ministers and had Mary beheaded in 1587.

In revenge Philip II decided to crush once and for all the Protestant power of the north and began to gather his ill-fated Armada, whereupon Francis Drake swept down upon Cadiz and destroyed part of the fleet before it was ready. His "singeing of the King of Spain's beard" postponed for a year the departure of the "Invincible Armada," which set out in 1588. From the beginning it was a case of incompetence and mismanagement compounded by bad luck. The Spanish idea of naval warfare was to bring rival ships together for what in effect was an infantry battle at sea. The heavy Spanish galleons, however, could not cope with the smaller and faster English vessels commanded by Drake and others. The English harried the Spanish ships through the English Channel on their way to the Netherlands, where the Armada was to pick up an army of invasion. But caught up in a powerful "Protestant Wind" from the south, the storm-tossed fleet never got there. It was swept into the North Sea instead, and what was left of it finally found its way home around the British Isles, leaving wreckage scattered on the shores of Scotland and Ireland.

Defeat of the Armada marked the beginning of English supremacy on the sea and cleared the way for English colonization. It was the climactic event of Elizabeth's reign, and it brought to a crescendo the surging patriotism that had been born of the epic conflict with Spain. The great literature of the Elizabethan age reflected a spirit of confidence and pride. The historical plays of William Shakespeare, especially, celebrated the glories of the House of Tudor and linked them to the spirit of the nation: "This blessed plot, this earth, this realm, this England." England was in the springtime of her power, filled with a youthful zest for new worlds and new wonders that were opening up before the nation.

ENGLISH EXPLORATIONS   A significant figure in channeling this energy was Richard Hakluyt the Younger, an Oxford clergyman, who as a youth was inspired by the example of his cousin, the elder Richard Hakluyt, to collect and publish accounts of the great voyages of exploration. He set out systematically to read whatever accounts he could find in Latin, Greek, Italian, Spanish, Portuguese, French, and English. In the process he rescued some accounts from destruction. In 1582 Hakluyt brought out his first book, *Divers Voyages touching the discoverie of America,* and in the summer of the Armada he finished *The Principall Navigations, voiages and discoveries of the English Nation.*

Hakluyt, moreover, became an active promoter of colonization. In 1584, at the request of Sir Walter Raleigh, he prepared for the queen *A Discourse of Western Planting* (first published three centuries later) in which he pleaded for colonies to accomplish diverse objects: to extend the reformed religion, to expand trade, to employ the idle, to supply England's needs from her own dominions, to provide bases in case of war with Spain, to enlarge the queen's revenues and navy, and to discover a Northwest Passage to the Orient.

While Hawkins and Drake ransacked the Spanish Main, other seamen renewed the search for the Northwest Passage, inspired by Sir Humphrey Gilbert's *A discourse of a Discoverie for a New Passage to Cataia.* Three voyages by Martin Frobisher (1476–1578) and three by John Davis (1585–1587) discovered new lands (and Eskimos) to the west of Greenland, but no passage. The history of English colonization must begin with Gilbert and his half-brother, Sir Walter Raleigh. In 1578 Gilbert, who had long been a confidant of the queen, secured a royal patent to possess and hold "heathen and barbarous landes countries and territories not actually possessed of any Christian prince or people." Significantly the patent guaranteed to Englishmen and their descendents in such a colony the rights and privileges of Englishmen "in suche like ample manner and fourme as if they were borne and personally residaunte within our sed Realme of England." And laws had to be "agreable to the forme of the lawes and pollicies of England." Gilbert, after two false starts, finally set out with a colonial expedition in 1583, intending to settle near Narragansett Bay. He landed in Newfoundland, took possession of the land for Elizabeth by right of John Cabot's discovery, read his commission to some mystified fishermen on the shore, and after losing his largest vessels, because the season was far advanced he resolved to return home with the other two. On the last day of his life he was seen with a book in his hand—probably Sir Thomas More's *Utopia,* which inspired his last recorded words. From the deck of his pinnace *The Squirrel,* Gilbert shouted across to the other ship the haunting words: "We are as near to heaven by sea as by land." The following night his ship vanished and was never seen again.

RALEIGH'S LOST COLONY The next year, 1584, Raleigh persuaded the queen to renew Gilbert's patent in his own name, and sent out Capts. Philip Amadas and Arthur Barlowe with an English-naturalized Portuguese pilot, Simon Ferdinando, to reconnoiter a site. Sailing by way of the West Indies, they came to the Outer Banks of North Carolina, which Verrazzano had visited sixty years before, found an inlet to Pamlico Sound, and discovered Roanoke Island, where the soil seemed fruitful and the natives friendly. The Outer Banks afforded some protection, and rivers to the interior encouraged dreams of a route to the Pacific. In 1585 Raleigh's first colony went out under the command of Sir Richard Grenville with Ralph Lane as governor. Grenville went via the West Indies, plundering Spanish vessels to help defray the cost, and left the colonists on Roanoke Island before returning to England. They survived a mild winter, but the following June friction with the natives led to a fight, and when Francis

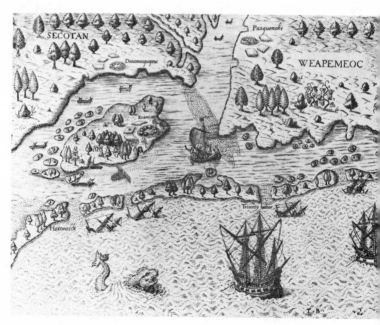

The English arrival at the Outer Banks. Roanoke Island is at left. The engraving is by Theodore de Bry, based on a drawing by John White. [Library of Congress]

Drake arrived to warn them of a threatened Spanish attack, the colonists decided to go home. Soon afterward Grenville returned, but not finding the colonists, left fifteen men behind to hold the fort and departed.

Raleigh immediately set about trying again, and in 1587 sponsored a colony of 117, including women and children, under Gov. John White. The plan was to pick up Grenville's men at Roanoke and proceed to Chesapeake Bay, since Roanoke was inaccessible to large vessels. But Simon Ferdinando, claiming the season was too far advanced—and probably eager to get on with plundering Spanish vessels—insisted that the colony remain at Roanoke. After a month in Roanoke, Governor White returned to England to get supplies, leaving behind his daughter Elinor and his grandaughter Virginia Dare, the first English child born in the New World. White, however, could not get back because of the war with Spain. He finally returned in 1590 to find the city of "Ralegh" abandoned and despoiled.

No trace of the colonists was ever found, nor any of the men Grenville left behind, and any theory as to their fate is only a wild surmise. Hostile Indians may have destroyed the colony, or hostile Spaniards—who certainly planned to attack—may have done the job. The only clue was one word carved on a doorpost, "Croatoan," the name of a friendly tribe of Indians and also of their island, the present Ocracoke. A romantic legend later developed that the colonists joined the Croatan Indians, finally were absorbed by them, and were among the ancestors of the present Lumbee Indians of Robeson County, North Carolina. There is no solid evidence for this, and while some may have gone south, the main body of colonists appears to have gone north to the southern shores of the Chesapeake Bay, as they had talked of doing, and lived there for some years until killed by Powhatan. But none of them was ever seen again. Unless some remnant of the Lost Colony did survive in the woods, there was still not a single Englishman in North America when Queen Elizabeth died in 1603.

FURTHER READING

Many scholars have at one time or another looked at pre-Columbian Amerindian life in the Western Hemisphere. Probably the most readable and comprehensive of the anthropological accounts is Harold E. Driver's *Indians of North America* (1970).° Alfred L.

° These books are available in paperback editions.

Kroeber's *Cultural and Natural Areas of Native North America* (1939) remains a fundamental guide for the dynamics of Indian culture. A good recent historical treatment is Alvin M. Joseph, Jr.'s *The Indian Heritage of America* (1968). A more topical use of the same material is Wilcomb E. Washburn's *The Indian In America* (1975).° Also useful is the ancient text by James Adair, *History of the American Indians, Particularly Those Nations Adjoining to the Mississippi, East and West Florida, Georgia, South and North Carolina, and Virginia* (1755, 1968).

Several works explore the theme of cultural conflict. Henry Warner Bowden's *American Indians and Christian Missions: Studies in Cultural Conflict* (1981) is short and interpretative. More theoretical is Richard Drinnon's *Facing West: The Metaphysics of Indian Hating and Empire Building* (1980).° Karen O. Kupperman's *Settling with the Indian: The Meeting of English and Indian Cultures in America, 1580–1640* (1980), stresses the racist nature of the conflict. Charles Gibson's *The Aztecs under Spanish Rule* (1964)° examines similar developments in Latin America, while Nathan Wachtel's *The Vision of the Vanquished* (1977) looks at the Indian point of view.

For evidence that Viking explorers came to North America before Columbus, see Frederick J. Pohl's *The Viking Settlements of North America* (1972) and Paul H. Chapman's *The Norse Discovery of America* (1981).° Michael A. Musmano's *Columbus Was First* (1966) counters such evidence. Interpretations of the conflicting evidence about early cultural contacts is presented in Carroll L. Riley et al. (eds.), *Man across the Sea: Problems of Pre-Columbian Contacts* (1971).

A number of fine overviews of European exploration are available. The most comprehensive are two volumes by Samuel E. Morison, *The European Discovery of America: The Northern Voyages*, A.D. 500–1600 (1971), and *The Southern Voyages*, A.D. 500–1600 (1974). Briefer, but a good outline of the forces of exploration, is John H. Parry's *The Age of Reconnaisance* (1963).° More specific are David B. Quinn's *North America from Earliest Discovery to First Settlements* (1977), John H. Parry's *The Spanish Seaborne Empire* (1966), and Charles R. Boxer's *The Portuguese Seaborne Empire* (1969). Scholarship on Columbus is best handled by Samuel E. Morison's *Columbus, Admiral of the Sea* (2 vols., 1942),° which was condensed into *Christopher Columbus, Mariner* (1956).°

The structure and form of European conquest and settlement is examined in Clarence H. Haring's *The Spanish Empire in America* (1947), which stresses the institutional framework of imperial government, and James Long's *Conquest and Commerce: Spain and England in the Americas* (1975), which compares the process of colonization of the two nations. See also William J. Eccles's *France in America* (1972)° and Charles Gipson's *Spain in America* (1966).° The most comprehensive view of how European mercantile tendencies led to "modernization" of the rest of the world is presented in Louis Hartz's *The Founding of New Society: Studies in the History of the United States, Latin America, South Africa, Canada, and Australia* (1964).

The English efforts which led to the Roanoke Island colony are documented in two books by David B. Quinn: *Raleigh and the British Empire*

(1947), and the aforementioned *England and the Discovery of America* (1974). For background on the motives for English exploration and settlement, consult Alfred L. Rowse's *The Expansion of Elizabethan England* (1955), John Phillips Kenyon's *Stuart England* (1978), and Carl Bridenbaugh's *Vexed and Troubled Englishmen, 1590–1642* (1968).° The link between English settlements like Roanoke and the Irish experience is explored in David B. Quinn's *The Elizabethans and the Irish* (1966). Robert R. Reynolds looks at the economic motivations which led to explorations in *Europe Emerges: Transition toward an Industrial World-Wide Society, 600–1750* (1961).

2

ENGLAND AND HER COLONIES

The England which Elizabeth bequeathed to her successor, like
the colonies it would plant, was a unique blend of elements. The
language and the people themselves mixed Germanic and Latin
ingredients. The Anglican church mixed Protestant theology and
Catholic forms in a way unknown on the continent. And the
growth of royal power paradoxically had been linked with the
rise of English liberties, in which even Tudor monarchs took
pride. In the course of their history the English people have displayed a genius for "muddling through," a gift for the pragmatic
compromise that defied logic but in the light of experience somehow worked.

THE ENGLISH BACKGROUND

Set off from the continent by the English Channel, that
"moat defensive to the house" in Shakespeare's words, England
had safe frontiers after the union of the English and Scottish
crowns in 1603. In her comparative isolation, England developed institutions to which the continent had few parallels, except perhaps among the Dutch. By 1600 the decline of feudal
practices was far advanced. The great nobles, decimated by the
Wars of the Roses, had been brought to heel by Tudor monarchs
and their ranks filled with men loyal to the crown. In fact the only
nobles left, strictly speaking, were those few peers of the realm
who sat in the House of Lords. All others were commoners, and
among their ranks the aristocratic pecking order ran through a
great class of landholding squires, distinguished mainly by their
wealth and bearing the simple titles of "esquires" and "gentlemen," as did many well-to-do townsmen. They in turn mingled

James I, the successor to Queen Elizabeth and the first of England's Stuart kings. [National Portrait Gallery, London]

IACOBVS D. G. MAGNÆ BRITANNIÆ FRANCIÆ
SCOTIÆ ET HYBERNIÆ REX ANNO M.D.C.X.X.I

freely and often intermarried with the classes of yeomen (small freehold farmers) and merchants.

ENGLISH LIBERTIES   It was to these middle classes that the Tudors looked for support and, for want of bureaucrats or a standing army, for local government. Chief reliance in the English counties was on the country gentlemen, who usually served without pay. Government therefore allowed a large measure of local initiative. Self-rule in the counties and towns became a habit—one that, along with the offices of justice of the peace and sheriff, English colonists took along as part of their cultural baggage.

Even the Tudors, who acted as autocrats, preserved the forms of constitutional procedure. In the making of laws the king's subjects consented through representatives in the House of Commons. By custom and practice the principle was established that the king taxed his subjects only with the consent of Parliament. And by its control of the purse strings Parliament would draw other strands of power into its hands. This structure of habit broadened down from precedent to precedent to form a constitution that was not written in one place, or for that matter, not fully written down at all. The *Magna Carta* of 1215, for instance, had been a statement of privileges wrested by certain nobles from the king, but it became part of a broader tradition that the people as a whole had rights which even the king could not violate.

A further buttress to English liberty was the great body of common law, which had developed since the twelfth century in royal courts established to check the arbitrary caprice of local nobles. Without laws to cover every detail, judges had to exercise their own ideas of fairness in settling disputes. Decisions once made became precedents for later decisions, and over the years a body of judge-made law developed, the outgrowth more of experience than of abstract logic. Through the courts the principle evolved that a subject could be arrested or his goods seized only upon a warrant issued by a court, and that he was entitled to a trial by a jury of his peers (his equals) in accordance with established rules of evidence.

ENGLISH ENTERPRISE   The liberties of Englishmen inspired a certain initiative and vigor of which prosperity and empire were born. The ranks of entrepreneurs and adventurers were constantly replenished by the young sons of the squirearchy, cut off from the estate which the oldest son inherited by the law of primogeniture (or first born). The growth of commerce featured at first the growth of the trade in woolen cloth built up after 1400 by the Company of Merchant Adventurers, which greatly expanded markets on the continent, working chiefly through Antwerp. The company was the prototype of the regulated company, actually a trade association of merchants who sold on their own accounts under the regulation of the company, which secured markets and privileges.

With time, however, investors formed joint-stock companies, ancestors of the modern corporation, in which stockholders shared the risks and profits, sometimes in a single venture but more and more on a permanent basis. When the cloth market became saturated in the mid-1500s, English merchants began to scan broader horizons for new outlets, new goods, new patterns of trade, and found themselves incurring greater risks. Some of the larger companies managed to get royal charters which entitled them to monopolies in certain areas and even governmental powers in their outposts: the Muscovy Company (1555), the Levant Company (1581), the Barbary Company (1585), the Guinea Company (1588), and the East India Company (1600). Companies like these would become the first instruments of colonization.

For all the vaunted glories of English liberty and enterprise, it was not the best of times for the common people of the realm. For more than two centuries serfdom had been on the way to extinction, as the feudal duties of serfs were commuted into rents. But while tenancy gave a degree of independence, it also gave landlords the ability to increase demands and, as the trade in woolen products grew, to enclose farmlands and evict the tenants in favor of sheep. The enclosure movement of the sixteenth century thus gave rise to the great numbers of sturdy beggars and rogues who people the literature of Elizabethan times and gained immortality in Mother Goose: "Hark, hark, the dogs do bark. The beggars have come to town." The problem was met only in part by Elizabethan poor laws which obligated each parish to care for its own (a practice passed on to the colonies), and the needs of this displaced population became another argument for colonial expansion—the more because the cloth market weakened and the nation's economy sought other outlets.

THE ENGLISH CIVIL WAR With the death of Elizabeth the Tudor line ran out and the throne fell to the first of the Stuarts, whose dynasty spanned most of the seventeenth century, a turbulent time during which, despite many distractions at home, the English planted an overseas empire. In 1603 James VI of Scotland, son of the ill-fated Mary, Queen of Scots, and great-great-grandson of Henry VII, became James I of England—as Elizabeth had planned. A man of ponderous erudition, James fully earned his reputation as the "wisest fool in all Christendom." He lectured Englishmen on every topic but remained blind to English traditions and sensibilities. Where the Tudors had wielded absolute power through constitutional forms, the learned James demanded a more consistent logic and advanced at every chance the theory of divine right, beginning with a lecture to his first Parliament. Where the Puritans hoped to find a Presbyterian ally, they found instead a testy autocrat. "No bishop, no king," he told them, and promised to "harry them out of the land." He even offended Anglicans by sensibly deciding to end Elizabeth's war with Catholic Spain—and old privateers by suppressing what had now become piracy.

Charles I, who succeeded his father in 1625, proved even more stubborn about royal prerogative, ruled without Parliament from 1628 to 1640, and levied taxes by royal decree. The archbishop of Canterbury, William Laud, directed a systematic persecution of Puritans but finally overreached himself when he tried to impose Anglican worship on Presbyterian Scots. In 1638 Scotland rose in revolt and in 1640 Charles called Parliament to

Charles I. [The Louvre, Paris]

rally support and raise money. The "Long Parliament" (new elections had been delayed now for twenty years) impeached Laud instead, condemned to death the king's chief minister, the earl of Strafford, and abolished the "prerogative courts" established by the crown. In 1642, when the king tried to arrest five members of Parliament, civil war broke out between the "Roundheads" who supported Parliament and the "Cavaliers" who supported the king.

In 1646 royalist resistance collapsed and parliamentary forces captured the king. Parliament, however, could not agree on a permanent settlement. A dispute arose between Presbyterians and Independents (who preferred a congregational church government), and in 1648 the New Model Army purged the Presbyterians, leaving a "Rump Parliament" which then instigated the trial and execution of Charles I on charges of treason.

Oliver Cromwell, commander of the army, became in effect a

military dictator, ruling first through a council chosen by Parliament (the Commonwealth) and after forcible dissolution of Parliament as Lord Protector (the Protectorate). Cromwell extended religious toleration to all except Catholics and Anglicans, but his arbitrary governance and his moralistic codes made the regime more and more unpopular. When, after his death in 1658, his son proved too weak to carry on, the army once again took control, permitted new elections for Parliament, and supported the restoration of the monarchy under Charles II, son of the martyred king, in 1660.

Charles accepted as terms of the Restoration settlement the principle that he must rule jointly with Parliament, and managed by tact or shrewd maneuvering to hold his throne. His younger brother, the duke of York, was less flexible. Succeeding as James II in 1685, he openly avowed Catholicism and assumed the same unyielding stance as the first two Stuarts. Englishmen could bear it so long as they expected one of his Protestant daughters, Mary or Anne, to succeed him, but in 1688 the birth of a son who would be reared a Catholic finally brought matters to a crisis. Leaders of Parliament invited Mary and her husband William of Orange, a Dutch prince, to assume the throne jointly, and James fled the country.

By this "Glorious Revolution" Parliament finally established its independence of royal control. Under the Bill of Rights, in 1689, William and Mary gave up the prerogatives of suspending laws, erecting special courts, keeping a standing army, or levying taxes except by Parliament's consent. They further agreed to frequent sessions and freedom of speech in Parliament, freedom of petition to the crown, and restrictions against excessive bail and cruel and unusual punishments. Under the Toleration Act of 1689 a degree of freedom of worship was extended to all Christians except Catholics and Unitarians, although dissenters from the established church still had few political rights. In 1701 the Act of Settlement ensured a Protestant succession through Queen Anne (1702–1727). And by the Act of Union in 1707 England and Scotland became the United Kingdom of Great Britain.

SETTLING THE CHESAPEAKE

During these eventful years all but one of the thirteen North American colonies and several more in the islands of the Caribbean had their start. After the ill-fated efforts of Gilbert and Raleigh, the joint-stock company of merchants and gentlemen became the chief vehicle of colonization. In 1606 James I

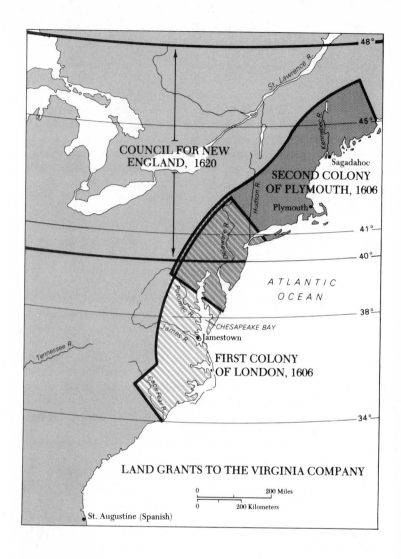

COUNCIL FOR NEW
ENGLAND, 1620

SECOND COLONY
OF PLYMOUTH, 1606

Sagadahoc

Plymouth

ATLANTIC
OCEAN

CHESAPEAKE BAY

Jamestown

FIRST COLONY
OF LONDON, 1606

LAND GRANTS TO THE VIRGINIA COMPANY

0   200 Miles

0   200 Kilometers

St. Augustine (Spanish)

St. Lawrence R.

Kennebec R.

Hudson R.

Delaware R.

Potomac R.

James R.

Tennessee R.

Cape Fear R.

48°

45°

41°

40°

38°

34°

chartered a Virginia Company with two divisions, the First Colony of London and the Second Colony of Plymouth. The London group could plant a settlement between the Thirty-fourth and Thirty-eighth Parallels, the Plymouth group between the Forty-first and Forty-fifth Parallels, and either between the Thirty-eighth and Forty-first Parallels, provided they kept a hundred miles apart. The stockholders expected a potential return from gold and other minerals; products, such as wine, citrus fruits, and olive oil, to free England from dependence on Spain; trade with the Indians; pitch, tar, potash, and other forest products needed for naval stores; and perhaps a passage to Cathay. Some investors dreamed of finding another Aztec or Inca Empire, but there were in fact relatively few Indians in eastern North America; some thought of a pirate base for plundering Spanish treasure ships. Few if any foresaw what the first English colony would actually become: a place to grow tobacco.

From the outset the pattern of English colonization would diverge from the Spanish. For one thing the English had a different model in their experience. The Spanish had retaken their homeland from the Moors and in the process worked out patterns of colonization later used in America. The English, after four centuries of sporadic intervention in Ireland, proceeded under Elizabeth to conquer the Irish by military force. While the interest in America was growing, the English were already involved in planting settlements, or "plantations" in Ireland. Within their own pale (or limit) of settlement the English set about reconstructing their familiar way of life insofar as possible. The term "wild Irish," which today seems more comic than serious, was then taken in dead earnest. The English went to Ireland, one historian said, with "a preconceived idea of a barbaric society and they merely tailored the Irishman to fit this ideological straitjacket." In English eyes, Irish Catholicism was mere paganism. What the English saw as a "savage nation" that lived "like beastes" could therefore be subjected without compunction. The same pattern would apply to the Indians of North America. In America, moreover, the English settled along the Atlantic seaboard, where the native populations were relatively sparse. There was no Aztec or Inca Empire to conquer and rule. Even without the example of Ireland, the colonists would have no alternative to setting up their own "pales" of settlement.

VIRGINIA In August 1607 the Plymouth Company landed about 100 men at Sagadahoc on the Kennebec River in Maine, but abandoned the site after a hard winter of Indian hostility, bungling, and short supplies. Meanwhile the London Company, under the vigorous lead of Sir Thomas Smith, a prominent merchant, had already planted the first permanent colony in Virginia. On December 20, 1606, three ships borrowed from the Muscovy Company—the *Susan Constant,* the *Godspeed,* and the *Discovery*—sailed out from the Thames River with about 144 men. On May 6, 1607, having traveled south via the West Indies to catch the trade winds, they sighted the capes of Chesapeake Bay. Following instructions, they chose a river with a northwest bend—in hope of a passage to Cathay—and settled about 100 miles from the sea to hide from marauding Spaniards. The river

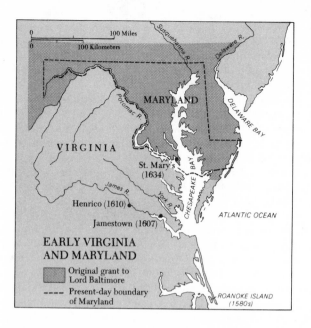

MARYLAND

VIRGINIA

St. Mary's
(1634)

Henrico (1610)

Jamestown (1607)

**EARLY VIRGINIA
AND MARYLAND**

Original grant to
Lord Baltimore

---- Present-day boundary
of Maryland

ATLANTIC OCEAN

*ROANOKE ISLAND
(1580s)*

100 Miles

100 Kilometers

they called the James, and the settlement, Jamestown. Contrary
to instructions to choose an island, they settled on a peninsula
where the 105 survivors could see any approach from downstream and defend a narrow neck of land against the Indians.
They were defenseless, however, from the mosquitoes of the
neighboring swamps.

The colonists set about building a fort, thatched huts, a store-
house, and a church. Capt. Christopher Newport explored the
James up to the falls near present Richmond, where he reached
the limits of tribes dominated by Powhatan, and then sailed
home, leaving the colonists perched on the edge of the wilderness. The colonists set to planting, but they were either townsmen unfamiliar with farming or, fully two-thirds of them,
"gentleman" adventurers who scorned manual labor. Ignorant of
woodlore, they could not exploit the abundant game and fish.
Supplies from England were undependable, although Newport
returned twice in 1608, and only John Smith's leadership and
their trade with the Indians, who taught them to grow maize, enabled them to survive.

The Indians of the region were loosely organized in what
Thomas Jefferson later called the "Powhatan Confederacy."
Neither that nor the title "emperor" which the English gave to
their *weroance* accurately conveys the structure of their society.
Powhatan, chief of the Pamunkey tribe, had merely extended an
insecure hegemony over some thirty tribes in the coastal area.

Despite occasional clashes with the colonists, the Indians adopted a stance of watchful waiting. The reason probably was that Powhatan at first hoped for trade and alliance with new-comers who might serve his purposes, and realized too late their growing design to possess the country.

The colonists, as it happened, had more than a match for Pow-hatan in Capt. John Smith, a man of humble origins but rare powers, a soldier of fortune whose tales of exploits in eastern Europe are so extravagant as to strain belief, except that they stand up wherever they can be checked against other evidence. When the colonists opened their sealed instructions, they found that Smith, who had quarreled with the expedition's leaders and had been clapped into chains on board ship, was to be a member of the governing council. The council was at first beset by dis-agreement and vacillation, but by force of will and ability Smith was soon in charge. With the colonists on the verge of starvation, he imposed discipline, forced all to work on pain of expulsion, bargained with the Indians, fought off a season of gold fever, ex-plored and mapped the Chesapeake region. Despite his efforts, however, only 53 of the 120 were alive at the end of 1608.

In 1609 the Virginia Company moved to reinforce the James-town colony. A new charter redefined the colony's boundaries

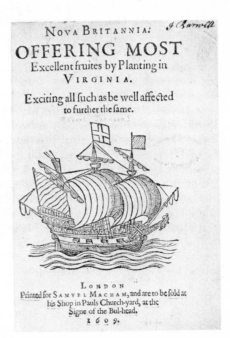

One of the Virginia Company's attempts to attract settlers to Jamestown. [Library of Congress]

NOVA BRITANNIA:

OFFERING MOST
Excellent fruites by Planting in
VIRGINIA.

Exciting all such as be well affected
to further the same.

LONDON
Printed for SAMVEL MACHAM, and are to be sold at
his Shop in Pauls Church-yard, at the
Signe of the Bul-head.
1609.

and replaced the largely ineffective council with an all-powerful governor whose council was only advisory. In a dramatic promotion the company lured new subscribers from all ranks of society and attracted new settlers with the promise of free land after seven years of labor. The company in effect had given up hope of prospering except through the sale of lands which would rise in value as the colony grew. The governor, the noble Lord De La Warr (Delaware), sent as interim governor Sir Thomas Gates. In May 1609 Gates set out with a fleet of nine vessels and about 500 passengers and crew. On the way Gates was shipwrecked on Bermuda, where he and the other survivors wintered in comparative ease, subsisting on fish, fowl, and wild pigs. (Their story was transformed by William Shakespeare into his play *The Tempest*.)

Part of the fleet did reach Jamestown, however, and deposited some 400 settlers, who overwhelmed the remnant of about 80. These leaderless settlers, said one observer, included "many unruly gallants packed thether by their friends to escape il destinies." But their destinies were "il" indeed. All chance that John Smith might control things was lost when he suffered a gunpowder burn and sailed back to England in October 1609. The consequence was anarchy and the "starving time" of the winter of 1609–1610, during which most of the colonists, weakened by hunger, fell prey to pestilence. By May, when Gates and his companions made their way to Jamestown on two small ships painfully built in Bermuda, only about 60 remained alive. All poultry and livestock (including horses) had been eaten, and one man was even said to have dined on his wife. Jamestown was falling into ruins, the Indians had turned hostile, and the decision was made to give it up.

In June 1610, as the colonists made their way down the river, Lord Delaware providentially arrived with three ships and 150 men, whereupon instead of leaving Virginia, the colonists returned to Jamestown and hived off the first new settlements upstream at Henrico (Richmond) and two more downstream near the mouth of the river. It was a critical turning point for the colony, whose survival required a combination of stern measures and not a little luck. Effective leadership came with Delaware, and after his departure, under his deputies. In 1611 Thomas Gates took charge and established a strict system of *Lawes Divine, Moral, and Martiall,* inaccurately called "Dale's Code," after Thomas Dale who enforced them as marshal. Severe even by the standards of a ruthless age, the code enforced a militaristic discipline needed for survival.

Under Governors Dale (1614–1616) and Samuel Argall

(1617–1618) the colony limped along until it gradually found a reason for being: tobacco. In 1612 John Rolfe had begun to experiment with the harsh and biting Virginia tobacco. Eventually he got hold of some seed for the more savory Spanish varieties, and by 1616 the weed had become an export staple. Meanwhile Rolfe had made another contribution to stability by marrying Pocahontas, the daughter of Powhatan. Pocahontas had been a familiar figure in the streets of Jamestown almost from the beginning. In 1607, then only twelve, she figured in perhaps the best-known story of the settlement, the rescue of John Smith, who attributed to his own charm and English superiority what was perhaps the climax to a ritual threat of execution, a bit of play-acting to impress Smith with Powhatan's authority. In 1613, however, on a foray to extort corn from the Indians, Dale's men had captured Pocahontas and held her for ransom. To fend off the crisis, Rolfe proposed marriage to Pocahontas, Powhatan agreed, and a wary peace ensued. Distinguished Virginians still boast of their descent from the Indian "princess."

Sir Edwin Sandys, a prominent member of Parliament, replaced Thomas Smith as head of the company in 1618 and set about a series of reforms. First of all he inaugurated a new headright policy. Anybody who bought a share in the company at $12\frac{1}{2}$ shillings, or anybody who could transport himself to Virginia, could have fifty acres, and fifty more for any servants he might send or bring. The following year, 1619, was memorable in several ways. The company now relaxed the tight regimen of the *Lawes* and promised that the settlers should have the "rights of Englishmen," including a representative assembly. A new governor, Sir George Yeardley, arrived with instructions to put the new order into effect, and on July 30, 1619, the first General Assembly of Virginia, including the governor, six councilors, and twenty-two burgesses, met in the church at Jamestown and deliberated for five days, "sweating & stewing, and battling flies and mosquitoes." It was an eventful year in two other respects. The promoters also saw a need to send out wives for the men who, Sir Edwin Sandys noted, "By defect thereof (as is credibly reported) stay there but to get something and then return for England." During 1619 a ship arrived with ninety young women, to be sold to likely husbands of their own choice for the cost of transportation (about 125 pounds of tobacco). And a Dutch man-of-war, according to an ominous note in John Rolfe's diary, stopped by and dropped off "20 Negars," the first blacks known to have reached English America. It would be another year before the fabled *Mayflower* came.

THE INCONVENIENCIES

THAT HAVE HAPPENED TO SOME PER-
SONS WHICH HAVE TRANSPORTED THEMSELUES

from *England* to *Virginia*, vvithout prouisions necessary to sustaine themselues, hath
greatly hindred the Progresse of that noble Plantation: For prevention of the like disorders
heereafter, that no man suffer, either through ignorance or misinformation; it is thought requisite to publish this short declaration: wherein is contained a particular of such neces-
saries, as either priuate families or single persons shall haue cause to furnish themselues with, for their better
support at their first landing in *Virginia*; whereby also greater numbers may receiue in part,
directions how to prouide themselues.

Apparrell.

	li.	s.	d.
One Monmouth Cap	00	01	10
Three falling bands		01	03
Three shirts		07	06
One waste-coate		02	02
One suite of Canuase		07	06
One suite of Frize		10	00
One suite of Cloth		15	00
Three paire of Irish stockins		04	—
Foure paire of shooes		08	08
One paire of garters		00	10
One doozen of points		00	03
One paire of Canuase sheets		08	00
Seuen ells of Canuase, to make a bed and boulster, to be filled in *Virginia* 8 s.			
One Rug for a bed 8. s. which with the bed seruing for two men, halle is	08	00	
Fiue ells coorse Canuase, to make a bed at Sea for two men, so besiilled with straw, iiij.s.			
One coorse Rug at Sea for two men, will cost vj.s. is for one	05	00	
	04	00	00

Apparrell for one man, and so after the rate for more.

Tooles.

	li.	s.	d.
Fiue broad howes at 2.s. a piece		10	—
Fiue narrow howes at 16.d. a piece		06	08
Two broad Axes at 3.s.8.d. a piece		07	04
Fiue felling Axes at 18.d. a piece		07	06
Two steele hand sawes at 16.d. a piece		02	08
Two two-hand sawes at 5. s. a piece		10	—
One whip-saw, set and filed with box, file, and wrest		10	—
Two hammers 12.d. a piece		02	00
Three shouels 18.d. a piece		04	06
Two spades at 18.d. a piece		03	—
Two augers 6.d. a piece		01	00
Sixe chissels 6.d. a piece		03	00
Two percers stocked 4.d. a piece		00	08
Three gimlets 2.d. a piece		00	06
Two hatchets 21.d. a piece		03	06
Two frowes to cleaue pale 18.d.		03	00
Two hand-bills 20. a piece		03	04
One grindlestone 4.s.		04	00
Nailes of all sorts to the value of		02	00
Two Pickaxes		03	—
	06	02	08

For a family of 6. persons and so after the rate for more.

Victuall.

	li.	s.	d.
Eight bushels of Meale	02	00	00
Two bushels of peafe at 3.s.		06	00
Two bushels of Oatemeale 4.s. 6.d.		09	00
One gallon of *Aquauitae*		02	06
One gallon of Oyle		03	06
Two gallons of Vineger 1. s.		02	00
	03	03	00

For a whole yeere for one man, and so for more after the rate.

Houshold Implements.

	li.	s.	d.
One Iron Pot		00	07
One kettle		06	—
One large frying pan		02	06
One gridiron		01	06
Two skillets		05	—
One spit		02	—
Platters, dishes, spoones of wood		04	—
	01	08	00

For a family of 6. persons, and so for more or lesse after the rate.

Armes.

	li.	s.	d.
One Armour compleat, light		17	00
One long Peece, fiue foot or fiue and a halfe, neere Musket bore	01	02	—
One sword		05	—
One belt		01	—
One bandaleere		01	06
Twenty pound of powder		18	00
Sixty pound of shot or lead, Pistoll and Goose shot		05	00
	03	09	06

For one man, but if halfe of your men haue armour it is sufficient so that all haue Peeces and swords.

	li.	s.	d.
For Suger, Spice, and fruit, and at Sea for 6.men	00	12	06
So the full charge of Apparrell, Victuall, Armes, Tooles, and houshold stuffe, and after this rate for each person, will amount vnto about the summe of	13	10	—
The passage of each man is	06	00	—
The fraight of these prouisions for a man, will bee about halfe a Tun, which is	01	10	—
So the whole charge will amount to about	20	00	00

Nets, hookes, lines, and a tent must be added, if the number of people be greater, as also some hire, &c.
And this is the vsuall proportion that the Virginia Company doe bestow vpon their Tenants which they send.

Whosoeuer transports himselfe or any other at his owne charge vnto *Virginia*, shall for each person so transported before Midsummer 1625. haue to him and his heires for euer fifty Acres of Land vpon a first, and fifty Acres vpon a second diuision.

Imprinted at London by FELIX KYNGSTON. 1622.

The Virginia Company recommended that prospective settlers bring to America these "provisions necessary to sustain themselves." At bottom is the company's new headright policy. [New York Public Library]

Despite its successes the company again fell upon evil days. Sandys quarreled with other leaders in the company, and in 1622 Powhatan's brother and successor, Opechancanough, led a concerted uprising which killed 347, including John Rolfe. Some 14,000 people had migrated to the colony since 1607, but the population in 1624 stood at a precarious 1,132. Despite the broad initial achievements of the company, after about 1617 a handful of insiders had engrossed large estates and began to monopolize the indentured workers. In a tobacco boom of those years some made fortunes, but most of the thousands sent out died before they could prove themselves. At the behest of Sandys's opponents, the king appointed a commission to investigate, and on its recommendation a court dissolved the company. Virginia became a royal colony.

The king did not renew instructions for an assembly, but his governors found it impossible to rule the troublesome Virginians without one, and annual assemblies met after 1629, although not recognized by the crown for another ten years. After 1622, relations with the Powhatan Confederates continued in a state of what the governor's council called "perpetual enmity" until the aging Opechancanough staged another concerted attack in 1644. The English suffered as many casualties as they had twenty-two years before, but put down the uprising with such ferocity that nothing quite like it happened again.

Sir William Berkeley, who arrived as governor in 1642, presided over the colony's growth for most of the next thirty-four years. The brawling populace of men on the make over which he held sway was a far cry from the cultivated gentry of the next century. But among them were the Byrds, Carters, Masons, and Randolphs who made the fortunes that nurtured the celebrated aristocrats of later generations.

MARYLAND In 1634, ten years after Virginia became a royal colony, a neighboring settlement appeared on the northern shores of Chesapeake Bay, the first proprietary colony, granted to Lord Baltimore by Charles I and named Maryland in honor of Queen Henrietta Maria. Sir George Calvert, the first Lord Baltimore, had announced in 1625 his conversion to Catholicism and sought the colony as a refuge for English Catholics who were subjected to discriminations at home. He had in fact undertaken to colonize Newfoundland in 1623 under a previous grant, but that colony was abandoned after a successful clash with the French followed by the severe winter of 1628–1629. Calvert had tried Virginia too. In October 1629 he had landed with his family and some followers at Jamestown, but was ordered to leave because he refused to take the Oaths of Allegiance and Supremacy to the monarch.

Nevertheless he kept the favor of King Charles and sought a charter in the region, which was issued in 1632 after his death. His son, Ceilius Calvert, the second Lord Baltimore, actually founded the colony. The charter, which set a precedent for later proprietary grants, gave the recipient the same powers bestowed upon the bishop of Durham in the past. In a region near the Scottish border, the warlike bishop had ruled almost as an independent monarch, but the charter specified that the laws must be in accordance with those of England. References to religion were vague except for a mention that chapels should be established according to the ecclesiastical law of England.

In 1634 Calvert planted the first settlement at St. Mary's on a small stream near the mouth of the Potomac. St. Mary's in fact was already there, a native settlement purchased from friendly Indians along with the cleared fields around it. Calvert brought Catholic gentlemen as landholders, but a majority of the servants from the beginning were Protestants. The charter gave Calvert power to make laws with the consent of the freemen (all property holders). The first legislative assembly met in 1635, and divided into two houses in 1650, with governor and council sitting separately. This was instigated by the predominantly Protestant freemen—largely servants who had become landholders, or immigrants from Virginia. The charter also empowered the proprietor to grant manorial estates, and Maryland had some sixty before 1676, but the Lords Baltimore soon found that to draw settlers they had to offer farms. Because of their flexibility, the Calverts bent rather than broke in the prevailing winds. Ousted from the proprietorship only for brief periods under Cromwell and William III, they continued even then to hold their property rights and coined a fortune in America before the end of the colonial period. The colony was meant to rely on mixed farming, but its fortunes, like those of Virginia, soon came to depend on tobacco.

SETTLING NEW ENGLAND

The Virginia Company of Plymouth never got back to colonization after the Sagadahoc failure in 1607, although it did bestir itself to hire John Smith as an explorer. After his return from a visit in 1614 Smith published *A Description of New England* (1616) and thus named the region. Having watched the London Company's transition from commerce to real estate, the leader of the Plymouth Company, Sir Ferdinando Gorges, reorganized his moribund enterprise into the Council for New England (1620), which had the right to issue land grants between the Fortieth and Forty-eighth Parallels.

PLYMOUTH The first permanent settlers landed in New England by no design of the council, which had some notion of creating vast feudal domains for its members. In fact they landed there by no design of their own—at least none that they acknowledged.

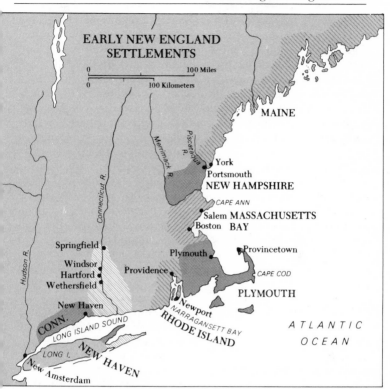

EARLY NEW ENGLAND
SETTLEMENTS

0   100 Miles

0   100 Kilometers

MAINE

Merrimack R.

Piscataqua R.

Connecticut R.

York
Portsmouth
NEW HAMPSHIRE

CAPE ANN

Salem MASSACHUSETTS
Boston BAY

Hudson R.

Springfield

Windsor
Hartford
Wethersfield

Plymouth

Providence

Provincetown

CAPE COD

PLYMOUTH

New Haven

CONN.

LONG ISLAND SOUND

Newport
NARRAGANSETT BAY
RHODE ISLAND

NEW HAVEN

LONG I.

New Amsterdam

ATLANTIC
OCEAN

They meant to go to Virginia, they said. The Pilgrims who established Plymouth colony belonged to the most extreme and uncompromising sect of Puritans, the Separatists, who had severed all ties with the Church of England. They stemmed from a congregation established in 1602 at Scrooby in eastern England, members of which had slipped away to Holland in 1607 to escape persecution. The Calvinistic Dutch granted them asylum and toleration, but restricted them mainly to unskilled labor. After ten years in Leyden they had wearied of the struggle. Watching their children gradually turn into Dutchmen, drifting away to become sailors, soldiers, or worse, so that "their posterity would be in danger to degenerate and be corrupted," they longed for English ways and the English flag. If they could not have them at home, perhaps they might transplant them to the New World. King James would not promise outright toleration if they set up a colony, but did agree to leave them alone, or as he put it, to "connive at them."

The Leyden group got the support of London merchants, led by Thomas Weston, who secured a land patent from the Virginia Company and set up a joint-stock company. In July 1620 a group of thirty-five Pilgrims led by William Bradford left Leyden on the *Speedwell.* At Southampton, England, a larger ship, the *Mayflower,* and a larger group of colonists joined them. At Plymouth, however, they had to abandon the leaky *Speedwell* and in September they crammed the *Mayflower* with their party of 101, both "saints" and "strangers," the latter including John Alden, a cooper, and Miles Standish, a soldier hired to organize their defenses. A stormy voyage led them in November to Cape Cod, far north of Virginia. Heading south, they encountered rough waters and turned back to seek safety at Provincetown. "Being thus arrived at safe harbor, and brought safe to land," William Bradford wrote in his history, *Of Plymouth Plantation,* "they fell upon their knees and blessed the God of Heaven who had brought them over the vast and furious ocean, and delivered them from all the perils thereof, again to set their feet on the firm and stable earth, their proper element." Exploring parties then scouted Cape Cod Bay and hit upon a place John Smith had called Plymouth for their settlement. Since they were outside the jurisdiction of any organized government, forty-one of the Pilgrim Fathers entered into a formal agreement to abide by laws made by leaders of their own choosing—the Mayflower Compact of November 21, 1620.

On December 26 the *Mayflower* reached Plymouth harbor and stayed there until April to give shelter and support while the Pilgrims raised and occupied their dwellings amid the winter snows. Nearly half the colonists died of exposure and disease, but friendly relations with the neighboring Wampanoag Indians proved their salvation. In March 1621 an Indian named Samoset walked into the settlement and later introduced Squanto, who spoke English and showed the colonists how to grow maize. A few years earlier Squanto had been kidnapped aboard a passing English ship and sold into slavery in Spain, whence he had somehow found his way back to England and, aboard a trading ship, back home, where he found himself to be the sole survivor of the Pawtuxet tribe, which had been wiped out by a pestilence in 1617. By autumn the Pilgrims had a bumper crop of corn, a flourishing fur trade, and a supply of lumber for shipment. To celebrate they held a harvest feast in company with Chief Massasoit and the Wampanoags. But after the ship *Fortune* arrived with thirty-five new colonists, the enlarged group again faced hunger before a food supply arrived in the spring. To make matters worse, on the way home the *Fortune* lost its cargo of furs and lumber to a French privateer.

But the colony soon stabilized. In 1621 it got a land patent from the Council for New England. Two years later it gave up its original communal economy to the extent that each settler was to provide for his family from his own land. A group of settlers bought out the sponsoring merchants in 1626 and promised to pay the purchase price in nine annual installments, although final settlement was delayed until 1648. In 1630 Governor Bradford secured a new title, the "Bradford Patent," from the Council for New England, which confirmed possession and defined the boundaries more clearly.

Throughout its separate existence, until absorbed into Massachusetts in 1691, the Plymouth colony remained in the anomalous position of holding a land grant but no charter of government from any English authority. The government grew instead out of the Mayflower Compact, which was neither exactly a constitution nor a precedent for later constitutions, but rather the obvious recourse of a group who had made a covenant (or agreement) to form a church and who believed that God had made a covenant with men to provide a way to salvation. Thus the civil government grew naturally out of the church government, and the members of each were identical at the start. The signers of the compact at first met as the General Court, which chose the governor and his assistants (or council). Later others were admitted as members, or "freemen," but only church members were eligible. Eventually, as the colony grew, the General Court became in 1639 a body of representatives from the various towns.

Plymouth Colony's population never rose above 7,000, and after ten years it was still overshadowed by its larger neighbor, Massachusetts Bay Colony. Plymouth's area, Cape Cod and the neighboring mainland, had relatively poor land, lacked ready access to furs from the interior, and was not in the best location for fisheries. But its imprint on the national mind would be greater than its size would warrant—William Bradford's unpretentious history, *Of Plymouth Plantation* (completed in 1651) brought the colony vividly to life. And Plymouth invented Thanksgiving—at least later generations persuaded themselves that its 1621 harvest festival was the first Thanksgiving.

During the decade of the 1620s a scattering of settlements appeared along the neighboring coasts, mainly fishing posts occupied only in season, plus a few rugged hermits like Samuel Maverick, who engaged in fishing, fur trading, and sometimes a little farming on his island in Massachusetts Bay. The Pilgrims got their first neighbors when Thomas Weston, who had helped them get a start, sent about fifty "rude and lusty fellows" via Plymouth to Wessagussett (now Weymouth), but that lasted only one winter. Another try by one Captain Wollaston at Mount Wollaston (now part of Quincy) likewise failed, and Wollaston moved to Virginia. He left behind Thomas Morton, who persuaded some thirty men to stay in what he renamed Merry Mount. There, only twenty-five miles from Plymouth, Morton's company of Indian traders brought Renaissance England to the New World, "drinking and dancing about" a maypole, in Governor Bradford's words, "inviting the Indean women for their consorts, dancing and frisking together . . . and worse practices." But his chief sin was selling the Indians firewater and firearms. It was all too much for the Pilgrims, who sent Miles Standish ("Captaine Shrimpe," in Morton's satiric account) to seize the reprobate and send him back to England in 1628.

MASSACHUSETTS BAY   Massachusetts Bay Colony, the Puritan Utopia, had its genesis in one of the fishing posts near Plymouth. In 1623 a group of Dorchester merchants with a patent from the Council for New England set up a permanent fishing village on Cape Ann. For three years they occupied the site of the present Gloucester, but the venture proved unprofitable and the promoters withdrew. In 1626 a remnant of about thirty moved down to Naumkeag (later Salem) under the leadership of Roger Conant, a devout Puritan. Back in Dorchester the Rev. John White, a moderate Puritan and a leading force in the Gloucester settlement, held to his hope for a Christian mission to the English fishermen and Indians along the coast. In answer to White's appeal, a group of Puritans and merchants formed the New England Company in 1628, and got a land patent from the Council for New England. Then to confirm its legality the company turned to Charles I, who issued a charter in 1629 under the new name of Massachusetts Bay Company.

The New England Company already had sent new settlers to Salem, including John Endecott as governor. Leaders of the company at first looked upon it mainly as a business venture, but a majority faction led by John Winthrop, a well-to-do lawyer from East Anglia recently discharged from a government job, resolved to use the colony as a refuge for persecuted Puritans and as an instrument for building a "wilderness Zion" in America. The charter had one fateful omission: the usual proviso that the company maintain its home office in England. Winthrop's group therefore decided to take the charter with them, thereby transferring the entire government of the colony to Massachusetts Bay, where they hoped to ensure Puritan control. By the Cambridge Agreement of 1629 twelve leaders resolved to migrate on these conditions, and the company's governing body agreed.

In March 1630 the *Arbella*, with Gov. John Winthrop and the charter aboard, embarked with six other ships for Massachusetts. In a sermon, "A Model of Christian Charity," delivered on board the *Arbella*, Winthrop told his fellow Puritans "we must consider that we shall be a city upon a hill"—an example to all people. By the end of 1630 seventeen ships bearing 1,000 more arrived. As new settlers poured in, Salem was joined by a new settlement, Charlestown, where Winthrop moved, and soon Mystic, Newton, Watertown, and Dorchester. Boston, on the Shawmut Peninsula, became the chief city and capital. The *Arbella* migrants thus proved but the vanguard of a massive movement, the Great Migration, that carried some 40,000–50,000 Englishmen to the New World over the next decade, fleeing persecution and economic depression at home. They went not only to New England and the Chesapeake, but now also to new English settlements in the Lesser Antilles: St. Christopher (first settled in 1624), Barbados (1627), Nevis (1632), Montserrat (1632), and Antigua (1632). The West Indian islands started out to grow tobacco but ended up in the more profitable business of producing cane sugar.

The transfer of the Massachusetts charter, whereby an English trading company evolved into a provincial government, was a unique venture in colonization. Power in the company rested with the General Court, which elected the governor and assistants. The General Court consisted of shareholders, called freemen (those who had the "freedom of the company"), but of those who came, few besides Winthrop and his assistants had such status. This suited Winthrop and his friends, but then 108 more settlers asked to be admitted as freemen. Rather than risk trouble, the inner group invited applications and finally admitted 118 in 1631. A further provision was made at that time that only church members, a limited category, could become freemen.

At first the freemen were limited to the choice of assistants who chose the governor and deputy governor. The procedure violated provisions of the charter, but Winthrop kept the document hidden and few knew of the exact provisions. In the Watertown Protest of 1632, the people of one town objected to paying taxes levied by the governor and assistants "for fear of bringing themselves and posterity into bondage." Winthrop rebuked

THE

OATH
OF A
FREE-MAN

I A.B. being by Gods Providence an Inhabitant and FREEMAN within the Iurifdiction of this Commonwealth; doe freely acknowledge myfelfe to be fubject to the Government thereof.

AND therefore doe here fweare by the Great and Dreadful NAME of the Everliving GOD, that I will be true and faithfull to the fame, and will accordingly yield affiftance & fupport thereunto with my perfon and eftate as in equity I am bound; and will alfo truly endeavour to maintaine& preferve all the liberties &priviledges thereof, fubmitting myfelfe to the wholefome Lawes & Orders made and eftablifhed by the fame. +++ AND further that I will not Plot or practife any evill againft it, or confent to any that fhall fo doe: but will timely difcover and reveal the fame to lawfull authority now here eftablifhed, for the fpeedy preventing thereof.

MOREOVER I doe folemnly bind myfelfe in the fight of GOD, that when I fhall be called to give my voyce touching any fuch matter of this State in which FREEMEN are to deale +++ I will give my vote and fuffrage as I fhall judge in mine own confcience may beft conduce and tend to the publicke weale of the body without refpect of perfon or favour of any man.
So help me GOD in the LORD IESVS CHRIST.

Printed at **Cambridge** in New England:
by Order of the Generall Courte:
Moneth the Firft - **1639**

The Oath of a Free-Man: "I will give my vote and suffrage as I shall judge in mine own conscience . . ." (1639). [American Antiquarian Society]

them, but that year restored to the body of freemen election of the governor and his deputy. Controversy simmered for two more years until 1634, when each town sent two delegates to Boston to confer on matters coming before the General Court. There they demanded to see the charter, which Winthrop reluctantly produced, and they read that the power to pass laws and levy taxes rested in the General Court. Winthrop argued that the body of freemen had grown too large, but when it met, the General Court responded by turning itself into a representative body with two or three deputies to represent each town. They also chose a new governor, and Winthrop did not resume the office until three years later.

A final stage in the evolution of the government, a two-house legislature, came in 1644 when, according to Winthrop, "there fell out a great business upon a very small occasion." The "small occasion" involved a classic melodrama which pitted a poor widow against a well-to-do merchant over ownership of a stray sow. The General Court, being the supreme judicial as well as legislative body, was the final authority in the case. Popular sympathy and the deputies favored the widow, a Mrs. Sherman, but the assistants disagreed. The case was finally settled out of court, but the assistants feared being outvoted on some greater occasion. They therefore secured a separation into two houses and Massachusetts thenceforth had a bicameral assembly, the deputies and assistants sitting apart, with all decisions requiring a majority in each house.

Thus over a period of fourteen years the Massachusetts Bay Company, a trading corporation, was transformed into the governing body of a commonwealth. Membership in a Puritan church replaced the purchase of stock as the means of becoming a freeman, which was to say, a voter. The General Court, like Parliament, became a representative body of two houses, the House of Assistants corresponding roughly to the House of Lords, the House of Deputies to the House of Commons. The charter remained unchanged, but practice under the charter was quite different from the original expectation.

RHODE ISLAND   More by accident than design Massachusetts became the staging area for the rest of New England as new colonies grew out of religious quarrels within the fold. Puritanism created a volatile mixture: on the one hand the search for God's will could lead to a stubborn orthodoxy; on the other hand it could lead troubled consciences to diverse, radical, even bizarre convictions. Young Roger Williams, who arrived in 1631, was among the first to cause problems, ironically because he was the purest of Puritans, troubled by the failure of Massachusetts Nonconformists to repudiate the Church of England. He held a brief pastorate in Salem, then tried Separatist Plymouth, where according to Governor Bradford he "began to fall into strange opinions," specifically questioning the king's right to grant Indian lands "under a sin of usurpation of others' possession," and returned to Salem. Williams's belief that a true church must have no truck with the unregenerate led him eventually to the absurdity that no true church was possible, unless perhaps consisting of his wife and himself—and he may have had doubts about her.

But bizarre as Williams's beliefs may have been, they led him to principles that later generations would honor for other reasons. The purity of the church required complete separation of church and state and freedom from coercion in matters of faith. Williams therefore questioned the authority of government to impose an oath of allegiance and rejected laws imposing religious conformity. Such views were too advanced even for the radical church of Salem, which finally removed him, whereupon Williams retorted so hotly against churches that were "ulcered and gangrened" that the General Court in 1635 banished him to England. Governor Winthrop, however, out of personal sympathy, permitted him to slip away with a few followers among the Narragansett Indians, whom he had befriended. In the spring of 1636 Williams established the town of Providence at the head of Narragansett Bay, the first permanent settlement in Rhode Island.

Anne Hutchinson fell into dispute with the Puritan leaders for different reasons. The articulate wife of a well-to-do settler, she called groups together in her home to discuss the sermons of the Rev. John Cotton. In the course of the talks it began to appear that she held to a belief in an inner light from the Holy Spirit. Only Cotton, it seemed, along with her brother-in-law, the Rev. John Wheelwright, preached the appropriate "covenant of grace"; the others had a "covenant of works." Her adversaries likened her beliefs to the Antinomian heresy, technically a belief that one is freed from the moral law by the dispensation of grace in the gospel. The important point here was that Mrs. Hutchinson offended authority. Upon being hauled before the General Court, she was lured into convicting herself by claiming direct divine inspiration—blasphemy to the orthodox. Banished in 1638, she too took refuge in Narragansett country with a group of followers under William Coddington, who founded Pocasset (Portsmouth) on Aquidneck Island. Eventually she went to Long Island, under Dutch jurisdiction, and died there in an Indian attack in 1643. Her fate, Winthrop wrote, was "a special manifestation of divine justice."

When dissentions split Portsmouth, Coddington founded Shawomet (Warwick) on the mainland below Providence, and another Massachusetts outcast, Samuel Gorton, established Newport at the southern end of Aquidneck. Thus the colony of Rhode Island and Providence Plantations grew up in Narragansett Bay. It was a disputatious lot of dissenters who agreed mainly on one thing: that the state had no right to coerce belief. In 1640 they formed a confederation and in 1644 secured their first charter—from the Puritan Parliament. Williams lived until 1683, an active and beloved citizen of the commonwealth he founded in a society which, during his lifetime at least, lived up to his principles of religious freedom and a government which rested on the consent of the people.

CONNECTICUT   Connecticut had a more orthodox start in groups of Puritans seeking better lands and access to the fur trade farther west. In 1633, ignoring Fort Good Hope which the Dutch had established near the present-day site of Hartford, a group from Plymouth settled Windsor, ten miles farther up the Connecticut River. In 1636, activated by the leadership of Thomas Hooker, three entire church congregations from Watertown, Dorchester, and Newton (now Cambridge) trekked westward by the "Great Road," driving their hogs and cattle like the westering pioneers of a later day, and moved respectively to the Connecticut River towns of Wethersfield, Windsor, and Hartford, which earlier arrivals had laid out the previous year. A fourth group, from Roxbury, founded Springfield. Meanwhile in 1635 John Winthrop, Jr., had planted another town at the mouth of the river—Saybrook, named after its two proprietors, Lord Saye and Sele and Lord Brooke, who had acquired a grant from the Council for New England.

For a year the settlers in the river towns were governed under a commission from the Massachusetts General Court, but finding that only Springfield lay within Massachusetts, the inhabitants of Wethersfield, Windsor, and Hartford organized the self-governing colony of Connecticut in 1637. The impulse to organize came when representatives of the towns met to consider ways of meeting the danger of attack from the Pequot Indians, who lived east of the river. Before the end of the year the Pequots had attacked Wethersfield, and the settlers, with help from Massachusetts, responded with ferocity, surprising and burning the chief Pequot town on the Mystic River and slaughtering some 400 men, women, and children; stragglers were sold into slavery. All but a remnant of the Pequots perished in the holocaust.

In 1639 the Connecticut General Court adopted the "Fundamental Orders of Connecticut," a series of laws which provided for a government like that of Massachusetts, except that voting was not limited to church members. New Haven had by then appeared within the later limits of Connecticut. A group of English Puritans, led by their minister John Davenport and the wealthy merchant Theophilus Eaton, had migrated first to Massachusetts and then, seeking a place to establish themselves in commerce, to New Haven on Long Island Sound in 1638. Mostly city dwellers, they found themselves reduced to hardscrabble farming, despite their intentions. The New Haven colony became the most rigorously Puritan of all. Like all the other offshoots of Massachusetts, it too lacked a charter and maintained a self-governing independence until 1662, when it was absorbed into Connecticut under the terms of that colony's first royal charter.

NEW HAMPSHIRE AND MAINE   To the north of Massachusetts, most of what are now New Hampshire and Maine was granted in 1622 by the Council for New England to Sir Ferdinando Gorges and Capt. John Mason and their associates. In 1629 Mason and Gorges divided their territory at the Piscataqua River, Mason taking the southern part which he named New Hampshire. The first settlement had already appeared at Rye in 1623, the same year as the Gloucester fishing settlement. It remains uncertain whether Rye was deserted or merged with a colony later founded nearby at Strawberry Bank, and still later known as Portsmouth. In the 1630s Puritan immigrants began filtering in, and in 1638 the Rev. John Wheelwright, one of Anne Hutchinson's group, founded Exeter. Maine consisted of a few scattered and small settlements, mostly fishing stations, the chief of them being York.

An ambiguity in the Massachusetts charter brought the proprietorships into doubt, however. The charter set the boundary three miles north of the Merrimack River and the Bay colony took that to mean north of the river's northermost reach, which gave it a claim on nearly the entire Gorges-Mason grant. During the English time of troubles in the early 1640s Massachusetts took over New Hampshire, and in the 1650s extended its authority to the scattered settlements in Maine. This led to lawsuits with the heirs of the proprietors and in 1677 English judges and the Privy Council decided against Massachusetts in both cases. Two years later New Hampshire became a royal colony, but Massachusetts bought out the Gorges heirs and continued to control Maine as its proprietor. A new Massachusetts charter in 1691 finally incorporated Maine into Massachusetts.

THE ENGLISH CIVIL WAR IN AMERICA

Before 1640 English settlers in New England and around Chesapeake Bay had established two great beachheads on the

Oliver Cromwell, England's Lord Protector from 1653 until his death in 1658. [British Information Service]

Atlantic coast, separated by the Dutch colony of New Netherland in between. After 1640, however, the struggle between king and Parliament distracted attention from colonization and migration dwindled to a trickle of emigrants for more than twenty years. During the time of civil war and Cromwell's Puritan dictatorship the struggling colonies were left pretty much to their own devices, especially in New England where English Puritans saw little need to intervene. In 1643 four of the New England colonies—Massachusetts, Plymouth, Connecticut, and New Haven—looked to their own safety by forming the New England Confederation. The purpose was mainly joint defense against the Dutch, French, and Indians, but the colonies agreed also to support the Christian faith, to render up fugitives, and to settle disputes through the machinery of the Confederation. Two commissioners from each colony met annually to transact business. In some ways the Confederation behaved like a sovereign power. It made treaties with New Netherland and French Acadia, and in 1653 voted a war against the Dutch who were supposedly stirring the Indians against Connecticut. Massachusetts, far from the scene of trouble, failed to cooperate, however, and the Confederation was greatly weakened by the inaction of its largest member. The commissioners nevertheless continued to meet annually until 1684, when Massachusetts lost its charter.

Virginia and Maryland remained almost as independent as New England. At the behest of Gov. William Berkeley, the Virginia Burgesses in 1649 denounced the execution of Charles and recognized his son, Charles II, as the lawful king. In 1652, however, the Assembly yielded to parliamentary commissioners backed by a parliamentary fleet and overruled the belligerent governor. In return for the surrender the commissioners let the Assembly choose its own council and governor, and the colony grew rapidly in population during its years of independent government—some of the growth came from the arrival of royalists who found a friendly haven in the Old Dominion, despite its capitulation to the Puritans.

The parliamentary commissioners who won the submission of Virginia proceeded to Maryland, where the proprietary governor faced particular difficulties with his Protestant majority, largely Puritan but including some earlier refugees from Anglican Virginia. At Governor Stone's suggestion the Assembly had passed, and the proprietor had accepted, the Maryland Toleration Act of 1649, an assurance that Puritans would not be molested in their religion. In 1652 Stone yielded to the commissioners, who nevertheless removed him temporarily, revoked the Toleration Act, and deprived Lord Baltimore of his governmental rights, though not of his lands and revenues. Still, the more extreme Puritan elements were dissatisfied and a brief clash in 1654 brought civil war to Maryland, deposing the governor. But the Calverts had a remarkable skill at retaining favor. Oliver Cromwell took the side of Lord Baltimore and restored him to full rights in 1657, whereupon the Toleration Act was reinstated. The act deservedly stands as a landmark to human liberty, albeit enacted more out of expediency than conviction, and although it limited toleration to those who professed belief in the Holy Trinity.

Although Cromwell let the colonies go their own way, he was not indifferent to the nascent empire. He fought trade wars with the Dutch and harassed England's traditional enemy, Catholic Spain, in the Caribbean. In 1655 he sent out an expedition which conquered Jamaica from the Spaniards, thereby improving the odds for English privateers and pirates who pillaged Spanish ships—and often any others that chanced by.

The Restoration of King Charles II in England was followed by an equally painless restoration of previous governments in the colonies. The process involved scarcely any change, since little had occurred under Cromwell. The Virginia Assembly gladly restored Governor Berkeley to his office, an act soon confirmed by the crown. The king promptly confirmed Lord Baltimore in his rights, which Cromwell had already restored. Emigration rapidly expanded population in both colonies. Fears of reprisals against Puritan New England proved unfounded, at least for the time being. Agents hastily dispatched by the colonies won reconfirmation of the Massachusetts charter in 1662 and the very first royal charters for Connecticut and Rhode Island in 1662 and 1663. All three retained their status as self-governing corporations. Plymouth still had no charter, but went unmolested. New Haven, however, disappeared as a separate entity, absorbed into the colony of Connecticut.

SETTLING THE CAROLINAS

The Restoration of the Merry Monarch opened a new season of enthusiasm for colonial expansion, directed mainly by royal favorites. Within twelve years the English had conquered New Netherland, had settled Carolina, and very nearly filled out the shape of the colonies. In the middle region formerly claimed by the Dutch, four new colonies sprang into being: New York, New Jersey, Pennsylvania, and Delaware. Without exception the new colonies were proprietary, awarded by the king to men who had remained loyal, or had contributed to his restoration, or in

EARLY SETTLEMENTS IN THE SOUTH

one case to whom he was indebted. In 1663 he granted Carolina to eight True and Absolute Lords Proprietors: Sir John Colleton, a Barbadian planter and prime mover of the enterprise; George Monk, the duke of Albemarle, Cromwell's army commander who engineered the Restoration; Edward Hyde, earl of Clarendon; Sir Anthony Ashley-Cooper, later earl of Shaftesbury; Lord John Berkeley and his brother, Gov. William Berkeley of Virginia; William Craven, earl of Craven; and Sir George Carteret. The list is nearly a complete rollcall of the movers and shakers in Restoration expansion. Six of the eight were connected with the Royal African and Hudson's Bay Companies. Two—Carteret and Lord Berkeley—became the proprietors of New Jersey, and six, including Berkeley and Carteret, became proprietors of the Bahamas. Five served on the Council of Trade, six on the Council for Foreign Plantations, both important committees of the Privy Council.

NORTH CAROLINA Carolina was from the beginning made up of two widely separated areas of settlement, which finally became separate colonies. The northernmost part, long called Albemarle, had been entered as early as the 1650s by stragglers who drifted southward from Virginia. For half a century Albemarle remained a remote scattering of settlers along the shores of Albemarle Sound, isolated from Virginia by the Dismal Swamp and lacking easy access for ocean-going vessels. For many years its reputation suffered from the belief that it served as a rogue's harbor for the offscourings of Virginia. Later the aristocratic William Byrd, who helped survey the dividing line between Virginia and North Carolina, dubbed the neighboring colony Lubberland: "Surely there is no place in the world where the inhabitants lived with less labor than in North Carolina. . . . When the weather is mild, they stand leaning with both their arms upon the cornfield fence and gravely consider whether they had best go and take a small beat at the hoe but generally find reasons to put it off. . . ." Albemarle had no governor until 1664 when Sir William Berkeley exercised proprietary authority to appoint William Drummond, no assembly until 1665, and not even a town until a group of French Huguenots founded the village of Bath in 1704.

SOUTH CAROLINA The proprietors neglected Albemarle from the outset, and focused on more promising sites to the south. They proposed to find settlers who had already been seasoned in the colonies, and from the outset Barbadians showed a lively inter-

*Advertisement for
settlers showing the
proprietors' interest in
South Carolina. [Univer-
sity of North Carolina]*

est. Colleton had connections in Barbados, where the rise of
large-scale sugar production had persuaded small planters to try
their luck elsewhere. Sir Anthony Ashley-Cooper finally spurred
the enterprise by persuading his colleagues to take on more of
the financial burden of settlement. In 1669 three ships left London with about 100 settlers recruited in England. The expedition
sailed first to Barbados, to pick up more settlers, then north to
Bermuda. The goal was Port Royal, at what is now the southern
tip of South Carolina, but the settlers decided to go farther north
to put more distance between themselves and Spanish St. Augustine. The choice fell on a place several miles up the Ashley
River, where Charles Town remained from 1670 to 1680, when
it was moved across and downstream to Oyster Point, overlooking Charleston Harbor where, as proud Charlestonians later
claimed, the Ashley and Cooper Rivers "join to form the Atlantic
Ocean."

The government of this colony rested on one of the most curious documents of colonial history, the "Fundamental Constitutions of Carolina," drawn up by Lord Ashley with the help of his
secretary, John Locke. Its cumbersome frame of government and

A view of Charles Town, South Carolina. [New York Public Library]

its provisions for a nobility of proprietors, landgraves, and cassiques had little effect in the colony except to encourage a practice of large land grants, but from the beginning smaller "headrights" were given to every immigrant who paid his own way. The provision which had greatest effect was a grant of religious toleration, designed to encourage immigration, which gave South Carolina a greater degree of indulgence (extending even to Jews and heathens) than either England or any other colony except Rhode Island, and when it was established, Pennsylvania.

For two decades the South Carolina proprietors struggled to find a staple crop. Indeed the colonists at first had trouble providing their own subsistence. The first profitable enterprise was the Indian trade developed by Dr. Henry Woodward, who had left an expedition to live among the Indians and learn their languages four years before the founding of Charles Town. Through his contacts with the coastal tribes of Cusabos and Coosas, later with the Westoes along the Savannah River, enterprising colonists built up a flourishing trade in deerskins and redskins. Ambitious Barbadians, case-hardened by African slavery in the tropics, dominated the colony and did not scruple at organizing a major trade in Indian slaves, whom the Westoes obligingly drove to the coast for shipment to the West Indians. The first major export other than furs and slaves was cattle, and a staple crop was not developed until the introduction of rice in the 1690s. Meanwhile the continuing Indian trade led to repeated troubles with the proprietors, who tried in vain to regulate Indian affairs and stabilize the colony. Ultimately the struggle would lead to a rebellion against proprietary rule and an appeal to the crown to take charge. South Carolina became a separate royal colony in

1719. North Carolina remained under proprietary rule for ten more years, until the proprietors surrendered their governing rights to the crown in 1729.

Settling the Middle Colonies and Georgia

NEW NETHERLAND BECOMES NEW YORK Charles II resolved early to pluck out that old thorn in the side of the English colonies— New Netherland. The Dutch colony was older than New England, and had been planted when the two Protestant powers enjoyed friendly relations in opposition to Catholic Spain. The Dutch East India Company (organized in 1620) had hired an English captain, Henry Hudson, to seek the elusive passage to Cathay. Coasting North America in 1609, Hudson had discovered Delaware Bay and explored the river named for him, to a point probably beyond Albany where he and a group of Mohawks made merry with brandy. From the contact stemmed a lasting trade relation between the Dutch and the Iroquois nations, a group of whom had met a hostile reception from the French explorer Champlain the year before. In 1614 the Dutch established fur-trading posts on Manhattan Island and upriver at Fort Orange (later Albany). Ten years later a newly organized West India Company began permanent settlement, the first on Governor's Island. In 1626 Gov. Peter Minuit purchased Man-

The earliest view of Fort New Amsterdam, at the southern tip of Manhattan, around 1636–1639. [New York Public Library]

hattan from the resident Indians and Fort Amsterdam appeared at the lower end of the island. The village of New Amsterdam, which grew up around the fort, became the capital of New Netherland.

Dutch settlements gradually dispersed in every direction where furs might be found. They moved not only into surrounding locales like Staten Island and Long Island, but north around Fort Orange, south around Fort Nassau on the Delaware, and eastward to Fort Good Hope on the Connecticut River, which was soon surrounded by New England settlers and eventually surrendered to them in 1653. In 1638 a Swedish trading company established Fort Christina at the site of the present Wilmington and scattered a few hundred settlers up and down the Delaware River. The Dutch, at the time allied to the Swedes in the Thirty Years' War, made no move to challenge the claim until 1655, when a force outnumbering the entire Swedish colony subjected them without bloodshed to the rule of New Netherland. The chief contribution of the short-lived New Sweden to American culture was the idea of the log cabin, which the Swedes and a few Finnish settlers with them had brought over from the woods of Scandinavia.

The West India Company was interested mainly in the fur trade and less in agricultural settlements. In 1629, however, the company provided that any stockholder might obtain a large estate (a patroonship) if he peopled it with fifty adults within four years. The patroon was obligated to supply cattle, tools, and buildings. His tenants, in turn, paid him rent, used his grist mill, gave him first option on surplus crops, and submitted to a court he established. It amounted to transplanting the feudal manor into the New World, and met with as little luck as similar efforts in Maryland and South Carolina. Volunteers for serfdom were hard to find when there was land available elsewhere, and the only successful patroonship was that of Kiliaen van Rensselaer, a pearl merchant of Amsterdam, who secured lands covering what are now two counties around Albany. Most settlers took advantage of the company's provision that one could have as farms (*bouweries*) all the lands one could improve.

The government of the colony was under the almost absolute control of a governor sent out by the company, subject to little check from his council or from the directors back in Holland. The three successors to Minuit—Wouter Van Twiller, William Kieft, and Peter Stuyvesant—proved stubborn autocrats, either corrupt or inept, especially at Indian relations. They depended on a small professional garrison for defense, and the inhabitants (including a number of English on Long Island) betrayed almost total indifference in 1664 when Governor Stuyvesant called them to arms against a threatening British fleet. Almost defenseless, old soldier Peter Stuyvesant blustered and stomped about on his wooden leg, but finally surrendered without a shot and stayed on quietly at his farm in what had become the colony of New York.

The plan of conquest had been hatched by the king's brother, the duke of York and Albany, later King James II. As lord high admiral and an investor in the African trade, York had already engaged in harassing Dutch shipping and forts in Africa. When he and his advisors counseled that New Netherland could easily be reduced, Charles II simply granted the region to his brother as proprietor, permitted the hasty gathering of a force, and the English transformed New Amsterdam into New York and Fort Orange into Albany, replaced Stuyvesant with Col. Richard Nicolls, and held the country thereafter, except for a brief Dutch reoccupation in 1673–1674. The Dutch, however, left a permanent imprint on the land and the language: the Dutch vernacular faded away but place names like Block Island, Wall Street (the original wall was for protection against Indians), Broadway (Breede Wegh) remained, along with family names like Rensselaer, Roosevelt, and Van Buren. The Dutch presence lingered in the Dutch Reformed church; in words like boss, cooky, crib, snoop, stoop, spook, and kill (for creek); in the legendary Santa Claus, Rip Van Winkle, and the picturesque Dutch governors, preserved in the satirical caricatures of Washington Irving's *Knickerbocker History*.

NEW JERSEY   Shortly after the conquest, still in 1664, the duke of York granted his lands between the Hudson and the Delaware Rivers to Sir George Carteret and Lord John Berkeley (brother of Virginia's governor), and named the territory for Carteret's native island of Jersey. The New Jersey proprietorship then passed through a sequence of incredible complications. In 1674 Berkeley sold his share to a Quaker leader Edward Byllynge, whose affairs were so encumbered that their management fell to three trustees, one of whom was William Penn, another prominent Quaker. In 1676 by mutual agreement the colony was divided by a diagonal line into East and West New Jersey, with Carteret taking the east—a division that corresponded to New Jersey's status later as hinterland and commuter bedroom for New York and Philadelphia. Finally in 1682 Carteret sold out to a group of twelve, including Penn, who in turn brought into

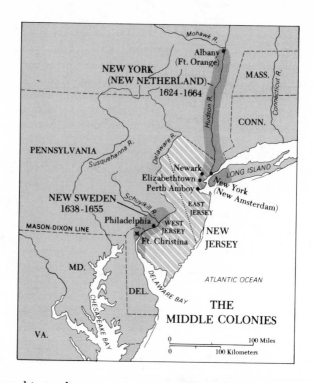

The map shows:

Mohawk R.

Albany
(Ft. Orange)

NEW YORK
(NEW NETHERLAND)
1624-1664

MASS.

Hudson R.

Connecticut R.

CONN.

PENNSYLVANIA

Susquehanna R.

Delaware R.

Newark

Elizabethtown
Perth Amboy

LONG ISLAND

New York
(New Amsterdam)

NEW SWEDEN
1638-1655

Schuylkill R.

EAST
JERSEY

MASON-DIXON LINE

Philadelphia

WEST
JERSEY

NEW
JERSEY

Ft. Christina

MD.

DEL.

DELAWARE BAY

ATLANTIC OCEAN

THE
MIDDLE COLONIES

CHESAPEAKE BAY

VA.

0   100 Miles
0   100 Kilometers

partnership twelve more proprietors, for a total of twenty-four!
In East New Jersey, peopled at first by perhaps 200 Dutch who
had crossed the Hudson, new settlements gradually arose: some
disaffected Puritans from New Haven founded Newark, Carteret's brother brought a group to found Elizabethtown (Elizabeth), and a group of Scots founded Perth Amboy. In the west,
which faces the Delaware, a scattering of Swedes, Finns, and
Dutch remained, soon to be overwhelmed by swarms of English
Quakers. In 1702 East and West Jersey were united as a royal
colony.

PENNSYLVANIA AND DELAWARE   The Quaker sect, as the Society of
Friends was called in ridicule, was the most influential of many
radical groups that sprang from the turbulence of the English
Civil War. Founded by George Fox about 1647, the Quakers
carried further than any other group the doctrine of individual
inspiration and interpretation—the "inner light," they called it.
Discarding all formal sacraments and formal ministry—each
spoke only as the spirit moved him—they refused deference to
persons of rank, used the familiar "thee" and "thou" in addressing everyone, refused to take oaths because that was contrary to

Scripture, and embraced pacifism. Quakers were subjected to persecution—often in their zeal they seemed to invite it—but never inflicted it on others. Their toleration extended to complete religious freedom for all, of whatever belief or disbelief, and to the equality of sexes and the full participation of women in religious affairs.

In 1673 George Fox had returned from an American visit with the vision of a Quaker commonwealth in the New World and had infected others with his idea. The entrance of Quakers into the New Jersey proprietorships had encouraged Quakers to migrate, especially to the Delaware River side. And soon, across the river, arose Fox's "Holy Experiment," William Penn's Quaker Commonwealth, the colony of Pennsylvania. William Penn was the son of Admiral Sir William Penn who had supported Parliament in the Civil War and led Cromwell's conquest of Jamaica but later helped in the Restoration. Young William was reared as a proper gentleman, but as a student at Oxford had turned to Quakerism. His father disowned him, but after a reconciliation, sent him off to France to get his mind on other things. It worked for a while, but Penn later came back to the faith.

A Quaker meeting. Note the presence of women, evidence of Quaker views on the equality of the sexes. [Museum of Fine Arts, Boston]

Upon his father's death he inherited the friendship of the Stuarts and a substantial estate, including a claim of £16,000 his father had lent the crown. Whether in settlement of the claim or out of simple friendship he got from Charles II in 1681 proprietary rights to a tract extending westward from the Delaware for five degrees of longitude and from the "beginning" of the forty-third degree on the north to the "beginning" of the fortieth degree on the south. The land was named, at the king's insistence, for Penn's father: Pennsylvania (literally Penn Woods). The boundary overlapped lands granted to both New York and Maryland. The New York boundary was settled on the basis of the duke of York's charter at 42° North, but the Maryland boundary remained in question until 1767 when a compromise line (nineteen miles south of the Fortieth Parallel) was surveyed by Charles Mason and Jeremiah Dixon—the celebrated Mason-Dixon Line.

When Penn assumed control there was already a scattering of Dutch, Swedish, and English settlers on the west bank of the Delaware, but Penn was soon making vigorous efforts to bring in more settlers. He published glowing descriptions of the colony, which were translated into German, Dutch, and French. They were favorably received, especially by members of Pietist sects whose beliefs paralleled those of the Quakers. By the end of 1681 Penn had about 1,000 settlers in his province, and in October of the next year arrived himself with 100 more. By that time a town was growing up at the junction of the Schuylkill and Delaware Rivers, which Penn called Philadelphia (the City of Brotherly Love). Because of the generous terms on which Penn offered land, because indeed he offered aid to emigrants, the colony grew rapidly.

Indian relations were unusually good from the beginning, because of the Quakers' friendliness and because of Penn's careful policy of purchasing land titles from the Indians. Penn even took the trouble to learn the language of the Delawares, something few white men even tried. For some fifty years the settlers and the natives lived side by side in peace, in relationships of such trust that Quaker farmers sometimes left their children in the care of Indians when they were away from home.

The government, which rested on three Frames of Government promulgated by Penn in 1682, 1683, and 1701, resembled that of other proprietary colonies, except that the councilors as well as the assembly were elected by the freemen (taxpayers and property owners) and the governor had no veto—although Penn did. "Any government is free . . . where the laws rule and the people are a party to the laws," Penn wrote in the 1682 Frame of Government. He hoped to show that a government could run in accordance with Quaker principles, that it could maintain peace and order without oaths or wars, that religion could flourish without an established church and with absolute freedom of conscience. Because of its tolerance, Pennsylvania became a refuge not only for Quakers but for a variety of dissenters—as well as Anglicans—and early reflected the ethnic mixture of Scotch-Irish and Germans that became common to the middle colonies and the southern backcountry. Penn himself stayed only two years in the colony, and although he returned in 1699 for two more years, he continued at home the life of an English gentleman—and Quaker.

In 1682 the duke of York also granted Penn the area of Delaware, another part of the Dutch territory. At first Delaware became part of Pennsylvania, but after 1701 was granted the right to choose its own assembly. From then until the American Revolution it had a separate assembly, but had the same governor as Pennsylvania.

GEORGIA   Georgia was the last of the British continental colonies to be established, half a century after Pennsylvania. In 1663, despite Spanish claims in the area, Charles II had granted the area from the Thirty-first to Thirty-sixth Parallels to the Carolina proprietors, but in 1732 George II gave the land between the Savannah and Altamaha Rivers to the twenty-one trustees of Georgia. In two respects Georgia was unique among the colonies; it was set up as both a philanthropic experiment and as a military buffer against Spanish Florida. Gen. James E. Oglethorpe, who accompanied the first colonists as resident trustee, represented both concerns: as a soldier who organized the defenses, and as a philanthropist who championed prison reform and sought a colonial refuge for the poor and persecuted.

In 1733 a band of 120 colonists founded Savannah near the mouth of the Savannah River. Carefully laid out by Oglethorpe, the old town with its geometrical pattern and its numerous little parks remains a monument to the city planning of a bygone day. A group of Protestant refugees from Salzburg began to arrive in 1734, followed by a number of Germans and German-speaking Moravians and Swiss, who made the colony for a time more German than English. The addition of Scottish Highlanders, Portuguese Jews, Welsh, Piedmontese, and others gave the early colony a cosmopolitan character much like that of its neighbor across the river.

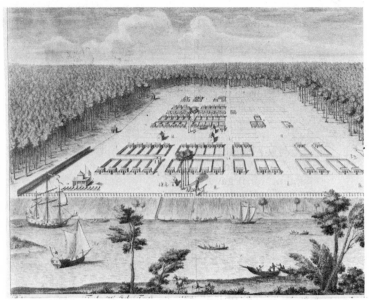

A view of Savannah in 1734. The town's layout was carefully planned.
[The Mariners' Museum, Newport News, Va.]

As a buffer against Florida the colony succeeded, but as a philanthropic experiment it failed. Efforts to develop silk and wine production had little success. Land holdings were limited to 500 acres, rum was prohibited, and the importation of slaves forbidden, partly to leave room for servants brought on charity, partly to ensure security. But the utopian rules soon collapsed. The regulations against rum and slavery were widely disregarded, and finally abandoned in 1742 and 1749 respectively. By 1759 all restrictions on landholding were removed.

In 1753 the trustees' charter expired and the province reverted to the crown. As a royal colony Georgia acquired for the first time an effective government. The province developed slowly over the next decade, but grew rapidly in population and wealth after 1763. Instead of wine and silk, Georgians exported rice, indigo, lumber, naval stores, beef, and pork, and carried on a lively trade with the West Indies. Georgia's products fitted well into the British economic system and Georgians prospered. The colony, which got off to such a late start, had become a roaring success.

Thriving Colonies

Sir John Seeley, a British historian of a later date, once wrote that England acquired an empire "in a fit of absence of mind." The determined propaganda of Richard Hakluyt and his disciples, the elaborate plans of Gilbert, Raleigh, and their successors, tend to belie such a claim, but the record of the colonies almost validates it.

In the abstract it seems an unlikely way to build an empire, but after a late start the English outstripped both the French and the Spanish in the New World. The lack of plan was the genius of English colonization, for it gave free rein to a variety of human impulses. The centralized control imposed by the monarchs of Spain and France got them off the mark more quickly but eventually led to their downfall because it hobbled innovation and responsiveness to new circumstances. The British acted by private investment and with a minimum of royal control. Not a single colony was begun at the direct initiative of the crown. In the English colonies poor immigrants had a much greater chance of getting at least a small parcel of land. The English, unlike their rivals, welcomed people from a variety of nationalities and dissenting sects who came in search of a new life or a safe harbor. And a degree of self-government made the English colonies more responsive to new circumstances—if sometimes stalled by controversy.

The compact pattern of English settlement contrasted sharply with the pattern of Spain's far-flung conquests or France's far-reaching trade routes to the interior by way of the St. Lawrence and Mississippi Rivers (discussed in Chapter 4). Geography reinforced England's bent for concentrated occupation and settlement of its colonies. The rivers and bays which indented the coasts served as veins of communication along which colonies first sprang up, but no great river offered a highway to the far interior. About a hundred miles back in Georgia and the Carolinas, and nearer the coast to the north, the "fall line" of the rivers presented rocky rapids which marked the head of navigation and the end of the coastal plain. About a hundred miles beyond that, and farther back in Pennsylvania, stretched the rolling expanse of the Piedmont, literally the foothills. And the final backdrop of English America was the Appalachian Mountain range, some 200 miles from the coast in the south, reaching down to the coast at points in New England, with only one significant break—up the Hudson-Mohawk Valley of New York. For 150 years the farthest outreach of settlement stopped at the slopes of the mountains.

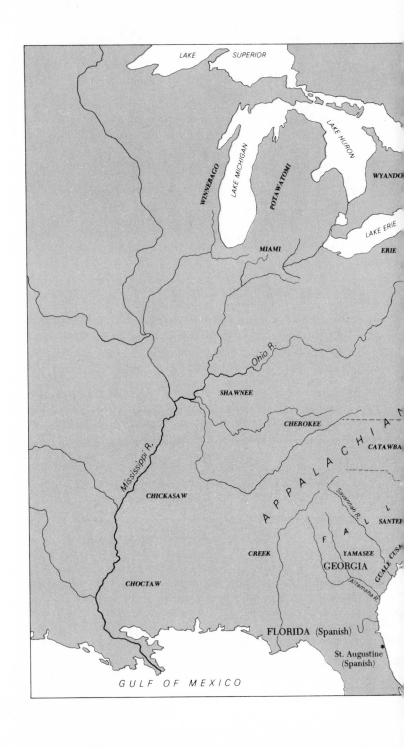

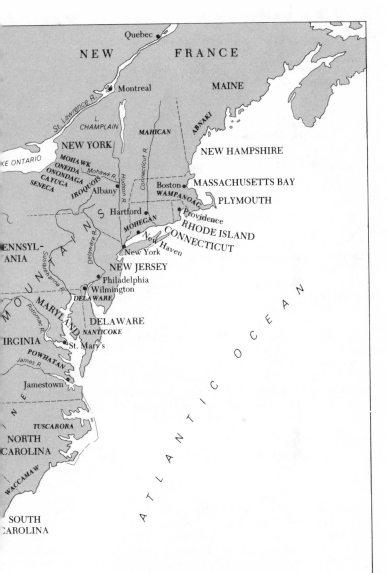

EUROPEAN SETTLEMENTS AND
INDIAN TRIBES IN EARLY AMERICA

0   200 Miles

0   200 Kilometers

To the east lay the wide expanse of ocean, which served as a highway for the transit of civilization from Europe to America, but also as a barrier beyond which civilization took to new paths in a new environment.°

FURTHER READING

Several general interpretations handle the sweep of English settlement during the early colonial period. The first volume of Charles M. Andrews's *The Colonial Period of American History* (1934–1937) is detailed and comprehensive. Shorter and more interpretative are Daniel J. Boorstin's *The Americans: The Colonial Experience* (1958),° David Hawke's *The Colonial Experience* (1966), and John E. Pomfret and Floyd M. Shumway's *The Founding of the American Colonies, 1583–1600* (1970). Pomfret and Shumway put the most emphasis on the early settlement patterns. Worth consultation are relevant passages from the fifteen-volume *The British Empire before the Revolution* (1936–1970), by Lawrence H. Gipson.

As noted in Chapter 1 Carl Bridenbaugh's *Vexed and Troubled Englishmen, 1500–1642* (1968)° helps explain why so many sought a new home in a strange land. Vital to perceiving how social conditions produced turmoil is Peter Laslett's *The World We Have Lost* (1965).° A study of the political institutions of the time is Wallace Notestein's *The English People on the Eve of Colonization, 1603–1630* (1951). English constitutional traditions and their effect on the colonists are examined in Julian H. Franklin's *John Locke and the Theory of Sovereignty* (1978) and Davis S. Lovejoy's *The Glorious Revolution in America* (1972).° John Phillips Kenyon documents the internal dynamics of English politics in *Stuart England* (1978).°

Carl Bridenbaugh's *Jamestown, 1544–1699* (1980), traces the English experience on the Chesapeake. P. L. Barbour's *The Three Worlds of Captain John Smith* (1964) is full of interesting detail. Alden Vaughn's *American Genesis: Captain John Smith and the Founding of America* (1975) is shorter. The early chapters of Edmund S. Morgan's *American Slavery / American Freedom* (1975)° also shed light on the English experience in Virginia.

George Langdon's *Pilgrim Colony: A History of New Plymouth, 1620–1691* (1966), focuses on the development of the second American settlement. Still useful and enlightening is William Bradford's narrative of the Pilgrim experience, *Of Plymouth Plantation,** edited in 1952 by Samuel E. Morison.

Scholarship abounds on the development of Puritanism. To learn about the English roots of the movement, see Charles H. and Katherine George's *The Protestant Mind of the English Reformation* (1961). More

° These books are available in paperback editions.

analytical and psychological is Michael Walzer's *The Revolution of the Saints: A Study in the Origins of Radical Politics* (1965).° The works of Perry Miller demonstrate how Puritan ideology evolved once transplanted to the New World. See especially Miller's *The New England Mind* (2 vols.; 1939, 1954).° More concise, yet complex and rewarding, is his *Errand into the Wilderness* (1964).° The problem of translating idea into governance is treated in Edmund S. Morgan's *The Puritan Dilemma: The Story of John Winthrop* (1958)° and George L. Haskin's *Law and Authority in Early Massachusetts* (1960).

The problem of dissent in a theocracy is handled in works on the establishment of other New England colonies. Start with Edmund S. Morgan's *Roger Williams, The Church, and the State* (1967).° Further explanation can be found in Emery Battis's *Saints and Sectarians: Anne Hutchinson and the Antinomian Controversey in Massachusetts Bay Colony* (1962). The religious theme in the settlement of Connecticut is also handled in Mary J. A. Jones's *Congregational Commonwealth* (1968).

No comprehensive work explores the overall pattern of settlement of the Middle Colonies, yet good scholarship exists for each colony. Thomas J. Condon's *New York Beginnings: The Commercial Origins of New Netherlands* (1968) examines the Dutch connection. The influence of Quakers can be studied through Gary B. Nash's *Quakers and Politics: Pennsylvania, 1681–1726* (1968), and Edwin B. Bronner's *William Penn's "Holy Experiment"* (1962). Also helpful are volumes on the early history of each colony. Consult Michael Kammen's *Colonial New York* (1975), Joseph E. Illick's *Colonial Pennsylvania* (1976), John E. Pomfret's *Colonial New Jersey* (1973), and John A. Munroe's *A History of Delaware* (1979).

Settlement of the areas along the south Atlantic is traced in William F. Craven's *The Southern Colonies in the Seventeenth Century, 1607–1689* (1949),° and Clarence L. Ver Steeg's *Origins of the Southern Mosaic* (1975). Aubrey C. Land et al., *Law, Society, and Politics in Early Maryland* (1977), explore early Maryland. The early chapters of Hugh Lefler and William S. Powell's *Colonial North Carolina* (1973) and M. Eugene Sirman's *Colonial South Carolina* (1966) cover the activities of the Lords Proprietors. To study Olgethorpe's aspirations, consult Paul S. Taylor's *Georgia Plan: 1732–1752* (1972).

3

COLONIAL WAYS OF LIFE

THE SHAPE OF EARLY AMERICA

POPULATION GROWTH   England's first footholds in America were bought at a fearful price. The beachhead in Virginia, one historian pointed out, "cost far more casualties, in proportion to numbers engaged, than did the conquest of any of the Japanese-held islands in World War II." But once the seasoning time was past and the colony was on its feet, Virginia and all its successors grew at a prodigious rate. After Virginia put down the last major Indian uprising in 1644, its population quadrupled from about 8,000 to 32,000 over the next thirty years, then more than doubled, to 75,000, by 1704. Throughout the mainland colonies the yearly growth rate during the eighteenth century ran about 3 percent. In 1625 the English colonists numbered little more than 2,000 in Virginia and Plymouth together; by 1700 the population in the colonies was perhaps 250,000, and during the eighteenth century it doubled at least every twenty-five years. By 1750 the number had passed 1 million; by 1775 it stood at about 2.5 million. In 1700 the English at home outnumbered the colonists by about 20 to 1; by 1775, on the eve of the American Revolution, the ratio was about 3 to 1.

The prodigious increase of colonial population did not go unnoticed of course. In 1770 Ezra Stiles, the future president of Yale College, predicted in his diary that English would "become the vernacular Tongue of more people than any one Tongue on Earth, except the Chinese." Benjamin Franklin of Pennsylvania, a keen observer of many things, published in 1751 his *Observations Concerning the Increase of Mankind* in which he pointed out two facts of life which distinguished the colonies from Europe: land was plentiful and cheap; labor was scarce and dear. Just the opposite conditions prevailed in the Old World. From this reversal of conditions flowed many if not most of the changes which European culture underwent in the New World—not the least being that good fortune beckoned the immigrant and induced the settlers to replenish the earth with large families. Where labor was scarce, children could lend a hand, and once they were grown could find new land for themselves if need be. Colonists tended, as a result, to marry and start new families at an earlier age.

THE BIRTH RATE   At the time many English women never married at all, and those who did often waited until their mid or later twenties, and men until even later. But in England women outnumbered men, while in the first waves of colonial settlement the sex ratio was reversed. The result was that the average age at marriage for colonial women dropped to twenty or twenty-one, for men to twenty-five or twenty-six, and the birth rate rose accordingly, since those who married earlier had time for about two additional pregnancies during the childbearing years. Later a gradual reversion to a more even sex ratio brought the average age at marriage back toward the European norm. Even so, given the better economic prospects in the colonies, a greater number of American women married and the birth rate remained higher

Mr. John Freake, *and* Mrs. Elizabeth Freake and Baby Mary. *Elizabeth married John at age nineteen; Mary, born when Elizabeth was thirty-two, was the Freake's eighth and last child. [The Worcester Art Museum]*

than in Europe, probably around 45–50 births per 1,000 women per year in the colonies in contrast to about 28 per 1,000 in Europe.

THE DEATH RATE What was equally important, however, was a startlingly lower death rate in the New World. Infants generally had a better chance to reach maturity, and adults had a better chance to reach old age. In seventeenth-century New England, apart from childhood mortality, men would expect to reach seventy and women nearly that age. The difference was less because of what Massachusetts Gov. William Shirley called the "Healthfulness of the Climates on this Continent" than because of the character of the settlements. Since the land was more bountiful, famine seldom occurred after the first year, and while the winters were more severe than in England, firewood was plentiful. Being younger on the whole—the average age in the colonies in 1790 was sixteen!—Americans were less susceptible to disease than were Europeans. More widely scattered, they were also less exposed to disease. This began to change, of course, as population centers grew and trade and travel increased. By the mid–eighteenth century the colonies were beginning to have levels of contagion much like those in Europe. In 1735–1737, for instance, a diphtheria epidemic swept the northern colonies, taking the lives of thousands. In this case the lack of previous ex-

94. Gravestone of Mary Briant and children by an unidentified artist. The epitaph reads HERE LYES Y [the] BODY / OF Mᵣˢ MA·RY BRI·ANᵀ / WIFE OF Mʳ THO·MAS / BRI·ANT WHO DYED / NO-UEMBER THE 30ᵗʰ / 1724 AGED 39 YEAREˢ / & IN HAR ARMS DOTH / LYE Y CORPS OF TWO / LOVELY BABES BORN / OF HAR 8 DAYS BE·FORᵉ / HAR DEATH ONE A SOⁿ / NATHAⁿᵉˡ DYED Y DAY / BEFORE HAR A DAUGHᵗʳ / NAMᵉᴰ HANˣᴬᴴ DYED A FEW OURˢ AFᵗᵉʳ HAR. 1724. Norwell, Massachusetts. Slate, 29" x 23¼".

The death rate in colonial America was relatively low, but Mary Briant's gravestone bears testimony to the ever-present spectre of childhood mortality. [The Warder Collection]

posure now left the young especially vulnerable for want of a chance to develop immunity.

The greatest variations on these patterns occurred in the earliest testing times of the southern colonies. During the first century after the Jamestown settlement, down to about 1700, a high rate of mortality and a chronic shortage of women meant that the population increase there could be sustained only by immigration. In the southern climate English settlers proved vulnerable to malaria, dysentery, and a host of other diseases. The mosquito-infested rice paddies of the Carolina tidewater were notoriously unhealthy. And ships which docked at the Chesapeake tobacco plantations brought in with their payloads unseen cargoes of smallpox, diphtheria, and other infections. Given the higher mortality, families were often broken by the early death of parents. One consequence was to throw children on their own at an earlier age. Another was probably to make the extended family support network, if not the extended household, more important in the South.

SEX RATIOS AND THE FAMILY   Whole communities of religious or ethnic groups migrated more often to the northern colonies than to the southern, bringing more women in their company. There was no mention of any women at all among the first arrivals at Jamestown. Virginia's seventeenth-century sex ratio of two or three white males to each female meant that many men never married, although nearly every adult woman did. Counting only the unmarried, the ratio went to about eight men for every woman. In South Carolina around 1680 the ratio stood at about three to one, but since about three-quarters of the women were married, it was something like seven to one for singles.

A population made up largely of bachelors without strong ties to family and to the larger community made for instability of a high order in the first years. And the high mortality rates of the early years further loosened family ties. While the first generations in New England proved to be long-lived, and many more children there knew their grandparents than in the motherland, young people in the seventeenth-century South were apt never to see their grandparents and in fact to lose one or both of their parents before reaching maturity. But after a time of seasoning, immunities built up. Eventually the southern colonies reverted to a more even sex ratio and family sizes approached those of New England. In eighteenth-century Virginia, Col. William Byrd of Westover asserted, matrimony thrived "so excellently" that an "Old Maid or an Old Bachelor are as scarce among us and reckoned as ominous as a Blazing Star." And early marriage remained common. The most "antique Virgin" Byrd knew was his own daughter, of about twenty.

Survival was the first necessity and for the 90–95 percent of colonists who farmed, a subsistence or semi-subsistence economy remained the foundation of being. Life moved more by the rhythms of the seasons, the rising and setting of the sun, than by the dictates of the clock. Not only food, but shelter, implements, utensils, furnishings, and clothing had to be made at home from the materials at hand. As the primary social and economic unit, the family became a "little commonwealth" which took on functions performed by the community in other times and places. Production, religion, learning, health care, and other activities centered around the home. Fathers taught their sons by example how to farm, hunt, and fish. Mothers taught their daughters how to tend to the chickens, the gardens, and the countless household chores that fell to the women of that time. Extended kinship ties added meaning to life and stability to communities. Such lineal family values tended to inhibit the constant mobility (social and geographic) and risk-taking so often assumed to be a peculiarly American characteristic.

Though colonists began in the early years to manifest such traditional American traits as practicality, acquisitiveness, restlessness, and a propensity for violence, it would be far too easy to read back into colonial times exaggerated notions of American individualism. Whatever the changes to be wrought by environment, the earliest settlers were transplanted Europeans whose ideas and practices adjusted to new circumstances only by degrees. Clusters of ethnic and religious groups which sprang up, such as the "tribal cult" of Puritans in New England, or the settlements of Germans in Pennsylvania, suggest that European values persisted in the New World for some time. Conditions in America did cause changes in family life, the implications of which social historians have only begun to work out, but this much seems clear. The conjugal unit, or nuclear family of parents and children, was not a new development in the colonies but the familiar arrangement in both England and America. The household that included an extended family of three or more generations was rare, although given the greater life span, large networks of kinship ties did develop. These networks included servants attached to households, who were often young kinspeople apprenticed to learn a trade.

THE SOCIAL HIERARCHY   The earliest settlers also brought in their cultural baggage certain fixed ideas of hierarchy and rank that had been part of their culture. People of the lower orders deferred to their "betters" almost without question. Devereux Jarratt, son of a carpenter and later an Episcopal evangelist, recalled that in the Virginia of his youth: "We were accustomed to look upon, what were called *gentle folks,* as beings of a superior order. . . . Such ideas of the differences between *gentle* and *simple,* were, I believe, universal among all of my rank and age. . . ." John Winthrop, looking out from a higher station in life, asserted it to be God's will that "in all times some must be rich, some poore, some high and eminent in power and dignitie, others meane and in subjection." But from Jamestown onward persons of "meane" birth like John Smith revealed rare qualities when confronted with the wilderness. The breadth of opportunity to be plucked from danger impelled settlers to shake off the sense of limitations that haunted the more crowded lands of Europe. J. Hector St. John de Crevecoeur, a French immigrant, wrote from his New York farm in the 1780s: "A European, when he first arrives, seems limited in his intentions, as well as in his views; but he very suddenly alters his scale; . . . he no sooner breathes our air than he forms schemes, and embarks in designs he never would have thought of in his own country."

Still, the new experience of social mobility took some getting used to. The fear lingered that it threatened the equilibrium of society, and efforts persisted to keep the "meaner sort" in their place. But attempts to regulate dress as the outward sign of social class ran up against a human weakness for finery. Even in Puritan New England, which got an undeserved credit for austerity, the scorn of fancy dress was reserved mainly for those who affected to rise above their station. In 1651 the Massachusetts General Court declared its "utter detestation and dislike" that persons of mean condition "should take upon them the garb of gentlemen." and prescribed fines for those with estates of less than £200 who wore gold or silver lace or silver buttons and other such finery.

WOMEN IN THE COLONIES   The status of women too altered in the new conditions of life. The acute shortage of women in the early years made them the more highly valued, and by many accounts brought subtle improvements in their status—a condition which tended to move with successive frontiers westward. The general labor shortage meant that both women and children were treated more indulgently than in the Europe of their times, not that their standing in the law or in their assigned roles in society was drastically altered. "Here, as in England," the historian Julia Cherry Spruill wrote, "women were without political rights, and generally wives were legal nonentities" whose property the husband controlled—although single women and widows had practically the same legal rights as men.

Despite the conventional mission of women to serve in the domestic sphere, the scarcity of labor opened new lines of action. Quite a few women by necessity or choice went into gainful occupations. In the towns they commonly served as tavern hostesses and shopkeepers, but occasional notices in colonial papers listed women also in such employments as doctors, printers, upholsterers, glaziers, painters, silversmiths, tanners, and shipwrights—often but not always widows carrying on their husbands' trade. Some managed plantations, again usually carrying on in the absence of husbands. One exceptional early case was "Mistress Margarett Brent, Spinster," of Maryland, who arrived in 1638 with two brothers and a sister. All four came on their own ventures, the Mistresses Brent bringing in servants and patenting large tracts of land. Margaret Brent ran her plantation so well that her brothers entrusted their affairs to her in their absence. As executrix of Gov. Leonard Calvert's estate she settled his complex affairs and arranged to pay the local militia and avert a mutiny. As "his Lordship's Attorney" she boldly demanded a vote in the Assembly the better to see after his affairs. The governor, in response, acknowledged her gifts, but denied her re-

Prudence Punderson's needlework The First, Second, and Last Scene of Mortality *(c. 1776), illustrating the domestic path, from cradle to coffin, followed by most colonial women.* [Connecticut Historical Society]

quest. When she became perhaps the first American suffragette, she had overstepped the bounds of acceptance.

The colonists everywhere had much in common. But as the land filled with population behind the frontier, the differences of geography and climate, and the diverse human elements entering the New World, produced ways of life that differed from north to south, from east to west. New England evolved into a center of fishing and commerce, the Puritan and the Yankee; the southern colonies into the land of tobacco and rice, the country gentleman and the black slave; the Middle Colonies into the colonial "breadbasket" of wheat and barley, the home of the Quaker, the Dutchman, and the Scotch-Irish.

SOCIETY AND ECONOMY IN THE SOUTHERN COLONIES

STAPLES The southern colonies had one unique advantage—the climate. They could grow exotic staples (market crops) that withered in northern latitudes and were prized by the mother country. Virginia, as Charles I put it, was "founded upon smoke." Within four years of John Rolfe's first experiments the passion for the "joviall weed" reached such heights that Gov. Thomas Dale required two acres of corn as a prerequisite for growing it. By 1619 production had reached 20,000 pounds, and in the year of the Glorious Revolution, 1688, it was up to 18 million pounds.

After 1690 rice was as much the staple in South Carolina as tobacco in Virginia or sugar in Barbados. The process of its naturalization is obscure. One cherished story is that the colony conjured the industry from a single bag of seed from Madagascar, but there are other stories of seed from India and Africa (black slaves, already familiar with rice growing in Africa, may have taught whites their method) and there is solid evidence that the Lords Proprietors planned experiments with rice from the beginning. From whatever source the rice came, the rise and fall of tidewater rivers made the region ideally suited to a crop which required alternate flooding and draining of the fields. In 1699 the young colony exported at least 366 tons of rice, according to the customs collector Edward Randolph.

Much later, in the 1740s, another exotic staple appeared—indigo, the blue dyestuff which found an eager market in the British woolens industry. An enterprising young lady named Eliza Lucas, daughter of the governor of Antigua, produced the first crop on her father's Carolina plantation, left in her care when she was only seventeen. She thereby founded a major industry, and as the wife of Charles Pinckney, later brought forth a major dynasty which flourished in the golden age of Charleston.

From the southern woods came harvests of lumber and naval stores (tar, pitch, and turpentine) as well. From their early leadership in the latter trade North Carolinians would later derive the nickname of Tar Heels. In the interior a fur trade flourished, and in the Carolinas, a cattle industry that pretokened the later industry on the Great Plains—with cowboys, roundups, brandings, and long drives to market.

English customs records showed that for the years 1698–1717 South Carolina and the Chesapeake colonies bought English goods averaging £154,000 in value annually, and sent back American goods averaging £246,000 leaving a balance of £92,000 in favor of the colonies. But the balance was more than offset by "invisible" charges: freight payments to shipper, profits, commissions, storage charges, and interest payments to English merchants, insurance premiums, inspection and customs duties, and outlays to purchase indentured servants and slaves. Thus began a pattern that would plague the southern staple-crop system into the twentieth century. Planter investments went into land and slaves while the profitable enterprises of shipping, trade, investment, and manufacture fell under the sway of outsiders.

LAND   Land could be had almost for the asking throughout the colonial period, although many a frontier squatter who succumbed to the lure ignored the formalities of getting a deed. In colonial law land titles rested ultimately upon grants from the crown, and in colonial practice the evolution of land policy in the first colony set patterns that were followed everywhere save in New England. In 1614 when Governor Dale gave each of the Virginia Company's colonists three acres for his own use, it was the beginning of a policy that every colonist could claim a plot of his own. In 1618 the company, lacking any assets other than land, promised each investor a fifty-acre "share-right" for £12.10s, and each settler a "headright" for paying his own way or for bringing in others. When Virginia became a royal colony in 1624, the headright system continued to apply, administered by the governor and his council. Lord Baltimore adopted the same practice in Maryland, and successive proprietors in the other southern and middle colonies adopted variations on the plan.

As time passed certain tracts were put up for sale and throughout the colonies special grants (often sizable) went to persons of rank or persons who had performed some meritorious service, such as fighting the Indians. Since land was plentiful and population desired, the rules tended to be generously interpreted and carelessly applied. With the right connections, persons or companies might engross handsome estates and vast speculative tracts in the interior, looking toward future growth and rising land values. From the beginning of colonization—in fact before the beginning—the real-estate boomer was a stock figure in American history, and access to power was often access to wealth. But by the early 1700s acquisition of land was commonly by purchase under more or less regular conditions of survey and sale by the provincial government. The later national land surveys followed the southern practice.

The first grants were made without any conditions attached, but at an early date the crown and proprietors decided to recover something from the giveaways by the levy of annual quit-rents on the land. In the Middle Ages such payments would quit (release) the tenant from military and other duties to his lord. In the New World, however, such levies had no roots in a feudal tradition and came to be a point of chronic protest, resistance, and evasion. But they remained on the books.

Some promoters of colonization, including Ferdinando Gorges, Lord Baltimore, and the Lords Proprietors of Carolina, had dreams of reviving the feudal manor in the New World. Their plans went awry, it is commonly said, because of the New World environment. With land aplenty, there was little call to volunteer for serfdom. Yet in unexpected ways the southern colonies gave rise to something analogous, a new institution with a new name: the plantation. The word originally carried the meaning of colony. The plantations in the New World were the colonies and planters were the settlers who had "planted" them. Gradually the name attached itself to individual holdings of large size.

If one distinctive feature of the South's staple economy was a good market in England, another was a trend toward large-scale production. Those who planted tobacco soon discovered that it quickly exhausted the soil, thereby giving an advantage to the planter who had extra fields to rotate in beans and corn or to leave fallow. With the increase of the tobacco crop, moreover, a fall in prices meant that economies of scale might come into play —the large planter with lower cost per unit might still make a profit. Gradually he would extend his holdings along the river-fronts, and thereby secure the advantage of direct access to the ocean-going vessels that moved freely up and down the water-

An idyllic view of a tidewater plantation. Note the easy access to ocean-going vessels. [Metropolitan Museum of Art]

ways of the Chesapeake, discharging goods from London and taking on hogsheads of tobacco. So easy was the access in fact that the Chesapeake colonies never required a city of any size as a center of commerce, and the larger planters functioned as merchants and harbormasters for their neighbors.

LABOR   If the planter found no volunteers for serfdom, and if wage labor was scarce and expensive, one could still purchase an indentured servant for £6 to £30 (a substantial sum, which in much of the seventeenth and eighteenth centuries would equal perhaps 900 to 5,000 pounds of tobacco) and get his labor for a term of years. Voluntary indentured servitude accounted for probably half the arrivals of white settlers in all the colonies outside New England. The name derived from the indenture, or contract, by which a person could bind himself to labor in return for transportation to the New World. Usually one made the contract with a shipmaster who would then sell it to a new master upon arrival. Not all went voluntarily. The London underworld developed a flourishing trade in "kids" and "spirits," who were enticed or spirited into servitude. On occasion orphans were bound off to the New World; from time to time the mother country sent convicts into colonial servitude, the first as early as 1617. After 1717, by act of Parliament, convicts guilty of certain crimes could escape the hangman by "transportation." Most of these, like Moll Flanders, the lusty heroine of Daniel Defoe's novel, seem to have gone to the Chesapeake. And after 1648 political and military offenders met a like fate, beginning with some captives of the Parliamentary armies.

In due course, however, the servant reached the end of his term, usually after four to seven years, claimed the freedom dues set by custom and law—some money, tools, clothing, food—and took up land of his own. And with the increase of the colonies, servants had a wider choice of destination. Pennsylvania became more often the chosen land, "one of the best poor man's countries in the world," in the verdict of Judge William Allen.

SLAVERY But captive Africans, although they might cost a bit more, had no choice and served for life. Slavery, long a dying institution in Europe, had undergone a revival in Spanish America a full century before the Jamestown colony. It gradually evolved in the Chesapeake after 1619, when a Dutch vessel dropped off twenty Negroes in Jamestown. Some of the first were treated as indentured servants, with a limited term, and achieved freedom and landownership. They themselves sometimes acquired slaves and white indentured servants. But gradually, with rationalizations based on color difference or heathenism, the practice of perpetual slavery became the custom of the land. Evidence that

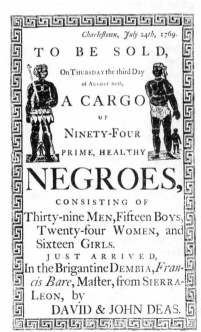

Advertisement for the sale of slaves—men, boys, women, and girls. [American Antiquarian Society]

in 1640 blacks were being held in hereditary life service appears in Virginia court records. In 1660 and 1661, and 1663 in Maryland, the colonial Assembly recognized slavery by laws that later expanded into elaborate and restrictive slave codes. In South Carolina, by contrast, Barbadians after 1670 simply transplanted the institution of slavery full-blown from the Caribbean before they discovered its value in the rice paddies, where indentured servants could hardly be enticed to work in the mud and heat.

The sugar islands of the French and British Antilles and the cane fields of Portuguese Brazil had the most voracious appetite for human cargoes, using them up in the tropical heat and miasmas on the average within seven years. By 1675 the English West Indies had over 100,000 slaves while the colonies in North America had only about 5,000. But as the staple crops became established on the American continent, the demand for slaves grew. And as readily available lands diminished, Virginians were less eager to bring in indentured servants who would lay claim to them at the end of their service. Though British North America took less than 5 percent of the total slave imports to the Western Hemisphere during the more than three centuries of that squalid traffic—399,000 out of some 9,566,000—it offered better chances for survival if few for human fulfillment. The natural increase of black immigrants in America approximated that of whites by the end of the colonial period.

Negro slavery was recognized in the laws of all the colonies, but flourished in the Tidewater South—one colony, South Carolina, had a black majority through most of the eighteenth century. By one estimate, about 40 percent of the slaves imported into North America came in through Sullivan's Island in Charleston Harbor, which was to black Americans what New York's Castle Garden and Ellis Island were later to millions of European immigrants or San Francisco's Angel Island to Asians. To say that black Africans made up the largest single group of non-English immigrants to the colonies, however, would be to ignore the great ethnic diversity of unwilling arrivals from lands as remote from each other as Angola and Senegambia, the west coast of Africa, and the area around the hump in between. About half the total came from Congo-Angola and the Bight of Biafra, and nearly all the rest from the Atlantic coast up to Senegambia. Thrown indiscriminately together, people who spoke Mandingo, Wolof, Ibo, Hausa, Kongo, and countless other tongues added to those who spoke various European and Indian languages to make the most relentless melting pot. As a result, diverse peoples developed a new identity as Afro-Americans, though not without leaving obscurely entwined in the fabric of American culture

The survival of African culture among American slaves is evident in this late–eighteenth-century painting of a South Carolina plantation. The musical instruments, pottery, and clothing are of African origin, probably Yoruba. [The Abby Aldridge Rockefeller Folk Art Center, Williamsburg, Va.]

more strands of African heritage than historians and anthropologists can ever disentangle. Among the more obvious were new words that entered the language, such as tabby, tote, cooter, goober, yam, banana, and the names of the Coosaw, Peedee, and Wando Rivers.

Most of the slaves were fated to become fieldhands, but not all did. Blacks from the lowlands of Africa used their skills as boatmen in the coastal waterways. Some had linguistic skills that made them useful interpreters. Others tended cattle and swine in the wilderness, or hacked away at the forests and operated sawmills. In a land which had to construct itself they became skilled artisans: blacksmiths, carpenters, coopers, bricklayers, and the like. Some of the more fortunate entered domestic service.

Slavery and the growth of a biracial South had economic, political, and cultural effects far into the future, and set America on the way to significant conflicts. Questions about the beginnings still have a bearing on the present. Did a deep-rooted color prejudice lead to slavery, for instance, or did the existence of slavery produce the prejudice? Clearly slavery evolved because of the desire for a supply of controlled labor, and Englishmen fell in with a trade established by the Portuguese and Spanish more than a century before—the very word "Negro" is Spanish for "black." But while Englishmen often enslaved Indian captives, they did not bring their white captives into slavery. Color was the crucial difference, or at least the crucial rationalization.

One historian has marshalled evidence that the seeds of slavery were already planted in Elizabethan attitudes. Englishmen associated the color black with darkness and evil; they stamped the different appearance, behavior, and customs of Africans as "savagery." At the very least such perceptions could soothe the consciences of people who trade in human flesh. On the other hand most of the qualities which colonial Virginians imputed to blacks to justify slavery were the same qualities that Englishmen assigned to their own poor to explain *their* status: their alleged bent for laziness, improvidence, treachery, and stupidity, among other shortcomings. Similar traits, moreover, were imputed by ancient Jews to the Canaanites and by the Mediterranean peoples of a later date to the Slavic captives sold among them. The names Canaanite and Slav both became synonymous with slavery—the latter lingers in our very word for it. Such expressions would seem to be the product of power relationships and not the other way around. Dominant peoples repeatedly assign ugly traits to those they bring into subjection.

THE GENTRY   By the early eighteenth century Virginia and South Carolina were moving into the golden age of the Tidewater gentry, leaving the more isolated and rustic colony of North Carolina as "a valley of humiliation between two mountains of conceit." The first rude huts of Jamestown had given way to frame and brick houses. Some of the seventeenth-century homes, like Governor Berkeley's Green Springs or Nathaniel Bacon's "Castle," were spacious, but even the most prosperous generally lived in houses of four to seven small rooms. It was only as the seventeenth century yielded to the eighteenth that the stately country seats in the Georgian, or "colonial," style began to emerge along the banks of the great rivers: Tuckahoe, Stratford, Westover, Berkeley, Carter's Grove, Nomini Hall, and others which still stand as monuments to a graceful age. The great mansions, flanked by storehouses and servants' quarters, characteristically faced both ways, looking down to the waterfront dock and the expanse of river, and to a landward front where a drive from the road led up to the imposing steps and doorways. In South Carolina the mansions along the Ashley, Cooper, and Wando, or along the tidal creeks that set the Sea Islands imperceptibly off from the mainland, came to be noted for

The Westover mansion (1730), built in Virginia by William Byrd II.
[Museum of Modern Art]

their spacious gardens and avenues of moss-hung live oaks. The Charleston town houses of the gentry varied the Georgian style by turning their sides to the street and adding to their fronts long piazzas in the West Indian style to catch the sea breezes.

The new aristocracy patterned its provincial lifestyle after that of the English country gentlemen. The great houses became centers of sumptuous living and legendary hospitality to neighbors and passing strangers. In their zest for the good life the planters kept in touch with the latest refinements of London style and fashion, living on credit extended for the next year's crop and the years' beyond that, to such a degree that in the late colonial period Thomas Jefferson called the Chesapeake gentry "a species of property annexed to certain English mercantile houses." Dependence on outside capital became a chronic southern problem lasting far beyond the colonial period.

In season the carriages of the Chesapeake elite rolled to the villages of Annapolis and Williamsburg, and the city of Charleston became the center of political life and high fashion where the new-issue aristocrats could reel and roister for days on end and patronize the taverns, silversmiths, cabinetmakers, milliners, and tailors. Through much of the year the outdoors beckoned planters to the pleasures of hunting and fishing and horsemanship. Gambling on horse races, cards, and dice became consuming passions for men and women alike. But a cultivated few courted high culture with a diligence that violated genteel indulgence. William Byrd II of Westover pursued learning with the same passion that he pursued the ladies, if not with the same flourish. He built a library of some 3,600 volumes and often rose early to keep up his Latin, Greek, and Hebrew. Robert "King" Carter of Nomini Hall practiced music several hours a day. The

Pinckneys of the Carolina low country, when they were at home, practiced their musical instruments and read from such authors as Vergil, Milton, Locke, Addison, Pope, and Richardson. Such families commonly sent their sons—and often their daughters— abroad for an education, usually to England, sometimes to France.

RELIGION   The first colonists in Virginia brought with them the Rev. Robert Hunt, an Anglican minister, but only in Virginia (1619) and Maryland (1692) was the Church of England established (tax supported) before the end of the seventeenth century. In the early eighteenth century it became the established church in all the South—and some counties of New York and New Jersey, despite the presence of many dissenters. In the new environment, however, the Anglican church evolved into something quite unlike the state church of England. The scattered population and the absence of bishops made centralized control difficult. After 1632 the bishop of London held theoretical jurisdiction over the colonial churches, but regulation was generally entrusted to governors more concerned with political matters.

In practice therefore, if not in theory, the Anglican churches became as independent of any hierarchy as the Congregationalists of New England. Governance fell to lay boards of vestrymen, who chose the ministers, and usually held them on a tight rein by granting short-term contracts. In Virginia ministerial salaries depended on the taxes paid in the parish, and in 1662 were set uniformly at the value of 13,333 pounds of leaf; the salary therefore fluctuated with the price of tobacco. Often the parishes were too large for an effective ministry. Isolated chapels might have lay readers and get only infrequent visits by clergymen. Standards were often lax, and the Anglican clergy around the Chesapeake became notorious for its "sporting parsons," addicted to foxhunting, gambling, drunkenness, and worse. Some parishes went for long periods without ministers: ordination by a bishop could be had only in England, and the pay was too uncertain.

No bishop ever resided in the colonies, and only a bishop could ordain ministers or confirm members, a fact which of itself caused a falling off. Certain functions of supervision and discipline, however, could be delegated to "commissaries," the first and most noted of whom was James Blair, who brought some order into Virginia's church affairs after 1689. At his death in 1743 only two parishes lacked ministers. Commissary Thomas Bray, appointed to Maryland in 1696, spent less than a year in the colony during which he established a library in nearly every parish, but was more significant for work back in England which led King William to charter the Society for the Propagation of the Gospel in Foreign Parts (the SPG, sometimes called the "Venerable Society"). The first missionary of the SPG arrived in South Carolina on Christmas Day 1702; from then until 1783 the SPG sponsored a total of 309 missionaries, who worked especially in New England and the Middle Colonies where the Anglican church was weakest. The missionaries kept up a sporadic agitation to have a bishop assigned to the colonies, but none ever was. Opposition came from various quarters: most of the colonists were dissenters; some in England feared that the appointment of bishops might make the colonies more independent, some in the colonies that it would make them less so; commercial and landed interests feared that it might make the colonies less attractive to dissenters, and so inhibit growth.

SOCIETY AND ECONOMY IN NEW ENGLAND

TOWNSHIPS   By contrast to the seaboard planters who transformed the English manor into the southern plantation, the Puritans transformed the English village into the New England town. Land policy in New England had a stronger social and religious purpose than elsewhere. Towns shaped by English precedent and Puritan policy also fitted the environment of a rockbound land, confined by sea and mountains and unfit for large-scale cultivation.

Neither headrights nor quitrents ever took root in New England. There were cases of large individual grants, but the standard system was one of township grants to organized groups. A group of settlers, often gathered already into a church, would petition the General Court for a town (what elsewhere was commonly called a "township") then divide it according to a rough principle of equity—those who invested more or had larger families might receive more land—retaining some pasture and woodland in common and holding some for later arrivals. In some early cases the towns arranged each settler's land in separate strips after the medieval practice, but with time land was commonly divided into separate farms to which landholders would move out, away from the close-knit village. And still later, by the early eighteenth century, the colonies used their remaining land as a source of revenue by selling townships to proprietors whose purpose, more often than not, was speculation and resale.

This colonial woodcut suggests the tremendous effort required by basic farming in New England. [New York Public Library]

ENTERPRISE   The life of the New England farmer was typically a hardscrabble subsistence. Simply clearing the glacier-scoured soil of rocks might require sixty days of hard labor per acre. The growing season was short, and no exotic staples grew in that hard climate. If the town resembled the English village, the crops too were those familiar to the English countryside: wheat, barley, oats, some cattle and swine, and where the woodland predators could be killed off—especially on islands like Nantucket or Martha's Vineyard—sheep grazed on the land. By the end of the seventeenth century New England farmers were developing some surpluses for export but never any staples that met the demands of the English market.

With virgin forests ready for conversion into masts, lumber, and ships, and rich fishing grounds that stretched northward to Newfoundland, it is little wonder that New Englanders turned to the sea for livelihood—the fisheries in fact antedated settlement by more than a century. The Chesapeake region afforded a rich harvest of oysters, but New England by its proximity to waters frequented by cod, mackerel, halibut, and other varieties became the more important maritime center. Marblehead, Salem, Ipswich, and Charlestown early became important commercial fishing towns. Whales too abounded in New England waters and supplied whale oil for lighting and lubrication, as well as ambergris, a secretion used in perfumes. New England ships eventually were chasing whales from Baffin Bay to Antarctica and out across the Pacific.

The fisheries, unlike the farms, supplied a staple of export to Europe, while lesser grades of fish went to the West Indies as food for slaves. Fisheries encouraged the development of ship-building, and experience at seafaring spurred commerce which led to wider contacts in the Atlantic world and a certain cosmo-politanism which clashed with more provincial aspects of the Pu-ritan utopia.

Abundant forests near the shore yielded lumber, masts, pitch, and tar, and as early as July 4, 1631, John Winthrop launched a ship of sixty tons, the *Blessing of the Bay*, which marked the be-ginning of an American merchant marine. By the mid–seven-teenth century shipyards had developed at Boston, Salem, Dorchester, Gloucester, Portsmouth, and other towns. New England remained the center of shipbuilding throughout the co-lonial period. Lumber provided not only raw material for ships but a prime cargo. As early as 1635 what may have been the first sawmill appeared at Portsmouth, New Hampshire. Sawmills soon abounded throughout the colonies, often together with gristmills using the same source of waterpower.

TRADE Commercially the colonies by the end of the seventeenth century had become part of a great North Atlantic connection, trading not only with the British Isles and the British West Indies, but also—and often illegally—with Spain, France, Por-tugal, Holland, and their colonies from America to the shores of Africa. Out of necessity the colonists had to import manufac-

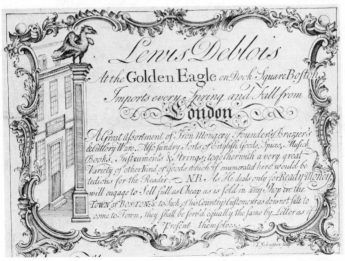

A Boston merchant's trade card (1757). Note the manufactured goods imported from London, to be sold "full as cheap as is sold in any shop in the town of Boston." [Winterthur Museum]

106 · Colonial Ways of Life

tured goods from Britain and Europe: hardware, machinery, paint, instruments of navigation, various household items. The function of the colonies as a market for English goods was important to the mother country. The central problem for the colonies was to find the means of paying for the imports—the eternal problem of the balance of trade.

The mechanism of trade in New England and the Middle Colonies differed from that of the South in two respects: their lack of staples to exchange for English goods was a relative disadvantage, but the abundance of their own shipping and mercantile enterprise worked in their favor. After 1660, in order to protect English agriculture and fisheries, the English government raised prohibitive duties against certain major exports of these colonies: fish, flour, wheat, and meat, while leaving the door open to timber, furs, and whale oil. Consequently New York and New England in the years 1698–1717 bought more from England than they sold there, incurring an unfavorable trade balance of about £66,000 sterling.

The northern colonies met the problem partly by using their own ships and merchants, thus avoiding the "invisible" charges for trade and transport, and by finding other markets for the sta-

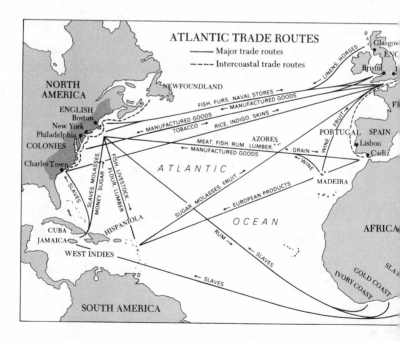

ATLANTIC TRADE ROUTES

ples excluded from England, thus acquiring goods or bullion to pay for imports from the mother country. American lumber and fish therefore went to southern Europe, Madeira, and the Azores for money or in exchange for wine; lumber, rum, and provisions went to Newfoundland; and all of these and more went to the West Indies, which became the most important outlet of all. American merchants could sell fish, bread, flour, corn, pork, bacon, beef, and horses to West Indian planters who specialized in sugarcane. In return they got money, sugar, molasses, rum, indigo, dyewoods, and other products, much of which went eventually to England. This gave rise to the famous "triangular trade" (more a descriptive convenience than a rigid pattern) in which New Englanders shipped rum to the west coast of Africa and bartered for slaves, took the slaves on the "Middle Passage" to the West Indies, and returned home with various commodities including molasses, from which they manufactured rum. In another version they shipped provisions to the West Indies, carried sugar and molasses to England, and returned with manufactured goods from Europe.

The generally unfavorable balance of trade left a chronic shortage of hard money, which drifted away to pay for imports and invisible charges. Since England restricted the export of bullion, such coins as found their way to the colonies were mostly foreign: the Portuguese johannes (or "joe") and moidore, the French pistole, and most important of all, the Spanish piece of eight (eight reals) or the Spanish milled dollar which later took its place—the ancestor of the American dollar. Colonists reckoned in terms of English pounds, shillings, and pence, but it has been said that they were more a medium of expression than a medium of exchange.

Various expedients met the shortage of currency: the use of wampum or commodities, the monetary value of which colonial governments tried vainly to set by law. From 1652 to 1684 Massachusetts coined silver "pine tree" shillings, but lost the right after the loss of its charter in 1684. Promissory notes of individuals or colonial treasurers often passed as a crude sort of paper money. Most of the colonies at one time or another issued bills of credit, on promise of payment later (hence the dollar "bill"), and after South Carolina took the lead in 1712, most set up land banks which issued paper money for loans to farmers on the security of their lands, which were mortgaged to the banks. Colonial farmers began to recognize that an inflation of paper money led to an inflation of crop prices, and therefore asked for more and more paper. Thus began in colonial politics what was to become a recurrent issue in later times, the question of currency inflation. Wherever the issue arose, debtors commonly favored growth in the money supply, which would make it easier for them to settle accounts, whereas creditors favored a limited money supply, which would increase the value of their capital. In 1741, therefore, in response to influential creditors of Massachusetts, Parliament extended the Bubble Act of 1720 to the colonies. That act, passed in response to speculative frauds in England like the South Sea Bubble, outlawed joint-stock companies not authorized by Parliament. Ten years later, in 1751, Parliament outlawed legal tender paper money in New England, and in 1764 throughout the colonies.

RELIGION   It has been said that in New England one was never far from the smell of fish and brimstone. The Puritans for many years had a bad press. By the standards of later ages they were judged bigots, but they had come to America to escape error, not to tolerate it in their New Zion. And the picture of the dour Puritan, hostile to anything that gave pleasure, is false. Puritans, especially those of the upper class, wore colorful clothing, enjoyed secular music, and imbibed prodigious quantities of rum. "Drink is in itself a good creature of God," said the Rev. Increase Mather, " . . . but the abuse of drink is from Satan." The architecture and household articles of Puritan New England have a continuing aesthetic appeal. The things of the world, in the Puritan view, were made by God and to be enjoyed by man. Sin lay not so much in their use as in their misuse. At the same time man had an obligation to work in this world, and worldly success was important.

The Puritans who settled Massachusetts, unlike the Separatists of Plymouth, proposed only to form a purified version of the Anglican church. They believed that they could remain loyal to the Church of England, the unity of church and state, and the principle of compulsory uniformity. But their remoteness from England led them directly, in fact very quickly, to a congregational form of church government identical with that of the Pilgrim Separatists, and for that matter little different from the practice of southern Anglicans.

Certain things in the Puritan faith were pregnant with meaning for the future. In the Puritan's version of Calvin's theology God had voluntarily entered into a covenant, or contract, with men through which his creatures could secure salvation. By analogy, therefore, an assembly of true Christians could enter into a church covenant, a voluntary union for the common worship of

God. From this it was a fairly short step to the idea of a voluntary union for purposes of government. The history of New England affords examples of several such limited steps towards constitutional government: the Mayflower Compact, the Cambridge Agreement of John Winthrop and his followers, the Fundamental Orders of Connecticut, and the informal arrangements whereby the Rhode Island settlers governed themselves until they secured a charter in 1663.

The covenant theory contained certain germs of democracy in both church and state, but democracy was no part of Puritan political science which, like so much else in Puritan belief, began with original sin. Because of man's depravity government became necessary for his restraint. "If people be governors," asked the Rev. John Cotton, "who shall be governed?" The Puritan was dedicated to seeking not the will of the people but the will of God. The ultimate source of authority was the Bible, God's revelation to man. But the Bible had to be known by right reason, which was best applied by those trained to the purpose. Hence most Puritans deferred to an intellectual elite for a true knowledge of God's will. Church and state were but two aspects of the same unity, the purpose of which was to carry out God's will on earth. The New England way might thus be summarized in the historian Perry Miller's phrase as a kind of "dictatorship of the regenerate."

The church exercised a pervasive influence over the life of the town, but unlike the Church of England it had no temporal power. Thus while Puritan New England has often been called a theocracy, the church technically was entirely separated from the state—except that the residents were taxed for its support. And if not all inhabitants were church members, they were impelled, indeed required, to be present for church services. So complete was the consensus of church member and nonmember alike that the closely knit communities of New England have been called peaceable kingdoms. It was a peace, however, under which there bubbled a volcano of soul-searching.

The Puritan lived anything but what Plato had called "the unexamined life." He was assailed by doubts, by a fear of falling away, by the haunting fear that despite his best outward efforts he might not be one of God's elect. Add that to the long winters which kept the family cooped up during the dark, cold months, and one has a formula for seething resentments and recriminations which, for the sake of peace in the family, had to be projected outward toward neighbors. The New Englanders of those peaceable kingdoms therefore built a reputation as the most litigious people on the face of God's earth, continually quarreling over fancied slights, business dealings, and other issues, and building in the process a flourishing legal profession.

SOCIAL STRAINS   All the while, social strains were growing in the community, a consequence of population pressure on the land. In the close-knit towns of New England the fragmentation of family ties seems to have been slowed by the peculiar circumstances of the community. Studies of Andover, Dedham, and Plymouth, Massachusetts, among other towns, suggest that at least in the seventeenth century family ties grew stronger and village life more cohesive than in the homeland. The conjugal unit prevailed, but intermarriage of families blurred the line between family and community. And among the first settlers, fathers exercised strong patriarchal control over their sons through their control of the land. They kept the sons in the town, not letting them set up their own households or get title to their farmland until they reached middle age.

In New England as elsewhere the tendency was to subdivide the land among all the children. But by the eighteenth century, with land scarcer, the younger sons were either getting control of property early or else moving on. Often the younger male children were forced out, with family help and blessings, to seek land elsewhere or new kinds of work in the commercial cities. With the growing pressure on land in the settled regions, poverty was becoming visible in what had once seemed a country of unlimited opportunity.

The emphasis on a direct accountability to God, which lay at the base of all Protestant theology, itself caused a persistent tension and led believers to challenge authority in the name of private conscience. Massachusetts repressed such heresy in the 1630s, but it resurfaced during the 1650s among Quakers and Baptists, and in 1659–1660 the colony hanged four Quakers who persisted in returning after they were expelled. These acts caused such revulsion—and an investigation by the crown—that they were not repeated, although heretics continued to face harassment and persecution.

More damaging to the Puritan Utopia was the increasing worldliness of New England, which placed growing strains on church discipline. More and more children of the "visible saints" found themselves unable to give the required testimony of regeneration. In 1662 an assembly of ministers at Boston accepted the "Half-Way Covenant," whereby baptized children of church members could be admitted to a "halfway" membership and secure baptism for their own children in turn. Such members, however, could neither vote nor take communion. A further blow to Puritan hegemony came with the Massachusetts royal charter of 1691, which required toleration of dissenters and based the right to vote on property rather than on church membership.

The strains which built up in Massachusetts's transition from Puritan utopia to royal colony reached an unhappy climax in the witchcraft hysteria at Salem Village (later Danvers) in 1692. The general upheaval in the colony's political, economic, social, and religious life was compounded in that locale by a conflict of values between a community rooted in the subsistence farm economy and the thriving port of Salem proper.

Seething insecurities in the community made it receptive to accusations by adolescent girls that they had been bewitched. Before the hysteria ran its course ten months later, nineteen people (including some men) had been hanged, one man pressed to death by heavy stones, and more than 100 others jailed. The fascination of horror has drawn a disproportionate amount of attention to the witchcraft delusions. It should be noted, however, that most people in the Western world at that time believed in witches who served the devil and his demons. But nearly everybody responsible for the Salem executions later recanted and nothing quite like it happened in the colonies again. In Europe witches were still being executed in the eighteenth century.

SOCIETY AND ECONOMY IN THE MIDDLE COLONIES

AN ECONOMIC MIX Both geographically and culturally the Middle Colonies stood between New England and the South, blending their own influences with elements derived from the older regions on either side. In so doing they more completely reflected the diversity of colonial life and more fully foreshadowed the pluralism of the later American nation than the regions on either side. Their crops were those of New England but more bountiful, owing to better land and a longer growing season, and they developed surpluses of foodstuffs for exports to the plantations of the South and the West Indies: wheat, barley, oats, and other cereals, flour, and livestock. Three great rivers—the Hudson, Delaware, and Susquehanna—and their tributaries gave the Middle Colonies a unique access to their backcountry and to the fur trade of the interior, where New York and Pennsylvania long enjoyed friendly relations with the Iroquois, Delaware, and other tribes of the area. As a consequence the region's commerce rivaled that of New England, and indeed Philadelphia eventually supplanted Boston as the largest city of the colonies.

Land policies followed the headright system of the South, with all the later embellishments of favoritism to influential speculators. One of the most successful of these was James Logan, a man of staggering erudition, secretary to William Penn, then Pennsylvania commissioner of property and holder of numerous other offices from which positions of influence he set himself up as one of the leading merchants and landholders—and owner of the largest private library—in the colonies. In New York the early royal governors, especially Lord Cornbury, went him one better. They carried forward, in practice if not in name, the Dutch device of the patroonship, granting to influential favorites vast estates on Long Island and up the Hudson and Mohawk Valleys. These realms most nearly approached the Old World manor, self-contained domains farmed by tenants who paid feudal dues to use the landlords' mills, warehouses, smokehouses, and wharfs. But with free land elsewhere, New York's population languished and the new waves of immigrants sought the promised land of Pennsylvania.

AN ETHNIC MIX In the makeup of their population the Middle Colonies stood apart from both the mostly English Puritan settlements and the biracial plantation colonies to the South. In New York and New Jersey, for instance, Dutch culture and language lingered for some time to come, along with the Dutch Reformed church. Up and down the Delaware River the few Swedes and Finns, the first settlers, were overwhelmed by the influx of English and Welsh Quakers, followed in turn by the Germans and Scotch-Irish.

The Germans came mainly from the Rhineland Palatinate, which had been devastated and impoverished first in the Thirty Years' War (1618–1648), then in the repeated wars of Louis XIV (1667–1713). Penn's brochures on the bounties of Pennsylvania circulated in German translation, and his promise of religious freedom brought a response from persecuted sects, especially the Mennonites, German Baptists whose beliefs resembled those of the Quakers. In 1683 Francis Daniel Pastorius brought a group of Mennonites to found Germantown near Philadelphia. They were but the vanguard of a swelling migration in the eighteenth century which included Lutherans, Reformed Calvinists, Moravians, Dunkers, and others, a large proportion of whom paid their way as indentured servants, or "redemptioners," as

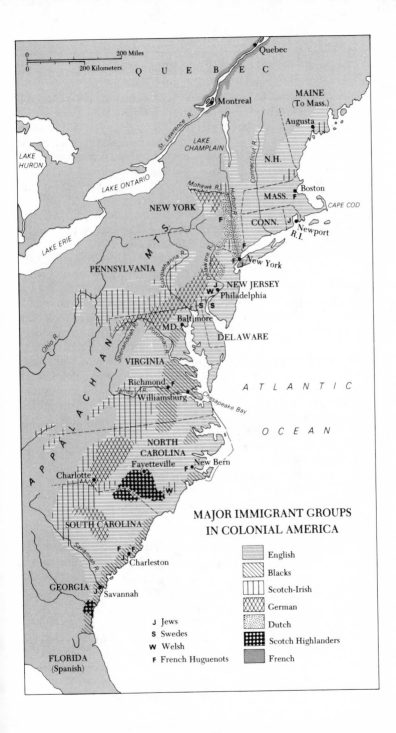

MAJOR IMMIGRANT GROUPS
IN COLONIAL AMERICA

	English
	Blacks
	Scotch-Irish
	German
	Dutch
	Scotch Highlanders
	French

J Jews
S Swedes
W Welsh
F French Huguenots

0 ___ 200 Miles
0 ___ 200 Kilometers

QUEBEC

Quebec

Montreal

LAKE HURON

LAKE ONTARIO

LAKE ERIE

LAKE CHAMPLAIN

St. Lawrence R.

Mohawk R.

Connecticut R.

Hudson R.

MAINE
(To Mass.)

Augusta

N.H.

MASS.

Boston

CAPE COD

CONN.

Newport
R.I.

NEW YORK

New York

PENNSYLVANIA

Susquehanna R.

Delaware R.

NEW JERSEY

Philadelphia

Baltimore

MD.

DELAWARE

Ohio R.

Shenandoah R.

Potomac R.

VIRGINIA

Richmond

Williamsburg

James R.

Chesapeake Bay

ATLANTIC

OCEAN

NORTH
CAROLINA

Fayetteville

New Bern

Charlotte

SOUTH CAROLINA

Savannah R.

Charleston

GEORGIA

Savannah

FLORIDA
(Spanish)

APPALACHIAN MTS.

they were commonly called. Back of Philadelphia they created a belt of settlement in which the "Pennsylvania Dutch" (a corruption of *Deutsch*, meaning German) predominated, and a channel for the dispersion of German population through the colonies.

The Scotch-Irish began to arrive later and moved still farther out in the backcountry. "Scotch-Irish" is an enduring misnomer for Ulster Scots, Presbyterians transplanted to confiscated lands in Northern Ireland to give that country a more Protestant tone. The Ulster plantation dated from 1607–1609, the years when Jamestown was fighting for survival. A century later the Ulster Scots were on the move again, in flight from economic disaster caused by English tariffs, especially the Woolens Act of 1699. This time they looked mainly to Pennsylvania.

The Germans and Scotch-Irish became the largest non-English elements in the colonies, but other groups enriched the diversity of population in New York and the Quaker colonies: French Huguenots (Calvinists whose privilege of toleration was revoked in 1685), Irish, Welshmen, Swiss, Jews, and others. New York had inherited from the Dutch a tradition of toleration which had given the colony a motley population before the English conquest: French-speaking Walloons and Frenchmen, Germans, Danes, Portuguese, Spaniards, Italians, Bohemians, Poles, and others, including some New England Puritans. The Protestant Netherlands had given haven to the Sephardic Jews expelled from Spain and Portugal, and enough of them found their way into New Netherland to found a synagogue there.

What could be said of Pennsylvania as a refuge for the persecuted might be said as well of Rhode Island and South Carolina, which practiced a similar religious toleration. Newport and Charleston, like New York and Philadelphia, became centers of minuscule Jewish populations. French Huguenots made their greatest mark on South Carolina, more by their enterprise than by their numbers, and left implanted in the life of the colony such family names as Huger, Porcher, DeSaussure, Legare, Lanneau, and Lesesne. A number of Highland Scots came directly from their homeland rather than by way of Ulster, especially after suppression of a rebellion in 1745 on behalf of the Stuart pretender to the throne, "Bonnie Prince Charlie." A large group of them went to Fayetteville, North Carolina, where Gaelic-speaking Scots settled beside Lumbee Indians who had spoken English for nearly a century.

The eighteenth century was the great period of expansion and population growth in British North America, and during those years a large increase of the non-English stock took place. A rough estimate of the national origins of the white population, based on linguistic analysis of family names in the census of 1790, found it to be 60.9 percent English, 14.3 percent Scots and Scotch-Irish, 8.7 percent German, 5.4 percent Dutch, French, and Swedish, 3.7 percent Irish, and 7 percent miscellaneous or unassigned. If one adds to the 3,172,444 whites in the first census the 756,770 nonwhites, not even considering uncounted Indians, it seems likely that little more than half the populace, and perhaps fewer, could trace their origins to England. Of the blacks about 75 percent had been transported from the bend of African coastline between the Senegal and Niger Rivers; most of the rest came from Congo-Angola.

THE BACKCOUNTRY   Pennsylvania in the eighteenth century became the great distribution point for the diverse ethnic groups of European origin, just as the Chesapeake and Charleston became the distribution points for African peoples. Before the mid–eighteenth century, population in the Pennsylvania backcountry was coming up against the Appalachian barrier and, following the line of least resistance, the Scotch-Irish and Germans filtered southward across western Maryland, down the Shenandoah valley of Virginia, and on into the Carolina and Georgia backcountry. Germans were first in the upper Shenandoah Valley, and to the south of them Scotch-Irish filled the lower valley. Migrants of both stocks continued to move into the Carolina and Georgia backcountry, while others found their way up from Charleston.

Along the fringes of the frontier were commonly found the Scotch-Irish, who had acquired in their homeland and in Ulster a stubborn fighting spirit that brooked no nonsense from the "savages" of the woods. And out on the cutting edge life might be in that "state of nature" described by Thomas Hobbes: "poor, nasty, brutish, and short." It was a lonely life of scattered settlements, isolated log cabins set on plots of land which the pioneer owned or at least occupied, furnished with crude furniture hacked out with axe and adze and pieced together with pegs. The frontier regions bred a rough democracy, because most people were on a nearly equal status, and instilled a stubborn individualism in people who got accustomed to deciding things for themselves. With time, of course, neighborhoods grew up within visiting distance, animal and Indian trails broadened into wagon roads, crossroads stores grew up into community gathering places where social intercourse could be lubricated with the whiskey that was omnipresent on the Scotch-Irish frontier.

The backcountry of the Piedmont, and something much like it on up to northern New England (Maine, New Hampshire, and what would become Vermont), became a fourth major region that stretched the length of the colonies across the abstract imaginary boundaries which separated the political units. Government was slow to reach these remote settlements, and the system of "every man for himself" sometimes led frontier communities into conditions of extreme disorder.

COLONIAL CITIES

During the seventeenth century the colonies remained in comparative isolation, evolving subtly distinctive ways and unfolding separate histories. Boston and New York, Philadelphia and Charleston were more likely to keep in closer touch with London than with each other. The Carolina upcountry had more in common with the Pennsylvania backcountry than either had with Charleston or Philadelphia. Colonial cities faced outward to the Atlantic. Since commerce was their chief reason for being, they hugged the coastline or, like Philadelphia, sprang up on streams where ocean-going vessels could reach them. Never holding more than 10 percent of the colonial population, they exerted an influence in commerce, politics, and civilization generally out of proportion to their size.

Five major port cities outdistanced the rest. By the end of the colonial period Philadelphia, with some 30,000 people (counting adjacent suburbs), was the largest city in the colonies and second only to London in the British Empire. New York, with about 25,000, ranked second, Boston numbered 16,000, Charles Town 12,000, and Newport 11,000. Falling in a range of about 8,000 down to 4,000 were secondary ports and inland towns like New Haven and Norwich, Connecticut; Norfolk; Baltimore; Lancaster, Pennsylvania; Salem; New London; Providence; and Albany.

THE SOCIAL AND POLITICAL ORDER   The upper crust of urban society were the merchants who bartered the products of American farms and forests for the molasses and rum of the West Indies, the wines of Madeira, the manufactured goods of Europe, and the slaves of Africa. Their trade in turn stimulated the activities of rum distilling, ropewalks, sail lofts, instrumentmakers, and ship chandlers who supplied vessels leaving port. After the merchants, who constituted the chief urban aristocracy, came a middle class of craftsmen, retailers, innkeepers, and small jobbers who met a variety of needs. And at the bottom of the pecking order were sailors, unskilled workers, and some artisans.

Class stratification in the cities became more pronounced as time went by. One study of Boston found that in 1687 the richest 15 percent of the population owned 52 percent of the taxable wealth; by 1771 the top 15 percent owned about two-thirds and the top 5 percent owned some 44 percent of the wealth. In Philadelphia the concentration of wealth was even more pronounced.

Problems created by urban growth are nothing new. Colonial cities had problems of traffic which required not only paved streets and lighting but regulations to protect children and animals in the streets from reckless riders. Regulations restrained citizens from creating public nuisances by tossing their garbage into the streets. Fires that on occasion swept through closely packed buildings led to preventive standards in building codes, restrictions on burning rubbish, and the organization of volunteer and finally professional fire companies. Crime and violence made necessary more police protection than the constable and watch duty which at first was required of ordinary citizens. And in cities the poor became more visible than in the countryside. Colonists brought with them the English principle of public responsibility. The number of Boston's poor receiving public assistance rose from 500 in 1700 to 4,000 in 1736, New York's from

Fighting a fire in colonial New York, from the certificate of the Hand in Hand Fire Company, New York (1762). [New York Public Library]

250 in 1698 to 5,000 in the 1770s. Most of it went to "outdoor" relief in the form of money, food, clothing, and fuel, but almshouses also appeared in colonial cities.

Town governments were not always equal to their multiple tasks. Of the major cities, Boston and Newport had the common New England system of town meetings and selectmen, while New York after 1791 had an elected council responsive to the citizens, although its major and other officials were still appointed by the governor. Philadelphia, however, fell under a self-perpetuating closed corporation in which the common run of citizens had no voice, and colonial Charles Town never achieved status as a municipal corporation at all, but remained under the thumb of the South Carolina Assembly.

CITY LIFE IN THE COLONIES   Little of the colonial population lived far from the navigable streams, except in the interior. The first roads were likely to be Indian trails, which themselves often followed the tracks of bison and perhaps the ancient mastodon through the forests. The trails widened with travel, then became roads by order of provincial and local authorities. Land travel at first had to go by horse or by foot. The first stagecoach line for the public, opened in 1732, linked Burlington and Perth Amboy, New Jersey, connecting by water to Philadelphia and New York, respectively. That same year a guidebook published in Boston, Thomas Prince's *The Vade Mecum for America,* gave roads connecting from Boston through Providence, New York, Philadelphia, and eventually on to Williamsburg and Charleston, with connecting branches. From the main ports good roads might reach thirty or forty miles inland, but all were dirt roads subject to washouts and mudholes. There was not a single hard-surfaced road during the entire colonial period, aside from city streets.

Taverns were an important adjunct of colonial travel, since movement by night was too risky, and they became social and political centers to which the local people repaired to learn news from travelers, to discuss the current issues, to socialize, drink, and gamble. Postal service through the seventeenth century was almost nonexistent—people entrusted letters to travelers or sea captains. Massachusetts set up a provincial postal system in 1677, and Pennsylvania in 1683. In 1691 King William favored Thomas Neale with a monopoly of postal service in Massachusetts, New York, and Pennsylvania, and Neale's deputy, Andrew Hamilton of Philadelphia, established a weekly service from Portsmouth, New Hampshire, to Philadelphia. The system proved unprofitable though, and Neale abandoned his monopoly in 1707. Under a Parliamentary Law of 1710, however, the postmaster of London was authorized to name a deputy in charge of the colonies and a system eventually extended the length of the Atlantic seaboard. Benjamin Franklin, who served as deputy-postmaster from 1753 to 1774, speeded up the service with shorter routes and night-traveling post riders, and increased the volume by inaugurating lower rates.

More reliable deliveries gave rise to newspapers in the eighteenth century. The first printing press was set up at Cambridge, Massachusetts, in 1638, in connection with Harvard College; it produced mainly religious tracts and sermons. The first newspaper to endure was the Boston *News-Letter* (1704), which started when William Campbell, postmaster of Boston, began writing letters to friends around Massachusetts to keep them informed of current events. Before 1745 twenty-two newspapers had been started, seven in New England, ten in the Middle Colonies, five in the South, including the *American Weekly Mercury* (1719) of Philadelphia; the *New England Courant* (1721) of Boston published by James Franklin, older brother of Benjamin; Ben's own *Pennsylvania Gazette* (acquired 1729), the *South Carolina Gazette* (1732) published by former Franklin printers Thomas Whitmarsh and Louis Timothy, John Peter Zenger's New York *Weekly Journal* (1733), and the *Virginia Gazette* (1736).

An important landmark in the progress of freedom of the press was Zenger's trial for seditious libel for publishing criticisms of New York's governor, William Cosby. Imprisoned for ten months and brought to trial in 1735, he was defended by the aged Andrew Hamilton of Philadelphia, whose cleverness made him perhaps the original "Philadelphia lawyer." The established rule in English common law held that one might be punished for criticism which fostered "an ill opinion of the government." The jury's function was only to determine whether or not the defendant had published the opinion. Hamilton startled the court with his claim that Zenger had published the truth—which the judge ruled an unacceptable defense. Cosby was so unpopular, however, that the jury considered the attacks on him true and held the editor not guilty. The libel law remained standing as before, but editors thereafter were emboldened to criticize officials more freely. No more such cases of any consequence arose.

THE ENLIGHTENMENT

DISCOVERING THE LAWS OF NATURE   It was the cities that, through their commercial contacts, through their newspapers, and through many-fold activities, became the centers for the dissemination of fashion and ideas. In the world of ideas a new fashion was abroad: the Enlightenment. During the first century of English colonization the settlers' contemporaries in Europe went through a scientific revolution in which the old Ptolemaic view of an earth-centered universe was overthrown by the new heliocentric (sun-centered) system of Polish astronomer Nicolaus Copernicus. A climax to the revolution came with Sir Isaac Newton's *Principia* (*Mathematical Principles of Natural Philosophy*, 1687), which set forth his theory of gravitation. Newton had, in short, hit upon the design of a mechanistic universe moving in accordance with natural laws which could be grasped by human reason and explained by mathematics.

By analogy from Newton's world machine one could reason that natural laws governed all things—the orbits of the planets and also the orbits of human relations: politics, economics, and society. Reason could make men aware, for instance, that the natural law of supply and demand governed economics or that natural rights to life, liberty, and property determined the limits and functions of government.

Much of enlightened thought could be reconciled with established beliefs—the idea of natural law existed in Christian theology, and religious people could reason that the worldview of Copernicus and Newton simply showed forth the glory of God. Puritan leaders accepted Newtonian science from the start. Yet if one carried the idea to its ultimate logic, one might find God eliminated or at best reduced to the position of a remote Creator —as the French *philosophe* Voltaire put it, as master clockmaker who planned the universe and set it in motion. Evil in the world, one might reason further, resulted not from original sin and innate depravity so much as from an imperfect understanding of the laws of nature. Man, John Locke argued in his *Essay on Human Understanding* (1690), is largely the product of his environment, the human mind a blank tablet on which experience is written. The evils of a corrupt society therefore might corrupt the mind. The way to improve both society and human nature was by the application and improvement of Reason—which was the highest Virtue (enlightened thinkers often capitalized both words).

THE ENLIGHTENMENT IN AMERICA Whether or not one pursued all this to the outermost reaches of its logic, such ideas affected the climate of thought in the eighteenth century. The premises of Newtonian science and the Enlightenment, moreover, fitted the

American experience. In the New World people no longer moved in the worn grooves of tradition that defined the roles of priest or peasant or noble. Much of their experience had already been with observation, experiment, and the need to think anew. America was therefore receptive to the new science. Anybody who pretended to a degree of learning revealed a curiosity about *natural philosophy*, and some carried it to considerable depth.

John Winthrop, Jr. (1606–1676), three times governor of Connecticut, wanted to establish industries and mining in America. These interests led to his work in chemistry and membership in the Royal Society of London. He owned probably the first telescope brought to the colonies. His cousin, John Winthrop IV (1714–1779), was a professional scientist, Hollis Professor of Mathematics and Natural Philosophy at Harvard, who introduced to the colonies the study of calculus and ranged over the fields of astronomy, geology, chemistry, and electricity. Cadwallader Colden, last royal governor of New York, studied and wrote in the fields of botany and physics. David Rittenhouse of Philadelphia, a clockmaker, became a self-taught scientist who built two orreries and probably the first telescope made in America. John Bartram of Philadelphia spent a lifetime traveling and studying American plant life, and gathered in Philadelphia a botanical garden now part of the city's park system.

FRANKLIN'S INFLUENCE   Benjamin Franklin stood apart from all these men as the person who epitomized the Enlightenment, in the eyes of both Americans and Europeans, more than any other single person. It was fitting that Franklin came from Pennsylvania, which in the eyes of Voltaire had fulfilled the Quaker virtues of toleration and simplicity. William Penn, Voltaire wrote, had "brought to the world that golden age of which men talk so much and which probably has never existed anywhere except in Pennsylvania." Franklin came from the ranks of the common man and never lost the common touch, a gift that accounted for his success as a publisher. Born in Boston in 1706, son of a candle and soap maker, apprenticed to his older brother, a printer, Franklin ran away at the age of seventeen. In Philadelphia, before he was twenty-four he owned a print shop where he edited and published the *Pennsylvania Gazette*, and when he was twenty-seven he brought out *Poor Richard's Almanac*, still mined for its homely maxims on success and happiness. Before he retired from business at the age of forty-two, Franklin, among other achievements, had founded a library, invented a stove, set up a fire com-

Benjamin Franklin as a leading figure in the Enlightenment. The electrical storm alludes to his famous experiments with electricity. [Philadelphia Museum of Art]

pany, helped start the academy which became the University of Pennsylvania, and started a debating club which grew into the American Philosophical Society. After his early retirement he intended to devote himself to public affairs and the sciences.

The course of events allowed him less and less time for science, but that was his passion. Franklin's *Experiments and Observations on Electricity* (1751) went through many editions in several languages and established his reputation as a leading thinker and experimenter. His speculations extended widely to the fields of medicine, meteorology, geology, astronomy, physics, and other aspects of science. He invented the Franklin stove, the lighting rod, and a glass harmonica for which Mozart and Beethoven composed. In his travels as colonial agent to London and later American ambassador to France, his insatiable curiosity led to suggestions (some of them later adopted) for improvements in ship design. Franklin's university had been the printshop, and the triumph of this untutored genius further confirmed the Enlightenment trust in the powers of Nature.

EDUCATION IN THE COLONIES The heights of abstract reasoning, of course, were remote from the everyday concerns of most colonists. For the colonists at large, education in the traditional ideas and manners of society—even literacy itself—remained primarily the responsibility of family and church, and one not always accepted. The modern conception of universal free education as a responsibility of the state was a slow growth and failed to win universal acceptance until the twentieth century. Yet there is evidence of a widespread concern almost from the beginning that steps needed to be taken lest the children of settlers grow up untutored in the wilderness.

Conditions in New England proved most favorable for the establishment of schools. The Puritan emphasis on Scripture reading, which all Protestants shared in some degree, implied an obligation to ensure literacy. The great proportion of highly educated people in Puritan New England (Massachusetts probably had a greater proportion of college graduates in the early seventeenth century than in the twentieth) ensured a common respect for education. And the compact towns of that region made schools more feasible than among the scattered people of the southern colonies. In 1635 the inhabitants of Boston established the Boston Latin Grammar School, which had a distinguished career to the twentieth century, and the same year the General Court voted to establish a college which, begun in 1638, grew into Harvard University. In 1647 the colony enacted the famous "ye olde deluder Satan" Act (designed to thwart the Evil One) which required every town of fifty or more families to set up a grammar school (a Latin school that could prepare a student

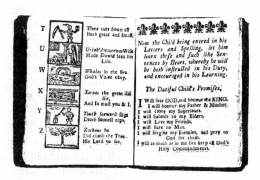

A New England primer (1727). From books such as this, the New England child was "both instructed in his Duty, and encouraged in his learning." [New York Public Library]

for college). Although the act was widely evaded, it did signify a serious purpose to promote education. Massachusetts Bay set an example which the rest of New England emulated.

The Dutch in New Netherland were nearly if not equally as active as the New England Puritans, and more active than the English who succeeded them after 1664. In Pennsylvania the Quakers never heeded William Penn's instructions to establish public schools, but did respect the usefulness of education and financed a number of private schools teaching practical as well as academic subjects. In the southern colonies efforts to establish schools were hampered by the more scattered populations, and in parts of the backcountry by indifference and neglect. Some of the wealthiest planters and merchants of the Tidewater sent their children to England or hired tutors, who in some cases would also serve the children of neighbors. In some places wealthy patrons or the people collectively managed to raise some kind of support for "old field" schools and academies at the secondary level.

THE GREAT AWAKENING

STIRRINGS   In the new currents of learning and the Enlightenment, however, many people seemed to be drifting away from the old moorings of piety. And if the Lord had allowed great Puritan and Quaker merchants of Boston and Philadelphia to prosper, the haunting fear arose that the devil had lured them into the vain pursuit of worldly gain. Intellectually the educated classes were falling into deism and skepticism. And out along the fringes of settlement there grew up a great backwater of the unchurched, people who had no minister to preach or administer sacraments or perform marriages, who fell into a primitive and sinful life, little different from the heathens who lurked in the woods. Charles Woodmason, an Anglican divine, called the backcountry preachers in the Carolinas "ignorant wretches, who cannot write." A Baptist communion service was to him like "A Gang of frantic Lunatics broke out of Bedlam." By the 1730s the sense of falling-away had prepared the time for a revival of faith, the Great Awakening, a wave of evangelism that within a few years swept the colonies from one end to the other, America's first mass movement.

In 1734–1735 a rehearsal for the event came in a remarkable spiritual refreshing that occurred in the congregation of Jon-

The Rev. Jonathan Edwards awoke many congregants to their plight in sermons such as "Sinners in the Hands of an Angry God."
[Yale University Art Gallery]

athan Edwards, a Congregationalist minister of Northampton in western Massachusetts. Edwards's vivid descriptions of the torments of hell and the delights of heaven inspired his congregants. About the same time William Tennant arrived from Ulster and in Neshaminy, Pennsylvania, set up a "Log College" for the education of ministers to serve the Scotch-Irish Presbyterians around Philadelphia. The Log College specialized in turning out zealots who scorned complacency and proclaimed the need for revival.

The catalyst of the Great Awakening, however, was a twenty-seven-year-old Anglican minister, George Whitefield, whose reputation as an evangelist preceded him to the colonies. In the autumn of 1739 he arrived in Philadelphia, and late in that year preached to crowds of as many as 6,000 around Philadelphia. After visiting in Georgia, he made a triumphal procession northward to New England, drawing great crowds and releasing "Gales of Heavenly Wind" that dispersed sparks throughout the colonies. Young and magnetic, possessed of a golden voice, a dramatic actor in the pulpit who impersonated the agonies of the damned and the joys of the regenerate, he swept audiences with his unparalleled eloquence. Even the skeptical Ben Franklin, who went to see the show in Philadelphia, found himself so carried away that he emptied his pockets into the collection plate —perhaps the highest possible tribute to Whitefield's persuasiveness. The core of his message was the need to experience a "new birth"—the need for a sudden and emotional moment of conversion and salvation—and the dangers of an unconverted ministry which had not experienced such rebirth.

Imitators sprang up everywhere, some of whom carried the language and histrionics to extremes. Graduates of the Log College denounced the "pharisaical preachers" who were themselves unconverted. The Rev. James Davenport, an itinerant Congregationalist of New England, set about stomping on the devil. The churched and unchurched flocked to the meetings, and seized of the terror and ecstacy, groveled on the floor or lay unconscious on the benches, to the chagrin of more decorous churchgoers. One never knew, the more traditional clergymen warned, whence came these enthusiasms—perhaps they were delusions sent by the Evil One to discredit the true faith.

PIETY AND REASON   Everywhere the Awakening brought splits, especially in the more Calvinistic churches. Presbyterians divided into the "Old Side" and "New Side"; Congregationalists into "Old Lights" and "New Lights." New England would never be the same. The more traditional clergy found its position being undermined as church members chose sides and either dismissed their ministers or deserted them. Many of the "New Lights" went over to the Baptists, and others flocked to Presbyterian or, later, Methodist groups, which in turn divided and subdivided into new sects.

New England Puritanism was now finally divided. The precarious tension in which the Founders had held the elements of piety and reason was now sundered. Jonathan Edwards, the great theologian of the Awakening and perhaps of all American history, led the movement toward piety and justified the emotional extravagance of the conversion experience as something beyond the ability of the human frame to stand without physical manifestation. But he was an intellectual, himself never given to those excesses nor to the histrionics of Whitefield. Edwards's magnum opus was an elaborate theological reconciliation of Calvinism and the Enlightenment: *Of Freedom of the Will* (1754). Indeed, one curious and paradoxical sequel of the revival was the growth in New England churches of the "New Divinity," which spun out the ramifications of the revival theology in such recondite fashion that whole congregations got lost in the fog. In consequence New England was infiltrated more and more by Baptists, Presbyterians, Anglicans, and other denominations, but the revival tradition which had its chief theologian in New England paradoxically scored its most lasting victories along the chaotic frontiers of the middle and southern colonies.

In the more sedate churches of Boston, moreover, the principle of reason got the upper hand in a reaction against the excesses of revival emotion. Bostonian ministers like Charles Chauncey and Jonathan Mayhew assumed the lead in preaching a doctrine of rationality. They reexamined Calvinist theology and found it too forbidding and irrational that men could be forever damned by predestination. The rationality of Newton and Locke, the idea of natural law, crept more and more into their sermons. They were already on the road to Unitarianism and Universalism.

In reaction to taunts that the "born-again" ministers lacked learning, the Awakening gave rise to the denominational colleges that became so characteristic of American higher education. The three colleges already in existence had grown earlier from religious motives: Harvard, founded in 1636, because the Puritans dreaded "to leave an illiterate ministry to the church when our present ministers shall lie in the dust"; the College of William and Mary, in 1693, to serve James Blair's purpose of strengthening the Anglican ministry; and Yale College, in 1701, set up to serve the Puritans of Connecticut, who felt that Harvard was drifting from the strictest orthodoxy. The Presbyterian College of New Jersey, later Princeton University, was founded in 1746 as successor to William Tennent's Log College. In close succession came King's College (1754) in New York, later Columbia University, an Anglican institution; the College of Rhode Island (1764), later Brown University, Baptist; Queen's College (1766), later Rutgers, Dutch Reformed; and Congregationalist Dartmouth (1769), the outgrowth of an earlier school for Indians. Among the colonial colleges only the University of Pennsylvania, founded as the Philadelphia Academy in 1754, arose from a secular impulse.

The Great Awakening, like the Enlightenment, set in motion currents that still flow in American life. It implanted permanently in American culture the evangelical principle and the endemic style of revivalism. The movement weakened the status of the old-fashioned clergy and encouraged the believer to exercise his own judgment, and thereby weakened habits of deference generally. By adding to the proliferation of denominations it added to the need for toleration of dissent. But in some respects the counterpoint between the Awakening and the Enlightenment, between the principles of piety and reason, paradoxically led by different roads to similar ends. Both emphasized the power and right of the individual to judge things for himself, and both aroused millennial hopes that America would become the promised land in which men might attain to the perfection of piety or reason, if not of both.

FURTHER READING

Scholarship in colonial social history traditionally offers a varied fare. Since most works concentrate on specific themes and particular locales, a comprehensive social analysis of the 1600s awaits its historian. Timothy H. Breen's *Puritans and Adventurers: Change and Persistance in Early America* (1980)° traces the steadfastness of early settlement patterns in both the northern and southern colonies, but concentrates on Virginia and Massachusetts. James A. Henretta's *The Evolution of American Society, 1700–1815* (1973),° brings together much recent research on the eighteenth century. Sketches of everyday life and social conditions appear in the overviews listed in Chapter 2, particularly Daniel Boorstin's *The Americans: The Colonial Experience* (1958).° Richard F. Hofstadter's *America At 1750: A Social Portrait* (1971)° is valuable for the later colonial period.

Until recently Puritan communities received the bulk of scholarly attention. Studies of the New England town include Darrett B. Rutman's *Winthrop's Boston: Portrait of a Puritan Town, 1630–1649* (1965);° Summer Powell's *Puritan Village* (1963),° on the origins and social structure of Sudbury, Mass.; Kenneth A. Lockridge's *A New England Town: The First One Hundred Years* (1970),° which looks at the relationship of family and authority in Dedham, Mass.; Philip Greven's *Four Generations: Population, Land, and Family in Colonial Amherst, Massachusetts* (1970);° and Paul Boyer and Stephen Nissenbaum's *Salem Possessed* (1974),° which conects the famous witch trials to changes in community structure and economic base.

All five books just listed stress patterns of structural development in Massachusetts during the seventeenth century. Broader in cultural interpretation are Richard S. Dunn's *Puritans and Yankees: The Winthrop Dynasty of New England, 1630–1717* (1982),° Timothy H. Breen's *The Character of the Good Ruler: Puritan Political Ideals in New England, 1630–1730* (1982),° and E. Digby Baltzell's *Puritan Boston and Quaker Philadelphia* (1982).° For an interdisciplinary approach, see John Demos's *Entertaining Satan: Witchcraft and the Culture of Early New England* (1982).° For a comparison of the Puritans and the Pilgrims, see John Demos's *A Little Commonwealth: Family Life in Plymouth Colony* (1970).°

The descendants of these early settlers are described in Michael Zuckerman's *Peaceable Kingdoms: Massachusetts Towns in the Eighteenth Century* (1970),° Edward Cook's *Fathers of the Towns: Leadership and Community Structure in Eighteenth Century New England* (1976), and Robert A. Gross's *The World of the Minutemen* (1976).°

For the social history of the southern colonies, see William F. Craven's *The Southern Colonies in the Seventeenth Century* (1949).° Valuable for the eighteenth century is Carl Bridenbaugh's *Myths and*

° These books are available in paperback editions.

Realities: Societies of the Colonial South (1963),° which advances the idea that more than one "South" was developing.

The best southern social history is intertwined with analysis of the origins of slavery. Begin with Edmund S. Morgan's *American Slavery / American Freedom: The Ordeal of Colonial Virginia* (1975),° which examines the impact of social structure, environment, and labor patterns in a biracial context. Peter H. Wood weaves a similar social mosaic for South Carolina in *Black Majority: Negroes in Colonial South Carolina from 1670 through the Stono Rebellion* (1974).° More specific on the racial nature of the origins of slavery are Winthrop Jordan's *White over Black: American Attitudes toward the Negro, 1550–1812* (1968),° and David B. Davis's *The Problem of Slavery in Western Culture* (1966).° The mechanics of the slave market are handled in Philip D. Curtin's *The Atlantic Slave Trade* (1969).° Black viewpoints are also presented in Gerald Mullin's *Flight and Rebellion: Slave Resistance in Eighteenth Century Virginia* (1972),° and Timothy H. Breen and Stephen Innes's *"Myne Own Ground": Race and Freedom on Virginia's Eastern Shore, 1640–1676* (1980),° a short and insightful work on free blacks. Lewis C. Gray's *History of Agriculture in the Southern United States to 1860* (vol. 1, 1933) handles the specifics of plantation agriculture. David W. Galenson's *White Servitude in Colonial America* (1981) looks at the indentured labor force.

Patterns of trade during the colonial period have principally been approached from the mercantile viewpoint. James F. Shepherd and Gary M. Walter, in *The Economic Rise of Early America* (1979), emphasize the connection between maritime commerce and interior development. Problems with the monetary system are treated in Curtis P. Nettels's *The Money Supply of the American Colonies before 1720* (1934). Trade connections with Europe are stressed in Ralph Davis's *Rise of the Atlantic Economy* (1973).° How the staple tobacco affected both commerce and cultivation can be studied in Jacob M. Price's *France and the Chesapeake* (2 vols.; 1973). The interaction of trade and politics in America's first cities is the subject of Carl Bridenbaugh's *Cities in the Wilderness* (1955) and Gary B. Nash's *The Urban Crucible* (1979).°

Land policies and the Turner thesis have also received recent attention. Charles S. Grant's *Democracy in the Connecticut Frontier Town of Kent* (1961)° challenges the interpretation that frontier settlements enjoyed a greater degree of equality. James T. Lemon explores land holding patterns in one county of Pennsylvania in *The Best Poor Man's Country* (1972).° The impact of land pressures and tenancy is explored in P. O. Walker's *Land and People* (1978) and Sung Bok Kim's *Landlord and Tenant in Colonial New York* (1978). The political implications of land pressures are documented for the Middle Colonies in Patricia Bonomi's *A Factious People* (1971).° The ethnic composition of landholders is studied in Robert V. Wells's *The population of the British Colonies before 1776* (1975).

An overview of cultural patterns is provided in Louis B. Wright's *Cultural Life of the American Colonies, 1607- 1763* (1957).° Henry F. May's *The Enlightenment in America* (1976)° examines intellectual trends. For the role of Benjamin Franklin in American culture, consult first the full-length biographies by Carl Van Doren, *Benjamin Franklin* (1938), and Charles G. Sellers, Jr., *Benjamin Franklin in Portraiture* (1962). Shorter but instructive is Verner W. Crane's *Benjamin Franklin and a Rising People* (1954). Franklin's reputation as a scientist is treated in Alfred O. Aldridge's *Franklin and His French Contemporaries* (1957). Lawrence Cremin's *American Education: The Colonial Experience, 1607–1783* (1970),° surveys educational development at several levels. Joseph J. Ellis's *The New England Mind in Transition: Samuel Johnson of Connecticut, 1696–1772* (1973), examines the role religion played in the development of higher education.

A concise introduction to the events and repercussions of the Great Awakening is J. M. Bumsted and John E. Van de Wetering's *What Must I Do To Be Saved?* (1976). Studies of the revival which concentrate on New England include Richard Bushman's *From Puritan to Yankee: Character and Social Order in Connecticut* (1967)° and C. C. Goen's *Revivalism and Separtism in New England, 1740–1800* (1962). Alan Heimert's *Religion and the American Mind from the Great Awakening to the Revolution* (1966) emphasizes the relationships of faith and belief to later political behavior. The political impact of the new religious enthusiasm in Virginia is handled in Rhys Isaac's *The Transformation of Virginia, 1740–1790* (1982).° Perry Miller analyzes Jonathan Edward's theological influence in *Jonathan Edwards* (1958). More recent is Patricia J. Tracy's *Jonathan Edwards, Pastor* (1980),° which stresses the Northampton minister's relations to his community. To understand the conflicts of authority between dissenters and the established churches in the colonies, consult Carl Bridenbaugh's *Mitre and Sceptre: Transatlantic Faiths, Ideas, Personalities, and Politics, 1689–1775* (1962), William G. McLoughlin's *Isaac Backus and the American Pietistic Tradition* (1967), and Charles S. Bolton's *Southern Anglicanism: The Church of England in Colonial South Carolina* (1982).

4

THE IMPERIAL PERSPECTIVE

In 1757, 150 years after the Jamestown beginnings, Edmund Burke wrote: "The settlement of our colonies was never pursued upon any regular plan; but they were formed, grew, and flourished, as accidents, the nature of the climate, or the dispositions of private men happened to operate." Burke's statement was true. For the better part of the seventeenth century England remained too disrupted by the running struggle between Parliament and the Stuarts ever to perfect either a colonial policy or effective agencies of imperial control. Intervention in colonial affairs was a matter of ad hoc commissions, experimentation, and "muddling through," a practice at which the British had a certain skill and not little luck. Slowly a plan of colonial administration emerged after the Restoration and began to fall into a semblance of order under William III, but even so it fell short of coherence and efficiency.

ENGLISH ADMINISTRATION OF THE COLONIES

Throughout the colonial period the king stood as the source of legal authority in America, and titles derived ultimately from royal grants. All colonies except Georgia got charters from the king before the Glorious Revolution, and thus before the crown lost supremacy to Parliament. The colonies therefore continued to stand as "dependencies of the crown" and the important colonial officials held office at the pleasure of the crown. And Georgia's status conformed to the established practice.

The king exercised his authority through the Privy Council, a body of some thirty to forty advisors appointed by and responsible solely to him, and this group became the first agency of colonial supervision. But the Privy Council was too large and too burdened to keep track of the details. So in 1634 Charles I entrusted colonial affairs to eleven members, the Lords Commissioners for Plantations in General, with William Laud, archbishop of Canterbury, as its head. The Laud Commission grew in part out of the troubles following the dissolution of the Virginia Company and in part out of Laud's design to impose political and religious conformity on New England. In 1638 his commission ordered Massachusetts to return its charter and answer charges that colonial officials had violated the provisions. Sir Ferdinando Gorges, appointed governor-general of New England, planned to subdue the region by force if necessary, and might have nipped the Puritan experiment in the bud except for the troubles at home which prevented further action.

The Civil War in England, which lasted from 1641 to 1649, was followed by Cromwell's Puritan Commonwealth and Protectorate, and both gave the colonies a respite from efforts at royal control. A Parliamentary Council for the Colonies, set up in 1643, and various Parliamentary committees and commissions, never exercised more than a shadowy authority. Puritan New England was naturally well disposed toward the Parliamentary cause, and in 1652 Cromwell dispatched an expedition to the colonies which forced the West Indies, Virginia, and Maryland to recognize Parliamentary authority but left them otherwise unmolested.

THE MERCANTILE SYSTEM If Cromwell showed little concern for colonial administration, he had a lively concern for colonial trade, which had fallen largely to Dutch shipping during the upheavals in England. Therefore in 1651 Parliament adopted a Navigation Act which excluded nearly all foreign shipping from the English and colonial trade. It required that all goods imported into England or the colonies must arrive on English ships and that the majority of the crew must be English. In all cases colonial ships and crews qualified as English. The act excepted European goods, which might come in ships of the country which produced the goods, but only from the place of origin or the port from which they were usually shipped.

On economic policy, if nothing else, Restoration England under Charles II took its cue from Cromwell. The New Parliament quickly adopted and then elaborated the mercantile system he had effected. The mercantile system, or mercantilism, became in the seventeenth and eighteenth centuries the operative theory of all major European powers—although the term itself was a later invention—and more than a trace of it remains in national policies today. In a world of national rivalries, the reasoning went, power and wealth went hand in hand. To be strong a state should be wealthy. To be wealthy it should enlarge its stores of gold and silver. To get and keep gold and silver the state should limit foreign imports and preserve a favorable balance of trade. And to accomplish these things the state should encourage manufacturers, through subsidies and monopolies if need be; it should develop and protect its own shipping; and it should make use of colonies as sources of raw materials and markets for its own finished goods. Mercantilists held that the total of the world's wealth, as reflected in the total stock of gold and silver, remained essentially fixed. All that changed was the nation's share of that stock. The theory lacked a conception of what today is a commonplace—that economic growth might enlarge wealth regardless of gold and silver.

Next came the Navigation Act of 1660, which amounted to a reenactment of Cromwell's act of 1651, but with a new twist. Ships' crews now had to be not half but three-quarters English, and certain enumerated articles were to be shipped only to England or other English colonies. These were things needed but not produced by the mother country. The list included at first tobacco, cotton, indigo, ginger, rustick and other dyewoods, and sugar. Later the enumeration expanded to include, among other things, rice, naval stores, hemp, masts and yards, copper ores, and furs. Not only did England (and the colonies) become the only outlet for these colonial exports, but three years later the Navigation Act of 1663 sought to make England the funnel through which all colonial imports had to be routed as well. The act was sometimes called the Staple Act because it made England the staple (market or trade center) for goods sent to the colonies. Everything shipped from Europe to America had to stop off in England, be landed, and pay duty before reshipment. There were few exceptions: only servants, horses, and provisions from Scotland; wine from Madeira and the Azores; and salt for fisheries. A third major act rounded out the trade system. The Navigation Act of 1673 (sometimes called the Plantation Duty Act) required that every captain loading enumerated articles give bond to land them in England, or if they were destined for another colony, that he pay on the spot a duty roughly equal to that paid in England.

ENFORCING THE NAVIGATION ACTS The Navigation Acts set forth policy in provisions that were simple and straightforward enough. And they supplied a convenient rationale for a colonial system: to serve the economic needs of the mother country. Their enforcement in scattered colonies was something else again, however. So in the age of Charles II a bureaucracy of colonial administrators began to emerge, but it took shape slowly, and in fact never achieved full delineation. After the Restoration of 1660, supervision of colonial affairs fell once again to the Privy Council, or rather to a succession of its committees. In 1675, however, Charles II introduced some order into the chaos when he designated certain privy councilors the Lords of Trade and Plantations, whose name reflects the overall importance of economic factors. The Lords of Trade were to make the colonies abide by the mercantile system and to seek out ways to make them more profitable to England and the crown. To these ends they served as the clearinghouse for all colonial affairs, building up an archive and a bureaucracy of colonial experts supervised by their secretary, William Blathwayte. By advice rather than by direct authority, at least in theory, they named governors, wrote or reviewed the governors' instructions, and handled all reports and correspondence dealing with colonial affairs.

Within five years of the Plantation Duty Act, between 1673 and 1678, collectors of customs appeared in all the colonies and in 1683 a surveyor-general of the customs in the American colonies was named. The most notorious of these, insofar as the colonists were concerned, was Edward Randolph, the first man to make an entire career in the colonial service and the nemesis of

William Burgis's view of Boston shows the importance of shipping and its regulation in the colonies, especially Massachusetts Bay. [Winterthur Museum]

insubordinate colonials for a quarter century. Randolph's first assignment was as courier from the Lords of Trade. He arrived at Boston in June 1676 to demand that Massachusetts send agents to answer complaints that it had usurped the proprietary rights in New Hampshire and Maine. More was at stake, however. Since the Restoration the colony had ignored gentle hints that it bring its practices more in line with fundamental elements of the Restoration compromise. Massachusetts had accepted the formality of conducting judicial proceedings in the king's name. It dragged its heels, however, on adopting an Oath of Allegiance, repealing laws counter to English law, allowing use of the Anglican *Book of Common Prayer,* or making property instead of church membership the voting test. The expanding commercial interests of New England counseled prudence and accommodation, but the Puritan leaders harbored a persistent distrust of Stuart designs on their Wilderness Zion.

After a brief stay, Randolph submitted a report bristling with hostility. The Bay Colony had not only ignored royal wishes, it had tolerated violations of the Navigation Acts, refused appeals from its courts to the Privy Council, and had operated a mint in defiance of the king's prerogative. Massachusetts officials had told him, Randolph reported, "that the legislative power is and abides in them solely to act and make laws by virtue" of their charter. Continuing intransigence from Massachusetts led the Lords of Trade to begin legal proceedings against the colonial charter in 1678, although the issue remained in legal snarls for another six years. Meanwhile Randolph returned in 1680 to establish the royal colony of New Hampshire, then set up shop as the king's collector of customs in Boston, whence he dispatched repeated accounts of colonial recalcitrance. Eventually, in 1684, the Lords of Trade won a court decision which annulled the charter of Massachusetts.

THE DOMINION OF NEW ENGLAND   Temporarily, its government was placed in the hands of a special royal commission. Then in 1685 Charles II died, to be succeeded by his brother, the duke of York, as James II, the first Catholic sovereign since the death of Queen Mary in 1558. Plans long maturing in the Lords of Trade for a general reorganization of colonial government fitted very well the autocratic notions of James II, who asserted his prerogatives more forcefully than his brother and seemed to have less fear that he might have "to embark on his travels" again. The new king therefore readily approved a proposal to create a Dominion of New England and to place under its sway all colonies down through New Jersey. Something of the sort might have been in store for Pennsylvania and the southern colonies as well if the reign of James II had lasted longer. In that case the English colonies might have found themselves on the same tight leash as the colonies of Spain or France.

The Dominion was to have a government named altogether by royal authority, a governor and council who would rule without any assembly at all. The royal governor, Sir Edmond Andros, who had already served briefly as governor of New York, appeared in Boston in 1686 to establish his rule, which he soon extended over Connecticut and Rhode Island, and in 1688 over New York and the Jerseys. Andros was a soldier, accustomed to taking—and giving—orders. He seems to have been honest, efficient, and loyal to the crown, but totally without tact in circumstances which called for the utmost diplomacy—the uprooting of long-established institutions in the face of popular hostility.

His measures inspired increasing resentment, especially in Massachusetts. Taxation was now levied without the consent of the General Court, and when residents of Ipswich, led by the Rev. John Wise, protested against taxation without representation, a number of them were imprisoned or fined. Andros suppressed town governments. He proceeded to establish enforcement of the trade laws and subdue smuggling with the help of Edward Randolph, that omnipresent servant of the crown. And most ominous of all, Andros and his lieutenants took over one of the Puritan churches for Anglican worship in Boston. Puritan leaders believed, with good reason, that he proposed to break their power and authority. Andros might have found a moderate party in the prosperous and comfortable merchants, concerned for their businesses perhaps more than for their religion, but his enforcement of the Navigation Acts enraged them as well.

In any case the Dominion was scarcely established before word came of the Glorious Revolution of 1688–1689. James II in the homeland, like Andros in New England, had aroused resentment by arbitrary measures and, what was more, by openly parading his Catholic faith. The birth of a son, sure to be reared a Catholic, put the opposition on notice that James's system would survive him. The Catholic son, rather than the Protestant daughters, Mary and Anne, would be next in line for the throne. Parliamentary leaders, their patience exhausted, invited Mary and her husband, the Dutch stadtholder, William of Orange, to assume the throne as joint monarchs. James, his support dwindling, fled the country.

THE GLORIOUS REVOLUTION IN AMERICA   When news reached Boston that William had landed in England, Boston staged its own Glorious Revolution, as bloodless as that in England. Andros and his councilors were arrested and Massachusetts reverted to its former government. In rapid sequence the other colonies that had been absorbed into the Dominion followed suit. All were permitted to retain their former status except Massachusetts and Plymouth which, after some delay, were united under a new charter in 1691 as the royal colony of Massachusetts Bay. In New York, however, events took a different course. There, Francis Nicholson, serving as Andros's lieutenant-governor, was deposed by a group led by a German immigrant, Jacob Leisler, who assumed the office of governor pending word from England. When ambiguous letters came from William authorizing a continuation of the government, Leisler believed that they gave him power, and for two years he kept the province under his control with the support of the militia which had mobilized to overthrow Nicholson. Finally, in 1691, the king appointed a new governor, but an unfortunate tragedy ensued, which turned upon misunderstandings and poor timing. Leisler hesitated to turn over authority, and on this pretext the new governor charged him with treason. Leisler and his son-in-law, Jacob Milborne, were hanged on May 16, 1691. Four years too late, in 1695, Parliament exonerated them of all charges. For years to come Leisler and anti-Leisler factions would poison the political atmosphere of New York.

No effort was made to resume the disastrous policy of the Dominion of New England, but a remnant of that design, so to speak, was salvaged in the policy of bringing more colonies under royal control to the extent that the crown appointed the governor. Massachusetts was first, in 1691. New York kept the status of royal colony it had achieved upon the accession of James II. In Maryland after the Glorious Revolution, a local rebellion against the Catholic proprietor gave the occasion to appoint a royal governor in 1691. Maryland, however, reverted to proprietary status in 1715 after the fourth Lord Baltimore became Anglican. Pennsylvania had an even briefer career as a royal colony, 1692–1694, before reverting to Penn's proprietorship. New Jersey became royal in 1702, South Carolina in 1719, North Carolina in 1729, and Georgia in 1752.

The Glorious Revolution had significant long-term effects on American history in that the Bill of Rights and Toleration Act, passed in 1689, influenced attitudes and the course of events in the colonies even though they were not legally binding there.

And what was more significant for the future, the overthrow of James II set an example and a precedent for revolution against the monarch. In defense of that action the philosopher John Locke published his *Two Treatises on Government* (1690), which had an enormous impact on political thought in the colonies. The *First Treatise* refuted theories of the divine right of kings. The more important *Second Treatise* set forth Locke's contract theory of government. People were endowed with certain natural rights, the reasoning went—basically the rights to life, liberty, and property. Without government, in a state of nature, such rights went without safeguard. Hence men came together and by mutual agreement established governments among themselves. Kings were parties to such agreements, and bound by them. When they violated the rights of the people, therefore, the people had the right—in extreme cases—to overthrow the monarch and change their government.

The idea that governments emerged by contract out of a primitive state of nature is of course hypothetical, not a documented account of events. What Locke was seeking, as the historian Carl Becker put it, was "not the historical origin, but the rational justification, of government." But in the American experience governments had actually grown out of contractual arrangements such as he described: for instance, the Mayflower Compact, the Cambridge Agreement, the Fundamental Orders of Connecticut. The royal charters themselves constituted a sort of contract between the crown and the settlers. Locke's writings in any case appealed to colonial readers, and his philosophy probably had

John Locke. [National Portrait Gallery, London]

more influence in America than in England. It might be an over-statement, but a plausible case can be made that Locke's theories established a tradition, a consensus within which American institutions operated by almost universal consent, at least from the time of independence and to some extent before. Other works of political philosophy which had a wide influence in the colonies were James Harrington's *Oceana* (1656), a republican utopia, and Algernon Sidney's *Discourse on Government* (1698).

AN EMERGING COLONIAL SYSTEM   The accession of William and Mary brought on a recapitulation and refinement of the existing Navigation Acts and administrative system. In 1696 two developments created at last the semblance, and to some degree the reality, of a coherent colonial system. First, the Navigation Act of 1696, "An Act for preventing Frauds and regulating Abuses in the Plantation Trade," restated the existing restrictions on colonial commerce but added certain provisions designed to tighten the enforcement: a special oath by governors to enforce the Navigation Acts, the use by customs officials of "writs of assistance" (general search warrants which did not have to specify the place to be searched), and the trial of accused violators in Admiralty Courts, which Edward Randolph had recommended because juries habitually refused to convict. Admiralty cases were decided by judges whom the governors appointed.

Second, also in 1696, by executive order William III created the Board of Trade (Lords Commissioners of Trade and Plantations) to take the place of the Lords of Trade and Plantations. The new board included eight privy councilors and additional members from outside. Colonial officials were required to report to the board, and its archives constitute the largest single collection of materials on colonial relations with the mother country from that time on.

The functions of the Board of Trade, which continued through the remainder of the colonial period, were again primarily advice and policy-making. Since its main purpose was to make the colonies serve the mother country's economy, the board investigated the enforcement of the Navigation Acts, and recommended ways to limit colonial manufactures and to encourage the production of raw materials. In 1705, for instance, at the board's behest Parliament enacted a bounty for the production of naval stores, ship timber, masts, and hemp. Similar payments were later extended to encourage the production of rice, indigo, and other commodities. The board examined all colonial laws and made recommendations for their disallowance by the crown.

In all, 8,563 colonial laws eventually were examined and 469 of them were actually disallowed. The board also made recommendations for official appointments in the colonies.

SALUTARY NEGLECT   From 1696 to 1725 the board met regularly and worked vigorously toward subjecting the colonies to a more efficient royal control. After 1725, however, the board entered a period of relative inactivity. After the death of Queen Anne the throne went in turn to the Hanoverian monarchs, George I (1714–1727) and George II (1727–1760), German princes who were next in the Protestant line of succession by virtue of descent from James I. Under these monarchs, the cabinet (a kind of executive committee in the Privy Council) emerged as the central agency of administration. Robert Walpole, as first minister (1721–1742), deliberately followed a policy of not rocking the boat lest he endanger the Hanoverian settlement, a policy which Edmund Burke later called "a wise and salutary neglect." The board became chiefly an agency of political patronage, studded with officials who took an interest mainly in their salaries. Under the earl of Halifax the board experienced a revival after 1748, and from 1752 to 1761 actually had power to appoint colonial governors, but generally decreased in significance thereafter.

In the course of the eighteenth century other administrative agencies and offices became involved in certain aspects of colonial government. The most important of these was the secretary of state for the Southern Department. After about 1700 he was the chief administrative official with supervision over colonial matters. Royal governors were responsible to him for colonial defense and military matters. At the same time the secretary had responsibility for Mediterranean affairs and relations with France and Spain, which of course often involved colonial matters—and colonial wars. But the secretary was too busy with diplomacy to give sustained attention to the colonies, and indeed none showed much energy, except the elder William Pitt, who held the office while also first minister. The duke of Newcastle, who served (1727–1748) during the decades of salutary neglect, was, according to a contemporary, a man who lost an hour in the morning every day and spent the rest of the day running around trying to find it.

COLONIAL GOVERNMENTS

Government within the colonies, like colonial policy, evolved without plan, but colonial governments at least had in the English government a body of precedent to fall back on. In broad outline the governor, council, and assembly in each colony corresponded to the king, lords, and commons of the mother country. At the outset all the colonies except Georgia had begun as projects of trading companies or feudal proprietors holding charters from the crown, but eight colonies eventually relinquished or forfeited their charters and became royal provinces. In these the governor was named by the crown. In Maryland, Pennsylvania, and Delaware he remained the choice of a proprietor, although each had an interim period of royal government. Connecticut and Rhode Island remained the exceptions, the last of the corporate colonies, which elected their own governors to the end of the colonial period. In the corporate and proprietary colonies, and in Massachusetts, the charter served as a rough equivalent to a written constitution. Rhode Island and Connecticut in fact kept their charters as state constitutions after independence. Over the years certain anomalies appeared, as colonial governments diverged from that of England. On the one hand the governors retained powers and prerogatives which the king had lost in the course of the seventeenth century. On the other hand the assemblies acquired powers, particularly with respect to appointments, which Parliament had yet to gain.

POWERS OF THE GOVERNORS   The crown never vetoed acts of Parliament after 1707, but the colonial governors still held an absolute veto and the crown could disallow (in effect, veto) colonial legislation by action of the Board of Trade. With respect to the assembly, the governor still had the power to determine when and where it would meet, to prorogue (adjourn or recess) sessions, and to dissolve the assembly for new elections or to postpone elections indefinitely at his pleasure. The crown, however, was pledged to summon Parliament every three years and call elections at least every seven, and could not prorogue sessions. The royal or proprietary governor, moreover, nominated for life appointment the members of his council (except in Massachusetts, where they were chosen by the lower house) and the council functioned as both the upper house of the legislature and the highest court of appeal within the colony. With respect to the judiciary, in all but the charter colonies the governor still held the prerogative of creating courts and of naming and dismissing judges, powers explicitly denied the king in England. The assemblies, however, generally made good their claim that courts should be created only by legislative authority, although the crown repeatedly disallowed acts to grant judges life tenure in order to make them more independent.

As chief executive the governor could appoint and remove officials, command the militia and naval forces, grant pardons, and as his commission often put it, "execute everything which doth and of right ought to belong to the governor"—which might cover a multitude of powers. In these things his authority resembled the crown's, for the kings still exercised executive authority and had the power generally to name all administrative officials. This often served as a powerful means of royal influence in Parliament, since the king could appoint members or their friends to lucrative offices. And while the arrangement might seem to another age a breeding ground for corruption or tyranny, it was often viewed in the eighteenth century as a stabilizing influence, especially by the king's friends. But it was an influence less and less available to the governors. On the one hand colonial assemblies nibbled away at their power of appointment; on the other hand the authorities in England more and more drew the control of colonial patronage into their own hands.

POWERS OF THE ASSEMBLIES Unlike the governor and council, chosen by an outside authority, the colonial assembly represented an internal choice. Whether called the House of Burgesses (Virginia), of Delegates (Maryland), of Representatives (Massachusetts), or simply Assembly, the lower houses were chosen by popular vote in counties or towns or, in South Carolina, parishes. Although the English Toleration Act of 1689 did not apply to the colonies, religious tests for voting tended to be abandoned thereafter (the Massachusetts charter of 1691 so specified) and the chief restriction left was a property qualification, based on the notion that only men who held a "stake in society" could vote responsibly. Yet the property qualifications generally set low hurdles in the way of potential voters. Property holding was widespread, and a greater proportion of the population could

Currency issued by Massachusetts Bay. Colonial assemblies grew powerful through their control of the purse. [American Antiquarian Society]

vote in the colonies than anywhere else in the world of the eighteenth century.

Women, children, and blacks were excluded—as a matter of course—and continued to be excluded for the most part into the twentieth century, but the qualifications excluded few adult free white males. Virginia, which at one time permitted all freemen to vote, in the eighteenth century required only the ownership of 25 acres of improved land or 100 acres of wild land (available from speculators for a total of about £3), or the ownership of a "house" and part of a lot in town, the ownership of a £50 estate, or a service in a five-year apprenticeship in Williamsburg or Norfolk. Qualifications for membership in the assembly ran somewhat higher, and in an age which still held to habits of deference, officeholders tended to come from the more well-to-do —a phenomenon not unknown today—but there were exceptions. One unsympathetic colonist observed in 1744 that the New Jersey Assembly "was chiefly composed of mechanicks and ignorant wretches; obstinate to the last degree." In any case, gentlefolk who ran for office found then as now that a certain respect for the sensibilities of humbler men paid off in votes.

Colonial politics of the eighteenth century recapitulated English politics of the seventeenth. In one case there had been a tug of war between king and Parliament, ending with the supremacy of Parliament, confirmed by the Glorious Revolution. In the other case colonial governors were still trying to wield prerogatives which the king had lost in England, a fact of which the assemblies were fully informed. They also knew all the arguments for the "rights" and "liberties" of the people and their legislative bodies, and against the dangers of despotic power. A further anomaly in the situation was the undefined relationship of the colonies to Parliament. The colonies had been created by authority of the crown and their governmental connections ran to the crown, yet Parliament on occasion passed laws which applied to the colonies, and were tacitly accepted by the colonies.

By the early eighteenth century the assemblies, like Parliament, held two important strands of power—and they were perfectly aware of the parallel. First, they held the power of the purse string in their right to vote on taxes and expenditures. Second, they held the power to initiate legislation and not merely, as in the early history of some colonies, the right to act on proposals from the governor and council. These powers they used to pull other strands of power into their hands when the chance presented itself. Governors were held on a tight leash by the assembly's control of salaries, his and others, which were voted annually and sometimes not at all. Only in four southern colonies did governors have some freedom from this coercion. In South Carolina and Georgia they were paid from crown funds, and in North Carolina and Virginia out of permanent funds drawn from colonial revenues: an export tax of two pence per hogshead of tobacco in Virginia and the more uncertain returns from quit-rents in North Carolina.

But even in those colonies the assemblies controlled other appropriations, and by refusing to vote money forced governors to yield up parts of the traditional executive powers. Assemblies, because they controlled finance, demanded and often got the right to name tax collectors and treasurers. Then they stretched the claim to cover public printers, Indian agents, supervisors of public works and services, and other officers of the government. By specifying how appropriations should be spent they played an important role even in military affairs and Indian relations, as well as other matters. Indeed in the choice of certain administrative officers they pushed their power beyond that of Parliament in England, where appointment remained a crown prerogative.

All through the eighteenth century the assemblies expanded their power and influence, sometimes in conflict with the governors, sometimes in harmony with them, and often in the course of routine business, passing laws and setting precedents the collective significance of which neither they nor the imperial authorities fully recognized. Once established, however, these laws and practices became fixed principles, parts of the "constitution" of the colonies. Self-government became first a habit, then a "right."

Troubled Neighbors

The English conquest of North America would have been a different story, maybe a shorter and simpler story, had the English first encountered a stronger Indian presence. Instead, in the coastal regions they found scattered and mutually hostile groups which were subject to a policy of divide and conquer. Some, perhaps most, of the Indians guessed at the settlers' purpose quickly, like those, Powhatan told John Smith, who "who do inform me your coming is not for trade, but to invade my people and possess my country." But tempted by trade goods or the promise of alliances, or intimidated by a show of force, they let things drift until the English were too entrenched to push back into the sea.

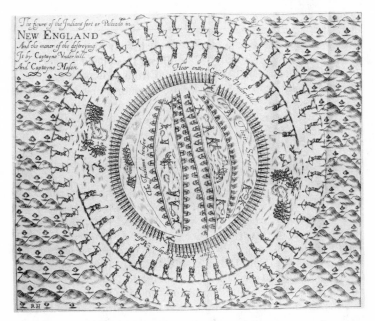

The Puritans and their Indian allies, the Narragansetts, mount a ferocious attack on the Pequots at Mystic, Connecticut (1637). [The Library Company of Philadelphia]

During the first half of the seventeenth century the most severe tests of the colonists' will to prevail came with the Virginia troubles of 1622 and 1644 and Connecticut's Pequot War of 1637. In both colonies Indian leaders had a desperate sense of last-chance efforts to save their lands; in both they failed. For the Pequots the results were virtual extermination—Puritan savagery in killing and enslaving Pequots was so great as to offend even the Englishmen's allies, the Narrangansetts, who had never seen such total war. In Virginia, according to a census taken in 1669, only eleven of twenty-eight tribes described by John Smith in 1608 and only about 2,000 of some 30,000 Indians remained in the colony. Indian resistance had been broken for the time.

Then in the mid-1670s both New England and Virginia went through another time of troubles: an Indian war in New England, and in Virginia a civil war masquerading as an Indian war. For a long time in New England the Indian fur trade had contributed to peaceful relations, but the growth of settlement and the decline of the animal population was reducing the eastern tribes to relative poverty. Colonial government encroached repeatedly, forcing Indians to acknowledge English laws and customs, including Puritan codes of behavior, and to permit English arbitration of disputes. On occasion colonial justice imposed fines, whippings, and worse. At the same time Puritan missionaries reached out to the tribes and one, John Eliot, translated the Bible into the Algonquian language. By 1675, several thousand converts had settled in special "praying Indian" towns.

CONFLICTS WITH THE INDIANS   The spark that set New England ablaze was struck by the murder of one Sassamon, a "praying Indian" who had attended Harvard, later strayed from the faith while serving King Philip of the Wampanoag tribe, and then returned to the Christian fold. King Philip (Metacomet to the Wampanoags) was a son of Chief Massasoit, who had early befriended the Pilgrims. Now King Philip became their enemy when Plymouth Colony tried and executed three Wampanoags for the murder of Sassamon. In retaliation the tribesmen attacked the settlement of Swansea on the fringes of Plymouth.

Thus began "King Philip's War," which the land-hungry leaders of Connecticut and Massachusetts quickly enlarged by attacking the peaceful Narragansetts at their chief refuge in Rhode Island—a massacre the Rhode Island authorities were helpless to prevent. From June to December 1675, Indian attacks ravaged the interior of Massachusetts and Plymouth, and guerrilla war continued through 1676. At one point Indians put to the torch a town within twenty miles of Boston. Finally, depleted supplies and the casualty toll wore down Indian resistance. In August Philip himself was tracked down and killed. The rest was a matter of mopping up pockets of resistance, but fighting went on until 1678 in New Hampshire and Maine. New England might have perished if King Philip had formed an effective coalition, but his failure to do so was typical of Indian wars. Indians who survived the slaughter had to submit to colonial authority and accept confinement to ever-dwindling plots of land.

BACON'S REBELLION   The news from New England added to tensions among settlers strung out into the interior of Virginia, and contributed to the tangled events thereafter known as Bacon's Rebellion. Virginia had the makings of trouble at the time in depressed tobacco prices and in the crowds of freed servants who found the best lands already taken. Just before the outbreak, Gov. William Berkeley had remarked in a letter: "How miserable that man is that Governes a People where six parts of seaven at least are Poore, Endebted, Discontented and Armed." And, he might have added, greedily eyeing lands north of the York River guaranteed to the Chesapeake tribes in 1646.

The discontent turned to violence in July 1675 when a petty squabble between a frontier planter and the Doeg Indians on the Potomac led to the murder of the planter's herdsman, and in turn retaliation by frontiersmen who killed ten or more Doegs and, by mistake, fourteen Susquehannocks. Soon a force of Virginia and Maryland militiamen laid siege to the Susquehannocks, murdered in cold blood five chieftans who came out for a parley, and then let the enraged survivors get away to take their revenge on frontier settlements. Scattered attacks continued on down to the James, where Nathaniel Bacon's overseer was killed.

By then, their revenge accomplished, the Susquehannocks pulled back. What followed had less to do with a state of war than with a state of hysteria. Berkeley proposed that the assembly support a series of forts along the frontier. But that would not slake the thirst for revenge—nor would it open new lands to settlement. Besides, it would be expensive. Some thought Berkeley was out to preserve a profitable fur trade, although there is no evidence that he was deeply involved personally. At this point in May 1676 Nathaniel Bacon assumed command of a group of frontier vigilantes. The twenty-nine-year-old Bacon had been in Virginia only two years, but he had been well set up by an English father relieved to get him out of the country. He was also a member of the governor's council. Later historians would praise him as "The Torchbearer of the Revolution" and leader of the

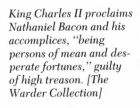

King Charles II proclaims Nathaniel Bacon and his accomplices, "being persons of mean and desperate fortunes," guilty of high treason. [The Warder Collection]

first struggle of common man versus aristocrat, of frontier versus tidewater. Instead he was the spoiled son of a rich squire who had a talent for trouble, who led punitive expeditions against peaceful Indians, and whose main achievement was to persuade the friendly. Occaneechees to destroy a small band of Susquehannocks just before he treacherously slaughtered the Occaneechees themselves.

After that the events had little to do with Indians, except some friendly Pamunkeys, who also felt Bacon's wrath. Bacon was early in the line of one hoary American tradition. Indians, he said, were "all alike," and therefore apparently fair game. Hoping to rally support against Bacon, Governor Berkeley called elections for a new assembly, which met in June 1676. Bacon was elected, had a brief reconciliation with Berkeley, and rejoined the governor's council, but failed to get the commission he demanded as commander of the militia. He fled Jamestown, aroused his own men to intimidate Berkeley, and eventually attacked and burned Jamestown in September only to fall ill and die of swamp fever a month later.

Berkeley quickly regained control and subdued the leaderless rebels. In the process he hanged twenty-three of them and confiscated several estates. In London, report had it, King Charles II said: "That old fool has hang'd more men in that naked Country than he had done for the Murther of his Father." For such severity the king recalled Berkeley to England and a royal commission made treaties of pacification with the remaining Indians, some of whose descendants still live on tiny reservations guaranteed them in 1677. One consequence of the fighting, however, was to open new lands to the colonists and to confirm the power of an inner group of established landholders who sat in the council.

The more powerful tribes all along had been back in the interior: mainly the Iroquois Confederation of the Hudson and Mohawk Valleys, the Cherokees of the southern Appalachians and foothills, and the Creeks farther south. By the time settlement pressed against these lands the English beachheads had grown into a formidable power. But the Indians had grown in strength too. Thrust suddenly by European traders from the Stone Age into the Iron Age, they had adopted into their cultures firearms, steel knives, iron utensils, and alchohol, and into their populations survivors of the eastern tribes. During the first century of settlement they had also learned the subtleties of international diplomacy, weighing the relative advantages of English, French, and Spanish trade goods and alliances, and learning to play the balance-of-power games that the great powers played in Europe.

NEW FRANCE   Permanent French settlement in the New World began the year after the Jamestown landing, far away in Québec where the explorer Samuel de Champlain unfurled the *fleur-de-lis* on the shores of the St. Lawrence River in 1608, and three years later at Port Royal, Acadia (later Nova Scotia). While Acadia remained a remote outpost, New France expanded well beyond Québec, from which Champlain pushed his explorations up the great river and into the Great Lakes as far as Lake Huron, and southward to the lake which still bears his name. There, in 1609, he joined a band of Huron and Ottawa allies in a fateful encounter, fired his arquebus into the ranks of their Iroquois foes, and kindled an enmity which pursued New France to the end. Shortly afterward the Iroquois had a more friendly meeting with Henry Hudson near Albany, and soon acquired their own firearms from Dutch, and later English, traders. Thenceforth the Iroquois stood as a buffer against any French designs to move toward the English of the Middle Colonies, and as a constant menace on the flank of the French waterways to the interior.

Until his death in 1653 Champlain governed New France under a sequence of trading companies, the last being the Company of a Hundred Associates which the king's minister, Cardinal Richelieu, formed in 1627 of men chosen for their close loyalty to the crown. The charter imposed a fatal weakness that hobbled New France to its end. The company won a profitable monopoly of the fur trade, but it had to limit the population to French Catholics. Neither the enterprising, seafaring Huguenots of coastal France nor foreigners of any faith could populate the country. Great seigneurial land grants went to persons who promised to bring settlers to work the land under feudal tenure. The colony therefore remained a scattered patchwork of dependent peasants, Jesuit missionaries, priests, soldiers, officials, and *coureurs de bois* (literally, runners of the woods) who ranged the interior in quest of furs.

In 1663 King Louis XIV and his chief minister, Jean Baptiste Colbert, changed New France into a royal colony and pursued a plan of consolidation and stabilization. Colbert dispatched new settlers, including shiploads of young women to lure disbanded soldiers and *coureurs de bois* into settled matrimony. He sent out tools and animals for farmers, nets for fishermen, and tried to make New France self-sufficient in foodstuffs. The population grew from about 4,000 in 1665 to about 15,000 in 1690. Still, Louis de Buade, Count Frontenac, who was governor from 1672 to 1682 and 1689 to 1698, held to a grand vision of French empire in the interior, spurring on the fur traders and missionaries and converting their outposts into military stations in the wilderness: Fort Detroit appeared at the far end of Lake Erie, Fort Michilimackinac at the far end of Lake Huron.

FRENCH LOUISIANA   From the Great Lakes explorers moved southward. In 1673 Louis Joliet and Père Marquette, a Jesuit priest, ventured into Lake Michigan, up the Fox River from Green Bay, then down the Wisconsin to the Mississippi, and on as far as the Arkansas River. Satisfied that the great river flowed to the Gulf of Mexico, they turned back for fear of meeting with Spaniards. Nine years later, in 1682, Robert Cavalier, sieur de la Salle, went all the way to the Gulf and named the country Louisiana after the king.

Settlement of the Louisiana country finally began in 1699 when Pierre le Moyne, sieur d'Iberville, landed a colony at Biloxi, Mississippi. In 1702 the main settlement was moved to Mobile Bay and in 1710 to the present site of Mobile, Alabama. In 1717 Louisiana annexed the Illinois villages near Fort Louis (1690–1691), settled originally from Canada. For nearly half a century the chief mover and shaker in Louisiana was Jean Baptiste le Moyne, sieur de Bienville, a younger brother of d'Iberville. Bienville arrived with the first settlers in 1699, when he was only eighteen, and left the colony for the last time in 1743, when he was sixty-two. Sometimes called the "Father of Louisiana," he served periodically as governor or acting governor and always as advisor during those years. In 1718 he founded New Orleans, which became the capital in 1722. Louisiana, first a proprietary and then a corporate colony, became a royal province in 1732.

"France in America had two heads," the historian Francis Parkman wrote, "one amid the snows of Canada, the other amid the canebrakes of Louisiana." The French thus had one enormous advantage: access to the great water routes which led to the heartland of the continent. Because of geography as well as deliberate policy, however, French America remained largely a howling wilderness inhabited by a mobile population of traders, trappers, missionaries—and, mainly, Indians. In 1750 when the English colonies numbered about 1.5 million, the French population was no more than 80,000. Yet in some ways the French had the edge on the British. They offered European goods in return for furs, encroached far less upon Indian lands, and so won allies against the English who came to possess the land. French governors could mobilize for action without any worry about quarreling assemblies or ethnic and religious diversity. The British may have had the edge in population, but their separate colo-

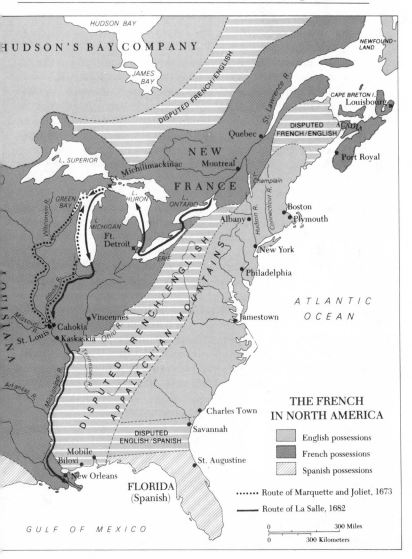

HUDSON BAY

HUDSON'S BAY COMPANY

NEWFOUND-
LAND

JAMES
BAY

DISPUTED FRENCH/ENGLISH

CAPE BRETON I.
Louisbourg

St. Lawrence R.

Quebec

DISPUTED
FRENCH/ENGLISH

ACADIA

Port Royal

NEW

L. SUPERIOR

Michilimackinac   Montreal

FRANCE

L.
Champlain

Connecticut R.

Boston
Plymouth

GREEN
BAY

L.
HURON

L. ONTARIO

Albany

Hudson R.

Wisconsin R.

L.
MICHIGAN

Ft.
Detroit

ERIE

New York

Illinois R.

DISPUTED FRENCH/ENGLISH

Philadelphia

ATLANTIC
OCEAN

Missouri R.

Vincennes

APPALACHIAN MOUNTAINS

Cahokia
St. Louis   Kaskaskia

Jamestown

Ohio R.

Tennessee R.

LOUISIANA

Arkansas R.

Mississippi R.

**THE FRENCH
IN NORTH AMERICA**

Charles Town

Savannah

DISPUTED
ENGLISH/SPANISH

Mobile
Biloxi

St. Augustine

English possessions

French possessions

Spanish possessions

New Orleans

FLORIDA
(Spanish)

•••••• Route of Marquette and Joliet, 1673

——— Route of La Salle, 1682

GULF   OF   MEXICO

0   300 Miles

0   300 Kilometers

nies often worked at cross purposes. The Middle Colonies, for
instance, protected by the Iroquois buffer, could afford to ignore
the French threat—for a long time at least. Whenever conflict
threatened, colonial assemblies seized the time to extract new
concessions from their governors. Colonial merchants, who built
up a trade supplying foodstuffs to the French, persisted in smuggling supplies even in wartime.

THE COLONIAL WARS

Colonists of the two nations came into conflict from the beginning of settlement. The Acadians clashed with Englishmen in Maine, across the Bay of Fundy, and suspiciously eyed the *Bostonnais*. Only a thin stretch of woods separated New England from Québec and Montréal, and an English force briefly occupied Québec from 1629 to 1632. Between New York and Québec, Lake Champlain supplied an easy water route for invasion in either direction, but the Iroquois stood athwart the path. Farther south the mountainous wilderness widened into an almost impenetrable buffer. On the northernmost flank, the isolated Hudson's Bay Company offered British competition for the fur trade of the interior, and both countries laid claim to Newfoundland. On the southernmost flank, the British and French jockeyed for position in the Caribbean sugar islands.

But for most of the seventeenth century the two continental empires developed in relative isolation from each other, and for most of that century the homelands remained at peace with each other. After the Restoration, Charles II and James II pursued a policy of friendship with Louis XIV—and secretly took pensions from His Catholic Majesty. The Glorious Revolution of 1688, however, worked an abrupt reversal in English diplomacy. William III, the new king, as stadtholder of the Dutch Republic, had fought a running conflict against the ambitions of Louis XIV in the Netherlands and the German Palatinate. His ascent to the throne brought England almost immediately into a Grand Coalition against Louis in the War of the League of Augsburg, sometimes called the War of the Palatinate, known in the colonies simply as King Williams's War (1689–1697), the first of four great European and intercolonial wars over the next sixty-four years: the War of the Spanish Succession (Queen Anne's War, 1701–1713); the War of the Austrian Succession (King George's War, 1744–1748); and the Seven Years' War (the French and Indian War, which lasted nine years in America, 1754–1763). In all except the last, which the historian Lawrence Gipson called the "Great War for Empire," the battles in America were but a sideshow to greater battles in Europe, where British policy riveted on keeping a balance of power against the French. The alliances shifted from one fight to the next, but Britain and France were pitted against each other every time.

KING WILLIAM'S WAR   In King William's War scattered fighting occurred in the Hudson Bay posts, most of which fell to the

French, and in Newfoundland, which fell to a French force under d'Iberville, soon to be the founder of Louisiana. The French aroused their Indian allies to join in scattered raids along the northern frontier, beginning with a surprise attack which destroyed Schenectady, New York, in the winter of 1690. In Massachusetts, Capt. William Phips, about to become the first royal governor, got up an expedition which took Acadia. New York's acting governor, Jacob Leisler, laid plans with agents from Massachusetts, Plymouth, and Connecticut for concerted attacks on Québec. But a New England expedition via the St. Lawrence bogged down in futility when the New York contingent failed to show up. The New York expedition via Lake Champlain never got under way for want of support from other colonies or the Iroquois allies, who refused to move in the face of a smallpox outbreak. The war finally degenerated into a series of frontier raids and ended ingloriously with the Treaty of Ryswick (1697), which returned the colonies to their prewar status.

QUEEN ANNE'S WAR   But fighting resumed only five years later. In 1700 the Spanish crown passed to Philip of Anjou, grandson of Louis XIV and potential heir to the throne of France. Against this new threat to the balance of power—a possible union of France and Spain—William III organized a new alliance, but the War of the Spanish Succession began after his death and was known to the colonists as Queen Anne's War. This time the Iroquois, tired of fighting the French, remained neutral and the French respected New York's immunity from attack. The brunt of this war therefore fell on New England and South Carolina. In Charleston the colonists raised a force which destroyed the Spanish town of St. Augustine in 1702, but withdrew after failing to reduce its fort of San Marcos. In 1706 Charleston fought off a counterattack, and for the next seven years a sporadic border war raged between South Carolina and Florida, the English with Yemassee and Creek allies taking the war nearly to St. Augustine.

South Carolina's Indian allies in fact constituted most of a force which responded to North Carolina's call for help in the Tuscarora War (1711–1713). The Tuscaroras, a numerous people who had long led a settled life in the Tidewater, suddenly found their lands invaded in 1709 by Germans and Swiss under Baron de Graffenried, who founded New Bern. The war began when the Tuscaroras fell upon the new settlements with devastating effect. It ended with even more devastating effect when slave merchants of South Carolina mobilized their Indian allies to kill about 1,000 Tuscaroras and enslave another 700. The survivors found refuge in the north, where they became the sixth nation of the Iroquois Confederacy.

In New England the exposed frontier from Maine to Massachusetts suffered repeated raids during Queen Anne's War. In the winter of 1704 the villages of Wells, Maine, and Deerfield, Massachusetts, were sacked by French and Indian forces, and the settlers were either slaughtered or taken on desperate marches through the snow to captivity among the Indians or the Canadians. Once again Port Royal fell in 1710, and once again a British force moved upriver toward Québec, but gave up the effort after eight transports ran aground. Things went better for the English in the Caribbean, where they took control of St. Christopher, and in Europe, where John Churchill, duke of Marlborough, led allied forces to brilliant victories in Germany and the Netherlands.

In the complex Peace of Utrecht (1713) England accepted Philip of Anjou as king of Spain, but only with the proviso that he renounce the throne of France. England also took from Spain the stronghold of Gibraltar and the island of Minorca. Louis XIV gave up most of his claims in Germany and recognized British title to the Hudson Bay, Newfoundland, Acadia (now Nova Scotia), and St. Christopher, as well as the British claim to sovereignty over the Iroquois (nobody consulted the Iroquois). The French renounced any claim to special privileges in the commerce of Spanish or Portuguese America. Spain agreed not to transfer any of its American territory to a third party, and granted to the British the *asiento,* a contract for supplying Spanish America 4,800 slaves annually over a period of thirty years and the right to send one ship a year to the great fair at Porto Bello in Panama—concessions which opened the door for British smuggling, a practice which grew into a major cause of friction and, eventually, of renewed warfare.

In the South the frontier flared up once more shortly after the war. The former Yemassee and Creek allies, outraged by the continuing advance of settlement, attacked the Charleston colony. The Yemassee War of 1715 was the southern equivalent of King Philip's War in New England, a desperate struggle which threatened the colony's very existence. Once again, however, the Indians were unable to present a united front. The Cherokees remained neutral for the sake of their fur trade and the defeated Yemassees retired into Florida or mingled with the Creeks who retreated beyond the Chattahoochee River, leaving open the country in which the new colony of Georgia appeared eighteen years later.

KING GEORGE'S WAR BEGINS   In the generation of nominal peace after Queen Anne's War the European colonists jockeyed for position, intrigued with the Indians, and set up fortified posts at strategic points in the wilderness. The third great international war began in 1739 with a preliminary bout between England and Spain, called the War of Jenkins' Ear in honor of an English seaman who lost an ear to a Spanish guardacosta and exhibited the shriveled member as part of a campaign to arouse London against Spain's rudeness to smugglers. The war began with a great British disaster, a grand expedition against Porto Bello in Panama, for which thousands of colonists volunteered and in which many died of yellow fever. One of the survivors, Lawrence Washington of Virginia, memorialized the event by naming his estate Mount Vernon, after the ill-starred but popular admiral in command. Along the southern frontier the new colony of Georgia, less than a decade old, now served its purpose as a military buffer. Gen. James Oglethorpe staged a raid on St. Augustine and later fought off Spanish counterattacks against Frederika, but Charleston remained secure.

In 1744 France entered the war, which merged with another general European conflict, the War of the Austrian Succession, or King George's War in the colonies. Once again border raids flared along the northern frontier. Gov. William Shirley of Massachusetts mounted an expedition under William Pepperell of Maine, a prominent merchant with a genius for management, and reduced the French Fort Louisbourg on Cape Breton after a lengthy siege. It was a costly conquest, but the war ended in stalemate. In the Treaty of Aix-la-Chappelle (1748) the British exchanged Louisbourg for Madras, which the French had taken in India.

In the brief respite that followed before the climactic struggle, the focus of attention turned to the Ohio Valley. French penetration had moved westward by the Great Lakes and down the Mississippi, but the Ohio, with short portages from Lake Erie to its headwaters, would make a shorter connecting link for French America. But during the 1740s fur traders from Virginia and Pennsylvania had begun to penetrate into that disputed region. Some 300 of them operated in the country by 1749, according to the French commander of Fort Miami, south of Detroit. Not far behind were the Pennsylvania and Virginia land speculators. "The English," one French agent warned the Indians, "are much less anxious to take away your peltries than to become masters of your lands." Pennsylvania, because of the Quaker impulse, gave less support to its speculators than Virginia, which laid claim to the country through a quirk in the 1609 charter which described boundaries leading "westward and Northwestward" to the South Sea; it was their northern boundary, they said, which led "Northwestward." Virginians had organized several land companies, most conspicuously the Ohio Company, to which the king granted 200,000 acres along the upper Ohio in 1749, with a promise of 300,000 more. The company forthwith dispatched a Pennsylvania frontiersman to seek out the best lands.

The French resolved to act before the British advance became a dagger pointed at the continental heartland. In 1749 Celoron de Blainville proceeded down the Alleghany and Ohio Rivers to spy out the land, woo the Indians, and bury leaden plates with inscriptions stating the French claim. Magic engravings hardly made the soil French, but in 1753 a new governor, the Marquis Duquesne, arrived in Canada and set about making good on the claim with a chain of forts in the region.

THE FRENCH AND INDIAN WAR When news of these trespasses reached Williamsburg, Governor Dinwiddie sent out an emissary to warn off the French. An ambitious young adjutant-general of the Virginia militia, Maj. George Washington, whose older brothers owned a part of the Ohio Company, volunteered for the mission. With a few companions, Washington made his way to Fort LeBoeuf and returned with a polite but firm refusal. Dinwiddie then sent one Capt. William Trent with a small force to erect a fort at the strategic fork where the Alleghany and Monongahela Rivers meet to form the great Ohio. No sooner was Trent started than a larger French force appeared, ousted him, and proceeded to build Fort Duquesne on the same strategic site. Meanwhile Washington had been organizing a force of volunteers, and in the spring of 1754 he went out with an advance guard and a few Indian allies. Near Great Meadows they fell into a skirmish with a French detachment. Who fired first is unknown, and perhaps irrelevant, but it marked the first bloodshed of a long—and finally decisive—war which reached far beyond America. Washington fell back with his prisoners and hastily constructed a stockade, Fort Necessity, which soon fell under siege by a larger force from Fort Duquesne. On July 4, 1754, Washington surrendered and was permitted to withdraw with his survivors. With that disaster in the backwoods a great world war had begun, but Washington came out of it with his reputation intact—and he was world-famous at the age of twenty-two.

Back in London the Board of Trade already had taken notice of the growing conflict in the backwoods, and had called a meeting in Albany, New York, of commissioners from all the colonies as

Benjamin Franklin saw the importance of uniting the colonies against the French in 1754. His symbol of the need to unite would become popular again twenty years later, when the colonies faced a different threat. [Historical Society of Pennsylvania]

far south as Maryland to confer on precautions. The Albany Congress (June 19 to July 10, 1754), which was sitting when the first shots sounded at Great Meadows, ended with little accomplished. The delegates conferred with Iroquois chieftains and sent them away loaded with gifts in return for some half-hearted promises of support. The congress is remembered mainly for the Plan of Union worked out by a committee under Benjamin Franklin and adopted by unanimous vote of the commissioners. The plan called for a chief executive, a kind of supreme governor to be called the President-General of the United Colonies, appointed and supported by the crown, and a supreme assembly called the Grand Council, with forty-eight members chosen by the colonial assemblies. This federal body would oversee matters of defense, Indian relations, and trade and settlement in the west, and would levy taxes to support its programs.

It must have been a good plan, Franklin reasoned, since the assemblies thought it gave too much power to the crown and the crown thought it gave too much to the colonies. At any rate the assemblies either rejected or ignored the plan, and the Board of Trade never had to face a decision. Only two substantive results came out of the congress. Its idea of a supreme commander for British forces in America was adopted, as was its advice that New Yorker William Johnson, a friend of the Iroquois, be made British superintendent of the northern Indians.

In London the government decided to force a showdown in

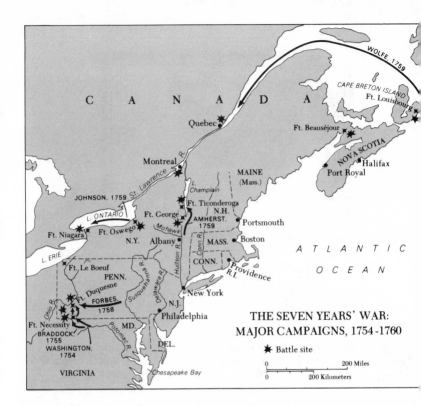

THE SEVEN YEARS' WAR:
MAJOR CAMPAIGNS, 1754-1760

★ Battle site

0   200 Miles
0   200 Kilometers

America, but things went badly at first. In 1755 the British fleet failed to halt the landing of reinforcements in Canada, but scored one success in Nova Scotia with the capture of Fort Beauséjour and then buttressed their hold on the country by expelling most of its French population. Some 5,000–7,000 Acadians who refused to take an oath of allegiance were scattered through the colonies from Maine to Georgia. Impoverished and homeless, many of them by desperate expedients found their way to French Louisiana, where they became the "Cajuns" (a corruption of "Acadians") whose descendants still preserve the language of Molière along the remote bayous.

The backwoods, however, became the scene of one British disaster after another over the next three years. In 1755 a new British commander-in-chief, Gen. Edward Braddock, arrived in Virginia with two regiments of regulars. With the addition of some colonial troops, including Washington as a volunteer staff officer, Braddock hacked a road through the wildernesses from the upper Potomac to the vicinity of Fort Duquesne. Hauling heavy artillery to invest the French fort, along with a wagon train of supplies, Braddock's men achieved a great feat of military logistics, and were on the verge of success when, seven miles from Fort Duquesne, the surrounding woods suddenly came alive with Indians and Frenchmen in Indian costume. Beset on three sides by concealed enemies, the wagon train broke down in blind panic and the British forces retreated in disarray, abandoning most of their artillery and supplies. Braddock lost his life in the encounter, and his second in command retreated with the remaining British regulars to the safety of Philadelphia.

After that, Indian attacks flared up along the frontier. Among the first to seize the chance to even old scores were the Delawares, once befriended by Penn, later cheated out of their lands by his successors. Scotch-Irish and German refugees fled eastward as the Delawares burned, killed, and pillaged in their settlements. Pennsylvania Quakers, stubbornly pacifist, insisted that compromise was still possible, but finally, under British pressure, bent their principles only to the extent of withdrawing from the Pennsylvania Assembly and letting the war party vote the money and measures needed to fight back.

A WORLD WAR   For two years war raged along the frontier without becoming the cause of war in Europe. In 1756, however, the colonial war merged with what became the Seven Year's War in

A 1755 cartoon boasts of British superiority to the French. The British lion at left stands over "his dominions"—Ohio, Virginia, Nova Scotia— protecting them from invasion. [Library of Congress]

Europe. There, Empress Maria Theresa of Austria, still brooding over the loss of territory in the last conflict, worked a diplomatic revolution by bringing Austria's old enemy France, as well as Russia, into an alliance against Frederick the Great of Prussia. Britain, ever mindful of the European balance of power, now deserted Austria to ally with Frederick. The onset of war brought into office a new British government with the popular and eloquent William Pitt as war minister. Pitt's ability and assurance ("I know that I can save England and no one else can") instilled confidence at home and abroad. The grandson of "Diamond" Pitt, once governor of Madras in India, Pitt committed his main forces to the war for overseas empire while providing subsidies to Frederick, who was desperately fighting off attacks from three sides.

Soon the force of British sea power began to cut off French reinforcements and supplies to the New World—and the trading goods with which they bought Indian allies. Pitt improved the British forces, gave command to young men of ability, and carried the battle to the enemy. In 1758 the tides began to turn. Fort Louisbourg fell. The Iroquois, sensing the turn of fortunes, pressed their dependents, the Delawares, to call off the frontier attacks. Gen. John Forbes organized a new expedition against Fort Duquesne and pushed a new wilderness road directly westward from Philadelphia. Having learned caution from Braddock's defeat, he kept his scouts alert on his flanks and proceeded slowly to set up supply posts along the way and send out emissaries to court the Indians. When he finally reached his goal, the outnumbered French chose discretion as the better part of valor, burned Fort Duquesne, and deserted the scene. On the site arose the British Fort Pitt, and later the city of Pittsburgh.

In 1759 the war reached its climax in a three-pronged offensive against Canada, along what had become the classic invasion routes: via Niagara, Lake Champlain, and up the St. Lawrence. British forces were earmarked for each. On the Niagara expedition British forces were joined by a group of Iroquois under William Johnson, who commanded the capture of Fort Niagara after the British commander fell in the field. The loss of Niagara virtually cut the French lifeline to the interior. On Lake Champlain Gen. Jeffrey Amherst took Fort George and Fort Ticonderoga, then paused to refortify and await reinforcements for an advance northward.

Meanwhile the most decisive battle was shaping up at Québec. Commanding the expedition up the St. Lawrence was Gen. James Wolfe, a dedicated professional soldier who at the age of thirty-three had already spent more than half his life in military

The decisive British assault on Québec (1759). [National Army Museum, London]

service. For two months Wolfe probed the defenses of Québec, seemingly impregnable on its fortified heights and defended by alert forces under Gen. Louis Joseph de Montcalm. Finally Wolfe found a path by which he led his force up the cliffs behind Québec under cover of darkness on the night of September 12–13 and emerged on the Plains of Abraham, athwart the main roads to the city. There, in a set battle more like the warfare of Europe than the skirmishes of the backwoods, his forces waited out the French advance until it was within close range, then loosed a simultaneous volley followed by one more which devastated the French ranks—and ended French power in North America for all time. News of the victory was clouded by the word of Wolfe's—and Montcalm's—death in the battle, but it reached London along with similar reports from India, where Gen. Robert Clive of the East Indian Company had reduced French outposts one by one, secured Bengal, and established the base for an expanding British control of India. It was the *annus mirabilis*, the miraculous year 1759, during which Great Britain secured an empire on which the sun never set.

The war dragged on until 1763, but the rest was a process of mopping up. Montréal, the last important vestige of French control in North America, fell in 1760, and while the frontiers remained active with the scattered Indian raids, the game was up for the French. In the South, where little significant action had occurred, the Cherokee nation flared into belated hostility, but Jeffrey Amherst, dispatched now to Charleston, moved toward the mountains with a force of British regulars and provincials and broke Cherokee resistance in 1761. In the North, just as peace

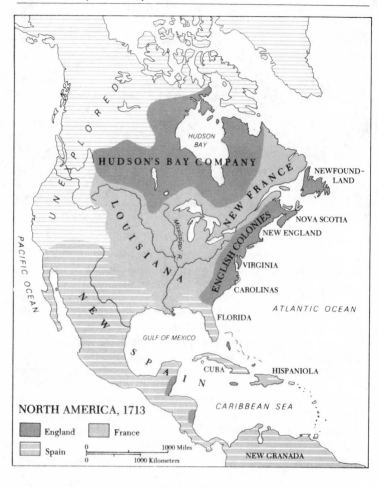

HUDSON BAY

HUDSON'S BAY COMPANY

NEWFOUND-LAND

NEW FRANCE

NOVA SCOTIA

NEW ENGLAND

U N E X P L O R E D

L O U I S I A N A

Mississippi R.

ENGLISH COLONIES

VIRGINIA

CAROLINAS

PACIFIC OCEAN

ATLANTIC OCEAN

N E W

FLORIDA

S P A I N

GULF OF MEXICO

CUBA

HISPANIOLA

NORTH AMERICA, 1713

CARIBBEAN SEA

England

France

Spain

1000 Miles

1000 Kilometers

NEW GRANADA

was signed, a chieftain of the Ottawas, Pontiac, conspired to confederate all the Indians of the frontier and launched a series of attacks that were not finally suppressed until 1764, after the backwoods had been ablaze for ten years.

Just six weeks after the capture of Montréal in 1760 King George II died and his grandson ascended to the throne as George III. George III resolved to take a more active role than his Hanoverian predecessors. Under the guidance of his former tutor and chief advisor, the Scottish earl of Bute, he resolved to seek peace and forced Pitt out of office. Pitt had wanted to carry the fight to the enemy by declaring war on Spain before the

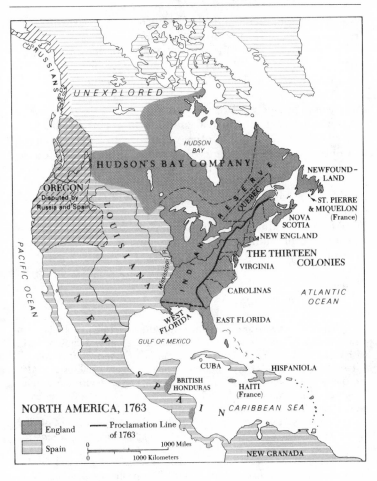

NORTH AMERICA, 1763

England
Spain

Proclamation Line of 1763

0   1000 Miles

0   1000 Kilometers

French could bring that other Bourbon monarchy into the conflict. He was forestalled, but Spain belatedly entered in 1761 and during the next year met the same fate as the French: in 1762 British forces took Manila in the Philippines and Havana in Cuba.

THE PEACE OF PARIS   An end to war came in the Peace of Paris of 1763. Bute as first minister accepted a more generous settlement than Pitt was willing to do, but nevertheless it was a peace that ended French power in North America and all but eliminated it in India, where France retained only a few trading posts. In America Britain took all French North American possessions east of the Mississippi River, and all of Spanish Florida, east and west. France ceded Louisiana to Spain in compensation for Spain's loss of the Floridas. This left France no territory on the continent of North America. In the West Indies France gave up Tobago, Dominica, Grenada, and St. Vincent. British power reigned supreme over North America east of the Mississippi, but a fatal irony would pursue the British victory.

In gaining Canada the British government put in motion a train of events that would end twenty years later with the loss of all the rest of British America. France, humiliated in 1763, thirsted for revenge. In London, Benjamin Franklin, agent for the colony of Pennsylvania, 1764–1775, found the French minister inordinately curious about America and suspected him of wanting to ignite the coals of controversy. Less than three years after Franklin left London, and only fifteen years after the conquest of New France, he would be in Paris arranging an alliance on behalf of Britain's rebellious colonists.

Further Reading

The student with a serious interest in the structure of colonial government and the global context of colonial development should begin with Charles M. Andrew's *The Colonial Period of American History* (vol. 4, 1938), which details the evolution of the British imperial system. Also see the relevant volumes of Lawrence H. Gipson's *The British Empire before the American Revolution* (1936–1970) to place the British colonies in the context of European imperial politics. Other works which cover much the same ground are George L. Beer's *The British Colonial System* (1908) and Leonard W. Labaree's *Royal Government in America* (1930).

The economics motivating colonial policies are covered in Eli Heckscher's *Mercantilism* (2 vols.; 1935). The problems of colonial customs administration are explored by George L. Beer's *The English Navigation Acts* (1939) and Thomas C. Barrow's *Trade and Empire* (1967). Michael G. Hall's *Edward Randolph and the American Colonies* (1969)° examines the same problems through the career of one imperial official.

The effect of imperial policies on colonial politics is covered in A. G. Olson's *Anglo-American Politics, 1660–1775* (1973), which traces the rise of party-like factions on the provincial level. For details on conflicts between those factions and the Crown, see Ian K. Steele's *Politics of Colonial Policy: The Board of Trade in Colonial Administration, 1696–1720* (1968). Jerome R. Reich's *Leisler's Rebellion* (1953) looks at the factional nature of that dispute. A good account of Bacon's Rebellion is found in Edmund S. Morgan's *American Slavery / American Freedom:*

° These books are available in paperback editions.

The Ordeal of Colonial Virginia (1975).° The Andros crisis is treated in Viola F. Barnes's *The Dominion of New England* (1923). Other views of Crown-colonial relations include Wilcomb E. Washburn's *The Governor and the General* (1957), which emphasizes Crown concerns over management of Indian affairs, and Stephen Webb's *The Governors-General* (1977), which argues that the Crown was more concerned with military administration than commercial regulation.

Historians of early Indian wars have taken several different approaches to the topic. Richard Slotkin's *Regeneration through Violence* (1973)° links the colonists' treatment of Indians with later national character traits. Alden Vaughan defends the treatment of Indians by the Puritans in *New England Frontier: Puritans and Indians, 1620–1675* (1965).° Francis Jennings counters this thesis in *The Invasion of America* (1975).° Allen Trelease documents the viewpoints of provincial officials in *Indian Affairs in Colonial New York: The Seventeenth Century* (1960). Other interesting works include George Hunt's *The Wars of the Iroquois* (1940)° and Douglas E. Leach's *Flintlock and Tomahawk: New England in King Phillip's War* (1958).°

A good introduction to the imperial phase of the colonial conflicts is Howard H. Peckman's *The Colonial Wars, 1689–1762* (1964). More analytical is Douglas E. Leach's *Arms for Empire: A Military History of the British Colonies in North America* (1973). Paul E. Kopperman's *Braddock at the Monongahela* (1976) is a good biography of that unfortunate general. The viewpoint of the French can be learned through William J. Eccles's *The Canadian Frontier, 1534–1760* (1969), and Charles E. O'Neill's *Church and State in French Colonial Louisiana* (1966). No understanding of these wars is complete without reading the majestic works of Francis Parkman, *France and England in North America*. The most rewarding single volume is *Montcalm and Wolfe* (1885).°

5

FROM EMPIRE TO INDEPENDENCE

THE HERITAGE OF WAR

Seldom if ever since the days of Elizabeth had England thrilled with such pride as in the closing years of the Great War for Empire. The victories of 1759 had delivered Canada and India to British control. In 1760 the young and vigorous George III ascended to the throne and confirmed once again the Hanoverian succession. Even the downfall of Pitt, who lost favor in 1761, failed to check the momentum of his war machine, which ousted the Spanish from Manila and Havana in 1762. And in 1763 the Peace of Paris, even though it brought England less than Pitt would have liked, confirmed the possession of a great new empire.

The colonists shared in the ebullience of patriotism. But the moment of euphoria was all too brief. It served to mask festering resentments and new problems which were the heritage of the war. Underneath the pride in the British Empire an American nationalism was maturing. Ben Franklin foresaw a time, he said, when the capital of the British Empire would be on the Hudson instead of the Thames. But Americans were beginning to think and speak of themselves more as Americans than as English or British. With a great new land to exploit, they could look to the future with confidence. They had a new sense of importance after starting and fighting a vast world war with such success. Some harbored resentment, justified or not, at the haughty air of British soldiers and slights received at their hands, and many in the early stages of the war lost their awe of British soldiers who were at such a loss in frontier fighting. Those feelings became all the stronger as they lost the need of further protection against the foreign enemy.

Imperial forces, nevertheless, had borne the brunt of the war and had won it for the colonists, who had supplied men and materials reluctantly, and who persisted in trading with the enemy. Molasses in the French West Indies, for instance, continued to draw New England ships like flies. The trade was too important for the colonists to give up, but more than Pitt could tolerate, although he put up with the colonies' reluctance to support even their own forces. Along with patrols, one important means of disrupting this trade was the use of "writs of assistance," general search warrants that allowed officers to enter any place during daylight hours to seek evidence of illegal trade. When the death of George II invalidated the writs in 1760, Boston merchants hired James Otis to fight in the courts against renewal. He lost, but in the process advanced the radical precept that any act of Parliament which authorized such "instruments of slavery" was against the British Constitution, against natural equity, and therefore void.

Neither at Albany in 1754 nor later in the war had the colonies been able, or even seriously sought, to form a concerted plan of action. They had relied on the imperial authorities to name a commander-in-chief, to formulate strategy, to bear most of the cost, and to set up superintendents of Indian affairs north and south. The assemblies had used the exigencies of war, though, to extract still more power from the governors and turn themselves more than ever into little parliaments. When the war ended Virginia was still embroiled in what came to be called the "parson's cause." Since the seventeenth century the Virginia clergy had been paid in tobacco, but after a crop failure in 1755 the legislature converted payment to cash at two pence per pound of tobacco—well below the market price of about six pence. After the Privy Council disallowed the Two Penny Act in 1759, several clergymen brought suit for full payment at market value. In the most celebrated suit, that of James Maury in Hanover County, a young lawyer named Patrick Henry swayed the jury against Maury with his logic that the king's disallowing a beneficial law had broken the compact with his people and had forfeited all right to obedience. The jury awarded the Reverend Maury one pence.

The peace which secured an empire laid upon the British ministry a burden of new problems. How should they manage the defense and governance of the new possessions? What disposition should they make of the western lands? How were they to service an unprecedented debt of nearly £140 million built up during the war, and bear the new burdens of administration and defense? And—the thorniest problem of all, as it turned out—

what role should the colonies play in all this? The problems were of a magnitude and complexity to challenge men of the greatest statemanship and vision, but those qualities were rare among the ministers of George III.

British Politics

In the British politics of the day nearly everybody who was anybody called himself a Whig, even King George. Whig had been the name given to those who opposed James II, led the Glorious Revolution of 1688, and secured the Protestant Hanoverian succession in 1714. By the time of the Glorious Revolution even their Tory adversaries had had enough of James II, but the Tories continued to bear the stigma of support for the Stuart cause and their influence waned. The Whigs were the champions of liberty and parliamentary supremacy, but with the passage of time Whiggism had drifted into complacency and leadership settled upon an aristocratic elite of the Whig gentry. This dominant group of landholding families was concerned mostly with the pursuit of personal place and advantage, and with local questions rather than great issues of statecraft. In the absence of party organization, parliamentary politics hinged on factions bound together by personal loyalties, family connections, and local interests, and on the pursuit of royal patronage.

In the administration of government an inner "Cabinet" of the

King George III, at age thirty-three. [Courtauld Institute of Art]

king's ministers had been supplanting the unwieldy Privy Council as the center of power ever since the Hanoverian succession. The kings still had the prerogative of naming their ministers, and they used this prerogative to form coalitions of men who controlled enough factions in the House of Commons to command majorities for the government's measures, though the king's ministers were still technically responsible to the king rather than to parliamentary majorities. George III resolved to take a more active role in the process than the first two Georges, who had abandoned initiative to the great Whig families—George I in part because he barely spoke English.

In 1761 the new king made the earl of Bute, a Scottish lord, his first minister. Bute held the trust of the king as a longtime confidant and political mentor, but as a lord he was disqualified from the House of Commons and had little influence there. In 1763, moreover, just as the great war came to an end, Bute wearied of parliamentary intrigues and stepped aside. For the remainder of that decade the king turned first to one and then to another leader, ministries came and went, and the government fell into instability just as the new problems of empire required solutions. Ministries rose and fell because somebody offended the king, or because somebody's friend failed to get a job. Colonial policy remained marginal to the chief concerned of British politics. The result was first inconsistency and vacillation, followed by stubborn inflexibility.

WESTERN LANDS

No sooner was peace arranged in 1763 than events thrust the problem of the western lands upon the government in an acute form. The Indians of the Ohio region, half unable to believe that their French friends were helpless and fully expecting the reentry of English settlers, grew restless and receptive to the warnings of the visionary Delaware Prophet and his disciple, Pontiac, chief of the Ottawa. In May 1763 Pontiac's effort to seize Fort Detroit was betrayed and failed, but the western tribes joined Pontiac's conspiracy to reopen frontier warfare and within a few months wiped out every British post in the Ohio region except Detroit and Fort Pitt. A relief force under Col. Henry Bouquet lifted the siege of Fort Pitt in August and Pontiac abandoned the attack on Detroit in November, but the outlying settlements suffered heavy losses before British forces could stop the attacks. Pontiac himself did not agree to peace until 1766.

THE PROCLAMATION OF 1763 To keep the peace, the ministers in London reasoned, further settlement could wait another day. The immediate need was to stop Pontiac's warriors and reassure the Indians. There were influential fur traders, moreover, who preferred to keep the wilderness as a game preserve. The pressure for expansion might ultimately prove irresistable—British and American speculators were already dazzled by the prospects—but there would be no harm in a pause while things settled down and a new policy evolved. The king's ministers therefore brought forward, and in October the king signed, the Royal Proclamation of 1763, drafted by the earl of Shelburne, head of the Board of Trade. The order drew a Proclamation Line along the crest of the Appalachians beyond which settlers were forbidden to go and colonial governors were forbidden to authorize surveys or issue land grants. It also established the new British colonies of Quebec and East and West Florida, the last two consisting mainly of small settlements at St. Marks and St. Augustine respectively, now peopled mainly by British garrisons.

The line did not long remain intact. In 1768 the chief royal agents for Indian affairs north and south negotiated two treaties, at Fort Stanwix, New York, and at Hard Labor, South Carolina, by which the Iroquois and Cherokees gave up their claims to lands in the Ohio region—a strip in western New York, a large area of southwestern Pennsylvania, and between the Ohio and the Tennessee farther south. In 1770, by the Treaty of Lochaber, the Cherokees agreed to move the line below the Ohio still farther westward. Land speculators, including Benjamin Franklin, Sir William Johnson, and a number of British investors, soon formed a syndicate and sought a vast domain covering most of present West Virginia and eastern Kentucky, where they proposed to establish the colony of Vandalia. The Board of Trade lent its support, but the formalities were not completed before Vandalia vanished in the revolutionary crisis.

SETTLERS PUSH WEST Regardless of the formalities, hardy backwoodsmen pushed on over the ridges; by 1770 the town of Pittsburgh had twenty log houses and a small village had appeared on the site of Wheeling. In 1769 another colony was settled on the Watauga River by immigrants from southwestern Virginia, soon joined by settlers from North Carolina. The Watauga colony turned out to be within the limits of North Carolina, but so far removed from other settlements that it became virtually a separate republic under the Watauga Compact of 1772; North Carolina took it into the new district of Washington in 1776.

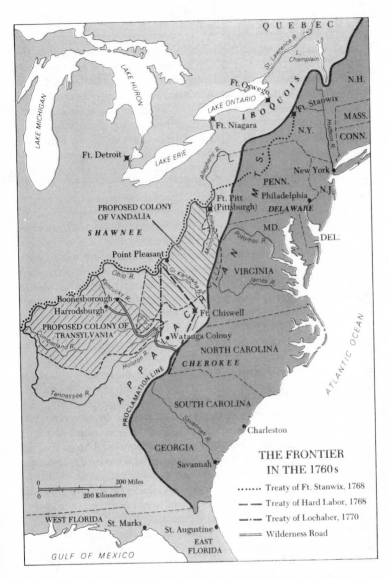

THE FRONTIER
IN THE 1760s

•••••• Treaty of Ft. Stanwix, 1768
— — Treaty of Hard Labor, 1768
—•— Treaty of Lochaber, 1770
═══ Wilderness Road

Another opening came south of the Ohio into the dark and bloody ground of Kentucky, which had been something of a neutral hunting ground shared by the northern and southern tribes. The Shawnees, who lived north of the Ohio, still claimed rights there despite the Iroquois and Cherokee concessions. In 1774 conflicts on the northwestern frontier of Virginia led the last royal governor, Lord Dunmore, to organize two expeditions against the Shawnees. In a battle at Point Pleasant, where the Kanawha empties into the Ohio, Gen. Andrew Lewis fought off an attack and the defeated war chiefs of the Shawnees forced their leader, Cornstalk, to surrender their claims. James Harrod of Pennsylvania soon rebuilt his settlement at Harrodsburg which had been destroyed during the fighting, and Judge Richard Henderson of North Carolina formed a plan to settle the area on a larger scale. He organized the Transylvania Company in 1774, and in 1775 bought from the Cherokees a dubious title to the land between Kentucky and Cumberland Rivers. Next he sent out a band of men under the most famous frontiersman of them all, Daniel Boone, to cut the Wilderness Road from the upper Holston River via the Cumberland Gap in southwestern Virginia on up to the Kentucky River. Along this road settlers moved up to Boonesborough and Henderson set about organizing a government for his colony of Transylvania. But his claim was weak. Transylvania sent a delegation to the Continental Congress, which refused to recieve it, and in 1776 Virginia responded to a petition from the Harrodsburg settlers and organized much of present Kentucky into a county of Virginia.

GRENVILLE AND THE STAMP ACT

GRENVILLE'S COLONIAL POLICY Meanwhile, as Shelbourne was drafting the Proclamation of 1763, a new ministry had begun to grapple with the problems of imperial finances. The new chief minister, George Grenville, first lord of the Treasury, was a man much like the king: industrious, honest, meticulous, and obtuse. His opinions, the king himself observed, were "seldom formed from any other motives than such as may be expected to originate in the mind of a clerk in a counting house." Grenville apparently took without question the need for redcoats to defend the frontier, although the colonies had been left mostly to their own devices before 1754. But he faced estimates of £300,000 annually for American defense, on top of an already staggering debt. He had already tried to find new revenues at home, one result being a cider tax so unpopular that it helped to drive him briefly out of office. It would not be the last time that British or American officials would learn that taxes on drink, fortified or otherwise, stirred deadly passions.

With the large tax burden at home and a much lighter one in the colonies, Grenville reasoned that the Americans were obli-

George Grenville, first lord of
the treasury, whose tax policy
aroused colonial opposition.
[Christ Church, Oxford]

gated to share the cost of their own defense. As he began to tot
up the accounts he learned that the American customs service
spent £8,000 to collect only a fourth that amount in revenue.
Clearly evasion and inefficiency, not to mention corruption,
were rampant, and the service needed tightening. Grenville directed absentee customs agents to pack themselves off to America
and cease hiring deputies. He issued stern orders to colonial officials and set the navy to patrolling the coasts. In Parliament he
secured an Act for the Encouragement of Officers Making Seizures (1763) which set up a new vice-admiralty court in Halifax
with jurisdiction over all the colonies, a court which had no
juries of colonists sympathetic to smugglers. The old habits of
salutary neglect in the enforcement of the Navigation Acts were
coming to an end, causing no little annoyance to American shippers.

Strict enforcement of the old Molasses Act of 1733 posed a
serious threat to New England's mercantile prosperity, which in
turn created markets for British goods. The sixpence duty had
been set prohibitively high, not for purposes of revenue but to
prevent trade with the French sugar islands. Yet the rum distilleries consumed more molasses than the British West Indies provided, and as Gov. Francis Bernard of Massachusetts wrote to the
king: "Even illegal trade, where the balance is in favor of British
subjects, makes its final return to Great Britain." Grenville recognized that the sixpence duty, if enforced, would be ruinous to
a major colonial enterprise, and put through a new Revenue Act
of 1764, commonly known as the Sugar Act, which cut the duty

in half, from sixpence to threepence. This, he reasoned, would reduce the temptation to smuggle or to bribe the customs officers. In addition the Sugar Act levied new duties on imports of foreign textiles, wines, coffee, indigo, and sugar. The act, Grenville estimated, would bring in about £45,000 a year which would go "toward defraying the necessary expenses of defending, protecting, and securing, the said colonies and plantations." For the first time Parliament had adopted duties frankly designed to raise revenues in the colonies and not merely incidental to regulation of trade.

One other measure in Grenville's new design of colonial policy had an important impact on the colonies: the Currency Act of 1764. The colonies faced a chronic shortage of hard money, which kept going out to pay debts in England. To meet the shortage they resorted to issuing their own paper money. British creditors, however, feared payment in a depreciated currency. To alleviate their fears, Parliament in 1751 had forbidden the New England colonies to make their currency legal tender. Now Grenville extended the prohibition to all the colonies. The result was a decline in the value of existing paper money, since nobody was obligated to accept it in payment of debts, even in the colonies. The deflationary impact of the Currency Act, combined with new duties and stricter enforcement, delivered a severe shock to a colonial economy already suffering a postwar business decline.

THE STAMP ACT   But Grenville's new design was still incomplete. The Sugar Act would defray only a fraction of the cost of maintaining the 10,000 troops to be stationed in the colonies. Grenville announced when he introduced the act that he had in mind still another measure to raise money in America, a stamp tax. Early in 1765 he presented his plan to agents of the colonies in London. They protested unanimously, but had no response to his request for an alternative. And neither he nor they seemed to have any inkling of the storm it would arouse. Benjamin Franklin, representing four colonies, even proposed one of his friends as a stamp agent.

On February 13, 1765, Grenville laid his proposal before Parliament. It aroused little interest or debate. Only three speeches were delivered in opposition, but one of them included a fateful phrase. Col. Isaac Barré, who had served with Wolfe at Québec, said that British agents sent out to the colonies had "caused the blood of these sons of liberty to recoil within them." Nevertheless the act passed the Commons by a vote of 205 to 49. The act

A British revenue stamp (1765).
[Library of Congress]

created revenue stamps ranging in cost from threepence to £6, and required that they be fixed to printed matter and legal documents of all kinds: newspapers, pamphlets, broadsides, almanacs, bonds, leases, deeds, licenses, insurance policies, ship clearances, college diplomas, even dice and playing cards. The requirement would go into effect on November 1, 1765.

In March 1765 Grenville put through the measure that completed his design, the Quartering Act, in effect still another tax. This act required the colonies to supply British troops with provisions and to provide them barracks or submit to their use of inns and vacant buildings. It applied to all colonies, but affected mainly New York, headquarters of the British forces.

WHIG IDEOLOGY IN THE COLONIES The cumulative effect of Grenville's measures raised colonial suspicions to a fever. Unwittingly this plodding minister of a plodding king had stirred up a storm of protest and set in train a profound and searching exploration of English traditions and imperial relations. If anything, the colonists were more impregnated with Whiggery than the English. They had absorbed it from the polemics of John Trenchard and Thomas Gordon, authors of *Cato's Letters* (1720–1723), Joseph Addison's play *Cato* (1713), Viscount Bolingbroke, Algernon Sidney, the histories of Paul Rapin and Catherine Macaulay, and above all from John Locke's justification of the Glorious Revolution, his *Two Treatises on Government* (1690). They knew that English history had been a struggle by Parliament to preserve life, liberty, and property against royal tyranny.

They also knew from their religious heritage and by what Patrick Henry called "the lamp of experience" that human nature is corruptible and lusts after power. The safeguard against abuses, in the view of those who called themselves "True Whigs," was not to rely on human goodness but to check power with power. And the British Constitution had embodied these principles in a mixed government of kings, lords, and commons, each serving as a check on the others. Even on the continent of Europe enlightened philosophers looked with admiration upon English liberties. A character in Mozart's opera, *The Abduction from the Seraglio*, announced: "I am an Englishwoman, born to freedom." The French writer Montesquieu, in his *Spirit of the Laws*, mingled the idea of a mixed government (king, lords, commons) with his own notion of the separation of powers (executive, legislative, judicial). The colonists, like Montesquieu, embraced the Enlightenment philosophy of natural law and natural rights. But if the Enlightenment found lodgment in their minds, the Whig interpretation of history and human nature was built into their bones. In the end it saved them from the facile optimism and the pursuit of utopia which would lure the French revolutionaries into the horrors of the Terror.

But in 1764 and 1765 it seemed to the colonists that Grenville had loosed upon them the very engines of tyranny from which Parliament had rescued England in the seventeenth century, and by imposition of that very Parliament! A standing army was the historic ally of despots, and now with the French gone and Pontiac subdued, several thousand soldiers remained in the colonies: to protect the colonists or to subdue them? It was beginning to seem clear that it was the latter. Among the fundamental rights of Englishmen were trial by jury and the presumption of innocence, but vice-admiralty courts excluded juries and put the burden of proof on the defendant. Most important, Englishmen had the right to be taxed only by their elected representatives. Parliament claimed that privilege in England, and the colonial assemblies had long exercised it in America. Now Parliament was out to usurp the assemblies' power of the purse strings.

THE QUESTION OF REPRESENTATION   In a flood of colonial pamphlets, speeches, and resolutions, debate on the Stamp Tax turned mainly on the point expressed in a slogan familiar to all Americans: "no taxation without representation," a cry that had been raised years before in response to the Molasses Act of 1733. In 1764 James Otis, now a popular leader in the Massachusetts assembly, set fourth the argument in a pamphlet, *The Rights of the British Colonists Asserted and Proved*. Grenville had one of his subordinates, Thomas Whately, prepare an answer which developed the ingenious theory of "virtual representation." If the colonies had no vote in Parliament, neither did most Englishmen who lived in boroughs that had developed since the last appointment. Large cities had grown up which had no right to elect a member, while old boroughs with little or no population still returned members. Nevertheless each member of Parliament represented the interests of the whole country and indeed the whole empire. Charleston, for instance, had fully as much representation as Manchester, England.

To the colonists virtual representation was nonsense, justified neither by logic nor by their own experience. In America, to be sure, the apportionment of assemblies failed to keep pace with the westward movement of population, but it was based more nearly on population and—in contrast to British practice—each member was expected to live in the district he represented. In a pamphlet widely circulated during 1765 Daniel Dulany, a young lawyer of Maryland, suggested that even if the theory had any validity for England, where the interests of electors might be closely tied to those of nonelectors, it had none for colonists 3,000 miles away, whose interests differed and whose distance from Westminster made it impossible for them to influence members. James Otis went more to the heart of the matter. If such considerable places as Manchester, Birmingham, and Sheffield were not represented, he said, "they ought to be."

PROTEST IN THE COLONIES   Soon after passage of the Stamp Act, Benjamin Franklin wrote back to his radical friend Charles Thomson in Philadelphia: "We might as well have hindered the sun's setting. But since 'tis down . . . let us make as good a night of it as we can." In reply Thomson predicted "the works of darkness" in the night. The Stamp Act became the chief target of colonial protest. The Sugar Act affected mainly New England, but the Stamp Act imposed a burden on all the colonists who did any kind of business. And it affected most of all the articulate elements in the community: merchants, planters, lawyers, printer-editors—all strategically placed to influence opinion.

Through the spring and summer of 1765 popular resentment found outlet in mass meetings, parades, bonfires, and other demonstrations. The protest enlisted farmers, artisans, laborers, businessmen, dock workers, and seamen alarmed at the disruption of business. Lawyers, editors, and merchants like Christopher Gadsden of Charleston and John Hancock of Boston took the lead or lent support. In North Carolina Governor Tryon reported the mobs to be composed of "gentlemen and planters." They began to assume a name adopted from Colonel Barré's speech: Sons of Liberty. They met underneath "Liberty Trees"—in Boston a great elm on Hanover Square, in Charleston a live oak in Mr. Mazyck's pasture. They erected "Liberty poles" topped by the Phrygian liberty cap, the ancient Roman *pileus* which was presented to freed slaves. One day in mid-August, nearly three months before the effective date of the Stamp Act, an effigy of Boston's stamp agent Andrew Oliver swung from the Liberty Tree and in the evening a mob carried it through the streets, destroyed the stamp office, and used the wood to burn the effigy. Somewhat later another mob sacked the home of Lt.-Gov. Thomas Hutchinson and the local customs officer. Oliver, thoroughly shaken, resigned his commission and stamp agents throughout the colonies felt impelled to follow his example.

By November 1, its effective date, the Stamp Act was a dead letter. Business went on without the stamps. Newspapers appeared with the skull and crossbones in the corner where the stamp belonged. After passage of the Sugar Act a movement had begun to boycott British goods. Now the adoption of non-importation agreements became a universal device of propaganda and pressure on British merchants. Sage and sassafras took the place of tea. Homespun garments became the fashion as symbols of colonial defiance.

The general revolt gave impulse to the idea of colonial unity, as colonists discovered that they had more in common with each other than with London. In May, long before the mobs went into action, the Virginia House of Burgesses had struck the first blow against the Stamp Act in the Virginia Resolves, a series of resolutions inspired by young Patrick Henry's "torrents of sublime eloquence." Virginians, the burgesses declared, were entitled to the rights of Englishmen, and Englishmen could be taxed only by their own representatives. Virginians, moreover, had always been governed by laws passed with their own consent. Newspapers spread the resolutions throughout the colonies, along with even more radical statements that were kept out of the final version, and other assemblies hastened to copy Virginia's example. On June 8, 1765, the Massachusetts House of Representatives issued a circular letter inviting the various assemblies to send delegates to confer in New York on appeals for relief from the king and Parliament.

Nine responded, and from October 7 to 25 the Stamp Act Congress of twenty-seven delegates conferred and issued expressions of colonial sentiment: a Declaration of the Rights and Grievances of the Colonies, a petition to the king for relief, and a petition to Parliament for repeal of the Stamp Act. The delegates acknowledged that the colonies owed a "due subordination" to Parliament, but they questioned "whether there be not a material distinction . . . between the necessary exercise of Parliamentary jurisdiction in general Acts, for the amendment of the Common Law and the regulation of trade and commerce throughout the whole empire, and the exercise of that jurisdiction by imposing taxes on the colonies." Parliament, in short, might have powers to legislate for the regulation of the empire, but it had no right to levy taxes, which were a free gift granted by the people through their representatives.

REPEAL OF THE ACT   The storm had scarcely broken before Grenville's ministry was out of office, dismissed not because of the colonial turmoil but because they had fallen out with the king over the distribution of offices. In July 1765 the king installed a new minister, the marquis of Rockingham, leader of the "Rockingham Whigs," the "old Whig" faction which included men like Barré and Edmund Burke who sympathized with the colonists' views. Rockingham resolved to end the quarrel by repealing the Stamp Act, but he needed to move carefully in order to win a ma-

The Repeal, or the Funeral Procession of Miss Americ-Stamp *(1766).*
Grenville carries the dead Stamp Act in its coffin. In the background,
trade with America starts up again. [John Carter Brown Library, Brown
University]

jority. Simple repeal was politically impossible without some affirmation of parliamentary authority. When Parliament assembled early in the year, William Pitt demanded that the Stamp Act be repealed "absolutely, totally, and immediately," but urged that Britain's authority over the colonies "be asserted in as strong terms as possible," except on the point of taxation. Rockingham steered a cautious course, and seized upon the widespread but false impression that Pitt accepted the principle of "external" taxes on trade but rejected "internal" taxes within the colonies. Benjamin Franklin, summoned before Parliament for interrogation in what was probably a rehearsed performance, helped to further the false impression that this was the colonists' view as well, an impression easily refuted by reference to the colonial resolutions of the previous year.

In March 1766 Parliament passed the repeal, but in order to pacify Grenville's following without offending the Pitt supporters, Rockingham accepted the Declaratory Act, which asserted the full power of Parliament to make laws binding the colonies "in all cases whatsoever." It was a cunning evasion which made no concession with regard to taxes, but made no mention of them either. It left intact in the minds of many members the impression that a distinction had been drawn between "external" and "internal" taxes, and that impression would have fateful consequences for the future. For the moment, however, the Declaratory Act seemed little if anything more than a gesture to save face. Amid the rejoicing and relief on both sides of the Atlantic there were no omens that the quarrel would be reopened within a year. To be sure, the Sugar Act remained on the books, but Rockingham reduced the molasses tax from three pence to one pence, less than the cost of a bribe.

FANNING THE FLAMES

But the king continued to have his ministers play musical chairs. Rockingham fell for the same reasons as Grenville, a quarrel over appointments, and the king invited Pitt to form a ministry including the major factions of Parliament and rewarded him with the title of earl of Chatham. Burke compared the coalition to pigs gathered at a trough. The ill-matched combination would have been hard to manage even if Pitt had remained in charge, but the old warlord began to slip over the fine line between genius and madness, leaving direction to the indolent duke of Grafton, who headed the cabinet after Pitt resigned in 1768. For a time in 1767 the guiding force in the ministry was

Charles Townshend, chancellor of the Exchequer, whose "abilities were superior to those of all men," according to Horace Walpole, "and his judgement below that of any man." The erratic Townshend took advantage of Pitt's absence to reopen the question of colonial taxation and seized upon the notion that "external" taxes were tolerable to the colonies—not that he believed it for a moment.

THE TOWNSHEND ACTS In May and June 1767 Townshend put his plan through the House of Commons and in September he died, leaving behind a bitter legacy: the Townshend Acts. First, he set out to bring the New York assembly to its senses. That body had defied the Quartering Act and refused to provide billets or supplies for the king's troops. Parliament, at Townshend's behest, suspended all acts of the assembly until it yielded. New York protested but finally caved in, inadvertently confirming the suspicion that too much indulgence had encouraged colonial bad manners. Townshend followed up with the Revenue Act of 1767, which levied duties ("external taxes") on colonial imports of glass, lead, paints, paper, and tea. Third, he set up a Board of Customs Commissioners at Boston, the colonial headquarters of smuggling. Finally, he reorganized the Vice-Admiralty Courts, providing four in the continental colonies—at Halifax, Boston, Philadelphia, and Charleston.

Christian Remick's watercolor of the Boston Commons shows British troops encamped. [New York Public Library]

The Townshend duties were something of a success on the ledger books, bringing in revenues of £31,000 at a cost of about £13,000. But the intangible costs were greater. For one thing the duties taxed goods exported from England, indirectly hurting British manufacturers, and had to be collected in colonial ports, increasing collection costs. But the greater cost was a new drift into ever-greater conflict. The Revenue Act of 1767 posed a more severe threat to colonial assemblies than Grenville's taxes, for Townshend proposed to apply these moneys to pay governors and other officers and release them from dependence on the assemblies.

DICKINSON'S *LETTERS*   The Townshend Acts took the colonists by surprise, and the storm gathered more slowly than it had two years before. But once again citizens resolved to resist, to boycott British goods, to wear homespun, to develop their own manufactures. Once again the colonial press spewed out expressions of protest, most notably the essays of John Dickinson, a Philadelphia lawyer who hoped to resolve the dispute by persuasion. Late in 1767 his twelve *Letters of a Pennsylvania Farmer* (as he chose to style himself) began to appear in the *Pennsylvania Chronicle*, from which they were copied in other papers and in pamphlet form. His argument simply repeated with greater detail and more elegance what Daniel Dulany and the Stamp Act Congress had already said. The colonists held that Parliament might regulate commerce and collect duties incidental to that purpose, but it had no right to levy taxes for revenue whether they were internal or external. Dickinson used the language of moderation throughout. "The cause of Liberty is a cause of too much dignity to be sullied by turbulence and tumult," he argued. The colonial complaints should "speak at the same time the language of affliction and veneration."

SAMUEL ADAMS AND THE SONS OF LIBERTY   But the affliction grew and the veneration waned. British ministers could neither conciliate moderates like Dickinson nor cope with firebrands like Samuel Adams of Boston, who was now emerging as the supreme genius of revolutionary agitation. Adams, a Harvard graduate, son of a moderately well-off family, had run down the family brewery and failed at everything else except politics. At Harvard he had chosen as the subject for his master's degree "whether it be lawful to resist the Supreme Magistrate, if the Commonwealth be otherwise preserved." Now he was obsessed with the conviction that Parliament had no right to legislate at all for the colonies, that Massachusetts must return to the spirit of its Puritan founders and defend itself from a new design against its liberties.

While other men tended their private affairs, Adams was whipping up the Sons of Liberty and organizing protests in the Boston town meeting and the provincial assembly. Early in 1768 he and James Otis formulated another Massachusetts Circular Letter, which the assembly dispatched to the other colonies. The letter restated the illegality of parliamentary taxation, warned that the new duties would be used to pay colonial officials, and invited the support of other colonies. In London the earl of Hillsborough, just appointed to the new office of secretary of state for the colonies, only made bad matters worse. He ordered the assembly to withdraw the letter. The assembly refused, by a vote of 92 to 17, and was dissolved. The consequence was simply more discussion of the need for colonial cooperation. In Charleston the John Wilkes Club drank toasts to the antirescinders, the "glorious ninety-two."

Among Townshend's legacies the new Board of Customs Commissioners at Boston offered still more confirmation of Adams's suspicions. Customs officers had been unwelcome in Boston since the arrival of Edward Randolph a century before. But the irascible Randolph at least had the virtue of honesty. His successors cultivated the fine art of what one historian has called "customs racketeering." Under the Sugar Act, collectors profited from illegal cargoes and exploited technicalities. One diabolical ploy was to neglect certain requirements, then suddenly insist on a strict adherence. In May 1768 they set a trap for Sam Adams's friend and patron John Hancock, a well-to-do merchant. On the narrow ground that Hancock had failed to post a bond before loading his sloop *Liberty* (always before he had posted bond after loading) they seized the ship. A mob gathered to prevent its unloading. The commissioners towed the ship to Castle William in the harbor and called for the protection of British troops. In September 1768 two regiments of redcoats arrived in Boston. Clearly they were not there to protect the frontiers. On the day the soldiers arrived, a convention of delegates from Massachusetts towns declared their "aversion to an unnecessary Standing Army, which they look upon as dangerous to their Civil Liberty."

To members of Parliament the illegal convention smacked of treason, but it gave them little reason to believe that any colonial jury would ever convict the likes of Sam Adams. Consequently by formal resolution Parliament recommended that the king get information on "all treasons, or misprison of treason" committed in Massachusetts and appoint a special commission to judge the evidence under a forgotten act passed during the reign of Henry VIII by which the accused could be taken to England for trial. The king never acted on the suggestion, but the threat was unmistakable. In mid-May 1769 the Virginia assembly passed a new set of resolves reasserting its exclusive right to tax Virginians, challenging the constitutionality of an act which would take a man across the ocean for trial, and calling upon the colonies to unite in the cause. Virginia's governor promptly dissolved the assembly, but the members met independently, dubbed themselves a "convention" after Boston's example, and adopted a new set of nonimportation agreements. Once again, as with the Virginia Resolves against the Stamp Act, most of the other assemblies followed the example.

In London events across the Atlantic still evoked only marginal interest. The king's long effort to reorder British politics to his liking was coming to fulfillment, and that was the big news. In 1769 new elections for Parliament finally produced a majority of the "King's Friends," held to his cause by pelf and patronage. And George III found a minister to his taste in Frederick, Lord North, the plodding chancellor of the Exchequer who had replaced Townshend. In 1770 the king dismissed the Grafton coalition and installed a cabinet of the King's Friends, with North as first minister. North, who venerated the traditions of Parliament, was no stooge for the king, but the two worked in harmony.

THE BOSTON MASSACRE The impact of colonial boycotts on English commerce had persuaded Lord North to modify the Townshend Acts, just in time to halt a perilous escalation of conflict. The presence of soldiers in Boston had been a constant provocation. Bostonians copied the example of the customs officers and indicted soldiers on technical violations of local law. Crowds heckled and ridiculed the "lobster backs." On March 5, 1770, in the square before the customs house, a group began taunting and snowballing the sentry on duty. His call for help brought Capt. Robert Preston with reinforcements. Then somebody rang the town firebell, drawing a larger crowd to the scene. At their head was Crispus Attucks, a runaway mulatto slave who had worked for some years on ships out of Boston. Finally one soldier was knocked down, rose to his feet, and fired into the crowd. When the smoke cleared away five people lay on the ground dead or dying and eight more were wounded. The cause of resistance now had its first martyrs, and the first to die was the runaway

A broadside published by the Boston Gazette *describes "The* BLOODY
MASSACRE *. . . in King Street, Boston" (March 1770). Paul Revere's
engraving illustrates the Massacre. The coffins bear the initials of those
killed. [New-York Historical Society]*

slave, Crispus Attucks. Gov. Thomas Hutchinson, at the insistence of a mass meeting in Faneuil Hall, moved the soldiers out of town to avoid another incident. Those involved in the shooting were indicted for murder, but they were defended by John Adams, Sam's cousin, who thought they were the victims of circumstance, provoked, he said, by a "motley rabble of saucy boys, negroes and mulattoes, Irish teagues and outlandish Jack tars." All were acquitted except two, who got light punishment for manslaughter.

News of the Boston Massacre sent shock waves up and down the colonies. "No previous outrage had given a general alarm," wrote Mercy Otis Warren in her *History of the American Revolution* (1805). The incident "created a resentment which emboldened the timid" and "determined the wavering." But late in April news arrived that Parliament had repealed all the Townshend duties save one. The cabinet, by a fateful vote of five to four, had advised keeping the tea tax as a token of parliamentary authority. Colonial diehards insisted that pressure should be kept on British merchants until Parliament gave in altogether, but the nonimportation movement soon faded. Parliament, after all, had given up the substance of the taxes, with one exception, and much of the colonists' tea was smuggled in from Holland anyway.

For two years little more was done to disturb relations. Discontent simmered down and suspicions began to fade on both sides of the ocean. The Stamp Act was gone, as were all the Townshend duties except that on tea, and Lord Hillsborough disclaimed any intent to seek further revenues. But most of the Grenville-Townshend innovations remained in effect: the Sugar Act, the Currency Act, the Quartering Act, the Vice-Admiralty Courts, the Boards of Customs Commissioners. The redcoats had left Boston but they remained nearby and the British navy still patrolled the coast. Each remained a source of irritation and the cause of occasional incidents. There was still tinder awaiting a spark, and colonial patriots remained alert to resist new impositions.

DISCONTENT ON THE FRONTIER

Through the years of agitation, parts of the backcountry had stirred with quarrels that had nothing to do with the Stamp and Townshend Acts. Rival land claims to the east of Lake Champlain pitted New York against New Hampshire, and the Green

Mountain Boys led by Ethan Allen against both. Eventually the denizens of the area would simply set up shop on their own, as the state of Vermont, created in 1777 although not recognized as a member of the Union until 1791. In Pennsylvania sporadic quarrels broke out with land claimants who held grants from Virginia and Connecticut, whose boundaries under their charters overlapped those granted to William Penn, or so they claimed. A more dangerous division in Pennsylvania arose when a group of frontier ruffians took the law into their own hands. Outraged at the lack of frontier protection during Pontiac's rebellion because of Quaker influence in the assembly, a group called the "Paxton Boys" took revenge by the massacre of peaceful Conestoga Indians in Lancaster County, then threatened the so-called Moravian Indians, a group of Moravian converts near Bethlehem. When the Moravian Indians took refuge in Philadelphia, some 1,500 Paxton Boys marched on the capital, where Benjamin Franklin talked them into returning home by promising that more protection would be forthcoming.

Farther south, frontiersmen of South Carolina had similar complaints about the lack of settled government and the need for protection against horse thieves, cattle rustlers, and Indians. The backcountrymen organized societies called "Regulators" to administer vigilante justice in the region and refused to pay taxes until they got effective government. In 1769 the assembly finally set up six new circuit courts in the region and revised the fees, but still did not respond to the backcountry's demand for representation.

In North Carolina the protest was less over the lack of government than over the abuses and extortion inflicted by appointees from the eastern part of the colony. Farmers felt especially oppressed at the refusal either to issue paper money or to accept produce in payment of taxes, and in 1768 organized as Regulators to resist. Efforts to stop seizures of property and other court proceedings led to more disorders and an enactment, the Johnston Bill, which made the rioters guilty of treason. In the spring of 1771 Gov. William Tryon led 1,200 militiamen into the Piedmont center of Regulator activity. There he met and defeated some 2,000 ill-organized Regulators in the Battle of Alamance, which cost eight killed on each side. One insurgent, James Few, was executed on the battlefield. Twelve others were convicted of treason and six hanged. While this went on, Tryon's men ranged through the backcountry forcing some 6,500 Piedmont settlers to sign an oath of allegiance.

In South Carolina, while Regulators protested in the interior, tensions between the colony and the imperial authorities never quite broke. There, in 1769, the very year the assembly was responding to the backcountry demands, it also voted £1,500 for the radical Bill of Rights Society in England to pay the debts of the government's outspoken critic, John Wilkes. When the king's ministers instructed the governor and council to assert themselves in the matter, royal government in South Carolina reached an impasse. The assembly passed its last annual tax law in 1769, and after 1771 passed no legislation at all.

A WORSENING CRISIS

Two events in June 1772 broke the period of quiescence in the quarrels with the mother country. Near Providence, Rhode Island, a British schooner, the *Gaspee*, patrolling for smugglers, accidentally ran aground. Under cover of darkness a crowd from the town boarded the ship, removed the crew, and set fire to the vessel. A commission of inquiry was formed with authority to hold suspects (for trial in England, it was rumored, under that old statute of Henry VIII), but nobody in Rhode Island seemed to know anything about the affair. Four days after the burning, on June 13, 1772, Gov. Thomas Hutchinson told the Massachusetts assembly that his salary thenceforth would come out of the customs revenues. Soon afterward word came that judges of the Superior Court would be paid from the same source, and no longer be dependent on the assembly for their income. The assembly expressed a fear that this portended "a despotic administration of government."

The existence of the *Gaspee* commission, which bypassed the courts of Rhode Island, and the independent salaries for royal officials in Massachusetts both suggested to the residents of other colonies that the same might be in store for them. The discussion of colonial rights and parliamentary encroachments gained momentum once again. To keep the pot boiling, in November 1772 Sam Adams got the Boston Town Meeting to form a committee of correspondence which issued a statement of rights and grievances and invited other towns to do the same. Committees of correspondence sprang up across Massachusetts and spread into other colonies. In March 1773 the Virginia assembly proposed the formation of such committees on an intercolonial basis, and a network of the committees spread across the colonies, keeping in touch, mobilizing public opinion, and keeping colonial resentments at a simmer. In unwitting tribute to their effectiveness,

Daniel Leonard, a Massachusetts loyalist, called the committees "the foulest, subtlest, and most venomous serpent ever issued from the egg of sedition."

THE BOSTON TEA PARTY Lord North soon provided them with the occasion to bring resentment from a simmer to a boil. In May 1773 he undertook to help some friends through a little difficulty. North's scheme was a clever contrivance, perhaps too clever, designed to bail out the East India Company which was foundering in a spell of bad business. The company had in its British warehouses some 17 million pounds of tea. Under the Tea Act of 1773 the government would refund the British duty of twelve pence per pound on all that was shipped to the colonies and collect only the existing three pence duty payable at the colonial port. By this arrangement colonists could get tea more cheaply than Englishmen could, for less even than the black-market Dutch tea. North, however, miscalculated in assuming that price alone would govern colonial reaction. And he erred even worse by permitting the East India Company to serve retailers directly though its own agents or consignees, bypassing the wholesalers who had handled it before. Once that kind of monopoly was established, colonial merchants began to wonder, how soon would the precedent apply to other commodities?

The committees of correspondence, with strong support from colonial merchants, alerted people to the new danger. The government was trying to purchase acquiescence with cheap tea. Before the end of the year large consignments went out to major colonial ports. In New York and Philadelphia popular hostility forced company agents to resign. With no one to receive the tea, it went back to England. In Charleston it was unloaded into warehouses—and later sold to finance the Revolution. In Boston, however, Governor Hutchinson and Sam Adams resolved upon a test of will. The ships' captains, alarmed by the radical opposition, proposed to turn back. Hutchinson, two of whose sons were among the consignees, refused permission until the tea was landed and the duty paid. On November 30, gathered in Old South Church, the Boston Town Meeting warned officials not to assist the landing, although they were legally bound to seize the cargo after twenty days in port, which expired on December 16. On that night a group of men hastened from the hall to Griffin's Wharf where, thinly disguised as Mohawk Indians, they boarded the three ships and threw the tea overboard—cheered on by a crowd along the shore. Like those who had burned the *Gaspee*, they remained parties unknown—except to hundreds of Boston-

Destruction of tea in Boston Harbor, December 16, 1773. [American Antiquarian Society]

ians. One participant later testified that Sam Adams and John Hancock were there—he had exchanged the countersign with Hancock: an Indian grunt followed by "me know you." About £15,000 worth of tea went to the fishes.

Given a more deft response from London the Boston Tea Party might easily have undermined the radicals' credibility. Many people, especially merchants, were aghast at the wanton destruction of property. A town meeting in Bristol, Massachusetts, condemned the action. Ben Franklin called on his native city to pay for the tea and hasten into sackcloth and ashes. But the British authorities had reached the end of patience. "The colonists must either submit or triumph," George III wrote to Lord North, and North hastened to make the king's judgment a self-fulfilling prophecy.

THE COERCIVE ACTS   In March 1774 North laid before Parliament four measures to discipline Boston, and Parliament enacted them in April. The Boston Port Act closed the port from June 1, 1774, until the tea was paid for. An Act for the Impartial Administration of Justice let the governor transfer to England the trial of any official accused of committing an offense in the line of duty—no more redcoats would be tried on technicalities. A new Quartering Act directed local authorities to provide lodging for soldiers, in private homes if necessary. Finally, the Massachusetts Government Act made the colony's council and law-enforcement officers all appointive; sheriffs would select jurors and no town meeting could be held without the governor's consent, except for the annual election of town officers. In May, Gen. Thomas Gage arrived to replace Hutchinson as governor and assume command of British forces.

The actions were designed to isolate Boston and make an example of the colony. Instead they hastened development of a movement for colonial unity. "Your scheme yields no revenue," Edmund Burke had warned Parliament; "it yields nothing but discontent, disorder, disobedience. . . ." At last, it seemed to colonists, their worst fears were being confirmed. If these "Intolerable Acts," as the colonists labeled the Coercive Acts, were not resisted, the same thing would be in store for the other colonists. Still further confirmation of British designs came with news of the Quebec Act, passed in June. The Quebec Act set up a totally unrepresentative government to the north under an appointed governor and council, and gave a privileged position to the

A 1774 engraving representing the tumultuous events in America. Lord North, with the Boston Port Bill in his pocket, pours tea down America's throat. America spits it back. Looking on (at left) are Spain and France, with interest, and (at right) the English military, with concern. [New York Public Library]

Catholic church. The measure was actually designed to deal with the peculiar milieu of a colony peopled mainly by Frenchmen, unused to representative assemblies, but it seemed merely another indicator of designs for the rest of the colonies. What was more, the act placed within the boundaries of Quebec the western lands north of the Ohio River, lands in which Pennsylvania, Virginia, and Connecticut had charter claims. Soon afterward came an announcement of new regulations which restricted sale of ungranted lands in the colonies and provided for relatively high quitrents on such lands.

Meanwhile colonists rallied to the cause of Boston, taking up collections and sending provisions. In Williamsburg, when the Virginia assembly met in May, a young member of the Committee of Correspondence, Thomas Jefferson, proposed to set aside June 1, the effective date of the Boston Port Act, as a day of fasting and prayer in Virginia. The governor immediately dissolved the assembly, whose members retired down Duke of Gloucester Street to the Raleigh Tavern and drew up a resolution for a "Continental Congress" to make representations on behalf of all the colonies. Similar calls were coming from Providence, New York, Philadelphia, and elsewhere, and in June the Massachusetts assembly suggested a meeting at Philadelphia, in September. Shortly before George Washington left to represent Virginia at the meeting, he wrote to a friend: " . . . the crisis is arrived when we must assert our rights, or submit to every imposition, that can be heaped upon us, till custom and use shall make us as tame and abject slaves, as the blacks we rule over with such arbitrary sway."

THE CONTINENTAL CONGRESS On September 5, 1774, the First Continental Congress assembled in Philadelphia's Carpenter's Hall. They numbered fifty-five in all, elected by provincial congresses or irregular conventions, and representing twelve continental colonies, all but Georgia, Quebec, Nova Scotia, and the Floridas. Peyton Randolph of Virginia was elected president and Charles Thomson, "the Sam Adams of Philadelphia," became secretary, but not a member. The Congress agreed to vote by colonies, although Patrick Henry urged the members to vote as individuals on the grounds that they were not Virginians or New Yorkers or whatever, but Americans. In effect the delegates functioned as a congress of ambassadors, gathered to concert forces on common policies and neither to govern nor rebel but to adopt and issue a series of resolutions and protests.

The Congress gave serious consideration to a plan of union introduced by Joseph Galloway of Pennsylvania. His proposal followed closely the plan of the Albany Congress twenty years before; to set up a central administration of a governor-general appointed by the crown and a grand council chosen by the assemblies to regulate "general affairs." All measures dealing with America would require approval of both this body and Parliament. The plan was defeated only by a vote of six to five. Meanwhile a silversmith from Boston, Paul Revere, had come riding in from Massachusetts with the radical Suffolk Resolves, which Congress proceeded to endorse. Drawn up by Joseph Warren and adopted by a convention in Suffolk County, the resolutions declared the Intolerable Acts null and void, called upon Massachusetts to arm for defense, and called for economic sanctions against British commerce.

In place of Galloway's plan the Congress adopted a Declaration of American Rights which conceded only Parliament's right to regulate commerce and those matters which were strictly imperial affairs. It proclaimed once again the rights of Englishmen, denied Parliament's authority with respect to internal colonial affairs, and proclaimed the right of each assembly to determine the need for troops within its own province. In addition Congress sent the king a petition for relief and issued addresses to the people of Great Britain and the colonies. Finally it adopted the Continental Association of 1774 which recommended that every county, town, and city form committees to enforce a boycott on all British goods. In taking its stand Congress had adopted what later would be called the dominion theory of the British Empire, a theory long implicit in the assemblies' claim to independent authority but more recently formulated in two widely circulated pamphlets by James Wilson of Pennsylvania (*Considerations on the Nature and Extent of the Legislative Authority of the British Parliament*) and Thomas Jefferson of Virginia (*Summary View of the Rights of British America*). Each had argued that the colonies were not subject to Parliament but merely to the crown; each like England itself was a separate realm, a point further argued after Congress adjourned in the *Novanglus Letters* of John Adams, published in Massachusetts. Another congress was called for May 1775.

In London few members of Parliament were ready to comprehend, much less accept, such "liberal and expanded thought," as Jefferson called it. In the House of Lords, William Pitt, earl of Chatham, did urge acceptance of the American view on taxation, however, and suggested a compromise under which the Continental Congress might vote a revenue for the crown. In the

Commons, Edmund Burke, in a brilliant speech on conciliation, urged merely an acceptance of the American view on taxation as consonant with English principles. The real question, he argued, was "not whether you have the right to render your people miserable; but whether it is not your interest to make them happy."

But neither house was in a mood for such points. Instead they declared Massachusetts in rebellion, forbade the New England colonies to trade with any nation outside the empire, and excluded New Englanders from the North Atlantic fisheries. Lord North's Conciliatory Resolution, adopted February 27, 1775, was as far as they would go. Under its terms, Parliament would refrain from any but taxes to regulate trade and would grant to each colony the duties collected within its boundaries provided the colonies would contribute voluntarily to a quota for defense of the empire. It was a formula, Burke said, not for peace but for new quarrels.

SHIFTING AUTHORITY

But events were already moving beyond conciliation. All through the later months of 1774 and early 1775 the patriot defenders of American rights were seizing the initiative. The uncertain and unorganized Loyalists, if they did not submit to nonimportation agreements, found themselves confronted with persuasive committees of "Whigs," with tar and feathers at the ready. In October 1774 the Massachusetts House of Representatives, meeting in defiance of Governor Gage, restyled itself the Provincial Congress and named John Hancock head of a Committee of Safety with power to call up the militia. The militia, as much a social as a military organization in the past, now took to serious drill in formations, tactics, and marksmanship, and organized special units of Minute Men ready for quick mobilization. Everywhere royal officials were losing control as provincial congresses assumed authority and colonial militias organized, raided military stores, gathered arms and gunpowder. In Massachusetts the authority of General Gage scarcely extended beyond Boston.

LEXINGTON AND CONCORD   On April 14 Gage received secret orders from the earl of Dartmouth, who had replaced Hillsborough as colonial secretary, to proceed against the "open rebellion" that existed in the colony, even at the risk of conflict. Leaders of the provincial congress, whom Gage was directed to arrest, were mostly beyond his reach, but Gage decided to move

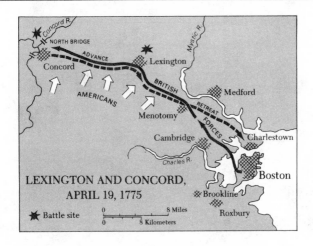

LEXINGTON AND CONCORD,
APRIL 19, 1775

★ Battle site

0   8 Miles
0   8 Kilometers

quickly against the militia's supply depot at Concord, about twenty miles away. On the night of April 18 Lt.-Col. Francis Smith and Maj. John Pitcairn of the marines gathered 700 men on Boston Common and set out by way of Lexington. But local patriots got wind of the plan, and Boston's Committee of Safety sent Paul Revere and William Dawes by separate routes on their famous ride to spread the alarm. Revere reached Lexington about midnight and alerted John Hancock and Sam Adams, who were hiding there. Joined by Dawes and Dr. Samuel Prescott, who had been visiting in Lexington, he rode on toward Concord. A British patrol intercepted the trio, but Prescott got through with the warning.

At dawn on the morning of April 19 the British advance guard found Capt. John Parker and about seventy Minute Men lined up on the village green at Lexington. Parker, lacking specific orders, had left the road to Concord unobstructed, and apparently intended only a silent protest, but Pitcairn rode onto the green ordering the militia to disperse. The Americans had already begun quietly backing away when somebody fired a shot and the British soldiers loosed a volley into the Minute Men, leaving eight dead (including Parker) and ten wounded. The British officers hastily got their men under control and back on the road to Concord. There the Americans already had carried off most of their stores, but the British destroyed what they could—including a Liberty Pole. At Concord's North Bridge the growing American forces inflicted fourteen casualties on a British platoon, and about noon Smith began marching his forces

(Above): *Amos Doolittle's 1775 engraving shows Major Pitcairn directing the fire of British troops on the Minute Men at Lexington. [New York Public Library]* (Below): *Doolittle here shows American farmers firing on the British as they retreat to Boston. [New York Public Library]*

back to Boston. The road back had turned into a gauntlet as the embattled farmers from "every Middlesex village and farm" sniped from behind stone walls, trees, barns, houses, all the way back to Charlestown peninsula. By nightfall the survivors were safe under the protection of the fleet and army at Boston, having lost 273 men along the way, the Americans 95.

THE SPREADING CONFLICT When the Second Continental Congress convened at Philadelphia on May 10, 1775, Boston was under siege by the Massachusetts militia, commanded by Gen. Artemus Ward. On the very day that Congress met, Fort Ticonderoga in New York was surprised and taken by a force of "Green Mountain Boys" under Ethan Allen of Vermont and Massachusetts volunteers under Benedict Arnold of Connecticut, who held a commission from the Massachusetts Committee of Safety. The British yielded, Allen said, to his demand "in the name of the great Jehovah and the Continental Congress." Two days later the force took Crown Point, north of Ticonderoga.

The Continental Congress, with no legal authority and no resources, met amid reports of spreading warfare and had little choice but to assume the de facto role of a revolutionary government. The Congress accepted a request that it "adopt" the motley army gathered around Boston and on June 15 named George Washington to be general and commander-in-chief of a Continental Army. In the original organizational plan, four major-generals and eight brigadiers were commissioned. To support the enterprise Congress resorted to a familiar colonial expedient, paper money, and voted to issue $2 million with the colonies pledged to redemption in proportion to their population.

On June 17, the very day that Washington got his commission, the colonials and British force engaged in their first major fight, the Battle of Bunker Hill. While Congress deliberated, both American and British forces in and around Boston had grown. Militiamen from Rhode Island, Connecticut, and New Hampshire joined in the siege. British reinforcements included three major-generals—Sir William Howe, Sir Henry Clinton, and John Burgoyne—who brought Gage belated orders to proceed against Concord. On the day before the battle American forces began to fortify the high ground of Charlestown peninsula, overlooking Boston. Breed's Hill was the battle location, nearer to Boston than Bunker Hill, the site first chosen (and the source of the battle's erroneous name). Gage, at the urging of Henry Clinton, ordered a frontal assault, with British forces moving in formation against murderously accurate fire from the militiamen. On the third attempt, when the colonials began to run out of gunpowder, a bayonet charge ousted them. The British took the high ground, but at the cost of 1,054 casualties among about 2,000 men. The colonials lost about 400 in casualties and prisoners.

When Washington arrived to take charge things had again reached a stalemate, and so remained through the winter, until early March. At that time American forces occupied Dorchester

Heights to the south and brought the city under threat of bombardment with cannon and mortars. Gen. William Howe, who had long since replaced Gage as British commander, reasoned that discretion was the better part of valor and retreated by water to Halifax, Nova Scotia. The last British forces, along with fearful American Loyalists, embarked on March 17, 1776, which Boston afterward celebrated as Evacuation Day—a double holiday for the Boston Irish. By that time British power had collapsed nearly everywhere, and the British forces faced not the suppression of a rebellion but the reconquest of a continent.

While Boston remained under siege the Continental Congress held to the dimming hope that compromise was still possible. On July 5 and 6, 1775, the delegates issued two major documents: an appeal to the king thereafter known as the Olive Branch Petition, and a Declaration of the Causes and Necessity of Taking Up Arms. The Olive Branch Petition, written by John Dickinson, professed continued loyalty to George III and begged him to restrain further hostilities pending a reconciliation. The Declaration, also largely Dickinson's work, traced the controversy, denounced the British for the unprovoked assault at Lexington, and rejected independence but affirmed the colonists' purpose to fight for their rights rather than submit to slavery. When the Olive Branch Petition reached London the outraged king refused even to look at it. On August 22 he ordered the army at Boston to regard the colonists "as open and avowed enemies." The next day he issued a proclamation of rebellion.

Before the end of July 1775 the Congress authorized an attack on Québec in the vain hope of rallying support from the French inhabitants. One force, under Richard Montgomery, advanced by way of Lake Champlain; another, under Benedict Arnold, struggled through the Maine woods. Together they held Québec under siege from mid-September until their final attack was repulsed on December 30, 1775. Montgomery was killed in the battle and Arnold wounded.

In the South, Virginia's Governor Dunmore raised a Loyalist force, including slaves recruited on promise of freedom, but met defeat in December 1775. After leaving Norfolk he returned on January 1, 1776, and burned most of the town. In North Carolina, Loyalist Scottish Highlanders, joined by some former Regulators, were dispersed by a Patriot force at Moore's Creek Bridge. The Loyalists had set out for Wilmington to join an expeditionary force under Lord Cornwallis and Sir Henry Clinton. That plan frustrated, the British commanders decided to attack Charleston instead, but the Patriot militia there had partially finished a palmetto log fort on Sullivan's Island (later named in honor of its commander, Col. William Moultrie). When the British fleet attacked on June 28, 1776, the spongy palmetto logs absorbed the naval fire and Fort Moultrie's cannon returned it with devastating effect. The fleet, with over 200 casualties and every ship damaged, was forced to retire. South Carolina honored the palmetto by putting it on the state flag.

As the fighting spread north into Canada and south into Virginia and the Carolinas, the Continental Congress assumed, one after another, the functions of government. As early as July 1775 it appointed commissioners to negotiate treaties of peace with Indian tribes and organized a Post Office Department with Benjamin Franklin as postmaster-general. In October it authorized formation of a navy, in November a marine corps. A committee appointed in November began to explore the possibility of foreign aid. In March 1776 the Continental Navy raided Nassau in the Bahamas, and Congress further authorized privateering operations against British vessels. But the delegates continued to hold back from the seeming abyss of independence. Yet through late 1775 and early 1776 word came of one British action after another that proclaimed rebellion and war. In December 1775 a Prohibitory Act declared the colonies closed to all commerce, and word came that the king and cabinet were seeking mercenaries in Europe, and getting them in Germany. Eventually almost 30,000 Germans served, about 17,000 of them from the principality of Hesse-Kassel, and "Hessian" became the name applied to them all. Parliament remained deaf to the warnings of Burke, Pitt, John Wilkes, Charles James Fox, and other members that reconquest would not only be costly in itself but that the effort might lead to another great war with France and Spain.

COMMON SENSE   In January 1776 Thomas Paine's pamphlet *Common Sense* was published anonymously in Philadelphia. Paine had arrived there thirteen months before. Coming from a humble Quaker background, Paine had distinguished himself chiefly as a drifter, a failure in marriage and business. At age thirty-seven he set sail for America with a letter of introduction from Benjamin Franklin and the purpose of setting up a school for young ladies. When that did not work out, he moved into the political controversy as a freelance writer, and with *Common Sense* proved himself the consummate revolutionary rhetorician. Until his pamphlet appeared the squabble had been mainly with Parliament. Paine directly attacked allegiance to the monarchy which had remained the last frayed connection to Britain, and refocused the hostility previously vented on Parliament. The common sense of the matter, it seemed, was that King George III and the King's Friends bore the responsibility for the malevolence toward the colonies. Monarchy, Paine boldly proclaimed, rested upon usurpation; its origins would not bear looking into. One honest man, he said, was worth more "than all the crowned ruffians that ever lived." Americans should consult their own interests, abandon George III, and declare their independence: "The blood of the slain, the weeping voice of nature cries,'TIS TIME TO PART."

INDEPENDENCE

Within three months more than 100,000 copies were in circulation. "*Common Sense* is working a powerful change in the minds of men," George Washington said. "A few more flaming arguments as Falmouth and Norfolk and the principles of *Common Sense* will not leave many in doubt." A visitor to North Carolina's Provincal Congress could "hear nothing praised but *Common Sense* and independence." One by one the provincial governments authorized their delegates in Congress to take the final step: Massachusetts in January, South Carolina in March, Georgia and North Carolina in April, Virginia in May. On June 7 Richard Henry Lee of Virginia moved a resolution "that these

The Continental Congress votes Independence, July 2, 1776. [American Antiquarian Society]

United Colonies are, and of right ought to be, free and independent states. . . ." Lee's resolution passed on July 2, a date that
"will be the most memorable epoch in the history of America,"
John Adams wrote to his wife Abigail. The memorable date, however, became July 4, 1776, when Congress adopted Thomas Jefferson's Declaration of Independence, a statement of political
philosophy which remains a dynamic force to the present day.

JEFFERSON'S *DECLARATION*   Jefferson's summary of the prevailing
political sentiment, prepared on behalf of a committee of John
Adams, Benjamin Franklin, Roger Sherman, and Robert R. Livingston, was an eloquent restatement of John Locke's contract
theory of government, the theory in Jefferson's words that governments derived "their just Powers from the consent of the
people," who were entitled to "alter or abolish" those which denied their "unalienable rights" to "life, Liberty, and the pursuit
of Happiness." The appeal was no longer simply to "the rights of
Englishmen" but to the broader "laws of Nature and Nature's
God." But at the same time the Declaration implicitly suported
the theory that the British Empire was a federation united only
through the crown. Parliament, which had no proper authority
over the colonies, was never mentioned by name. The enemy
was a king who had "combined with others to subject us to a jurisdiction foreign to our constitution, and unacknowledged by
our laws. . . ." The document set forth "a history of repeated
injuries and usurpations, all having in direct object the establishment of an absolute Tyranny over these States." The
"Representatives of the United States of America," therefore,
declared the thirteen "United Colonies" to be "Free and Independent States."

"WE ALWAYS HAD GOVERNED OURSELVES"   So it had come to this,
thirteen years after Britain acquired domination of North America. Historians have been fruitful in advancing theories and explanations: trade regulation, the restrictions on western lands,
the tax burden, the burden of debts to British merchants, the fear
of an Anglican bishop, the growth of a national consciousness,
the lack of representation in Parliament, ideologies of Whiggery
and the Enlightenment, the evangelistic impulse, Scottish moral
philosophy, the abrupt shift from a mercantile to an "imperial"
policy after 1763, class conflict, revolutionary conspiracy. Each
of them separately and all of them together are subject to challenge, but each contributed something to collective grievances
that rose to a climax in a gigantic failure of British statesmanship.
A conflict between British sovereignty and American rights had

Jefferson's draft of the Declaration of Independence. [Library of Congress] come to a point of confrontation that adroit statesmanship might have avoided, sidestepped, or outflanked. Irresolution and vacillation in the British ministry finally gave way to the stubborn determination to force an issue long permitted to drift. The colonists, conditioned by the Whig interpretation of history, saw these developments as the conspiracy of a corrupted oligarchy —and finally, they decided, of a despotic king—to impose an "absolute Tyranny."

Perhaps the last word on how it came about should belong to an obscure participant, Levi Preston, a Minute Man of Danvers, Massachusetts. Asked sixty-seven years after Lexington and Concord about British oppressions, he responded, as his young interviewer reported later: " 'What were they? Oppressions? I didn't feel them.' 'What, were you not oppressed by the Stamp Act?' 'I never saw one of those stamps, and always understood that Governor Bernard put them all in Castle William. I am certain I never paid a penny for one of them.' 'Well, what then about the tea-tax?' 'Tea-tax! I never drank a drop of the stuff; the boys threw it all overboard.' 'Then I suppose you had been reading Harrington or Sidney and Locke about the eternal principles of liberty.' 'Never heard of 'em. We read only the Bible, the Catechism, Watts's Psalms and Hymns, and the Almanack.' 'Well, then, what was the matter? and what did you mean in going to the fight?' 'Young man, what we meant in going for those redcoats was this: we always had governed ourselves, and we always meant to. They didn't mean we should.' "

FURTHER READING

Interpretations of America's path to independence have displayed some of the most influential scholarship of recent times. Jack P. Greene, ed., *The Reinterpretation of the American Revolution* (1968),° brings together many of the recent theories. Also valuable are Stephen G. Kurtz and James H. Hutson, eds., *Essays on the American Revolution* (1973),° and Alfred T. Young, ed., *The American Revolution: A Radical Interpretation* (1976).° Young is particularly good for further reading on political conflicts such as the Regulator controversy.

Narrative surveys of the events covered in this chapter include John C. Miller's *Origins of the American Revolution* (1943) and Lawrence H. Gipson's *The Coming of the Revolution* (1954),° the latter a condensation of material from a multivolume study of British imperial policy. The

° These books are available in paperback editions.

early chapters of Robert Middlekauff's *The Glorious Cause: The American Revolution, 1763–1789* (1982), are also helpful.

The perspective of Great Britain remains important for understanding why revolution erupted. Sir Lewis Namier's *England in the Age of the American Revolution* (1961)° provides a sound introduction for both politics and society. More emphasis is put on politics in George H. Guttridge's *English Whiggism and the American Revolution* (1963) and John Brewer's *Party Ideology and Popular Politics at the Accession of George III* (1976). Studies of relations between the Mother Country and its colonies include R. R. Palmer's *The Age of the Democratic Revolution: A Political History of Europe and America, 1760–1800* (2 vols.; 1959, 1964), Ian R. Christie and Benjamin W. Labaree's *Empire or Independence, 1760–1776* (1976),° and Bernard Donoughue's *British Politics and the American Revolution: The Path to War* (1964). J. A. Ernest's *Money and Politics in America, 1755–1775* (1973), deals with fiscal policy.

How Americans came to an intellectual justification for revolt is traced in Bernard Bailyn's *The Ideological Origins of the American Revolution* (1967),° and in the opening chapters of Gordon S. Wood's *The Creation of the American Republic, 1776–1787* (1969).° To understand how these views deterred the outbreak of violence for so long, see Pauline Maier's *From Resistance to Revolution: Colonial Radicals and the Development of American Opposition to Great Britain, 1765–1776* (1972).° Biographical studies of the men who held such views include John C. Miller's *Sam Adams* (1936), Richard R. Beeman's *Patrick Henry* (1974), Merrill Petersen's *Thomas Jefferson and the New Nation* (1970),° Dumas Malone's *Jefferson, The Virginian* (1948),° Peter Shaw's *The Character of John Adams* (1976),° Eric Foner's *Tom Paine and Revolutionary America* (1976),° and Pauline Maier's *The Old Revolutionaries: Political Lives in the Age of Samuel Adams* (1980).°

A number of books deal with specific events in the chain of crises. Edmund S. and Helen Morgan's *Prologue to Revolution: The Stamp Act Crisis* (1953)° gives the colonial perspective on that crucial event, while P. D. G. Thomas's *British Politics and the Stamp Act Crisis* (1975) emphasizes imperial motives. Also valuable are Benjamin W. Larabee's *The Boston Tea Party* (1964)° and Hiller Zobel's *The Boston Massacre* (1970).° Carl Becker's *The Declaration of Independence* (1922)° remains the best introduction to the events in Philadelphia. Also valuable is the relevant chapter in Merrill Jensen's *The Founding of a Nation* (1968). More interpretative about the contents of the Declaration is Garry Wills's *Inventing America: Jefferson's Declaration of Independence* (1978).°

Colony-level studies also give a clearer perspective to the events of the Revolution. A traditional standard is Carl Becker's *The History of Political Parties in the Province of New York, 1760–1776* (1909). More recent are Patricia U. Bonomi's *A Factious People: Politics and Society in Colonial New York* (1971),° James H. Hutson's *Pennsylvania Politics, 1746–1770: The Movement for Royal Government and its Consequences* (1972), Rhys Isaac's *The Transformation of Virginia, 1740–1790*

(1982),° A. Roger Ekirch's *"Poor Carolina": Politics and Society in Colonial North Carolina, 1729–1776* (1981), William Pencok's *War, Politics, and Revolution in Provincial Massachusetts* (1981), and Edward Countryman's *A People in Revolution: The American Revolution and Political Society in New York, 1760–1790* (1981).

The events across the Appalachians are chronicled concisely by Jack M. Sosin in *The Revolutionary Frontier* (1967). Michael A. Lafaro's *The Life and Adventures of Daniel Boone* (1978) presents a brief but thorough account of that pioneer.

Military affairs in the early phases of the war are handled in John Shy's *Toward Lexington: The Role of the British Army in the Coming of the Revolution* (1965)° and Don Higginbotham's *The War for American Independence* (1971),° as well as other works listed in Chapter 6. In particular, see the early chapters of Charles Royster's *A Revolutionary People at War* (1979)° for the link between rebellion and ideology.

6 ✒

THE AMERICAN REVOLUTION

1776: Washington's Narrow Escape

On July 2, 1776, the day that Congress voted for independence, British redcoats landed on the undefended Staten Island. They were the vanguard of a gigantic effort to reconquer America and the first elements of an enormous force that gathered around New York Harbor over the next month. By mid-August Gen. William Howe, with the support of a fleet under his older brother, Admiral Richard, Lord Howe, had some 32,000 men at his disposal, including 9,000 "Hessians"—the biggest single force ever mustered by the British in the eighteenth century. Washington had expected the move and transferred most of his men from Boston, but could muster only about 19,000 Continentals and militiamen. With such a force New York was indefensible, but Congress wanted it held, and in making gestures of resistance Washington exposed his men to entrapments from which they escaped more by luck and Howe's caution than by any strategic genius of the American commander. Washington was still learning his trade, and the New York campaign afforded some expensive lessons.

FIGHTING IN NEW YORK AND NEW JERSEY The first conflicts took place on Long Island, where the Americans wanted to hold Brooklyn Heights, from which the city might be bombarded. In late August, however, Howe inflicted heavy losses in preliminary battles and forced Washington to evacuate Long Island to reunite his dangerously divided forces. A timely rainstorm, with winds and tides, kept the British fleet out of the East River and made possible a withdrawal to Manhattan under cover of darkness.

George Washington, commander-in-chief of the Continental Army. [Washington/Custis/Lee Collection, Washington and Lee University]

After their success on Long Island the brothers Howe sought a parley with commissioners from the Continental Congress. At the Staten Island Peace Conference on September 11 they met with Benjamin Franklin, John Adams, and Edmund Rutledge, but it soon became clear that the Howes were empowered, in effect, only to negotiate a surrender. Pardons were offered to those who returned to British allegiance and vague promises of fair treatment were advanced—but only after all "extralegal" congresses and conventions were dissolved. The Americans chose to fight on against the odds.

The odds were overwhelming, and they might have been decisive if Howe had moved quickly to pen Washington in lower Manhattan. The main American force, however, withdrew northward to the mainland and retreated slowly across New Jersey and over the Delaware River into Pennsylvania. In the retreat marched a volunteer, Thomas Paine. Having opened an eventful year with his pamphlet *Common Sense*, he composed in Newark *The American Crisis* (the first of several *Crisis* papers) which now appeared in Philadelphia:

> These are the times that try men's souls: The summer soldier and the sunshine patriot will, in this crisis, shrink from the service of his country; but he that stands it **NOW** deserves the love and thanks of man and woman. Tyranny, like Hell, is not easily conquered. Yet we have this consolation with us, that the harder the conflict, the more glorious the triumph.

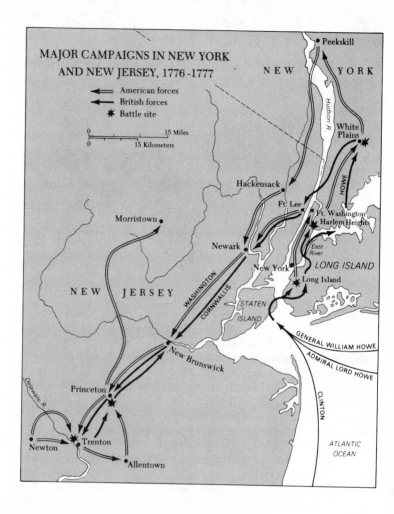

MAJOR CAMPAIGNS IN NEW YORK
AND NEW JERSEY, 1776-1777

⟵ American forces
⟵ British forces
✳ Battle site

0   15 Miles
0   15 Kilometers

N E W   Y O R K

Peekskill

Hudson R.

White Plains

HOWE

Hackensack

Ft. Lee

Ft. Washington
Harlem Heights

Morristown

Newark

East River

LONG ISLAND

New York

Long Island

N E W   J E R S E Y

WASHINGTON

CORNWALLIS

STATEN ISLAND

GENERAL WILLIAM HOWE

ADMIRAL LORD HOWE

CLINTON

New Brunswick

Princeton

Delaware R.

Newton

Trenton

Allentown

ATLANTIC OCEAN

The pamphlet, ordered read in the Revolutionary camps, resolved by its eloquence the hesitation of many and helped restore the shaken morale of the Patriots—as events would soon do
more decisively.

General Howe, firmly ensconced in New York (which the British held throughout the war), established outposts in New Jersey
and to the east at Newport, and settled down to wait out the
winter. But Washington was not yet ready to go into winter
quarters. Instead he daringly seized the initiative. On Christmas
night 1776 he slipped across the icy Delaware with some 2,400
men (an episode immortalized in the heroic and fanciful painting
of Emmanuel Leutze) and near dawn at Trenton surprised a gar-

rison of 1,500 Hessians still befuddled from too much holiday cheer. It was a total rout from which only 500 royal soldiers escaped death or capture. At nearby Princeton on January 3 the Americans met and drove off three regiments of British redcoats, and finally took refuge in winter quarters at Morristown, in the hills of northern Jersey. The campaigns of 1776 had ended, after repeated defeats, with two minor victories which inspirited the Patriot cause. Howe had missed his great chance, indeed several chances, to bring the rebellion to a speedy end.

AMERICAN SOCIETY AT WAR

THE LOYALISTS Before Trenton, General Howe may have thought that Washington's army was on the verge of collapse and that he need not embitter the colonials and endanger the future restoration by inflicting needless casualties. During the summer and fall of 1776, in fact, New Jersey civilians assumed that the rebellion was collapsing and thousands hastened to sign an oath of allegiance. But the British setbacks at Trenton and Princeton reversed the outlook, and with the British withdrawal New Jersey quickly went back under insurgent control. Through most of the war, in New Jersey and in other colonies, the British would be chasing that elusive will-o'-the-wisp, the Tory majority that Loyalists kept telling them was out there waiting only for British regulars to show the flag.

That the Loyalists were numerous is evident from the departure during or after the war of roughly 100,000 of them, or more than 3 percent of the total population. One plausible estimate had it that opinion was about evenly divided three ways among Patriots or Whigs (as the revolutionaries called themselves), Tories (as Patriots called the Empire Loyalists), and an indifferent middle swayed mostly by the better organized and more energetic radicals. A more likely guess, taking note of the trouble both sides had with recruitment, would be that the middle ground was held by a majority of the populace. Neither side showed great enthusiasm for the struggle. And there was a like division in British opinion. The aversion of so many Englishmen to the war was one reason for the government's hiring German mercenaries, the "Hessians."

The historian Wallace Brown has estimated the total number of Loyalists to have been no more than 7.6–18 percent of the total white adult population. Toryism was "a distinctly urban and seaboard phenomenon" with a clear "commercial, officeholding, and professional bias." But Tories came from all walks of life. Governors, judges, and other royal officials were almost totally loyal; colonial merchants might be tugged one way or the other, depending on how much they had benefited or suffered from mercantilist regulation; the great planters were swayed one way by dependence on British bounties, another by their debts to British merchants. In the backcountry of New York and the Carolinas many humble folk rallied to the crown. Where planter aristocrats tended to be Whig, as in North Carolina, backcountry farmers (many of them recently Regulators) leaned to the Tories. Calculations of self-interest, of course, did not always govern. Sentiment and conviction could be, and often were, the roots of loyalty.

THE MOMENTUM OF WAR   The American Revolution has ever since seemed to most Americans a fight between the Americans and the British, but the War for Independence was also very much a civil war which set brother against brother and divided such families as the Randolphs of Virginia, the Morrises of Pennsylvania, and the Otises of Massachusetts. Benjamin Franklin's illegitimate son, William Temple, royal governor of New Jersey, was a Tory. The fratricidal hate that often goes with civil war gave rise to some of the most bloodcurdling atrocities in the backcountry of New York and Pennsylvania and in Georgia where Tory Rangers and their Indian allies went marauding against frontier Whigs. Whigs responded in kind against units of Loyalist militia or regulars. Once begun, the retaliation and counterretaliation of guerrilla warfare developed a momentum of its own.

In few places, however, were there enough Tories to establish control without the presence of British regulars, and nowhere for very long. Time and again the British forces were frustrated by both the failure of Loyalists to materialize in strength and the collapse of Loyalist militia units once regular detachments pulled out. Even more disheartening was what one British officer called "the licentiousness of the troops, who committed every species of rapine and plunder," and thereby converted potential friends into enemies. British and Hessian regulars, brought up in a hard school of warfare, tended to treat all civilians as hostile. Loyalist militiamen, at the same time, where loath to let any rebel sympathizers slip back into passivity, and so prodded them into active hostility. On the other side the Patriot militia kept springing to life whenever redcoats appeared nearby, and all adult white males, with few exceptions, were obligated under state law to serve when called. With time even the most apathetic would be pressed into a commitment, if only to turn out for drill. And sooner or later nearly every colonial county was touched by military action that would call for armed resistance. The war itself, then, whether through British and Loyalist behavior or the call of the militia, mobilized the apathetic majority into at least an appearance of support for the American cause. This commitment, even if sham, could seldom be reversed once made.

MILITIA AND ARMY   Americans were engaged in the kind of fighting that had become habitual when they were colonists. To repel an attack, the militia somehow materialized; the danger past, it evaporated. There were things to take care of at home and no time for concern about other battles over the horizon. They "come in, you cannot tell how," George Washington said in exasperation, "go, you cannot tell when, and act you cannot tell where, consume your provisions, exhaust your stores, and leave you at last at a critical moment." The militia was usually best at bushwhacking. All too often the green troops would panic in a formal line of battle, and so were commonly placed in the front ranks in the hope that they would get off a shot or two before they turned tail.

The Continental Army, by contrast, was on the whole well trained and dependable, whipped into shape by such foreign volunteers as the marquis de Lafayette and the baron von Steuben. Although some 230,000 enlistees passed through the army, many of those were repeaters who came in for tenures as brief as three months. Washington's army fluctuated in size from around 10,000 troops to as high as 20,000 and as low as 5,000. At times he could put only 2,000–3.000 in the field. Line regiments were

Soldiers in the Continental Army. [The Anne S. K. Brown Military Collection]

organized, state by state, and the states were supposed to keep them filled with volunteers, or conscripts if need be, but Washington could never be sure that his requisitions would be met.

PROBLEMS OF FINANCE AND SUPPLY   The same uncertainty beset the army and Congress in their quest for supplies. None of the states came through with more than a part of its share, and Congress reluctantly let army agents take supplies directly from farmers in return for Quartermaster Certificates, which promised future payment. Congress managed to raise some $9 million from the domestic sale of bonds, some $11 million from foreign loans, and about $6 million in requisitions on the states. Since these totals were far short of the war's cost the only expedient left was paper money. In June 1775 Congress began the issuance of Continental currency and kept the printing presses running until nearly $250 million was outstanding before the end of 1779. The states issued about another $200 million. By 1780 the Continental dollar had depreciated so badly that Congress called in the notes, taking them for payments in place of silver at ratio of $40 in paper to $1 in silver. Over $100 million came in under that proviso, but new notes were issued in their place to the amount of about $4.5 million.

With goods scarce and money so plentiful, prices in terms of "Continentals" rose sharply. During the winter of 1777–1778 Washington's men would suffer terribly, less because of actual shortages than because farmers preferred to sell for British gold and silver. Congress did better at providing munitions than at providing other supplies. In 1777 Congress established a government arsenal at Springfield, Massachusetts, and during the war states offered bounties for the manufacture of guns and powder. Still, most munitions were supplied either by capture during the war or by importation from France, where the government was all too glad to help rebels against its British archenemy.

During the harsh winter at Morristown (1776–1777) Washington's army very nearly disintegrated as enlistments expired and deserters fled the hardships. Only about 1,000 Continentals and a few militiamen stuck it out. With the spring thaw, however, recruits began arriving to claim the bounty of $20 and 100 acres of land offered by Congress to those who would enlist for three years or for the duration of the conflict, if less. With some 9,000 regulars Washington began sparring and feinting with Howe in northern New Jersey. Howe had been maturing other plans, however, and so had other British officers.

1777: Setbacks for the British

Divided counsels, overconfidence, poor communications, and vacillation plagued British planning for the campaigns of 1777. After the removal of General Gage during the siege of Boston, there was no commander-in-chief. Guy Carleton held an independent command in Canada, but it transpired that he was not even in charge of plans for his own theater. Instead his subordinate, the vainglorious "Gentleman Johnny" Burgoyne, had rushed back to London at the end of 1776 with news of Carleton's cautious withdrawal from Ticonderoga. In London, Burgoyne won the ear of Lord George Germain, the secretary of state for the colonies, who endorsed Burgoyne's plan and put him in command of the northern armies. Burgoyne proposed to advance southward to the Hudson while another force moved eastward from Oswego down the Mohawk Valley. Howe, meanwhile, could lead a third force up the Hudson from New York City. This three-pronged offensive would bisect the colonies along the Hudson River line.

Howe in fact had proposed a similar plan, combined with an attack on New England, and had he stuck to it, might have cut the colonies in two and delivered them a disheartening blow. But he changed his mind and decided to move against the Patriot capital, Philadelphia, expecting that the Pennyslvania Tories would then rally to the crown and secure the colony. Germain had approved that plan too, confident that some 3,000 troops left in New York would be enough to divert Patriot strength from Burgoyne. Howe and Germain, it turned out, were both wrong in their expectations. Howe, moreover, finally decided to move on Philadelphia from the south, by way of Chesapeake Bay, and that put his forces even father away from Burgoyne.

Howe's plan succeeded, up to a point. He took Philadelphia—or as Benjamin Franklin put it, Philadelphia took him. The Tories there proved less numerous than he expected. Washington, sensing Howe's purpose, withdrew most of his men from New Jersey to meet the new threat. At Brandywine Creek, south of Philadelphia, Howe pushed Washington's forces back on September 11 and eight days later occupied Philadelphia. Washington counterattacked against a British encampment at Germantown on October 4, but reinforcements from Philadelphia under Gerneral Lord Cornwallis arrived in time to repulse the attack. Washington retired into winter quarters at Valley Forge

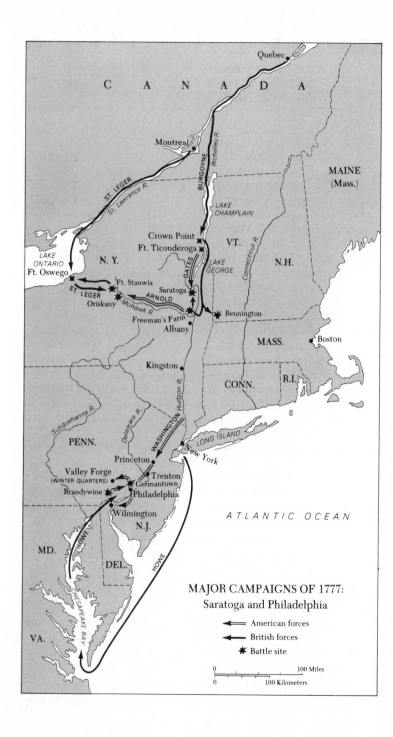

Quebec

C A N A D A

MAINE
(Mass.)

Montreal

Richelieu R.

ST. LEGER

St. Lawrence R.

BURGOYNE

LAKE
CHAMPLAIN

Connecticut R.

Crown Point
Ft. Ticonderoga

VT.

N.H.

LAKE
ONTARIO

N. Y.

GATES

LAKE
GEORGE

Ft. Oswego

Ft. Stanwix

Saratoga

ST. LEGER

ARNOLD

Oriskany

Mohawk R.

Freeman's Farm

Bennington

MASS.

Boston

Albany

Kingston

Hudson R.

CONN.

R.I.

Susquehanna R.

Delaware R.

WASHINGTON

LONG ISLAND

PENN.

Princeton

New York

Valley Forge
(WINTER QUARTERS)

Trenton
Germantown
Philadelphia

Brandywine

Wilmington

ATLANTIC OCEAN

HOWE

N.J.

MD.

DEL.

HOWE

MAJOR CAMPAIGNS OF 1777:
Saratoga and Philadelphia

CHESAPEAKE BAY

VA.

American forces

British forces

Battle site

0   100 Miles

0   100 Kilometers

while Howe and his men remained for the winter in the relative comfort of Philadelphia, twenty miles away. But Howe had gained a pyrrhic victory, while Burgoyne to the north was stumbling into disaster.

SARATOGA Burgoyne moved southward along the Richlieu River toward Lake Champlain with about 9,500 men, and sent Lt.-Col. Barry St. Leger westward with a band of 900 regular, Tories, and Canadian scouts. At Oswego they picked up nearly a thousand Iroquois allies and headed eastward for Albany. The American army in the north, like Washington's army at Morristown, had dwindled during the winter, and when Burgoyne brought cannon to Mount Defiance, overlooking Fort Ticonderoga, the Continentals prudently abandoned the fort but with substantial loss of powder and supplies. An angry Congress thereupon removed Gen. Philip Schuyler from command of the northern forces and replaced him with Horatio Gates, a favorite of the New Englanders. Fortunately for the American forces Burgoyne delayed at Ticonderoga while reinforcements of Continentals and militia arrived from the south and from New England.

Before Gates arrived, Burgoyne had already experienced two serious reversals. At Oriskany, New York, on August 6, a band of militia repulsed an ambush by St.Leger's Tories and Indians, and gained time for Benedict Arnold to bring a thousand Continentals to the relief of Fort Stanwix. St. Leger's Indians, convinced they faced an even greater force than they actually did, deserted him, and the Mohawk Valley was secured for the Patriot forces. To the east, at Bennington, Vermont (August 16) a body of New England militia repulsed a British foraging party with heavy losses. American reinforcements continued to gather, and after two sharp battles at Freeman's Farm (September 19 and October 7) Burgoyne pulled back to Saratoga, where Gates's forces surrounded him. On October 17,1777, Burgoyne capitulated. By the terms of the surrender his 5,000 soldiers laid down their arms on their word that they would embark for England, under parole (or promise) not to participate further in the war—a genial eighteenth-century practice that saved a lot of upkeep on prisoners-of-war. American leaders, however, feared that the returned prisoners would only be replaced by others stationed in England, and reneged on this agreement. Some of the Hessians were released to assume American residence but the main forces were taken away as prisoners to Virginia. Burgoyne himself was permitted to go home.

ALLIANCE WITH FRANCE   On December 2 news of the American triumph reached London; two days later it reached Paris, where it was celebrated almost as if it were a French victory. It was a signal awaited by both French officials and American agents there. The French foreign minister, the comte de Vergennes, had watched the developing Anglo-American crisis with great anticipation. In September 1775 he had sent a special agent to Philadelphia to encourage the colonists and hint at French aid. In November of that year the Continental Congress set up a Committee of Secret Correspondence, later called the Committee for Foreign Affairs, a forerunner of the State Department. The committee employed Massachusetts colonial agent Arthur Lee as its envoy in London. Then in March 1776 it sent Silas Deane, a Connecticut merchant, to buy munitions and other supplies and inquire about French aid. In September 1776 the committee named Deane, Lee, and Benjamin Franklin its commissioners to France.

In May 1776 the French took their first step toward aiding the colonists. King Louis XVI turned over a million livres to Pierre Augustin Caron de Beaumarchais (author of *The Barber of Seville* and *The Marriage of Figaro*) for clandestine help to the Americans. Assuming the guise of Roderigue Hortalez and Company, ostensibly a trading enterprise, Beaumarchais was soon guiding fourteen ships with war matériel to America; most of the Continental Army's powder in the first years of the war came from this source. The Spanish government added a donation, but soon established its own supply company in Bilbao: Don Diego de Gardoqui and Sons. When the word from Saratoga arrived, Beaumarchais got so carried away in his haste to tell Louis XVI that he wrecked his carriage.

Vergennes now saw his chance to strike a sharper blow at France's enemy and entered into serious negotiations with the American commissioners. On February 6, 1778, they signed two treaties; a Treaty of Amity and Commerce, in which France recognized the United States and offered trade concessions, including important privileges to American shipping, and a Treaty of Alliance. Under the latter both agreed, first, that if France entered the war, both countries would fight until American independence was won; second, that neither would conclude a "truce or peace" without "the formal consent of the other first obtained"; and third, that each guaranteed the other's possessions in America "from the present time and forever against all other powers." France further bound herself to seek neither Canada nor other British possessions on the mainland of North America.

Vergennes at first tried to get Spain to act with him. When she hesitated he took the plunge alone. By June 1778 British vessels had fired on French ships and the two nations were at war. In 1779, after extracting French promises to help her get back territories taken by the British in the previous war, including Gibraltar, Spain entered the war as an ally of France, but not of the United States. In 1780 Britain declared war on the Dutch, who persisted in a profitable trade with the French and Americans. The embattled farmers at Concord had indeed fired the "shot heard round the world." Like Washington's encounter with the French in 1754, it was the start of another world war, and the fighting now spread to the Mediterranean, Africa, India, the West Indies, and the high seas.

1778: Both Sides Regroup

After Saratoga, Lord North knew that the war was unwinable, but the king refused to let him either resign or make peace. North did propose a gesture of conciliation, but his ministry and Parliament moved in such a dilatory fashion that the Franco-American Alliance was signed before the gesture could be made. On March 16, 1778, the House of Commons finally adopted a program which in effect granted all the American demands prior to independence. Parliament repealed the Townshend tea duty, the Massachusetts Government Act, and the Prohibitory Act, and authorized a peace commission which the earl of Carlisle was appointed to head. Further delays followed before the Carlisle Commission reached Philadelphia in June, a month after Congress had ratified the French treaties. The Congress refused to begin any negotiations until independence was recognized or British forces withdrawn, neither of which the commissioners could promise.

Unbeknownst to the Carlisle commissioners, the crown had already authorized the evacuation of Philadelphia, a withdrawal which further weakened what little bargaining power they had. After Saratoga, General Howe had resigned his command and Sir Henry Clinton had replaced him, with orders to pull out of Philadelphia, and if necessary, New York, but to keep Newport. He was to supply troops for an attack on the French island of St. Lucia and send an expedition to Georgia. In short, he was to take a defensive stand except in the South, where the government believed a latent Tory sentiment in the backcountry needed only the British presence for its release. The ministry was right, up to a point, but the sentiment turned out once again, as in other theaters of war, to be weaker that it seemed.

For Washington's army at Valley Forge the winter had been a season of suffering greater than the previous winter at Morristown. While the great diplomatic achievement was maturing in Paris, the American force, encamped near Philadelphia, endured cold, hunger, and disease. Many deserted or resigned their commissions. Washington had to commandeer foodstuffs. The winter was marked by dissension in Congress and the army, and by some sentiment to make Washington the scapegoat for the Patriots' plight. Despite rumors of a movement to replace him, there seems never to have developed any concerted effort to do so. One incident, which went down in history as the "Conway Cabal," apparently never amounted to anything more than a letter in which Gen. Thomas Conway criticized Washington and hinted at his hope that Horatio Gates would replace the commanding general. Gates disavowed any connection with the affair, except as recipient of the letter. Conway himself resigned from the service and later apologized to Washington after being wounded by another officer in a duel resulting from the affair.

As winter drew to an end the army's morale was strengthened by promises from Congress of extra pay and bonuses after the war, its spirit revived by the good news from France, and its fighting trim sharpened by the Prussian baron von Steuben who began to drill it in March. As General Clinton withdrew his forces eastward toward New York, Washington began to move out in pursuit across New Jersey. On June 28 he caught up with the British at Monmouth Court House and engaged them in an indecisive battle, with about 300 casualties on either side. Clinton then slipped away into New York while Washington took up a position at White Plains, north of the city. From that time on the northern theater, scene of the major campaigns and battles in the first years of the war, settled into a long stalemate, interrupted by minor and mostly inconclusive engagements.

ACTIONS ON THE FRONTIER   The one major American success of 1778 occurred far from the New Jersey battlefields, out to the west where British garrisons at Forts Niagara and Detroit had set frontier Tories and Indians to raiding western settlements. At Detroit Col. William Hamilton won the sobriquet "hair buyer" for his offers to pay for American scalps. Early in 1778 young George Rogers Clark took 175 frontiersmen and a flotilla of flatboats down the Ohio River, marched through the woods, and on the evening of July 4 took Kaskaskia by surprise. The French inhabitants, terrified at first, "fell into transports of joy" at news of the French alliance. Within a month, and without bloodshed,

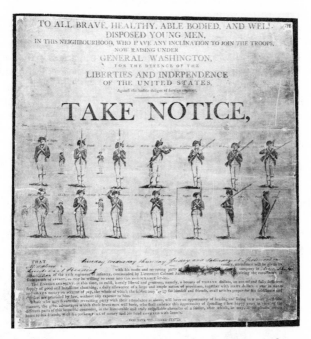

*Recruiting soldiers for the Continental Army. An appeal to
those interested in "viewing the different parts of this
beautiful continent, in the honourable and truly respectable
character of a soldier," and then returning home "with his
pockets FULL of money and his head COVERED with laurels."
[Historical Society of Pennsylvania]*

Clark took Cahokia (opposite St. Louis), Vincennes, and some
minor outposts in what he now called the County of Illinois in the
state of Virginia. After the British retook Vincennes in December, Clark marched his men (almost half French volunteers)
through icy rivers and flooded prairies, sometimes in water neck
deep, and laid siege to an astonished British garrison there. Then
Clark, the hardened woodsman, tomahawked Indian captives in
sight of the fort to show that the British afforded no protection.
He spared the British captives when they surrendered, however,
including the notorious Colonel Hamilton. Clark is often credited with having conquered the West for the new nation, but
there is no evidence that the peace negotiators in 1782 knew
about his exploit.

While Clark's captives traveled eastward to Williamsburg, a
much larger punitive expedition moved against the Iroquois

country. On July 3, 1778, as Clark neared Kaskaskia, hundreds of
Tory Rangers and Senecas (reputedly the most ferocious of the
Iroquois) swept down from Fort Niagara into the Wyoming Valley of Pennsylvania, annihilated some "regular"and militia defenders, and took more than 200 scalps. The Tories and Indians
continued to terrorize frontier settlements all through the summer until a climatic attack in November ravaged Cherry Valley,
only fifty miles from Albany, New York. In response to the frontier outcries the Continental Congress instructed Washington to
chastise the Iroquois. The task was entrusted to an expedition of
4,000 men under Gen. John Sullivan and James Clinton. At
Newtown (now Elmira) Sullivan met and defeated the only serious opposition on August 29, 1779, and proceeded to carry out
Washington's instruction that the Iroquois country be not
"merely overrun but destroyed."

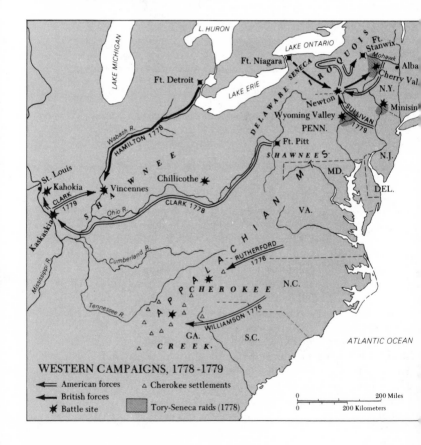

WESTERN CAMPAIGNS, 1778-1779

← American forces   △ Cherry settlements

← British forces

★ Battle site   Tory-Seneca raids (1778)

0   200 Miles

0   200 Kilometers

The American force devastated about forty Seneca and Cayuga villages together with their orchards and food stores. So ruthless and complete was the destruction that large numbers of the Indians were thrown completely upon their British allies for scant supplies from Fort Niagara. The action broke the power of the Iroquois federation for all time, but it did not completely pacify the frontier. Sporadic encounters with various tribes of the region continued to the end of the war.

A similar fate befell the Cherokees farther south. In early 1776 a delegation of northern Indians—Shawnees, Delawares, and Mohawks—talked the Cherokees into striking at frontier settlements in Virginia and the Carolinas. Swift retaliation followed. In August, South Carolina forces burned the lower Cherokee towns and destroyed all the corn they could get their hands on. Virginia and North Carolina forces brought a similar destruction upon the middle and upper towns. Once again, in 1780, a Virginia–North Carolina force wrought destruction on Cherokee towns lest the Indians go to the aid of General Cornwallis, killing twenty-nine and burning over 1,000 towns and 50,000 bushels of corn, along with other supplies. By weakening the major Indian tribes along the frontier, the American Revolution, among its other results, cleared the way for rapid settlement of the trans-Appalachian West.

THE WAR IN THE SOUTH

At the end of 1778 the focus of British action shifted suddenly to the south. The whole region from Virginia to the Carolinas had been free from any major action for over two years. Now the British would test King George's belief that a sleeping Tory power in the South needed only the presence of a few regulars to awaken it. So Lord George Germain conveyed to General Clinton His Majesty's plan to take Savannah and roll northward gathering momentum from the Loyalist countryside. For a while the idea seemed to work, but it ran afoul of two things: first, the Loyalist strength was less than estimated; and second, the British forces behaved so harshly as to drive even loyal men into rebellion.

SAVANNAH AND CHARLESTON   In November 1778, in accord with the king's desire, Clinton dispatched 3,500 men from New York and New Jersey under Lt.-Col. Archibald Campbell to join Gen. Augustin Prevost's Florida Rangers in attacking Savannah. So small was the defending force of Continentals and militia that Campbell quickly overwhelmed the Patriots and took the town. Almost as quickly, with the help of Prevost, Campbell brushed aside opposition in the interior; Gov. James Wright returned and reestablished the royal government in Georgia. There followed a byplay of thrust and parry between Prevost and South Carolina forces. Prevost finally drove toward Charleston, his redcoats plundering plantation houses along the way. The pillage so delayed his army that in May 1779 Prevost fetched up against impregnable defenses on Charleston Neck and narrowly escaped entrapment by Gen. Benjamin Lincoln's Continentals.

The seesaw campaign took a major turn when General Clinton brought new naval and land forces southward to join a massive amphibious attack which bottled up General Lincoln on the Charleston peninsula. On May 12, 1780, Lincoln was compelled to surrender the city and its 5,500 defenders, the largest army surrendered since Saratoga and the greatest single American loss of the war. At this point Congress, against Washington's advice, turned to the victor of Saratoga, Horatio Gates, to take command and sent him south. Charles Lord Cornwallis, dispatched with one of three columns to subdue the Carolina interior, surprised Gates's force at Camden, South Carolina, and threw his new army into a rout, led by Gates himself all the way back to Hillsborough, North Carolina, 160 miles away. It had come to pass as Gates's friend and neighbor Charles Lee had warned after Saratoga: "Beware that your Northern laurels do not turn to Southern willows."

THE CAROLINAS   Cornwallis had South Carolina just about under control, but his cavalry leaders Banastre Tarleton and Patrick Ferguson, who mobilized Tory militiamen, overreached themselves in their effort to subdue the Whigs. "Tarleton's Quarters" became bywords for savagery, because "Bloody Tarleton" gave little quarter to vanquished foes. Ferguson sealed his own doom when he threatened to march over the mountains and hang the leaders of the Watauga country. Instead the "overmountain men" went after Ferguson and, allied with other backcountry Whigs, caught him and his Tories on Kings Mountain, just inside South Carolina. There, on October 7, 1780, they devastated his force of about 1,100. By then feelings were so strong that American irregulars continued firing on Tories trying to surrender and later inflicted indiscriminate slaughter on Tory prisoners. Kings Mountain, and unaccustomed victory, is sometimes called the turning point of the war in the South. Its effect, by proving that

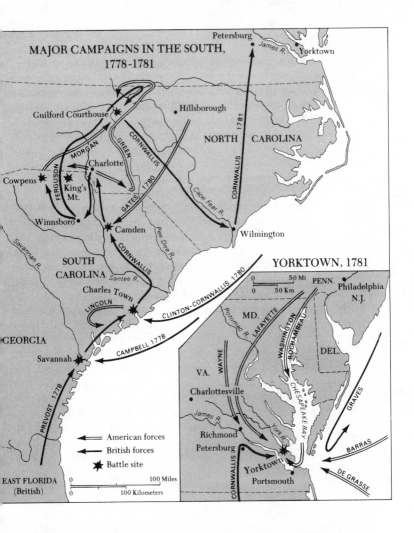

MAJOR CAMPAIGNS IN THE SOUTH, 1778–1781

YORKTOWN, 1781

American forces
British forces
★ Battle site

the British were not invincible, was to embolden small farmers to join guerrilla bands under partisan leaders like Francis Marion, "the Swamp Fox."

While the overmountain men were closing on Ferguson, Congress had chosen a new commander for the southern theater, Gen. Nathanael Greene, the "fighting Quaker" of Rhode Island. A man of infinite patience, skilled at managing men and saving supplies, careful to avoid needless risks, he was suited to a war of attrition against the British forces. From Charlotte, where he arrived in December, Greene moved his army eastward toward the Pee Dee River, to a site picked by his engineer, the Polish volunteer Thaddeus Kosciuszko. As a diversion he sent Gen. Daniel Morgan with about 700 men on a sweep to the west of Cornwallis's headquarters at Winnsboro. Taking a position near Cowpens, Morgan found himself swamped by militia units joining him faster than he could provide for them. Tarleton caught Morgan and his men on January 17, 1781, with the rain-swollen Broad River at their backs—a position Morgan took deliberately to force the green militiamen to stand and fight. Once the battle was joined, Tarleton mistook a readjustment in the American line for a militia panic, and rushed his men into a destructive fire. Tarleton and a handful of cavalry escaped, but more than 100 of his men were killed and more than 700 taken prisoner.

Morgan then fell back into North Carolina linked up with Greene's main force at Guilford Court House (now Greensboro), and then led Cornwallis on a wild goose chase up to the Dan River where, once the Americans had crossed, the British could not follow. His supplies running low, Cornwallis drew back to Hillsborough. When reinforcements of militiamen from Virginia and the Carolinas arrived, Greene returned to Guilford Court house and offered battle on March 15, 1781. There he placed his militiamen at the front of the line, asking them only to fire three shots before they drew back. As he feared, they fled the field, but in the process drew the pursuing redcoats into an enfilading fire from either side. Having inflicted heavy losses, Greene prudently withdrew to fight another day. Cornwallis was left in possession of the field, but at a cost of nearly 100 men killed and more than 400 wounded. In London, when the word arrived, parliamentary leader Charles James Fox echoed King Pyrrhus: "Another such victory and we are undone."

Cornwallis marched off toward the coast at Wilmington to lick his wounds and take on new supplies. Greene then resolved to go back into South Carolina in the hope of drawing Cornwallis after him or forcing the British to give up the state. There he joined forces with the guerrillas already active on the scene, and in a series of brilliant actions kept losing battles while winning the war: "We fight, get beat, rise, and fight again," he said. By September he had narrowed British control in the Deep South to Charleston and Savannah, although for more than a year longer Whigs and Tories slashed at each other in murderous backcountry actions.

Meanwhile Cornwallis had headed north away from Greene, reasoning that Virginia must be eliminated as a source of reinforcement before the Carolinas could be subdued. In May 1781 he marched north into Virginia. There, since December, Benedict Arnold, now a British general, was engaged in a war of maneuver with American forces under Lafayette and von Steuben. Arnold, until the previous September, had been American commander at West Point; there he nursed grievances over an official reprimand for extravagances as commander of reoccupied Philadelphia, and plotted to sell out the American stronghold to the British. The American capture of the British go-between, Maj. John Andre, revealed Arnold's plot. Forewarned, Arnold joined the British in New York while the hapless Andre was hanged as a spy.

YORKTOWN When Cornwallis linked up with Arnold at Petersburg, their combined forces rose to 7,200, far more than the small American force there. British raiders went out deep into Virginia, and one sortie by Tarleton nearly captured Governor Jefferson and his legislature at Charlottesville. When American reinforcements arrived under Anthony Wayne, captor of Stony Point in 1779, Cornwallis moved back toward the coast to establish contact with New York. In a fatal miscalculation, he picked Yorktown as a defensible site. There seemed to be little reason to worry about a siege, with Washington's main land force attacking New York and the British navy in control of American waters.

To be sure, there was a small American navy, but it was no match for the British fleet. Washington had started it with some fishing vessels during the siege of Boston, but American privateers, acting under state or Continental authority, proved far more troublesome. Most celebrated then and after were the exploits of Capt. John Paul Jones, who crossed the Atlantic in 1778 with his sloop of war *Ranger* and gave the British navy some bad moments in its home waters. In France, Benjamin Franklin got Jones an old Indiaman which the captain named the *Bonhomme Richard* in honor of Franklin's Poor Richard. Off England's Flamborough Head on September 23, 1779, Jones won a desperate battle with the British frigate *Serapis*, which he captured and occupied before his own ship sank. This was the occasion for his stirring and oft-repeated response to a British demand for surrender: "I have not yet begun to fight."

Still, such heroics were little more than nuisances to the British. But at a critical point, thanks to the French navy, the British lost control of the Chesapeake waters. For three years Washington had waited to get some military benefit from the French alliance. In 1780 the French finally landed a force of about 6,000 at Newport, which the British had given up to concentrate on the South, but the French army under the comte de Rochambeau sat there for a year, blockaded by the British fleet. But in 1781 the elements for combined action suddenly fell into place. In May, as

Cornwallis moved into Virginia, Washington persuaded Rochambeau to join forces for an attack on New York. The two armies linked up in July, but before they could strike at New York, word came from the West Indies that Admiral De Grasse was bound for the Chesapeake with his entire French fleet and some 3,000 soldiers. Washington and Rochambeau immediately set out toward Yorktown, all the while preserving the semblance of a flank movement against New York.

On August 30 De Grasse's fleet reached Yorktown and landed his troops to join Lafayette's force already watching Cornwallis. On September 6, the day after a British fleet under Admiral Thomas Graves appeared, De Grasse gave battle and forced Graves to give up his effort to relieve Cornwallis, whose fate was quickly sealed. Graves departed four days later for repairs in New York. De Grasse then sent ships up the Chesapeake to ferry down Washington's and Rochambeau's armies, which brought the total allied forces to more than 16,000, or better than double the size of Cornwallis's army. The siege began on September 28. On October 14 two major redoubts guarding the left of the British line fell to French and American attackers, the latter led by Washington's aide Alexander Hamilton. A British counterattack on October 16 failed to retake them, and later that day a squall forced Cornwallis to abandon a desperate plan to escape across the York River. On October 17, 1781, three years to the day after Saratoga, he sued for peace, and on October 19 the British force of almost 8,000 marched out, their colors cased. Gen. Benjamin Lincoln, captured at Charleston, later returned in a prisoner exchange and now Washington's second in command, directed them to the field of surrender as the band played somber tunes along with the English nursery rhyme, "The World Turned Upside Down":

> If buttercups buzzed
> after the bee;
> If boats were on land,
> Churches on sea;
> If ponies rode men,
> and grass ate the cow;
> If cats should be chased,
> into holes by the mouse;
> If mammas sold their babies,
> To gypsies for half a crown;
> If summer were spring
> And the other way round;
> Then all the world would be upside down.

Broadside celebrating America's victory at Yorktown. [Winterthur Museum]

NEGOTIATIONS

Whatever lingering hopes of victory the British may have harbored vanished at Yorktown. "O God, it's all over," Lord North groaned at news of the surrender. On February 27, 1782, the House of Commons voted against further prosecution of the war and on March 5 passed a bill authorizing the crown to make peace. On March 20 Lord North resigned and a new ministry was made up of the old friends of the Americans headed by the duke of Rockingham, who had brought about repeal of the Stamp Act. The new colonial minister, Lord Shelburne, became chief minister after Rockingham's death in September, and directed negotiations with American commissioners.

As early as 1779 the Continental Congress had authorized John Adams to conduct peace negotiations, but he and Vergennes were at odds almost from the beginning, and the French foreign minister used his influence in Philadelphia to get a new five-man commission with instructions to rely on Vergennes for advice. Only three members of the commission were active, however: Adams, who was on state business in the Netherlands;

John Jay, minister to Spain; and Franklin, already in Paris. Thomas Jefferson stayed home because of his wife's fatal illness, and Henry Laurens, held prisoner in the Tower of London after capture on the high seas, arrived late in the negotiations. Franklin and Jay did most of the work. In April 1782 Lord Shelburne sent a special representative, Richard Oswald, to Paris for conversations with Franklin. When Jay arrived, however, he was still smarting from snubs he had received in Madrid and intensely suspicious of Vergennes.

The French commitment to Spain complicated matters. Spain and the United States were both allied with France, but not with each other. America was bound by its alliance to fight on until the French made peace, and the French were bound to help the Spanish recover Gibraltar from England. Unable to deliver Gibraltar, or so the tough-minded Jay reasoned, Vergennes might try to bargain off American land west of the Appalachians in its place. Jay's distrust quickened when Vergennes's secretary informally suggested just such a bargain and left secretly for London. Fearful that the French were angling for a separate peace with the British, Jay persuaded Franklin to play the same game. Ignoring their instructions to consult fully with the French, they agreed to further talks provided Oswald were authorized "to treat with the Commissioners appointed by the Colonys, under the title of Thirteen United States." On November 30, 1782, the talks produced a preliminary treaty with Great Britain. If it violated the spirit of the alliance, it did not violate the strict letter of the treaty with France, for Vergennes was notified the day before it was signed and final agreement still depended on a Franco-British settlement.

THE PEACE OF PARIS   Early in 1783 France and Spain gave up on Gibraltar and reached an armistice. The final signing of the Peace of Paris came on September 3, 1783. In accord with the bargain already struck, Great Britain recognized the independence of the United States and agreed to a Mississippi River boundary to the west. Both the northern and southern borders left ambiguities that would require further definition in the future. Florida, as it turned out, passed back to Spain—along with the island of Minorca in the Mediterranean. France regained Senegal in Africa and the island of Tobago in the West Indies, both of which she had lost in 1763. The British further granted Americans the "liberty" of fishing off Newfoundland and in the St. Lawrence Gulf, and the right to dry their catches on the unsettled coasts of Labrador, Nova Scotia, and the Magdalen Islands. On the matter

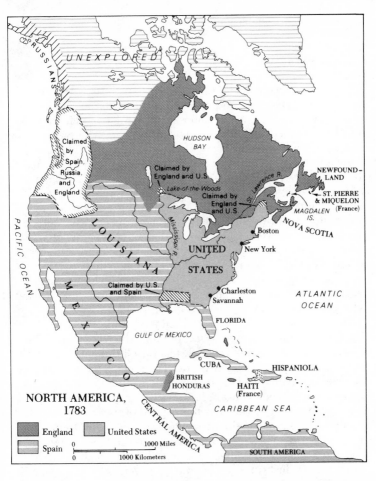

NORTH AMERICA, 1783

UNEXPLORED

RUSSIANS

HUDSON BAY

Claimed by Spain, Russia, and England

Claimed by England and U.S.

Lake-of-the-Woods

Claimed by England and U.S.

St. Lawrence R.

NEWFOUND-LAND

ST. PIERRE & MIQUELON (France)

MAGDALEN IS.

NOVA SCOTIA

PACIFIC OCEAN

LOUISIANA

Mississippi R.

UNITED STATES

Boston

New York

Claimed by U.S. and Spain

Charleston

Savannah

ATLANTIC OCEAN

MEXICO

FLORIDA

GULF OF MEXICO

CUBA

HISPANIOLA

BRITISH HONDURAS

HAITI (France)

CENTRAL AMERICA

CARIBBEAN SEA

■ England ▨ United States ▨ Spain

0 ____ 1000 Miles
0 ____ 1000 Kilometers

SOUTH AMERICA

of debts, the best the British could get was a promise that British merchants should "meet with no legal impediment" in seeking to collect them. And on the tender point of Loyalists whose property had been confiscated, the negotiators agreed that Congress would "earnestly recommend" to the states the restoration of confiscated property. Each of the last two points was little more than a face-saving gesture for the British.

On November 24 the last British troops left New York City, and on December 4 they evacuated Staten Island and Long Island. That same day Washington took leave of his officers at Fraunces Tavern in New York. On December 23 he appeared before the Continental Congress, meeting in Annapolis, to resign his commission. Before the end of the next day he was back at Mount Vernon, home in time for Christmas.

THE POLITICAL REVOLUTION

REPUBLICAN IDEOLOGY   The Americans had won their War for Independence. Had they undergone a political revolution as well? One answer was given years later by John Adams: "The Revolution was affected before the war commenced. The Revolution was in the minds and hearts of the people. . . . This radical change in the principles, opinions, sentiments, and affections of the people, was the real American Revolution." A movement which began as a struggle for the rights of Englishmen had become a fight for independence in which those rights found expression in governments which were new yet deeply rooted in the colonial experience and the prevailing viewpoints of Whiggery and the Enlightenment. Such ideas as the contract theory of government, the sovereignty of the people, the separation of powers, and natural rights found their way quickly, almost automatically, into the new frames of government that were devised while the fight went on—amid other urgent business.

The American Revolution was unique, Louis Hartz wrote in *The Liberal Tradition in America*, not for "the freedom to which it led, but the established feudal structure it did not have to destroy." Unlike France, Alexis de Tocqueville later said, the Americans did not have to "endure a democratic revolution." In a sense they had been born free, and they saw their revolution as in the main a defense of their liberty and property against what seemed a tyrannical and corrupt government. Still, the revolutionary controversies forced Americans to think out things once taken as a matter of course. Political thinking had to catch up with colonial institutions and practices, but once that process began it carried a momentum of its own.

The very idea of republican government was a far more radical departure in that day of kings and emperors than it would seem to later generations. The idea was rooted in that radical element of British Whiggery which a later historian labeled the eighteenth-century Commonwealthmen, a group which invoked the spirit of republican thinkers in Cromwell's England, the late Roman Republic, and classical antiquity. In the focus of republican thinking Americans began to see themselves in a new light, no longer the rustic provincials in a backwater of European culture but rather the embodiment of the virtue so long praised by intellectuals. "Those who labor in the earth," Jefferson wrote in his *Notes on the State of Virginia* (1781), "are the chosen people of God, if ever He had a chosen people, whose breasts He has

made His peculiar deposit for substantial and genuine virtue."
As free citizens of a republic, unshackled by dependence on the
favor of the court, the American would cast off corruptions of the
Old World and usher in a new reign of liberty and bliss, not only
for themselves but for all mankind. Reality, of course, was bound
to fall short of such millennial hopes, but the republican ideal
served to focus and reinforce the new American vision.

NEW STATE CONSTITUTIONS   At the onset of the fighting every colony saw the departure of governors and other officials, and
usually the expulsion of Loyalists from the assemblies, which
then assumed power as provincial "congresses" or "conventions." But they were acting as revolutionary bodies without any
legal basis for the exercise of authority. In two of the states this
presented little difficulty. Connecticut and Rhode Island, which
had been virtually little republics as corporate colonies, simply
purged their charters of any reference to colonial ties. Massachusetts followed their example until 1780. In the other states
the prevailing notions of social contract and popular sovereignty
led to written constitutions which specified the framework and
powers of government. One of the lessons of the Revolution, it
seemed, had been that one should not rely on the vague body of
law and precedent which made up the unwritten constitution of
Britain. The colonies in fact had had written constitutions in the
form of their charters. Constitution making got under way even
before independence. In May 1776 Congress advised the colonies to set up new governments "under the authority of the people." At first the authority of the people was exercised by
legislature which simply adopted constitutions and promulgated
them. But they had little more status than ordinary statutory law,
it could be argued, since the people had no chance to express
their wishes directly.

When the Massachusetts assembly hastily submitted a constitution to the towns for approval, however, it was rejected. Massachusetts thereupon invented what became a standard device
for American constitution making: a body separate from and superior to the legislature to exercise the people's sovereignty. In
1779–1780 Massachusetts elected a special convention, chosen
for the specific purpose of making a constitution. The invention
of the constitutional convention was an altogether original contribution to the art of government, and one that other states copied. The resultant document went out to the town meetings with
the provision that two-thirds or more would have to ratify it,
which they did. The Massachusetts Constitution of 1780 de-

clared: "The body politic is formed by a voluntary association of individuals; it is a social compact, by which the whole people covenants with each citizen, and each with the whole people that all shall be governed by certain laws for the common good."

The first state constitutions varied mainly in detail. They formed governments much like the colonial governments, with elected governors and senates instead of appointed governors and councils. Generally they embodied, sometimes explicitly, a separation of powers as a safeguard against abuses, and generally they included a Bill of Rights which protected the time-honored rights of petition, freedom of speech, trial by jury, freedom from self-incrimination, and the like. Most tended to limit the powers of governors and increase the powers of·the legislatures, which had led the people in their quarrels with the colonial governors. Pennsylvania went so far as to eliminate the governor and upper house of the legislature altogether, and operated until 1790 with a unicameral legislature limited only by a house of "censors" who reviewed its work every five years.

THE ARTICLES OF CONFEDERATION   The central government, like the state governments, grew out of an extralegal revolutionary body. The Continental Congress exercised governmental powers by common consent and without any constitutional sanction before March 1781. In a sense it had much the character of a diplomatic congress, composed of delegates named annually by the state legislatures. Plans for a permanent frame of government were started very early, however. Richard Henry Lee's motion for independence included a call for a plan of confederation. As early as July 12, 1776, a committee headed by John Dickinson produced a draft constitution, the "Articles of Confederation and Perpetual Union." For more than a year Congress debated the articles in between more urgent matters and finally adopted them on November 15, 1777, subject to ratification by all the states. All states ratified promptly except Maryland, which stubbornly insisted that the seven states claiming western lands should cede them to the authority of Congress. Maryland did not relent until early 1781, when Virginia gave up its claims under the old colonial charter to the vast region north of the Ohio River. New York had already given up a dubious claim based on its "jurisdiction" over the Iroquois, and the other states eventually gave up their charter claims, although Georgia did not until 1802.

When the Articles of Confederation became effective in March 1781 they did little more than legalize the status quo.

"The United States in Congress Assembled" had a multitude of responsibilities but little authority to carry them out. It had full power over foreign affairs and questions of war and peace; it could decide disputes between the states; it had authority over coinage, postal service, and Indian affairs, and responsibility for the government of the western territories. But it had no power to enforce its resolutions and ordinances upon either states or individuals. And it had no power to levy taxes, but had to rely on requisitions which state legislatures could ignore at their will.

The states, after their battles with Parliament, were in no mood for a strong central government. The Congress in fact had less power than the colonists had once accepted in Parliament, since it could not regulate interstate and foreign commerce. For certain important acts, moreover, a special majority was required. Nine states had to approve measures dealing with war, privateering, treaties, coinage, finances, or the army and navy. Amendments to the articles required unanimous ratification by all the states. The Confederation had neither an executive nor a judicial branch; there was no administrative head of government (only the president of the Congress, chosen annually) and no federal courts.

THE SOCIAL REVOLUTION

On the general frame of government there was in America a consensus—the forms grew so naturally out of experience and the prevalent theories. On other points, however, there was disagreement. As the historian J. Franklin Jamieson put it, in what might be taken almost as a general law of revolutions: "The stream of revolution, once started, could not be confined within narrow banks, but spread abroad upon the land." The more conservative Patriots would have been content to replace royal officials with the rich, the well-born, and the able, and let it go at that. But more radical elements, which had been quickened by the long agitations, raised the question not only of home rule but who shall rule at home, to cite the oft-quoted phrase of the historian Carl Becker.

EQUALITY AND ITS LIMITS   The spirit of equality borne by the Revolution found outlet in several directions, one of which was simply a weakening of old habits of deference. One Colonel Randolph of Virginia told of being in a tavern when a rough group of farmers came in, spitting and pulling off their muddy boots without regard to the sensibilities of the gentlemen present: "The spirit of independence was converted into equality," Randolph wrote, "and every one who bore arms, esteems himself upon a footing with his neighbors. . . . No doubt each of these men considers himself, in every respect, my equal." No doubt each did.

What was more, participation in the army or militia activated and politicized people who had taken little interest in politics before. The large number of new political opportunities that opened up led more ordinary citizens into participation than ever before. The social base of the new legislatures was much broader than that of the old assemblies.

Men fighting for their liberty found it difficult to justify the denial to others of the rights of suffrage and representation. The property qualifications for voting, which already admitted an overwhelming majority of white males, were lowered still further. In Pennsylvania, Delaware, North Carolina, Georgia, and Vermont any taxpayer could vote, although commonly office-holders had to meet higher property requirements. Men who had argued against taxation without representation found it hard to justify denial of proportionate representation for the back-country, which generally enlarged its presence in the legislatures. New men thrown up by the revolutionary turmoil often replaced older men, some of whom had been Loyalists. More often than not the newcomers were men of lesser property. Some states concentrated much power in a legislature chosen by a wide suffrage, but not even Pennsylvania went quite so far as universal manhood suffrage. Others, like New York and Maryland, took a more conservative stance.

New developments in land tenure which grew out of the Revolution extended the democratic trends of suffrage requirements. Confiscations resulted in the seizure of Tory estates by all the state legislatures. Some were quite large, such as the estates of the Penn family, of Lord Fairfax in Virginia, and James DeLancey in New York. William Pepperrell of Maine lost a spread on which he could ride for thirty miles. These lands, however, were of small consequence in contrast to the unsettled lands formerly at the disposal of crown and proprietors, now in the hands of popular assemblies, much of which was used for bonuses to veterans of the war. Western lands, formerly closed by the Proclamation of 1763 and the Quebec Act of 1774, were soon thrown open for settlers.

THE PARADOX OF SLAVERY   The revolutionary principles of liberty and equality, moreover, had clear implications for the enslaved blacks. Jefferson's draft of the Declaration had indicted the king for having violated the "most sacred rights of life and liberty of a distant people, who never offended him, captivating them into slavery in another hemisphere," but the clause was struck out "in complaisance to South Carolina and Georgia." The clause was in fact inaccurate in completely ignoring the implication of American slaveholders and slavetraders in the traffic. Before the Revolution, only Rhode Island, Connecticut, and Pennsylvania had halted the importation of slaves. After independence all the states except Georgia stopped the traffic, although South Carolina later reopened it.

Black soldiers or sailors were present at most of the major battles, from Lexington to Yorktown; some were on the Loyalist side. Lord Dunmore, governor of Virginia, anticipated a general British policy in 1775 when he promised freedom to slaves, as well as indentured servants, who would bear arms for the Loyalist cause. Taking alarm at this, General Washington at the end of 1775 reversed an original policy of excluding blacks from American forces—except the few already in militia companies—and Congress quickly approved. Only two states, South Carolina and Georgia, held out completely against the policy, but by a rough estimate few if any more than about 5,000 were admitted to the American forces in a total of about 300,000, and most of those were free blacks from northern states. They served mainly in white units, although Massachusetts did organize two all-black companies and Rhode Island one. Slaves who served in the cause of independence got their freedom and in some cases land bounties. But the British army, which freed probably tens of thousands, was a greater instrument of emancipation than the American forces. Most of the newly freed blacks found their way to Canada or to British colonies in the Caribbean.

In the northern states, which had fewer slaves than the southern, the doctrines of liberty led swiftly to emancipation for all either during the fighting or shortly afterward. Vermont's Constitution of 1777 specifically forbade slavery. The Massachusetts Constitution of 1780 proclaimed the "inherent liberty" of all, and a court decision in 1783 freed one Quock Walker on the grounds that slavery could not legally exist under that provision. Elsewhere north of the Mason-Dixon line gradual emancipation became the device for freeing the slaves. Pennsylvania in 1780 provided that all children born thereafter to slave mothers would become free at age twenty-eight. In 1784 Rhode Island provided freedom for all born thereafter, at age twenty-one for males, eighteen for females. New York lagged until 1799 in granting freedom to mature slaves born after enactment, but an

Elizabeth Freeman (Mumbet). A former slave, Elizabeth Freeman won her freedom in a Massachusetts court by claiming that the "inherent liberty" of all applied to slaves as well. [Massachusetts Historical Society]

act of 1817 set July 4, 1827, as the date for emancipation of all remaining slaves.

South of Pennsylvania the potential consequences of emancipation were so staggering—South Carolina had a black majority—that whites refused to be stampeded by abstract philosophy. Yet even there slaveholders like Washington, Jefferson, Patrick Henry, and others were troubled. "I am not one of those . . ." Henry Laurens of South Carolina wrote his son, "who dare trust in Providence for defense and security of their own liberty while they enslave and wish to continue in slavery thousands who are as well entitled to freedom as themselves." Jefferson wrote in his *Notes on Virginia* (1785): "Indeed I tremble for my country when I reflect that God is just; that his justice cannot sleep forever." But he, like many other white southerners, was riding the tiger and did not know how to dismount. The furthest antislavery sentiment carried the southern states was to relax the manumission laws under which owners might free their slaves.

THE STATUS OF WOMEN The logic of liberty applied to the status of women as much as to that of blacks, but wrought even less change in their sphere. Women joined in prewar campaigns to boycott British goods—in fact their support was essential to success in that cause. The war drew women at least temporarily into new pursuits. They plowed fields, kept shop, and melted down pots and pans to make shot. Esther Reed of Philadelphia organized a ladies' association which raised money to provide comforts for the troops. The fighting was man's work, but women served the armies in various support roles, such as handling supplies and serving as couriers. Wives often followed their husbands to camp, and on occasion took their places in the line, as Margaret Corbin did at Fort Washington when her husband fell at his artillery post, or Mary Ludwig Hays (better known as Molly Pitcher) did when hers collapsed of heat fatigue. An exceptional case was that of Deborah Sampson, who joined a Massachusetts regiment as Robert Shurtleff and served from 1781 to 1783 by the "artful concealment" of her sex.

Early in the struggle, on March 31, 1776, Abigail Adams wrote to her husband John: "In the new Code of Laws which I suppose it will be necessary for you to make I desire you would remember the Ladies. . . . Do not put such unlimited power into the hands of the Husbands." Since men were "Naturally Tyrannical," she wrote, "why then, not put it out of the power of the vicious and the Lawless to use us with cruelty and indignity with impunity." Otherwise, "If particular care and attention is not paid to the Ladies we are determined to foment a Rebellion, and will not hold ourselves bound by any Laws in which we have no voice, or Representation." Husband John replied playfully: "We have been told that our Struggle has loosened the bands of Government every where." But Abigail's letter offered the "first Intimation that another Tribe more numerous and powerful than all the rest were grown discontented." But he continued: "Depend upon it, we know better than to repeal our Masculine systems."

And one is hard put to find evidence that the legal status of women benefited from equalitarian doctrine. There is local evidence that in parts of New England divorces were easier to get, but married women still forfeited control of their own property to their husbands, and women gained no political rights except in one state, apparently by accident. New Jersey's state constitu-

Abigail Adams, in a portrait by Gilbert Stuart. [National Gallery of Art]

tion of 1776 defined voters as all "free inhabitants" who could meet property requirements, and some women began voting in the 1780s and continued to do so until 1807, when the state disfranchised both women and blacks. Although some limited advances were made in education, it was a slow process. The chief contribution of the Revolution seems to have been less in substantive gains for women than in a growing willingness to challenge old shibboleths, in the spirit of Abigail Adams. In an essay "On the Equality of the Sexes" (written in 1779, published in 1790), Judith Sargent Murray wrote: "We can only reason from what we know, and if an opportunity of acquiring knowledge hath been denied us, the inferiority of our sex cannot fairly be deduced from thence." Some groundwork was being laid for future battles, but meaningful victories in the cause of equality between the sexes remained in the future.

FREEDOM OF RELIGION   The Revolution also set in motion a transition from the toleration of religious dissent to a complete freedom of religion in the separation of church and state. The Anglican church, established in five colonies and parts of two others, was especially vulnerable because of its association with the crown and because dissenters outnumbered Anglicans in all the states except Virginia. And all but Virginia removed tax support for the church before the fighting was over. In 1776 the Virginia Declaration of Rights guaranteed the free exercise of religion, and in 1786 the Virginia Statute of Religious Freedom (written by Thomas Jefferson) declared that: "no man shall be compelled to frequent or support any religious worship, place or ministry whatsoever," that none should in any way suffer for his religious opinions and beliefs, "But that all men shall be free to profess, and by argument to maintain, their opinions in matters of religion."

New England, with its Puritan heritage, was in less haste to disestablish the Congregational church, although the rules were already being relaxed enough by the 1720s to let Quakers and Baptists assign their tax support to their own churches. New Hampshire finally discontinued tax support for its churches in 1817, Connecticut in 1818, Maine in 1820, and Massachusetts in 1833. Certain religious requirements for officeholding lingered here and there on the law books: Massachusetts and Maryland required a declaration of Christian faith; Delaware had a Trinitarian test; New Jersey and the Carolinas held that officeholders must be Protestants. But in most cases these requirements disappeared before many more years.

In churches as well as in government the Revolution set off a period of constitution making, as some of the first national church bodies emerged. In 1784 the Methodists, who at first were an offshoot of the Anglicans, came together in a general conference at Baltimore under Bishop Francis Asbury. The Anglican church, rechristened Episcopal, gathered in a series of meetings which by 1789 had united the various dioceses in a federal union under Bishop Samuel Seabury of Connecticut; in 1789 also the Presbyterians held their first general assembly in Philadelphia. The following year, 1790, the Catholic church had its first bishop in the United States when John Carroll was named bishop of Baltimore. Other churches would follow in the process of coming together on a national basis.

EMERGENCE OF AN AMERICAN CULTURE

For all the weakness of the central government, the Revolution generated a nascent sense of common nationality. At the time of the French and Indian War Andrew Burnaby, an English traveler, observed: "Fire and water are not more heterogeneous than the different colonies in North America. Nothing can exceed the jealousy . . . which they possess in regard to each other." But the Revolution taught Americans to think "continentally," as Alexander Hamilton put it. As early as the Stamp Act Congress of 1765, Christopher Gadsden, leader of the Charleston radicals, had said: "There ought to be no New England man, no New Yorker, known on the Continent; but all of us Americans." In the first Continental Congress Patrick Henry asserted that such a sense of identity had come to pass: "The distinctions between Virginians, Pennsylvanians, New Yorkers, and New Englanders are no more. I am not a Virginian but an American."

The concrete experience of the war reinforced the feeling. Soldiers who went to fight in other states inevitably broadened their horizons. John Marshall, future chief justice, served first in the Virginia militia and then in the Continental Army in the middle states and endured the winter of 1777–1778 at Valley Forge. He later wrote: "I found myself associated with brave men from different states who were risking life and everything valuable in a common cause. I was confirmed in the habit of considering America as my country and Congress as my government." American nationalism, like American independence, was the creation of the Revolution.

At the same time the Revolution itself marked the start of a national tradition, one that would ultimately reach back and incorporate colonial heroes in its legends. The Revolution produced symbols of unity in, for instance, the Declaration of Independence and the flag, designed by Francis Hopkinson, a Philadelphia lawyer and poet, and a pantheon of heroes whose deeds and whose stirring cries echoed down the years: Sgt. William Jasper's vaulting the palmetto fort on Sullivan's Island to retrieve the fallen flag; Patrick Henry's exhorting his countrymen to choose liberty or death; Nathan Hale's speaking his perhaps apocryphal last words before the British hanged him for a spy: "I only regret that I have but one life to lose for my country." It detracted not a bit from the effect of those cries that both paraphrased lines from Addison's *Cato* nor that William Prescott's admonition at Bunker Hill not to fire "until you see the whites of their eyes" echoed Frederick the Great. And at least some were American originals: John Parker's telling the Minute Men at Lexington, "Don't fire unless fired upon, but if they mean to have a war let it begin here!"; John Paul Jones's defiantly responding to the call for surrender, "I have not yet begun to fight!"; or Richard Henry Lee's postwar tribute to the dead Washington, "first in war, first in peace, and first in the hearts of his countrymen."

ARTS IN THE NEW NATION   The marquis de Chastellux, a French aristocrat who fought in the cause, thought the Revolution in America had generated "more heroes than she [America] has marble and artists to commemorate them." The Revolution provided the first generation of native artists with inspirational subjects. It also filled them with high expectations that individual freedom would release creative energies and vitalize both commerce and the arts. The hope that America would become the future seat of empire and the arts had excited the colonials at least since the appearance of the Anglican divine George Berkeley's celebrated "Verses on the Prospect of Planting Arts and Learning in America" (published in 1752), which included the oft-quoted line: "Westward the course of empire takes its way." Nathaniel Ames's *Almanac* for 1758 took up the theme in unmeasured terms: "The Curious have observed, that the Progress of Humane Literature (like the Sun) is from the East to the West." Soon the course of the arts and sciences would alter the face of the land. "O! Ye unborn Inhabitants of America," the *Almanac* continued, "when your Eyes behold the sun after he has rolled the seasons round for two or three centuries more, you will know that in Anno Domini 1758, we dream'd of your Times."

At the Princeton commencement in 1771 two graduating seniors and budding young authors, Philip Freneau and Hugh Henry Brackenridge, classmates of James Madison and Aaron Burr, presented "A Poem on the Rising Glory of America" in which they reviewed once again the westward transit of culture and foretold in America "the final stage . . . of high invention and wond'rous art, which not the ravages of time shall waste." The Revolution itself raised expectations yet higher. As David Ramsay put it in his *History of the American Revolution* (1789), the conflict with England "gave a spring to the active powers of the inhabitants, and set them on thinking, speaking and acting, in a line far beyond that to which they had been accustomed." The result, one historian has noted, was a sudden efflorescence of the arts: "By the time the country inaugurated its first president in 1789" it had also produced "its first novel, first epic poem, first composer, first professionally acted play, first actor and dancer, first museum, its first important painters, musical-instrument makers, magazine engravers—indeed most of the defining features of traditional high culture."

If, as it happened, no American artist of the time quite measured up to the highest expectations, many of them in the inspiration of the moment chose patriotic themes and celebrated the new nation. Ironically, the best American painters of the time spent all or most of the Revolution in England, studying with Benjamin West of Pennsylvania and John Singleton Copley of

Charles Willson Peale founded the world's first popular museum of natural science and art. Peale began the museum in his Philadelphia home in 1784. His idea of opening a museum to all was revolutionary. [Elise Peale Patterson de Gelpi-Toro]

Massachusetts, both of whom had set up shop in London before the outbreak. Even John Trumbull, who had served in the siege of Boston and the Saratoga campaign, somehow managed a visit to London during the war before returning to help his brother supply the Continentals. Later he adopted patriotic themes in *The Battle of Bunker Hill*, and his four panels in the Capitol Rotunda at Washington: *The Declaration of Independence, The Surrender of General Burgoyne, The Surrender of General Cornwallis*, and *The Resignation of General Washington*. Charles Willson Peale, who fought at Trenton and Princeton and survived the winter at Valley Forge, produced a virtual portrait gallery of Revolutionary War figures. Over twenty-three years he painted George Washington seven times from life and produced in all sixty portraits of him. Peale's portrait of Washington after the battle of Princeton (painted in 1779) is believed to be the most faithful representation of the general at the time of the War of Independence.

The poet John Trumbull (cousin of the painter) produced perhaps the most successful creative work on the Revolution in *M'Fingal* (1776), a mock heroic satire on American Tories. At the time its ironic tone suited the public temper less than *Common Sense*, but it went through many editions after the war. Joel Barlow, associated with Trumbull in a literary group called the Hartford Wits, later composed an ambitious patriotic epic, *The Vision of Columbus* (1787), enlarged and revised as *The Columbiad* (1807), designed to show America as "the noblest and most elevated part of the earth." Widely hailed at the time as an instant classic, it was pretentious and almost unreadable. Barlow is better remembered for *The Hasty Pudding* (1796), a mock epic which celebrated American simplicity in contrast to Old World sophistication. The Revolution-era poems of Philip Freneau, such as his elegy "To the Memory of Brave Americans," "Eutaw Springs," and "The Memorable Victory of Paul Jones," capture better than any others the patriotic emotions of the war.

EDUCATION The most lasting effect of postwar nationalism may well have been its mark on education. In the colonies there had been a total of nine colleges, but once the Revolution was over, eight more sprang up in the 1780s and six in the 1790s. Several of the revolutionary state constitutions had provisions for state universities. Georgia's was the first chartered, in 1785, but the University of North Carolina (chartered in 1789) was the first to open, in 1795. An interest in general systems of public schools stirred in some of the states, especially in Pennsylvania and Virginia. Jefferson worked out an elaborate plan for a state system that would provide a rudimentary education for all, and higher levels of education for the talented, up through a state university. The movement for public education, however, would reach fruition much later. At the time, and well into the next century, no state would have a system of schools in the present-day sense.

Education played an important role in broadening and deepening the sense of nationalism, and no single element was as important, perhaps as the spelling book, an item of almost universal use. Noah Webster of Hartford, while teaching at Goshen, New York, prepared an elementary speller published in 1783. By 1890 more than 60 million copies of his "Blue Back Speller" had been printed, and the book continued to sell well into the twentieth century. In his preface Webster issued a cultural Declaration of Independence: "The country," he wrote, "must in some future time, be as distinguished by the superiority of her literary improvements, as she already is by the liberality of her civil and ecclesiastical constitutions." Volume II of Webster's *Grammatical Institute*, a grammar, appeared in 1784, and Volume III, a reader, in 1785, crammed with selections from the speeches of Revolutionary leaders who, he said, were the equals of Cicero and Demosthenes. Other titles, *The American Spelling Book* (the "Blue Back") and *An American Selection of Lessons in Reading and Speaking*, pursued a growing fashion in textbooks of using the word American in the title: American arithmetics as well as spellers appeared. Jedediah Morse, author of *American Geography* (1789), said that the country needed its own textbooks so that the people would not be affected with monarchical and aristocratic ideas.

In a special sense American nationalism was the embodiment of an idea. This first new nation, unlike the rising nations of Europe, was not rooted in antiquity. Its people save the Indians, had not inhabited it over the centuries, nor was there any nation of a common descent. "The American national consciousness," Hans Kohn wrote in *The Idea of Nationalism*, " . . . is not a voice crying out of the depth of the dark past, but is proudly a product of the enlightened present, setting its face resolutely toward the future." And American nationalism embodied a universal idea, with implications for all the world.

Many people, at least since the time of the Pilgrims, had thought America to be singled out for a special identity, a special mission. Jonathan Edwards said God had singled out America as "the glorious renovator of the world," and still later John Adams proclaimed the opening of America "a grand scheme and design in Providence for the illumination and the emancipation of the slavish part of mankind all over the earth." The mission had subtly changed, but it was still there. It was now a call to lead the way for all mankind toward liberty and equality. Meanwhile, however, Americans had to come to grips with more immediate problems created by their new nationhood.

FURTHER READING

The war of the Revolution is the subject of many good surveys. Two which scholars use often are Don Higginbotham's *The War of American Independence* (1971)° and John R. Alden's *The American Revolution, 1775–1783* (1954). Military history buffs should also turn to Christopher Ward's *The War of the Revolution* (2 vols.; 1952) for its details of maneuvers and its clear maps. Another perspective is provided by memoirs and reports of the actual participants in George F. Scheer and Hugh Rankin's *Rebels and Redcoats* (1957).° Briefer accounts are found in Howard Peckham's *The War for Independence* (1958)° and Willard M. Wallace's *Appeal to Arms* (1951).° The British side of the conflict is handled by Piers MacKesy in *The War for America* (1964). Action at sea is the subject of Gardner W. Allen's *A Naval History of the American Revolution* (2 vols.; 1913). Perceptive analysis of the values and goals which led Americans to fight appears in Don Higginbotham, ed., *Reconsiderations on the American Revolution* (1978), as well as John Shy's *A People Numerous and Armed* (1976),° Charles Royster's *A Revolutionary People at War* (1979),° and Lawrence D. Cress's *Citizens in Arms* (1982).

Biographical studies of the major military figures include James T. Flexner's *George Washington in the American Revolution* (1968), Ira D. Gruber's *The Howe Brothers and the American Revolution* (1972),° William Willcox's *Portrait of a General: Sir Henry Clinton in the War of Independence* (1964), Franklin Wickwire's *Cornwallis and the War of Independence* (1970), Samuel E. Morison's *John Paul Jones: A Sailor's Biography* (1959),° Theodore Thayer's *Nathanael Greene: Strategist of the American Revolution* (1960), and Don Higginbotham's *Daniel Morgan: Revolutionary Rifleman* (1961). Material on George Rogers Clark can be found in Jack Sosin's *The Revolutionary Frontier, 1763–1783* (1967).

Why some Americans remained loyal to the Crown is the subject of Bernard Bailyn's *The Ordeal of Thomas Hutchinson* (1974),° Robert M. Calhoon's *The Loyalists in Revolutionary America* (1973), and William H. Nelson's *The American Tory* (1962).° Paul H. Smith's *Loyalists and Redcoats* (1964) traces the military role of the Tories, and Wallace Brown's *The King's Friends* (1965) argues that the loyalists came from all classes of colonial society.

Edmund S. Morgan's *The Birth of the Republic, 1763–1789* (1956),°

° These books are available in paperback editions.

provides a concise introduction to the political events which led rebellious colonists to form a new nation. Herbert Aptheker's *The American Revolution, 1763–1783* (1960), gives a Marxist interpretation to the same events. A more detailed focus on the ideology of Republicanism is in Gordon S. Wood's *The Creation of the American Republic, 1776–1787* (1969).° Merrill Jensen's *The Articles of Confederation* (1940)° is a good introduction to the first attempt at nation forming. Also see a more recent work by Jensen, *The American Revolution within America* (1974). State-level studies of revolutionary politics include some of the works cited for Chapter 5, as well as the following: Fletcher Greene's *Constitutional Developments in the South Atlantic States* (1930), Jackson Turner Main's *The Upper House in Revolutionary America, 1763–1788* (1967) and *The Sovereign States, 1775–1783* (1973), and Robert Brown's *Middle Class Democracy and the Revolution in Massachusetts, 1691–1780* (1955).°

The effort to trace the social effects of the Revolution goes back at least to James F. Jameson's, *The American Revolution Considered as a Social Movement* (1925).° Richard B. Morris's *The American Revolution Reconsidered* (1967)° works at updating and modifying Jameson. A radical view of the social conflicts of the period is found in some of the essays in Alfred Young (ed.), *The American Revolution* (1976).° Jackson Turner Main's *The Social Structure of Revolutionary America* (1965)° looks at the quantitative evidence for the emergence of social equality, while Rhys Isaac's *The Transformation of Virginia, 1740–1790* (1982),° examines the social conflicts in that pivotal state. The question of disestablishment and religious liberty is treated in essays by Sidney Mead, *The Lively Experiment* (1963). Relevant chapters in Winthrop Jordan's *White over Black* (1968)° address the issue of emancipation during the Revolutionary period. One of the few recent community-level studies of change is Robert A. Gross's *The Minute Men and Their World* (1976).° Mary Beth Norton's *Liberty's Daughters* (1980)° documents the role women played in securing independence, and Lynne Withey's *Dearest Friend: A Life of Abigail Adams* (1981) portrays the role played by one very important Revolutionary woman. Joy and Richard Buel's *The Way of Duty: A Woman and Her Family in Revolutionary America* (1984) shows the impact of the Revolution on the lives of a remarkable New England family.

The standard introduction to diplomacy remains Samuel F. Bemis's *The Diplomacy of the American Revolution* (1935).° Richard B. Morris's *The Peacemakers* (1965)° examines more closely the negotiations for the Treaty of Paris, and William C. Stinchcombe details the events of American diplomats in *The American Revolution and the French Alliance* (1969).

7

SHAPING A FEDERAL UNION

Speaking to his fellow graduates at the Harvard commencement in 1787, young John Quincy Adams lamented "this critical period" when the country was "groaning under the intolerable burden of . . . accumulated evils." More than a century later the popular writer and lecturer John Fiske used the same phrase, the "critical period," as the title for a history of the United States under the Articles of Confederation. For many years it was the fashion among historians to dwell upon the weaknesses of the Confederation and the "accumulated evils" of the time to the neglect of the major achievements.

The Congress of the Confederation, to be sure, had little if any more governmental authority than the United Nations would have 200 years later. "It could ask for money but not compel payment," as one historian wrote, "it could enter into treaties but not enforce their stipulations; it could provide for raising of armies but not fill the ranks; it could borrow money but take no proper measures for repayment; it could advise and recommend but not command." In foreign affairs and the domestic economy the Congress was virtually helpless to cope with problems of diplomacy and postwar depression which would have challenged the resources of a much stronger government. It was not easy to find men of stature to serve in such a body, and often hard to gather a quorum of those who did. Yet in spite of its handicaps the Confederation Congress somehow managed to keep afloat and to lay important foundations for the future. It concluded the Peace of Paris in 1783. It created the first executive departments. And it formulated principles of land distribution and territorial government which guided expansion ultimately all the way to the Pacific coast.

Throughout most of the War for Independence the Congress remained distrustful of executive power. It assigned administrative duties to its committees and thereby imposed an almost intolerable burden on conscientious members. At one time or another John Adams, for instance, served on some eighty committees. In 1781, however, anticipating ratification of the Articles of Confederation, Congress began to set up three departments: Foreign Affairs, Finance, and War, in addition to a Post Office Department which had existed since 1775. Each was to have a single head responsible to Congress. For superintendent of finance Congress chose Robert Morris, a prominent Philadelphia merchant who by virtue of his business connections and a talent for financial sleight-of-hand brought a semblance of order into the federal accounts. The other departments had less success to their credit, and indeed lacked executive heads for long periods. The first secretary for foreign affairs, Robert R. Livingston, left that post in May 1783 and was not replaced by John Jay until the following summer. Given enough time and stability, however, Congress and the department heads might have evolved something like the parliamentary cabinet system. As it turned out, these agencies were the beginnings of the government departments that came into being later under the Constitution.

FINANCE   But as yet there was neither president nor prime minister, only the presiding officer of Congress and its secretary, Charles Thomson, the "Sam Adams of Philadelphia," who served continuously from 1774 to 1789. The closest thing to an executive head of the Confederation was Robert Morris, who as superintendent of finance in the final years of the war became the most influential figure in the government, and who had ideas of making both himself and the Confederation more powerful. He envisioned a coherent program of taxation and debt management to make the government financially stable; "a public debt supported by public revenue will prove the strongest cement to keep our confederacy together," he confided to a friend. It would wed to the support of the federal government the powerful influence of the public creditors. Morris therefore welcomed the chance to enlarge the debt by issuing new securities in settlement of wartime claims. Because of the government's precarious finances, these securities brought only ten to fifteen cents on the dollar, but with a sounder treasury—certainly with a tax power

Robert Morris, the most influential figure in the Confederation government, in a portrait by Charles Willson Peale. [Independence National Historical Park Collection]

—they could be expected to rise in value, creating new capital with which to finance banks and economic development.

In 1781, as part of his overall plan, Morris secured a congressional charter for the Bank of North America, which would hold federal deposits, lend money to the government, and issue banknotes that would be a stable currency. A national bank, it was in part privately owned and was expected to turn a profit for Morris and other shareholders, in addition to performing a public service. But his program depended ultimately on a secure income for the government, and foundered on the requirement of unanimous approval for amendments to the Articles of Confederation. During the war he nearly got for Congress the power to levy a 5 percent import duty, but Rhode Island's refusal to ratify an amendment stood in the way. Once the war was over the spur of military need was gone. Local interests and the fear of a central authority—a fear strengthened by the recent quarrels with king and Parliament—hobbled action.

To carry their point, Morris and his nationalist friends in 1783 risked a dangerous gamble. Washington's army, encamped at Newburgh on the Hudson River, had grown restless in the final winter of the war. Their pay was in arrears as usual, and past experience gave them reason to fear that claims to bounties and life pensions for officers might never be honored once their services were no longer needed. In January 1783 a delegation of officers appeared in Philadelphia with a petition for redress. Soon they found themselves drawn into a scheme to line up the army and public creditors with nationalists in Congress and confront the states with the threat of a coup d'état unless they yielded more power to Congress. Horatio Gates and other high officers were drawn into the network and circulated an inflammatory address against any further "milk and water" petitions. Alexander Hamilton, congressman from New York and former aide to General Washington, sought to bring his old commander into the plan.

Washington sympathized with the purpose. If congressional powers were not enlarged, he had told a friend, "the band which at present holds us together, by a very feeble thread, will soon be broken, when anarchy and confusion must ensue." But Washington was just as deeply convinced that a military coup would be both dishonorable and dangerous. When he learned that some of the plotters had planned an unauthorized meeting of officers, he summoned a meeting first and confronted the issue. Drawing his spectacles from his pocket, he began: "I have grown not only gray but blind in the service of my country." When he had finished his dramatic and emotional address, his officers, with Gates in the chair, unanimously adopted resolutions denouncing the recent "infamous propositions" and the Newburgh Conspiracy came to a sudden end. By the middle of June all those who had enlisted for the duration were furloughed with three months' pay in the personal notes of Superintendent Morris, and Washington awaited the British evacuation of New York with a skeleton force serving time enlistments.

A body of Pennsylvania recruits provided a sorry aftermath to the quiet dispersal. Their pay in arrears, about eighty militiamen mutinied, marched from Lancaster to Philadelphia, and with reinforcements from regiments there, conducted a threatening demonstration in front of Independence Hall. When state authorities failed to provide a guard, for fear the militia would join the mutiny, the Congress after three days fled to Princeton, later adjourned to Annapolis, then Trenton, and in 1785 finally settled in New York. Moving from place to place, often unable to muster a quorum, the Congress struggled on with growing futility. An amendment to give Congress power to levy duties for twenty-five years, proposed in 1783, met the same fate as the previous amendment. In 1784 Morris resigned as superintendent of finance and a committee took charge once again.

The Confederation never did put its finances in order. The Continental currency had long since become a byword for worthlessness. It was never redeemed. The debt, domestic and foreign, grew from $11 million to $28 million as Congress paid off citizens' and soldiers' claims. Each year Congress ran a deficit on its operating expenses. Since the Confederation remained unable to pay off its securities, some of the states agreed to assume the burden of their citizens. They accepted in payment of taxes and imposts the indents (certificates) which Congress issued in lieu of interest payments—and Congress then took back the indents in payment of requisitions on the states, up to a fourth of the total amount due. Some of the states accepted federal securities in payment for state securities or for land. The foreign debt alone ran up to $11 million, but in spite of everything, Congress somehow managed to find the money to pay interest on loans from Dutch bankers and kept open a line of credit at least from that source.

LAND POLICY   The one source from which Congress might hope ultimately to draw an independent income was the sale of western lands. But throughout the Confederation period that income remained more a fleeting promise of the future than an accomplished fact. The Confederation nevertheless dealt more effectively with the western lands than with anything else. There Congress had direct authority, at least on paper. Thinly popu-

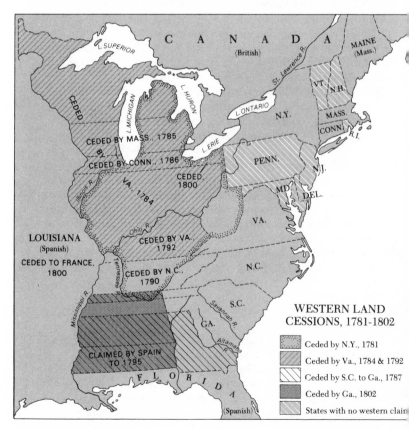

WESTERN LAND
CESSIONS, 1781-1802

Ceded by N.Y., 1781
Ceded by Va., 1784 & 1792
Ceded by S.C. to Ga., 1787
Ceded by Ga., 1802
States with no western claim

lated by Indians, Frenchmen, and a growing number of American squatters, the region north of the Ohio River had long been the site of overlapping claims by colonies and speculators. The Revolution itself had been brought on in no small part by disagreement over western lands and British feelings that the colonies should be taxed for their administration and defense. In 1784 Virginia's cession of lands north of the Ohio was complete, and by 1786 all states had abandoned their claims in the area except for a 120-mile strip along Lake Erie, which Connecticut held until 1800 as its "Western Reserve," in return for giving up its claims in the Wyoming Valley of Pennsylvania.

As early as 1779 Congress had made a basic commitment in principle not to pursue a colonial policy in the future national domain. The delegates resolved instead that western lands ceded by the states "shall be . . . formed into distinct Republican states," equal in all respects to other states. Between 1784 and 1787 policies for the development of the West emerged in three major ordinances of the Confederation Congress. These documents, which rank among its most positive achievements—and among the most important in American history—set precedents that the United States followed in its expansion all the way to the Pacific. Thomas Jefferson in fact was prepared to grant self-government from an early stage, when settlers would meet and choose their own officials. Under the ordinance of 1784, when the population equaled that of the smallest existing state the territory would achieve full statehood. Congress, however, rejected Jefferson's specific provision for ten future states with bizarre if melodious names like Assenissipia and Cherronesus, although three of the suggestions later turned up on the map with only slight alteration: Michigania, Illinoia, and Washington.

In the Land Ordinance of 1785 the delegates outlined a plan of land surveys and sales which would eventually stamp a rectangular pattern on much of the nation's surface, a pattern still visible from the air in many parts of the country because of the layout of roads and fields. Wherever Indian titles had been extinguished, the Northwest was to be surveyed into townships six miles square along east-west and north-south lines. Each township in turn was divided into 36 lots (or sections) one mile square (or 640 acres). The 640-acre sections were to go at auction for no less than $1 per acre or $640 total, and without provision for credit. Such terms favored land speculators, of course, since few dirt farmers had that much money or were able to cultivate that much land. In later years new land laws would make smaller plots available at lower prices, but in 1785 Congress was faced with an

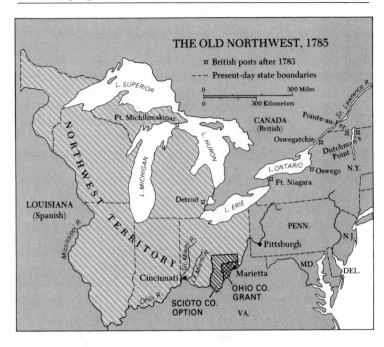

THE OLD NORTHWEST, 1785

¤ British posts after 1783
--- Present-day state boundaries

0   300 Miles
0   300 Kilometers

L. SUPERIOR

NORTHWEST TERRITORY

Ft. Michilimakinac

CANADA
(British)

Pointe-au-Fer

St. Lawrence R.

Oswegatchie

Dutchman's
Point

L. HURON

L. MICHIGAN

L. ONTARIO

Oswego   N.Y.

Ft. Niagara

Detroit

L. ERIE

LOUISIANA
(Spanish)

PENN.

Pittsburgh

N.J.

Mississippi R.

Gt. Miami R.

Lt. Miami R.

Cincinnati

Marietta

MD

DEL.

OHIO CO.
GRANT

SCIOTO CO.
OPTION

Ohio R.

VA.

empty treasury. In each township, however, Congress did reserve the income from the sixteenth section for the support of schools—a significant departure at a time when public schools were rare.

In seven ranges to the west of the Ohio River, an area in which recent treaties had voided Indian titles, surveying began. But before any land sales occurred a group of speculators from New England presented Congress a seductive offer. Organized in Boston under the leadership of Gen. Samuel Parsons the group took the name of the Ohio Company and sent the Rev. Manasseh Cutler to present their plan. He proved a persuasive lobbyist, and in 1787 Congress voted a grant of 1.5 million acres for about $1 million in certificates of indebtedness to Revolutionary War veterans. The arrangement had the dual merit, Cutler argued, of reducing the debt and encouraging new settlement and sales. Further, to ensure passage the lobbyist cut in several congressmen on another deal, the Scioto Company, which got an option on 5 million acres more. In April 1788 the Ohio Company's first settlers floated downstream from Pittsburgh on a flatboat aptly named the *May-flower* and established Marietta. The Scioto Company never took up its option, but that did not prevent its

European agent, the poet Joel Barlow, from selling lands it did not own—with the help of an Englishman named, of all things, Playfair! In 1790 several hundred French settlers arrived only to find that they had no title to the lands they had supposedly bought. A sympathetic Congress relieved their distress by voting them a grant of land. In 1788 a New Jersey speculator named John Cleves Symmes got an option on lands between the Great and the Little Miami Rivers and soon had Cincinnati and several other villages under way.

A TOWNSHIP IN THE OLD NORTHWEST

6	5	4	3	2	1
7	8	9	Income reserved for school support		
18	17	16	15	14	13
19	20	21	22	23	24
30	29	28	27	26	25
31	32	33	34	35	36

Numbering system adopted in 1796

A township is 36 square miles

A section is 1 square mile (640 acres)

THE NORTHWEST ORDINANCE   Spurred by the plans for land sales and settlement, Congress drafted a new and more specific frame of territorial government to replace Jefferson's ordinance of 1784. The new plan backed off from Jefferson's recommendation of early self-government. Because of the trouble that might be expected from squatters who were clamoring for free land, the Northwest Ordinance of 1787 required a period of colonial tutelage. At first the territory fell subject to a governor, a secretary, and three judges, all chosen by Congress. Eventually there would be three to five territories in the region, and when any one had 5,000 free male adults it could choose an assembly and Congress would name a council of five from ten names proposed by the assembly. The governor, named by the central authority, would have a veto and so would Congress. The resemblance to the old royal colonies is clear, but there were two significant differences. For one, the Ordinance anticipated statehood when any territory's population reached 60,000. For another, it included a bill of rights which guaranteed religious freedom, representation in proportion to population, trial by jury, habeus corpus, and the application of common law. And finally, the Ordinance excluded slavery permanently from the Northwest—a proviso Jefferson had failed to get accepted in his Ordinance of 1784. This proved a fateful decision. As the progress of emancipation in the existing states gradually freed all slaves above the Mason-Dixon line, the Ohio River boundary of the Old Northwest extended the line between freedom and slavery all the way to the Mississippi.

In the lands south of the Ohio River a different line of development occurred. Title to the western lands remained with Georgia, North Carolina, and Virginia for the time being, but settlement proceeded at a far more rapid pace during and after the Revolution, despite the Indians' fierce resentment of encroachments on their hunting grounds. Substantial centers of population grew up around Harrodsburg and Boonesboro in the Kentucky Blue Grass and along the Watauga, Holston, and Cumberland Rivers, as far west as Nashborough (Nashville). In the Southwest active movements for statehood arose early. North Carolina tentatively ceded its western claims in 1784, whereupon the Holston settlers formed the short-lived state of Franklin, which became little more than a bone of contention between rival speculators until North Carolina reasserted control in 1789, shortly before the cession of its western lands became final.

Indian claims too were being extinguished. The Iroquois and Cherokees, badly battered during the Revolution, were in no position to resist encroachments. By the Treaty of Fort Stanwix (1784) the Iroquois were forced to cede land in western New York and Pennsylvania. In the Treaty of Hopewell (1785) the Cherokees gave up all claims in South Carolina, much of western North Carolina, and large portions of present-day Kentucky and Tennessee. Also in 1785 the major Ohio tribes gave up their claim to most of Ohio, except for a chunk bordering the western part of Lake Erie. The Creeks, pressed by the state of Georgia to cede portions of their lands in 1784–1785, went to war in the summer of 1786 with covert aid from Spanish Florida. But when Spanish aid diminished, the Creek chief Alexander McGillivray traveled to New York and in 1791 finally struck a bargain which gave the Creeks favorable trade arrangements with the United States, but did not restore the lost lands.

TRADE AND THE ECONOMY   In its economic life, as in planning westward expansion, the young nation dealt with difficult problems vigorously. Congress had little to do with achievements in the economy but neither could it bear the blame for a depression that wracked the country for several years during the transition to independence, the result of the war and separation from the British Empire. In New England and much of the backcountry fighting seldom interrupted the tempo of farming, and the producers of foodstuffs especially benefited from rising prices and wartime demands. The southern Tidewater suffered a loss of slave labor, much of it carried off by the British. Returns from indigo and naval stores declined with the loss of British bounties, but in the long run rice and tobacco benefited from an enlarged foreign market for their products.

Merchants suffered far more wrenching adjustments than the farmers. Cut out of the British mercantile system, they had to find new outlets for their trade. Circumstances that impoverished some enriched those who financed privateers, supplied the armies on both sides, and hoarded precious goods while demand and prices soared. By the end of the war a strong sentiment for free trade had developed in both Britain and America. In the memorable year 1776 the Scottish economist Adam Smith brought out *The Wealth of Nations*, a classic manifesto against mercantilism. Some British statesmen embraced the new gospel, but the public and Parliament still clung to the conventional wisdom of mercantilism for many years to come.

British trade with America did resume, and American ships were allowed to deliver American products and return to the United States with British goods. American ships could not carry British goods anywhere else, however. The pent-up demand for familiar goods created a bull market in exports to America, fueled by British credits and the hard money that had come into America from foreign aid, the expenditures of foreign armies, or wartime trade and privateering. The result was a quick cycle of boom and bust, a buying spree followed by a currency shortage and economic troubles that lasted several years.

In colonial days the chronic deficit in trade with Britain could be offset by the influx of coins from trade with the West Indies. Now American ships found themselves excluded altogether from the British West Indies, and therefore from the old triangular trades. But the islands still demanded wheat, fish, lumber, and other products from the mainland, and American shippers had not lost their talent for smuggling, at which the islanders connived. Already American shippers had begun exploring new outlets, and by 1787 their seaports were flourishing more than ever. Freed from the old colonial restraints, they now had the run of the seven seas. Trade treaties opened new markets with the Dutch (1782), Swedes (1783), Prussians (1785), and Moroccans (1787), and American shippers found new outlets on their own in Europe, Africa, and Asia. The most spectacular new development, if not the largest, was trade with China. It began in 1784–1785, when the *Empress of China* sailed from New York to Canton and back, around the tip of South America. Profits from its cargo of silks and tea encouraged the outfitting of other ships which carried ginseng root and other American goods to exchange for the luxury goods of the Orient.

The dislocations in trade and the need for readjustment, one historian noted, "produced bitter complaints in the newspapers and led to extravagant charges against both state and central governments, but in no case do the records of imports and exports and ship tonnages bear out the cries of havoc." By 1790 American commerce and exports had far out run the trade of the colonies. American merchants had more ships than before the war. Agricultural exports were twice what they had been. Although most of the exports were the products of American forests, fields, and fisheries, during and after the war more Americans had turned to small-scale manufacturing, mainly for domestic markets. By 1787, when Tench Coxe of Philadelphia, a promoter of manufactures, set out to summarize major American enterprises, he ended with dozens of products from ships and ironwork to shoes, textiles, and soap.

DIPLOMACY The achievements of the flourishing young nation are more visible in hindsight than they were at the time. Until 1787 the shortcomings and failures remained far more apparent —and the advocates of a stronger central government were extremely vocal on the subject. In diplomacy, despite the achievement of trade treaties by 1787 with France, Holland, Sweden, Prussia, and Morocco, there remained the nagging problems of relations with Great Britain and Spain, both of which still kept posts on United States soil and intrigued with Indians and white settlers in the West. The British, despite the peace treaty of 1783, held on to a string of forts from Lake Champlain to Michilimackinac. From these they kept a hand in the fur trade and a degree of influence with the Indian tribes whom they were suspected of stirring up to make sporadic attacks on the frontier. They gave as a reason for their continued occupation the failure of Americans to pay their debts, conveniently ignoring the point that the peace treaty had included only a face-saving gesture which committed Congress to recommend that the states place no legal impediment in the way of their collection. Impediments continued, nonetheless. A common question in Virginia, George Mason said, was: "If we are now to pay the debts due to British merchants, what have we been fighting for all this while?"

Another major irritant was the confiscation of Loyalist property. Under the peace treaty Congress was obligated to stop persecutions, to guarantee immunity for twelve months during which Loyalists could return and wind up their affairs, and to recommend that the states return confiscated property. Persecutions, even lynchings, of Loyalists still occurred until after the end of the war. Some Loyalists returned unmolested, however, and once again took up their lives in their former homes. By the end of 1787, moreover, all the states at the request of Congress had rescinded the laws that were in conflict with the peace treaty.

The British refused even to dispatch an ambassador to the new nation before 1791. As early as 1785, however, the United States took the initiative by sending over that confirmed rebel, John Adams, as ambassador to the Court of St. James's. He was politely received by George III himself, but spent three years in futile efforts to settle the points at issue: mainly the forts, debts, and the property rights of Loyalists. Unknown to Adams the British even toyed with the idea of annexing Vermont through intrigues with the Allen brothers, Ethan and Levi. The area, claimed by New Hampshire, had been awarded by the Privy Council to New York, but the influential Allen brothers, with large land claims at stake, ignored the ruling, then took the lead in organizing the state of Vermont in 1777. When Congress refused to recognize Vermont for fear of offending New York, the Allens began dickering with the British. Eventually, however, nothing came of it all. New York gave up its claim in 1790 and Vermont became the fourteenth state in 1791.

With Spain the chief points at issue were the southern boundary and the right to navigate the Mississippi. According to the preliminary treaty with Britain the United States claimed a line as far south as the Thirty-first Parallel; Spain held out for the line running eastward from the mouth of the Yazoo River (at 32° 22′ N), which she claimed as the traditional boundary—and which would have been the boundary if Britain had retained Florida. Spanish forces, which had taken Natchez from the British during the war, continued to occupy that town in territory claimed by the United States. The American treaty with Britain had also specified the right to navigate the Mississippi River to its mouth, but the international boundary ran down the middle of the river most of its length and the river was entirely within Spanish Louisiana in its lower reaches. The right to navigation was a matter of importance because of the growing settlements in Kentucky and Tennessee, but in 1784 Louisiana's Governor Miro closed the river to American commerce and began to intrigue with the Creeks, Choctaws, Chickasaws, and other Indians of the Southwest against the frontiersmen, and with the frontiersmen against the United States. Gen. James Wilkinson, a Kentucky land speculator, further enriched himself with Spanish gold in return for promises to conspire for secession of the West and perhaps its annexation by Spain. But Wilkinson was a professional slyboots, with an instinct for trouble, whose loyalties ran mainly to his own pocketbook. And he was not the only man on the make who was double-dealing with the Spaniards.

In 1785 the Spanish government sent as its ambassador to the United States Don Diego de Gardoqui, whose father's trading company had been the front for Spanish aid during the Revolution. Gardoqui entered into lengthy but fruitless negotiations with John Jay, the secretary for foreign affairs, whom he had first met in Madrid during the war. Jay had instructions to get free navigation of the Mississippi and the Spanish acceptance of the 31° boundary; Gardoqui had instructions not to give them. But he did ply Jay and his wife with gifts and flattery. Finally, in hope of getting trade concessions from Spain, Jay sought permission from Congress to give up navigation of the Mississippi—an idea planted by Gardoqui in the knowledge that it would be divisive. It was granted, but only by a vote of seven to five, with the southern states holding out against such a sacrifice in the interest of northern merchants. Since the ratification of a treaty required the vote of nine states, the negotiations collapsed and the issues remained unsettled for nearly another decade.

THE CONFEDERATION'S PROBLEMS The problems of trans-Appalachian settlers, however, seemed remote from the everyday concerns of most Americans. What touched them more closely were the economic dislocations and the currency shortage. Merchants who found themselves excluded from old channels of imperial trade began to agitate for reprisals. State governments, in response, laid special tonnage duties on British vessels and special tariffs on the goods they brought. But state action alone failed to work for want of uniformity. British ships could be diverted to states whose duties were less restrictive. Efforts to meet this problem by taxing British goods that flowed across state lines created an impression that states were involved in commercial

A North Carolina hundred-dollar bill (1778). Rampant inflation during the Revolution reduced the value of paper money, creating economic problems the Confederation could not solve. [American Antiquarian Society]

war with each other, although the duties seldom affected American goods. The need, it seemed to commercial interests, was for a central power to regulate trade. In 1784 Congress proposed to amend the Articles of Confederation so as to permit uniform navigation acts, but Rhode Island and North Carolina objected. The amendment, like all others, failed of ratification—not for want of support but for want of unanimity.

Mechanics and artisans who were developing an infant industry with products ranging from crude iron nails to the fine silver bowls of Paul Revere wanted to go further, to take reprisals against British goods as well as British ships. They sought, and in various degrees obtained from the states, tariffs against foreign goods that competed with theirs. The country would be on its way to economic independence, they argued, if only the specie that flowed into the country had been invested in domestic manufactures instead of being paid out for foreign goods. Nearly all the states gave some preference to American goods, but again the lack of uniformity in their laws put them at cross purposes, and so urban mechanics along with merchants were drawn into the movement for a stronger central government in the interest of uniform regulation.

The shortage of cash gave rise also to some more immediate demands for paper currency as legal tender, for postponement of tax and debt payments, for laws to "stay" the foreclosure of mortgages. Farmers, who had profited during the war, found themselves squeezed by depression and mounting debts while merchants sorted out and opened up their new trade routes. Creditors demanded hard money, but specie was in short supply—and paper money was almost nonexistent after the depreciation of the Continental currency. The result was an outcry for relief, and around 1785 the demand for paper money became the most divisive issue in state politics. Debtors demanded it, and in some cases, most notably South Carolina, merchants supported it because in that state they could use the paper but did not have to take it in payment of old debts. In Pennsylvania public creditors demanded paper as a device to collect their claims against the state. Paper, they reasoned, was better than nothing. Creditors elsewhere generally opposed such action, however, because it was likely to mean payment in a depreciated currency.

In 1785–1786, seven states provided for issues of paper money. In spite of the cries of calamity at the time the money never seriously depreciated in Pennsylvania, New York, and South Carolina. It served in five states—Pennsylvania, New York, New Jersey, South Carolina, and Rhode Island—as a means of credit to hard-pressed farmers through state loans on farm mortgages. It was variously used to fund state debts and to pay off the claims of veterans. North Carolina used some of it to buy tobacco for sale abroad to raise specie, but in that case swindlers bilked the state with overpriced leaf and collected veterans' claims with forged certificates.

Sharp depreciation finally discredited the issue in the Tar Heel state, which was second in notoriety only to Rhode Island, where the debtor party ran wild. In 1786 the Rhode Island legislature issued £100,000 in paper, the largest issue of any state in proportion to population, and declared it legal tender in payment of all debts. Creditors fled the state to avoid being paid in worthless paper, merchants closed their doors while mobs rioted against them, and a "forcing act" denied trial by jury and levied fines against anyone who refused to take the money at face value. Eventually a test case reached the state's supreme court, and in *Trevett v. Weeden* (1787) the court ruled the law unconstitutional. The case stands as a landmark, the first in which a court exercised the doctrine of judicial review in holding a state law unconstitutional. The forcing act was then repealed and the legal tender clause finally repealed in 1789.

SHAYS'S REBELLION   Newspapers throughout the country ran accounts of developments in Rhode Island, and that little common-

Daniel Shays and Job Shattuck, leaders of the revolt of western Massachusetts farmers against tax and debt policy (1787). [National Portrait Gallery, Smithsonian Institution]

wealth, stubbornly cross-grained since the days of Roger Williams, became the prime example of democracy run riot—until its hotspur neighbor, Massachusetts, provided the final proof (some said) that the country was poised on the brink of anarchy: Shays's Rebellion. There the trouble was not too much paper money but too little, and too much taxation. After 1780 Massachusetts had remained in the grip of a rigidly conservative regime. Ever-larger poll and land taxes were levied to pay off a heavy debt, held mainly by wealthy creditors in Boston, and the taxes fell most heavily upon beleaguered farmers and the poor in general. When the legislature adjourned in 1786 without providing either paper money or any other relief from taxes and debts, three western counties erupted into spontaneous revolt. Armed bands closed the courts and prevented foreclosures, and a tatterdemalion "army" under Daniel Shays, a destitute farmer and war veteran, advanced upon the federal arsenal at Springfield in January 1787.

A small militia force, however, scattered the approaching army with a single volley of artillery which left four dead. Gen. Benjamin Lincoln, arriving soon after with reinforcements from Boston, routed the remaining Shaysites at Petersham. The Shaysites nevertheless had a victory of sorts. The state legislature omitted direct taxes the following year, lowered court fees, and exempted clothing, household goods, and tools from the debt process. But a more important consequence was the impetus the rebellion gave to conservatism and nationalism.

Rumors, at times deliberately inflated, blew up out of all proportion a pathetic rebellion of desperate men. The rebels were linked to the conniving British and accused of seeking to pillage the wealthy. What was more, the rebellion set an ominous example. "There are combustibles in every State," Washington wrote, "which a spark might set fire to." Of the disorders he asked: "Good God! Who, besides a Tory, could have foreseen, or a Briton predicted them?" The answer, of course, was nearly every political philosopher of the Whig or Enlightened persuasion who was dear to the men of the Revolution. Anarchy, they taught, was the nemesis of republics, mob rule the sequel to unchecked democracy. Shays therefore was the harbinger of greater evils to come unless the course of events were altered. Not that all the leaders of the time agreed. Jefferson was, if anything, too complacent. From his post in Paris, where one of history's great bloodbaths would soon take place, he wrote to a friend back home: "The tree of liberty must be refreshed from time to time with the blood of patriots and tyrants."

CALLS FOR A STRONGER GOVERNMENT   The advocates of a stronger central authority already had gained momentum from the adversities of the times. Public creditors, merchants, and mechanics had a self-interest in a stronger central government, and many public-spirited men saw it as the only alternative to anarchy. Gradually they were breaking down the ingrained fear of a tyrannical central authority with the evidence that tyranny might come from other quarters. And one thing readers of another century must remember, conditioned as we are to see potential conflict between human rights and property rights, is that the American of the eighteenth century considered the security of property to be the foundation stone of liberty. What the eighteenth-century American might forget, however, was that the Shaysites were fighting in defense of their property too.

Already, well before the outbreaks in New England, the nationalist movement had come to demand a convention to revise the Articles of Confederation. Such a convention had been the subject of fruitless discussions in Congress, initiated by Charles Pinckney of South Carolina, but the initiative finally came from an unexpected quarter. In March 1785 commissioners from the states of Virginia and Maryland had met at Mount Vernon upon Washington's invitation to settle outstanding questions about the navigation of the Potomac and Chesapeake Bay. Washington had a personal interest in the river flowing by his door: it was a potential route to the West, with its upper reaches close to the upper reaches of the Ohio, where his military career had begun thirty years before. The delegates agreed on interstate cooperation, and Maryland suggested a further pact with Pennsylvania and Delaware to encourage water communication between the Chesapeake and the Ohio River; the Virginia legislature agreed, and at Madison's suggestion invited all thirteen states to send delegates for a general discussion of commercial problems. Nine states named representatives, but those from only five appeared at the Annapolis Convention in September 1786—Maryland itself failed to name delegates and neither the New England states nor the Carolinas and Georgia were represented. Apparent failure was turned into success, however, by the alert Alexander Hamilton, representing New York, who presented a resolution for still another convention in Philadelphia to consider all measures necessary "to render the constitution of the Federal Government adequate to the exigencies of the Union."

ADOPTING THE CONSTITUTION

THE CONSTITUTIONAL CONVENTION After stalling for several months Congress fell in line on February 21, 1787, with a resolution endorsing as "expedient" a convention "for the sole and express purpose of revising the Articles of Confederation." By then five states had already named delegates; before the meeting six more states had acted. New Hampshire delayed until June and its delegates arrived in July. Independent-minded Rhode Island kept aloof throughout. On the appointed date (May 14, 1787) only the delegates from Pennsylvania and Virginia were present, but twenty-nine delegates from nine states began work on May 25. Altogether seventy-three men were elected by the state legislatures, fifty-five attended at one time or another, and after four months thirty-nine signed the Constitution they had drafted.

The durability and flexibility of that document testify to the remarkable quality of the men who made it, an assembly of "demi-gods" according to Jefferson, who was himself absent as a diplomat in France. They were surprisingly young: forty-two was the average age, although they ranged from the twenty-seven-year-old Jonathan Dayton of New Jersey to the eighty-one-year-old Benjamin Franklin, president of the state of Pennsylvania. They were even more surprisingly mature and foresighted: many of them were widely read in history, law, and political philosophy, familiar with the writings of Vattel, Locke, and Montesquieu, aware of the confederacies of the ancient world, and at the same time practical men of experience, tested in the fires of the Revolution. "Experience must be our only guide," John Dickinson said. "Reason may mislead us." Washington and

Franklin were the most famous of them at the time, and both, especially Washington, lent prestige and inspired confidence. More active in the debates were James Madison, the ablest political philosopher in the group; George Mason, author of the Virginia Bill of Rights; the witty and eloquent Gouverneur Morris and James Wilson of Pennsylvania, the latter one of the ablest lawyers in the colonies and next in importance in the convention only to Washington and Madison; Roger Sherman of Connecticut; and Elbridge Gerry of Massachusetts. Conspicuous by their absence were John Adams and Thomas Jefferson, then serving in London and Paris, and during most of the convention, Alexander Hamilton, since he could not vote once his two states'-rights colleagues from New York had gone home for good.

The delegates' differences on political philosophy for the most part fell within a narrow range. On certain fundamentals they generally agreed: that government derived its just powers from the consent of the people, but that society must be protected from the tyranny of the majority; that the people at large must have a voice in their government, but that checks and balances must be provided to keep any one group from arrogating power; that a stronger central authority was essential, but that all political power was easily subject to abuse. They believed that even the best of men were selfish by nature, and they harbored few illusions that government could be founded altogether upon a trust in goodwill and virtue. Since governments existed to restrain men, James Madison said, their very existence was "a reflection upon human nature." Yet by a careful arrangement of checks and balances, by checking power with power, the Founding Fathers hoped to devise institutions that could somehow constrain the sinfulness of individuals.

THE VIRGINIA AND NEW JERSEY PLANS   At the outset the delegates made Washington their president by unanimous vote, and William Jackson their secretary. One of the first decisions was to meet behind closed doors, in order to discourage outside pressures and speeches to the galleries. The secrecy of the proceedings was remarkably well kept, and since Jackson's journal was a skeleton record of motions and votes, knowledge of the debates comes mainly from extensive notes kept by James Madison. It was Madison, too, who drafted the proposals which set the framework of the discussions. These proposals, which came to be called the "Virginia Plan," were presented on May 29 by Edmund Randolph, governor of the state and delegate to the convention. The Virginia plan embodied a revolutionary proposal for the delegates to scrap their instructions to revise the Articles of Confederation and to submit an entirely new document to the states. The plan proposed separate legislative, executive, and judicial branches, and a truly national government to make laws binding upon individual citizens and to coerce states as well. Congress would be divided into two houses, a lower house chosen by popular vote and an upper house chosen by the lower house from nominees of the state legislatures. Congress could disallow state laws under the plan and would itself define the extent of its and the states' authority.

On June 15 William Paterson submitted the alternative New Jersey or small-state plan, which proposed to keep the existing structure of Congress, but to give it power to levy taxes and regulate commerce and authority to name a plural executive (with no veto) and a Supreme Court. The different plans presented the convention with two major issues: whether to amend the Articles or draft a new document, and whether to have congressional representation by states or by population. On the first point the Convention voted, June 19, to work toward a national government as envisioned by the Virginians. On the powers of this government there was little disagreement save in detail. Experience with the Articles had persuaded the delegates that an effective government, as distinguished from a confederation, needed the power to levy taxes, to regulate commerce, to raise an army and navy, and to make laws binding upon individual citizens. The lessons of the 1780s suggested to them, moreover, that in the interest of order and uniformity the states must be denied certain powers: to issue money, to abrogate contracts, to make treaties or wage war, to levy tariffs or export duties.

Disagreement then turned less on philosophy than on geography. The first clash in the convention involved the issue of representation. Delegates from the larger states generally favored the Virginia plan, which would give them greater representation; those from the smaller states rallied behind the New Jersey plan, which would preserve an equal vote to each state. In hindsight the issue was a false one, since differing interests have seldom ranged the states into blocs according to size, but at the time it was the most divisive single question to rise in the convention and one that might have wrecked the whole enterprise had it not been resolved. The solution was the "Great Compromise," sometimes called the "Connecticut Compromise," proposed by Roger Sherman, which gave both groups their way. The larger states won apportionment by population in the House of Representatives; the smaller states got equality in the Senate, but with the vote there by individuals and not by states.

Geographic division cut another way in a struggle between northern and southern delegates which turned upon slavery and the regulation of trade, an omen of sectional controversies to come in future years. Southerners, with slaves so numerous in their states, wanted them counted as part of the population in determining the number of their representatives. Northerners were happy enough to have slaves counted in deciding each state's share of direct taxes but not for purposes of representation. On this issue the Confederation Congress had supplied a handy precedent when it sought an amendment to make population rather than land values the standard for requisitions. The proposed amendment to the Articles would have counted three-fifths of the slaves. The delegates, with little dissent, agreed to incorporate the same three-fifths ratio in the new Constitution as a basis for apportioning both representatives and direct taxes. A more sensitive issue was presented by an effort to prevent the central government from stopping the foreign slave trade. Again, since slavery had not yet become the overriding issue it later became, the question was fairly readily settled by establishing a time limit. "The morality or wisdom of slavery," said Oliver Ellsworth of Connecticut, "are considerations belonging to the states themselves." Congress could not forbid the foreign slave trade before 1808, but could levy a tax of $10 a head on all slaves imported. In both provisions, a sense of delicacy dictated the use of euphemisms. The Constitution spoke of "free Persons" and "all other persons," of "such persons as any of the States Now existing shall think proper to admit," and of persons "held to Service of Labor." The odious word "slavery" did not appear in the Constitution until the Thirteenth Amendment (1865) abolished the "peculiar institution" by name.

The final decision on the slave trade was linked to a compromise on the question of the broader congressional power to regulate commerce. Northern states, where the merchant and shipping interests were most influential, were prepared to give Congress unlimited powers, but the southerners feared that navigation acts favoring American shipping might work at the expense of getting southern commodities to the market by reducing foreign competition with northern shippers. Southerners therefore demanded that navigation acts be passed only by a two-thirds vote, but finally traded this demand for a prohibition on congressional power to levy export taxes and for a twenty-year, instead of a ten-year, delay on power to prohibit the slave trade.

THE SEPARATION OF POWERS   Their essential agreement on the need for a new frame of government kept the delegates from lapsing into quarelling factions: they were determined to seek accomodation. The details of governmental structure, while causing disagreement, occasioned far less trouble than the basic issues pitting the large and small states, the northern and southern states. Existing state constitutions, and the convention's resolve to disperse power with checks and balances, encouraged a consensus on the separation of powers among legislative, executive, and judicial branches. The American version of checks and

Signing the Constitution, September 17, 1787. *Thomas Pritchard Rossiter's painting shows George Washington presiding over what Thomas Jefferson called "an assembly of demi-gods." [Independence National Historical Park Collection]*

balances did not correspond to the old Whig model which separated powers among British commons, lords, and king, since Americans had neither lords nor a king—and the new document would specifically forbid titles of nobility—but there were parallels. The Founding Fathers expected the lower house to be closest to the people from whom they rose by election every two years. The upper house, chosen by state legislatures, was at one remove from the voters. Staggered terms of six years further isolated senators from the passing fancies of public passion by preventing the choice of a majority in any given year. Senators were expected to be, if not an American House of Lords, at least something like the colonial councils, a body of dignitaries advising the president as the councils had advised the governors.

And the president was to be an almost kingly figure. He was subject to election every four years, but his executive powers corresponded to those which British theory still extended to the king; in practice his powers actually exceeded the monarch's powers. This was the sharpest departure from the recent experience in state government, where the office of governor had commonly been downgraded because of the recent memory of struggles with the colonial executives. The president had a veto over acts of Congress, subject to being overridden by a two-thirds vote in each house, although the royal veto had long since fallen into complete disuse. He was commander-in-chief of the armed forces, and responsible for the execution of the laws. He could make treaties with the advice and consent of two-thirds of the Senate. He had power to appoint diplomats, judges, and other officers with the consent of a Senate majority. He was instructed to report annually on the state of the nation and was authorized to recommend legislation, a provision which presidents eventually would take as a mandate to form and promote extensive programs. Unlike the king, however, he could be removed for cause, by action short of revolution. The House could impeach (indict) him—and other civil officers—on charges of treason, bribery, or "other high crimes and misdemeanors," and the Senate could remove him by a two-thirds vote upon conviction. The presiding officer at the trial of a president would be the chief justice, since the usual presiding officer of the Senate (the vice-president) would have a personal stake in the outcome.

The convention's nationalists—men like Madison, James Wilson, and Hamilton—wanted to strengthen the independence of the executive by entrusting the choice to popular election. At least in this instance the nationalists, often accused of being the aristocratic party, favored a bold new departure in democracy.

But an elected executive was still too far beyond the American experience. Besides, a national election would have created enormous problems of organization and voter qualification. Wilson suggested instead that the people of each state choose presidential electors equal to the number of their senators and representatives. Others proposed that the legislators make the choice. Finally, late in the convention, it was voted to let the legislature decide the method in each state. Before long nearly all the states were choosing the electors by popular vote, and the electors were acting as agents of party will, casting their votes as they had pledged before the election. This method was contrary to the original expectation that the electors would deliberate and make their own choices.

On the third branch of government, the judiciary, there was surprisingly little debate. Both the Virginia and New Jersey plans had called for a Supreme Court, which the Constitution established, providing specifically for a chief justice of the United States and leaving up to Congress the number of other justices. The only dispute was on courts "inferior" to the Supreme Court, and that too was left up to Congress. Although the Constitution nowhere authorized the courts to declare laws void when they conflicted with the Constitution, the power of judicial review was almost surely intended by the framers, and was soon exercised in cases involving both state and federal laws. Article VI declared the federal constitution, federal laws, and treaties to be the "supreme law of the land," state laws or constitutions to the contrary notwithstanding. At the time the advocates of states' rights thought this a victory, since it eliminated the proviso in the Virginia plan for Congress to settle all conflicts with state authority. As it turned out the clause became the basis for an important expansion of judicial review.

While the Constitution extended vast new powers to the national government, the delegates' mistrust of unchecked power is apparent in repeated examples of countervailing forces: the separation of the three branches of government, the president's veto, the congressional power of impeachment and removal, the Senate's power over treaties and appointments, the courts' implied right of judicial review. In addition the new frame of government reserved to the states large areas of undivided sovereignty—a reservation soon made explicit by amendment —and specifically forbade Congress to pass bills of attainder (legislative acts depriving persons of property) or ex post facto laws (laws adopted after the event to make past deeds criminal).

The most glaring defect of the Articles of Confederation, the rule of unanimity which defeated every effort to amend them, led the delegates to provide a less forbidding though still difficult method of amending the new Constitution. Amendments could be proposed either by two-thirds vote of each house or by a convention especially called upon application of two-thirds of the legislatures. Amendments could be ratified by approval of three-fourths of the states acting through their legislatures or special conventions. The national convention has never been used, however, and state conventions have been called only once—to ratify the repeal of the Eighteenth Amendment (the Prohibition amendment).

THE FIGHT FOR RATIFICATION The old rule of unanimity, if applied to ratification of the Constitution itself, would almost surely have doomed its chances at the outset. The final article of the original Constitution therefore provided that it would become effective upon ratification by nine states (not quite the three-fourths majority required for amendment). Conventions were specified as the proper agency for ratification, since legislatures might be expected to boggle at giving up any of their powers. The procedure, insofar as it bypassed the existing Articles of Confederation, constituted a legal revolution, but it was one in which the Confederation Congress joined. After fighting off efforts to censure the convention for exceeding its authority, the Congress submitted its work to the states on September 28, 1787.

The first nationwide political struggle of United States history, or rather thirteen separate struggles over the same issue, began in the fall of 1787. Advocates of the new Constitution, who might properly have been called Nationalists, assumed the more reassuring name of Federalists. Opponents, who really favored more of a federal system, became Antifederalists. The initiative which the Federalists took in assuming their name was characteristic of the whole campaign. They got the jump on their critics. Their leaders, who had been members of the convention, were already familiar with the document and the arguments on each point. They were not only better prepared but better organized, and on the whole, made up of the more articulate elements in the community.

Much ink has been spilled by historians in debating the motivation of the advocates of the new Constitution. For more than a century the tendency prevailed to idolize the Founding Fathers who created what the nineteenth-century British statesman William Gladstone called "the most wonderful work ever struck off at a given time by the brain and purpose of man." In 1913, however, Charles A. Beard's book *An Economic Interpretation of the Constitution* advanced the amazing thesis that the Philadelphia "assembly of demi-gods" was made up of humans who had a selfish interest in the outcome. They held large amounts of depreciated government securities and otherwise stood to gain from the power and stability of the new order.

Beard argued that the delegates represented an economic elite of those who held mainly "personalty" against those who held mainly "realty." The first group was an upper crust of lawyers, merchants, speculators in western lands, holders of depreciated government securities, and creditors generally whose wealth was mostly in "paper": mortgages, stocks, bonds, and the like. The second group consisted of small farmers and planters whose wealth was mostly in land and slaves. The holders of western lands and government bonds stood to gain from a stronger government. Creditors generally stood to gain from the prohibitions against state currency issues and against the impairment of contract, provisions clearly aimed at the paper money issues and stay laws (granting stays, or postponements, on debt payments) then effective in many states.

Beard's thesis was a useful antidote to hero worship, and still contains a germ of truth, but he rested his argument too heavily on the claim that holders of personalty predominated in the convention. Most of the delegates, according to evidence unavailable to Beard, had no compelling stake in paper wealth, and most were far more involved in landholding. After doing exhaustive research into the actual holdings of the Founding Fathers, the historian Forrest McDonald announced in his book *We the People: The Economic Origins of the Constitution* that Beard's "economic interpretation of the Constitution does not work." Many prominent nationalists, including the "Father of the Constitution," James Madison himself, had no bonds, western lands, or much other personalty. Some opponents of the Constitution, on the other hand, held large blocks of personalty. McDonald did not deny that economic interests figured in the process, but they functioned in a complex interplay of state, sectional, group, and individual interests which turned largely on how well people had fared under the Confederation.

There is evidence, however, in the voting and in the makeup of the ratifying conventions of divisions between "localist" and "cosmopolitan" elements, as the historian Jackson T. Main labeled them, who held to opposing worldviews because of their contrasting experiences. The localist tended to be a person "of narrow horizons—most often rural and sparsely educated—whose experience is limited to his own neighborhood," whereas the cosmopolitan was a person "of broad outlook, usually urban, urbane, and well-educated, who has traveled widely and has had extensive contacts with the world because of his occupation, the offices he has held, or his interests."

A large proportion of the localists were, to be sure, small farmers, but their leaders were often men of substance who were temperamentally or ideologically opposed to centralization. Two decades before Beard's interpretation appeared, the historian O. G. Libby had mapped out the vote on ratification state by state and had observed that a line drawn fifty miles inland from Maine to Georgia would separate "pretty accurately" the Federalist tidewater from the Antifederalist interior. In general the idea works. Small farmers and frontiersmen saw little to gain from the promotion of interstate commerce and much to lose from prohibitions on paper money and stay laws, and many of

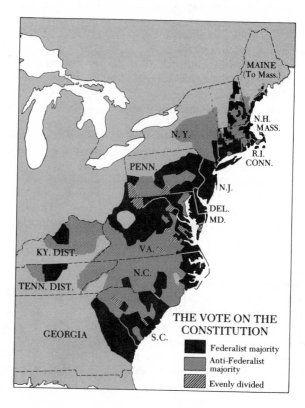

THE VOTE ON THE
CONSTITUTION

■ Federalist majority

▨ Anti-Federalist
majority

▨ Evenly divided

them feared that an expansive land policy was likely to favor speculators.

There were, however, some notable exceptions. Some farmers in New Hampshire and western Massachusetts, for instance, felt they had an interest in promoting interstate commerce up and down the Connecticut River. In Virginia the Shenandoah Valley, running northeastward, encouraged strong ties with Maryland and Pennsylvania. Some parts of the frontier looked to a stronger government for defense against Indians: in the state of Georgia, for instance, fear of the Creek Indians motivated unanimous ratification by a state convention eager to promote a stronger central government—which, as it turned out, soon reached an understanding with the Creeks.

Charles A. Beard hardly made a new discovery in finding that people are selfish, but it would be simplistic to attribute all human action to hidden economic interest. One must give some credence to the possibility that people mean what they say and are often candid about their motives, especially in large matters of public affairs. The most notable circumstance of the times in fact was that, unlike so many revolutions, the American Revolution led not to general chaos and terror but, in the words of the social critic Hannah Arendt, to "a spontaneous outbreak of constitution-making." From the 1760s through the 1780s there occurred a prolonged debate over the fundamental issues of government which in its scope and depth—and in the durability of its outcome—is without parallel.

THE FEDERALIST   Among the supreme legacies of that debate was *The Federalist*, a collection of essays originally published in the New York press between October 1787 and July 1788. Instigated by Alexander Hamilton, the eighty-five articles published under the name "Publius" included about thirty by James Madison and five by John Jay. The authorship of some remain in doubt. Written in support of ratification, the essays defended the principle of a supreme national authority, but at the same time sought to reassure doubters that the people and the states had little reason to fear usurpations and tyranny by the new government. In perhaps the most famous single essay, No. Ten, Madison argued that the very size and diversity of the country would make it impossible for any single faction to form a majority which could dominate the government. Republics, the conventional wisdom of the times insisted, could work only in small, homogeneous countries like Switzerland and the Netherlands. In larger countries they would descend into anarchy and tyranny through the influence of factions. Quite the contrary, Madison insisted. Given a balanced federal polity they could work in large and diverse countries probably better. "Extend the sphere," he wrote, "and you take in a greater variety of parties and interests; you make it less probable that a majority of the whole will have a common motive to invade the rights of other citizens. . . ."

The Federalists did try to cultivate a belief that the new union would contribute to prosperity, in part to link their movement with the economic recovery already under way. The Antifederalists, however, talked more of the dangers of power in terms that had become familiar during the long struggles with Parliament and the crown. They noted the absence of a Bill of Rights protecting the rights of individuals and states. They found the process of ratification highly irregular, as it was—indeed illegal under the Articles of Confederation. Patrick Henry "smelt a rat" from the beginning. Not only did he refuse to attend the Constitutional Convention, he demanded later that it be investigated as a conspiracy. The Antifederalist leaders—men like Henry and Richard Henry Lee of Virginia, George Clinton of New York, Sam Adams and Elbridge Gerry of Massachusetts, Luther Martin of Maryland—were often men whose careers and reputations had been established well before the Revolution. The Federalist leaders, on the other hand, were more likely to be younger men whose careers had begun in the Revolution and who had been "nationalized" in the fires of battle—men like Hamilton, Madison, and Jay.

The disagreement between the two groups, however, was more over means than ends. Both sides for the most part agreed that a stronger national authority was needed, and that it required an independent income to function properly. Both were convinced that the people must erect safeguards against tyranny, even the tyranny of the majority. Few of its supporters liked the Constitution in its entirety, but felt that it was the best obtainable; few of its opponents found it unacceptable in its entirety. Once the new government had become an accomplished fact, few diehards were left who wanted to undo the work of the Philadelphia convention.

THE DECISION OF THE STATES Ratification gained momentum before the year 1787 was ended, and several of the smaller states were among the first to act, apparently satisfied that they had gained all the safeguards they could hope for in equality of representation in the Senate. Delaware's convention was first, and ratified the Constitution unanimously on December 7; Pennsylvania approved by 46 to 23 on December 12; New Jersey on December 18 and Georgia on January 2 were unanimous; Connecticut voted in favor, 128 to 40, on January 9. Massachusetts, still sharply divided in the aftermath of Shays's Rebellion, was the first state in which the outcome was close. There the Federalists carried the day by winning over two hesitant leaders of the popular party. They dangled before John Hancock the possibility of becoming vice-president, and won the acquiescence of Samuel Adams when they agreed to recommend amendments designed to protect human rights, including one that would specifically reserve to the states all powers not granted to the new government. Massachusetts approved, by 187 to 168 on February 6. Maryland ratified on April 26, by 63 to 11; South Carolina on May 23, by 149 to 73. In New Hampshire one session had failed to agree, and the Federalists had won a delay during which they mobilized greater strength. On June 21, 1788, the reassembled delegates voted ratification by 57 to 47.

New Hampshire was the ninth to ratify, and the Constitution could now be put into effect, but the union could hardly succeed without the approval of Virginia, the largest state, or New York, the third largest, which occupied a key position geographically. Both states had a strong opposition. In Virginia Patrick Henry

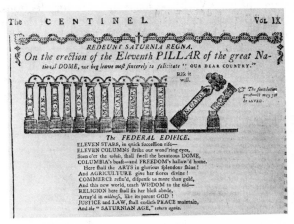

This cartoon from the August 2, 1788, Massachusetts Centinel *announces New York's vote to ratify the Constitution. It took almost two years for Rhode Island to complete "the beauteous* DOME.*" [New-York Historical Society]*

became the chief spokesman of backcountry farmers who feared the powers of the new government, but wavering delegates were won over by the same strategem as in Massachusetts. When it was proposed that the convention should recommend a Bill of Rights, Edmund Randolph, who had refused to sign the finished document, announced his conversion to the cause. Virginia's convention ratified on June 25, by a vote of 89 to 79. In New York, as in New Hampshire, Hamilton and the other Federalists worked for a delay, in the hope that action by New Hampshire and Virginia would persuade the delegates that the new framework would go into effect with or without New York. On July 26, 1788, they carried the day by the closest margin thus far, 30 to 27. North Carolina and Rhode Island remained the only holdouts, and North Carolina stubbornly withheld action until amendments composing a Bill of Rights were actually submitted by Congress. On November 21, 1789, North Carolina joined the new government, which was already under way, 194 to 77. Rhode Island, true to form, continued to hold out, and did not relent until May 29, 1790. Even then the vote was the closest of all, 34 to 32.

Upon notification that New Hampshire had become the ninth state to ratify, the Confederation Congress began to draft plans for an orderly transfer of power. On September 13, 1788, Congress adopted an ordinance which placed the seat of the new government in New York and fixed the date for elections: January 7, 1789, for choice of electors; February 4 for their balloting. March 4, 1789, was the date set for the meeting of the new Congress. Each state would set the date for electing its first members. On October 10, 1788, the Confederation Congress transacted its last business and passed into history.

"Our constitution is in actual operation," the elderly Ben Franklin wrote to a friend; "everything appears to promise that it will last; but in this world nothing is certain but death and taxes."

Further Reading

The traditional view that multiple crises led America from Confederation to Constitution began with John Fiske's *The Critical Period of American History* (1888). Merrill Jensen's *The New Nation* (1950) presents a more recent, "consensus" view that downplays the extent of crisis. Overviews of the political events of the 1780s can be found in

Jensen's *The Articles of Confederation* (1940),° and Andrew C. McLaughlin's *The Confederation and the Constitution* (1962).° Relevant chapters of Gordon S. Wood's *The Creation of the American Republic, 1776–1787* (1969),° trace the changing contours of political philosophy during these years. The behavior of Congress is the subject of both H. James Henderson's *Party Politics in the Continental Congress* (1974) and Jack N. Rakove's *The Beginnings of National Politics* (1979).°

More specific treatments of the events of the 1780s are Frederick W. Marks III's *Independence on Trial* (1973), which deals with the problems of foreign commerce among the various states, and E. James Ferguson's *The Power of the Purse: A History of American Public Finance, 1776–1790* (1961), which analyzes the difficulties of putting together a credit system. Clarence L. Van Steeg's biography, *Robert Morris: Revolutionary Financier* (1954),° examines the role of that central figure.

To understand what individual states faced during the period, see Richard P. McCormick's *Experiment in Independence: New Jersey in the Critical Period, 1781–1789* (1950), and Florence Parker Simister's *The Fire's Center: Rhode Island in the Revolutionary Era, 1763–1790* (1978). Robert S. Taylor's *Western Massachusetts in the Revolution* (1954) and Marion L. Starkey's *A Little Rebellion* (1955) provide background on Shays's Rebellion. A brief account of the state of Franklin is in Noel B. Gerson's *Franklin: America's Lost State* (1968). For a view of public sentiment during the period, see Joseph J. Ellis's *After the Revolution: Profiles of American Culture* (1979),° as well as Oscar and Lillian Handlin's *A Restless People: America in Rebellion, 1770–1787* (1982).

As noted in the text, Charles A. Beard's *An Economic Interpretation of the Constitution* (1913)° remained powerfully influential for more than a generation. More recent challenges to Beard include Robert E. Brown's *Charles Beard and the Constitution* (1956)° and Forrest McDonald's *We the People: The Economic Origins of the Constitution* (1958).° Also helpful is McDonald's *E Pluribus Unum: The Formation of the American Republic, 1776–1790* (1965).° Other interpretations are found in Leonard W. Levy (ed.), *Essays on the Making of the American Constitution* (1969), Merrill Jensen's *Making of the American Constitution* (1964), and Robert E. Brown's *Reinterpretation of the Formation of the American Constitution* (1963). Catherine Drinker Bowen's *Miracle at Philadelphia* (1966)° is a readable narrative of the convention proceedings.

Recent scholarship treats both sides of the ratification argument. The best introduction to the Federalist viewpoint remains in their own words, edited by Benjamin F. Wright, *The Federalist* (1961). Garry Wills's *Explaining America: The Federalist* (1981)° provides an interpretation of what they wrote. Biographies of Federalist writers are also helpful, among them Jacob Ernest Cook's *Alexander Hamilton* (1982), Forrest McDonald's *Alexander Hamilton: A Biography* (1979),° and Irving Brant's *James Madison: The Nationalist, 1780–87* (1948).

Most recently Herbert J. Storing and Murray Day have completed a

° These books are available in paperback editions.

multivolume compendium of the anti-Federalist documents. Their slim, but incisive, introduction is *What the Anti-Federalists Were For* (1981). Also see Robert A. Rutland's *The Ordeal of the Constitution: The Anti-Federalists and the Ratification Struggle of 1787–1788* (1966) and Jackson Turner Main's *The Anti-Federalists: Critics of the Constitution, 1781–1788* (1961).° For the Bill of Rights which emerged from the ratification struggles, see Robert A. Rutland's *The Birth of the Bill of Rights, 1776–1791* (1955).

For discussions of the problem of slavery in forming the Constitution, see the relevant sections of Donald Robinson's *Slavery in the Structure of American Politics, 1765–1820* (1982),° and James McGregor Burns's *The Vineyard of Liberty: The American Experiment* (1982).°

8

THE FEDERALISTS:
WASHINGTON AND ADAMS

A New Government

On the appointed date, March 4, 1789, the new Congress of the United States, meeting in New York, could muster only eight senators and thirteen representatives. A month passed before both chambers gathered a quorum. Only then could the temporary presiding officer of the Senate count the ballots and certify the foregone conclusion that George Washington, with sixty-nine votes, was the unanimous choice of the electoral college for president. John Adams, with thirty-four votes, the second-highest number, became vice-president.

Washington's journey from Mount Vernon to New York, where he was inaugurated on April 30, turned into a triumphal procession which confirmed the universal confidence he commanded, and the hopeful expectancy with which the new experiment was awaited. But Washington himself confessed to feeling like "a culprit who is going to his place of execution," burdened with dread that so much was expected of him. When he delivered the inaugural address he trembled visibly and at times seemed barely able to make out the manuscript in front of him.

SYMBOLS OF AUTHORITY   The task before the president and the Congress was to create a government anew. From the Confederation Washington inherited but the shadow of a bureaucracy: a foreign office with John Jay and two clerks; a Treasury Board with little or no treasury; a secretary of war with an army of 672 officers and men, and no navy at all; a dozen or so clerks who had

Mary Varick's sampler celebrates George Washington's inauguration as president of the United States in 1789. [Museum of the City of New York]

served the old Congress; a heavy debt and almost no revenue, and no machinery for collecting one. There was an acute realization that anything done at the time would set important precedents for the future. Even the question of an etiquette appropriate to the dignity and authority of the new government occupied Congress to a degree that later Americans (and not a few at the time) would regard as absurd. A committee of Congress went so far as to suggest for a presidential title "His Highness, the President of the United States and Protector of Rights of the Same." A solemn discussion of the issue in Congress ended happily when the House of Representatives addressed the chief executive simply by his constitutional title: "President of the United States." One irreverent wag in the Congress suggested privately that a form of address appropriate to the vice-president's appearance would be "Your Rotundity."

The Congress nevertheless agreed with John Vining of Delaware, who said on the floor of the House: "there are cases in which generosity is the best economy, and no loss is ever sustained by a decent support of the Magistrate. A certain appearance of parade and external dignity is necessary to be supported." To that end Congress set the president's salary at $25,000, an income far above that of any other official and probably all but a few Americans. The president obliged them with a show of pomp and circumstance. On public occasions he ap-

A 1790 reception at President Washington's house in New York. The formality of the occasion fit the man, and, many thought, the newly created office. [The Brooklyn Museum]

peared in a coach drawn by four horses, sometimes six, escorted by liveried retainers. He held formal dinners for "official characters and strangers of distinction," but took no invitations himself. Every Tuesday from 3 to 4 p.m. he held a formal levee, clothed in black velvet, his hair in full dress, powdered and gathered, wearing yellow gloves and a finely polished sword, holding a cocked hat with cockade and feather. Visiting in Boston, Washington stubbornly declined to visit Gov. John Hancock until Hancock paid a call on him, thus making the point that a president takes precedence over a mere governor. Mixed emotions greeted the show of ceremony. Some members of Congress continued to fear that another president might make "that bold push for the throne" predicted by Patrick Henry. The antimonarchists did stop a move to stamp coins with the head of the incumbent president—preferring an emblem of Liberty instead.

GOVERNMENTAL STRUCTURE   More than matters of punctilio occupied the First Congress, of course. In framing the structure of government it was second in importance only to the Constitutional Convention itself. During the summer of 1789 Congress authorized executive departments, corresponding in each case to those already formed under the Confederation. To head the Department of State Washington named Thomas Jefferson, recently back from his mission to France. As head of the Department of War, Gen. Henry Knox continued in substantially the same position he had occupied since 1785. To head the Department of the Treasury, Washington picked his old wartime aide Alexander Hamilton, now a prominent lawyer in New York. The new position of attorney-general was occupied by Edmund Randolph, former governor of Virginia. Unlike the other three Randolph headed no department but served as legal advisor to the government, and on such a meager salary that he was expected to continue a private practice on the side. Almost from the beginning Washington routinely called these men to sit as a group for discussion and advice on matters of policy. This was the origin of the president's cabinet, an advisory body for which the constitution made no formal provision—except insofar as it provided for the heads of departments.

The structure of the court system, like that of the executive departments, was left to Congress, except for a chief justice and Supreme Court. Congress determined to set the membership of the highest court at six: the chief justice and five associate justices. There was some sentiment for stopping there and permitting state courts to determine matters of federal law, but the Congress decided in favor of thirteen Federal District Courts. From these, appeals might go to one of three Circuit Courts, composed of two Supreme Court justices and the district judge, meeting twice a year in each district. Members of the Supreme Court, therefore, became intinerant judges riding the circuit during a good part of the year. All federal cases originated in the District Court, and if appealed on issues of procedure or legal interpretation, went to the Circuit Courts and from there to the Supreme Court. There were only two exceptions, both specified in the Constitution: the Supreme Court had original jurisdiction in cases involving states or foreign ambassadors, ministers, and consuls. As the first chief justice Washington named John Jay, who served until 1795.

THE BILL OF RIGHTS   In the House of Representatives James Madison made a Bill of Rights one of the first items of business. The lack of such provisions had been one of the Antifederalists' major objections to the Constitution as originally proposed. While at first Madison believed that the absence of a Bill of Rights made little difference (events proved him wrong), he recognized the need to allay the fears of Antifederalists and to meet the moral obligation imposed by those ratifying conventions which had approved the Constitution with the understanding that amendments would be offered. In all 210 amendments had been suggested. From the Virginia proposals Madison drew the first eight amendments, modeled after the Virginia Bill of Rights which George Mason had written in 1776. These all provided safeguards for certain fundamental rights of individuals. The Ninth and Tenth Amendments addressed themselves to the demand for specific statements that the enumeration of rights in the Constitution "shall not be construed to deny or disparage others retained by the people" and that "powers not delegated to the United States by the Constitution, nor prohibited by it to the states, are reserved to the States respectively, or to the people." The Tenth Amendment was taken almost verbatim from the Articles of Confederation. The House adopted, in all, seventeen amendments; the Senate, after conference with the House, adopted twelve; the states in the end ratified ten, which constitute the Bill of Rights, effective December 15, 1791.

RAISING A REVENUE   Revenue was the government's most critical need and the Congress, at Madison's lead, undertook a revenue measure as another of the first items of business. Madison proposed a modest duty for revenue only, but the demands of manufacturers in the northern states for higher duties to protect them from foreign competition forced a compromise. Madison's proposed ad valorem duty of 5 percent (of the goods' value) applied to most items, but reached 7 1/2 percent on certain listed items, and specific duties as high as 50 percent were placed on thirty items: steel, nails, hemp, molasses, ships, tobacco, salt, indigo, and cloth among them. Madison linked the tariff to a proposal for a mercantile system which would levy extra tonnage duties on foreign ships, an especially heavy duty on countries which had no commercial treaty with the United States.

Madison's specific purpose was to levy economic war against Great Britain, which had no such treaty but had more foreign trade with the new nation than any other country. Northern businessmen, however, were in no mood for a renewal of economic pressures, for fear of disrupting the economy. Secretary of the Treasury Hamilton agreed with them. In the end the only discrimination built into the Tonnage Act of 1789 was between American and all foreign ships: American ships paid a duty of 6¢ per ton; American-built but foreign-owned ships paid 30¢; and foreign-built and owned ships paid 50¢ per ton. The disagreements created by the trade measures were portents of quarrels yet to come: whether foreign policy should favor Britain or France, and the more persistent question of whether tariff and tonnage duties should penalize farmers with higher prices and freight rates in the interest of northern manufacturers and ship-owners. The latter in turn became a sectional question of South versus North.

HAMILTON'S VISION OF AMERICA

But the first provision for a revenue, linked as it was to other issues, was but the beginning of the effort to get the country on a sound financial basis. In finance, with all its broad implications for policy in general, it was Alexander Hamilton who, in the words of the historian Joseph Charles, more than any other man "bent the twig and inclined the tree." The first secretary of the treasury was in a sense the protégé of the president, a younger man who had been his aide during four years of the Revolution. Born out of wedlock on the island of Nevis, deserted by a ne'er-do-well father, Hamilton was left an orphan on St. Croix at thirteen by the death of his mother. With the help of friends and relatives, Hamilton found his way at seventeen to New York, attended King's College (later Columbia University), entered the revolutionary agitations as speaker and pamphleteer, and joined the service, where he came to the attention of the commander. "George Washington was an aegis essential to me," Hamilton wrote later, after the president's death. Married to the daughter of Gen. Philip Schuyler, he studied law, passed the bar examination, established a legal practice in New York, and became a self-made aristocrat, serving as collector of revenues and member of

Alexander Hamilton in 1796.
[National Portrait Gallery,
Smithsonian Institution]

the Confederation Congress. An early convert to nationalism, he had a big part in promoting the Constitutional Convention. A hero of the siege of Yorktown, he remained forever after a frustrated military genius, hungry for greater glory on the field of battle.

In a series of classic reports submitted to Congress in the two years from January 1790 to December 1791, Hamilton outlined his program for government finances and the economic development of the United States. The reports were soon adopted, with some alterations in detail but little in substance. The only exception was the last of the series, the Report on Manufactures, and that one outlined a neomercantilist program which eventually would become government policy, whatever brave talk of laissez-faire might accompany it.

ESTABLISHING THE PUBLIC CREDIT   Hamilton submitted the first and most important of his reports to the House of Representatives on January 14, 1790, at the invitation of that body. This First Report on the Public Credit, as it has since been called, was the cornerstone of the Hamiltonian program. It recommended two things mainly: first, funding of the federal debt at face value, which meant that the government's creditors could turn in securities for new interest-bearing bonds; and second, the federal government's assumption of state debts from the Revolution to the amount of $21 million. The report raised a multiplicity of issues about the national and state debts, and provided the material for lengthy discussions and debates before its substance was adopted on August 4, 1791. Then in short order came three more reports: on December 13, 1790, a Second Report on Public Credit, which included a proposal for an excise tax on distilled spirits to aid in raising revenue to cover the nation's debts (Hamilton meant this tax also to establish the precedent of an excise tax, and to rebuke elements that had been least friendly to his program). On the following day another report from Hamilton recommended a national bank, a revival of the Robert Morris idea that had led to the Bank of North America. On January 28, 1791, the secretary suggested a national mint—which was established the following year. And finally, on December 5, 1791, as the culmination of his basic reports, the Report on Manufactures proposed an extensive program of government aid and encouragement to the development of manufacturing enterprises.

Each of Hamilton's reports excited vigorous discussion and disagreement. His program was substantially the one Robert Morris had urged upon the Confederation a decade before, and one which Hamilton had strongly endorsed at the time. "A national debt," Hamilton had written Morris in 1781, "if it is not excessive, will be to us a national blessing; it will be a powerful cement of our union. It will also create a necessity for keeping up taxation to a degree which without being oppressive, will be a spur to industry; remote as we are from Europe and shall be from danger, it were otherwise to be feared our popular maxims would incline us to great parsimony and indulgence." Payment of the national debt, in short, would be not only a point of national honor and sound finance, ensuring the country's credit for the future; it would also be an ocasion to assert a national taxing power and thus instill respect for the authority of the national government.

Few in Congress would dispute this logic, although a number of members had come expecting at least some degree of debt repudiation to lessen the burden. What troubled them more were questions of simple equity, questions which Hamilton took pains to anticipate and answer in the First Report itself. Since many of the bonds had fallen into the hands of speculators, especially after the appearance of the First Report sent agents of speculators (including members of Congress) scurrying to buy them up, was it fair that the original purchasers, who had been forced into selling their bonds at a reduced price, should lose the benefit of the restoration of governmental credit? Hamilton answered the argument on both practical and moral grounds. Not only would it be impossible to judge who might have benefited from selling bonds and investing the proceeds in more productive ways, but speculators were entitled to consideration for the risk they had taken and the faith they had shown in the government.

SECTIONAL DIFFERENCES EMERGE   It was on this point, however, that Madison, who had been Hamilton's close ally in the movement for a stronger government, broke with him for the second time (their first break had been over the issue of tonnage duties), and as in the first case the difference here had ominous overtones of sectionalism. Madison did not question that the debt should be paid; he was troubled, however, that speculators and "stock-jobbers" would become the chief beneficiaries, and troubled further by the fact that the far greater portion of the debt was held north of the Mason-Dixon line. Madison, whom Hamilton had expected to take the lead for his program in the House, therefore advanced an alternative plan to give a larger share to the first owners than to the later speculators. "Let it be a liberal one in favor of the present holders," he suggested. "Let them have the highest price which has prevailed in the market; and let the residue belong to the original sufferers." Madison's opposition touched off a vigorous debate, but Hamilton carried his point by a margin of three to one when the House brought it to a vote.

Madison's opposition to the assumption of state debts got more support, however, and set up a division more clearly along sectional lines. The southern states, with the exception of South Carolina, had whittled down their debts. New England, with the largest unpaid debts, stood to be the greatest beneficiary of the assumption scheme. Rather than see Virginia victimized, Madison held out an alternative. Why not, he suggested, have the government assume state debts as they stood in 1783 at the conclusion of the peace? Debates over this issue deadlocked the whole question of debt funding and assumption through much of 1790.

A resolution finally came when Hamilton accosted Thomas Jefferson on the steps of the president's home and suggested a compromise with the Virginians. The next evening, at a dinner arranged by Jefferson, Hamilton and Madison reached an understanding. In return for northern votes in favor of locating the permanent capital on the Potomac, Madison pledged to seek enough southern votes to pass the assumption, with the further arrangement that those states with smaller debts would get in effect outright grants from the federal government to equalize the difference. With these arrangements enough votes were secured to carry Hamilton's funding and assumption schemes. The capital would be moved to Philadelphia for ten years, after which time it would be settled at a Federal City on the Potomac, the site to be chosen by the president. In August 1790 Congress finally passed the legislation for Hamilton's plan.

A NATIONAL BANK   By this vast program of funding and assumption Hamilton had called up from nowhere, as if by magic, a great sum of capital. As he put it in his original report, a national debt "answers most of the purposes of money." Transfers of government bonds, once the debt was properly funded, would be "equivalent to payments in specie." This feature of the program was especially important in a country which had, from the first settlements, suffered a shortage of hard money and in which foreign coins circulated widely for another half century. But having established the public credit, Hamilton moved on to a related measure essential to his vision of national greatness. He called for the creation of a national bank, which by issuance of banknotes (paper money) might provide a uniform circulating medium. Government bonds held by the bank would back up the value of its new banknotes, needed as a medium of exchange because of the chronic shortage of specie. The national bank, chartered by Congress, would remain under governmental surveillance, but private investors would purchase four-fifths of the $10 million capital and name twenty of the twenty-five directors; the government would take the other fifth of the capital and name five directors. Government bonds would be received in payment for three-fourths of the stock in the bank, and the other fourth would be payable in gold and silver.

The bank, Hamilton explained, would serve many purposes. Its notes would become a stable circulating currency, uniform in value because redeemable in gold and silver upon demand. Moreover, the bank would provide a source of capital for loans to fund the development of business and commerce. Bonds, which might otherwise be stowed away in safes, would instead become the basis for a productive capital in the form of banknotes available for loan at low rates of interest, the "natural effect" of which would be "to incease trade and industry." What is more, the existence of the bank would serve certain housekeeping needs of the government: a safe place to keep its funds, a source of "pecuniary aids" in sudden emergencies, and the ready transfer of

The first Bank of the United States in Philadelphia. Proposed by Hamilton, the bank opened in 1791. [Library of Congress]

funds to and from branch offices by means of bookkeeping entries which would obviate the tedious "transportation and re-transportation" of metals for payment of bills and taxes.

Once again Madison rose to lead the opposition. Madison could find no authority in the Constitution for such a bank. He himself had proposed in the Constitutional Convention a grant of power to charter corporations, but no specific provisions had been adopted. That was enough to raise in President Washington's mind serious doubts as to the constitutionality of the measure, which Congress passed fairly quickly over Madison's objections. Before signing the bill into law, therefore, the president sought the advice of his cabinet and found there an equal division of opinion. The result was the first great and fundamental debate on constitutional interpretation. Should there be a strict or a broad construction of the document? Were the powers of Congress only those explicitly stated or were there others implied by the language of the Constitution? The argument turned chiefly on Article 1, Section 8, which authorized Congress to "make all laws which shall be necessary and proper for carrying into execution the foregoing Powers."

Such language left room for serious disagreement and led to a direct confrontation between Jefferson, with whom Attorney-General Edmund Randolph agreed, and Hamilton, who had the support of Secretary of War Henry Knox. Jefferson pointed to the Tenth Amendment, which reserved to the states and the people powers not delegated to Congress. "To take a single step beyond the boundaries thus specially drawn around the powers of Congress, is to take possession of a boundless field of power, no longer susceptible of any definition." A bank might be a convenient aid to Congress in collecting taxes and regulating the currency, but it was not, as Article 1, Section 8, specified, *necessary*.

Hamilton had not expected the constitutionality of the bank to become a decisive issue, and in his original report had neglected the point, but he was prepared to meet his opponents on their own ground. In a lengthy report to the president, Hamilton insisted that the power to charter corporations was included in the sovereignty of any government, whether or not expressly stated. The word "necessary," he explained, often meant no more than "needful, requisite, incidental, useful, or conducive to." And in a classic summary, he expressed his criterion on constitutionality: "This criterion is the *end*, to which the measure relates as a *mean*. If the *end* be clearly comprehended within any of the specified powers, collecting taxes and regulating the currency, and if the measure have an obvious relation to that *end*, and is not forbidden by any particular provision of the Constitution, it may safely be deemed to come within the compass of the national authority. . . ."

The president, influenced by the fact that the matter under consideration came within the jurisdiction of the secretary of the treasury, accepted Hamilton's argument and signed the bill. And he had indeed, in Jefferson's words, opened up "a boundless field of power" which in coming years would lead to a further broadening of implied powers with the approval of the Supreme Court. Under John Marshall the Court would eventually adopt Hamilton's words almost verbatim. On July 4, 1791, the bank's stock was put up for sale and in what seemed to Jefferson a "delirium of speculation" was sold within a few hours, with hundreds of buyers turned away. It cost the government itself nothing until later, for its subscription of $2 million was immediately returned by the bank in a loan of the same amount, with ten years for repayment.

ENCOURAGING MANUFACTURES But Hamilton's imagination and his ambitions for the new country remained unexhausted. In the last of his great reports, the Report on Manufactures, he set in place the capstone of his design, an argument for the active encouragement of manufacturing to provide productive uses for the new capital he had created by his funding, assumption, and banking schemes. A reading of this report will lay to rest any idea that the Founding Fathers abandoned mercantilism to embrace the newfangled laissez-faire attitudes of Adam Smith. "The extreme embarrassments of the United States during the late War, from an incapacity of supplying themselves, are still matter of keen recollection," Hamilton wrote. Multiple advantages would flow from the development of manufactures: the diversification of labor in a country given over too exclusively to farming; greater use of machinery; work for those not ordinarily employed, such as women and children; the promotion of immigration; a greater scope for the diversity of talents in business; a more ample and various field for enterprise; and a better domestic market for the products of agriculture.

To secure his ends Hamilton was ready to use the means to which other countries had resorted, and which he summarized: protective tariffs, or in Hamilton's words, "protecting duties," which in some cases might be put so high as to be prohibitive; restraints on the export of raw materials; bounties and premiums to encourage certain industries; tariff exemptions for the raw mate-rials of manufacturing, or "drawbacks" (rebates) to manufac-turers where duties had been levied for revenue or other purposes; encouragements to inventions and discoveries; regula-tions for the inspection of commodities; and finally, the encour-agement of internal improvements in transportation, the development of roads, canals, and navigable streams.

Some of his tariff proposals were enacted in 1792. Otherwise the program was filed away—but not forgotten. It became an ar-senal of arguments for the advocates of manufactures in years to come, in Europe as well as in America. An outline can hardly do justice to what was a complex state paper which anticipated and attempted to demolish all counterarguments, among them the ominous question which kept arising with Hamilton's schemes: "Ideas of a contrariety of interests between the northern and southern regions of the Union," which he found "in the Main as unfounded as they are mischievous." If, as seemed likely from experience and circumstances, the northern and middle states should become the chief scenes of manufacturing, they would create robust markets for agricultural products, some of which the southern states were peculiarly qualified to produce. North and South would both benefit, he argued, as commerce moved between these regions more than along the established channels across the Atlantic, thus strengthening the Union: "every thing tending to establish *substantial* and *permanent order* in the affairs of a Country, to increase the total mass of industry and opulence, is ultimately beneficial to every part of it."

HAMILTON'S ACHIEVEMENT Largely owing to the skillful Hamil-ton, whom a close student of the Federalist period called "the greatest administrative genius in America, and one of the great-est administrators of all time," the Treasury Department, which employed half or more of the civil servants at the time, was es-tablished on a basis of integrity and efficiency. The Revolution-ary War debt was put on the way to retirement, a "Continental" became worth something after all (if only at a ratio of 100 to 1 in payments to the government), the credit of the government was secure, government securities sold at par, and foreign capital began to flow in once again. And prosperity, so elusive in the 1780s, began to flourish once again, although President Wash-ington cautioned against attributing "to the Government what is due only to the goodness of Providence."

Still, the suspicion would not die down that Hamilton's was a program designed to promote a class and sectional interest, and some even thought a personal interest. There is, however, no evidence that Hamilton benefited personally in any way from his program, although Assistant Treasury Secretary William Duer, unbeknownst to Hamilton, did leak word of the funding and assumption message to favored friends in time for them to reap a speculative harvest from the rise in values. Duer himself later became involved in deals which landed him in prison. There is no reason to believe that Hamilton's conscious aim was to benefit either a section or a class at the expense of the government. He was inclined toward a truly nationalist outlook. As a result of his early years in the islands he lacked the background of narrow localism that most of his contemporaries shared to some degree, although his failure to take that factor into full account was one of his weaknesses. Indeed he would have favored a much stronger central government, including a federal veto on state action, even a constitutional monarchy if that had been practicable. But, ironically, given his background of illegitimacy and poverty, Hamilton believed that throughout history a minority of the strong dominated the weak. There was always a ruling group, perhaps military or aristocratic, and Hamilton had the wit to see now the rising power of commercial capitalism. He was in many ways a classic Whig who, like Britain's ruling oligarchy of the eighteenth century, favored government by the rich and well-born. The mass of the people, he once said "are turbulent and changing; they seldom judge or determine right." And once, in his cups, he went further: "Your people, sir, is a great beast!" To tie the government closely to the rich and the well-born, then, was but to secure the interest of good government and to guard the public order against the potential turbulence which always haunted him.

Hamilton's achievement, however, was to tie more closely to the government those who were already on its side—and to overlook, or even antagonize, those who had their doubts. Hamilton never came to know the people of the small villages and farms, the people of the frontier. They were absent from his world, despite his own humble beginnings in the islands. And they, along with the planters of the South, would be at best only indirect beneficiaries of his programs. Below the Potomac the Hamiltonian vision excited little enthusiasm except in South Carolina, which had a large state debt to be assumed and a sizable concentration of mercantile interests at Charleston. There was, in short, a vast number of people who were drawn into opposition to Hamilton's new engines of power. In part they were southern, in part backcountry, and in part a politically motivated faction opposing Hamilton in New York.

THE REPUBLICAN ALTERNATIVE

In this split over the Hamiltonian program lay the seeds of the first political parties of national scope. Hamilton became the embodiment of the party known as the Federalists; Madison and Jefferson became the leaders of those who took the name Republican and thereby implied that the Federalists really aimed at a monarchy. Parties were slow in developing, or at least in being acknowledged as legitimate. All the political philosophers of the age deplored the spirit of party or faction. The concept of a loyal opposition, of a two-party system as a positive good, was yet to be formulated. Parties, or factions, as eighteenth-century Englishmen and colonists knew them, were bodies of men bent upon self-aggrandizement through the favor of the government. They smelled of jobbery and corruption. So it cannot be said that either side in the disagreement over national policy deliberately set out to create a party system, which indeed would not be firmly established nor widely accepted as a public good until the next century was more than a quarter spent.

But there were important differences of both philosophy and self-interest which simply would not dissolve. At the outset Madison, who had collaborated with Hamilton in the movement for a national government and the writing of *The Federalist,* assumed leadership of Hamilton's opponents in the Congress. The states meant more to Madison than to Hamilton, who would as soon have seen a consolidated central government. And Madison, like Thomas Jefferson, was rooted in Virginia, where opposition to the funding schemes flourished. In December 1790 the Virginia Assembly bluntly protested Hamilton's funding schemes in a resolution drafted by Patrick Henry: "In an agricultural country like this . . . to erect, and concentrate, and perpetuate a large monied interest . . . must in the course of human events produce one or other of two evils, the prostration of agriculture at the feet of commerce, or a change in the present from of federal government, fatal to the existence of American liberty. . . . Your memorialists can find no clause in the Constitution authorizing Congress to assume the debts of the States!" To Hamilton this was "the first symptom of a spirit which must either be killed, or will kill the Constitution of the United States."

After the compromise which had assured passage of the funding and assumption, Madison and Jefferson moved into ever more irreconcilable opposition to Hamilton's policies: his move to place an excise tax on whiskey, which laid a burden especially on the trans-Appalachian farmers whose grain went into that potable and portable liquid; his proposal for the bank; and his report on manufactures. Against the last two both men raised constitutional objections. As the differences developed, hostility between Jefferson and Hamilton grew and festered, to the distress of President Washington. Jefferson, the temperamentally shy and retiring secretary of state, then emerged as the leader of the opposition to Hamilton's policies; Madison continued to direct the opposition in Congress.

JEFFERSON'S AGRARIAN VIEW Thomas Jefferson, twelve years Hamilton's senior, was in almost every respect his opposite. In contrast to Hamilton, the careerist, the self-made aristocrat, Jefferson was to the manor born, son of a successful surveyor and land speculator, his mother a Randolph, from one of the First Families in Virginia. In contrast to Hamilton's ordered intensity, Jefferson conveyed a certain sense of aristocratic carelessness and a breadth of cultivated interests that ranged perhaps more widely in science, the arts, and the humanities than those of any contemporary, even Franklin. Jefferson read or spoke seven languages. He was an architect of some distinction (Monticello, the Virginia Capitol, the University of Virginia are monuments to his talent), a man who understood mathematics and engineering, an inventor, an agronomist. In his *Notes on Virginia* (1785) he displayed a knowledge of geography, paleontology, zoology, botany, and archeology. He collected paintings and sculpture. He knew music and practiced the violin, although some wit said only Patrick Henry played it worse.

Thomas Jefferson, in a portrait by Rembrandt Peale (1800). [White House Collection]

Philosophically, Hamilton and Jefferson personified the two poles of a great dialectic that formed the character of the Union in the first generation under the Constitution, and defined certain fundamental issues of American life which still echo two centuries later. Hamilton foresaw a diversified capitalistic economy, agriculture balanced by commerce and industry, and was thus the better prophet. Jefferson feared the growth of cities which would be filled with crowds and divided into a capitalistic aristocracy on the one hand and a depraved proletariat on the other. Hamilton feared anarchy and loved order; Jefferson feared tyranny and loved liberty.

What Hamilton wanted for his country was a strong central government, run by the rich and well-born actively encouraging capitalistic enterprise. What Jefferson wanted was a republic of yeoman farmers: "Those who labor in the earth," he wrote, "are the chosen people of God, if ever he had a chosen people, whose breasts He has made His peculiar deposit for genuine and substantial virtue." Where Hamilton was the old-fashioned English Whig, Jefferson, who spent several years in France, was the enlightened *philosophe*, the natural radical and reformer who attacked the aristocratic relics of entail and primogeniture in Virginia; opposed an established church; proposed an elaborate plan for public schools; prepared a more humane criminal code; and was instrumental in eliminating slavery from the Old Northwest, although he kept the slaves he had inherited. On his tomb were finally recorded the achievements of which he was proudest: author of the Declaration of Independence and the Virginia Statute of Religious Freedom, and founder of the University of Virginia.

Jefferson set forth his vision of what America should be in his *Notes on Virginia* in 1785: "While we have land to labor then, let us never wish to see our citizens occupied at a work-bench, or twirling a distaff. . . . For the general operations of manufacture, let our work-shops remain in Europe. It is better to carry provisions and materials to work-men there, than bring them to the provisions and materials, and with them their manners and principles. . . . The mobs of great cities add just so much to the support of pure government, as sores do to the strength of the human body."

PARTY DISPUTES   The one thing that Jefferson and Hamilton had in common, it seemed, was their mutual enmity, which began with disagreement in the cabinet and soon became widely visible in a journalistic war of words between two editors with the curiously similar names of Fenno and Freneau. John Fenno's *Gazette of the*

United States, founded in 1789, "to endear the General Government to the people," became virtually the official administration organ, extolling Hamilton and his policies at every opportunity, and holding contracts for government printing. Philip Freneau, poet and journalist, was enticed to Philadelphia from New York in 1791 to found the *National Gazette* and given a sinecure as translator for Jefferson's Department of State. Each man was compromised by his connection, but each loyally supported his benefactor out of real conviction.

In their quarrel Hamilton unwittingly identified Jefferson more and more in the public mind as the leader of the opposition to his policies; Madison was still a relatively obscure congressman whose central role in the Constitutional Convention was yet unknown. In the summer of 1791 Jefferson and Madison set out on a "botanizing" excursion up the Hudson, a vacation which many Federalists feared was a cover for consultations with Gov. George Clinton, the Livingstons, and Aaron Burr, leaders of the faction in New York which opposed the aristocratic party of the De Lanceys, Van Rensselaers, and Philip Schuyler, Hamilton's father-in-law. While the significance of that single trip was blown out of proportion, there did ultimately arise an informal alliance of Jeffersonian Republicans in the south and New York which would become a constant if sometimes awkward feature of the party and its successor, the Democratic party.

Still, there was no opposition to Washington, who longed to end his exile from Mount Vernon and even began preparing a farewell address, but was urged by both Hamilton and Jefferson to continue in public life. He was the only man who could transcend party differences and hold things together with his unmatched prestige and the infinite confidence the American people placed in him. In 1792 Washington was unanimously reelected, but in the scattering of second votes the Republican Clinton got fifty electoral votes to Adams's seventy-seven.

CRISES FOREIGN AND DOMESTIC

In Washington's second term the problems of foreign relations came to center stage, brought there by the consequences of the French Revolution, which had begun during the first months of Washington's presidency. Americans followed events in France with almost universal sympathy, up to a point. By the spring of 1792, though, the hopeful experiment in liberty, equality, and fraternity had transmogrified itself into a monster that plunged France into war with Austria and Prussia and began devouring its own children along with its enemies in the Terror of 1793–1794.

After the execution of King Louis XVI in January 1793, Great Britain entered into the coalition of monarchies at war with the French Republic. For the next twenty-two years Britain and France were at war, with only a brief respite, until the final defeat of French forces under Napoleon in 1815. The war presented Washington, just beginning his second term, with an awkward decision. By the treaty of 1778 the United States was a perpetual ally of France, obligated to defend her possessions in the West Indies. But Americans wanted no part of the war; on this much Hamilton and Jefferson could agree. Hamilton had a simple and direct answer to this problem: simply declare the alliance invalid because it was made with a government that no longer existed. Jefferson preferred to delay and use the alliance as a bargaining point with the British. But in the end Washington followed the advice of neither. Taking a middle course, on April 22, 1793, the president issued a neutrality proclamation that evaded even the word "neutrality." It simply declared the United States "friendly and impartial toward the belligerent powers" and warned American citizens that "aiding or abetting hostilities" or other unneutral acts might be prosecuted.

CITIZEN GENÊT At the same time, Washington accepted Jefferson's argument that the United States should recognize the new French government (becoming the first country to do so) and receive its new ambassador, Citizen Edmond Charles Genêt. Early in 1793 Citizen Genêt landed at Charleston, where he immediately organized a Jacobin Club, officially recognized in Paris by his fellow radicals. Along the route to Philadelphia the enthusiastic reception accorded by his sympathizers gave Genêt an inflated notion of his potential, not that he needed encouragement. In Charleston he began to authorize privateers to bring in British prizes, and in Philadelphia he continued the process. He intrigued with frontiersmen and land speculators, including George Rogers Clark, with an eye to an attack on Spanish Florida and Louisiana, and issued military commissions in an Armée du Mississippi and an Armée des Florides.

Genêt quickly became an embarrassment even to his Republican friends. Jefferson decided that the French minister had overreached himself when he violated a promise not to outfit a captured British ship as a privateer and sent out the *Little Sarah*, rechristened the *Petite Democrate*. When, finally, Genêt threatened in a moment of anger to appeal his cause directly to the American people over the head of their president, the cabinet unanimously agreed that he had to go and in August 1793 Washington demanded his recall. Meanwhile a new party of radicals had gained power in France and sent over its own minister, Citizen Fauchet, with a warrant for Genêt's arrest. Instead of returning to risk the guillotine, Genêt sought asylum, married the daughter of Governor Clinton, settled down as a country gentleman on the Hudson, and died years later an American citizen.

Genêt's foolishness and the growing excesses of the French radicals were fast cooling American support for their revolution. To Hamilton's followers it began to resemble their worst nightmares of democratic anarchy and infidelity. The French made it hard even for Republicans to retain sympathy, but they swallowed hard and made excuses. "The liberty of the whole earth was depending on the issue of the contest," the genteel Jefferson wrote, "and . . . rather than it should have failed, I would have seen half the earth devastated." Nor did the British make it easy for Federalists to rally to their side. Near the end of 1793 they informed the American government that they intended to occupy their northwest posts indefinitely and announced Orders in Council under which they seized the cargoes of American ships with provisions for or produce from the French islands. Given the offenses by both sides, it is hard to comprehend the degree to which the French and British causes polarized American opinion and the two parties. In the contest, it seemed, one either had to be a Republican and support liberty, reason, and France, or become a Federalist and support order, faith, and Britain. And the division gave rise to some curious anomalies: slaveholding planters joined the yelps for Jacobin radicals who dispossessed their aristocratic counterparts in France, and rang the tocsin in protest against British seizures of New England ships; Massachusetts shippers still profited from the British trade and kept quiet. Boston, once a hotbed of revolution, became a bastion of Federalism.

JAY'S TREATY   Early in 1794 the Republican leaders in Congress were gaining support for a plan of commercial retaliation to bring the British to their senses, when the British gave Washington a timely opening for a settlement. They announced abandonment of the Orders under which American brigs and schooners were being seized in wholesale lots, and on April 16, 1794, Washington named Chief Justice John Jay as a special envoy to Great Britain. Jay left with instructions to settle all major issues:

to secure British abandonment of the western posts, reparations for the losses of American shippers, compensation for slaves carried away in 1783, and a commercial treaty which would legalize American commerce with the British West Indies.

Jay entered the negotiations with his bargaining power compromised by both Federalists and Republicans. In Philadelphia Hamilton indiscreetly told the British minister that the United States had no intention of joining the Armed Neutrality recently formed by Scandinavian countries to uphold neutral rights. In Paris the new American minister, James Monroe, spoke before the National Assembly and embraced both its president and its revolution. The British in turn demanded from Jay greater assurances that America would keep neutral.

To win his objectives, Jay was obliged in fact to be more than neutral and to concede the British definition of neutral rights. He accepted the principles that naval stores were contraband, that provisions could not go in neutral ships to enemy ports, and the "Rule of 1756" by which trade with enemy colonies prohibited in peacetime could not be opened in wartime. Britain also gained most-favored-nation treatment in American commerce and a promise that French privateers would not be outfitted in American ports. Finally, Jay conceded that the old American debts to British merchants would be adjudicated and paid by the American government. In return for these concessions he won three important points: British evacuation of the northwest posts by 1796, reparations for the seizures of American ships and cargoes in 1793–1794, and legalization of trade with the British West Indies. But the last of these (Article XII) was so hedged with restrictions that the Senate eventually struck it from the treaty. Only ships of seventy tons or less could enter the trade, and the United States had to promise not to re-export any molasses, sugar, coffee, cocoa, or cotton. Jay, of course, knew nothing of the future importance of the cotton gin Eli Whitney had just invented.

A public outcry of rage greeted the terms of the treaty when they were leaked and published in the Philadelphia *Aurora*. Even Federalist shippers, ready for settlement on almost any terms, were disappointed at the limitations on their privileges in the West Indies. But much of the outcry was simply expression of disappointment by Republican partisans who sought an escalation of conflict with "perfidious Albion." Some of it was the outrage of Virginia planters at the concession on debts to British merchants and the failure to get reparations for lost slaves. Given the limited enthusiasm of Federalists—Washington himself

John Jay hanged in effigy by opponents to his treaty (1795). [The Warder Collection]

wrestled with doubts over the treaty—Jay remarked he could travel across the country by the light of his burning effigies. Yet the Senate debated the treaty in secret, and in the end quiet counsels of moderation prevailed. Without a single vote to spare, Jay's Treaty got the necessary two-thirds majority on June 24, 1795, with Article XII (the provision regarding the West Indies) expunged. Washington still hesitated but finally signed the treaty as the best he was likely to get and out of fear that subsequent escalation of conflict caused by a refusal would throw the United States into the role of a French satellite. In the House opposition to the treaty went so far as to demand that the president produce all papers relevant to the treaty, but the president refused on the grounds that treaty approval was solely the business of the Senate. He thereby set an important precedent of executive privilege (a term not used at the time), and the House finally relented, supplying the money to fund the treaty on a close vote.

THE FRONTIER STIRS   Other events also had an important bearing on Jay's Treaty, adding force to its settlement of the Canadian frontier and strengthening Spain's conviction that she too needed to reach a settlement of long-festering problems along the southwestern frontier. While Jay was haggling in London, frontier conflict with Indians was moving toward a resolution. Early in 1790 the northwestern tribes routed an American army under Gen. Josiah Harmar along the Maumee River. The next year Gen. Arthur St. Clair, governor of the Northwest Territory, gathered an army of militiamen and "men collected from the streets . . . from the stews and brothels of the cities," and went out to meet an even worse disaster. On November 4, 1791, the Indians surprised the American camp along the Wabash, singled out the officers, few of whom survived, and threw the militia into panic. Only about half of his men escaped unhurt. St. Clair himself, disabled by gout and propped up with pillows in a wagon to watch battle, barely escaped. The defeat resulted in the first congressional investigating committee, which finally put the blame on contractors who failed to supply the army properly.

Conditions along the northwestern frontier, on down into Kentucky, remained unsettled for three more years. Finally Washington named General Wayne, known as "Mad Anthony" since the storming of Stony Point in 1779, to head another expedition. In the fall of 1793 Wayne marched into Indian country with some 2,600 men, built Fort Greenville, and with reinforcements from Kentucky went on the offensive in 1794. On August, 4, 1794, the Indians, reinforced by some Canadian militia, at-

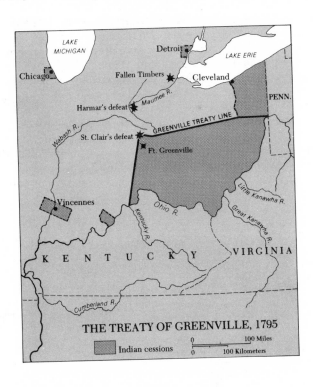

THE TREATY OF GREENVILLE, 1795

Indian cessions

tacked Wayne's force at the Battle of Fallen Timbers, but this time the Americans were ready and repulsed them with heavy losses, after which American detachments laid waste their fields and villages. Dispersed and decimated, they finally agreed to the Treaty of Greenville, signed in August 1795. In the treaty, at the cost of a $10,000 annuity, the United States bought from twelve tribes the rights to the southeastern quarter of the Northwest Territory (now Ohio and Indiana) and enclaves at the sites of Vincennes, Detroit, and Chicago.

THE WHISKEY REBELLION Wayne's forces were still mopping up after the Battle of Fallen Timbers when the administration resolved on another show of strength in the backcountry against the so-called Whiskey Rebellion. Hamilton's excise tax on strong drink, levied in 1791, had excited strong feeling along the frontier since it taxed a staple crop of the very people who had the least to gain from Hamilton's program. Their grain was more easily transported to market in concentrated liquid form than in bulk. The tax was another part of Hamilton's scheme to pick the pockets of the poor to enrich fat speculators, as the frontiersmen saw it. All through the backcountry from Georgia to Pennsylvania and beyond, the tax gave rise to resistance and evasion. In the summer of 1794 the rumblings of discontent broke into open rebellion in the four western counties of Pennsylvania, where vigilantes organized to terrorize revenuers and taxpayers. They blew up the stills of those who paid the tax, robbed the mails, stopped court proceedings, and in a meeting held at Braddock's Field, threatened an assault on Pittsburgh. On August 7, 1794, President Washington issued a proclamation ordering them home and calling out 12,900 militiamen from Virginia, Maryland, Pennsylvania, and New Jersey. Getting no response from the "Whiskey Boys," he issued a proclamation on September 24 for suppression of the rebellion.

Robert Johnson resigns his commission as collector of the whiskey tax in Pittsburgh, 1794. [Carnegie Library, Pittsburgh]

Under the command of Gen. Henry Lee, a force larger than any Washington had ever commanded in the Revolution marched out from Harrisburg across the Alleghenies with Hamilton in their midst, itching to smite the insurgents. To his disappointment the rebels vaporized like rye mash when the heat was applied, and the troops met with little more opposition than a few liberty poles. By dint of great effort and much marching they finally rounded up twenty prisoners whom they paraded down Market Street in Philadelphia and clapped into prison. Eventually two of these were found guilty of treason, but were pardoned by Washington on the grounds that one was a "simpleton" and the other "insane." The government had made its point and gained "reputation and strength," according to Hamilton, by suppressing a rebellion which, according to Jefferson, "could never be found," but it was at the cost of creating or confirming new numbers of Republicans who scored heavily in the next Pennsylvania elections. Nor was it the end of whiskey rebellions, which continued in an unending war of wits between moonshiners and revenuers down to the day of twentieth-century rum-runners in hopped-up stock cars.

PINCKNEY'S TREATY   While these stirring events were transpiring in the Keystone State, Spain was suffering some setbacks to her schemes farther south. Spanish intrigues among the Creeks, Choctaws, Chickasaws, and Cherokees were keeping up the same turmoil the British fomented along the Ohio. Washington had sought to buy peace by payment of $100,000 and a commission as brigadier-general to the Creek chief, Alexander McGillivray, the half-blooded son of a Scottish trader, but it was to no avail. In 1793, therefore, John Sevier and some settlers from East Tennessee took it upon themselves to teach the proud Cherokees a lesson by leveling a few of their villages, and in 1794 James Robertson with some Tennesseans from around Nashville smote them again, burning and killing without pity.

The collapse of Spain's own designs in the west combined with Britain's concessions to the north to give some second thoughts to the Spanish, who were preparing to make peace with the French and switch sides in the European war. Among the more agreeable fruits of Jay's talks, therefore, were new parleys with the Spanish government, culminating in the Treaty of San Lorenzo (1795) in which the Spanish Government conceded every substantial point at issue. United States Minister Thomas Pinckney won acceptance of a boundary at the Thirty-first Parallel, free navigation of the Mississippi, the right to deposit goods at

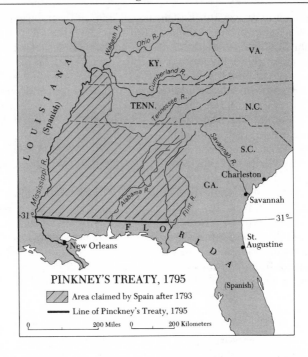

PINKNEY'S TREATY, 1795

Area claimed by Spain after 1793

Line of Pinckney's Treaty, 1795

0   200 Miles   0   200 Kilometers

New Orleans for three years with promise of renewal, a commission to settle American claims against Spain, and a promise on each side to refrain from inciting Indian attacks on the other. Ratification of the Pinckney Treaty ran into no opposition at all.

Now that Jay and Pinckney had settled things with Britain and Spain, and General Wayne in the Northwest and the Tennessee settlers to the south had smashed the Indians, the West was open for a renewed surge of settlers. New lands, ceded by the Indians in the Treaty of Greenville, revealed Congress once again divided on land policy. There were two basic viewpoints on the matter, one that the public domain should serve mainly as a source of revenue, the other that it was more important to accommodate settlers with low prices, maybe free land, and get the country settled. In the long run the evolution of policy would be from the first toward the second viewpoint, but for the time being the government's need for revenue took priority.

Opinions on land policy, like other issues, separated Federalists from Republicans. Federalists involved in speculation might prefer lower land prices, but the more influential Federalists like Hamilton and Jay preferred to build the population of the eastern states first, lest the East lose political influence and lose a labor force important to the future growth of manufactures. Men of their persuasion wanted high land prices to enrich the treasury, sale of relatively large parcels of land to speculators rather than small amounts to actual settlers, and the development of compact settlements. In addition to his other reports, Hamilton had put out one on the public lands in which he emphasized the need for governmental revenues. Jefferson and Madison at this point were prepared reluctantly to go along for the sake of reducing the national debt, but Jefferson expressed the hope for a plan by which the lands could be more readily settled. In any case, he suggested, frontiersmen would do as they had done before: "They will settle the lands in spite of everybody." The Daniel Boones of the West, always moving out beyond the settlers and surveyors, were already proving him right.

But for the time Federalist policy prevailed. In the Land Act of 1796 Congress resolved to extend the rectangular surveys ordained in 1785, but it doubled the price to $2 per acre, with only a year in which to complete payment. Half the townships would

A farm newly cleared and settled in the West (1793). [New York Public Library]

go in 640-acre sections, making the minimum cost $1,280, and alternate townships would be sold in blocks of eight sections, or 5,120 acres, making the minimum cost $10,240. Either was beyond the means of most ordinary settlers, and a bit much even for speculators who could still pick up state lands at lower prices. By 1800 government land offices had sold fewer than 50,000 acres under the act. Continuing pressures from the West led to the Land Act of 1800 (introduced by a nonvoting territorial delegate from Indiana named William Henry Harrison) which reduced the minimum sale to 320 acres and spread the payments over four years. Thus with a down payment of $160 one could get a farm. All lands went for the minimum price if they did not sell at auction within three weeks. Under the Land Act of 1804 the minimum unit was reduced to 160 acres, which became the traditional homestead, and the price per acre went down to $1.64.

WASHINGTON'S FAREWELL By 1796 President Washington had decided that two terms in office were enough. Tired of the political quarrels and the venom of the partisan press, he was ready to retire once and for all to Mount Vernon. He would leave behind a formidable record of achievement: the organization of a national government with demonstrated power, establishment of the national credit, the recovery of territory previously withheld by Britain and Spain, stabilization of the northwestern frontier, the admission of three new states: Vermont (1791), Kentucky (1792), and Tennessee (1796). With the help of Jay and especially Hamilton, Washington set about preparing a valedictory address, using a draft prepared by Madison four years before.

Washington's Farewell Address, dated September 17, 1796, was not delivered as a speech. It was first published in the Philadelphia *Daily American Advertiser* two days later. It stated first his resolve to decline being considered for a third term. After that, most of the message dwelled on domestic policy, and particularly on the need for unity among the American people in backing their new government. Washington decried the spirit of sectionalism. "In contemplating the causes which may disturb our union," he wrote in one prescient passage, "it occurs as a matter of serious concern that any ground should have been furnished for characterizing parties by geographical discriminations—*Northern* and *Southern*, *Atlantic* and *Western*—whence designing men may endeavor to excite a belief that there is a real difference of local interests and views." He decried as strongly the spirit of party, while acknowledging a body of opinion that parties were "useful checks upon the administration of the government, and serve to keep alive the spirit of liberty." From the natural tendency of men there would always be enough spirit of party, however, to serve that purpose. The danger was partisan excess: "A fire not to be quenched, it demands a uniform vigilance to prevent its bursting into a flame, lest, instead of warming, it should consume."

In foreign relations, he said, America should show "good faith and justice toward all nations" and avoid either "an habitual hatred or an habitual fondness" for other countries. Europe, he noted, "has a set of primary interests which to us have none or a very remote relation. Hence she must be engaged in frequent controversies, the causes of which are essentially foreign to our concerns." The United States should keep clear of those quarrels. It was, moreover, "our true policy to steer clear of permanent alliances with any portion of the foreign world." A key word here is "permanent." Washington enjoined against any further permanent arrangements like that with France, still technically in effect. He did not speak of "entangling alliances"—that phrase would be used by Thomas Jefferson in his first inaugural address—and in fact specifically advised that "we may safely trust to temporary alliances for extraordinary emergencies."

Washington himself had not escaped the "baneful effects" of the party spirit, for during his second term the Republican press came to link him with the Federalist partisans. For the first time in his long career Washington was subjected to sustained, and often scurrilous, criticism. According to Benjamin F. Bache, grandson of Franklin and editor of the Philadelphia *Aurora,* the president was "a man in his political dotage" and "a supercilious tyrant." Washington never responded to such abuse in public but in private he went into towering rages. The effect of such abuse was to hasten his resolve to retire. On the eve of that event the *Aurora* proclaimed that "this day ought to be a Jubilee in the United States. . . . If ever a nation was debauched by a man, the American Nation has been debauched by Washington."

THE ADAMS YEARS

With Washington out of the race, the United States had its first partisan election for president. The logical choice of the Federalists would have been Washington's protégé Hamilton, the chief architect of their programs. But like many a later presidential candidate, Hamilton was not "available," however willing. His policies had left scars and made enemies. Nor did he suffer fools gladly, a common affliction of Federalist leaders, including the man on whom the choice fell. In Philadelphia, a caucus of Federalist congressmen chose John Adams as heir apparent with Thomas Pinckney of South Carolina, fresh from his triumph in Spain, as nominee for vice-president. The Republicans drafted Jefferson (any other choice would have been a surprise) and added geographical balance with Aaron Burr of New York, an ally of Clinton.

The rising strength of the Republicans, largely due to the smouldering resentment of Jay's Treaty, very nearly swept Jefferson into office, and perhaps would have but for the public appeals of the French ambassador Adet for his election—an action which, like the indiscretions of Citizen Genêt, backfired. Then, despite a Federalist majority among the electors, Alexander Hamilton thought up an impulsive scheme which very nearly threw the election away after all. Between Hamilton and Adams there had been no love lost since the Revolution, when Adams

THE PROVIDENTIAL DETECTION

An anti-Republican cartoon shows the American eagle arriving just in time to stop Thomas Jefferson from burning the Constitution on the "Altar to Gallic Despotism." [American Antiquarian Society]

had joined the movement to remove Hamilton's father-in-law, General Schuyler, from command of the Saratoga campaign. Thomas Pinckney, Hamilton thought, would be more subject to influence than the strong-minded Adams. He therefore sought to have South Carolina Federalists withhold a few votes from Adams and bring Pinckney in first. The Carolinians more than co-operated—they divided their vote between Pinckney and Jefferson—but New Englanders got wind of the scheme and dropped Pinckney. The upshot of Hamilton's intrigue was to cut Pinckney out of both offices and put Jefferson back in the capital as vice-president with sixty-eight votes, second to Adams's seventy-one.

Adams had behind him a distinguished career as a Massachusetts lawyer, a leader in the revolutionary movement and the Continental Congress, a diplomat in France, Holland, and Britain, and as vice-president. In two treatises on politics, the three-volume *Defense of the Constitution of Government of the United States* (1787–1788) and the less formidable *Discourse on Davila*° (1790), he had formally committed to paper a political philosophy that put him somewhere between Jefferson and Hamilton. He shared neither the one's faith in the common people nor the other's fondness for an aristocracy of "paper wealth . . . the madness of the many for the profit of the few." He favored the classic mixture of aristocratic, democratic, and monarchical elements though his use of "monarchical" interchangeably with "executive" exposed him to the attacks of Republicans who saw a monarchist in every Federalist. At times, in his manner and appearance, Adams was made out by his enemies to be a pompous ass, but his fondness for titles and protocol arose from a reasoned purpose to exploit men's "thirst for distinction." He was always haunted by a feeling that he was never properly appreciated—and he may have been right. He tried to play the role of disinterested executive which he outlined in his philosophy. And on the overriding issue of his administration, war and peace, he kept his head when others about him were losing theirs—probably at the cost of his reelection.

WAR WITH FRANCE Adams inherited from Washington his cabinet —the precedent of changing personnel with each new administration had not yet been set—and with them a party division, for three of the department heads looked to Hamilton for counsel: Timothy Pickering at State, Oliver Wolcott at the Treasury, and

°An Italian historian.

John Adams. [Adams National Historic Site, Quincy, Mass.]

Joseph McHenry at the War Department. Adams also inherited a menacing quarrel with France, a by-product of the Jay Treaty. When Jay accepted the British position that food supplies and naval stores—as well as war matériel—were contraband subject to seizure, the French reasoned that American cargoes in the British trade were subject to the same interpretation and loosed their corsairs in the West Indies with even more devastating effect than the British had in 1793–1794. By the time of Adams's inauguration in 1797 the French had plundered some 300 American ships, and had broken diplomatic relations. As ambassador to Paris, James Monroe had become so pro-French and so hostile to the Jay Treaty that Washington had felt impelled to remove him for his indiscretions. France then had refused to accept Monroe's replacement, Charles Cotesworth Pinckney, and ordered him out of the country.

Adams immediately acted to restore relations in the face of an outcry for war from the "High Federalists," including Secretary of State Pickering. Hamilton, to whom the group generally looked as their leader, agreed with Adams on this point and approved his last-ditch effort for a settlement. In October 1797 C. C. Pinckney returned to Paris with John Marshall and Elbridge Gerry (a Massachusetts Republican) for further negotiations. After long, nagging delays, the three commissioners were accosted by three French counterparts (whom Adams labeled X, Y, and Z in his report to Congress), agents of Foreign Minister Talleyrand, a past master of the diplomatic shakedown. The three delicately let it be known that negotiations could begin only if there were a loan of $12 million, a bribe of $250,000 to the five directors then heading the government, and suitable apologies for remarks recently made in Adams's message to Congress.

Such bribes were common eighteenth-century diplomatic practice—Washington himself had bribed a Creek chieftain and ransomed American sailors from Algerian pirates, each at a cost of $100,000—but Talleyrand's price was high merely for a promise to negotiate. The answer, according to the commissioners' report, was "no, no, not a sixpence." When the XYZ Affair broke in Congress and the public press, this was translated into the more stirring slogan first offered as a banquet toast by Robert Goodloe Harper: "Millions for defense but not one cent for tribute." And the expressions of hostility toward France rose to a crescendo—even the most partisan Republicans were hard put to make any more excuses, and many of them joined a cry for war. An undeclared naval war in fact raged in the West Indies (with some engagements in the Mediterranean and Indian Ocean) from 1798 to 1800, but Adams resisted a formal declaration of war. The French would have to bear the onus for that. Congress, however, authorized the capture of armed French ships, suspended commerce with France, and renounced the alliance of 1778, which was already a dead letter. Adams used the occasion to strengthen American defenses.

An American navy had ceased to exist at the end of the Revolution. Except for revenue cutters of the Treasury Department, no armed ships were available when Algerian brigands began to war on American commerce in 1794. As a result Congress had authorized the arming of six ships. These were incomplete in 1796 when Washington bought peace with the Algerians, but Congress allowed work on three to continue: the *Constitution*, the *United States*, and the *Constellation*, all completed in 1797. In 1798 Congress authorized a new Department of the Navy, headed first by Benjamin Stoddert, a Baltimore merchant. By the end of 1798 the number of naval ships had increased to twenty and by the end of 1799 to thirty-three. But before the end of 1798 an undeclared naval war had begun in the West Indies with the French capture of the American schooner *Retaliation* off Guadeloupe in November 1798.

While the naval war went on, a new army was authorized in 1798 as a 10,000-man force to serve three years. Adams called Washington from retirement to be its commander, agreeing to Washington's condition that he name his three chief subordinates. Washington sent in the names of Hamilton, Charles C. Pinckney, and Henry Knox. In the old army the three ranked in precisely the opposite order, but Washington insisted that Hamilton be his second in command. Adams relented, but resented the slight to his authority as commander-in-chief. The rift among Federalists thus widened further. Because of Washington's age, the choice meant that Hamilton would command the army in the field, if it ever took the field. But recruitment went slowly until well into 1799, by which time all fear of French invasion was dispelled. Hamilton continued to dream of imperial glory, though, planning the seizure of Louisiana and the Floridas to keep them out of French hands, even the invasion of South America, but these remained Hamilton's dreams.

Peace overtures began to come from Talleyrand even before the naval war was fully under way. In the autumn of 1798 Elbridge Gerry returned from Paris with the word. Adams decided to act on the information and took it upon himself, without consulting the cabinet, to name the American minister to the Netherlands, William Vans Murray, special envoy to Paris. The Hamiltonians, infected with a virulent attack of war fever, fought the nomination but finally compromised, in face of Adams's threat to resign, on a commission of three. Adams named Chief Justice Oliver Ellsworth and Gov. William R. Davie of North Carolina to accompany Murray. After a long delay they left late in 1799 and arrived to find themselves confronting a new government under First Consul Napoleon Bonaparte. By the Convention of 1800 they got the best terms they could from the triumphant Napoleon. In return for giving up all claims of indemnity for American losses they got the suspension of the French alliance and the end of the quasi-war. The Senate ratified, contingent upon outright abrogation of the alliance, and the agreement became effective on December 21, 1801.

THE WAR AT HOME   The real purpose of the French crisis all along, the more ardent Republicans suspected, was to create an excuse to put down the domestic opposition. The Alien and Sedition Acts of 1798 lent credence to their suspicions. These four measures, passed in the wave of patriotic war fever, limited freedom of speech and the press, and the liberty of aliens. Proposed by the High Federalists in Congress, they did not originate with Adams but had his blessing. Three of the four acts reflected hostility to foreigners, especially the French and Irish, a large number of whom had become active Republicans and were suspected of revolutionary intent. The Naturalization Act changed from five to fourteen years the residence requirement for citizenship. The Alien Act empowered the president to expel "dangerous" aliens on pain of imprisonment. The Alien Enemy Act authorized the president in time of declared war to expel or imprison enemy aliens at will. Finally, the Sedition Act defined as high misdemeanor any combination or conspiracy against legal measures of the government, including interference with federal officers and insurrection or riot. What is more, the law forbade writing, publishing, or speaking anything of "a false, scandalous and malicious" nature against the government or any of its officers.

Considering what Federalists and Republicans said about each other, the act, applied rigorously, could have caused the imprisonment of nearly the whole government itself. But the purpose was transparently partisan, designed to punish Republicans whom Federalists could scarcely distinguish from Jacobins and traitors. To be sure, perfervid Republican journalists were resorting to scandalous lies and misrepresentations, but so were Federalists; it was a time when both sides seemed afflicted with paranoia. But the fifteen indictments brought, with ten convictions, were all directed at Republicans and some for trivial matters. In the very first case Luther Baldwin of New Jersey was fined $100 for wishing out loud that the wad of a salute cannon might hit President Adams in his rear. The most conspicuous targets of prosecution were Republican editors, including Thomas Cooper, James Callender, and William Duane. Another target was a congressman, Matthew Lyon of Vermont, a rough-and-tumble Irishman who published censures of Adams's "continual grasp for power" and "unbounded thirst for ridiculous pomp, foolish adulation, and selfish avarice." For such libels Lyon got four months and a fine of $1,000, but from his cell he continued to write articles and letters for the Republican papers. The few convictions under the act only created martyrs to the cause of freedom of speech and the press, and exposed the vindictiveness of Federalist judges.

Lyon and the others based a defense on the unconstitutionality of the Sedition Act, but Federalist judges were scarcely inclined to entertain such notions. It ran against the Republican grain, anyway, to have federal courts assume the authority to declare laws unconstitutional. To offset the Alien and Sedition Acts, therefore, Jefferson and Madison conferred and brought forth drafts of what came to be known as the Kentucky and Virginia Resolutions. These passed the legislatures of the two states in November and December 1798, while further Kentucky Resolutions, adopted in November 1799, responded to counterresolutions from northern states. These resolutions, much alike in their arguments, denounced the Alien and Sedition Acts as unconstitutional and advanced what came to be known as the state compact theory. Since the Constitution arose as a compact among the states, the resolutions argued, it followed logically that the states should assume the right to say when Congress had exceeded its

Republican Rep. Matthew Lyon and the Connecticut Federalist Roger Griswald go at each other on the floor of the House (1798). Lyon soon became a target of the Sedition Act. [New York Public Library]

powers. The Virginia Resolutions, drafted by Madison, declared that states "have the right and are in duty bound to interpose for arresting the progress of the evil." The second set of Kentucky Resolutions, in restating the states' right to judge violations of the Constitution, added: "That a nullification of those sovereignties, of all unauthorized acts done under color of that instrument, is the rightful remedy."

The doctrines of interposition and nullification, revised and edited by later theorists, were destined to be used for causes unforeseen by the authors of the Kentucky and Virginia Resolutions. Years later Madison would disclaim the doctrine of nullification as developed by John C. Calhoun, but his own doctrine of "interposition" would resurface as late as the 1950s as a device to oppose racial integration. At the time, it seems, both men intended the resolutions to serve chiefly as propaganda, the opening guns in the political campaign of 1800. Neither Kentucky nor Virginia took steps to nullify or interpose its authority against enforcement of the Alien and Sedition Acts. Instead both called upon the other states to help them win a repeal. Jefferson counseled against any thought of violence, which was "not the

kind of opposition the American people will permit." He assured
fellow Virginian John Taylor that "the reign of witches" would
soon end, that it would be discredited by the arrival of the tax
collector more than anything else.

In 1798 Congress had imposed a direct tax on houses, land,
and slaves. The Alien and Sedition Acts touched comparatively
few individuals, but the tax reached every property holder in the
country. In eastern Pennsylvania the general discontent with the
tax reached the stage of armed resistance in Fries's Rebellion, an
incident that scarcely deserves so impressive a name. John Fries,
a Pennsylvania Dutch auctioneer, had led a group of armed men
to force the release of two tax evaders imprisoned at Bethlehem.
To suppress this "insurrection" President Adams sent army regulars and militiamen into Northampton County. But like the
Whiskey Rebellion five years before, the insurrection evaporated. The soldiers found not a rebellion but John Fries conducting an auction. He was arrested and brought to trial with two
others on inflated charges of treason. The three men were found
guilty twice, a second trial having been granted on appeal, and
twice sentenced to hang. President Adams, however, decided
that the men had not committed treason and granted them a pardon along with a general pardon to all participants in the affair.

REPUBLICAN VICTORY Thus as the presidential election of 1800
approached, grievances were mounting against Federalist policies: taxation to support an army that had little to do but chase
Pennsylvania farmers, the Alien and Sedition Acts which cast the
Republicans in the role of defending liberty, the lingering fears
of "monarchism," the hostilities aroused by Hamilton's programs, the suppression of the Whiskey Rebellion, and Jay's
Treaty. When Adams decided for peace in 1800, he probably
doomed his one chance for reelection: a wave of patriotic war
fever with a united party behind him. His decision gained him
much goodwill among the people at large, but left the Hamiltonians unreconciled and his party divided. In May 1800 the Federalists summoned enough unity to name as their candidates
Adams and C. C. Pinckney, brother of Thomas Pinckney, who
ran in 1796; they agreed to cast all their electoral votes for both.
But the Hamiltonians continued to snipe at Adams and his policies. Soon after his renomination Adams removed two of them
from his cabinet—Secretary of State Timothy Pickering and Secretary of War James McHenry—replacing them with two Virginians: John Marshall and Samuel Dexter. Hamilton struck back
with a pamphlet questioning Adams's fitness to be president, cit-

ing his "disgusting egotism." Intended for private distribution among Federalist leaders, the pamphlet reached the hands of Aaron Burr, who put it in circulation.

Jefferson and Burr, as the Republican candidates, once again represented the alliance of Virginia and New York. Jefferson, perhaps even more than Adams, became the target of villification as a Jacobin and an atheist. His election, people were told, would bring "dwellings in flames, hoary hairs bathed in blood, female chastity violated . . . children writing on the pike and halberd." Jefferson kept quiet, refused to answer the attacks, and directed the campaign by mail from his home at Monticello. He was advanced as the farmers' friend, the champion of states' rights, frugal government, liberty, and peace.

Adams proved more popular than his party, whose candidates generally fared worse than the president, but the Republicans edged him out by seventy-three electoral votes to sixty-five. The decisive states were New York and South Carolina, either of whom might have given the victory to Adams. But in New York

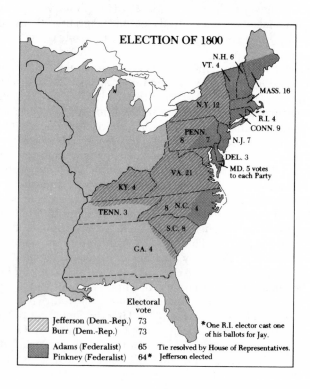

ELECTION OF 1800

N.H. 6
VT. 4
MASS. 16
N.Y. 12
R.I. 4
CONN. 9
PENN.
8   7
N.J. 7
DEL. 3
MD. 5 votes to each Party
VA. 21
KY. 4
TENN. 3
8 N.C. 4
S.C. 8
GA. 4

Electoral vote

Jefferson (Dem.-Rep.)   73
Burr (Dem.-Rep.)   73

Adams (Federalist)   65
Pinkney (Federalist)   64*

*One R.I. elector cast one of his ballots for Jay.

Tie resolved by House of Representatives. Jefferson elected

Burr's organization by vigorous activity won control of the legislature, which cast the electoral votes. In South Carolina, Charles
Pinckney (cousin to the Federalist Pinckneys) won over the legislature by well-placed promises of Republican patronage. Still,
the result was not final, for Jefferson and Burr had tied with seventy-three votes each, and the choice of the president was
thrown into the House of Representatives, where Federalist die-
hards tried vainly to give the election to Burr. This was too much
for Hamilton, who opposed Jefferson but held an even lower
opinion of Burr. Burr refused to assent to the Federalist movement, but neither would he renounce it. Eventually the deadlock
was broken when a confidant of Jefferson assured James A.
Bayard of Delaware that Jefferson would refrain from wholesale
removals of Federalists and uphold the new fiscal system. Bayard
resolved to vote for Jefferson, and several other Federalists
agreed simply to cast blank ballots, permitting Jefferson to win
without any of them actually having to vote for him.

Before the Federalists relinquished power on March 4, 1801,
their "lame duck" Congress passed the Judiciary Act of 1801.
This act provided that the next vacancy on the Supreme Court
should not be filled, created sixteen Circuit Courts with a new
judge for each, and increased the number of attorneys, clerks,
and marshals. Before he left office Adams named John Marshall
to the vacant office of Chief Justice and appointed good Federalists to all the new positions, including forty-two justices of the
peace for the new District of Columbia. The Federalists, defeated and destined never to regain national power, had in the
words of Jefferson "retired into the judiciary as a stronghold."

FURTHER READING

The best introduction to the early Federalists remains John C.
Miller's *The Federalist Era, 1789–1800* (1960).° Where Miller stresses
narrative detail, more recent works analyze the ideological debates
among the nation's first leaders. Richard Buel, Jr.'s *Securing the Revolution: Ideology in American Politics, 1789–1815* (1972),° and John
Zvesper's *Political Philosophy and Rhetoric: A Study of the Origins of
American Party Politics* (1977) trace the persistence of ideas first fostered during the Revolutionary crisis. Older but valuable studies of the
early parties include Joseph Charles's *The Origins of the American Party
System* (1956),° Richard Hofstadter's *The Idea of a Party System* (1969),

°These books are available in paperback editions.

and William D. Chambers's *Political Parties in a New Nation, the American Experience, 1776–1809* (1963).

The 1790s may be best understood through the views and behavior of national leaders. Among the studies of Federalist leaders are a number of biographies of Alexander Hamilton: Jacob Ernest Cook's *Alexander Hamilton* (1982), Forrest McDonald's *Alexander Hamilton: A Biography* (1979),° Gerald Stourzh's *Alexander Hamilton and the Idea of a Republican Government* (1970), Broadus Mitchell's *Alexander Hamilton: The National Adventure, 1788–1804* (1962), and John C. Miller's *Alexander Hamilton: Portrait in Paradox* (1959). For the nation's first president, consult the two volumes by James T. Flexner, *George Washington and the New Nation* (1969) and *George Washington: Anguish and Farewell* (1972). Forrest McDonald's *The Presidency of George Washington* (1974) is also helpful. The second president is handled in Page Smith's *John Adams* (2 vols.; 1962), Martin J. Dauer's *The Adams Federalists* (1969), and Stephen G. Kurtz's *The Presidency of John Adams: The Collapse of Federalism, 1795–1800* (1957).

The opposition viewpoint is the subject of Lance Banning's *The Jeffersonian Persuasion: Evolution of a Party Ideology* (1978). Noble E. Cunningham, Jr.'s *The Jeffersonian Republicans: The Formation of Party Organization, 1789–1801* (1957),° and Lawrence S. Kaplan's *Jefferson and France* (1967) help clarify political views. Biographies include Irving Brant's *James Madison: Father of the Constitution, 1787–1800* (1950), and Merrill Petersen's *Thomas Jefferson and the New Nation* (1970).°

State-level studies illuminate how the conflicts spread beyond the national capital. Consult Harry Tinkcom's *The Republicans and Federalists in Pennsylvania, 1790–1801: A Study in National Stimulus and Local Response* (1950), Paul Goodman's *The Democratic-Republicans of Massachusetts: Politics in a Young Republic* (1964), Alfred F. Young's *The Democratic Republicans of New York: The Origins, 1763–1797* (1967), and Norman Risjord's *Chesapeake Politics, 1781–1800* (1978).

The study of Federalist foreign policy begins with the work of Samuel F. Bemis: *Jay's Treaty* (1923) and *Pinckney's Treaty* (1926).° More recent is Jerald A. Combs's *The Jay Treaty* (1970). Surveys include Lawrence S. Kaplan's *Colonies into Nation: American Diplomacy, 1763–1801* (1972), Paul A. Varg's *Foreign Policies of the Founding Fathers* (1963), and Felix Gilbert's *To the Farewell Address: Ideas of Early American Foreign Policy* (1961). Albert H. Bowman's *Struggle for Neutrality* (1974) is more interpretative. Alexander De Conde breaks down foreign policies in the two Federalist administrations in *Entangling Alliance: Politics and Diplomacy under George Washington* (1958) and *The Quasi-War: The Politics and Diplomacy of the Undeclared War with France, 1797–1801* (1966).

Specific domestic issues are handled in several works. Leland D. Baldwin's *Whiskey Rebels: The Story of a Frontier Uprising* (1939) treats that incident. Patricia Watlingon's *The Partisan Spirit* (1972) examines the Kentucky Resolutions. Harry Ammon looks at the domestic conflicts engendered by *The Genet Mission* (1973).° The treatment of Indians in the old Northwest is handled in Richard H. Kohn's *Eagle and Sword: The Federalists and the Creation of the Military Establishment in America, 1783–1802* (1975). For the Alien and Sedition Acts, consult James Morton Smith's *Freedom's Fetters: The Alien and Sedition Laws and American Civil Liberties* (1956)° and Leonard W. Levy's *Legacy of Suppression: Freedom of Speech and Press in Early American History* (1960). Daniel Sisson's *The American Revolution of 1800* (1974) and Morton Borden's *The Federalism of James A. Bayard* (1955) are good on the election of 1800. The bureaucratic perspective is found in Leonard D. White's *The Federalists: A Study in Administrative History* (1948).°

9

REPUBLICANISM:
JEFFERSON AND MADISON

A NEW CAPITAL

On March 4, 1801, Thomas Jefferson became the first president to be inaugurated in the new Federal City, Washington, District of Columbia. The location of the city on the Potomac had been the fruit of Jefferson's and Madison's compromise with Hamilton on the assumption of state debts. Choice of the site had been entrusted to President Washington, who picked a location upstream from Mount Vernon and reaching from the village of Georgetown, Maryland, which it included, to the East Branch (now the Anacostia River). The District of Columbia at first took in land on the Virginia side of the Potomac, making it precisely ten miles by ten, but that portion was later ceded back to Virginia. In 1791 Maj. Pierre L'Enfant, a French engineer who had served in the Revolution, drew up the original plan for the district. Followed in its essence, the design called for a gridwork of parallel streets overlaid with diagonal avenues which radiated from various centers, most conspicuously Jenkins's Hill (site of the Capitol) and the site of the Executive Mansion, which faced each other along the length of Pennsylvania Avenue. L'Enfant also planned a third focus for the site of the Supreme Court, symbolizing the three branches of government, but that part of the plan was later abandoned, and the Court long occupied a room in the Capitol basement.

In accordance with the requirement of Congress, work progressed on the public buildings and the city during the 1790s,

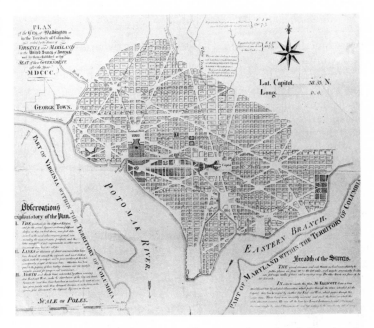

This Plan of the City of Washington *shows L'Enfant's detailed gridwork pattern of "Grand Avenues and Streets" (1800). [New York Public Library]*

and President Adams moved into his new home in September 1800. Abigail arrived at the "great castle" in October. It was "in a beautiful situation" with a view of the Potomac and Alexandria, but all the rooms were new and unfinished. By November the Adams family had to keep thirteen fires daily, she said, "or sleep in wet and damp places." Nearby Georgetown, D.C., where Abigail was obliged to market, was "the very dirtyest hole . . . for a place of any trade, or respectability of inhabitants." When Jefferson took office, Washington was still an unprepossessing array of buildings around two centers, Capitol Hill and the Executive Mansion. Between them was a swampy wilderness traversed by the Tiber River and by Pennsylvania Avenue, still full of stumps and mud holes, but with a stone walkway which offered a vantage from which to shoot ducks, snipe, partridge, and, after rains, the perch in the Tiber River! The Congress, having met in eight different towns and cities since 1774, had at least found a permanent home, but as yet enjoyed few amenities. There were only a few sad houses, "most of them small miserable huts," according to Oliver Wolcott, Adams's secretary of the treasury. To a

French acquaintance Sen. Gouverneur Morris wrote: "We lack here only houses, wine cellars, learned men, amiable women, and other trifles to make our city perfect . . . it is the best city in the world to live in—in the future." There were two places of amusement, one a racetrack, the other a theater filled with "tobacco smoke, whiskey breaths, and other strenches, mixed up with the effluvia of stables, and miasmas of the canal. . . . " Practically deserted much of the year, the town came to life only when Congress assembled.

JEFFERSON IN OFFICE

The inauguration of Jefferson befitted the surroundings. The new president left his lodgings and walked two blocks to the unfinished Capitol, entered the Senate chamber and took the oath from Chief Justice John Marshall, read his inaugural address in a barely audible voice, and returned to his boarding house for dinner and the common table. John Adams was absent. He had quietly slipped away, which was just as well according to his descendant, the historian Henry Adams, since "he would have seemed, in his successor's opinion, as little in place as George III would have appeared at the inauguration of President Washington." A tone of simplicity and conciliation ran through Jeffer-

Republican victory banner. The American eagle proclaims Jefferson president, and John Adams "No More." [Smithsonian Institution]

son's inaugural address, its seeming artlessness the product of three laborious drafts: "We are all Republicans—we are all Federalists. If there be any among us who would wish to dissolve this Union or to change its republican form, let them stand undisturbed as monuments of the safety with which error of opinion may be tolerated where reason is left free to combat it."

After this eloquent affirmation of freedom, he proceeded to a ringing affirmation of republican govenment: "I know, indeed, that some honest men fear that a republican government cannot be strong; that this government is not strong enough. But would the honest patriot, in the full tide of successful experiment, abandon a government which has so far kept us free and firm, on the theoretic and visionary fear that this government, the world's best hope, may by possibility want energy to preserve itself? I trust not. I believe this, on the contrary, the strongest government on earth. I believe it is the only one where every man . . . would meet invasions of the public order as his own personal concern. Sometimes it is said that man cannot be trusted with the government of himself. Can he, then, be trusted with the government of others? Or have we found angels in the form of kings to govern him? Let history answer this question."

Jefferson's "happy faculty of condensing whole chapters into aphorisms," as one of his biographers put it, was displayed in his summary of the "essential principles" that would guide his administration: "Equal and exact justice to all men. . . ; peace commerce, and honest friendship with all nations, entangling alliances with none. . . ; freedom of religion; freedom of the press; and freedom of person, under the protection of the habeas corpus; and trial by juries impartially selected. . . . The wisdom of our sages and the blood of our heroes have been devoted to their attainment."

The deliberate display of republican simplicity at Jefferson's inauguration would become the style of his administration. He took pains to avoid the occasions of pomp and circumstance which had characterized Federalist administrations and which to his mind suggested the trappings of kingship. Presidential messages went to Congress in writing lest they resemble the parliamentary speech from the throne. The practice also allowed Jefferson, a notoriously bad public speaker, to exploit his skill as a writer.

Jefferson discarded the coach and six in which Washington and Adams had gone to state occasions and rode about the city on horseback, often by himself. But this was, at least in part, therapy recommended by a doctor, and in part because Washington's

A watercolor of the president's house in 1800. Jefferson called it "big enough for two emperors, one pope, and the grand lama in the bargain." [The Warder Collection]

rutted streets were hardly the place for a carriage. The formal levee was abandoned for an informal weekly reception to which all were invited. Dinners at the White House were held around a circular table, so that none should take precedence, and at social affairs the new president simply ignored the rules of protocol for what he called the rule of *pele mele,* in which the only custom observed was that the ladies went ahead of the men. "When brought together in society, all are perfectly equal," Jefferson said.

It was not that Jefferson had ceased to be the Virginia gentleman, nor that he had abandoned elegant manners or the good life. The cuisine of his French chef and the wines for his frequent dinners strained his budget to the point that he had to borrow money and he left office with a debt which was to pursue him the rest of his life. The dinners also strained the patience of British Minister Anthony Merry, who had already taken umbrage at being received by a president "standing in slippers down at the heels, and both pantaloons, coat and underclothes indicative of an indifference to appearance." Perhaps it was a calculated slight to the minister of George III, who had behaved rudely when the author of the Declaration was presented to him in 1786.

Jefferson liked to think of his election as the "Revolution of 1800," but the margin had been close and the policies which he followed were more conciliatory than revolutionary. That they suited the vast majority of the people is attested to by his overwhelming reelection in 1804. Perhaps the most revolutionary thing about Jefferson's presidency was the orderly transfer of power in 1801, an uncommon event in the world of that day.

"The changes of administration," a Washington lady wrote in her diary, "which in every age have most generally been epochs of confusion, villainy and bloodshed, in this our happy country take place without any species of distraction, or disorder." Jefferson placed in policy-making positions men of his own party, and was the first president to pursue the role of party leader, assiduously cultivating congressional support at his dinner parties and otherwise. It was a role he had not so much sought as fallen into; he still shared the eighteenth-century distrust of the party spirit. In the cabinet the leading fixtures were Secretary of State James Madison, a longtime neighbor and political collaborator, and Secretary of the Treasury Albert Gallatin, a Pennsylvania Republican whose financial skills had won him the respect of Federalists. In an effort to cultivate Federalist New England, Jefferson chose men from that region for the positions of attorney-general, secretary of war, and postmaster-general.

In lesser offices, however, Jefferson refrained from wholesale removal of Federalists, preferring to wait until vacancies appeared, a policy which led to his rueful remark that vacancies obtained "by death are few; by resignation, none." But the pressure from Republicans was such that he often yielded and removed Federalists, trying as best he could to assign some other than partisan causes for the removals. In one area, however, he managed to remove the offices rather than the appointees. In 1802 Congress repealed the Judiciary Act of 1801, and so abolished the circuit judgeships and other offices to which Adams had made his "midnight appointments." A new judiciary act restored to six the number of Supreme Court justices, and set up six circuit courts, each headed by a justice.

MARBURY V. MADISON   It was in the judiciary, however, that Jefferson suffered the chief setbacks of his first term, especially in the case of *Marbury v. Madison*, a case of little intrinsic significance but one which set a precedent of great import. The case involved the appointment of one William Marbury as Justice of the peace in the District of Columbia. Marbury's commission, signed by President Adams two days before he left office, was still undelivered when Madison took office as secretary of state, and Jefferson directed him to withhold it. Marbury then sued for a court order (a writ of mandamus) directing Madison to deliver his commission. The Court's unanimous opinion, written by John Marshall, held that Marbury was entitled to his commission, but then denied that the Court had jurisdiction in the case. Section 13 of the Judiciary Act of 1789, which gave the Court original jurisdiction in mandamus proceedings, was unconstitutional, the court ruled, because the Constitution specified that the Court should have original jurisdiction only in cases involving ambassadors or states. With one bold stroke Marshall avoided an awkward confrontation with an administration which might have defied his order and at the same time established the precedent that the Court could declare a federal law invalid on the grounds that it violated provisions of the Constitution. The precedent of judicial review was not followed again for fifty-four years, but the principle was fixed for want of a challenge.

PARTISAN SQUABBLES The decision, about which Jefferson could do nothing, confirmed his fear of the judges' tendency to "throw an anchor ahead, and grapple further hold for future advances of power." In 1804 Republicans finally determined to use the impeachment power against two of the most partisan Federalist judges, and succeeded in ousting one of the two. The Republican House brought impeachments against District Judge John Pickering of New Hampshire and Justice Samuel Chase. Pickering was clearly insane, not a high crime or misdemeanor, but he was also given to profane and drunken harangues from the bench, which the Senate quickly decided was. In any event he was incompetent.

The case against Justice Chase, a much bigger matter, was less cut and dried. That he was highhanded and intemperate there was no question. Chase had presided at the sedition trials of two Republican editors, ordering a marshal to strike off the jury panel "any of those creatures or persons called democrats," and once attacked the Maryland consitution from the bench because it granted manhood suffrage, under which "our republican Constitution will sink into a mobocracy." But neither Jefferson nor the best efforts of John Randolph of Roanoke as prosecutor for the House could persuade two-thirds of the senators that Chase's vindictive partisanship constituted "high crimes and misdemeanors." His removal indeed might have set off the partisanship of Republicans in a political carnival of reprisals. His acquittal discouraged further efforts at impeachment, however, which Jefferson pronounced a "farce," after the failure to remove Chase.

DOMESTIC REFORMS Aside from these setbacks, however, Jefferson for a while had things pretty much his own way. His first term was a succession of triumphs in both domestic and foreign affairs. He did not set out to dismantle Hamilton's program root and branch. Under Gallatin's tutoring he learned to accept the national bank as an essential convenience, and did not push a measure for the bank's repeal which more dogmatic Republicans sponsored. It was too late of course to undo Hamilton's funding and debt assumption operations, but none too soon in the opinion of both Jefferson and Gallatin to set the resultant debt on the way to extinction. At the same time Jefferson insisted on the repeal of the whiskey tax and other Federalist excises. Gallatin, former champion of the "whiskey boys" in Pennsylvania politics, had a change of heart after he took over the treasury, but Jefferson was adamant. The excises were repealed in 1802 and Jefferson won the undying gratitude of bibulous backwoodsmen.

Without the excises, frugality was all the more necessary to a government dependent for revenue chiefly on customs duties and the sale of western lands. Happily for Gallatin's treasury, both flourished. The tragedy of war that had engulfed Europe brought a continually increasing traffic to American shipping and thus revenues to the customs. And settlers flocked into the western lands, which were coming more and more within their reach. The admission of Ohio to statehood in 1803 increased to seventeen the number of states.

By the "wise and frugal government" promised in the inaugural, Jefferson and Gallatin reasoned, the United States could live within its income, like a prudent husbandman. The basic formula was simple: cut back expenses on the military. A standing army was a menace to a free society anyway, and therefore should be kept to a minimum and defense left, in Jefferson's words, to "a well-disciplined militia, our best reliance in peace, and for the first moments of war, till regulars may relieve them. . . ." The navy, which the Federalists had already reduced after the quasi-war with France, ought to be reduced further. Coastal defense, Jefferson argued, should rely on fortifications and a "mosquito fleet" of small gunboats.

In 1807 the record of Jeffersonian reforms was crowned by an act which outlawed the foreign slave trade as of January 1, 1808, the earliest date possible under the Constitution. At the time South Carolina was the only state that still permitted the trade, having reopened it in 1803. But for years to come an illegal traffic would continue. By one informal estimate perhaps 300,000 slaves were smuggled in between 1808 and 1861.

THE BARBARY PIRATES   Issues of foreign relations intruded on Jefferson early in his term. Events in the Mediterranean quickly gave him second thoughts about the need for a navy. On the Barbary Coast of North Africa the rulers of Morocco, Algeria, Tunis, and Tripoli had for years filled their coffers by means of piracy and extortion. After the Revolution American shipping in the Mediterranean became fair game, no longer protected by British payments of tribute. The new American government yielded up protection money too, first to Morocco in 1786, then to the others in the 1790s. In May 1801, however, the pasha of Tripoli upped his demands and declared war on the United States by the symbolic gesture of chopping down the flagpole at the United States Consulate. Rather than give in to this, Jefferson sent warships to blockade Tripoli, and a wearisome warfare dragged on until 1805, punctuated in 1804 by the notable exploit of Lt. Stephen Decatur who slipped into Tripoli harbor by night and set fire to the frigate *Philadelphia,* which had been captured (along with its crew) after it ran aground. Before the war ended William Eaton, consul at Tunis, staged an unlikely land invasion of Tripoli from Egypt. With fifteen United States Marines, about forty Greek soldiers, and some restless Arabs, he advanced across the desert and took Derna. But in 1805 the pasha settled for $60,000 ransom and released the crew of the *Philadelphia* (mostly British subjects) whom he had held hostage more than a year. It was still tribute, but less than the $300,000 the pasha had demanded at first, and much less than the cost of the war.

THE LOUISIANA PURCHASE   It was an inglorious end to a shabby affair, but well before it was over events elsewhere had conspired to produce the greatest single achievement of the Jefferson administration, the Louisiana Purchase of 1803, which more than doubled the territory of the United States by bringing into its borders the entire Mississippi Valley west of the river itself. Louisiana, settled by the French, had been ceded to Spain in 1763. Since that time the dream of retaking Lousiana had stirred in the minds of Frenchmen. In 1800 Napoleon Bonaparte secured its return in exchange for a promise (never-fulfilled) to set up a Spanish princess and her husband in Italy as rulers of an enlarged Tuscany. When unofficial word of the deal reached Washington in May 1801, Jefferson hastened Robert R. Livingston, the new minister to France, on his way. Spain in control of the Mississippi outlet was bad enough, but Napoleon in control could only mean serious trouble. "There is on the globe one single spot the possessor of which is our natural and habitual enemy," Jefferson wrote Livingston. "The day that France takes possession of New Orleans . . . we must marry ourselves to the British fleet and nation," not at all the happiest prospect Jefferson ever faced.

Livingston had instructions to talk the French out of it, if it was not too late. If Louisiana had become French he should try to get West Florida (once part of French Louisiana) either from France or with French help. Late Secretary of State Madison told him to seek a price for New Orleans and the Floridas, but Spain still held the Floridas, as it turned out. On into 1803 long and frustrating talks dragged out. Early that year James Monroe was made minister plenipotentiary to assist Livingston in Paris, but no sooner had he arrived in April than Napoleon's minister, Talleyrand, surprised Livingston by asking if the United States would like to buy the whole of Louisiana. Livingston, once he could regain his composure, snapped at the offer.

Napoleon's motives in the whole affair can only be surmised. At first he seems to have thought of a New World empire, but that plan took an ugly turn in French Sainte Domingue (later Haiti). There during the 1790s the revolutionary governments of France had lost control to a black revolt. In 1802, having just patched up the temporary Peace of Amiens with the British, Napoleon thought to improve the occasion by sending a force to subdue the island. By a ruse of war the French captured the black leader, Toussaint l'Ouverture, but then fell victim to guerrilas and yellow fever. Napoleon's plan may have been discouraged too by the fierce American reaction when the Spanish governor of Louisiana closed the Mississippi to American traffic in October 1802, on secret orders from Madrid. In the end Napoleon's purpose seems to have been simply to cut his losses, turn a quick profit, mollify the Americans, and go back to reshaping the map of Europe.

By the treaty of cession, dated April 30, 1803, the United States paid 60 million francs, approximately $11¼ million, for Louisiana. By a separate agreement the United States also agreed to assume French debts owed to American citizens up to 20 million francs, or $3¾ million—making the total price about $15 million. In defining the boundaries of Louisiana the treaty was vague. Its language could be stretched to provide a tenuous claim on Texas and a much stronger claim on West Florida, from Baton Rouge on the Mississippi past Mobile to the Perdido River on the east. When Livingston asked about the boundaries, Talleyrand responded: "I can give you no direction. You have made a noble bargain for yourselves, and I suppose you will make the most of it." Napoleon himself observed: "If an obscurity did not exist, perhaps it would be good policy to put it there."

The turn of events had indeed presented Jefferson with a noble bargain, a great new "empire of liberty," but also with a constitutional dilemma. Nowhere did the Constitution provide for or even mention the purchase of territory. By a strict construction, which Jefferson had professed, no such power existed. Jefferson at first thought to resolve the matter by amendment, but his advisers argued against delay lest Napoleon change his mind. The power to purchase territory, they reasoned, resided in the power to make treaties. Jefferson relented, trusting, he said, "that the good sense of our country will correct the evil of loose construction when it shall produce ill effects." New England Federalists boggled at the prospect of new states that would probably strengthen the Jeffersonian party and centered their fire on a proviso that the inhabitants be "incorporated in the Union" as citizens. In a reversal that foretokened many future reversals on constitutional issues, Federalists found themselves arguing strict construction of the Constitution while Republicans brushed aside such scruples in favor of implied power.

In October 1803 the Senate ratified the treaty by an overwhelming vote of 26 to 6. Both houses of Congress voted the necessary money and made provision for the govenment of the new territory. On December 20, 1803, Gov. William C. C. Clairborne and Gen. James Wilkinson took formal possession of Louisiana from a French agent who had taken over from Spanish authorities only three weeks before. For the time the Spanish kept West Florida, but within a decade it would be ripe for the plucking. In 1808 Napoleon put his brother on the throne of Spain. With the Spanish colonial administration in disarray, American settlers in 1810 staged a rebellion in Baton Rouge and proclaimed the Republic of West Florida, quickly annexed and occupied by the United States as far eastward as the Pearl River. In 1812 the state of Louisiana absorbed the region—still known as the Florida parishes. In 1813, with Spain itself a battlefield for French and British forces, General Wilkinson took over the rest of West Florida, now the Gulf coast of Mississippi and Alabama. Legally, the American government has claimed ever since, all these areas were included in the original Louisiana Purchase.

EXPLORING THE CONTINENT As an amateur scientist long before he was president, Jefferson had nourished an active curiosity about the Louisiana country, its geography, its flora and fauna, its prospects for trade. In January 1803 he asked Congress for money to send an exploring expedition to the far northwest, beyond the Mississippi, in what was still foreign territory. Congress approved and Jefferson assigned as commanders Meriwether Lewis, who as the president's private secretary had been groomed for the job, and another Virginian, William Clark, the much younger brother of George Rogers Clark.

During the winter of 1803–1804 a party of soldiers gathered at St. Louis and in May 1804 the "Corps of Discovery," numbering nearly fifty, set out to ascend the Missouri River. Six months later, near the Mandan Sioux villages in what was later North Dakota, they built Fort Mandan and wintered there in relative comfort, sending back downriver a barge loaded with specimens such as the prairie dog, previously unknown to science, and the magpie, previously unknown in America. Jefferson kept the great horns of a wapiti to display at Monticello. In the spring they added to the main party a French guide, who was little help, and his remarkable Shoshone wife, Sacajawea ("Canoe Launcher"),

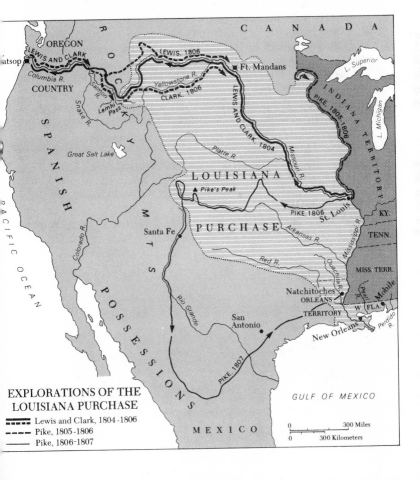

EXPLORATIONS OF THE LOUISIANA PURCHASE

▬▬▬ Lewis and Clark, 1804-1806
▬ ▬ ▬ Pike, 1805-1806
───── Pike, 1806-1807

an enormous help as interpreter and go-between with the Indians of the region, and set out once again upstream. At the head of the Missouri they took the north fork, thenceforth the Jefferson River, crossed the continental divide at Lemhi Pass and in dugout canoes descended the Snake and Columbia Rivers to the Pacific. Near the later site of Astoria at the mouth of the Columbia they built Fort Clatsop in which they spent another winter. The following spring they headed back by almost the same route, and after a swing through the Yellowstone country returned to St. Louis in September 1806, having been gone nearly two and a half years.

No longer was the Far West unknown country. Although it was nearly a century before a good edition of the *Journals of Lewis and Clark* appeared in print, many of their findings came out piecemeal, including an influential map in 1814. Convinced that they had found a practical route for the China trade, Lewis and Clark were among the last to hold out hope for a water route through the continent. Their reports of friendly Indians and abundant pelts attracted traders and trappers to the region very quickly, and also gave the United States a claim to the Oregon country by right of discovery and exploration. It would have strained the genius even of a Talleyrand to extend a claim to the Louisiana country beyond the Rocky Mountains.

From the Journals of Lewis and Clark, *this is Clark's sketch of a Chinook alâkân, or candlefish, discovered on February 24, 1806. [The Warder Collection]*

While Lewis and Clark were gone, Jefferson sent other explorers up the Ouachita and Red Rivers, but with little profit to geographical knowledge. More important were the travels of Lt. Zebulon Pike. Sent out by General Wilkinson in 1805–1806 to find the source of the Mississippi River, he mistakenly picked a tributary, later discoveries showed, but contributed to knowledge of the upper Mississippi Valley. Then, during 1806–1807, he went out to the headwaters of the Arkansas River as far as Colorado, discovered Pike's Peak but failed in an attempt to climb it, and made a roundabout return by way of Santa Fe, courtesy of Spanish soldiers who captured his party. Pike's account, while less reliable and less full than that of Lewis and Clark, appeared first and gave Americans their first overall picture of the Great Plains and Rocky Mountains. It also contributed to the widespread belief that the arid regions of the West constituted a Great American Desert, largely unfit for human habitation.

POLITICAL SCHEMES   Jefferson's policies, including the Louisiana Purchase, brought him almost solid support in the South and West. Even New Englanders were moving to his side. By 1809 John Quincy Adams, the son of the second president, would become a Republican! Die-hard Federalists read the handwriting on the wall. The acquisition of a vast new empire in the west would reduce New England to insignificance in political affairs, and along with it the Federalist cause. Under the leadership of Sen. Timothy Pickering, a group of Massachusetts bitter-enders called the Essex Junto began to think about secession from the Union, an idea that would simmer in certain New England circles for another decade. Rather than accede to a Union formed in the image of Jeffersonian Republicanism, they would withdraw.

Soon they hatched a scheme to link New York with New England and contacted Vice-President Aaron Burr, who had been on the outs with the Jeffersonians long since and who was, as ever, ready for subterranean schemes. Their plan depended on Burr's election as governor of New York. In April 1804, however, Burr was overwhelmed by the regular Republican candidate. The extreme Federalists it turned out, could not even hold members of their own party to the plan, which Hamilton bitterly opposed on the grounds that Burr was "a dangerous man, and one who ought not to be trusted with the reins of government." When Hamilton's remarks appeared in the public press, Burr's demand for an explanation led to a duel at Weehawken, New Jersey, in which Hamilton was mortally wounded. Hamilton personally opposed dueling but his romantic streak and sense of honor compelled him to demonstrate his courage, long since established beyond any question at Yorktown. He went to his death, as his son had done in a similar affair the previous year, determined not to fire at his opponent. Burr was unhampered by such scruples. The death of Hamilton ended both Pickering's scheme and Burr's political career— but not his intrigues.

Meanwhile the presidential campaign of 1804 got under way when a congressional caucus of Republicans on February 25 renominated Jefferson and chose George Clinton for vice-president. Opposed by the Federalists Charles Coteworth Pinckney and Rufus King, Jefferson and Clinton won 162 of 176 electoral votes. Only Connecticut and Delaware recorded solid opposition. Jefferson's policy of conciliation had made him a national rather than a sectional candidate. With some pride, Jefferson said in his second inaugural address that he had carried out the general policies announced in the first: "The suppression of unnecessary offices, of useless establishments and expenses, enabled us to discontinue our internal taxes. . . . What farmer, what mechanic, what laborer ever sees a tax-gatherer of the United States?"

DIVISIONS IN THE REPUBLICAN PARTY

RANDOLPH AND THE *TERTIUM QUID*   "Never was there an administration more brilliant than that of Mr. Jefferson up to this period," said John Randolph of Roanoke. "We were indeed in the full tide of successful experiment." But the Republican landslide had a sequel that would often follow such victories in later years. Freed from a strong opposition—Federalists made up only a quarter of the new Congress—the majority began to lose some of its cohesion. Cracks appeared in the Republican facade, portents of major fissures that would finally split the party as the Federalists faded into oblivion. Ironically, John Randolph of Roanoke, a Jeffersonian mainstay in the first term, became the most conspicious of the dissidents. A brilliant but erratic Virginian, left frustrated by a hormonal deficiency, given to fits of insanity in his later years, gifted with a talent for invective delivered in a shrill soprano voice, the Virginia congressman flourished best in opposition. Few of his colleagues had the stomach for one of his tongue-lashings.

Randolph, too much a loner for leadership, was spokesman for a shifting group of "Old Republicans," whose adherence to party principles had rendered them more Jeffersonian than Jefferson

The mercurial John Randolph of Roanoke, in a silhouette drawn from life by William H. Brown. [New York Public Library]

himself. Their philosopher was John Taylor of Carolina, a Virginia planter-pamphleteer whose fine-spun theories of states' rights and strict construction had little effect at the time but delighted the logic-choppers of later years. Neither Randolph nor Taylor could accept his leader's pragmatic gift for adjusting principle to circumstance.

Randolph first began to smell a rat in the case of the Yazoo Fraud, a land scheme which originated in Georgia but entangled speculators from all over. In 1795 the Georgia legislature had sold to four land companies, in which some of the legislators were involved, 35 million acres in the Yazoo country (Mississippi and Alabama) for $500,000 (little more than a penny an acre). A new legislature rescinded the sale the following year, but not before some of the land claims had been sold to third parties. When Georgia finally ceded her western lands to federal authority in 1802, Jefferson sought a compromise settlement of the claims but Randolph managed to block passage of the necessary measures and in the ensuing quarrels was removed as Speaker of the House. The snarled Yazoo affair plagued the courts and Congress for another decade. Finally, in the case of *Fletcher v. Peck* (1810), Chief Justice Marshall ruled that the original sale, however fraudulent, was a legal contract. The repeal impaired the obligation of contract and was therefore unconstitutional. Final settlement came in 1814 when Congress awarded $4.2 million to the speculators.

Randolph's definitive break with Jefferson came in 1806,

when the president sought an appropriation of $2 million for a thinly disguised bribe to the French to win their influence in persuading Spain to yield the Floridas to the United States. "I found I might co-operate or be an honest man—I have therefore opposed and will oppose them," Randolph said. Thereafter he resisted Jefferson's initiatives almost out of reflex. Randolph and his colleagues were sometimes called "Quids," or the *Tertium Quid* (the "third something"), and their dissents gave rise to talk of a third party, neither Republican nor Federalist. But they never got together. Some of the dissenters in 1808 backed James Monroe against Madison for the presidential succession, but the campaign quickly fizzled.

THE BURR CONSPIRACY John Randolph may have got enmeshed in dogma, but Aaron Burr was never one to let principle stand in the way. Born of a distinguished line of Puritans, including grandfather Jonathan Edwards, he cast off the family Calvinism early to pursue the main chance—and the women. Sheer brilliance and opportunism carried him to the vice-presidency. With a leaven of discretion he might easily have become heir-apparent to Jefferson, but a taste for intrigue was the tragic flaw in his character. Caught up in dubious schemes of Federalist die-hards in 1800 and again in 1804, he ended his political career once and for all when he killed Hamilton.

Searching then for new worlds to conquer, he turned to the West, and before he left office as vice-president he hatched the scheme that came to be known as the Burr Conspiracy. Just what he was up to probably will never be known, because Burr himself very likely was keeping some options open. He may have been getting up an expedition to conquer Mexico—some American freebooters had already pounced on Texas—or West Florida; he perhaps was out to organize a secession of Louisiana and set up an independent republic. On various pretexts he won the ear of the British and Spanish ministers in Washington (with whom he planted hints of a coup d'état in Washington), a variety of public figures in the East, and innumerable westerners, including two future presidents (William Henry Harrison and Andrew Jackson), and that noblest villain of them all, Gen. James Wilkinson, now governor of the Louisiana Territory but still in the pay of the Spanish government.°

In the summer of 1805 Burr sailed on a flatboat downriver all the way to New Orleans, propounding different schemes, lining

°The present state of Louisiana was then the Territory of Orleans. Wilkinson governed the rest of the Louisiana Purchase.

Aaron Burr, the brilliant but erratic vice-president. [New Jersey Historical Society]

up adventurers and dupes. By the summer of 1806 he was in Lexington, Kentucky, recruiting for an expedition to take up a land claim he had purchased in Arkansas, a likely staging area for a military enterprise or a fallback position if things went wrong. He arranged, but did not actually attend, the assembling of men, boats, and supplies on an island belonging to one of his confederates, a rich Irish refugee named Harmon Blennerhassett. Off they went, some sixty strong, to be joined downstream by Burr. But by now Burr's adventure had a cast of thousands, which was bound to cause talk. Rumors began to reach Jefferson, and in November 1806 so did a letter from Wilkinson warning of "a deep, dark, wicked and wide-spread conspiracy." Wilkinson was double-dealing with Spain and America, but Jefferson never suspected him of being anything but a patriot.

In January 1807, as Burr neared Natchez with his motley crew, he learned that Wilkinson had betrayed him and that Jefferson had ordered his arrest. He cut out cross-country toward Pensacola, but was caught and taken off to Richmond for a trial, which, like the conspiracy, had a stellar cast. Charged with treason by the grand jury, Burr was brought for trial before Chief Justice Marshall, then riding circuit. The issue revealed both Marshall and Jefferson at their partisan worst. Marshall was convinced that the "hand of malignity" was grasping at Burr, while Jefferson, determined to get a conviction at any cost, published relevant affidavits in advance and promised pardons to conspirators who helped convict Burr. Marshall in turn was so indiscreet as to attend a dinner given by the chief defense counsel at which Burr himself was present.

The case established two major constitutional precedents. First, Jefferson ignored a subpoena requiring him to appear in court with certain papers in his possession. He refused, as Washington had refused, to submit papers to the Congress on grounds of executive privilege. Both believed that the independence of the executive branch would be compromised if the president were subject to a court writ, a position since sustained by law. The second major precedent was the rigid definition of treason. On this Marshall adopted the strictest of constructions. Treason under the Constitution consists of "levying war against the United States or adhering to their enemies" and requires "two witnesses to the same overt act" for conviction. Since the prosecution failed to produce two witnesses to an overt act of treason by Burr, the jury brought in a verdict of not guilty.

Whether or not Burr escaped his just deserts, Marshall's strict construction of the Constitution protected the United States, as the authors of the Constitution clearly intended, against the capricious judgments of "treason" that governments through the centuries have used to terrorize dissenters. As to Burr, with further charges pending, he skipped bail and took refuge in France, but returned unmolested in 1812 to practice law in New York. He survived to a virile old age. At age eighty, shortly before his death, he was divorced on grounds of adultery.

War in Europe

Oppositionists of whatever stripe were more an annoyance than a threat to Jefferson. The more intractable problems of his second term were created by the renewal of the European war in 1803, which helped resolve the problem of Louisiana but put more strains on Jefferson's desire to avoid "entangling alliances" and the quarrels of Europe. In 1805 Napoleon's smashing defeat of Russian and Austrian forces at Austerlitz made him the master of western Europe. The same year Lord Nelson's defeat of the French and Spanish fleets in the Battle of Trafalgar secured Britain's control of the seas. The war resolved itself into a battle of elephant and whale, Napoleon dominant on land, the British dominant in the water, neither able to strike a decisive blow at the other, and neither restrained by an overly delicate sense of neutral rights or international law.

HARASSMENT BY BRITAIN AND FRANCE For two years after the renewal of hostilities things went well for American shipping, which took over trade with the French and Spanish West Indies.

But in the case of the *Essex* (1805), a British prize court ruled that the practice of shipping French and Spanish goods through American ports while on their way elsewhere did not neutralize enemy goods. Such a practice violated the British rule of 1756 (laid down by the British courts during the Seven Years' War) under which trade closed in time of peace remained closed in time of war. Goods shipped in violation of the rule, the British held, were liable to seizure at any point under the doctrine of continuous voyage. In 1807 the commercial provisions of Jay's Treaty expired and James Monroe, ambassador to Great Britain, failed to get a renewal satisfactory to Jefferson. After that, the British interference with American shipping increased, not just to keep supplies from Napoleon's continent but also to hobble competition with British merchantmen.

In a series of Orders in Council adopted in 1806 and 1807 the British ministry set up a paper blockade of Europe from Copenhagen to Trieste. Vessels headed for continental ports had to get licenses and accept British inspection or be liable to seizure. Napoleon retaliated with his "Continental System," proclaimed in the Berlin Decree of 1806 and the Milan Decree of 1807. In the first he declared a blockade of the British Isles and in the second he ruled that neutral ships which complied with British regulations were subject to seizure when they reached continental ports. The situation presented American shippers with a dilemma. If they complied with the demands of one side they were subject to seizure by the other.

It was humiliating, but the prospects for profits were so great that shippers ran the risk. For seamen the danger was heightened by a renewal of the practice of impressment. The use of press gangs to kidnap men in British (and colonial) ports was a long-standing method of recruitment for the British navy. The seizure of British subjects from American vessels became a new source of recruits, justified on the principle that British subjects remained British subjects for life: "Once an Englishman, always an Englishman." Mistakes might be made, of course, since it was sometimes hard to distinguish British subjects from native Americans; indeed a flourishing trade in fake citizenship papers had arisen in American ports. The humiliation of impressment was mostly confined to merchant vessels, but on at least two occasions before 1807 vessels of the American navy had been stopped on the high seas and seamen removed.

In the summer of 1807 the British *Leopard* accosted the American frigate *Chesapeake* off Norfolk, just outside territorial waters, and after its captain refused to be searched, the *Leopard* fired upon the *Chesapeake* at the cost of three killed and eighteen

Jefferson's Embargo, pictured here as a pesky snapping turtle (Ograbme), stops a tobacco trader. [New York Public Library]

wounded. The *Chesapeake*, unready for battle, was forced to strike its colors. A British search party seized four men, one of whom was later hanged for desertion from the British navy. Soon after the *Chesapeake* limped back into Norfolk, the Washington *Federalist* editorialized: 'We have never, on any occasion, witnessed the spirit of the people excited to so great a degree of indignation, or such a thirst for revenge. . . .'' Public wrath was so aroused that Jefferson could have had war on the spot. Had Congress been in session, he might have been forced into war. But Jefferson, like Adams before him, resisted the war fever and suffered politically as a result.

THE EMBARGO   Jefferson resolved to use public indignation as the occasion for an effort at "peaceable coercion." In December 1807, in response to his request, Congress passed the Embargo Act, which stopped all export of American goods and prohibited American ships from clearing for foreign ports. The constitutional basis of the embargo was the power to regulate commerce, which in this case Republicans interpreted broadly as the power to prohibit commerce. "Let the example teach the world that our firmness equals our moderation," said the *National Intelligencer*, "that having resorted to a measure just in itself, and adequate to its object, we will flinch from no sacrifices which the honor and good of the nation demand from virtuous and faithful citizens."

But Jefferson's embargo was a failure from the beginning for want of a will to make the necessary sacrifices. The idealistic spirit which had made economic pressures effective in the prerevolutionary crises was lacking. Trade remained profitable despite the risks, and violation of the embargo was almost laughably easy. Enforcement was lax, and loopholes in the act permitted ships to clear port under the pretense of engaging in coastal trade or whaling, or under an amendment passed a few months after the act, for the purpose of bringing home American property stored in foreign warehouses. Some 800 ships left on such missions, but few of them returned before the embargo expired. Trade across the Canadian border flourished. As it turned out, France was little hurt by the act. Napoleon in fact exploited it to issue the Bayonne Decree (1808), which ordered the seizure of American ships in continental ports on the pretext that they must be British ships with false papers. Or if they truly were American, Napoleon slyly noted, he would be helping Jefferson enforce the embargo. Some British manufacturers and workers were hurt by the lack of American cotton, but they carried little weight with the government, and British shippers benefited. With American ports closed, they found a new trade in Latin American ports thrown open by the colonial authorities when Napoleon occupied the mother countries of Spain and Portugal.

The coercive effect was minimal, and the embargo revived the moribund Federalist party in New England, which renewed the charge that Jefferson was in league with the French. The em-

This 1807 Federalist cartoon compares Washington, on the left, to Jefferson, on the right. Washington is flanked by the British lion and the American eagle, while Jefferson is flanked by a snake and a lizard. Below Jefferson are volumes by French philosophers. [New-York Historical Society]

bargo, one New Englander said, was "like cutting one's throat to cure the nosebleed." At the same time agriculture in the south and west suffered for want of outlets for grain, cotton, and tobacco. After fifteen months of ineffectiveness, Jefferson finally accepted failure and on March 1, 1809, signed a repeal of the embargo shortly before he relinquished the "splendid misery" of the presidency.

In the election of 1808 the succession passed to another Virginian, Secretary of State James Madison. Presidential trial balloons for James Monroe and George Clinton, launched by the Quids, never got off the ground, and Jefferson used his influence in the caucus of Republican congressmen to win the nomination for Madison. Clinton was again the candidate for vice-president. The Federalists, backing Charles Cotesworth Pinckney and Rufus King of New York, revived enough as a result of the embargo to win 47 votes to Madison's 122.

THE DRIFT TO WAR   Madison was entangled in foreign affairs from the beginning. Still insisting on neutral rights and freedom of the seas, he pursued Jefferson's policy of "peaceful coercion" by different but no less ineffective means. In place of the embargo Congress had substituted the Non-Intercourse Act, which reopened trade with all countries except France and Great Britain and authorized the president to reopen trade with whichever of these gave up its restrictions. British Minister David M. Erskine assured Madison's secretary of state that Britain would revoke its restrictions on June 10, 1809. With that assurance, Madison reopened trade with Britain, but Erskine had acted on his own and the foreign secretary, repudiating his action, recalled him. Nonintercourse resumed, but it proved as ineffective as the embargo. In the vain search for an alternative, Congress on May 1, 1810, reversed its ground and adopted a measure introduced by Nathaniel Macon of North Carolina, Macon's Bill No. 2, which reopened trade with the warring powers but provided that if either dropped its restrictions nonintercourse would be restored with the other.

This time Napoleon took a turn at trying to bamboozle Madison. Napoleon's foreign minister, the duc de Cadore, informed the American minister in Paris that he had withdrawn the Berlin and Milan Decrees, but the carefully worded Cadore letter had strings attached: revocation of the decrees depended on withdrawal of the British Orders in Council. The strings were plain to see, but either Madison misunderstood or, more likely, went along in hope of putting pressure on the British. The British refused to give in, but Madison clung to his policy despite Napoleon's continued seizure of American ships. The seemingly hopeless effort did indeed finally work. With more time, with more patience, with a transatlantic cable, Madison's policy would have been vindicated without resort to war. On June 16, 1812, the British foreign minister, facing economic crisis, announced revocation of the Orders in Council. Britain preferred not to risk war with the United States on top of its war with Napoleon. But on June 1 Madison had asked for war, and by mid-June the Congress concurred.

THE WAR OF 1812

CAUSES   The main cause of the war—the demand for neutral rights—seems clear enough. Neutral rights were the main burden of Madison's war message and the main reason for a mounting hostility toward the British. Yet the geographical distribution of the vote for war raises a troubling question. The preponderance of the vote for war came from members of Congress representing the agricultural regions from Pennsylvania southward and westward. The maritime states of New York and New England, the region that bore the brunt of British attacks on American trade, gave a majority against the declaration of war. One explanation for this seeming anomaly is simple enough. The farming regions were afflicted by the damage to their markets for grain, cotton, and tobacco, while New England shippers made profits in spite of British restrictions.

Other plausible explanations for the sectional vote, however, include frontier Indian depredations which were blamed on the British, western land hunger, and the desire for new lands in Canada and the Floridas. Indian troubles were endemic to a rapidly expanding West. Land-hungry settlers and speculators kept moving out ahead of government surveys and sales in search of fertile acres. The constant pressure to open new lands repeatedly forced or persuaded Indians to sign treaties they did not always understand, causing stronger resentment among tribes that were losing more and more of their lands. It was an old story, dating from the Jamestown settlement, but one that took a new turn with the rise of two Shawnee leaders, Tecumseh and his twin brother Tenskwatawa, "the Prophet."

Tecumseh, according to Gov. William Henry Harrison of the Indian Territory, was "one of those uncommon geniuses, which spring up occasionally to produce revolutions and overturn the order of things." He saw with blazing clarity the consequences of Indian disunity, and set out to form a confederation of tribes to

Tecumseh, the Shawnee leader who tried to unite the tribes in defense of their land. He was killed in 1813 at the Battle of the Thames. [Museum of Natural History]

defend Indian hunting grounds, insisting that no land cession was valid without the consent of all tribes since they held the land in common. His brother supplied the inspiration of a religious revival, calling upon the Indians to worship the "Master of Life," to resist the white man's firewater, and lead a simple life within their means. By 1811 Tecumseh had matured his plans and headed south to win the Creeks, Cherokees, Choctaws, and Chickasaws to his cause.

Governor Harrison saw the danger. He gathered a force and set out to attack Tecumseh's capital on the Tippecanoe River, Prophet's Town, while the leader was away. On November 7, 1811, the Indians attacked Harrison's encampment on the Tippecanoe River, although Tecumseh had warned against any fighting in his absence. The Shawnees were finally repulsed in a bloody engagement which left about a quarter of Harrison's men dead or wounded. Only later did Harrison realize that he had inflicted a defeat on the Indians, who had become demoralized and many of whom had fled to Canada. Harrison then burned their town and destroyed all its stores. Tecumseh's dreams went up in smoke, and Tecumseh himself fled to British protection in Canada.

The Battle of Tippecanoe reinforced suspicions that the British were inciting the Indians. Actually the incident was mainly Harrison's doing. With little hope of help from war-torn Europe, Canadian authorities had steered a careful course, discouraging warfare but seeking to keep the Indians' friendship and fur trade. To eliminate the Indian menace, frontiersmen reasoned, they needed to remove its foreign support. The province of Ontario was like a pistol pointed at the United States. Conquest of Canada would accomplish a twofold purpose. It would eliminate British influence among the Indians and open a new empire for land-hungry Americans. It was also the only place, in case of war, where the British were vulnerable to American attack. East Florida, still under the Spanish flag, posed a similar menace. Spain was too weak or unwilling to prevent sporadic Indian attacks across the frontier. The British too were suspected of smuggling through Florida and intriguing with the Indians on the southwest border.

One historian of the quarrels with Britain has suggested that "scholars have overemphasized the tangible, rational reasons for action and . . . have given too little heed to such things as national pride, sensitivity, and frustration, although the evidence for this sort of thing leaps to the eye." Madison's drift toward war was hastened by the rising temperature of war fever. In the Congress which assembled in November 1811 a number of new members from southern and western districts began to ring the changes, holding forth on "national honor" and British perfidy. Among them were Henry Clay of Kentucky, who became Speaker of the House, Richard M. Johnson of Kentucky, Felix Grundy of Tennessee, and John C. Calhoun of South Carolina. John Randolph of Roanoke christened them the "War Hawks." After they entered the House, Randolph said "We have heard but one word —like the whip-poor-will, but one eternal monotonous tone—Canada! Canada! Canada!"

PREPARATIONS As it turned out, the War Hawks would get neither Canada nor Florida. For James Madison had carried into war a country that was ill-prepared both financially and militarily. In 1811, despite earnest pleas from Treasury Secretary Gallatin, Congress had let the twenty-year charter of the Bank of the United States expire. A combination of strict-constructionist Republicans and anglophobes, who feared the large British interest in the bank, did it in. Also, state banks were often mismanaged, resulting in deposits lost through bankruptcy. Trade had approached a standstill and tariff revenues had declined. Loans were needed for about two-thirds of the war costs while northeast opponents to the war were reluctant to lend money. Government bonds were difficult to float.

War had been likely for nearly a decade, but Republican economy had prevented preparations. When, finally, late in 1811 the administration decided to fill up the army to its authorized strength of 10,000 and add an additional force of 10,000, Madison still faced the old arguments against the danger of a standing army. Sen. William B. Giles of Virginia, one of the Old Republicans, suggested an additional force of 25,000 to serve five years. His purpose was to embarrass the administration, because such a volunteer force probably could not be raised and would strain the country's resources. The War Hawks nevertheless supported the measure, and in a law passed on January 9, 1812, increased the authorized force to 35,000. But when the war began the army numbered only 6,700 men, ill-trained, poorly equipped, and led by poorly prepared officers. The senior officers were still in large part veterans of the Revolution. The ranking general, Henry Dearborn, was a veteran of Bunker Hill, sixty-one at the outbreak of war.

The navy, on the other hand, was in comparatively good shape, with able officers and trained men whose seamanship had been tested in the fighting against France and Tripoli. Its ships were well outfitted and seaworthy—all sixteen of them. In the first year of the war it was the navy that produced the only American victories in isolated duels with British vessels, but their effect was mainly an occasional lift to morale. Within a year the British had blockaded the coast, except for New England where they hoped to cultivate antiwar feeling, and most of the little American fleet was bottled up in port.

THE WAR IN THE NORTH The only place where the United States could effectively strike at the British was Canada. Only once, however, had a war in that arena proved decisive, late in the French and Indian War, when Wolfe took Quebec and strangled the French Empire in America. A similar instinct for the jugular was Madison's best hope: a quick attack on Quebec or Montreal would cut Canada's lifeline, the St. Lawrence River. Instead the old history of the indecisive colonial wars was repeated, for the last time.

Instead of striking directly at the lifeline, the administration opted for a three-pronged drive against Canada: along the Lake Champlain route toward Montreal, with Gen. Henry Dearborn in command; along the Niagara River, with forces under Gen. Stephen Van Rensselaer; and into Upper Canada from Detroit, where Gen. William Hull and some 2,000 men arrived in early July. In Detroit, Hull deliberated and vacillated while his position worsened and the news arrived that Fort Michilimackinac, isolated at the head of Lake Huron, had surrendered on July 17. British Gen. Isaac Brock cleverly played upon Hull's worst fears. Gathering what redcoats he could to parade in view of Detroit's defenders, Brock let it be known that thousands of Indian allies were at the rear and that once fighting began he would be unable to control them. Fearing massacre, Hull surrendered his entire force on August 16, 1812.

Along the Niagara front, General Van Rensselaer was more aggressive than Hull. On October 13 an advance party of 600

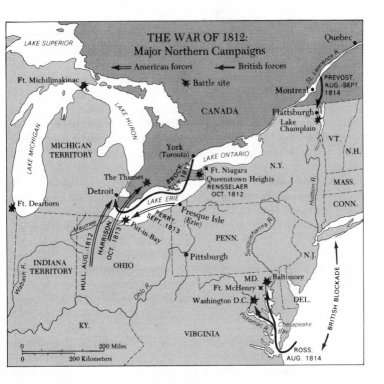

THE WAR OF 1812:
Major Northern Campaigns

⟵ American forces ⟵ British forces

✳ Battle site

LAKE SUPERIOR

Quebec

Ft. Michilimakinac

Montreal

PREVOST,
AUG.-SEPT.
1814

CANADA

Plattsburgh
Lake
Champlain

MICHIGAN
TERRITORY

York
(Toronto)

LAKE ONTARIO

VT.

N.H.

The Thames

Ft. Niagara
Queenstown Heights
RENSSELAER
OCT. 1812

N.Y.

MASS.

Detroit

LAKE ERIE

CONN.

Ft. Dearborn

Presque Isle
(Erie)

Put-in-Bay

PENN.

INDIANA
TERRITORY

OHIO

Pittsburgh

N.J.

MD.

Baltimore

Ft. McHenry

KY.

Washington D.C.

DEL.

Chesapeake
Bay

VIRGINIA

ROSS,
AUG. 1814

BRITISH BLOCKADE

0   200 Miles
0   200 Kilometers

Americans crossed the Niagara River, and worked their way up
the bluffs on the Canadian side to occupy Queenston Heights.
The stage was set for a major victory, but the New York militia
refused to reinforce Van Rensselaer's men on the claim that their
military service did not obligate them to leave the country. They
complacently remained on the New York side and watched their
outnumbered countrymen be mowed down by a superior force
on the other side.

On the third front, the old invasion route via Lake Champlain,
the trumpet once more gave an uncertain sound. At first, when
word came that British had revoked the Orders in Council, General Dearborn accepted a temporary armistice. On November 19
he finally led his army north from Plattsburg toward Montreal.
He marched them up to the border, where the militia once again
stood on its alleged constitutional rights and refused to cross, and
then marched them down again.

Madison's navy secretary now pushed vigorously for American
control of inland waters. At Presque Isle (Erie), Pennsylvania,
twenty-eight-year-old Commodore Oliver H. Perry, already a
fourteen-year veteran who had seen action against Tripoli, was
fetching up hardware from Pittsburgh and building a squadron

from the wilderness lumber. By the end of the summer Perry had achieved superiority and set out in search of the British, whom he found at Put-in Bay, near the mouth of the Sandusky, on September 10, 1813. Perry refused to quit when his flagship was shot out from under him. He transferred to another vessel, carried the battle to the enemy, and finally accepted surrender of the entire British squadron. To Gen. William Henry Harrison he sent the long-awaited message: "We have met the enemy and they are ours."

American naval control of waters in the region soon made Upper Canada (north of Lake Erie) untenable to the British. They gave up Detroit in September, and were dissuaded from falling back all the way to the Niagara only by the protests of Tecumseh and his Indian allies. When they took a defensive stand at the Battle of the Thames (October 5), General Harrison inflicted a defeat which eliminated British power in Upper Canada and released the Northwest from any further threat. In the course of the battle, Tecumseh fell and his dream of Indian unity died with him.

THE WAR IN THE SOUTH In the Southwest too the war flared up in 1813. In April, before moving north, Gen. James Wilkinson had occupied the remainder of Spanish West Florida, where British agents had been active, on the claim that it was part of the Louisiana Purchase. In July 1813 a group of American settlers clashed with the Creeks at Burnt Corn, north of Pensacola, and on August 30 the Creeks attacked Fort Mims, on the Alabama River above Mobile, killing almost half the people in the fort. The news found Andrew Jackson home in bed recovering from a street brawl with Thomas Hart Benton, later senator from Missouri. As major-general of the Tennessee militia, Jackson summoned about 2,000 volunteers and set out on a campaign which utterly crushed the Creek resistance. The decisive battle came on March 27, 1814, at the Horseshoe Bend of the Tallapoosa River, in the heart of the upper Creek country. In the Treaty of Fort Jackson signed that August, the Creeks ceded two-thirds of their lands to the United States, including part of Georgia and most of Alabama.

Four days after the Battle of Horsehoe Bend, Napoleon's empire collapsed. Now free to deal with America, the British developed a threefold plan of operations for 1814. They would launch a two-pronged invasion of America via Niagara and Lake Champlain to increase the clamor for peace in the Northeast, extend the naval blockade to New England, subjecting coastal towns to raids, and seize New Orleans to cut the Mississippi River, lifeline of the West. Uncertainties about the peace settlement in Europe, however, prevented the release of British veterans for a wholesale descent upon the New World. War weariness, after a generation of conflict, countered the British thirst for revenge against the former colonials. British plans were stymied also by the more resolute young commanders Madison had placed in charge of strategic areas by the summer of 1814.

MACDONOUGH'S VICTORY   The main British effort was planned for the invasion via Lake Champlain. From the north Gen. George Prevost, governor-general of Canada, advanced with the finest army yet assembled on American soil: fifteen regiments of regulars, plus militia and artillerymen, a total of about 15,000. The front was saved only by Prevost's vacillation and the superb ability of Commodore Thomas Macdonough, commander of the American naval squadron on Lake Champlain. A land assault might have take Plattsburg and forced Macdonough out of his protected position nearby, but England's army bogged down while its flotilla engaged Macdonough in a deadly battle on September 11.

The British concentrated superior firepower from the flagship, the *Confiance,* on Macdonough's ship, the *Saratoga.* With

John Bull making a new Batch of ships to send to the lakes. *The figure at the right tells John Bull, "If you send all you've got to the Lakes, it will only make fun for the Yankeys to take them." [New York Public Library]*

his starboard battery disabled, Macdonough executed a daring maneuver known as "winding ship." He turned the *Saratoga* around while at anchor and brought its undamaged port broadside into action with devastating effect. The *Saratoga* was so damaged that it had to be scuttled, but the battle ended with the entire British flotilla either destroyed or captured. After reading the news, the duke of Wellington informed the British ministry: "That which appears to me to be wanting in America is not a general, or a general officer and troops, but a naval superiority on the Lakes." Lacking this advantage the duke thought the British had no right "to demand any concession of territory from America."

FIGHTING IN THE CHESAPEAKE Meanwhile, however, American forces suffered the most humiliating experience of the war, the capture and burning of Washington, D.C. With attention focused on the Canadian front, the Chesapeake Bay offered the British a number of inviting targets, including Baltimore, now the fourth-largest city in America. Under the command of Gen. Robert Ross, a British force landed without opposition in June at Benedict, Maryland, and headed for Washington, forty miles away. To defend the capital the Americans had a force of about 7,000, including only a few hundred regulars and 400 sailors. At Bladensburg, Maryland, the American militia melted away in the face of the smaller British force. Only Commodore Joshua Barney's sailors held firm, pounding the British with five twenty-four-pound guns, but the sailors were forced to retire after half an hour.

On the evening of August 24, 1814, the British marched unopposed into Washington, where British officers ate a meal prepared for President and Mrs. Madison, who had joined the other refugees in Virginia. The British then burned the White House, the Capitol, and all other government buildings except the Patent Office. A tornado the next day compounded the damage, but a violent thunderstorm dampened both the fires and the enthusiasm of the British forces, who left to prepare a new assault on Baltimore.

The attack on Baltimore was a different story. With some 13,000 men, chiefly militia, some of them stragglers from Bladensburg, American forces fortified the heights behind the city. About 1,000 men held Fort McHenry, on an island in the harbor. The British landed at North Point, where an advance group of American militia inflicted severe casualties, including a mortal wound to General Ross. When the British finally came into sight of the city on September 13, they halted in the face of American defenses. All through the following night the fleet bombarded Fort McHenry to no avail, and the invaders abandoned the attack on the city as too costly to risk. Francis Scott Key, a Washington lawyer, watched the siege from a vessel in the harbor. The sight of the flag still in place at dawn inspired Key to draft the verses of "The Star Spangled Banner." Later revised and set to the tune of an English drinking song, it was immediately popular and eventually became the national anthem.

THE BATTLE OF NEW ORLEANS   The British failure at Baltimore followed by three days their failure on Lake Champlain, and their offensive against New Orleans had yet to run its course. Along the Gulf coast Andrew Jackson had been busy shoring up the defenses of Mobile and New Orleans. In November, without authorization, he invaded Spanish Florida and took Pensacola to end British intrigues there. Back in Louisiana by the end of November, he began to erect defenses on the approaches to New Orleans, anticipating a British approach by the interior to pick up Indian support and control the Mississippi. Instead the British

THE WAR OF 1812: Major Southern Campaigns

⇐= American forces   ✳ Battle site
◄— British forces

fleet, with some 7,500 European veterans under Gen. Sir Edwin Pakenham, entered Lake Borgne to the east of New Orleans, and eventually reached a level plain on the banks of the Mississippi just south of New Orleans.

Pakenham's painfully careful approach—he waited until all his artillery was available—gave Jackson time to throw up earth works bolstered by cotton bales for protection. It was an almost invulnerable position, but Pakenham, contemptuous of Jackson's array of frontier militiamen, Creole aristocrats, free Negroes, and pirates, rashly ordered his veterans forward in a frontal assault at dawn on January 8, 1815. His redcoats ran into a murderous hail of artillery shells and deadly rifle fire. Before the British withdrew about 2,000 had died on the field, including Pakenham himself, whose body, pickled in a barrel of rum, was returned to the ship where his wife awaited news of the battle.

The Battle of New Orleans occurred after a peace treaty had already been signed, but this is not to say that it was an anticlimax or that it had no effect on the outcome of the war, for the treaty was yet to be ratified and the British might have exploited to advantage the possession of New Orleans had they won it. But the battle assured ratification of the treaty as it stood, and both governments acted quickly.

This engraving of Pakenham's death at the Battle of New Orleans (January 8, 1815) is based on a painting done at the scene. [New York Public Library]

THE TREATY OF GHENT   Peace efforts had begun in 1812 even before hostilities got under way. The British, after all, had repealed their Orders in Council two days before the declaration of war and confidently expected at least an armistice. Secretary of State Monroe, however, told the British that they would have to give up the outrage of impressment as well. Meanwhile Czar Alexander of Russia offered to mediate the dispute, hoping to relieve the pressure on Great Britain, his ally against France. Madison then sent Albert Gallatin and James Bayard to join John Quincy Adams, American ambassador to Russia, in St. Petersburg. They arrived in July 1813, but the czar was at the warfront, and they waited impatiently until January 1814, but then the British refused mediation. England soon offered to negotiate directly, however. In February, Madison appointed Henry Clay and Jonathan Russell to join the other three commissioners in talks which finally got under way in the Flemish city of Ghent in August.

In contrast to the array of talent gathered in the American contingent, the British diplomats were nonentities, really messengers acting for the Foreign Office, which was more concerned with the effort to remake the map of Europe at the Congress of Vienna. The Americans had more leeway to use their own judgment, and sharp disagreements developed which had to be patched up by Albert Gallatin. The sober-sided Adams and the hard-drinking, poker-playing Clay, especially, rubbed each other the wrong way. The American delegates at first were instructed to demand abandonment of impressment and paper blockades, and to get indemnities for seizures of American ships. The British opened the discussions with demands for territory in New York and Maine, removal of American warships from the Great Lakes, an autonomous Indian buffer state in the Northwest, access to the Mississippi River, and abandonment of American fishing rights off Labrador and Newfoundland. If the British insisted on such a position, the Americans informed them, the negotiations would be at an end.

But the British were stalling, awaiting news of victories to strengthen their hand. They withdrew the demand for an Indian buffer state and substituted *uti possidetis* (retention of occupied territory) as a basis for settlement. This too was rejected. The Americans countered with a proposal for the *status quo ante bellum* (the situation before the war). The news of American victory on Lake Champlain arrived in October and weakened the British resolve. Their will to fight was further weakened by a continuing power struggle at the Congress of Vienna, by the eagerness of

British merchants to renew trade with America, and by the war-weariness of a tax-burdened public. The British finally decided that the game was not worth the candle. One by one demands were dropped on both sides until the envoys agreed to end the war, return the prisoners, restore the previous boundaries, and to settle nothing else. The questions of fisheries and disputed boundaries were referred to commissions for future settlement. The Treaty of Ghent was signed on Christmas Eve 1814.

THE HARTFORD CONVENTION   While the diplomats converged on a peace settlement, an entirely different kind of meeting took place in Hartford, Connecticut. An ill-fated affair, the Hartford Convention represented the climax of New England's dissaffection with "Mr. Madison's war." New England had managed to keep aloof from the war and extract a profit from illegal trading and privateering. New England shippers monopolized the import trade and took advantage of the chance to engage in active trade with the enemy. After the fall of Napoleon, however, the British extended their blockade to New England, occupied Maine as far as the Penobscot River, and conducted several raids along the coast. Even Boston seemed threatened. Instead of rallying to the American flag, however, Federalists in the Massachusetts legislature on October 5, 1814, voted for a convention of New England states to plan independent action. The Constitution, they said, "has failed to secure to this commonwealth, and as they believe, to the Eastern sections of this Union, those equal rights and benefits which are the greatest objects of its formation."

On December 15 the Hartford Convention assembled with delegates chosen by the legislatures of Massachusetts, Rhode Island, and Connecticut, with two delegates from Vermont and one from New Hampshire: twenty-two in all. The convention included an extreme group, Timothy Pickering's "Essex Junto," who were prepared for secession from the Union, but it was controlled by a more moderate group led by Harrison Gray Otis, interested only in a protest in language reminiscent of Madison's Virginia Resolutions of 1798. As the ultimate remedy for their grievances they proposed seven constitutional amendments designed to limit Republican influence: abolishing the three-fifths compromise, requiring a two-thirds vote to declare war or admit new states, prohibiting embargoes lasting more than sixty days, excluding the foreign-born from federal offices, limiting the president to one term, and forbidding successive presidents from the same state.

Their call for a later convention in Boston carried the unmistakable threat of secession if the demands were ignored. Yet the threat quickly evaporated. When messengers from Hartford reached Washington, they found the battered capital celebrating the good news from Ghent and New Orleans. The consequence was a fatal blow to the Federalist party, which never recovered from the stigma of disloyalty and narrow provincialism stamped on it by the Hartford Convention.

THE WAR'S AFTERMATH   Conveniently forgotten in the celebrations of peace were the calamities to which the Jeffersonian neglect of national defense had led. For all the fumbling ineptitude with which the War of 1812 was fought, it generated an intense feeling of patriotism. Despite the standoff with which it ended at Ghent, the American public came out of the war with a sense of victory, courtesy of Andrew Jackson and his men at New Orleans. Remembered were the heroic exploits of American frigates in their duels with British ships. Remembered too were the vivid words of the dying Capt. James Lawrence on the *Chesa-*

The War of 1812 created a new feeling of nationalism: "We Owe Allegiance to No Crown." [Collection of Davenport West, Jr.]

peake ("Don't give up the ship") and Oliver H. Perry on Lake Erie ("We have met the enemy and they are ours"), and the stirring stanzas of "The Star Spangled Banner." Under Republican leadership the nation had survived a "Second War of Independence" against the greatest power on earth, and emerged with new symbols of nationhood and a new pantheon of heroes. After forty years of independence, it dawned on the world that the new republic might be here to stay, and that it might be something more than a pawn in European power games.

As if to underline the point, Congress authorized a quick and decisive blow at the pirates of the Barbary Coast. During the War of 1812 the dey of Algiers had once again set about plundering American ships on the claim that he was getting too little tribute. On March 3, 1815, little more than two weeks after the Senate ratified the Peace of Ghent, Congress authorized hostilities against the pirates. On May 10 Capt. Stephen Decatur sailed from New York with ten vessels. In the Mediterranean he first seized two Algerian ships and then sailed boldly into the harbor of Algiers. On June 30, 1815, the dey of Algiers agreed to cease molesting American ships and to give up all United States prisoners. In July and August Decatur's show of force induced similar treaties from Tunis and Tripoli. This time there was no tribute; this time, for a change, the Barbary pirates paid indemnities for the damage they had done. This time victory put an end to the piracy and extortion in that quarter, permanently.

One of the strangest results of a strange war and its aftermath was a reversal of roles by the Republicans and Federalists. Out of the wartime experience the Republicans had learned some lessons in nationalism. Certain needs and inadequacies revealed by the war had "Federalized" Madison, or perhaps "re-Federalized" the Father of the Constitution. Perhaps, Madison reasoned, a peacetime army and navy would not be such an unmitigated evil. Madison now preferred to keep something more than a token force. The lack of a national bank had added to the problems of financing the war. Now Madison wanted it back. The rise of new industries during the war led to a clamor for increased tariffs. Madison went along. The problems of overland transportation in the West had revealed the need for internal improvements. Madison agreed, but on that point kept his constitutional scruples. He wanted a constitutional amendment. So while Madison embraced nationalism and broad construction of the Constitution, the Federalists took up the Jeffersonians' position of states' rights and strict construction. It was the first great reversal of roles in constitutional interpretation. It would not be the last.

FURTHER READING

One of the classics of American history remains the survey of the Republican years found in Henry Adams's *History of the United States during the Administration of Thomas Jefferson* [and] *James Madison* (9 vols.; 1889–1891). Marshall Smelser's *The Democratic Republic, 1801–1815* (1968),° presents a more modern overview. Closer attention to the Jeffersonians themselves is paid by Noble E. Cunningham, Jr.'s *The Republicans in Power: Party Operations, 1801–1809* (1963). James S. Young's *The Washington Community 1800–1828* (1966)° provides an interesting approach to both the mechanics of Jeffersonian politics and the design of the new national capital. Also helpful is Morton Borden's *Parties and Politics in the Early Republic, 1789–1815* (1967).°

Students of Jefferson have been assiduous and productive. The standard modern biography is the multivolume work by Dumas Malone, *Jefferson and His Times* (6 vols.; 1948–1981).° Malone covers this period in *Jefferson, The President* (2 vols.; 1970, 1974).° Forrest McDonald's *The Presidency of Thomas Jefferson* (1976) and Merrill Petersen's *Thomas Jefferson and the New Nation* (1970)° present shorter, yet incisive, views. Fawn Brodie's *Thomas Jefferson: An Intimate Biography* (1974)° takes a psychological approach to a complex man. Good introductions to the life of Jefferson's friend and successor are found in Ralph Ketcham's *James Madison* (1971) and Irving Brant's *The Fourth President: A Life of James Madison* (1970). Raymond Walters, Jr.'s *Albert Gallatin: Jeffersonian Financier and Diplomat* (1957)° assesses both Jeffersonian presidents and studies one of their chief allies. Another look at the Jeffersonian influence is Robert E. Shalhope's *John Taylor of Caroline: Pastoral Republican* (1980).

David Hackett Fischer's *The Revolution of American Conservatism: The Federalist Party in the Era of Jeffersonian Democracy* (1965),° Shaw Livermore, Jr.'s *The Twilight of Federalism: The Disintegration of the Federalist Party* (1962), and Linda K. Kerber's *Federalists in Dissent* (1970)° document how the Federalists behaved while out of power. James M. Banner's *To the Hartford Convention* (1970) analyzes their opposition to the War of 1812. A regional study is James H. Broussard's *The Southern Federalists, 1800–1816* (1979).

Events of the Jeffersonian years are given greater detail in more specialized studies. The concept of judicial review and the courts can be studied in Richard Ellis's *The Jeffersonians and the Judiciary* (1971)° and Charles G. Haines's *The American Doctrine of Judicial Supremacy* (1932). The most comprehensive work on John Marshall remains Albert J. Beveridge's *The Life of John Marshall* (4 vols.; 1919). For the Louisiana Purchase, consult E. Wilson Lewis's *Louisiana in French Diplomacy, 1759–1804* (1934), and Alexander De Conde's *The Affairs of Louisiana* (1976). Bernard De Voto (ed.), *The Journals of Lewis and Clark* (1953), is highly readable but Bernard W. Sheehan's *Seeds of Ex-*

°These books are available in paperback editions.

tinction: *Jeffersonian Philanthrophy and the American Indian* (1973)° is more analytical about the Jeffersonians and the opening of the West. Thomas P. Abernethy's *The Burr Conspiracy* (1954) and Milton Lomask's *Aaron Burr: The Years from Princeton to Vice President, 1756–1805* (1979) and *The Conspiracy and the Years of Exile, 1805–1836* (1982) trace the career of that remarkable American.

Bradford Perkins's *Prologue to War: England and the United States, 1805–1812* (1961),° concentrates on the diplomacy of the Jeffersonian years. More specific is Burton Spivak's *Jefferson's English Crisis: Commerce, the Embargo, and the Republican Revolution* (1979). Lawrence S. Kaplan's *Jefferson and France: An Essay on Politics and Political Ideas* (1967) is also insightful. Jefferson's first diplomatic decisions are treated in Ray W. Irwin's *Diplomatic Relations of the United States and the Barbary Powers* (1931). A review of the events which brought on war in 1812 is presented in Robert A. Rutland's *Madison's Alternatives: The Jeffersonian Republicans and the Coming of War, 1805–1812* (1975). Also helpful are Roger H. Brown's *The Republic in Peril: 1812* (1964)° and Julius W. Pratt's *Expansionists of 1812* (1925). Accounts of the military conflicts are found in J. K. Mahan's *The War of 1812* (1972), Reginald Horseman's *The War of 1812* (1969), and Harry L. Coles's *The War of 1812* (1965).° Two recent works which concentrate on specific aspects of the war are Alan Lloyd's *The Torching of Washington: The War of 1812* (1975) and Robert V. Remini's *Andrew Jackson and the Course of American Empire, 1767–1821* (1977).° Samuel F. Bemis's *John Quincy Adams and the Foundations of American Foreign Policy* (1949)° and F. L. Engleman's *The Peace of Christmas Eve* (1962) handle the peace negotiations.

10

NATIONALISM AND SECTIONALISM

ECONOMIC NATIONALISM

When did the United States become a nation? There is no easy answer to the question, for a sense of nationhood was a gradual growth and one always subject to cross-currents of localism, sectionalism, and class interest, as indeed it still is. Americans of the colonies and the early republic by and large identified more closely with the local community and at most the province or state in which they resided than with any larger idea of empire or nation. Among the colonies there was no common tie equal to the connection between each and the mother country. The Revolution gave rise to a sense of nationhood, but that could hardly be regarded as the dominant idea of the Revolution. Men who, like Hamilton, were prepared to think continentally, strengthened the federal Union by the Constitution, but Jefferson's "Revolution of 1800" revealed the countervailing forces of local and state interest. Jefferson himself, for instance, always spoke of Virginia as "my country."

Immediately after the War of 1812, however, there could no longer be any doubt that an American nation existed. Nationalism found expression in economic policy and culture after 1815. An abnormal economic prosperity after the war led to a feeling of well-being and enhanced the prestige of the national government. Jefferson's embargo ironically had given impulse to the factories that he abhorred. The policy of "peaceful coercion" followed by the wartime constraints on trade had caused capital in New England and the middle states to drift from commerce toward manufacturing. The idea became more prevalent that the strength of the country was dependent on a more balanced economy. After a generation of war, shortages of farm commodities in

Samuel Slater's cotton-spinning mill at Pawtucket, Rhode Island, pictured here between 1810 and 1819. Mills like this proliferated after the War of 1812. [Rhode Island Historical Society]

Europe forced up the prices of American products and stimulated agricultural expansion, indeed a wild speculation in farmlands. Southern cotton, tobacco, and rice came to account for about two-thirds of American exports. At the same time planters and farmers could buy in a postwar market which was being flooded with cheap English goods. The new American manufacturers would seek protection from this competition.

President Madison, in his first annual message to Congress after the war, recommended several steps toward strengthening the government: better fortifications, a standing army and a strong navy, a new national bank, effective protection of the new infant industries, a system of canals and roads for commercial and military use, and to top it off, a great national university. "The Republicans have out-Federalized Federalism," Josiah Quincy of Massachusetts remarked. Congress responded by authorizing a standing army of 10,000 and strengthening the navy as well.

THE BANK OF THE UNITED STATES   The trinity of economic nationalism—proposals for a second national bank, protective tariff, and internal improvements—inspired the greatest controversies of the time. After the national bank expired in 1811 the country had fallen into a financial muddle. State-chartered banks mushroomed with little or no control and their banknotes flooded the channels of commerce with money of uncertain value, which often was not accepted at par. And this was the money on which Americans depended. When the national bank liquidated its resources, it had to return about $7 million in gold to English investors, while most of the hard money remaining in the country found its way into New England banks because of the flourishing manufacturing and commercial economy there. Because hard money had been so short during the war, many state banks had suspended specie payments in redemption of their notes, thereby depressing the value of these notes further. The absence of the central bank had been a source of financial embarrassment to the government, which had neither a ready means of floating loans nor of transferring funds across the country.

Madison and most younger Republicans salved their constitutional scruples with a dash of pragmatism. The issue, Madison said, had been decided "by repeated recognitions . . . of the validity of such an institution in acts of the legislative, executive, and judicial branches of the Government, accompanied by . . . a concurrence of the general will of the nation." In 1816 Congress adopted over the protest of Old Republicans provision for a new Bank of the United States. Modeled after Hamilton's bank, it differed chiefly in that it was capitalized at $35 million instead of $10 million. Once again the charter ran for twenty years, once again the government owned a fifth of the stock and named five of the twenty-five directors, and again the bank served as the government depository. Its banknotes were accepted in payments to the government. In return for its privileges the bank had to take care of the government's funds without charge, lend the government $5 million on demand, and pay the government a cash bonus of $1.5 million.

The debate on the bank was noteworthy because of the leading roles played by the great triumvirate of John C. Calhoun of South Carolina, Henry Clay of Kentucky, and Daniel Webster of New Hampshire, later of Massachusetts. Calhoun, still in his youthful phase as a War Hawk nationalist, introduced the measure and pushed it through, justifying its constitutionality by the congressional power to regulate the currency, and pointing to the need for a uniform circulating medium. Clay, who had been in on the kill when Hamilton's bank expired in 1811, now confessed that he had failed to foresee the evils that resulted, and asserted that circumstances had made the bank indispensible. Webster, on the other hand, led the opposition of the New England Federalists, who did not want the banking center moved from Boston to Philadelphia. Later, after he moved from New Hampshire to Massachusetts, he would return to Congress as the champion of a much stronger national power, while events would carry Calhoun in the other direction.

A PROTECTIVE TARIFF   The shift of capital from commerce to manufactures, begun during the embargo, had speeded up during the war. Peace in 1815 brought a sudden renewal of cheap British imports, and gave impetus to a movement for the protection of infant industries. The self-interest of the manufacturers, who as yet had little political impact, was reinforced by a patriotic desire for economic independence from Britain. Spokesmen for New England shippers and southern farmers opposed the movement, but both sections had sizable minorities who believed that the promotion of industry was vital to both sectional and national welfare.

The Tariff of 1816, the first intended more for the protection of industry against foreign competition than for revenue, passed by a comfortable majority. The South and New England registered a majority of their votes against the bill, but the middle states and Old Northwest cast only five negative votes altogether. Nathaniel Macon of North Carolina opposed the tariff and defended the Old Republican doctrine of strict construction. The power to protect industry, Macon said, like the power to establish a bank, rested on the doctrine of implied powers; Macon worried that implied powers might one day be used to abolish slavery. The minority of southerners who voted for the tariff, led by William Lowndes and John C. Calhoun of South Carolina, had good reason to expect that the South might itself become a manufacturing center. South Carolina was then developing a relatively diversified economy which included a few textile mills. According to the census of 1810, the southern states had approximately as many manufactures as New England. Within a few years New England moved ahead of the South, and Calhoun went over to Macon's views against protection. The tariff then became a sectional issue, with manufacturers, food growers, wool, sugar, and hemp growers favoring higher tariffs, while planters and shipping interests favored lower duties.

INTERNAL IMPROVEMENTS   The third major issue of the time was internal improvements: the building of roads and the development of water transportation. The war had highlighted the shortcomings of existing facilities. Troop movements through the western wilderness proved very difficult. Settlers found that unless they located near navigable waters, they were cut off from trade and limited to a frontier subsistence.

The federal government had entered the field of internal improvements under Jefferson, who went along with some hesitation. He and both of his successors recommended a constitutional amendment to give the federal government undisputed

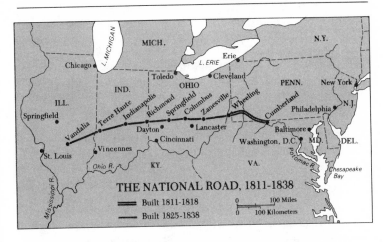

THE NATIONAL ROAD, 1811-1838
Built 1811-1818
Built 1825-1838

power in the field, but lacking that, the constitutional grounds for federal action rested mainly on provision for national defense and expansion of the postal system. In 1803, when Ohio became a state, Congress decreed that 5 percent of the proceeds from land sales in the state would go to building a National Road from the Atlantic coast into Ohio and beyond as the territory developed. In 1806 Jefferson signed a measure for a survey, and construction of the National Road got under way in 1811. By 1818 it was open from Cumberland, Maryland, to Wheeling on the Ohio River. Construction stopped temporarily during the business panic of 1819, but by 1838 the road extended all the way to Vandalia, Illinois.

In 1817 John C. Calhoun put through the House a bill to place in a fund for internal improvements the $1.5 million bonus the Bank of the United States had paid for its charter, as well as all future dividends on the government's bank stock. Once again opposition centered in New England and the South, which expected to gain least, and support came largely from the West, which badly needed good roads. On his last day in office Madison vetoed the bill. Sympathetic to its purpose, he could not overcome his "insuperable difficulty . . . in reconciling the bill with the Constitution" and suggested instead a constitutional amendment. Internal improvements remained for another hundred years, with few exceptions, the responsibility of states and private enterprise. Then and later Congress supported river and harbor improvements, and scattered post roads, but nothing of a systematic nature. The federal government did not enter the field on a large scale until passage of the Federal Highways Act of 1916.

"Good Feelings"

JAMES MONROE   As Madison approached the end of a turbulent tenure he, like Jefferson, turned to a fellow Virginian, another secretary of state, as his successor: James Monroe. The Old Republicans, who had started a presidential campaign for Monroe in 1808, now turned to William H. Crawford of Georgia, who had replaced Gallatin at the Treasury. In the Republican caucus Monroe won the nomination, then overwhelmed his Federalist opponent, Rufus King of New York, 183 to 34 in the electoral college. The "Virginia Dynasty" continued. Like three of the four presidents before him, Monroe was a Virginia planter, but with a difference: Monroe came from the small-planter group. At the outbreak of the Revolution he was just beginning college at William and Mary. He joined the army at the age of sixteen, fought with Washington at Trenton, and was a lieutenant-colonel when the war ended. Later he studied law with Jefferson and absorbed Jeffersonian principles at the master's feet.

Monroe never showed the profundity of his Republican predecessors in scholarship or political theory, but what he lacked in intellect he made up in dedication to public service. His soul, Jefferson said, if turned inside out, would be found spotless. Monroe served in the Virginia assembly, as governor of the state, in the Confederation Congress and United States Senate, and as minister to Paris, London, and Madrid. Under Madison he had served as secretary of state, and twice doubled as secretary of

James Monroe, portrayed as he entered the presidency in 1816. [National Portrait Gallery, Smithsonian Institution]

war. Monroe, with his powdered wig, cocked hat, and knee-breeches, was the last of the revolutionary generation to serve in the White House and the last president to dress in the old style.

To the postwar generation there was an air of nostalgic solidity about him, even though little more than twenty years before, as minister to Paris, he had defended the French radicals during their bloodiest exploits. Firmly grounded in Republican principles, he was never quite able to keep up with the onrush of the new nationalism. He accepted as accomplished fact the bank and the protective tariff, but during his tenure there was no further extension of economic nationalism. Indeed there was a minor setback. He permitted the National (or Cumberland) Road to be carried forward, but in his veto of Cumberland Road Bill (1822) denied the authority of Congress to collect tolls for its repair and maintenance. Like Jefferson and Madison, he also suggested a constitutional amendment to remove all doubt about federal authority in the field of internal improvements, and in his last year in office did sign the General Survey Bill of 1824, which authorized estimates of roads and canals needed for military, commercial, and postal purposes.

Whatever his limitations, Monroe surrounded himself with some of the strongest and ablest young Republican leaders. John Quincy Adams became secretary of state. William Crawford of Georgia, his rival for the presidency, continued in office as secretary of the treasury. John C. Calhoun headed the War Department after Henry Clay refused the position in order to remain Speaker of the House. The new administration found the country in a state of well-being: America was at peace and the economy was flourishing. Soon after the inauguration Monroe embarked on a goodwill tour of New England. In Boston, lately a hotbed of wartime dissent, a Federalist paper, the *Columbian Centinel*, ran a general comment on the president's visit under the heading "Era of Good Feelings." The label became a popular catch-phrase for Monroe's administration, and one that historians seized upon later. Like many a maxim, it conveys just enough truth to be sadly misleading. A resurgence of factionalism and sectionalism erupted just as the postwar prosperity collapsed in the Panic of 1819.

For two years, however, general harmony reigned, and even when the country's troubles revived, little of the blame sullied the name of Monroe. In 1820 he was reelected without opposition, even without needing nomination. The Federalists were too weak to put up a candidate, and the Republicans did not bother to call a caucus. Monroe got all the electoral votes except for three absentions and one vote from New Hampshire for John Quincy Adams. The Republican party was dominant, or perhaps more accurately, was following the Federalists into oblivion. In the general political contentment the first party system was fading away, but rivalries for the succession soon commenced the process of forming new parties.

IMPROVING RELATIONS WITH BRITAIN   Adding to the prevailing contentment after the war was a growing rapprochement with the recent enemy. Trade relations with Britain (and India) were restored by a Commercial Convention of 1815, which eliminated discriminatory duties on either side. The Peace of Ghent had left unsettled a number of minor disputes, but in the sequel two important compacts—the Rush-Bagot Agreement of 1817 and the Convention of 1818—removed several potential causes of irritation. In the first, effected by an exchange of notes between Acting Secretary of State Richard Rush and British Minister Charles Bagot, the threat of naval competition on the Great Lakes vanished with an arrangement to limit naval forces there to several revenue cutters. Although the exchange made no reference to the land boundary between the countries, its spirit gave rise to the tradition of an unfortified border, the longest in the world.

The Convention of 1818 covered three major points. The northern limit of the Louisiana Purchase was settled by extending the national boundary along the Forty-ninth Parellel west from Lake of the Woods to the crest of the Rocky Mountains. West of that point the Oregon country would be open to joint occupation, but the boundary remained unsettled. The right of Americans to fish off Newfoundland and Labrador, granted in 1783, was acknowledged once again.

The chief remaining problem was Britain's exclusion of American ships from the West Indies in order to reserve that lucrative trade for British ships. The Commercial Convention of 1815 did not apply there, and after the War of 1812 the British had once again closed the door. This remained a chronic irritant, and the United States retaliated with several measures. Under a Navigation Act of 1817, importation of West Indian produce was restricted to American vessels or vessels belonging to West Indian merchants. In 1818 American ports were closed to all British vessels arriving from a colony that was legally closed to vessels of the United States. In 1820 Monroe approved an act of Congress which specified total nonintercourse, in British vessels, with all British-American colonies, even in goods taken to England and reexported. The rapprochement with Britain therefore fell short of perfection.

JACKSON TAKES FLORIDA   The year 1819 was one of the more fateful years in American history, a time when a whole sequence of developments came into focus. The bumptious new nationalism reached a climax with the acquisition of Florida and the extension of the southwestern boundary to the Pacific, and with three major decisions of the Supreme Court. But nationalism quickly began to run afoul of domestic cross-currents that would set up an ever-widening swirl in the next decades. In the calculus of global power, it was perhaps long since reckoned that Florida would some day pass to the United States. Spanish sovereignty was more a technicality than an actuality, and extended little beyond St. Augustine on the east coast and Pensacola and St. Marks on the Gulf. The thinly held province had been a thorn in the side of the United States during the recent war, a center of British intrigue, a haven for Creek refugees, who there were beginning to take the name Seminole (runaway or separatist), and a harbor for runaway slaves and criminals. Florida also stood athwart the outlets of several important rivers flowing to the Gulf.

Spain was almost powerless at that point because of both internal and colonial revolt, and unable to enforce its obligations under the Pinckney Treaty of 1795 to pacify the frontiers. In 1816 American forces came into conflict with a group of escaped slaves who had taken over a British fort on the Appalachicola River. Seminoles who challenged the legality of Creek land cessions were soon fighting white settlers in the area. In November 1817 Americans burned the Seminole border settlement of Fowltown, killed four of its inhabitants, and dispersed the rest across the border into Florida.

At this point Secretary of War Calhoun authorized a campaign against the Seminoles, and summoned General Jackson from Nashville to take command. Jackson's orders allowed him to pursue the offenders into Spanish territory, but not to attack any Spanish post. A man of Jackson's direct purpose naturally felt hobbled by such a restriction, so he wrote to President Monroe that if the United States wanted Florida he could wind up the whole thing in sixty days. All he needed was private, unofficial word, which might be sent through Tennessee Rep. John Rhea. Soon afterward Jackson indeed got a letter from Rhea, and claimed that it transmitted cryptically the required authority, although Monroe always denied any such intention. The truth about the Rhea letter, which Jackson destroyed (at Monroe's request, he said), remains a mystery.

In any case, when it came to Spaniards or Indians, no white Tennessean—certainly not Andrew Jackson—was likely to bother with technicalities. Jackson pushed eastward through Florida, reinforced by Tennessee volunteers and a party of friendly Creeks, taking the Spanish post at St. Marks, and skirmishing with the Seminoles, destroying their settlements, and pursuing them to the Suwannee River. Two of their leaders, the prophet Francis and Chief Homollimico, Jackson hanged without any semblance of a trial. For two British intriguers in the area, a trader named Alexander Arbuthnot and a former British officer, Robert Ambrister, he convened a court-martial, but to the same end. Both had befriended the Seminoles, and Ambrister at least had offered them military training. In any case Jackson was convinced that the two were at the root of all the trouble, and the evidence did not much matter. Arbuthnot was hanged; Ambrister shot. Having mopped up the region from the Appalachicola to the Suwannee, Jackson then turned west and seized Pensacola, appointed one of his colonels civil and military governor of Florida, and returned home to Nashville. The whole thing had taken about four months; the Florida panhandle was in American hands by the end of May 1818.

The news created consternation in both Madrid and Washington. Spain demanded the return of its territory, reparations, and the punishment of Jackson, but Spain's impotence was plain for all to see. Monroe's cabinet was at first prepared to disavow Jackson's action, especially his direct attack on Spanish posts. Calhoun, as secretary of war, was inclined, at least officially, to discipline Jackson for disregard of orders—a stand which caused bad blood between the two men later—but privately confessed a certain pleasure at the outcome. In any case a man as popular as Jackson was almost invulnerable. And he had one important friend at court, Secretary of State John Quincy Adams, who realized that Jackson had strengthened his hand in negotiations already under way with the Spanish minister, Luís de Onís y Gonzalez. American forces withdrew from Florida, but negotiations resumed with the knowledge that the United States could take Florida at any time.

The fate of Florida was a foregone conclusion. Adams now had his eye on a larger purpose, a definition of the western boundary of the Louisiana Purchase and—his boldest stroke—extension of a boundary to the Pacific coast. In lengthy negotiations Adams gradually gave ground on claims to Texas, but stuck to his de-

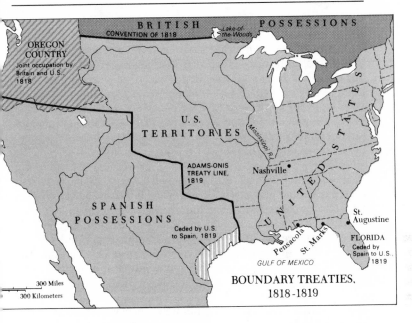

BRITISH POSSESSIONS

CONVENTION OF 1818

Lake-of-the-Woods

OREGON COUNTRY
Joint occupation by Britain and U.S. 1818

U.S. TERRITORIES

Mississippi R.

ADAMS-ONIS TREATY LINE, 1819

Nashville

UNITED STATES

SPANISH POSSESSIONS

Ceded by U.S. to Spain, 1819

St. Augustine

Pensacola St. Marks

FLORIDA
Ceded by Spain to U.S. 1819

GULF OF MEXICO

300 Miles
300 Kilometers

BOUNDARY TREATIES, 1818-1819

mand for a transcontinental line. Agreement finally came early in 1819. Spain ceded all of Florida in return for American assumption of private American claims against Spain up to $5 million. The western boundary of the Louisiana Purchase would run along the Sabine River and then in stair-step fashion up to the Red River, along the Red, and up to the Arkansas River. From the source of the Arkansas it would go north to the Forty-second Parallel and thence west to the Pacific coast. A dispute over land claims held up ratification for another two years, but those claims were revoked and final ratifications were exchanged in 1821. Florida became a territory, and its first governor briefly was Andrew Jackson. In 1845 Florida eventually achieved statehood.

"A FIREBELL IN THE NIGHT"

THE PANIC OF 1819 Adams's Transcontinental Treaty was a triumph of foreign policy and the climactic event of the postwar nationalism. Even before it was signed in February 1819, however, two thunderclaps signaled the end of the brief "Era of Good Feelings" and gave warning of stormy weather ahead. The two portents were the financial Panic of 1819 and the controversy over statehood for Missouri. The occasion for the panic was the sudden collapse of cotton prices in the Liverpool market. At one point in 1818 cotton had soared to 32 1/2 cents a pound. The pressure of high prices forced British manufacturers to turn to cheaper East Indian cotton. It proved unsatisfactory, but only after severe damage had been done in American markets. In 1819 cotton averaged only 14.3 cents per pound at New Orleans. The price collapse in cotton was the catalytic event that set off a decline in the demand for other American goods, and suddenly revealed the fragility of the prosperity that followed the War of 1812.

Since 1815 a speculative bubble had grown with expectations that expansion would go on forever. But American industry began to run into trouble finding markets for its goods. Even the Tariff of 1816 had not been enough to eliminate British competition. What was more, businessmen, farmers, and land jobbers had inflated the bubble with a volatile expansion of credit. The sources of this credit were both government and banks. Under the Land Law of 1800 the government extended four years' credit to those who bought western lands. After 1804 one could buy as little as 160 acres at a minimum price of $1.64 per acre (although in auctions the best lands went for more). In many cases speculators took up large tracts, paying one-fourth down, and then sold them to settlers with the understanding that the settlers would pay the remaining installments. With the collapse of prices, and then of land values, both speculators and settlers found themselves caught short.

The inflation of credit was compounded by the reckless practices of state banks. To enlarge their loans they issued banknotes far beyond their means of redemption, and at first were under little pressure to promise redemption in specie. Even the second Bank of the United States, which was supposed to introduce some order, was at first caught up in the mania. Its first president, William Jones, had been a disaster at the Treasury, and seen his own business just go bankrupt. Jones yielded to the contagion of get-rich-quick fever that was sweeping the country.

Under the bank's charter its own stockholders were expected to pay a fourth of their subscription in specie. But with specie going at a premium, the hard-pressed stockholders were permitted to pay their last two installments in promissory notes secured by the value of their own stock. The proliferation of branches combined with little supervision from Philadelphia to carry the bank into the same reckless extension of loans that state banks had pursued. In 1819, just as alert businessmen began to take

The second Bank of the United States. [Historical Society of Pennsylvania]

alarm, a case of extensive fraud and embezzlement in the Baltimore branch came to light. The upshot of the disclosure was Jones's resignation, his replacement by Langdon Cheves, former congressman from South Carolina, and the establishment of a sounder policy.

Cheves reduced salaries and other costs, postponed dividends, restrained the extension of credit, and presented for redemption the state banknotes that came in, thereby forcing the wildcat banks to keep specie reserves. Cheves rescued the bank from near-ruin, but only by putting heavy pressure on state banks. State banks in turn put pressure on their debtors, who found it harder to renew old loans or get new ones. In 1823, his job completed, Cheves relinquished his position to Nicholas Biddle of Philadelphia. The Cheves policies were the result rather than the cause of the Panic, but they were anathema to debtors who found it all the more difficult to meet their obligations. Hard times lasted about three years, and the bank took much of the blame in the popular mind. The Panic passed, but resentment of the bank lingered. It never fully regained the confidence of the South and the West.

THE MISSOURI COMPROMISE   Just as the Panic was breaking over the country, another cloud appeared on the horizon, the onset of a sectional controversy over slavery. By 1819 it happened that the country had an equal number of slave and free states, eleven of each. The line between them was defined by the southern and western boundaries of Pennsylvania and the Ohio River. Although slavery still existed in some places north of the line, it was on the way to extinction there. Beyond the Mississippi, however, no move had been made to extend the dividing line across the Louisiana Purchase territory, where slavery had existed from the days when France and Spain had colonized the area. At the time the Missouri Territory embraced all of the Louisiana Purchase except the state of Louisiana (1812) and the Arkansas Territory (1819). In the westward rush of population, the old French town of St. Louis became the funnel through which settlers pushed on beyond the Mississippi. These were largely settlers from the south who brought their slaves with them.

In February 1819 the House of Representatives confronted legislation enabling Missouri to draft a state constitution, its population having passed the minimum of 60,000. At that point Rep. James Tallmadge, Jr., a congressman from New York, introduced a resolution prohibiting the further introduction of slaves into Missouri, which had some 10,000 in 1820, and providing freedom at age twenty-five for those born after the territory's admission as a state. Tallmadge's motives remain obscure, but may have been very simply a moral aversion to slavery or perhaps a political aversion to having slavery and three-fifths compromise extended any farther beyond the Mississippi River. After brief but fiery exchanges, the House passed the amendment on an almost strictly sectional vote and the Senate rejected it by a similar tally, but with several northerners joining in the opposition. With population at the time growing faster in the north, a balance between the two sections could be held only in the Senate. In the House, slave states had 81 votes while free states had 105; a balance was unlikely ever again to be restored in the House.

Congress adjourned in March, postponing further debate until the regular session in December. When the debate came, it was remarkable for the absence of moral argument, although repugnance to slavery and moral guilt about it were never far from the surface. The debate turned on the constitutional issue. Congress, Rufus King of New York asserted, was empowered to forbid slavery in Missouri as the Confederation Congress had done in the Northwest Territory. William Pinckney of Maryland asserted that the states were equal and that Congress could not bind a state. Southern leaders argued further that under the Fifth Amendment, slaveholders could not be denied the right to carry their property into the territory, which would be deprivation of property without due process of law. Henry Clay and others expressed a view, which Jefferson and Madison now shared, that the expansion and dispersal of slavery would ameliorate the condition of the slaves. Most of the constitutional arguments that would reverberate in later quarrels over slavery were already present in the argument over Missouri, but the moral issue of bondage had not yet reached the fevered condition it would later achieve, since few were yet prepared to defend slavery as a posi-

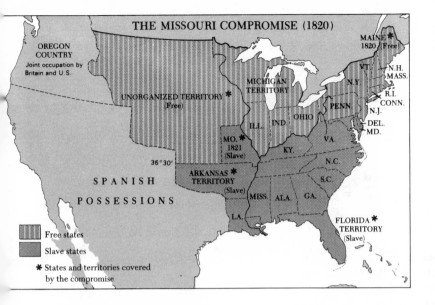

THE MISSOURI COMPROMISE (1820)

OREGON COUNTRY
Joint occupation by Britain and U.S.

UNORGANIZED TERRITORY *
(Free)

MICHIGAN TERRITORY

MAINE *
1820 (Free)

VT.
N.H.
MASS.
N.Y.
R.I.
CONN.
PENN.
N.J.
OHIO
DEL.
MD.
ILL. IND.
MO. *
1821
(Slave)
VA.
KY.
N.C.
36°30'
ARKANSAS *
TERRITORY
(Slave)
S.C.
SPANISH
MISS. ALA. GA.
POSSESSIONS
LA.
FLORIDA *
TERRITORY
(Slave)

Free states
Slave states
* States and territories covered by the compromise

tive good. In fact the general abhorrence of slavery was still strong enough that during 1820 Congress defined the illegal foreign slave trade as piracy, subjecting those engaged in it to the death penalty. This penalty was not actually imposed, however, until the outbreak of the Civil War.

Maine's application for statehood made it easier to arrive at an agreement. Since colonial times Maine had been the northern province of Massachusetts. The Senate linked its request for separate statehood with Missouri's and voted to admit Maine as a free state and Missouri as a slave state, thus maintaining the balance in the Senate. Sen. Jesse B. Thomas of Illinois further extended the compromise by an amendment to exclude slavery from the rest of the Louisiana Purchase north of 36° 30', Missouri's southern border. Slavery thus would continue in the Arkansas Territory and be excluded from the remainder of the area. But that was country which Zebulon Pike's and Stephen Long's reports had persuaded the public was the Great American Desert, unlikely ever to be settled. For this reason the arrangement seemed to be a victory for the slave states. The House at first refused to accept the arrangement, but the question went to a conference committee of the two houses for which Speaker Henry Clay had carefully chosen malleable members who accepted the Senate compromise. By a very close vote it passed the House on March 2, 1820.

Once that issue was settled, however, another problem arose.

Henry Clay's compromise deflected a confrontation on the expansion of slavery. Clay is portrayed here in 1822. [Library of Congress]

The proslavery elements which dominated Missouri's constitutional convention inserted in the new state constitution a proviso excluding free Negroes and mulattoes from the state. This clearly violated the requirement of Article IV, Section 2, of the Constitution: "The Citizens of each State shall be entitled to all Privileges and Immunities of Citizens in the Several States." Free Negroes were citizens of many states, including the slave states of North Carolina and Tennessee where, until the mid-1830s, they also voted.

The renewed controversy threatened final approval of Missouri's admission until Henry Clay, now beginning to earn his later title of the "Great Compromiser," formulated a "Second Missouri Compromise." Admission of Missouri as a state depended on assurance from the Missouri legislature that it would never construe the offending clause in such a way as to sanction denial of privileges that citizens held under the Constitution. It was one of the more artless dodges in American history, for it required the legislature to affirm that the state constitution did not mean what it clearly said, but the compromise worked. The Missouri legislature duly adopted the pledge, but qualified it by denying that the legislature had any power to bind the people of the state. On August 10, 1821, President Monroe proclaimed the admission of Missouri as the twenty-fourth state. For the time the controversy was settled. "But this momentous question," the aging Thomas Jefferson wrote to a friend after the first compromise, "like a firebell in the night awakened and filled me with terror. I considered it at once as the knell of the Union."

JUDICIAL NATIONALISM

JOHN MARSHALL, CHIEF JUSTICE   Meanwhile nationalism was still flourishing in the Supreme Court, where another Virginian, Chief Justice John Marshall, preserved Hamiltonian Federalism for another generation. Marshall, survivor of the Revolution, was among those who had been forever nationalized by the experience. In later years he said: "I was confirmed in the habit of considering America as my country and Congress as my government." The habit persisted through a successful legal career punctuated by service in Virginia's legislature and ratifying convention, as part of the "**XYZ**" mission to France, and as a member of Congress. Never a judge before he became chief justice in 1801, he established the power of the Supreme Court by the force of his mind and his determination. His influence was scarcely lessened when Jefferson and Madison filled vacancies on the Court with William Johnson (1804) of South Carolina and Joseph Story (1811) of Massachusetts. Once confirmed and beyond the reach of presidents, these Republican justices fell under the spell of Marshall. Story became a close collaborator.

During Marshall's early years on the Court (altogether he served thirty-four years) he affirmed the principle of judicial review. In *Marbury v. Madison* (1803) and *Fletcher v. Peck* (1810) the Court first struck down a federal law and then a state law as unconstitutional. In the cases of *Martin v. Hunter's Lessee* (1816) and *Cohens v. Virginia* (1821) the Court assumed the right to

Chief Justice John Marshall, pillar of judicial nationalism. [Library of Congress]

take appeals from state courts on the grounds that the Constitution, laws, and treaties of the United States could be kept uniformly the supreme law of the land only if the Court could review decisions of state courts. In the first case the Court overruled Virginia's confiscation of Loyalist property because this violated treaties with Great Britain; in the second it upheld Virginia's right to forbid the sale of lottery tickets.

PROTECTING CONTRACT RIGHTS   In the fateful year 1819 came two more decisions of major importance in checking the states and building the power of the central government: *Dartmouth College v. Woodward*, and *McCulloch v. Maryland*. The Dartmouth College case involved an attempt by the New Hampshire legislature to alter a charter granted Dartmouth by George III in 1769 under which the trustees became a self-perpetuating board. In 1816 the state's Republican legislature, offended by this relic of monarchy and even more by the Federalist majority on the board, placed Dartmouth under a new board named by the governor. The original trustees sued, lost in the state courts, but with Daniel Webster as counsel won on appeal to the Supreme Court. The charter, Marshall said for the Court, was a valid contract which the legislature had impaired, an act forbidden by the Constitution. This implied a new and enlarged definition of contract which seemed to put private corporations beyond the reach of the states that chartered them. But thereafter states commonly wrote into charters and general laws of incorporation provisions making them subject to modification. Such provisions were then part of the "contract."

STRENGTHENING THE FEDERAL GOVERNMENT   Marshall's single most important interpretation of the constitutional system came in the case of *McCulloch v. Maryland*. McCulloch, a clerk in the Baltimore branch of the Bank of the United States, failed to affix state revenue stamps to banknotes as required by a Maryland law taxing the notes. Indicted by the state, McCulloch, acting for the bank appealed to the Supreme Court, which handed down a unanimous judgment upholding the power of Congress to charter the bank and denying any right of the state to tax the bank. In a lengthy opinion Marshall examined and rejected Maryland's argument that the federal government was the creature of sovereign states. Instead, he argued, it arose directly from the people acting through the conventions which ratified the Constitution. While sovereignty was divided between the states and the national government, the latter, "though limited in its powers, is supreme within its sphere of action."

Marshall then went on to endorse the doctrine of broad construction and implied powers set forth by Hamilton in his bank message of 1791. The "necessary and proper" clause, he argued, did not mean "absolutely indispensable." The test of constitutionality he summed up in almost the same words as Hamilton: "Let the end be legitimate, let it be within the scope of the constitution, and all means which are appropriate, which are plainly adapted to that end, which are not prohibited, but consistent with the letter and spirit of the constitution, are constitutional."

The state's effort to tax the bank conflicted with the supreme law of the land. One great principle which "entirely pervades the constitution," Marshall wrote, was "that the constitution and the laws made in pursuance thereof are supreme: that they control the constitution and laws of the respective states, and cannot be controlled by them." The tax therefore was unconstitutional for "the power to tax involves the power to destroy"—which was precisely what the legislatures of Maryland and several other states had in mind with respect to the bank.

REGULATING INTERSTATE COMMERCE   Marshall's last great decision, *Gibbons v. Ogden* (1824), established national supremacy in regulating interstate commerce. In 1808 Robert Fulton and Robert Livingston, who pioneered commercial use of the steamboat, got

This 1810 lithograph shows Fulton's steamboat The Clermont, *going up the Hudson from New York to Albany. [New York Public Library]*

from the New York legislature the exclusive right to operate steamboats on the state's waters. From them in turn Aaron Ogden got the exclusive right to navigation across the Hudson between New York and New Jersey. Thomas Gibbons, however, operated a coastal trade under a federal license and came into competition with Ogden. On behalf of a unanimous Court, Marshall ruled that the monopoly granted by the state conflicted with the federal Coasting Act under which Gibbons operated. Congressional power to regulate commerce, the Court said, "like all others vested in Congress, is complete in itself, may be exercised to its utmost extent, and acknowledges no limitations other than are prescribed in the constitution." The opinion stopped just short of stating an exclusive federal power over commerce, and later cases would clarify the point that states had a concurrent jurisdiction so long as it did not come into conflict with federal action. For many years there was in fact little federal regulation, so that in striking down the monopoly created by the state Marshall had opened the way to extensive development of steamboat navigation and, soon afterward, steam railroads. Economic expansion was often consonant with judicial nationalism.

NATIONALIST DIPLOMACY

THE NORTHWEST   In foreign affairs, too, nationalism continued to be an effective force. Within two years after final approval of Adams's Transcontinental Treaty, the secretary of state was able to draw another important transcontinental line. In 1819 Spain had abandoned her claim to the Oregon country above the Forty-second Parallel. Russia, however, had claims along the Pacific coast as well. In 1741 Vitus Bering, in the employ of Russia, had explored the strait which now bears his name, and in 1799 the Russian-American Company had been formed to exploit the resources of Alaska. Some Russian outposts reached as far south as the California coast. In September 1821 the Russian czar issued an *ukase* (proclamation) claiming the Pacific coast as far south as 51°, which in the American view lay within the "Oregon country." In 1823 Secretary of State Adams contested "the right of Russia to any territorial establishment on this continent." The American government, he informed the Russian minister, assumed the principle "that the American continents are no longer subjects for any new European colonial establishments." The upshot of his protest was a treaty signed in 1824 whereby Russia accepted the line of 54° 40′ as the southern boundary of its claim. In 1825 a similar agreement between Russia and Britain gave the Oregon country clearly defined boundaries, although it was still subject to joint occupation by the United States and Great Britain under their agreement of 1818.

LATIN AMERICA   Adams's disapproval of further colonization also had clear implications for Latin America. One consequence of the Napoleonic wars and French occupation of Spain and Portugal had been a series of wars of liberation in Latin America. Within little more than a decade after the flag of rebellion was first raised in 1811, Spain had lost its entire continental empire. All that was left were the islands of Cuba, Puerto Rico, and Santo Domingo. The only continental possessions left to European powers, 330 years after Columbus, were Russian Alaska, Canada, British Honduras, and Dutch, French, and British Guiana.

That Spain could not regain her empire seems clear enough in retrospect. The British navy would not permit it because Britain's trade with the area was too important. For a time, however, the temper of Europe after Napoleon was to restore "legitimacy" everywhere. The great European peace conference, the Congress of Vienna (1814–1815), returned that continent, as nearly as possible, to its status before the French Revolution and set out to make the world safe for monarchy. To that end the major powers (Great Britain, Prussia, Russia, and Austria) set up the Quadruple Alliance (it became the Quintuple Alliance after France entered in 1818) to police the continent. In 1821 the Alliance, with Britain dissenting, authorized Austria to put down liberal movements in Italy. The British government was no champion of liberal revolution, but neither did it feel impelled to police the entire continent. In 1822, when the allies met in the Congress of Verona, they authorized France to suppress the constitutionalist movement in Spain and restore the authority of Ferdinand VII. At that point the British withdrew from the Concert of Europe, which in a few more years fell apart in a dispute over support of Greek rebellion against the Turks.

THE MONROE DOCTRINE   But in 1823 French troops crossed the Spanish border, put down the rebels, and restored King Ferdinand VII to absolute authority. Rumors began to circulate that France would also try to restore Ferdinand's "legitimate" power over Spain's American empire. Monroe and Secretary of War Calhoun were alarmed at the possibility, although John Quincy Adams took the more realistic view that such action was unlikely.

After the break with the Quadruple Alliance, British Foreign Minister George Canning sought to reach an understanding with the American minister to London that the two countries jointly undertake to forestall action by the Quadruple Alliance against Latin America. Monroe at first agreed, with the support of his sage advisors Jefferson and Madison.

Adams, however, urged upon Monroe and the cabinet the independent course of proclaiming a unilateral policy against the restoration of Spain's colonies. "It would be more candid," Adams said, "as well as more dignified, to avow our principles explicitly to Russia and France, than to come in as a cock-boat in the wake of the British man-of-war." Adams knew that the British navy would stop any action by the Quadruple Alliance in Latin America and he suspected that the alliance had no real intention to intervene anyway. The British wanted, moreover, the United States to agree not to acquire any more Spanish territory, including Cuba, Texas, or California, and Adams preferred to avoid such a commitment.

Indeed unbeknownst to Adams at the time Canning had already procured from French Foreign Minister Jules de Polignac a statement which renounced any purpose to reconquer or annex the former Spanish colonies. The Polignac Agreement was still unknown in the United States when Monroe incorporated the substance of Adams's views in his annual message to Congress on December 2, 1823. The Monroe Doctrine, as it was later called, comprised four major points: (1) that "the American continents . . . are henceforth not to be considered as subjects for future colonization by any European powers"; (2) the political system of European powers was different from that of the United States, which would "consider any attempt on their part to extend their system to any portion of this hemisphere as dangerous to our peace and safety"; (3) the United States would not interfere with existing European colonies; and (4) the United States would keep out of the internal affairs of European nations and their wars.

At the time the statement drew little attention either in the United States or abroad. Canning was more chagrined than anything else, since he had already achieved Monroe's objective two months before in the Polignac Agreement. In time the Monroe Doctrine, not even so called until 1852, became one of the cherished principles of American foreign policy, but for the time being it slipped into obscurity for want of any occasion to invoke it. In spite of Adams's affirmation, the United States came in as a cock boat in the wake of the British man-of-war after all, for the effectiveness of the doctrine depended on British naval supremacy. The doctrine had no standing in international law. It was merely a statement of intent by an American president to the Congress, and did not even draw enough interest at the time for European powers to renounce it.

ONE-PARTY POLITICS

Almost from the start of Monroe's second term the jockeying for the presidential succession had begun. Three members of Monroe's cabinet were active candidates: Calhoun, Crawford, and Adams. Henry Clay, longtime Speaker of the House, hungered and thirsted after the office. And on the fringes of the Washington scene a new force appeared in the person of Sen. Andrew Jackson, the scourge of the British, Spaniards, Creeks, and Seminoles, the epitome of what every frontiersman admired. All were Republicans, for again no Federalist stood a chance, but they were competing in a new political world, complicated by the cross-currents of nationalism and sectionalism. With only one party there was in effect no party, for there existed no generally accepted method for choosing a "regular" candidate.

PRESIDENTIAL NOMINATIONS Selection by congressional caucus, already under attack in 1816, had disappeared in the wave of unanimity which reelected Monroe in 1820 without the formality of a nomination. The friends of Crawford sought in vain to breathe life back into "King Caucus," but only sixty-six congressmen appeared in answer to the call. They duly named Crawford for president and Albert Gallatin for vice-president, but the endorsement was so weak as to be more a handicap than an advantage. Crawford was in fact the logical successor to the Virginia dynasty, a native of the state though a resident of Georgia. He had flirted with nationalism, but swung back to states' rights and strict construction, and assumed leadership of a faction, called the Radicals, which included Old Republicans and those who distrusted the nationalism of Adams and Calhoun. Crawford's candidacy was a forlorn cause from the beginning, for the candidate had been stricken in 1823 by some unknown disease which left him half-paralyzed and half-blind. His friends protested that he would soon be well but he never did fully recover.

Long before the rump caucus met on February 14, 1824, indeed for two years before, the country had broken out in a rash of presidential endorsements by legislatures and public meetings.

On July 20, 1822, the Tennessee legislature named Andrew Jackson. In March 1824 a mass meeting of Pennsylvanians in Harrisburg added their endorsement and Jackson, who had previously kept silent, responded that while the presidency should not be sought, it could not with propriety be declined. The same meeting named Calhoun for vice-president, and Calhoun accepted. The youngest of the candidates, he was content to retire from the presidential contest and take second place for the time being. Meanwhile the Kentucky legislature named its favorite son, Clay, on November 18, 1822. The Massachusetts legislature named Adams in 1824.

Of the four candidates only two had clearly defined programs, and the outcome was an early lesson in the danger of being committed on the issues too soon. Crawford's friends emphasized his devotion to the "principles of 1798," states' rights and strict construction. Clay, on the contrary, took his stand for the "American System," which he outlined in a lengthy speech to the House on March 30–31, 1824: he favored the national bank, the protective tariff, and a national program of internal improvements to bind the country together and build its economy. Adams was close to Clay, openly dedicated to internal improvements but less strongly committed to the tariff. Jackson, where issues were concerned, remained an enigma and carefully avoided commitment. His managers hoped that, by being all things to all men, Jackson could capitalize on his popularity as the hero of New Orleans.

THE "CORRUPT BARGAIN" The outcome turned on personalities and sectional allegiance more than on issues. Adams, the only northern candidate, carried New England, the former bastion of Federalism, and most of New York's electoral votes. Clay took Kentucky, Ohio, and Missouri. Crawford carried Virginia, Georgia, and Delaware. Jackson swept the Southeast, plus Illinois and Indiana, and with Calhoun's support, the Carolinas, Pennsylvania, Maryland, and New Jersey. All candidates got scattered votes elsewhere. In New York, where Clay was strong, his supporters were outmaneuvered in the legislature, which still chose the presidential electors. Martin Van Buren, trying to hold the old Virginia–New York axis for Crawford, also lost out to the Adams forces under Thurlow Weed.

The result was inconclusive in both the electoral vote and the popular vote, wherever the state legislature permitted the choice of electors by the people. In the electoral college Jackson had 99, Adams 84, Crawford 41, Clay 37. In the popular vote it ran about the same: Jackson 154,000, Adams 109,000, Crawford 47,000, and Clay 47,000. Whatever might have been said about the outcome, one thing seemed apparent. It was a defeat for Clay's American System: New England and New York opposed him on internal improvements; the South and Southwest on the protective tariff. Sectionalism had defeated the national program, yet the advocate of the American System now assumed the role of president-maker, since the election was thrown into the House of Representatives, where Speaker Clay's influence was decisive. Clay had little trouble in choosing, since he regarded Jackson as unfit for the office. He kept his own counsel until near the end, then threw his support to Adams. The final vote in the House, which was by state, carried Adams to victory with thirteen votes to Jackson's seven and Crawford's four.

It was a pyrrhic victory, for the result was to unite Adams's foes and to cripple his administration before it got under way. There is no evidence that Adams entered into any bargain with Clay to win his support, but the charge was made and widely believed after Adams made Clay his secretary of state, and thus put him in the office from which three successive presidents had risen. Adams's Puritan conscience could never quite ovecome its sense of guilt at the maneuverings that were necessary to gain his election, but a "corrupt bargain" was too much out of character for credence. Yet credence it had with a large number of people, and on that cry a campaign to elect Jackson next time was launched almost immediately after the 1824 decision. The Crawford people, including Martin Van Buren, the "Little Magician" of New York politics, soon moved into the Jackson camp.

JOHN QUINCY ADAMS'S PRESIDENCY   John Quincy Adams was one of the ablest men and finest intellects ever to enter the White House, but he sadly lacked the common touch and the politician's gift for maneuver. He firmly refused to play the game of patronage, on the simple grounds that it would be dishonorable to dismiss "able and faithful political opponents to provide for my own partisans." In four years he removed only twelve officeholders. His first annual message to Congress was a grandiose blueprint for national development, set forth in such a blunt way that it became a disaster of political ineptitude. In the boldness and magnitude of its conception, the Adams plan outdid both Hamilton and Clay. The central government, the president said, should promote internal improvements, set up a national university, finance scientific explorations, build astronomical observatories ("lighthouses of the skies"), reform the patent laws, and

John Quincy Adams, a president of great intellect but without the common touch, in a portrait by Thomas Sully. [New York State Bureau of Historic Sites]

create a new Department of the Interior. Ample powers to do all these things existed in "the power to exercise exclusive legislation in all cases whatsoever over the District of Columbia; . . . to lay and collect taxes, duties, imposts, and excises, to pay the debts and provide for the common defense and general welfare of the United States. . . . " In general terms he proposed "laws promoting the improvement of the agriculture, commerce, and manufactures, the cultivation and encouragement of the mechanic and of the elegant arts, the advancement of literature, and the progress of the sciences, ornamental and profound. . . . "

To refrain from using these powers "would be treachery to the most sacred of trusts." Officers of the government, he said, should not "fold up our arms and proclaim to the world that we are palsied by the will of our constituents. . . . " Whatever grandeur of conception the message had, it was obscured by an unhappy choice of language. For a minority president to demean the sovereignty of the voter was tactless enough. For the son of John Adams to cite the example "of the nations of Europe and of their rulers" was downright suicidal. At one fell swoop he had revived all the Republican suspicions of the Adamses. To the aging Jefferson his message seemed like Federalism run riot, looking to "a single and splendid government of an aristocracy, founded on banking institutions, and moneyed incorporation under the guise and cloak of . . . manufactures, commerce, and navigation, riding and ruling over the plundered ploughman and beggared yeomanry." Jefferson did not see, though, that

Adams's presidential message was the beginning of the definition of a new party system. The minority who cast their lot with Adams and Clay were turning into National-Republicans; the opposition, the growing party of Jacksonians, were the Democratic-Republicans, who would eventually drop the name Republican and become Democrats.

Adams's headstrong plunge into nationalism and his refusal to play the game of politics condemned his administration to utter frustration. Congress ignored his domestic proposals, and in foreign affairs the triumphs that he had scored as secretary of state had no sequels. In relations with Britain Adams had overreached himself by a "Perilous experiment" begun when he was secretary of state. By trying to force upon the British acceptance of American shipping on the same basis as British shipping in the West Indies, he passed up a chance for compromise on favorable terms, with the result that American shipping was banned altogether in 1826.

Before the year 1826 was out, Adams faced a showdown with the state of Georgia and meekly backed off. The affair began in 1825 when a federal Indian commissioner signed the fraudulent Treaty of Indian Springs with a group of Creek chieftains by which the Creeks lost 4.7 million acres in Georgia. Adams at first signed the treaty, but on further inquiry withdrew it and worked out the somewhat less stringent Treaty of Washington in 1826. The Georgia legislature denounced this annulment of the previous treaty as invalid and, by some obscure reasoning, called it a violation of states' rights. Gov. George M. Troup mobilized the Georgia militia and notified Adams that the state would repel with force any attempt to void the earlier treaty. At this the administration simply abandoned the Creeks to their fate. The Cherokees were next on the agenda, but by the time Georgia got around to them, there was a president who supported the land grabbers.

The climactic effort to discredit Adams came on the tariff issue. The Panic of 1819 had given rise to action for a higher tariff in 1820, but the effort failed by one vote in the Senate. In 1824 the advocates of protection renewed the effort, with greater success. The Tariff of 1824 favored the Middle Atlantic and New England manufacturers with higher duties on woolen, cotton, iron, and other finished goods. Clay's Kentucky won a tariff on hemp, and a tariff on raw wool brought the wool-growing interests to the support of the measure. Additional revenues were provided by duties on sugar, molasses, coffee, and salt. The tariff on raw wool was in obvious conflict with that on manufactured woolens, but the two groups got together and reached an agreement. A bill to raise further the wool and woolens duties failed in 1827 only by the tie-breaking vote of Vice-President Calhoun, who was in retreat from his prior support of the tariff.

At this point the supporters of Jackson saw a chance to advance their candidate by an awkward piece of political skulduggery. The plan, as later divulged by one of its authors, John Calhoun, was to present a bill with such outrageously high tariffs on raw materials that the manufacturers of the East would join the commercial interests there and with the votes of the agricultural South and Southwest defeat the measure. In the process Jackson men in the Northeast could take credit for supporting the tariff, and Jackson men, wherever it best fitted their interests, could take credit for opposing it—while Jackson himself remained in the background. John Randolph saw through the ruse. The bill, he asserted, "referred to manufactures of no sort or kind, but the manufacture of a President of the United States." The measure served that purpose, but in the process Calhoun was hoist on his own petard. The idea was a shade too clever, and Calhoun calculated neither upon the defection of Van Buren, who supported a crucial amendment to satisfy the woolens manufacturers, nor upon the growing strength of manufacturing interests in New England. Daniel Webster, now a senator from Massachusetts, explained that he was ready to deny all he had said against the tariff because New England had built up her manufactures on the understanding that the protective tariff was a settled policy.

When the bill passed on May 11, 1828, it was Calhoun's turn to explain his newfound opposition to the gospel of protection, and nothing so well illustrates the flexibility of constitutional principles as the switch in positions by Webster and Calhoun. Back in his study at Fort Hill, Calhoun prepared the *South Carolina Exposition and Protest* (1828), which was issued anonymously along with a series of resolutions by the South Carolina legislature. In that document Calhoun set forth the right of a state to nullify an act of Congress which it found unconstitutional.

JACKSON SWEEPS IN   Thus far the stage was set for the election of 1828, which might more truly be called a revolution than that of 1800. But if the issues of the day had anything to do with the election, they were hardly visible in the campaign, in which politicians on both sides reached depths of scurrilousness that had not been plumbed since 1800. Jackson was denounced as a hot-tempered and ignorant barbarian, a co-conspirator with Aaron

This anti-Jackson cartoon, published during the 1828 campaign, shows him as a frontier ruffian. [New-York Historical Society]

"Jackson is to be President, and you will be HANGED."

Burr, a participant in repeated duels and frontier brawls, a man whose fame rested on his reputation as a killer, a man whom Thomas Jefferson himself had pronounced unfit because of the rashness of his feelings—a remark inspired by Jackson's brief tenure in the Senate in 1797. In addition to that, his enemies dredged up the old story that Jackson had lived in adultery with his wife Rachel before they had been legally married; in fact they had lived together for two years in the mistaken belief that her divorce from a former husband was final. The worry over this humiliation and her probable reception in Washington may have contributed to an illness from which she died before Jackson took office, and it was one thing for which he could never forgive his enemies.

The Jacksonians, however, got in their licks against Adams, condemning him as a man who had lived his adult life on the public treasury, who had been corrupted by foreigners in the courts of Europe, and who had allegedly delivered up an American girl to serve the lust of Czar Alexander I. They called him a gambler and a spendthrift for having bought a billiard table and a set of chessmen for the White House, and a puritanical hypocrite for despising the common people and warning Congress to ignore the will of its constituents. He had finally reached the presidency, the Jacksonians claimed, by a corrupt bargain with Henry Clay.

In the campaign of 1828 when, the historian George Danger-

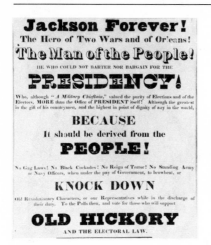

Jackson Forever!

The Hero of Two Wars and of Or'eans!

The Man of the People!

HE WHO COULD NOT BARTER NOR BARGAIN FOR THE

PRESIDENCY!

Who, although "*A Military Chieftain*," valued the purity of Elections and of the Electors, **MORE** than the Office of **PRESIDENT** itself! Although the greatest in the gift of his countrymen, and the highest in point of dignity of any in the world,

BECAUSE

It should be derived from the

PEOPLE!

No Gag Laws! No Black Cockades! No Reign of Terror! No Standing Army or Navy Officers, when under the pay of Government, to browbeat, or

KNOCK DOWN

Old Revolutionary Characters, or our Representatives while in the discharge of their duty. To the Polls then, and vote for those who will support

OLD HICKORY

AND THE ELECTORAL LAW.

This 1828 handbill identifies Jackson, "The Man of the People," with the democratic impulse of the time. [New-York Historical Society]

field said, "to betray an idea was almost to commit a felony," Jackson held most of the advantages. As a military hero he had some claim on patriotism. As a son of the West he was almost unbeatable there. As a planter and slaveholder he had the trust of southern planters. Debtors and local bankers who hated the national bank turned to Jackson. Not least of all, Jackson benefited from a spirit of democracy in which the commonality were no longer satisfied to look to their betters for leadership, as they had done in the lost world of Thomas Jefferson. It had become politically fatal to be labeled an aristocrat. Jackson's coalition now included even a seasoning of young Federalists—James Buchanan of Pennsylvania, Rober B. Taney of Maryland, William Drayton of South Carolina—eager to shed the stigma of aristocracy and get on in the world.

Since the Revolution and especially since 1800 manhood suffrage had been gaining ground. The traditional story has been that a surge of Jacksonian Democracy came out of the West like a great wave, supported mainly by small farmers, leading the way for the East. But there were other forces working in the older states toward a wider franchise: the revolutionary doctrine of equality, and the feeling on the parts of the workers, artisans, and small merchants of the towns, as well as small farmers and landed grandees, that a democratic ballot provided a means to combat the rising commercial and manufacturing interests. From the beginning Pennsylvania had opened the way to the ballot box with a taxpayers' franchise; by 1790 Georgia and New Hampshire had similar arrangements. Vermont, in 1791, became the first state with manhood suffrage, having first adopted it in 1777. Kentucky, admitted in 1792, became the second. Tennessee (1796) had only a light taxpaying qualification. New Jersey in 1807, and Maryland and South Carolina in 1810, abolished property and taxpaying requirements, and the new states of the West after 1815 came in with either white manhood suffrage or a low taxpaying requirement. Connecticut (1818), Massachusetts (1821), and New York (1821) all abolished their property requirements.

Along with the broadening of the suffrage went a liberalization of other features of government. Representation was reapportioned more nearly in line with population. An increasing number of officials, even judges, were named by popular vote. Final disestablishment of the Congregational church in New England came in Vermont (1807), New Hampshire (1817), Connecticut (1818), Maine (1820), and Massachusetts (1834). In 1824 six state legislatures still chose the presidential electors. By 1828 the popular vote prevailed in all but South Carolina and Delaware, and by 1832 in all but South Carolina.

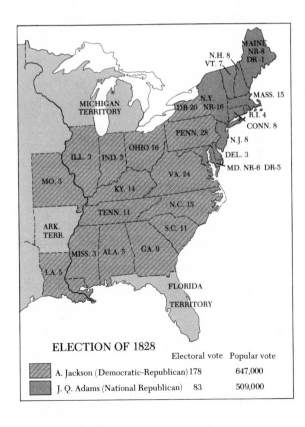

ELECTION OF 1828

		Electoral vote	Popular vote
	A. Jackson (Democratic-Republican)	178	647,000
	J. Q. Adams (National Republican)	83	509,000

The spread of the suffrage brought a new type of politician to the fore, the man who had special appeal to the masses or knew how to organize the people for political purposes, and who became a vocal advocate of the people's right to rule and the mystical concept that the voice of the people was the voice of God. Jackson fitted the ideal of this new political world, a leader sprung from the people rather than an aristocratic leader of the people, a frontiersman of humble origin who had scrambled up by will and tenacity, a fighter, a defender of the liberties of the people, a man who made no pretence of profound learning. "Adams can write," went one of the campaign slogans, "Jackson can fight." He could write too, but he once said that he had no respect for a man who could think of only one way to spell a word.

When the returns came in, it was clear that Jackson had won by a comfortable margin. The electoral vote was 178 to 83, and the popular vote (the figures vary) was about 647,000 to 509,000. Adams won all of New England, except for one of Maine's nine electoral votes, sixteen of the thirty-six from New York and six of the eleven from Maryland. All the rest belonged to Jackson.

FURTHER READING

A standard overview of the Era of Good Feelings remains George Dangerfield's *The Awakening of American Nationalism, 1815–1828* (1965).° Dangerfield also wrote *The Era of Good Feelings* (1952).° John Mayfield's *The New Nation, 1800–1845* (1981),° also treats events of this period. The gathering sense of a national spirit, hindered by an equally growing sectionalism, can be traced in Daniel J. Boorstin's *The Americans: The National Experience* (1965)° and in Paul C. Nagel's *One Nation Indivisible: The Union in American Thought, 1776–1861* (1964).

Background on the American System is handled in Frank W. Taussig's *The Tariff History of the United States* (1931) and in J. Van Fenstermaker's *The Development of American Commercial Banking, 1782–1837* (1965). Also good are the relevant chapters in Bray Hammond's *Banks and Politics in America from the Revolution to the Civil War* (1957).° George R. Taylor discusses internal improvements in *The Transportation Revolution, 1815–1860* (1951).° Phillip D. Jordan's *The National Road* (1948) concentrates on development of that internal project. Murray N. Rothbard's *The Panic of 1819* (1951) examines economics on the frontier. An overview of all the economic trends of the period is Douglass C.

°These books are available in paperback editions.

North's *The Economic Growth of the United States, 1790–1860* (1961).°

The political temper of the times is treated in biographical studies of principal figures: Harry Ammon's *James Monroe: The Quest for National Identity* (1971), Glyndon Van Deusen's *The Life of Henry Clay* (1937),° Clement Eaton's *Henry Clay and the Art of American Politics* (1957), Samuel F. Bemis's *John Quincy Adams and the Union* (1956), Richard W. Current's *John C. Calhoun* (1963), and C. C. Mooney's *William H. Crawford, 1772–1834* (1974). James S. Young's *The Washington Community, 1800–1828* (1961),° analyzes group leadership on the national level.

Diplomatic relations after 1812 are surveyed in several works, including C. C. Griffith's *The United States and the Disruption of the Spanish Empire* (1937) and Frank Thistlethwaite's *The Anglo-American Connection in the Early Nineteenth Century* (1959).° Ernest R. May's *The Making of the Monroe Doctrine* (1975) and Dexter Perkins's *A History of the Monroe Doctrine* (1963) provide clues to the formation of that policy.

In addition to works on the judiciary cited in Chapter 9, the following may also be consulted: Charles G. Haines's *The Role of the Supreme Court in American Government and Politics, 1789–1835* (1944), Robert K. Faulkner's *The Jurisprudence of John Marshall* (1968), Donald O. Dewey's *Marshall vs. Jefferson: The Background of Marbury v. Madison* (1970),° and Leonard Baker's *John Marshall: A Life at Law* (1974).°

Background on Andrew Jackson can be obtained from works cited in Chapter 11. The campaign which brought Jackson to the White House is analyzed in Robert V. Remini's *The Election of Andrew Jackson* (1963). Grant Foreman's *Indian Removal: The Emigration of the Five Civilized Tribes of Indians* (1932) and William W. Freehling's *Prelude to Civil War: The Nullification Controversy in South Carolina, 1816–1836* (1966)° treat specific issues of Jackson's first term.

11 ~

THE JACKSONIAN IMPULSE

SETTING THE STAGE

INAUGURATION Inauguration Day, March 4, 1829, came in a welcome spell of balmy weather after a bitterly cold winter. For days before, visitors had been crowding the streets and rooming houses of Washington in hope of seeing the people's hero take office. When Jackson emerged from his lodgings, dressed in black out of respect to his late wife Rachel, a great crowd filled both the east and west slopes of Capitol Hill. After Chief Justice Marshall administered the oath, the new president delivered his inaugural address in a voice so low that few of the crowd could hear a word of it. It mattered little, for Jackson's advisers had eliminated anything that might give offense. On the major issues of the tariff, internal improvements, and the Bank of the United States, Jackson remained enigmatic. Only a few points foreshadowed policies that the new chief executive would pursue: he favored retirement of the national debt, a proper regard for states' rights, a "just" policy toward Indians, and rotation in office, which he pronounced "a leading principle in the republican creed"—a principle his enemies would dub the "spoils system."

To that point all proceeded with dignity. Francis Scott Key, who witnessed the spectacle, declared: "It is beautiful, it is sublime!" After his speech Jackson mounted his horse and rode off to the White House, where a reception was scheduled for all who chose to come. The boisterous party that followed evoked the climate of turmoil that seemed always to surround Jackson. The crowd pushed into the White House, surged through the rooms, jostled the waiters, broke dishes, leaped on the furniture—all in an effort to shake the president's hand or at least get a glimpse of him. Surrounded by a group of his friends, the president soon

All creation Going to the White House. *The scene following Jackson's inauguration, according to satirist Robert Cruikshank.* *[Library of Congress]*

made his escape by a side door and went back to his lodgings for the night. Somebody then had the presence of mind to haul tubs of punch out on the White House lawn, where the unruly crowd followed. To Justice Story, "the reign of 'King Mob' seemed triumphant."

APPOINTMENTS AND POLITICAL RIVALRIES   To the office seekers who made up much of the restless crowd at the inaugural, some of Jackson's words held out high expectations that he planned to turn the rascals out and let the people rule. So it seemed when Jackson set forth a reasoned defense of rotation in office. The duties of government were reasonably simple, he said. Democratic principles supported the idea that a man should serve a term in government, then return to the status of private citizen, for officeholders who stayed too long became corrupted by a sense of power. And democracy, he argued, "is promoted by party appointments by newly elected officials." Jackson hardly foresaw how these principles would work out in practice, and it would be misleading to link him too closely with the "spoils system," which took its name from an 1832 partisan assertion by Democratic Sen. William L. Marcy of New York: "To the victor belong the spoils." Jackson in fact behaved with great moderation compared to the politicians of New York and Pennsylvania, where the spoils of office nourished extensive political machines. And a number of his successors made many more partisan appointments. During his first year in office Jackson replaced only about 9 percent of the appointed officials in the federal government, and during his entire term fewer than 20 percent were replaced.

Jackson relied very little on his appointments to the cabinet, which had little influence as an advisory group. More powerful was a coterie of men who had the president's ear and were soon dubbed his "Kitchen Cabinet." Among these, only Secretary of State Martin Van Buren headed a department, but most of the others were on the public payroll in some capacity. These included Amos Kendall of Kentucky, a former partisan of Clay, Isaac Hill of New Hampshire, and Duff Green, editor of the *United States Telegraph,* which had supported both Calhoun and Jackson. Others in the group from time to time included William B. Lewis of Tennessee, who had worked to make Jackson president, and Jackson's nephew and secretary, Andrew Jackson Donelson. The most influential members seem to have been Kentuckians Amos Kendall and Frank Blair, Sr., editor of the administration newspaper, the *Globe.*

Jackson's administration was from the outset a house divided between the partisans of Van Buren of New York and Vice-President Calhoun of South Carolina. Much of the political history of the next few years would turn upon the rivalry of the two, as each man jockeyed for position as the heir apparent to Jackson. It soon became clear in the political infighting for the succession that Van Buren held most of the advantages, foremost among them his skill at timing and tactics. As John Randolph put it, Van Buren always "rowed to his objective with muffled oars." Jackson, new to political administration, leaned heavily on him for advice and for help in soothing the ruffled feathers of rejected office seekers. Van Buren had perhaps more skill at maneuver than Calhoun, and certainly more freedom of maneuver since his home base of New York was more secure politically than Calhoun's base in South Carolina.

THE EATON AFFAIR   Van Buren also had luck on his side. Fate had quickly handed him a trump card: the succulent scandal of the Peggy Eaton affair. Peggy Eaton was the lively daughter of an Irish innkeeper, William O'Neale, whose place had been a Washington hangout for politicians, including at times Senators Jackson and Eaton of Tennessee. She was the widow of a navy purser named Timberlake, whose death (capital gossip had it) was a suicide brought on by her affair with Senator Eaton. Her marriage to Eaton, three months before he entered the cabinet, had scarcely made an honest woman of her in the eyes of the proper ladies of Washington. Floride Calhoun, the vice-president's wife, pointedly snubbed her, and cabinet wives followed suit. Even Mrs. A. J. Donelson withdrew as White House hostess rather than accept a fallen woman.

Peggy's plight reminded Jackson of the gossip which had pursued his own Rachel, and he pronounced Peggy "chaste as a virgin." To a friend he wrote: "I did not come here to make a Cabinet for the Ladies of this place, but for the Nation." Despite the cabinet members' discomfort at Jackson's open displeasure, the cabinet members were unable to cure their wives of what Van Buren dubbed "the Eaton Marlaria." Van Buren, however, was a widower, and therefore free to lavish on poor Peggy all the attention that Jackson thought was her due. The bemused John Quincy Adams looked on from afar and noted in his diary that Van Buren had become the leader of the party of the frail sisterhood. Mrs. Eaton herself finally wilted under the chill, began to refuse invitations, and withdrew from society. The outraged Jackson came to link Calhoun with what he called a conspiracy, and drew even closer to Van Buren.

INTERNAL IMPROVEMENTS While capital society weathered the chilly winter of 1829–1830, Van Buren prepared some additional blows to Calhoun. It was easy to bring Jackson into opposition to internal improvements and thus to federal programs with which Calhoun had long been identified: the Bonus Bill of 1817, the General Survey Bill of 1824, and Calhoun's own report on internal improvements made when he was secretary of war. Jackson did not oppose roadbuilding per se, but he had the same constitutional scruples as Madison and Monroe about federal aid to local projects. In 1830 the Maysville Road Bill, passed by Congress, offered Jackson a happy chance for a dual thrust at both Calhoun and Clay. The bill authorized the government to buy stock in a road from Maysville to Clay's hometown of Lexington. The road lay entirely within the state of Kentucky, and though part of a larger scheme to link up with the National Road via Cincinnati, it could be viewed as a purely local undertaking. On that ground Jackson vetoed the bill as unconstitutional, to widespread popular acclaim.

But a foolish consistency about internal improvements was never Jackson's hobgoblin any more than it was his predecessors'. While Jackson continued to oppose federal aid to local projects, he supported interstate projects, such as the national road, as well as roadbuilding in the territories, and rivers and harbors bills, the "pork barrels" from which every congressman tried to pluck a morsel for his district. Even so, Jackson's attitude set an important precedent, on the eve of the railroad age, for limiting federal initiative in internal improvements. Railroads would be built altogether by state and private capital at least until 1850. And except for scattered post roads, the federal government did not aid roadbuilding again until 1916, with the coming of the automobile.

NULLIFICATION

CALHOUN'S THEORY   There is a fine irony to Calhoun's plight in the Jackson administration, for Calhoun was now in midpassage from his early phase as a War Hawk nationalist to his later phase as a states'-rights sectionalist—and open to thrusts on both flanks. Circumstances in his home state had brought on this change. Suffering from agricultural depression, South Carolina lost almost 70,000 people to emigration during the 1820s, and was fated to lose nearly twice that number in the 1830s. Most South Carolinians blamed the protective tariff, which tended to raise the price of manufactured goods and, insofar as it discouraged the sale of foreign goods in the United States, reduced the ability of British and French traders to acquire the American money and bills of exchange with which to buy American cotton. This worsened problems of low cotton prices and exhausted lands. The South Carolinians' malaise was further compounded by a growing reaction against the criticism of slavery. Hardly had

John C. Calhoun. A War Hawk nationalist during the 1810s and 1820s, Calhoun was now becoming a states'-rights sectionalist. [National Archives]

the country emerged from the Missouri controversy when Charleston was thrown into panic by the Denmark Vesey slave insurrection of 1822, though the Vesey plot was nipped before it erupted. The unexpected passage of the Tariff of Abominations (1828) left Calhoun no choice but to join those in opposition or abandon his home base.

Calhoun's *South Carolina Exposition and Protest* (1828), written in opposition to that tariff, actually had been an effort to check the most extreme states'-rights advocates with a fine-spun theory in which nullification stopped short of secession from the Union. The statement, unsigned by its author, accompanied resolutions of the South Carolina legislature against the tariff. Calhoun, it was clear, had not entirely abandoned his earlier nationalism. His object was to preserve the Union by protecting the minority rights which the agricultural and slaveholding South claimed. The fine balance he struck between states' rights and central authority, ironically, was not as far removed from Jackson's own philosophy as it might seem, but growing tension between the two men would complicate the issue. Jackson, in addition, was determined to draw the line at any defiance of federal law.

Nor would Calhoun's theory permit any state to take up such defiance lightly. The procedure of nullification, whereby a state could in effect repeal a federal law, would follow that by which the original thirteen states had ratified the Constitution. A special state convention, like the ratifying conventions embodying the sovereign power of the people, could declare a federal law null and void because it violated the Constitution, the original compact among the states. One of two outcomes would then be possible. Either the federal government would have to abandon the law or it would have to get a constitutional amendment removing all doubt as to its validity. The immediate issue was the constitutionality of a tariff designed mainly to protect American industries against foreign competition. The South Carolinians argued that the Constitution authorized tariffs for revenue only.

THE WEBSTER-HAYNE DEBATE   South Carolina had proclaimed its dislike for the impost, but had postponed any action against its enforcement, awaiting with hope the election of 1828 in which Calhoun was the Jacksonian candidate for vice-president. The state anticipated a new tariff policy from the Jackson administration. There the issue stood until 1830, when the great Hayne-Webster debate sharpened the lines between states' rights and the Union. The immediate occasion for the debate, however, was the question of public lands. Late in 1829 Sen. Samuel A. Foot of Connecticut, an otherwise obscure figure, proposed an inquiry looking toward restriction of land sales in the West. When the Foot Resolution came before the Senate in January, Thomas Hart Benton of Missouri denounced it as a sectional attack designed to hamstring the settlement and development of the West so that the East might keep a supply of cheap factory labor. Robert Y. Hayne of South Carolina took Benton's side. Hayne saw in the issue a chance to strengthen the alliance of South and West that the vote for Jackson reflected. Perhaps by supporting a policy of cheap lands in the West the southerners could get in return western support for lower tariffs. The government, said Hayne, endangered the Union by any policy that would impose a hardship upon one section to the benefit of another. The use of public lands as a source of revenue to the central government would create "a fund for corruption—fatal to the sovereignty and independence of the states."

Daniel Webster of Massachusetts rose to defend the East. Denying that the East had ever shown an illiberal policy toward the West, he rebuked those southerners who, he said, "habitually speak of the Union in terms of indifference, or even of disparagement." Hayne had raised the false spectre of "Consolidation!—That perpetual cry, both of terror and delusion—consolidation!" Federal moneys, Webster argued, were not a source of corruption but a source of improvement. At this point the Foot Resolution and the issue of western lands vanished from sight. Webster had adroitly shifted the grounds of debate, and lured Hayne into defending states' rights and upholding the doctrine of nullification instead of pursuing coalition with the West.

Hayne took the bait. After some personal thrusts, in which he harked back to Webster's early career as a Federalist, he launched into a defense of the "South Carolina Exposition," appealed to the example of the Virginia and Kentucky Resolutions of 1798, and called attention to the Hartford Convention in which New Englanders had taken much the same position against majority measures as South Carolina did. The Union was created by a compact of the states, he argued, and the federal government could not be the judge of its own powers, else its powers would be unlimited. Rather, the states remained free to judge when their agent had overstepped the bounds of its constitutional authority. The right of state interposition was "as full and complete as it was before the Constitution was formed."

In rebuttal to the state-compact theory, Webster defined a nationalistic view of the Constitution. From the beginning, he asserted, the American Revolution had been a crusade of the united colonies rather than of each separately. True sovereignty resided in the people as a whole, for whom both federal and state governments acted as agents in their respective spheres. If a single state could nullify a law of the general government, then the Union would be a "rope of sand," a practical absurdity. Instead the Constitution had created a Supreme Court with the final jurisdiction on all questions of constitutionality. A state could neither nullify a federal law nor secede from the Union. The practical outcome of nullification would be a confrontation leading to civil war.

Hayne may have had the better of the argument historically in advancing the state-compact theory, but the Senate galleries and much of the country at large thrilled to the eloquence of "the Godlike Daniel." His peroration became an American classic, reprinted in school texts and committed to memory by generations of schoolboy orators: "When my eyes shall be turned to behold, for the last time, the sun in heaven, may I not see him shining on the broken and dishonored fragments of a once glorious Union. . . . Let their last feeble and lingering glance, rather, behold the gorgeous ensign of the republic . . . blazing on all its ample folds, as they float over the sea and over the land . . . Liberty and Union, now and forever, one and inseparable." In the practical world of coalition politics Webster had the better of the

Massachusetts Sen. Daniel Webster in G. P. A. Healy's painting of the Webster-Hayne debate. [Boston Art Commission]

argument, for the Union and majority rule meant more to westerners, including Jackson, than the abstractions of state sovereignty and nullification. As for the public lands, the Foot Resolution was soon defeated anyway. And whatever one might argue about the origins of the Union, its evolution would more and more validate Webster's position.

THE RIFT WITH CALHOUN As yet, however, the enigmatic Jackson had not spoken out on the issue. The nullificationists had given South Carolina's electoral vote to him as well as to Calhoun in 1828. Jackson, like Calhoun, was a slaveholder, albeit a westerner, and might be expected to sympathize with South Carolina, his native state. Soon all doubt was removed, at least on the point of nullification. On April 13, 1830, the Jefferson Day Dinner was held in Washington to honor the birthday of the former president. It was a party affair, but the Calhounites controlled the arrangements with an eye to advancing their own doctrine. Jackson and Van Buren were invited as a matter of course, and the two agreed that Jackson should present a toast which would indicate his opposition to nullification. When his turn came, after twenty-four toasts, many of them extolling states' rights, Jackson raised his glass and, pointedly looking at Calhoun, announced: "Our Union—It must be preserved!" (At the behest of Senator Hayne the first words were later published as "Our Federal Union.") Calhoun, who followed, trembled so that he spilled some of the amber fluid from his glass (according to Van Buren), but tried quickly to retrieve the situation with a toast to "The Union, next to our liberty most dear! May we all remember that it can only be preserved by respecting the rights of the States and distributing equally the benefit and the burthen of the Union!" But Jackson had set off a bombshell which exploded the plans of the states'-righters.

Nearly a month afterward a final nail was driven into the coffin of Calhoun's presidential ambitions. On May 12, 1830, Jackson saw a letter from William H. Crawford giving final confirmation to reports that had been reaching him of Calhoun's stand in 1818, when as secretary of war the South Carolinian had proposed to discipline Jackson for his Florida invasion. A tense correspondence between Jackson and Calhoun followed, and ended with a curt note from Jackson cutting it off. "Understanding you now," Jackson wrote on May 30, 1830, "no further communication with you on this subject is necessary."

One result of the growing rift between the men was the appearance of a new administration paper. Duff Green's *United States Telegraph,* for two years the administration organ, was too closely allied with Calhoun. Jackson and his "Kitchen Cabinet" arranged to have Francis Preston Blair, Sr., of Kentucky, move to Washington and set up the Washington *Globe*, the first issue of which appeared before the end of 1830. Another result was a cabinet shakeup by Jackson, who was resolved to remove all Calhoun partisans. According to a plan contrived by Van Buren, he and Secretary of War Eaton resigned, offering as their reason a desire to relieve Jackson of the embarrassment of awkward controversy. Jackson in turn requested and got resignations of the others, except Postmaster-General William T. Barry. Before the end of the summer of 1831 the president had a new cabinet entirely loyal to him.

Jackson then named Van Buren minister to London, pending Senate approval. The friends of Van Buren now importuned Jackson to repudiate his previous intention of only serving one term. It might have been hard, they felt, to get the nomination in 1832 for the New Yorker, who had been charged with intrigues against Calhoun, and the still-popular Carolinian might yet have carried off the prize. Jackson relented and in the fall of 1831 announced his readiness for one more term, with the idea of returning Van Buren from London in time to win the presidency in 1836. But in January 1832, when the Senate reconvened, Van Buren's enemies opposed his appointment as minister, and gave Calhoun, as vice-president, a chance to reject the nomination by a tie-breaking vote. "It will kill him, sir, kill him dead," Calhoun told Sen. Thomas Hart Benton. Benton disagreed: "You have broken a minister, and elected a Vice-President." So, it turned out, he had. Calhoun's vote against Van Buren provoked popular sympathy for the New Yorker, who would soon be nominated to succeed Calhoun.

Now that his presidential hopes were blasted, Calhoun came forth as the public leader of the nullificationists. These South Carolinians thought that, despite Jackson's gestures, tariff rates remained too high. Jackson, who accepted the principle of protection, nevertheless had called upon Congress in 1829 to modify duties by reducing tariffs on goods "which cannot come in competition with our own products." Late in the spring of 1830 Congress lowered duties on such consumer products as tea, coffee, salt, and molasses. In all it cut about $4.5 million from something over $20 million in tariff revenue. That and the Maysville veto, coming at about the same time, mollified a few South Carolinians, but nullifiers regarded the two actions as "nothing but sugar plums to pacify children." By the end of 1831 Jackson was calling for further reductions to take the wind out of the nullificationists' sails, and the tariff of 1832, pushed through by now

Rep. John Quincy Adams, cut revenues another $5 million, again mainly on unprotected items. Average tariff rates were about 25 percent, but rates on cottons, woolens, and iron remained up around 50 percent.

THE SOUTH CAROLINA ORDINANCE   In the South Carolina state elections of October 1832, all attention centered on the nullification issue. The nullificationists took the initiative in organization and agitation, and the Unionist party was left with a distinguished leadership but only small support, drawn chiefly from the merchants of Charleston and the yeoman farmers of the upcountry. A special session of the legislature in October called for the election of a state convention. The convention assembled at Columbia on November 19 and on November 24 overwhelmingly adopted an ordinance of nullification which repudiated the tariff acts of 1828 and 1832 as unconstitutional and forbade collection of the duties in the state after February 1, 1833. The reassembled legislature then provided that any citizen whose property was seized by federal authorities for failure to pay the duty could get a state court order to recover twice its value. The legislature also chose Hayne as governor and elected Calhoun to succeed him as senator. Calhoun promptly resigned as vice-president in order to defend nullification on the Senate floor.

JACKSON'S FIRM RESPONSE   In the crisis South Carolina found itself standing alone, despite the sympathy expressed elsewhere. The Georgia legislature called for a southern convention, but dismissed nullification as "rash and revolutionary." Alabama pronounced it "unsound in theory and dangerous in practice"; Mississippi stood "firmly resolved" to put down nullification. Jackson's response was measured and firm, but not rash—at least not in public. In private he threatened to hang Calhoun and all other traitors—and later expressed regret that he had failed to hang at least Calhoun. In his annual message on December 4, 1832, Jackson announced his firm intention to enforce the tariff, but once again urged Congress to lower the rates. On December 10 he followed up with his Nullification Proclamation, drafted by Secretary of State Edward Livingston, a document which characterized the doctrine as an "impractical absurdity." Jackson said in part: "I consider, then, the power to annul a law in the United States, assumed by one state, incompatible with the existence of the Union, contradicted expressly by the letter of the Constitution, unauthorized by its spirit, inconsistent with every principle on which it was founded, and destructive of the great object for which it was formed." He appealed to the people of his native state not to follow false leaders: "The laws of the United States must be executed. I have no discretionary power on the subject; my duty is emphatically pronounced in the constitution. Those who told you that you might peaceably prevent their execution, deceived you; they could not have been deceived themselves. . . . Their object is disunion. But be not deceived by names. Disunion by armed force is treason."

CLAY'S COMPROMISE   Jackson sent Gen. Winfield Scott to Charleston Harbor with reinforcements of federal soldiers, who were kept carefully isolated in the island posts at Fort Moultrie and Castle Pinckney to avoid incidents. A ship of war and seven revenue cutters appeared in the harbor, ready to enforce the tariff before ships had a chance to land their cargoes. The nullifiers mobilized the state militia while unionists in the state organized a volunteer force. In January 1833 the president requested from Congress a "Force Bill," specifically authorizing him to use the army to compel compliance with federal law in South Carolina. Under existing legislation he already had such authority, but this affirmation would strengthen his hand. At the same time he gave his support to a bill in Congress which would have lowered duties to a maximum of 20 percent within two years. The nullifiers postponed enforcement of their ordinances in anticipation of a compromise. Passage of the bill depended on the support of Henry Clay, who finally yielded to those urging him to save the day. On February 12, 1833, he brought forth a plan to reduce the tariff gradually until 1842, by which time no rate would be more than 20 percent. It was less than South Carolina would have preferred, but it got the nullifiers out of the corner into which they had painted themselves.

On March 1, 1833, the compromise tariff and the Force Bill passed Congress and the next day Jackson signed both. The South Carolina Convention then met and rescinded its nullification, and in a face-saving gesture, nullified the Force Bill, for which Jackson no longer had any need. Both sides were able to claim victory. Jackson had upheld the supremacy of the Union and South Carolina had secured a reduction of the tariff.

JACKSON'S INDIAN POLICY

On Indian affairs Jackson's attitude was the typically western one, that Indians were better off out of the way. Jackson had already done his part in the Creek and Seminole Wars to chastise them and separate them from their lands. By the time of his election in 1828 he was fully in accord with the view that a "just, humane, liberal policy toward Indians" dictated moving them onto the plains west of the Mississippi. The policy was by no means new or original with Jackson; the ideal had emerged gradually after the Louisiana Purchase in 1803. It had been formally set forth in 1823 by Calhoun, as secretary of war, and by now was generally accepted, that a permanent solution to the Indian "problem" would be their removal and resettlement in the "Great American Desert," which white men would never covet since it was thought fit mainly for horned toads and rattlesnakes.

INDIAN REMOVAL   In response to Jackson's message, Congress in 1830 approved the Indian Removal Act and appropriated $500,000 for the purpose. Jackson's presidency saw some ninety-four removal treaties negotiated, and by 1835 Jackson was able to announce that the policy had been carried out or was in process of completion for all but a handful of Indians. The policy was effected with remarkable speed, but even that was too slow for state authorities in the South and Southwest. Unlike the Ohio Valley–Great Lakes region, where flow of white settlement had constantly pushed the Indians westward before it, in the Old Southwest settlement moved across Kentucky and Tennessee and down the Mississippi, surrounding the Creeks, Choctaws,

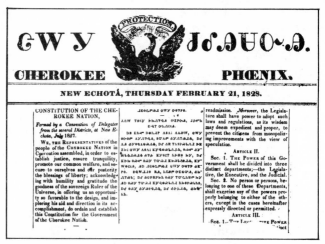

The first issue of the Cherokee Phoenix *published the Constitution of the Cherokee nation, which embraced "the lands solemnly guaranteed and reserved forever to the Cherokee Nation by the Treaties concluded with the United States." [American Antiquarian Society]*

Chickasaws, Seminoles, and Cherokees. These tribes of the area had over the years taken on many of the features of white society. The Cherokees even had such appurtenances of "white civilization" as a constitution, a written language, and black slaves.

Most of the northern tribes were too weak to resist the importunings of Indian commissioners who, if necessary, used bribery and alcohol to woo the chiefs, and if sometimes the tribesmen rebelled, there was, on the whole, remarkably little resistance. In Illinois and Wisconsin Territory an armed clash sprang up from April to August 1832, which came to be known as the Black Hawk War, when the Sauk and Fox under Chief Black Hawk sought to reoccupy some lands they had abandoned in the previous year. Facing famine and hostile Sioux west of the Mississippi, they were simply seeking a place to get in a corn crop. The Illinois militia mobilized to expel them, chased them into Wisconsin Territory, and inflicted a gruesome massacre of women and children as they tried to escape across the Mississippi. The Black Hawk War came to be remembered later, however, less because of the atrocities inflicted on the Indians than because the participants included two native Kentuckians later pitted against each other; Lt. Jefferson Davis of the regular army and Capt. Abraham Lincoln of the Illinois volunteers.

In the South two nations, the Seminoles and Cherokees, put up a stubborn resistance. The Seminoles of Florida fought a protracted guerrilla war in the Everglades from 1835 to 1842. But most of the vigor went out of their resistance after 1837, when their leader Osceola was seized by treachery under a flag of truce to die a prisoner at Fort Moultrie in Charleston Harbor. After 1842 only a few hundred Seminoles remained, hiding out in the swamps. Most of the rest had been removed to the West.

THE CHEROKEES' TRAIL OF TEARS   The Cherokees had by the end of the eighteenth century fallen back into the mountains of northern Georgia and western North Carolina, onto land guaranteed to them in 1791 by treaty with the United States. But when Georgia ceded its western lands in 1802 it did so on the ambiguous condition that the United States extinguish all Indian titles within the state "as early as the same can be obtained on reasonable terms." In 1827 the Cherokees, relying on their treaty rights, adopted a constitution in which they said pointedly that they were not subject to any other state or nation. In 1828 Georgia responded with a law that after June 1, 1830, the authority of state law would extend over the Cherokees living within the boundaries of the state.

The discovery of gold in 1829 whetted the whites' appetite for Cherokee lands and brought bands of rough prospectors into the country. The Cherokees sought relief in the Supreme Court, but in *Cherokee Nation v. Georgia* (1831) John Marshall ruled that the Court lacked jurisdiction because the Cherokees were a "domestic dependent nation" rather than a foreign state in the meaning of the Constitution. In 1830 a Georgia law required whites in the territory to get licenses authorizing their residence there, and to take an oath of allegiance to the state. Two New England missionaries among the Indians refused and were sentenced to four years at hard labor. On appeal their case reached the Supreme Court as *Worcester v. Georgia* (1832) and the court held that the national government had exclusive jurisdiction in the Cherokee country and the Georgia law was therefore unconstitutional.

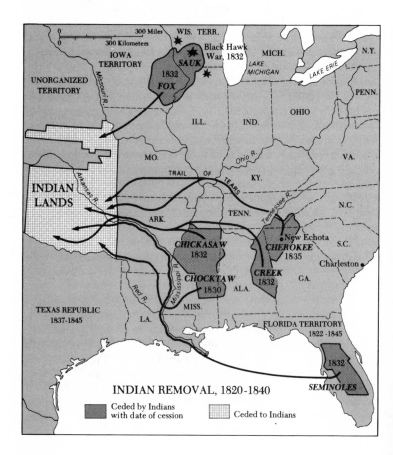

INDIAN REMOVAL, 1820-1840

Ceded by Indians with date of cession

Ceded to Indians

Six years earlier Georgia had faced down President Adams when he tried to protect the rights of the Creeks. Now Georgia faced down the Supreme Court with the tacit consent of another president. Jackson is supposed to have said privately: "Marshall has made his decision, now let him enforce it!" Whether or not he actually put it so bluntly, Jackson did nothing to enforce the decision. In the circumstances there was nothing for the Cherokees to do but give in and sign a treaty, which they did in 1835. They gave up their lands in the Southeast in exchange for lands in the Indian Territory west of Arkansas, $5 million from the federal government, and expenses for transportation. By 1838 the Cherokees had departed on the "trail of tears" westward, following the Choctaws, Chickasaws, and Creeks on a journey marked by the cruelty and neglect of soldiers and private contractors, and scorn and pilferage by whites along the way. A few held out in the mountains and got a reservation from the state of North Carolina; thenceforth they were the "eastern band" of the Cherokees. A scattered few of the others remained in the Southeast, especially mixed-blood Creeks who could pass for white.

The Bank Controversy

THE BANK'S OPPONENTS   The overriding national issue in the campaign of 1832 was neither Jackson's Indian policy nor South Carolina's obsession with nullification. It was the question of rechartering the Bank of the United States. On the bank issue, as on others, Jackson had made no public commitment, but his personal opposition to the bank was already formed. Jackson had absorbed the western attitude of hostility toward the bank after the Panic of 1819, and held to a conviction that it was unconstitutional no matter what Marshall had said in *McCulloch v. Maryland*. Banks in general had contributed to a speculative mania, and Jackson, suspicious of all banks, preferred a hard-money policy. The general felt in his bones that the bank was wrong and did not need to form his opinions out of an intimate knowledge of banking. He was in fact blissfully ignorant of the subject.

Under the management of Nicholas Biddle the Bank of the United States had prospered and grown. Coming from a well-to-do Philadelphia family, Biddle had previously followed a career as editor, diplomat, and politician. He had little acquaintance with business when Monroe appointed him a government director of the bank, but he proved a quick study and by the time he replaced Langdon Cheves as president of the bank in 1823 Biddle was well versed in banking. The bank had worked to the benefit of business and performed the important function of supplying a stable currency by its policy of forcing state banks to keep a specie reserve (gold or silver) behind their notes. But arrayed against the bank were powerful enemies: some of the state and local banks which had been forced to reduce their note issues, debtor groups which suffered from the reduction and businessmen and speculators "on the make" who wanted easier credit. States'-rights groups questioned the bank's constitutionality, though Calhoun, who had sponsored the original charter and valued the bank's function of regulating the currency, was not among them. Financiers of New York's Wall Street resented the supremacy of the bank on Philadelphia's Chestnut Street. Many westerners and workingmen, like Jackson, felt in their bones that the bank was, in Thomas Hart Benton's words, a "Monster," a monopoly controlled by a few of the wealthy with power which was irreconcilable with a democracy. "I think it right to be perfectly frank with you," Jackson told Biddle in 1829. "I do not dislike your Bank any more than all banks. But ever since I read the history of the South Sea Bubble I have been afraid of banks." This struck Biddle as odd, since he regarded his conservative policies as a safeguard against speculative manias like the eighteenth-century "South Sea Bubble," in which thousands of British investors had been fleeced. Jackson was perhaps right in his instinct that the bank lodged too much power in private hands, but mistaken in his understanding of the bank's policies.

Biddle at first tried to conciliate Jackson and appointed a number of Jackson men to branch offices of the bank. In his first annual message (1829), though, Jackson questioned the bank's constitutionality and asserted (whatever the evidence to the contrary) that it had failed to maintain a sound and uniform currency. Jackson talked of a compromise, perhaps a bank completely owned by the government with its operations confined chiefly to government deposits, its profits payable to the government, and its authority to set up branches in any state dependent on the state's wishes. But Jackson would never commit himself on the precise terms of compromise. Some of Jackson's cabinet members cautiously favored the bank, but the opposition of Amos Kendall and Francis P. Blair in the Kitchen Cabinet influenced him more. The bank's survival was left up to Biddle.

BIDDLE'S RECHARTER EFFORT   Its twenty-year charter would run through 1836, but Biddle could not afford the uncertainty of waiting until then for a renewal. Biddle pondered whether to force the issue of recharter before the election of 1832 or after. On this point leaders of the National Republicans, especially Clay and Webster (who was counsel to the bank as well as a senator), argued that the time to move was before the election. Clay, already the candidate of the National Republicans, proposed to make the bank the central issue of the presidential canvass. Friends of the bank held a majority in Congress, and Jackson would risk loss of support in the election if he vetoed a renewal. But they failed to grasp the depth of prejudice against the bank, and succeeded mainly in handing to Jackson a popular issue on the eve of the election.

Both houses passed the recharter by comfortable margins, but without the two-thirds majority needed to override a veto. On July 10, 1832, Jackson vetoed the bill, sending it back to Congress with a ringing denunciation of monopoly and special privilege. In a message written largely by his confidant Amos Kendall, Jackson argued that the bank was unconstitutional, whatever the Court and Congress said. "Each public officer who takes an oath to support the Constitution swears that he will support it as he understands it, and not as it is understood by others. . . . The opinion of the judges has no more authority over Congress than the opinion of Congress had over the judges, and on that point the President is independent of both." Besides, there were sub-

This caricature shows King Andrew Jackson trampling the Constitution, internal improvements, and the U.S. Bank. Opponents considered Jackson's Maysville veto and bank veto abuses of power. [Library of Congress]

stantive objections aside from the question of constitutionality. Foreign stockholders in the bank had an undue influence. The bank had shown favors to members of Congress and exercised an improper power over state banks. The bill, he argued, demonstrated that "Many of our rich men have not been content with equal protection and equal benefits, but have besought us to make them richer by act of Congress." An effort to overrule the veto failed in the Senate; a vote of 22 to 19 for the bank fell far short of the needed two-thirds majority. Thus the stage was set for a nationwide financial crisis.

CAMPAIGN INNOVATIONS   The presidential campaign, as usual, was under way early, the nominations having been made before the bank veto, two in fact before the end of 1831. For the first time a third party entered the field. The Anti-Masonic party was, like the bank, the object of strong emotions then sweeping the new democracy. The group had grown out of popular hostility toward the Masonic order, members of which were suspected of having kidnapped and murdered a bricklayer of Batavia, New York, for revealing the "secrets" of his lodge. Opposition to a fraternal order was hardly the foundation on which to build a lasting party, but the Anti-Masonic party had three important "firsts" to its credit: in addition to being the first third party, it was the first party to hold a national nominating convention and the first to announce a platform, all of which it accomplished in September 1831 when it nominated William Wirt of Maryland for president.

The major parties followed its example by holding national conventions of their own. In December 1831 the delegates of the National Republican party assembled in Baltimore to nominate Henry Clay for president and John Sergeant of Pennsylvania, counsel to the bank and chief advocate of the recharter strategy, for vice-president. Jackson endorsed the idea of a nominating convention for the Democratic party (the name Republican was now formally dropped) to demonstrate popular support for its candidates. To that purpose the convention, also meeting at Baltimore, adopted the two-thirds rule for nomination (which prevailed until 1936), and then named Martin Van Buren as Jackson's running mate. The Democrats, unlike the other two parties, adopted no formal platform at their first convention, and relied to a substantial degree on hoopla and the personal popularity of the president to carry their cause.

The outcome was an overwhelming endorsement of Jackson in the electoral college by 219 votes to 49 for Clay, and a less overwhelming but solid victory in the popular vote, by 688,000 to

530,000. William Wirt carried only Vermont, with several electoral votes. South Carolina, preparing for nullification and unable to stomach either Jackson or Clay, delivered its eleven votes to Gov. John Floyd of Virginia.

REMOVAL OF GOVERNMENT DEPOSITS   Jackson took the election as a mandate to proceed further against the bank. He asked Congress to investigate the safety of government deposits in the bank, since one of the current rumors told of empty vaults, carefully concealed. After a committee had checked, the Calhoun and Clay forces in the House of Representatives united in the passage of a resolution affirming that government deposits were safe and could be continued. The resolution passed, by chance, on March 2, 1833, the same day that Jackson signed the compromise tariff and Force Bill. With the nullification issue out of the way, however, Jackson was free to wage his unrelenting war on the bank, that "hydra of corruption," which still had nearly four years to run on its charter. Despite the House study and resolution, Jackson now resolved to remove all government deposits from the bank.

When Secretary of the Treasury McLane opposed removal of the government deposits and suggested a new and modified version of the bank, Jackson shook up his cabinet. He kicked McLane upstairs to head the State Department, which Edward Livingston left to become minister to France. To take McLane's place at the Treasury he chose William J. Duane of Philadelphia, but by some oversight Jackson failed to explore Duane's views fully or advise him of the presidential expectations. Duane was antibank, but he was consistent in his convictions. Dubious about banks in general, he saw no merit in removing deposits from the Monster for redeposit in countless state banks. Jackson might well have listened to Duane's warnings that such action would lead to speculative inflation, but the old general's combative instincts were too much aroused. He summarily dismissed Duane and moved Attorney-General Taney to the Treasury, where the new secretary gladly complied with the presidential wishes, which corresponded to his own views.

The procedure was to continue drawing on governmental accounts with Biddle's Bank, and to deposit all new governmental receipts in state banks. By the end of 1833 there were twenty-three state banks which had the benefit of governmental deposits, "pet banks" as they came to be called. The sequel to Jackson's headlong plunge into finance, it soon turned out, was the precise opposite of what he had sought. As so often happens

The Downfall of Mother Bank. In this pro-Jackson cartoon of 1833, the bank crumbles and Jackson's opponents flee in the face of the heroic president's removal of government deposits. [New-York Historical Society]

with complex public issues, dissatisfaction had become focused on a symbol. In this case the symbol was the "Monster of Chestnut Street," which had been all along the one institution able to maintain some degree of order in the financial world. The immediate result of Jackson's action was a contraction of credit by Biddle's bank in order to shore up its defenses against the loss of deposits. By 1834 the tightness of credit was creating complaints of business distress, which was probably exaggerated by both sides in the bank controversy for political effect: Biddle to show the evil consequences of the withdrawal of deposits, Jacksonians to show how Biddle abused his power.

The contraction brought about by the bank quickly gave way, however, to a speculative binge encouraged by the deposit of government funds in the pet banks. With the restraint of Biddle's bank removed, the state banks gave full rein to their wildcat tendencies. (The term "wildcat," used in this sense, originated in Michigan, where one of the fly-by-night banks featured a panther, or wildcat, on its worthless notes.) New banks mushroomed, printing banknotes with abandon for the purpose of lending to speculators. Sales of public lands rose from 4 million acres in 1834 to 15 million in 1835 and to 20 million in 1836. At the same time the states plunged heavily into debt to finance the building of roads and canals, inspired by the success of New York's Erie Canal. By 1837 total state indebtedness had soared to $170 million, a very large sum for this time. The supreme irony of Jackson's war on the bank then was that it preceded a speculative mania that dwarfed even the South Sea Bubble.

FISCAL MEASURES   The new bubble reached its greatest extent in 1836, when a combination of events conspired suddenly to deflate it. Most important among these were the Distribution Act, passed in June 1836, and the Specie Circular of July 1836. Distribution of the government's surplus funds had long been a pet project of Henry Clay. One of its purposes was to eliminate the surplus thus removing one argument for cutting the tariff. Much of the surplus, however, was brought in by the "land office business" in western real estate, and was therefore in the form of banknotes that had been issued to speculators. Many westerners thought that the solution to the surplus was simply to lower the price of land; southerners preferred to lower the tariff—but such action would now upset the compromise achieved in the tariff of 1833. For a time the annual surpluses could be applied to paying off the government debt, but the debt, reduced to $7 million by 1832, was entirely paid off by January 1835.

Still the federal surplus continued to mount. Clay again proposed distribution, but Jackson had constitutional scruples about the process. Finally, a compromise was worked out whereby the government would distribute most of the surplus as loans to the states. To satisfy Jackson's scruples the funds were technically "deposits," but in reality they were never demanded back. Distribution was to be in proportion to each state's representation in the two houses of Congress, and was to be paid out in quarterly installments, beginning January 1, 1837.

About a month after passage of the Distribution Act came the Specie Circular of July 11, 1836, issued by the secretary of the treasury at Jackson's order. With that document the president belatedly applied his hard-money conviction to the sale of public lands. According to his order, the government after August 15 would accept only gold and silver in payment for lands—with the exception that for a brief time banknotes would be accepted for parcels up to 320 acres when bought by actual settlers or residents of the state in which the sale was made. The purposes declared in the circular were to "repress frauds," to withhold support "from the monopoly of the public lands in the hands of speculators and capitalists," and to discourage the "ruinous extension" of banknotes and credit.

Irony dogged Jackson to the end on this matter. Since few actual settlers could get their hands on specie, they were now left all the more at the mercy of speculators for land purchases. Both the distribution and the Specie Circular put many state banks in a precarious plight. The distribution reduced their deposits, or at least threw things into disarray by shifting them from bank to bank, and the increased demand for specie put an added strain on the supply of gold and silver.

BOOM AND BUST   But the boom and bust of the 1830s had causes larger even than Andrew Jackson, causes that were beyond his control. The inflation of mid-decade was rooted not in a prodigal expansion of banknotes, as it seemed at the time, but by an increase of specie flowing in from England and France, and especially from Mexico, for investment and for the purchase of American cotton and other commodities. At the same time British credits enabled Americans to buy British goods without having to export specie. Meanwhile the flow of hard cash to China, where silver had been much prized, declined. The Chinese now took in payment for their goods British credits which they could in turn use to cover rapidly increasing imports of opium from British India.

Contrary to appearances, therefore, the reserves of specie in American banks kept pace with the increase of banknotes, despite reckless behavior on the part of some banks. But by 1836 a tighter British economy caused a decline in British investments and in British demand for American cotton just when the new western lands were creating a rapid increase in cotton supply. Fortunately for Jackson, the Panic of 1837 did not break until he was out of the White House and safely back at the Hermitage. His successor would serve as the scapegoat.

In May 1837 New York banks suspended specie payments on their banknotes and fears of bankruptcy set off runs on banks around the country, many of which were soon overextended. A brief recovery followed in 1838, stimulated in part by a bad wheat harvest at home which forced the British to buy American wheat. But by 1839 that stimulus had passed. The same year a bumper cotton crop overloaded the market and a collapse of cotton prices set off a depression from which the economy did not fully recover until the mid-1840s.

Van Buren and the New Party System

THE WHIG COALITION   Before the crash, however, the Jacksonian Democrats reaped a political bonanza. Jackson had downed the dual monsters of nullification and the bank, and the people loved him for it. But out of the political wreckage that Jackson had inflicted on his opponents they began in 1834 to pull together a new coalition of diverse elements united chiefly by their hostility to Jackson. The imperial demeanor of that champion of democracy had given rise to the name of "King Andrew I"! His followers therefore were "Tories," supporters of the king, and his opponents took unto themselves the hallowed title of "Whigs," a name sanctioned by its honorable connotations in the American Revolution. This diverse coalition clustered around its center, the National Republican party of J. Q. Adams, Clay, and Webster. Into the combination came remnants of the Anti-Masons and Democrats who for one reason or another were alienated by Jackson's stands on the bank or state's rights. Of the forty-one Democrats in Congress who had voted to recharter the bank, twenty-eight had joined the Whigs by 1836.

Whiggery always had about it an atmosphere of social conservatism and superiority. The core Whigs were the supporters of Henry Clay, men whose vision was quickened by the vistas of his "American System." In the South the Whigs enjoyed the support of the urban banking and commercial interests, as well as their planter associates, owners of most of the slaves in the region. In the West, farmers who valued internal improvements joined the Whig ranks. Most states'-rights supporters eventually dropped away, and by the early 1840s the Whigs were becoming more clearly the party of Henry Clay's nationalism, even in the South. Throughout their two decades of strength the Whigs were a national party, strong both North and South, and a cohesive force for Union.

THE ELECTION OF 1836 By the presidential election of 1836 a new two-party system was emerging out of the Jackson and anti-Jackson forces, a system that would remain in fairly even balance for twenty years. In May 1835, eighteen months before the election, the Democrats held their second national convention and nominated Jackson's handpicked successor, Vice-President Martin Van Buren, the Red Fox of Kinderhook. The Whig coalition, united chiefly in its opposition to Jackson, held no convention but adopted a strategy of multiple candidacies, hoping to throw the election into the House of Representatives. The result was a free-for-all reminiscent of 1824, except that this time one candidate stood apart from the rest. It was Van Buren against the field. The Whigs put up three favorite sons: Daniel Webster, named by the Massachusetts legislature; Hugh Lawson White, chosen by anti-Jackson Democrats in the Tennessee legislature; and Wil-

Martin Van Buren, the "Little Magician." [Library of Congress]

liam Henry Harrison of Indiana, nominated by a predominantly Anti-Masonic convention in Harrisburg, Pennsylvania. In the South the Whigs made heavy inroads on the Democratic vote by arguing that Van Buren would be soft on antislavery advocates and that the South could trust only a southerner—i.e., White—as president.

In the popular vote Van Buren outdistanced the entire Whig field, with 765,000 votes to 740,000 votes for the Whigs, most of which were cast for Harrison. Van Buren had 170 electoral votes, Harrison 73, White 26, and Webster 14. In South Carolina, where the legislature still chose the electors, anti-Jackson Democrats threw 11 votes to Willie P. Mangum of North Carolina (soon to be a Whig himself).

Martin Van Buren, the eighth president, was the first of Dutch ancestry and at the age of fifty-five the first born under the Stars and Stripes. Son of a tavernkeeper in Kinderhook, New York, he had been schooled in a local academy, read law, and entered politics. Although he kept up a limited practice of law, he had been for most of his adult life a professional politician, so skilled in the arts of organization and manipulation that he came to be known as the "Little Magician." In New York politics he became leader of an organization known as the "Albany Regency," which backed his election as senator and later as governor. In 1824 he supported Crawford, then switched to Jackson in 1828, but continued to look to the Old Republicans of Virginia as the southern anchor of his support. After a brief tenure as governor of New York he resigned to join the cabinet, and because of Jackson's favor became minister to London and then vice-president.

THE PANIC OF 1837 Van Buren owed much of his success to good luck, to having backed the right horse, having been in the right place at the right time. But once he had climbed to the top of the greasy pole, luck suddenly deserted him. Van Buren had inherited Jackson's favor and a good part of his following, but he also inherited a financial panic. An already precarious economy was tipped over into crisis by depression in England, which resulted in a drop in the price of cotton from 17½¢ to 13½¢ a pound, and caused English banks and investors to cut back their commitments in the New World and refuse extensions of loans. This was a particularly hard blow since much of America's economic expansion depended on European—and mainly English—capital. On top of everything else, in 1836 there had been a failure of the wheat crop, the export of which in good years helped offset the drain of payments abroad. As creditors hastened to foreclose, the inflationary spiral went into reverse. States curtailed ambitious plans for roads and canals, and in many cases felt impelled to repudiate their debts. In the crunch a good many of the wildcat banks succumbed, and the government itself lost some $9 million it had deposited in pet banks.

Van Buren's advisors and supporters were inclined to blame speculators and bankers but at the same time to expect that the evildoers would get what they deserved in a healthy shakeout that would bring the economy back to stability. Van Buren did not believe that he or the government had any responsibility to rescue hard-pressed farmers or businessmen, or to provide public relief. He did feel obliged to keep the government itself in a healthy financial situation, however. To that end he called a special session of Congress in September 1837 which quickly voted to postpone indefinitely the distribution of the surplus because of a probable upcoming deficit, and also approved an issue of Treasury notes to cover immediate expenses.

AN INDEPENDENT TREASURY But Van Buren devoted most of his message to his idea that the government cease risking its deposits in shaky banks and set up an Independent Treasury. Under this the government would keep its funds in its own vaults and do business entirely in hard money. Van Buren was opposed to the "bleeding of private interests with the operations of public business." The founders of the republic had "wisely judged that the less government interferes with private pursuits the better for the general prosperity." Webster's response typified the Whig reaction: "I feel . . . as if this could not be America when I see schemes of public policy proposed, having for their object the

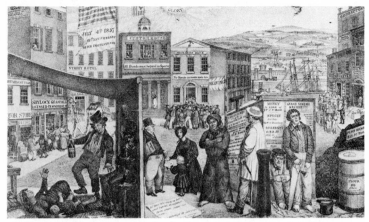

THE TIMES. *The panic at the bank, the closed factory, and the beggars in the street all depict the effects of the depression of 1837, according to this anti-Jacksonian lithograph.* [Library of Congress]

convenience of Government only, and leaving the people to shift for themselves." The Whiggish approach, presumably, would have been some kind of Hamiltonian program of government promotion of economic development, perhaps in the form of tariff or currency legislation. Good Jacksonians disapproved of such programs, at least when they were run from Washington.

Passage of the Independent Treasury was held up by opposition from a combination of Whigs and conservative Democrats who feared deflation. It took Van Buren several years of maneuvering to get what he wanted. Calhoun signaled a return to the Democratic fold, after several years of flirting with the Whigs, when he came out for the Independent Treasury. Van Buren gained western support by backing a more liberal land policy. He finally got his Independent Treasury on July 4, 1840. Although it lasted little more than a year before the Whigs repealed it in 1841, it would be restored in 1846.

The drawn-out hassle over the Treasury was only one of several that kept Washington preoccupied through the Van Buren years. A flood of petitions for Congress to abolish slavery and the slave trade in the District of Columbia brought on tumultuous debate, especially in the House of Representatives. Border incidents growing out of a Canadian insurrection in 1837 and a dispute over the Maine boundary kept British-American animosity at a simmer, but Gen. Winfield Scott, the president's ace trouble-shooter, managed to keep the hotheads in check along the border. These matters will be discussed elsewhere, but basic to the spreading malaise of the time was the depressed condition of the economy that lasted through Van Buren's entire term. Fairly or not, the administration became the target of growing discontent. The president won renomination easily enough, but could not get the Democratic convention to agree on his vice-presidential choice, which the convention left up to the Democratic electors.

THE "LOG CABIN AND HARD CIDER" CAMPAIGN The Whigs got an early start on their campaign when they met at Harrisburg, Pennsylvania, on December 4, 1839, to choose a candidate. Clay expected 1840 to be his year and had soft-pedaled talk of his American System in the interest of building broader support. Although he led on the first ballot, the convention was of a mind to look for a Whiggish Jackson, as it were, a military hero who could enter the race with few known political convictions or enemies. One possibility was Winfield Scott, but the delegates finally turned to William Henry Harrison, victor at the battle of Tippecanoe, former governor of the Indiana territory, briefly congressman and senator from Ohio, more briefly minister to Columbia. Another advantage of Harrison's was that the Anti-Masons liked him. To rally their states'-rights wing the Whigs chose for vice-president John Tyler of Virginia, a close friend of Clay.

The Whigs had no platform. That would have risked dividing a coalition united chiefly by opposition to the Democrats. But they had a slogan, "Tippecanoe and Tyler too," that went trippingly

In front of his log cabin, Old Tippecanoe pours the cider for cheering supporters. Jackson and Van Buren try to stop the flow. [New-York Historical Society]

on the tongue. And they soon had a rousing campaign theme which a Democratic paper unwittingly supplied them when the Baltimore *Republican* declared sardonically "that upon condition of his receiving a pension of $2,000 and a barrel of cider, General Harrison would no doubt consent to withdraw his pretensions, and spend his days in a log cabin on the banks of the Ohio." The Whigs seized upon the cider and log cabin symbols to depict Harrison as a simple man sprung from the people. Actually he sprang from one of the first families of Virginia and lived in a commodious farmhouse.

Substituting spectacle for argument, the Whig "Log Cabin and Hard Cider" campaign featured such sublime irrelevancy as the country had never seen before. Portable log cabins rolled through the streets along with barrels of potable cider to the tune of catchy campaign songs in support of

> The iron-armed soldier, the true-hearted soldier,
> The gallant old soldier of Tippecanoe.

His sweating supporters rolled huge victory balls along the highways to symbolize the snowballing majorities. All the devices of hoopla were mobilized: placards, emblems, campaign buttons, floats, effigies, transparencies, great rallies, and a campaign newspaper, *The Log Cabin*. Building on the example of the Jacksonians' campaign to discredit John Quincy Adams, the Whigs pictured Van Buren, who unlike Harrison came of humble origins as an aristocrat living in luxury at "the Palace":

> Let Van from his coolers of silver drink wine,
> And lounge on his cushioned settee;
> Our man on his buckeye bench can recline
> Content with hard cider is he!

The campaign left one lasting heritage in the American language, a usage now virtually worldwide. The expression "O.K." began as an abbreviation for "Old Kinderhook," an affectionate name for Van Buren, whose supporters organized "O.K. Clubs" during the campaign. The Whigs gave the initials a jocular turn and a new meaning when they attributed them to Andrew Jackson's creative spelling. Jackson had marked certain papers with the initials, he was said to have told Amos Kendall, to signify that they were "oll korrect." Thereafter Whig cider barrels carried the same seal of approval.

"We have taught them to conquer us!" the *Democratic Review*

ELECTION OF 1840

	Electoral vote	Popular vote
W. H. Harrison (Whig)	234	1,275,000
Van Buren (Democrat)	60	1,128,000

lamented. The Whig party had not only learned its lessons well, it had learned to improve on its teachers in the art of campaigning. "Van! Van! Is a Used-up Man!" went one of the campaign refrains, and down he went by the thumping margin of 234 votes to 60 in the electoral college. In the popular vote it was closer: 1,275,000 for Old Tip, 1,128,000 for Van Buren.

ASSESSING THE JACKSON YEARS

The Jacksonian impulse had altered American politics permanently. Longstanding ambivalence about political parties had been purged in the fires of political conflict, and mass political parties had arrived to stay. They were now widely justified as a positive good. By 1840 both parties were organized down to the precinct level, and the proportion of adult white males who voted in the presidential election nearly tripled, from 26.5 percent in 1824 to 78.0 percent in 1840. That much is beyond dispute, but the phenomenon of Jackson, the great symbol for an

Andrew Jackson in 1845.
Jackson died shortly after this
daguerrotype was taken.
[Library of Congress]

age, has inspired among historians conflicts of interpretation as spirited as those among his supporters and opponents at the time. Jackson's personality itself seemed a compound of contradictions. His first major biographer concluded from conflicting evidence that Jackson "was a patriot and a traitor. He was one of the greatest of generals, and wholly ignorant of the art of war. A writer brilliant, elegant, eloquent, without being able to compose a correct sentence or spell words of four syllables. The first of statesmen, he never devised, he never framed a measure. He was the most candid of men, and was capable of the profoundest dissimulation. A most law-defying, law-obeying citizen. A stickler for discipline, he never hesitated to disobey his superior. A democratic aristocrat. An urbane savage. An atrocious saint."

Interpretations of his policies, their sources, and their consequences have likewise differed. The earliest historians of the Jackson era belonged largely to an eastern elite nurtured in a "Whiggish" culture, men who could never quite forgive Jackson for the spoils system which in their view excluded from office the fittest and ablest. A later school of "progressive" historians depicted Jackson as the leader of a vast democratic movement which welled up in the West and mobilized a farmer-labor alliance to sweep the "Monster" bank into the dustbin of history. Some historians recently have focused attention on local power struggles in which the great national debates of the time often seem empty rhetoric or at most snares to catch the voters. One view of Jackson makes him out to be essentially a frontier nabob, an opportunist for whom democracy "was good talk with which to win the favor of the people. . . ."

Another school has emphasized the importance of cultural-ethnic identity in deciding party loyalties. Jackson, according to this view, revitalized the Jeffersonian alliance of Virginia and New York, of individualistic southern planters and those elements of the North who stood outside the strait-laced Yankee culture created mainly by people of English origin. Though the political effects of ethnic identities were complex, in large measure such out-groups as the Scotch-Irish and the Catholic Irish felt more comfortable with the more tolerant Democratic party. If valid for the northern states, however, the cultural-ethnic interpretation needs qualification in the light of southern experience. Ethnic identities in the South had faded with the decline of immigration after the Revolution, but the South developed in the 1840s as vigorous a party division as the North.

There seems little question that, whatever else Jackson and his supporters had in mind, they followed an ideal of republican virtue, of returning to the Jeffersonian Arcadia of the Old Republic in which government would leave people largely to their own devices. In the Jacksonian view the alliance of government and business was always an invitation to special favors and an eternal source of corruption. The bank was the epitome of such evil. The right policy for government, at the national level in particular, was to refrain from granting special privileges and to let free competition in the marketplace regulate the economy.

In the bustling world of the nineteenth century, however, the idea of a return to agrarian simplicity was a futile exercise in nostalgia. Instead, laissez-faire policies opened the way for a host of aspiring entrepreneurs eager to replace the established economic elite with a new order of laissez-faire capitalism. And in fact there was no great conflict in the Jacksonian mentality between the farmer or planter who delved in the soil and the independent speculator and entrepreneur who won his way by other means. Jackson himself was all these things. What the Jacksonian mentality could not foresee was the degree to which, in a growing country, unrestrained enterprise could lead on to new economic combinations, centers of gigantic power largely independent of governmental regulation. But history is forever pursued by irony. Here the ultimate irony would be that the laissez-faire rationale for republican simplicity eventually became the justification for the growth of unregulated centers of economic power far greater than any ever wielded by Biddle's bank.

FURTHER READING

A survey of events covered in the chapter can be found in Glyndon Van Deusen's *The Jacksonian Era, 1828–1848* (1959).° The first of the modern interpretations of the Jacksonian period is Arthur M. Schlesinger, Jr.'s *The Age of Jackson* (1945),° which emphasizes the role played by antibusiness interests in the agrarian South and the urban North. Richard Hofstadter's *The American Political Tradition and the Men Who Made It* (1948)° challenges this thesis. Lee Benson's *The Concept of Jacksonian Democracy* (1964)° examines the ethnocultural basis for New York's politics of the common man. John W. Ward's *Andrew Jackson: Symbol for an Age* (1955)° assesses Jackson's impact on the psychology of mass politics. Also helpful is Marvin Meyer's *The Jacksonian Persuasion: Politics and Belief* (1960).° Robert Kelley treats these themes in two works: *The Transatlantic Persuasion: The Liberal-Democratic Mind in the Age of Gladstone* (1969) and *The Cultural Pattern in American Politics: The First Century* (1979). Edward E. Pessen's *Jacksonian America: Society, Personality, and Politics* (1978)° provides a recent overview of these arguments.

An introduction to development of political parties of the 1830s is in Richard P. McCormick's *The Second American Party System: Party Formation in the Jacksonian Era* (1966).° Richard Hofstadter's *The Idea of a Party System* (1969)° traces the roots of the theories of political opposition which carried over from the first party system. In addition to the work by Benson, illuminating case studies include Ronald P. Formisano's *The Birth of Mass Political Parties: Michigan, 1827–1861* (1971), Douglass T. Miller's *Jacksonian Aristocracy: Class and Democracy in New York, 1830–1860* (1967), and Harry L. Watson's *Jacksonian Politics and Community Conflict: The Emergence of the Second American Party System in Cumberland County, North Carolina* (1981).

Biographies of Jackson include Robert V. Remini's *Andrew Jackson* (1966),° which can serve as a good introduction. Also consult the two-volume work by Remini, *Andrew Jackson and the Course of American Empire, 1767–1821* (1977), and *Andrew Jackson and the Course of American Freedom, 1822–1832* (1981). A critical work is James C. Curtis's *Andrew Jackson and the Search for Vindication* (1976).° Marquis James's *Andrew Jackson: Portrait of a President* (1937) is more sympathetic. For Jackson's successor, consult Robert V. Remini's *Martin Van Buren and the Making of the Democratic Party* (1959) and James C. Curtis's *The Fox at Bay* (1970).

The political philosophies of those who came to oppose Jackson are treated in Daniel Walker Howe's *The Political Culture of the American Whigs* (1979). Biographies of leading Whigs include Charles M. Wiltse's *John C. Calhoun* (3 vols.; 1944–1951), Clement Eaton's *Henry Clay and*

°These books are available in paperback editions.

the Art of American Politics (1957), and Sydney Nathans's *Daniel Webster and Jacksonian Democracy* (1973).

A number of scholars have concentrated on the economics and finance of the period. An overview is found in Peter Temin's *The Jacksonian Economy* (1969).° Bray Hamond's *Banks and Politics in America from the Revolution to the Civil War* (1957) provides extensive background for the 1830s controversy. Robert V. Remini's *Andrew Jackson and the Bank War* (1967)° stresses the political differences. Thomas P. Govan's *Nicholas Biddle: Nationalist and Public Banker* (1959) provides a perspective from the anti-Jackson side. John McFaul's *The Politics of Jacksonian Finance* (1972) is a more recent treatment of all sides of the issue. Two studies of the impact of the bank controversy are William G. Shade's *Banks or No Banks: The Money Question in the Western States, 1832–1865* (1973), and James Roger Sharp's *The Jacksonians versus the Banks: Politics in the States after the Panic of 1837* (1970).

Among the best of all scholarship on the Jacksonian years is William W. Freehling's *Prelude to Civil War: The Nullification Controversy in South Carolina, 1816–1836* (1966).° Leonard D. White's *The Jacksonians: A study in Administrative History, 1829–1861* (1954),° examines the spoils system. Ronald N. Satz's *American Indian Policy in the Jacksonian Era* (1975) surveys that tragedy. Other studies of Indian affairs include Arthur H. DeRosier, Jr.'s *The Removal of the Choctaw Indians* (1970)° and Michael P. Rogin's *Fathers and Children: Andrew Jackson and the Subjugation of the American Indian* (1975). The question of rising inequality in American cities is treated in Edward E. Pesson's *Riches, Class, and Power before the Civil War* (1973) and Douglas T. Miller's *The Birth of Modern America, 1820–1850* (1970). Michael Feldberg's *The Turbulent Era: Riot and Disorder in Jacksonian America* (1980) discusses the ramifications of inequality.

12

THE DYNAMICS OF GROWTH

AGRICULTURE AND THE NATIONAL ECONOMY

COTTON "We are greatly, I was about to say fearfully, growing," John C. Calhoun told his congressional colleagues in 1816 when he introduced his Bonus Bill for internal improvements. His prophetic sentence expressed both the promise of national greatness and the threat of divisions that would blight Calhoun's own ambition. But in the brief period of good feelings after the War of 1812, it was opportunity that seemed most conspicuously visible to Americans everywhere, and nowhere more than in Calhoun's native South Carolina. The reason was cotton, the new staple crop of the South, which was spreading from South Carolina and Georgia into the new lands of Mississippi and Alabama, where Andrew Jackson had recently chastised the Creeks, and on into Louisiana and Arkansas. Jackson himself had been set up as a cotton planter at The Hermitage, near Nashville, Tennessee, since the mid-1790s.

Cotton had been used from ancient times, but the Industrial Revolution and its spread of textile mills created a rapidly growing market for the fluffy staple. Cotton had remained for many years rare and expensive because of the need for hand labor to separate the lint from the tenacious seeds of most varieties. But by the mid-1780s in coastal Georgia and South Carolina a long-staple "sea island" cotton was being grown commercially which could easily be separated from its shiny black seeds by squeezing it through rollers. Sea-island cotton, like the rice and indigo of the colonial Tidewater, had little chance, though, in the soil and climate of the upcountry. And the green seed of the upland cotton clung to the lint so stubbornly that the rollers crushed the seed and spoiled the fiber. One person working all day could manage to separate little if any more than a pound by hand. Cotton could not yet be king.

The rising cotton kingdom of the lower South came to birth at a plantation called Mulberry Hill in coastal Georgia, the home of Mrs. Nathanael Greene, widow of the Revolutionary War hero. At Mulberry Hill discussion often turned to the promising new crop and to speculation about better ways to remove the seeds. In 1792, on the way to a job as a tutor in South Carolina, young Eli Whitney, recently graduated from Yale, visited fellow graduate Phineas Miller, was was overseer at Mulberry Hill. Catherine Greene noticed her visitor's mechanical aptitude, which had been nurtured in boyhood by the needs of a Massachusetts farm. When she suggested that young Whitney devise a mechanism for removing the seed from upland cotton, he mulled it over and solved the problem in ten days. In the spring of 1793, his job as a tutor quickly forgotten, Whitney had a working model of a cotton gin.

By chance one of Mrs. Greene's daughters had bought some iron wire for a bird cage. Whitney used the wire to make iron pins which he inserted into a cylinder. When rotated, the cylinder passed cotton fiber through slots in an iron guard and the seeds dropped into a box below. Rotating brushes on the other side served as a doffer, removing the fiber as it passed through. With it one man could separate fifty times as much cotton as he could by hand. The device was an "absurdly simple contrivance," too much so as it turned out. A simple description was all any skilled worker needed to make a copy, and by the time

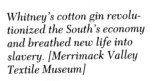

Whitney's cotton gin revolutionized the South's economy and breathed new life into slavery. [Merrimack Valley Textile Museum]

Whitney and Miller had secured a patent in 1794 a number of copies were already in use. Consequently the two men were never able to make good on the promise of riches that the gin offered, and spent most of their modest gains in expensive lawsuits. Improved models soon appeared. The use of a saw-toothed cylinder proved more effective than the original pins, and that device —which had occurred to Whitney at the start—appeared on the market as one of many designs contesting for patent rights.

Although Whitney realized little from his idea, he had unwittingly begun a revolution. Green-seed cotton first engulfed the upcountry hills of South Carolina and Georgia, and after the War of 1812 migrated into the former Creek, Choctaw, and Chickasaw lands to the west. Cotton production soared. Slavery had found a new and profitable use. Indeed thereafter slavery became almost synonymous with the Cotton Kingdom in the popular view. Planters migrated westward with their gangs of workers in tow, and a profitable trade began to develop in the sale of slaves from the coastal South to the West. The cotton culture became a way of life that tied the Old Southwest to the coastal Southeast in a common interest.

Not the least of the cotton gin's revolutionary consequences, although less apparent at first, was that cotton became almost immediately a major export commodity. Cotton exports averaged about $9 million in value from 1803 to 1807, about 22 percent of the value of all exports; from 1815 to 1819 they averaged over $23 million or 39 percent of the total, and from the mid-1830s to 1860 accounted for more than half the value of all exports. For the national economy as a whole, one historian asserted: "Cotton was the most important proximate cause of expansion." The South supplied the North both raw materials and markets for manufactures. Income from the North's role in handling the cotton trade then provided surpluses for capital investment. It was once assumed that the South supplied the Northwest with markets for foodstuffs, but recent research shows the Cotton Belt to have been self-sufficient in foodstuffs. The more likely explanation of growth in the Northwest now seems to be its own growing urban markets for foodstuffs, which supplemented the export market for grain.

FARMING THE WEST The westward flow of planters and their slave gangs to Alabama and Mississippi during these flush times was paralleled by another migration through the Ohio Valley and the Great Lakes region, where the Indians had been steadily pushed westward until the risk was minimal. "Old America seems to be

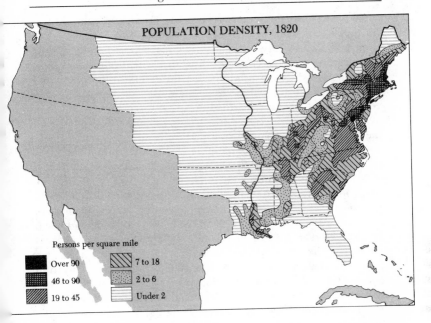

POPULATION DENSITY, 1820

Persons per square mile

Over 90
46 to 90
19 to 45
7 to 18
2 to 6
Under 2

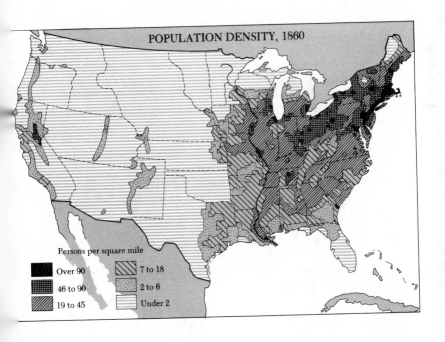

POPULATION DENSITY, 1860

Persons per square mile

Over 90
46 to 90
19 to 45
7 to 18
2 to 6
Under 2

breaking up and moving westward," an English traveler, Morris Birkbeck, observed in 1817 as he watched the migrants make their way along westward roads in Pennsylvania. Family groups, stages, light wagons, riders on horseback made up "a scene of bustle and business, extending over three hundred miles, which is truly wonderful." In 1800 some 387,000 settlers were counted west of the Atlantic states; by 1801, 1,338,000 lived over the mountains; by 1820, 2,419,000. By 1860 more than half the nation's expanded population resided in trans-Appalachia, and the restless movement had long since spilled across the Mississippi and touched the shores of the Pacific.

North of the expanding cotton belt in the Gulf states, the fertile woodland soils, riverside bottom lands, and black loam of the prairies drew farmers from the rocky lands of New England and the leached, exhausted soils of the Southeast. A new land law of 1820, passed after the Panic of 1819, eliminated the credit provisions of the 1800 act but reduced the minimum price from $1.64 to $1.25 per acre and the minimum plot from 160 to 80 acres. The settler could get a place for as little as $100, and over the years the proliferation of state banks made it possible to continue buying on credit. Even that was not enough for westerners who began a long—and eventually victorious—agitation for further relaxation of the land laws. They favored preemption, the right of squatters to purchase land at the minimum price, and graduation, the progressive reduction of the price on lands that did not sell.

Success came ultimately with two acts of Congress. Under the Preemption Act of 1830, a renewable law made permanent in the Preemption Act of 1841, squatters could stake out claims ahead of the land surveys and later get 160 acres at the minimum price of $1.25. In effect the law recognized a practice enforced more often than not by frontier vigilantes. Under the Graduation Act of 1854, which Sen. Thomas Hart Benton had plugged since the 1820s, prices of unsold lands were to go down in stages until the lands could sell for 12½¢ per acre after thirty years.

The progress of settlement followed the old pattern of girdling trees, clearing land, and settling down at first to a crude subsistence. The development of effective iron plows greatly eased the backbreaking job of breaking the soil. As early as 1797 Charles Newbold had secured a patent on an iron plow, but a superstition that iron poisoned the soil prevented much use until after 1819, when Jethro Wood of Scipio, New York, developed an improved version with separate parts that could be replaced without buying a whole new plow complete. The prejudice against iron suddenly vanished, and the demand for plows grew so fast that

Wood, like Whitney, could not supply the need and spent much of his remaining fifteen years fighting against patent infringements. The iron plow was a special godsend to those farmers who first ventured into the sticky black loams of the treeless prairies. Further improvements would follow in later years, including John Deere's steel plow (1837) and the chilled-iron and steel plow of John Oliver (1855).

TRANSPORTATION AND THE NATIONAL ECONOMY

NEW ROADS The pioneer's life of crude subsistence eventually gave way to staple farming for cash income, as markets for foodstuffs grew both in the South and Northwest. Improvements in transportation were beginning to make possible the development of a national market. As settlers moved west the demand went back east for better roads. In 1795 the Wilderness Road, along the trail blazed by Daniel Boone twenty years before, was opened to wagon traffic, thereby easing the route through the Cumberland Gap into Kentucky and along the Knoxville and Old Walton Roads, completed the same year, into Tennessee. "Stand at Cumberland Gap," Frederick Jackson Turner wrote years later, "and watch the procession of civilization marching single file—the buffalo following the trail to the salt springs, the Indian,

The primitive condition of American roads is evident in this early–nineteenth-century watercolor. [Museum of Fine Arts]

the fur-trader and hunter, the cattle-raiser, the pioneer farmer
—and the frontier has passed by." South of these roads there
were no such major highways. South Carolinians and Georgians
pushed westward on whatever trails or rutted roads had appeared.

To the northeast a movement for graded and paved roads
(macadamized with crushed stones packed down) gathered momentum after completion of the Philadelphia-Lancaster Turnpike in 1794 (the term derives from a pole or pike at the tollgate,
turned to admit the traffic). By 1821 some 4,000 miles of turnpikes had been completed, mainly connecting eastern cities, but
western traffic could move along the Frederick Pike to Cumberland and thence along the National Road, completed to Wheeling on the Ohio in 1818, and to Vandalia, Illinois, by about
mid-century; along the old Forbes Road from Philadelphia to

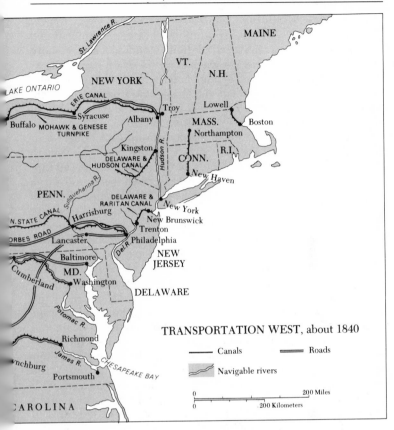

TRANSPORTATION WEST, about 1840

——— Canals   === Roads

〰 Navigable rivers

0 ——————— 200 Miles
0 ——————— 200 Kilometers

Pittsburgh; and along the Mohawk and Genesee Turnpike from the Massachusetts line through Albany to Buffalo, whence one could take ship for points on the Great Lakes.

RIVER TRANSPORT   Once turnpike travelers had reached the Ohio they could float westward in comparative comfort. At Pittsburgh, Wheeling, and other points the emigrants could buy flatboats, commonly of two kinds: an ark with room for living quarters, possessions, and perhaps some livestock; or a keelboat —similar but with a keel. For large flatboats—a capacity of forty tons was common—crews were available for hire. At the destination the boat could be used again or sold for lumber. In the early 1820s an estimated 3,000 flatboats went down the Ohio every year, and for many years after that the flatboat remained the chief conveyance for heavy traffic downstream.

By the early 1820s the turnpike boom was giving way to new developments in water transportation: the river steamboat and the barge canal, which carried bulk commodities far more cheaply than did Conestoga wagons on the National Road. As early as 1787 John Fitch had launched a steamboat on the Delaware River, and in 1790 had one that carried passengers from Philadelphia to Trenton on a regular schedule, but technical problems continued to frustrate Fitch and other inventors. No commercially successful steamboat appeared until Robert Fulton and Robert R. Livingston sent the *Clermont* up the Hudson to Albany in 1807. After that the use of the steamboat spread rapidly to other eastern rivers, and in 1811 Nicholas Roosevelt, a business associate of Fulton, launched a sidewheeler, the *New Orleans*, at Pittsburgh and sent it down the Ohio and Mississippi; thus began an era of steamboat transportation that opened nearly half a continent to water traffic. The *New Orleans* itself thereafter plied between New Orleans and Natchez, but in 1815 the *Enterprise*, built by Henry Shreve, went all the way from New Orleans up the Ohio and another fifty miles up the Monongahela. In 1818 the *Walk-in-the-Water*, the first steamboat on Lake Erie, began a regular nine-day schedule between Buffalo and Detroit.

By 1836, 361 steamboats were registered to navigate the western waters. As the boats reached ever farther up the tributaries that connected to the main artery of the Mississippi, their design evolved toward the familiar "steamboat Gothic," the glorified keelboat which one wit called "an engine on a raft with $11,000 worth of jig-saw work." By the 1840s shallow-draft ships that traveled *on* rather than *in* the water carried 50–100 tons of freight on twenty-four-inch drafts. These steam-powered rafts, the scorn of ocean-going salts, became the basis of the rivermen's boast that they could navigate a heavy dew, that they were "so built that when the river is low and the sandbars come out for air, the first mate can tap a keg of beer and run the boat four miles on the suds." These boats ventured into far reaches of the Mississippi Valley, up such rivers as the Wabash, the Monongahela, the Cumberland, the Tennessee, the Missouri, and the Arkansas.

The miracle of these floating palaces became one of the romantic epics of America. The tradition was fixed early. In 1827 a lyrical writer for Cincinnati's *Western Monthly Review* let himself go with a description of the "fairy structures of oriental gorgeousness and splendor . . . rushing down the Mississippi . . . or plowing up between the forests . . . bearing speculators, merchants, dandies, fine ladies, everything real and everything af-

The sumptuous interior of the steamboat Princess. *[Anglo-American Art Museum, Louisiana State University]*

fected in the form of humanity, with pianos, and stocks of novels, and cards, and dice, and flirting, and love-making, and drinking, and champagne, and on the deck, perhaps, three hundred fellows, who have seen alligators and neither fear whiskey, nor gunpowder. A steamboat, coming from New Orleans, brings to the remotest villages of our streams, and the very doors of the cabins, a little Paris, a section of Broadway, or a slice of Philadelphia, to a ferment in the minds of our young people, the innate propensity for fashions and finery."

The prosaic flatboat, however, still carried to market most of the western wheat, corn, flour, meal, bacon, ham, pork, whiskey, soap and candles (the by-products of slaughterhouses), lead from Missouri, copper from Michigan, wood from the Rockies, and ironwork from Pittsburgh. But the steamboat, by bringing two-way traffic to the Mississippi Valley, created a continental market and an agricultural empire which became the new breadbasket of America. Farming evolved from a subsistence level to the ever-greater production of valuable staples. Along with the new farmers came promoters, speculators, and land-boomers. Villages at strategic trading points along the streams evolved into centers of commerce and urban life. The port of New Orleans grew in the 1830s and 1840s to lead all others in exports.

But by then the Erie Canal was drawing eastward much of the trade that once went down to the Gulf. In 1817 the New York

Flatboats in tow along the Erie Canal. The scene depicted is around 1830–1832. [New York Public Library]

legislature endorsed Gov. De Witt Clinton's dream of connecting the Hudson River with Lake Erie and authorized construction. Eight years later, in 1825, the canal was open for its entire 350 miles from Albany to Buffalo; branches soon put most of the state within reach of the canal. After 1828 the Delaware and Hudson Canal linked New York with the anthracite fields of northeastern Pennsylvania. The speedy success of the New York system inspired a mania for canals that lasted more than a decade and resulted in the completion of about 3,000 miles of waterways by 1837. But no canal ever matched the spectacular success of the Erie, which rendered the entire Great Lakes region an economic tributary to the port of New York. With the further development of canals spanning Ohio and Indiana from north to south, much of the upper Ohio Valley also came within the economic sphere of New York.

RAILROADS The Panic of 1837 and the subsequent depression cooled the fever quickly. States which had borrowed heavily to finance canals in some cases had to repudiate their debts. The holders of repudiated bonds were left without recourse. Meanwhile a new and more versatile form of transportation was gaining on the canal: the railroad. Vehicles that ran on iron rails had long been in use, especially in mining, but now came a tremen-

dous innovation—the use of steam power—as the steam locomotive followed soon after the steamboat. As early as 1814
George Stephenson had built the first practical one in England.
In 1825, the year the Erie Canal was completed, the world's first
commercial steam railway began operations in England. By the
1820s the port cities of Baltimore, Charleston, and Boston were
alive with schemes to tap the hinterlands by rail.

On July 4, 1828, Baltimore got the jump on other cities when
Charles Carroll, the last surviving signer of the Declaration of
Independence, laid the first stone in the roadbed of the Baltimore and Ohio (B&O) Railroad. By 1832 the road reached
seventy-three miles west of Baltimore. The Charleston and
Hamburg Railroad, started in 1831 and finished in 1833, was at
that time the longest railroad under single management in the
world. It reached westward 136 miles to the hamlet of Hamburg,
opposite Augusta, where Charleston merchants hoped to divert
traffic from the Savannah River. Boston by 1836 had fanned out
three major lines to Lowell, Worcester, and Providence.

By 1840 the railroads, with a total of 3,328 miles, had outdistanced the canals by just two miles. Over the next twenty years,
though, railroads grew nearly tenfold to cover 30,626 miles;
more than a third of this total was built in the 1850s. Several
major east-west lines appeared, connecting Boston to Albany
and Albany with Buffalo; combined in 1853, these lines became
the New York Central. In 1851 the Erie Railroad spanned southern New York; by 1852 the Pennsylvania Railway connected
Philadelphia and Pittsburgh; in 1853 the B&O finally reached
Wheeling on the Ohio. By then New York had connections all
the way to Chicago, and in two years to St. Louis. Before 1860
the Hannibal and St. Joseph had crossed the state of Missouri.
Farther south, despite Charleston's early start on both canals and
railroads and despite the brave dream of a line to tap western
commerce at Cincinnati, the network of railroads still had many
gaps in 1860. By 1857 Charleston, Savannah, and Norfolk connected by way of lines into Chattanooga and thence along a single line to Memphis, the only southern route that connected the
east coast and the Mississippi. In 1860 the North and South had
only three major links: at Washington, Louisville, and Cairo, Illinois.

The proliferation of trunk lines had by then supplemented the
earlier canals to create multiple ties between the Northwest and
Northeast. But it was still not until the eve of the Civil War that
railroads surpassed canals in total haulage: in 1859 they carried a
little over 2 billion ton-miles compared to 1.6 billion on canals.

THE GROWTH
OF RAILROADS,
1850

—— Railroads in 1850

Travel on the early railroads was a chancy venture. Iron straps on top of wooden rails, for instance, tended to work loose and curl up into "snakesheads" which sometimes pierced railway coaches. The solution was the iron T-rail, introduced in 1831 and soon standard equipment on the best roads, but the strap-iron rail remained common because wood was so cheap. Wood was used for fuel too, and the sparks often caused fires along the way or damaged passengers' clothing. An English traveler, Harriet Martineau, reported seeing a lady's shawl ignited on one trip. She found in her own gown thirteen holes "and in my veil, with which I saved my eyes, more than could be counted." Creation of the "spark arrester" and the use of coal relieved but never overcame the hazard. Until after 1860 brakes had to be operated manually, crude pin-and-link couplings were used, and adequate springs were unknown. Different track widths often forced passengers to change trains until a standard gauge became national in 1882. Land travel, whether by stagecoach or train, was a

THE GROWTH
OF RAILROADS,
1860

—— Railroads in 1860
■■■ Principal east-west lines

jerky, bumpy, wearying ordeal. An early stage rider on the
Forbes Road said he alternately walked and rode and "though
the pain of riding exceeded the fatigue of walking, yet . . . it refreshed us by varying the weariness of our bodies."

Water travel, where available, offered far more comfort, but
railroads gained supremacy over other forms of transport because of their economy, speed, and reliability. By 1859 railroads
had reduced the cost of transportation services by $150–$175
million, accounting for a social saving that amounted to some 4
percent of the gross national product. By 1890 the saving would
run up to almost 15 percent. Railroads provided indirect benefits
by encouraging settlement and the expansion of farming. During
the antebellum period the reduced costs brought on by the
railroads aided the expansion of farming more than manufacturing, since manufacturers in the Northeast, especially New England, had better access to water transportation. The railroads'
demand for rail iron and equipment of various kinds, however,

The New-York Central Rail Road connected Albany with New England and "All Points West, Northwest, and Southwest." "Well ventilated Sleeping Cars" afforded "travelers the luxury of a Night's Sleep." [American Antiquarian Society]

did provide an enormous market for the industries that made these capital goods. And the ability of railroads to operate year round in all kinds of weather gave them an advantage in carrying finished goods too.

OCEAN TRANSPORT For ocean-going traffic the start of service on regular schedules was the most important change of the early 1800s. In the first week of 1818 ships of the Black Ball Line inaugurated a weekly transatlantic packet service to and from New York and Liverpool. Beginning with four ships in all, the Black Ball Line thereafter had one ship leaving each port monthly at an announced time. With the business recovery in 1822 the packet business grew in a rush. Runs to London and Le Havre were added, and by 1845 some fifty-two transatlantic lines ran square-riggers on schedule from New York, with three regular sailings per week. Many others ran in the coastwide trade, to Charleston, Savannah, New Orleans, and elsewhere.

In the same year, 1845, came a great innovation with the building of the first clipper ship, the *Rainbow*, designed by Donald McKay. The clippers, built for speed, long and narrow with enormous sail areas, cut a dashing figure during their brief day of glory, which lasted less than two decades. In 1854 the *Flying Cloud* took eighty-nine days and eight hours to make the distance from New York to San Francisco, a speed that steamships took several decades to equal. But clippers, while fast, lacked ample cargo space, and after the Civil War would give way to the steamship.

The use of steam on ocean-going vessels lagged behind the development of steam riverboats because of the greater technological problems involved. The first steamship to cross the Atlantic, the *Savannah*, used steam power for only eighty hours during a twenty-seven day voyage from Savannah to Liverpool, relying on sails for most of the trip. It ended its days as a sailing vessel, stripped of its engines. On April 23, 1838, the British and American Steamship Navigation Company's ship *Sirius* arrived in New York, and another steamship, the *Great Western*, came in later the same day, but it would be another ten years before steamships began to threaten the sailing packets.

THE ROLE OF GOVERNMENT   The massive internal improvements of the era were the product of both governmental and private initiatives, sometimes undertaken jointly and sometimes separately. Private investment accounted for nearly all the turnpikes in New England and the middle states. Elsewhere states invested heavily in turnpike companies and in some cases, notably South Carolina and Indiana, themselves built and owned the turnpikes. Canals were to a much greater extent the product of state investment, and more commonly state-owned and operated. The Panic of 1837, however, caused states to pull back and leave railroad development mainly to private corporations. Most of the railroad capital came from private sources. Still, government had an enormous role in railroad development. Several states of the South and West built state-owned lines, such as Georgia's Eastern and Atlantic, completed from Atlanta to Chattanooga in 1851, although they generally looked to private companies to handle actual operations and in some cases sold the lines. States and localities along the routes invested in railroad corporations and granted loans; states were generous in granting charters and tax concessions.

The federal government helped too, despite the constitutional scruples of some against direct involvement. The government bought stock in turnpike and canal companies, and after the success of the Erie, extended land grants to several western states for the support of canal projects. Congress provided for railroad surveys by government engineers, and during 1830–1848 reduced the tariff duties on iron used in railroad construction. In 1850 Sen. Stephen A. Douglas of Illinois and others prevailed on Congress to extend a major land grant to support a north-south line connecting Chicago with Mobile. Grants of three square miles on alternate sides for each mile of railroad subsidized the building of the Illinois Central and the Mobile and Ohio Railroads. Regarded at the time a special case, the 1850 grant set a precedent for other bounties that totaled about 20 million acres by 1860—a small amount compared to the grants for transcontinental lines in the Civil War decade.

THE GROWTH OF INDUSTRY

While the South and West developed the agricultural basis for a national economy, the Northeast was laying foundations for an industrial revolution. Technology in the form of the cotton gin, the harvester, and improvements in transportation had quickened agricultural development and to some extent decided its direction. But technology altered the economic landscape even more profoundly by giving rise to the factory system.

EARLY TEXTILE MANUFACTURES   At the end of the colonial period manufacturing remained in the household or handicraft stage of development, or at best the "putting-out" stage, in which the merchant capitalist would distribute raw materials (say, leather patterns for shoes) to be worked up at home, then collected and sold. In 1815 *Niles' Weekly Register* described the town of Mount Pleasant, Ohio, with a population of barely over 500, as having some thirty-eight handicraft shops, including blacksmiths and bakers, and eight more shops engaged in tanning, textiles, and railmaking. Farmers themselves had to produce much of what they needed in the way of crude implements, shoes, and clothing, and in their crude workshops inventive genius was sometimes nurtured. As a boy Eli Whitney had set up a crude forge and manufactured nails in his father's rural workshop. The tran-

New England Factory Village, *around 1830.* [*New York State Historical Association*]

sition from such production to the factory was a slow process, but one for which a base had been laid before 1815.

In the eighteenth century Great Britain had jumped out to a long head start in industrial production, one that other countries were slow to overcome. The foundations of Britain's advantage were: the development of iron smelting by coke when sufficient wood was lacking; the invention of the steam engine by Thomas Newcomen in 1705 and its improvement by James Watt in 1765; and a series of inventions that mechanized the production of textiles, including John Kay's flying shuttle (1733), James Hargreaves's spinning jenny (1764), Richard Arkwright's "water frame" (1769), and Samuel Crompton's spinning mule (1779). The last could do the work of 200 spinners. Britain also carefully guarded its hard-won secrets, forbidding the export of machines or descriptions of them, even restricting the departure of informed mechanics. But the secrets could not be kept. In 1789 Samuel Slater arrived from England with the plan of Arkwright's water frame in his head. He contracted with Moses Brown, an enterprising merchant-manufacturer in Rhode Island, to build a mill in Pawtucket, and in this little mill, completed in 1790, nine children turned out a satisfactory cotton yarn, which was then worked up by the putting-out system. In 1793 the Schofield brothers, Englishmen from Yorkshire built the first woolens mill at Byfield, Massachusetts.

The beginnings in textiles were slow and faltering until Jefferson's embargo in 1807 and the War of 1812 restricted imports and encouraged the merchant capitalists of New England to switch their resources into manufacturing. New England, it happened, had one distinct advantage in that the fall line and the water power it provided stood near the coast where water transportation was also readily available. In 1813 Francis Cabot Lowell and a group of wealthy merchants known as the Boston Associates formed the Boston Manufacturing Company. At Waltham, Massachusetts, they built the first factory in which the processes of spinning and weaving by power machinery were brought under one roof, mechanizing every process from raw material to finished cloth. By 1815 textile mills numbered in the hundreds. A flood of British imports after the War of 1812 dealt a temporary setback to the infant industry, but the foundations of textile manufacture were laid, and they spurred the growth of garment trades and a machine-tool industry to build and service the mills.

TECHNOLOGY IN AMERICA Meanwhile American ingenuity was adding other bases for industrial growth. Oliver Evans of Philadelphia was a frustrated pioneer who had the misfortune to be ahead of his time. As a teenager he had been fascinated by steam engines but could not find the backing to pursue his ideas for steamboats and locomotives. As early as 1785 he built an automatic mill in which grain introduced at one end came out flour at the other, but could not get millers interested in trying it. Success eluded him until 1804, when he developed a high-pressure steam engine adapted to a variety of uses in ships and factories.

The practical bent of Americans was one of the outstanding traits noted by foreign visitors. In Europe, where class consciousness prevailed, Tocqueville wrote, men confined themselves to "the arrogant and sterile researches of abstract truths, whilst the social condition and institutions of democracy prepare them to seek immediate and useful practical results of the sciences." In 1814 Dr. Jacob Bigelow, a Harvard botanist, began to lecture on "The Elements of Technology," a word he did much to popularize. In his book of the same title he argued that technology constituted the chief superiority of moderns over the ancients, effecting profound changes in ways of living. Benjamin Silliman, Yale's first professor of chemistry, emphasized the application of science in his classes, publications (he founded the *American Journal of Science* in 1818), and public lectures.

One of the most striking examples of the connection between pure research and innovation, however, was in the researches of Joseph Henry, a Princeton physicist. His work in electromagnetism provided the basis for Samuel F. B. Morse's invention of the telegraph and for electrical motors later on. In 1846 Henry became head of the new Smithsonian Institution, founded with a bequest from the Englishman James Smithson "for the increase and diffusion of knowledge among men." The year 1846 also saw the founding of the American Association for the Advancement of Science.

It would be difficult to exaggerate the importance of science and technology in changing the ways people live. All aspects of life—the social, cultural, economic, and political—were and are shaped by it. Thomas Ewbank, a commissioner of patents in the mid–nineteenth century, pondered technology in reports widely publicized through Horace Greeley's New York *Tribune.* Ewbank, an English immigrant and hydraulic engineer, noted in his first report "a singular vagary" in the human mind, the delusion that the more abstract the study the nearer to the Great Spirit, "whereas God is the greatest of workers—the chief of artificers." Ewbank also emphasized the democratic implications of the machine which, he said, would bring equal opportunity within reach by reducing the costs of both necessities and luxuries.

Invention often brought about completely new enterprises, the steamboat and the railroad being the most spectacular, without which the pace of development would have been slowed immeasurably. Most basic inventions were imports from Europe. Preservation of food by canning, for instance, was unknown before the early nineteenth century when Americans learned of a new French discovery that food stayed fresh when cooked in airtight containers. By 1820 major canneries were in existence in Boston and New York. At the end of the 1830s glass containers were giving way to the "tin can" (tin-plated steel) brought in from England, and eventually used to market Gail Borden's new invention—a process for condensed milk. Among the other outstanding American originals were Cyrus Hall McCormick of Virginia and Obed Hussey of Massachusetts, who separately invented practical reapers for grain at about the same time, a development as significant to the Northwest as the cotton gin was to the South. Hussey got a patent in 1833, McCormick in 1834. Competition between the two brought a rapid growth in the industry, but McCormick finally emerged on top because he had the foresight in 1847 to put his main plant at Chicago near the emerging wheat belt and the wit to accept improvements more quickly than Hussey.

A spate of inventions in the 1840s foretokened future changes

"In this Field, July 25, 1831, will be Tried a new Patent Grain Cutter, worked by horsepower, invented by C. H. McCormick." [The Science Museum, London]

in American life. In 1844 Charles Goodyear patented a process for vulcanizing rubber. In the same year the first intercity telegraph message was transmitted from Baltimore to Washington on the device Morse had invented back in 1832. The telegraph was slow to catch on at first, but seventeen years after that demonstration, with the completion of connections to San Francisco, an entire continent had been wired for instant communications. In 1846 Elias Howe invented the sewing machine, soon improved by Allen B. Wilson and Isaac Merritt Singer. The sewing machine, incidentally, was one invention that slowed the progress of the factory. Since it was adapted to use in the home, it gave the "putting-out" system a new lease on life in the clothing industry.

Examples can do no more than hint at the magnitude of change in technology and manufacturing. A suggestive if flawed measure of this change was the growing number of patents issued. During the first twenty-one years of the Patent Office, 1790–1811, the number issued averaged only 77 per year; from 1820 to 1830 the average was up to 535; during the 1840s it was 646; and during the 1850s the number suddenly quadrupled to an average of 2,525 per year.

THE LOWELL SYSTEM   Before the 1850s the factory still had not become typical of American industry. Handicraft and domestic production (putting-out) remained common. In many industries they stayed for decades the chief agencies of growth. Hatmaking in Danbury, Connecticut, and shoemaking in eastern Massachusetts, for instance, grew mainly by the multiplication of small shops and their gradual enlargement. Not until the 1850s did either begin to adopt power-driven machinery, usually a distinctive feature of the factory system.

The factory system sprang full-blown upon the American scene at Waltham, Massachusetts, in 1813, in the plant of the Boston Manufacturing Company. In 1822 its promoters, the Boston Associates, developed a new center at a village, renamed Lowell, where the Merrimack River fell thirty-five feet. At this "Manchester of America" the Merrimack Manufacturing Company developed a new plant similar to the Waltham mill. Another sprang up in 1823 at Chicopee and before 1850 textile mills appeared at many other places in Massachusetts, New Hampshire, and Maine. By 1850, as good waterpower locations were occupied, steam power was becoming common in textile manufacture.

Companies organized on the Waltham plan produced by 1850 a fifth of the nation's total output of cotton cloth. The chief features of this plan were large capital investment, the concentration of all processes in one plant under unified management, and specialization in a relatively coarse cloth requiring minimum skill by the workers. In the public mind, however, the system then and afterward was associated above all with the recruitment of young women from New England farms who lived in dormitories while they worked in the mills. The system offered reassurance to parents by providing strait-laced discipline supervised by respectable housemothers, regular curfews, and compulsory church attendance. Many women were drawn by the chance to escape the routine of farm life and to earn money which might be used to help the family or improve their own circumstances. Despite their twelve-hour day and seventy-hour week some of them found the time and energy to form study groups, publish a literary magazine, and attend lectures by Ralph Waldo Emerson and other luminaries of the era. Foreign travelers were almost universally charmed by the arrangement. It was hardly an idyllic existence, but few if any of the young women saw their work as a lifetime career. It was, rather, at worst a temporary burden, at best a preparation for life or an exciting interlude before settling into the routine of domesticity.

It was but an interlude in the history of American labor too. The "Lowell girls" drew attention less because they were typical than because they were special. An increasingly common pattern for industry was the family system, sometimes called the Rhode

A label for cloth "made and printed by the Merrimack Manufacturing Co., Lowell, Mass." Women such as those at left typically worked twelve-hour days, seventy-hour weeks. [Merrimack Valley Textile Museum]

Island or Fall River system, which prevailed in textile manufactures outside of northern New England. Factories that relied on waterpower often rose in unpopulated areas, and part of their construction included tenements or mill villages. Whole families might be hired, the men for heavy labor, the women and children for the lighter work. The system promoted paternalism. Employers dominated the life of the mill villages, often setting rules of good behavior. Wages under the system are hard to establish, for employers often paid in goods from the company store. The hours of labor often ran from sunup to sunset, and longer in winter—a sixty-eight- to seventy-two-hour week. Such hours were common on the farms of the time, but in factories the work was more intense and offered no seasonal let-up. The labor of children, common on the farm, excited little censure from communities still close to the soil. A common opinion at the time regarded the provision of gainful employment for the women and children of the lower orders as a community benefit.

CORPORATIONS AND INDUSTRY   In manufacturing the corporate form of organization caught on slowly. Manufacturing firms usually took the form of individual proprietorships, family enterprises, or partnerships. The success of the Boston Associates at Waltham and Lowell, and the growth of larger units, particularly in textiles, brought the corporate device into greater use. But until 1860 most manufacturing was carried on by unincorporated enterprises.

The corporate organization was more common for banking, turnpike, canal, and railroad companies, since many then believed that the form should be reserved for such quasi-public and quasi-monopolistic functions. The irregular practices of "wildcat" banks gave corporations a bad name throughout the period. Corporations were regarded with suspicion as the beneficiaries of special privileges, as threats to individual enterprises. "The very object of the act of incorporation is to produce inequality, either in rights, or in the division of property," the lawyer-economist Daniel Raymond wrote in 1820. "*Prima facie*, therefore, all money corporations, are detrimental to national health. They are always for the benefit of the rich, and never for the poor." It would be many years before corporations came to be widely regarded as agencies of free enterprise.

Banks of the time supplied mainly short-term commercial loans and long-term secured loans, but even before 1815 some of them had become active as investment banks—that is, they would take government or private securities in wholesale lots and put them on the market. The New York Stock Exchange, started in 1817, soon became the chief exchange for these securities, and the Boston Stock Exchange was the one on which manufacturing securities were traded before the Civil War. Most of the capital that financed new factories through the purchase of securities came from profits made earlier in commerce. New England's head start in commerce fueled its head start in factories. Foreign investments were important in building the canals and railroads, but contributed little to manufacturing. The same was true of investments by the states.

As late as 1860 the United States was still preponderantly rural and agricultural. Industry was heavily concentrated in the Northeast. In southern New England, especially its coastal regions, and along the Hudson and Delaware Rivers, the concentration of industry rivaled that in any of the industrialized parts of Britain and exceeded that in most parts of the European continent.

In the 1860 Census of Manufactures cotton textiles stood ahead of all other categories in rank order of value added (value of product minus value of raw material). Recognizing the primacy of the fiber in exports as well, the census report began with these words: "The growth of the culture and manufacture of cotton in the United States constitutes the most striking feature of the industrial history of the last fifty years." In all, American industry in 1860 employed 1,311,000 workers in 140,000 establishments; with a capital investment of just over $1 billion, output amounted to $1.886 billion (up significantly from 1810's

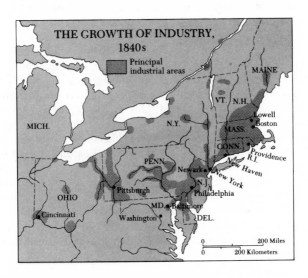

THE GROWTH OF INDUSTRY, 1840s

total output of $149 million), of which the value added by manufacturing was $854 million.

INDUSTRY AND CITIES   The rapid growth of commerce and industry impelled a rapid growth of cities. Using the census definition of "urban" as places with 8,000 inhabitants or more, the proportion of urban population grew from 3.3 percent in 1790 to 16.1 percent in 1860. Modern cities have served three major economic functions: they have been centers of trade and distribution, centers of manufacturing, and centers of administration. Until near the mid–nineteenth century American cities grew mainly in response to the circumstances of transportation and trade. Because of their strategic locations the four great Atlantic seaports of New York, Philadelphia, Baltimore, and Boston held throughout the antebellum period the relative positions of leadership they had gained by the end of the Revolution. New Orleans became the nation's fifth-largest city from the time of the Louisiana Purchase. Its focus on cotton exports, to the neglect of imports, however, caused it eventually to lag behind its eastern competitors. New York outpaced both its competitors and the nation as a whole in its population growth. By 1860 it was the first American city to reach the size of more than a million, largely because of its superior harbor and its unique access to commerce.

Pittsburgh, at the head of the Ohio, was already a center of iron production by 1800, and Cincinnati, at the mouth of the Little Miami, soon surpassed all other centers of meatpacking, with pork a specialty. Louisville, because it stood at the falls of the Ohio, became an important stop for trade and remained so after the short Louisville and Portland Canal bypassed the falls in 1830. On the Great Lakes the leading cities also stood at important breaking points in water transportation: Buffalo, Cleveland, Detroit, Chicago, and Milwaukee. Chicago was especially well located to become a hub of both water and rail transportation on into the trans-Mississippi West. During the 1830s St. Louis tripled in size mainly because most of the trans-Mississippi fur trade was funneled down the Missouri River. By 1860 St. Louis and Chicago were positioned to challenge Boston and Baltimore for third and fourth places.

Before 1840 commerce dominated the activities of major cities, but early industry often created new concentrations of population at places convenient to waterpower of raw materials. During the 1840s and 1850s, however, the stationary steam engine and declining transportation costs more and more offset the

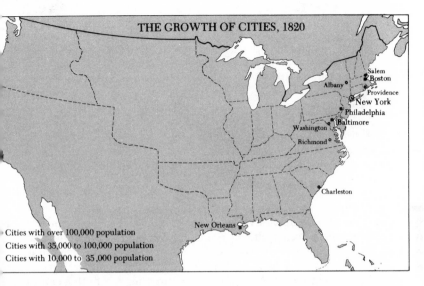

THE GROWTH OF CITIES, 1820

Salem
Boston
Albany
Providence
New York
Philadelphia
Baltimore
Washington
Richmond

Charleston

New Orleans

Cities with over 100,000 population
Cities with 35,000 to 100,000 population
Cities with 10,000 to 35,000 population

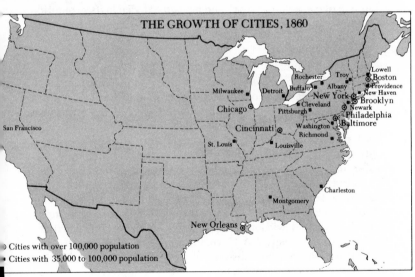

THE GROWTH OF CITIES, 1860

Lowell
Troy
Rochester
Boston
Milwaukee   Detroit   Buffalo   Albany   Providence
New Haven
Chicago   Cleveland   New York   Brooklyn
Pittsburgh   Newark
Cincinnati   Philadelphia
Washington   Baltimore
St. Louis   Louisville   Richmond

San Francisco

Charleston

Montgomery

New Orleans

Cities with over 100,000 population
Cities with 35,000 to 100,000 population

St. Louis in the 1850s, looking east toward the Mississippi River. [Chicago Historical Society]

advantages of locations near waterpower and resources, and the attractions of older cities were enhanced: pools of experienced labor, capital, warehousing and trading services, access to information, the savings of bulk purchasing and handling, and the many amenities of city life. Urbanization thus was both a consequence of economic growth and a positive force in its promotion.

IMMIGRATION

For all the new economic growth, one basic condition of American life carried over beyond the mid–nineteenth century: land remained plentiful and relatively cheap, while labor was scarce and relatively dear. A decline in the birth rate coinciding with the onset of industry and urbanization influenced this condition. The United States became a strong magnet to immigrants, offering them chances to take up farms in the country or jobs in the cities. Glowing reports from early arrivals who made good reinforced romantic views of America opportunity and freedom. "Tell Miriam," one immigrant wrote back, "there is no sending children to bed without supper, or husbands to work without dinner in their bags." A German immigrant in Missouri wrote home applauding the "absence of overbearing soldier, haughty clergymen, and inquisitive tax collectors."

During the forty years from the outbreak of the Revolution until the end of the War of 1812 immigration had slowed to a trickle. The wars of the French Revolution and Napoleon restricted travel until 1815. Within a few years, however, packet lines had begun to cross the north Atlantic, and competing shippers who needed westbound payloads kept the transatlantic fares as low as $30 per person. One informed estimate had it that from 1783 to 1819 total arrivals numbered about 250,000, or something under 7,000 per year. In 1820, when the govenment began to keep records, the number was 8,385. Thereafter the pace followed just behind the growth of business. For two decades the numbers rose steadily: 10,199 in 1825, 23,322 in 1830, 84,066 in 1840. After 1845 the tempo picked up rapidly. During the 1830s total arrivals had numbered fewer than 600,000. In the 1840s almost three times as many, or 1.7 million, immigrated, and during the 1850s 2.6 million more. In 1850 the annual count went above 300,000 for the first time, then rose annually to a peak of 427,833 in 1854, a figure not equaled before 1880. The years from 1845 to 1854 saw the greatest proportionate influx of immigrants in American history, 2.4 million, or about 14.5 percent of the total population in 1845.

THE IRISH In 1860 more than one of every eight persons in America was foreign born. The largest groups among them, by far, were 1.6 million Irish, 1.3 million Germans, and 588,000 British (mostly English). The Catholic Irish were the most conspicuous new element in the population. Ireland had long seethed with discontent at British rule, British landlords, and British taxes to support the Church of England. What sent the Irish fleeing their homeland was a chronic depression that set in with the nineteenth century. By the 1830s their numbers in America were growing annually, and after an epidemic of potato rot in 1845 brought famine, the flow of Irish immigrants rose to a flood. The Irish disaster coincided with the end of depression and a rising tempo of business in the United States. In 1847 Irish arrivals numbered above 100,000 and stayed above that level for eight years, reaching a peak of 221,000 in 1851.

The Irish were mostly tenant farmers, but their experience had left them little taste for farm work and little money to travel or buy land. Great numbers of them hired on with construction gangs building the canal and railways—about 3,000 set to work on the Erie Canal as early as 1818. Few immigrants of any origin found their way into the South, but the Irish who did sometimes found work with planters who preferred not to risk valuable slaves at hazardous tasks. For the most part, however, the Irish congregated in the eastern cities, in or near their port of entry. Generally they worked as domestic servants or unskilled laborers, and clustered together in shanty-towns and around

Catholic churches, both of which became familiar features of the urban scene.

Experienced at organized resistance to rent and tax collectors, the Irish formed blocs of voters and found their way into American politics more quickly than any other immigrant group. Drawn mainly to the party of Jefferson and Jackson, "the party of the common man," they set a pattern of identification with the Democrats that other ethnic groups by and large followed. They also stimulated the growth of the Catholic church with their numbers and their more aggressive spirit. Years of persecution had instilled in them a fierce loyalty to the doctrines of the church.

THE GERMANS When the new wave of German migration got under way in the 1830s there were still large enclaves of Germans in Pennsylvania and Ohio who preserved their language and cultures, and in the Old World style, clustered in agricultural villages. The new German migration peaked just a few years after the Irish, in 1854 when 215,000 arrived. Unlike the Irish, the Germans included fair numbers of independent farmers, skilled workers, and shopkeepers who arrived with some means to get themselves established in skilled labor or on the land. Three major centers of new settlement developed in Missouri and southwestern Illinois (around St. Louis), in Texas (near San Antonio), and in Wisconsin (especially around Milwaukee). The German migrants also included a large number of professional people, some of them refugees from the failure of liberal revolution in Germany, among whom was Carl Schurz, later senator from Missouri. The larger German communities developed traditions of good food, beer, and music along with German *Turnvereine* (gymnastic societies), sharpshooter clubs, fire engine companies, and kindergartens (introduced by Mrs. Carl Schurz).

A Turnvereine *in Cincinnati (1850). [Cincinnati Historical Society]*

THE BRITISH, SCANDINAVIANS, AND CHINESE   Among the British immigrants too were large numbers of professionals, independent farmers, and skilled workers. Some British workers, such as Samuel Slater, helped transmit the technology of British factories into the United States. Two other groups that began to arrive in some number during the 1840s and 1850s were but the vanguard of greater numbers to come later. Annual arrivals from Scandinavia did not exceed 1,000 until 1843, but by 1860 a total of 72,600 Scandinavians lived in America. The Norwegians and Swedes gravitated to Wisconsin and Minnesota where the climate and woodlands reminded them of home. By the 1850s the sudden development of California was bringing in Chinese who, like the Irish in the East, did the heavy work of construction. Infinitesimal in numbers until 1854, the Chinese in America numbered 35,500 by 1860.

NATIVISM   America had always been a land of immigrants, but the welcome accorded them had often been less than cordial. For many natives these waves of strangers in the land posed a threat of unknown tongues and mysterious ways. The greatest single group of newcomers were the Irish, who were mostly Catholic. The Germans too included many Catholics. This massive increase naturally aroused antagonisms which were rooted in the Protestant tradition of hostility to "popery" and aggravated by job competition in the cities where immigrants gathered. A militant Protestantism growing out of revivals in the early nineteenth century heated up the climate of opinion. There were fears of radicalism among the Germans and of voting blocs among the Irish, but above all hovered the menace of unfamiliar religious practices. Catholic authoritarianism was widely perceived as a threat to hard-won liberties, religious and political. The convenience of this, for political adventurers and fanatics, was that the Catholic church in most places remained small enough to be attacked with impunity.

In the 1830s nativism was conspicuously on the rise. Pointing to the Catholic missions sponsored by European groups, and to the pope's trappings of monarchy in Italy, overheated patriots envisaged conspiracy and subversion in America. Samuel F. B. Morse, already at work on his telegraph, took time out from his painting and inventing to write two books demonstrating his theory that Catholicism in America was a plot of foreign monarchs to undermine American liberty before its revolutionary message affected their own people. In 1836 he ran for mayor of New York on a Native American ticket, and his books went through numerous editions. But the literature of conspiracy could scarcely compete with a profitable trade in books which, in the guise of attacking evil, exploited salacious fantasies of sex in Catholic nunneries.

At times this hostility rekindled the spirit of the wars of religion. In 1834 a series of anti-Catholic sermons by Lyman Beecher and others aroused feelings to the extent that a mob attacked and burned the Ursuline Convent in Charlestown, Massachusetts. In 1844 armed clashes between Protestants and Catholics in Philadelphia ended with about 20 killed and 100 injured. Sporadically, the nativist spirit took organized form in groups that proved their patriotism by hating foreigners and Catholics.

As early as 1837 a Native American Association was formed at Washington, but the most significant such group was the Order of the Star Spangled Banner, founded in New York in 1849. Within a few years this group had grown into a formidable third party. In July 1854 delegates from thirteen states gathered to form the American party, which had the trappings of a secret fraternal order. Members pledged never to vote for any foreign-born or Catholic candidate. When asked about the organization, they were to say "I know nothing." In popular parlance the American party became the Know-Nothing party. For a season it

Americans Shall Rule America. *This 1856 sketch satirizes Baltimore nativists out to bully German and Irish immigrants.*
[Maryland Historical Society]

seemed that the American party might achieve major-party status. In state and local campaigns during 1854 the Know-Nothings carried one election after another. In November they swept the Massachusetts legislature, winning all but two seats in the lower house. That fall they elected more than forty congressmen. For a while they threatened to control New England, New York, and Maryland, and showed strength elsewhere, but the movement collapsed when slavery became the focal issue of the 1850s.

The Know-Nothings demanded the exclusion of immigrants and Catholics from public office and extension of the period for naturalization from five to twenty-one years, but the party never gathered the political strength to effect such legislation. Nor did Congress act during the period to restrict immigration in any way. The first federal law on immigration, passed in 1819, enacted only safety and health regulations regarding supplies and the number of passengers on immigrant ships. This and subsequent acts designed to protect immigrants from overcrowding and unsanitary conditions were, however, poorly enforced.

IMMIGRANT LABOR After 1840 immigration became critical to the dynamics of growth. The increase in population it brought contributed to economic growth and demand, whether the newcomer took up land or went into the city. The readiness of immigrant and native alike to go where jobs beckoned was important to rapid growth. By meeting the demand for cheap, unskilled labor immigrants made a twofold contribution. They moved into jobs vacated or bypassed by those who went into the factories; they themselves made up a pool of labor from which in time factory workers were drawn.

In New England the large numbers of Irish workers, accustomed to hard treatment, spelled the end of the "Lowell girls." By 1860 immigrants made up more than half the labor force in New England mills. Even so, their price was generally higher than that of the women and children who worked to supplement family incomes, and the flood of immigration never rose fast enough to stop the long-term rise in wages. So factory labor continued to draw people from the countryside. Work in the cities offered higher real wages than work on the farm, which kept manufacturers alert for ways to cut their labor costs by improving machines. The cost of labor also put a premium on mass production of low-priced goods for a mass market. Artisans who emphasized quality and craftsmanship for a custom trade found it hard to meet such competitive conditions. Many artisans in fact found that their skills were going out of style. Some took work as craftsmen in factories, while others went into small-scale manufacturing or shopkeeping, and some bought homesteads to practice their skills in the West.

ORGANIZED LABOR

EARLY UNIONS Few workers of the period belonged to unions, but in the 1820s and 1830s a growing fear that they were losing status led artisans of the major cities into intense activity in labor politics and unions. As early as the colonial period craftsmen had formed fraternal and mutual benefit societies, much like the medieval guilds, through which they regulated a system for training apprentices. These organizations continued to flourish well into the national period. After the Revolution, however, organizations of journeymen carpenters, masons, shipfitters, tailors, printers, and cordwainers (as shoemakers were called) became concerned with wages, hours, and working conditions and began to back up their demands with such devices as the strike and the closed shop. These organizations were local, often largely social in purpose, and frequently lasted only for the duration of the dispute. The longest-lived was Philadelphia's Federated Society of Journeymen Cordwainers, which flourished from 1794 to 1806.

Early labor unions faced serious legal obstacles. Unions were prosecuted as unlawful conspiracies. In 1806, for instance, Philadelphia shoemakers were found "guilty of a combination to raise their wages." The decision broke the union. Such precedents were used for many years to hamstring labor organizations until the Massachusetts Supreme Court made a landmark ruling in the case of *Commonwealth v. Hunt* (1842). In this case Chief Justice Shaw ruled that forming a trade union was not in itself illegal nor was a demand that employers hire only members of the union.

Until the 1820s labor organizations took the form of local trade unions, confined to one city and one craft. During the ten years from 1827 to 1837 organization on a larger scale began to take hold. Philadelphia, in 1827, had the first city central, formed after the carpenters had lost a strike for the ten-hour day. The Mechanics' Union of Trade Associations included carpenters, shoemakers, bricklayers, glaziers, and other groups associated for the purpose of pooling resources. In the mid-1830s still wider organizations were attempted. In 1834 the National Trades' Union was set up in the effort to federate the city societies. At the same time national craft unions were established by the shoemakers, printers, combmakers, carpenters, and hand-

THE TRIAL

T. Wharton 567903

Journeymen

BOOT & SHOEMAKERS

OF PHILADELPHIA,

ON AN INDICTMENT

FOR A COMBINATION AND CONSPIRACY

TO RAISE THEIR WAGES.

TAKEN IN SHORT-HAND,
BY THOMAS LLOYD.

PHILADELPHIA:

PRINTED BY B. GRAVES, NO. 40, NORTH FOURTH-STREET,
FOR T. LLOYD, AND B. GRAVES.

1806.

Early labor unions were hampered by legal obstacles. These boot and shoemakers were found guilty of a "conspiracy to raise their wages." [New York Public Library]

loom weavers, but all the national groups and most of the local ones vanished in the economic collapse of 1837.

LABOR POLITICS   With the removal of property qualifications for voting nearly everywhere, labor politics flourished briefly. In this, as in other respects, Philadelphia was in the forefront. A Working Men's party, formed there in 1828, gained the balance of power in the city council that fall. This success inspired other Working Men's parties in New York, Boston, and about fifteen states. In 1829 the New York party elected the head of the carpenters' union to the state legislature. The Working Men's parties were broad reformist groups devoted to the interests of labor. But they admitted to their ranks many who were not workers by any strict definition, and their leaders were mainly reformers and small businessmen. The labor parties faded quickly for a variety of reasons: the inexperience of labor politicians, which left the parties prey to manipulation by political professionals; the fact that some of their causes were espoused also by the major parties; and their vulnerability to attack on grounds of extreme radicalism or dilettantism. Additionally, they often splintered into warring factions, limiting their effectiveness.

Once the parties had faded, however, many of their supporters found their way into a radical wing of the Jacksonian

Democrats. This wing became the Equal Rights party and in 1835 acquired the name "Locofocos" when their opponents from New York City's regular Democratic organization, Tammany Hall, turned off the gas lights at their meeting and the Equal Rights supporters produced candles, lighting them with the new friction matches known as Locofocos. The Locofocos soon faded as a separate group, but endured as a radical faction within the Democrat party.

While the labor parties elected few candidates they did succeed in drawing notice to their demands, many of which attracted the support of middle-class reformers. Above all they carried on an agitation for free public education and the abolition of imprisonment for debt, causes that won widespread popular support. The labor parties and unions actively promoted the ten-hour day. In 1836 President Jackson established the ten-hour day at the Philadelphia Navy Yard in response to a strike, and in 1840 President Van Buren extended the limit to all government offices and projects. In private jobs the ten-hour day became increasingly common, although by no means universal, before 1860. Other reforms put forward by the workingman's parties included mechanics' lien laws, to protect workers against nonpayment of wages; reform of a militia system which allowed the rich to escape service with fines but forced the poor to face jail terms; the abolition of "licensed monopolies," especially banks; measures to ensure hard money and to protect workers against inflated banknote currency; measures to restrict competition from prison labor; and the abolition of child labor.

LABOR AND REFORM After the Panic of 1837 the nascent labor movement went into decline, and during the 1840s the focus of its radical spirit turned toward the promotion of cooperative societies. During the 1830s there had been sporadic efforts to provide self-employment through producers' cooperatives, but the movement began to catch on after the iron molders of Cincinnati set up a successful shop in 1848. Soon the tailors of Boston had a cooperative workshop which employed thirty to forty men. New York was an especially strong center, with cooperatives among tailors, shirtmakers, bakers, shoemakers, and carpenters. Consumer cooperatives became much more vigorous and involved more people. The New England Protective Union, formed in 1845, organized a central purchasing agency for co-op stores and by 1852 was buying more than $1 million worth of goods while affiliated stores were doing in excess of $4 million in trade. Both the producers' and consumers' movement benefited from the support of Associationists, who saw it as a possible first step on the road to utopia, but more people probably were drawn to the movement for practical reasons: to reduce their dependence on employers or to reduce the cost of purchases. After peaking in the early 1850s, however, cooperatives went into decline. The high mobility of Americans and the heterogenous character of the population as immigration increased created unfavorable conditions. Insufficient capital and weak, inexperienced management also plagued the cooperative movement.

THE REVIVAL OF UNIONS   The high visibility of reform efforts, however, should not obscure the continuing activity of unions, which began to revive with improved business conditions in the early 1840s. Still, the unions remained local, weak, and given to sporadic activity. Often they came and went with a single strike. The greatest single labor dispute before the Civil War came on February 22, 1860, when shoemakers at Lynn and Natick, Massachusetts, walked out for higher wages. Before the strike ended it had spread through New England, involving perhaps twenty-five towns and 20,000 workers. It stood out also as a strike the workers won. Most of the employers agreed to wage increases and some also agreed to recognize the union as a bargaining agent.

This reflected the growing tendency of workers to view their unions as permanent. Workers emphasized union recognition and regular collective bargaining agreements. They shared a growing sense of solidarity. In 1852 the National Typographical Union revived the effort to organize skilled crafts on a national scale. Others followed: the Hat Finishers National Association in 1854, the Journeymen Stone Cutters Association in 1855, the National Union of Iron Molders in 1859. By 1860 about twenty such organizations had appeared, although none was strong enough as yet to do much more than hold national conventions and pass resolutions.

JACKSONIAN INEQUALITY

During the years before the Civil War the United States had begun to develop a distinctive working class, most conspicuously in the factories and the ranks of common labor, often including many Irish or German immigrants. More and more craftsmen, aware that they were likely to remain wage earners, became receptive to permanent unions. But the American legend of "rags to riches," the image of the self-made man, was a durable myth. "In America," Tocqueville wrote, "most of the rich men were formerly poor." Speaking to the Senate on the tariff in 1832, Henry Clay said that almost all the successful factory owners he knew were "enterprising self-made men, who have whatever wealth they possess by patient and diligent labor." The legend had just enough basis in fact to lend credence. John Jacob Astor, the wealthiest man in America, worth more than $20 million at his death in 1848, came of humble if not exactly destitute origins. Son of a minor official in the Duchy of Baden, he arrived in 1784 with little or nothing, made a fortune first on the western fur trade, then parlayed that into a large fortune in New York real estate. But his and similar cases were more exceptional than common.

Researches by Edward Pessen on the rich in major eastern cities show that while men of moderate means could sometimes run their inheritances into fortunes by good management and prudent speculation, those who started with the handicap of poverty and ignorance seldom made it to the top. In 1828 the top 1 percent of New York's families (owning $34,000 or more) held 40 percent of the wealth, and the top 4 percent held 76 percent. Similar circumstances prevailed in Philadelphia, Boston, and other cities.

A supreme irony of the times was that the "age of the common man," "the age of Jacksonian Democracy," seems actually to have been an age of increasing social rigidity. Years before, the colonists had brought to America conceptions of a social hierarchy which during the eighteenth century corresponded imperfectly with the developing reality. In the late eighteenth century, slavery aside, American society probably approached equality more closely than any population its size anywhere else in the world. During the last half of the 1700s, the historian Jackson T. Main has argued, social mobility was higher than either before or since. By the time popular egalitarianism caught up with reality, reality was moving back toward greater inequality.

Why this happened is difficult to say, except that the boundless wealth of the untapped frontier narrowed as the land was occupied and claims on various opportunities were staked out. Such developments took place in New England towns even before the end of the seventeenth century. But despite growing social distinctions, it seems likely that the white population of America, at least, was better off than the general run of European peoples. New frontiers, geographical and technological, raised the level of material well-being much as a rising tide raises boats of all sizes.

FURTHER READING

On economic developments in the nation's early decades, see W. Elliott Brownlee's *Dynamics of Ascent: A History of the American Economy* (1979), which provides the most current overview. Older, yet still valuable, are Stuart Bruchey's *The Roots of American Economic Growth, 1607–1861* (1965),° Douglass C. North's *The Economic Growth of the United States, 1790–1860* (1961),° and Thomas C. Cochran and William Miller's *The Age of Enterprise: A Social History of Industrial America* (1961).°

The resilient classic on transportation as a basis for growth is George R. Taylor's *The Transportation Revolution, 1815–1861* (1951).° Specialized accounts of water travel and trade are Erik F. Haites, James Mak, and Gary M. Walter's *Western Rivers Transportation: The Era of Early Internal Improvements* (1975), Walter Havighurst's *Voices on the River: The Story of the Mississippi Water Ways* (1964), Ronald Shaw's *Erie Water West: A History of the Erie Canal* (1966), and Carter Goodrich's *Government Promotion of Canals and Railroads, 1800–1890* (1960). Scholarly works concentrating on railroads include John F. Stover's *Iron Road to the West: American Railroads in the 1850s* (1978), Albert Fishlow's *American Railroads and the Transformation of the American Economy* (1965), and Robert W. Fogel's *Railroads and American Economic Growth* (1964). Phillip D. Jordan's *The National Road* (1948) treats one of the first government transportation projects. For background on the merchant marine, consult Samuel E. Morison's *Maritime History of Massachusetts, 1789–1860* (1921), and A. H. Clark's *The Clipper Ship Era* (1910).

Concurrent with transportation innovations was industrial growth. Thomas C. Cochran's *Frontiers of Change: Early Industrialism in America* (1981)° is a recent survey. The business side of industrial growth can be studied in the surveys cited above, as well as in Elisha P. Douglass's *The Coming of Age of American Business* (1971) and Edwin M. Dodd's *American Business Corporations until 1860* (1954). The impact of technology is traced in David J. Jeremy's *Transatlantic Industrial Revolution: The Diffusion of Textile Technologies between Britain and America* (1981), Nathan Rosenberg's *Technology and American Economic Growth* (1972),° H. J. Habakkuk's *American and British Technology in the Nineteenth Century* (1962),° and Merritt R. Smith's *Harper's Ferry Armory and the New Technology: The Challenge of Change* (1977).

What Americans thought about the changes wrought by technology and industry is surveyed in Joseph Dorfman's *The Economic Mind in American Civilization* (vols. 1–4, 1946–1959). Richard D. Brown's *Modernization: The Transformation of American Life, 1600–1865* (1976),° assesses the impact of technology on living patterns. How American values were affected by the new industrial system is assessed in John F. Kasson's

°These books are available in paperback editions.

Civilizing the Machine: Technology and Republican Values in America, 1776–1900 (1977),° and Leo Marx's *The Machine in the Garden: Technology and the Pastoral Ideal in America* (1964).° Roger Burlingame's *The March of the Iron Men* (1960) gauges the role of technology in American social history, and Paul Johnson's *A Shopkeepers Millennium: Society and Revivals in Rochester, New York, 1815–1837* (1978),° studies the role religion played in the emerging industrial order.

The attitude of the worker during this time of transition is surveyed in Joseph G. Rayback's *A History of American Labor* (1966).° More narrative in treatment are John R. Commons's *A History of Labour in the United States* (vol. 1, 1918) and Norman Ware's *The Industrial Worker, 1840–1860* (1924). Edward E. Pessen's *Most Uncommon Jacksonians: The Radical Leaders of the Early Labor Movement* (1967)° concentrates on political reactions. Detailed case studies of working communities include Anthony F. C. Wallace's *Rockdale: The Growth of an American Village in the Early Industrial Revolution* (1978),° Thomas Dublin's *Women at Work: The Transformation of Work and Community in Lowell, Massachusetts, 1826–1860* (1979),° Alan Dawley's *Class and Community: The Industrial Revolution in Lynn* (1976),° and Bruce Laurie's *The Working People of Philadelphia, 1800–1850* (1980).

For introductions to the development of urbanization, see Sam Bass Warner, Jr.'s *The Urban Wilderness* (1972),° Richard C. Wade's *The Urban Frontier* (1964), and Howard P. Chudacoff's *The Evolution of American Urban Society* (1981). A recent valuable case study is Edward K. Spann's *The New Metropolis: New York, 1840–1857* (1981). Studies of the origins of immigration include Oscar Handlin's *The Uprooted* (1951),° Phillip Taylor's *The Distant Magnet: European Emigration to the USA* (1971),° Carl Wittke's *The Irish in America* (1956), Robert Ernest's *Immigrant Life in New York City, 1825–1863* (1949), and Jay P. Dolan's *The Immigrant Church: New York's Irish and German Catholics, 1815–1865* (1975). Ray Billington's *The Protestant Crusade, 1800–1860* (1938), examines nativist sentiments toward the immigrants. Walter E. Hugins's *Jacksonian Democracy and the Working Class* (1960) surveys the Working-Men's party and Locofocos of New York City.

13

AN AMERICAN RENAISSANCE: ROMANTICISM AND REFORM

RATIONAL RELIGION

The American novelist Nathaniel Hawthorne once lamented "the difficulty of writing a romance about a country where there is no shadow, no antiquity, no mystery, no picturesque and gloomy wrong. . . . Romance and poetry, ivy, lichens, and wall-flowers, need ruin to make them grow." Unlike nations of the Old World, rooted in shadow and mystery, in historic cultures and traditions, the United States had been rooted in the ideas of the Enlightenment. Those ideas, most vividly set forth in Jefferson's Declaration, had in turn a universal application. In the eyes of many if not most citizens, the "first new nation" had a mission to stand as an example to the world, much as John Winthrop's "city upon a hill" had once stood as an example to erring humanity. The concept of mission in fact still carried spiritual overtones, for the religious fervor quickened in the Great Awakening had reinforced the idea of national purpose. In turn the sense of high calling infused the national character with an element of perfectionism—and an element of impatience when reality fell short of expectations. The combination brought major reforms and advances in human rights. It also brought disappointments that could fester into cynicism and alienation.

DEISM The currents of the Enlightenment and the Great Awakening, now mingling, now parting, flowed on into the nineteenth century. By the turn of the century both had worked changes in the Calvinist orthodoxy of American religion. Many leaders of the Revolutionary War era, like Jefferson and Franklin, became deists, even while nominally attached to existent churches. Deism, which arose in eighteenth-century Europe, simply carried the logic of Sir Isaac Newton's world machine to its logical conclusion. The God of the deist, the Master Clockmaker in Voltaire's words, had planned the universe, built it, and then set in motion. But men, on their own, by the use of reason might grasp the natural laws which govern the universe. Deism tended to be a benevolent force. Thomas Paine in *The Age of Reason* (1794) defined religious duties as "doing justice, loving mercy and endeavoring to make our fellow creatures happy," a message of Quaker-like simplicity. But ever the controversialist, Tom Paine felt obliged to assail the "superstition" of the Scriptures and the existing churches—"human inventions set up to terrify and enslave mankind and monopolize power and profit." Orthodox churchmen could hardly distinguish such doctrine from atheism.

The old Puritan churches around Boston ironically proved most vulnerable to the logic of the Enlightenment. A strain of rationalism had run through Puritan belief all along in its stress on the need for right reason to interpret the Scriptures. Boston's progress from Puritanism to prosperity had persuaded many rising families that they were anything but sinners in the hands of an angry God. Drawn toward less strenuous doctrines, some went back to the traditional rites of the Episcopal church. More of them simply dropped or qualified their adherence to Calvinism while remaining in the Congregational churches.

UNITARIANISM   By the end of the eighteenth century they were drifting into Unitarianism, a belief which emphasized the oneness of God and put reason and conscience ahead of creeds and confessions. One stale jest had it that Unitarians believed in the fatherhood of God, the brotherhood of man, and the neighborhood of Boston. Boston was very much the center of the movement and it flourished chiefly within Congregational churches which kept their standing in the established order until controversy began to smoke them out.

It began in 1805 with the election of a liberal clergyman, Henry Ware, as Hollis Professor of Divinity at Harvard, followed by the choice of four more liberal professors in as many years. In protest against Unitarian Harvard, the Rev. Jedediah Morse, the noted geographer, led a movement to establish Andover Theological Seminary as a center of orthodoxy. Thereafter more and more liberal churches accepted the name of Unitarian.

William Ellery Channing of Boston's Federal Street Church emerged as the chief spokesman for the liberal position. "I am surer that my rational nature is from God," he said, "than that any book is an expression of his will." A "Conference of Liberal Ministers," formed in 1820, became in 1826 the American Unitarian Association with 125 churches (all but 5 of them in Massachusetts) including 20 of the 25 oldest Calvinist churches in the United States. That same year, when the Presbyterian minister Lyman Beecher moved to Boston, he lamented: "All the literary men of Massachusetts were Unitarian; all the trustees and professors of Harvard College were Unitarian, all the elite of wealth and fashion crowded Unitarian churches."

UNIVERSALISM   A parallel movement, Universalism, attracted a different social stratum: workers and the more humble. In 1779 John Murray, who had come from England as a missionary for the new doctrine, founded the first Universalist church at Gloucester, Massachusetts. In 1794 a Universalist convention in Philadelphia organized the sect. Universalism held to a belief in the salvation of all men and women, while holding intact most Calvinist doctrines. God, they taught, was too merciful to condemn anyone to eternal punishment. True believers could escape altogether through Christ's atonement; the unregenerate would suffer in proportion to their sins, but eventually all souls would come into harmony with God. "Thus, the Unitarians and Universalists were in fundamental agreement," wrote one historian of religion, "the Universalists holding that God was too good to damn man; the Unitarians insisting that man was too good to be damned."

THE SECOND AWAKENING

For all the impact of rationalism, however, Americans remained a profoundly religious people. There was, Alexis de Tocqueville asserted, "no country in the world where the Christian religion retains a greater influence over the souls of men than in America." Around 1800 a revival of faith began to manifest itself. Soon it grew into a Second Awakening. An early exemplar of the movement, Timothy Dwight, became president of Yale College in 1795 and set about to purify a place which, in Lyman Beecher's words, had turned into "a hotbed of infidelity," where students openly discussed French radicalism, deism, and perhaps things even worse. Like his grandfather, Jonathan Edwards,

"Pope Timothy" had the gift of moving both mind and spirit, of reaching both the lettered and the unlettered. The result was a series of revivals that swept the student body and spread to all New England as well. "Wheresoever students were found," wrote a participant in the 1802 revival, "the reigning impression was, 'surely God is in this place.' "

After the founding in 1808, Jedediah Morse's Andover Seminary reinforced orthodoxy and the revival spirit so forcefully that its location came to be known as "Brimstone Hill." "Let us guard against the insidious encroachments of *innovation*—that evil and beguiling spirit which is now stalking to and fro in the earth, seeking whom it may devour." To avoid the fate of Harvard, Morse and his associates made professors give their assent to an Andover Creed of double-distilled Calvinism. The religious intensity and periodic revivals at Andover and Yale had their counterparts in many colleges for the next fifty years, since most were under the control of evangelical denominations. Hampden-Sydney College in Virginia had in fact got the jump on New England with a revival in 1787 which influenced many leaders of the awakening in the South.

REVIVALS ON THE FRONTIER   In its frontier phase the Second Awakening, like the first, generated great excitement and strange manifestations. It gave birth, moreover, to a new institution, the camp meeting, in which the fires of faith were repeatedly rekindled. Missionaries found ready audiences among lonely frontiersmen hungry for a sense of community. Among the

While Methodist preachers address the crowd at this camp meeting, a man in the foreground is overcome with religious ecstacy. [Library of Congress]

established sects, the Presbyterians were entrenched among the Scotch-Irish from Pennsylvania to Georgia. They gained further from the Plan of Union worked out in 1801 with the Congregationalists of Connecticut and later other states. Since the two groups agreed on doctrine and differed mainly on the form of church government, they were able to form unified congregations and call a minister from either church. The result through much of the Old Northwest was that New Englanders became Presbyterians by way of the "Presbygational" churches.

The Baptists had a simplicity of doctrine and organization which appealed to the common people of the frontier. Since each congregation was its own highest authority, a frontier congregation need appeal to no hierarchy before setting up shop and calling a minister or naming one of their own. Sometimes whole congregations moved across the mountains as a body. As Theodore Roosevelt described it in *The Winning of the West:* "Baptist preachers lived and worked exactly as their flocks. . . . they cleared the ground, split rails, planted corn, and raised hogs on equal terms with their parishioners."

But the Methodists may have had the most effective method of all, the circuit rider who sought out people in the most remote areas with the message of salvation as a gift free for the taking. The system began with Francis Asbury, the founder. "When he came to America," a biographer wrote, "he rented no house, he hired no lodgings, he made no arrangements to board anywhere, but simply set out on the Long Road, and was traveling forty-five years later when death caught up with him." By the 1840s the Methodists had grown into the largest Protestant church in the country, with over a million members.

The frontier phase of the Second Awakening got its start in Logan County, Kentucky, an area notorious as a Rogue's Harbor, a refuge of thieves and cutthroats. James McGready, a Presbyterian minister of Pennsylvania Scotch-Irish background, arrived there in 1796 after threats drove him out of the North Carolina Piedmont, where he was accused of running people distracted with his revivals. He had been influenced in his course by the Hampden-Sydney revival. Over the next few years he prepared a way for the Lord in the West. In 1800 a Methodist preacher named John McGee conducted a meeting in the neighborhood. So much excitement attended his preaching that other meetings were held near each of McGready's three churches and through the summer people came from far and wide, prepared to stay on the grounds for several days. Among those drawn to the Logan County, or Cumberland, Revival was Barton W. Stone, minister of two Presbyterian churches in Bourbon County. He soon began to preach the revival in his own churches and the result was the greatest of all camp meetings at Cane Ridge. During August 1801 the preachings drew great crowds variously estimated at from 10,000 to 25,000.

The Great Revival spread quickly through the West and into more settled regions back east. Camp meetings came to be held typically in late summer or fall, when crops could be laid-by temporarily. People came from far and wide, camping in wagons, tents, brush arbors or crude shacks. Mass excitement swept up even the most stable onlookers and the spirit moved participants to strange manifestations. Some went into cataleptic trances, others contracted the "jerks," laughed the "holy laugh," babbled in unknown tongues, danced like David before the Ark of God, or got down on all fours and barked like dogs to "tree the Devil." More sedate and prudent believers thought such rousements might be the work of the devil, out to discredit the true faith. But to dwell on the bizarre aspects of the camp meetings would be to distort an institution that offered social outlet to an isolated people, that brought a more settled community life through the churches that grew out of it, that spread a more democratic faith among the common people. Indeed with time camp meetings became much more sedate and dignified affairs.

THE "BURNED-OVER DISTRICT" But little wonder that regions swept by such fevers might be compared to forests devastated by fire. Western New York state all the way from Lake Ontario to the Adirondacks achieved the name of the "Burned-Over District" long before 1821, when a "mighty baptism of the Holy Ghost" overwhelmed a young lawyer in the town of Adams. The spirit went through him "in waves and waves of liquid love," Charles Grandison Finney wrote years later. The next day he announced a new profession: "I have a retainer from the Lord Jesus Christ to plead his case," he told a caller. In 1823 the St. Lawrence Presbytery ordained Finney and for the next decade he subjected the Burned-Over District to yet another scorching.

Finney went on to become the greatest single exemplar of revivalism and, some would argue, the very inventor of professional revivalism. The saving of souls did not have to wait for a miracle, he argued; it could come from careful planning. Nor did Finney shrink from comparing his methods to those of politicians who used advertising and showmanship to get attention. The revivalist planned carefully to arouse excitement, not for its own sake but to rivet attention on the Word. "New measures are necessary from time to time to awaken attention and bring the gospel to bear on the public mind." To those who challenged such use of emotion Finney had a frank answer: "The results justify my methods." Finney carried the methods of the frontier revival into the cities of the East and as far as Great Britain.

Untrained in theology, Finney read the Bible, he said, as he would a law book, and worked out his own theology of free will. His gospel combined faith and good works: one led to the other. "All sin consists in selfishness," he said, "and all holiness or virtue, in disinterested benevolence." Regeneration therefore was "a change from selfishness to benevolence, from having a supreme regard to one's own interest to an absorbing and controlling choice of the happiness and glory of God's Kingdom."

In 1835 Finney took the chair of theology in the new Oberlin College, founded by pious New Englanders in Ohio's Western Reserve. Later he served as its president. From the start Oberlin radiated a spirit of reform predicated on faith; it was the first college in America to admit either women or Negroes, and it was a hotbed of antislavery doctrine. Finney himself, however, held that men must be reformed from within, and cautioned against political action. In this, he held to a view which deeply influenced American social thought and action, a view which the historian John L. Thomas called romantic perfectionism: "Since social evils were simply individual acts of selfishness compounded, . . . it followed that . . . deep and lasting reform . . . meant an educational crusade based on the assumption that

Ohio's Oberlin College was the first in America to admit women or blacks. This graduating class is from the later nineteenth century. [Oberlin College Archives]

when a sufficient number of individual Americans had seen the light, they would automatically solve the country's social problems."

On the other hand the ardor aroused by revivals led to narrow sectarian bickerings, repeated schisms, and the phenomenon known as "come-outism" which further multiplied the sects—a phenomenon almost always noted by foreign travelers. James McGready's first revivals in Kentucky, for instance, created a tremendous demand for preachers which the Cumberland Presbytery met by ordaining men who lacked proper educational credentials. After a prolonged quarrel with the Kentucky Synod, the revivalists formed the Cumberland Presbyterian church to which McGready himself adhered before he returned to a more orthodox faith. Likewise, when the synod began to investigate two ministers connected with Barton W. Stone's Cane Ridge Revival, Stone and others pulled out in 1803 and adopted the name "Christian Church"—a name they claimed had no sectarian bias. Each congregation was independent and recognized no other authority than the Bible. A similar movement arose independently in western Pennsylvania in 1809 led by Thomas and Alexander Campbell. The Campbellites, like the Stonites, adopted the name "Christian" and the practice of baptism by immersion. In 1832 a movement started in Lexington, Kentucky, to unite these churches as the Disciples of Christ—a name that came to be used interchangeably with Christian church.

THE MORMONS   The Kentucky sects remained pretty much within the bounds of previous experience. The Burned-Over District, by contrast, gave rise to several new departures, of which the most important was the Church of Jesus Christ of Latter Day Saints, or the Mormons. The founder, Joseph Smith, Jr., born in Vermont, was the fourth child of wandering parents who finally settled in the village of Palmyra, New York. In 1820 young Smith (then fourteen) had a vision of "two Personages, whose brightness and glory defy all description." They identified themselves as the Savior and God the Father and cautioned him that all existing beliefs were false. About three years later the angel Moroni led Smith to the hill of Gumorah (its ancient name), where he found the Book of Mormon engraved on golden tablets in "reformed Egyptian." Later, with the aid of the magic stones Urim and Thummim, he rendered into English what he found to be a lost section of the Bible. This was the story of ancient Hebrews who had inhabited the New World and to whom Jesus had made an appearance.

After a slow start the church, founded April 6, 1830, gathered converts by the thousands. From the outset the Mormon saints upset the "gentiles" with their close pattern of community and their assurance of righteousness. In their search for a refuge from persecution the Mormons moved from New York to Kirtland, Ohio, then to several places in Missouri, and finally in 1839 to Nauvoo, Illinois, where they settled and grew in number for some five years. Through bloc voting they soon gathered political power in the Illinois state house, but eventually offended both major parties with their demands. In 1844 a crisis arose when dissidents accused Smith of justifying polygamy and published in the *Nauvoo Expositor* an exposé of polygamy in theory and practice. When Smith tried to suppress the paper, the upshot was a schism in the church, a gathering movement in the neighboring counties to attack Nauvoo, and the arrest of Smith and his brother Hyrum. On June 27, 1844, an anti-Mormon lynch mob stormed the feebly defended jail and took out and shot both Joseph and Hyrum Smith.

In Brigham Young, successor to Joseph Smith and president of the Quorum of the Twelve, the Mormons found a leader of uncommon qualities: strong-minded, intelligent, and decisive. After the murder of the founder, Young patched up an unsure peace with the neighbors by promising to plan an early exodus from Nauvoo, Illinois. Before that year was out Young had chosen the place, sight unseen, from promotional literature on the West. It lay near the Great Salt Lake, guarded by mountains to the east and north, deserts to the west and south, yet itself fed by mountain streams of melted snow—"Truly a bucolic region," in John Charles Frémont's words. Despite its isolation, moreover, it was close enough to the Oregon Trail for the saints to prosper by trade with passing gentiles.

Brigham Young trusted God, but believed in making preparations—no wandering in the wilderness for the Mormon Moses. As a result, the Mormon trek was better organized and less burdensome than most of the overland migrations of the time. Early in 1846 a small band crossed the frozen Mississippi into Iowa to set up the Camp of Israel, the first in a string of way stations along the route. By the fall of 1846 all 15,000 of the migrants had reached the prepared winter quarters on the Missouri River, where they paused until the first bands set out the next spring for the Promised Land. The first arrivals at Salt Lake in July 1847 found only "a broad and barren plain hemmed in by mountains . . . the paradise of the lizard, the cricket and the rattlesnake." But by the end of 1848 the Mormons had developed an efficient

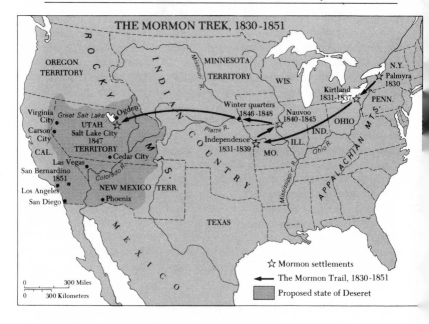

THE MORMON TREK, 1830-1851

OREGON TERRITORY

ROCKY

INDIAN

Missouri R.

MINNESOTA TERRITORY

WIS.

N.Y.

☆ Palmyra 1830

Kirtland 1831-1837

PENN.

Virginia City

Great Salt Lake Ogden

UTAH

Carson City

Salt Lake City 1847

TERRITORY

CAL.

Cedar City

Platte R.

Winter quarters 1846-1848

COUNTRY

Nauvoo 1840-1845

OHIO

Independence 1831-1839

IND.

ILL.

Ohio R.

MO.

Las Vegas

San Bernardino 1851

Colorado R.

Los Angeles

San Diego

NEW MEXICO TERR.

Phoenix

MTS.

APPALACHIAN MTS.

Mississippi R.

MEXICO

TEXAS

☆ Mormon settlements

◀━━ The Mormon Trail, 1830-1851

Proposed state of Deseret

0   300 Miles

0   300 Kilometers

irrigation system and over the next decade, by cooperative labor, they brought about the greening of the desert. The Mormons had scarcely arrived when their land became part of the United States. They organized at first their own state of Deseret (meaning "land of the honey bee," according to Young) with ambitious boundaries that reached the Pacific in southern California. But the Utah Territory, which Congress created, afforded them almost the same control with Gov. Brigham Young the chief political and theocratic authority.

MILLENNIALISM   In the 1840s the Burned-Over District was once more swept by religious fervor, this time centered on millennialism and spiritualism. One William Miller, a Baptist farmer-preacher in upstate New York near the Vermont line, had become persuaded that the signs of the times pointed to an early Second Advent of Christ. The year 1843, which Miller called the last sure "year of time," brought widespread excitement and religious delusions. Miller had set no exact date, but when 1843, passed, some of his followers set October 22, 1844, as the date of the second coming. Even after that final disappointment Miller and others held to the belief that the millennium was near, however wrong their mathematics. In 1845 a loose organization was formed, which grew into the Advent Christian Association, from which in 1846 the Seventh Day Adventists broke away on the question of observing the Jewish Sabbath instead of the new Lord's Day.

Hard on the heels of the Millerite frenzy came the craze of "spirit-rapping" which began with Kate and Margaret Fox, daughters of a farmer near Rochester. In 1848 strange knocking sounds in the house began to keep their family awake. The girls soon identified the sounds as messages from the spirit world. As the word spread, the curious gathered for their revelations, and the Fox sisters were launched on a professional career of demonstrations as far away as England. Before long spirit mediums by the hundreds were staging seances, communicating with the dead, and spreading the vogue through spiritualist magazines.

This revival of faith was very much attuned to the rising democratic belief in the power and wisdom of the common man, with its preference for heart over head. No one expressed the hopefulness of this belief better that President Andrew Jackson:

> I believe that man can be elevated; man can become more and more endowed with divinity; and as he does he becomes more God-like in his character and capable of governing himself. Let us go on elevating our people, perfecting our institutions, until democracy shall reach such a point of perfection that we can acclaim with truth that the voice of the people is the voice of God.

ROMANTICISM IN AMERICA

Another great victory of heart over head was the romantic movement in thought, literature, and the arts. By the 1780s a revolt was brewing in Europe against the well-ordered world of the Enlightened thinkers. Were there not, after all, more things in this world than reason and logic can box up and explain: moods, impressions, feelings; mysterious, unknown, and half-seen things? A clear and lucid idea, organized and understandable, might well be superficial. Americans took readily to the romantics' emphasis on individualism, idealizing now the virtues of the common man, now the idea of original or creative genius in the artist, the author, or the great personality.

Where the Enlightened had scorned the Middle Ages, the romantic now looked back to the period with fascination. America, lacking a feudal history, nonetheless had an audience for the novels of Sir Walter Scott and copied the Gothic and even more exotic styles in architecture. More congenial to the American scene were the new themes in art. In contrast to well-ordered classical scenes, romantic artists such as Thomas Cole (1801–1848) and Thomas Doughty (1793–1856) preferred wild and misty landscapes which often evoked more than they showed.

The German philosopher Immanuel Kant gave the movement a summary definition in the title of his *Critique of Pure Reason* (1781), an influential book which emphasized the limits of human science and reason in explaining the universe. People have conceptions of conscience and beauty, the romantics believed, and religious impulses too strong to be dismissed as illusions. Where science can neither prove nor disprove, people are justified in having faith. The impact of such ideas was stated succinctly by a historian of American cultural life: "By degrees intuitive knowledge, during the period 1770–1830, took on validity equal to, or superior to, rational knowledge."

TRANSCENDENTALISM The most intense expression of such thought came in the Transcendentalist Movement of New England, which drew its name from its emphasis on those things which transcended (or rose above) the limits of reason. Transcendentalism, said its chronicler O. B. Frothingham, assumed "certain fundamental truths not derived from experience, not susceptible of proof, which transcend human life, and are perceived directly and intuitively by the human mind." If transcendentalism drew much from Kant, it was also rooted in New England Puritanism, to which it owed a pervasive moralism, and had a close affinity with the Quaker doctrine of the inner light. The inner light, a gift from God's grace, was transformed into intuition, a faculty of man's mind.

An element of mysticism had always lurked in Puritanism, even if viewed as a heresy—Anne Hutchinson, for instance, had been banished for claiming direct revelation. The reassertion of mysticism had something in common, too, with the meditative religions of the Orient—with which New England now had a flourishing trade. Transcendentalists steeped themselves in the teachings of Buddha, the Mohammedan Sufis, the Upanishads, and the Bhagavadgita.

In 1836 an informal discussion group soon named the Transcendental Club began to meet from time to time at the homes of members in Boston and Concord. A floating group, it drew at different times clergymen such as Theodore Parker, George Ripley, and James Freeman Clarke; writers such as Henry Thoreau,

Bronson Alcott, Jones Very, Nathaniel Hawthorne, and Orestes Brownson; and learned women like Elizabeth and Sophia Peabody and Margaret Fuller, who edited the group's quarterly review, *The Dial* (1840–1844), for two years before the duty fell to Ralph Waldo Emerson, soon to become the acknowledged high priest of transcendentalism.

EMERSON   More than any other person, Emerson spread the Transcendentalist gospel across the country. Sprung from a line of New England ministers, he set out to be a Unitarian parson, then quit before he was thirty. After travel to Europe, where he met such literary lights as Wordsworth, Coleridge, and Carlyle (a lifelong correspondent), Emerson settled in Concord to take the life of an essayist, poet, and popular speaker on the lecture circuit. On the road he took up a new ministry preaching the good news of optimism, self-reliance, and man's unlimited potential.

Emerson's lectures and writings hold the core of the Transcendentalist worldview. His notable lecture delivered at Harvard in 1837 "The American Scholar," essentially summarized his first book *Nature*, published the previous year. In that lecture he urged his hearers to put aside their awe of European culture and explore their own new world. It was "our intellectual Declaration of Independence," said Oliver Wendell Holmes, Sr. Emerson's lecture on "The Over-soul" set forth a kind of pantheism, in which the souls of all men commune with the great universal soul, of which they are part and parcel. His essay on "Self-Reliance" (1841) has a timeless appeal to youth with its message of individualism and the cultivation of one's personality. Like most of Emerson's writings, it is crammed with quotable quotes:

Ralph Waldo Emerson, author of Nature, *America's "intellectual Declaration of Independence." [The Warder Collection]*

Whoso would be a man, must be a nonconformist. . . . Nothing is at last sacred but the integrity of your own mind. . . . It is easy in the world to live after the world's opinion; it is easy in solitude to live after our own; but the great man is he who in the midst of a crowd keeps with perfect sweetness the independence of solitude. . . . A foolish consistency is the hobgoblin of little minds, adored by little statesmen and philosophers and divines. . . . Speak what you think in hard words and tomorrow speak what tomorrow thinks in hard words again, though it contradict everything you said today. . . . To be great is to be misunderstood.

THOREAU Emerson's friend and Concord neighbor, Henry David Thoreau, practiced the self-reliance that Emerson preached. "If a man does not keep pace with his companion," Thoreau wrote, "perhaps it is because he hears a different drummer." And Thoreau marched to a different drummer all his life. After Harvard, where he exhausted the resources of the library in gargantuan bouts of reading, and after a brief stint as a teacher in which he got in trouble by his preference for persuasion over discipline, Thoreau settled down to eke out a living through his family's cottage industry of pencil making. But he made frequent escapes to drink in the beauties of nature. Not for him the contemporary scramble for wealth. "The mass of men," he wrote, "lead lives of quiet desperation."

His first book, *A Week on the Concord and Merrimack Rivers* (1849), used the story of a boat trip with his brother as the thread on which to string his comments on life and literature. The second, *Walden, or Life in the Woods* (1854), used an account of his experiment in self-sufficiency to much the same purpose. On July 4, 1845, Thoreau took to the woods to live in a cabin he had built beside Walden Pond. He was out to demonstrate that a person could free himself from the products of commercialism and industrialism. His purpose was not to lead a hermit's life, but to test the possibilities. He would return to town to dine with his friends, and although he used manufactured lime to caulk his walls, he gathered clamshells and made enough himself to show it could be done. "I went to the woods because I wished to live deliberately," he wrote, ". . . and not, when I came to die, discover that I had not lived."

While Thoreau was at Walden the Mexican War broke out. Believing it an unjust war to advance the cause of slavery, he refused payment of his state poll tax as a gesture of opposition, for which he was put in jail (only for one night; an aunt paid the tax). The incident was so trivial as to be almost comic, but out of it grew the classic essay "Civil Disobedience" (1849) which was

*Henry David Thoreau, author
of the American classics*
Walden *and "Civil Disobedience." [The Warder Collction]*

later to influence the passive-resistance movements of Mahatma
Gandhi in India and Martin Luther King in the American South.
"If the law is of such a nature that it requires you to be an agent of
unjustice to another," Thoreau wrote, "then, I say, break the
law. . . ."

The broadening ripples of influence more than a century after
Thoreau's death show the impact a contemplative man can have
on the world of action. Although both men lent their voices to
worthy causes, Thoreau, like Emerson, shied away from involvement in public life. The Transcendentalists primarily supplied
the force of an idea: men must follow their consciences. If these
thinkers attracted only a small following among the public at
large in their own time, they had much to do with pushing along
reform movements and were the quickening force for a generation of writers that produced the first great classic age of American literature.

THE FLOWERING OF AMERICAN LITERATURE

HAWTHORNE Nathaniel Hawthorne, the supreme artist of the
New England group, never shared the sunny optimism of his
neighbors nor their belief in reform. A sometime resident of
Concord, but a native and longtime resident of Salem, he was
haunted by the knowledge of evil bequeathed to him by his Puritan forebears—one of whom had been a judge at the Salem
witchcraft trial. After college at Bowdoin, he worked for some
time in obscurity in Salem, gradually began to place a few stories,

Nathaniel Hawthorne, in the center, with his publishers Ticknor and Fields. [The Warder Collection]

and finally emerged to a degree of fame with his collection of *Twice-Told Tales* (1837). In these, as in most of his later work, his themes were the examination of sin and its consequences: pride and selfishness, secret guilt, selfish egotism, the impossibility of rooting sin out of the human soul. His two greatest novels explored such burdens. In *The Scarlet Letter* (1850) Hester Prynne, an adulteress tagged with a badge of shame by the Puritan authorities, won redemption by her suffering, while the Rev. Arthur Dimmesdale was destroyed by his gnawing guilt and Roger Chillingworth by his obsession with vengeance.

The flowering of New England featured, too, a foursome of poets who shaped the American imagination in a day when poetry was still accessible to a wide public: Henry Wadsworth Longfellow, John Greenleaf Whittier, Oliver Wendell Holmes, Sr., and James Russell Lowell. But a fifth, Emily Dickinson, the most original of the lot, remained a recluse in the family home in Amherst. Only two of her poems had been published (anonymously) before her death in 1886 and the full corpus of her work remained unknown for years after that.

The half-decade of 1850–1855 saw the publication of *Representative Men* by Emerson, *Walden* by Thoreau, *The Scarlet Letter* and *The House of the Seven Gables* by Nathaniel Hawthorne, *Moby-Dick* by Herman Melville, and *Leaves of Grass* by Walt Whitman. As the critic F. O. Mathiessen wrote in his book *American Renaissance:* "You might search all the rest of American literature without being able to collect a group of books equal to these in imaginative quality."

It had been little more than thirty years since the noted British critic Sydney Smith asked in 1820: "In the four quarters of the

Globe, who reads an American book?" Quoted out of context, the question rubbed Americans the wrong way, but Smith, an admirer of American institutions, foresaw a future flowering in the new country. He did not have long to wait, for within a year Washington Irving's *The Sketch Book* (1820), James Fenimore Cooper's *The Spy* (1821), and William Cullen Bryant's *Poems* (1821) were drawing wide notice in Britain as well as in America. Bryant's energies were drawn into journalism by his need to earn a living. As editor of the New York *Evening Post* he wielded an important influence in American life. He is remembered as a poet mainly for two poems of his youth: "Thanatopsis" and "To a Waterfowl." But Irving and Cooper went on to greater literary triumphs, and made New York for a time the national literary capital.

IRVING AND COOPER   Irving in fact stood as a central figure in the American literary world from the time of his satirical *Diedrich Knickerbocker's A History of New York* (1809) until his death fifty years later. He showed that an American could, after all, make a career of literature, and was a confidant and advocate of numerous other writers. During those years a flood of histories, biographies, essays, and stories poured from his pen. A talented writer, Irving was the first to show that authentic American themes could draw a wide audience. Yet, as Melville later noted, he was less a creative genius than an adept imitator. Even the most "American" of his stories, "Rip Van Winkle" and "The Legend of Sleepy Hollow," drew heavily on German folk tales.

Cooper, a country gentleman, got his start as a writer on a bet with his wife that he could write a better novel than one they had just read. *Precaution* (1820) was an imitative story of manners in English high society, but the following year he brought out *The Spy* (1821), a historical romance based on a real incident of the American Revolution. In 1823 Cooper in *The Pioneers* introduced Natty Bumppo, an eighteenth-century frontiersman destined to be the hero of five novels known collectively as *The Leather-Stocking Tales*. Natty Bumppo, a deadshot also known as Hawkeye, and his Indian friend Chingachgook, the epitome of the noble savage, took a place among the most unforgettable heroes of world literature. The tales of man pitted against nature in the backwoods, of hairbreadth escapes and gallant rescues, were the first successful romances of frontier life and models for the later cowboy novels and movies set in the Far West. In addition to the backwoods tales, Cooper also was the virtual creator of the sea novel in *The Pilot* (1823), another romance of the Revolution.

Edgar Allen Poe, perhaps the most inventive American writer of the period. [American Antiquarian Society]

POE AND THE SOUTH   By the 1830s and 1840s new major talents had come on the scene. Edgar Allan Poe, a native of Boston but reared in Virginia, was arguably America's most inventive genius in the first half of the century, and probably the most important American writer of the times in the critical esteem of Europeans. Poe's success had many dimensions. As a critic, he argued that the object of poetry was beauty (not truth) and that the writer should calculate his effect on the reader with precision. To that end he favored relatively short poems and stories, and wrote only one novel in his brief career. His poems, such as "The Raven," exemplified his theory, and although relatively few in number, won great fame. He was moreover a master of gothic horror in the short story and the inventor of the detective story and its major conventions. But the tormented, hard-drinking wanderer that Poe became hardly fit his countrymen's image of the proper man of letters.

Neither did a group of southern writers who came to be called the southwestern humorists. With stories of the backwoods from Georgia westward they exploited frontier tall tales and the raw, violent life of the region. Their number included Davy Crockett, a sort of real-life Natty Bumppo, George Washington Harris, whose hero Sut Lovingood lived up to his name, and Johnson Jones Hooper, author of *Some Adventures of Captain Simon Suggs* (1845), about a peerless con man whose motto became a national joke: "It is good to be shifty in a new country." Augustus Baldwin Longstreet, author of *Georgia Scenes* (1835), would hardly be remembered but for his stories about Ransy Sniffle and other examples of backwoods low life. Dismissed at the time as subliterary amusement, southwestern humor was later raised to the level of high art by Mark Twain.

Among southern authors, William Gilmore Simms best exemplified the genteel man of letters. Editor and writer in many genres, he had a prodigious output of poems, novels, histories, biographies, essays, short stories, and drama. He gained a wide audience with *Guy Rivers* (1834), first of a series of "Border Romances" set in frontier Georgia, but the peak of his achievement was in two novels published in 1835: *The Yemassee*, a story of Indian war in 1715, and *The Partisan*, first of seven novels about the Revolution in South Carolina. In his own time he was the preeminent southern author and something of a national figure, but he finally dissipated his energies in politics and the defense of slavery. He went down steadily in critical esteem, and most critics would agree with his own epitaph, that he had "left all his better works undone."

The duc de La Rochefoucauld-Liancourt, who visited the south in the 1790s, noted some cultural characteristics that continued to prevail in the nineteenth century: "In spite of the Virginian love for dissipation, the taste for reading is commoner there among men of the first class than in any other part of America; but the populace is perhaps more ignorant there than elsewhere." The readers of "the first class," however, tended to take their cues in literary and aesthetic matters from London or New York. They usually read English and northern authors to the neglect of their own, and took northern rather than southern magazines. And "men of the first class" who read widely tended to look upon literature as ornamental and a less praiseworthy activity than the high arts of oratory and statesmanship.

MELVILLE Those southerners who followed the literary preferences of the North are likely to have passed over the work of Herman Melville, whose literary reputation went into a decline after his initial successes. In the twentieth century Melville's good reputation was dramatically revived, elevating him into the literary pantheon occupied by only the finest American authors. Born of distinguished ancestry on both sides, Melville suffered a sharp reversal of fortunes when his father died a bankrupt, and after various odd jobs, he shipped out as a seaman at age twenty. Some time later, after eighteen months aboard a whaler, he fetched up in the South Seas and jumped ship with a companion in the Marquesas Islands. After several weeks spent with a friendly tribe in the valley of the Typees, he signed onto an Aus-

Whaling off the Acushnet. *Melville's experiences on the ship informed his great novel,* Moby-Dick *(1851). [Peabody Museum of Salem]*

tralian whaler, jumped ship again in Tahiti, and finally returned home as a seaman aboard a frigate of the United States Navy. An embroidered account of his exotic adventures in *Typee* (1846) became an instant popular success, which he repeated in *Omoo* (1847), based on his stay in Tahiti.

So many readers took his accounts as fictional (as in part they were) that Melville was inspired to write novels of nautical adventures, and scored two successes after an initial failure. Then just five years after his first success, he produced one of the world's great novels in *Moby-Dick* (1851). In the story of Captain Ahab and his obsessive quest for the white whale which had caused the loss of his leg, Melville explored the darker recesses of the soul just as his good friend Hawthorne had done. The book was aimed at two audiences. On one level it was a ripping good yarn of adventure on the high seas. But Ahab's single-minded mission to slay the evildoer turned the captain himself into a monster of destruction who sacrificed his ship, his crew, and himself to his folly, leaving as the one survivor the narrator of the story. Unhappily, neither the public nor the critics at the time accepted the novel on either level. After that Melville's career wound down into futility. He supported himself for years with a job in the New York Custom House and turned to poetry, much of which, especially the Civil War *Battle-Pieces* (1866), gained acclaim in later years.

WHITMAN   Walt Whitman of Brooklyn had from the age of twelve worked mainly as a handyman and newspaperman, and remained relatively obscure until the first edition of *Leaves of Grass* (1855) caught the eye of contemporaries. Emerson found it "the most extraordinary piece of wit and wisdom that America has yet contributed," and greeted Whitman "at the beginning of a great career, which yet must have had a long foreground somewhere, for such a start"—an endorsement Whitman brazenly seized upon to promote the book. Yet it was appropriate that Emerson should endorse it for Whitman had taken to heart his argument that an American poet must exploit great American themes. The two greatest influences on him, Whitman said, were hearing Italian opera and reading Emerson: "I was simmering, simmering, simmering; Emerson brought me to a boil."

Whitman's life thereafter was in large measure given to "hackling" at his gargantuan *Leaves of Grass,* enlarging and reshaping it in successive editions. The growth of the book he identified with the growth of the country, which he proclaimed in all its variety. "I hear America singing," he wrote, "the varied carols I hear." He sounded his "barbaric yawp over the roofs of the world," and wrote unabashedly:

> Do I contradict myself?
> Very well then I contradict myself,
> (I am large, I contain multitudes.)

While he celebrated America, he also set out to "celebrate myself and sing myself."

To his Victorian generation Whitman was a startling figure with his frank reminders of sexuality and "the body electric," which were not without homoerotic overtones. And he stood out from the pack of fellow writers in rejecting the idea that woman's proper sphere was a supportive and dependent role, just as he rejected the "empty dish, gallantry."

Later, during the Civil War, Whitman went to Washington to see about his injured brother. The injury was slight, but "the good gray poet" stayed on to visit the sick and wounded, to serve as attendant and nurse when needed. Out of his wartime service came *Drum Taps* (1865), containing his masterpiece of the 1860s, an elegy on the death of Lincoln: "When lilacs first in the dooryard bloomed." In much of his prose Whitman vigorously defended democracy. In the postbellum *Democratic Vistas* (1871) he summoned Americans to higher goals than materialism.

THE POPULAR PRESS The renaissance in literature came at a time of massive expansion in the popular press. The steam-driven Napier press, introduced from England in 1825, could print 4,000 sheets of newsprint in an hour. Richard Hoe of New York improved on it, inventing in 1847 the Hoe Rotary Press, which printed 20,000 sheets an hour. Like many advances in technology, this was a mixed blessing. The high cost of such a press made it harder for a man of small means to break into publishing. On the other hand it expedited production of cheap newspapers, magazines, and books—which were often cheap in more ways than one.

The New York *Sun*, in 1833 the first successful penny daily, and others like it, often ignored the merely important in favor of scandals and sensations, true or false. James Gordon Bennett, a native of Scotland, perfected this style on the New York *Herald*, which he founded in 1835. His innovations drew readers by the thousands: the first Wall Street column, the first society page (which satirized the well-to-do until it proved more gainful to show readers their names in print), pictorial news, telegraphic news, and great initiative in getting scoops. Eventually, however, the *Herald* suffered from dwelling so much on crime, sex, and depravity in general.

The chief beneficiary of a rising revulsion was the New York *Tribune*, founded as a Whig organ in 1841. Horace Greeley, who became the most important journalist of the era, announced that it would be a cheap but decent paper avoiding the "matters which have been allowed to disgrace the columns of our leading Penny Papers." And despite occasional lapses, Greeley's "Great Moral Organ" typically amused its readers with wholesome human-interest stories. Greeley also won a varied following by plugging the reforms of the day—those few he did not espouse he reported nonetheless. Socialism, land reform, feminism, abolitionism, temperance, the protective tariff, internal improvements, improved methods of agriculture, vegetarianism, spiritualism, trade unions—all got a share of attention. The *Tribune*, moreover, set a new standard in reporting literary news. Margaret Fuller briefly served as critic; in 1856 the *Tribune* became the first daily to have a regular book-review column. For a generation it was probably the most influential paper in the country. By 1860 its weekly edition had a national circulation of 200,000. The number of newspapers around the country grew from about 1,200 in 1833 to about 3,000 in 1860.

Magazines found a growing market too. Periodicals of the eighteenth century typically had brief lives, but *The Port Folio* (1801–1827) of Philadelphia lasted an unusually long time. A monthly literary review edited at one time by Nicholas Biddle, it gave much attention to politics as well, from a Federalist view-point. *Niles' Weekly Register* (1811–1849) of Baltimore and Washington, founded by the printer Hezekiah Niles, was an early version of the twentieth-century news magazine. Niles got credit for accurate reports on the War of 1812 and made a reputation for good and unbiased coverage of public events—all of which make it a basic source for historians. The *North American Review* of Boston (1815–1940), started by a young graduate of Harvard, achieved high standing among scholarly readers. Its editor adorned the journal with materials on American history and biography. It also featured coverage of European literature.

More popular and more widely circulated than the others was *Graham's Magazine* of Philadelphia (1826–1858). Started as *The Casket: Flowers of Literature, Wit and Sentiment*, the magazine became a highly profitable enterprise after George R. Graham bought it in 1839, spicing it up with a "magazinish" style in contrast to the heavy review style of the day and decorating it with original artwork. As a result of the liberal payment he offered, Graham published the best authors of the day: Bryant, Longfellow, Cooper, Lowell, and Poe all appeared in its pages.

Harpers' Magazine (1850–present), originally the organ of the publishers Harper and Brothers, went Graham one better. Instead of showing that liberal rewards to authors paid off, the publisher built on a practice already profitable in book publishing—pirating the output of popular English writers in the absence of an international copyright agreement. Gradually, however, faced with an outcry against the practice, *Harpers'* instituted payment and published original material by American authors. *Frank Leslie's Illustrated Newspaper* (1855–1922) in New York used large and striking pictures to illustrate its material, and generally followed its founder's motto: "Never shoot over the heads of the people." *Leslie's* and a vigorous competitor of somewhat higher quality, *Harper's Illustrated Weekly* (1857–1916), appeared in time to provide a thoroughgoing pictorial record of the Civil War.

The boom in periodicals gave rise to more journals directed to specialized audiences. Worthy of mention, among others, are such magazines as *Godey's Lady's Book* (1830–1898), *The Southern Literary Messenger* (1834–1864), *Hunt's Merchants' Magazine* (1839–1870), *DeBow's Commercial Review of the South and West* (1846–1880), and *The American Farmer* (1819–1897), the first important agricultural journal. The new methods of production and distribution gave a boost to the book market as well. The publisher Samuel Goodrich estimated gross sales of

Without the protection of international copyright laws (not enacted until the late nineteenth century), many British authors found their works pirated by unscrupulous American publishers. With book sales growing, this cartoon of an "American Bookman Scalping an English Author" became more apt. [Punch, London]

books in America at $2 million in 1820, $12 million in 1850, and nearly $20 million in 1860. From 1820 to 1850, he estimated, moreover, books by American authors increased their share of the market from about a third to about two-thirds.

EDUCATION

EARLY PUBLIC SCHOOLS Literacy was surprisingly widespread, given the condition of public education. By 1840, according to census data, some 78 percent of the total population and 91 percent of the white population could read and write. Ever since the colonial period, in fact, Americans had the highest literacy rate in the Western World. Most children learned their letters from church or private "dame" schools, formal tutors, or from their families. When Abraham Lincoln came of age, he said, he did not know much. "Still, somehow, I could read, write and cipher to the rule of three, but that was all." At that time, about 1830, no state had a school system in the modern sense, although Massachusetts had for nearly two centuries required towns to maintain schools. Some major cities had the resources to develop real systems on their own. The Public School Society of New York, for instance, built a model system of free schools in the city, with state aid after 1815. In 1806 the society introduced the Lancasterian schools (after Joseph Lancaster, an English Quaker) in which teachers used monitors to instruct hundreds of pupils at once. By 1853 when the state took over its properties the society had provided schooling for more than 600,000 pupils.

A scattered rural popularion, however, did not lend itself so readily to the development of schools. In 1860, for instance, Louisiana had a population density of 11 per square mile, Virginia 14, while Massachusetts had 127. In many parts of the country, as in South Carolina after 1811, the state provided some aid to schools for children of indigent parents, but such institutions were normally stigmatized as "pauper schools," to be shunned by the better sort.

Beginning with Connecticut as early as 1750, and New York in 1782, most states built up "literary" or school funds—an idea which gained momentum when Ohio, upon achieving statehood in 1803, also got the sixteenth section of each township as endowment for education. The funds were applied to various purposes—usually at first to aid local schools either public or private.

By the 1830s the demand for public schools was rising fast. Reformers argued that popular government presupposed a literate and informed electorate. With the lowering of barriers to the ballot box the argument carried all the more force. Workers wanted free schools to give their children an equal chance. In 1830 the Working Men's party of Philadelphia resolved in favor of "a system of education that shall embrace equally all the children of the state, of every rank and condition." Education, it was argued, would be a means of reform. It would improve manners and at the same time lessen crime and poverty. Opposition was minor, but when it came it was from taxpayers who held education to be a family matter and from those church groups which maintained schools at their own expense.

Horace Mann of Massachusetts stood out in the early drive for statewide school systems. Trained as a lawyer, Mann sponsored through the legislature the creation of a state board of education, which he then served as secretary. Mann went on to sponsor many reforms in Massachusetts, including the first state-supported normal school for teachers, teacher-training institutes for refresher courses, a state association of teachers, and a minimum school year of six months. He made his twelve annual reports into instruments of propaganda for public education. In these papers he explored problems of methods, curriculum, school management, and much more. His final report in 1848 defended the school system as the way to social stability and equal opportunity. It had never happened, he argued, and never could happen, that an educated people could be permanently poor. "Education then, beyond all other devices of human origin, is a great equalizer of the conditions of men—the balance wheel of the social machinery."

In the South the state of North Carolina led the way. There Calvin H. Wiley played a role like that of Mann, building from a law of 1839 which provided support to localities willing to tax themselves for the support of schools. As the first state superintendent of public instruction he traveled to every county drumming up support for the schools. By 1860, as a result of his activities, North Carolina enrolled more than two-thirds of its white school population for an average term of four months. But the educational pattern in the South continued to reflect the aristocratic pretensions of the region: the South had a higher percentage of college students than any other region, but a lower percentage of public school students. And the South had some 500,000 white illiterates, more than half the total number in the country.

For all the effort, conditions for public education were seldom ideal. Funds were insufficient for buildings, books, and equipment; teachers were poorly paid, and often so poorly prepared as to be little ahead of their charges in the ability to read, write, and cipher. In many a rural schoolhouse the teacher's first task was to thrash the huskiest youth in the class in order to encourage the others. The teachers, consequently, were at first mostly men, often young men who did not regard teaching as a career but as a means of support while preparing for a career as a lawyer or preacher, or as part-time work during slack seasons on the farm. With the encouragement of educational reformers, however, teaching was beginning to be regarded as a profession. As the schools multiplied and the school term lengthened, women increasingly entered the field.

Still, given the condition of their preparation, teachers were heavily dependent on textbooks and publishers were happy to oblige them. The most common texts were Noah Webster's *Blue-Backed Spellers* and a series of six graded *Eclectic Readers* which William Holmes McGuffey, a professor and university president in Ohio, began to bring out in 1836 and completed in 1857. His books taught children to recite "Twinkle, Twinkle,

Little Star," "The Boy Stood on the Burning Deck," "The Boy Who Cried Wolf," and the patriotic words of Washington, Patrick Henry, Webster, and Clay. The readers were replete with parables designed to instill thrift, morality, and patriotism. At the same time they carried selections from the masters of English prose and verse.

Most students going beyond the elementary grades went to private academies, often subsidized by church and public funds. Such schools, begun in colonial days, multiplied until there were in 1850 more than 6,000 of them. In 1821 the Boston English High School opened as the first free public secondary school, set up mainly for students not going on to college. By a law of 1827 Massachusetts required a high school in every town of 500; in towns of 4,000 or more the school had to offer Latin, Greek, rhetoric, and other college preparatory courses. Public high schools became well established in school systems only after the Civil War. In 1860 there were barely 300 in the whole country.

POPULAR EDUCATION   Beyond the schools there grew up many societies and institutes to inform the general public: mechanics' and workingmen's "institutes," "young men's associations," "debating societies," "literary societies," and such. Outstanding in the field was the Franklin Institute, founded at Philadelphia in 1824 to inform the public mainly in the fields of science and industry. Similar institutes were sponsored by major philanthropists like Lowell in Boston, Peabody in Baltimore, and Cooper in New York. Some cities offered evening classes to those who could not attend day schools. The most widespread and effective means of popular education, however, was the lyceum movement, which aimed to diffuse knowledge through public lectures. Professional agencies provided speakers and performers of all kinds, in literature, science, music, humor, travel, and other fields. Most of the major savants of the age at one time or another rode the lecture circuit: Emerson, Melville, Lyman Beecher, Daniel Webster, Harriet Beecher Stowe, Louis Agassiz, Benjamin Silliman.

Akin to the lyceum movement and ultimately reaching more people was the movement for public libraries. Benjamin Franklin's Philadelphia Library Company (1731) had given impulse to the growth of subscription or association libraries. In 1803 Salisbury, Connecticut, opened a free library for children and in 1833 Peterborough, New Hampshire, established a tax-supported library open to all. The opening of the Boston Public Library in 1851 was a turning point. By 1860 there were approximately 10,000 public libraries (not all completely free) housing some 8 million volumes.

HIGHER EDUCATION   The postrevolutionary proliferation of colleges continued after 1800 with the spread of small church schools and state universities. Nine colleges had been founded in the colonial period, all of which survived; but not many of the fifty that sprang up between 1776 and 1800 lasted. Among those that did were Hampden-Sydney, Charleston, Bowdoin, and Middlebury, all of which went on to long and fruitful careers. Of the seventy-eight colleges and universities in 1840, fully thirty-five had been founded after 1830, almost all as church schools. A postrevolutionary movement for state universities flourished in those southern states which had had no colonial university. Federal policy abetted the spread of universities into the West. When Congress granted statehood to Ohio in 1803, it set aside two townships for the support of a state university and kept up that policy in other new states.

The coexistence of state and religious schools, however, set up conflicts over funding and curriculum. Beset by the need for funds, as colleges usually were, denominational schools often competed with tax-supported schools. Regarding curricula, the new Awakening led many of the church schools to emphasize theology at the expense of science and the humanities. On the other hand America's development required broader access to education and programs geared to vocations. The University of Virginia, "Mr. Jefferson's University," founded in 1819 within sight of Monticello, introduced in 1826 a curriculum which reflected Jefferson's own view that education ought to combine pure knowledge with "all the branches of science useful *to us, and at this day.*" The model influenced the other new state universities of the South and West.

Technical education grew slowly. The United States Military Academy at West Point, founded in 1802, trained a limited number of engineers. More were trained by practical experience with railroad and canal companies, and apprenticeship to experienced technologists. Similarly, most aspiring lawyers went to "read law" with an established attorney, and doctors served their apprenticeships with practicing physicians. Francis Wayland, president of Brown University, remarked that there were forty-two theological schools and forty-seven law schools, but none to provide "the agriculturalist, the manufacturer, the mechanic, and the merchant with any kind of professional preparation." There were few schools of this sort before 1860, but a

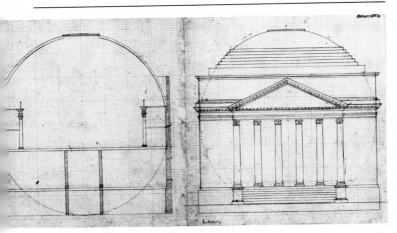

Jefferson's design for the rotunda at the University of Virginia, founded in 1819. [University of Virginia Manuscript Department]

promise for the future came in 1855 when Michigan and Pennsylvania each established an agricultural and mechanical college, now Michigan State and Pennsylvania State.

Elementary education for girls, where available for boys, met with general acceptance, but training beyond that level did not. Many men and women thought higher education unsuited to woman's destiny in life. Some did argue that education would make better wives and mothers, but few were ready yet to demand equality on principle. Progress began with the academies, some of which taught boys and girls alike. Good "female seminaries" like those founded by Emma Willard at Troy, New York (1824), and Mary Lyon at Mount Holyoke, Massachusetts (1836), prepared the way for women's colleges. Many of them, in fact, grew into such colleges, but Georgia Female College (later Wesleyan) at Macon, chartered in 1836, first offered women the A.B. in 1840. The work in female seminaries usually differed from the courses in men's schools, giving more attention to the social amenities and such "embellishments" as music and art. Vassar, opened at Poughkeepsie, New York, in 1865, is usually credited with being the first women's college which gave priority to academic standards. Oberlin College in Ohio, founded in 1833, opened as both a biracial and a coeducational institution. Its first women students were admitted in 1837. In general the West gave the greatest impetus to coeducation, with state universities in the lead.

SOME MOVEMENTS FOR REFORM

Alexis de Tocqueville, a French traveler who wrote a classic report on American society, *Democracy in America* (1835), commented on many things, including the role of education in the United States. Another matter caught his special attention: nothing, he wrote, "in my view, more deserves attention than the intellectual and moral associations in America." During his extended visit in 1831 he heard that 100,000 men had pledged to abstain from alcohol. At first he thought it was a joke. Why should these abstemious citizens not quietly drink water by their own firesides? Then he understood that "Americans of all ages, all stations to life and all types of dispositions are forever forming associations. There are not only commercial and industrial associations in which all take part, but others of a thousand different types—religious, moral, serious, futile, very general and very limited, very large and very minute."

Emerson spoke for his generation, as he so often did, when he asked: "What is man born for, but to be a Reformer, a Remaker of what man has made?" The urge to eradicate evil from nineteenth-century America had its roots in the ubiquitous sense of mission, which in turn drew upon rising faith in the perfectibility of man. Belief in perfectibility had both evangelical and liberal bases. Transcendentalism, the spirit of which infected even those unfamiliar with the philosophy, offered a romantic faith in the individual and the belief that human intuition led to right thinking.

Few things escaped the ministrations of the reformers, however trivial or weighty: observance of the Sabbath, dueling, crime and punishment, the hours and conditions of work, poverty, vice, care of the handicapped, pacifism, foreign missions, temperance, women's rights, the abolition of slavery. Some crusaders challenged a host of evils; others focused on pet causes. Dr. William Alcott of Massachusetts, for example, insisted that "a vegetable diet lies at the basis of all reforms." The greatest dietary reformer of the age, however, was Sylvester Graham, who started as a temperance speaker in 1830 and moved on to champion a natural diet of grains, vegetables, and fruits, and abstinence from alcohol, coffee, tea, tobacco, and many foods. The Graham cracker is one of the movement's legacies to later times. Graham's ideas evolved into a way of life requiring proper habits of dress, hygiene, sex, and mind. The movement became a major industry, sponsoring health clubs, camps, sanitariums, magazines, and regular lecture tours by Graham, "the Peristaltic Persuader."

TEMPERANCE The temperance crusade, at which Tocqueville marvelled, was perhaps the most widespread of all, with the possible exception of the public school movement. The cause drew its share of spoilsports, but it also drew upon concern with a real problem. The census of 1810 reported some 14,000 distilleries producing 25 million gallons of spirits each year. With a hard-drinking population of just over 7 million, the "alcoholic republic" was producing well over three gallons per year for every man, woman, and child, not counting beer, wine, and cider. And the census takers no doubt missed a few stills. William Cobbett, an English reformer who traveled in the United States, noted in 1819 that one could "go into hardly any man's house without being asked to drink wine or spirits, even *in the morning.*"

The movement for temperance rested on a number of arguments. First and foremost was the demand of religion that "sol-

Intemperance was an important step on the way of evil, leading to "everlasting Punishment." [Library of Congress]

diers of the cross" lead blameless lives. The bad effects of distilled beverages on body and mind were noted by the respected physician Benjamin Rush as early as 1784. The dynamic new economy, with factories and railroads moving on strict schedules, made tippling by the labor force a far greater problem than it had been in a simple economy. Humanitarians emphasized the relations between drinking and poverty. Much of the movement's propaganda focused on the sufferings of innocent mothers and children. "Drink," said a pamphlet from the Sons of Temperance, "is the prolific source (directly or indirectly) of nearly all the ills that afflict the human family."

In 1826 a group of ministers in Boston organized the American Society for the Promotion of Temperance. The society worked through lecturers, press campaigns, prize essay contests, and the formation of local and state societies. A favorite device was to ask each person who took the pledge to put by his signature a T for Total Abstinence. With that a new word entered the language: "teetotaler."

In 1833 the society called a national convention in Philadelphia where the American Temperance Union was formed. The convention revealed internal tensions, however: Was the goal moderation or total abstinence, and if the latter, abstinence merely from ardent spirits or also from wine, cider, and beer? Should the movement work by persuasion or by legislation? Like nearly every movement of the day, temperance had a wing of perfectionists who rejected counsels of prudence. They would brook no compromise with Demon Rum, and carried the day with a resolution that the liquor traffic was morally wrong and ought to be prohibited by law. The union, at its spring convention in 1836, called for abstinence from all alcoholic beverages —a pyrrhic victory that caused moderates to abstain from the movement instead.

The demand for the prohibition of alcoholic beverages led in the 1830s and thereafter to experiments with more stringent regulations and local option laws. In 1838 Massachusetts forbade the sale of spirits in lots of less than fifteen gallons, thereby cutting off sales in taverns and to the poor—who could not handle it as well as their betters, or so their betters thought. After repeal of the law in 1840, prohibitionists in Massachusetts turned to the towns, about a hundred of which were dry by 1845. In 1839 Mississippi restricted sales to no less than a gallon, but the movement went little further in the South. In 1846 Maine enacted a law against sales of less than twenty-eight gallons; five years later Maine forbade the manufacture or sale of *any* intoxicants. By 1855 thirteen states had such laws. Rum-soaked New England had gone legally dry, along with New York and parts of the Midwest. But most of the laws were poorly drafted and vulnerable to court challenge. Within a few years they survived only in northern New England. Still, between 1830 and 1860 the temperance agitation drastically reduced the per-capita consumption of alcohol.

PRISONS AND ASYLUMS   The sublime optimism of the age, the liberal belief that people are innately good and capable of improvement, brought major changes in the treatment of prisoners, the handicapped, and dependent children. Public institutions arose dedicated to the treatment and cure of social ills. Earlier these had been "places of last resort," David Rothman wrote in *The Discovery of the Asylum.* Now they "became places of first resort, the preferred solution to the problems of poverty, crime, delinquency, and insanity." Removed from society, the needy and deviant could be made whole again. Unhappily, this ideal kept running up against the dictates of convenience and economy. The institutions had a way of turning into breeding grounds of brutality and neglect.

In the colonial period prisons were usually places for brief confinement before punishment, which was either death or some kind of pain or humiliation: whipping, mutilation, confinement in stocks, ducking, branding, and the like. A new attitude began to emerge after the Revolution. American reformers argued against the harshness of the penal code and asserted that the certainty of punishment was more important than its severity. Society, moreover, would benefit more from the prevention than the punishment of crime. The Philadelphia Society for Alleviating the Miseries of Public Prisons, founded in 1787, took the lead in spreading the new doctrines. Gradually the idea of the penitentiary developed. It would be a place where the guilty experienced penitence and underwent rehabilitation, not just punishment.

An early model of the new system, widely copied, was the Auburn Penitentiary, commissioned by New York in 1816. The prisoners at Auburn had separate cells and gathered for meals and group labor. Discipline was severe. The men were marched out in lock step and never put face to face or allowed to talk. But prisoners were at least reasonably secure from abuse by other prisoners. The system, its advocates argued, had a beneficial effect on the prisoners and saved money since the workshops supplied prison needs and produced goods for sale at a profit. By 1840 there were twelve prisons of the Auburn type.

It was still more common, and the persistent curse of prisons, for inmates to be thrown together willy-nilly. In an earlier day of corporal punishments jails housed mainly debtors. But as practices changed, debtors found themselves housed with convicts. In New York City, investigation showed about 2,000 debtors confined during 1816, as many as 600 at one time. Of the annual total, over 1,000 were held for debts less than $50, 700 for debts under $25. Without provision for food, furniture, or fuel, the debtors would have expired but for charity. The absurdity of the system was so obvious that the tardiness of reform seems strange. New York in 1817 made $25 the minimum for which one could be imprisoned, but no state eliminated the practice altogether until Kentucky acted in 1821. Ohio acted in 1828 and other states gradually fell in line, but it was still more than three decades before debtors' prisons became a thing of the past.

The reform impulse naturally found outlet in the care of the insane. The Philadelphia Hospital (1752), one of the first in the country, had a provision in its charter that it should care for "lunaticks," but before 1800 few hospitals provided care for the mentally ill. There were in fact few hospitals of any kind. The insane were merely confined at home with hired keepers or in jails and almshouses. In the years after 1815, however, asylums which housed the disturbed separately from criminals began to appear. Early efforts led to such optimism that a committee reported to the Massachusetts legislature in 1832 that with the right treatment "insanity yields with more readiness than ordinary diseases." These high expectations gradually faded with experience.

The most important figure in arousing the public conscience to

Dorothea Dix, one of the most influential of American reformers. [Schlesinger Library, Radcliffe College]

the plight of these unfortunates was Dorothea Lynde Dix. A Boston schoolteacher called upon to instruct a Sunday school class at the East Cambridge House of Correction in 1841, she found there a roomful of insane persons completely neglected and left without heat on a cold March day. She then commenced a two-year investigation of jails and almshouses in Massachusetts. In a memorial to the state legislature in 1843 she began "I tell what I have seen," and went on to report "the *present* state of insane persons confined within the Commonwealth, in *cages, closets, cellars, stalls, pens! Chained, naked, beaten with rods, and lashed into obedience!*" Keepers of the institutions charged "slanderous lies," but she got the support of leading reformers and won a large appropriation. From Massachusetts she carried her campaign throughout the country and abroad. By 1860 she had gotten twenty states to heed her advice. Of Dorothea Dix it was truly said that "Few persons have ever had such far-reaching effect on public policy toward reform."

WOMEN'S RIGHTS   While Dorothea Dix stood out as an example of the opportunity reform gave middle-class women to enter public life, Catherine Beecher, a leader in the education movement and founder of women's schools in Connecticut and Ohio, published a guide prescribing the domestic sphere for women. *A Treatise on Domestic Economy* (1841) became the leading handbook of what historians have labeled the "cult of domesticity." While Beecher upheld high standards in women's education, she also accepted the prevailing view that "woman's sphere" was the home and argued that young women should be trained in the domestic arts. Her guide, designed for use also as a textbook, led prospective wives and mothers through the endless rounds from Monday washing to Saturday baking, with instructions on health, food, clothing, cleanliness, care of domestics and children, gardening, and hundreds of other household details. Such duties, Beecher emphasized, should never be taken as "petty, trivial or unworthy" since "no statesman . . . had more frequent calls for wisdom, firmness, tact, discrimination, prudence, and versatility of talent."

The social custom of assigning the sexes different roles of course did not spring full-blown into life during the nineteenth century. In earlier agrarian societies sex-based functions were closely tied to the household and often overlapped. As the more complex economy of the nineteenth century matured, economic production came to be increasingly separated from the home, and the home in turn became a refuge from the cruel world outside, with separate and distinctive functions. Some have argued that the home became a trap for women, a prison that hindered fulfillment. But others have noted that it often gave women a sphere of independence in which they might exercise a degree of initiative and leadership. The so-called cult of true womanhood idealized woman's moral role in civilizing husband and family.

The status of women remained much as it had been in the colonial era. Legally, a woman was disfranchised, denied control of her property and even of her children. A wife could not make a will, sign a contract, or bring suit in court without her husband's permission. Her legal status was like that of a minor, a slave, or a free Negro. The organized movement for women's rights in fact had its origins in 1840, when the American antislavery movement split over the question of women's right to participate. American women decided then that they needed to organize on behalf of their own emancipation too.

In 1848 Lucretia Mott and Elizabeth Cady Stanton decided to call a convention to discuss "the social, civil, and religious condition and rights of women." The hastily called Seneca Falls Convention, the first of its kind, issued on July 19, 1848, a clever paraphrase of Jefferson's Declaration, the Declaration of Sentiments, mainly the work of Mrs. Stanton. The document proclaimed the self-evident truth that "all men and women are created equal," and the attendant resolutions said that all laws which placed woman "in a position inferior to that of men, are contrary to the great precept of nature, and therefore of no force or authority."

From 1850 until the Civil War the women's rights leaders held annual conventions, and carried on a program of organizing, lecturing, and petitioning. The movement had to struggle in the face of meager funds and antifeminist women and men. What success the movement had was due to the work of a few undaunted women who refused to be overawed by the odds against them. Susan B. Anthony, already active in temperance and antislavery groups, joined the crusade in the 1850s. As one observer put it, Mrs. Stanton "forged the thunderbolts and Miss Anthony hurled them." Both were young when the movement started and both lived into the twentieth century, focusing after the Civil War on demands for woman suffrage. Many of the feminists like Stanton, Lucretia Mott, and Lucy Stone had supportive husbands, and the movement won prominent male champions like Emerson, William Ellery Channing, and William Lloyd Garrison. Editor Horace Greeley gave the feminists sympathetic attention in the New York *Tribune*. The fruits of the movement were slow to ripen. The women did not gain the ballot, but there were some legal gains. The state of Mississippi, seldom regarded as a hotbed

Elizabeth Cady Stanton (left) and Susan B. Anthony. Mrs. Stanton "forged the thunderbolts and Miss Anthony hurled them." [The Warder Collection]

of reform, was in 1839 the first to grant married women control over their property; by the 1860s eleven more states had such laws, and other rights followed.

Still, the only jobs open to educated women in any numbers were nursing and teaching, both of which extended the domestic roles of health care and nurture into the world outside. Both brought relatively lower status and pay than "man's work" despite the skills, training, and responsibility involved. Against the odds, a hardy band of women carved out professional careers. With the rapid expansion of schools, women moved into the teaching profession first. If women could be teachers, Susan Anthony asked, why not lawyers or doctors? Harriet Hunt of Boston was a teacher who, after nursing her sister through a serious illness, set up shop in 1835 as a self-taught physician and persisted in medical practice although twice rejected by Harvard Medical School. Voted into Geneva Medical College in western New York as a joke, Elizabeth Blackwell of Ohio had the last laugh when she finished at the head of her class in 1849. She founded the New York Infirmary for Women and Children and later had a long career as a professor of gynecology in the London School of Medicine for Women.

An intellectual prodigy among women of the time—the derisory term was "bluestocking"—was Margaret Fuller. A precocious child, she was forced-fed education by a father who set her at Latin when she was six. As a young adult she moved in the literary circles of Boston and Concord, edited the *The Dial* for two years, and became literary editor and critic for Horace Greeley's New York *Tribune*. From 1839 to 1844 she conducted "conversations" with the cultivated ladies of Boston. From this

Margaret Fuller, an influential American intellectual. [Metropolitan Museum of Art]

classroom-salon emerged many of the ideas that went into her book *Woman in the Nineteenth Century* (1845), a plea for removal of all intellectual and economic disabilities. Minds and souls were neither masculine nor feminine, she argued. Genius had no sex. "What woman needs," she wrote, "is not as a woman to act or rule, but as a nature to grow, as an intellect to discern, as a soul to live freely and unimpeded, to unfold such powers as were given her when we left our common home."

UTOPIAN COMMUNITIES   The quest for utopia flourished in the climate of reform. "We are all a little mad here with numberless projects of social reform," Emerson wrote to Thomas Carlyle in 1840. "Not a reading man but has a draft of a new community in his pocket." Drafts of new communities had long been an American passion, at least since the Puritans set out to build a Wilderness Zion. The visionary communes of the nineteenth century often had purely economic and social objectives, but those that were rooted in religion proved most durable. An early instance, an offshoot of the Mennonites in 1732, the Ephrata Community in Pennsylvania practiced an almost monastic life into the early nineteenth century. Founder Johann Conrad Beissel's emphasis on music left a lasting imprint on American hymnology. In 1803 George Rapp led about 600 Lutheran come-outers from Württemberg to Pennsylvania. They took the Bible literally, and like Beissel's group, renounced sex. Since the millennium was near they had to keep ready. No quarrel went unsettled overnight, and all who had sinned confessed to Rapp before sleeping. Industrious and disciplined, the Rappites prospered, and persevered to the end of the century.

Sixteen utopian communities sprang up between 1820 and

1830, forty-two in the palmy days from 1830 to 1850, ten more between 1850 and 1870—in all more than a hundred between 1800 and 1900. Among the most durable were the Shakers, officially the United Society of Believers, founded by Ann Lee Stanley (Mother Ann), who reached New York state with eight followers in 1774. Believing religious fervor a sign of inspiration from the Holy Ghost, they had strange fits in which they saw visions and prophesied. These manifestations later evolved into a ritual dance—hence the name Shakers. Shaker doctrine held God to be a dual personality: in Christ the masculine side was manifested, in Mother Ann the feminine element. Mother Ann preached celibacy to prepare Shakers for the perfection that was promised them. The church would first gather in the elect, and eventually in the spirit world convert and save all mankind.

Mother Ann died in 1784, but the group found new leaders. From the first community at Mount Lebanon, New York, the movement spread to new colonies in New England, and soon afterward into Ohio and Kentucky. By 1830 about twenty groups were flourishing. In Shaker communities all property was held in common. Governance of the colonies was concentrated in the hands of select groups chosen by the ministry, or "Head of Influence" at Mount Lebanon. To outsiders this might seem almost despotic, but the Shakers emphasized equality of labor and reward, and members were free to leave at will. The Shakers' farms yielded a surplus for the market. They were among the leading sources of garden seed and medicinal herbs, and many of their manufactures, including clothing, household items, and especially furniture, were prized for their simple beauty. By the mid–twentieth century, however, few members remained alive; they had reached the peak of activity in the years 1830–1860.

John Humphrey Noyes, founder of the Oneida Community, got religion at one of Charles G. Finney's revivals and entered the ministry. He was forced out, however, when he concluded that with true conversion came perfection and a complete release from sin. In 1836 he gathered a group of "Perfectionists" around his home in Putney, Vermont. Ten years later Noyes announced a new doctrine of complex marriage, which meant that every man in the community was married to every woman and vice versa. To outsiders it looked like simple promiscuity and Noyes was arrested. He fled to New York and in 1848 established the Oneida Community, which numbered more than 200 by 1851.

The group eked out a living with farming and logging until the mid-1850s, when the inventor of a new steel trap joined the community. Oneida traps were soon known as the best. The community then branched out into sewing silk, canning fruits, and making silver spoons. The spoons were so popular that, with the addition of knives and forks, tableware became the Oneida speciality. Community Plate is still made. In 1879, however, the community faced a crisis when Noyes fled to Canada to avoid prosecution for adultery. The members then abandoned complex marriage, and in 1881 decided to convert into a joint-stock company, the Oneida Community, Ltd. A similar fate overtook the Amana Society, or Community of True Faith, a German group that migrated to New York state in 1843 and on to Iowa in 1850. Eventually, in 1932, beset by the problems of the Great Depression, they incorporated as a joint-stock company making refrigerators and eventually a great variety of home appliances.

In contrast to these communities, Robert Owen's New Harmony was based on a secular principle. A British capitalist who worried about the social effects of the factory system, Owen built a model factory town, supported labor legislation, and set forth a scheme for a model community in his pamphlet *A New View of Society* (1813). Later he snapped at a chance to buy the Rappites' town of Harmony, Indiana, and promptly christened it New Harmony. In Washington an audience including President Monroe crowded the hall of the House of Representatives to hear Owen tell about his high hopes.

In 1825 a varied group of about 900 colonists gathered in New Harmony for a period of transition from Owen's ownership to the new system of cooperation. The group began to run the former Rappite industries, and after only nine months' trial Owen turned over management of the colony to a town meeting of all residents and a council of town officers. The high proportion of learned participants generated a certain intellectual electricity about the place. Schools sprang up quickly. Owen's two sons started a sprightly paper, the *New Harmony Gazette.* There were frequent lectures and social gatherings with music and dancing.

For a time it looked like a brilliant success, but New Harmony soon fell into discord. The *Gazette* complained of "grumbling, carping, and murmuring" members and others who had the "disease of laziness." The problem, it seems, was a problem common to reform groups. Every idealist wanted his own patented plan put into practice. In 1827 Owen returned from a visit to England to find New Harmony insolvent. The following year he dissolved the project and sold or leased the lands on good terms, in many cases to the settlers. All that remained he turned over to his sons, who remained and became American citizens.

The 1840s brought a flurry of interest in the ideas of Fourieristic socialism. Charles Fourier, a Frenchman, proposed to reorder society into small units, or "phalanxes," ideally of 1,620 members. All property would be held in common and each phalanx would produce that for which it felt itself best suited; the joy of work and communal living would supply the incentive. By example the phalanxes would eventually cover the earth and displace capitalism. Fourier remained a prophet without honor in his own country, but Arthur Brisbane's book *The Social Destiny of Man* (1840) brought Fourierism before the American public and Horace Greeley's New York *Tribune* kept it there.

Greeley was in such a hurry to try out the idea, however, that Brisbane thought him rash. Brisbane was right. The first community, the Sylvania Phalanx in northern Pennsylvania, founded with Greeley's help in 1842, lasted but a year. Sylvania picked up 2,300 acres of land at little cost because it was remote and infertile. During their only season about 100 members produced just eleven bushels of grain on the four acres of arable land. Greeley lost $5,000. In all some forty or fifty phalansteries sprang up, but lasted on the average about two years.

Brook Farm was surely the most celebrated of all the utopian communities because it had the support of Emerson, Lowell, Whittier, and countless other well-known literary figures of New England. Nathaniel Hawthorne, a member, later memorialized its failure in his novel *The Blithedale Romance* (1852). George Ripley, a Unitarian minister and Transcendentalist, conceived of Brook Farm as a kind of early-day "think tank," combining high thinking and plain living. The place survived, however, mainly because of an excellent community school that drew tuition-paying students from outside. In 1844 Brook Farm converted itself into a phalanstery, but when a new central building burned down on the day of its dedication in 1846, the community spirit expired in the embers.

Utopian communities, with few exceptions, quickly ran into futility. Soon after Hawthorne left Brook Farm he wrote: "It already looks like a dream behind me." His life there was "an unnatural and unsuitable, and therefore an unreal one." Such experiments, performed in relative isolation, had little effect on the real world outside, where reformers wrestled with the sins of the multitudes. Among all the targets of reformers' wrath, one great evil would finally take precedence over the others— human bondage. The paradox of American slavery coupled with American freedom, of "the world's fairest hope linked with man's foulest crime," in Herman Melville's words, would inspire the climactic crusade of the age, abolitionism, one that would ultimately move to the center of the political stage and sweep the nation into an epic struggle.

FURTHER READING

Few single-volume works cover the diversity of early American reform. A good start is Perry Miller's *The Life of the Mind in America: From the Revolution to the Civil War* (1966),° on the intellectual evolution which ran concurrent with reformist behavior. Russel B. Nye's *Society and Culture in America, 1830–1860* (1974), provides a wide-ranging survey. Everyday behavior is stressed more in Carl Bode's *The Anatomy of American Popular Culture, 1840–1861* (1959). On reform itself, consult Alice F. Tyler's *Freedom's Ferment: Phases of American Social History to 1860* (1944).°

Sydney E. Ahlstrom's *A Religious History of the America People* (1972) gives a solid survey of antebellum religious movements and developments. More interpretative is Martin E. Marty's *Righteous Empire: The Protestant Experience in America* (1970). Henry F. May traces the legacy of rationalist thinking in *The Enlightenment in America* (1976).° Theodore D. Bozeman's *Protestants in an Age of Science: The Baconian Ideal and Antebellum American Religious Thought* (1977) examines similar themes for a later period. The development of the rationalist-oriented sects is the subject of Daniel W. Howe's *The Unitarian Conscience: Harvard Moral Philosophy, 1805–1861* (1970), David P. Edgell's *William Ellery Channing: An Intellectual Portrait* (1955), and H. M. Morais's *Deism in Eighteenth Century America* (1934). Revivals are covered in Whitney R. Cross's *The Burned Over District* (1950),° John B. Boles's *The Great Revival* (1972), and William G. McLoughlin's *Modern Revivalism: Charles Grandison Finney to Billy Graham* (1959). Donald G. Mathews, in *Religion in the Old South* (1977),° dissects the concept of the evangelical mind.

For splinter sects, the scholarship is most voluminous on the Mormons. Consult Klaus J. Hansen's *Mormonism and the American Experience* (1981), Leonard Arrington's *Great Basin Kingdom* (1958), and Fawn M. Brodie's *No Man Knows My History: The Life of Joseph Smith* (1945).

Francis O. Matthiessen's *American Renaissance* (1941),° examines the literary history of the antebellum period. Good for the interpretive contents are Richard W. B. Lewis's *The American Adam: Innocence, Tragedy, and Tradition in the Nineteenth Century* (1955) and Charles Feidelson, Jr.'s *Symbolism and American Art* (1953). The best introduction to transcendentalist thought are the writings of the transcendentalists themselves, collected in Perry Miller (ed.), *The Transcendentalists* (1950).° Also see Gay Wilson Allen's *Waldo Emerson: A Biography* (1981)° and Joel Porte's *Representative Man: Ralph Waldo Emerson in His Time* (1979). For Emerson's protégé, see Walter Harding's *Thoreau: Man of Concord* (1960), Sherman Paul's *The Shores of America: Thoreau's Inward Exploration* (1961), and Richard LeBeaux's *Young Man*

°These books are available in paperback editions.

Thoreau (1977).° A recent treatment of the poet Whitman is Justin Kaplan's *Walt Whitman: A Life* (1980).° Henry Nash Smith's *Virgin Land: The American West as Symbol and Myth* (1950),° examines some important themes of the romantics. A solid introduction to antebellum newspapers is Frank L. Mott's *American Journalism* (1962), while Glyndon Van Deusen's *Horace Greeley, Nineteenth-Century Crusader* (1953) documents the life of that famous editor. Barbara Novak's *Nature and Culture: American Landscape and Painting, 1825–1875* (1980),° provides an overview of the Hudson River School.

Lawrence Cremin's *American Education: The National Experience, 1783–1876* (1980),° traces early school reform. Other views on the topic appear in Stanley K. Schultze's *The Culture Factory: Boston Public Schools, 1789–1860* (1973), Michael Katz's *The Irony of Early School Reform* (1968),° and Jonathan Messerli's *Horace Mann* (1972).

Ronald G. Walters's *American Reformers* (1978),° surveys the general bounds of the reform impulse. For temperance, see W. G. Rorabaugh's *The Alcoholic Republic: An American Tradition* (1979),° Frank L. Byrne's *Prophet of Prohibition: Neal Dow and His Crusade* (1961), and Clifford S. Griffin's *Their Brother's Keeper: Moral Stewardship in the United States, 1800–1865* (1960). For the religious context of reform, consult Carroll Smith-Rosenberg's *Religion and the Rise of the American City: The New York Mission Movement* (1971). On prison reform and other humanitarian projects, see David J. Rothman's *The Discovery of the Asylum* (1971),° Helen D. Marshall's *Dorothea Dix: Forgotten Samaritan* (1937), and Gerald N. Grob's *Mental Institutions in America* (1973).

The literature on feminism is both voluminous and diverse. Surveys of feminist history which extend into the antebellum period include Carl N. Degler's *At Odds: Women and Family in America from the Revolution to the Present* (1980),° William L. O'Neill's *Everyone Was Brave: The Rise and Fall of Feminism in America* (1970),° Gerda Lerner's *The Woman in American History* (1970), and Mary P. Ryan's *Womanhood in America* (1975).° More specific are Eleanor Flexner's *Century of Struggle: The Women's Rights Movement in the United States* (1975)° and Linda Gordon's *Woman's Body, Woman's Right: A Social History of Birth Control in America* (1976).° More particular to the antebellum period are Keith Melder's *The Beginnings of Sisterhood* (1977), Nancy Cott's *The Bonds of Womanhood: "Women's Sphere" in New England, 1780–1835* (1977),° Barbara J. Berg's *The Remembered Gate: Origins of American Feminism—The Woman and the City, 1800–1860* (1977), and Ellen C. DuBois's *Feminism and Suffrage: The Emergence of an Independent Women's Movement in America, 1848–1869* (1978).° Biographical studies include Alma Lutz's *Susan B. Anthony* (1959), Lois Banner's *Elizabeth Cady Stanton* (1980),° and Paula Blanchard's *Margaret Fuller: From Transcendentalism to Revolution* (1978).°

Michael Fellman's *The Unbounded Frame: Freedom and Community in Nineteenth Century Utopianism* (1973) and Mark Holloway's *Heavens on Earth* (1951) survey the utopian movements. J. F. C. Harrison's *Quest for the New Moral World: Robert Owen and the Owenites in Britain and*

America (1969); Robert O. Thomas's *The Man Who Would Be Perfect* (1977), on John Humphrey Noyes; Marin L. Carden's *Oneida* (1969); and Henri Desroche's *The American Shakers from Neo-Christianity to Pre-Socialism* (1971) all treat specific experiments. Also helpful is Lawrence Foster's *Religion and Sexuality: Three American Communal Experiments of the Nineteenth Century* (1981).

Perspectives on family life during the times of reforms can be gained from Milton Rugoff's *The Beechers: An American Family in the Nineteenth Century* (1981) and Mary P. Ryan's *Cradle of the Middle Class: The Family in Oneida Country, New York, 1790–1865* (1981).

14

MANIFEST DESTINY

The Tyler Years

When William Henry Harrison took office in 1841, elected like Jackson mainly on the strength of his military record and without commitment on issues, the Whig leaders expected him to be a figurehead. At first it did seem that he would be a tool in the hands of Webster and Clay. Webster became secretary of state and, while Clay preferred to stay in the Senate, the cabinet was filled with his friends. Within a few days of the inauguration there were signs of strain between Harrison and Clay, whose disappointment at missing the nomination had made him peevish and arrogant. But the enmity never had a chance to develop, for Harrison served the shortest term of any president—after the longest inaugural address. At the inauguration on a cold and rainy day he caught cold. The importunings of office seekers in the following month filled his days and sapped his strength. On April 4, 1841, exactly one month after the inauguration, he died of pneumonia.

Thus John Tyler of Virginia, the first vice-president to succeed on the death of a president, was to serve practically all of Harrison's term. And if there was ambiguity about where Harrison stood, there was none about Tyler. At age fifty-one he already had a long career behind him as legislator, governor, congressman, and senator, and was on record on all the important issues. At an earlier time he might have been called an Old Republican, stubbornly opposed to everything that was signified by Clay's American System—protective tariffs, a national bank, or internal improvements at national expense—and in favor of strict construction and states' rights. Once a Democrat, he had broken with Jackson's stand on nullification and his imperious use of executive authority. Tyler had been chosen to "balance" the ticket, with no belief that he would wield power. And to compound the irony, because he was known as a friend of Clay, his choice had been designed in part to pacify Clay's disappointed followers.

DOMESTIC AFFAIRS   Given more finesse on Clay's part, personal friendship might have enabled him to bridge the policy divisions among the Whigs. But for once, driven by disappointment and ambition, the "Great Pacificator" had lost his instinct for compromise. When Congress met in special session at the end of May 1841 Clay introduced, and the Whig majority passed, a series of resolutions designed to supply the platform which the party had evaded in the previous election. The chief points were repeal of the Independent Treasury, establishment of a third Bank of the United States, distribution to the states of proceeds from public land sales, and a higher tariff. Clay then set out to push his program through Congress. Despite the known views of Tyler, he remained hopeful. "Tyler dares not resist me. I will drive him before me," he said. Tyler, it turned out, was not easily driven.

By 1842 Clay's program was in ruins. He had failed to get a new bank, and distribution was abandoned with adoption of the high 1842 tariff. Even his successes were temporary—a Democratic Congress and president in 1846 restored the Independent Treasury and cut the tariff, leaving preemption (which legalized the frontier tradition of "squatter's rights") as the only major permanent achievement of the Whigs, something that had been no part of Clay's original scheme. If the program was in ruins, however, Clay's leadership of his party was fixed beyond question, and Tyler was left in the position of a president without a party.

FOREIGN AFFAIRS   In foreign relations, on the other hand, developments of immense significance were taking place. Several unsettled issues had arisen to trouble relations between Britain and the United States. In 1837 a forlorn insurrection in Upper Canada led to the seizure of the American steamboat *Caroline* by Canadians who set it afire and let it drift over Niagara Falls. In the course of the incident one American was killed. The British ignored all protests, but President Van Buren called out militia under Gen. Winfield Scott to prevent frontier violations in either direction. The issue faded until 1840 when Alexander McLeod, a Canadian, was arrested and brought to trial in New York state after he boasted of his participation in the incident and his responsibility for the killing. The British government now did admit that it had ordered destruction of the vessel and argued that McLeod could not be held personally responsible. The incident fortunately was closed when McLeod proved to have an air-tight alibi—he was miles away and his story had been nothing but barroom braggadocio.

Another issue involved the suppression of the African slave trade, which both the United States and Britain had outlawed in 1808. In August 1841 Prime Minister Palmerston asserted the right of British patrols off the coast of Africa to board and search vessels flying the American flag to see if they carried slaves, but the American government remembered the impressments and seizures during the Napoleonic Wars and refused to accept it. Relations were further strained late in 1841 when American slaves on a brig, the *Creole*, bound from Hampton Roads to New Orleans, mutinied and sailed into Nassau, where the British set them free. Webster demanded that the slaves be returned as American property, but the British refused.

Fortunately at this point a new British ministry under Sir Robert Peel decided to accept Webster's overtures for negotiations and sent Lord Ashburton to Washington. Ashburton was widely known to be friendly to Americans, and the talks proceeded smoothly. The Maine boundary was settled in what Webster later called "the battle of the maps." Webster settled for about seven-twelfths of the contested lands along the Maine boundary, and except for Oregon, which remained under joint occupation, he settled the other border disputes by accepting the existing line between the Connecticut and St. Lawrence rivers, and by compromising on the line between Lake Superior and the Lake of the Woods. This last was important because it gave the United States most of the Mesabi iron range, which was apparently known to

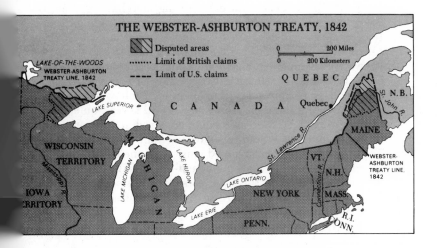

THE WEBSTER-ASHBURTON TREATY, 1842

Disputed areas
Limit of British claims
Limit of U.S. claims

0   200 Miles
0   200 Kilometers

LAKE-OF-THE-WOODS
WEBSTER-ASHBURTON
TREATY LINE, 1842

QUEBEC

N.B.

St. John R.

CANADA

Quebec

LAKE SUPERIOR

MAINE

WISCONSIN
TERRITORY

MICHIGAN

LAKE HURON

LAKE MICHIGAN

St. Lawrence R.

VT.

N.H.

WEBSTER-
ASHBURTON
TREATY LINE,
1842

Connecticut R.

IOWA
TERRITORY

Mississippi R.

LAKE ONTARIO

LAKE ERIE

NEW YORK

MASS.

R.I.

CONN.

PENN.

Tyler and Webster but not to Ashburton. The Webster-Ashburton treaty (1842) also provided for joint patrols off Africa to repress the slave trade.

MOVING WEST

In the early 1840s the American people were no more stirred by the quarrels of Tyler and Clay over such issues as banking, tariffs, and distribution, important as they were, than students of history would be at a later date. Nor was the pulse much quickened by the adjustment of boundaries supposedly settled in 1783. What stirred the blood was the mounting evidence that the "empire of freedom" was hurdling the barriers of the "Great American Desert" and the Rocky Mountains, reaching out toward the Pacific coast. In 1845 John Louis O'Sullivan, editor of the *United States Magazine and Democratic Review*, gave a name to this bumptious spirit of expansion. "Our manifest destiny," he wrote, "is to overspread the continent allotted by Providence for the free development of our yearly multiplying millions." Traders and trappers, as always, were the harbingers of empire, and an unguarded boundary was no barrier to their entering Mexican borderlands sparsely peopled and scarcely governed from the remote capital.

REACHING THE ROCKIES One of the first magnets to draw Americans was Santa Fe, a remote outpost of Spanish empire founded in the seventeenth century, the capital and trading center for a population of perhaps 60,000 in New Mexico. In September 1821 William Becknell, an enterprising merchant, gathered a party to head up the Arkansas River on a horse-trading expedition. Becknell and his men stumbled onto a group of Mexican soldiers who received them hospitably with the news that Mexico was newly independent and that American traders were welcome in Santa Fe, where Becknell sold his goods for Spanish silver dollars. His second expedition in 1822 followed a new desert route along the Cimarron River. Word spread quickly and every spring thereafter merchants gathered at Independence, Missouri, for the long journey of wagon trains along the Santa Fe Trail. The trade never involved more than one or two hundred merchants, but it was a profitable enterprise in which American goods were traded for the gold, silver, and furs of the Mexicans. In 1843 trouble over the Texas question caused the Mexican government to close the trade once again.

The Santa Fe traders had pioneered more than a new trail.

They showed that heavy wagons could cross the plains and penetrate the mountains, and they developed the technique of organized caravans for mutual protection. They also began to
discover the weakness of Mexico's control over its northern borderlands, and to implant in American minds their contempt for
the "mongrel" population of the region. From the 1820s on,
however, that population had begun to include a few Americans
who lingered in Santa Fe or Taos, using them as jumping-off
points for hunting and trapping expeditions northward and westward.

The more important avenue for the fur trade, however, was
the Missouri River with its many tributaries. The heyday of the
mountain fur trade began in 1822 when a Missouri businessman,
William H. Ashley, sent his first trading party to the upper Missouri. In 1825 Ashley devised the "rendezvous system," in
which trappers, traders, and Indians from all over the Rocky
Mountain country gathered annually at some designated place,
usually in or near the Grand Tetons, in order to trade. But by
1840 the great days of the western fur trade were over. The
streams no longer teemed with beavers. The country was
trapped out, and the animals were saved from extinction only by
the caprice of fashion, which now decreed that men's dress hats
should be made of silk rather than beaver skins. But during the
1820s and 1830s the trade had sired a uniquely reckless breed of
"mountain men," who deserted civilization for the pursuit of the
beaver, reverted to a primitive existence in the wilderness,
sometimes in splendid isolation, sometimes in the shelter of
primitive forts, and sometimes among the Indians. They were the
first to find their way around in the Rocky Mountains and they pioneered the trails over which settlers by the 1840s were beginning to flood the Oregon country and trickle across the border
into California.

THE OREGON COUNTRY Beyond the mountains the Oregon country stretched from the Forty-second Parallel north to 54° 40′,
between which Spain and Russia had given up their claims, leaving Great Britain and the United States as the only claimants.
Under the Convention of 1818 the two countries had agreed to
"joint occupation." Until the 1830s, however, joint occupation
had been a legal technicality, because the only American presence was the occasional mountain man who wandered into the
Pacific slope or the infrequent trading vessel from Boston, Salem,
or New York.

The effective impulse for American settlement came finally
from an unlikely source. In 1833 the *Christian Advocate and*

Herald, a Methodist journal, published a fanciful letter from William Walker, an educated Wyandot Indian. It told of western tribesmen who wanted the white man's "Book of Heaven" and missionaries to instruct them in the Christian faith. Soon every pulpit and church paper was echoing this fictitious request, and before the year was ended the Methodist Missionary Society had sent out the Rev. Jason Lee, who established a mission in the fertile Willamette Valley, south of the Columbia.

Lee sent back glowing reports and returned east to speak on the attractions of Oregon; his mission in the fertile Willamette Valley became the chief magnet for settlement. By the late 1830s a trickle of emigrants was flowing along the Oregon Trail. In 1841 and 1842 the first sizable wagon trains made the trip, and in 1843 the movement began to assume the proportions of mass migrations. That year about a thousand overlanders followed the trail westward from Independence, Missouri, along

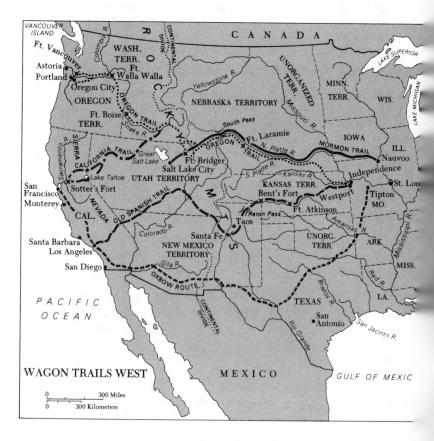

WAGON TRAILS WEST

the Platte River into Wyoming, through South Pass down to Fort Bridger (abode of a celebrated Mountain Man, Jim Bridger), then down the Snake River to the Columbia and along the Columbia to their goal in the Willamette Valley. By 1845 there were about 5,000 settlers in the region.

EYEING CALIFORNIA   California, thinly peopled by mission friars and Mexican rancheros, had drawn New England ships into an illegal traffic in sea-otter skins before the end of the eighteenth century. By the late 1820s American trappers wandered in from time to time and American ships began to enter the "hide and tallow" trade. The ranchos of California produced cowhide and beef tallow in large quantity and both products enjoyed a brisk demand, cowhides mainly for shoes and the tallow chiefly for candles. Ships from Boston, Salem, or New York, well stocked with trade goods, struggled southward around Cape Horn and northward to the customs office at the California capital of Monterey. From there the ships worked their way down the coast, stopping to sell their goods and take on return cargoes. Richard Henry Dana's *Two Years before the Mast* (1840), a classic account of his adventures as a seaman in the trade, brought the scene vividly to life for his many readers and focused their attention on the romance and the potential of California.

By the mid-1830s shippers began setting up agents on the scene to buy the hides and store them until a company ship arrived. One of these agents, Thomas O. Larkin at Monterey, was destined to play a leading role in the American acquisition of California. Larkin stuck pretty much to his trade, operating a retail business on the side, while others branched out and struck it rich in ranching. The most noteworthy of the alien nabobs, however, was not American, but Swiss. John A. Sutter had tried the Santa Fe trade first, then found his way to California via Oregon, Hawaii, and Alaska. In Monterey he persuaded the Mexican governor to give him land on which to plant a colony of Swiss emigrés.

At the juncture of the Sacramento and American Rivers (later the site of Sacramento) he built an enormous enclosure that guarded an entire village of settlers and shops. At New Helvetia (Americans called it Sutter's Fort), completed in 1843, no Swiss colony materialized, but the enclosure became the chief mecca for Americans bent on settling the Sacramento country. It stood at the end of what became the most traveled route through the Sierras, the California Trail which forked off from the Oregon Trail and led through the mountains south of Lake Tahoe. By the start of 1846 there were perhaps 800 Americans in California, along with some 8,000–12,000 Californios of Spanish descent.

John Charles Frémont, the Pathfinder. [Library of Congress]

The premier press agent for California, and the Far West generally, was John Charles Frémont, the Pathfinder—who found mainly paths that the Mountain Men showed him. In the early 1840s his new father-in-law, Missouri Sen. Thomas Hart Benton, arranged the explorations toward Oregon that made him famous. In 1842 he mapped the Oregon Trail beyond South Pass—and met Christopher Carson, one of the most knowledgeable of the mountain men, who became his frequent associate, and as Kit Carson, the most famous frontiersman after Daniel Boone. In 1843–1844 Frémont went on to Oregon, then made a heroic sweep down the eastern slopes of the Sierras, headed southward through the central valley of California, bypassed the mountains in the south, and returned via Great Salt Lake. His reports on both expeditions, published together in 1845, enjoyed a career rare for a government document. In numerous popular reprints they gained a wide circulation.

American presidents, beginning with Jackson, tried to acquire at least northern California, down to San Francisco Bay, by purchase from Mexico. Jackson reasoned that as a free state California could balance the future admission of Texas as a slave state. But Jackson's agent Anthony Butler had to be recalled after a clumsy effort to bribe Mexican officials. Tyler's minister to Mexico resumed talks, but they ended abruptly after a bloodless comic-opera conquest of Monterey by the commander of the American Pacific Fleet.

Rumors flourished that the British and French were scheming to grab California, though neither government had such intentions. Political conditions in Mexico left the remote territory in near anarchy much of the time, as governors came and went in rapid succession. Amid the chaos substantial Californios reasoned that they would be better off if they cut the ties to Mexico altogether. Some favored an independent state, perhaps under French or British protection. A larger group, led by a Sonoma cattleman, Mariano G. Vallejo, admired the balance of central and local authority in the United States and felt their interests might best be served by American annexation. By the time the Americans were ready to fire the spark of rebellion, there was little will to resist.

ANNEXING TEXAS

AMERICAN SETTLEMENTS Manifest Destiny was most clearly at work in the most accessible of all the Mexican borderlands, Texas. There more Americans were resident than in all the other coveted regions combined. Many claimed in fact, if with little evidence, that Texas had been part of the Louisiana Purchase, abandoned only when John Quincy Adams had accepted a boundary at the Sabine River in 1819. Adams himself, as president, tried to make up for the loss by offering to buy Texas for $1 million, but Mexico refused both that and a later offer of $5 million, from Jackson. Meanwhile, however, it was rapidly turning into an American province, for Mexico welcomed American settlers there.

First and foremost among the promoters of Anglo-American settlement was Stephen F. Austin, a resident of Missouri, who gained from Mexico confirmation of a huge land grant originally given to his father by Spanish authorities. Indeed before Mexican independence was fully won he had begun a colony on the lower Brazos River late in 1821 and by 1824 had more than 2,000 settlers on his lands. In 1825, under a National Colonization Law, the state of Coahuila-Texas offered large tracts to *empresarios* who promised to sponsor immigrants. Most of the newcomers were southern farmers drawn to rich new cotton lands going for only a few cents an acre. By 1830 the coastal region of eastern Texas had approximately 20,000 white settlers and 1,000 Negro slaves brought in to work the cotton.

At that point the Mexican government took alarm at the flood of strangers who threatened to engulf the province. A new edict forbade further immigration, and troops moved to the frontier to enforce the law. But illegal immigrants moved across the long border as easily as illegal immigrants would later cross over in the other direction. By 1835 the American population had grown to around 30,000, about ten times the number of Mexicans in Texas. Friction mounted in 1832 and 1833 as Americans organized conventions to demand a state of their own, separate from Coahuila. Instead of granting Texans their own state, General Santa Anna, who had seized power in Mexico, dissolved the national congress late in 1834, abolished the federal system, and became dictator of a centralized state. Texans rose in rebellion, summoned a convention which, like the earlier Continental Congress, adopted a "Declaration of Causes" for taking up arms, and pledged to fight for the old Mexican constitution. On March 2, 1836, however, the Texans declared their independence as Santa Anna approached with an army of conquest.

INDEPENDENCE FROM MEXICO   The Mexican army delivered its first blow at San Antonio, where it had already brought under seige a small Texas garrison holed up behind the adobe walls of an abandoned mission, the Alamo. On March 6, four days after the declaration of independence, the Mexican force of 4,000 launched a frontal assault and, taking fearful losses, finally swarmed over the walls and annihiliated the 187 Texans in the Alamo, including their commander William B. Travis and the frontier heroes Davy Crockett and Jim Bowie, slave smuggler and inventor of the Bowie knife. It was a complete victory, but a costly one. The defenders of the Alamo sold their lives at the cost of 1,544 Mexicans, and inspired the rest of Texas to fanatical resistance.

Commander-in-chief of the Texas forces was Sam Houston, a Tennessee frontiersman who had learned war under the tutelage of Old Hickory at Horseshoe Bend, had later represented the Nashville district in Congress, and had moved to Texas only

Sam Houston, president of the Republic of Texas before it was annexed by the United States. [Library of Congress]

three years before. Houston beat a strategic retreat eastward, gathering reinforcements as he went, including volunteer recruits from the United States. Just west of the San Jacinto River he finally paused near the site of the city that later bore his name, and on April 21 surprised a Mexican encampment there. The Texans charged, yelling "Remember the Alamo," overwhelmed the Mexican force within fifteen minutes, and took Santa Anna prisoner. The Mexican dictator bought his freedom at the price of a treaty recognizing Texan independence, with the Rio Grande as the boundary. The Mexican Congress repudiated the treaty, but the war was at an end.

THE MOVE FOR ANNEXATION   The Lone Star Republic then drafted a constitution, made Houston its first president, and voted almost unanimously for annexation to the United States as soon as the opportunity arose. Houston's old friend Jackson was still president, but even Old Hickory could be discreet when delicacy demanded it. The addition of a new slave state at a time when Congress was beset with abolitionist petitions threatened a serious sectional quarrel which might endanger the election of Van Buren. Worse than that, it raised the spectre of war with Mexico. Jackson kept his counsel and even delayed recognition of the Texas Republic until his last day in office. Van Buren shied away from the issue during his entire term as president.

Rebuffed in Washington, Texans turned their thoughts to a separate destiny. Under President Mirabeau Bonaparte Lamar, elected in 1838, they began to talk of expanding to the Pacific as a new nation that would rival the United States. France and Britain extended recognition and began to develop trade relations. Texas supplied them an independent source of cotton, new markets, and promised also to become an obstacle to American expansion. The British, who had emancipated slaves in their colonies in 1833, hoped Texans might embrace abolition as the price of guarantees against Mexico.

The Texans, however, had never abandoned their hopes of annexation. Reports of growing British influence created anxieties in the United States government and among southern slaveholders, who became the chief advocates of annexation. In 1843 Abel P. Upshur, Tyler's secretary of state, opened secret negotiations with Texas. Before the negotiations were far advanced, Upshur met an untimely death aboard a navy frigate when a cannon exploded, killing both him and the secretary of the navy. In April John C. Calhoun, the new secretary of state, completed a treaty which went to the Senate for ratification.

Calhoun chose this moment also to send the British minister,

Richard Pakenham, a letter instructing him on the blessings of slavery and stating that annexation of Texas was needed to foil the British abolitionists. Publication of the note fostered the claim that annexation was planned less in the national interest than to promote the expansion of slavery. It was so worded, Francis P. Blair wrote Jackson, as to "drive off every northern man from the support of the measure." Sectional division, plus fear of a war with Mexico, contributed to the Senate's overwhelming rejection of the treaty. Solid Whig opposition contributed more than anything to its defeat.

POLK'S PRESIDENCY

THE ELECTION OF 1844 Prudent leaders in both political parties had hoped to keep this divisive issue out of the 1844 campaign. Clay and Van Buren, the leading candidates, had reached the same conclusion about Texas: when the treaty was submitted to the Senate, they both wrote letters opposing annexation because it would create the danger of war. Both letters, dated three days apart, appeared in separate Washington newspapers on April 27, 1844. Clay's "Raleigh letter" (written while he was on a southern tour) added that annexation was "dangerous to the integrity of the Union . . . and not called for by any general expression of public opinion." The outcome of the Whig convention in Baltimore seemed to bear out his view. Party leaders showed no qualms about Clay's stance. The convention nominated him unanimously, and the Whig platform omitted any reference to Texas.

The Democratic convention was a different story. Van Buren's southern supporters, including Jackson, left him. Expansionist forces got the convention to adopt the two-thirds rule once again. It had served Van Buren's cause before, but this time it doomed his chances. With the convention deadlocked, on the eighth ballot the expansionists brought forward James K. Polk of Tennessee, and on the ninth ballot he became the first "dark horse" candidate to win a major-party nomination. The party platform took an unequivocal stand favoring expansion, and to win support in the North and West as well as the South it linked the questions of Oregon and Texas: "our title to the whole of the territory of Oregon is clear and unquestionable," the party proclaimed, and called for "the reoccupation of Oregon and the reannexation of Texas."

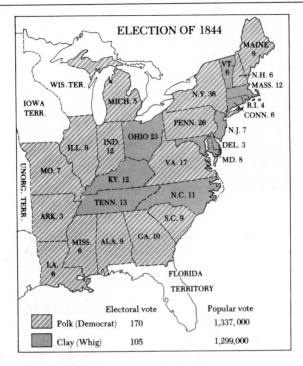

ELECTION OF 1844

	Electoral vote	Popular vote
Polk (Democrat)	170	1,337,000
Clay (Whig)	105	1,299,000

The combination of southern and western expansionism was a winning strategy, so popular that Clay began to hedge his statement on Texas. While he still believed the integrity of the Union the chief consideration, he had "no personal objection to the annexation of Texas" if it could be achieved "without dishonor, without war, with the common consent of the Union, and upon just and fair terms." His explanation seemed clear enough, but prudence was no match for spread-eagle oratory and the emotional pull of Manifest Destiny. The net result of Clay's stand was to turn more antislavery votes to the Liberty party, which increased its count from about 7,000 in 1840 to more than 62,000 in 1844. In the western counties of New York the Liberty party drew enough votes away from the Whigs to give the state to Polk. With New York, Clay would have carried the election by seven electoral votes. Polk won a narrow plurality of 38,000 popular votes nationwide (the first president to win without a majority) but a clear majority of the electoral college, 170 to 105.

"Who is James K. Polk?" the Whigs scornfully asked in the campaign. But the man was not as obscure as they implied. He

James Knox Polk, in a daguerrotype by Mathew Brady. [Library of Congress]

was a dark horse only in the sense that he was not a candidate before the convention. Born near Charlotte, North Carolina, trained in mathematics and the classics at the University of North Carolina, Polk had moved to Tennessee as a young man. A successful lawyer and planter, he had entered politics early, served fourteen years in Congress (four as Speaker of the House) and two as governor of Tennessee. Young Hickory, as his partisans liked to call him, had none of Jackson's charisma, but shared his prejudices and made up for his lack of color by stubborn determination and hard work, which destroyed his health during four years in the White House. March 4, 1845, was dark and rainy; Polk delivered his inaugural address to "a large assemblage of umbrellas," as John Quincy Adams described it. The speech was as colorless as the day, a recitation of Jeffersonian and Jacksonian principles in which Polk denounced protective tariffs, national banks, and implied powers, and again claimed title to Oregon.

POLK'S PROGRAM In domestic affairs Young Hickory hewed to the principle of the old hero, but the new Jacksonians subtly reflected the growing influence of the slaveholding South within the party. Abolitionism, Polk warned, could bring the dissolution of the Union. Antislavery northerners had already begun to drift away from the Democratic party, which New York Rep. Lemuel Stetson complained was coming to represent the slaveholding interest.

Soon after Polk took office he explained his objectives to the historian George Bancroft, his navy secretary. His major objectives were reduction of the tariff, reestablishment of the Independent Treasury, settlement of the Oregon question, and the acquisition of California. He got them all. The Tariff of 1846 replaced specific or flat duties with *ad valorem* (or percentage) duties and reduced the tariff to an average level of about 26.5 percent. In the same year Polk persuaded Congress to restore the Independent Treasury, which the Whigs had eliminated. Twice Polk vetoed internal improvement bills. In each case his blows to the American System of Henry Clay's Whigs satisfied the urges of the slaveholding South, but at the cost of annoying northern protectionists and westerners who wanted internal improvements.

THE STATE OF TEXAS But the chief focus of Polk's concern remained geographical expansion. He privately vowed to Bancroft his purpose of acquiring California, and New Mexico as well, preferably by purchase. The acquisition of Texas was already under way before Polk took office. President Tyler, taking Polk's election as a mandate to act, asked Congress to accomplish annexation by joint resolution, which required only a simple majority in each house and avoided the two-thirds Senate vote needed to ratify a treaty. Congress had read the election returns too, and after a bitter debate over slavery, the resolution passed by votes of 27 to 25 in the Senate and 120 to 98 in the House. Tyler signed the resolution on March 1, 1845, offering to admit Texas to statehood. The new state would keep its public lands but pay its own war debt, and with its own consent might be divided into as many as five states in the near future. A Texas convention accepted the offer in July, the voters of Texas ratified the action in October, and the new state formally entered the Union on December 29, 1845.

OREGON Meanwhile the Oregon issue heated up as expansionists aggressively insisted that Polk abandon previous offers to settle on the Forty-ninth Parallel and stand by the platform pledge to take all of Oregon. The bumptious expansionists were prepared to risk war with Britain while relations with Mexico were simultaneously moving toward the breaking point. "Fifty-four forty or fight," they intoned. "All of Oregon or none." In his inaugural address Polk declared the American title to Oregon "clear and unquestionable," but privately he favored a prudent compromise. War with Mexico was brewing; the territory up to 54°40′ seemed of less importance than Puget Sound or the ports of California, on which the British also were thought to have an eye. Since Monroe each administration had offered to extend the boundary along the Forty-ninth Parallel. In July 1845 Polk and Buchanan renewed the offer, only to have it refused by the British minister, Richard Pakenham.

Polk withdrew the offer and went back to his claim to all of Oregon. In the annual message to Congress at year's end, he asked for permission to give a year's notice that joint occupation would be abrogated, and revived the Monroe Doctrine with a new twist: "The people of *this continent* alone have the right to decide their own destiny." To a hesitant congressman he avowed that "the only way to treat John Bull was to look him straight in the eye."After a long and bitter debate Congress adopted the resolution, but Polk was playing a bluff game. War with Mexico seemed increasingly certain and Secretary of State Buchanan privately informed the British government that any new offer would be submitted to the Senate.

Fortunately for Polk the British government had no enthusiasm for war over that remote wilderness at the cost of profitable trade relations with the United States. From the British viewpoint, the only land in dispute all along had been between the Forty-ninth Parallel and the Columbia River. Now the fur trade

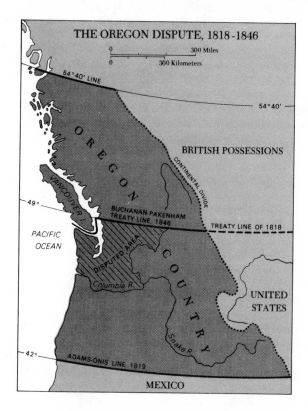

THE OREGON DISPUTE, 1818-1846

0   300 Miles
0   300 Kilometers

54°40′ LINE

54°40′

BRITISH POSSESSIONS

CONTINENTAL DIVIDE

OREGON

49°

VANCOUVER I.

BUCHANAN-PAKENHAM
TREATY LINE, 1846

TREATY LINE OF 1818

PACIFIC
OCEAN

DISPUTED AREA

Columbia R.

COUNTRY

UNITED
STATES

Snake R.

42°

ADAMS-ONIS LINE, 1819

MEXICO

of the region was a dying industry. In early June 1846 the British government submitted a draft treaty to extend the border along the Forty-ninth Parallel and through the main channel south of Vancouver Island. On June 15 Buchanan and British Minister Pakenham signed it, and three days later it was ratified in the Senate, where the only opposition came from a group of bitter-end expansionists representing the Old Northwest who wanted more. Most of the country was satisfied. Southerners cared less about Oregon than Texas, and northern business interests valued British trade more than they valued Oregon. Besides, the country was already at war with Mexico.

THE MEXICAN WAR

THE OUTBREAK OF WAR   Relations with Mexico had gone from bad to worse. On March 6, 1845, two days after Polk took office, the Mexican ambassador broke off relations and left for home to protest the annexation of Texas. When an effort at negotiation failed, Polk focused his efforts on unilateral initiatives. Already he was egging on American intrigues in California. On October 17, 1845, he had written Consul Thomas O. Larkin in Monterey that the president would make no effort to induce California into the Union, but "if the people should desire to unite their destiny with ours, they would be received as brethren." Larkin, who could take a hint, began to line up Americans and sympathetic Californios. Meanwhile Polk ordered American troops under Gen. Zachary Taylor to take up positions on the Rio Grande in the new state of Texas. These positions lay in territory that was doubly disputed: Mexico recognized neither the American annexation of Texas nor the Rio Grande boundary.

The last hope for peace died when John Slidell, sent to Mexico City to negotiate a settlement, finally gave up on his mission in March. After receiving him back in early May 1846, Polk resolved that he could achieve has purposes only by force. He sought and got the cabinet's approval of a war message to Congress. That very evening, May 9, the news arrived that Mexicans had attacked American soldiers north of the Rio Grande. Eleven Americans were killed, five wounded, and the remainder taken prisoner.

In his war message Polk could now take the high ground that the war was a response to aggression, a recognition that war had been forced upon the United States. "The cup of forbearance had been exhausted" before the incident; now, he said, Mexico "has passed the boundary of the United States, has invaded our territory, and shed American blood upon the American soil." The House quickly passed the war resolution, 174 to 14, the Senate on the next day by 40 to 2 with 3 abstentions, including Calhoun who feared that acquiring new territory would inflame the slavery issue. Polk signed the declaration of war on May 13. Both votes exaggerated the extent of support for the war. In the House twenty-seven members favored an amendment stating that the resolution should not be construed as approval of Polk's moving troops into the disputed area between the Nueces and the Rio Grande. The House authorized a call for 50,000 volunteers and a war appropriation of $10 million, but sixty-seven Whigs voted against that measure, another token of rising opposition to the war.

OPPOSITION TO THE WAR   In the Mississippi Valley, where expansion fever ran high, the war was immensely popular. The farther away from the scene of action, as a general rule, the less the enthusiasm for "Mr. Polk's War." Whigs ranged from lukewarm to hostile. John Quincy Adams, who voted against participation, called it "a most unrighteous war." and an obscure one-term congressman from Illinois named Abraham Lincoln, upon taking his seat in December 1847, began introducing "spot resolutions," calling on Polk to name the spot where American blood had been shed on American soil. If he were Mexican, Sen. Thomas Corwin of Ohio said, he would ask: "Have you not room in your own country to bury your dead men? If they come into mine, we will greet you, with bloody hands, and welcome you to hospitable graves."

Once again, as in 1812, New England was a hotbed of opposition, largely in the belief that this war was the work of "Land-Jobbers and Slave-Jobbers." As the Massachusetts poet James Russell Lowell put it in his *Biglow Papers*:

> They just want this Californy
>   So's to lug new slave-states in
> To abuse ye, an' to scorn ye,
>   An' to plunder ye like sin.

Some New England men, including Lowell, were ready to separate from the slave states, and the Massachusetts legislature formally pronounced the conflict a war of conquest. But before the war ended some antislavery men had a change of heart. Mexican territory seemed so unsuited to plantation staples that they endorsed expansion in hope of enlarging the area of free soil. Manifest Destiny exerted a potent influence even on those who opposed the war. *The Harbinger*, house organ of Brook Farm, managed to have it both ways. "This plundering aggression," the paper editorialized, "is monstrously iniquitous, but after all it seems to be completing a more universal design of Providence of extending the power and intelligence of advanced civilized nations."

PREPARING FOR BATTLE Both the United States and Mexico approached the war ill-prepared. American policy had been incredibly reckless, risking war with both Britain and Mexico while doing nothing to strenghten the armed forces until war came. At the outset of war the United States' regular army numbered barely over 7,000 in contrast to the Mexican force of 32,000. Before the war ended the American force grew to 104,000, of whom about 31,000 were regular army troops and marines. Most of these were six- and twelve-month volunteers from the West. Volunteer militia companies, often filled with frontier toughs, made up as raunchy a crew as ever graced the American military—innocent of uniforms, standard equipment, and discipline alike. One observer watched a band of such recruits with "torn and dirty shirts—uncombed heads—unwashed faces" trying to drill, "all hollowing, cursing, yelling like so many incarnate fiends." Repeatedly, despite the best efforts of the commanding generals, these undisciplined forces ran out of control in plunder, rape, and murder.

Nevertheless, being used to a rough-and-tumble life, they overmatched larger Mexican forces which had their own problems with training, discipline and munitions. Mexican artillery pieces were generally obsolete and the powder was so faulty that American soldiers could often dodge cannon balls that fell short and bounced ineffectively along the ground.

The United States entered the war without even a tentative plan of action. One had to be worked out hastily, and politics complicated things. What Polk wanted, Thomas Hart Benton wrote later, was "a small war, just large enough to require a treaty of peace, and not large enough to make military reputations, dangerous for the presidency." Winfield Scott, general-in-chief of the army, was both a Whig and politically ambitious. Nevertheless Polk named him at first to take charge of the Rio Grande front. When Scott fell into disputes with Secretary of War William L. Marcy, the exasperated Polk had Marcy withdraw the appointment. Scott, already known as "Old Fuss and Feathers" for his insistence on proper uniform, had also a genius for absurd turns of phrase. He began an indignant reply to Marcy with the remark that he got the secretary's letter as he "sat down to take a hasty plate of soup." One Washington wit promptly dubbed him Marshal Tureen.

There seemed now a better choice. Zachary Taylor's men had scored two victories over Mexican forces north of the Rio Grande, at Palo Alto (May 8) and Resaca de la Palma (May 9). On May 18 Taylor crossed over and occupied Matamoros, which a demoralized and bloodied Mexican army had abandoned. These quick victories brought Taylor instant popularity and the president responded willingly to the demand that he be made commander for the conquest of Mexico. "Old Rough and Ready" Taylor, a thickset and none-too-handsome man of sixty-one, seemed unlikely stuff from which to fashion a hero and impressed Polk as less of a political threat than Scott. Taylor acted at least as cautiously as Scott, awaiting substantial reinforcements and supplies before moving any deeper into Mexico. But without a major battle he had achieved Polk's main objective, the conquest of Mexico's northern provinces.

ANNEXATION OF CALIFORNIA   Along the Pacific coast, conquest was under way before definite news of the Mexican war arrived. Near the end of 1845 John C. Frémont brought out a band of sixty frontiersmen ostensibly on another exploration of California and Oregon. "Frémont's conduct was extremely mysterious," John A. Sutter wrote. "Flitting about the country with an armed body of men, he was regarded with suspicion by everybody." When José Castro, commandant at Monterey, ordered him out of the

Zachary Taylor, "Old Rough and Ready." This daguerrotype was made around the time of the Mexican War. [Chicago Historical Society]

Salinas Valley, he occupied the peak of Gavilan Mountain and defied the Mexicans to oust him, but soon changed his mind and headed for Oregon. In June 1846 Frémont and his men moved south into the Sacramento Valley. Americans in the area fell upon Sonoma on June 14, proclaimed William B. Ide president of the "Republic of California," and hoisted the hastily designed Bear Flag, a California Grizzly and star painted on white cloth— an idealized version of which became the state flag.

By the end of June Frémont had endorsed the Bear Flag Republic and set out for Monterey. Before he arrived, Commodore John D. Sloat of the Pacific Fleet, having heard of the outbreak of hostilities, sent a party ashore to raise the American flag and proclaim California a part of the United States. The Republic of California had lasted less than a month and most Californians of whatever origin welcomed a change that promised order in preference to the confusion of the unruly Bear Flaggers.

Before the end of July Commodore Robert F. Stockton replaced the ailing Sloat and began preparations to move against southern California. As senior officer on the scene, Sloat enlisted Frémont's band as the California Battalion and gave Frémont the rank of major. This group he sent down to San Diego too late to overtake the fleeing Mexican loyalists. In a more leisurely fashion, then, Stockton occupied Santa Barbara and Los Angeles. By mid-August resistance had dissipated. On August 17 Stockton declared himself governor, with Frémont as military commander in the north and Lieutenant Gillespie in the south.

By August another expedition was closing on Santa Fe. On August 18 Stephen Kearny and his men entered the Mexican town, whence an irresolute governor had fled with its defenders. After setting up a civilian governor, Kearny divided his remaining force, leading 300 dragoons west toward California in late September. On October 6 they encountered a band of frontiersmen under Frémont's old helper, Kit Carson, who was riding eastward with news that California had already fallen. Kearny sent 200 of his men back and with the remaining 100 pushed west with Carson serving as a reluctant guide.

But after Carson's departure from the coast, the picture had changed. In southern California, where most of the poorer Mexicans and Mexicanized Indians resented American rule, a rebellion broke out. By the end of October the rebels had ousted the token American force that remained in southern California. Kearny walked right into this rebel zone when he arrived. At San Diego he met up with Stockton and joined him in the reconquest of southern California, which they achieved after two brief

The Battle of the Plains of Mesa took place just before American forces entered Los Angeles. This sketch was made at the scene. [The Warder Collection]

clashes when they entered Los Angeles on January 10, 1847. Rebel forces capitulated on January 13.

TAYLOR'S BATTLES   Both California and New Mexico had been taken before Gen. Zachary Taylor fought his first major battle in northern Mexico. Having waited for more men and munitions, Taylor finally moved out of his Matamoros base in September 1846 and headed southward toward the heart of Mexico. His first goal was the fortified city of Monterrey, in Nuevo Leon, which he took after a five-day seige. Polk, however, was none too happy with the easy terms to which Taylor agreed, nor with Taylor's growing popularity. The whole episode merely confirmed the president's impression that Taylor was too passive to be trusted further with the major campaign. Besides, his victories, if flawed, were leading to talk of Taylor as the next Whig candidate for president.

But Polk's grand strategy was itself flawed. Having never seen the Mexican desert, Polk wrongly assumed that Taylor could live off the country and need not depend on resupply. Polk therefore misunderstood the general's reluctance to strike out across several hundred miles of barren land in front of Mexico City. The president was simply duped on another point. The old dictator Santa Anna, forced out in 1844, got word to Polk from his exile in Havana that in return for the right considerations he could bring about a settlement. Polk in turn assured the Mexican leader that Washington would pay well for any territory taken through a settlement. In August, after another overturn in the Mexican government, Santa Anna was permitted to pass through the American blockade into Vera Cruz. Soon he was again in command of the Mexican army and then was named president once more. The consequence of Polk's intrigue was to put perhaps the ablest Mexican general back in command of the enemy army, where he busily organized his forces to strike at Taylor.

By then another front had been opened and Taylor was consigned to inactivity. In October 1846 Polk and his cabinet decided to move against Mexico City by way of Vera Cruz. Polk would have preferred a Democratic general, but for want of a better choice named Winfield Scott to the field command. In January 1847 Taylor was required to give up most of his regulars to Scott's force gathering at Tampico. Taylor, miffed at his reduction to a minor role, disobeyed orders and advanced beyond Saltillo.

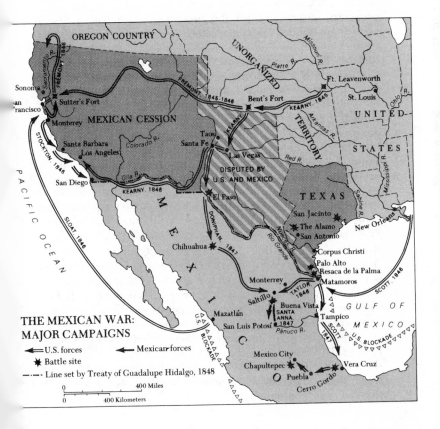

THE MEXICAN WAR:
MAJOR CAMPAIGNS

◄— U.S. forces   ◄— Mexican forces

★ Battle site

–·–· Line set by Treaty of Guadalupe Hidalgo, 1848

0   400 Miles

0   400 Kilometers

There, near the hacienda of Buena Vista, Santa Anna met Taylor's untested volunteers with a large but ill-trained and tired army. In the hard-fought Battle of Buena Vista (February 22–23, 1847) neither side could claim victory on the strength of the outcome, but Taylor was convinced that only his lack of regulars prevented him from striking a decisive blow. In any case it was the last major action on the northern front, and Taylor was granted leave to return home.

SCOTT'S TRIUMPH   The long-planned assault on the enemy capital had begun on March 9, 1847, when Scott's army landed on the beaches south of Vera Cruz. It was the first major amphibious operation by American military forces, carried out without loss. Vera Cruz surrendered on March 27 after a weeklong siege. Scott then set out on the route taken by Cortes more than 300 years before. Santa Anna tried to set a trap for him at the mountain pass of Cerro Gordo, but Scott's men took more than 3,000 prisoners, large quantities of equipment and provisions, and the Mexican president's personal effects.

On May 15 Scott's men entered Puebla, the second city of Mexico. There Scott lost about a third of his army. Men whose twelve-month enlistments had expired felt free to go home, leaving Scott with about 7,000 troops in all. There was nothing to do but hang on until reinforcements and new supplies came up from the coast. After three months, with his numbers almost doubled, Scott set out on August 7 through the mountain passes into the valley of Mexico, cutting his supply line to the coast. The aging duke of Wellington, following the campaign from afar, predicted: "is lost—he cannot capture the city and he cannot fall back upon his base."

But Scott directed a brilliant flanking operation around the lakes and marshes which guarded the eastern approaches to Mexico City, then another around the Mexican defenses at San Antonio. In the battles of Contreras and Churubusco (both on August 20) Scott's army overwhelmed Mexican defenses on the way to the capital. In those defeats Santa Anna lost a third of his forces and had to fall back within three miles of the city. In fighting renewed after a lull, two strong points guarding the western approaches to Mexico City fell in the Battles of Molino del Rey (September 8) and Chapultepec (September 12–13). On September 13 American forces entered Mexico City and within three days mopped up the remnants of resistance. At the National Palace a batallion of marines ran up the flag and occupied the "halls of Montezuma."

Winfield Scott takes Mexico City after his defeat of Santa Anna. [The Warder Collection]

THE TREATY OF GUADALUPE HIDALGO   After the fall of the capital, Santa Anna resigned and a month later left the country. Meanwhile Polk had appointed as chief peace negotiator Nicholas P. Trist, chief clerk of the State Department and a Virginia Democrat of impeccable partisan credentials. Trist was frustrated for want of anybody to negotiate with. In October Polk decided that the Mexican delays required a stronger stand and ordered Trist recalled, but before the message reached Mexico City things had changed. On November 11 the Mexican Congress elected an interim president, and on November 22 the new administration told Trist it had named commissioners to deal with him. Trist, having just received the recall notice, decided to go ahead with negotiations anyway. A sixty-five-page letter of justification did nothing to persuade Polk that he was anything but an "impudent and unqualified scoundrel," but Trist reasoned that it was better to continue than to risk a return of the war party or the disintegration of all government in Mexico.

Formal talks got under way on January 2, 1848, at the village of Guadalupe Hidalgo just outside the capital, and dragged out through the month. Finally Trist, fearing stronger orders from Washington at any time, threatened to end the negotiations and the Mexicans yielded. By the treaty of Guadalupe Hidalgo, signed on February 2, 1848, Mexico gave up all claims to Texas above the Rio Grande and ceded California and New Mexico to the United States. In return the United States agreed to pay

Mexico $15 million and assume the claims of American citizens against Mexico up to a total of $3¼ million.

Miffed that Trist had ignored his orders, Polk nevertheless had little choice but to submit the treaty to the Senate. A growing movement to annex all of Mexico had impelled him to hold out for more. But as Polk confided to his diary, rejecting the treaty would be too risky. If he should reject a treaty made in accord with his own original terms in order to gain more territory, "the probability is that Congress would not grant either men or money to prosecute the war." In that case he might eventually have to withdraw the army and lose everything. The treaty went to the Senate, which ratified it on March 10, 1848, by a vote of 38 to 14. By the end of July the last remaining American soldiers had boarded ship in Vera Cruz.

THE WAR'S LEGACIES The Mexican War had cost the United States 1,721 killed, 4,102 wounded, and far more, 11,155 dead of disease. The military and naval expenditures had been $97.7 million. For this price, and payments made under the treaty, the United States acquired more than 500,000 square miles of territory (more than a million counting Texas), including the great Pacific harbors of San Diego, Monterey, and San Francisco, with uncounted millions in mineral wealth. Except for a small addition by the Gadsden Purchase of 1853, these annexations rounded out the continental United States. Several important "firsts" are associated with the Mexican War: the first successful offensive war, the first major amphibious operation, the first occupation of an enemy capital, the first in which martial law was declared on foreign soil, the first in which West Point graduates played a major role, and the first reported by modern war correspondents like George W. Kendall of the New Orleans *Picayune*.

Manifest Destiny and images of the Golden West fired the imaginations of Americans, then and since. But the Mexican War somehow never became entrenched in the national legends. Within a few years it fell in the shadow of another and greater conflict, and was often recalled as a kind of preliminary bout in which Grant, Lee, and other great generals learned their trade as junior officers. The Mexican War never took on the dimensions of a moral crusade based on the defense of great principles. It was, transparently, a war of conquest provoked by a president bent on the acquisition of territory. One might argue that Polk merely hastened, and possibly achieved at less cost in treasure and human misery, what the march of the restless frontier would soon have achieved anyway. During one term in office he annexed to Jefferson's "of liberty" more land than Jefferson him-self, but the imperishable glamor that shone about the names of Caesar, Cortes, or Napoleon never brightened the name of Polk. For a brief season, however, the glory of conquest did shed luster on the names of Zachary Taylor and Winfield Scott. Despite Polk's best efforts, he had manufactured the next, and last two Whig candidates for president. One of them, Taylor, would re-place him in the White House, with the storm of sectional con-flict already on the horizon.

FURTHER READING

While no recent survey of Whig party history has been completed, Glyndon G. Van Deusen's *The Jacksonian Era* (1959),° Richard P. McCormick's *The Second American Party System* (1966),° and William R. Brock's *Parties and Political Conscience* (1979), as well as other works cited in Chapter 11, provide background on Whig programs and activi-ties. More focused on the values which inspired Whig programs is Daniel Walker Howe's *The Political Culture of the American Whigs* (1979). Rob-ert G. Gundersen's *The Log Cabin Campaign* (1957) examines the elec-tion of 1840. To understand more fully the Tyler administration, consult Oscar D. Lambert's *Presidential Politics in the United States, 1841–1844* (1936), and Robert J. Morgan's *A Whig Embattled* (1954). The border disputes of the period are covered in Albert B. Corey's *The Crisis of 1830–1842 in Canadian-American Relations* (1941).

Several works help interpret the concept of Manifest Destiny. Freder-ick Merk's *Manifest Destiny and Mission in American History* (1963)° and Edward M. Burns's *The American Idea of Mission: Concepts of National Purpose and Destiny* (1957) study the ideological background. Merk takes a more diplomatic slant in *The Monroe Doctrine and American Expansion, 1843–1849* (1966). Other works which explore the same themes are Norman A. Graebner's *Empire on the Pacific: A Study in American Continental Expansion* (1955), Albert K. Weinberg's *Manifest Destiny* (1936), and Henry Nash Smith's *Virgin Land* (1950).°

Ray A. Billington's *Westward Expansion* (1974) and *The Far Western Frontier, 1830–1860* (1956),° narrate well the story of pioneer move-ment. Bernard DeVoto's *Across the Wide Missouri* (1947) concentrates on the fur trappers and the Mountain Men. Robert L. Duffus's *The Santa Fe Trail* (1930) covers some of the same material. William H. Goetz-mann's *Army Exploration in the American West, 1803–1863* (1959), looks at the military involvement. A recent interpretation is John D. Unruh's *The Plains Across: The Overland Emigrants and the TransMissis-*

°These books are available in paperback editions.

sippi West, 1840–1860 (1978). Francis Parkman's *The Oregon Trail* (1849)° is an enduring classic on the subject.

Since California was the promised land for many, several scholars have concentrated on that area. Kevin Starr's *America and the California Dream, 1850–1915* (1973), is a good introduction. Also valuable are Leonard Pitt's *The Decline of the Californias* (1970), Walter Bean's *California: An Interpretative History* (1968), and Earl Pomeroy's *The Pacific Slope: A History* (1965). Pomeroy is also helpful for the early history of Oregon. How the Mormons came to Utah is covered in Wallace Stegner's *The Gathering of Zion: The Story of the Mormon Trail* (1964),° as well as works cited in Chapter 13.

The settlement of Texas is presented by William C. Binkley in *The Texas Revolution* (1952)° and *The Expansionist Movement in Texas, 1836–1850* (1925). Eugene C. Barker adds a nationalistic perspective in *Mexico and Texas, 1821–1835* (1928). Marquis James's *The Raven* (1929)° remains a fine biography of Sam Houston. The controversy over annexation is analyzed in David M. Pletcher's *The Diplomacy of Annexation: Texas, Oregon, and the Mexican War* (1973) and Frederick Merk's *Slavery and the Annexation of Texas* (1972).

Gene M. Brack's *Mexico Views Manifest Destiny, 1821–1846* (1975), takes Mexico's viewpoint on American designs on the West. The views of the expansionist president are gauged in Charles G. Sellers's *James K. Polk: Continentalist, 1843–1849* (1966), while John H. Schroeder's *Mr. Polk's War* (1973) is more critical. Surveys of the military conflict are provided in Otis Singletary's *The Mexican War* (1960)° and K. Jack Bauer's *The Mexican War, 1846–1848* (1974). Biographies of two leading generals are Charles W. Elliott's *Winfield Scott* (1937) and Holman Hamilton's *Zachary Taylor: Soldier of the Republic* (1941).

15

THE OLD SOUTH:
AN AMERICAN TRAGEDY

Myth, Reality, and the Old South

SOUTHERN MYTHOLOGY   Southerners, North Carolina editor Jonathan Daniels once wrote, are "a mythological people, created half out of dream and half out of slander, who live in a still legendary land." Most Americans, including southerners, carry an assorted mental baggage of myths about the South in which a variety of elements have been assembled. But the main burden of southern mythology is still carried in those images of the Old South set during the nineteenth-century sectional conflict, or in modernized versions of them: the Sunny South of the plantation tradition or the Benighted South of the Savage Ideal, the "dream" and the "slander."

The pattern of the first appeared full-blown at least as early as 1832 in John Pendleton Kennedy's romance, *Swallow Barn*. Every American is familiar with the euphoric pattern of kindly old massa with his mint julep on the white-columned piazza, happy "darkies" singing in fields perpetually white to the harvest, coquettish belles wooed by slender gallants underneath the moonlight and magnolias. The legend of the Southern Cavalier seemed to fulfill some psychic need for an American counterweight to the mental image of the grasping, money-grubbing Yankee.

But there are other elements in the traditional pattern. Off in the piney woods and erosion-gutted clay hills, away from gentility, dwelt a depraved group known as the poor white trash: the crackers; hillbillies; sand-hillers; squatters; rag, tag, and bobtail; po' buckra to the blacks. Somewhere in the pattern the respectable small farmer was lost from sight, perhaps neither romantic enough nor outrageous enough to fit in. He was absent too from the image of the Benighted South, in which the plantation myth simply appeared in reverse, as a pattern of corrupt opulence resting on human exploitation. Gentle old massa became the arrogant, haughty, imperious potentate, the very embodiment of sin, the central target of antislavery attack. He kept a seraglio in the slave quarters; he bred Negroes like cattle and sold them "down the river" to certain death in the sugar mills, separating families if that suited his purpose, while southern women suffered in silence the guilty knowledge of their men's infidelity. The "happy darkies" in this picture became white men in black skins, an oppressed people longing for freedom, the victims of countless atrocities, forever seeking a chance to follow the North Star to freedom. The masses of the white folks were, once again, poor whites, relegated to ignorance and degeneracy by the slavocracy.

THE SOUTHERN CONDITION   Everyone of course recognizes these pictures as overdrawn stereotypes, but as one historian has said, myths are made of tough stuff. Once implanted in the mind, they are hard to shake, partly because they have roots in reality. But to comprehend the distinctiveness of the Old South we must first identify the forces and factors that gave it a sense of unity. Efforts to do so usually turn on two lines of thought: the causal effects of environment (geography and climate), and the causal effects of human decisions and actions. The name of the historian Ulrich B. Phillips is associated with both. At the outset of his *Life and Labor in the Old South* (1929) Phillips wrote: "Let us begin by discussing the weather, for that has been the chief agency in making the South distinctive." It fostered the growing of staple crops, and thus the plantation system and black slavery. These things in turn brought sectional conflict and Civil War.

But while geography may render certain things possible and others impossible, explanations that involve human agency are more persuasive. In the 1830s Alexis de Tocqueville found the origins of southern distinctiveness in the institution of slavery. U. B. Phillips argued nearly a century later that with large numbers of blacks in the population, "the central theme" of southern history became "a common resolve indomitably maintained" by whites that they should retain their control. And this resolve in turn led to a sense of racial unity that muted class conflict among whites. But in the long run, the biracial character of the population influenced far more aspects of life than Phillips acknowledged. In making the culture of the South, W. J. Cash asserted in *The Mind of the South* (1941), "Negro entered into white man as profoundly as white man entered into Negro—subtly influencing every gesture, every word, every emotion and idea, every attitude." In shaping patterns of speech and folklore, of music and literature, black southerners immeasurably influenced and enriched the culture of the region.

The South differed from other sections too in its high proportion of native population, both white and black. Despite a great diversity of origins in the colonial population, the South drew few immigrants after the Revolution. One reason was that the main shipping lines went to northern ports; another, that the prospect of competing with slave labor was unattractive to immigrants. The South, one writer has said, "was created by the need to protected a peculiar institution from threats originating outside the region." After the Missouri Controversy of 1819–1821 the South became more and more a conscious minority, its population growth lagging behind that of other sections, its peculiar institution of slavery more and more an isolated and odious thing in Western civilization. Attitudes of defensiveness strongly affected its churches. The religious culture of the white South retreated from the liberalism of the Revolutionary War era into orthodoxy, which provided one line of defense against new doctrines of any kind, while black southerners found in a similar religious culture a refuge from the hardships of their lot, a promise of release on some future day of Jubilee.

Other ways in which the South was said to be different included its architecture, its peculiar work ethic, its penchant for the military, and its country-gentlemen ideal. One author, tongue in cheek, even suggested that the South was where the mule population was highest. The preponderance of farming remained a distinctive characteristic, whether pictured as the Jeffersonian yeoman living by the sweat of his brow or the lordly planter dispatching his slave gangs. In an agricultural society like the South there tended to be a greater "personalness" of human relations in contrast to the organized and contractual nature of relations in a more complex urban environment. But in the end what made the South distinctive was its people's belief, and other people's belief, that they *were* distinctive. Southernism, one historian asserted, was too elusive for a clear definition. "Poets," he wrote, "have done better in expressing the oneness of the South than historians in explaining it."

Cotton, the South's most important staple crop, being prepared for the gin on J. J. Smith's plantation, Beaufort, South Carolina, 1862. [Library of Congress]

STAPLE CROPS   The idea of the Cotton Kingdom is itself something of a mythic stereotype. Although cotton was the most important of the staple, or market, crops, it was a latecomer. Tobacco, the first staple crop, had earlier been the mainstay of Virginia and Maryland, and important in North Carolina. After the Revolution pioneers carried it over the mountains into Kentucky and as far as Missouri. Indigo, an important crop in colonial South Carolina, vanished with the loss of British bounties, but rice growing continued in a coastal strip that lapped over into North Carolina and Georgia. Rice growing was limited to the Tidewater because it required frequent flooding and draining of the fields, and along that sector of the coast the tides rose and fell six or seven feet. Since rice growing required substantial capital for floodgates, ditches, and machinery, its plantations were large and relatively few in number.

Sugar, like rice, called for a heavy capital investment in machinery to grind the cane, and was limited in extent because the cane was extremely susceptible to frost. An influx of refugees from the revolution in Haiti helped the development of a sugar belt centered along the Mississippi River above New Orleans. Some sugar grew in a smaller belt of eastern Texas. But it was always something of an exotic growth, better suited to a tropical climate. Since it needed the prop of a protective tariff, it produced the anomaly in southern politics of pro-tariff congressmen from Louisiana. Hemp had something of the same effect in the

Kentucky Blue Grass region and northwestern Missouri. Both flax and hemp were important to backcountry farmers at the end of the colonial era. Homespun clothing was most apt to be lin-sey-woolsey, a combination of linen and wool. But flax never de-veloped more than a limited commercial market, and that mostly for linseed oil. Hemp, on the other hand, developed commercial possibilities in rope and cotton baling cloth, although it suffered heavy competition from a higher quality Russian product.

Cotton, the last of the major staples, eventually outpaced all the others put together. At the end of the War of 1812 produc-tion was estimated at less than 150,000 bales; in 1860 it was re-ported at 3.8 million. Two things accounted for the growth: the voracious market in British and French textiles, and the cultiva-tion of new lands in the Southwest. Much of the story of the southern people—white and black—from 1820 to 1860 was their movement to fertile cotton lands farther west. The crop flourished best in the hot growing season of the Deep South. By 1860 the center of the cotton belt stretched from eastern North Carolina through the fertile Alabama-Mississippi black belts (so called for the color of both people and soil), on to Texas, and up the Mississippi Valley as far as southern Illinois. Cotton prices fell sharply after the Panic of 1837, and remained below 10¢ a pound through most of the 1840s, but they advanced above 10¢ late in 1855 and stayed there until 1860, reaching 15¢ in 1857—despite a business setback and a constantly increasing supply.

AGRICULTURAL DIVERSITY   The focus on cotton and the other cash crops has obscured the degree to which the South fed itself from its own fields. With 29.5 percent of the country's area in 1860, and 38.9 percent of its population, the slave states produced 52 percent of the nation's corn, 28.9 percent of the wheat, 19.2 percent of the oats, 19.4 percent of the rye, 10 percent of the white potatoes, and 94 percent of the sweet potatoes. The upper South in many areas practiced general farming in much the same way as the Northwest. Cyrus McCormick first tested his har-vester in the wheatfields of Virginia. Corn grew everywhere, but went less into the market than into local consumption by man and beast, as feed and fodder, as hoecake and grits. On many farms and plantations the rhythms of the growing season permit-ted the labor force to alternate attention between the staples and the food crops.

Livestock added to the diversity of the farm economy. The South had in 1860 half of the nation's cattle, over 60 percent of

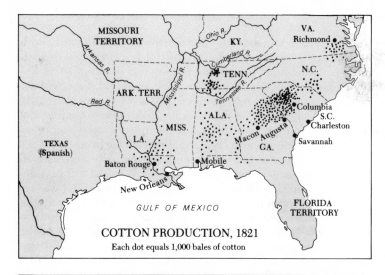

COTTON PRODUCTION, 1821
Each dot equals 1,000 bales of cotton

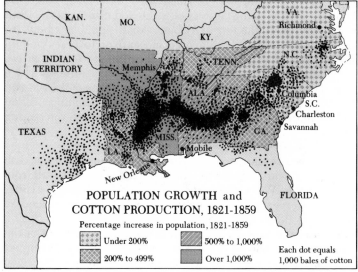

POPULATION GROWTH and COTTON PRODUCTION, 1821-1859

Percentage increase in population, 1821-1859

Under 200%	500% to 1,000%
200% to 499%	Over 1,000%

Each dot equals 1,000 bales of cotton

the swine, nearly 45 percent of the horses, 52 percent of the oxen, nearly 90 percent of the mules, and nearly a third of the sheep, the last mostly in the upper South. Cattle herding prevailed on the southern frontier at one time, and persisted in areas less suited to farming, such as the piney woods of the coastal plains, the Appalachians, and the Ozarks and their foothills. Plantations and farms commonly raised livestock for home consumption.

Yet the picture was hardly one of unbroken prosperity. The

South's staple crops quickly exhausted the soil, and open row crops like tobacco, cotton, and corn left the bare ground in between subject to leaching and erosion. Much of eastern Virginia by 1800 had abandoned tobacco, and in some places had turned to scrabbling wheat from the soil for the northern market. One ex-slave later recalled what he saw as a slave trader carried him across Virginia about 1805: "For several days we traversed a region, which had been deserted by the occupants—being no longer worth culture—and immense thickets of young red cedars now occupied the fields." In low-country South Carolina Sen. Robert Y. Hayne spoke of "Fields abandoned; and hospitable mansions of our fathers deserted. . . . " The older farming lands had trouble competing with the newer soils farther west. But when the Panic of 1837 ended the flush times of Alabama and Mississippi, farm prices everywhere remained low until the mid-1850s. Soon western lands too began to show wear and tear. By 1855 Sen. C. C. Clay was writing of his home country in northern Alabama: "Our small planters, after taking the cream off their lands . . . are going further west and south in search of other virgin lands which they may and will despoil and impoverish in like manner." This of course happened all along the frontier. "If the Old South had greater ruins than did the other sections,"historian Avery Craven insisted, "it was largely because it had been more successful in quickly and cheaply garnering the riches which Nature offered and spending them in the far-away markets where the comforts and luxuries of a more advanced life might be secured."

So the Southeast and then the Southwest faced a growing sense of economic crisis as the century advanced. Proposals to deal with it followed two lines. Some argued for agricultural reform, and others for diversification through industry and trade. Edmund Ruffin of Virginia stands out as perhaps the greatest of the reformers. After studying the chemistry of soils, he reasoned that most exhausted soils of the upper South had acid conditions which needed to be neutralized before they could become productive again. He turned his plantations into laboratories in which he discovered that marl from a shell deposit in eastern Virginia did the trick. His *Essay on Calcareous Manures* (1832) a Department of Agriculture expert pronounced at the end of the century the "most thoughtful piece of work on a special agricultural subject ever published in the English language." Such publications and farm magazines in general, however, reached but a minority of farmers, mostly the larger and more successful planters. The same was true of the agricultural associations which sprang up in the Old South, though some of these sponsored experimental farms and agricultural fairs which became fairly common by the 1840s and 1850s, reaching farmers with examples put before their very eyes.

MANUFACTURING AND TRADE By 1840 many thoughtful southerners reasoned that by staking everything on agriculture the region had wasted chances in manufacturing and trade. The census of 1810 had shown the South with more various and numerous manufactures than New England. The War of 1812 provided the South some stimulus for manufacturing, but the momentum was lost in the postwar flood of British imports. Then cotton growing swept everything before it. As the spread of landholding rendered concern with industry sporadic, the South became increasingly dependent on northern manufacturing and trade. Cotton and tobacco were exported mainly in northern vessels. In 1830 southern ship tonnage of 109,000 was less than a third of the North's 360,000; by 1860 the South's 855,000 was little more than a fifth of the North's 4 million. Southerners also relied on connections in the North for imported goods. The South became, economically if not formally, a kind of colonial dependency on the North.

The South's dependence on the North inspired a series of commercial conventions which commenced with a meeting at Augusta, Georgia, in 1837, and continued almost every year through the next two decades. The call for the first convention set forth a theme that would run through them all. The merchants of northern cities, it said, "export our immense valuable productions, and import our articles of consumption and from this agency they derive a profit which has enriched them . . . at our expense."

Along with the call for direct trade in southern ships went a movement for a more diversified economy, for native industries to balance agriculture and trade. Southern publicists called attention to the section's great resources: its raw materials, labor supply, waterpower, wood and coal, and markets. The chief vehicle for the advocates of economic development, and the leading economic journal of the South, came to be *The Commercial Review of the South and the Southwest*, edited by James D. B. De Bow.

De Bow's contemporary, William Gregg, began promoting textiles in South Carolina during the 1840s, when he bought into an early cotton mill near Edgefield and successfully reorganized it. After travels in New England, he wrote a series of articles for a Charleston paper advocating southern industrial development.

These pieces appeared in 1845 as a pamphlet: *Essays on Domestic Industry*. About a year later he began construction of the Graniteville Manufacturing Company. Built of native granite by local labor, the mill still survives. Adjoining the mill he built a model village with good homes, a school, library, churches, infirmary, and recreational facilities. The project was a success from the start, paying dividends in a few years of up to 8 percent.

In Richmond, Virginia, the Tredegar Iron Works grew into the most important single manufacturing enterprise in the Old South. Launched in 1837, the company in 1848 fell under the control of Joseph Reid Anderson, for several years its sales agent, before that a graduate of West Point and an army engineer. His military connections brought Tredegar contracts for cannon, shot, and shell, but the firm also made axes, saws, bridge materials, boilers, and steam engines, including locomotives. Unlike Gregg, Anderson used mainly slave workers, either hired from their owners or, more and more, owned by him outright.

Daniel Pratt of Alabama built Prattville, which grew into a model of diversified industry. Prattville ultimately had a gristmill, a shingle mill, a carriage factory, foundries, a tin mill, and a blacksmith shop. Pratt then launched into the iron business and coal mining, while on the side experimenting with vineyards and truck farming. Like Anderson he used both black and white labor; like Gregg he practiced paternalism. Profits from his company store went into churches, schools, a library, an art gallery, and a printing establishment—and into handsome dividends.

These men and others like them directed a program of industry that gathered momentum in the 1850s, and in its extent and diversity belied the common image of a strictly agricultural South. Manufactures were supplemented by important extractive industries such as coal, iron, lead, copper, salt, and gold, the

The Tredegar Iron Works in Richmond, Virginia. [Library of Congress]

last chiefly in North Carolina and Georgia. In manufacturing, altogether in 1860 the slave states had 22 percent of the country's plants, 17 percent of its labor, 20 percent of the capital invested, 17 percent of the wages generated, and 16 percent of the output, an impressive showing but still not up to the South's 29½ percent of the population. Also, southern industry was concentrated in the border states, which had many economic conditions in common with neighboring states of the North.

ECONOMIC DEVELOPMENT   There were two major explanations generally put forward for the lag in southern industrial development. First, blacks were presumed unsuited to factory work, perhaps because they could not adjust to the discipline of work by the clock. Second, the ruling orders of the Old South were said to have developed a lordly disdain for the practice of trade, because a certain aristocratic prestige derived from owning land and slaves, and from conspicuous consumption. But any argument that black labor was incompatible with industry simply flew in the face of the evidence, since factory owners bought or hired slave operatives for just about every kind of manufacture. Given the opportunity, a number of blacks displayed managerial skills as overseers. Nor should one take at face value the legendary indifference of aristocratic planters to the balance sheet. On the southwestern frontiers of the Cotton Kingdom, those who did fit that description became pathetic objects of humor, pushed aside by the hustlers.

More often than not the successful planter was a driving newcomer bent on maximizing profits. While the profitability of slavery has been a long-standing subject of controversy, in recent years economic historians, applying new tools of statistics and theory, have reached the conclusion that slaves on the average supplied about a 10 percent return on their cost. Slave ownership was, moreover, a reasonable speculation, for slave prices tended to move upward. By a strictly hardnosed and hardheaded calculation, investment in slaves and cotton lands was the most profitable investment available at the time in the South.

Despite the South's lag in trade and industry, incomes in the region fared well indeed, especially in the newer cotton lands of the Southwest. The census region comprising Arkansas, Louisiana, Texas, and the Indian Territory (later Oklahoma) had a higher per-capita income than any other census region in 1860, $184 to a national average of $128. Since these calculations included the total population, slave and free, some of the southwestern slaveholders clearly were rich beyond the dreams of avarice. The wealthiest regions at the time were the Southwest and the Northeast, which had a per-capita income of $181 in 1860. The new cotton lands and the expanding factories enjoyed the most dynamic growth of the time.

The notion that the South was economically backward emerged from the sectional quarrels of the times, in which southerners took a poorer-than-thou attitude, so to speak, in order to bolster their claims of northern exploitation. Antislavery elements also contributed to this notion by way of arguing the failure of a slave economy. It was true that in any comparison of the South with the North, the South usually came off second best. But in comparison with the rest of the world, the South as a whole was well off: its average per-capita income in 1860 ($103) was about the same as that of Switzerland, and was exceeded only by Australia, the North, and Great Britain, in that order.

WHITE SOCIETY IN THE SOUTH

If an understanding of the Old South must begin with a knowledge of social myths, it must end with a sense of tragedy. White southerners had won short-term gains at the costs of both long-term development and moral isolation in the eyes of the world. The concentration on land and slaves, and the paucity of cities and immigrants, deprived the South of the dynamic bases of innovation. The slaveholding South hitched its wagon not to a star, but to the world (largely British) demand for cotton, which had not slackened from the start of the Industrial Revolution. In the piping times of the late 1850s, it seemed that prosperity would never end. The South, "safely entrenched behind her cotton bags . . . can defy the world—for the civilized world depends on the cotton of the South," said a Vicksburg newspaper in 1860. "No power on earth dares to make war upon it," said James H. Hammond of South Carolina. "Cotton is king." The only perceived threat to King Cotton was the growing antislavery sentiment. The unperceived threat was an imminent slackening of the cotton market. The hey-day of expansion in British textiles was over by 1860, but by then the Deep South was locked into cotton production for generations to come.

THE PLANTERS   Although great plantations were relatively few in number, they set the tone of economic and social life in the South. What distinguished the plantation from the farm, in addition to its size, was the use of a large labor force, under separate control and supervision, to grow primarily staple crops for profit. A clear-cut distinction between management and labor set the planter apart from the small slaveholder, who often worked side by side with his bondsmen at the same tasks.

If, to be called a planter, one had to own 20 slaves, the South in 1860 numbered only 46,274 planters. Fewer than 8,000 owned 50 or more slaves, and the owners of over 100 numbered 2,292. The census enumerated only 11 with 500 and just 1 with as many as 1,000 slaves. Yet this small, privileged group tended to think of their class interest as the interest of the South, and to perceive themselves as community leaders in much the fashion of the English gentry. The planter group owned more than half the slaves, produced most of the cotton, tobacco, and hemp, and all of the sugar and rice. In a white population numbering just over 8 million in 1860, the total number of slaveholders came to only 383,637. But assuming that each family numbered five people, the whites with some proprietary interest in slavery came to 1.9 million, or roughly one-fourth of the white population. While the preponderance of southern whites belonged to the small-farmer class, the presumptions of the planters were seldom challenged. Too many small farmers aspired to rise in the world.

Often the planter did live in the splendor which legend attributed to him, with the wealth and leisure to cultivate the arts of hospitality, good manners, learning, and politics. More often the scene was less charming. Some of the mansions on closer inspection turned out to be modest houses with false fronts. A style of housing derived from the frontier log cabin grew to be surprisingly common. The one-room cabin would expand by the building of a second room with a sheltered open "dog trot" in the middle. As wealth increased, larger houses evolved from the plain log cabin and the dog trot grew into a central hall from the front

The Fairntosh plantation house, North Carolina. [North Carolina State Archives]

to the rear of the house. In larger houses halls to one or both sides might be added.

The planter commonly had less leisure than legend would suggest, for he in fact managed a large enterprise. At the same time he often served as the patron to whom workers appealed the actions of their foremen. The quality of life for the slaves was governed far more by the attitude of the master than by the formal slave codes, which were seldom enforced strictly except in times of troubles. The mistress of the plantation, like the master, seldom led a life of idle leisure. She was called upon to supervise the domestic household in the same way the planter took care of the business, to see after food, linens, housecleaning, the care of the sick, and a hundred other details. Mary Boykin Chesnut of South Carolina complained that "there is no slave like a wife."

THE MIDDLE CLASS   Overseers on the largest plantations generally came from the middle class of small farmers or skilled workers, or were younger sons of planters. Most aspired to become slaveholders themselves, and sometimes rose to that status, but others were constantly on the move in search of better positions. And their interests did not always coincide with the long-term interests of the planter. "Overseers are not interested in raising negro children, or meat, in improving land, or improving productive qualities of seed or animals," a Mississippi planter complained to Frederick Law Olmstead, a northern visitor. "Many of them do not care whether property has depreciated or improved, so they make a crop to boast of." Occasionally there were black overseers, but the highest management position to which a slave could aspire was usually that of driver or leader, placed in charge of a small group of slaves with the duty of getting them to work without creating dissension.

The most numerous white southerners were the middle-class yeoman farmers. W. J. Cash, in his classic *The Mind of the South*, called the small farmer "the man at the center." The most prosperous of these generally lived in the mountain-sheltered valleys from the Shenandoah of Virginia down to northern Alabama, areas with rich soil but without ready access to markets, and so less suitable for staple crops or slave labor. But the more numerous yeomen lived in the interstices of the plantation economy. Probably about 80 percent of them owned land. "Nearly all of them," Cash wrote, "enjoyed some measure of a kind of curious half-thrifty, half-shiftless prosperity—a thing of sagging rail fences, unpainted houses, and crazy barns which yet bulged with corn." The yeomen adapted from the planters certain traits of character. "The result was a kindly courtesy, a level eyed pride, an easy quietness, a barely perceptible flourish of bearing, which for all its obvious angularity and fundamental plainness, was one of the finest things the Old South produced."

THE "POOR WHITES"   But outside observers often had trouble telling yeomen apart from the true "poor whites," a degraded class crowded off into the pine barrens. Stereotyped views of southern society had prepared many travelers to see only planters and "poor whites," and many a small farmer living in rude comfort, his wealth concealed in cattle and swine off foraging in the woods, was mistaken for "white trash." The type was a familiar one from the frontier days, living on the fringes of polite society. William Byrd of Virginia found them in "Lubberland" (his name for North Carolina) as early as 1730, and in the literature of the South, both fiction and nonfiction, their descendants appeared right on down to the twentieth-century Jeeter Lester of *Tobacco Road* and the Snopeses of William Faulkner's novels. D. R. Hundley wrote in 1860: "There is no . . . method by which they can be weaned from leading the lives of vagrom-men, idlers, and squatters, useless to themselves and to the rest of mankind." They were characterized by a pronounced lankness and sallowness, given over to hunting and fishing, to hound dogs and moonshine whiskey.

Speculation had it that they were descended from indentured servants or convicts transported to the colonies, or that they were the weakest of the frontier population, forced to take refuge in the sand land, the pine barrens, and the swamps after having been pushed aside by the more enterprising and successful. But the problem was less heredity than environment, the consequence of infections and dietary deficiencies which gave rise to a trilogy of "lazy diseases": hookworm, malaria, and pellagra, all of which produced an overpowering lethargy. Many poor whites displayed a morbid craving to chew clay, from which they got the name "dirt eaters"; the cause was a dietary deficiency, although a folklore grew up about the nutritional and medicinal qualities of certain clays. Around 1900 modern medicine discovered the causes and cures for these diseases and by 1930 they had practically disappeared, taking with them many stereotypes of poor whites.

PROFESSIONALS AND OTHERS   "The social system of the South may be likened to a three-story white structure on a mudsill of black," as one historian put it. But that hardly exhausted the complexity of things. Manufacturers held their own with the planters, as did merchants, often called brokers or factors, who handled the planters' crops and acted as purchasing agents for their needs, supplying credit along the way. Professional people, including lawyers, doctors, and editors, stood in close relationship to the planter and merchant classes which they served and to which they sometimes belonged.

There was a degree of fluidity and social mobility in the class structure of the white South. Few indeed were the "cotton snobs" who lorded it over the lower orders. Planters were acknowledged as the social models and natural leaders of society by consensus. Planters risen from the ranks as often as not had close relatives still among the less well-to-do. Those who aspired to public office, especially, could not afford to take a lordly attitude, for every southern state by 1860 allowed universal white male suffrage. The voters, while perhaps showing deference to their "betters," could nevertheless pick and choose among them at election time.

Other groups stood farther from the mainstream. The mountain people of Appalachia engaged in subsistence farming, employed few or no slaves, and in attitude stood apart from the planter society, sometimes in open hostility toward it. Scattered in many of the flatland counties were small groups who sometimes fell even below the poor whites in the social scale. In some places the advance of the frontier had left behind pockets of Indians with whom passing whites and escaped slaves eventually mingled. The triple admixture of races produced islands of peoples known variously as brass ankles, Turks, redbones, yellow hammers, and Melungeons (derived apparently from "mélange," mixture).

BLACK SOCIETY IN THE SOUTH

"FREE PERSONS OF COLOR" Free Negroes, or "free persons of color," occupied an uncertain status, balanced somewhere between slavery and freedom, subject to legal restrictions not imposed on whites. In the seventeenth century a few blacks had been freed on the same basis as indentured servants. Over the years some slaves were able to purchase their freedom, while some gained freedom as a reward for service in American wars. Others were simply freed by conscientious masters, either in their wills, as in the case of George Washington, or during their lifetimes, as in the case of John Randolph. In one incredible case, a prince of the kingdom of Fita Jallon (in present-day Guinea), captured in warfare, turned up as a slave in Natchez, and after

A badge, issued in Charleston, South Carolina, to be worn by free blacks. [Charleston Museum]

some years managed to get a letter in Arabic to the sultan of Morocco, who intervened in his favor. In 1827, after thirty-nine years of slavery, he gained his freedom and returned to Africa.

The free persons of color included a large number of mulattoes. In urban centers like Charleston and especially New Orleans, "colored" society become virtually a third caste, a new people who occupied a status somewhere between black and white. Some of them built substantial fortunes and even became slaveholders. They often operated inns serving a white clientele. Jehu Jones, for instance, was the "colored" proprietor of one of Charleston's best hotels, which he bought in 1815 for $13,000. In Louisiana a mulatto, Cyprien Ricard, bought an estate with ninety-one slaves for $250,000. In Natchez William Johnson, son of a white father and mulatto mother, operated three barbershops and owned 1,500 acres of land and several slaves.

But such cases were rare. Free blacks more often were skilled artisans (blacksmiths, carpenters, cobblers), farmers, or common laborers. The increase in their numbers slowed as legislatures put more and more restrictions on the right to free slaves, but by 1860 there were 262,000 free blacks in the slave states, a little over half the national total of 488,000. They were most numerous in the upper South. In Maryland the number of free Negroes very nearly equaled the number still held in slavery; in Delaware free Negroes made up 91.7 percent of the black population.

THE TRADE IN SLAVES   The slaves stood at the bottom of the social hierarchy. From the first census in 1790 to the eighth in 1860 their numbers had grown from 698,000 to almost 4 million. The rise in the slave population came mainly through a natural increase, the rate of which was very close to that of whites at the time. When the African slave trade was outlawed in 1808, it

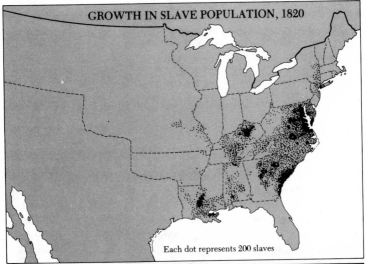

GROWTH IN SLAVE POPULATION, 1820

Each dot represents 200 slaves

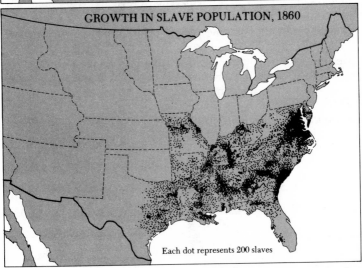

GROWTH IN SLAVE POPULATION, 1860

Each dot represents 200 slaves

seemed to many a step toward the extinction of slavery, but the expansion of the cotton belt, with its voracious appetite for workers, soon created such a vested interest in slaves as to dash such hopes. Shutting off the import of slaves only added to the value of those already present. Prices for prime fieldhands ranged between $300 and $400 in the 1790s, up to $1,000–$1,300 in the 1830s, peaked just before the onset of depression in 1837, and rose again in the great prosperity of the 1850s to $1,500-$2,000. Slaves with special skills cost even more.

The rise in slave value tempered some of the harsher features of the peculiar institution. Valuable slaves, like valuable livestock, justified some minimal standards of care. "Massa was purty good," one ex-slave recalled later. "He treated us jus' 'bout like you would a good mule." Another said his master "fed us reg'lar on good, 'stantial food, jus' like you'd tend to you hoss, if you had a real good one." Some owners hired wage laborers, often Irish immigrants, for ditching and other dangerous work rather than risk the lives of valuable slaves.

The end of the foreign slave trade gave rise to a flourishing domestic trade, with slaves moving mainly from the used-up lands of the Southeast into the booming new country of the Southwest. The trade peaked just before 1837, then slacked off, first because of depression, then because agricultural reform and recovery renewed the demand for slaves in the upper South. Many slaves moved south and west with their owners, but there also developed an organized business with brokers, slave pens, and auctioneers. Franklin and Armfield, the leading traders, had their offices and collecting pens in Alexandria, Virginia, where they fattened and spruced up slaves for the auction block. From Alexandria slave coffles moved overland through the Ohio Valley or down the Piedmont, making sales along the way. Other groups went out by sea to Wilmington, Charleston, Savannah, or directly to Mobile, New Orleans, and on to Natchez, a leading market for the new districts.

While the mainstream of the trade moved southwestward, every town of any size had public auctioneers and dealers willing to buy and sell slaves—along with other merchandise—or handle sales on a commission. The worst aspect of the slave trade was

Slave pens inside Pine, Birch & Co., dealers in slaves, Alexandria, Virginia. [Library of Congress]

Gathering Cotton on a South Carolina Plantation. *Sketch by William Waud. [The Historic New Orleans Collection]*

its breakup of families. Only Louisiana and Alabama (from 1852) forbade selling a child under ten from its mother, and no state forbade separation of husband from wife. Many such sales are matters of record, and although the total number is controversial, it took only a few to have a damaging effect on the morale of all.

PLANTATION SLAVERY The typical lot of the slave was plantation labor. More than half of all slaves in 1860 worked on plantations, and most of those were fieldhands. The best jobs were those of household servants and skilled workers, including blacksmiths, carpenters, and coopers. Others might get special assignments as, say, boatmen or cooks. Housing for the fieldhands was usually in simple one- or two-room wooden shacks with dirt floors, some without windows. Of food there was usually a rough sufficiency, but one slave recalled that "de flour dat we make the biscuits out of wus de third-grade shorts." A distribution of clothing commonly came twice a year, but shoes were generally provided only in winter. On larger plantations there was sometimes an infirmary and regular sick call, but most planters resorted to doctors mainly in cases of sickness. In a material way slaves probably fared about as well as the poor in the rest of the world, perhaps better than the peasants of eastern Europe.

To some extent, chiefly in the rice and tobacco belts, work was parceled out by the task. But more commonly fieldhands worked long hours from dawn to dusk, or "from kin [see] to kaint." The slave codes gave little protection from long hours. South Carolina's limit of fifteen hours in winter and sixteen in summer exceeded the hours of daylight most of the year. The slave codes adopted in each state concerned themselves mainly with the owner's interests, and subjected the slaves not only to his governance but to surveillance by patrols of county militiamen, who struck fear into the slave quarters by abusing slaves found at large without a good explanation. Evidence suggests that a majority of both planters and small farmers used the whip, which the slave codes authorized. The difference between a good owner and a bad one, according to one ex-slave, was the difference between one who did not "whip too much" and one who "whipped till he's bloodied you and blistered you."

The ultimate recourse of slaves was rebellion or flight, but most recognized the futility of such measures with whites wielding most of the power and weapons. In the nineteenth century only three slave insurrections drew much notice, and two of those were betrayed before they got under way. In 1800 a slave named Gabriel on a plantation near Richmond hatched a plot involving perhaps a thousand others in a scheme to seize key points in Richmond and start a general slaughter of whites. Twenty-five slaves involved in the plot were executed and ten others deported. The Denmark Vesey plot in Charleston, discovered in 1822, was the plan of a free black to fall upon the white population of the town, seize ships in the harbor, and make for Santo Domingo. In this case thirty-five were executed and thirty-four deported. Only the Nat Turner insurrection of 1831 in rural Southhampton County, Virginia, got beyond the planning stage. Turner, a black overseer, was also a religious exhorter who professed a divine mission in leading the movement. The revolt began when a small group killed Turner's master's household and set off down the road repeating the process at other farmhouses, where other slaves joined the marauders. Before it ended at least fifty-five whites were killed. Eventually trials resulted in seventeen hangings and seven deportations, but the militia killed large numbers of slaves indiscriminately in the process of putting down the rebels.

Slaves more often retaliated against oppression by malingering, by pretending literal-mindedness in following orders, or by outright sabotage. There were constraints on such behavior, however, for laborers would likely eat better on a prosperous plantation than on one they had reduced to poverty. And the shrewdest slaveholders knew that they would more likely benefit from holding out rewards than from inflicting pain. Plantations based on the profit motive fostered between slaves and owners mutual dependency as well as natural antagonism. And in an agrarian society where personal relations counted for much, blacks could win concessions which moderated the harshness of slavery, permitting them a certain degree of individual and community development.

FORGING THE SLAVE COMMUNITY To generalize about slavery is to miss elements of diversity from place to place and from time to time. The experience could be as varied as people are. Historians of slavery in recent years have transferred their perspectives from the institutional aspects of slavery to the human aspects: what it was like to be held in bondage. At its worst, the historian Stanley M. Elkins has argued, slavery, like the concentration camps of Nazi Germany, dehumanized its victims, and turned them into creatures who internalized their masters' image of them. The slave thus actually became what he seemed to whites to be, a "Sambo" who in Elkins's words "was docile but irresponsible, loyal but lazy, humble but chronically given to lying and stealing," an adult "full of infantile silliness" and "utter dependence and childlike attachment." Some slaves were no doubt so beaten down as to fit the description, but slave lore was too full of stories about "puttin' on ole massa" to permit the belief that Sambo was often anything more than a protective mask put on to meet the white folks' expectations—and not all slaves would demean themselves in that way.

Slaves were victims, there was no question about that. But to stop with so obvious a perception would be to miss an important story of endurance and achievement. If ever there was a melting pot in American history, the most effective may have been that in which Africans from a variety of ethnic, linguistic, and tribal origins fused into a new community and a new culture as Afro-Americans.

Recent scholarship on slavery has looked inside the slave community, once thought inaccessible, mainly by taking seriously firsthand accounts previously discounted as unreliable. Most useful among these have been the slave narratives, life stories of slaves and former slaves published in the 1800s. Among the more interesting are *The Narrative of the Life of Frederick Douglass* (1845) and *Twenty Years a Slave* (1853) by Solomon Northrup, a free man in the North who was kidnapped and sold south into slavery.

Members of the slave community were bound together in helping and protecting one another, which in turn created a sense of cohesion and pride. Slave culture incorporated many African survivals, especially in areas where whites were few.

Among the Gullah Negroes of the South Carolina and Georgia coast, a researcher found as late as the 1940s more than 4,000 words still in use from the languages of twenty-one African tribes. But the important point, as another researcher put it, was not survivals which served "as quaint reminders of an exotic culture sufficiently alive to render the slaves picturesquely different but little more." The point was one of transformations in a living culture. Elements of African cultures thus "have continued to exist . . . as dynamic, living, creative parts of life in the United States," and have interacted with other cultures in which they came in contact.

SLAVE RELIGION AND FOLKLORE Among the most important manifestations of slave culture was the slaves' religion, a mixture of African and Christian elements. Most Africans brought with them a concept of a Creator, or Supreme God, whom they could recognize in Jehovah, and lesser gods whom they might identify with Christ, the Holy Ghost, and the saints, thereby reconciling their earlier beliefs with the new Christain religion. Alongside the church they maintanied beliefs in spirits, many of them benign magic, and conjuring. Belief in magic is in fact a common human response to conditions of danger or helplessness. Conjurors plied a brisk trade in the slave community, and often exercised considerable influence by promising protection against floggings, separations, and other dangers.

But slaves found greater comfort in the church. Masters sought to instill lessons of humility and obedience, but blacks could identify their plight with that of the Israelites in Egypt or of the God who suffered as they did. And the ultimate hope of a better world gave solace in this one. Some owners openly encouraged religious meetings among their slaves, but those who were denied the open use of "praise houses" held "bush meetings" in secret. The preachers and exhorters who sprang up in the slave world commonly won the acceptance of the owners if only because efforts to get rid of them proved futile. The peculiar cadences of their exhortations, chants, and spirituals were to the whites at best exotic but fundamentally mystifying. The ecstatic "ring shout," in which the celebrants moved rhythmically in a circle, was not a dance—as whites tended to believe—because, the worshippers said, they never crossed their feet. Because slave religion was so widely misperceived by whites, one historian has called it the "invisible institution" of the antebellum South.

"African culture was much more resistant to the bludgeon of slavery than historians have hitherto suspected," John Blassingame wrote in *The Slave Community* (1972). African cultural forms influenced a music of great rhythmic complexity, forms of dance and body language, spirituals and secular songs, and folk tales. Among oppressed peoples humor often becomes a means of psychological release, and there was a lively humor in the West African "trickster tales" of rabbits, tortoises, or Anansi the spider—relatively weak creatures who outwitted stronger animals. Afro-American folklore tended to be realistic in its images of wish-fulfillment. Until after emancipation there were few stories of superhuman heroes like Davy Crockett or Mike Fink, except for tales about captive Africans who escaped slavery by flying back home across the ocean. For the most part whites remained strangely blind and deaf to the black culture around them.

THE SLAVE FAMILY   Whites showed much the same ambivalence toward the slaves' instinct for family life. Slave marriages had no legal status, but slaveowners generally seem to have accepted marriage as a stabilizing influence on the plantation. Sometimes they performed marriages themselves or had a minister celebrate a formal wedding with all the trimmings. A common practice was the "broomstick wedding," in which the couple was married by simply jumping over a broomstick, a custom of un-

Several generations of a family raised in slavery. Plantation of J. J. Smith, Beaufort, South Carolina, 1862. [Library of Congress]

certain origin. But whatever the formalities, the norm for the slave community as for the white was the nuclear family of parents and children, with the father regarded as head of the family. Slaves also displayed a lively awareness of the extended family of cousins. Most slave children were socialized into their culture through the nuclear family, which afforded some degree of independence from white influence.

Slaves were not always allowed to realize this norm. In some cases the matter of family arrangements was ignored or left entirely up to the slaves on the assumption that black females were simply promiscuous—a convenient rationalization for sexual exploitation, to which the presence of many mulattoes attested. The census of 1860 reported 412,000 persons of mixed ancestry in the United States, or about 10 percent of the Negro population, probably a drastic undercount. That planters and their sons took advantage of female slaves was widely admitted, and sometimes defended on the grounds that the practice protected the chastity of white women. "Like the patriarchs of old," wrote Mary Boykin Chesnut, a plantation mistress of South Carolina, "our men live all in one house with their wives and concubines." And, she observed, "any lady is ready to tell you who is the father of all the mulatto children in everybody's household but her own."

ANTISLAVERY MOVEMENTS

EARLY OPPOSITION TO SLAVERY   From the Revolution to the early 1830s, few southern whites showed much disposition to defend the peculiar institution. But in the oft-used figure of speech, they had the wolf by the ears and could not let go. Such scattered antislavery groups and publications as existed in those years in fact were found mainly in the upper South. In 1815, for instance, Charles Osborn, a Quaker preacher, founded the Tennessee Manumission Society, and in 1819 Elihu Embree began the *Manumission Intelligencer*, soon renamed *The Emancipator*, in Jonesboro, Tennessee. In 1821 Benjamin Lundy established in Ohio the *Genius of Universal Emancipation*, later published at Greenville, Tennessee, and Baltimore. In 1827 Lundy counted 106 emancipation societies, with 5,150 members, in the slave states and only 24, with 1,475 members, in the free states. The North Carolina Manumission Society held meetings as late as 1834. These groups and publications urged masters to free their slaves voluntarily.

The emancipation movement got a new thrust with the formation of the American Colonization Society in 1817. The society proposed to colonize freed slaves in Africa, or as one historian put it, "more truly, away from America." Its supporters included such prominent figures as James Madison, James Monroe, Henry Clay, John Marshall, and Daniel Webster, and it appealed to diverse opinions. Some backed it as an antislavery group, while others saw it as a way to bolster slavery by getting rid of potentially troublesome free Negroes. Articulate elements of the free black community denounced it from the start. About a month after the group's founding, when James Forten, a successful sailmaker and Revolutionary War veteran, called upon the assembled free blacks of Philadelphia to vote on the proposition, he got a long, tremendous "No" which, he wrote, "seemed as if it would bring down the walls of the building." America, the blacks insisted, was their native land.

In 1821, nevertheless, agents of the Society acquired from local chieftains in West Africa a parcel of land which became the nucleus of a new country. In 1822 the first freed slaves arrived there, and twenty-five years later the society relinquished control to the independent republic of Liberia. But given its uncertain purpose, the colonization movement fell between two stools. It got meager support from either antislavery or proslavery elements. In all, up to 1860 only about 15,000 blacks migrated to Africa, approximately 12,000 with the help of the Colonization Society. The number was infinitesimal compared to the number of slave births.

A certificate of membership in the New York City Colonization Society. Natives of Liberia welcome society members and a ship carrying freed slaves from America. [Oberlin College Archives]

FROM GRADUALISM TO ABOLITIONISM   Meanwhile in the early 1830s the antislavery movement took a new departure. Three dramatic events marked its transition from favoring gradualism to demanding the immediate end of slavery. In 1829 a pamphlet appeared in Boston: *Walker's Appeal . . . to the Colored Citizens of the World*. Its author, David Walker, born a free Negro in North Carolina, preached insurrection and violence as a proper response to the wrongs that blacks suffered. Over the next few years Walker circulated the pamphlet widely among blacks and white sympathizers. While free Negroes in parts of the South were known to have read it, the message appears to have reached few slaves.

Two other major events followed in close sequence during 1831. On January 1, William Lloyd Garrison began publication in Boston of a new antislavery newspaper, *The Liberator*. Garrison, who rose from poverty in Newburyport, Massachusetts, had been apprenticed to a newspaperman and had edited a number of papers. For two years he worked on Benjamin Lundy's *Genius of Universal Emancipation* in Baltimore, but became restless with Lundy's moderation. In the first issue of his new paper he renounced "the popular but pernicious doctrine of gradual emancipation" and vowed: "I will be as harsh as truth, and as uncompromising as justice. On this subject, I do not wish to think, or speak, or write, with moderation. . . . I am in earnest—I will not equivocate—I will not excuse—I will not retreat a single inch AND I WILL BE HEARD."

And he was heard, mainly at first because his language provoked outraged retorts from slaveholders who publicized the paper more than his own supporters did. Circulation in fact was never very large, but copies went to papers with much wider cir-

William Lloyd Garrison. [Metropolitan Museum of Art]

culations. In the South, literate blacks would more likely encounter Garrison's ideas in the local papers than in what few
copies of *The Liberator* found their way to them. Slaveholders'
outrage mounted higher after the Nat Turner insurrection in August 1831. Garrison, they assumed, bore a large part of the responsibility for the affair, but there is no evidence that Nat
Turner had ever heard of him, and Garrison said that he had not a
single subscriber in the South at the time. What is more, however
violent his language, Garrison was a pacifist, opposed to the use
of physical violence.

THE AMERICAN ANTI-SLAVERY SOCIETY   A period of organization followed these events. In 1832 Garrison and his followers set up the
New England Anti-Slavery Society. In 1833 two wealthy New
York merchants, Arthur and Lewis Tappan, founded a similar
group in their state and the same year took the lead in starting a
national society with the help of Garrison and a variety of other
antislavery people. They hoped to exploit the publicity gained
by the British antislavery movement, which that same year had
induced Parliament to end slavery, with compensation to slaveholders, throughout the British Empire.

The American Anti-Slavery Society conceded in its constitution the right of each state to legislate on its domestic institutions, but set a goal of convincing fellow citizens "that
Slaveholding is a heinous crime in the sight of God, and that the
duty, safety, and best interests of all concerned, require its *immediate abandonment*, without expatriation." The society went
beyond the issue of emancipation to argue that blacks should
"share an equality with the whites, of civil and religious privileges."

The group set about organizing a barrage of propaganda for its
cause, including periodicals, tracts, agents, lecturers, organizers,
and fund-raisers. Probably its most effective single agent was
Theodore Dwight Weld of Ohio, a convert and disciple of the
great evangelist Charles Grandison Finney. In 1834 Weld led a
group of students at Lane Theological Seminary in Cincinnati in
a protracted discussion of abolition. Efforts of its president,
Lyman Beecher, and the trustees to repress this interruption of
normal routine led to a mass secession from Lane and the start of
a new theological school at the recently opened Oberlin College.
The move won the financial and moral support of the Tappans.
Weld and a number of the "Lane rebels" set out to evangelize
the country for abolition. Weld earned the reputation of trouble-
maker and "the most mobbed man in the United States," but at
the same time he displayed a genius for turning enemies into dis-

ciples. In 1836 Weld conducted a New York training school for lecturers from which seventy apostles went out two by two to weave a network of abolitionist organizations across the North. Publications by Weld included *The Bible Against Slavery* (1837) and *American Slavery as It is: Testimony of a Thousand Witnesses* (1839), the latter including examples of atrocities against slaves gathered from news accounts. The book sold 100,000 copies in its first year.

THE MOVEMENT SPLITS As the movement spread, debates over tactics inevitably grew. The Garrisonians, mainly New Englanders, were radicals who felt that American society had been corrupted from top to bottom and needed universal reform. Garrison embraced just about every important reform movement that came down the pike in those years: antislavery, temperance, pacifism, and women's rights. Deeply affected by the perfectionism of the times, he refused to compromise principle for expediency, to sacrifice one reform for another. Abolition was not enough. He opposed colonization of freed slaves and stood for equal rights. He broke with the organized church, which to his mind was in league with slavery. The federal government, with its Fugitive Slave Law, was all the more so. The Constitution, he said, was "a covenant with death and an agreement with hell." Garrison therefore refused to vote. He was, however, prepared to collaborate with those who did or with those who disagreed with him on other matters.

Other reformers saw American society as fundamentally sound and concentrated their attention on purging it of slavery. Garrison struck them as an impractical fanatic. A showdown came in 1840 on the issue of women's rights. Women had joined the movement from the start, but quietly and largely in groups without men. The activities of the Grimké sisters brought the issue of women's rights forward. Sarah and Angelina Grimké, daughters of a prominent South Carolina family, had moved north to embrace antislavery and other reforms. Their publications included Angelina's *Appeal to the Christian Women of the South* (1836), calling on southern women to speak and act against slavery, and Sarah's *Letter on the Equality of the Sexes and the Condition of Women* (1838). Having attended Weld's school for antislavery apostles in New York (Sarah later married Weld), they set out speaking to women in New England and slowly widened their audiences to "promiscuous assemblies" of both men and women. Such unseemly behavior inspired the Congregational clergy of Massachusetts to pontificate in a pastoral letter: "If the vine . . . thinks to assume the independence and overshadowing nature of the elm, it will not only cease to bear fruit, but fall in shame and dishonor in the dust." But the Grimké sisters declined the role of clinging vines.

At the Anti-Slavery Society's meeting in 1840 the Garrisonians insisted on the right of women to participate equally in the organization, and carried their point. They did not commit the group to women's rights in any other way, however. Contrary opinion, mainly from the Tappans' New York group, ranged from outright antifeminism to simple fear of scattering shots on too many reforms. The New Yorkers broke away to form the American and Foreign Anti-Slavery Society. Weld, who had probably done more than anybody else to build the movement, declined to go with either group. Like the New Yorkers, he preferred to focus on slavery as the central evil of the times, but he could not accept their "anti-woman" attitude, as he saw it. Discouraged by the bickering, he drifted away from the movement he had done so much to build and into a long-term teaching career.

BLACK ANTISLAVERY   Antislavery men also balked at granting full recognition to black abolitionists of either sex. Often blindly patronizing, white leaders expected blacks to take a back seat in the movement. Not all blacks were easily put down, and most became exasperated at whites' tendency to value purity over results, to strike a moral posture at the expense of action. But despite the invitation to form separate black groups, black leaders were active in the white societies from the beginning. Three attended the organizational meeting of the American Anti-Slavery Society in 1833, and some became outstanding agents for the movement, notably the former slaves who could speak from firsthand experience. Garrison pronounced such men as Henry Bibb and William Wells Brown, both escapees from Kentucky, and Frederick Douglass, who fled Maryland, "the best qualified to address the public on the subject of slavery." Douglass, blessed with an imposing frame and a gift of eloquence, became the best known black man in America. "I appear before the immense assembly this evening as a thief and a robber," he told a Massachusetts group in 1842. "I stole this head, these limbs, this body from my master, and ran off with them." Fearful of capture after publishing his *Narrative of the Life of Frederick Douglass* (1845), he left for an extended lecture tour of the British Isles and returned two years later with enough money to purchase his freedom. He then started an abolitionist newspaper for blacks, the *North Star*, in Rochester, New York.

Douglass's *Narrative* was but the best known among a hundred or more such accounts. Escapees often made it out on their own

Frederick Douglass (left) and Sojourner Truth (right) were both leading abolitionists. [Library of Congress; New-York Historical Society]

—Douglass borrowed a pass from a free black seaman—but many were aided by the Underground Railroad, which grew in legend into a vast system to conceal runaways and spirit them to freedom, often over the Canadian border. Levi Coffin, a North Carolina Quaker who moved to Cincinnati and did help many fugitives, was the reputed president. Actually, there seems to have been more spontaneity than system about the matter, and blacks contributed more than was credited in the legend. Experience had conditioned escapees to distrust whites. One escapee recalled later: "We did not dare ask [for food], except when we found a slave's or a free colored person's house remote from any other, and then we were never refused, if they had food to give." A few intrepid refugees actually ventured back into slave states to organize escapes. Harriet Tubman, the most celebrated, went back nineteen times. Most refugees came from the upper South. Among the few who made it out of the Deep South, William and Ellen Craft of Macon, Georgia, devised one of the cleverest ruses. Being light-skinned she disguised herself as a decrepit planter accompanied north for medical aid by a faithful servant.

REACTIONS TO ANTISLAVERY Even the road north, many blacks found to their dismay, did not lead to the Promised Land. North of slavery, they encountered much of the discrimination and segregation that freed slaves would later encounter in the southern states. When Prudence Crandall of Connecticut admitted a black girl to her private school in 1833, she lost most of her white pupils. She held out in the face of insults, vandalism, and a law which made her action illegal, but closed the school after eighteen months and left the state. Garrison, Douglass, Weld, and other abolitionists had to face down hostile crowds who disliked blacks or found antislavery agitation bad for business. In 1837 a hostile mob killed the antislavery editor Elijah P. Lovejoy, in Alton, Illinois, giving the movement a martyr to both abolition and freedom of the press.

By then proslavery southerners, by seeking to suppress discussion of emancipation, had already given abolitionists ways to link antislavery with the cause of civil liberties for whites. In the summer of 1835 a mob destroyed several sacks of abolitionist literature in the Charleston post office. The postmaster had announced that he would not try to deliver such matter. Bitter debates in Congress ensued. President Jackson wanted a law against handling "incendiary literature," but Congress failed to oblige him. The postmaster-general, nevertheless, did nothing about forcing delivery.

One shrewd political strategy, promoted by Weld, was to deluge Congress with petitions for abolition in the District of Columbia. Most such petitions were presented by former President John Quincy Adams, elected to the House from Massachusetts in 1830. In 1836, however, the House adopted a rule to lay abolition petitions automatically on the table, in effect ignoring them. Adams, "Old Man Eloquent," stubbornly fought this "Gag Rule" as a violation of the First Amendment, and hounded its supporters until the Gag Rule was finally repealed in 1844.

Meanwhile, in 1840, the year of the schism in the antislavery movement, a small group of abolitionists called a convention in Albany, New York, and launched the Liberty party, with James G. Birney, one-time slaveholder of Alabama and Kentucky, as its candidate for president. Birney, converted to the cause by Weld, had tried without success to publish an antislavery paper in Danville, Kentucky. He then moved it to Ohio and in 1837 became executive secretary of the American Anti-Slavery Society. In the 1840 election he polled only 7,000 votes, but in 1844 his vote rose to 60,000, and from that time forth an antislavery party contested every national election until Abraham Lincoln won the presidency.

THE DEFENSE OF SLAVERY   Birney was but one among a number of southerners propelled north during the 1830s by the south's growing hostility to emancipationist ideas. Antislavery in the upper South had its last stand in 1831–1832 when the Virginia legislature debated a plan of gradual emancipation and colonization, then rejected it by a vote of 73 to 58. Thereafter, leaders of southern thought worked out an elaborate intellectual defense of slavery, presenting it as a positive good rather than, in the words of Tennessee's constitutional convention of 1834, "a great evil" that "the wisest heads and most benevolent hearts" had not been able to dispose of.

In 1832 Prof. Thomas R. Dew of the College of William and Mary published the most comprehensive defense of slavery produced to that time, his *Review of the Debate of the Virginia Legislature of 1831 and 1832*. In it he made the practical argument that the natural increase of the slave population would outrun any colonization effort. But he went on to justify slavery as required by the circumstances of southern life and the condition of human inequality, citing as authorities the Bible, Aristotle, and Edmund Burke.

The biblical argument became one of the most powerful. The evangelical churches, which had widely condemned slavery at one time, gradually turned proslavery. Ministers of all denominations joined in the argument. Had not the patriarchs of the Old Testament held bondsmen? Had not Noah, upon awakening from a drunken stupor, cursed Canaan, son of Ham, from whom the Negroes were descended? Had not Saint Paul advised servants to obey their masters and told a fugitive servant to return to his master? And had not Jesus remained silent on the subject, at least so far as the Gospels reported his words? In 1844–1845 disputes over slavery split two great denominations and led to the formation of the Methodist Episcopal Church, South, and the Southern Baptist Convention.

Another, and fundamental, feature of the proslavery argument developed a theory of the intrinsic inferiority of Negroes. Most whites, blind and deaf to the complexity of black culture, assumed that the evidence of their eyes and ears confirmed their own superiority. The weight of scientific opinion, which was not above prejudice on such matters, was on their side, but it is doubtful that many felt the need of science to prove what seemed so obvious to them. Stereotyping the poor and powerless as inferior is an old and seemingly ineradicable human habit. There was in fact a theory championed by Dr. Josiah C. Nott, a physician of Mobile, Alabama, that blacks were the product of a separate creation, but this challenged orthodox faith in the biblical account of creation and was generally rejected.

Other arguments took a more "practical" view of slavery. Not only was slavery profitable, it was a matter of social necessity. Jefferson, for instance, in his *Notes On Virginia* (1785), had argued that emancipated slaves and whites could not live together without risk of race war growing out of the recollection of past injustices. What is more, it seemed clear that blacks could not be expected to work under conditions of freedom. They were too shiftless and improvident, the argument went, and in freedom would be a danger to themselves as well as to others. White workmen, on the other hand, feared their competition. Whites were struck with fear too by the terrible example of the bloody rebellion in Santo Domingo.

In 1856 William J. Grayson of Charleston published a lengthy poem, *The Hireling and the Slave*, which defended slavery as better for the worker than the "wage slavery" of northern industry. George Fitzhugh of Virginia developed the same argument, among others, in two books: *Sociology for the South; or, The Failure of a Free Society* (1854) and *Cannibals All! or, Slaves Without Masters* (1857). Few if any socialists ever waxed more eloquent over the evils of industrial capitalism than these proslavery theorists. The factory system had brought abuses and neglect far worse than those of slavery. Slavery, Fitzhugh argued, was the truest form of socialism, for it provided security for the workers in sickness and old age, whereas workers in the North were exploited for profit and then cast aside without compunction. Men were not born equal, he insisted: "It would be far nearer the truth to say that some were born with saddles on their backs, and others booted and spurred to ride them—and the riding does them good." Fitzhugh argued for an organic, hierarchical society, much like the family, in which each had a place with both rights and obligations. Calhoun endorsed slavery with the more popular argument that it freed masters from drudgery to pursue higher things, and thus made possible a Greek democracy—or what one historian has more aptly tagged a "Herrenvolk [master race] democracy."

Within one generation such ideas had triumphed in the white South over the postrevolutionary apology for slavery as an evil bequeathed by the forefathers. Opponents of the orthodox faith in slavery as a positive good were either silenced or exiled. Freedom of thought in the Old South had become a victim of the nation's growing obsession with slavery.

FURTHER READING

Those interested in the problem of separating myth from reality in the southern experience should consult Patrick Gerster and William Cords (eds.), *Myth and Image in Southern History* (vol. 1, 1974)°, for

° These books are available in paperback editions.

various essays on the topic. William R. Taylor's *Cavalier and Yankee: The Old South and American National Character* (1961)° is also helpful. W. J. Cash's *The Mind of the South* (1940)° remains a classic on the subject.

I. A. Newby's *The American South* (1979), Monroe Billington's *The American South* (1971), and Clement Eaton's *A History of the Old South* (1975) offer good surveys of the antebellum period. More specific are Charles S. Syndnor's *The Development of Southern Sectionalism, 1819–1848* (1948),° and Avery O. Craven's *The Growth of Southern Nationalism, 1848–1860* (1953).°

The dominance of the plantation system is analyzed in Ulrich B. Phillips's *Life and Labor in the Old South* (1929)° and Lewis C. Gray's *History of Agriculture in the Southern United States to 1860* (vol. 2, 1933). Frank L. Owsley's *Plain Folk of the South* (1949)° argues that yeomen farmers were dominant in many aspects of antebellum agriculture. A Marxist analysis of the plantations system is Eugene Genovese's *The World the Slaveholders Made* (1969),° while Gavin Wright's *The Political Economy of the Cotton South* (1978)° is while more economic in approach.

A firsthand description of cotton growing in the South comes from Frederick Law Olmsted's *The Cotton Kingdom* (1861, 1953), based on his travels in the region just before the Civil War. The concept of agricultural reform is handled in Avery O. Craven's *Edmund Ruffin, Southerner* (1932),° and Betty L. Mitchell's *Edmund Ruffin, A Biography* (1981). The support system of merchants, factors, and bankers is described in both Harold Woodman's *King Cotton and His Retainers* (1968) and Lewis Atherton's *The Southern Country Store, 1800–1860* (1948). How southerners distributed their agricultural produce is the subject of Samuel Hilliard's *Hog Meat and Hoe Cake: Food Supply in the Antebellum South, 1840–1860* (1972).

Why southern industry lagged behind agriculture is treated in relevant chapters of Eugene Genovese's *The Political Economy of Slavery* (1962).° The life of a pioneer southern industrialist is documented in Broadus Mitchell's *William Gregg* (1928). Ernest Lander's *Antebellum Textiles in South Carolina* (1969) handles the origins of Piedmont cotton mills. Thomas Weiss and Fred Bateman's *A Deplorable Scarcity* (1981) explores the unfulfilled potential for southern industrial growth. Robert Starobin's *Industrial Slavery in the Old South* (1970)° and Claudia Goldin's *Urban Slavery in the South, 1820–1860* (1976), take opposing viewpoints on the use of bondsmen in nonagricultural labor.

The historiography of slavery and racism contains some of the most exciting and controversial scholarship in American letters. The first major work, U. B. Phillips's *American Negro Slavery* (1919), stressed a benign paternalism among planters. That view went generally unchallenged until Kenneth Stampp's *The Peculiar Institution* (1956)° showed how slaves resisted the oppression they faced. The idea of a creative black personality was challenged in Stanley Elkins's *Slavery: A Problem in American Intellectual Life* (1963).° More recent scholarship emphasizes the self-generative, dynamic character of black society under slavery. Harold Rawick's *From Sunup to Sundown* (1967), John W.

Blassingame's *The Slave Community: Plantation Life in the Antebellum South* (1972),° Eugene Genevese's *Roll, Jordan, Roll: The World the Slaves Made* (1974),° and Herbert Gutman's *The Black Family in Slavery and Freedom* (1976)° all stress the theme of a persisting and identifiable slave culture.

Most controversial has been the profitability of slavery. Harold A. Woodman handles the topic in *Slavery and the Southern Economy* (1966). Robert W. Fogel and Stanley L. Engerman sparked controversy with *Time on the Cross: The Economics of Negro Slavery* (1974),° which argues that not only did planters benefit from bondage, but that slaves themselves incorporated a Victorian work ethic based on incentives. Herbert Gutman reviews this controversy in *Slavery and the Numbers Game* (1975).°

Other recent works on slavery include R. C. Wade's *Slavery in the Cities* (1964), Leslie H. Owens's *This Species of Property* (1976),° Nathan I. Huggins's *Black Odyssey* (1977),° Lawrence W. Levine's *Black Culture and Black Consciousness: Afro-American Folk Thought from Slavery to Freedom* (1977),° Albert J. Raboteau's *Slave Religion: The "Invisible Institution" in the Antebellum South* (1978),° and Joel Williamson's *Miscegenation and Mulattoes in the United States* (1982). Much of the oral history used to construct some of the new concepts on slavery is in John W. Blassingame (ed.), *Slave Testimony* (1977).°

Quite a number of overviews of abolitionism are worth inspection. For background on the origins of antislavery thought in Western civilization, consult David Brion Davis's *The Problem of Slavery in Western Culture* (1966).° Other surveys include Louis Filler's *The Crusade against Slavery* (1960)° Merton L. Dillon's *The Abolitionists: The Growth of a Dissenting Minority* (1974),° Ronald G. Walters's *The Anti-Slavery Appeal* (1976), and James B. Stewart's *Holy Warriors: The Abolitionists and American Slavery* (1976).° Also valuable is a collection of documents edited by Donald G. Mathews, *Agitators for Freedom: The Abolitionist Movement* (1972).

For particular emphasis on the religious background of abolitionism, see Gilbert H. Barnes's *The Anti-Slavery Impulse* (1933), which imparts a central role to Theodore Dwight Weld. For a contrasting viewpoint, see Aileen S. Kraditor's *Means and Ends in Anti-Slavery Thought* (1967), with its stress on the role of the Garrisonians. More philosophical is Lewis Perry's *Radical Abolitionists: Anarchy and the Government of God in Anti-Slave Thought* (1973). A comparative approach is Lewis Perry and Michael Fellman (eds.), *Anti-Slavery Reconsidered: New Perspectives on the Abolitionists* (1979).

Numerous biographies of the leading abolitionists contribute to an understanding of the movement: Betty Fladefeld's *James Gillespie Birney: Slaveholder to Abolitionist* (1955), Walter M. Merrill's *Against Wind and Tide: A Biography of William Lloyd Garrison* (1963), John L. Thomas's *The Liberator: William Lloyd Garrison* (1963), Gerda Lerner's *The Grimké Sisters from South Carolina: Rebels against Slavery* (1967),° Bertram Wyatt-Brown's *Lewis Tappan and the Evangelical War against Slavery* (1969), James B. Stewart's *Joshua Giddings and the Tactics of*

Radical Politics (1970), and Robert Abzug's *Passionate Liberator: Theodore Dwight Weld and the Dilemma of Reform* (1980).°

The role free blacks played in the antislavery movement appears in Benjamin Quarles's *Black Abolitionists* (1969)°. Jane H. and William H. Pease also examine the role of black abolitionists in *They Who Would Be Free* (1974)°. The legend and the reality of the underground railroad is explored in Larry Gara's *The Liberty Line* (1961)°. A recent work on the leading black abolitionist is Arna Bontemps's *Free at Last: The Life of Frederick Douglass* (1971). Surveys of black history for the period include John Hope Franklin's *From Slavery to Freedom* (1974),° Leon F. Litwack's *North of Slavery: The Negro in the Free States, 1790–1860* (1961),° and Ira Berlin's *Slaves without Masters* (1975),° on southern free blacks.

The literature on white reaction to the antislavery movement includes Russel B. Nye's *Fettered Freedom: Civil Liberties and the Slavery Controversy* (1963), Leonard L. Richards's *"Gentlemen of Property and Standing": Anti-Abolition Mobs in Jacksonian America* (1970), and Thomas O. Morris's *Free Men All: The Personal Liberty Laws of the North, 1780–1861* (1974).

For the proslavery argument as it developed in the South, see William J. Cooper's *The South and the Politics of Slavery, 1828–1856* (1978),° and James Oakes's *The Ruling Race: A History of American Slaveholders* (1982).° Harvey Wish's *George Fitzhugh* (1943) examines the role of the leading southern apologist for slavery. The role which churches played in the argument appears in H. Shelton Smith's *In His Image, But. . . : Racism in Southern Religion, 1780–1910* (1972). Also helpful for the conflict within one denomination is Donald G. Mathews's *Methodism and Slavery* (1965). The problems leading southerners had in justifying slavery is explored in Drew G. Faust's *A Sacred Circle: The Dilemma of the Intellectual in the Old South, 1840–1860* (1977), and Carl N. Degler's *The Other South: Southern Dissenters in the Nineteenth Century* (1974).° How one family coped with ambiguous feelings about slavery is shown in Drew G. Faust's *James Henry Hammond and the Old South* (1982). Dickson D. Bruce, Jr., explores the white tendency toward a physical defense of slavery in *Violence and Culture in the Antebellum South* (1979). George M. Frederickson's *The Black Image in the White Mind* (1971)° examines a variety of racial stereotypes held by white southerners.

16

THE CRISIS OF UNION

SLAVERY IN THE TERRITORIES

John C. Calhoun and Ralph Waldo Emerson had little else in common, but both men sensed in the Mexican War the omens of a greater disaster. Mexico was "the forbidden fruit; the penalty of eating it would be to subject our institutions to political death," Calhoun warned. "The United States will conquer Mexico," Emerson conceded, "but it will be as the man swallows the arsenic. . . . Mexico will poison us." Wars, as both men knew, have a way of breeding new wars, often in unforseen ways. Like Britain's conquest of New France, the winning of the Southwest gave rise in turn to quarrels over newly acquired lands. In each case the quarrels set in train a series of disputes: Britain's crisis of empire had its counterpart in America's crisis of union.

THE WILMOT PROVISO The Mexican War was less than three months old when the seeds of a new conflict began to sprout. On Saturday evening, August 8, 1846, a sweltering House of Representatives reassembled to clear its calendar for adjournment. Polk had sent Congress that noon a hurried request for $2 million to expedite negotiations with Mexico. He expected little hindrance, since party discipline had already whipped through most of his program. But the House, resentful of Polk's triumphs, was ripe for revolt when a freshman Democrat from Pennsylvania, David Wilmot, stood up. He favored expansion, Wilmot explained, even the annexation of Texas as a slave state. But slavery had come to an end in Mexico, and if free soil should be acquired, "God forbid that we should be the means of planting this institution upon it." Drawing upon the words of the Northwest Ordinance, he offered a fateful amendment: in lands acquired from

Mexico, "neither slavery nor involuntary servitude shall ever exist in any part of said territory, except for crime, whereof the party shall first be duly convicted."

Within ten minutes an otherwise obscure congressman had immortalized his name. The Wilmot Proviso, although never a law, politicized slavery once and for all. For a generation, since the Missouri Controversy of 1819–1821, the issue had been lurking in the wings, kept there most of the time by politicians who feared its disruptive force. From that day forth, for two decades the question would never be far from center stage.

The first flurry of excitement passed quickly, however. The House adopted the Wilmot Proviso that Saturday night. The following Monday the Senate refused to concur and Congress adjourned without giving Polk his $2 million. When Congress reconvened in December Polk prevailed on Wilmot to withhold his amendment when he asked for the money again, but by then others were ready to take up the cause. When Preston King of New York revived the proviso he signaled a revolt by the Van Burenites in concert with the antislavery forces of the North. Once again the House approved the amendment. Once again the Senate refused. In March the House finally gave in, but in one form or another Wilmot's idea kept cropping up. Abraham Lincoln later recalled that during one term as congressman, 1847–1849, he voted for it "as good as forty times."

John C. Calhoun meanwhile devised a thesis to counter the proviso and set it before the Senate in four resolutions on February 19, 1847. The Calhoun Resolutions, which never came to a vote, argued that since the territories were the common possession of the states, Congress had no right to prevent any citizen from taking his slaves into them. To do so would violate the Fifth Amendment, which forbade Congress to deprive any person of life, liberty, or property without due process of law, and slaves were property. Thus by a clever stroke of logic Calhoun took that basic guarantee of liberty, the Bill of Rights, and turned it into a basic guarantee of slavery. The irony was not lost on his critics, but the point became established southern dogma— echoed by his colleagues and formally endorsed by the Virginia legislature.

Thomas Hart Benton of Missouri, himself a slaveholder but also a Jacksonian nationalist, found in Calhoun's resolutions a set of abstractions "leading to no result." Wilmot and Calhoun between them, he said, had fashioned a pair of shears. Neither blade alone would cut very well, but joined together they could sever the ties of union. Within another year Benton was complaining that the slavery issue had become like the plague of frogs in Pharaoh's Egypt, with "this black question, forever on the table, on the nuptial couch, everywhere."

POPULAR SOVEREIGNTY   Many others, like Benton, refused to be polarized, seeking to bypass the conflict that was brewing. President Polk was among the first to suggest extending the Missouri Compromise dividing free and slave territory at latitude 36° 30′ all the way to the Pacific. Sen. Lewis Cass of Michigan suggested that the citizens of a territory "regulate their own internal concerns in their own way," like the citizens of a state. Such an approach would combine the merits of expediency and democracy. It would take the issue out of the national arena and put it in the hands of those directly affected.

Popular sovereignty, or squatter sovereignty, as the idea was alternatively called, had much to commend it, including an ambiguity which improved the presidential prospects of Cass. Without directly challenging the slaveholders' access to the new lands, it promised to open them quickly to free farmers who would almost surely dominate the territories. With this tacit understanding the idea prospered in Cass's Old Northwest, where Stephen A. Douglas of Illinois and other prominent Democrats soon endorsed it. Popular sovereignty, they hoped, might check the magnetic pull toward the opposite poles of Wilmot and Calhoun.

When the Mexican War ended in 1848, the question of bondage in the new territories was no longer hypothetical—unless one reasoned, as many did, that their arid climate excluded plantation crops and therefore excluded slavery. For Calhoun, who leaned to that opinion, that was beside the point since the right to carry slaves into the territories was the outer defense line of the peculiar institution, not be yielded without opening the way to further assaults. In fact there is little reason in retrospect to credit the argument that slavery had reached its natural limits of expansion. Slavery had been adapted to occupations other than plantation agriculture. Besides, on irrigated lands, cotton later became a staple crop of the Southwest.

Nobody doubted that Oregon would become free soil, but it too was drawn into the maelstrom of controversy. Territorial status, pending since 1846, was delayed because its provisional government had excluded slavery. To concede that provision would imply an authority drawn from the powers of Congress, since a territory was created by Congress. Finally, a Senate committee proposed to let Oregon exclude slavery but to deny the territories of California and New Mexico any power to legislate at all on the subject, thus passing the issue to the courts. The question of slavery, previously outlawed under Mexican rule, could rise on appeal to the Supreme Court and thus be kept out of the political arena. The Senate accepted this but the House rejected it, and finally an exhausted Congress let Oregon organize without slavery, but postponed decision on the Southwest. Polk signed the bill on the principle that Oregon was north of 36°30′.

Polk had promised to serve only one term; exhausted by his labors and having reached his major goals, he refused to run again. In the Democratic convention Lewis Cass took an early lead and won nomination on the fourth ballot. The Democratic party had endorsed the author of squatter sovereignty, but its platform simply denied the power of Congress to interfere with slavery in the states and criticized all efforts to bring the question before Congress. The Whigs devised an even more artful shift. Once again, as in 1840, they passed over their party leader for a general, Zachary Taylor, whose fame and popularity had grown since the Battle of Buena Vista. He was a legal resident of Louisiana who owned more than a hundred slaves, an apolitical figure who had never voted in a national election. Once again, as in 1840, the party adopted no platform at all. While most of Taylor's support came from the South, Thurlow Weed and William H. Seward of New York had favored him and helped engineer a vice-presidential nomination for New Yorker Millard Fillmore.

THE FREE-SOIL COALITION But the antislavery impulse was not easily squelched. Wilmot had raised a standard to which a broad coalition could rally. Men who shied away from abolitionism could readily endorse the exclusion of slavery from the territories. The Northwest Ordinance and the Missouri Compromise supplied honored precedents. By doing so, moreover, one could strike a blow for liberty without caring about slavery itself, or about the slaves. One might simply want free soil for white farmers, while keeping the unwelcome blacks far away in the South, where they belonged. Free soil, therefore, rather than abolition, became the rallying point—and also the name of a new party.

Three major groups entered the free-soil coalition: rebellious Democrats, antislavery Whigs, and members of the Liberty party, which dated from 1840. Disaffection among the Democrats centered in New York, where the Van Burenite "Barnburners" squared off against the pro-administration "Hunkers" in a factional dispute which had as much to do with personal ambitions as with local politics. Each group gave the other its name, the one for its alleged purpose to rule or ruin like the farmer who burned his barn to get rid of the rats, the other for hankering or "hunkering" after office.

As their conflict grew, however, the Barnburners seized on the free-soil issue as a means of winning support. When the Democratic convention voted to divide the state's votes between contesting delegations, they bolted the party and named Van Buren as their candidate for president on a free-soil platform. Other Wilmot Democrats, including Wilmot himself, joined the revolt. Revolt among the Whigs centered in Massachusetts where a group of "conscience" Whigs battled the "cotton" Whigs. The latter, according to Charles Sumner, belonged to a coalition of northern businessmen and southern planters, "the lords of the lash and the lords of the loom." Conscience Whigs rejected the slaveholder, Taylor. The third group in the coalition, the abolitionist Liberty party, had already nominated Sen. John P. Hale of New Hampshire for president.

In August these groups—Barnburners, Conscience Whigs, and Liberty party men—organized the Free Soil party in a convention at Buffalo. Its presidential nomination went to Martin Van Buren by a close margin over Hale, while the vice-presidential nomination went to Charles Francis Adams, a Conscience Whig. The old Jacksonian and the son of John Quincy Adams made strange bedfellows indeed! The old Liberty party was rewarded with a platform plank which pledged the government to

*An 1848 Free Soil party banner.
The party's slogan was "Free Soil,
Free Labor, Free Speech."
[Library of Congress]*

abolish slavery whenever such action became constitutional, but the party's main principle was the Wilmot Proviso and it entered the campaign with the catchy slogan of "free soil, free speech, free labor, and free men."

Its impact on the election was mixed. The Free Soilers split the Democractic vote enough to throw New York to Taylor, and the Whig vote enough to give Ohio to Cass, but Van Buren's total of 291,000 votes was far below the popular totals of 1,361,000 for Taylor and 1,222,000 for Cass. Taylor won with 163 to 127 electoral votes, and both major parties retained a national following. Taylor took eight slave states and seven free; Cass just the opposite, seven slave and eight free.

STATEHOOD FOR CALIFORNIA Meanwhile a new dimension had been introduced into the question of the territories. On January 24, 1848, nine days before Trist signed the Mexican peace treaty, gold was discovered in California. The word spread quickly, and Polk's confirmation of the discovery in his last annual message, on December 5, 1848, turned the gold-fever into a worldwide contagion.

During 1849, by the best estimates, more than 80,000 persons reached California. Probably 55,000 went overland; the rest went by way of Panama or Cape Horn. Along the western slopes of the Sierra Nevada they thronged the valleys and canyons in a wide belt from LaPorte southward to Mariposa. The village of San Francisco, located near the harbor entrance Frémont had aptly named Golden Gate, grew rapidly into a city. The influx quickly reduced the Mexicans to a minority, and sporadic conflicts with the Indians of the Sierra Nevada foothills decimated the native peoples. In 1850 Americans already accounted for 68 percent of the population and there was a cosmopolitan array of "Sydney Ducks" from Australia, "Kanakas" from Hawaii, "Limies" from London, "Paddies" from Ireland, "Coolies" from China, and "Keskydees" from Paris (who were always asking "Qu'est-ce qu'il dit?").

Zachary Taylor did not remain an enigma for long. Born in Virginia, raised in Kentucky, he had been a soldier most of his adult life, with service in the War of 1812, the Black Hawk and Seminole Wars, as well as in Mexico. Constantly on the move, he had acquired a home in Louisiana and a plantation in Mississippi. Southern Whigs had rallied to his support, expecting him to uphold the cause of slavery. Instead they had turned up a southern man with Union principles, who had no more use for Calhoun's proslavery abstractions than Jackson had for his nullification doctrine. Innocent of politics Taylor might be, and to southern Whigs it was ominous that the antislavery Seward had his ear, but "Old Rough and Ready" had the direct mind of the soldier he was. Slavery should be upheld where it existed, he felt, but he had little patience with abstract theories about slavery in territories where it probably could not exist. Why not make California and New Mexico into states immediately, he reasoned, and bypass the whole issue?

But the Californians, in need of organized government, were already ahead of him. By December 1849, without leave of Congress, California had a free-state government in operation. New Mexico responded more slowly, but by June 1850 Americans there had adopted another free-state constitution. The Mormons around Salt Lake, meanwhile, drafted a basic law for the imperial state of Deseret, which embraced most of the Mexican Cession, including a slice of the coast from Los Angeles to San Diego.

In Taylor's annual message on December 4, 1849, he endorsed immediate statehood for California and enjoined Congress to "abstain from . . . those exciting topics of sectional character which have hitherto produced painful apprehensions in the public mind." The new Congress, however, was in no mood for simple solutions. For three weeks the House, where fifteen Free Soilers held the balance of power, remained snarled in an angry contest over the choice of a Speaker.

THE COMPROMISE OF 1850

THE GREAT DEBATE The spotlight, however, fell on the Senate, where a stellar cast enacted one of the great dramas of American politics, the Compromise of 1850: the great triumvirate of Clay, Calhoun, and Webster, with a supporting cast that included William H. Seward, Stephen A. Douglas, Jefferson Davis, and Thomas Hart Benton. Henry Clay once again took the role of "Great Pacificator," which he had played in the Missouri and nullification controversies. In January he presented a package of eight resolutions which wrapped up solutions to all the disputed issues. He proposed to (1) admit California as a free state, (2) organize the remainder of the Southwest without restriction as to slavery, (3) deny Texas its extreme claim to a Rio Grande boundary up to its source, (4) compensate Texas for this by assuming the Texas debt, (5) uphold slavery in the District of Columbia, but (6) abolish the slave trade across its boundaries, (7) adopt a more effective fugitive slave act, and (8) deny congressional authority to interfere with the interstate slave trade. His proposals, in substance, became the Compromise of 1850, but only after a prolonged debate, the most celebrated, if not the greatest, in the annals of Congress—and the final great debate for Calhoun, Clay and Webster. Calhoun, already dying, would be gone on March 31, and Clay and Webster two years later, in 1852.

On February 5–6 the aging Clay summoned all his resources of eloquence in a defense of the settlement. In the interest of "peace, concord and harmony" he called for an end to "passion, passion—party, party—and intemperance." California should be admitted on the terms that its own people had approved. As to the remainder of the new lands, he told northerners: "You have got what is worth more than a thousand Wilmot provisos. You have nature on your side. . . ." Secession, he warned southerners, would inevitably bring on war. Even a peaceful secession, however unlikely, would gain none of the South's demands. Slavery in the territories and the District, the return of fugitives—all would be endangered.

The debate continued sporadically through February, with Sam Houston rising to the support of Clay's compromise, Jefferson Davis defending the slavery cause on every point, and none rising to any effective defense of President Taylor's straightforward plan. Then on March 4 Calhoun left his sickbed to sit, a gaunt figure with his cloak draped about his shoulders, as Senator Mason of Virginia read the "sentiments" he had "reduced to writing."

"I have, Senators, believed from the first that the agitation of the subject of slavery would, if not prevented by some timely and effective measure, end in disunion," said Calhoun. Neither Clay's compromise nor Taylor's efforts would serve the Union. The South needed but an acceptance of its rights: equality in the territories, the return of fugitive slaves, and some guarantee of "an equilibrium between the sections." The last, while not spelled out in the speech, referred to Calhoun's notion of a "concurrent majority" by which each section could gain security through a veto power, perhaps through a dual executive, an idea which would be elaborated in his posthumous *Discourse on the Constitution*.

Three days later Calhoun returned to hear Daniel Webster. The assumption was widely held that the "godlike Daniel," long since acknowledged the supreme orator of an age of oratory, would stick to his mildly free-soil views. In a sense he did, but his central theme, as in the classic debate with Hayne, was the preservation of the Union: "I wish to speak today, not as a Massachusetts man, not as a Northern man, but as an American. . . . I speak today for the preservation of the Union. 'Hear me for my cause.'" The extent of slavery was already determined, he insisted, by the Northwest Ordinance, by the Missouri Compromise, and in the new lands by the law of nature. The Wilmot Proviso was superfluous: "I would not take pains to reaffirm an ordinance of nature nor to re-enact the will of God." Both sections, to be sure, had legitimate grievances: on the one hand the excesses of "infernal fanatics and abolitionists" in the North; and on the other hand southern efforts to expand slavery and southern slurs on northern workingmen. But "Secession! Peaceable secession! Sir, your eyes and mine are never destined to see that miracle." Instead of looking into such "caverns of darkness," let men "enjoy the fresh air of liberty and union." Let them look to a more hopeful future.

The March 7 speech was a supreme gesture of conciliation, and Webster had knowingly brought down a storm upon his head. New England antislavery leaders virtually exhausted the vocabulary of abuse against this new "Benedict Arnold" who had betrayed his section. John Greenleaf Whittier lamented in "Ichabod":

> So fallen! so lost! the light withdrawn
> Which once he wore!
> The glory from his gray hairs gone
> Forevermore!

But Webster had also revived hopes of compromise in both North and South. Agreement, wrote the New England historian George Ticknor, "will be mainly owing to the conciliatory tone taken by Mr. Webster." Georgia's Senator Toombs found "a tolerable prospect for a proper settlement of the slavery question, probably along the lines backed by Webster."

On March 11 William H. Seward, freshman Whig senator from New York, gave the antislavery reply to Webster. As the confidant of Taylor he might have been expected to defend the president's program. Instead he stated his own view that compromise with slavery was "radically wrong and essentially vicious." There was, he said, "a higher law than the Constitution," thus leaving some doubt, according to the historian David Potter, whether he was floor leader for Zachary Taylor or for God.

In mid-April a select Committee of Thirteen bundled Clay's suggestions (insofar as they concerned the Mexican cession) into one comprehensive bill, which the committee reported to the

Senate early in May. The measure was quickly dubbed the "Omnibus" bill because it resembled the contemporary vehicle that carried many riders. Taylor continued to oppose Clay's compromise and the two men came to an open break which threatened to split the Whig party wide open. Another crisis loomed when word came near the end of June that a convention in New Mexico was applying for statehood, with Taylor's support, and with boundaries that conflicted with the Texas claim to the east bank of the Rio Grande.

TOWARD A COMPROMISE On July 4 friends of the Union staged a grand rally at the base of the unfinished Washington Monument. Taylor went to hear Henry S. Foote, but lingered for other ceremonies in the hot sun. Back at the White House he quenched his thirst with iced water and milk, ate some cherries, cucumbers, or cabbage, and was stricken with cholera morbus (gastroenteritis). Five days later he was dead. The outcome of the sectional quarrel, had he lived, probably would have been different, whether for better or worse one cannot know. In a showdown Taylor had put everyone on notice that he would be as resolute as Jackson. "I can save the Union without shedding a drop of blood," he said. On the other hand a showdown might have provoked civil war ten years before it came, years during which the northern states gained in population and economic strength.

Taylor's sudden death, however, strengthened the chances of compromise. The soldier in the White House was followed by a politician, Millard Fillmore. The son of a poor farmer in upper New York, Fillmore had come up through the school of hard

Millard Fillmore. His support of the Compromise of 1850 helped the Union muddle through the crisis. [Library of Congress]

knocks. Largely self-educated, he had made his own way in the profession of law and the rough-and-tumble world of New York politics. Experience had taught him caution, which some thought was indecision, but he had made up his mind to support Clay's compromise and had so informed Taylor. It was a strange switch. Taylor, the Louisiana slaveholder, had been ready to make war on his native region; Fillmore, whom southerners thought was antislavery, was ready to make peace.

At this point young Sen. Stephen A. Douglas of Illinois, a rising star of the Democratic party, came to the rescue of Clay's faltering compromise. Never sanguine about the Omnibus, he had refused service on the Committee of Thirteen, and with Clay's consent, kept himself ready to lead an alternative strategy. His strategy was in fact the same one that Clay had used to pass the Missouri Compromise thirty years before. Reasoning that nearly everybody objected to one or another provision of the Omnibus, Douglas worked on the principle of breaking it up into six (later five) separate measures. Few members were prepared to vote for all of them, but from different elements Douglas hoped to mobilize a majority for each.

It worked. Thomas Hart Benton described the sequel. The separate items were like "cats and dogs that had been tied together by their tails four months, scratching and biting, but being loose again, every one of them ran off to his own hole and was quiet." By September 17 it was over, and three days later Fillmore had signed the last of the five measures into law. The Union had muddled through, and the settlement went down in history as the Compromise of 1850. For the time it defused an explosive situation and settled each of the major points at issue.

First, California entered the Union as a free state, ending forever the old balance of free and slave states. Second, the Texas and New Mexico Act made New Mexico a territory and set the Texas boundary at its present location. In return for giving up its claims east of the Rio Grande Texas was paid $10 million, which secured payment of the Texas debt and brought a powerful lobby of bondholders to the support of compromise. Third, the Utah Act set up another territory. The territorial act in each case omitted reference to slavery except to give the territorial legislature authority over "all rightful subjects of legislation" with provision for appeal to federal courts. For the sake of agreement the deliberate ambiguity of the statement was its merit. Northern congressmen could assume that territorial legislatures might act to exclude slavery on the unstated principle of popular sovereignty. Southern congressmen assumed that they could not.

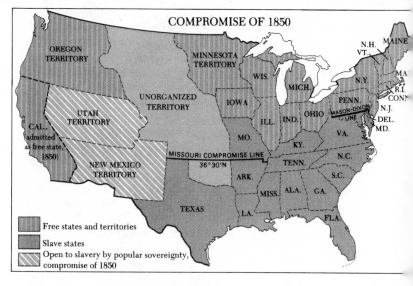

COMPROMISE OF 1850

OREGON TERRITORY

MINNESOTA TERRITORY

WIS.

MICH.

UNORGANIZED TERRITORY

IOWA

UTAH TERRITORY

CAL. (admitted as free state, 1850)

MO.

NEW MEXICO TERRITORY

MISSOURI COMPROMISE LINE 36°30'N

ARK.

TEXAS

LA.

ILL. IND. OHIO

KY.

TENN.

MISS. ALA. GA.

FLA.

PENN.

VA.

N.C.

S.C.

N.H. VT.

MAINE

N.Y.

MA

R.I.

CONN

N.J.

DEL.

MD.

MASON-DIXON LINE

Free states and territories

Slave states

Open to slavery by popular sovereignty, compromise of 1850

Fourth, a new Fugitive Slave Act put the matter wholly under federal jurisdiction and stacked the cards in favor of slave-catchers. Fifth, as a gesture to antislavery forces the slave trade, but not slavery itself, was abolished in the District of Columbia: more specifically, no slave could be brought into the District for the purpose of sale or be held in a depot for transfer and sale elsewhere. The spectacle of slave coffles passing through the streets of the capital was brought to an end. Calling these five measures the Compromise of 1850 was an afterthought. Actually they were the result less of a sectional bargain than of a parliamentary maneuver. They were nevertheless an accomplished fact, and a large body of citizens welcomed the outcome, if not with joy, at least with relief. Millard Fillmore's message to Congress in December 1850 pronounced the measures "a final settlement."

Still, doubts lingered that either North or South could be reconciled to the measures permanently. In the South the disputes of 1846–1850 had transformed the abstract doctrine of secession into a movement animated by such fire-eaters as Robert Barnwell Rhett of South Carolina, William Lowndes Yancey of Alabama, and Edmund Ruffin of Virginia.

But once the furies aroused by the Wilmot Provisio were spent, the compromise left little on which to focus a proslavery agitation. The state of California was an accomplished fact, and, ironically, tended to elect proslavery men to Congress. New Mexico and Utah were far away, and in any case at least hypothetically open to slavery. Both in fact adopted slave codes, but the census of 1860 reported no slaves in New Mexico and only twenty-nine in Utah. The Fugitive Slave Law was something else again. It was the one clear-cut victory for the cause of slavery, but a pyrrhic victory if ever there was one.

THE FUGITIVE SLAVE LAW   Southern intransigence had presented abolition its greatest gift since the Gag Rule, a new focus for agitation and one that was far more charged with emotion. The fugitive slave law did more than stack the deck in favor of slave-catchers; it offered a strong temptation to kidnap free Negroes by denying alleged fugitives a jury trial and by providing a fee of $10 for each fugitive delivered. In addition federal marshals could require citizens to help in enforcement; violators could be imprisoned up to six months and fined $1,000. Anson Burlingame of Massachusetts said it fixed the value of a Carolina slave at $1,000, of a Yankee soul at $5.

"This filthy enactment was made in the nineteenth century, by people who could read and write," Emerson marveled in his journal. He advised neighbors to break it "on the earliest occasion." The occasion soon arose in many places, if not in Emerson's Concord. Within a month of the law's enactment claims were filed in New York, Philadelphia, Harrisburg, Detroit, and

Practical Illustration of the Fugitive Slave Law. *Depicts the divisive effects of the law. [The Smithsonian Institution]*

other cities. Trouble soon followed. In Detroit only military force stopped the rescue of an alleged fugitive by an outraged mob in October 1850.

There were relatively few such incidents, however. In the first six years of the fugitive act only three fugitives were forcibly rescued from the slave-catchers. On the other hand probably fewer than 200 were remanded to bondage during the same years. More than that were rescued by stealth, often through the Underground Railroad. Still, the Fugitive Slave Act had tremendous effect in widening and deepening the antislavery impulse in the North.

UNCLE TOM'S CABIN   Antislavery forces found their most persuasive appeal not in the fugitive slave law but in the fictional drama of Harriet Beecher Stowe's *Uncle Tom's Cabin*, a combination of unlikely saints and sinners, stereotypes and melodramatic escapades—and a smashing commercial success. The long-suffering Uncle Tom, the villainous Simon Legree, the angelic Eva, the desperate Eliza taking her child to freedom across the icy Ohio —all became stock characters of the American imagination. Slavery, seen through Mrs. Stowe's eyes, subjected its victims either to callous brutality or, at the hands of indulgent masters, to the indignity of extravagant ineptitude and bankruptcy. It took time for the novel to work its effect on public opinion, however. Neither abolitionists nor fire-eaters represented their sections at the time. The country was enjoying a surge of prosperity, and the course of the presidential campaign in 1852 reflected a common desire to lay sectional quarrels to rest.

"The Greatest Book of the Age." Uncle Tom's Cabin, *as this advertisement indicates, was a tremendous commercial success.* [New-York Historical Society]

FOREIGN ADVENTURES

The Democrats, despite a fight over the nomination, had some success in papering over the divisions within their party. As their nominee for president they turned finally to Franklin Pierce of New Hampshire; William R. King of Alabama was nominated for vice-president. The platform pledged the Democrats to "abide by and adhere to a faithful execution of the acts known as the Compromise measures. . . . " The candidates and the platform generated a surprising reconciliation of the party's factions. Pierce rallied both the Southern Rights men and the Barnburners, who at least had not burned their bridges with the Democrats. The Free Soilers, as a consequence, mustered only 156,000 votes for John P. Hale in contrast to the 291,000 they got for Van Buren in 1848.

The Whigs were less fortunate. They repudiated the lackluster Fillmore, who had faithfully supported the Compromise, and once again tried to exploit martial glory. It took fifty-three ballots, but the convention finally chose Winfield Scott, the hero of Lundy's Lane and Mexico City, a native of Virginia backed mainly by northern Whigs, including Seward. The convention dutifully endorsed the Compromise, but with some opposition from the North. Scott, an able commander but politically inept, had gained a reputation for antislavery and nativism, alienating German and Irish ethnic voters. In the end Scott carried only Tennessee, Kentucky, Massachusetts and Vermont. Pierce overwhelmed him in the electoral college 254 to 42, although the popular vote was closer: 1.6 million to 1.4 million.

Pierce, an undistinguished but handsome and engaging figure, a former congressman, senator, and brigadier in Mexico, was, like Polk, touted as another "Young Hickory." But he turned out to be made of more pliable stuff, unable to dominate the warring factions of his party, trying to be all things to all men, but looking more and more like a "Northern man with Southern principles."

"YOUNG AMERICA" Foreign diversions now distracted attention from domestic quarrels. After the Mexican War the spirit of Manifest Destiny took on new life in an amorphous movement called "Young America." The Spirit of Young America was full of spread-eagle bombast, buoyant optimism, and enthusiasm for economic growth and territorial expansion. The dynamic force of American institutions would somehow transform the world. On February 21, 1848, just two days after word of the Mexican treaty reached Washington, an uprising in Paris signaled the liberal Revolutions of 1848, which set Europe ablaze. The Young Americans greeted that new dawn with all the ardor Jeffersonians had lavished on the first French Revolution. And when it all collapsed, the result seemed all the more to confirm the belief that Europe was, in the words of Stephen A. Douglas, "antiquated, decrepit, tottering on the verge of dissolution . . . a vast graveyard."

CUBA Closer to home, Cuba, one of Spain's earliest and one of its last possessions in the New World, continued to be an object of American concern. In the early 1850's a crisis arose over expeditions launched against Cuba from American soil. Spanish authorities retaliated against these provocations by harassment of American ships. In 1854 the Cuban crisis expired in one final outburst of braggadocio, the Ostend Manifesto. That year the Pierce administration instructed Pierre Soule, the minister in Madrid, to offer $130 million for Cuba, which Spain peremptorily spurned. Soule then joined the American ministers to France and Britain in drafting the Ostend Manifesto. It declared that if Spain, "actuated by stubborn pride and a false sense of honor refused to sell," then the United States must ask itself, "does Cuba, in the possession of Spain, seriously endanger our internal peace and existence of our cherished Union?" If so, "then, by every law, human and divine, we shall be justified in wresting it from Spain. . . ." Publication of the supposedly confidential dispatch left the administration no choice but to disavow what northern opinion widely regarded as a "slaveholders' plot." The last word on this and other such episodes perhaps should go to the staid London *Times*, which commented near the end of 1854: "The diplomacy of the United States is certainly a very singular profession."

So was the practice of filibustering which, again, was more bluster than action. Little wonder the word has come to suggest gas-bag as well as freebooter, and the double-meaning is appropriate for the 1850s. William Walker, a Tennessean by birth who went to California and began to fancy himself a new Cortés, reached his supreme moment in 1855 when the "grey-eyed man of destiny" sailed with sixty followers, "the immortals," to mix in a Nicaraguan civil war. Before the year was out he had made himself president of a republic which Franklin Pierce promptly recognized. Walker was deposed in 1857, and in 1860 was executed by a firing squad in Honduras.

DIPLOMATIC GAINS IN THE PACIFIC In the Pacific, however, American diplomacy scored some positive achievements. American trade with China dated from 1785, but was allowed only through the port of Canton. In 1844 the United States and China signed the Treaty of Wanghsia, which opened four ports, including Shanghai, to American trade and for the first time granted America "extraterritoriality," or special privileges, including the right of Americans to remain subject to their own law in certain areas. The Treaty of Tientsin (1858) opened eleven more ports and granted Americans the right to travel and trade throughout China. China quickly became a special concern of American Protestant missionaries as well. About fifty were already there by 1855, and for nearly a century China remained far and away the greatest mission field for Americans.

Japan meanwhile had remained for two centuries closed to American trade. Moreover, American whalers wrecked on the shores of Japan had been forbidden to leave the country. Mainly in their interest President Fillmore entrusted a special Japanese expedition to Commodore Matthew C. Perry, who arrived in Tokyo on July 8, 1853. Japan's actual ruler, the Tokugawa shogun, was already under pressure from merchants and the educated classes to seek wider contacts in the world. He agreed to deliver Perry's letter to the emperor. Negotiations followed, and in the Treaty of Kanagawa (March 31, 1854) Japan agreed to an American consulate, promised good treatment to castaways, and permitted visits in certain ports for supplies and repairs. Broad commercial relations came after the first envoy, Townsend Harris, negotiated the Harris Convention of 1858, which opened five ports to American trade and made certain tariff concessions. In 1860 a Japanese diplomatic mission, the first to enter a Western country, visited the United States for three months.

A Japanese view of Commodore Perry's landing in Yokohama Harbor.
[Library of Congress]

THE KANSAS-NEBRASKA CRISIS

During the 1850s the only land added to the United States was a barren stretch of some 30,000 square miles south of the Gila River in present New Mexico and Arizona. This Gadsden Purchase of 1853, which cost the United States $10 million, was made to acquire land offering a likely route for a Pacific railroad. The idea of building a railroad linking together the new continental domain of the United States, though a great national goal, spawned sectional rivalries in still another quarter and reopened the slavery issue. Among the many transcontinental routes projected, the four most important were the northern route from Milwaukee to the Columbia River, a central route from St. Louis to San Francsico, another from Memphis to Los Angeles, and a more southerly route from New Orleans to San Diego via the Gadsden Purchase.

DOUGLAS'S PROPOSAL   Stephen A. Douglas of Illinois had an even better idea: Chicago ought to be the eastern terminus. In 1852 and 1853 Congress debated and dropped several likely proposals. For various reasons, including terrain, climate, and sectional interest, Secretary of War Jefferson Davis favored the southern route and encouraged the Gadsden Purchase. Any other route, moreover, would go through the Indian country which stretched from Texas to the Canadian border.

Since 1845, therefore, Douglas and others had offered bills for

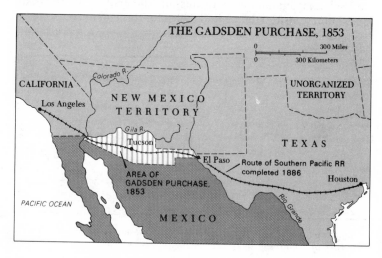

THE GADSDEN PURCHASE, 1853

a new territory in the lands west of Missouri and Iowa, bearing the Indian name Nebraska. In January 1854, as chairman of the committee on territories, Senator Douglas reported yet another Nebraska bill. Unlike the others this one included the entire unorganized portion of the Louisiana Purchase to the Canadian border. At this point fateful connections began to transform his proposal from a railroad bill to a proslavery bill. To carry his point Douglas needed the support of southerners, and to win that support he needed to make some concession on slavery. This he did by writing popular sovereignty into the bill in language which specified that "all questions pertaining to slavery in the Territories, and in the new states to be formed therefrom are to be left to the people residing therein, through their appropriate representatives."

It was a clever dodge since the Missouri Compromise would still exclude slaves until the territorial government had made a decision, preventing slaveholders from getting established before a decision was reached. Southerners quickly spotted the barrier and Douglas as quickly made two more concessions. He supported an amendment for repeal of the Missouri Compromise insofar as it excluded slavery north of 36°30′, and then agreed to organize two territories, Kansas, west of Missouri; and Nebraska, west of Iowa and Minnesota.

Douglas's motives are unclear. Railroads were surely foremost in his mind, but he was influenced also by his proslavery friend, Sen. David Atchison of Missouri, by the desire to win support for his bill in the South, by the hope that popular sovereignty would quiet the slavery issue and open the Northwest, or by a chance to split the Whigs. But he had blundered, had damaged his presidential chances, and had set his country on the road to civil war. The tragic flaw in his plan was his failure to gauge the depth of antislavery feelings. Douglas himself preferred that the territories become free. Their climate and geography excluded plantation agriculture, he reasoned, and he could not comprehend how people could get so wrought up over abstract rights. Yet he had in fact opened the possibility that slavery might gain a foothold in Kansas.

The agreement to repeal the Missouri Compromise was less than a week old before six antislavery congressmen published a protest, the "Appeal of the Independent Democrats." The tone of moral indignation which informed their protest quickly spread among those who opposed Douglas. The document arraigned his bill "as a gross violation of a sacred pledge," and as "part and parcel of an atrocious plot" to create "a dreary region of despotism, inhabited by masters and slaves." They called upon their fellow citizens to protest against this "atrocious crime."

Across the North editorials, sermons, speeches, and petitions echoed this indignation. What had been radical opinion was fast becoming the common view of people in the North. But Douglas had the votes and, once committed, forced the issue with tireless energy. President Pierce impulsively added his support. Southerners lined up behind Douglas, with notable exceptions like Texas Sen. Sam Houston, who denounced the violation of two solemn compacts: the Missouri Compromise and the confirmation of the territory to the Indians "as long as grass shall grow and water run." He was not the only one to think of the Indians, however. Federal agents were already busy extinguishing Indian titles. But Douglas and Pierce whipped reluctant Democrats into line (though about half the northern Democrats refused to yield), pushing the bill to final passage in May by 37 to 14 in the Senate and 113 to 100 in the House.

Very well, many in the North reasoned, if the Missouri Compromise was not a sacred pledge, then neither was the Fugitive Slave Act. On June 2 Boston witnessed the most dramatic demonstration against the act. After several attempts had failed to rescue a fugitive named Anthony Burns, a force of soldiers and marines marched him to a waiting ship through streets lined with people shouting "Kidnappers!" past buildings draped in black, while church bells tolled across the city. The event cost the federal government $14,000. Burns was the last to be returned from Boston, and was himself soon freed through purchase by the black community of Boston.

THE EMERGENCE OF THE REPUBLICAN PARTY   What John C. Calhoun had called the cords holding the Union together had already begun to part. The national church organizations of Baptists and Methodists, for instance, had split over slavery by 1845. The national parties, which had created mutual interests transcending sectional issues, were beginning to unravel under the strain. The Democrats managed to postpone disruption for yet a while, but their congressional delegation lost heavily in the North, enhancing the influence of the southern wing.

The strain of the Kansas-Nebraska Act, however, soon destroyed the Whig party. Southern Whigs now tended to abstain from voting while Northern Whigs moved toward two new parties. One was the new American (Know Nothing) party, which had raised the banner of native Americanism and the hope of serving the patriotic cause of Union. More Northern Whigs

joined with independent Democrats and Free Soilers in spontaneous antislavery coalitions with a confusing array of names, including "anti-Nebraska," "Fusion," and "People's party." These
coalitions finally converged in 1854 on the name "Republican,"
evoking the memory of Jefferson. The Know-Nothings and the
Republicans, paradoxically, appealed to overlapping constituencies. As the historian David Potter aptly pointed out, "much of
the rural, Protestant, puritan-oriented population of the North
was sympathetic to antislavery and temperance and nativism and
unsympathetic to the hard-drinking Irish Catholics."

"BLEEDING" KANSAS   After passage of the Kansas-Nebraska Act,
attention swung to the plains of Kansas where opposing elements
gathered to stage a rehearsal for civil war. All agreed that Nebraska would be free, but Kansas soon exposed the potential for
mischief in popular sovereignty. The ambiguity of the law, useful
to Douglas in getting it passed, only added to the chaos. The people of Kansas were "perfectly free to form and regulate their
domestic institutions in their own way, subject only to the Constitution." That in itself was subject to conflicting interpretations, but the law was completely silent as to the time of decision,
adding to each side's sense of urgency about getting control of
the territory.

The settlement of Kansas therefore differed from the usual pioneering efforts. Groups sprang up North and South to hurry
right-minded settlers westward. The first and best known was Eli
Thayer's New England Emigrant Aid Society. During 1855 and
1856 it sent fewer than 1,250 colonists, but its example encouraged other groups and individuals to follow suit. Southern efforts
of the same kind centered in Missouri, which was separated from
Kansas only by a surveyor's line. When Kansas's first governor,
Andrew H. Reeder of Pennsylvania, arrived in October 1854, he
found several thousand settlers already on the ground. He ordered a census and scheduled an election for a territorial legislature in March 1855. When the election took place, several
thousand "Border Ruffians" crossed over from Missouri and
swept the polls for proslavery forces. Reeder denounced the
vote as a fraud, but did nothing to alter the results. The legislature so elected expelled the few antislavery members, adopted a
drastic slave code, and made it a capital offense to aid a fugitive
slave and a felony even to question the legality of slavery in the
territory.

Free-state men rejected this "bogus" government and moved
directly toward application for statehood. In October 1855 a

constitutional convention, the product of an extralegal election, met in Topeka, drafted a state constitution excluding both slavery and free Negroes from Kansas, and applied for admission to the Union. By March 1856 a free-state "governor" and "legislature" were functioning in Topeka. But the prospect of getting any government to command general authority in Kansas seemed dim, and both sides began to arm. The Emigrant Aid Society was soon in the business of gun-running as well as helping settlers. The Rev. Henry Ward Beecher's name became especially identified with gun-running because of "Beecher's Bibles," rifles supplied by his congregation.

Finally, confrontation began to slip into conflict. In May 1856 a proslavery mob entered the free-state town of Lawrence and began a wanton destruction of property. They smashed newspaper presses and tossed them into the river, set fire to the free-state governor's home, stole property that was not nailed down, and trained five cannon on the Free State Hotel, destroying it.

The "sack of Lawrence" resulted in just one casualty, but the excitement aroused a fanatical free-soiler named John Brown,

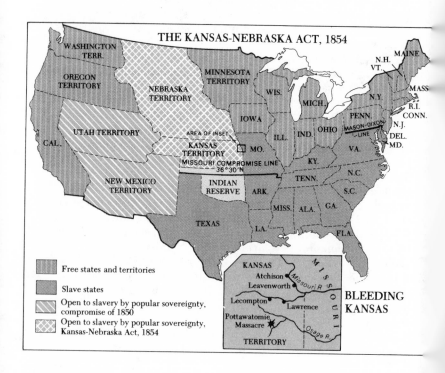

THE KANSAS-NEBRASKA ACT, 1854

Free states and territories

Slave states

Open to slavery by popular sovereignty, compromise of 1850

Open to slavery by popular sovereignty, Kansas-Nebraska Act, 1854

BLEEDING KANSAS

who had a history of instability. A minister with whom he stayed in Kansas described him later as one "impressed with the idea that God had raised him up on purpose to break the jaws of the wicked." Two days after the sack of Lawrence, Brown set out with four sons and three other men toward Pottawatomie Creek, site of a proslavery settlement, where they killed five men in cold blood, ostensibly as revenge for the deaths of free-state men. The Pottawatomie Massacre (May 24–25, 1856) set off a running guerrilla war in the territory which lasted through the fall when a new governor, John W. Geary of Pennsylvania, restored a semblance of order with the help of federal soldiers. Altogether, by the end of 1856 Kansas lost about 200 killed and $2 million in property destroyed.

VIOLENCE IN THE SENATE   Violence in Kansas spilled over into the rhetoric of Congress, where angry legislators began to trade recriminations, coming to the verge of blows. On May 22, the day after the sack of Lawrence, two days before the Pottawatomie Massacre, a sudden flash of violence on the Senate floor electrified the whole country. Just two days earlier Sen. Charles Sumner of Massachusetts had finished a speech on "The Crime against Kansas." Sumner, elected five years earlier by a coalition of Free Soilers and Democrats, was a complex mixture of traits: capable at once of eloquence and excess, a man of principle with limited tolerance for opinions different from his own. He had intended his speech to be "the most thorough philippic" ever heard.

What he produced was an exercise in pedantry and studied insult. The treatment of Kansas was "the rape of a virgin territory," he said, " . . . and it may be clearly traced to a depraved longing for a new slave State, the hideous offspring of such a crime. . . . " Sen. A. P. Butler of South Carolina became a special target of his censure. Like Don Quixote in choosing Dulcinea, Butler had "chosen a mistress . . . who . . . though polluted in the sight of the world, is chaste in his sight—I mean the harlot, Slavery." Sumner said that Butler betrayed "an incapacity of accuracy," a constant "deviation of truth."

Sumner's rudeness might well have discredited the man, if not his cause, had it not been for Preston S. Brooks, a congressman from Edgefield, South Carolina. For two days Brooks brooded over the insult to his uncle, Senator Butler. Knowing that Sumner would refuse a challenge to a duel, he considered but rejected the idea of taking a horsewhip to him. Finally, on May 22 he found Sumner writing at his Senate desk after an adjournment,

"Bully" Brooks's attack on Charles Sumner. The incident increased the strains on the Union. [New York Public Library]

accused him of libel against South Carolina and Butler, and commenced beating him about the head with a cane. Sumner, struggling to rise, wrenched the desk from the floor and collapsed.

Brooks had created a martyr for the antislavery cause. Like so many other men in those years, he betrayed the hotspur's gift for snatching defeat from the jaws of victory. For two and a half years Sumner's empty seat was a solemn reminder of the violence done to him. Some thought the senator was feigning injury, others that he really was physically disabled. In fact, although his injuries were bad enough, including two gashes to the skull, he seems to have suffered a psychosomatic shock which left him incapable of functioning adequately. When the House censured Brooks, he resigned, went home to Edgefield, and returned after being triumphantly reelected. His admirers showered him with new canes. Southerners who never would have done what Brooks did now hastened to make excuses for him. Northerners who never would have said what Sumner said now hastened to his defense. Men on each side, appalled at the behavior of the other, reasoned that North and South had developed into different civilizations, with incompatible standards of honor. "I do not see," Emerson confessed, "how a barbarous community and a civilized community can constitute one state. We must either get rid of slavery, or get rid of freedom."

SECTIONAL POLITICS   Within the span of five days in May "Bleeding Kansas," "Bleeding Sumner," and "Bully Brooks" had set the tone for another presidential year. The major parties could no longer evade the slavery issue. Already in February it had split the hopeful American party wide open. Southern delegates, with help from New York, killed a resolution to restore the Missouri Compromise, and nominated Millard Fillmore for president and Andrew Jackson Donelson for vice-president. Later, what was left of the Whig party endorsed the same candidates.

At its first national convention the new Republican party passed over its leading figure, William H. Seward, who was awaiting a better chance in 1860. Following the Whig tradition they sought out a military hero, John C. Frémont, the "Pathfinder" and leader in the conquest of California. The Republican platform owed much to the Whigs too. It favored a transcontinental railroad and, in general, more internal improvements. It condemned the repeal of the Missouri Compromise, the Democratic policy of expansion, and "those twin relics of barbarism— Polygamy and Slavery." The campaign slogan echoed that of the Free Soilers: "Free soil, free speech, and Frémont." It was the first time a major party platform had taken a stand against slavery.

The Republican position on slavery, the historian Eric Foner has argued, developed from an ideology of free labor. "Political anti-slavery was not merely a negative doctrine, an attack on southern slavery and the society built on it," Foner wrote; "it was an affirmation of the superiority of the social system of the North—a dynamic expanding capitalist society, whose achievements and destiny were almost wholly the result of the dignity and opportunities which it offered the average laboring man." Such a creed, he argued, could accommodate a variety of opinions on race, economics, or other issues, but it was "an ideology which blended personal and sectional interest with morality so perfectly that it became the most potent political force in the nation."

The Democrats, meeting two weeks earlier in June, had rejected Pierce, the hapless victim of so much turmoil. Douglas too was left out because of the damage done by his Kansas-Nebraska Act. The party therefore turned to its old wheelhorse, James Buchanan of Pennsylvania, who had long sought the nomination. The party and its candidate nevertheless hewed to the policies of Pierce. The platform endorsed the Kansas-Nebraska Act and nonintervention. Congress, it said, should not interfere with slavery in either states or territories. The party reached out to its newly acquired ethnic voters by condemning nativism and endorsing religious liberty.

The campaign of 1856 resolved itself into two sectional cam-

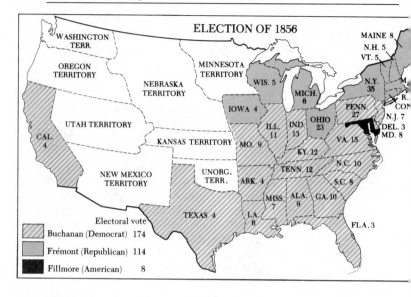

ELECTION OF 1856

WASHINGTON TERR.

OREGON TERRITORY

UTAH TERRITORY

CAL. 4

NEW MEXICO TERRITORY

NEBRASKA TERRITORY

MINNESOTA TERRITORY

WIS. 5

IOWA 4

KANSAS TERRITORY

UNORG. TERR.

TEXAS 4

MICH. 6

ILL. 11

MO. 9

ARK. 4

LA. 6

IND. 13

OHIO 23

KY. 12

TENN. 12

MISS. 7

ALA. 9

GA. 10

S.C. 8

N.C. 10

VA. 15

PENN. 27

FLA. 3

MAINE 8
N.H. 5
VT. 5
N.Y. 35
M.
R.
CON
N.J. 7
DEL. 3
MD. 8

Electoral vote

Buchanan (Democrat)   174

Frémont (Republican)   114

Fillmore (American)   8

paigns. The "Black Republicans" had few southern supporters, and only a handful in the border states, where fears of disunion held many Whigs in line. Buchanan thus went to the country as the candidate of the only remaining national party. Although Fillmore won a larger vote in the South than Scott had, the slave states were safe for Buchanan. Frémont swept the northernmost states, with 114 electoral votes, but Buchanan added five free states to his southern majority for a total of 174: Pennsylvania, New Jersey, Illinois, Indiana, and California, all but the last of which bordered on slave states.

Few presidents before Buchanan had a broader experience in politics and diplomacy. His career went back to 1815 when he started as a Federalist legislator in Pennsylvania before switching to Jackson in the 1820s. He had been over twenty years in Congress, minister to Russia and Britain, and Polk's secretary of state in between. His long quest for the presidency had been built on a southern alliance, and his political debts reinforced his belief that saving the Union depended on concessions to the South. Republicans belittled him as another "doughface" like Pierce, lacking the backbone to stand up to the southerners who dominated the Democratic majorities in Congress. His choice of four slave-state and only three free-state men for his cabinet seemed another bad omen.

THE DEEPENING SECTIONAL CRISIS

THE DRED SCOTT CASE   An old saying has it that troubles come in threes. In 1856 Lawrence, the Brooks-Sumner affair, and Pottawotamie came in quick succession. During Buchanan's first six months in 1857 he encountered the Dred Scott decision, new troubles in Kansas, and a business panic. On March 6, 1857, two days after the inauguration, the Supreme Court rendered a decision in the long-pending case of *Dred Scott v. Sandford.* Dred Scott, born a slave in Virginia about 1800, had been taken to St. Louis and sold to an army surgeon, Dr. John Emerson. In 1834 Emerson took him as body servant to Fort Armstrong, Illinois, then to Fort Snelling in Wisconsin Territory (later Minnesota), and finally returned him to St. Louis in 1838. After Emerson's death in 1843 Scott apparently had tried to buy his freedom. In 1846, with help from white friends, he brought suit in Missouri courts claiming that residence in Illinois and Wisconsin Territory had made him free. A jury decided in his favor, but the state supreme court ruled against him. When the case rose on appeal to the Supreme Court, the country anxiously awaited its opinion on the issue of slavery in the territories.

Each of the nine justices filed a separate opinion, except one who concurred with Chief Justice Taney. By different lines of reasoning seven justices ruled that Scott remained a slave. The aging Taney, whose opinion stood as the opinion of the Court, ruled that Scott lacked standing in court because he lacked citizenship. Taney argued that one became a federal citizen either by birth or by naturalization, which ruled out any former slave.

Dred Scott. The Supreme Court's decision on his suit for freedom fanned the flames of discord. [Missouri Historical Society]

He further argued that no state had ever accorded citizenship to Negroes—a statement demonstrably in error. At the time the Constitution was adopted, Taney further said, Negroes "had for more than a century been regarded as . . . so far inferior, that they had no rights which the white man was bound to respect."

To nail down further the definition of Scott's status, Taney moved to a second major question. Residency in a free state had not freed him since, in line with precedent, the decision of the state court governed. This left the question of residency in a free territory. On this point Taney argued that the Missouri Compromise had deprived citizens of property in slaves, an action "not warranted by the constitution." He strongly implied, but never said explicitly, that the compromise had violated the due process clause of the Fifth Amendment, as Calhoun had earlier argued. The upshot was that the Supreme Court had declared an act of Congress unconstitutional for the first time since *Marbury v. Madison* (1803), and a major act for the first time ever. Congress had repealed the Missouri Compromise in the Kansas-Nebraska Act three years earlier, but the decision now pointed a thrust at popular sovereignty. If Congress could not exclude slavery from the territories, then presumably slavery could not be lawfully excluded by any other means short of changing the constitution.

By this decision six justices of the Supreme Court had thought to settle a question which Congress had dodged ever since the Wilmot Proviso surfaced. But far from settling it, they had only fanned the flames of dissension. Little wonder that Republicans protested: the Court had declared their program unconstitutional. It had also reinforced the suspicion that the slavocracy was hatching a conspiracy. Were not all but one of the justices who joined Taney southerners? And had not Buchanan chatted with the chief justice at the inauguration and then urged the people to accept the early decision as a final settlement, "Whatever this may be"? (Actually, Buchanan already knew the outcome because two other justices had spilled the beans in private letters.) Besides, if Dred Scott were not a citizen and had no standing in court, there was no case before it. The majority ruling was an *obiter dictum*—a statement not essential to deciding the case and therefore not binding, "entitled to just so much moral weight as would be the judgment of a majority of those congregated in any Washington bar-room."

Proslavery elements, of course, greeted the court's opinion as binding. Now the fire-eaters among them were emboldened to yet another demand. It was not enough to deny Congress the right to interfere with slavery in the territories; Congress had an obligation to protect the property of slaveholders, making a federal slave code the next step. The idea, first broached by Alabama Democrats in the "Alabama Platform" of 1848, soon became orthodox southern doctrine.

THE LECOMPTON CONSTITUTION   Out in Kansas, meanwhile, the struggle continued. Just before Buchanan's inauguration the proslavery legislature called an election of delegates to a constitutional convention. Since no provision was made for a referendum on the constitution, Governor Geary vetoed the measure and the legislature overrode his veto. Geary resigned on the day Buchanan took office and the new president replaced him with Robert J. Walker. A native Pennsylvanian who made a political career in Mississippi and a former member of Polk's cabinet, Walker had greater prestige than his predecessors, and like contemporaries such as Houston of Texas, Foote of Mississippi, and Benton of Missouri, put the Union above slavery in his scale of values. In Kansas he scented a chance to advance the cause of both the Union and his party. Under popular sovereignty, fair elections would produce a state that was both free and Democratic. Walker arrived in May, and, with Buchanan's approval, pledged to the free-state elements that the new constitution would be submitted to a fair vote. But in spite of his pleas, he arrived too late to persuade free-state men to vote for convention delegates in elections they were sure had been rigged against them. Later, however, Walker did persuade the free-state leaders to vote in the October election of a new territorial legislature.

As a result a polarity arose between an antislavery legislature and a proslavery constitutional convention. The convention, meeting at Lecompton, drew up a constitution under which Kansas would become a slave state. A referendum on the document was cunningly contrived so that voters could not vote against the proposed constitution. They could only accept it "with slavery" or "with no slavery," and even the latter meant that property in slaves already in Kansas would "in no measure be interfered with." The vote was set for December 21, 1857, with rules and officials chosen by the convention.

Although Kansas had only about 200 slaves at the time, free-state men boycotted the election on the claim that it was rigged. At this point President Buchanan took a fateful step. Influenced by southern advisers and politically dependent upon southern congressmen, he decided to renege on his pledge to Walker and support the action of the Lecompton Convention. Walker resigned and the election went according to form: 6,226 for the constitution with slavery, 569 for the constitution without slavery. Meanwhile, Frederick P. Stanton of Tennessee, the acting governor, had convened the antislavery legislature, which called for another election to vote the Lecompton Constitution up or down. The result on January 4, 1858, was overwhelming: 10,226 against the constitution, 138 for the constitution with slavery, 24 for the constitution without slavery.

The combined results suggested a clear majority against slavery, but Buchanan stuck to his support of the Lecompton Constitution, driving another wedge into the Democratic party. Senator Douglas, up for reelection, could not afford to run as a champion of Lecompton. He broke dramatically with the president in a tense confrontation, but Buchanan persisted in trying to drive Lecompton "naked" through the Congress. In the Senate, administration forces held firm, and in March 1858 Lecompton was passed. In the House, enough anti-Lecompton Democrats combined to put through an amendment for a new and carefully supervised popular vote in Kansas. Enough senators went along to permit passage of the House bill. Southerners were confident the vote would favor slavery, because to reject slavery the voters would have to reject the constitution, which would postpone statehood until the population reached 90,000. On August 2, 1858, Kansas voters nevertheless rejected Lecompton by 11,300 to 1,788. With that vote Kansas, now firmly in the hands of its antislavery legislature, ended its main role in the sectional controversy.

THE PANIC OF 1857   The third crisis of Buchanan's first half year in office, a financial crisis, broke in August 1857. It was brought on by a reduction in demand for American grain caused by the end of the Crimean War (1854–1856), a surge in manufacturing which outran the growth of markets, and the continued weakness and confusion of the state banknote system. Failure of the Ohio Life Insurance and Trust Company on August 24, 1857, precipitated the panic, which was followed by a depression from which the country did not emerge until 1859.

Everything in those years seemed to get drawn into the vortex of sectional conflict, and business troubles were no exception. Northern businessmen tended to blame the depression on the Democratic Tariff of 1857, which had put rates at their lowest level since 1816. The agricultural South weathered the crisis better than the North. Cotton prices fell, but slowly, and world markets for cotton quickly recovered. The result was an exalted notion of King Cotton's importance to the world, and apparent confirmation of the growing argument that the southern system was superior to the free-labor system of the North.

DOUGLAS VS. LINCOLN   Amid the recriminations over Dred Scott, Kansas, and the depression, the center could not hold. The Lecompton battle put severe strains on the one substantial cord of Union left, the Democratic party. To many, Douglas seemed the best hope, one of the few remaining Democratic leaders with support in both sections. But now Douglas was being whipsawed between the extremes. Kansas-Nebraska had cast him in the role of "doughface." His opposition to Lecompton, the fraudulent fruit of popular sovereignty, however, had alienated him from Buchanan's southern junta. But for all his flexibility and opportunism, Douglas had convinced himself that popular sovereignty was a point of principle, a bulwark of democracy and local self-government. In 1858 he faced reelection to the Senate against the opposition of Buchanan Democrats and Republicans. The year 1860 would give him a chance for the presidency, but first he had to secure his home base in Illinois.

To oppose him Illinois Republicans named Abraham Lincoln of Springfield, former Whig state legislator and one-term congressman, a moderately prosperous small-town lawyer. Lincoln's early life had been the hardscrabble existence of the frontier farm. Born in a Kentucky log cabin in 1809, raised on frontier farms in Indiana and Illinois, the young Lincoln had the wit and will to rise above his beginnings. With less than twelve months of sporadic schooling he learned to read, studied such books as came to hand, and eventually developed a prose style as muscular as the man himself. He worked at various farm tasks, operated a ferry, and made two trips down to New Orleans as a flatboatman. Striking out on his own, he managed a general store in New Salem, Illinois, learned surveying, served in the Black Hawk War (1832), won election to the legislature in 1834 at the age of twenty-five, read law, and was admitted to the bar in 1836. As a Whig regular, he adhered to the philosophy of Henry Clay. He stayed in the legislature until 1842, and in 1846 won a term in Congress. After a single term he retired from active politics to cultivate his law practice.

In 1854 the Kansas-Nebraska debate drew him back into active politics. When Douglas appeared in Springfield to defend his stand, Lincoln spoke in refutation from the same platform. In Peoria he repeated the performance of what was known thereafter as the "Peoria Speech." This speech began the journey toward his appointment with destiny, preaching an old but oft-neglected doctrine: hate the sin but not the sinner.

> When Southern people tell us they are no more responsible for the origin of slavery, than we; I acknowledge the fact. When it is said that the institution exists; and that it is very difficult to get rid of it, in any satisfactory way, I can understand and appreciate the saying. . . .
>
> But all this, to my judgment, furnishes no more excuse for permitting slavery to go into our own free territory, than it would for reviving the African slave trade by law.

At first Lincoln held back from the rapidly growing new party, but in 1856 he threw in his lot with the Republicans, getting over 100 votes for their vice-presidential nomination, and gave some fifty speeches for the Frémont ticket in Illinois and nearby states. By 1858 he was the obvious choice to oppose Douglas himself, and Douglas knew he was up against a formidable foe. Lincoln resorted to the classic ploy of the underdog: he challenged the favorite to debate with him. Douglas had little relish for drawing attention to his opponent, but agreed to meet him in seven places around the state. Thus the legendary Lincoln-Douglas debates took place, August 21 to October 15.

At the time and since, much attention focused on the second debate, at Freeport, where Lincoln asked Douglas how he could reconcile popular sovereignty with the Dred Scott ruling that

A scene from Lincoln's 1858 senatorial campaign. The tall figure at the right of the doorway is Abraham Lincoln. [Library of Congress]

citizens had the right to carry slaves into any territory. Douglas's answer, thenceforth known as the Freeport Doctrine, was to state the obvious. Whatever the Supreme Court might say about slavery, it could not exist anywhere unless supported by local police regulations.

Douglas tried to set some traps of his own. It is standard practice, of course, to put extreme constructions upon an adversary's stand. Douglas intimated that Lincoln belonged to the fanatical sect of abolitionists who planned to carry the battle to the slave states, just as Lincoln intimated the opposite about Douglas. Douglas accepted, without any apparent qualms, the conviction of black inferiority which most whites, North and South, shared at the time, and sought to pin on Lincoln the stigma of advocating racial equality. The question was a hot potato, which Lincoln handled with caution. There was "A physical difference between the white and black races" and it would "forever forbid the two races living together on terms of social and political equality," he said. He simply favored the containment of slavery where it existed so that "the public mind shall rest in the belief that it is in the course of ultimate extinction." But the basic difference between the two men, Lincoln insisted, lay in Douglas's professed indifference to the moral question of slavery: "He says he 'don't care whether it is voted up or voted down' in the territories. . . . Any man can say that who does not see anything wrong in slavery, but no man can logically say it who does see a wrong in it; because no man can logically say he don't care whether a wrong is voted up or down. . . ."

If Lincoln had the better of the argument, at least in the long view, Douglas had the better of the election. The voters actually had to choose a legislature, which would then elect the senator. Lincoln men won the larger total vote, but its distribution gave Douglas the legislature, 54 to 41. As the returns trickled in from the fall elections in 1858—there was still no common election date—they recorded one loss after another for Buchanan men. When they were over, the administration had lost control of the House. But the new Congress would not meet in regular session until December 1859.

STORM WARNINGS   After the Lecompton fiasco the slavery issue was no longer before Congress in any direct way. The gradual return of prosperity in 1859 offered hope that the storms of the 1850s might yet pass. But the issue still haunted the public mind, and like sheet lightning on the horizon, warned that a storm was still pending. In the spring there were two warning flashes. The

Supreme Court finally ruled in the case of *Ableman v. Booth,* which had arisen in 1854 when an abolitionist editor in Milwaukee, Sherman M. Booth, roused a mob to rescue a fugitive slave. Convicted in federal court of violating the Fugitive Slave Act, he got the Wisconsin Supreme Court to order him freed on the ground that the act was unconstitutional. A unanimous Supreme Court made short work of Wisconsin's interposition. Chief Justice Taney's opinion denied the right of state courts to interfere and reaffirmed the constitutionality of the Fugitive Slave Act. The Wisconsin legislature in turn responded with states'-rights resolutions that faintly echoed the Virginia and Kentucky Resolutions of 1798–1799.

The episode, like others at the time, illustrated the significant fact that both North and South seized on nationalism or states' rights for their own purposes—neither was a point on which many men could claim consistency. Since the early 1840s the Garrisonian abolitionists had openly championed disunion, but they were a small, if vocal, minority in the North. In the South few denied a state's right to dissolve the bond of Union in the same way that the original states had ratified it. And as the South became increasingly a conscious minority, beset by antislavery forces and aware of its growing isolation in the Western world, more and more were willing to consider secession a possibility. By 1855, when Peru acted to abolish slavery, the peculiar institution was left only in Brazil, in the Spanish colonies of Cuba and Puerto Rico, in the Dutch colonies of Guiana and the West Indies, and in the American South.

JOHN BROWN'S RAID   For a season, however, sectional agitations were held in check. But in October 1859 John Brown once again surfaced. Since the Pottawatomie Massacre in 1856 Brown had led a furtive existence, engaging in fundraising and occasional bushwhacking. Finally, on October 16, 1859, he was ready for his supreme gesture. From a Maryland farm he crossed the Potomac with nineteen men, including five Negroes, and under cover of darkness occupied the federal arsenal in Harper's Ferry, Virginia (now West Virginia). His scheme was foredoomed from the start, and any attempt at a rational explanation probably misses the point. His notion seems to have been that he would arm the many slaves who would flock to his cause, set up a black stronghold in the mountains of western Virginia, and provide a nucleus of support for slave insurrections across the South. What he actually did was to take the arsenal by surprise, seize a few hostages, and sit there until he was surrounded and captured. He had even

John Brown. [The Warder Collection]

forgotten to bring food. Militiamen from the surrounding country rallied by the next afternoon, and the next evening Lt. Col. Robert E. Lee, U.S. Cavalry, arrived with his aide, Lt. J. E. B. Stuart, and a force of marines. On the morning of October 18 Brown refused a call to surrender and the marines stormed the arsenal and took Brown prisoner, with a painful wound. Altogether Brown's men killed four people (including one marine) and wounded nine. Of their own force, ten died (including two of Brown's sons), five escaped, and seven were captured.

Brown was turned over to Virginia authorities, quickly tried for treason against the state and conspiracy to incite insurrection, convicted on October 31, and hanged on December 2 at Charles Town. Six others died on the gallows later. If Brown had failed in his purpose—whatever it was—he had achieved two things. He had become a martyr for the antislavery cause, and he had set off panic throughout the slaveholding South. At his sentencing he delivered one of the classic American speeches: "Now, if it is deemed necessary that I should forfeit my life for the furtherance of the ends of justice, and mingle my blood further with the blood of my children and with the blood of millions in this slave country whose rights are disregarded by wicked, cruel, and unjust enactments, I say, let it be done."

When Brown, still unflinching, met his end, it was a day of solemn observances in the North. Prominent Republicans, including Lincoln and Seward, repudiated Brown's coup, but the discovery of Brown's correspondence revealed that he had enjoyed support among prominent antislavery leaders who, whether or not they knew at the time what they were getting into, later defended his deeds. "That new saint," Emerson said,

" . . . will make the gallows as glorious as the cross." Garrison, the lifelong pacifist, now wished "success to every slave insurrection at the South and in every slave country."

By far the gravest after-effect of Brown's raid was to leave southerners in no mood to distinguish between John Brown and the Republican party. The southern mind now merged those who would contain slavery with those who would drown it in blood. All through the fall and winter of 1859–1860 rumors of conspiracy and insurrection swept the region. Every northern visitor, commercial traveler, or schoolteacher came under suspicion, and many were driven out. "We regard every man in our midst an enemy to the institutions of the South," said the Atlanta *Confederacy*, "who does not boldly declare that he believes African slavery to be a social, moral, and political blessing." Francis Lieber, a German exile, political scientist, and dedicated nationalist, survived in discomfort for yet a while at the College of South Carolina. But relations between the sections reminded him of what Thucydides had said about the Peloponnesian War: "The Greeks did not understand each other any longer, though they spoke the same language."

THE CENTER COMES APART

The first session of the new Congress, which convened three days after the death of John Brown, confirmed Lieber's melancholy thought. The Democrats still controlled the Senate, but the House once again was thrown into deadlock over the choice of a Speaker. John Sherman of Ohio, the Republican candidate for Speaker, had committed the unforgivable sin in southern eyes of supporting the distribution of Hinton R. Helper's *The Impending Crisis of the South* (1857). Helper was a former North Carolinian who sought to demonstrate that slavery had impoverished nonslaveholding white southerners. The issue of "Helperism" kept enough votes from Sherman to prevent his selection. The House finally turned to William Pennington of New Jersey, an old Whig who supported the Fugitive Slave Act but also favored exclusion of slavery from the territories. He soon lined up with the Republicans. On the day after Pennington's election as Speaker, Jefferson Davis stood up in the Senate to introduce a set of resolutions for the defense of slavery, the main burden of which was a demand that the federal government extend "all needful protection" to slavery in the territories. Davis in effect asked for a federal slave code.

THE DEMOCRATS DIVIDE   Thus amid emotional hysteria and impossible demands the nation ushered in the year of another presidential election, destined to be the most fateful in its history. Four years earlier, in a moment of euphoria, the Democrats had settled on Charleston, South Carolina, as the site for their 1860 convention. Charleston in April, with the azaleas ablaze, was perhaps the most enticing city in the United States, but the worst conceivable place for such a meeting. It was a hotbed of extremist sentiment, and lacked adequate accommodations for the crowds thronging in. South Carolina itself had chosen a remarkably moderate delegation, but the extreme southern-rights men held the upper hand in the delegations from the Gulf states.

Douglas men preferred to stand by the platform of 1856, which simply promised congressional noninterference with slavery. Southern firebrands, however, were now demanding federal protection for slavery in the territories. Buchanan supporters, hoping to stop Douglas, encouraged the strategy. The platform debate reached a heady climax when the Alabama fire-eater Yancey informed the northern Democracy that its error had been the failure to defend slavery as a positive good. Sen. George E. Pugh of Ohio offered a blunt reply: "Gentlemen of the South," he said, "you mistake us—you mistake us. We will not do it."

When the southern planks lost, Alabama walked out of the convention, followed by the other Gulf states, Georgia, South Carolina (except for two stubborn upcountry Unionists), and parts of the delegations from Arkansas and Delaware. This pattern foreshadowed with some fidelity the pattern of secession, in which the Deep South left the Union first. The convention then decided to leave the overwrought atmosphere of Charleston and reassemble in Baltimore on June 18. The Baltimore convention finally nominated Douglas on the 1856 platform. The Charleston seceders met first in Richmond, then in Baltimore, where they adopted the slave-code platform defeated in Charleston, and named Vice-President John C. Breckinridge of Kentucky for president. Thus another cord of union had snapped: the last remaining national party.

LINCOLN'S ELECTION   The Republicans meanwhile gathered in Chicago, in a gigantic hall jocosely called the "Wigwam." There everything suddenly came together for "Honest Abe" Lincoln, "the Railsplitter," the uncommon common man. Lincoln had suddenly emerged in the national view during his senatorial campaign two years before, and had since taken a stance de-

Abraham Lincoln at the time of his nomination for the presidency. [Library of Congress]

signed to make him available for the nomination. He was strong enough on the containment of slavery to satisfy the abolitionists, yet moderate enough to seem less threatening than they were. In February 1860 he had gone east to address an audience of influential Republicans at the Cooper Union in New York, where he emphasized his view of slavery "as an evil, not to be extended, but to be tolerated and protected only because of and so far as its actual presence among us makes that toleration and protection a necessity."

Chicago provided surroundings which gave Lincoln's people many advantages. His managers, for instance, could pack the galleries with noisy supporters. They started out with little more support than the Illinois delegation, but worked to make Lincoln everybody else's second choice. William H. Seward was the early leader, but he had been tagged, perhaps wrongly, as an extremist for his earlier statements about an "irrepressible conflict" and a "higher law." On the first ballot Lincoln finished in second place. On the next ballot he drew almost even with Seward, and when he came within one and a half votes of a majority on the third count, Ohio quickly switched four votes to put him over the top. Later the same day Sen. Hannibal Hamlin of Maine, a former Democrat, became the vice-presidential nominee.

The platform foreshadowed future policy better than most. It denounced John Brown's raid as "among the gravest of crimes," and promised the "maintenance inviolate of the right of each state to order and control its own domestic institutions."the party reaffirmed its resistance to the extension of slavery, and in an effort to gain broader support, endorsed a protective tariff for manufacturers, a more liberal naturalization law, and internal improvements, including a Pacific railroad. With this platform Republicans made a strong appeal to eastern businessmen, western farmers, and the large immigrant population.

Both major conventions revealed that opinion tended to become more radical in the upper North and Deep South. Attitude followed latitude. In the border states a sense of moderation, perhaps due to a sense that the border areas would bear the brunt of any calamity, aroused the diehard Whigs there to make one more try at reconciliation. Meeting in Baltimore a week before the Republicans met in Chicago, they reorganized into the Constitutional Union party and named John Bell of Tennessee for president. Their only platform was "the Constitution of the Country, the Union of the States, and the Enforcement of the Laws."

Of the four candidates not one was able to command a national following, and the campaign resolved into a choice between Lincoln and Douglas in the North, Breckinridge and Bell in the South. One consequence of these separate campaigns was that each section gained a false impression of the other. The South never learned to distinguish Lincoln from the radicals; the North failed to gauge the force of southern intransigence—and in this Lincoln was among the worst. He stubbornly refused to offer the South assurances or to amplify his position, which he said was a matter of public record. The one man who tried to break through the veil that was falling between the sections was Douglas, who tried to mount a national campaign. Only forty-seven, but al-

The Carolina Clothing Depot's advertisement drums up business while beating the drums of disunion in South Carolina. [The Bettmann Archive]

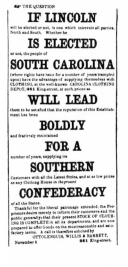

ready weakened by drink, ill-health, and disappointments, he wore himself out in one final glorious campaign. Early in October, at Cedar Rapids, Iowa, he got the news of Republican state victories from Pennsylvania and Indiana. "Mr. Lincoln is the next President," he said. "We must try to save the Union. I will go South." Down through the hostile areas of Tennessee, Georgia, and Alabama he carried appeals on behalf of the Union. "I do not believe that every Breckinridge man is a disunionist," he said, "but I do believe that every disunionist is a Breckinridge man." He was in Mobile when the election came.

By midnight of November 6 Lincoln's victory was clear. In the final count he had about 39 percent of the total popular vote, but a clear majority with 180 votes in the electoral college. He carried every one of the eighteen free states, and by a margin enough to elect him even if the votes for the other candidates had been combined. Among all the candidates, only Douglas had electoral votes from both slave and free states, but his total of 12 was but a pitiful remnant of Democratic Unionism. He ran last. Bell took Virginia, Kentucky, and Tennessee for 39 votes, and Breckinridge swept the other slave states to come in second with 72.

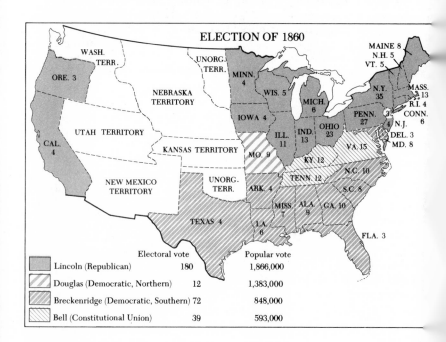

ELECTION OF 1860

	Electoral vote	Popular vote
Lincoln (Republican)	180	1,866,000
Douglas (Democratic, Northern)	12	1,383,000
Breckenridge (Democratic, Southern)	72	848,000
Bell (Constitutional Union)	39	593,000

A handbill announcing South Carolina's secession from the Union. [New York Public Library]

SECESSION OF THE DEEP SOUTH   Soon after the election the South Carolina legislature, which had assembled to choose the state's electors, set a special election for December 6 to choose delegates to a convention. In Charleston on December 20 the convention unanimously voted an Ordinance of Secession, declaring the state's ratification of the Constitution repealed and the union with other states dissolved. A Declaration of the Causes of Secession reviewed the threats to slavery, and asserted that a sectional party had elected to the presidency a man "whose opinions and purposes are hostile to slavery," who had declared "Government cannot endure permanently half slave, half free," and "that the public mind must rest in the belief that Slavery is in the course of ultimate extinction."

By February 1, 1861, six more states had declared themselves out of the Union. Texas was the last to act because its governor, staunch old Jacksonian Sam Houston, had refused to assemble the legislature for a convention call, but secessionist leaders called an irregular convention which authorized secession. Only there was the decision submitted to a referendum, which the secessionists carried handily. In some places the vote for delegates revealed a close division, especially in Georgia and Louisiana, but secession carried. On February 4, a convention of the seven states met in Montgomery; on February 7 they adopted a provisional constitution for the Confederate States of America, and two days later they elected Jefferson Davis its president. He was inaugurated February 18, with Alexander Stephens of Georgia as vice-president.

In all seven states of the southernmost tier a solid majority had voted for secessionist delegates, but their combined vote would not have been a majority of the presidential vote in November. What happened, it seemed, was what often happens in revolutionary situations: a determined and decisive group acted quickly in an emotionally charged climate and carried its program against a confused and indecisive opposition. Trying to decide whether or not a majority of the whites actually favored secession probably is beside the point—a majority were vulnerable to the decisive action of the secessionists.

BUCHANAN'S WAITING GAME   History is full of might-have-beens. A bold stroke, even a bold statement, by the president at this point might have changed things, but there was no Jacksonian flourish in Buchanan. Besides, a bold stroke might simply have hastened the conflict. No bold stroke came from Lincoln either, nor would he consult with the administration during the long months before his inauguration on March 4. He inclined all too strongly to the belief that secession was just another bluff and kept his public silence. Buchanan followed his natural bent, the policy on which he had built a career: make concessions, seek a compromise to mollify the South. In his annual message on December 3 Buchanan made a forthright argument that secession was illegal, but that he lacked authority to coerce a state. "Seldom have we known so strong an argument come to so lame and impotent a conclusion," the Cincinnati *Enquirer* editorialized. There was, however, a hidden weapon in the president's reaffirmation of a duty to "take care that the laws be faithfully executed" insofar as he was able. If the president could enforce the law upon all citizens, he would have no need to "coerce" a state. Indeed his position became the policy of the Lincoln administration, which fought a war on the theory that individuals but not states as such were in rebellion.

Buchanan held firmly to his resolve, with some slight stiffening by the end of December when secession became a fact and the departure of two southerners removed the region's influence in his cabinet. He would retain positions already held, but would make no effort to assert federal authority provocatively. As the secessionists seized federal property, arsenals, and forts, this policy soon meant holding to isolated positions at Fort Pickens in Pensacola Harbor, some remote islands off southern Florida, and Fort Sumter in Charleston Harbor. On the day after Christmas the small garrison at Fort Moultrie had been moved into the nearly completed Fort Sumter by Maj. Robert Anderson, a Kentucky Unionist. Anderson's move, designed to achieve both disengagement and greater security, struck South Carolina authorities as provocative, a violation of an earlier "gentleman's agreement" that the administration would make no changes in its arrangements, and commissioners of the newly "independent" state peremptorily demanded withdrawal of all federal forces. They had overplayed their hand. Buchanan's cabinet, with only one southerner left, insisted it would be a gross violation of duty, perhaps grounds for impeachment, for the president to yield. His backbone thus stiffened, he sharply rejected the South Carolina ultimatum to withdraw: "This I cannot do: this I will not do." His nearest approach to coercion was to dispatch a steamer, *Star of the West*, to Fort Sumter with reinforcements and provisions. As the ship approached Charleston Harbor, Carolina batteries at Fort Moultrie and Morris Island opened fire and drove it away on January 9. It was in fact an act of war, but Buchanan chose to ignore the challenge. He decided instead to hunker down and ride out the remaining weeks of his term, hoping against hope that one of several compromise efforts would yet prove fruitful.

LAST EFFORTS AT COMPROMISE   Forlorn efforts at compromise continued in Congress until dawn of inauguration day. On December 18 Sen. John J. Crittenden of Kentucky had proposed a series of amendments and resolutions the central features of which were the recognition of slavery in the territories south of 36° 30′; and guarantees to maintain slavery where it already existed. A Senate Committee of Thirteen named to consider the proposal proved unable to agree. A House Committee of Thirty-three under Thomas Corwin of Ohio adopted two concessions to the South: an amendment guaranteeing slavery where it existed and granting statehood to New Mexico, presumably as a slave state. But the committee finished by submitting a set of proposals without endorsing any of them. The fight for a compromise was carried to the floor of each house by Crittenden and Corwin, and subjected to intensive debate during January and February.

Meanwhile a Peace Conference met in Willard's Hotel in February at the call of the Virginia legislature. Twenty-one states sent delegates and former president John Tyler presided, but the convention's proposal, substantially the same as the Crittenden Compromise, failed to win the support of either house of Congress. The only compromise proposal that met with any success was Corwin's amendment to guarantee slavery where it existed. Many Republicans, including Lincoln, were prepared to go that far to save the Union, but they were unwilling to repudiate their stand against slavery in the territories. As it happened, after passing the House the amendment passed the Senate without a vote to spare, by 24 to 12, on the dawn of inauguration day. It would have become the Thirteenth Amendment, with the first use of the word "slavery" in the Constitution, but the states never ratified it. When a Thirteenth Amendment was ratified in 1865, it did not guarantee slavery—it abolished slavery.

FURTHER READING

Two works which survey the coming of the Civil War are Allan Nevins's *Ordeal of the Union* (2 vols.; 1947) and David M. Potter's *The Impending Crisis, 1848–1861* (1976).° Interpretive essays can be studied in Edwin C. Rozwenc (ed.), *The Causes of the American Civil War* (1972), and Eric Foner's *Politics and Ideology in the Age of the Civil War* (1980).°

Numerous works cover various aspects of the political crises of the 1850s. C. W. Morrison's *Democratic Politics and Sectionalism: The Wilmot Proviso Controversy* (1967) focuses on the initial dispute. Joseph G. Rayback's *Free Soil: The Election of 1848* (1970), Frederick J. Blue's *Free Soilers: Third Party Politics, 1848–1854* (1973), and William R. Brock's *Parties and Political Conscience: American Dilemmas, 1840–1850* (1979), all examine the disruption of the two-party balance. Holman Hamilton's *Prologue to Conflict: The Crisis and Compromise of 1850* (1964)° probes that crucial dispute. Michael F. Holt's *The Political Crisis of the 1850s* (1978)° traces the demise of the Whigs. Eric Foner provides a good introduction to how events and ideas combined to form a new political party in *Free Soil, Free Labor, Free Men: The Ideology of the Republican Party before the Civil War* (1970).° Michael F. Holt's *Forging a Majority: The Republican Party in Pittsburgh, 1848–1860* (1969), explores how ethnic tensions led to local political realignments. Also good on the Republicans is Hans L. Trefousse's *The Radical Republicans: Lincoln's Vanguard for Racial Justice* (1969) and David H. Donald's *Charles Sumner and the Coming of the Civil War* (1970).°

Robert W. Johansen's *Stephen A. Douglass* (1973) analyzes the issue of popular sovereignty, and Paul W. Gates details the violence in Kansas in *Fifty Million Acres: Conflicts over Kansas Land Policy, 1854–1890* (1954).° A more national perspective is provided in James A. Rawley's *Race and Politics: "Bleeding Kansas" and the Coming of the Civil War* (1969). Two works which treat the role played by one abolitionist in Kansas are James C. Malin's *John Brown and the Legend of Fifty-Six* (1970) and Stephen B. Oates's *To Purge This Land with Blood: A Biography of John Brown* (1970).° Also useful is Malin's *The Nebraska Question: 1852–1854* (1953).

° These books are available in paperback editions.

The links between foreign policy aims and the desire for slavery expansion can be studied in Robert E. May's *The Southern Dream of a Caribbean Empire* (1973), Basil Rauch's *American Interest in Cuba, 1848–1855* (1948), and E. S Wallace's *Destiny and Glory* (1957). America's Asian interests are explored in Tyler Dennett's *America in East Asia* (1941), Arthur Walworth's *Black Ships off Japan* (1946), and Alfred W. Griswold's *The Far Eastern Policy of the United States* (1938).

Stanley W. Campbell's *The Slave Catchers: Enforcement of the Fugitive Slave Law, 1840–1860* (1968), traces the problems caused by the Compromise of 1850. Richard H. Sewell's *Ballots for Freedom: Anti-Slavery Politics in the United States, 1847–1860* (1976),° and Louis Filler's *The Crusade against Slavery, 1830–1860* (1960),° stress the role of abolitionists. William J. Cooper's *The South and the Politics of Slavery, 1828–1865* (1978),° presents the opposing viewpoint. A wonderful primary document of antebellum attitudes is Harriet Beecher Stowe's *Uncle Tom's Cabin*, edited and annotated by Phillip Van Doren Stern (1964).° For details of the Dred Scott case, consult Don E. Fehrenbacher's *The Dred Scott Case: Its Significance in American Law and Politics* (1978).°

The growing alienation of southerners from national trends is explored in David M. Potter's *The South and the Sectional Conflict* (1968), Avery O. Craven's *The Growth of Southern Nationalism, 1848–1861* (1953), and Jesse T. Carpenter's *The South as a Conscious Minority* (1930). Studies of southern states include J. Mills Thornton III's *Politics and Power in a Slave Society: Alabama, 1800–1860* (1978),° Michael Johnson's *Toward a Patriarchial Society: The Secession of Georgia* (1977), Steven A. Channing's *Crisis of Fear: Secession in South Carolina* (1970),° and William L. Barney's *The Road to Secession: A New Perspective on the Old South* (1972)° and *The Secessionist Impulse: Alabama and Mississippi* (1974). Also consult R. A. Wooster's *The Secession Conventions of the South* (1962). How the North reacted is studied in Kenneth M. Stampp's *And the War Came: The North and the Secession Crisis, 1860–61* (1950).°

To gauge the role played by Lincoln in the coming crisis of war, see the biographies listed in Chapter 17. Particularly good for Lincoln during the 1850s is Don E. Fehrenbacher's *Prelude to Greatness* (1962).° Harry V. Jaffa's *Crisis of the House Divided* (1959) details the Lincoln-Douglas debates, and Richard N. Current's *Lincoln and the First Shot* (1963)° treats the Fort Sumter controversy.

17

THE WAR OF THE UNION

End of the Waiting Game

During the four long months between his election and in-auguration Lincoln would say little about future policies and less about past positions. "If I thought a *repetition* would do any good I would make it," he wrote to an editor in St. Louis. "But my judgment is it would do positive harm. The secessionists *per se,* believing they had alarmed me, would clamor all the louder." So he stayed in Springfield until February 11, 1861, biding his time. He then boarded a train for a long, roundabout trip, and began to drop some hints to audiences along the way. To the New Jersey legislature, which responded with prolonged cheering, he said: "The man does not live who is more devoted to peace than I am. . . . But it may be necessary to put the foot down." At the end of the journey he reluctantly yielded to rumors of plots against his life, passed unnoticed on a night train through Baltimore, and slipped into Washington before daybreak on February 23.

The ignominious end to his journey reinforced the fears of eastern sophisticates that the man lacked style. Lincoln, to be sure, lacked a formal education and training in the rules of eti-quette. His clothing was hardly modish, even for the times. His tall frame shambled awkwardly, and he had an unseemly pen-chant for funny stories. But the qualities that first called him to public attention would soon manifest themselves. His prose, at least, had style—and substance. So did his politics. What Hawthorne called his "Yankee shrewdness and not-to-be caughtness" guided him through the traps laid for the unwary in Washington. Whatever else people might think of him, they soon learned that he was not easily dominated.

618

LINCOLN'S INAUGURATION   Buchanan called for Lincoln at Willard's Hotel on a bright and blustery March 4. Together they rode in an open carriage to the Capitol, where Chief Justice Taney administered the oath on a platform outside the East Portico. At the start, Stephen A. Douglas reached out to hold Lincoln's hat as a gesture of unity. In his inaugural address Lincoln repeated views already on record by quoting from an earlier speech: "I have no purpose, directly or indirectly, to interfere with the institution of slavery in the States where it exists. I believe I have no lawful right to do so, and I have no inclination to do so."

But the immediate question had shifted from slavery to secession, and most of the speech emphasized Lincoln's view that "the Union of these States is perpetual." The Union, he asserted, was older than the Constitution itself, dating from the Articles of Association in 1774, "matured and continued" by the Declaration of Independence and the Articles of Confederation. But even if the United States were only a contractual association, "no State upon its own mere motion can lawfully get out of the Union." Lincoln promised to hold areas belonging to the government, collect duties and imposts, and deliver the mails unless repelled, but beyond that "there will be no invasion, no using of force against or among the people anywhere." The final paragraph, based on a draft by Seward, was an eloquent appeal for harmony:

> I am loath to close. We are not enemies, but friends. We must not be enemies. Though passion may have strained, it must not break, our bonds of affection. The mystic chords of memory, stretching from every battlefield and patriot grave to every living heart and hearthstone all over this broad land, will yet swell the chorus of the Union, when again touched, as surely they will be, by the better angels of our nature.

Lincoln not only entered office amid the gravest crisis yet faced by a president, but he also faced unusual problems of transition. Republicans, in power for the first time, crowded Washington, hungry for office. Four of the seven new cabinet members had been rivals for the presidency: William H. Seward at State, Salmon P. Chase at the Treasury, Simon Cameron at the War Department, and Edward Bates as attorney-general. Four were former Democrats and three were former Whigs. They formed a group of better than average ability, though most were so strong-minded they thought themselves better qualified to lead than Lincoln. It was only later than they were ready to acknowledge with Seward that "he is the best man among us."

THE FALL OF FORT SUMTER For the time being Lincoln's combination of firmness and moderation differed little in effect from his predecessor's stance. Harsh judgments of Buchanan's waiting game overlook the fact that Lincoln kept it going. Indeed his only other choices were to accept secession as an accomplished fact or to use force right away. On the day after he took office, however, word arrived from Charleston that time was running out. Major Anderson had supplies for a month to six weeks, and Fort Sumter was being surrounded by a Confederate "ring of fire." Most cabinet members favored evacuation of Fort Sumter and defense of Fort Pickens at Pensacola, where relief ships were already offshore.

Events moved quickly to a climax in the next two weeks. On April 4 Lincoln decided to reinforce Fort Pickens and resupply Fort Sumter. On April 6 he notified the governor of South Carolina that "an attempt will be made to supply Fort Sumter with provisions only. . . . " On April 9 President Jefferson Davis and his cabinet in Montgomery decided against permitting Lincoln to maintain the status quo. On April 11 Confederate Gen. Pierre G. T. Beauregard demanded a speedy surrender of Sumter. Major Anderson refused, but said his supplies would be used up in

The Fourth Regiment, Georgia Volunteer Army, Confederate States of America. These troops were guarding Fort Sumter in April 1861. [Library of Congress]

three more days. With the relief ships approaching, Anderson received an ultimatum to yield. He again refused, and at 4:30 A.M. on April 12 the first gun sounded at Fort Johnson on James Island, and Fort Sumter quickly came under a crossfire from Sullivan's and Morris Islands as well. After more than thirty hours, his ammunition exhausted, Anderson agreed to give up, and on April 14 he lowered his flag. The only fatalities, ironically, were two men killed in an explosion during a final salute to the colors, the first in a melancholy train of war dead.

The guns of Charleston signaled the end of the waiting game. On the day after Anderson's surrender, Lincoln called upon the loyal states to supply 75,000 militiamen to subdue a combination "too powerful to be suppressed by the ordinary course of judicial proceedings." Volunteers rallied around the flag at the recruiting stations. On April 19 Lincoln proclaimed a blockade of southern ports which, as the Supreme Court later ruled, confirmed the existence of war.

TAKING SIDES In the free states and the Confederate states the proclamation reinforced the patriotic fervor of the day. In the upper South it brought dismay, and another wave of secession which swept four more states into the Confederacy. Many in those states, like Jonathan Worth of North Carolina, abhorred both abolitionists and secessionists, but faced with a call for troops to suppress their sister states, decided to abandon the Union. Virginia acted first. Its convention had met intermittently since February 13; now it convened again and passed an ordinance of secession on April 17. On May 21 the Confederate Congress chose Richmond as its new capital, and the government moved there in June.

Three other states followed Virginia in little over a month: Arkansas on May 6, Tennessee on May 7, and North Carolina on May 20. The Tar Heel state, next to last to ratify the Constitution, was last in secession. All four of the holdout states, especially Tennessee and Virginia, had mountain areas where both slaves and secessionists were scarce and where Union sentiment ran strong. In Tennessee the mountain counties would supply more volunteers to the Union than to the Confederate cause. Unionists in western Virginia, bolstered by a Union army from Ohio under Gen. George B. McClellan, contrived a loyal government of Virginia which gave its consent to the formation of a new state. In 1863 Congress admitted West Virginia to the Union with a constitution that provided for gradual emancipation of the few slaves there.

Of the other slave states, Delaware, with but a token number of slaves, remained firmly in the Union, but Maryland, Kentucky, and Missouri went through bitter struggles for control. The secession of Maryland would have made Washington but a Union enclave within the Confederacy, and in fact Baltimore's mayor for a time did cut all connections to the capital. On April 19 a mob attacked the Sixth Massachusetts Regiment on its way through Baltimore and inflicted a toll of four dead and thirty-six wounded. To hold the state Lincoln took drastic measures of dubious legality: he suspended the writ of habeas corpus (under which judges could require arresting officers to produce their prisoners and justify their arrest) and rounded up pro-Confederate leaders and threw them in jail. The fall elections ended the threat of Maryland's secession by returning a solidly Unionist majority in the state.

Kentucky, native state of both Lincoln and Davis, home of Crittenden and Breckinridge, was torn by divided loyalties. But May and June elections for a state convention returned a thumping Unionist majority, and the state legislature proclaimed Kentucky's "neutrality" in the conflict. Lincoln recognized the strategic value of his native state, situated on the south bank of

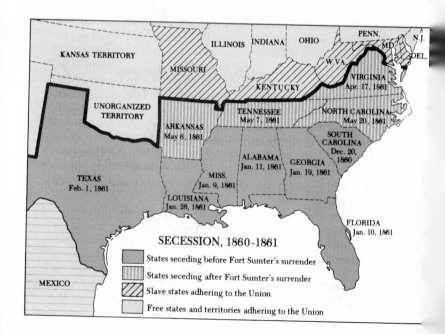

SECESSION, 1860-1861

States seceding before Fort Sumter's surrender

States seceding after Fort Sumter's surrender

Slave states adhering to the Union

Free states and territories adhering to the Union

the Ohio. "I think to lose Kentucky is nearly the same as to lose the whole game," he said. He promised to leave the state alone so long as the Confederates did likewise, and reassured its citizens that a war against secession was not a war against slavery. Kentucky's fragile neutrality lasted until September 3, when a Confederate force occupied Hickman and Columbus. Gen. Ulysses S. Grant then moved Union soldiers into Paducah, at the mouth of the Tennessee River. Kentucky, though divided in allegiance, for the most part remained with the Union. It joined the Confederacy, some have said, only after the war.

Lincoln's effort to hold a middle course in Missouri was upset by the maneuvers of less patient men in the state. Unionists there had a numerical advantage, but Confederate sympathies were strong and St. Louis had large numbers of both. For a time the state, like Kentucky, kept an uneasy peace. But elections for a convention brought an overwhelming Union victory, while a pro-Confederate militia under Gov. Claiborne F. Jackson began to gather near St. Louis. In the city Unionist forces rallied under Nathaniel Lyon and Francis P. Blair, Jr., brother of the postmaster-general, and on May 10 they surprised and disarmed the militia at its camp. Lyon pursued the pro-Confederate forces into the southwestern part of the state, and after a temporary setback at Wilson's Creek on August 10, in which Lyon lost his own life, the Unionists pushed the Confederates back again, finally breaking their resistance at the battle of Pea Ridge (March 6–8, 1862), just over the state line in Arkansas. Thereafter border warfare continued in Missouri, pitting rival bands of gunslingers who kept up their feuding and banditry for years after the war was over.

A "BROTHERS' WAR"   Robert E. Lee epitomized the agonizing choice facing many men of the border states. Son of "Lighthorse Harry" Lee, a Revolutionary War hero, and married to a descendant of Martha Washington, Lee had served in the United States Army for thirty years. Master of Arlington, an estate which faced Washington across the Potomac, he was summoned by Gen. Winfield Scott, another Virginian, and offered command of the Federal forces in the field. After a sleepless night pacing the floor, Lee told Scott that he could not go against his "country," meaning Virginia. He resigned his commission, retired to his estate, and soon answered a call to the Virginia—later the Confederate—service. The course of the war might have been different had Lee made another choice.

The conflict sometimes became literally a "brothers' war." At

Hilton Head, South Carolina, Percival Drayton commanded a Federal gunboat while his brother, Brig. Gen. Thomas F. Drayton, led Confederate land forces. Franklin Buchanan, who commanded the *Virginia* (formerly the *Merrimac*), sank the Union ship *Congress* with his brother on board. John J. Crittenden of Kentucky had a son in each army. J. E. B. Stuart of the Confederate cavalry was chased around the peninsula below Richmond by his Federal father-in-law, Philip St. George Cooke. Lincoln's attorney-general Edward Bates had a son in the Confederate army, and Mrs. Lincoln herself had a brother, three half-brothers, and three brothers-in-law in the Confederate forces.

Neither side was ready for war, not even for the kind that had been fought before. And certainly neither could foresee the consuming force of this one, with its total mobilization of men and materials. This first of "modern" wars brought into use devices and techniques never before employed on such a scale: railroad transport, artillery, repeating rifles, ironclad ships, the telegraph, balloons, the Gatling gun (a rudimentary machine-gun), trenches, and wire entanglements.

ECONOMIC ADVANTAGES If the South seceded in part out of a growing awareness of its minority status in the nation, a balance sheet of the sections in 1860 shows the accuracy of that perception. To begin, the Union held twenty-three states, including four border slave states; while the Confederacy had eleven, claiming also Missouri and Kentucky. Ignoring conflicts of allegiance within various states, which might roughly cancel each other out, the population count was about 22 million in the Union to 9 million in the Confederacy, and about 3½ million of the latter were slaves. The Union therefore had an edge of about four to one in potential manpower.

An even greater advantage for the North was its industry. In gross value of manufactures, the Union states had a margin of better than ten to one in 1860. The states which joined the Confederacy produced just under 7.4 percent of the nation's manufactures on the eve of conflict. What made the disparity even greater was that little of this was in heavy industry. The only iron industry of any size in the Confederacy was the Tredegar Iron Works in Richmond, which had long supplied the United States Army. Tredegar's existence strengthened the Confederacy's will to defend its capital. The Union states, in addition to making most of the country's shoes, textiles, and iron products, turned out 97 percent of the firearms and 96 percent of the railroad equipment produced in the nation. They had most of the trained mechanics, most of the shipping and mercantile firms, and the bulk of the banking and financial resources.

Even in farm production the northern states overshadowed the bucolic South, for most of the North's population was still rooted in the soil. As the progress of the war upset southern output, northern farms managed to increase theirs, despite the loss of workers to the army. The Confederacy produced enough to meet minimal needs, but the disruption of transport caused shortages in many places. One consequence was that the North produced a surplus of wheat for export at a time when drought and crop failures in Europe created a critical demand. King Wheat supplanted King Cotton as the nation's main export, the chief means of acquiring foreign money and bills of exchange to pay for imports from abroad.

The North's advantage in transport weighed heavily as the war went on. The Union had more wagons, horses, and ships than the Confederacy, and an impressive edge in railroads: about 20,000 miles to the South's 10,000. The actual discrepancy was even greater, for southern railroads were mainly short lines built to different gauges, and had few replacements for rolling stock which broke down or wore out. The Confederacy had only one east-west connection, between Memphis and Chattanooga. The latter was an important rail hub with connections via Knoxville into Virginia and down through Atlanta to Charleston and Savannah. The North, on the other hand, already had an intricate network. Three major lines gave western farmers an outlet to the eastern seaboard and greatly lessened their former dependence on the Mississippi River.

MILITARY ADVANTAGES   Against the weight of such odds the wonder was that the Confederacy managed to survive more than four years. Yet at the start certain things evened the odds. At first the South had more experienced military leaders. A number of circumstances had given rise to a military tradition in the South: the long-standing Indian danger, the fear of slave insurrection, an archaic punctilio about points of honor, and a history of expansionism. Military careers had prestige, and military schools multiplied in the antebellum years, the most notable West Points of the South being the Citadel and Virginia Military Institute. West Point itself drew many southerners, producing an army corps dominated by men from the region, chief among them Winfield Scott. Many northern West Pointers, like George B. McClellan and Ulysses S. Grant, dropped out of the service for civilian careers. A large proportion of the army's southern officers resigned their commissions to follow their states into the Confederacy. The head of the Louisiana Seminary of Learning and Military Academy (precursor of Louisiana State University), William Tecumseh Sherman, went the other way, rejoining the United States Army.

The general loyalty of the navy, which retained most of its southern officers, provided an important balance to the North's losses of army men. At the start Union seapower relied on about 90 ships, though only 42 were on active service and most were at distant stations. But under the able guidance of Secretary Gideon Welles and his assistant Gustavus V. Fox, the Union navy eventually grew to 650 vessels of all types. It never completely sealed off the South, but it raised to desperate levels the hazards of blockade running. On the inland waters navy gunboats and transports played an even more direct role in ultimately securing the Union's control of the Mississippi and its larger tributaries, which provided easy routes into the center of the Confederacy.

THE WAR'S EARLY COURSE   Amid the furies of passion after the fall of Fort Sumter, hearts lifted on both sides with the hope that the war might end with one sudden bold stroke, the capture of Washington or the fall of Richmond. Strategic thought at the time remained under the spell of Napoleon, holding that everything would turn on one climactic battle in which a huge force, massed against an enemy's point of weakness, would demoralize its armies and break its will to resist. Such ideas had been instilled in a generation of West Point cadets through their study of the baron de Jomini, a French interpreter of Napoleonic strategy, and the works of American strategists such as Henry W. Halleck's *Elements of Military Art and Science* (1846) and Dennis Mahan's *Elementary Treatise on Advance Guard, Out-Post, and Detachment Service of Troops . . .* (1847), commonly known by the short title *Out-Post*. But these ideas neglected the massive losses Napoleon had suffered, losses that finally turned his victories into defeat.

General Scott, the seventy-five-year-old commander of the Union army, saw a long road ahead. Being older—his career dated from the War of 1812—he fell under the Napoleonic spell less than others. He proposed to use the navy to blockade the long Atlantic and Gulf coastlines, and then to divide and subdivide the Confederacy by pushing southward along the main water routes: the Mississippi, Tennessee, and Cumberland Rivers. As word leaked out, the newspapers impatiently derided his "Anaconda" strategy, which they judged far too slow, indicative of the commander's old age and caution. To the end, however, the Anaconda strategy of attrition remained Union policy: there was no Napoleonic climax.

Like Lincoln, President Davis was under pressure to strike for a quick decision. Davis let the battle-hungry Gen. P. G. T. Beauregard hurry his main forces in Virginia to Manassas Junction, about twenty-five miles from Washington. Lincoln seems meanwhile to have been persuaded that Gen. Irwin McDowell's newly recruited army of some 30,000 might overrun the outnumbered Confederates and quickly march on to Richmond. But Gen. Joseph E. Johnston had another Confederate force of some 12,000 in the Shenandoah Valley around Winchester. These men slipped over the Blue Ridge and down the Manassas Gap Railroad. Most arrived on the scene the day before the battle.

On July 21, 1861, McDowell's forces encountered Beauregard's army dug in behind a little stream called Bull Run. The generals adopted markedly similar plans—each would turn the other's left. Beauregard's orders went astray, while the Federals nearly achieved their purpose early in the afternoon. Beauregard then rushed his reserves to meet the offensive, which reached its climax around the Henry House Hill. Amid the fury, Gen. Barnard Bee rallied his South Carolina volunteers by pointing to Thomas J. Jackson's brigade: "There stands Jackson like a stone wall." After McDowell's last assault had faltered, he de-

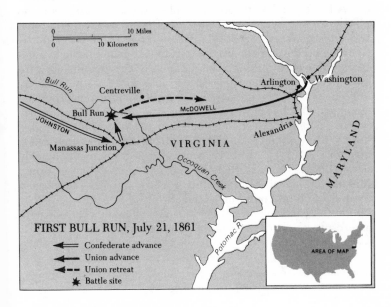

FIRST BULL RUN, July 21, 1861

⬅ Confederate advance
⬅ Union advance
⬅-- Union retreat
★ Battle site

cided that discretion was the better part of valor. An orderly retreat in battle is one of the most difficult of maneuvers, and as it happened, was too much for the raw Federal recruits. On the road back to Washington a bridge at Cub Run collapsed, and in the traffic jam that ensued, retreat turned into panic.

Fortunately for the Federals, the Confederates were about as demoralized by victory as the Federals by defeat. In any case a summer downpour the next day turned roads into sloughs. The quick decision for which both sides had reached proved beyond their grasp. Beauregard, however, was promoted to full general, one of five in the Confederate service, while the Union set about building Washington's defenses. To replace the hapless McDowell, Lincoln named Gen. George B. McClellan, fresh from his victories in western Virginia where he had secured the route of the Baltimore and Ohio Railroad.

Military Deadlock

MOBILIZING VOLUNTEERS   After the Battle of Bull Run (or Manassas)° both sides realized that the war would be more than a triumphant march. But even then mobilization was so haphazard that a Prussian general later remarked that the war was fought by little more than armed mobs on both sides. When secession came, the United States Army numbered only 16,400 men and officers, most of whom were out west. The army remained a separate and very small part of the Union forces. Both sides, in the time-honored American way of war, looked to militia and volunteers to beef up their armies, and in the beginning were swamped with lighthearted recruits.

Lincoln's first emergency call for 75,000 militiamen produced about 80,000, but most of these three-month men were nearly due to go home by the time of Bull Run. On May 3 Lincoln called for 45,000 volunteers in 40 regiments to serve for three years. So overwhelming was the response that 208 regiments quickly materialized. This was the beginning of a great volunteer army. Meeting in special session on July 4, 1861, Congress authorized a call for 500,000 more men, and after Bull Run added another 500,000. By the end of the year the first half million had enlisted, as a result mainly of state initiative and in many cases the efforts

---

°The Federals most often named battles for natural features, the Confederates for nearby towns, thus Bull Run (Manassas), Antietam (Sharpsburg), Stone's River (Murfreesboro), and the like.

of groups, towns, and even individuals who raised and equipped regiments. This pell-mell mobilization left the army with a large number of "political" officers, commissioned by state governors or elected by the recruits.

The Confederate record was much the same. The first mass enlistment put an even greater strain on limited means. By act of February 28, 1861, the Provisional Congress authorized President Davis to accept for terms of one year state troops or volunteer units offered by governors. On March 6 Davis was empowered to call 100,000 twelve-month volunteers and to employ state militia up to six months. In May, once the fighting had started, he was authorized to raise up to 400,000 three-year volunteers "without the delay of a formal call upon the respective states." Thus by early 1862, despite the leavening of three-year men, most of the veteran Confederate soldiers were nearing the end of their terms without having encountered much significant action. They were also resisting the incentives of bonuses and furloughs for reenlistment.

THE DRAFT   The Confederates were driven to adopt conscription first. By act of April 16, 1862, all male white citizens, eighteen to thirty-five, were declared members of the army for three years and those already in service were required to serve out three years. In September 1862 the upper age was raised to forty-five, and in February 1864 the age limits were further extended to cover all from seventeen to fifty, with those under eighteen and over forty-five reserved for state defense.

Comprehensive as the law appeared on its face, it was weakened in practice by two loopholes. First, a draftee might escape service either by providing an able-bodied substitute not of draft age or by paying $500 in commutation. Second, exemptions, designed to protect key civilian work, were all too subject to abuse by men seeking "bombproof" jobs. Exemption of state officials, for example, was flagrantly abused by governors like Joseph E. Brown of Georgia and Zebulon B. Vance of North Carolina, who were in charge of defining the vital jobs. The exclusion of teachers with twenty pupils inspired a sudden educational renaissance, and the exemption of one white man for each plantation with twenty or more slaves led to bitter complaints about "a rich man's war and a poor man's fight."

The Union took nearly another year to decide that volunteers would be too few once the first excitement had passed. Congress flirted with conscription in the Militia Act of July 1862, which invited states to draft 300,000 militiamen, but this move pro-

duced only about 65,000 soldiers. Then Congress offered bounties of $100 ($300 by 1864) for enlistments, but the system was
grossly abused by "bounty-jumpers" who would collect in one
place and then move on to enlist somewhere else.

Congress finally acted in March 1863 to draft men aged
twenty to forty-five. Exemptions were granted to specified federal and state officeholders and to others on medical or compas-
sionate grounds, but one could still buy a substitute or, for $300,
have his service commuted. An elaborate machinery of enforcement passed down quotas to states and districts; conscription was
used only where the number of volunteers fell short of the quota,
an incentive for communities to supplement the federal bounties. In both the North and the South conscription spurred men
to volunteer, either to collect bounties or to avoid the disgrace of
being drafted. Eventually the draft in the North produced only
46,000 conscripts and 118,000 substitutes, or about 6 percent of
the Union armies.

The draft flouted an American tradition of voluntary service
and was widely held to be arbitrary and unconstitutional. In the
South the draft also sullied the cause of states' rights by requiring
the exercise of a central power. It might have worked better had
it operated through the states, some of which had set up their
own drafts to meet the calls of President Davis. Governor Brown
of Georgia, who had one of the best records for raising troops at
first, turned into a bitter critic of the draft, pronouncing it unconstitutional and trying to obstruct its enforcement. Few of the
other governors gave it unqualified support, and Vice-President
Stephens remained unreconciled to it throughout the war.

Widespread opposition limited enforcement of the draft acts
both North and South. In New York City, which had long enjoyed commercial ties with the South, the announcement of a
draft lottery on July 11, 1863, led to a week of rioting in which
mobs turned on black scapegoats, lynched Negroes caught on
the streets, and burned down a Negro orphanage. The violence
and pillaging ran completely out of control; seventy-four persons
died, and an estimated $2 million in property was destroyed be-
fore soldiers brought from Gettysburg restored order.

As important as the problem of manpower were those of supply and logistics. If wars bring forth loyalty, they also bring forth
greed, and this war's pell-mell mobilization offered much room
for profiteering. Simon E. Cameron, the machine politician
whom Lincoln appointed secretary of war to round out his political coalition, tolerated wholesale fraud. Lincoln eased him out in
January 1862, and his successor, Edwin M. Stanton, brought
order and efficiency into the department. But he was never able

entirely to eliminate the plague of overcharging for shoddy goods.

NAVAL ACTIONS   After Bull Run, both sides mobilized for a longer war, and for the rest of 1861 into early 1862 the most important actions involved naval war and blockade. The one great threat to the Union navy proved to be short-lived. The Confederates in Norfolk fashioned an ironclad ship from an abandoned Union steam frigate, the *Merrimac*. Rechristened the *Virginia,* it ventured out on March 8, 1862, and wrought havoc among Union ships at the Chesapeake entrance. But as luck would have it, a new Union ironclad, the *Monitor,* arrived from New York in time to engage the *Virginia* on the next day. They fought to a draw and the *Virginia* returned to port, where the Confederates destroyed it when they had to give up Norfolk soon afterward.

Gradually the "anaconda" tightened its grip on the South. At Fortress Monroe, Virginia, Union forces under Benjamin F. Butler held the tip of the peninsula between the James and the York, the scene of much colonial and revolutionary history. The navy extended its bases farther down the coast in the late summer and fall of 1862. Ben Butler's troops then captured Hatteras Inlet on the Outer Banks of North Carolina in August, a foothold soon extended to Roanoke Island and New Bern on the mainland. In November 1861 a Federal flotilla appeared at Port Royal, South Carolina, pounded the fortifications into submission, and seized the port and nearby sea islands.

From there the navy's progress extended southward along the Georgia-Florida coast. To the north the Federals laid siege to Charleston; by 1863 Fort Sumter and the city itself had come under bombardment from Morris Island. In the spring of 1862 Flag Officer David Glasgow Farragut forced open the lower Mississippi and surprised New Orleans, which had expected any attack to come downstream. He won a surrender on May 1, then moved quickly to take Baton Rouge in the same way. An occupation force moved in under General Butler.

ACTIONS IN THE WEST   Except for the amphibious thrusts along the southern coast, little happened in the Eastern Theater (east of the Appalachians) before May 1862. The Western Theater (from the mountains to the Mississippi), on the other hand, flared up with several encounters and an important penetration of the Confederate states. In January, Gen. George H. Thomas cleared eastern Kentucky by a decisive defeat of the Confederates at Mill Springs. The main routes southward, however, lay farther west. There Confederate Gen. Albert Sidney Johnston had perhaps

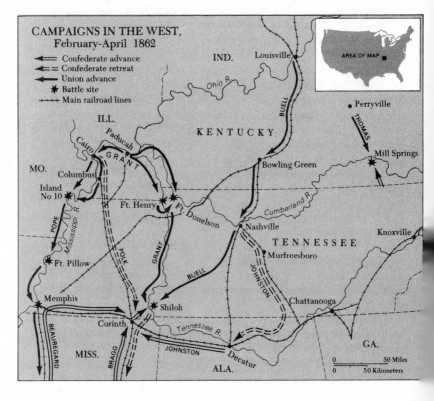

CAMPAIGNS IN THE WEST,
February-April 1862

◄═══ Confederate advance
◄═ ═ Confederate retreat
◄─── Union advance
✴ Battle site
+++++ Main railroad lines

AREA OF MAP

IND.   Louisville

Ohio R.

ILL.

KENTUCKY   Perryville

Cairo   Paducah   BUELL

MO.   GRANT   Bowling Green   Mill Springs

Columbus   THOMAS

Island   Ft. Henry   Cumberland R.   Knoxville
No 10   Ft. Donelson

POPE   Nashville

MISSISSIPPI R.   POLK   GRANT   TENNESSEE

Ft. Pillow   BUELL   Murfreesboro

Memphis   JOHNSTON   Chattanooga

BEAUREGARD   Corinth   Shiloh
Tennessee R.

MISS.   BRAGG   JOHNSTON   Decatur   GA.
0   50 Miles
ALA.   0   50 Kilometers

40,000 men stretched over some 150 miles, with concentrations
at Columbus and Bowling Green, Kentucky, each astride a major
north-south railroad. At the center, however, only about 5,500
men held Fort Henry on the Tennessee and Fort Donelson on the
Cumberland.

Early in 1862 Ulysses S. Grant made the first thrust against
Johnston's center. Moving out of Cairo and Paducah with a gunboat flotilla under Commodore Andrew H. Foote, he swung
southward up the Tennessee River toward Fort Henry. After a
pounding from the Union gunboats, Fort Henry fell on February
6. Grant then moved quickly overland to attack Fort Donelson,
while Foote ran his gunboats back to the Ohio and up the Cumberland. Donelson proved a harder nut to crack, but on February
16 it gave up with some 12,000 men. Grant's terms, "unconditional surrender," and his quick success sent a thrill through the
Union. U. S. "Unconditional Surrender" Grant had not only
opened a water route to Nashville, but had thrust his forces between the two strongholds of the western Confederates. A. S.
Johnston therefore had to give up his foothold in Kentucky and
abandon Nashville to Don Carlos Buell's Army of the Ohio (Feb-

ruary 25) in order to reunite his forces at Corinth, Mississippi, along the Memphis and Chattanooga Railroad.

SHILOH Thus, quickly, the Union regained most of Kentucky and western Tennessee, and stood poised to strike at the Deep South. On the Mississippi itself, Confederate strong points at Island No. 10 and at Fort Pillow fell on April 7 and 13 respectively, and Memphis on June 6, to a combined force under Commodore Foote and Gen. John Pope. Meanwhile Grant moved farther southward along the Tennessee River, hoping to link up with Buell's army near the southern border of Tennessee. At Pittsburg Landing, their rendezvous, Grant made a deadly mistake. While planning his attack on Corinth, he failed to set up defensive lines. The morning of April 6 the Confederates struck suddenly at Shiloh, a country church, and after a day of bloody confusion, pinned Grant's men against the river. But under the cover of gunboats and artillery at Pittsburg Landing, reinforcements from Buell's army arrived overnight. The next day the tide turned and the Rebels withdrew to Corinth, with Grant's army too battered to pursue.

Shiloh was the costliest battle in which Americans had ever engaged, although worse was yet to come. Combined casualties of nearly 25,000 exceeded the total dead and wounded of the Revolution, the War of 1812, and the Mexican War combined. Among the dead was Albert Sidney Johnston, an artery in his leg severed by a gunshot. The Union, too, lost for a while the full services of its finest general. Grant had been caught napping and was too shattered by his heavy losses to press the advantage. The Confederates had missed their chance to prevent Grant's linkage with Buell, but as at Bull Run, the victors were as demoralized by victory as the losers by defeat.

Gen. Henry W. Halleck, who first replaced Frémont in Missouri and then took overall command in the West, now arrived to take personal command of the Union forces in the field. He shelved Grant in an insignificant position as second in command, giving the troops Grant had been leading to George H. Thomas. Halleck, "Old Brains," the textbook strategist of offensive war, proved in the field to be unaccountably timid. Determined not to repeat Grant's mistake, he moved with profound caution on Corinth, taking at face value every inflated report of Rebel strength. But outnumbered better than two to one, P. G. T. Beauregard (Johnston's successor) abandoned Corinth to the Federals on May 30, falling back on Tupelo.

Halleck let slip the chance to overwhelm Beauregard. Instead, before being summoned back to Washington in June, he split up

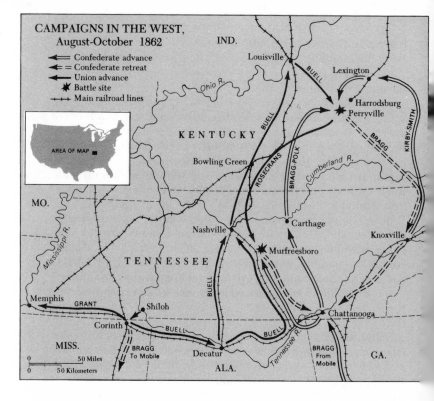

his army in several directions. Grant remained on the scene, guarding Corinth and other points. Buell withdrew to Nashville to prepare an offensive against Chattanooga. The Confederate force, commanded by Braxton Bragg after the loss of Corinth, moved via Mobile to Chattanooga. For the remainder of 1862 the chief action in the Western Theater was a series of inconclusive maneuvers and two sharp engagements. Bragg took his army to Kentucky, threatened Louisville, and was stopped by Buell's Army of the Ohio at Perryville on October 8. Kentuckians failed to rally to the Confederate flag and Bragg pulled back into Tennessee. Buell, meanwhile, under pressure to sever the rail line at Chattanooga, proved to be one of the many Union generals who Lincoln said had "the slows." The administration replaced him with William S. Rosecrans, who moved out of Nashville and met Bragg in the costly engagement at Murfreesboro (or Stone's River), December 31 to January 3, after which Bragg cleared out of central Tennessee and fell back on Chattanooga. But Lincoln still coveted eastern Tennessee both for its many Unionists and for its railroads, which he wanted to cut to get between the Rebels and their "hog and hominy."

MCCLELLAN'S PENINSULAR CAMPAIGN   The Eastern Theater, aside from the coastal operations, remained fairly quiet for nine months after Bull Run. When George B. McClellan took command in Washington after Bull Run, he vigorously set about getting men back to their units, getting them organized, and keeping them busy—in short, he built an army out of the fragments left from the first battle. In November, upon General Scott's retirement, which McClellan impatiently awaited, he became general-in-chief. The newspapers dubbed him Little Napoleon, and a photographer posed him with his right hand inside his jacket. But these impressions were misleading. On the surface McClellan exuded confidence and poise, and a certain flair for parade-ground showmanship. Yet his knack for organization never went much beyond that.

Time passed, the army grew, and McClellan kept building his forces to meet the superior numbers that always seemed to be facing him. His intelligence service, headed by the private detective Allen Pinkerton, tended to estimate enemy forces at double their actual size. Before moving, there was always the need to do this or that, to get 10,000 or 20,000 more men, always something. McClellan's Army of the Potomac was nine months in gestation after Bull Run, and then moved mainly because Lincoln insisted. In General Order No. 1, the president directed McClellan to begin forward movement by Washington's Birthday, February 22. The president's idea was that the army should move directly toward Richmond, keeping itself between the Confederate army and Washington. But McClellan had another idea, and despite his reluctance to move, very nearly pulled it off. The idea was to enter Richmond by the side door, so to speak, up the neck of land between the York and James Rivers, site of Jamestown, Williamsburg, and Yorktown, at the tip of which Federal forces already held Fortress Monroe, about seventy-five miles from Richmond.

Lincoln consented but specified, to McClellan's chargin, that a force be left under McDowell to guard Washington. In mid-March 1862 McClellan's army finally embarked. Advancing slowly up the thinly defended peninsula, taking no chances, McClellan brought Yorktown under siege from April 5 until May 4, when the Confederates slipped away, having accomplished their purpose of allowing Gen. Joseph E. Johnston to get his army in front of Richmond. Before the end of May McClellan's advance units sighted the church spires of Richmond. But his army was divided by the Chickahominy River, which splits the peninsula north and east of Richmond, and though Richmond lay south of the Chickahominy, part of the Confederate army was on the north bank to counter any southward move from Washington by McDowell.

McDowell, however, was delayed by more urgent matters, or what seemed so. President Davis, at the urging of military adviser Robert E. Lee, sent Stonewall Jackson into the Shenandoah Valley on what proved to be a brilliant diversionary action. From March 23 to June 9, Jackson and some 18,000 men pinned down two separate armies with more than twice his numbers by striking first at Frémont in the western Virginia mountains, then at Nathanial P. Banks at the northern end of the valley. While McDowell braced to defend Washington, Jackson hastened back to defend Richmond.

On May 31 Johnston struck at Union forces isolated on the south bank by the flooded river. In the battle of Seven Pines (Fair Oaks), only the arrival of reinforcements, who somehow crossed the swollen river, prevented a disastrous Union defeat. Both

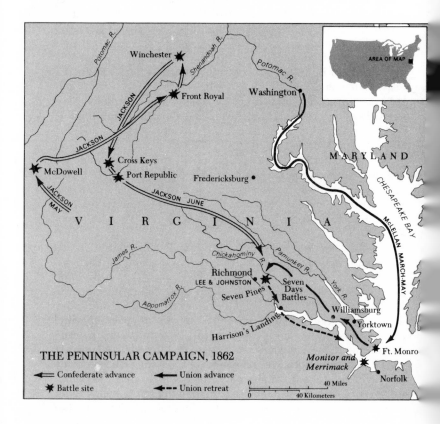

THE PENINSULAR CAMPAIGN, 1862

sides took heavy casualties, and General Johnston was severely wounded. At this point Robert E. Lee assumed command of the Army of Northern Virginia. Lee quickly sized up the situation. Reunited with the elusive Jackson, Lee would hit the Union forces north of the Chickahominy with everything he had, leaving a token force in front of Richmond.

On June 26, Lee and Jackson struck the Union's extreme right at Mechanicsville, and kept up the assault on successive days at Gaines' Mill, Savage's Station, and White Oak Swamp. As the Federals withdrew they inflicted heavy losses on the Rebels, frustrating Lee's purpose of crushing the right flank. McClellan managed to get his main forces on the south side of the river, and established a new base at Harrison's Landing on the James. Lee's final desperate attack came at Malvern Hill (July 1), where the Confederates suffered heavy losses from Union artillery and gunboats in the James. The Seven Days' Battles (June 25 to July 1) had failed to dislodge the Union forces. McClellan was still near Richmond, with good supply lines on the James River.

On July 9, when Lincoln visited McClellan's headquarters on the James, the general complained that the administration had failed to support him adequately and handed the president a strange document, the "Harrison's Landing Letter," in which, despite his critical plight, he instructed the president at length on war policies. It was ample reason to remove the general. Instead Lincoln returned to Washington and on July 11 called Henry Halleck from the west to take charge as general-in-chief, a post that McClellan had temporarily vacated.

SECOND BATTLE OF MANASSAS   The new high command decided to evacuate the peninsula, which had become the graveyard of the last hope for a short war. McClellan was ordered to leave the peninsula and join the Washington defense force, now under John Pope, for a new overland move on Richmond. As McClellan's Army of the Potomac began to pull out, Lee moved northward to strike at Pope before McClellan arrived. Once again he adopted an audacious stratagem. Dividing his forces, he sent Jackson on a sweep around Pope's right flank to attack his supply lines. At Cedar Mountain on August 9 Jackson pushed back an advance party under General Banks, and on August 26 issued suddenly down Thoroughfare Gap to seize and destroy the Federal supply base at Manassas Junction. At Second Bull Run (or Second Manassas), fought on almost the same site as the earlier battle, Pope assumed that he faced only Jackson, but Lee's main army by that time had joined in. On August 30 a crushing attack on Pope's flank by James Longstreet's corps of 30,000 drove the Federals from the field. In the next few days the Union forces pulled back into the fortifications around Washington, where McClellan once again took command and reorganized.

ANTIETAM   But Lee gave him little time. Still on the offensive, early in September he invaded western Maryland. His purpose was in part to get the fighting out of Virginia during harvest season, in part to score a victory on Union soil for the sake of prestige and possible foreign recognition. By a stroke of fortune a

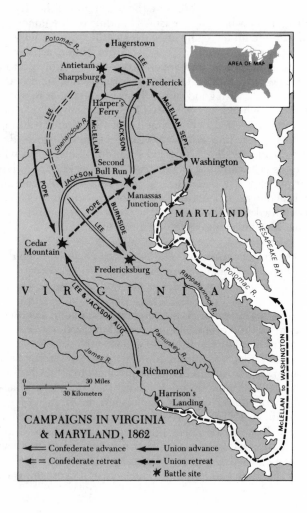

CAMPAIGNS IN VIRGINIA & MARYLAND, 1862

Lincoln and his staff at Antietam, 1862. [National Archives]

Union soldier picked up a bundle of cigars with an order from Lee wrapped around them. The paper revealed that Lee had again divided his army, sending Jackson off to take Harpers Ferry. But McClellan delayed, still worried about enemy strength, and Lee got most of his army back together behind Antietam Creek. On September 17, at the Battle of Antietam (Sharpsburg), just as the Confederate lines seemed ready to break, the last of Jackson's men arrived to bolster them. At this point McClellan backed away, letting Lee get away across the Potomac. Lincoln, discouraged by McClellan's failure to follow up, removed him once and for all and assigned him to recruiting duty in Trenton, New Jersey. McClellan would never again have a command.

FREDERICKSBURG   In his search for a fighting general Lincoln now made the worst choice of all. He turned to Ambrose E. Burnside, whose main achievements to that time had been to capture Roanoke Island and grow his famous side-whiskers. Burnside had twice before turned down the job on the grounds that he felt unfit for so large a command. But if the White House wanted him to fight, he would fight even in the face of oncoming winter. On December 13 he sent his men across the Rappahannock River to face Lee's forces, entrenched behind Fredericksburg on Marye's Heights. Confederate artillery and small-arms fire chewed up the blue columns as they crossed a mile of bottomland outside the town. Six times the Union's suicidal assaults melted under the murderous fire issuing from protected positions above and below them. After taking more than 12,000 casualties compared to fewer than 6,000 for the Confederates, Burnside retired across the river.

The year 1862 ended with forces in the East deadlocked and the Union advance in the West stalled since mid-year. Union morale reached a low ebb. Northern Democrats were calling for negotiated peace. At the same time Lincoln was under pressure from the Radicals of his own party who were pushing for more stringent war measures, questioning the competence of the president, and demanding the removal of Secretary of State Seward. Burnside was under fire from his own officers, some of whom were ready to testify publicly to his shortcomings.

But the deeper currents of the war were turning in favor of the Union: in a lengthening war its resources began to tell. In both the Eastern and Western Theaters the Confederate counterattack had been turned back. The year ended with forces under Rosecrans and Bragg locked in combat at Stone's River (Murfreesboro) in Tennessee. There again, after three more days of bloody stalemate, the Confederates fell back. And even while the armies clashed on that darkling plain in Tennessee, Lincoln by the stroke of a pen had changed the conflict from a war for the Union into a revolutionary struggle for abolition. On January 1, 1863, he signed the Emancipation Proclamation.

EMANCIPATION

It was the product of long and painful deliberation. In Lincoln's annual message of December 3, 1861, he had warned Congress to be "anxious and careful" that the war did not "degenerate into a violent and remorseless revolutionary struggle." At the outset he had upheld the promise of his party's platform to restore the Union but accept slavery where it existed. Congress too endorsed that position in the Crittenden-Johnson Resolutions which passed both houses soon after the Battle of Bull Run, with few dissenting votes. Once fighting began, the need to hold the border states dictated caution on the issue of emancipation. Beyond that, some other things deterred action. For one, Lincoln had to cope with a deep-seated racial prejudice in the North. Even the antislavery impulse derived often from the will to keep both slavery and blacks in the South. Lincoln himself harbored doubts about his authority to act so long as he clung to the view that the states remained legally in the Union. The only way around the problem would be to justify emancipation on the bases of military necessity and the president's war powers, as in fact John Quincy Adams had foreseen many years before.

Former slaves, or "contrabands," on Mr. Foller's farm, Cumberland Landing, Virginia, 1862. [Library of Congress]

A MEASURE OF WAR   The war forced the issue. Fugitive slaves began to turn up in Union camps. In May 1861 at Fortress Monroe, Virginia, Benjamin F. Butler declared them "contraband of war" and put them to work on his fortifications. "Contrabands" soon became a common name for runaways in Union lines. But John C. Frémont pressed the issue one step too far. As commander of the Department of the West, on August 30, 1861, he simply liberated the slaves of all who actively helped the Rebel cause, an action which risked unsettling the yet-doubtful border states. Lincoln demanded that Frémont conform to the Confiscation Act of 1861, which freed only those slaves used by Rebel military services, as Butler's first "contrabands" had been. On May 9, 1862, Gen. David Hunter declared free all slaves in South Carolina, Georgia, and Florida. He had no runaway slaves in his lines, he said, although some runaway masters had fled the scene. Lincoln quickly revoked the order, and took the brunt of the rising outrage among congressional Radicals.

Lincoln himself meanwhile edged toward emancipation. In March 1862 he proposed that federal compensation be offered any state which began gradual emancipation. The cost in the border states, he estimated, would about equal the cost of eighty-seven days of the war. The plan failed in Congress because of border-state opposition, but on April 16, 1862, Lincoln signed an act which abolished slavery in the District of Columbia, with compensation to owners; on June 19 another act excluded slavery from the territories, without offering owners compensation. A Second Confiscation Act, passed on July 17, liberated the slaves of all persons aiding the rebellion. Still another act forbade the army to help return runaways.

To save the Union, Lincoln finally decided, complete emancipation would be required for several reasons: slave labor bolstered the Rebel cause, sagging morale in the North needed the lift of a moral cause, and public opinion was swinging that way as the war dragged on. Proclaiming a war on slavery, moreover, would end forever any chance that France or Britain would suport the Confederacy. In July 1862 Lincoln first confided to his cabinet that he had in mind a proclamation that under his war powers would free the slaves of the enemy. At the time Seward advised him to wait for a Union victory in order to avoid any semblance of desperation.

The delay lasted through the long weeks during which Lee invaded Maryland and Bragg moved into Kentucky. As late as August 22, 1962, Lincoln responded to Horace Greeley's plea for emancipation: "My paramount object in this struggle is to save the Union and is not either to save or destroy slavery." The time to act finally came a month later, after Antietam. It was a dubious victory, but it did result in Lee's withdrawal. On September 22 Lincoln issued a preliminary Emancipation Proclamation, in which he repeated all his earlier stands: that his object was mainly to restore the Union and that he favored proposals for compensated emancipation and colonization. But the main burden of the document was his warning that on January 1, 1863, "all persons held as slaves within any state, or designated part of a state, the people whereof shall be in rebellion against the United States, shall be then, thenceforward and forever free."

In his annual message of December 1862 Lincoln once again raised the question of border-state compensation and ended with one of his most eloquent passages:

> We, even we here, hold the power and bear the responsibility. In giving freedom to the slave we assure freedom to the free—honorable alike in what we give and what we preserve. We shall nobly save or meanly lose the last, best hope of earth. Other means may succeed; this could not fail. The way is plain, peaceful, generous, just—a way which if followed the world will forever applaud and God must forever bless.

But this peroration was delivered with one eye to justifying the emancipation he had already promised. On January 1, 1863, Lincoln signed the second Emancipation Proclamation, giving effect to his promise of September, again emphasizing that this was a war measure based on his war powers. He also urged blacks to abstain from violence except in self-defense, and added that free blacks would now be received into the armed service of the

Two views of the Emancipation Proclamation. The Union view (top) shows a thoughtful Lincoln composing the Proclamation with the Constitution and the Holy Bible in his lap. The Confederate view (bottom) shows a demented Lincoln with his foot on the Constitution using an inkwell held by the devil. [Library of Congress]

United States. For all its eloquence, the document set forth its points in commonplace terms. *Die Presse*, a newspaper in far-away Austria, got the point better than many closer home: "Lincoln is a figure *sui generis* in history. No pathos, no idealistic flights of eloquence, no posing, no wrapping himself in the toga of history. The most formidable decrees which he hurls against the enemy and which will never lose their historic significance, resemble—as the author intends them to—ordinary summonses sent by one lawyer to another on the opposing side. . . . " But as Henry Adams wrote from the London embassy, the Proclamation had created "an almost convulsive reaction in our favour."

REACTIONS TO EMANCIPATION Among the Confederate states, Tennessee and the occupied parts of Virginia and Louisiana were exempted from its effect. The document, with few exceptions, freed no slaves who were within Union lines at the time, as cynics noted. Moreover, it went little further than the Second Confiscation Act. But these objections missed a point which black slaves readily grasped. "In a document proclaiming liberty," wrote the historian Benjamin Quarles, "the unfree never bother to read the fine print." Word spread quickly in the quarters, and in some cases masters learned of it first from their slaves. Though most slaves deemed it safer just to wait for the "day of jubilee" when Union forces arrived, some actively claimed their freedom. One spectacular instance was that of the black pilot Robert Smalls, who one night in May 1862 took over a small Confederate gunboat, the *Planter*, and sailed his family through Charleston Harbor out to the blockading Union fleet. Later he served the Union navy as a pilot and still later became a congressman.

BLACKS IN THE MILITARY From very early in the war Union commanders found "contrabands" like Smalls useful as guides to unfamiliar terrain and waterways, informants on the enemy, and at the very least common laborers. While menial labor by blacks was familiar enough, military service was something else again. Though not unprecedented, it aroused in whites instinctive fears. For more than a year the administration warily evaded the issue, although the navy began to enlist blacks before the end of 1861.

Even after Congress authorized the enlistment of Negroes in the Second Confiscation Act of July 1862, the administration ordered no general mobilization of black troops. It did, however, permit Gen. Rufus Saxton to raise five regiments in the Sea Island, forming the First South Carolina Volunteer Regiment under Col. Thomas Wentworth Higginson, which sallied forth in late 1862 on raids along the Georgia-Florida coast. On January 1, 1863, Lincoln's Emancipation Proclamation reaffirmed the policy that blacks could enroll in the armed services and sparked new efforts to organize all-black units. Gov. John A. Andrew swiftly mustered the Massachusetts Fifty-fourth Regiment as the first northern all-Negro unit, under Col. Robert Gould Shaw. Rhode Island and other states soon followed suit. In May the War Department authorized general recruitment of blacks all over the country.

By mid-1863 black units were involved in significant action in both the Eastern and Western Theaters. On July 18 the Massachusetts Fifty-fourth led a gallant if hopeless assault on Battery Wagner, at the entrance to Charleston Harbor. This action, and the use of Negro units in the Vicksburg campaign, did much to win acceptance for both black soldiers and for emancipation, at least as a proper strategem of war. Commenting on Union victories at Port Hudson and Milliken's Bend, Mississippi, Lincoln reported that "some of our commanders . . . believe that . . . the use of colored troops constitutes the heaviest blow yet dealt to the rebels, and that at least one of these important successes could not have been achieved . . . but for the aid of black soldiers."

Altogether, between 180,000 and 200,000 black Americans served in the Union army, providing around 10 percent of its total. Some 38,000 gave their lives. In the Union navy the 29,500 blacks accounted for about a fourth of all enlistments; of

Company E of the Fourth U.S. Colored Infantry. These determined soldiers helped defend Washington, D.C. [Library of Congress]

these more than 2,800 died. Not only black men but black women as well served in the war; Harriet Tubman and Susie King Taylor, for instance, were nurses with Clara Barton in the Sea Islands.

As the war entered its final months freedom emerged more fully as a legal reality. Three major steps occurred in January 1865 when both Missouri and Tennessee abolished slavery by state action and the House of Representatives passed an abolition amendment introduced by Sen. Lyman Trumbull of Illinois the year before. Upon ratification by three-fourths of the states, the Thirteenth Amendment became part of the Constitution on December 18, 1865, and removed any lingering doubts about the legality of emancipation. By then, in fact, slavery remained only in the border states of Kentucky and Delaware.

GOVERNMENT DURING THE WAR

Striking the shackles from 3.5 million slaves was a momentous social and economic revolution. But an even broader revolution got under way as power shifted from South to North with secession. Before the war southern congressmen had been able at least to frustrate the designs of both Free Soil and Whiggery. But once the secessionists abandoned Congress to the Republicans, a dramatic change occurred. The protective tariff, a transcontinental railroad, a homestead act—all of which had been stalled by sectional controversy—were adopted before the end of 1862. The National Banking Act followed in 1863. These were supplemented by the Morrill Land Grant Act (1862), which provided federal aid to state colleges of "agriculture and mechanic arts," and the Contract Labor Act (1864), which aided the importation of immigrant labor. All of these had great long-term significance.

UNION FINANCES   The more immediate problem for Congress was how to finance the war, because expenditures generally ran ahead of expectations while revenues lagged behind. Three expedients were open: higher taxes, issues of paper money, and borrowing. The higher taxes came chiefly in the form of the Morrill Tariff and excise duties which one historian said "might be described with a near approach to accuracy as a tax on everything." Excises taxed manufactures and the practice of nearly every profession. A butcher, for example, had to pay thirty cents for every head of beef he slaughtered, ten cents for every hog, five for every sheep. On top of the excises came an income tax which started in 1861 at 3 percent of incomes over $800 and increased in 1864 to a graduated rate rising from 5 percent of incomes over $600 to 10 percent of incomes over $10,000. To collect these the Revenue Act of 1862 created a Bureau of Internal Revenue.

But tax revenues trickled in so slowly—in the end they would meet 21 percent of wartime expenditures—that Congress in 1862 forced upon a reluctant Treasury Secretary Chase the expedient of printing paper money, backed up only by the proviso that it was legal tender for all debts. Beginning with the Legal Tender Act of February 1862, Congress ultimately authorized $450 million of the notes, which soon became known as "greenbacks" because of their color. The amount of greenbacks issued was limited enough to tide the Union over its financial crisis without causing the ruinous inflation which the unlimited issue of paper money caused in the Confederacy.

The net wartime issue of $431 million in greenbacks was only about a sixth of the total wartime indebtedness. From the beginning Chase had intended to rely for funds chiefly on the sale of bonds. Sales went slowly at first, although the issue of greenbacks, which depreciated in value against gold, encouraged the purchase of 6 percent bonds with the cheaper currency. But after October 1862 a Philadelphia banker named Jay Cooke (sometimes tagged "The Financier of the Civil War") mobilized a nationwide machinery of agents and patriotic propaganda for the sale of bonds. Eventually bonds amounting to more than $2 billion were sold, but not all by the ballyhoo of Jay Cooke and Company. New banks formed under the National Banking Act were required to invest part of their capital in the bonds, and encouraged to invest even more as security for the national banknotes they could issue.

For many businessmen wartime ventures brought quick riches which were made visible all too often in vulgar display and extravagance. "The world has seen its iron age, its silver age, its golden age and its brazen age," the New York *Herald* commented. "This is the age of shoddy . . . shoddy brokers in Wall Street, or shoddy manufacturers of shoddy goods, or shoddy contractors for shoddy articles for shoddy government. Six days a week they are shoddy businessmen. On the seventh day they are shoddy Christians." Not all the wartime fortunes, however, were made dishonestly. And their long-run importance was in promoting the capital accumulation with which American businessmen fueled later expansion. Wartime business laid the groundwork for the fortunes of such nabobs as Morgan, Rockefeller, Mellon, Carnegie, Stanford, Huntington, Armour, and Swift.

CONFEDERATE FINANCES   Confederate finances were a disaster from the start. Treasury Secretary Christopher Memminger was appointed more to give South Carolina a place in the cabinet than for his financial skill or tact. But even the most tactful genius might never have overcome popular reluctance, congressional stalling, and limited governmental structure, all of which hindered efforts to finance the Confederacy. In the first year of its existence the Confederacy levied export and import duties, but exports and imports were low. It enacted a tax of one-half of 1 percent on most forms of property, which should have yielded a hefty income, but the Confederacy farmed out its collection to the states, promising a 10 percent rebate on the take. The result was chaos. All but three states raised their quota by floating loans, which only worsened inflation.

In April 1863 Memminger extracted from the Confederate Congress a measure which, like Union excises, taxed nearly everything. A 10 percent tax in kind on all agricultural products did more to outrage farmers and planters than to supply the army, however. Enforcement was so poor and evasion so easy that the taxes produced only negligible amounts of depreciated currency.

Altogether, taxes covered no more than 5 percent of Confederate costs, perhaps less; bond issues accounted for less than 33 percent; and treasury notes more than 66 percent. The last resort, the printing press, was in fact one of the early resorts. The first issue of $1 million in treasury notes in February 1861 was only the beginning: $20 million was authorized in May and $100 million in August, launching the Confederacy on an extended binge for which the only cure was more of the same. Altogether the Confederacy turned out more than $1 billion in paper money. J.B. Jones, a clerk at the War Department in Richmond, reported in March 1864 a wild turkey offered in the market for $100, flour at $425 a barrel, home calls by doctors at $30, meal at $72 a bushel, and bacon at $10 a pound. Country folk were likely to have enough for subsistence, perhaps a little surplus to barter, but townspeople on fixed incomes were caught in a merciless squeeze.

CONFEDERATE DIPLOMACY   Civil wars often become international conflicts. The foundation of Confederate diplomacy in fact was the hope of help from the outside in the form of supplies, diplomatic recognition, or perhaps even intervention. The South indulged the pathetic expectation that diplomatic recognition would prove decisive, when in fact it more likely would have followed decisive victory in the field, which never came. An equally fragile illusion was the conviction that King Cotton, as an Atlanta newspaper affirmed, would "bring more wooing princes to the feet of the Confederate states than Penelope had."

Indeed, to help foreign leaders make up their minds, the Confederates imposed a voluntary embargo on shipments of cotton until the Union blockade began to strangle their foreign trade. European textile manufacturers meanwhile subsisted on the carryover from their purchase of the record crops of 1859 and 1860. By the time they needed cotton, it was available from new sources in Egypt, India, and elsewhere. Cotton textiles aside, the British economy was undergoing a boom from wartime trade with the Union and blockade-running into the Confederacy.

The first Confederate emissaries to England and France took hope when Foreign Minister Lord John Russell received them informally after their arrival in London in May 1861; they even got a promise from Napoleon III to recognize the Confederacy if Britain would lead the way. The key was therefore in London, but Russell refused to receive the Confederates again, partly because of Union pressures and partly out of British self-interest.

One incident early in the war threatened to upset British equanimity. In November 1861 Cap. Charles Wilkes's Union warship *San Jacinto* stopped a British mail packet, the *Trent*, and took into custody two Confederate commissioners, James. M. Mason and John Slidell, en route from Havana to Europe. Celebrated as a heroic deed by a northern public still starved for victories, the *Trent* affair roused a storm of protest in Britain. An ultimatum for the captives' release was delivered to Washington, confronting Lincoln and Seward with an explosive crisis. But the interference with a neutral ship on the high seas violated long-settled American principle, and Seward finally decided to face down popular clamor and release Mason and Slidell, much to their own chagrin. As martyrs in Boston's Fort Warren they were more useful to their own cause than they could ever be in London and Paris.

In contrast to the futility of King Cotton diplomacy, Confederate commissioners scored some successes in getting supplies. The most spectacular feat was James D. Bulloch's procurement of Confederate raiding ships. Although British law forbade the sale of warships to belligerents, Bulloch contrived to have the ships built and then, on trial runs, to escape to the Azores or elsewhere for outfitting with guns. In all, eighteen such ships were activated and saw action in the Atlantic, Pacific, and Indian Oceans, where they sank hundreds of Yankee ships and threw terror into the rest. The most spectacular of the Confederate raiders were the first two, the *Florida* and the *Alabama*, which took thirty-eight and sixty-four prizes respectively.

A much greater threat to Union seapower came when Bulloch contracted with England's Laird Shipyard for fast ironclad ships with pointed prows. Named the "Laird rams," they were meant to smash the Union's wooden vessels, break its blockade, and maybe even attack northern ports. Perhaps in response to news of Union victories at Gettysburg and Vicksburg, however, the British government decided to hold the Laird rams in port. Thereafter the British showed little disposition to ignore Confederate transgressions, although one Rebel raider, the *Shenandoah*, did escape British port in October 1864, and was still burning Yankee whalers in the Bering Sea as late as July 1865, when a passing British ship brought word that the war was over.

UNION POLITICS AND CIVIL LIBERTIES   On the home fronts there was no moratorium on politics, North or South. Within his own party Lincoln faced a Radical wing composed mainly of prewar abolitionists. By the end of 1861 they were getting restless with the policy of fighting solely to protect the Union. The congressional Joint Committee on the Conduct of the War, created December 20,1861, became an instrument of their cause. Led by men like Thaddeus Stevens and George W. Julian in the House, and Charles Sumner, Benjamin F. Wade (the chairman), and Zachariah Chandler in the Senate, they pushed for confiscation and emancipation, and a more vigorous prosecution of the war. Still, the greater body of Republicans backed Lincoln's more cautious approach. And the party was generally united on economic policy.

The Democratic party was set back by the loss of its southern wing and the death of its leader, Stephen A. Douglas, in June 1861. By and large, northern Democrats supported a war for the "Union as it was" before 1860 giving reluctant support to war policies but opposing wartime restraints on civil liberties and the new economic legislation. "War Democrats" like Sen. Andrew Johnson and Secretary of War Edwin M. Stanton fully supported Lincoln's policies, however, while a Peace Wing of the party preferred an end to the fighting, even at risk to the Union. An extreme fringe of the Peace Wing even flirted with outright disloyalty. The "Copperheads," as they were called, organized secret orders with such names as Sons of Liberty for purposes that were none too clear and often suspect. They were strongest in states such as Ohio, Indiana, and Illinois, all leavened with native southerners, some of whom were pro-Confederate.

Coercive measures against disloyalty were perhaps as much a boost as a hindrance to Democrats, who took up the cause of civil liberty. Early in the war Lincoln assumed the power to suspend the writ of habeas corpus and subjected "disloyal" persons to martial law—often just on vague suspicion. The Constitution said only that it should be suspended in cases of rebellion or invasion, but congressional leaders argued that Congress alone had authority to act, since the provision fell in Article 1, which deals with the powers of Congress. When Congress, by the Habeas Corpus Act of March 1863, finally authorized the president to suspend the writ, it required officers to report the names of all arrested persons to the nearest district court, and provided that if the grand jury found no indictment, those arrested could be released upon taking an oath of allegiance.

There were probably more than 14,000 arrests made without a writ of habeas corpus. One celebrated case arose in 1863 when Federal soldiers hustled Clement L. Vallandigham out of his home in Dayton, Ohio. Brought before a military commission, Ohio's most prominent Copperhead was condemned to confinement for the duration of the war because he had questioned arbitrary arrests. The muzzling of a political opponent proved such an embarrassment to Lincoln that he commuted the sentence, but only by another irregular device, banishment behind the Confederate lines. Vallandigham eventually found his way to Canada. In 1863 he ran as Democratic candidate for governor *in absentia*, and in 1864 slipped back into the country. He was left alone at Lincoln's order, took part in the Democratic national convention, and ultimately proved more of an embarrassment to the Democrats than to the president.

In the midterm elections of 1862, the Democrats exploited war weariness and resentment of Lincoln's war measures to gain a startling recovery, though not control of Congress. At their 1864 national convention in Chicago the Democrats called for an armistice to be followed by a national convention which would restore the Union. They named Gen. George B. McClellan as their candidate, but McClellan distanced himself from the peace platform by declaring that agreement on Union would have to precede peace.

Radical Republicans, who still regarded Lincoln as soft on treason, trotted out two candidates, first Salmon P. Chase, who failed to get the support of his own state, then John C. Frémont, but too late. Lincoln outmaneuvered them at every turn, and without public announcement of a choice, brought about the vice-presidential nomination of Andrew Johnson, a War Democrat from Tennessee, on the "National Union" ticket, so named to minimize partisanship. As the war dragged on through 1864, with Grant taking heavy losses in Virginia, Lincoln fully expected to lose. Then Admiral Farragut's capture of Mobile in August and Sherman's capture of Atlanta on September 2 turned the tide. McClellan carried only New Jersey, Delaware, and Kentucky, with 21 electoral votes to Lincoln's 212, and 1 million popular votes (45 percent) to Lincoln's 2.2 million (55 percent).

CONFEDERATE POLITICS   Unlike Lincoln, Jefferson Davis never had to contest a presidential election. Both Davis and Vice-President Stephens, named first by the Provisional Congress, were elected without opposition in 1861 and began single terms of six years on Washington's Birthday, February 22, 1862. But discontent flourished as things went from bad to worse, and came very close to home in the Richmond bread riot of April 2, 1863, which ended only when Davis himself persuaded the mob to disperse. After the congressional elections of 1863, the second and last in the confederacy, about a third of the legislators were antiadministration. Although parties as such did not figure in the elections, it was noteworthy that many ex-Whigs and other opponents of secession were chosen.

Davis, like Lincoln, had to contend with dissenters. Large pockets of Union loyalists appeared in the German counties of Texas, the hill country of Arkansas, and most of all along the Appalachian spine that reached as far as Alabama and Georgia. Many Unionists followed their states into the Confederacy reluctantly, and were receptive to talk of peace. They were less troublesome to Davis, however, than the states'-rights men who had embraced secession and then guarded states' rights against the Confederacy as zealously as they had against the Union. Georgia under Gov. Joseph E. Brown, and to a lesser degree North Carolina under Gov. Zebulon B. Vance, were strongholds of such sentiment, which prevailed widely elsewhere as well. They challenged, among other things, the legality of conscription, taxes on farm produce, and above all the suspension of habeas corpus. Never mind that Davis, the legal-minded leader of a revolution, never suspended habeas corpus until granted congressional authority on February 27, 1862, and then did so sparingly. Vice-President Alexander Stephens carried on a running battle against

Davis's effort to establish "military despotism," left Richmond to sulk at his Georgia home for eighteen months, and warned the Georgia legislature in 1864, on the eve of Sherman's march, against the "siren song, 'Independence first and liberty afterwards.' " The ultimate failure of the Confederacy has been attributed to many things. One of many ironies was that the fight for slavery suffered from a doctrinaire defense of liberty. Among other things, the Confederacy died of dogma.

THE FALTERING CONFEDERACY

In 1863 the hinge of fate began to close the door on the brief career of the Confederacy. After the Union disaster at Fredericksburg, Lincoln's search for a general turned to one of Burnsides's disgruntled lieutenants, Joseph E. Hooker, whose pugnacity had given him the name of "Fighting Joe." Hooker took over the Army of the Potomac near the end of January. After the appointment, Lincoln wrote his new commander, "there are some things in regard to which, I am not quite satisfied with you." Hooker had been saying the country needed a dictator, and word reached Lincoln. "Only those generals who gain successes can set up dictators," the president wrote. "What I now ask of you is military success, and I will risk the dictatorship." But the risk was not great. Hooker was no more able than Burnside to deliver the goods. He failed the test at Chancellorsville, May 1–5.

CHANCELLORSVILLE   With a force of perhaps 130,000, the largest Union army yet gathered, and a brilliant plan, he suffered a loss of control, perhaps a failure of nerve, at the critical juncture. Lee, with perhaps half that number, staged what became a textbook classic of daring and maneuver. Hooker's plan was to leave his base, opposite Fredericksburg, on a sweeping movement upstream across the Rappahannock and Rapidan to flank Lee's position. John N. Sedgwick was to cross below the town for a major diversion with 40,000 men. Lee, however, leaving about 10,000 men at Marye's Heights, pulled his main forces back to meet Hooker. At Chancellorsville, after a preliminary skirmish, Lee divided his army again, sending Jackson with more than half the men on a long march to hit the enemy's exposed right flank.

On May 2, toward evening, Jackson surprised the right flank at the edge of a wooded area called the Wilderness, throwing things into chaos, but the fighting died out in confusion as dark-

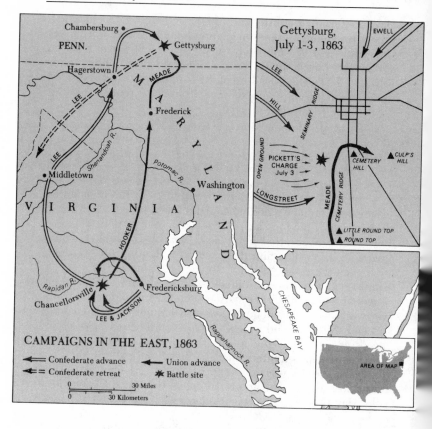

Gettysburg,
July 1-3, 1863

PICKETT'S
CHARGE
July 3

CAMPAIGNS IN THE EAST, 1863

← Confederate advance   ← Union advance
←= Confederate retreat   ✳ Battle site

0   30 Miles
0   30 Kilometers

AREA OF MAP

ness fell. The next day, while Jeb Stuart held Hooker at bay, Lee
had to turn around and fend off Sedgwick, who had stormed
Marye's Heights and advanced on Lee's rear. Lee struck him and
counterattacked on May 3–4, after which Sedgwick recrossed
the Rappahannock. The following day Hooker did the same, although he was still left in a strong position. It was the peak of
Lee's career, but Chancellorsville was his last significant victory.
And his costliest: the South suffered some 12,000 casualties and
more than 1,600 killed, among them Stonewall Jackson, mistakenly felled by his own men upon his return from a reconnaisance.

VICKSBURG   While Lee held the Federals at bay in the East, they
had resumed a torturous advance in the West. Since the previous
fall Ulysses Grant had been groping his way toward Vicksburg,

which along with Port Hudson, Louisiana, was one of the last two Rebel strongholds on the Mississippi. Located on a bluff 200 feet above the river, Vicksburg had withstood naval attacks and a downriver expedition led by William T. Sherman, which had stormed Chickasaw Bluffs north of the city in December. Because the rail lines were vulnerable to hit-and-run attacks, Grant resolved to use naval supply lines downriver. He positioned his army about fifteen miles north of the city, but the Delta region there was laced with bayous which baffled efforts to reach the goal. At first Grant thought to use these waterways to advantage, and during the winter he made bold efforts along two routes. Well to the north, opposite Helena, Arkansas, he blasted a hole in the levee and floated gunboats and transports through to the Tallahatchie River. There ensued a strange progress along winding waterways choked with vegetation and covered by overhanging branches, where the Union navy stood in danger of capture by the Confederate army. That effort, and a similar try up Steele's Bayou farther south, was soon abandoned.

Grant finally gave up the idea of a northern approach. He crossed over to Louisiana at Milliken's Bend, and while the navy ran gunboats and transports past the Confederate batteries at

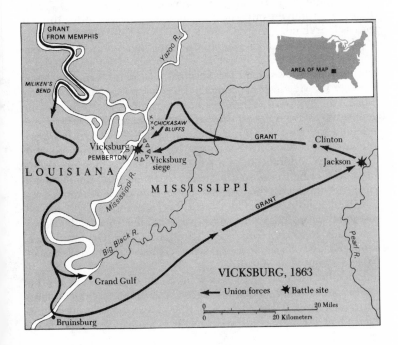

Vicksburg, he moved south to meet them, crossed back, and fetched up on dry ground south of Vicksburg at the end of April. From there Grant adopted a new expedient. He would forget supply lines and live off the country. John C. Pemberton, Confederate commander at Vicksburg, thoroughly baffled, was further confused by two diversions: a feint by General Sherman at Chickasaw Bluffs and a cavalry raid by Col. Benjamin Grierson, who cut a swath through central Mississippi with fewer than 1,000 men and reentered Union lines at Baton Rouge. Grant himself swept eastward on a campaign which Lincoln later called "one of the most brilliant in the world," took Jackson, where he seized or destroyed supplies, then turned westward and on May 18 emerged from the "tunnel" he had entered two weeks before to pin Pemberton's army of 30,000 inside Vicksburg.

GETTYSBURG   The plight of Vicksburg put the Confederate high command in a quandary. Joseph E. Johnston, now in charge of the western forces but with few men under his personal command, would have preferred to focus on the Tennessee front and thereby perhaps force Grant to relax his grip. Robert E. Lee had another idea for a diversion. If he could win a victory on northern soil he might do more than just relieve the pressure at Vicksburg. In June he moved into the Shenandoah Valley and northward across Maryland.

Hooker followed, keeping himself between Lee and Washington, but demoralized by defeat at Chancellorsville and quarrels with Halleck, he turned in his resignation. On June 28 Maj.-Gen. George C. Meade took command. Neither side chose Gettysburg, Pennsylvania, as the site for the climactic battle, but a Confederate party entered the town in search of shoes and encountered units of Union cavalry on June 30. The main forces quickly converged on that point. On July 1 the Confederates pushed the Federals out of the town, but into stronger positions on high ground to the south. Meade hastened reinforcements to his new lines along the heights; on the map these resembled an inverted fishhook with Culp's Hill and Cemetery Hill curved around the top, and Cemetery Ridge extended three miles down the shank to Round Top and Little Round Top. On July 2 Lee mounted assaults at both the extreme left and right flanks of Meade's army, but in vain.

On July 3 Lee staked everything on one final assault on the Union center on Cemetery Ridge. Confederate artillery raked the ridge, but with less effect than intended. About 2 P.M. 15,000 men of Gen. George E. Pickett's command emerged from

Harvest of Death. *T. H. O'Sullivan's grim photograph of the dead at Gettysburg. [Library of Congress]*

the woods west of Cemetery Ridge and began their advance across open ground commanded by Union artillery. It was as hopeless as Burnside's assault at Fredericksburg. Only 5,000 of Pickett's men finally reached the ridge, and the few who got within range of hand-to-hand combat were quickly overwhelmed.

With nothing left to do but retreat, on July 4 Lee's dejected army, with about a third of its number gone, began to slog back through a driving rain. They had failed in all their purposes, not the least being to relieve the pressure on Vicksburg. On that same July 4 Pemberton reached the end of his tether and surrendered his entire garrison of 30,000 men, whom Grant paroled and permitted to go home. Four days later the last remaining Confederate stronghold on the Mississippi, Port Hudson, under siege since May by Union forces, gave up. "The father of waters," Lincoln said, "flows unvexed to the sea." The Confederacy was irrevocably split, and had Meade pursued Lee he might have delivered the *coup de grace* before the Rebels could get back across the flooded Potomac.

CHATTANOOGA The third great Union victory of 1863 occurred in fighting around Chattanooga, the railhead of eastern Tennessee and gateway to northern Georgia. In the late summer Rosecrans's Union army moved southeastward from Murfreesboro, and Bragg pulled out of Chattanooga to gain room for maneuver. Rosecrans took the city on September 9 and then rashly pursued Bragg into Georgia, where his forces met the Confederates at Chickamauga. The battle (September 19–20) had the makings of a Union disaster, since it was one of the few times when the Confederates had a numerical advantage (about 70,000 to 56,000). On the second day Bragg smashed the Federal right, and only the stubborn stand of the left under George H. Thomas (thenceforth "the Rock of Chickamauga") prevented a general rout. The battered Union forces fell back into Chattanooga, while Bragg cut the railroad from the west and held the city virtually under siege from the heights to the south and east.

Rosecrans seemed stunned and apathetic, but Lincoln urged him to hang on: "If we can hold Chattanooga, and East Tennessee, I think rebellion must dwindle and die." Following the Con-

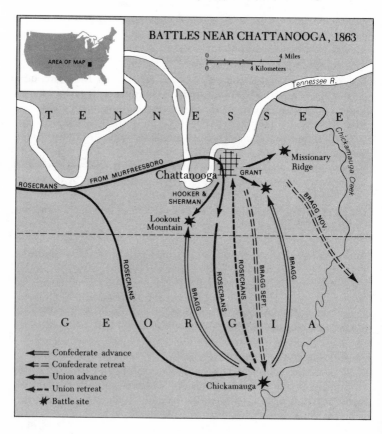

BATTLES NEAR CHATTANOOGA, 1863

Gen. Ulysses S. Grant. [Library of Congress]

federate example the Union command sent Joe Hooker with reinforcements from Virginia, Grant and Sherman with more from the west. Grant, given overall command of the West on October 16, pushed his way into Chattanooga a few days later, forcing open a supply route as he came. He replaced Rosecrans, putting Thomas in command. On November 24 the Federals began to move, with Hooker and Sherman hitting the Confederate flanks at Lookout Mountain and Signal Hill while Thomas created a diversion at the center. Hooker took Lookout Mountain in what was mainly a feat of mountaineering, but Sherman was stalled. On the second day of the battle Grant ordered Thomas forward to positions at the foot of Misssionary Ridge. Successful there, but still exposed, the men spontaneously began to move on up toward the crest 400 to 500 feet above. They might well have been cut up badly, but the Rebels were unable to lower their big guns enough and in the face of thousands swarming up the hill they panicked and fled.

Bragg was unable to get his forces together until they were many miles to the south, and the Battle of Chattanooga was the end of his active career. Jefferson Davis, who had backed him against all censure, reluctantly replaced him with Johnston and called Bragg back to Richmond as an advisor. Soon after the battle the Federals linked up with Burnside, who had taken Knoxville, and proceeded to secure their control of Eastern Tennessee, where the hills were full of Unionists.

Chattanooga had another consequence. If the battle was won by the rush on Missionary Ridge, against orders, the victory nonetheless confirmed the impression of Grant's genius. Lincoln had at last found his general. In March 1864 Grant arrived in Washington to assume the rank of lieutenant-general and a new position as general-in-chief. Halleck became chief-of-staff and continued in his role as channel of communication between the president and commanders in the field. Within the Union armies at least, a modern command system was emerging; the Confederacy never had a unified command.

The Confederacy's Defeat

The main targets now were Lee's army in Virginia and Johnston's in Georgia. Grant personally would accompany Meade, who retained direct command over the Army of the Potomac; operations in the West were entrusted to Grant's longtime lieutenant, William T. Sherman. As Sherman put it later, "he was to go for Lee, and I was to go for Joe Johnston. That was his plan."

GRANT'S PURSUIT OF LEE They began to go for both of them in May, while lesser offensives kept the Confederates occupied all across the map. The Army of the Potomac, numbering about 115,000 to Lee's 65,000, moved south across the Rappahannock and the Rapidan into the Wilderness, where Hooker had come to grief in the Battle of Chancellorsville. In the Battle of the Wilderness (May 5–6) the armies fought blindly through the woods, the horror and suffering of the scene heightened by crackling brush fires. Grant's men took heavier casualties than the Confederates, but the Rebels were running out of replacements. Always before, Lee's adversaries had pulled back to nurse their wounds, but Grant slid off to his left and continued his relentless advance, now toward Spotsylvania Court House.

There Lee's advance guard barely arrived in time to stall the movement and the armies settled down for five days of bloody warfare, May 8–12, in which the Federals failed to break the Confederate center, the "Bloody Angle." Before it was over Grant sent word back to Halleck: "I propose to fight it out along this line if it takes all summer." But again Grant slid off to his left, tested Lee's defenses along the North Anna River (May 16–23), and veered off again over the Pamunkey and back to the scenes of McClellan's Peninsula Campaign. There, along the Chickaho-

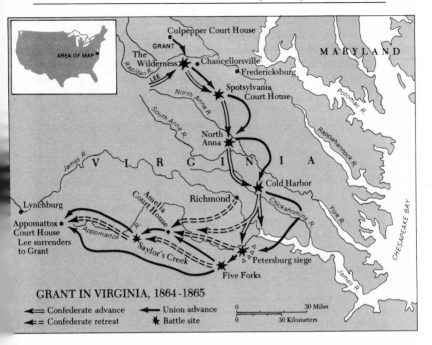

AREA OF MAP

Culpepper Court House

GRANT

The Wilderness • Chancellorsville

Rapidan R. • Fredericksburg

LEE

North Anna R. Spotsylvania Court House

South Anna R.

MARYLAND

Potomac R.

Rappahannock R.

James R. V I R G I N I A

North Anna

Cold Harbor

Lynchburg Amelia Court House Richmond Chickahominy R.

Appomattox Court House Lee surrenders to Grant

Appomattox R.

Saylor's Creek

Petersburg siege

York R.

CHESAPEAKE BAY

Five Forks James R.

GRANT IN VIRGINIA, 1864-1865

⟸ Confederate advance ⟵ Union advance 0   30 Miles
⟸= Confederate retreat ★ Battle site 0   30 Kilometers

miny, occurred the pitched battle of Cold Harbor (June 1–3). Battered and again repulsed, Grant cut away yet again. For several days Lee lost sight of the Federals while they crossed the James on a pontoon bridge and headed for Petersburg, the junction of railroads into Richmond from the south.

Petersburg was thinly held by Confederates under Beauregard, but before Grant could bring up his main force Lee's men moved into the defenses. Grant dug in for a siege along lines that extended for twenty-five miles above and below Petersburg. On July 30 a huge mine exploded in a tunnel under the Confederate line. In the ensuing Battle of the Crater, the soldiers who were supposed to exploit the opening milled around aimlessly in the pit while Rebels shot them like fish in a pond. For nine months the two armies faced each other down while Grant kept pushing toward his left flank to break the railroad arteries that were Lee's lifeline. He would fight it out along *this* line all summer, all autumn, and all winter, generously supplied by Union vessels moving up the James while Lee's forces, beset by hunger, cold, and desertion, wasted away. Petersburg had become Lee's prison while disasters piled up for the Confederacy elsewhere.

SHERMAN'S MARCH   When Grant headed south, so did Sherman—toward the railroad hub of Atlanta, with 90,000 men against Joe Johnston's 60,000. Sherman's campaign, like Grant's, developed into a war of maneuver, but without the pitched battles. As Grant kept slipping off to his left, Sherman kept moving to his right, but Johnston was always one step ahead of him—turning up in secure positions along the North Georgia ridges, drawing him farther from his Chattanooga base, harassing his supply lines with Joe Wheeler's cavalry, and keeping his own main force intact. But Johnston's skillful use of Fabian tactics caused an impatient President Davis finally to replace him with the combative but reckless John B. Hood. Three times in eight days Hood lashed out, first at Peachtree Creek (July 20) on the Union center, then at the Battle of Atlanta (July 22) to the east, and Ezra Church (July 28) to the west, each time meeting a bloody rebuff. Sherman at first resorted to a siege of Atlanta, then slid off to the right again, cutting the rail lines below Atlanta. Hood evacuated on September 1, but kept his army intact.

Sherman now laid plans for a march through central Georgia where no organized armies remained. Hood meanwhile had hatched an equally audacious plan. He would cut away to northern Alabama and push on into Tennessee, forcing Sherman into

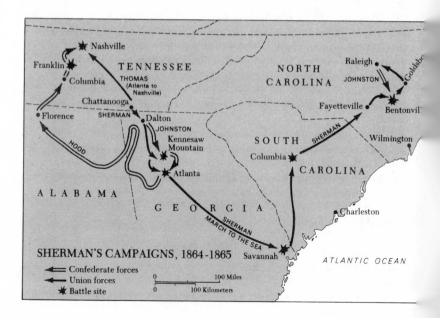

SHERMAN'S CAMPAIGNS, 1864-1865

Confederate forces
Union forces
★ Battle site

0 ___ 100 Miles
0 ___ 100 Kilometers

ATLANTIC OCEAN

William Tecumseh Sherman.
[National Archives]

pursuit. Sherman refused to take the bait, although he did send
Thomas back to Tennessee to keep watch with 30,000 men. So
the curious spectacle unfolded of the main armies moving off in
opposite directions. But it was a measure of the Confederates'
plight that Sherman could cut a swath across Georgia with impunity while Hood was soon outnumbered again. In the Battle of
Franklin (November 30), Hood sent his army across two miles of
open ground. Six waves broke against the Union lines, leaving
the ground strewn with Confederates. Total Rebel casualties
numbered 6,000. With what he had left, Hood dared not attack
Nashville, nor did he dare withdraw for fear of final disintegration. Finally, in the Battle of Nashville (December 15–16),
Thomas broke and scattered what was left of the Confederate
Army of Tennessee. The Confederate front west of the Appalachians had collapsed, leaving only Nathan Bedford Forrest's cavalry and a few other scattered units in the field, mainly around
Mobile.

During all this Sherman was marching through Georgia, pioneering the modern practice of total war against a people's resources and against their will to resist. On November 15, 1864,
he destroyed Atlanta's warehouses and railroad facilities while
spreading fires consumed about a third of the city. The Union
army moved out in four columns over a front twenty to sixty
miles wide, living off the land and destroying any stores or provisions that might serve Confederate forces. Bands of stragglers
and deserters from both armies joined in looting along the flanks,
while Joe Wheeler's cavalry destroyed Rebel stores to keep
them out of enemy hands. When, after a month, Sherman
fetched up near Savannah he had cut a swath of desolation 250

Robert E. Lee. Mathew Brady took this photograph in Richmond eleven days after Lee's surrender at Appomattox. [Library of Congress]

miles long. On December 21 Sherman marched into Savannah, and three days later Lincoln got a dispatch tendering the city as a Christmas gift.

Pushing across the river into that "hell-hole of secession," South Carolina, his men wrought even greater destruction. More than a dozen towns were consigned to the flames in whole or part, including the state capital of Columbia, captured February 17. On the day Sherman entered Columbia, Charleston's defenders abandoned the city and pulled north to join an army which Joseph E. Johnston was desperately pulling together. Johnston was able to mount one final attack on Sherman's left wing at Bentonville (March 19–20), but that was his last major battle.

APPOMATTOX During this final season of the Confederacy, Grant kept pushing, probing, and battering the Petersburg defenses. Raids by Philip H. Sheridan had desolated Lee's breadbasket in the Shenandoah Valley, and winter left his men on short rations. News of Sherman's progress added to the gloom and the impulse to desert. By March the Confederate lines had thinned out to about 1,000 men per mile. Lee began to lay plans to escape and join Johnston in North Carolina. At Five Forks (April 1, 1865) Grant finally cut the last rail line to Petersburg, and the next day Lee abandoned Richmond and Petersburg in a desperate flight toward Lynchburg and rails south. President Davis gathered what archives and treasure he could and made it out by train ahead of the advancing Federals, only to be captured on May 10 at Irwinton, Georgia, by James H. Wilson's Union cavalry, which had been ranging across Mississippi and Alabama.

By then the Confederacy was already dead. Lee moved out with Grant in hot pursuit, and soon found his escape route cut by forces under Sheridan. On April 9 (Palm Sunday) he met Grant in the parlor of the McLean home at Appomattox to tender his surrender, four years to the day after Davis and his cabinet decided to attack Fort Sumter. Grant, at Lee's request, let the Rebel officers keep their side arms and permitted soldiers to keep private horses and mules. On April 18, Johnston surrendered to Sherman at the Bennett house near what would soon be the thriving tobacco town of Durham. On May 4 at Citronelle, Alabama, General Taylor surrendered the remaining forces east of the Mississippi to General Canby, leaving only the forces under Edmund Kirby Smith west of the river. On May 26 Kirby Smith capitulated to Canby at New Orleans.

In Charleston, the Confederate "holy of holies," the first occupation troops to arrive in February were black units, including the Third and Fourth South Carolina Regiments, some of whom had been among the city's slaves in 1860. It was little more than four years since the secession convention had met at Institution Hall, not quite five years since the disruption of the Democratic party in the same building. Soon after the occupation the War Department began plans for a massive celebration at Fort Sumter on the fourth anniversary of its fall. On April 14, 1865, the fort filled with dignitaries, including William Lloyd Garrison and Henry Ward Beecher, the orator of the day, and a few hundred black soldiers brought out by the *Planter*, the boat on which Capt. Robert Smalls had fled slavery two years before. At noon Major Anderson ran up the flag he had lowered just four years previously, while gaily decorated ships and all the forts in the harbor sounded a salute.

The same day President Lincoln spent the afternoon discussing postwar policy with his cabinet. That night Mr. and Mrs. Lincoln went to the theater.

FURTHER READING

The most comprehensive treatment of the Civil War period is Allan Nevins's *The War for the Union* (4 vols.; 1959–1971). Also good for an overview are James G. Randall and David Donald's *The Civil War and Reconstruction* (1969) and James M. McPherson's *Ordeal by Fire: The Civil War and Reconstruction* (1982). The many military histories by

Bruce Catton are extremely readable; begin with *This Hallowed Ground* (1956).°

More interpretative treatments are William L. Barney's *Flawed Victory* (1975)° and Peter Prish's *The American Civil War* (1975). Principal themes of the period are discussed in David Donald (ed.), *Why the North Won the War* (1960),° Irwin Unger's *Essays on the Civil War and Reconstruction* (1970), and Eric Foner's *Politics and Ideology in the Age of the Civil War* (1980).°

The Civil War period is also blessed with a number of firsthand accounts of personal experiences. Among the better are C. Vann Woodward (ed.), *Mary Chestnutt's Civil War* (1981),° and Robert M. Myers (ed.), *The Children of Pride* (1972).° Stephen Crane's *The Red Badge of Courage* (1895)° remains a literary classic of the conflict. Also revealing are MacKinley Kantor's *Andersonville* (1955)° and Michael Shaara's *The Killer Angels* (1969),° about Gettysburg. The life of the common soldier is well treated by Bell I. Wiley in *The Life of Johnny Reb* (1943)° and *The Life of Billy Yank* (1952).° The values held by the soldiers on both sides are explored in Michael Barton's *Good Men: The Character of Civil War Soldiers* (1981).

For emphasis on the South, turn first to Emory M. Thomas's *The Confederate Nation* (1979).° Older, but still reliable, is Clement Eaton's *A History of the Southern Confederacy* (1954). More interpretive is Emory M. Thomas's *The Confederacy as a Revolutionary Experience* (1971),° which looks at the problems of states'-rights doctrine. Also helpful is Henry S. Commager's *The Defeat of the Confederacy* (1964). Stress on the role of Confederate leadership is provided in E. M. Coulter's *The Confederate States of America, 1861–65* (1950), and Frank VanDiver's *Their Tattered Flags* (1965). The most recent work on the president of the Confederacy is Clement Eaton's *Jefferson Davis* (1977). Thomas L. Connelly and Archer Jones also deal with Davis in *The Politics of Command* (1973). Rudolph Von Abele's *Alexander Stephens* (1946) is good for the interpretation of Confederate politics. Also see Thomas B. Alexander and Richard E. Beringer's *The Anatomy of the Confederate Congress* (1972). Background on problems of supply can be gleaned from Charles B. Dew's *Ironmaker to the Confederacy* (1966) and Frank VanDiver's *Ploughshares into Swords* (1952).

Shelby Foote's *The Civil War* (3 vols.; 1958–1973) gives the most thorough treatment of the military conflict from the southern perspective. The war in the Eastern Theater is handled in the several biographies of Robert E. Lee, among them Douglass S. Freeman's *Lee: A Biography* (4 vols.; 1934–1935) and Thomas L. Connelly's *Marble Man* (1971).° The war in the West is the subject of Thomas L. Connelly's *Army of the Heartland: The Army of Tennessee, 1861–62* (1967) and *Autumn of Glory: The Army of Tennessee, 1862–65* (1971). Studies of other generals include Hal Bridges's *Lee Maverick General: Daniel Harvey Hill* (1962), Frank VanDiver's *Mighty Stonewall* (1957), Grady McWhiney's *Braxton Bragg and the Confederate Defeat* (1969), Robert L. Kerby's *Kirby-*

° These books are available in paperback editions.

Smith's Confederacy (1972), and Richard M. Murray's *John Bell Hood and the War for Southern Independence* (1982). A cultural interpretation of Confederate military behavior is Grady McWhiney's *Attack and Die* (1982).

Treatments of northern politics during the war include David Donald's *Charles Sumner and the Rights of Man* (1971),° Harold M. Hyman's *A More Perfect Union* (1973),° and Allan G. Bogue's *The Earnest Men: Republicans of the Civil War Senate* (1981). Diplomatic relations with Europe are covered in Glyndon G. Van Deusen's *William Henry Seward* (1967) and Martin B. Duberman's *Charles Francis Adams* (1961).°

The central political figure, Abraham Lincoln, is the subject of many books. Good single-volume biographies are Stephen B. Oates's *With Malice toward None* (1979)° and Benjamin P. Thomas's *Abraham Lincoln* (1952). Carl Sandburg's *Lincoln: The War Years* (4 vols.; 1939)° gives the fullest treatment of his presidential career. Varying interpretations of Lincoln can be found in David Donald's *Lincoln Reconsidered* (1956)° and Richard N. Current's *The Lincoln Nobody Knows* (1958). Also valuable is the chapter on Lincoln in Daniel Walker Howe's *The Political Culture of the American Whigs* (1979).

The emphasis is also on Lincoln in a number of works dealing with northern military strategy. Most voluminous is Kenneth P. Williams's *Lincoln Finds a General* (5 vols.; 1949–1959). A fine interpretive work is T. Harry Williams's *Lincoln and His Generals* (1952). Biographical studies of the northern military leaders include T. Harry Williams's *McClellan, Sherman and Grant* (1962), Lloyd Lewis's *Sherman* (1932), and William S. McFeely's *Grant: A Biography* (1981).° A review of the careers of all the Eastern Theater commanders appears in Bruce Catton's *The Army of the Potomac* (3 vols.; 1951–1954). Naval operations are detailed in Virgil C. Jones's *The Civil War at Sea* (3 vols.; 1960–1962), and John Niven's *Gideon Welles: Lincoln's Secretary of the Navy* (1973).

Life behind the battle lines is the topic of several works. Emerson D. Fite's *Social and Industrial Conditions in the North during the Civil War* (1910) remains the standard introduction. Political dissent is handled in Frank L. Klement's *The Copperheads in the Middle West* (1960). Paul C. Gates treats the disruption of farming in *Agriculture and the Civil War* (1965). Mary E. Massey's *Bonnet Brigades* (1966) examines the contributions of women. Adrian Cook's *The Armies of the Streets* (1974) analyzes the antidraft riots of New York City, and Eugene C. Murdock's *One Million Men* (1971) examines reaction to the draft in general. The views of northern intellectuals is the subject of George Frederickson's *The Inner Civil War* (1965).°

How the emancipated slave fared during the war has drawn recent scholarly attention. The standard overview is Benjamin Quarles's *The Negro in the Civil War* (1953).° The career of the black soldier is found in Dudley T. Cornish's *The Sable Arm* (1966). Willie Lee Rose's *Rehearsal for Reconstruction: The Port Royal Experiment* (1964)° and Louis Gerteis's *From Contraband to Freedman: Federal Policy toward Southern Blacks, 1861–1865* (1973), both trace the federal government's policies. For Lincoln's viewpoint, see Lawanda Cox's *Lincoln and Black Freedom:*

A Study in Presidential Leadership (1981). The Confederate viewpoint is handled in Robert F. Durden's *The Gray and the Black* (1972). Peter Kolchin's *First Freedom* (1972) examines what blacks themselves thought, as does Leon F. Litwack in the early chapters of *Been in the Storm So Long* (1979).°

18

RECONSTRUCTION: NORTH AND SOUTH

THE WAR'S AFTERMATH

In the spring of 1865 the weary war was over, a war whose cost in casualties was greater than all foreign wars down to World War II, and in proportion to population, greater than all other American wars down to the present day. At this frightful cost some old and tenacious issues were finally resolved. As the historian David Potter so graphically put it, "slavery was dead, secession was dead, and six hundred thousand men were dead." American nationalism emerged triumphant, its victory ratified in 1869 when the Supreme Court stamped its approval on the decision of arms. In the case of *Texas v. White,* the Court firmly denied any legality to Rebel state governments while it affirmed the existence of "an indestructible Union, composed of indestructible states." Pursued at first to preserve that Union, the war had turned into a crusade for the total abolition of chattel slavery. Before the end of 1865 all but two border states had voted emancipation. Ratification of the Thirteenth Amendment in December 1865 ended the remnants of slavery in Delaware and Kentucky and overrode any lingering doubts about the legitimacy of Lincoln's Emancipation Proclamation.

DEVELOPMENT IN THE NORTH   The war had been, in the words of Charles and Mary Beard, a Second American Revolution. It was more truly a social revolution than the War of Independence, for it reduced the once-dominant power of planter agrarians in the national councils and elevated that of the "captains of industry."

It is easy to exaggerate the profundity of this change, but government did become subtly more friendly to businessmen and unfriendly to those who would probe into their activities. The Republican Congress had delivered on the major platform promises of 1860, which had cemented the allegiance of northeastern businessmen and western farmers to the party of free labor.

In the absence of southern members, Congress had passed the Morrill Tariff of 1861 which, with later revisions, brought the average level of duties up to about double what it had been on the eve of conflict. The National Banking Act of 1863, reframed in 1864, created a uniform system of banking and banknote currency, and helped to finance the war. Under laws of 1862 and 1864 Congress guaranteed that the first transcontinental railroad would run along a north-central route from Omaha to Sacramento, and donated public lands and public bonds to ensure its financing. In the Homestead Act of 1862, moreover, Congress voted free homesteads of 160 acres to actual settlers who occupied the land for five years, and in the Morrill Land Grant Act of the same year conveyed to each state 30,000 acres of public land per member of Congress from the state, the proceeds from the sale of which went to colleges of "agriculture and mechanic arts."

DEVASTATION IN THE SOUTH   The South, where most of the fighting had occurred, offered a sharp contrast to the victorious North. Along the path of the army led by General Sherman, Carl Schurz reported in 1866, the countryside still "looked for many miles like a broad black streak of ruin and desolation." Columbia, South Carolina, said another observer, was "a wilderness of ruins," Charleston a place of "vacant houses, of widowed women, of rotting wharves, of deserted warehouses, of weed-wild gardens, of miles of grass-grown streets, of acres of pitiful and voiceless barrenness." In the valley of the Tennessee, the British visitor Robert Somers reported: "The trail of war is visible . . . in burnt-up gin houses, ruined bridges, mills, and factories." The border states of Missouri and Kentucky had gone through a guerrilla war which lapsed into postwar anarchy perpetrated by marauding bands of bushwackers turned bank robbers, such as the notorious Younger brothers, Coleman and Jim, and the even more notorious James boys, Frank and Jesse.

Property values had collapsed. Confederate bonds and money became worthless, railroads and rolling stock were damaged or destroyed. Stores of cotton which had escaped destruction were seized as Confederate property or in forfeit of federal taxes. Emancipation at one stroke wiped out perhaps $4 billion in-

Virginia's Capitol, designed by Thomas Jefferson, looms over the ruins of Richmond, Virginia, April 1865. [Library of Congress]

vested in human flesh and left the labor system in disarray. The great age of expansion in the cotton market was over. Not until 1879 would the cotton crop again equal the record crop of 1860; tobacco production did not regain its prewar level until 1880; the sugar crop of Louisiana not until 1893; and the old rice industry of the Tidewater and the hemp industry of the Kentucky Blue Grass never regained their prewar status.

LEGALLY FREE, SOCIALLY BOUND   The newly freed slaves suffered most of all. According to Frederick Douglass, the black abolitionist, the former bondsman "was free from the individual master but a slave of society. He had neither money, property, nor friends. He was free from the old plantation, but he had nothing but the dusty road under his feet. He was free from the old quarter that once gave him shelter, but a slave to the rains of summer and the frosts of winter. He was turned loose, naked, hungry, and destitute to the open sky."

According to a former Confederate general, recently freed blacks had "nothing but freedom." [Library of Congress]

Even dedicated abolitionists in large part shrank from the measures of land reform that might have given the freedmen more self-support and independence. Citizenship and legal rights were one thing, wholesale confiscation and land distribution quite another. Instead of land or material help the freedmen more often got what the historian Leon Litwack called "the moral and economic injunctions and shibboleths that were standard fare in nineteenth-century American society: success came ultimately to the hard-working, the sober, the honest, and the educated, to those individuals who engaged in 'faithful industry,' practiced 'judicious economy,' cultivated habits of thrift and temperance, made their homes 'models of neatness,' and led moral, virtuous, Christian lives."

In 1865 Rep. George Julian of Indiana and Sen. Charles Sumner of Massachusetts proposed to give freedmen forty-acre homesteads carved out of Rebel lands taken under the Confiscation Act of 1862. But their plan for outright grants was replaced by a program of rentals since, under the law, confiscation was effective only for the lifetime of the offender. Discussions of land distribution, however, fueled rumors that freedmen would get "forty acres and a mule," a slogan that swept the South at the end of the war. Its source remains unknown, but the aspirations which gave rise to it are clear enough. As one black man in Mississippi put it: "Gib us our own land and we take care ourselves; but widout land, de ole massas can hire us or starve us, as dey please." More lands were seized as "abandoned lands" under an act of 1864, and for default on the direct taxes which Congress levied in 1861 and 1862, than under the Confiscation Act. The most conspicuous example of confiscation was the estate of Robert E. Lee and the Custis family, which became Arlington National Cemetery, but larger amounts were taken in the South Carolina Sea Islands and elsewhere. Some of these lands were sold to freedmen, some to Yankee speculators.

THE FREEDMEN'S BUREAU   On March 3, 1865, Congress set up within the War Department the Bureau of Refugees, Freedmen, and Abandoned Lands, to provide "such issues of provisions, clothing, and fuel" as might be needed to relieve "destitute and suffering refugees and freedmen and their wives and children." The Freedmen's Bureau would also take over abandoned and confiscated land for rental in forty-acre tracts to "loyal refugees and freedmen," who might buy the land at a fair price within three years. But the amount of such lands was limited. Under Gen. Oliver O. Howard as commissioner, and assistant commis-

Sketch of a primary school set up by the Freedmen's Bureau, Vicksburg, Mississippi, 1866. [The Historic New Orleans Collection]

sioners in each state of the former Confederacy, agents were entrusted with negotiating labor contracts (something new for both freedmen and planters), providing medical care, and setting up schools, often in cooperation with northern agencies like the American Missionary Association and the Freedmen's Aid Society. The bureau had its own courts to deal with labor disputes and land titles, and its agents were further authorized to supervise trials involving Negroes in other courts.

This was as far as Congress would go. Beyond such temporary measures of relief, no program of reconstruction ever incorporated much more than constitutional and legal rights for freedmen. These were important in themselves, of course, but the extent to which even these should go was very uncertain, to be settled more by the course of events than by any clear-cut commitment to equality.

THE BATTLE OVER RECONSTRUCTION

The problem of reconstruction arose first at the very beginning of the Civil War, when the western counties of Virginia refused to go along with secession. In 1861 a loyal state government of Virginia was proclaimed at Wheeling and this government in turn consented to the formation of a new state called West Virginia, duly if irregularly admitted to the Union in 1863. The loyal government of Virginia under Gov. Francis H. Pierpont then carried on from Alexandria, its reach limited to that part of the state which the Union controlled. As Union forces advanced into the South, Lincoln in 1862 named military governors for Tennessee, Arkansas, and Louisiana. By the end of the following year he had formulated a plan for regular governments in those states and any others that might qualify.

LINCOLN'S PLAN AND CONGRESS'S RESPONSE   Acting under his pardon power, President Lincoln issued on December 8, 1863, a Proclamation of Amnesty and Reconstruction under which any Rebel state could form a Union government whenever a number equal to 10 percent of those who had voted in 1860 took an oath of allegiance to the Constitution and Union and received a presidential pardon. Participants also had to swear support for laws and proclamations dealing with emancipation. Excluded from the pardon, however, were certain groups: civil and diplomatic officers of the Confederacy; high officers of the Confederate army and navy; judges, congressmen, and military officers of the United States who had left their posts to aid the rebellion; and those accused of failure to treat captured Negro soldiers and their officers as prisoners of war.

Under this plan loyal governments appeared in Tennessee, Arkansas, and Louisiana, but Congress recognized them neither by representation nor in counting the electoral votes of 1864. In the absence of any specific provisions for reconstruction in the Constitution, there was disagreement as to where authority properly rested. Lincoln claimed the right to direct reconstruction under Article II, Section 2, which set forth the presidential pardon power, and also under Article IV, Section 4, which imposed an obligation on the United States to guarantee each state a republican form of government. Republican congressmen, however, argued that Article IV, Section 4, implied a power of Congress to act. The first congressional plan for reconstruction appeared in the Wade-Davis Bill, sponsored by Sen. Benjamin Wade of Ohio and Rep. Henry Winter Davis of Maryland, which proposed much more stringent requirements than Lincoln had. In contrast to Lincoln's 10 percent plan, the Wade-Davis Bill required that a majority of white male citizens declare their allegiance and that only those who could take an "ironclad" oath (required of federal officials since 1862) attesting to their *past* loyalty could vote or serve in the state constitutional conventions. The conventions, moreover, would have to abolish slavery, exclude from political rights high-ranking civil and military officers of the Confederacy, and repudiate debts incurred "under the sanction of the usurping power."

Passed during the closing day of the session, the bill was subjected to a pocket veto by Lincoln, who refused to sign it but issued an artful statement that he would accept any state which preferred to present itself under the congressional plan. The sponsors responded by issuing to the newspaper the Wade-Davis Manifesto, which accused the president, among other sins, of usurping power and attempting to use readmitted states to ensure his reelection.

Lincoln's last public words on reconstruction came in his last public address, on April 11, 1865. Speaking from the White House balcony, he pronounced the theoretical question of whether the Confederate states were in the Union "bad as the basis of a controversy, and good for nothing at all—a mere pernicious abstraction." These states were simply "out of their proper practical relation with the Union," and the object was to get them "into their proper practical relation." It would be easier to do this by merely ignoring the abstract issue: "Finding themselves safely at home, it would be utterly immaterial whether they had been abroad." At a cabinet meeting on April 14, Lincoln proposed to get state governments in operation before Congress met in December. Secretary Gideon Welles later reported him to have said: "There were men in Congress who, if their motives were good, were nevertheless impracticable, and who possessed feelings of hate and vindictiveness in which he did not sympathize and could not participate." He wanted "no persecution, no bloody work."

THE ASSASSINATION OF LINCOLN That evening Lincoln went to Ford's Theater and his rendezvous with death. Shot by John Wilkes Booth, a crazed actor who thought he was doing something for the South, the president died the next morning in a room across the street. Accomplices had also targeted Vice-President Johnson and Secretary of State Seward. Seward and four others, including his son, were victims of severe but not fatal stab wounds. Johnson escaped injury, however, because his chosen assassin got cold feet and wound up in the barroom of Johnson's hotel. Had he been murdered, the presidency would have gone to a man whose name is virtually unknown today: Lafayette Sabine Foster, president pro tem of the Senate, a moderate Republican from Connecticut.

Martyred in the hour of victory, Lincoln entered into the national mythology even while the funeral train took its mournful burden north to New York and westward home to Springfield. The nation extracted a full measure of vengeance from the conspirators. Pursued into Virginia, Booth was trapped and shot in a burning barn. Three collaborators were brought to trial by a military commission and hanged, along with Mrs. Mary Surratt, at whose boarding house they had plotted. Against her the court had no credible evidence of complicity. Three others got life sentences, including a Maryland doctor who set the leg Booth had broken when he jumped to the stage. A stagehand at Ford's Theater got six years. All were eventually pardoned by President Johnson, except one who died in prison. The doctor achieved lasting fame by making common a once obscure expression. His name was Mudd. Apart from those cases, however, there was only one other execution in the aftermath of war: Henry Wirz, who commanded the infamous prison at Andersonville, Georgia, where Union prisoners were probably more the victims of war conditions than of deliberate cruelty.

JOHNSON'S PLAN   Lincoln's death suddenly elevated to the White House Andrew Johnson of Tennessee, a man whose state was still in legal limbo and whose party affiliation was unclear. He was a War Democrat who had been put on the Union ticket in 1864 as a gesture of unity. Of humble origins like Lincoln, Johnson had moved as a youth from his birthplace in Raleigh, North Carolina, to Greeneville, Tennessee, where he became proprietor of a moderately prosperous tailor shop. Self-educated with the help of his wife, he had made himself into an effective orator of the rough-and-tumble school, and had become an advocate of the yeomanry against the privileges of the aristocrats. He was one of the few southern men who championed a homestead act. He had served as mayor, congressman, governor, and senator, then as military governor of Tennessee before he became vice-president.

Andrew Johnson. [Library of Congress]

Some of the most advanced Radicals at first thought Johnson, unlike Lincoln, to be one of them—an illusion created by Johnson's gift for strong language. "Treason is a crime and must be punished," he had said. "Treason must be made infamous and traitors must be impoverished." Ben Wade was carried away with admiration. "Johnson, we have faith in you," he said. "By the gods, there will be no trouble now in running this government." But Wade would soon find him as untrustworthy as Lincoln, if for different reasons. Johnson's very loyalty to the Union sprang from a strict adherence to the Constitution. Given to dogmatic abstractions which were alien to Lincoln's temperament, he nevertheless arrived by a different route at similar objectives. The states should be brought back into their proper relation to the Union not by ignoring as a pernicious abstraction the theoretical question of their status, but because the states and the Union were indestructible. And like many other whites, he found it hard to accept the growing Radical movement toward suffrage for blacks. By May he was saying "there is no such thing as reconstruction. Those States have not gone out of the Union. Therefore reconstruction is unnecessary."

Johnson's plan of Reconstruction thus closely resembled Lincoln's. A new Proclamation of Amnesty (May 29, 1865) added to those Lincoln excluded from pardon everybody with taxable property worth more than $20,000. These were the people Johnson believed had led the South into secession. But special applications for pardon might be made by those in the excluded groups, and before the year was out Johnson had issued some 13,000 such pardons. In every case Johnson ruled that pardon, whether by general amnesty or special clemency, restored one's property rights in land. He defined as "confiscated" only lands already sold under court decree. This included lands set aside by General Sherman's expansive Special Field Order No. 15, which had allocated for the exclusive use of freed Negroes a coastal strip thirty miles wide from Charleston south to the St. John's River in Florida.

Johnson's rulings nipped in the bud an experiment in land distribution that had barely begun. More than seventy years later one Thomas Hall, born a slave in Orange County, North Carolina, spoke bluntly of his dashed hopes: "Lincoln got the praise for freeing us, but did he do it? He give us freedom without giving us any chance to live to ourselves and we still had to depend on the southern white man for work, food and clothing, and he held us through our necessity and want in a state of servitude but little better than slavery." Later, a South Carolina Land Commission, established by the Radical state government in 1869, distributed lands to more than 5,000 black families. One black community in the upcountry, Promised Land, still retained its identity more than a century later, an obscure reminder of what might have been.

On the same day that Johnson announced his amnesty, he issued another proclamation which applied to his native state of North Carolina, and within six more weeks came further edicts for the other Rebel states not already organized by Lincoln. In each a native Unionist became provisional governor with authority to call a convention elected by loyal voters. Lincoln's 10 percent requirement was omitted. Johnson called upon the conventions to invalidate the secession ordinances, abolish slavery, and repudiate all debts incurred to aid the Confederacy. Each state, moreover, was to ratify the Thirteenth Amendment. Lincoln had privately advised the governor of Louisiana to consider a grant of suffrage to some blacks, "the very intelligent and those who have fought gallantly in our ranks." In his final public address he publicly endorsed a limited black suffrage. Johnson repeated Lincoln's advice. He reminded the provisional governor of Mississippi, for example, that the state conventions might "with perfect safety" extend suffrage to blacks with education or with military service so as to "disarm the adversary"—the adversary being "radicals who are wild upon Negro franchise."

The state conventions for the most part met Johnson's requirements, although South Carolina and Mississippi did not repudiate their debt and the new Mississippi legislature refused to ratify the Thirteenth Amendment. Presidential agents sent south to observe and report back for the most part echoed General Grant's finding after a two-month tour: "I am satisfied that the mass of thinking men of the south accept the present situation of affairs in good faith." But Carl Schurz of Missouri found "an *utter absence of national feeling* . . . and a desire to preserve slavery . . . as much and as long as possible." The discrepancy between the two reports is perhaps only apparent: southern whites accepted the situation because they thought so little had changed after all. Emboldened by Johnson's indulgence they ignored his counsels of expediency. Suggestions of Negro suffrage were scarcely raised in the conventions, and promptly squelched when they were.

SOUTHERN INTRANSIGENCE   When Congress met in December, for the first time since the end of the war, it had only to accept the accomplished fact that state governments were functioning in the South. But there was the rub. Southern voters had acted with extreme disregard of northern feelings. Among the new members presenting themselves were Georgia's Alexander H. Stephens, late vice-president of the Confederacy, now claiming a seat in the Senate, four Confederate generals, eight colonels, six cabinet members, and a host of lesser Rebels. That many of them had counseled delay in secession, like Stephens, or actually opposed it until it happened, made little difference given the temper of the times. The Congress forthwith excluded from the roll call and denied seats to all members from the eleven former Confederate states. It was too much to expect, after four bloody years, that Unionists would welcome Rebels like prodigal sons.

Furthermore, the action of southern legislatures in passing repressive Black Codes seemed to confirm Schurz's view that they intended to preserve slavery as nearly as possible. The codes extended to blacks certain rights they had not hitherto enjoyed, but universally set them aside as a separate caste subject to special restraints. Details varied from state to state, but some provisions were common. Existing marriages, including common-law marriages, were recognized, and testimony of Negroes was accepted in cases involving Negroes—in six states in all cases. Blacks could hold property. They could sue and be sued in the courts. On the other hand Negroes could not own farm lands in Mississippi or city lots in South Carolina. In some states they could not carry firearms without a license to do so.

The codes' labor provisions seemed to confirm the worst suspi-

Slavery Is Dead (?) *Thomas Nast's cartoon suggested that, in 1866, slavery was only legally dead.* [Harper's Weekly]

cions. Blacks were required to enter into annual labor contracts, with provision for punishment in case of violation. Dependent children were subject to compulsory apprenticeship and corporal punishment by masters. Vagrants were punished with severe fines and could be sold into private service if unable to pay. To many people it indeed seemed that slavery was on the way back in another guise. The new Mississippi penal code virtually said so: "All penal and criminal laws now in force describing the mode of punishment of crimes and misdemeanors committed by slaves, free negroes, or mulattoes are hereby re-enacted, and decreed to be in full force against all freedmen, free negroes and mulattoes."

Faced with such evidence of southern intransigence, moderate Republicans drifted more and more toward Radical views. Having excluded southern members, the new Congress set up a Joint Committee on Reconstruction, with nine members from the House and six from the Senate, to gather evidence and submit proposals. Headed by the moderate Sen. William Pitt Fessenden, the committee fell under greater Radical influence as a parade of witnesses testified to the Rebels' impenitence. Initiative on the committee fell to determined Radicals who knew what they wanted: Ben Wade of Ohio, George W. Julian of Indiana, Henry Wilson of Massachusetts, Zachary Chandler of Michigan, James M. Ashley of Ohio—and most conspicuously of all, Thaddeus Stevens of Pennsylvania and Charles Sumner of Massachusetts.

THE RADICALS   Their motivations were mixed, and perhaps little purpose is served in attempting to sort them out. Purity of motive is rare in an imperfect world. Most Radicals had been connected with the antislavery cause. While one could be hostile to both slavery and blacks, many whites approached the question of Negro rights with a humanitarian impulse. Few could escape the bitterness bred by the long and bloody war, however, or remain unaware of the partisan advantage that would come to the Republican party from Negro suffrage. But the party of Union and freedom, after all, could best guarantee the fruits of victory, they reasoned, and Negro suffrage could best guarantee Negro rights.

The growing conflict of opinion brought about an inversion in constitutional reasoning. Secessionists—and Johnson—were now arguing that their states had remained in the Union, and some Radicals were contriving arguments that they had left the Union after all. Rep. Thaddeus Stevens spun out a theory that the Confederate states were now conquered provinces, subject to the absolute will of the victors. Sen. Charles Sumner advanced a

Two leading Radicals: Sen. Charles Sumner (left) and Rep. Thaddeus Stevens. [Library of Congress; National Archives]

thesis that the southern states, by their pretended acts of secession, had in effect committed suicide and reverted to the status of unorganized territories subject to the will of Congress. But few ever took such ideas seriously. Republicans converged instead on the "forfeited rights theory" first advanced by Rep. Samuel Shellabarger of Ohio and later embodied in the report of the Joint Committee on Reconstruction. This theory held that the states as entities continued to exist, but by the acts of secession and war had forfeited "all civil and political rights under the constitution." And Congress was the proper authority to determine conditions under which such rights might be restored.

JOHNSON'S BATTLE WITH CONGRESS   A long year of political battling remained, however, before this idea triumphed. Radical views had gained a majority in Congress, if one not yet large enough to override presidential vetoes. But the critical year 1866 saw the gradual waning of Johnson's power and influence; much of this was self-induced, for he betrayed as much addiction to "pernicious abstraction" as any Radical. Johnson first challenged Congress in February, when he vetoed a bill to extend the life of the Freedmen's Bureau. The measure, he said, assumed that wartime conditions still existed, whereas the country had returned "to a state of peace and industry." No longer valid as a war measure, the bill violated the Constitution in several ways. It made the federal government responsible for the care of indigents. It was passed by a Congress in which eleven states were denied seats. And it used vague language in defining the "civil rights and immunities" of Negroes. The Congress soon moved to correct that particular defect, but for the time being Johnson's prestige remained sufficiently intact that the Senate upheld his veto.

Three days after the veto, however, Johnson undermined his already weakening prestige with a gross assault on Radical leaders during an impromptu speech on Washington's Birthday. The Joint Committee on Reconstruction, he said, was "an irresponsible central directory" which had repudiated the principle of an indestructible Union and accepted the legality of secession by entertaining conquered-province and state-suicide theories. From that point forward moderate Republicans backed away from a president who had opened himself to counterattack. He was "an alien enemy of a foreign state," Stevens declared. He was "an insolent drunken brute," Sumner asserted—and Johnson was open to the charge because of an incident at his vice-presidential inauguration. Weakened by illness at the time, he had taken a belt of brandy to get him through the ceremony and, under the influence of fever and alcohol, had become incoherent.

In mid-March 1866 Congress passed the Civil Rights Act, which Sen. Lyman Trumbull of Illinois had introduced along with the Freedmen's Bureau Bill. A response to the Black Codes, this bill declared that "all persons born in the United States and not subject to any foreign power, excluding Indians not taxed," were citizens entitled to "full and equal benefit of all laws." The grant of citizenship to native-born blacks, Johnson fulminated, went beyond anything formerly held to be within the scope of federal power. It would, moreover, "foment discord among the races." This time, on April 9, 1866, Congress overrode the presidential veto. On July 16 it enacted a revised Bureau Bill, again overriding a veto. From that point on Johnson steadily lost ground.

THE FOURTEENTH AMENDMENT   To remove all doubt about the constitutionality of the new Civil Rights Act, which was justified as implementing freedom under the Thirteenth Amendment, the Joint Committee recommended a new amendment which passed Congress on June 16, 1866, and was ratified by July 28, 1868. The Fourteenth Amendment, however, went far beyond the Civil Rights Act. It merits close scrutiny because of its broad impact on subsequent laws and litigation. In the first section it did four things: it reaffirmed state and federal citizenship for persons born or naturalized in the United States, it forbade any *state* (the word "state" was important in later litigation) to abridge the "privileges and immunities" of citizens; to deprive any *person* (again an important term) of life, liberty, or property without "due process of law"; or to deny any person "the equal protection of the laws." The last three of these clauses have been the subject of long and involved lawsuits resulting in applications not widely, if at all, foreseen at the time. The "due process clause" has come in the twentieth century to mean that state as well as federal power is subject to the Bill of Rights, and the "due process clause" has been used to protect corporations, as legal "persons," from "unreasonable" regulation by the states. Other provisions of the amendment had less far-reaching effect. Section 4 specified that the debt of the United States "shall not be questioned," but declared "illegal and void" all debts contracted in aid of the rebellion. Section 5 specified the power of Congress to pass laws enforcing the amendment.

Johnson's home state was among the first to ratify. In Tennessee, which had harbored probably more Unionists than any other Confederate state, the government had fallen under Radical control. Gov. W. G. "Parson" Brownlow, in reporting the results to the secretary of the Senate, added: "Give my respects to the dead dog of the White House." His words afford a fair sample of the growing acrimony on both sides of the reconstruction debates. In May and July bloody race riots in Memphis and New Orleans added fuel to the flames. Both incidents amounted to indiscriminate massacres of blacks by local police and white mobs. The carnage, Radicals argued, was the natural fruit of Johnson's policy. "Witness Memphis, witness New Orleans," Sumner cried. "Who can doubt that the President is the author of these tragedies?"

RECONSTRUCTING THE SOUTH

THE TRIUMPH OF CONGRESSIONAL RECONSTRUCTION   As 1866 drew to an end, the congressional elections promised to resolve differences in the direction of policy. In August Johnson's friends staged a National Union Convention in Philadelphia. Men from Massachusetts and South Carolina marched down the aisle arm in arm to symbolize national reconciliation. The Radicals countered with a convention of their own and organized a congressional campaign committee to coordinate their propaganda. Johnson responded with a stumping tour of the Midwest, a "swing around the circle," which turned into an undignified contest of vituperation. Subjected to heckling and attacks on his integrity, Johnson responded in kind. "I have been called Judas Iscariot and all that," he said in St. Louis. "If I have played the Judas, who has been my Christ that I have played the Judas with? Was it Thad Stevens? Was it Wendell Phillips? Was it Charles Sumner?" Johnson may have been, as Secretary Seward claimed, the best stump speaker in the country. The trouble was, as Secretary Welles responded, the president ought not to be a stump speaker. It tended to confirm his image as a "ludicrous boor" and "drunken imbecile," which Radical papers projected. When the returns came in, the Republicans had well over a two-thirds majority in each house, by counts of 42 to 11 in the Senate and 143 to 49 in the House, a comfortable margin with which to override any presidential vetoes.

The Congress in fact enacted a new program even before new members took office. Two acts passed in January 1867 extended the suffrage to Negroes in the District of Columbia and the territories. Another law provided that the new Congress would meet on March 4 instead of the following December, depriving Johnson of a breathing spell. On March 2, 1867, two days before the old Congress expired, it passed three basic laws of congressional reconstruction over Johnson's vetoes: the Military Reconstruction Act, the Command of the Army Act (an amendment to an army appropriation), and the Tenure of Office Act.

The first of the three acts prescribed new conditions under which the formation of southern state governments should begin all over again. The other two sought to block obstruction by the president. The Army Act required that all orders from the commander-in-chief go through the headquarters of the general of the army, then Ulysses S. Grant, who could not be reassigned outside Washington without the consent of the Senate. The Radicals had faith in Grant, who was already leaning their way. The Tenure of Office Act required the consent of the Senate for the president to remove any officeholder whose appointment the Senate had to confirm in the first place. The purpose of at least some congressmen was to retain Secretary of War Edwin M. Stanton, the one Radical sympathizer in Johnson's cabinet, but an ambiguity crept into the wording of the act. Cabinet officers, it said, should serve during the term of the president who appointed them—and Lincoln had appointed Stanton, although, to be sure, Johnson was serving out Lincoln's term.

The Military Reconstruction Act, often hailed or denounced as the triumphant victory of "Radical" Reconstruction, actually fell short of a thoroughgoing radicalism. It emerged, the historian Michael Les Benedict wrote, "only after furious tugging and hauling among various Republican factions." As first reported from the Reconstruction committee by Stevens, it would have given military commanders in the South ultimate control over law enforcement and would have left open indefinitely the terms of future restoration. More moderate elements, however, pushed through the "Blaine amendment," which scrapped the prolonged national control under which Radicals hoped to put through the far more revolutionary program of reducing the Rebel states to territories, plus programs of land confiscation and education. With the Blaine amendment in place the Reconstruction program boiled down to little more than a requirement that southern states accept black suffrage and ratify the Fourteenth Amendment. Years later Albion W. Tourgée, after a career as a carpetbagger in North Carolina, wrote: "Republicans gave the ballot to men without homes, money, education, or security, and then told them to use it to protect themselves. . . . It was cheap patriotism, cheap philanthropy, cheap success!"

The act began with a pronouncement that "no legal state governments or adequate protection for life and property now exists in the rebel States. . . . " One state, Tennessee, which had ratified the Fourteenth Amendment, was exempted from the application of the act. The other ten were divided into five military districts, and the commanding officer of each was authorized to keep order and protect the "rights of persons and property." To that end he might use military tribunals in place of civil courts when he judged it necessary. The Johnson governments remained intact for the time being, but new constitutions were to be framed "in conformity with the Constitution of the United States," in conventions elected by male citizens twenty-one and older "of whatever race, color, or previous condition." Each state constitution had to provide the same universal male suffrage. Then, once the constitution was ratified by a majority of voters and accepted by Congress, and once the state legislature had ratified the Fourteenth Amendment, and once the amendment became part of the Constitution, any given state would be entitled to representation in Congress once again. Persons excluded from officeholding by the proposed amendment were also excluded from participation in the process.

Johnson reluctantly appointed military commanders under the act, but the situation remained uncertain for a time. Some people expected the Supreme Court to strike down the act, and for the time being no machinery existed for the new elections.

Congress quickly remedied that on March 23 with the Second Reconstruction Act, which directed the commanders to register for voting all adult males who swore they were qualified. A Third Reconstruction Act, passed on July 19, directed registrars to go beyond the loyalty oath and determine each person's eligibility to take it, and also authorized district commanders to remove and replace officeholders of any existing "so-called state" or division thereof. Before the end of 1867 new elections had been held in all the states but Texas.

Having clipped the president's wings, the Republican Congress moved a year later to safeguard its program from possible interference by the Supreme Court. In two important cases during 1866 the Court had shown a readiness to question certain actions. In *Ex parte Milligan* it struck down the wartime conviction of an Indiana Copperhead tried by court-martial for conspiracy to release and arm Rebel prisoners. The civil courts, the opinion noted, were duly operating in the area, which was far from the front. In *Cummings v. Missouri* the Court ruled void, as *ex post facto*, a Missouri statute which excluded ex-Confederates from certain professions. In *Ex parte Garland* (1867) it made a similar ruling against a test oath which barred ex-Confederates from practice before the Court. On the other hand it had evaded decision on two suits which directly challenged military Reconstruction, *Mississippi v. Johnson* and *Georgia v. Stanton,* on the ground that the suits involved political questions. Nevertheless, another case arising from Mississippi, *Ex parte McCardle,* raised the issue in a different form. McCardle, a Vicksburg editor arrested for criticizing General Ord's administration of the Fourth Military District, sought release under the Habeas Corpus Act of 1867. Congress responded on March 27, 1868, by simply removing the power of the Supreme Court to review cases arising under the law, which Congress clearly had the right to do under its power to define the Court's appellate jurisdiction (Article III, Section 2). The Court accepted this curtailment on the same day it affirmed the notion of an "indestructible Union" in *Texas v. White* (1869). In that case it also asserted the right of Congress under Article IV, Section 4, to reframe state governments.

THE IMPEACHMENT AND TRIAL OF JOHNSON   Congress's move to restrain the Supreme Court preceded by just two days the trial of the president in the Senate on an impeachment brought in by the House. Johnson, though hostile to the congressional program, had gone through the motions required of him. He continued, however, to pardon former Confederates in wholesale lots and replaced several district commanders whose Radical sympathies offended him. He and his cabinet members, moreover, largely ignored the Test Oath Act of 1862 by naming former Confederates to post offices and other federal positions. Nevertheless a lengthy investigation by the House Judiciary Committee, extending through most of the year 1867, failed to convince the House that grounds for impeachment existed.

The occasion for impeachment came when Johnson deliberately violated the Tenure of Office Act in order, he said, to test its constitutionality in the courts. Secretary of War Stanton had become a thorn in the president's side, refusing to resign despite his disagreements with the president's policy. On August 12, 1867, during a recess of Congress, Johnson suspended Stanton and named General Grant in his place. Grant's political stance was ambiguous at the time, but his acceptance implied cooperation with Johnson. When the Senate refused to confirm Johnson's action, however, Grant returned the office to Stanton. The president thereupon named Gen. Lorenzo Thomas as secretary of war after a futile effort to interest Gen. William T. Sherman. Three days later, on February 24, 1868, the House voted impeachment, to be followed by specific charges. In due course a special committee of seven brought in its report.

Of the eleven articles of impeachment, eight focused on the charge that he had unlawfully removed Stanton and had failed to give the Senate the name of a successor. Article 9, the "Emory article," accused the president of issuing orders directly to Gen. William H. Emory in violation of the Army Act. The last two in effect charged him with criticizing Congress by "inflammatory and scandalous harangues" and by claiming that the Congress was not legally valid without southern representatives. But Article 11 accused Johnson of "unlawfully devising and contriving" to violate the Reconstruction Acts, contrary to his obligation to execute the laws. At the least, Johnson had tried to obstruct Congress's will while observing the letter of the law.

The Senate trial opened on March 5 and continued until May 26, with Chief Justice Salmon P. Chase presiding. Seven managers from the House, including Thaddeus Stevens and Benjamin F. Butler, directed the prosecution. The president was spared the humiliation of a personal appearance, and was ably represented by Attorney-General Henry Stanbery, William H. Evarts, Benjamin R. Curtis, and William S. Groesbeck. The defense counsel shrewdly insisted on narrowing the trial to questions that would be indictable offenses under the law, and steered the

Johnson, impeached by the House, barely survived his trial in the Senate. [Harper's Weekly, *April 11, 1868*]

questions away from Johnson's manifest wish to frustrate the will of Congress. Such questions, they contended, were purely political in nature. In the end enough Republican senators, the "recusants," joined their pro-Johnson colleagues to prevent conviction. On May 16 the crucial vote came on Article 9: 35 votes guilty and 19 not guilty, one vote short of the two-thirds needed to convict. On Articles 2 and 3 the vote was exactly the same, and the trial adjourned.

In a parliamentary system Johnson probably would have been removed as leader of the government long before then. But by deciding the case on the narrowest grounds, the Senate made it unlikely that any future president could ever be removed except for the gravest personal offenses, and almost surely not for flouting the will of Congress in his execution of the laws. Impeachment of Johnson was in the end a great political mistake, for the failure to remove the president was damaging to Radical morale and support. Nevertheless the Radical cause did gain something. To blunt the opposition, Johnson agreed not to obstruct the process of Reconstruction, named as secretary of war Gen. John M. Schofield, who was committed to enforcing the new laws, and sent to Congress the new Radical constitutions of Arkansas and South Carolina. Thereafter his obstruction ceased and Radical Reconstruction got under way.

REPUBLICAN RULE IN THE SOUTH In June 1868 Congress agreed that seven states had met the conditions for readmission, all but

Virginia, Mississippi, and Texas. Congress rescinded Georgia's admission, however, when the state legislature expelled twenty-eight black members on the pretext that the state constitution had failed to specify their eligibility, and seated some former Confederate leaders. The military commander of Georgia then forced the legislature to reseat the Negro members and remove the Confederates, and the state was compelled to ratify the Fifteenth Amendment before being admitted in July 1870. Mississippi, Texas, and Virginia had returned earlier in 1870, under the added requirement that they too ratify the Fifteenth Amendment. This amendment, submitted to the states in 1869, ratified in 1870, forbade the states to deny any person the vote on grounds of race, color, or previous condition of servitude.

Long before the new governments were established, Republican groups began to spring up in the South, chiefly under the aegis of the Union League, founded at Philadelphia in 1862 to promote support for the Union. Emissaries of the league enrolled Negroes and loyal whites, initiated them into the secrets and rituals of the order, and instructed them "in their rights and duties." The league emphasized the display of such symbols as the Bible, the flag, the Constitution, and the Declaration of Independence. The sign of recognition was the recital of the "four Ls": Lincoln, Liberty, Loyal, League. Agents of the Freedmen's Bureau, northern missionaries, teachers, and soldiers aided the cause and spread its influence. When the time came for political action, they were ready. In October 1867, for instance, on the eve of South Carolina's choice of convention delegates, the league reported eighty-eight chapters, which claimed to have enrolled almost every adult black male in the state.

BLACKS IN SOUTHERN POLITICS   It was the new role of Negroes in politics on which attention focused then and afterward. If largely illiterate and inexperienced in the rudiments of politics, they were little different from millions of whites enfranchised in the age of Jackson or immigrants herded to the polls by political bosses in New York and other cities after the war. Some freedmen frankly confessed their disadvantages. Beverly Nash, a black delegate in the South Carolina convention of 1868, told his colleagues: "I believe, my friends and fellow-citizens, we are not prepared for this suffrage. But we can learn. Give a man tools and let him commence to use them, and in time he will learn a trade. So it is with voting."

Brought suddenly into politics in times that tried the most skilled of statesmen, a surprising number of blacks rose to the occasion. Yet it would be absurd to claim, in the phrase of the times, that the "bottom rail" ever got on top. To call what happened "black Reconstruction" is to exaggerate black influence, which was limited mainly to voting, and to overlook the large numbers of white Republicans, especially in the mountain areas of the upper South. Only one of the new conventions, South Carolina's, had a black majority, 76 to 41. Louisiana's was evenly divided between blacks and whites, and in only two other conventions were more than 20 percent of the members black: Florida's, with 40 percent, and Virginia's, with 24 percent. The Texas convention was only 10 percent and North Carolina's 11 percent—but that did not stop a white newspaper from calling it "Ethiopian minstrelsy, Ham radicalism in all its glory," a body consisting of "baboons, monkeys, mules, Tourgee, and other jackasses."

In the new state governments, any Negro participation was a novelty, but no black man ever served as governor and few as judges. There were two Negro senators in Congress, Hiram Revels and Blanche K. Bruce, both from Mississippi, and fourteen black members of the House during Reconstruction. Among these were some of the ablest congressmen of the time. Blacks served in every state legislature, but only in South Carolina did they ever make up a majority in both houses and that only for two years.

CARPETBAGGERS AND SCALAWAGS The top positions in southern state governments went for the most part to white Republicans, whom the opposition whites soon labeled "carpetbaggers" and "scalawags," depending on their place of birth. The men who al-

Hiram R. Revels. Senator from Mississippi, Revels was also a Methodist minister and, later, president of Alcorn College. [Library of Congress]

legedly came south with all their belongings in carpetbags to
pick up the political pelf were more often than not men who had
arrived as early as 1865 or 1866, drawn south by the hope of economic opportunity and by other attractions that many of them
had seen in Union service. Many were teachers or preachers who
came on missionary endeavors. Albion W. Tourgée, for instance, a
badly wounded Union veteran, moved to North Carolina in
1865, seeking a milder climate for reasons of health. He invested
$5,000 in a nursery, and promptly lost it. He would have needed
a fine crystal ball indeed to see two years in advance the chance
for political office under the Radical program. As it turned out,
he served in the state constitutional convention of 1868 and later
as a state judge.

The "scalawags," or native white Republicans, were even
more reviled and misrepresented. Most had opposed secession,
forming a Unionist majority in many mountain counties as far
south as Georgia and Alabama, and especially in the Tennessee
hills. Not a few in both hills and flatlands attested to the power of
what has been labeled "persistent Whiggery." Old Whigs often
found Republican economic policies to be in keeping with Henry
Clay's American System. Unionists, whether Whig or Democratic before the war, and even some secessionists, agreed with
Georgia's Joseph E. Brown, confederate governor and later
Democratic senator: "The statesman like the businessman
should take a practical view of questions as they arise." For the
time a practical view dictated joining the Republicans. Mississippi's James L. Alcorn, wealthy planter and former Whig, was
among the prominent whites who joined the Republicans in the
hope of moderating Radical policies. Such men were ready to
concede Negro suffrage in the hope of influencing Negro voters.
Alcorn became the first Republican governor of Mississippi.

THE REPUBLICAN RECORD   The new state constitutions were objectionable to adherents of the old order more because of their origins than because of their contents, excepting their provisions
for Negro suffrage and civil rights. Otherwise the documents
were in keeping with other state constitutions of the day, their
provisions often drawn from the basic laws of northern states.
Most remained in effect for some years after the end of Radical
control, and later constitutions incorporated many of their features. Conspicuous among Radical innovations were such steps
toward greater democracy as requiring universal manhood suffrage, reapportioning legislatures more nearly according to population, and making more state offices elective.

Given the circumstances in which the Radical governments arose and the intense hostility which met them, they made a surprisingly good record of positive achievement. For the first time in most of the South they established state school systems, however inadequate and ill-supported at first. The testimony is almost universal that Negroes eagerly sought education for themselves and their children. Some 600,000 black pupils were in schools by 1877. State governments under the Radicals gave more attention than ever before to poor relief and to public institutions for the disadvantaged and handicapped: orphanages, asylums, institutions for the deaf, dumb, and blind of both races. Public roads, bridges, and buildings were repaired or rebuilt. Blacks achieved new rights and opportunities that would never again be taken away, at least in principle: equality before the law, and the right to own property, carry on business, enter professions, attend schools, and learn to read and write.

In the annals of Reconstruction, partisan historians long denounced the Republican regimes for unparalleled corruption and abuse. That abuses proliferated in those years there is no question. Public money and public credit were often voted to privately owned corporations, especially railroads, under conditions which invited influence-peddling. But governmental subsidies were common before and after Reconstruction, especially for transportation, and the extension of public aid had general support among all elements, including the Radicals and their enemies. Contracts were let at absurd prices and public officials took their cut. Taxes and public debt rose in every state. Yet the figures of taxation and debt hardly constitute an unqualified indictment of Radical governments, since they then faced unusual and inflated costs for the physical reconstruction of public works in the South. Most states, moreover, had to float loans at outrageous discounts, sometimes at 50–75 percent of face value, because of uncertain conditions.

Nor, for that matter, were the breaches of public morality limited to the South or to Republicans. The Democratic Tweed Ring at the time was robbing New York City of more than $75 million, while the Republican "Gas Ring" in Philadelphia was lining its pockets. In national politics it was the time of the Crédit Mobilier, the Whiskey Ring, and other scandals that plagued the Grant administration. Corruption was neither invented by the Radical regimes, nor did it die with them. In Louisiana, the carpetbag governor Henry C. Warmoth found a certain Latin zest in the game: "Why," he said, "down here everybody is demoralized. Corruption is the fashion." In three years Louisiana's printing bill ran to $1.5 million, about half of which went to a newspaper belonging to young Warmoth, who left office with a tidy nest egg and settled down to a long life as a planter. But a later Democratic state treasurer, Maj. E. A. Burke, who decamped for Tegucigalpa in 1890 with the accounts over $1 million short, far outstripped Warmoth's record or anybody else's. About the same time Mississippi's Democratic state treasurer was found to have embezzled over $315,000. During Republican rule in Mississippi, on the other hand, there was no evidence of major corruption.

WHITE TERROR The case of Mississippi strongly suggests that whites were hostile to Republican regimes less because of their corruption than their inclusion of blacks. Most white southerners remained unreconstructed, so conditioned by slavery that they were unable to conceive of blacks as citizens or even free agents. In some places hostility to the new regimes took on the form of white terror. The prototype of terrorist groups was the Ku Klux Klan, first organized in 1866 by some young men of Pulaski, Tennessee, as a social club with the costumes, secret ritual, and mumbo-jumbo common to fraternal groups. At first a group of Merry Andrews devoted to practical jokes, the founders eventually realized, as two of them wrote in a later account, that they "had evoked a spirit from 'the vasty deep' [which] would not down at their bidding." Pranks turned into intimidation of blacks and white Republicans, and the KKK and imitators like Louisiana's Knights of the White Camellia spread rapidly across the South in answer to the Union League. Klansmen rode about the

Two "carpetbaggers" hanged by the Klan, in the Tuscaloosa Independent Monitor, *1868. [Alabama State Department of Archives and History]*

countryside hiding under masks and robes, spreading horren-
dous rumors, issuing threats, harassing assertive Negroes, and
occasionally running amok in violence and destruction. "Typically the Klan was a reactionary and racist crusade against equal
rights which sought to overthrow the most democratic society or
government the South had yet known," wrote its historian, Allan
W. Trelease. During its brief career it "whipped, shot, hanged,
robbed, raped, and otherwise outraged Negroes and Republicans across the South in the name of preserving white civilization."

Militia groups formed by the Radical regimes were hardly able
to cope with the underground tactics of the Klan, although their
presence may have prevented worse violence. Congress struck
back with three Enforcement Acts (1870–1871) to protect
Negro voters. The first of these measures levied penalties on
persons who interfered with any citizen's right to vote. A second
placed the election of congressmen under surveillance by federal election supervisors and marshals. The third (the Ku Klux
Klan Act) outlawed the characteristic activities of the Klan—
forming conspiracies, wearing disguises, resisting officers, and
intimidating officials—and authorized the president to suspend
habeas corpus where necessary to suppress "armed combinations." President Grant, in October 1871, singled out nine counties in upcountry South Carolina as an example, suspended
habeas corpus, and pursued mass prosecutions which brought an
abrupt halt to the Klan outrages. Elsewhere the Justice Department carried out a campaign of prosecution on a smaller scale,
while a congressional committee gathered testimony on Klan activity which ran to twelve volumes. The program of federal enforcement broke the back of the Klan, whose outrages declined
steadily as conservative southerners resorted to more subtle
methods.

CONSERVATIVE RESURGENCE   The Klan in fact could not take credit
for the overthrow of Republican control in any state. Perhaps its
most important effect, Allen Trelease suggested, was to weaken
Negro and Republican morale in the South and strengthen in the
North a growing weariness with the whole "southern question."
Yankees had other fish to fry anyway. Onrushing expansion into
the West, Indian wars, economic growth, and political controversy over the tariff and the currency distracted attention from
southern outrages. Republican control in the South gradually
loosened as "Conservative" parties—Democrats used that name
to mollify former Whigs—mobilized the white vote. Scalawags,
and many carpetbaggers, drifted away from the Radical ranks

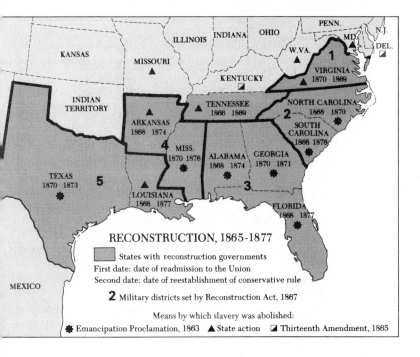

RECONSTRUCTION, 1865-1877

☐ States with reconstruction governments
First date: date of readmission to the Union
Second date: date of reestablishment of conservative rule

2 Military districts set by Reconstruction Act, 1867

Means by which slavery was abolished:
✹ Emancipation Proclamation, 1863   ▲ State action   ◪ Thirteenth Amendment, 1865

under pressure from their white neighbors. Few of them had joined the Republicans out of concern for Negro rights in the first place.

Republican control collapsed in Virginia and Tennessee as early as 1869, in Georgia and North Carolina in 1870, although there was a Republican governor in North Carolina until 1876. Reconstruction lasted longest in the Deep South states with the heaviest Negro population, where whites abandoned Klan masks for barefaced intimidation in paramilitary groups like the Mississippi Rifle Club and the South Carolina Red Shirts. By 1876 Radical regimes survived only in Louisiana, South Carolina, and Florida, and these all collapsed after the elections of that year. Later Daniel H. Chamberlain, the last carpetbag governor of South Carolina, told William Lloyd Garrison that "the uneducated negro was too weak, no matter what his numbers, to cope with the whites."

THE GRANT YEARS

GRANT'S ELECTION   Ulysses S. Grant, who presided over this fiasco, brought to the presidency less political experience than any man who ever occupied the office, except perhaps Zachary Taylor, and arguably less political judgment than any other. But in 1868 the rank-and-file voter could be expected to support "the Lion of Vicksburg" because of his record as a war leader. Both parties wooed him, but his falling-out with President Johnson pushed him toward the Republicans and built trust in him among the Radicals. They were, as Thad Stevens said, ready to "let him into the church." Impeachment proceedings were still in progress when the Republicans gathered in Chicago to name their candidate. Grant was the unanimous choice and House Speaker Schuyler Colfax of Indiana became his running mate. The platform endorsed the Reconstruction policy of Congress, congratulating the country on the "assured success" of the program. One plank cautiously defended Negro suffrage as a necessity in the South, but a matter each northern state should settle for itself. Another urged payment of the national debt "in the utmost good faith to all creditors," which meant in gold. More important than the platform were the great expectations of a soldier-president and his slogan: "Let us have peace."

The Democrats took an opposite position on both Reconstruction and the debt. The Republican Congress, the platform charged, instead of restoring the Union, had "so far as in its power, dissolved it, and subjected ten states, in the time of profound peace, to military despotism and Negro supremacy." As to the public debt, the party endorsed Rep. George H. Pendleton's "Ohio idea" that since most bonds had been bought with depreciated greenbacks, they should be paid off in greenbacks unless they specified payment in gold. With no conspicuously available candidate in sight, the convention turned to Horatio Seymour, war governor of New York and chairman of the convention. His friends had to hustle him out of the hall to prevent his withdrawal. With Francis P. Blair of Missouri in the second place on the ticket, the Democrats made a closer race of it than showed up in the electoral vote. Eight states, including New York and New Jersey, went for Seymour. While Grant swept the electoral college by 214 to 80, his popular majority was only 307,000 out of a total of over 5.7 million votes. More than 500,000 black voters accounted for Grant's margin of victory.

EARLY APPOINTMENTS   Grant had proven himself a great leader in the war, but in the White House he seemed blind to the political forces and influence peddlers around him. He was awe-struck by men of wealth and unaccountably loyal to some who betrayed his trust. The historian Henry Adams, who lived in Washington at the time, noted that to his friends "Grant appeared as intermittent energy, immensely powerful when awake, but passive and plastic in repose. . . . They could never measure his character or be sure when he would act. They could never follow a mental process in his thought. They were not sure that he did think." His conception of the presidency was "Whiggish." The chief executive carried out the laws; in the formulation of policy he passively followed the lead of Congress. This approach endeared him at first to party leaders, but it left him at last ineffective and others disillusioned with his leadership.

At the outset Grant consulted nobody on his cabinet appointments. Some of his choices indulged personal whims; others simply betrayed bad judgment. In some cases appointees learned of their nomination from the newspapers. The first secretary of state, former Rep. Elihu B. Washburne, an old friend from Illinois, served an honorific term of one week before going to his destined post as minister to France. Secretary of the Navy Adolph E. Borie was a casual dinner-table acquaintance and political contributor. A. T. Stewart, a wealthy merchant nominated as secretary of the treasury, was ineligible because of a law which barred anyone in "trade or commerce." As time went by Grant betrayed a fatal gift for losing men of talent and integrity from his cabinet. Secretary of State Hamilton Fish of New York turned out to be a happy exception; he guided foreign policy throughout the Grant presidency.

At first it looked as if Grant's free-wheeling style of choosing a cabinet signaled a sharp departure from the spoils system. But once Grant had taken care of his friends and relatives, he began to take care of party leaders. Cabinet members who balked at the procedure were soon eased out. This strengthened a nascent movement for a merit system in the civil service, modeled on systems recently adopted in Great Britain, Germany, and France. Grant finally approved a measure to set up a commission to look into the matter in 1872, a good gesture in a political year. The group duly brought in recommendations which in turn were duly shelved and forgotten once the election was over.

THE GOVERNMENT DEBT   The "sound money" men had more success than the reformers. They claimed that Grant's election had been a mandate to save the country from the Democrats' "Ohio idea." The underlying purpose of the movement to pay off the government debt in greenbacks was to bring about an inflation of the currency. Many debtors and aggressive businessmen rallied to the cause of "easy money," joined by a large number of Radicals who thought a combination of high tariffs and easy money would bring about more rapid economic growth. But creditors stood to gain from payment in gold, and they had the greater influence in Republican circles. They also had the benefit of a strong Calvinistic tendency in the public mind to look upon the cause of hard money as a moral one; depreciated currency was somehow a fraud. In his inaugural address Grant endorsed payment of the debt in gold not as a point of policy but as a point of national honor. On March 18, 1869, the Public Credit Act endorsing that principle became the first act of Congress he signed. Under the Refunding Act of 1870 the Treasury was able to replace 6 percent Civil War bonds with a new issue promising 4–5 percent in gold.

But whatever Grant's convictions respecting a "sound currency," he was not ready to risk a sharp contraction of the greenbacks in circulation. After the war the Treasury had assumed that the $400 million in greenbacks would be retired from circulation. To that end in 1866 Congress gave the Treasury discretionary power to begin the process at a rate of $10 million in the first six months and $4 million a month thereafter. In 1868, however, "soft money" elements in Congress stopped the process, leaving $356 million outstanding. There matters stood when Grant took office.

REFORM AND SCANDAL   Long before Grant's first term was out, a reaction against the Reconstruction measures, and against incompetence and corruption in the administration, had incited mutiny within the Republican ranks. Open revolt broke out first in Missouri where Carl Schurz, a German immigrant and war hero, led a group which elected a governor with Democratic help in 1870 and sent Schurz to the Senate. In 1872 the Liberal Republicans (as they called themselves) held a national convention at Cincinnati which produced a compromise platform condemning the party's southern policy and favoring civil service reform, but remained silent on the protective tariff. The meeting, moreover, was stampeded toward an anomalous presidential candidate: Horace Greeley, editor of the New York *Tribune*, a strong protectionist, and longtime champion of just about every reform of his times. His image as a visionary eccentric was complemented by his record of hostility to Democrats, whose support the Liberals needed. The Democrats nevertheless swallowed the pill and gave their nomination to Greeley as the only hope of beating Grant.

The result was a foregone conclusion. Republican regulars duly endorsed Radical Reconstruction and the protective tariff.

Grant still had seven carpetbag states in his pocket, generous support from business and banking interests, and the stalwart support of the Radicals. Above all he still evoked the imperishable glory of Missionary Ridge and Appomattox. Greeley, despite an exhausting tour of the country—still unusual for a presidential candidate—carried only six southern and border states and none in the North. Greeley's wife had died during the campaign, and worn out with grief and fatigue, he too was gone three weeks after the election.

Within less than a year of his reelection Grant was adrift in a cesspool of scandal. The first hint of scandal had touched Grant in the summer of 1869, when the crafty Jay Gould and the flamboyant Jim Fisk connived with the president's brother-in-law, Abel R. Corbin, to corner the gold market. Gould concocted an argument that the government should refrain from selling gold on the market because a rise in gold prices would raise temporarily depressed farm prices. Grant apparently smelled a rat from the start, but was seen in public with the speculators. Corbin convinced his associates that the president had bought the argument. As the rumor spread on Wall Street, gold rose from $132 to $163 an ounce. When Grant finally persuaded Corbin to pull out of the deal, Gould began quietly selling out. Finally, on "Black Friday," September 24, 1869, Grant ordered the Treasury to sell a large quantity of gold and the bubble burst. Fisk got out by repudiating his agreements and hiring thugs to intimidate his creditors. "Nothing is lost save honor," he said.

During the campaign of 1872 the public first learned about the financial buccaneering of the Crédit Mobilier, a construction company which had milked the Union Pacific Railroad for exorbitant fees to line the pockets of insiders who controlled both firms. Rank-and-file Union Pacific shareholders were left holding the bag. Rep. Oakes Ames had distributed Crédit Mobilier shares at bargain rates where, he said, "it will produce much good to us." The beneficiaries had included Speaker Schuyler Colfax, later vice-president, and Rep. James A. Garfield, later president. This chicanery had transpired before Grant's election in 1868, but it touched a number of prominent Republicans. Of thirteen members of Congress involved, only two were censured by a Congress which, before it adjourned in March 1873, voted itself a pay raise from $5,000 to $7,500—retroactive, it decided, for two years. A public uproar forced repeal, leaving the raises voted the president ($25,000 to $50,000) and Supreme Court justices.

Even more odious disclosures soon followed, and some in-

The People's Handwriting on the Wall. *An 1872 engraving comments on the corruption engulfing Grant. [Library of Congress]*

volved the president's cabinet. Secretary of War W. W. Belknap, it turned out, had accepted bribes from Indian traders at army posts in the West. He was impeached, but resigned in time to elude trial by the Senate. Post-office contracts, it was revealed, went to carriers who offered the highest kickbacks. Secretary of the Treasury W. A. Richardson had awarded a commission of 50 percent for the collection of overdue taxes by John D. Sanborn, a political friend of Massachusetts Rep. Benjamin F. Butler. In St. Louis a "Whiskey Ring" bribed tax collectors to bilk the government of millions in revenue. Grant's private secretary, Orville Babcock, was enmeshed in that scheme, taking large sums of money and other valuables in return for inside information. Before Grant's second term ended, the corruption crossed the Atlantic when Gen. Robert Schenck, minister to London, unloaded worthless stock in "Emma Mines" on gullible Britons. Only a plea of diplomatic immunity and a sudden exit spared him from British justice. There is no evidence that Grant himself was ever involved in, or that he personally profited from, any of the fraud, but his poor choice of associates earned him the public censure that was heaped upon his head.

PANIC AND REDEMPTION Economic distress followed close upon public scandal. Contraction of the money supply and expansion of the railroads into sparsely settled areas had made investors cautious. During 1873 the market for railroad bonds turned sour as some twenty-five roads defaulted on their interest payments before the end of August. The investment banking firm of Jay Cooke and Company, unable to sell the bonds of the Northern Pacific Railroad, financed them with short-term deposits in hope that a European market would develop. But in 1873 the opposite happened when a financial panic in Vienna forced many financiers to unload American stocks and bonds. Caught short, Cooke and Company went bankrupt on September 18, 1873. The ensuing stampede forced the stock market to close for ten days. The Panic of 1873 set off a depression that lasted for six years, the longest and most severe that Americans had yet suffered, marked by widespread bankruptcies, unemployment, and a drastic slowdown in railroad building.

Hard times and scandals hurt Republicans in the midterm elections of 1874. The Democrats won control of the House of Representatives and gained in the Senate. The new Democratic House immediately launched inquiries into the scandals and unearthed further evidence of corruption in high places. The panic meanwhile focused attention once more on greenback currency.

Since greenbacks were valued less than gold, they had become the chief circulating medium. Most people spent greenbacks first and held their gold or used it to settle foreign accounts, which drained much gold out of the country. The postwar retirement of greenbacks had made for tight money. To relieve deflation and stimulate business, therefore, the Treasury reissued $26 million in greenbacks previously withdrawn, raising the total in circulation to about $382 million.

For a time the advocates of easy money were riding high. Early in 1874 they pushed through a bill to issue greenbacks up to the wartime level of $400 million. Here the administration drew the line, however. Grant vetoed the bill in April and in his annual message of December 1874 called for the gradual resumption of specie payments—that is, the redemption of greenbacks in gold. This would make greenbacks "good as gold" and raise their value to a par with the gold dollar. In January, before the Republicans gave up control of the House, Congress obliged by passing the Resumption Act of 1875. The redemption in specie began on January 1, 1879, after the Treasury had built a gold reserve for the purpose and reduced the value of greenbacks in circulation.

THE COMPROMISE OF 1877   Grant, despite everything, was eager to run again in 1876, but the recent scandals discouraged any challenge to the two-term tradition. James G. Blaine of Maine, late Speaker of the House, emerged as the Republican front-runner, but he too bore the taint of scandal. Letters in the possession of James Mulligan of Boston linked Blaine to some dubious railroad dealings. Blaine cajoled Mulligan into turning over a packet of letters, from which he read to Congress selected passages exonerating him. But the performance was a shade too clever. It left doubts which were strengthened by the disclosure of still other "Mulligan letters" that found their way into print.

The Republican convention in Cincinnati therefore eliminated Blaine and several other hopefuls in favor of Ohio's favorite son, Rutherford B. Hayes. Three times elected governor of Ohio, most recently as an advocate of sound money, Hayes had also made a name as a civil service reformer. But his chief virtue was that he offended neither Radicals nor reformers. As Henry Adams put it, he was "a third rate nonentity, whose only recommendation is that he is obnoxious to no one." The vice-presidential nod went to William A. Wheeler of New York.

The Democratic convention in St. Louis was abnormally harmonious from the start. The nomination went on the second ballot to Samuel J. Tilden, millionaire corporation lawyer and reform governor of New York who had directed a campaign to overthrow first the Tweed Ring in New York City and then another ring in Albany which had bilked the state of millions. The convention named Thomas A. Hendricks of Indiana for vice-president.

The campaign generated no burning issues. Both candidates favored the trend toward conservative rule in the South. During one of the most corrupt elections ever, both candidates favored civil service reform. In the absence of strong differences, Democrats waved the Republicans' dirty linen. In response, Republicans waved the bloody shirt, which is to say that they engaged in verbal assaults on former Confederates and the spirit of Rebellion. The phrase "waving the bloody shirt" originated at the impeachment trial of President Johnson when Benjamin F. Butler, speaking for the prosecution, displayed the bloody shirt a Mississippi carpetbagger had been wearing when hauled out of bed and beaten by Ku Kluxers. Reporting such atrocities came to be known to Democrats as "grinding the outrage mills." "Our strong ground," Hayes wrote to Blaine, "is the dread of a solid South, *rebel rule*, etc., etc. . . . It leads people away from 'hard times,' which is our deadliest foe."

On the night of the election early returns pointed to a victory for Tilden, but Republican National Chairman Zachariah Chandler refused to concede. As it fell out, Tilden had 184 electoral votes, just one short of a majority, but Republicans claimed nineteen doubtful votes from Florida, Louisiana, and South Carolina, while Democrats laid a counterclaim to Oregon. But the Republicans had clearly carried Oregon. In the South the outcome was less certain, and given the fraud and intimidation perpetrated on both sides, nobody will ever know what might have happened if, to use a slogan of the day, "a free ballot and a fair count" had prevailed. As good a guess as any may be, as one writer suggested, that the Democrats stole the election first and the Republicans stole it back.

In all three of the disputed southern states rival canvassing boards sent in different returns. In Florida, Republicans conceded the state election, but in Louisiana and South Carolina rival state governments also appeared. The Constitution offered no guidance in this unprecedented situation. Even if Congress was empowered to sort things out, the Democratic House and the Republican Senate proved unable to reach an agreement.

Finally, on January 29, 1877, the two houses decided to set up a special Electoral Commission which would investigate and report back its findings. It had fifteen members, five each from the House, the Senate, and the Supreme Court. Members were so chosen as to have seven from each major party with Justice David Davis of Illinois as the swing man. Davis, though appointed to the Court by Lincoln, was no party regular and was in fact thought to be leaning toward the Democrats. Republicans who voted for the commission, James A. Garfield said, were "fair-minded asses" who thought that "truth is always half way between God and the Devil." The panel appeared to be stacked in favor of Tilden.

But as it turned out, the panel got restacked the other way. Short-sighted Democrats in the Illinois legislature teamed up with minority Greenbackers to name Davis their senator. Davis accepted, no doubt with a sense of relief. From the remaining justices, all Republicans, the panel chose Joseph P. Bradley to fill the vacancy. The decision on each state went by a vote of 8 to 7, along party lines, in favor of Hayes. After much bluster and threat of filibuster by Democrats, the House voted on March 2 to accept the report and declare Hayes elected by an electoral vote of 185 to 184.

Critical to this outcome was the defection of southern Democrats who had made several informal agreements with the Republicans. On February 26, 1877, a bargain was struck at the Wormley House, a Washington hotel, between prominent Ohio Republicans, including Sen. John Sherman and Rep. James A.

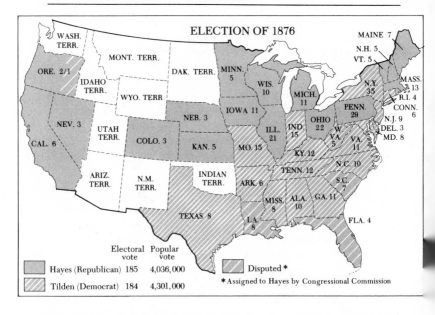

ELECTION OF 1876

	Electoral vote	Popular vote
Hayes (Republican)	185	4,036,000
Tilden (Democrat)	184	4,301,000

Disputed *

*Assigned to Hayes by Congressional Commission

Garfield, and powerful southern Democrats, including Sen. John Brown Gordon of Georgia and Rep. L. Q. C. Lamar of Mississippi. The Republicans promised that, if elected, Hayes would withdraw federal troops from Louisiana and South Carolina, letting the Republican governments there collapse. In return the Democrats promised to withdraw their opposition to Hayes, to accept in good faith the Reconstruction amendments, and to refrain from partisan reprisals against Republicans in the South.

With this agreement in hand, southern Democrats could justify deserting Tilden because this so-called Compromise of 1877 brought a final "redemption" from the "Radicals" and a return to "home rule," which actually meant rule by white Democrats. Other, more informal promises, less noticed by the public, bolstered the Wormley House agreement. Hayes's friends pledged more support for Mississippi levees and other internal improvements, including federal subsidy for a transcontinental railroad along a southern route. Southerners extracted a further promise that Hayes would name a white southerner as postmaster-general, the cabinet position with the most patronage jobs at hand. In return, southerners would let Republicans make James A. Garfield Speaker of the new House.

THE END OF RECONSTRUCTION   After Hayes took office, most of these promises were either renounced or forgotten. They had served their purpose of breaking the crisis. In April, Hayes withdrew federal troops from the state houses in Louisiana and South Carolina, and the Republican governments there collapsed— along with much of Hayes's claim to legitimacy. Hayes chose a Tennessean, former Confederate David M. Key, as postmaster-general. But after southern Democrats failed to permit the choice of Garfield as Speaker, Hayes expressed doubt about any further subsidy for railroad building, and none was voted.

As to southern promises regarding the civil rights of blacks, only a few Democratic leaders such as Wade Hampton and Francis T. Nicholls, the new governors of South Carolina and Louisiana, remembered them for long. Over the next three decades those rights crumbled under the pressure of white rule in the South and the force of Supreme Court decisions narrowing the application of the Reconstruction amendments. The Compromise of 1877, viewed in the light of its consequences, might justly bear the label which one historian gave it: "The betrayal of the Negro." But "betrayal" implies that a promise was made in the first place, and Reconstruction never offered more than an uncertain commitment to equality before the law. Yet it left an enduring legacy, the Thirteenth, Fourteenth, and Fifteenth Amendments—not dead but dormant, waiting to be warmed back into life.

FURTHER READING

Over time the various interpretations of Reconstruction have made that period "a dark and bloody ground" for historians. Those interested in following the interplay of interpretation might first turn to works of fiction to understand how the adversaries line up. Albion W. Tourgée's *A Fool's Errand* (1880, 1966)° provides a northern carpetbagger's idealistic view, while Thomas Dixon's *The Clansman* (1905)° applauds the defeated South's heroic casting off of the tyranny of corrupt occupation. This pro-southern viewpoint came to dominate professional scholarship as well after 1900. William A. Dunning's *Reconstruction, Political and Economic, 1865–1877* (1907), sets the tone for numerous monographs sympathetic to white southern suffering under "black rule."

Among the early challengers to the Dunning school are Charles and Mary Beard, whose sweeping *Rise of American Civilization* (1927) assigns largely economic motives to the actors in Reconstruction politics. Howard Beale's *The Critical Year* (1930) sees the Radical Republicans as fanatics who served business interests, and Andrew Johnson as a commonsensical mediator in the controversies of 1866. Among the strongest

°These books are available in paperback editions.

challengers of the pro-southern view is W. E. B. Du Bois's *Black Reconstruction* (1935), which maintains that the Republicans held valid ideals in their defense of freedmen rights.

The civil rights movement of the 1950s and 1960s brought new freshness to the topic. Among the surveys which reflect a new sympathy for the aims of the Radicals and the plight of freedmen are John Hope Franklin's *Reconstruction after the Civil War* (1961) and Kenneth M. Stampp's *The Era of Reconstruction* (1964).° More detailed, but equally valuable, are Rembert W. Patrick's *The Reconstruction of the Nation* (1967), James G. Randall and David Donald's *Civil War and Reconstruction* (1969), and James M. McPherson's *Ordeal by Fire: The Civil War and Reconstruction* (1982).

More specialized works give closer scrutiny to the aims of the principal political figures. William B. Hesseltine's *Lincoln's Plan of Reconstruction* (1960) argues that the president planned postwar policy in the same pragmatic fashion as he directed the Civil War. Peyton McCrary's *Abraham Lincoln and Reconstruction* (1978) deals with the Lincoln policies as they were carried out in Louisiana. Claude G. Bower's *The Tragic Era* (1929) is sympathetic to Johnson, while Eric McKitrick's *Andrew Johnson and Reconstruction* (1960),° John H. and LaWanda C. Cox's *Politics, Principle, and Prejudice* (1963), and William R. Brock's *An American Crisis* (1963) sharply criticize the behavior of a president who obstructed Republican policies. Why Johnson was impeached is detailed in Michael L. Benedict's *The Impeachment of Andrew Johnson* (1973)° and H. L. Trefousse's *Impeachment of a President* (1975).

Recent scholars have been far more sympathetic to the aims and motives of the Radical Republicans. Surveys of congressional behavior are Hans F. Trefousse's *The Radical Republicans* (1969)° and Herman Belz's *Reconstructing the Union* (1969). Clearest in dealing with the ideology of these Radicals is Michael L. Benedict's *A Compromise of Principle: Congressional Republicans and Reconstruction* (1974). Biographies of Radical leaders include Fawn M. Brodie's *Thaddeus Stevens* (1959)° and David Donald's *Charles Summer and the Rights of Man* (1970).° For an emphasis on the relations of the courts and these congressmen, consult Stanley I. Kutler's *The Judicial Power and Reconstruction Policies* (1968) or Charles Fairman's *Reconstruction and Reunion* (1971).

The intransigence of southern white attitudes is examined in Michael Perman's *Reunion without Compromise* (1973) and Joe G. Taylor's *Louisiana Reconstructed* (1974). Allen W. Trelease's *White Terror* (1971) covers the various organizations which practiced vigilante tactics, chiefly the Ku Klux Klan. The difficulties former planters had in adjusting to the new labor system are documented in James L. Roark's *Masters without Slaves* (1977).°

Numerous works have appeared on the freedmen's experience in the South. Start with Leon Litwack's *Been in the Storm So Long* (1979),° which wonderfully covers the transition from slavey to freedom. Among the best state-level studies are those dealing with South Carolina blacks. Willie Lee Rose's *Rehearsal for Reconstruction* (1964)° examines Union efforts to define the social role of former slaves during wartime emancipation. Joel Williamson's *After Slavery* (1965)° argues that South Carolina freedmen took an active role in pursuing their political and economic rights. A study of Alabama freedmen—Peter Kolchin's *First Freedom* (1974)—should also be consulted. The role of the Freedman's Bureau is explored in George R. Bentley's *A History of the Freedman's Bureau* (1955), William S. McFeely's *Yankee Stepfather: O. O. Howard and the Freedman* (1980),° and Robert C. Morris's *Reading, 'Riting and Reconstruction: The Education of Freedmen in the South, 1861–1870* (1981).

The role of white Republicans in one southern state in the immediate postwar years is traced in William C. Harris's *The Day of the Carpetbagger: Republican Reconstruction in Mississippi* (1979). The land confiscation issue is discussed in Eric Foner's *Politics and Ideology in the Age of the Civil War* (1980),° Beth Bethel's *Promiseland* (1981) on a South Carolina black community, and Janet S. Hermann's *The Pursuit of a Dream* (1981)° on the Davis Bend experiment.

The politics of corruption outside the South is depicted in Allan Nevin's *Hamilton Fish: The Inner History of the Great Administration* (1936) and William S. McFeeley's *Grant: A Biography* (1981).° The influence of Horace Greeley in postwar politics is treated in Eric S. Lunde's *Horace Greeley* (1980). The political maneuvers of the election of 1876 and the resultant crisis and compromise are explained in C. Vann Woodward's *Reunion and Reaction* (1966)° and William Gillette's *Retreat from Reconstruction, 1869–1879* (1979).°

19

NEW FRONTIERS:
SOUTH AND WEST

THE NEW SOUTH

A FRESH VISION The major prophet of a New South emerged in an improbable setting—at New York's most elegant restaurant, Delmonico's—where on December 21, 1886, the New England Society of New York held its annual dinner to commemorate the landing of the Pilgrims at Plymouth Rock. The main speaker of the evening was Henry Woodfin Grady, thirty-six-year-old editor of the Atlanta *Constitution,* who had gained notice with his vivid reports of the recent Charleston earthquake. Grady's topic was "The New South," and his eloquent words became certainly the most celebrated statement of the New South Creed, a classic speech that multitudes of schoolboy orators in the South would commit to memory.

In plain yet almost poetic language, Grady set forth the vision that inspired a generation of southerners: "The Old South rested everything on slavery and agriculture, unconscious that these could neither give nor maintain healthy growth. The new South presents a perfect democracy, the oligarchs leading in the popular movement—a social system compact and closely knitted, less splendid on the surface, but stronger at the core—a hundred farms for every plantation, fifty homes for every palace—and a diversified industry that meets the complex need of this complex age."

Many prophets had gone before Grady and still others stood with him as major spokesmen for the New South Creed. In the aftermath of the Civil War these men, and Yankee patrons like William D. "Pig Iron" Kelly of Pennsylvania, preached with evangelical fervor the gospel of industry. The Confederacy, they reasoned, had lost because it relied too much on King Cotton. In the future the South must follow the North's example and industrialize. From that central belief flowed certain corollaries: that a more diversified and efficient agriculture would be a foundation for economic growth, that more widespread education especially vocational training, would promote material success, and that sectional peace and racial harmony would provide a stable environment for economic growth.

By the late 1870s, with Reconstruction over and the panic of 1873 forgotten, a mood of progress permeated the editorials and the speeches of the day. The mood found material expression in a series of industrial fairs whose prototype was Atlanta's International Cotton Exposition of 1881. Organized in response to the call of a Boston capitalist, Edward Atkinson, the exposition would, according to a prospectus, show how the South could become "prosperous in its own right through a liberal development of its own resources." To that end the displays featured machinery for spinning and weaving, and showed the best applications of power. In all some 1,113 exhibits from thirty-three states, the District of Columbia, and six foreign countries were mounted, at an expense of more than $2 million.

ECONOMIC GROWTH   The first and chief fruit of the New South zealots was an expansion of the area's textile production that got under way in the 1880s and eventually overtook the older New

White Oak Cotton Mills, Greensboro, North Carolina. These women are measuring, sewing, and finishing denim. [Brown Brothers]

England industry by the 1920s. In the New South, as in New England and Old England, cotton textiles were the harbingers of the Industrial Revolution. Already in the 1870s new cotton mills had begun to dot the landscape of the Carolina Piedmont, where their promotion generated an almost revivalistic fervor. From 1880 to 1900 the number of cotton mills in the South grew from 161 to 400, the number of mill workers (among whom women and children outnumbered the men) increased fivefold, and the consumption of cotton went up nearly tenfold, from 182,000 bales to 1,479,000. This development was the product mainly of southern capital and southern labor at the outset, though later the decline of the textile industry in New England contributed labor and capital to the South.

Tobacco growth also increased significantly, entering a new era with the development of two varieties of the weed: burley, which appeared in 1864 in southern Ohio, and bright leaf, which was grown on otherwise infertile soils and cured by a charcoal process discovered by a slave in 1839. Knowledge of the bright-leaf type remained chiefly local until, in what seemed a misfortune, Union soldiers swarmed over central North Carolina in 1865.

One victim of their looting was John Ruffin Green, whose bright-leaf tobacco factory was ransacked by soldiers loitering around Durham's Station. Within a few weeks orders began to pour in to Green's factory for the Best Flavored Spanish Smoking Tobacco "that did not bite." With this revival, Green adopted as his trademark a bull's head similar to that on Coleman's mustard, made in Durham, England. It did not take long for Green and his successors to make the image of Bull Durham ubiquitous, so much so that years later Mark Twain, who was not above embellishing a good story, claimed that when he visited Egypt he never got a clear view of the pyramids for the Bull Durham signs.

Even more important in the rise of tobacco and Durham was the Duke family, whose story started at a nearby farm. At the end of the Civil War, the story goes, old Washington Duke had a capital of fifty cents obtained from a Yankee soldier for a souvenir Confederate five-dollar bill. He took a barnful of tobacco, and with the help of his three sons, beat it out with hickory sticks, stuffed it in bags labeled "Pro Bono Publico," hitched up two mules to his wagon, and set out across the state, selling bright leaf as he went. From that start success followed quickly. By 1872 the Dukes had a factory producing 125,000 pounds of leaf annually, and Washington Duke prepared to settle down and enjoy success. His son Buck (James Buchanan Duke), however, had the same drive that animated the Carnegies and Rockefellers of that

PARALLEL BAR,   WALKING,

W. DUKE SONS & CO.
THE LARGEST CIGARETTE
MANUFACTURERS IN THE WORLD.

From the "Sporting Girls" series of trade cards,
W. Duke Sons & Co. These cards were inserted
in cigarette packs to promote sales. [W. Duke &
Co. Papers, Manuscript Department, Duke
University Library]

day. Buck Duke recognized early that the industry was "half smoke and half ballyhoo" and poured large sums into advertising schemes, such as the cigarette coupons for which one could get an album in color entitled "Sporting Girls." Duke also squeezed competitors by underselling them in their own markets, and by cornering the supply of ingredients like glycerin and licorice. Eventually his competitors were ready to take the hint that they join forces, and in 1890 Duke brought most of them into the American Tobacco Company, which controlled nine-tenths of the nation's cigarette production and by 1904 about three-fourths of all tobacco production in the United States. In 1911 the Supreme Court found the company in violation of the Sherman Anti-Trust Act and ordered it broken up, but by then Duke had found new worlds to conquer in hydroelectric power and aluminum.

Systematic use of other natural resources brought into the New South that area along the Applachian Mountain chain from West Virginia to Alabama. Coal production in the South (including West Virginia) grew from 4.6 million tons in 1875 to 49.3 million tons by 1900. At the southern end of the mountains, Birmingham, Alabama, sprang up during the 1870s in the shadow of Red Mountain, so named for its iron ore, and soon tagged itself the "Pittsburgh of the South." Birmingham's close proximity to coal, iron, and limestone gave it a strong advantage over Chattanooga, which had a meteoric career as an iron center after the war.

With growth came a need for housing, and thus after 1870 lumbering became a ubiquitous industry in the South. Lumber camps and little "peckerwood" mills sprang up all across the mountains and flatlands. By the turn of the century their product, mainly southern pine, had outdistanced textiles in value. Tree cutting seemed to know no bounds. It went on and on, despite the ecological devastation it caused. In time the industry would be saved only by the warm climate, which fostered quick renewal, and the rise of scientific forestry, which had its beginnings on George Vanderbilt's Biltmore Estate near Asheville, North Carolina. Here Dr. Carl Alvin Schenck opened the nation's first school of forestry in 1898.

The South still had far to go to achieve the "diversified industry" that Grady envisioned in the mid-1880s, but a profusion of other products poured from southern plants: phosphate fertilizers from coastal South Carolina and Florida; oysters, vegetables, and fruits from widespread canneries; ships, including battleships, from the Newport News Shipbuilding and Drydock Company; leather products; wagons and buggies; liquors and beverages; paper in small quantities; clay, glass, and stone products.

At the turn of the century two great forces that would impel an even greater industrial revolution were already on the horizon: petroleum in the Southwest and hydroelectric power in the Southeast. The Corsicana field in Texas had been opened in 1895, and in 1901 the Spindletop gusher would bring a great bonanza. Local powerplants dotted the map by the 1890s. Richmond, Virginia, had the nation's first electric streetcar system in 1888, and Columbia, South Carolina, had the first electrically powered cotton mill in 1894. The greatest advance would begin in 1905 when Buck Duke's Southern Power Company set out to develop entire river valleys in the Carolinas.

AGRICULTURE, OLD AND NEW   At the turn of the century, however, most of the South was still undeveloped, at least by northeastern standards. The typical southerner was less apt to be tending a loom or forge than, as the saying went, facing the eastern end of a westbound mule. King Cotton survived the Civil War and expanded over new acreage even as its export markets leveled off. The old tobacco belts of Virginia and Kentucky now reached across North Carolina and touched South Carolina. Louisiana cane sugar, probably the most war-devastated of all crops, flourished again by the 1890s. In 1885 Seaman A. Knapp, an agriculturist from New York by way of Iowa, moved to Louisiana and developed a new rice belt on behalf of an English land company, using machinery imported from the wheatfields. In the process Knapp invented the demonstration methods of agricultural education, which showed farmers the most productive methods on selected plots of land, with the aim of teaching by example.

Knapp later used the demonstration method to fight the boll weevil in Texas. His work led eventually to the national system of county farm and home demonstration agents. In the old rice belt of coastal South Carolina and elsewhere truck farming sprang up with the advent of the railroads and refrigerator cars. Vegetables from the Sea Islands, strawberries from Louisiana, and citrus fruits from Florida combined with other produce to create a cash crop second only to cotton.

In 1880 the poet Sidney Lanier, in one of the perennial essays on "The New South," claimed that "The New South means small farming." The "quiet rise of the small farmer" was "the notable circumstance of the period, in comparison with which noisier events signify nothing." But the growth of small farming remained a statistical illusion. Farms of all sizes were more numerous because new acreage came into cultivation, even in the seaboard states. The census, moreover, counted tenant and sharecropper plots as separate farms.

Sharecropping and tenancy became increasingly prevalent in the aftermath of emancipation, but they seldom produced the self-sufficiency that Lanier envisioned. The sharecropper, who had nothing to offer the landowner but his labor, tilled the land in return for supplies and a share of the crop, generally about half. The tenant farmer, hardly better off, might offer the planter a mule, a plow, and perhaps his own line of credit with the country store, and therefore might claim a larger share, commonly three-fourths of the cash crop and two-thirds of the subsistence crop, which was mainly corn. There were, moreover, infinite variations that ranged from cash rental at best to outright peon-

Black sharecroppers, ca. 1880–1890. [Brown Brothers]

age at worst. From the standpoint of efficiency the system approached the worst conceivable, for the tenant lacked incentive to care for the land and the owner had little chance to supervise the work. In addition the system bred a morbid suspicion on both sides, and the folklore of the rural South was replete with stories of tenants who remained stubbornly shiftless and improvident, and landlords who kept books with crooked pencils.

The crop lien system was equally flawed. At best, it supplied credit where cash was scarce. Country merchants furnished supplies in return for liens (or mortgages) on farmers' crops. To a few tenants and small farmers who seized the chance, the credit offered a way out, but to most it offered only a hopeless cycle of perennial debt. The merchant, who assumed great risks, generally charged markups and interest which ranged, according to one farmer, "from 24 percent to grand larceny." The merchant, like the planter (often the same man), demanded a cash crop that could be readily sold at harvest time. For all the wind and ink expended on preachments of diversification, the routines of tenancy and sharecropping yielded only with difficulty to other arrangements because the marketing, supply, and credit systems were still geared to a staple crop, usually cotton. The stagnation of rural life held millions, white and black, in bondage to privation and ignorance.

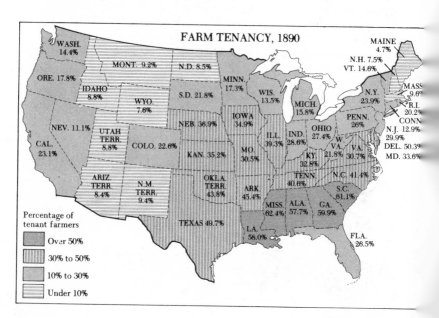

FARM TENANCY, 1890

Percentage of tenant farmers

- Over 50%
- 30% to 50%
- 10% to 30%
- Under 10%

WASH. 14.4%
MONT. 9.2%
N.D. 8.5%
MAINE 4.7%
N.H. 7.5%
VT. 14.6%
ORE. 17.8%
IDAHO 8.8%
WYO. 7.8%
S.D. 21.8%
MINN. 17.3%
WIS. 13.5%
MICH. 15.8%
N.Y. 23.9%
MASS. 9.6%
R.I. 20.2%
NEV. 11.1%
UTAH TERR. 8.8%
COLO. 22.6%
NEB. 36.9%
IOWA 34.9%
ILL. 39.3%
IND. 28.6%
OHIO 27.4%
PENN. 26%
CONN. 29.9%
N.J. 12.9%
DEL. 50.3%
MD. 33.6%
CAL. 23.1%
ARIZ. TERR. 8.4%
N.M. TERR. 9.4%
KAN. 35.2%
MO. 30.5%
KY. 32.8%
W. VA.
VA. 30.7%
OKLA. TERR. 43.8%
ARK. 45.4%
TENN. 40.6%
N.C. 41.4%
S.C. 61.1%
TEXAS 49.7%
MISS. 62.4%
ALA. 57.7%
GA. 59.9%
LA. 58.0%
FLA. 26.5%

THE BOURBON REDEEMERS   In politics, despite the South's formal democracy, habits of deference still prevailed. "Every community," Union officer John DeForest noted in postwar South Carolina, "had its great man, or its little great man, around whom his fellow citizens gather when they want information, and to whose monologues they listen with a respect akin to humility." DeForest called him the "Central Monkey." After Reconstruction, southern politics was dominated by small coteries of "Central Monkeys" collectively known to history as Bourbons. Like the French Bourbons, the royal family which, Napoleon said, forgot nothing and learned nothing in the ordeal of revolution, the southern Bourbons were said to have forgotten nothing and learned nothing in the ordeal of Civil War. Yet the term, according to one historian, is one of "the most indefinable words ever used to describe Southern persons, places, and things, either solid or liquid."

The word functioned mainly as a hateful epithet, and few could glory in it. But their Republican, Independent, and Populist adversaries fixed the label so firmly in the vocabulary of the times that Bourbon came to signify the leaders of the Democratic party, whether they were real mossbacks or, more commonly, champions of an industrial New South who, if they had forgotten nothing, had at least learned something. They may have worshipped at the shrine of the old order, but they embraced a new order of economic development.

These Bourbons of the New South perfected a political alliance with eastern conservatives and an economic alliance with eastern capitalists. They generally pursued a policy of laissez-faire, except for the tax exemptions and other favors they offered to business. They avoided political initiatives, making the transition from Republican rule to Bourbon rule less abrupt than is often assumed. The Bourbons' favorable disposition toward the railroads was not unlike that of the Radicals. The Louisiana Lottery, a state lottery established during Reconstruction as a private monopoly, paid for "Redemption" from Republican rule in the state and was rewarded by Bourbons with a renewed tenure, written into the state constitution. And despite their reputation for honesty, Bourbon officeholders were occasionally caught with their fingers in the till.

Being basically antigovernment and haunted by the war, the Bourbons made a cardinal virtue of retrenchment. Their parsimony spelled austerity for public services, including the school systems started during Reconstruction. In 1871 the South Atlantic states were spending $10.27 per pupil; by 1880 the figure was down to $6.00 and in 1890 it still stood at $7.63. In 1901 Charles W. Dabney, an educational leader of the time, summarized conditions at the turn of the century: "In the Southern states, in schoolhouses costing an average of $276 each, under teachers receiving an average salary of $25 a month, we are giving children in actual attendance only 5 cents' worth of education a day for eighty-seven days only in the year." Illiteracy rates at the time ran at about 12 percent of the native white population and 50 percent of the black population.

Private philanthropy, however, did help to keep southern schools afloat. In 1867 George Peabody, a London banker born in Massachusetts, established the Peabody Fund for Education, which was to spend some $3.6 million on public schools by 1914, when it was dissolved and most of its capital transferred to the George Peabody College for Teachers, established in 1875 in Nashville. Aid from the Peabody Fund was supplemented by the $1 million in the John F. Slater Fund, established in 1882 by a donor in Connecticut and earmarked for Negro schools. J. L. M. Curry, onetime soldier, preacher, teacher, and politician, became the general agent of both the Peabody and the Slater Funds. A very active man, Curry pursued an extensive program of speaking and building support for education. He set up teachers' associations and started some of the first summer schools for teachers, and in general tried to foster exemplary schools.

The urge to economize created in the penal system one of the darkest blots on the Bourbon record: convict leasing. Necessity gave rise to the practice immediately after the Civil War; economy dictated its continuance. The destruction of prisons and the chaotic poverty of state treasuries combined with the demand for cheap labor on the railroads, in the mines, and in lumber and turpentine camps, to make the leasing of convict labor a way for southern states to avoid expenses and even bring in profits. The burden on the states of detaining criminals grew after the war because freedmen, who as slaves had been subject to the discipline of masters, were now subject to the criminal law. Convict leasing, in the absence of state supervision, allowed inefficiency, neglect, and disregard for human life to proliferate.

The Bourbons scaled down not only expenditures but also the public debt, and by a simple means—they repudiated a vast amount of debt in all the former Confederate states except Florida and Mississippi. The corruption and extravagance of Radical rule were commonly advanced as justification for the process, but repudiation did not stop with Reconstruction debts. Altogether nine states reprediated more than half of what they owed, or nearly $130 million out of an estimated total of $247.6 million. The Bourbons, who respected the sancity of property, were not of one mind about the process, however, and in Virginia their leaders honored the state debt so zealously, and at such cost to public services, that they were temporarily ousted by an Independent rebellion, the Readjuster party.

There are elements of diversity in the Bourbon record, however. Despite their devotion to economy, these parsimonious regimes, so ardently devoted to laissez-faire, did respond to the demand for commisssions to regulate the rates charged by railroads for commercial transport. They established boards of agriculture, boards of public health, agricultural experiment stations, agricultural and mechanical colleges, normal schools and women's colleges, even state colleges for Negroes. Nor will any simplistic interpretation encompass the variety of Bourbon leaders. The Democratic party of the time was a mongrel coalition which threw Old Whigs, Know Nothings, Unionists, secessionists, businessmen, small farmers, hillbillies, planters, and even some Republicans together in alliance against the Reconstruction Radicals. Democrats therefore, even those who willynilly bore the Bourbon label, often heard different drummers.

The effects of Radical and Bourbon rule in the South. This 1880 cartoon shows the South staggering under the oppressive weight of military Reconstruction (left) and flourishing under the "Let 'Em Alone Policy" of Hayes and the Bourbons (right). [The Granger Collection]

And once they got control, the conflicts inherent in any coalition began to assert themselves so that Bourbon regimes never achieved complete unity in philosophy or government.

Independent movements cropped up in all the southern states, endorsing a variety of proposals including debt repudiation, inflation, usury laws, and antimonopoly laws. Locally they fought Bourbon Democrats over fencing laws (poor farmers preferred to let their scrub stock forage for itself), patronage, and issues of corruption. On occasion they joined forces with third parties like the Greenbackers, and sometimes they elected local officials and congressmen. In Tennessee the division became so acute that the Republicans elected a governor in 1880. In Virginia, where the rebels sought reduction of the state debt, a Readjuster party captured the legislature in 1879, elected a governor in 1881, and sent their leader, William E. Mahone, to the United States Senate.

For a brief time there emerged a wholesale collaboration between Republicans and Independents, which Chester A. Arthur promoted after he became president in the fall of 1881. The policy failed to make headway, however, because Republicans had little in common with the Independents except their opposition to the Democrats, and because the Republican machinery in the South had already been devastated by the overthrow of Reconstruction and by President Hayes's policy of reconciliation with the Bourbons immediately afterward. The Republicans maintained a secure foothold only in the Blue Ridge and Smoky Mountains, "the great spine of Republicanism which runs down the back of the South," where stubborn white Unionists passed the faith on to later generations.

Perhaps the ultimate paradox of the Bourbons' rule was that these paragons of white supremacy tolerated a lingering black voice in politics and showed no haste about raising the barriers of racial separation. A number of them harbored at least some element of patrician benevolence toward blacks. The old slaveowner, said a South Carolina editor, "has no desire to browbeat, maltreat, and spit upon the colored man"—clearly in part because the slaveowner saw in freedmen no threat to his status. Blacks sat in the state legislatures of South Carolina until 1900 and of Georgia until 1890; some of these black representatives were Democrats. The South sent black congressmen to Washington in every election down to 1900 except one, though they always represented gerrymandered districts into which most of the state's black voters had been thrown. Under the Bourbons the disfranchisement of black voters remained inconsistent, a local matter brought about mainly by fraud and intimidation, but it occurred enough to ensure white control.

A like flexibility applied to other areas of race relations. The color line was drawn less strictly than it would be in the twentieth century. In some places, to be sure, racial segregation appeared before the end of Reconstruction, especially in schools, churches, hotels and rooming houses, and private social relations. In places of public accommodation such as trains, depots, theaters, and soda fountains, however, discrimination was more capricious. In 1885 a black journalist, T. McCants Stewart, reported from his native state of South Carolina that he rode first-class cars on the railroads and in the streets, was served at saloons and soda fountains, saw Negroes dining with whites at train stations, and saw a black policeman arrest a white man on the streets of Columbia. Fifteen years later such scenes would be rare.

DISFRANCHISING BLACKS During the 1890s the attitudes that permitted such moderation eroded swiftly. One reason was political. The rise of the Populist party divided the white vote to such an extent that in some places the black vote became the balance of power. Populists made a play for black votes and brought blacks prominently into their councils. "You are kept apart," Georgia's Tom Watson told black and white farmers, "in order that you may be separately fleeced." The Bourbons' reponse to all this was to revive the race issue, which they exploited with seasoned finesse, all the while controlling for their ticket a good part of the black vote in plantation areas. Nevertheless the Bourbons soon argued that the black vote be eliminated completely from southern elections. It was imperative, Gov. Murphy J. Foster told the Louisiana legislature in 1894, that "the mass of ignorance, vice and venality without any proprietary interest in the State" be denied the vote. Some leaders of the farmers hoped that disfranchisement of Negroes would make it possible for whites to divide politically without raising the spectre of "Negro domination."

But since the Fifteenth Amendment made it impossible to disfranchise Negroes as such, the purpose was accomplished indirectly with devices such as poll taxes, head taxes, and literacy tests. Some opposed such devices because they also caught up poor whites in the net. But this white opposition was neutralized by providing loopholes in the literacy tests through which illiterate whites could slip. The Senate buried one last effort to protect black voters in 1890, when Rep. Henry Cabot Lodge sponsored a bill authorizing federal supervisors of elections to pass on the qualifications of excluded voters. Northern sentiment seemed unwilling to support any interference, and the bill failed.

Mississippi led the way to near-total disfranchisement of blacks. The state called a constitutional convention in 1890, while the Lodge Bill was still under consideration, for the express purpose of changing the suffrage provisions of the old Radical constitution of 1868. The Mississippi plan set the pattern that seven more states would follow over the next twenty years. First, a residence requirement—two years in the state, one year in the election district—eliminated those tenants who were in the habit of moving yearly in search of a better chance. Second, voters were disqualified if convicted of certain crimes. Third, all taxes, including a poll tax, had to be paid by February 1 of election year, which left plenty of time to lose the receipt before the fall vote. This proviso fell most heavily on the poor, most of whom were black. Fourth and finally, all voters had to be literate. The alternative, designed as a loophole for whites otherwise disqualified, was an "understanding" clause. The voter, if unable to read the Constitution, could qualify by being able to "understand" it—to the satisfaction of the registrar. Fraud was thus institutionalized rather than eliminated by "legal" disfranchisement.

In other states, variations on the Mississippi plan added a few flourishes. In 1895 South Carolina tacked on the proviso that owning property assessed at $300 would qualify an illiterate voter. In 1898 Louisiana invented the "grandfather clause," which allowed illiterates to qualify if their fathers or grandfathers had been eligible to vote on January 1, 1867, when blacks were still excluded. Negro educator Booker T. Washington sent the convention a sarcastic telegram expressing hope that "no one clothed with state authority will be tempted to perjure and degrade himself by putting one interpretation upon it for the white man and another for the black man. . . ." By 1910 Georgia, North Carolina, Virginia, Alabama, and Oklahoma had all adopted the grandfather clause. The effectiveness of these measures can be seen in a few sample figures. Louisiana in 1896 had 130,000 black voters registered, and in 1900, 5,320. Alabama in 1900 had 121,159 literate Negro males over twenty-one, according to the census; only 3,742 were registered to vote.

More significant than the technical devices for disfranchisement was the futility of attempting to overcome them. The literacy test in fact never had much to do with literacy. It was simply a device that could be used, fraudulently if need be, to exclude blacks. The fraud that had once prevailed at the ballot box was simply moved back one step to the registration process. Years later, when the Republican Calvin Coolidge got 1,000 votes in

South Carolina, Sen. Cole Blease remarked: "I do not know where he got them. I was astonished to know that they were cast and shocked to know that they were counted." Every southern state, moreover, adopted a statewide Democratic primary between 1896 and 1915, which became the only meaningful election outside isolated areas of Republican strength. With minor exceptions, the Democratic primaries excluded black voters altogether.

SEGREGATION SPREADS "Jim Crow" segregation followed hard on disfranchisement and in some states came first. The symbolic target at first was the railway train. In the 1880s it was still common practice for American trains to have first- and second-class cars, which afforded a degree of racial segregation by the difference in cost. In 1885, nevertheless, George Washington Cable noted that in South Carolina Negroes "ride in first class cars as a right" and "their presence excites no comment." From 1875 to 1883 in fact any racial segregation violated a federal Civil Rights Act, which forbade discrimination in places of public accommodation. But in 1883 the Supreme Court ruled on seven *Civil Rights Cases* involving discrimination against Negroes by corporations or individuals. The Court held, with only one dissent, that the force of federal law could not extend to individual action because the Fourteenth Amendment, which provided that "no State" could deny citizens the equal protection of the laws, stood as a prohibition only against state action.

"Jim Crow," a stock character in the old minstrel shows, became a synonym for racial segregation in the twentieth century. Dan Rice developed the character in the 1830s. [New York Public Library]

This left as an open question the constitutionality of state laws *requiring* separate facilities under the rubric of "separate but equal," a slogan popular with the New South prophets. In 1881 Tennessee had required railroads in the state to maintain separate first-class cars for blacks and whites. In 1888 Mississippi went a step further by requiring passengers, under penalty of law, to occupy the car set aside for their race. When Louisiana followed suit in 1890, the law was challenged in the case of *Plessy v. Ferguson*, which the Supreme Court decided in 1896. The test case originated in New Orleans when Homer Plessy, an octoroon, refused to leave a white car when asked to do so. He was convicted, and the case rose on appeal to the Supreme Court. The Court's majority opinion, written by Justice Henry Billings Brown, a native of Massachusetts, said that segregation laws "have been generally, if not universally recognized as within the competency of state legislatures in the exercise of their police power." The sole dissenter was John Marshall Harlan, a former slaveholder and Whig Unionist from Kentucky, who had written the only dissent in the *Civil Rights Cases*. "In my opinion," Harlan wrote, "the judgment this day rendered will, in time, prove to be quite as pernicious as the decision made by this tribunal in the Dred Scott Case." The Plessy ruling, he predicted, would "stimulate aggressions, more or less brutal, upon the admitted rights of colored citizens. . . ."

Very soon the principle of segregation extended into every area of southern life, including street railways, hotels, restaurants, hospitals, recreations, sports, and employment. If an activity was overlooked by the laws, it was not overlooked in custom and practice. The editor of the Richmond *Times* expressed the prevailing view in his remark on January 12, 1900: "It is necessary that this principle be applied in every relation of Southern life. God Almighty drew the color line and it cannot be obliterated. The negro must stay on his side of the line and the white man must stay on his side, and the sooner both races recognize this fact and accept it, the better it will be for both."

As for the "aggressions, more or less brutal," which Harlan foretold, they were already routine when he pronounced his dissent. From the days of slavery race relations had operated in a context of force and violence. The period of growing discrimination at the turn of the century was one of the worst. In the decade from 1890 to 1899 lynchings in the United States averaged 187.5 per year, 82 percent of which occurred in the South; from 1900 to 1909 they averaged 92.5 per year, 92 percent in the South. Whites constituted 32.2 percent of the victims during the first period, only 11.4 percent in the latter. Edgar Gardner

Murphy, a young Episcopal priest in Montgomery, said that extremists had proceeded "from an undiscriminating attack upon the Negro's ballot to a like attack upon his schools, his labor, his life—from the contention that no Negro shall vote to the contention that no Negro shall learn, that no Negro shall labor, and (by implication) that no Negro shall live."

WASHINGTON AND DU BOIS   A few brave souls, black and white, spoke out against the new dispensations, but by and large blacks had to accommodate them as best they could. To be sure, the doctrine of "separate but equal" did open some doors, such as those to black schools, that had once been closed entirely. Some blacks even began to make a virtue of necessity. The chief spokesman for this philosophy was Booker T. Washington, the black prophet of the New South Creed. Born in Virginia of a slave mother and a white father, Washington had fought extreme adversity to get an education at Hampton Institute, one of the postwar missionary schools, and then to build at Tuskegee, Alabama, a leading college for Negroes. Washington argued that American Negroes should first establish an economic base for their advancement. He insisted that Negroes should focus "upon the everyday practical things of life, upon something that is needed to be done, and something which they will be permitted to do in the community in which they reside." In his speech at the Atlanta Cotton States and International Exposition in 1895, which propelled him to fame, Washington advised fellow blacks: "Cast down your bucket where you are—cast it down in making friends . . . of the people of all races by whom we are surrounded. Cast it down in agriculture, mechanics, in commerce, in domestic service, and in the professions." He conspicuously

Booker T. Washington. [New York Public Library]

W. E. B. Du Bois. [The Warder Collection]

omitted politics and let fall an oblique endorsement of segregation: "In all things that are purely social we can be as separate as the five fingers, yet one as the hand in all things essential to mutual progress."

Some people bitterly criticized Washington in his lifetime and after for making a bad bargain: the sacrifice of broad education and of civil rights for the dubious acceptance of white conservatives. W. E. B. Du Bois led blacks in this criticism of Washington. A native of Massachusetts whose bearing suggested the hauteur of a Boston Brahmin, Du Bois once said defiantly that he was born "with a flood of Negro blood, a strain of French, a bit of Dutch, but thank God! no 'Anglo-Saxon.' " Du Bois first experienced southern racial practices as an undergraduate at Fisk University in Nashville, a missionary school which emphasized liberal education. Later he took a Ph.D. in history from Harvard and briefly attended the University of Berlin. In addition to an active career in racial protest he left a distinguished record as a scholar and author. On the faculty of Atlanta University he began in 1896 a series of annual Conferences on Negro Problems which produced some of the earliest sociological research in the South.

Washington, Du Bois argued, preached "a gospel of Work and Money to such an extent as apparently almost completely to overshadow the higher aims of life." The education of Negroes, he argued, should not be merely vocational but should nurture leaders willing to bid defiance to segregation and discrimination. Du Bois called Washington's 1895 speech "The Atlanta Compromise" and argued that it had made Washington the leader of his race by the choice of whites.

MYTH AND THE NEW SOUTH   Du Bois wanted to see a New South for blacks, one sharply different from the Old. But the connections between the New and Old South were strong. One connection was ideological. The champions of a New South used the romantic myth of an Old South to bolster their creed while still deploring the backwardness created by slavery and agrarianism. The juxtaposition of old and new was manifested in the offices of the Atlanta *Constitution,* where one could find both Henry Grady, prophet of a New South, and Joel Chandler Harris, creator of Uncle Remus, a character who in turn epitomized the dutiful "darkies" that inhabited the postwar romances of the Old South, along with kindly old massa and his mint julep, the winsome belle, and the gallant suitor.

These New South spokesmen used the Old South myth not because it offered an example for the future, but because it salved the wounds of defeat, bolstered self-esteem, gave a sense of identity, and blunted sectional enmity. By the end of the 1880s the image of the New South itself was moving into the realm of myth, as Paul M. Gaston argued in his book *The New South Creed* (1970). The New South movement's "legacy to the twentieth century was a pattern of belief in which Southerners could see themselves and their section as rich, successful, and just. . . . This picture of a New South had the double effect of ameliorating the bleak realities of the present and winning approbation and respect from the world outside."

The ultimate achievement of the New South prophets and their allies, the Bourbons, was that like all lasting conservative movements they reconciled tradition with innovation. Their relative moderation in racial policy, at least before the 1890s, allowed them to accommodate just enough of the new to disarm adversaries and keep control. By accommodating themselves to the growth of industry, the Bourbons led the South into a new economic era, but without sacrificing what the historian Francis B. Simkins called "the pageantry and rhetoric of the sentimental South." Bourbon rule left a permanent mark on the South, for as C. Vann Woodward has noted, "it was not the Radicals nor the Confederates but the Redeemers who laid the lasting foundations in matters of race, politics, economics and institutions for the modern South."

THE NEW WEST

For vast reaches of western America the great epics of Civil War and Reconstruction were remote events hardly touching the lives of Indians, trappers, miners, and Mormons scattered through the plains and mountains. There the march of Manifest

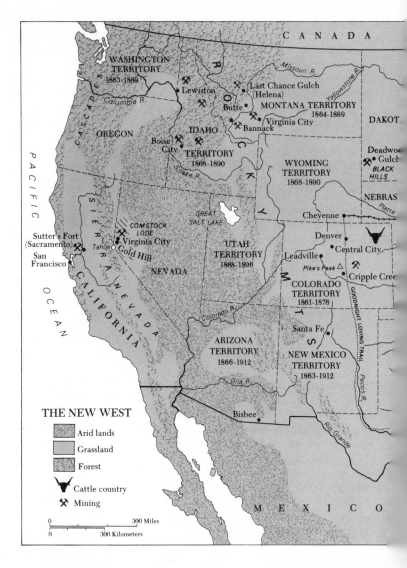

THE NEW WEST

- Arid lands
- Grassland
- Forest
- Cattle country
- Mining

0 _____ 300 Miles
0 _____ 300 Kilometers

Destiny continued on its inexorable course. In the second tier of trans-Mississippi states—Iowa, Kansas, Nebraska—and in western Minnesota, the last frontier of farmers was now pressing out onto the Great Plains. From California the miners' frontier scattered enclaves east through the mountains at one new strike after another. From Texas the nomadic cowboys migrated northward into the plains and across the Rockies into the Great Basin. Now there were two frontiers of settlement, east and west, and even a third on the south; in another generation there would be none.

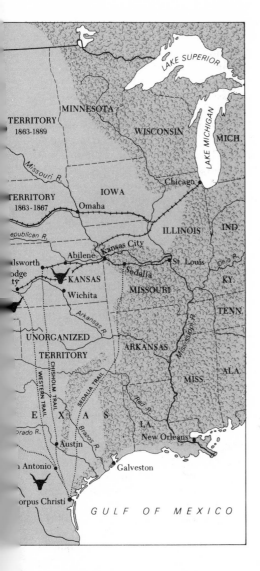

After one final great rush the occupation of the continent would be complete, less than three centuries following the first beachhead at Jamestown.

As settlement moved west, the environment gradually altered. There was no line at which it suddenly changed, but the pathfinders who ventured beyond about 98° West longitude encountered a radically different environment. About two-fifths of the nation's land area was arid, swept by dry winds which had surrendered their moisture successively to the Pacific coastal ranges, the Sierra Nevadas and Cascades, and the Rockies. As Walter Prescott Webb wrote in *The Great Plains*, it was as if "east of the Mississippi civilization stood on three legs—land, water, and timber; west of the Mississippi not one but two of these legs were withdrawn—water and (for want of water) timber—and civilization was left on one leg—land." The scarcity of water and timber rendered useless or impossible the familiar accoutrements of the pioneer: the axe, the log cabin, the rail fence, and the accustomed methods of tilling the soil.

For a long time the region had been called the Great American Desert, a barrier to cross on the way to the Pacific, unfit for human habitation and therefore, to white Americans, the perfect refuge for Indians. But that pattern changed in the last half of the nineteenth century as a result of new finds of gold, silver, and other minerals, completion of transcontinental railroads, destruction of the buffalo, the collapse of Indian resistance, the rise of the range-cattle industry, and the dawning realization that the arid region need not be a sterile desert. With the use of what water was available, techniques of dry farming and irrigation could make the land fruitful after all.

MINING THE WEST   The miners' frontier was in fact not so much a frontier as a scattering of settlements in parts unsuitable for farming, such as steep mountainsides, remote highlands, and barren deserts. The California argonauts of '49 set the typical pattern in which the sudden disorderly rush of prospectors to the new find was quickly followed by the arrival of the campfollowers, a motley crew of sutlers, saloonkeepers, wild women, card sharps, hustlers, and assorted desperadoes, out to mine the miners. Then if the new field panned out, the forces of respectability slowly worked their way in. An era of lawlessness gave place to vigilante rule and, finally, a stable community.

As mining became more dependent on capital, the day of the individual prospector began to wane. The Forty-niners first got at the gold by sifting off dirt and gravel through "placer" mining or "panning," or diverting a stream through a "sluice box" or "long tom." But once the rich diggings tailed off, efficient mining required shafts sunk into the ground or crushing mills built to extract the precious metal locked in quartz. The wild rush then gave way to organized enterprise and the "sourdoughs" either moved on, settled down to work for the bosses, or took up farming in the vicinity.

The drama of the 1849 gold rush was reenacted time and again in the following three decades. Though the California fever had

A sluice box used by gold miners in Auburn Ravine near Virginia City, 1852. [California State Library]

passed by 1851, and no big strikes were made for seven years, new finds in Colorado and Nevada revived hopes for riches. Along Cherry Creek, not far from Pike's Peak in Colorado, a prospecting party found promise of gold in 1858, and stories of success there brought perhaps 100,000 "Fifty-niners" into the country by June 1859, only to find that the rumors had been greatly exaggerated. Wagons that headed west with the legend "Pike's Peak or Bust!" on their sides were soon rumbling back with the sardonic message "Busted, by gosh." Still, a few mines proved out, some new arrivals took up farming to exploit high prices for farm goods in Denver and other mining centers, and the census of 1860 showed 35,000 still in the region. And new discoveries kept occurring: near Central City in 1859, at Leadville in the 1870s, and the last important strikes in the West, again gold and silver, at Cripple Creek in 1891–1894. During these years farming and grazing had given the economy a stable base, and Colorado had become the "Centennial State" in July 1876.

While the early rushers were crowding around Pike's Peak, the Comstock Lode was discovered at Gold Hill, Nevada. H. T. P. Comstock, "Old Pancake," a one-time mountain man, had drifted to the Carson River diggings opened in 1856. Possessed of a glib tongue, he talked his way into a share in a new discovery made by two other prospectors in 1859 and gave it his own name. The lode produced not only gold but a troublesome "blue earth" that turned out to contain silver. Nearby, James Finney, known as "Old Virginia," located a lead to the Ophir vein and gave his nickname to nearby Virginia City. Neither man had the foresight to develop his claim; both sold out for tiny sums what proved to be the two richest fields in the West. Within twenty years the Comstock Lode alone had yielded more than $300 million from shafts that reached hundreds of feet into the mountainside. In 1861 Nevada became a territory and in 1864 the state of Nevada was admitted in time to give its three electoral votes to Lincoln.

The Spaniards had found silver in New Mexico, but mining in Arizona began during the Civil War, when many of Col. James H. Carleton's California volunteers, going to meet a Confederate foray into New Mexico, deserted to the promising mining country near the Colorado River. In both Arizona and Montana the most important mineral proved to be neither gold nor silver, but copper. The richest copper mines included the Anaconda mine in Butte, Montana, and the Phelps-Dodge mine near Bisbee, Arizona.

The last great strike before the Cripple Creek find of the 1890s occurred in 1874–1875 in the Black Hills of South Dakota, which belonged by treaty to the Sioux Indians. Deadwood, the site of the strike, earned brief glory as the refuge of some of the West's most notorious desperadoes: "Calamity Jane," "Wild Bill Hickock," and a host of others. But in Deadwood, as elsewhere, when the gold and silver lodes ran out there was often little to support life in an arid, infertile terrain. The Virginia Citys, the Auroras, the Gold Hills, and others turned into ghost towns until the twentieth century, when shrewd promoters found a new bonanza in mining tourists.

The growing demand for orderly government in the West led to the hasty creation of new territories, and eventually the admission of a host of new states. After Colorado was admitted in 1876, however, there was a long hiatus because of the party divisions in Congress. Democrats were reluctant to create states out of territories that were heavily Republican. After the sweeping Republican victory of 1888, however, Congress admitted the Dakotas, Montana, and Washington in 1889, and Idaho and Wyoming in 1890, completing a tier of states from coast to coast. Utah entered in 1896, after the Mormons abandoned the practice of polygamy, Oklahoma in 1907, and in 1912 Arizona and New Mexico finally rounded out the forty-eight continental states.

THE INDIAN WARS As the frontier pressed in from east and west, relentless greed and duplicity pursued the Indians into what was supposed to be their last refuge. Mounted on horses which were a legacy of the Spaniards, perhaps 250,000 Indians in the Great

Plains and mountain regions lived mainly off the herds of buffalo which provided food and, from their hides, clothing and shelter. No sooner was the Jacksonian removal policy complete than the onrush of migration in the 1840s began to crowd the Indians' land. Emigrants crossing to Oregon, California, Utah, and Santa Fe came into contact and sometimes into conflict with them. In 1851 the chiefs of the principal plains tribes were gathered at Fort Laramie, where they agreed to accept more or less definite tribal borders and to leave the emigrants unmolested on their trails. It soon became easier to force one tribe to cede its lands without arousing the others, for the Indians could never realize the old dream of Tecumseh, a unified resistance.

From the early 1860s until the late 1870s the frontier was ablaze with Indian wars, and intermittent outbreaks continued through the 1880s. The first serious trouble developed in Minnesota, where a volunteer militia had taken the place of army garrisons fighting in the Civil War. Fighting started in 1862 when a band of Sioux braves, aroused by recent land cessions, killed five whites near New Ulm. Some of the Sioux fled to the west, but others remained and wrought havoc on the frontier, killing or capturing some 1,000 whites until the militia in overwhelming force drove them back and inflicted a devastating revenge. Out of 400 Indians captured, 300 were sentenced to death and eventually 38 were hanged in a mass execution the day after Christmas, 1862.

In Colorado, where chiefs of the Cheyennes and Arapahoes accepted a treaty banishing them westward, protesting braves began sporadic raids on the trails and mining camps. In 1864 the territorial governor persuaded most of the warring Indians to gather at Fort Lyon on Sand Creek, where they were promised protection. Despite this promise, Col. J. M. Chivington's militia fell upon an Indian camp flying the American flag and a white flag of truce, slaughtering 450 peaceful Indians—men, women, and children. Gen. Nelson A. Miles called it the "foulest and most unjustifiable crime in the annals of America." Chivington, a former Methodist minister, later exhibited his personal collection of 100 scalps in Denver. In 1865 the survivors surrendered unconditionally and gave up their Sand Creek reservation for lands farther west.

With other scattered battles erupting, in 1865 a congressional committee began to gather evidence on the grisly Indian wars and massacres. Its 1867 *Report on the Condition of the Indian Tribes* led to an act to establish an Indian Peace Commission charged with ending the Sioux War and removing the causes of

Indian wars in general. Congress decided this was best accomplished at the expense of the Indians, by persuading them to take up life on out-of-the-way reservations. This solution, in short, was to continue the persistent encroachment on Indian hunting grounds.

In October 1867 a conference at Medicine Creek Lodge, Kansas, ended with an agreement that the Kiowa, Comanche, Arapahoes, and Cheyennes would accept lands in western Oklahoma. Smaller tribes from the southern Plains later got reservations in the same area. In the following spring a conference at Fort Laramie resulted in peace with the Sioux, who agreed to settle within the Black Hills reservation in Dakota Territory. But Indian resistance in the southern Plains continued until the Red River War of 1874–1875. In a winter campaign of relentless pursuit, General Sheridan scattered the Indians and finally brought them to terms in the spring of 1875.

By then trouble was brewing once again in the north. In 1874, Gen. George A. Custer led an exploring expedition into the Black Hills, accompanied by gold seekers who began to find what they were after. Miners were soon filtering into the Sioux hunting grounds despite promises that the army would keep them out. The army had done little to protect the Indian lands, but when orders came to move against wandering bands of Sioux hunting on the range according to their treaty rights, the army moved vigorously. After several indecisive encounters, General Custer found the main encampment of Sioux and their Cheyenne allies on the Little Big Horn River. Separated from the main body of his men, Custer and a detachment of 200 were surrounded by a body of warriors numbering about 2,500 and completely annihilated.

But the Battle of the Little Big Horn was only one incident in this war. Instead of following up their victory, the Indians threw away their advantage in celebration and renewed hunting. When the army regained the offensive, the Indians began to melt away into the isolated wilderness. Chief Sitting Bull escaped into Canada, only to return to the Sioux reservation several years later. Crazy Horse was captured and murdered by his guard. The remaining Sioux were forced to give up their hunting grounds and the gold fields around Deadwood in return for payments. When a peace commission imposed this settlement Chief Spotted Tail said: "Tell your people that since the Great Father promised that we should never be removed, we have been moved five times. . . . I think you had better put the Indians on wheels and you can run them about wherever you wish."

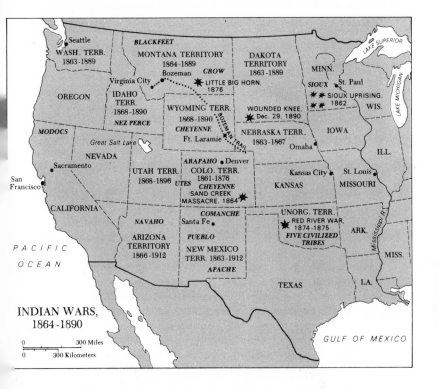

INDIAN WARS,
1864-1890

0 ____ 300 Miles
0 ____ 300 Kilometers

In the Rockies and westward the same story of hopeless resistance was repeated. The Blackfeet and Crows had to leave their homes in Montana. In a war along the California-Oregon boundary the Modocs held out for six months in 1871–1872 before they were overwhelmed. In 1879 the Utes were forced to give up their vast territories in western Colorado after a brief battle. In Idaho the peaceful Nez Perces finally refused to surrender lands along the Salmon River. Chief Joseph tried to avoid war, but when some unruly braves started a fight, he directed a masterful campaign against overwhelming odds, one of the most spectacular feats in the history of Indian warfare. After a retreat of 1,500 miles, through mountains and plains, across the Yellowstone region and through the Bitterroot Mountains of Montana, he was finally caught thirty miles short of the Canadian border, and exiled to Oklahoma.

In his character the heroic Joseph embodied the image of nobility. He maintained strict discipline among his followers, countenanced no scalpings or outrages against civilians, bought supplies which he could have confiscated, and kept his dignity to the end. His eloquent speech of surrender was an epitaph to the warriors's last stand against the march of empire: "I am tired of fighting. Our chiefs are killed. Looking Glass is dead. Toohoolhoolzote is dead. The old men are all dead. . . . I want to have time to look for my children, and see how many of them I can find. . . . Hear me, my chiefs! I am tired. My heart is sick and sad. From where the sun now stands I will fight no more forever."

A generation of Indian wars virtually ended in 1886 with the capture of Geronimo, a chief of the Chiricahua Apaches, who had fought encroachments in the Southwest for fifteen years. But there would be one tragic epilogue. Late in 1888 Wovoka (or "Jack Wilson"), a Paiute in western Nevada, fell ill and in a delirium imagined he had visited the spirit world where he learned of a deliverer coming to rescue the Indians and restore their lands. To hasten the day, he said, they had to take up a ceremonial dance at each new moon. The Ghost Dance craze fed upon old legends of a coming Messiah and spread rapidly. In 1890 the Sioux took it up with such fervor that it alarmed white authorities. An effort to arrest Sitting Bull led to his death and shortly afterward, on December 29, 1890, a bloodbath at Wounded Knee, South Dakota. An accidental rifle discharge led nervous soldiers to fire into a group of Indians who had come to surrender. Nearly 200 Indians and 25 soldiers died in the "Battle of Wounded Knee." The Indian wars had ended with characteristic brutality.

Over the long run the collapse of Indian resistance resulted as much from the killing off of the buffalo herds on which they subsisted as from direct suppression. White hunters felled buffaloes for sport, sometimes firing from train windows for the joy of see-

"Chief Joseph" of the Nez Perce tribe. [The Smithsonian Institution]

Geronimo (seated, left foreground) and his Apache tribesmen in council with the U.S. Army, 1886. [Library of Congress]

ing them die. Systematic slaughter of the buffalo began in the 1870s to satisfy the fashion of buffalo robes and overcoats in the East. By the mid-1880s the herds had reached the verge of extinction.

Most frontiersmen had little tolerance for moralizing on the Indian question. Easterners who were far removed from frontier dangers took a different view. The slaughter of the Indian wars was immensely unpopular. In his annual message of 1877 President Hayes echoed the protest: "Many, if not most, of our Indian wars have had their origin in broken promises and acts of injustice on our part." Statesmen and churchmen spoke out against mistreatment of Indians. In the 1880s Helen Hunt Jackson, a novelist and poet, focused attention on the Indian cause in *A Century of Dishonor* (1881) and *Ramona* (1884), the latter a novel about wrongs inflicted on the California Indians.

INDIAN POLICY Indian policy gradually became more benevolent, but this did little to alleviate the plight of the Indians and actually helped to destroy the remnants of their cultures. The reservation policy inaugurated by the Peace Commission in 1867 did little more than extend a practice that dated from colonial Virginia. Partly humanitarian in motive, this policy also saved money: it cost less to house and feed Indians on reservations than it did to fight them. And one Indian commissioner wrote candidly: "That these reservations will cause any considerable annoyance to the whites we do not believe. They consist, for the most part, of ground unfitted for cultivation, but suited to the peculiar habits of the Indians." Mistakes would be made, of course. Too late it was discovered that the Utes and Osage and some other tribes were left sitting atop rich stores of oil and natural gas.

Well-intentioned reformers sought to "Americanize" the aborigines by dealing with them as individuals rather than as tribes. The fruition of reform efforts came in the Dawes Severalty Act of 1887. Sponsored by Henry M. Dawes of Massachusetts, the act proposed to introduce the Indians to individual land ownership and agriculture. The Dawes Act permitted the president to divide the lands of any tribe and grant 160 acres to each head of family and lesser amounts to others. To protect the Indian in his property, the government held it in trust for twenty-five years, after which the owner won full title and became a citizen. Under the Burke Act of 1906 Indians who took up life apart from their tribes became citizens immediately. Members of the tribes granted land titles became subject to state and federal laws like all other persons. In 1901 citizenship was extended to the Five Civilized Tribes of Oklahoma, and in 1924 to all Indians.

But the more it changed, the more Indian policy remained the same. Despite the best of intentions, the Dawes Act struck a double blow at the Indians. It created an opportunity for more land spoliation, and it disrupted what remained of the traditional cultures. Dawes himself had foreseen the result, but defended his bill as an effort to salvage something for the Indians. Few others had such foresight, except land grabbers and students of Indian "ethnology," the forerunners of the study of anthropology. Lewis H. Morgan, a leading authority, pronounced the Indian "entirely incapable" of dealing with the whites on an individual basis. The result, he predicted, would be "that in a very short time he would divest himself of every foot of land and fall into poverty." And so it happened. Those lands not distributed to Indian families were sold, while others were lost to land sharks because of the Indians' inexperience with private ownership, or simply their powerlessness in the face of fraud. Between 1887 and 1934 they lost an estimated 86 million of their 130 million acres. Most of what remained was unsuited to agriculture.

CATTLE AND COWBOYS While the West was being taken from the Indians, cattle entered the grasslands where the buffalo had roamed, and the cowboy enjoyed his brief heyday, fading then into the folklore of the Wild West along with the sourdoughs, the desperadoes, and the Plains Indians. From colonial times, especially in the South, cattle raising had been a common enterprise just beyond the fringe of settlement. In many cases the early slaves took care of the livestock. Later, in the West, Negro cowboys were still a common sight, although they were lost from view in the novels and "horse operas" which pictured a lily-white frontier. Much of the romance of the open-range cattle industry derived from its Mexican roots. The Texas longhorns and the cowboys' horses had in large part descended from stock brought over by the Spaniards, and many of the industry's characteristics had been worked out in Mexico first: the cowboy's saddle, his chaps (*chaparajos*) to protect the legs, his spurs, and his lariat.

For many years wild cattle competed with the buffalo in the Spanish borderlands. Natural selection and contact with "Anglo" scrub cattle produced the Texas longhorns: lean and rangy, they were noted more for speed and endurance than for providing a choice steak. They had little value, moreover, because the largest markets for beef were too far away. Occasionally they were driven to market in Austin, Galveston, or New Orleans, and some even to the gold fields of California, Arizona, and Colorado. At the end of the Civil War, perhaps as many as 5 million roamed the grasslands of Texas, still neglected—but not for long. In the upper Mississippi valley, where herds had been depleted by the war, cattle prices ranged from $30 to $50 a head, while the Texas cattle could be had just for the effort of rounding them up.

So the cattle drives began anew after the Civil War, but on a scale far greater than before. In 1866 a large herd set out for Sedalia, Missouri, the western terminus of the Missouri-Pacific Railroad. But that route proved unsuitable because it was subject to raids by postwar bushwhackers, obstructed by woodlands, and opposed by Arkansas and Missouri farmers. New opportunities arose as railroads pushed farther west where cattle could be driven through relatively vacant lands. Joseph G. McCoy, an Illinois livestock dealer, realized the possibilities and showed the way. Officers of the Missouri-Pacific, to whom he turned first, brushed him off as a crank. The result, he later claimed, was that St. Louis took second place to Chicago as a livestock and packing center. The Kansas Pacific finally approved a lenient contract with McCoy, which they later tried to repudiate because they had not foreseen his enormous profits. Another road, the Hannibal and St. Joe, gave McCoy connections to Chicago.

McCoy chose Abilene, Kansas, as the terminus and laid out a trail as far south as Corpus Christi. Abilene was then a sleepy village of about a dozen shacks with so little business that the saloonkeeper raised prairie dogs as curiosities to sell tourists. But the town had water and grass. McCoy threw up stock pens, barns, loading chutes, and a hotel to house the cowboys. In September 1867 the first shipment went to Chicago. Abilene was the first of the great cowtowns, which in their brief day rivaled the mining camps for lawlessness. "On the surface," Walter P. Webb wrote, "Abilene was corruption personified. Life was hectic, raw, lurid, awful. But the dance hall, the saloon, and the red light, the dissonance of immoral revelry punctuated by pistolshots, were but the superficialities. . . . If Abilene excelled all later cowtowns in wickedness, it also excelled them in service, —the service of bartering the beef of the South for the money of the North." As the railroads moved west, so did the cowtowns and the trails. Ellsworth, Wichita, Newton City, Baxter Springs, and Dodge City, all in Kansas, succeeded Abilene, while farther north arose Oglalla, Nebraska, Cheyenne, Wyoming, and Miles City, Montana.

The flush times of the cowtown soon passed, however, and many reverted to sleepy villages with occasional "boot hills" as reminders of the hell-roaring times. The long cattle drives played out too because they were economically unsound. The dangers of the trail, the wear and tear on men and cattle, the charges levied on drives across Indian Territory, and the advance of farms across the trails combined to persuade cattlemen that they could best function near the railroads. As railroads spread out into Texas and the Plains, the cattle business spread with

NOTICE!

TO THIEVES, THUGS, FAKIRS
AND BUNKO-STEERERS,
Among Whom Are

J. J. HARLIN, alias "OFF WHEELER;" SAW DUST
CHARLIE, WM. HEDGES, BILLY THE KID,
Billy Mullin, Little Jack, The
Cuter, Pock-Marked Kid, and
about Twenty Others:

If Found within the Limits of this City
after TEN O'CLOCK P. M., this Night,
you will be Invited to attend a GRAND
NECK-TIE PARTY,

Lawlessness in the West. [The N. H. Rose Collection]

them over the High Plains as far as Montana and on into Canada.

In the absence of laws governing the range, the cattlemen worked out a code of action largely dictated by circumstances. As a rule the man who staked out a claim, or simply made good his occupation of a stream bank, controlled the grasslands as far back as the next divide since land was useless without access to water. Cowboys would "ride the line" to keep the cattle off the next ranch and conduct spring and fall roundups to separate the mixed herds. In 1873 Joseph Glidden, a farmer of De Kalb, Illinois, invented the first effective barbed-wire, which ranchers used to fence off their claims at relatively low cost. More often than not these were parts of the public domain to which they had no valid title. In 1878 an eastern promoter, John W. "Bet-a-Million" Gates, one of the early agents for Glidden, gave a persuasive demonstration of the barbed-wire in San Antonio. Skeptical cattlemen discovered that their meanest longhorns shied away from the fence which, as Gates put it, was light as air, stronger than whiskey, and cheaper than dirt. Orders poured in, and Gates eventually put together a virtual monopoly in the American Steel and Wire Company. The coming of barbed-wire finally ended the open, free range.

The greatest boom in the range-cattle trade came in the early 1880s, when eastern and European capitalists began to pour money into the "Beef Bonanza." Cattle growing, like mining, entered a season of wild speculation, and then evolved from a romantic adventure into a prosaic business, often a corporate business. A combination of factors conspired to end the open-range industry. Farmers kept crowding in and laying out homesteads on the open range, waging "barbed-wire wars" with cattlemen by either cutting the cattlemen's fences or policing their own. The boundless range was beginning to be overstocked by 1883, and expenses mounted as stock breeders formed associations to keep intruders out of overstocked ranges, to establish and protect land titles, to deal with railroads and buyers, to fight prairie fires, and to cope with rustlers and predatory beasts. The rise of sheep herding by 1880 caused still another conflict with the cattlemen. Warfare between defenders of the bovine and ovine species gradually faded, however, as the sheep for the most part found refuge in the high pastures of the mountains, leaving the grasslands of the Plains to the cattlemen. A final blow to the open-range industry came with two unusually severe winters in 1886 and 1887, followed by ten long years of drought.

For those who survived all the hazards of the range, the response to these problems was to establish legal title and fence in the lands, restrict the herds to a reasonable size, and provide shelter and hay against the rigors of winter. The cowboy settled into a more sedentary existence. Even in the heroic days his life had been a lonely, wearisome affair, the romance of which lay mainly in the pages of books like Owen Wister's *The Virginian* (1902), in which the hero utters the famous line: "When you call me that, *smile!*" Within two short decades, 1866–1886, the glory was ended; it was always more in the eye of the beholder than anywhere else.

FARMERS AND THE LAND Among the legendary figures of the West, the sodbusters projected an unromantic image in contrast to the sourdoughs and cowboys, the Cavalry and the Indians. After 1865, on paper at least, the land laws offered favorable terms to the farmer. Under the old Preemption Act of 1841, if he could locate a claim before the government surveys, he could after six months get 160 acres for $1.25 an acre. Under the Homestead Act of 1862 he could either realize the old dream of free land simply by staking out a claim and living on it for five years, or buy the land at $1.25 an acre after six months. But the land legislation of earlier days was predicated upon an entirely different environment from that of the Plains, and the laws never completely adjusted to the fact that much of the land was suited only for cattle. Cattlemen were forced to garner land by gradual acquisition from homesteaders or land grant railroads.

In the 1870s two new laws at least recognized the shortage of water and timber in the New West. The Timber Culture Act of 1873 permitted any settler to get an additional 160 acres if he maintained 40 acres of woodland for ten years. The act benefited a few farmers of the eastern Plains, but it was subject to such widespread fraud that it was repealed in 1891. The Desert Land Act of 1877 authorized the sale of 640-acre tracts at $1.25 an acre to settlers who irrigated the land within three years. But the act ignored the facts that 640 acres was often not enough to sustain agriculture in arid regions, and that irrigation works were too costly for most settlers. The Timber and Stone Act of 1878 made available 160-acre tracts for $2.50 an acre in areas "unfit for civilization," mostly in California, Nevada, Oregon, and Washington. This amounted to a virtual giveaway of great natural resources in timber and stone which were far more valuable than their purchase price.

The unchangeable fact of aridity, rather than new land laws, shaped institutions in the New West. Where farming was impossible the cattlemen simply established hegemony by control of the water, regardless of the laws. The land laws probably could not have been better designed for fraud and misuse if that had been their purpose. The supposed settler could build a dollhouse, twelve by fourteen inches, and swear that a dwelling "twelve by fourteen" stood on the homestead. He might pour out a bucket of water and swear that the land was irrigated. Better yet, he could just perjure himself without bothering with such rigmarole.

Belated legislative efforts to develop irrigable lands finally achieved a major success when the Newlands Reclamation Act (after the aptly named Sen. Francis G. Newlands of Nevada) of 1901 set up the Bureau of Reclamation. The proceeds of public land sales in sixteen states became a fund for irrigation works, and the Reclamation Bureau set about building such major projects as Boulder (later Hoover) Dam on the Nevada-Arizona line, Roosevelt Dam in Arizona, Elephant Butte Dam in Idaho, and Arrowrock Dam in New Mexico.

But the stubborn problem of water remained, rendering much of the west's land useless for field crops. The area in which rainfall averaged ten to twenty inches per year was marginal, but with the techniques of "dry farming" could support such crops as sorghums, kaffir corn, and Turkey wheat. Certain varieties of spring and winter wheat grew at the times of greatest rainfall. The eastern Plains from Minnesota and North Dakota down to Texas emerged as the wheat belt, the new breadbasket of the nation, and behind wheat the corn belt and corn-hog combination edged westward.

The lands of the New West, as on previous frontiers, passed to their ultimate owners more often from private hands than directly from the government. Much of the 274 million acres claimed under the Homestead Act passed quickly to cattlemen or speculators, and thence to settlers. The land-grant railroads got some 200 million acres of the public domain in the twenty years from 1851 to 1871, and sold much of this land to build population and traffic along the lines. The New West of cattlemen and farmers was in fact largely the product of the railroads.

For the first arrivals on the sod-house frontier, life was a grim struggle with adversity and monotony. As the railroads arrived bearing lumber from the wooded regions, farmers could leave their dugouts and homes of "Kansas brick" to build more familiar frame houses. New machinery helped open fresh opportunities for farmers. Back in 1837 John Deere of Illinois had developed the steel-faced plow and moldboard that conquered the clinging humus of the prairie. But its high cost encouraged further exper-

Sod-house farm, Nebraska, 1887. [Nebraska State Historical Society]

iments, and in 1868 James Oliver of Indiana made a successful chilled-iron plow. With further improvements his "sod buster" was ready for mass production by 1878, easing the task of breaking the shallow but tough grass roots of the Plains. Improvements and new inventions in threshing machines, hay mowers, planters, manure spreaders, cream separators, and other devices lightened the burden of labor but added to the capital outlay of the farmer.

In some parts of the West the gigantic "bonanza farms" with machinery for mass production became the marvels of the age, the new corporate plantations complete with mechanized slaves. On one farm in North Dakota, 13,000 acres of wheat made a single field. "You are in a sea of wheat," a bedazzled visitor wrote in 1880. "The railroad train rolls through an ocean of grain. . . . We encounter a squadron of war chariots . . . doing the work of human hands. . . . There are twenty-five of them in this one brigade of the grand army of 115, under the marshalship of this Dakota farmer." Publicized out of proportion to their significance, the bonanza farms disintegrated in the decade of drought after 1885. The land often remained in the same hands, however, operated now on a tenant basis.

The small farmers who diversified their crops fared better, especially those who stayed in the eastern Plains. But even they, to make a go of it, had to make concessions to size. To get a start on a family homestead, the historian Allen G. Bogue estimates, required a minimum capital investment of $1,000. And while the overall value of farm lands and farm products increased in the late nineteenth century, the small farmer did not keep up with the march of progress. His numbers grew, but decreased in proportion to the population at large. Wheat, like cotton in the antebellum period, provided the great export crop which evened America's balance of payments and spurred economic growth. But for a variety of reasons the individual farmer failed to prosper. Something was amiss, he began to reason, and by the decade of the 1890s he was in open revolt against the powers that be.

"THE FRONTIER HAS GONE" American life reached an important juncture in the postbellum years. After the 1890 population count, the superintendent of the census noted that he could no longer locate as before a continuous frontier line beyond which population thinned out to less than two per square mile. This fact inspired the historian Frederick Jackson Turner to develop the influential frontier thesis, first outlined in his paper "The Significance of the Frontier in American History," delivered to the American Historical Association in 1893. "The existence of an area of free land," Turner wrote, "its continuous recession, and the advance of American settlement westward, explain American development." The frontier had shaped the national character in striking ways. It was

> to the frontier [that] the American intellect owes its striking characteristics. That coarseness and strength combined with acuteness and acquisitiveness; that practical, inventive turn of mind, quick to

Oklahoma Territory, 1889. These open-air law and land offices suggest Americans' "masterful grasp of material things" and "restless, nervous energy," which Turner attributed to the frontier experience. [University of Oklahoma Library]

find expedients; that masterful grasp of material things, lacking in the artistic but powerful to effect great ends; that restless, nervous energy; that dominant individualism, working for good and for evil, and withal that buoyancy and exuberance which comes with freedom—these are traits of the frontier, or traits called out elsewhere because of the existence of the frontier.

In 1893 he wrote, "four centuries from the discovery of America, at the end of a hundred years under the Constitution, the frontier has gone and with its going has closed the first period of American history."

FURTHER READING

The concept of the "New South" is explored in Paul W. Gaston's *The New South Creed: A Study in Southern Mythmaking* (1970).° W. J. Cash comments on the boosterism of postwar southerners in *The Mind of the South* (1941).° Biographies of the region's leading proselytizers include Raymond B. Nixon's *Henry W. Grady: Spokesman of the New South* (1969), Joseph F. Wall's *Henry W. Watterson: Reconstructed Rebel* (1956), and John M. Cooper's *Walter Hines Page: The Southerner as American, 1855–1918* (1977).

Scholarship on the textile industry, which formed the heart of New South aspirations, includes Patrick J. Hearden's *Independence and Empire: The New South's Cotton Mill Campaign, 1865–1901* (1982), Dwight G. Billings's *Planters in the Making of a "New South": Class, Politics, and Development in North Carolina, 1865–1900* (1979), and David Carlton's *Mill and Town in South Carolina, 1880–1920* (1982).° For developments in the tobacco industry, consult Robert F. Durden's *The Dukes of Durham, 1865–1929* (1975). For the iron industry, consult Carl V. Harris's *Political Power in Birmingham, 1871–1921* (1977). John F. Stover's *The Railroads of the South* (1955) covers the growth in transportation.

The cultural dimenson of the New South is explored in Daniel J. Singal's *The Conflict Within: From Victorian to Modernist Thought in the South, 1919–1945* (1982).° The religious nature of postwar culture is treated in Charles R. Wilson's *Baptized in Blood: The Religion of the Lost Cause, 1865–1920* (1980), and Thomas L. Connelly's *God and General Longstreet: The Lost Cause and the Southern Mind* (1982). For Bourbon politics after Reconstruction, see Jack P. Maddox's *The Virginia Conservatives, 1867–1879* (1970), and William J. Cooper, Jr.'s *The Conservative Regime: South Carolina, 1877–1900* (1968).°

C. Vann Woodward's *The Strange Career of Jim Crow* (1974)° remains a classic on southern race relations. Some of Woodward's points are challenged in Howard N. Rabinowitz's *Race Relations in the Urban South, 1865–1900* (1978). Other views on race relations are treated in

°These books are available in paperback editions.

August Meier's *Negro Thought in America: Racial Ideologies in the Age of Booker T. Washington, 1880–1915* (1963). The attitudes of the two principal black leaders are defined in Louis R. Harlan's *Booker T. Washington: The Making of a Black Leader, 1865–1901* (1972),° and Elliott M. Rudiwick's *W. E. B. Du Bois: Propagandist of Negro Protest* (1969). J. Morgan Kousser's *The Shaping of Southern Politics: Suffrage Restriction and Establishment of the One-Party South, 1880–1910* (1974), handles disfranchisement.

Race is also a chief component of works on postwar developments in farming. Roger Ransom and Richard Sutch's *One Kind of Freedom: The Economic Consequences of Emancipation* (1977),° Robert W. Higgs's *Competition and Coercion: Blacks in the American Economy, 1865–1914* (1977), Jay R. Mandle's *The Roots of Black Poverty: The Southern Plantation Economy after the Civil War* (1978),° and Jonathan Wiener's *Social Origins of the New South: Alabama, 1860–1865* (1978), all examine the origins of sharecropping.

Both regions surveyed in this chapter receive attention in overall interpretations of post–Civil War development. Robert H. Wiebe's *The Search for Order, 1877–1920* (1968),° and Louis M. Hacker's *The Course of American Economic Development* (1970)° portray the hinterlands as extensions of the more dominant northeastern and midwestern states. C. Vann Woodward also develops the theme of a "colonial economy" in *Origins of the New South, 1877–1913* (1951),° a work which is also the best introduction to the New South. Another overview of the region is John S. Ezell's *The South since 1865* (1975). Overviews of the settlement of the Great Desert include Frederick Merk's *History of the Western Movement* (1978),° and more specifically, Howard R. Lamar's *The Far Southwest, 1846–1912* (1966).

The Turner thesis is best presented by Frederick Jackson Turner himself in *The Frontier in American History* (1920). Ray A. Billington, in his *Frederick Jackson Turner* (1973), analyzes the thesis, and in *Westward Expansion* (1967) applies it. Thomas D. Clark's *Frontier America: The Story of the Westward Movement* (1969) disclaims the centrality of Turner's thesis. A more cultural treatment of the subject of the frontier is Henry Nash Smith's *Virgin Land: The American West as Symbol and Myth* (1950).°

Quite a bit of recent scholarship examines the realities of life among western cowboys. Terry G. Jordan's *Trails to Texas: Southern Roots of Western Cattle Ranching* (1981) finds cowboy origins along the Atlantic seaboard. David Day's *Cowboy Culture: A Saga of Five Centuries* (1981) traces the roots further back. Other studies of various aspects of the cattle trade include J. M. Shagg's *The Cattle Trading Industry* (1973) and Robert R. Dystra's *The Cattle Towns* (1968).°

The sodbusters also have their scholars. Fred A. Shannon's *The Farmer's Last Frontier* (1963),° Gilbert C. Fite's *The Farmer's Frontier, 1865–1900* (1963), and Allen G. Bogue's *From Prairie to Corn Belt* (1963) each details the harsh Great Plains life. The views of important participants are analyzed in Joanna L. Stratton's *Pioneer Women: Voices from the Kansas Frontier* (1981).° Paul W. Gates's *History of Public Land*

Development (1968) concentrates on the effects of the Homestead Law on settlement patterns.

Works which deal with western miners include Rodman W. Paul's *Mining Frontiers of the Far West, 1848–1880* (1963),° and Duane A. Smith's *Rocky Mountain Mining Camps* (1967). Michael P. Molane's *The Battle for Butte: Mining and Politics on the Northern Frontier, 1884–1906* (1981), presents a case study of the copper industry.

The best introduction to the history of the Plains Indians remains Wilcomb E. Washburn's *The Indian in North America* (1975).° The Indian conflict with the encroaching white man is explored in Dee Brown's *Bury My Heart at Wounded Knee* (1970)° and Robert M. Utley's *Last Days of the Sioux Nation* (1963). The white perspective on the issue is presented in Francis Paul Prucha's *American Indian Policy in Crisis: Christian Reformers and the Indians, 1865–1900* (1976), Robert M. Utley's *Frontier Regulars: The United States Army and the Indian* (1973),° and Robert F. Berkhofer, Jr.'s *The White Man's Indian: Images of the American Indian from Columbus to the Present* (1978).° A psychological interpretation of an Indian fighter is in Charles K. Hofling's *Custer and the Little Big Horn: A Psychobiographical Inquiry* (1981).

20

THE RISE OF BIG BUSINESS

THE POSTBELLUM ECONOMY

ECONOMIC EFFECTS OF THE CIVIL WAR   America's rise as an industrial giant in the late nineteenth century is a fact of towering visibility. It has led all too easily to the judgement that the demands created by the Civil War powered a "takeoff" in economic growth and that the legislative program of the Republicans at the same time unleashed business, allowing it to guide and continue the process. The Civil War connection seemed to many so obvious as to exclude the need for detailed proof.

But the highly visible success of wartime profiteers in arms and supplies, of speculators in various markets, and of such nabobs as investment banker Jay Cooke, who got rich selling Treasury bonds, have overshadowed the actual setbacks that marked the wartime economy. Estimates of production and income for the nineteenth century prepared by the economic historian Robert E. Gallman have cast much doubt on the conventional story. "Between 1839 and 1899," Gallman wrote, "total commodity output [from farm and factory] increased elevenfold, or at an average decade rate of slightly less than 50 percent. Actual rates varied fairly widely, high rates appearing during the decades ending with 1854 and 1884 and a very low rate during the decade ending with 1869." The decade of the 1860s was the only one in which, on a per-capita basis, output actually decreased, North and South.

Figures for specific goods tend to show the same effect in these years. The output of copper, railroad track, cotton, and woolen textiles all showed the lag. Most surprising of all, pig iron production, which grew 17 percent from 1855 to 1860 (despite a depression in 1857) and 100 percent from 1865 to 1870, grew only 1 percent during the war years. The Civil War, sometimes called the "first modern war," was in large part unmechanized. Rifles, bayonets, sabers, artillery, and ammunition consumed relatively little iron, and army railroads offset only partially the drop in civilian construction. Production declined largely because of unsettled wartime conditions and the loss of southern markets.

Professor Gallman's figures also show that commodity output grew at an annual rate of 4.6 percent from 1840 to 1860, and at a rate of 4.4 percent from 1870 to 1900. Other long-term trends, such as the shift toward manufacturing, seem to have remained relatively constant, except during the 1860s, when the growth of manufactured goods averaged only 2.0 percent per year. In the light of this evidence, economic growth in the 1800s seems now to have been a sustained process, interrupted by the depressions of 1819, 1839, 1857, 1873, and 1893, and by the Civil War.

The postwar expansion, which started from a relatively high base and moved the economy to even higher levels, may have been fueled indirectly by the Civil War. Wartime inflation as usual transferred income to those owning property and making profits, while entrepreneurs forced to save by the war contributed to the immediate postwar period of speculation. It is not clear, though, that postwar Republican policies contributed uniquely to economic expansion. The National Banking Act created a sounder currency, but its effects on the economy were ambiguous. Government aid in building the great transcontinental and regional railroads simply continued the encouragement to railroads long offered by state and federal government. The postwar climate of favoritism to business was but slightly strengthened by the defeat of southern agrarianism. Postwar tariffs also had ambiguous effects, hampering foreign competitors but discouraging American exports. The emotional lift of victory provided an important, if indirect, spur to the economy. After the war Sen. John Sherman of Ohio wrote to his brother, the famous general: "The truth is the close of the war with our resources unimpaired gives an elevation, a scope to the ideas of leading capitalists far higher than anything ever undertaken in this country. They talk of millions as confidently as before of thousands."

BUILDING THE TRANSCONTINENTAL RAILROADS Whatever the explanation, the fact remains that between 1869 and 1899 the population nearly trebled, farm production more than doubled, and the value of manufactures grew sixfold (in constant prices). Basic to this economic transition was the growth of railroads. They were the first big business, the first magnet for the great financial markets, and the first industry to develop a large-scale management bureaucracy. The railroads opened the West, connected raw materials to factories and markets, and in so doing created a national market. At the same time they were themselves gigantic markets for iron, steel, lumber, and other capital goods.

The renewal of railroad building after the Civil War increased the total mileage in roads from 30,600 in 1862 to 53,000 in 1870 and 94,000 by 1880. During the 1880s, the great decade of railroad building, mileage leaped to 167,000 by 1890 and then grew to 199,000 by 1900. Most of this construction filled out the network east of the Mississippi, but the most spectacular exploits were the great transcontinental lines built across the plains and mountains. Running through sparsely settled lands the roads promised little quick return, but they served the national purpose of binding the country together and so received a generous public bounty. Until 1850 constitutional scruples had constrained federal aid, although many states had subsidized railroads within their borders, but in 1850 Stephen Douglas secured from Congress a grant of public lands to subsidize two north-south roads connecting Chicago and Mobile: the Illinois Central and the Mobile and Ohio. Over the next twenty years federal land grants, mainly to transcontinentals, amounted to a net figure of some 129 million acres. In addition to land the railroads received financial aid from federal, state, and local governments. Altogether, according to one railroad authority, the roads got about $707 million in cash and $335 million in land.

Before the Civil War, sectional differences over routes held up the start of a transcontinental line. Secession finally permitted passage of the Pacific Railway Bill, which Lincoln signed into law on July 1, 1862. The act authorized a line along a north-central route, to be built by the Union Pacific railroad westward from Omaha and the Central Pacific railroad eastward from Sacramento. As amended in 1864, the act donated to these two corporations twenty sections of land per mile of track, in alternating blocs of railroad and government property, and loans of $16,000, $32,000, and $48,000 per mile, depending on the difficulty of the terrain. Security for the loans after 1864 was a second mortgage on the property, which permitted the roads to float their own bonds secured by a first mortgage.

Both roads began construction during the war, but most of the work was done after 1865 as the companies raced to build most of the line and get most of the subsidy. Under Gen. Grenville

Dodge, who became chief engineer in 1866, the Union Pacific pushed across the plains at a rapid pace, piercing the Rockies through Cheyenne Pass. The work crews, with large numbers of ex-soldiers and Irish immigrants as laborers, had to cope with bad roads, water shortages, alternately hot and cold weather, and Indian marauders. The moveable encampments with their retinue of sutlers, gamblers, and prostitutes, were aptly dubbed "Hell-on-wheels." Construction was hasty and much of it so flimsy that it had to be redone later, but the Union Pacific pushed on to its rendezvous with the Central Pacific.

The Central Pacific was the brainchild of the engineer Theodore P. Judah, but it was organized and, after Judah's untimely death, dominated by the Sacramento shopkeepers who made an indelible imprint on their state as the California "Big Four": Charles Crocker, Mark Hopkins, Collis P. Huntington, and Leland Stanford, who was elected governor in 1862. The Central Pacific used mainly Chinese crews and early encountered the Sierra massif, but cut through by way of Dutch Flat and Donner Pass to more level country in Nevada. The Union Pacific had built 1,086 miles to the Central Pacific's 689 when the race ended on the salt plains of Utah near Ogden, at Promontory Point. There, on May 10, 1869, Leland Stanford drove a gold spike which symbolized the road's completion as the telegraph lines signaled the taps of the hammer to a celebrating nation.

It was twelve years before the next transcontinental was completed, when the Atchison, Topeka and Santa Fe made contact

Union Pacific Railroad announces the "Great Event," the opening of the nation's first transcontinental line. For "Gold, Silver, and Other Miners, Now is the time to seek your Fortunes" in the West. [Union Pacific Railroad Museum Collection]

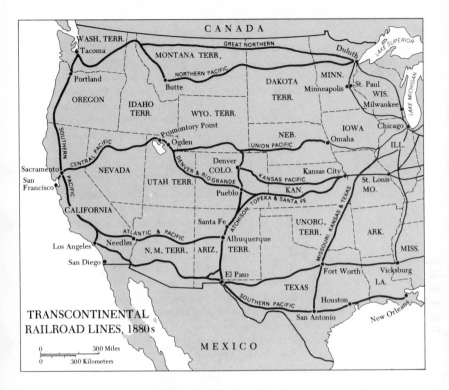

with the Big Four's Southern Pacific at the Needles in southern California. The Santa Fe built on to San Diego by 1884. Meanwhile the Southern Pacific, which had absorbed the Central Pacific, built on by way of Yuma to El Paso in 1882, where it made connections to St. Louis and New Orleans. To the north the Northern Pacific had connected Lake Superior with Portland by 1883, and ten years later the Great Northern, which James J. Hill had slowly and carefully extended westward from Minneapolis, thrust its way through Marias Pass and on to Tacoma—and Hill did it without a land grant. Thus before the turn of the century five trunk lines existed, supplemented by connections which afforded other transcontinental routes. In 1909 another trunk line was completed: the Chicago, Milwaukee, St. Paul, and Pacific.

FINANCING THE RAILROADS   The financial practices attending the construction was enough to give railroading a bad name. The financial doings of railroad men in fact gave rise to the label of "robber barons," an epithet soon extended to the "captains of industry" as well. The building of both the Union Pacific and Central Pacific was accompanied by shameless profiteering through construction companies, controlled by insiders, which drained off the resources of the railroad companies. The Crédit Mobilier Company, according to a congressional investigation, bought congressmen like sacks of potatoes and charged the Union Pacific $94 million for construction that cost at most $44 million. In one year, 1868, a holder of Crédit Mobilier stock took dividends that amounted to 230 percent in Union Pacific bonds and 515 percent in Union Pacific stock, on top of 60 percent in cash. The Credit and Finance Corporation, controlled by the California Big Four, did almost as well, taking the Central Pacific for $79 million, of which an estimated $36 million was profit. When the same men began building the Southern Pacific northward and southward, then eastward to El Paso, the Western Development Company looted the new road just as effectively. The vast economic and political power wielded by the four men in California was lambasted by Frank Norris in a novel entitled *The Octopus*, but the book could not alter the facts. Each of the Big Four at his death left an estate of $40 million or more.

In the long run, nevertheless, the federal government recovered much if not all of its investment in transcontinentals and accomplished the purpose of linking the country together. The Union Pacific, for example, repaid in full its second mortgage loan in 1897. The roads increased incalculably the value of the alternate sections of land that remained in government hands, and until 1946 the government shipped freight and military personnel over land-grant roads at half fare.

The transcontinentals were trunk lines from the start, but in the East trunk lines were formed by continued expansion and combination. Eastern lines, like those in the West, were subject to financial buccaneering, which centered first on the Erie Railroad, the favorite prey of manipulators. Prince of the railroad buccaneers was Jay Gould, a secretive trickster who developed on a grand scale the fine art of buying up run-down railroads, making cosmetic improvements, paying dividends out of capital, and selling out at a profit, meanwhile using corporate treasuries for personal speculation and judicious bribes. Ousted by a reform group after having looted the Erie, Gould moved on to bigger things in western roads and a variety of other corporations, including Western Union. Nearly every enterprise he touched was either compromised or ruined, while Gould was building a fortune that amounted to $100 million upon his death at age fifty-six.

Few railroad fortunes were built in those free-wheeling times by methods of pristine purity, but compared to such as Gould, most railroaders were giants of probity. They at least took some interest in the welfare of their companies, if not always in that of the public. Cornelius Vanderbilt, called "Commodore" by virtue of his early exploits in steamboating, stands out among the railroad barons. Already rich before the Civil War, he decided to give up the hazards of wartime shipping and move his capital into land transport. Under his direction the first of the major eastern consolidations took form. Back in 1853 the New York Central Railroad had brought eleven roads into a line that paralleled the Erie Canal from Albany to Buffalo. For connections into New York City, however, it depended on two other lines, especially when river steamboats quit running in winter. In 1862 Vanderbilt began to secure control of these, first the New York and Harlem, then the Hudson River line. He may have been after the Central from the start, but in any case it soon fell into his hands. In 1867, as a result of disagreements over money owed the Hudson River line by the Central, Vanderbilt refused to transfer any traffic to and from his Hudson lines to the Central. Driven to the wall by Vanderbilt, the Central's stockholders conceded him a controlling interest. When protest arose at his embargo on traffic, he asked innocently: "Can't I do what I want with my own?"

In December 1867 he became president of the Central and soon combined it with the other lines. Next he tried to corner the stock of his chief competitor, the Erie, but Daniel Drew, Jim Fisk, and Jay Gould beat him there by the simple expedient of printing new stock faster than he could buy it. In 1873, however, he bought the Lake Shore and Michigan Southern road, which gave his lines connections into Chicago. After the Commodore's death in 1877, his son William Henry extended the Vanderbilt lines to include more than 13,000 miles in the Northeast. By similar acts of acquisition and combination about two-thirds of the nation's railroad mileage fell under the control of only seven major groups.

ADVANCES IN MANUFACTURING   The story of manufacturing after the Civil War shows much the same pattern of expansion and merger in both old and new industries. The Patent Office, which had recorded only 276 inventions during its first decade of existence, the 1790s, registered 234,956 in the decade of the 1890s. And whether or not necessity was the mother of invention, invention was the mother of new industries—and new departures in old ones. New processes in steelmaking and refining, for instance, were the foundation of the Carnegie and Rockefeller enterprises. The refrigerator car made it possible for the beef, mutton, and pork of the New West to reach a national market, giving rise to the great packinghouse enterprises of Gustavus V. Swift in Chicago and Philip D. Armour in Minneapolis. The use of corrugated rollers to crack the hard spicy wheat of the Plains provided impetus to the flour milling that centered in Minneapolis under the control of the Pillsburys, Washburns, and Crosbys. Technological improvements in papermaking, which occurred first in Europe, made it possible to satisfy the appetite of continuous-action roller presses with cheap paper made from woodpulps. Glassmaking became a mechanized industry. In 1884 tobacco manufacturing moved into a new stage when the Duke interests employed a machine to roll cigarettes.

The list of industrial innovations can be extended indefinitely: barbed-wire, farm implements, George Westinghouse's air brake for trains (1868), steam turbines, gas distribution and electrical devices, Christopher Schole's typewriter (1867), J. W. McGaffey's vacuum cleaner (1869), and countless others. Before the end of the century the internal combustion engine and the motion picture, each the work of many hands, were laying foundations for new industries of the twentieth century.

These advances in technology altered the lives of ordinary people far more than the activities of the political or intellectual realms. In no field was this more true than in the applications of electricity to communications and power. Few if any inventions of the times could rival the importance of the telephone, which Alexander Graham Bell patented in 1876 and demonstrated at the Philadelphia Centennial Exposition the same year. In 1877 he staged a conversation between Boston and New York. To promote the new device the inventor and his supporters formed the Bell Telephone Association, out of which grew in 1879 the National Bell Telephone Company. Almost from the beginning the Bell interests had to defend their patent against competitors. The most dangerous threat came from Western Union which, after turning down a chance to buy Bell's "toy," employed Thomas Edison to develop an improved version. Edison's telephone became the prototype of the modern instrument, with its separate transmitter and receiver. But Bell had a prior claim on the basic principle and Western Union, rather than risk a legal defeat, sold its rights and properties for a tidy sum, clearing the way for the creation of a monopoly. In 1885 the Bell interests, led by Theodore N. Vail, organized the American Telephone and Telegraph Company. By 1899 it was a holding company, capitalized at $120 million, in control of forty-nine licensed subsidiaries and itself an operating company for long-distance lines.

EDISON'S INVENTIONS In the rise of electrical industries the name of Thomas Alva Edison stands above that of other inventors. He started his career at an early age as a railway news butcher, selling papers and candies on trains, soon learned telegraphy, and began making improvements in that and other areas. In 1876, at quarters in Menlo Park, New Jersey, Edison went full-time into the "invention business"; eleven years later he moved into enlarged quarters in West Orange, New Jersey. He invented the phonograph in 1877, the first successful incandescent light bulb in 1879, and altogether through his invention factories created or perfected hundreds of new devices and processes including the storage battery, dictaphone, mimeograph, dynamo, electric transmission, and the motion picture. In 1882, with the backing of J. P. Morgan, the Edison Electric Illuminating Company began to supply current to eighty-five customers from its Pearl Street Station in New York City, beginning the great electric utility industry. A number of companies making light bulbs merged into the Edison General Electric Company in 1888. Financially secure, Edison retired from business to devote full-time once again to invention.

The use of direct current limited Edison's lighting system to a radius of about two miles. To get more distance required an alternating current, which could be transmitted at high voltage and then stepped down by transformers. George Westinghouse, inventor of the air brake, developed the first alternating-current system in 1886 and manufactured the equipment through the Westinghouse Electric Company. Edison resisted the new method on the ground that it was too dangerous, but just as Edison's instrument supplanted Bell's first telephone, the Westing-

Thomas Edison in his laboratory. [Photoworld]

house system won the "Battle of the Currents," and the Edison companies had to switch over. After the invention of the alternating-current motor in 1888 by Nikola Tesla, a Croatian immigrant, Westinghouse acquired and improved the motor and worked a revolution by enabling factories to disperse widely. They no longer had to cluster around waterfalls and coal supplies.

Edison and Westinghouse were rare examples of inventors with the luck and foresight to get rich from the industries they created. The great captains of industry were more often pure entrepreneurs, men skilled mainly in organizing and promoting industry. Three stand out both for their achievements and for their special contributions: John D. Rockefeller, for his innovations in organization; Andrew Carnegie, for his own achievements in organization and for contributions to the philosophical rationale for entrepreneurial activity; and J. Pierpont Morgan, for his development of investment banking.

Entrepreneurs

ROCKEFELLER AND THE OIL TRUST   Born in New York state, Rockefeller moved as a youth to Cleveland, where railroad and ship connections provided a strategic location for servicing the oil fields of western Pennsylvania, which were later found to extend into Ohio and West Virginia. Oil had long been known to exist in the region. One branch of the Allegheny River was called Oil Creek, from which farmers skimmed off the stuff to grease their wagon wheels. Medicine men bottled it and claimed it had miraculous curative powers. One of these men, "Doc" Samuel M. Kier, distilled what he called "carbon oil" for use in a lamp burner, but the resulting odor made it impractical. The problem remained unsolved until the late 1850s when Yale's Dr. Benjamin Silliman, Jr., at the behest of a local promoter, showed that the oil could be refined into a good illuminant (kerosene) which served also for heating and cooking. The promoter, George Henry Bissell, set a friend to drilling on his lease near Titusville, Pennsylvania, where in 1859 the first well was struck, producing oil at a rate of twenty-five barrels a day. This proved the start of a great industry, based at first mainly on the sale of kerosene.

In economic importance the Pennsylvania oil rush far outweighed the California gold rush of just ten years before. If it duplicated many of the earlier scenes of disorder, it ended by

Drums of oil leaving Rouseville, Pennsylvania, by train. Rouseville was one of the centers of the Pennsylvania oil rush. [Drake Well Museum]

yielding more wealth. Well before the end of the Civil War derricks checkered the area and refineries sprang up in Pittsburgh and Cleveland. Of the two cities, Cleveland had the edge in transportation, and John D. Rockefeller made the most of it. He started as a bookkeeper, but before age twenty-one was already a partner in a wholesale house. While other young men were going off to war, Rockefeller moved into the oil business. In 1860, sent out by business friends to look over the Pennsylvania fields, he advised against the risks of sinking wells, but saw that refining, a strategic bottleneck, promised great profits at little risk. In 1862 he backed a refinery started by his friend, Samuel Andrews. He then quit merchandising to form a partnership with Andrews, and in 1867 added H. M. Flagler to create the firm of Rockefeller, Flagler, and Andrews. In 1870 Rockefeller incorporated his various interests as the Standard Oil Company of Ohio, capitalized at $1 million.

Rockefeller was already the largest refiner, but as he put it, "the butcher, the baker, and the candlestick maker began to refine oil." As a result, "the price went down and down until the trade was ruined." Rockefeller resolved to bring order out of chaos, which is to say he decided to weed out the competition. Soon a useful device presented itself. In 1872 Rockefeller acquired the South Improvement Company, which he made the marketing agent for a large percentage of his oil shipments. By controlling this traffic, he gained clout with the railroads, which gave him large rebates on the standard rates in order to keep his business. In some cases they even gave him information on competitors' shipments. Rockefeller then approached his Cleveland competitors and offered to buy them out at his own price. Most of them saw the wisdom of this course. As Rockefeller put it, "the conditions were so chaotic [i.e., competitive] that most of the refiners were very desirous to get out of the business." By 1879 Standard Oil had come to control 90–95 percent of the oil refining in the country.

Much of Rockefeller's success was based on his determination to "pay nobody a profit." Instead of depending on the products or services of other firms, Standard undertook to make its own barrels, cans, staves, and whatever else it needed. In economic terms this was vertical integration. The company kept large amounts of cash reserves to make it independent of banks in case of a crisis. In line with this policy, Rockefeller set out also to control his transportation needs. By 1879 most of the pipelines in the Appalachian field had come under United Pipe Lines Company, a Standard subsidiary. With Standard owning most of the pipelines leading to railroads, plus the tank cars and the oil-storage facilities, it was able to dissuade the railroads from servicing eastern competitors. Those competitors who insisted on holding out then faced a giant marketing organization capable of driving them to the wall with price wars.

Eventually, in order to consolidate scattered business interests under a more efficient control, Rockefeller and his friends resorted to the legal device of the trust. Long established in law to enable one or more people to manage property belonging to others, such as children or the mentally incompetent, the trust now was used for a new purpose—centralized control of business. Since Standard Oil of Ohio was not permitted to hold property out of state, it began in 1872 to place properties or companies acquired elsewhere in trust, usually with Henry M. Flagler, company secretary. This became impractical, however, since the death of the trustee would endanger the trust. To get around this problem, in 1882 all of the thirty-seven stockholders in various Standard Oil enterprises conveyed their stock to nine trustees, getting "trust certificates" in return. The nine trustees were thus empowered to give central direction to all the Standard companies.

The original plan, never fully carried out, was to organize a Standard Oil Company in each state in which the trust did business. But the trust device, widely copied in the 1880s, proved legally vulnerable to prosecution under state laws prohibiting monopoly or restraint of trade. In 1892 the Supreme Court of Ohio ordered the Standard Oil Trust dissolved. For a while the company maintained a unified control by the simple device of interlocking directorates, through which the board of directors of one company was made identical or nearly so to the boards of the others. Gradually, however, Rockefeller took to the idea of the holding company: a firm which controlled other companies by holding all or at least a majority of their stock. The Pennsylvania Railroad had adopted the device as early as 1870; American Bell Telephone did the same in 1880. New Jersey favored the device under a law enacted in 1888 and clarified in the 1890s. In 1899 Rockefeller brought his empire under the direction of the Standard Oil Company of New Jersey, a holding company. Though less vulnerable to prosecution under state law, some holding companies proved vulnerable to the Sherman Anti-Trust Act of 1890. (This story will be told later.) Meanwhile the term "trust" had become so fixed in the public lexicon that it was used to describe large combinations under holding companies as well.

CARNEGIE'S GOSPEL OF WEALTH Andrew Carnegie, like Rockefeller, experienced the untypical rise from poverty to riches that came to be known in those days as "the typical American success story." Born in Dunfermline, Scotland, son of a hand weaver who fell upon hard times, he migrated in 1848 with his family to Allegheny, Pennsylvania. Then thirteen, he started out as a bobbin boy in a textile mill at wages of $1.20 per week. At fourteen he was getting $2.50 per week as a telegraph messenger and im-

Andrew Carnegie, apostle of "The Gospel of Wealth." [Carnegie Library, Pittsburgh]

proved himself in his spare time by learning to read messages by ear. Soon he was promoted to telegrapher and in 1853 became personal secretary and telegrapher to Thomas Scott, then district superintendent of the Pennsylvania Railroad and later its president. When Scott moved up, Carnegie moved into his job and was soon on his way. During the Civil War, when Scott became assistant secretary of war in charge of transportation, Carnegie went with him, developed a military telegraph system, and personally helped evacuate the wounded from Bull Run.

Carnegie kept on moving—from telegraphy to railroading to bridge building and then to iron and steel making. He used personal connections and borrowed money to enter these fields, usually moving into the next one before dropping the last. Tom Scott got Carnegie started in investments with a hot tip on American Express stock. Carnegie mortgaged his mother's home to buy it. A chance venture in the Pennsylvania oilfields, which Rockefeller shunned, netted Carnegie a gusher. Because of his help in promoting sleeping cars, he got an eighth share in the venture, after which he bought into the Iron City Forge Company and organized the Keystone Bridge Company. He then persuaded officials of the Pennsylvania Railroad to finance his plan to make bridges for the road.

In 1865 Carnegie quit the railroad to devote full time to his own interests. These were mainly in iron and bridge building, but the versatile entrepreneur also made money in oil and sold railroad bonds in Europe. In 1872 he netted $150,000 on one trip, and on that trip met Sir Henry Bessemer, inventor of a new process of steelmaking. The next year Carnegie resolved to concentrate on steel, or as he put it, to put all his eggs in one basket and then watch that basket. He began first the J. Edgar Thompson Steel Works, which he shrewdly named after the head of the Pennsylvania Railroad. In addition to the Bessemer process, Carnegie soon began using the open-hearth process, developed first in Germany. As competitors arose, Carnegie picked them off one by one. In 1882 when the Pittsburgh Bessemer Steel Company ran into labor troubles and slackening demand, Carnegie bought out their almost-new Homestead works approximately at cost. When the Duquesne Bessemer Steel Company ran afoul of a smear campaign describing their rails as unsafe, Carnegie bought them out at less than cost—and in bonds which were paid off in five years out of profits from the Duquesne plant. By 1900 Carnegie Steel was paying dividends of $40 million.

Carnegie was never a technical expert on steel. He was a promoter, salesman, and organizer with a gift for finding and using men of expert ability. He always insisted on up-to-date machinery and equipment, and shrewdly used times of recession to expand more cheaply.

In much of this Carnegie was a typical businessman of the time, if abler and luckier than most. But he stands out from the lot especially as a thinker who fashioned and publicized a philosophy for big business, a conservative rationale that became deeply implanted in the conventional wisdom of Americans. Carnegie argued that however harsh their methods at times, the captains of industry were on the whole public benefactors. At thirty-three he confided to his diary an ambition to retire early and devote his time to self-improvement, to being a "distributor" of wealth (he disliked the word "philanthropy"), and perhaps to public service. He did finally achieve that goal, but not until age sixty-five. Meanwhile, however, he found time to write articles for current magazines and to produce a modest shelf of books.

His best remembered piece was an essay, "Wealth," published by the *North American Review* in 1889, and retitled "The Gospel of Wealth" when reprinted in the *Pall Mall Gazette* of London. In this basic statement of his philosophy Carnegie drew upon the ideas of Charles Darwin and especially Darwin's English interpreter Herbert Spencer, who had invented the phrase "survival of the fittest." In the evolution of society, Carnegie argued, the contrast between the millionaire and the laborer measures the distance society has come. "Not evil, but good, has come to the race from the accumulation of wealth by those who have the ability and energy that produces it." The process had been costly in many ways, but the law of competition was "best for the race, because it insures the survival of the fittest in every department."

Carnegie then moved on to a sermon on the proper uses of wealth. Carnegie professed no religious faith, but surely had absorbed from his Presbyterian origins the Christian doctrine of stewardship. A rich man could leave his fortune to his children, Carnegie said, but experience suggested that this was not always wise or even kind. He might leave it at his death for public uses, but in his absence it would likely be misused. The best way to dispense a fortune was to administer it during one's lifetime for the public good. One should first set an example of humble living—in Carnegie's case this included Skibo Castle in Scotland—and provide for his dependents, then consider the rest a trust fund for the public good. One should avoid alms-giving, but rather provide means for people to help themselves by supporting universities, libraries, hospitals, parks, halls for meetings and concerts, swimming baths, and church buildings—in that order. To his credit, Carnegie meant it, devoting his wealth to many such benefactions and to the cause of world peace. Rockefeller too gave many gifts, mainly to education and medicine, but apparently at least in part because he was persuaded it would make for good public relations.

Carnegie's gospel of wealth found widespread acceptance in the late nineteenth century's worship of success, an attitude of respect for the self-made man that owed perhaps more to the *Autobiography* of Benjamin Franklin and the sayings of Franklin's Poor Richard than to Charles Darwin and his interpreters. The popularity of such attitudes was shown by the market for inspirational literature touting the ancient verities of thrift, integrity, and hard work. Among the sages of that school none was better known than Horatio Alger, whose very name became a byword for success. A Unitarian minister in New York, he wrote novels for boys, mostly about poor boys who made good, with titles like *Ragged Dick* (1867), *Luck and Pluck* (1869), and *Tattered Tom* (1871). More often than not, however, Horatio Alger heroes made it, like Carnegie, by winning the favor of some well-placed man. William Makepeace Thayer's biographies of self-made men such as Franklin, Lincoln, and Grant became the nonfiction counterparts to Alger's novels. On the Chautauqua circuit the star was Russell Conwell, a Baptist minister who delivered his lecture, "Acres of Diamonds," more than 6,000 times. The message was that opportunity, in effect acres of diamonds, was at everybody's doorstep. "I say, get rich, get rich." It was a social and Christian duty.

J. P. MORGAN, THE FINANCIER   J. Pierpont Morgan, who was born to wealth and increased it enormously, was about as far from being a Horatio Alger hero as one could get. Born in Connecticut, he was the son of Junius Spencer Morgan, partner in the banking house of George Peabody and Company of London, which later became J. S. Morgan and Company. Young Pierpont attended preparatory school in Switzerland and the University of Gottingen in Germany, where he proved so adept at mathematics that a chance was held out to him to become a professor. It was a skill not without its uses for a young financier. After a brief apprenticeship, he was sent in 1857 to work in a New York firm which represented his father's London firm, and in 1860 set himself up as its New York agent under the name of J. Pierpont Morgan and Company. This firm, under various names, chan-

J. Pierpont Morgan. [The Pierpont Morgan Library]

neled much European capital into the country and grew into a financial power in its own right.

Morgan was an investment banker, which meant that he was engaged in a marketing operation. He would buy corporate shares and bonds wholesale and then sell them at a profit, much as other merchants would market, say, hardware, but on a larger scale. The growth of large corporations put Morgan's and other investment firms in a more and more strategic position in the economy. The financial world began to take notice in 1869 when Morgan actually beat the wily Jay Gould and Jim Fisk in a fight to control a New York railroad. Other major signs of his growing stature came in 1872 when Morgan was able quietly to sell a large bloc of New York Central stock in England before the news could adversely affect the American markets, and in 1873 when he secured the division of a Treasury loan with Jay Cooke and Company, which had held a virtual monopoly on the sale of government bonds since the Civil War.

Railroads were the key to the times and they became a special concern of Morgan's; he picked up and reorganized one line after another. After the Panic of 1893 Morgan took over the Erie, Philadelphia and Reading, the Northern Pacific, and organized the Southern Railway; he already had a hand in the Vanderbilt and Pennsylvania lines. Since the investment business depended on the general good health of client companies, investment bankers became involved in the operation of their clients' firms, demanding places on boards of directors and helping to shape their fiscal dealings. By these means bankers could influence company policies, which, technicians often argued, resulted in heavy emphasis on fiscal matters to the detriment of technical innovation. Eventually people were speaking of the "money trust," the greatest trust of all, with its hand in all kinds of other enterprises.

To Morgan, however, the stability brought by his operations was plain common sense. The railroad people and other businessmen, if unrestrained, acted like anarchists. Morgan, the historian Joseph F. Wall wrote,"felt that the American economy should ideally be like a company organizational chart, with each part in its proper place, and the lines of authority clearly designated. He did not really believe in the free-enterprise system, and like the most ardent socialists, he hated the waste, duplication, and clutter of unrestrained competition." In this view, the difference between the Morgans and Rockefellers on one side and the socialists on the other was chiefly over who would control the system, "the state or an oligopoly." While most Americans loudly professed belief in the "American system" of free enterprise, Wall wrote, "a few men like Morgan, with an efficiency and power that the socialists could never achieve in America, went about in their quiet way, building combines and trusts and interlocking directorates that would forever eliminate that wasteful competitive system."

Morgan's crowning triumph was consolidation of the steel industry, to which he was introduced by his interests in railroading. In 1898 a rapid series of mergers in the iron and steel industry was brought on mainly by two groups: one centered on the American Steel and Wire Company, formed by William H. Moore and John W. "Bet-a-Million" Gates, both longtime speculative plungers; the other group comprised the Morgan interests, chiefly the National Tube Company and the Federal Steel Company, headed by Judge Elbert Gary, who urged Morgan to buy out Carnegie and the other interests.

In 1901 Carnegie sold out to Morgan at his own price, which came to nearly $500 million, of which his personal share was nearly $300 million. In rapid succession Morgan added the Moore-Gates interests and the Rockefeller holdings in both the Mesabi ore range and a Great Lakes ore fleet. Altogether the new United States Steel Corporation, a holding company for these varied interests, was capitalized at $1.4 billion, a total that was heavily watered (well above the company's actual assets) but was soon made solid by large profits. The new giant was a marvel of the new century, the first billion-dollar corporation, the climactic event in that age of consolidation. By 1904, the financial writer John Moody recorded in *The Truth about the Trusts*, there were some 318 industrial trusts capitalized at over $7 billion,

*A lavish dinner celebrated the merger of the Carnegie and Morgan
interests into U.S. Steel in 1901. These executives are seated at a table
shaped like a huge rail. [Carnegie Library, Pittsburgh]*

with nearly 5,300 distinct plants. Of these trusts, 236, holding
five-sixths of the capital, had incorporated since January 1, 1898,
most under New Jersey law.

ADVANCES FOR LABOR

THE DISTRIBUTION OF WEALTH   Accompanying the spread of such
industrial combinations was a rising standard of living for most
people. If the rich were still getting richer, a lot of other people
were at least better off, and the pre–Civil War trend toward even
higher concentrations of wealth slacked off. This, of course, is far
from saying that disparities in the distribution of wealth had disappeared. One set of estimates by Robert E. Gallman has it that
in both 1860 and 1900 the richest 2 percent of American families owned more than a third of the nation's physical wealth,
while the top 10 percent owned almost three-fourths and all the
nation's physical assets were in the hands of half its families.
Studies of social mobility in towns across the country show,
moreover, that while the rise from rags to riches was rare, "upward mobility both from blue-collar to white-collar callings and
from low-ranked to high-ranked manual jobs was quite common."

The continuing demand for unskilled or semi-skilled workers
meanwhile was filled by new groups entering the workforce at
the bottom: immigrants above all, but also growing numbers of

women and children. Because of a long-term decline in prices and the cost of living, real wages and earnings in manufacturing went up about 50 percent between 1860 and 1890, and another 37 percent from 1890 to 1914. By latter-day standards, however, working conditions then were dreary indeed. At the turn of the century the average hourly wage in manufacturing was 21.6¢, and average annual earnings were $490. The average work week was fifty-nine hours, which amounted nearly to six ten-hour days, but that was only an average. Most steelworkers put in a twelve-hour day, and as late as the 1920s a great many worked a seven-day or eighty-four-hour week. Oil and pipeline crews were still doing such stints into the 1930s.

A NEW SOCIAL WORLD   Rising wages in no way discount the high social costs of industrialization. In the crowded tenements that grew up in major cities the death rates ran substantially higher than in the countryside. Factories often maintained poor health and safety conditions. In 1913, for instance, there were some 25,000 factory fatalities and some 700,000 injuries that required at least four weeks' disability—more than half the number of American casualties in World War I. A fundamental social fact in this new bureaucratic world was the dependence of ever-larger numbers of people on the machinery and factories of owners whom they seldom if ever saw. In the simpler world of small shops, workers and employers could enter into close personal relationships; the larger corporation, on the other hand, was likely governed by a bureaucracy in which ownership was separate from management.

The coming of the railroads was basic to this development. The roads, the business historian Alfred Chandler wrote, "caused entrepreneurs to integrate and subdivide their business activities and to hire salaried managers to monitor and coordinate the flow of goods through their enlarged enterprises." What Chandler called the "visible hand" of management increasingly replaced the "invisible hand" which in Adam Smith's theory guided the marketplace through multitudes of individual decisions. As an old formulation had it, the corporation "has no soul to be damned and no body to be kicked." Much of the social history of the modern world in fact turns on the transition from a world of personal relationships to one of impersonal and contractual relationships.

DISORGANIZED PROTEST   In these circumstances it was far more difficult for thousands and millions of workers to organize for mutual benefit than for a few captains of industry to organize for profit. Public opinion was likely to respect property rights more than any right that inhered in labor. Many businessmen held to the viewpoint that a "labor supply" was simply another commodity to be procured at the lowest possible price.

Among workers still rooted in an agrarian world the idea of durable unions was slow to take hold. Immigrant workers came from many cultures and spoke many tongues. Many if not most saw their jobs as transient, the first rung on the ladder to success. They hoped to move on to a homestead, or having made their fortunes, to return to the old farms of their European homelands. With or without unions, though, workers often staged impromptu strikes in response to grievances such as wage cuts. But impromptu action often led to violence, and three violent incidents of the 1870s colored much of the public's view of labor unions thereafter.

The decade's early years saw a reign of terror in the eastern Pennsylvania coal fields, attributed to an Irish group called the Molly Maguires. Taking their name from an Irish patriot who had directed violent resistance against the British, the group aimed to right perceived wrongs against Irish workers by such methods as intimidation, beatings, and killings. Their actions excited high emotions which were reflected in later chronicles depicting them as either heroic defenders of the workingman in a genuine class war, or early practitioners of labor racketeering. The terrorism reached its peak in 1874–1875. In the meantime Franklin P. Gowen, president of a railroad which owned a number of the mines, had hired Pinkerton detectives to stop the movement. James McParlan, the most effective of the agents who infiltrated the Mollies, produced enough evidence to indict the leaders of the movement. At trials in 1876 twenty-four of the Molly Maguires were convicted. Ten of them were hanged. The trials also resulted in a wage reduction in the mines and the final destruction of the Miners' National Association, a weak union the Mollies had infiltrated. Later investigations have shown that agents of the mine operators themselves stirred up some of the trouble. Nobody came out of the affair smelling like a rose, except perhaps a few Catholic priests who, at some risk to themselves, urged their Irish brethren to abjure violence and secret societies.

THE RAILROAD STRIKE OF 1877 Far more significant, because more widespread, was the Great Railroad Strike of 1877, the first major interstate strike. For many people it raised the spectre of a social revolution led by workers, like the short-lived Paris Commune of 1871. Wage cuts caused the walkout. After the Panic of 1873 the major rail lines in the East had cut wages, and then in 1877 effected another 10 percent cut. This cut went into effect on July 16, and the next day most of the railroad workers at Martinsburg, West Virginia, walked out and blocked the tracks. Without organized direction, however, their movement degenerated into a mob which burned and plundered railroad property.

Walkouts and demonstrations of sympathy spread spontaneously from Cumberland, Maryland, to Chicago and San Francisco. The greatest outbreak began at Pittsburgh on July 19, when the Pennsylvania Railroad put on "double-headers" (long trains pulled by two locomotives) in order to reduce crews. Public sympathy for the strikers was so great at first that local militiamen, called out to suppress them, instead fraternized with them. But militiamen from Philadelphia were called, and after dispersing one crowd at the cost of twenty-six lives, found themselves besieged in the railroad's roundhouse, where the commander disbanded them and advised them to escape as best they could. Looting and rioting went on for another day until the frenzy wore itself out. Public opinion, sympathetic at first, tended to blame the strikers for the violence. Eventually the workers, lacking organized bargaining power, had no choice but to drift back to work. Everywhere the strikes failed.

In California, however, they indirectly gave rise to a political movement. At San Francisco's "Sand Lot" a meeting to express

The railroad strike of 1877. Railroad workers in Pittsburgh reacted violently to wage cuts. [Carnegie Library, Pittsburgh]

sympathy for the strikers ended with attacks on some passing Chinese. Within a few days sporadic anti-Chinese riots led to a mob attack on Chinatown. Depression had hit the West Coast especially hard, and the Chinese were a handy scapegoat for the frustrations of the time. Soon an Irish immigrant, Dennis Kearney, organized the "Workingmen's Party of California" mainly on the platform of Chinese exclusion. A gifted agitator, himself only recently naturalized, he harangued the "sand lotters" about the "foreign peril" and assaulted the rich for exploiting the poor —sometimes at gatherings beside their mansions on Nob Hill. In 1878 his new party won a good number of seats in a state constitutional convention, but managed to incorporate in the state's basic law little more than ineffective attempts to regulate the railroads. The workingmen's movement peaked in 1879 when it elected many members of the new legislature and the mayor of San Francisco. Kearney lacked the gift for building a durable movement, but as his party went to pieces his anti-Chinese theme became a national issue, and in 1882 Congress voted to prohibit Chinese immigration for ten years.

TOWARD PERMANENT UNIONS   Meanwhile efforts to build a permanent union movement had begun to bear fruit. Earlier efforts, in the 1830s and 1840s, had largely been dominated by reformers with schemes that ranged from free homesteads to utopian socialism. But the 1850s had seen the beginning of "job-conscious" unions in certain skilled trades: first the National Typographical Union (1852), then the Stone Cutters (1853), Hat Finishers (1854), Iron Molders (1859), and Machinists and Blacksmiths (1859). By 1860 there were about twenty such unions, and during the Civil War, because of the demand for labor, such unions grew in strength and numbers.

Until after the war, however, there was no overall federation of these groups. In August 1866 some seventy-seven delegates organized the National Labor Union at a convention in Baltimore and chose as their leader William H. Sylvis, a Philadelphian who headed the Iron Molders. Essentially the NLU comprised congresses of delegates from labor and reform groups more interested in political and social reform than in bargaining with employers. The groups espoused such ideas as the eight-hour day, workers' cooperatives, greenbackism, and equal rights for women and blacks. In 1869 Sylvis died suddenly, still only forty-one, after which trade union support fell away quickly. Only a remnant of reformers was left in 1872 when the union reorganized as the National Labor Reform party, but its candidate for president, Justice David Davis of Illinois, withdrew and the movement collapsed. The National Labor Union cannot be put down as a total failure, however. It was influential in persuading Congress to enact an eight-hour day for federal employees and to repeal the Contract Labor Law, which had been passed during the Civil War to encourage the importation of labor. The union, moreover, undertook to encourage the organization of black workers, but with little success.

THE KNIGHTS OF LABOR Before the National Labor Union collapsed, another group had emerged which soon claimed national standing, the Noble and Holy Order of the Knights of Labor. The name betokened a tendency to copy the forms of fraternal orders and to evoke the aura of medieval guilds. The founder of the Knights of Labor, Uriah S. Stephens, a Philadephia tailor, was a habitual "joiner" involved with several secret orders, including the Masons. His early training for the Baptist ministry also affected his outlook. Secrecy, he felt, along with a semi-religious ritual, would protect members against retaliation and at the same time create a sense of solidarity.

In 1869, with Stephens as leader, nine Philadelphia tailors founded the order. At first it grew slowly, but in 1873 formed the first district assembly in the Philadelphia area. During the years of depression, as other unions collapsed, it spread more rapidly and in 1878 its first General Assembly established a national organization. Its preamble and platform endorsed the reforms advanced by previous workingmen's groups, including producers' and consumers' cooperatives, homesteads, bureaus of labor statistics, mechanics' lien laws (to ensure payment of salaries), elimination of convict-labor competition, the eight-hour day, and greenbacks. One plank in the platform, far ahead of the times, called for equal pay for equal work by both sexes.

Throughout its existence the Knights emphasized reform measures and preferred boycotts to strikes as a way to put pressure on employers. The constitution of the order allowed as members all who had ever worked for wages except lawyers, doctors, bankers, and those who sold liquor. Theoretically it was one big union of all workers regardless of race, color, creed, or sex, skilled and unskilled. Each local assembly was to be formed on such a basis, but in practice some local and district assemblies were organized on a craft basis, such as the telegraphers and cigarmakers. Above these stood the General Assembly, a General Executive Board, and at the head of the organization a Grand Master Workman.

Stephens was the first elected to this office, but he stepped down in 1879 to protest a relaxation of secrecy. Secret labor groups had become suspect after the Molly Maguires, and had been the objects of the Catholic church's disapproval for some time. When the General Assembly allowed local and district groups to emerge into the open, Stephens gave way to Terence V. Powderly, the thirty-year-old mayor of Scranton, Pennsylvania. Born of Irish immigrant parents, Powderly had become a switchtender at sixteen but soon moved into the machine shop. In many ways he was unsuited to the new job. At once mayor, head of the Knights, county health officer, and part-owner and manager of a grocery store, he had too many irons in the fire. He was physically frail, sensitive to criticism, and indecisive at critical moments. He was temperamentally opposed to strikes, and when they did occur, did not always back up the local groups involved. Yet the Knights owed their greatest growth to strikes that occurred under his leadership.

In the mid-1880s the union had a meteoric rise. In 1884 a successful strike against wage cuts in the Union Pacific shops at Denver led many railroad workers to form new assemblies. Then, in 1885, the Knights scored a startling victory over Jay Gould. Late the previous year and early in 1885 Gould had cut wages on the Missouri, Kansas, and Texas and Wabash roads. A spontaneous strike on these lines in February 1885 spread to Gould's Missouri-Pacific, and as organizers from the Knights of Labor moved in, Gould restored the wage cuts. In June another strike on the Wabash against the firing of union members brought another victory. These successes allowed the Knights to grow rapidly from about 100,000 members to more than 700,000 in 1886, a memorable year in the history of organized labor for several reasons.

One was that the Knights peaked and then went into rapid decline. Jay Gould, taken by surprise in 1885, set a trap for the Knights in 1886. He spoke favorably of unions, expressed his wish that all railroad workers were organized, but in February 1886 he provoked another strike by firing a foreman in the Texas-Pacific shops at Marshall, Texas. When the Knights struck, Gould refused arbitration and hired Pinkerton agents to harass strikers and keep the trains running. On May 4 the Knights had to call off the strike. The organization was further damaged by an incident in Chicago that very night, with which the Knights had little to do but which provoked widespread revulsion against labor groups in general.

THE HAYMARKET AFFAIR The Haymarket Affair grew indirectly out of agitation for the eight-hour day. The lead on this issue had been taken by a little-known organization with an unwieldy name, forerunner to the American Federation of Labor, the Federation of Organized Trades and Labor Unions of the United States and Canada. In 1884 this group had set May 1, 1886, as the deadline for the eight-hour day in all trades. Powderly declined to join the federation in a call for strikes on that day, but some assemblies of the Knights did. Chicago became the center of the movement, and on May 3 the International Harvester plant became the site of an unfortunate clash between strikers and policemen in which one striker was killed.

Leaders of a minuscule anarchist movement in Chicago scheduled an open meeting the following night at Haymarket Square to protest the killing. After listening under a light drizzle to lengthy speeches promoting socialism and anarchism, the crowd was beginning to break up when a group of policemen arrived and called upon the meeting to disperse. At that point somebody threw a bomb at the police, killing one and wounding others. The police responded by firing into the crowd. In a trial marked by prejudice and hysteria, seven anarchist leaders were sentenced to death despite the lack of any evidence linking them to the bomb-thrower, whose identity was never established. Of these, two were reprieved and some years later pardoned, one committed suicide in prison, but four were actually hanged. All but one of the group were German-speaking, but that one, Albert Parsons, held a membership card in the Knights of Labor.

Despite his best efforts, Powderly could never dissociate in the public mind the Knights from the anarchists. He clung to leadership until 1893, but after that the union evaporated and by the turn of the century it was but a memory. A number of problems accounted for the Knights' decline other than widespread fantasies of radicalism: a leadership devoted more to reform than to the nuts and bolts of organization, the failure of the Knights' cooperative enterprises, and a preoccupation with politics which led the Knights to sponsor labor candidates in hundreds of local elections. They won a surprising number of races in 1886, but their political efforts proved in the end to be a flash in the pan. The Knights may be credited with some lasting achievements among them the creation of the federal Bureau of Labor Statistics in 1884 as well as several state bureaus; the Foran Act of 1885 which, though weakly enforced, penalized employers who imported contract labor (an arrangement similar to the indentured servitude of colonial times in which workers were committed to a term of labor in exchange for transportation to America); and a national law enacted in 1880 for the arbitration of labor disputes.

The Knights by example also spread the idea of unionism and initiated a new type of union organization: the industrial union, an industry-wide union of the skilled and unskilled, begun in special assemblies of railway and telegraph workers. Industrial unions would have the power to match that of the organized concentrations of capital, but not for some time.

The craft unions were successful earlier. They organized workers who shared special skills, such as typographers or cigarmakers. In 1881 the Federation of Organized Trades and Labor Unions came into being as a group similar to the old National Labor Union; it was primarily an association of national craft unions but with representation of state and local assemblies as well. The craft unions were at first inclined to cooperate with the Knights, but the two groups were organized on different principles. Leaders of the crafts feared that joining with the unskilled would mean a loss of their separate craft identities and a loss of the bargaining power held by skilled workers.

GOMPERS AND THE AFL   As it turned out, however, the main threat to the Federation came from another direction when the Knights themselves organized a few special assemblies along craft lines. An effort by the Knights' District Assembly 49 to organize a separate union in the New York cigar trade led the Cigarmakers International Union to call for stronger unity among the existing craft unions. In May 1886 delegates from twenty craft unions met in Philadelphia and called on the Knights to cease organizing in trades for which a national union already existed. When the Knights failed to heed the suggestion, a second conference met at Columbus, Ohio, and organized the American Federation of Labor (AFL). In structure it differed from the Knights in that it was a federation of national organizations, each of which retained a large degree of autonomy. The structure, it was sometimes said, was typically American because it followed the federal model of the Constitution; actually it followed very closely the model of the British Trades Union Congress.

Samuel Gompers served as president of the AFL from its start until his death in 1924 with only one year's interruption. Born in London of Dutch-Jewish ancestry, Gompers came to the United States as a teenager, joined the Cigarmakers Union in 1864, and became president of his New York local in 1877. This background was significant. The Cigarmakers were the intellectuals of the labor movement; to relieve the tedium of their task, they hired young men to read aloud as they worked, and debated such weighty topics as socialism and Darwinism. But Gompers and

Samuel Gompers, head of the
American Federation of Labor.
[AFL-CIO]

other leaders of the union focused on concrete economic gains,
avoiding involvement with utopian ideas or politics. "At no time
in my life," Gompers once said, "have I ever worked out a definitely articulated economic theory." Adolph Strasser head of the
Cigarmakers, put it more strongly: "We have no ultimate ends,"
he told a Senate hearing. "We are going on from day to day. We
are fighting only for immediate objects—objects that can be realized in a few years."

Such job-consciousness became the policy of the AFL under
Gompers, whose lifetime concern was the effectiveness of the
federation. He hired organizers to spread unionism, and worked
as a diplomat to prevent overlapping unions and to settle jurisdictional disputes. The federation represented workers in matters of national legislation and acted as a sounding board for their
cause. On occasion it exercised its power to request from
members dues for the support of strikes. Gompers, it turned out,
was temperamentally more fitted than Powderly for the rough-
and-tumble world of unionism. He had a thick hide, liked to talk
and drink with the boys in the back room, and did not shy off
from using the strike to achieve labor's objectives. His preference, though, was to achieve these objectives by trade agreements including provisos for union recognition in the form of
closed shops (which could hire only union members) or union-
preference shops (which could hire others only if no union
members were available).

One great objective which Gompers achieved at least in principle was making the eight-hour day standard. In 1889 the AFL
voted to revive its May Day demonstrations for the eight-hour
day abandoned after the Haymarket Affair. But within a few
years the demonstrations underwent a curious change. In July

1889 the founding congress of the Socialist International in Paris voted to sponsor demonstrations for the eight-hour day worldwide. Later, these evolved into demonstrations for general worker demands, labor solidarity, and socialism. Still later, Communists took up the May Day celebrations and, in the supreme irony, paraded their armor through Moscow to observe a holiday which, its origins forgotten, began with an American demand for the eight-hour day.

The AFL at first grew slowly, but by 1890 it had already surpassed the Knights of Labor in membership. By the turn of the century it claimed 500,000 members in affiliated unions; in 1914, on the eve of World War I, it had 2 million and in 1920 reached a peak of 4 million. But even then it embraced less than 15 percent of the nonagricultural workers, and all unions, including the unaffiliated railroad brotherhoods, accounted for little more than 18 percent of these workers. Organized labor's strongholds were in transportation and the building trades. Most of the larger manufacturing industries, including steel, textiles, tobacco, and packing houses remained almost untouched. Gompers never frowned on industrial unions, and several became important affiliates of the AFL: the United Mine Workers, the International Ladies' Garment Workers, and the Amalgamated Clothing Workers. But the AFL had its greatest success in organizing skilled workers.

THE HOMESTEAD STRIKE Two violent incidents in the 1890s nipped the emerging industrial union movement, and set it back for forty years to come—the Homestead Steel Strike of 1892 and the Pullman Strike of 1894. The Amalgamated Association of Iron and Steel Workers, founded in 1876, had by 1891 a membership of more than 24,000 and was probably the largest craft union at that time. But it excluded the unskilled and had failed to organized the larger steel plants. The Homestead Works at Pittsburgh was an important exception. There the union had enjoyed friendly relations with the Carnegie company until H. C. Frick became its president in 1889. A showdown was delayed, however, until 1892 when the union contract came up for renewal. Andrew Carnegie, who had expressed sympathy for unions in the past, had gone to Scotland and left matters in the hands of Frick. Carnegie, however, knew what was afoot: a cost-cutting reduction in the number of workers through the use of labor-saving devices, and a deliberate attempt to smash the union.

As negotiations dragged on, the company announced it would treat with workers as individuals unless an agreement was reached by June 29. A strike, or more properly a lockout of unionists, began on that date. Even before the negotiations ended, Frick had hired as plant guards 300 Pinkerton detectives whose specialty was union-busting. But on the morning of July 6, when the Pinkertons came up the Monongahela River on barges, unionists were waiting behind breastworks on shore. Who fired the first shot remains unknown, but a battle broke out in which six workers and three Pinkertons died. In the end the Pinkertons surrendered and were marched away, subjected to taunts from crowds in the street. Six days later the state militia appeared at the plant. The strike dragged on until November, but by then the union was dead at Homestead. It did not help the labor cause that anarchist Alexander Berkman tried to help out by killing Frick. Armed with both knife and gun he still botched the job, although he wounded the company president severely.

THE PULLMAN STRIKE The Pullman Strike of 1894 involved a dispute at the "model" town of Pullman, Illinois, which housed workers of the Pullman Palace Car Company. The idyllic appearance of the town was deceptive. Employees were required to live there, pay rents and utility costs higher than in nearby towns, and buy goods from company stores. During the Depression of 1893 George Pullman laid off 3,000 of 5,800 employees, and cut wages 25–40 percent, but not his rents and other charges. When Pullman fired three members of a grievance committee, a strike began on May 11, 1894. Pullman workers had been joining the American Railway Union, founded the previous year by Eugene V. Debs. Once secretary-treasurer of the Brotherhood of Locomotive Firemen, Debs had decided that such brotherhoods were too exclusive and set out to organize an industrial union to include all railway workers. Late in June union workers ceased to handle Pullman cars and by the end of July had tied up most of the roads in the Midwest.

The roads brought strikebreakers from Canada and elsewhere, instructing them to connect mail cars to Pullman cars so that interference with Pullman cars meant also interference with the mails. Attorney-General Richard Olney swore in 3,400 special deputies to keep the trains running, and when clashes occurred between these and some of the strikers, lawless elements exploited the situation to repeat some of the scenes of the 1877 strike. Finally, on July 3 President Grover Cleveland answered an appeal from the railroads that he send federal troops into the Chicago area, where the strike was centered. Illinois Gov. John Peter Altgeld insisted that the state could keep order, but Cleveland claimed authority and a duty to ensure delivery of the mails. "If it takes every dollar in the Treasury and every soldier in the United States to deliver a postal card in Chicago," he vowed, "that postal card should be delivered."

Meanwhile Olney had got an injunction from the federal district court forbidding any interference with the mails or any combination to restrain interstate commerce; the principle was that a strike or boycott violated the Sherman Anti-Trust Act. On July 13 the union called off the strike and on the same day Debs was cited for violating the injunction and sentenced to six months in jail. The Supreme Court upheld the decree in the case of *In re Debs* (1895) on broad grounds of national sovereignty: "The strong arm of the national government may be put forth to brush away all obstructions to the freedom of interstate commerce or the transportation of the mails." Debs served his term, during which time he read deeply in socialist literature, and emerged to devote the rest of his life to that cause.

SOCIALISM AND THE UNIONS   The major American unions, for the most part, never allied themselves with the socialists as many European labor movements did. But socialist ideas had been abroad in the country at least since the time Robert Owen visited America in the 1820s. Marxism, a strain of socialism, was imported mainly by German immigrants. Karl Marx's International Workingmen's Association, the First International, founded in 1864, inspired a few affiliates in the United States. In 1872, at Marx's urging, the headquarters was moved from London to New York as a precaution against the growing influence of anarchists in the movement. In 1876 the First International expired, but the next year followers of Marx in America organized the Socialist Labor party, a group so heavily made up of immigrants that German was its official language in the first years. The movement gained little notice before the rise of Daniel DeLeon in the 1890s. As editor of its paper, *The People*, he became the dominant figure in the party. A native of the Dutch West Indies, DeLeon had studied law and lectured for some years at Columbia University. DeLeon proposed to organize industrial unions with a socialist purpose, and to build a political party which would abolish the state once it gained power, after which the unions of the Socialist Trade and Labor Alliance would become the units of control. His ideas seem to have influenced Lenin, leader of the Bolshevik Revolution of 1917, but DeLeon preached revolution at the ballot box, not by violence.

Debs was more successful at building a socialist movement in

America. To many, DeLeon seemed doctrinaire and inflexible. Debs, however, built his new party by following a method now traditional in the United States: he formed a coalition, one which embraced viewpoints ranging from moderate reform to doctrinaire Marxism. In 1897 Debs organized the Social Democratic party from the remnants of the American Railway Union, and got over 4,000 votes as its candidate for president in 1900. In 1901 his followers joined a number of secessionists from DeLeon's party, led by Morris Hillquit of New York, to set up the Socialists Party of America. In 1904 Debs polled over 400,000 votes as the party's candidate for president and more than doubled that to almost 900,000 votes in 1912, or 6 percent of the popular vote. In 1910 the Socialists of Milwaukee elected Emil Seidel mayor and sent Victor Berger to Congress.

By 1912 the party seemed well on the way to becoming a permanent fixture in American politics. Thirty-three cities had Socialist mayors, including Berkeley, California; Butte, Montana; Flint and Jackson, Michigan; as well as Milwaukee. The party sponsored five English daily newspapers, eight foreign-language dailies, and a number of weeklies and monthlies. Its support was not confined to urban workers and intellectuals. In the Southwest the party built a sizable grass-roots following among farmers and tenants. Oklahoma, for instance, had in 1910 more paid-up party members than any other state except New York, and in 1912 gave 16.5 percent of its popular vote to Debs, a greater proportion than any other state. But the party reached its peak in 1912. During World War I it was wracked by disagreements over America's participation, and was split thereafter by desertions to the new Communist party. A brief revival during the Great Depression served only to interrupt, not halt, its decline.

THE WOBBLIES   During the years of Socialist party growth there emerged a parallel effort to revive industrial unionism, led by the Industrial Workers of the World (IWW). The chief base for this group was the Western Federation of Miners, organized at Butte, Montana, in 1893. Over the next decade the Western Federation was the storm-center of violent confrontation with unyielding bosses who mobilized private armies against it at Leadville and Cripple Creek in Colorado, in the Coeur d'Alenes of Idaho, and elsewhere. In June 1905 the founding convention of the IWW drew a variety of people who opposed the AFL's philosophy. Debs participated, although many of his comrades preferred to work within the AFL. DeLeon was of course happy at

"One Big Union." The Arlington, Virginia, branch of the Industrial Workers of the World. [Archives of Labor and Urban Affairs, Wayne State University]

this chance to strike back at craft unionism. A radical manifesto issued from the meetings, arguing that the IWW "must be founded on the class struggle, and its general administration must be conducted in harmony with the recognition of the irrepressible conflict between the capitalist class and the working class."

But the IWW waged class war better than it articulated class ideology. Like the Knights of Labor, it was designed to be "One Big Union," including all workers, skilled or unskilled. Its roots were in the mining and lumber camps of the West, where unstable conditions of employment created a large number of nomadic workers, to whom neither the AFL's pragmatic approach nor the socialists' political appeal held much attraction. The revolutionary goal of the Wobblies, as they came to be called, was an idea labeled syndicalism by its French supporters: the ultimate destruction of the state and its replacement by one big Union. "We have been *naught*—We shall be *All!*" went their version of the *Internationale*. "The industrial Union Shall be the Human Race." But just how it would govern remained vague.

Like other radical groups it was split by sectarian disputes. Because of policy disagreements all the major founders withdrew, first the Western Federation of Miners, then Debs, then DeLeon. William D. "Big Bill" Haywood of the Western Federation remained, however, and as its leader held the group together. But the Wobblies were reaching out to the fringe elements of least power and influence, chiefly the migratory workers of the West and the ethnic groups of the East. Always ambivalent about diluting their revolutionary principles, they scorned the usual labor agreements, even when they participated in them. Consequently they engaged in spectacular battles with capital but scored few victories, the largest of which was a textile strike at Lawrence, Massachusetts, in 1912, which ended with wage raises, overtime pay, and other benefits. But the next year a strike of silk workers at Paterson, New Jersey, ended in disaster, and the IWW entered a rapid decline.

The IWW was effectively destroyed during World War I, when most of its leaders were jailed for conspiracy because of their militant opposition to the war. Big Bill Haywood fled to the Soviet Union, where he died and was honored by burial in the Kremlin wall. But the IWW, decried as a conduit for alien ideas, was actually an American original, born of the rough-and-tumble world of western miners and migrants. The Wobblies left behind a rich folklore of nomadic working stiffs and bindlebums, martyrs like the Swedish songster and labor organizer Joe Hill, framed (so the faithful assumed) for murder and executed in Utah, and the folk music of *The Little Red Song Book*, rediscovered by singers of a later generation.

FURTHER READING

All surveys of the Gilded Age deal extensively with developments in business and labor. Consult the relevant chapters in Robert H. Wiebe's *The Search for Order, 1877–1920* (1966),° John A. Garraty's *The New Commonwealth, 1877–1890* (1968),° and Samuel P. Hays's *The Response to Industrialism, 1885–1914* (1957).° Other works deal more strictly with the development of commerce. They include Howard M. Jones's *The Age of Energy: Varieties of American Experience, 1865–1915* (1970),° Thomas C. Cochrane and William Miller's *The Age of Enterprise* (1942),° Edward C. Kirkland's *Industry Comes of Age* (1961), and Glenn Porter's *The Rise of Big Business, 1860–1910* (1973).° Of particular interest are Sidney Fine's *Laissez-Faire and the General-Welfare State: A Study of Conflict in American Thought, 1865–1901* (1956), which gauges public opinion about the effects of business, and Alfred D. Chandler's *The Visible Hand: The Managerial Revolution in American Business* (1977),° which details the strategies of the early corporate managers. Also useful is Douglass C. North's quantitative *Growth and Welfare in the American Past* (1966).°

Scholarship on the growth of transportation includes George R. Taylor and Irene D. Neu's *The American Railroad Network, 1861–1890*

°These books are available in paperback editions.

(1956), Robert W. Fogel's *Railroads and American Economic Growth* (1964), and John F. Stover's *The Life and Decline of the American Railroad* (1970). Matthew Josephson's *The Robber Barons* (1934)° denounces the methods used by men like Jay Gould, while Thomas C. Cochrane's *The Railroad Leaders* (1953) is more sympathetic to the entrepreneurs as a group. Gabriel Kolko's *Railroads and Regulation, 1877–1916* (1965),° argues that the entrepreneurs themselves sought regulation.

For an overview of the entrepreneurial leaders, consult Jonathan Hughes's *The Vital Few* (1966). Allen Nevins's *Study in Power: John D. Rockefeller, Industrialist and Philanthropist* (1953), and David F. Hawke's *John D.: The Founding Father of the Rockefellers* (1980) scrutinize that vital individual. Harold F. Williamson and Arnold R. Daum et al., in *The American Petroleum Industry* (2 vols.; 1959–1963), also treat Rockefeller's rise to power. In the iron and steel sector, Peter Temin's *Iron and Steel in Nineteenth Century America: An Economic Inquiry* (1964) surveys development, while Harold Livesay's *Andrew Carnegie and the Rise of Big Business* (1975)° treats the titan of the steel mills. The best available biographies of J. P. Morgan are Andrew Sinclair's *Corsair: The Life of J. Pierpont Morgan* (1981) and George Wheeler's *Pierpont Morgan and Friends: The Anatomy of a Myth* (1973).

Nathan Rosenberg's *Technology and American Economic Growth* (1972) and Elting E. Morison's *From Know-How to Nowhere: The Development of American Technology* (1974) document the growth of invention during the period. More specific are Matthew Josephson's *Edison* (1959), which emphasizes the innovations which came from Edison's laboratory, and R. V. Bruce's *Alexander Graham Bell and the Conquest of Solitude* (1973), which stresses the social impact of technology.

The best introduction to the justification for business growth is Richard Hofstadter's *Social Darwinism in American Thought* (1959). Irwin G. Wyler's *The Self-Made Man in America* (1964) treats the Horatio Alger myth. Robert G. McCloskey's *American Conservatism in the Age of Enterprise* (1951)° and James Weinstein's *The Corporate Ideal in the Liberal State* (1960)° critically analyze laissez-faire capitalism.

Much of the recent scholarship on labor in the Gilded Age stresses the traditional values and the culture of work which the workforce brought to the factory. Herbert G. Gutman's *Work, Culture, and Society in Industrializing America* (1976)° best introduces these themes. Also helpful are Daniel T. Rodgers's *The Work Ethic in Industrial America, 1850–1920* (1974), and Daniel Nelson's *Managers and Workers: Origins of the New Factory System in the United States, 1880–1920* (1975).° Two brief surveys which have chapters on the Gilded Age are Joseph G. Rayback's *A History of American Labor* (1959)° and Henry Pelling's *American Labor* (1959). More specific to the Gilded Age is Melvyn Dubofsky's *Industrialism and the American Worker, 1865–1920* (1975).° David Montgomery, in *Beyond Equality: Labor and the Radical Republicans, 1862–1872* (1975),° and *Workers' Control in America: Studies in the History of Work, Technology, and Labor Struggles* (1979), analyzes the evolution of the work environment.

As for labor groups, Gerald N. Grob's *Workers and Utopia* (1961)° examines the difference in outlook between the Knights of Labor and the American Federation of Labor. For the Knights, see Terence V. Powderly's autobiography, *Thirty Years of Life and Labor, 1859–1889* (1890), and Melton McLaurin's *The Knights of Labor in the South* (1978). Two recent works on the leader of the AFL are Harold C. Livesay's *Samuel Gompers and Organized Labor in America* (1978)° and Stuart Kaufman's *Samuel Gompers and the Origins of the American Federation of Labor* (1978). To trace the rise of socialism among organized workers, see Nick Salivatore's *Eugene V. Debs: Citizen and Socialist* (1983) and Patrick Renshaw's *The Wobblies: The Story of Syndicalism in the United States* (1967).

In addition to the relevant essays in the Gutman volume, Gilded Age strikes and strikers are handled in Daniel Walkowitz's *Worker City, Company Town: Iron and Cotton Worker Protest in Troy and Cahoes, New York, 1855–1884* (1978).

21

THE EMERGENCE OF
MODERN AMERICA

AMERICA'S MOVE TO TOWN

EXPLOSIVE URBAN GROWTH   The frontier was a safety valve, Frederick Jackson Turner said in his influential thesis on America. Its cheap lands afforded a release for the population pressures mounting in the cities. If there was such a thing as a safety valve in his own time, however, he had it just backward. The flow of population toward the city was greater than toward the west, and "country came to town" epitomized the American people better than the occasional city "dude" who turned up in cow country. Much of the westward movement in fact was itself an urban movement, spawning new towns near the mining digs or at the railheads, forming in the arid regions what a later historian would call an "oasis civilization." More often than not, western towns anticipated settlement. They supplied headquarters for the land boomers and services for the hinterlands. On the Pacific coast a greater portion of the population was urbanized than anywhere else; its major concentrations were around San Francisco Bay at first, and then in Los Angeles, which became a boom town after the arrival of the Southern Pacific and Santa Fe Railroads in the 1880s. Remarkably, its salubrious climate and clean air were among Los Angeles's chief selling points. Seattle grew quickly, first as the terminus of three transcontinental railroad lines, and by the end of the century as the staging area for the Yukon gold rush. Minneapolis, St. Paul, Omaha, Kansas City, and Denver were no longer the mere villages they had been in 1860. The

South, too, produced new towns: Durham and Birmingham, which were centers of tobacco and iron manufactures, and Houston, which handled cotton and cattle, and soon, oil.

Trade and transportation had been the city builders of the past. Eight of the nine cities that by 1860 had passed 100,000 in population were ports, and the ninth (Brooklyn) was a suburb to the largest port. By the late nineteenth century no city could hope to thrive without at least one railroad, and most could boast a cluster of railroads. But it was the explosion in industry that powered the growth of new cities during this period. Industry brought huge concentrations of labor, and both required the proliferation of services that became synonymous with city life.

The emergence of the major cities was completed during the years from 1860 to 1910. After that, new cities sprang up only in unusual circumstances: Miami was the product of tourism brought by the coastal railroad, while Tulsa was the product of an oil boom. In those fifty years, population in incorporated towns of 2,500 or more grew from 6.2 million to 44.6 million, or from 19.8 to 45.7 percent of the nation's total population. After 1920 more than half the nation's population would be urban.

While the Far West had the greatest proportion of urban population, the Northeast had far greater numbers of people in the teeming cities north of the Ohio River and east of the Mississippi. There the situation that Jefferson had so dreaded was coming to pass: the people "piled high up on one another in the cities," and worse, these people increasingly were landless, tool-less, and homeless—an urban proletariat with nothing but their labor to sell. By 1900 more than 90 percent of the residents in Manhattan lived in rented homes or tenements. In Boston, Fall River, Jersey City, Memphis, four-fifths of the inhabitants were renters.

The cities expanded both vertically and horizontally to absorb their huge populations. In either case progress in the means of conveyance played an important role: the elevator, the streetcar, and before the end of the century the first automobiles. The first safety elevator, which would not fall if the rope or cable broke, was developed in 1852 by Elisha Graves Otis. In 1889 the Otis Elevator Company installed the first electric elevator, which made possible the erection of taller buildings. Before the 1860s few structures had gone higher than three or four stories.

Another support for the vertical city came from the engineers who developed cast-iron and steel-frame construction. Much of the impulse to new design centered in Chicago, which had to re-build after the great fire of 1871. There William LeBaron Jenney built a metal skeleton for the ten-story Home Life Insurance

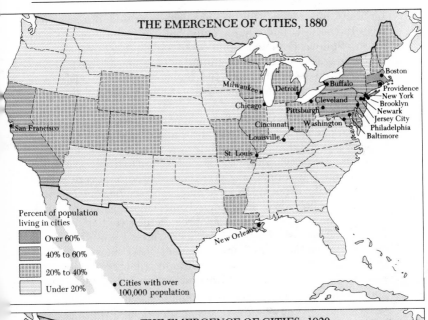

THE EMERGENCE OF CITIES, 1880

Boston
Providence
New York
Brooklyn
Newark
Jersey City
Philadelphia
Baltimore

Milwaukee
Detroit
Buffalo
Chicago
Cleveland
Pittsburgh
Cincinnati
Washington
Louisville
St. Louis

San Francisco

New Orleans

Percent of population
living in cities

Over 60%
40% to 60%
20% to 40%
Under 20%

• Cities with over
100,000 population

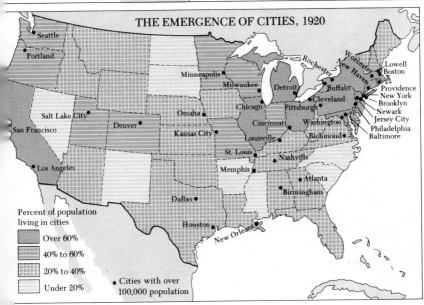

THE EMERGENCE OF CITIES, 1920

Seattle
Portland

Worcester
New Haven
Lowell
Boston
Rochester
Providence
New York
Brooklyn
Newark
Jersey City
Philadelphia
Baltimore

Minneapolis
Milwaukee
Detroit
Buffalo
Chicago
Cleveland
Pittsburgh
Omaha
Cincinnati
Washington
Salt Lake City
Denver
Kansas City
Louisville
Richmond
San Francisco
St. Louis
Nashville
Memphis
Los Angeles
Atlanta
Birmingham
Dallas
Houston
New Orleans

Percent of population
living in cities

Over 60%
40% to 60%
20% to 40%
Under 20%

• Cities with over
100,000 population

building, finished in 1885. Other architects added a sense of style to the new techniques. Louis Sullivan, whose motto was "Form Follows Function," pioneered a plain functional style in reaction against elaborate Victorian decoration. Other popular architectural styles included the Romanesque, with elaborate stone and masonry, the Italian Renaissance style, and the neo-classical.

Before the 1890s the chief sources of urban transport were either animals or steam. Horse- and mule-drawn streetcars had appeared in antebellum cities, but they were slow and cumbersome, and cleaning up after the animals added to the cost. Animal power, like the automobile later, contributed to severe pollution, but in its own way. In 1873 San Francisco became the first city to use cable cars which clamped onto a moving underground cable driven by a central power source. In the twentieth century it would become the last to use cable cars, after a few other cities tried and gave them up. Some cities used steam-powered trains on elevated tracks, but by the 1890s electric trolleys were replacing these. The electrical traction system in Richmond, Virginia, completed by Frank J. Sprague in 1888, is generally regarded as the first successful trolley system in a city of any size. Such systems spread rapidly, and in some places mass-transit companies began to dig underground passages for their cars. Around the turn of the century subway systems began to function in Boston, New York, and Philadelphia. Advances in bridge building through the use of steel and the perfection of the steel-cable

Carson, Pirie, Scott & Co. Louis Sullivan designed this Chicago store, built in the 1890s. [Chicago Architectural Photo Company]

The Elevated Rail Road, looking north on Eighth Avenue in New York City, 1883. Here, mass transit preceded urban growth. [Library of Congress]

suspension bridge also enlarged the reach of commuters. The marvels of the age were James B. Eads's cantilevered steel bridge over the Mississippi at St. Louis (1874) and John A. and Washington Roebling's cable-supported Brooklyn Bridge (1883), which linked Brooklyn to Manhattan.

The spread of mass transit made it possible now for large numbers of people to become commuters, and a growing middle class (working people often could not afford even the nickel fare) retreated to quieter tree-lined "streetcar suburbs" whence they could travel into the central city for business or entertainment. The pattern of urban growth often became a sprawl, however, since it took place usually without plan, in the interest of a fast buck, and without thought to the need for parks and public services. But some cities and developers had the wit to look ahead. New York in the early 1850s had set up a park commission which hired Frederick Law Olmsted as superintendent to plan Central Park. Olmsted later planned parks and even new subdivisions in San Francisco, Brooklyn, Chicago, and other cities.

CITY PLANNING   Chicago's World Fair, the Columbian Exposition of 1893–1894, gave impetus to a "city beautiful" movement. The fair was of such size that a whole new city had to be built on Chicago's South Side lakefront and supplied with a complex of services. Olmsted helped with the choice of a site, and the planning brought together leading architects and engineers. One planning session was called "the greatest meeting of artists since the fifteenth century."

The success of what visitors took to calling the "White City" stirred a new interest in city planning. Among the early fruits of the enthusiasm was a project to commemorate Washington, D.C.'s centennial in 1900 by completing L'Enfant's plan for a mall from the Capitol to the Potomac and the landscaping of Rock Creek Park. New civic centers sprang up in San Francisco, Cleveland, and Chicago, and new riverfront and lakefront plans in Harrisburg and Chicago. Hartford created the first city-planning commission in 1907, and in 1916 the American City Planning Institute, a professional organization of planners, met for the first time.

CITY PROBLEMS AND POLITICS   Although housing conditions in the mill villages of the New South could be bad indeed, one observer who saw laborers going to work through the pine woods at Lyman, South Carolina, noted the contrast to "the stuffy, crowded subways and the crowded elevated" of the metropolis. But workers in the big cities often had no choice other than crowded tenements, most of which were poorly designed. The new dumbbell tenements that began to appear in New York in the late 1870s derived their name from their shape: a narrow airshaft on either side at the middle made possible, even for a building crowded into a standard 25- by 100-foot lot, at least a small window in every room, giving some measure of light and ventilation. By the time the state adopted a stricter tenement law in 1901 the dumbbells had spread across the city. In 1900 Manhattan numbered 42,700 tenements which housed almost 1.6 million people, an average of 33.58 residents per building. Before the day of high-rise apartments this represented an extremely high density. Other cities were less densely populated, but the spread of slums with urban growth created immense problems of health and morale.

The sheer size of these cities helped create a new politics. Since individuals could hardly provide for themselves such necessary services as transit, paving, water, sewers, street lighting and cleaning, and fire and police protection, they came increasingly to rely on city government for these things. Before city agencies took over these functions, operating with some degree of efficiency, they were handled by local political bosses who traded in patronage favors, and graft. Big-city machines were not altogether sinister in their effects: they provided food and money for the poor, fixed problems at city hall, and generally helped immigrants in their adjustment to a new life. Martin Lomasney, a ward boss in Boston, said: "There's got to be in every ward somebody that any bloke can come to—no matter what he's done—

Overcrowding in New York. Jacob Riis took this photograph of a tenement on Bayard Street in 1889. [Museum of the City of New York]

and get help. Help, you understand, none of your law and justice, but help.''

In return the political professionals felt entitled to some reward for having done the grubby work of the local organization. George Washington Plunkitt, for instance, a power in Tammany Hall (New York City's Democratic organization) at the turn of the century, saw nothing wrong with a little honest graft. "Well, I'm tipped off, say, that they're going to lay out a new park at a certain place. . . . I go to that place and buy up all the land I can in the neighborhood. . . . Ain't it perfectly honest to charge a good price and make a profit on my investment and foresight?'' Dishonest graft would consist of ''robbin' the city treasury or levyin' blackmail on disorderly houses or workin' in with the gamblers and lawbreakers.'' For his own epitaph Plunkitt proposed: "He Seen His Opportunitities, and He Took 'Em.''

MOVING FROM COUNTRY TO CITY   But whatever the problems of the cities, the wonder of their glittering new arc and electric lights, their streetcars, telephones, amusements, newspapers and magazines, and a thousand other things exerted a magnetic lure on the youth of the farms. Hamlin Garland told in his autobiography, *A Son of the Middle Border,* of his mixed sense of dread and wonder at first visiting Chicago with his brother. The city first appeared from the train window enveloped in clouds of smoke, ''the soaring banners of the great and gloomy inland metropolis, whose dens of vice and houses of greed had been so often reported to me.'' Later the two young men wandered the streets: ''Everything interested us. The business section so sordid to others was grandly terrifying to us. . . . Nothing was commonplace, nothing was ugly to us.''

Luck and Pluck. *The young hero of Horatio Alger's story leaves his home in the country for the city where, with some luck and pluck, he will make good.* [New York Public Library]

The new cities threw into stark contrast the frustration of unending toil, the isolation and loneliness of country life. In times of rural depression thousands left for the cities in search of the opportunity that Horatio Alger and other writers of success literature dangled before their eyes. The exodus from the countryside was especially evident in the East, where the census documented the shift in population from country to city, and stories began to appear of entire regions where buildings were abandoned and going to ruin, where the wilderness was reclaiming farms that had been wrested from it during the previous 250 years.

THE NEW IMMIGRATION

AMERICA'S PULL   Newcomers to the cities arrived not only from the surrounding hinterland but from Europe as well. European immigrants also were often moving from country to city, and increasingly from the great agricultural areas of eastern and southern Europe directly to the foremost cities of America. They gathered in these cities in order to live with others of like language, customs, and religion, and also because they lacked the means to go west and take up farms. Though cities of the South and West (excepting the Far West) drew their populations mainly from the native-born of their regions, American cities as a whole drew more residents from abroad. During the peak decade of immigration, 1900–1910, 41 percent of the urban newcomers arrived from abroad, while 29.8 percent were native Americans, 21.6 percent were the products of natural increase, and 7.6 percent lived in areas annexed to the cities.

Ethnic neighborhoods, "Little Italys," "Hunkertowns," "Chinatowns," sometimes populated by those from a single province or town, preserved familiar ways and shielded newcomers from the shocks of a strange culture. Such communities grew to be so large they soon overshadowed their Old World counterparts. In 1890 four out of five New Yorkers were foreign-born, a higher proportion than any other city in the world. It had twice as many Irish as Dublin, as many Germans as Hamburg, and half as many Italians as Naples. "A map of the city, colored to designate nationalities," Jacob Riis (a native of Denmark) wrote in *How the Other Half Lives* (1890), "would show more stripes than . . . a zebra, and more colors than any rainbow." In 1893 Chicago claimed the largest Bohemian (Czech) community in the world, and by 1910 the size of its Polish population ranked behind only Warsaw and Lodz.

This nation of immigrants continued to draw new inhabitants for much the same reasons as always, and from much the same strata of society. Immigrants came in flight from famine or the grinding lack of opportunity in their native lands. They fled racial, religious, and political persecution, or the imposition of compulsory military service. Yet one historian has claimed that "the desire to get cheap labor, to take in passenger fares, and to sell land have probably brought more immigrants than the hard conditions of Europe, Asia, and Africa have sent."

More immigrants probably were pulled by America's promise than were pushed by conditions at home. American industries, seeking cheap labor, kept agents abroad and at American ports to solicit members of depressed groups. Railroads, eager to sell land and build up the traffic on their lines, put out tempting propaganda in a medley of languages. Many of the western and southern states set up official bureaus and agents to attract immigrants. Under the Contract Labor Law of 1864 the federal government itself encouraged immigration by providing a lien on the immigrant's wages in order to pay for his or her passage. The law was repealed in 1868, but not until 1885 did the government forbid companies to import contract labor, which had put immigrant workers under the control of their employers. Domestic service and some skilled occupations were exempted from the ban, and evasion was easy.

From 1820 (when by requirement of Congress official statistics on immigration began to be kept) to 1900 about 20 million immigrants entered American ports, more than half of them coming after the Civil War. The tide of immigration rose from just under 3 million in the 1870s to more than 5 million in the 1880s, then fell to a little over 3.5 million in the depression dec-

Immigrants about to arrive at New York's Ellis Island in 1906. [Library of Congress]

ade of the 1890s, and rose to its high-water mark of 8.8 million in the first decade of the new century. The numbers declined to 5.7 million in the 1910s and 4.1 million in the 1920s, after which official restrictions cut the flow of immigration down to a negligible level.

A NEW WAVE   During the 1880s the continuing search for cheap labor combined with renewed persecutions in eastern Europe to bring a noticeable change in the source of immigration, one fraught with meaning for American social history. Before 1880 immigrants were mainly of Teutonic and Celtic origin, hailing from northern and western Europe. But by the 1870s there were signs of a change. The proportion of Latin, Slavic, and Jewish peoples from southern and eastern Europe rose sharply. After 1890 these groups made up a majority of the newcomers, and by the first decade of the new century they formed 70 percent of the immigrants to this country. Among these new immigrants were Italians, Hungarians, Czechs, Slovaks, Poles, Serbs, Croats, Slovenes, Russians, Rumanians, and Greeks—all people of markedly different cultural and language stocks from those of western Europe, and most followers of different religions, including Judaism and Catholicism.

THE NATIVIST RESPONSE   Many Americans of native stock saw the new immigration as a threat, not as an enrichment of American culture. The "clannishness" of these new ethnic communities posed a problem of assimilation far more complex than that which had once alarmed Benjamin Franklin, whose colonial Pennsylvania had only to assimilate Germans and Ulster Scots to a still-formative culture. The new immigrants found in America attitudes like those of Prof. Ellwood P. Cubberley of Stanford University, who called them "Illiterate, docile, lacking in self-reliance and initiative, and not possessing the Anglo-Teutonic conceptions of law, order, and government. . . ." The undercurrent of nativism so often present in American culture now surfaced mainly in anti-Catholic, and secondarily anti-Semitic, sentiments. The Catholic church in America, long dominated by the English-speaking Irish, now became a polyglot group all the more subject to misunderstanding and persecution. Similarly, Russian and Polish Jews came from a far different tradition than the Sephardic and German Jews who preceded them. Their unruly beards, long black coats, and their distinctive language, Yiddish, made them seem almost as strange to old Jewish stock as to other Americans.

More than religious prejudice underlay hostility toward the latest newcomers. Cultural differences confirmed in the minds of nativists the assumption that the Nordic peoples of the old immigration were superior to the Slavic and Latin peoples of the new immigration. Many of the new immigrants were illiterate, and more appeared so because they could not speak English. Some

An immigrant family, Ellis Island, New York, ca. 1910. The unfamiliar ways of immigrants from southern and eastern Europe reawakened nativist sentiment in America. [Library of Congress]

resorted to crime in order to survive in the new land, encouraging suspicions that criminals were being quietly helped out of Europe just as they had once been transported from England to the colonies. Italians from Sicily knew the tradition of Mafia, which bred a spirit of defiance to law and its enforcers. In the early 1890s vendettas among Italian gangs in New Orleans led to the murder of the police chief and the lynching of eleven Italian suspects, an incident which convinced many that the new immigrants were criminals.

The success of the Irish in city politics was emulated by the newer groups, who also thereby offended the sensibilities of well-born natives. Political and social radicals turned up among these immigrant groups in sufficient numbers to encourage nativists to blame labor disputes on alien elements. Such charges harbored a fine irony, however, because mainline labor organizations generally favored restricting immigration to keep down the competition for jobs. Employers sometimes used immigrants as strikebreakers; those who came from peasant origins, and were unfamiliar with strikes, were apt as not to think they were merely taking jobs that others had abandoned. Employers also learned quickly that a babel of tongues could confound unity of action among workers.

A resurgence of nativism in the 1880s was marked by the growth of groups devoted to saving the country from imaginary papal conspiracies. The most successful of these nativist groups, the American Protective Association, operated mainly in Protestant strongholds of the upper Mississippi Valley. Its organizer, Henry F. Bowers of Clinton, Iowa, seemed addicted to paranoid fantasies of Catholic conspiracies, and was especially concerned to keep the public schools free from Jesuit control. The movement grew slowly until 1893, when keen leaders took advantage of a severe depression to draw large numbers of the frustrated to its ranks. The APA soon vanished, swallowed up in the Populist and free-silver agitations, but while it lasted it promoted restricted immigration, more stringent naturalization requirements, refusal to employ aliens or Catholics, and the teaching of the "American" language in the schools.

IMMIGRATION RESTRICTION The movement to restrict immigration had little success beyond the exclusion of certain individuals deemed undesirable. In 1875, for instance, a new law refused entry to prostitutes and to convicts whose sentences had been remitted in other countries on condition they leave. In 1882 a more general law added lunatics, idiots, and persons likely to become public charges, and over the years other specific undesirables joined the list. In 1891 Rep. Henry Cabot Lodge of Massachusetts took up the cause of excluding illiterates—a measure that would have affected most of the new immigration. Bills embodying the restriction were vetoed by three presidents on the ground that they penalized people for lack of opportunity: Cleveland in 1897, Taft in 1913, and Wilson in 1915 and 1917. The last time, however, Congress overrode the veto.

The one group specifically excluded as a nationality were the Chinese, who were victims of everything the European immigrants suffered, plus color prejudice as well. By 1880 there were some 75,000 Chinese in California, about one-ninth of the population. Their nemesis there was himself an immigrant (from Ireland), Dennis Kearney, leader of the Working Men's party. Many white workers resented the Chinese for accepting lower wages, but their greatest sin, the New York *Nation* opined, was perpetuating "those disgusting habits of thrift, industry, and self-denial."

Exclusion of the Chinese was prevented by the Burlingame Treaty, which in 1868 gave China most-favored-nation status (the same as the best conceded to any other country) with respect to travel and immigration. But by 1880 the urgent need for railway labor had ebbed, and a new treaty with China permitted the United States to "regulate, limit, and suspend" Chinese immigration. In 1882 President Arthur vetoed a twenty-year suspension of immigration from China as actually a prohibition, but accepted a ten-year suspension. This was periodically extended until it was made permanent in 1904.

Chinese immigrants are unfairly excluded from the United States in this 1882 cartoon by Thomas Nast. [The Warder Collection]

April 1, 1882

E Pluribus Unum (Except the Chinese).

PUBLIC EDUCATION

THE SPREAD OF SCHOOLS   The spread of public education helped quicken the emergence of a new America. "The spirit of American institutions is to be looked for in the public schools to a greater degree than anywhere else," wrote William T. Harris, the superintendent of St. Louis schools, philosopher, and proponent of graded schools and professional administration. By the time Harris wrote this in his annual report for 1871, America's commitment to public education was well nigh universal, though performance often fell short of the ideal.

The growing importance of public education is evident in statistics compiled by the national commissioner of education, whose office was created in 1867. In 1870 there were 6.8 million pupils in public schools; by 1920 the number had risen to 21.6 million. The percentage of school-age children in attendance went from 57 to 78 during these years, expenditures from $63 million to over $1 billion, and expenditures per pupil from $9 to $48. City schools quickly became schools of several rooms and separate grades with a teacher for each. In rural areas one-room schools lingered on into the twentieth century, when good roads made it possible to bus children to "consolidated schools." Despite these signs of progress, educational leaders all too often had to struggle against a pattern of political appointments, corruption, and incompetence in the public schools.

The spread of secondary schools accounted for a good bit of the increased enrollment in public schools. In antebellum America private academies prepared those who intended to enter college. At the beginning of the Civil War there were only about 100 public high schools in the whole country, but in the next decades their number grew rapidly to about 800 in 1880 and 6,000 at the turn of the century. Their curricula at first copied the academies' emphasis on higher mathematics and classical languages, but the public schools gradually accommodated their programs to those not going on to college, devising vocational training in such arts as bookkeeping, typing, drafting, and the actual use of tools.

VOCATIONAL TRAINING   Vocational training was most intensely promoted after the Civil War by missionary schools for blacks such as Hampton Institute in Virginia, which trained Booker T. Washington, founder of Tuskegee Institute in Alabama. Another major prophet of the movement was Prof. Calvin M. Woodward

The beginnings of Tuskegee Institute. These three buildings first housed the school, an early leader in providing vocational training for blacks. [Library of Congress]

of St. Louis, who in setting up a school of engineering found his students woefully inept at the use of simple tools. He called on the public schools to teach manual skills as well as more abstract knowledge. Prodded by the National Society for the Promotion of Industrial Education, high schools installed workshops for training in carpentry, printing, drafting, bricklaying, and machine work, and for home management, or "home economics," as well. Under the Smith-Hughes Act of 1917 the national government provided dollar-matching grants for such programs.

Congress had supported vocational training at the college level for many years. The Morrill Act of 1862 granted each state warrants for 30,000 acres per representative and senator, the income from which was to be applied to teaching agriculture and the mechanic arts in what came to be known as the "land-grant colleges." In 1890 a Second Morrill Act began the practice of making federal grants to these colleges. Their outreach, first attempted in Farmers' Institutes, greatly expanded with the rise of the demonstration technique perfected by Seaman A. Knapp, "schoolmaster to American agriculture." In 1903, about a decade after the Mexican boll weevil crossed the Rio Grande, Knapp set up near Terrell, Texas, a demonstration of the best techniques then known to fight the pest. From this beginning, with the support of the Rockefellers' General Education Board, the demonstration technique spread rapidly as a means of getting knowledge into the field. The Smith-Lever Act of 1914 subsidized a permanent Extension Service of county demonstration agents who worked closely with land-grant colleges and state agricultural experiment stations.

HIGHER EDUCATION   American colleges at this time, whether church schools or state "universities," sought to instill discipline, morality, and a curriculum heavy on mathematics and the classics (and in church schools, theology), along with ethics and rhetoric. History, modern languages and literature, and some science were tolerated, although laboratory work would likely be limited to a professor's demonstration to his class. The ill-assorted collection of books that passed for libraries drove faculties to take refuge in textbooks, which often represented the limits of their own knowledge. The college teacher was all too apt to be a young man seeking temporary refuge or a broken-down preacher seeking safe harbor. In 1871 a writer in *The Galaxy* called the typical professor "nondescript, a jack of all trades, equally ready to teach surveying and Latin eloquence, and thankful if his quarter's salary is not docked to whitewash the college fence." A case in point, the versatile J. L. M. Curry of Richmond College, sometime congressman, soldier, preacher, and lawyer, taught English, philosophy, and international and constitutional law. An even more heroic scholar at Columbia University taught mental and moral philosophy, English literature, history, political economy, and logic. One cannot help thinking that the subject matter must have run thin somewhere.

Nevertheless the increasing demand for higher learning drove the college student population up from 52,000 in 1870 to 157,000 in 1890 and to 600,000 in 1920. During the same years the number of institutions rose from 563 to 998 and then to 1,041, and the number of faculty from 5,553 to 15,809 to 48,615. To accommodate the diverse needs of these growing numbers, colleges moved away from rigidly prescribed courses toward an elective system. In 1866 Washington College in Virginia, under its president, Robert E. Lee, adopted electives, and after 1869 Harvard College did so under its young president Charles W. Eliot. The new approach allowed students to favor their strong points and colleges to expand their scope to include all knowledge instead of a few set disciplines. But as Henry Cabot Lodge complained, it also allowed students to "escape without learning anything at all by a judicious selection of unrelated subjects taken up only because they were easy or because the burden imposed by those who taught them was light."

Women's access to higher education improved markedly in

the period. Before the Civil War some colleges had already gone coeducational, and state universities in the West were commonly open to women from the start. But colleges in the South and East fell in line very slowly. Of the women's colleges, Vassar (1865) was the first to teach by the same standards as the best of the men's colleges, though it had to maintain a Preparatory Department for twenty-three years to upgrade poorly prepared entrants. In 1875 two more excellent women's schools appeared in Massachusetts: Wellesley and Smith, the latter being the first to set the same admission requirements as men's colleges. The older women's colleges moved fast to upgrade their standards in the same way.

The dominant new trend in American higher education after the Civil War was the rise of the graduate school. The versatile professors of the old school had a knowledge more broad than deep. With some notable exceptions they engaged in little research, nor were they expected to advance the frontiers of knowledge. But gradually more and more Americans experienced a different system at the German universities, where training was more systematic and focused. After the Civil War the German system became the basis for the modern American university. Yale awarded its first Ph.D. in 1861, and Harvard its first in 1872.

The Johns Hopkins University, opened in Baltimore in 1876, set a new precedent by making graduate work its chief concern. The graduate students gathered in seminar rooms or laboratories, where under the guidance of an experienced scholar they learned a craft, much as journeymen had in the medieval guilds. The crowning achievement, signifying admission to full membership in the craft, was a masterpiece—in this case the Ph.D. dissertation, which it was expected would make an original contribution to knowledge. Clark University at Worcester, Massachusetts, founded in 1887 under the guidance of the prominent psychologist G. Stanley Hall, followed the model of Johns Hopkins. In the early 1890s two more major universities were founded to spread the gospel of Germanic education. The first, established by railroad magnate Leland Stanford (and named after his son, Leland Stanford, Jr.), opened at Palo Alto, California, in 1891, and the following year the University of Chicago, endowed by oil baron John D. Rockefeller, began operation. Meanwhile other established institutions, including Harvard, Columbia, Cornell, Michigan, and Wisconsin, also set up graduate schools, and by 1900 American universities annually conferred upward of 300 doctorates. The Ph.D. was fast becoming the ticket of admission to the guild of professors.

THE RISE OF PROFESSIONALISM   The Ph.D. revolution, moreover, was but one aspect of a growing emphasis on professionalism, with its imposition of standards, licensing of practitioners, and accreditation of professional schools. The number of professional schools grew rapidly in fields such as theology, law, medicine, dentistry, pharmacy, and veterinary medicine. While these fields accounted for 60 schools in 1850, there were 146 in 1875 and 283 in 1900. Growth in numbers brought pressures for higher standards. At Harvard in 1870 one could qualify for a medical degree by attending two lecture courses for four months, proving three years of medical experience, and passing a simple examination. Harvard President Eliot then insisted on requiring three years of class attendance, together with laboratory and clinical work. In 1870 the Harvard Law School developed a rough equivalent to the laboratory by introducing the "case method," which required students to dig out the rules for themselves.

Along with advanced schooling went a movement for licensing practitioners in certain fields. The first state licensing law for dentistry, for instance, came in 1868, for pharmacy in 1874, for veterinary medicine in 1886, for accounting in 1896, and for architecture in 1897. By 1894 twenty-one states held standard examinations for doctors, and fourteen others recognized only graduates from accredited medical schools. Licensing benefited the public by certifying competence in a given field, but it also benefited members of the profession by limiting competition.

A Red Sox home game, 1897. Professional baseball became a major attraction in the late nineteenth century. [Library of Congress]

Learned and professional associations now began to proliferate. Earlier societies, such as the American Association for the Advancement of Science (1848), which had seemed specialized enough, made way for still more specialized groups such as the American Chemical Society (1876), the American Ornithologists' Union (1883), and the National Statistical Association (1888). Modern-language scholars organized in 1883, American historians in 1884, economists in 1885, political scientists in 1889, folklorists in 1888, and all sponsored meetings and journals to keep members in touch with developments in the field. A host of commonplace and simple jobs entered the ranks of the "professions," including barbering, playing baseball, and planning vacations.

THEORIES OF SOCIAL CHANGE

Every field of thought in the postbellum years felt the impact of Charles Darwin's *On the Origin of Species* (1859), which argued that existing species, including humanity itself, had evolved through a long process of "natural selection" from less complex forms of life. Those species adapted to survival by reason of quickness, shrewdness, or other advantages reproduced their kind, while others fell by the wayside. The idea of species evolution shocked those of conventional religious views by contradicting a literal interpretation of the creation stories in Genesis. Heated arguments arose among scientists and clergymen, and the two leading scientists at Harvard took opposing positions, with Asa Gray defending Darwin's theory against Louis Agassiz's denial of its validity. Some of the faithful rejected Darwin's doctrine, while others found their faith severely shaken not only by evolutionary theory but also by the urging of professionals to apply the critical standards of scholarship to the Bible itself, and by the study of comparative religion, which found parallels to biblical stories and doctrines in other faiths. Most of the faithful, however, came to reconcile science and religion. Men like Joseph Le Conte, a scientist at the University of California, and James McCosh, a theologian and president of Princeton, came to view evolution as the Divine Will, as one of the secondary causes through which God worked.

SOCIAL DARWINISM   Though Darwin's theory applied only to biological phenomena, other thinkers drew broader inferences from it. The temptation to apply evolutionary theory to the social world proved irresistible. Darwin's fellow Englishman Herbert

Spencer became the first major prophet of Social Darwinism, and an important influence on American thought. Spencer, whose first works anticipated Darwin, brought forth in eight weighty tomes his *System of Synthetic Philosophy* (1862–1893), an effort to embrace all fields of knowledge within an overall system of Darwinian evolution. He argued that human society and institutions, like organisms, passed through the process of natural selection, which resulted, in Spencer's phrase, in the "survival of the fittest." For Spencer, social evolution implied progress, ending "only in the establisment of the greatest perfection and the most complete happiness."

If, as Spencer believed, society naturally evolved for the better, then the right of the individual to do as he pleased was inviolable, and organized interference with the process of social evolution was a serious mistake. This view amounted to a more ponderous version of Carnegie's "Gospel of Wealth"; it used biological laws to justify the workings of the free market. Social Darwinism implied a governmental policy of hands-off; it decried the regulation of business, the graduated income tax, sanitation and housing regulations, and even protection against medical quacks. All these would only impede progress by contributing to the survival of the unfit. The only acceptable charity was voluntary, and even that was of dubious value. Spencer warned that "fostering the good-for-nothing at the expense of the good, is an extreme cruelty."

Accumulated wealth was the best evidence of fitness. Successful businessmen and corporations were the engines of progress. If small business were crowded out by trusts and monopolies, that too was part of the process. Thus John D. Rockefeller told his Baptist Sunday school class: "The growth of a large business is merely a survival of the fittest. . . . The American Beauty rose can be produced in the splendor and fragrance which bring cheer to its beholder only by sacrificing the early buds which grow up around it. This is not an evil tendency in business. It is merely the working-out of a law of nature and a law of God."

The ideas of Darwin and Spencer were quickly popularized in America. John Fiske, a historian and lecturer, was one of the chief spokesmen for Social Darwinism, writing copiously and speaking to audiences all over the country. In 1872 Edward Livingston Youmans founded *Popular Science Monthly,* which soon became the chief medium for popularizing Darwinism. That same year Darwin's chief academic disciple, William Graham Sumner, took up the new chair of political and social science at Yale. Trained for the ministry and formerly an Episcopal rector, he was given to preaching the gospel of natural selection under titles such as *What Social Classes Owe to Each Other* (1883) and "The Absurd Effort to Make the World Over" (1894).

Sumner's most lasting contribution, made in his book *Folkways* (1907), was to argue that social conditions were set by the working of tradition, or the customs of a community, and not by reason or natural laws. The implication here too was that it would be a mistake for government to interfere with established customs in the name of ideals of equality or natural rights. Democracy, according to Sumner, was a condition based not on reason but on customs arising from the availability of much free land in America. As available land diminished, customs would slowly change, showing democracy to be merely a temporary condition.

REFORM DARWINISM   The influence of Darwin and Spencer over the American mind did not go without challenge. Social Darwinism itself was partly a defense against critics of industrial society. Reform found its major philosopher in an obscure Washington civil servant, Lester Frank Ward, who had fought his way up from poverty and never lost his empathy for the underdog. Ward's book *Dynamic Sociology* (1883) singled out one product of evolution that previous pundits had neglected, the human brain. Man, unlike the animals, had a mind that was "telic," that could shape his ends and purposes. Far from being the helpless pawn of evolution, Ward argued, humanity could improve its situation by reflecting upon it and then acting. People thus had reached a stage at which they could control the process of evolution. The competition extolled by Sumner was in fact highly wasteful, and so was the natural competitive process: plant or cattle breeding, for instance, could actually improve on the results of natural selection.

Ward's Reform Darwinism challenged Sumner's conservative Social Darwinism, holding that cooperation, not competition, would better promote progress. Sumner's "irrational distrust of government" might have been justified in an earlier day of autocracy, but no longer under a representative system. Government could become the agency of progress by striving to reach two main goals: to ameliorate poverty, which impeded the development of the mind, and to promote the education of the masses. "Intelligence, far more than necessity," Ward wrote, "is the mother of invention," and "the influence of knowledge as a social factor, like that of wealth, is proportional to the extent of its distribution." Intellect, rightly informed by science, could plan successfully. In the benevolent "sociocracy" of the future, legislatures would function mainly to sanction decisions worked out in the sociological laboratory.

REALISM IN FACT AND FICTION

HISTORY AND THE SOCIAL SCIENCES The pervasive effect of Darwinism in late nineteenth-century America was comparable to the effect of romanticism in the first part of the century. Like the earlier reaction against the Enlightenment's praise of reason, the trend in social thought now was, as one scholar put it, the "revolt against formalism," that is, a turn against abstract logic and toward concrete reality. The revolt had two salient features: its emphasis on history, on looking to the past for explanations, and its interest in investigating reality broadly through a variety of the social sciences. A succinct expression of the first feature as applied to the law lay in the book by Oliver Wendell Holmes, Jr., *The Common Law* (1881). "The life of the law has not been logic; it has been experience," Holmes explained. And experience was history. "The law embodies the story of a nation's development through many centuries," Holmes wrote, "and it cannot be dealt with as if it contained only the axioms and corollaries of a book of mathematics."

In the milieu of Darwinism the study of history flourished. The historian, like the biologist, studied the process of development, but in the origins and the evolution of society. Under the influence of German scholarship, and the new emphasis on science, history aspired to become "scientific." This meant examining documents and manuscripts critically, using external and internal evidence to determine validity and relevancy. The ideal of the scientific historian was to reproduce history with perfect objectivity, as Leopold von Ranke suggested, as it actually was—a noble if unreachable goal. At the new Johns Hopkins University, Herbert Baxter Adams instilled into a whole generation of historians the "germ theory" of history, which held that the truth about things was to be found in their origins. For most American institutions the germ theory led to the forests of ancient Germany. Frederick Jackson Turner, a student of Adams's, carried to his work on the American frontier his teacher's approach to history as an evolutionary process of adaptation.

Henry Adams spent half a long lifetime in vain quest for the "laws" of history, and ended with the chilling thought that human history was a cycle marked by the accelerating capture and dissipation of energy, so that standards of living rose sharply, but with disruptive effects. "Power leaped from every atom," he wrote. "Man could no longer hold it off. . . . The railways alone approached the carnage of war; automobiles and fire-arms ravaged society, until an earthquake became almost a nervous relaxation." There was much to be said for the new rigor in historical study, less to be said for a growing notion in academe that literary style was irrelevant to the science of history. But Henry Adams presided over a happy marriage of science with art in his nine-volume *History of the United States during the Administrations of Jefferson and Madison* (1889–1891).

Lester Frank Ward's achievements in *Dynamic Sociology* (1883) qualified him as the father of American sociology, but he, like many others, thought of the book as a broad synthesis of the social studies. It fell to Albion W. Small, head of the department at the University of Chicago, to define the field specifically. In his *General Sociology* (1905) Small confined it to the scientific analysis of social phenomena with emphasis on groups in human society. As founder and editor of the *American Journal of Sociology* (1895–present) Small wielded a strong influence in turning sociology from abstract speculation to the study of actual human relations. Theory, once all there was to sociology, gave way to a multitude of special interests: population, the family, ethnic groups, social class, public opinion, and social movements, to name but a few.

Economists made the same transition from abstract theory to the study of actual conditions. This transition was reflected in the statement of principles of the American Economics Association, founded in 1885 by a group of young scholars including Richard T. Ely, Simon Patten, and John Bates Clark. These economists looked "not so much to speculation as to historical and statistical study of actual conditions of economic life for the satisfactory accomplishment of [economic] study" and upheld the state "as an agency whose positive assistance is one of the indispensable conditions of human progress." Simon Patten, an economist at the University of Pennsylvania, argued that the economic problem would soon no longer be scarcity, since modern technology would make possible a surplus of goods, but distribution: how best to distribute goods and services. Wesley C. Mitchell of Columbia and the New School for Social Research carried further the "revolt against formalism" in economics by pioneering the statistical study of business cycles and economic trends.

PRAGMATISM   Around the turn of the century the evolutionary idea found expression in a philosophical principle set forth in mature form by William James in his book *Pragmatism: A New Name for Some Old Ways of Thinking*. James, a professor of philosophy and psychology at Harvard, like Lester Frank Ward was concerned with the role of ideas in the process of evolution. Truth, to James, arose from the testing of new ideas, the value of which lay in their practical consequences. Similarly, scientists could test the validity of their ideas in the laboratory, and judge their import by their applications. James applied the principles of pragmatism even to religion in *Varieties of Religious Experience* (1902), where he noted that prayer in some cases seemed to raise the energy and potential of an individual, making prayer a true and valid experience for those people. Pragmatism reflected a quality often looked upon as genuinely American: the inventive, experimental spirit.

John Dewey, who would become the chief philosopher of pragmatism after James, preferred the term "instrumentalism," by which he meant that ideas were instruments, especially of social reform. Dewey, unlike James, threw himself into movements for the rights of labor and women, the promotion of peace, and the reform of education. Dewey believed that education was the process through which society would gradually progress toward the end of economic democracy. Dewey became the founder of an experimental laboratory school at the University of Chicago in 1895 and the prophet of what was later labeled "progressive education." He emphasized the teaching of history, geography, and science in order to enlarge the child's personal experience. Dewey also pointed out that social conditions had so changed that schools had to find ways to inculcate values once derived from participation in family and community activities. Another important goal of the schools was to keep habits plastic and flexible to prepare children for a changing world. They needed not just knowledge but a critical intelligence to cope with a complex, modern world.

THE LOCAL COLORISTS   American literature responded in different ways to the changes in American life and thought. The local color movement, which emerged after the Civil War, reflected a reunited nation engrossed with the diversity of its peoples and cultures. This movement also expressed the nostalgia of a people moving from a rural to an urban culture and longing for those places where the old verities survived. In California Bret Harte, the editor of the *Overland Monthly,* burst upon the national consciousness in the late 1860s with colorful stories of the gold country such as "The Outcasts of Poker Flat," "The Luck of Roaring Camp," and his best known poem, "Plain Language from Truthful James," about the "Heathen Chinee." Hamlin Garland, in *Main Traveled Roads* (1891), pictured the hardscrabble existence of farmers and their wives in his native country, the upper Midwest from Wisconsin to the Dakotas. Sarah Orne Jewett depicted the down-easters of her native Maine, most enduringly in the stories and sketches collected in *The Country of the Pointed Firs* (1896), while Mary E. Wilkins Freeman wrote stories of village life in Vermont and Massachusetts gathered in *A Humble Romance* (1887) and other works.

Once the passions of war and Reconstruction were spent, the South became for many northern readers an inexhaustible gallery of quaint types. George Washington Cable exploited the local color of the quaint Louisiana Creoles and Cajuns in *Old Creole Days* (1879), *The Grandissimes* (1880), *Madame Delphine* (1881), and other books. Joel Chandler Harris, a newsman and columnist, wove authentic Afro-American folk tales into the unforgettable stories of Uncle Remus, gathered first in *Uncle Remus: His Songs and His Sayings* (1880). Few Americans, whether they have read the stories or not, can long remain ignorant of the wonderful tar-baby or the brier patch.

TWAIN, HOWELL, AND JAMES   The best of the local colorists could find universal truths in local life, but Samuel Langhorne Clemens (Mark Twain) transcended them all. A native of Missouri, Clemens was forced to work from the time he was twelve, becoming first a printer and then a Mississippi riverboat pilot. When the Civil War shut down the river traffic, he briefly joined a Confederate militia company, then accompanied his brother Orion to Nevada, where he wrote for the *Territorial Enterprise*. He moved on to California in 1864, where he first gained widespread notice with his tall tale of the gold country, "The Jumping Frog of Cala-

Samuel Langhorne Clemens, or Mark Twain. [Mark Twain Memorial, Hartford, Conn.]

veras County" (1865). In 1867 the San Francisco *Alta Californian* staked him to a tour of the Mediterranean, and his humorous reports on the trip, revised and collected into *Innocents Abroad* (1869), established him as a funny man much in demand on the lecture circuit. With the success of *Roughing It* (1871), an account of his western years, he moved to Hartford and was able to set up as a full-time author and lecturer.

Clemens was the first great American writer born and raised west of the Appalachians. His early writings accentuated his western background, but for his greatest books he drew heavily upon his boyhood in a border slave state and the tall-tale tradition of southwestern humor. In *The Adventures of Tom Sawyer* (1876) he evoked in fiction the prewar Hannibal, Missouri, where his own boyhood was cut so short. Its story of childhood adventures is firmly etched on the American memory. *Life on the Mississippi* (1883), based on articles written eight years before, drew upon what Clemens remembered as his happiest days as a young riverboat pilot before the war.

Twain's masterpiece, *The Adventures of Huckleberry Finn* (1884), created unforgettable characters in Huck Finn, his shiftless father, Nigger Jim, the Widow Douglas, the "King," and the "Duke." The product of an erratic upbringing, Huck Finn embodied the instinct of every red-blooded American boy to "light out for the territory" whenever polite society set out to civilize him. Huck's effort to help his friend Jim escape bondage expressed well the moral dilemmas imposed on everyone by slavery. Many years later another great American writer, Ernest Hemingway, would claim that "All modern literature comes from one book by Mark Twain, called *Huckleberry Finn.*"

Twain wrote other memorable books, but nothing to equal those three. Like many humorists he had a broad streak of pessimism. He preferred to laugh rather than gaze into the abyss, but eventually the laughter stopped. Speculative investments bankrupted him during the Panic of 1893 and sent him back to the lecture circuits. Then his oldest daughter died of meningitis and his wife went into a long decline. His later writings, many not published before his death, expressed despair about what Clemens took to calling "that damned human race," but he himself remained a revered national treasure. As his friend William Dean Howells observed, he was unique among his contemporaries: "Emerson, Longfellow, Lowell, Holmes—I knew them all and all the rest of our sages, poets, seers, critics, humorists; they were like one another and like other literary men; but Clemens was sole, incomparable, the Lincoln of our literature."

Howells himself was unique, for no other American writer ever so dominated the scene as literary arbiter. Born in Ohio, he went to Boston in 1867 and soon became editor of the influential *Atlantic Monthly*. He left that post in 1881 to devote himself to novel writing, but later served better than two decades as a columnist and critic for *Harper's Monthly*. Howells proclaimed the doctrine of realism, a sort of literary version of scientific history's effort to reproduce the past as it actually happened. He wrote that realism "was nothing more or less than the truthful treatment of . . . the motives, the impulses, the principles that shape the life of actual men and women." The realist commonly wrote of the middle class in a simple and direct language, taking a pragmatic, objective point of view.

Howells wrote novels, plays, travel books, criticism, essays, biography, and autobiography. Amid the varied output of a long and productive life, *The Rise of Silas Lapham* (1885) stands out as his most famous novel. In it Howells presented a sympathetic portrayal of a *nouveau riche* manufacturer from the West, and one of the earliest fictional treatments of an American businessman. Soon after its publication, however, at the height of his career, Howells felt that "the bottom had dropped out" of his life. Converted to socialism by reading Tolstoy, horrified by the "civic murder" of the Haymarket anarchists, he entered a new phase. In *A Hazard of New Fortunes* (1890) he offered less sympathetic views of businessmen, included scenes of squalor and misery in the Bowery, and introduced a German-American socialist who lost his life in a police beating during a violent streetcar strike.

The third major literary figure of the times, Henry James, moved in a world far different from those of Clemens or Howells. Brother of the pragmatist philosopher William James, Henry spent most of his adult life as a voluntary expatriate in London, where he produced elegant novels that for the first time explored the international society of Americans in Europe. In novels such as *Daisy Miller* (1878), *Portrait of a Lady* (1881), *The Ambassadors* (1903), and *The Golden Bowl* (1904), James explored the tensions that developed between direct, innocent, and idealistic Americans (most often young women) and sophisticated, devious Europeans. James typically wrote of the upper classes, and his stories turned less on plot than on moral dilemmas. His intense exploration of the inner selves of his characters brought him the titles of "father of the psychological novel" and "biographer of fine consciences." What was more, he could produce spine-tingling ghost stories such as "The Turn of the Screw"

(1898) and "The Jolly Corner" (1907). In his later work he pioneered the technique of removing the author from the reader's awareness, becoming "invisible," as T. S. Eliot said, a technique commonplace among later authors.

LITERARY NATURALISM   During the 1890s the naturalists emerged as a new literary school, the heralds of twentieth-century modernism. Naturalism reacted against realism as realism had reacted against romanticism. The naturalists imported scientific determinism into literature, viewing man as part of the animal world, prey to natural forces and internal drives without control or full knowledge of them. From Darwin, their greatest inspiration, they drew biological determinism, from Newton a mechanistic determinism, and from Karl Marx a type of historical determinism. Frank Norris, who drew inspiration from the French novelist Emile Zola, pictured in *McTeague* (1899) the degeneration of a San Francisco dentist and his wife into madness, driven by greed, violence, and lust. Norris's *The Octopus* (1901), first of an unfinished trilogy on the lives of wheat farmers, presented the attempt of railroad owners to squeeze out the ranchers from the wheatfields of California. Stephen Crane in *Maggie: A Girl of the Streets* (1893) and *The Red Badge of Courage* (1895) pictured people caught up in situations beyond their control. *Maggie* depicted a girl driven to prostitution and death amid scenes so sordid that Crane had to finance publication himself. *The Red Badge of Courage,* his masterpiece, told the story of a young man going through his baptism of fire in the Civil War, and evoked nobility and courage amid the ungovernable carnage of war. Crane himself had had no experience of battle, which made his achievement the more remarkable.

Two of the naturalists achieved a degree of popular success: Jack London and Theodore Dreiser. Jack London of California was both a professed socialist and a believer in the philosopher Friedrich Nietzsche's doctrine of the superman. In adventure stories like *Call of the Wild* (1903) and *The Sea Wolf* (1904) London celebrated the triumph of brute force and the will to survive. He reinforced his point about animal force in the *Call of the Wild* by making his protagonist not a superman but a superdog who reverted to the wild in Alaska and ran with a wolf pack.

Theodore Dreiser shocked the genteel public probably more than the others with protagonists who sinned without remorse and without punishment. *Sister Carrie* (1900), a companion piece to *Maggie,* departed from it in having Carrie Meeber survive illicit loves and go on to success on the stage. In *The Finan-*

cier (1912) and *The Titan* (1914) Dreiser pictured in Frank Cowperwood (modeled on the Chicago speculator Charles T. Yerkes) a sexual athlete and a man of elemental force who rose to a dominant position in business and society. *An American Tragedy* (1925), generally regarded as Dreiser's masterpiece, pictured a less successful young man driven by the desire for sex and money to murder his pregnant mistress in order to marry wealth. He eventually was convicted and executed.

SOCIAL CRITICISM   Behind their dogma of determinism the naturalists harbored intense outrage at human misery. Other writers addressed themselves more directly to protest and reform. Henry George, a California printer and journalist, was suddenly struck on a visit to New York by the contrast the city offered between wealth and poverty. "Once, in daylight, and in a city street, there came to me a thought, a vision, a call. . . . And there and then I made a vow." The vow was to seek out the cause of poverty in the midst of progress. Back in California, the spectacle of land boomers grabbing choice sites brought George a new insight. The basic problem, he reasoned, was the unearned increment in wealth that came to those who owned the land. The fruit of his thought, *Progress and Poverty* (1879), a thick and difficult book, started slowly but by 1905 had sold about 2 million copies in several languages.

George held that everyone had as much right to the use of the land as to the air she breathed. Nobody had a right to the value that accrued from the land, since that was created by the community, not by its owner. Labor and capital, on the other hand, did have a just claim on the wealth they produced. One justifiable solution to the problem of unearned wealth was to socialize all property in land, but that would have been too disruptive. Better simply to tax the unearned increment in the value of the land, or the rent. George's "single-tax" idea was intended to free capital and labor from paying tribute for the land, and to put to use lands previously held out of production by speculators. George's idea was widely propagated and actually affected tax policy here and there, but his influence on the thinking of the day came less from his "single-tax" panacea than from the paradox he posed in his title, *Progress and Poverty.*

The journalist and freelance writer Henry Demarest Lloyd addressed himself to what many found a more vital issue than Henry George's, not the monopoly in land but industrial monopoly. His best known book, *Wealth Against Commonwealth* (1894), drew on more than a decade of studying the Standard Oil

Company. Lloyd, like Lester Frank Ward, saw the key to progress in cooperation rather than competition. Economic activities in their cooperative aspects demonstrated a civilizing process; Lloyd argued that "the spectacle of the million or more employees of the railroads . . . dispatching trains, maintaining tracks, collecting fares and freights . . . is possible only where civilization has reached a high average of morals and culture. . . ." But those in charge of the machinery of industry were concerned only with wealth, not with promoting civilization. "Of gods, friends, learning, of the uncomprehended civilization they overrun, they ask but one question: How much? What is a good time to sell? What is a good time to buy?" To avoid destruction, civilization required changes. The cooperative principle should be applied "to all toils in which private sovereignty has become through monopoly a despotism over the public." Where monopoly had developed, it should be transferred to public operation in the public interest. In 1903, just before his death, Lloyd joined the Socialist party.

Thorstein Veblen brought to his social criticism a background of formal training in economics and a purpose of making economics more an evolutionary or historical science. By all accounts he taught miserably, even inaudibly, and seldom held a job for long, but he wrote brilliantly. In his best known work, *The Theory of the Leisure Class* (1899), he examined the pecuniary values of the middle classes and introduced phrases that have since become almost clichés: "conspicuous consumption" and "conspicuous leisure." With the advent of industrial society, Veblen argued, property became the conventional basis of reputation. For the upper classes, moreover, it became necessary to consume time nonproductively as evidence of the ability to afford a life of leisure. In this and later works such as *The Theory of Business Enterprise* (1904) and *The Engineers and the Price System* (1921), Veblen held that the division between industrial experts and business managers was widening to a dangerous point. The businessman's interest in profits combined with his ignorance of productive efficiency to produce wasteful organization and a failure to realize the full potential of modern technology.

Edward Bellamy's *Looking Backward, 2000–1887* (1888) typified another genre of reform literature, the utopian novel. In Bellamy's futuristic story, a Bostonian who falls asleep in 1887 awakens in the year 2000 to find that the millennium has genuinely arrived. More than a hundred years in the future Julian West discovers a society transformed. The revolution which led to political equality has led on, by the democratic method, to a

"Nationalist" society of economic equality under socialism. Everybody gets an equal share of the national product and labor is shared by the simple method of reducing the hours for distasteful jobs until someone is willing to do the work. All this is accomplished by public control under national planning. The book enjoyed a temporary vogue, became a bestseller, and led to the founding of Nationalist Clubs, numbering 163 by 1891. The popularity of Bellamy's book gave rise to a spate of utopian novels, and some antiutopian ones depicting model societies gone wrong.

THE SOCIAL GOSPEL

RISE OF THE INSTITUTIONAL CHURCH The churches responded slowly to the mounting social criticism, for American Protestantism had become one of the main props of the established order. The Rev. Henry Ward Beecher, pastor of the fashionable Plymouth Congregational Church in Brooklyn, preached success, Social Darwinism, and the unworthiness of the poor. Rudyard Kipling in 1899 reported a visit to a church in Chicago where the minister pictured "a heaven along the lines of the Palmer House (but with all the gilding real gold, and all the plate-glass diamond). . . . One sentence . . . caught my delighted ear. It was apropos of some question of the Judgment, and ran: 'NO! I tell you God doesn't do business that way!'"

As the middle classes moved out to the streetcar suburbs, their churches followed. In the years 1868–1888, for instance, seventeen Protestant churches abandoned the areas below Fourteenth Street in Manhattan. In the center of Chicago 60,000 residents had no church, Protestant or Catholic. Where churches became prosperous they fell easily under the spell of respectability and Social Darwinism. Working-class people sometimes felt out of place in opulent edifices with stained-glass windows: "opera-singing churches," revivalist Dwight L. Moody called them.

Many churches responded to the growing secularism of the time by undertaking earthly functions in addition to saving souls. The institutional church devoted most of its resources to community service and care for the unfortunate. The Young Men's Christian Association had entered the United States from England in 1850s and grew rapidly after 1870; the Salvation Army, founded in London in 1876, entered the United States four years later.

Churches in urban districts began to develop institutional features that were more social than strictly religious in function. Before the Civil War William A. Muhlenberg, an Episcopal minister in New York, organized St. Luke's Hospital and St. Johnland, a rural settlement in the Hudson Valley, as a refuge for slum dwellers. In the postbellum years this kind of work spread as church buildings acquired gymnasiums, libraries, lecture rooms, and other facilities for social programs. By 1894 there were enough such churches to form the Open and Institutional Church League. St. George's Episcopal Church exemplified the success of the institutional church: when it first offered institutional features in 1882 it had 75 members; by 1897 it had over 4,000 members. Russell Conwell's Baptist Temple in Philadelphia included, among other features, a night school for working people which grew into Temple University.

RELIGIOUS REFORMERS   The involvement of Conwell, a leading spokesman for the gospel of success, signified that the institutional movement might be consistent with a conservative outlook. But other church leaders built upon the institutional movement by preaching what came to be called the social gospel. One of the earliest, Washington Gladden of Columbus, Ohio, managed to preach the social gospel from the pulpit of a middle-class Congregational church. The new gospel in fact expressed the social conscience of the middle class. Gladden accepted the new ideas of evolution and textual criticism of the Bible, which he said relieved him of defending the literal truth of the story of Jonah and the whale. In *Working People and Their Employers* (1878), *Applied Christianity* (1886), and numerous other books, Gladden set forth the idea that true Christianity lies not in rituals, dogmas, or even in the mystical experience of God, but in the principle that "Thou shalt love thy neighbor as thyself." Christian law should govern the operation of industry, with worker and employer united in serving each other's interest. He argued for labor's right to organize, and complained that the class distinctions of society had invaded and split congregations as well.

The acknowledged intellectual leader of the social gospel movement, however, was the Baptist Walter Rauschenbusch, professor at the Colgate-Rochester Theological Seminary—appropriately located in the unofficial capital of the old Burnt-Over District. In *Christianity and the Social Crisis* (1907) and other works he developed a theological basis for the movement in the Kingdom of God. This kingdom existed in the churches themselves, but it embraced far more than these: "It is the Christian transfiguration of the social order. The church is one social institution alongside of the family, the industrial organization of society, and the State. The Kingdom of God is in all these, and realizes itself through them all. . . ." The church was indispensable to religion, but "the greatest future awaits religion in the public life of humanity."

THE CATHOLIC CHURCH   In the postbellum years Catholics remained inhibited from support of the new social movements by the *Syllabus of Errors* (1864), issued by Pope Pius IX, which declared erroneous such current ideas as progress, liberalism, rationalism, and socialism. James Cardinal Gibbons of Baltimore was instrumental, however, in moderating the effects of the *Syllabus*. In 1886 he forestalled an official condemnation of the Knights of Labor, which had abandoned secrecy and was headed by a Catholic, Terence Powderly. Gibbons also prevented the listing of *Progress and Poverty* on the *Index of Forbidden Books*. The church's outlook altered drastically in 1891 when Pope Leo XIII issued his encyclical, *Rerum novarum* ("Of modern things"). This new expression of Catholic social doctrine upheld private property as a natural right but condemned capitalism where it had imposed poverty and degredation on workers. It upheld the right of Catholics to join labor unions and socialist movements insofar as these were not antireligious. But American Catholics for the most part remained isolated from reform movements until the twentieth century, though they themselves were among the victims of the slums.

EARLY EFFORTS AT URBAN REFORM

THE SETTLEMENT HOUSE MOVEMENT   While preachers of the social gospel dispensed inspiration, dedicated reformers attacked the problems of the slums from residential and community centers called settlement houses. The movement sprang from the example of Toynbee Hall, founded in London's Whitechapel industrial district, where an English vicar, Samuel A. Barrett, invited students to join him in "settling" in a deprived section. Stanton Coit, an early American visitor, established the Neighborhood Guild on New York's Lower East Side in 1886. By 1900 perhaps a hundred settlement houses existed, some of the best known being Jane Addams's and Ellen Starr's Hull House in Chicago (1889), Jane E. Robbins's and Jean Fine's College Settlement in New York (1889), Robert A. Woods's South End House in Boston (1891), and Lillian Wald's Henry Street Settlement in New York.

Jane Addams. [New York Public Library]

The settlement houses were populated mainly by idealistic middle-class young people, a majority of them college-trained women who found the world unready to employ them except in nurturing roles. Settlement workers sought to broaden the horizons and improve the lives of slum dwellers in diverse ways. At Jane Addams's Hull House, for instance, workers sought to draw the neighborhood children into clubs and kindergartens, and a day nursery served the infant children of working mothers. The program gradually expanded as Hull House sponsored health clinics, lectures, music and art studios, an employment bureau, men's clubs, training in skills such as bookbinding, a gymnasium, and a savings bank. The Hull House Players helped initiate the Little Theater movement. Jane Addams and other settlement house leaders realized, however, that the spreading slums made their work as effective as bailing out the ocean with a teaspoon. They therefore spoke out and organized political support for housing laws, public playgrounds, juvenile courts, mothers' pensions, workmen's compensation laws, and legislation against child labor. Lillian Wald promoted the establishment of the federal Children's Bureau in 1912 and Jane Addams, for her work in the peace movement, received late in her life the Nobel Peace Prize for 1931.

The settlement house movement was not all of one piece, however. Critics accused settlements of subtle and not-so-subtle forms of social control, and of attempts to assimilate the poor to middle-class standards. The cultural gap between middle-class social workers and slum dwellers could often lead to misunderstanding, and in the effort to "Americanize" immigrants, the settlement houses and agencies of education sometimes lacked sensitivity to the values of other cultures. But on balance their contributions were more positive than negative. By the end of the century both the Catholic church and Jewish agencies were taking up the settlement house movement.

THE WOMEN'S SUFFRAGE MOVEMENT   Settlement house workers, insofar as they were paid, of course made up but a fraction of all gainfully employed women. With the growth of population the number of employed women steadily increased, as did their percentage of the labor force and of the total female population. The greatest leaps forward came in the decades of the 1880s and the 1900s, both of which were also peak decades of immigration, a correlation which can be explained by the immigrant's need for income. The number of employed women went from over 2.6 million in 1880 to 4 million in 1890, then from 5.1 million in 1900 to 7.8 million in 1910. "Between 1880 and 1900 the employment of women in most parts of the economy became an established fact," wrote one historian. "This was surely the most significant event in the modern history of women." Through all those years domestic work remained the largest category of employment for women; teaching and nursing also remained among the leading fields. The main change was that clerical work (bookkeeping, stenographic work, and the like) and sales jobs became increasingly available to women.

These changes in occupational status had little connection with the women's rights movement, which increasingly focused on the issue of suffrage. Immediately after the Civil War, Susan B. Anthony, a seasoned veteran of the movement though still in her forties, demanded that the Fourteenth Amendment include a guarantee of the vote for women as well as black males. She made little impression on the defenders of masculine prerogative, however, who kept intact the notion that women belonged in the domestic sphere. "Their mission is at home, by their blandishments and their love to assuage the passions of men as they come in from the battle of life . . ." said New Jersey's Senator Frelinghuyson. "It will be a sorry day for this country when those vestal fires of love and piety are put out."

In 1869 the unity of the women's movement was broken in a manner reminiscent of the antislavery rift three decades before. The question once again was whether or not the movement should concentrate on one overriding issue. Anthony and Elizabeth Cady Stanton founded the National Woman Suffrage Association to promote a woman suffrage amendment to the constitution, but they looked upon suffrage as but one among many feminist causes to be promoted as well. Later that same year Lucy Stone, Julia Ward Howe, and other leaders formed the American Woman Suffrage Association, which focused single-mindedly on the suffrage as the first and basic reform.

It would be another half century before the battle could be won, and the long struggle for referenda and state legislation on the issue focused the women's cause ever more on the primary objective of the vote. In 1890, after three years of negotiation, the rival groups united as the National American Woman Suffrage Association, with Elizabeth Cady Stanton as president for two years, to be followed by Susan B. Anthony until 1900. The work thereafter was carried on by a new generation, led by Anna Howard Shaw and Carrie Chapman Catt. Over the years the movement slogged its way to some local and some partial victories, as a few states granted woman suffrage in school board or municipal elections, or bond referenda. In 1869 the Territory of Wyoming granted full suffrage to women, and after 1890 retained woman suffrage as a state. Three other western states soon followed suit: Colorado in 1893, Utah and Idaho in 1896. But woman suffrage lost in a California referendum in 1896 by a dishearteningly narrow margin of 27,000 votes.

The movement remained in the doldrums thereafter until the cause won a Washington state referendum by a two-to-one margin in 1910, and then carried California by a close majority of 3,500 in 1911. The following year three more western states—Arizona, Kansas, and Oregon—joined in to make a total of nine western states with full suffrage. In 1913 Illinois granted women presidential and municipal suffrage. Not until New York acted in 1917 did a state east of the Mississippi adopt universal suffrage. In 1878 California's Sen. A. A. Sargent introduced the "Anthony Amendment," which remained before Congress until 1896 and then vanished until 1913. It was word for word the woman suffrage amendment eventually ratified, but that triumph required another schism in the movement brought on by a new generation of militants who had been fired up by the direct action of the British suffragists (see Chapter 26).

Despite the focus on the vote, women did not confine their public work to that issue. In 1866 a Young Women's Christian Association, a parallel to the YMCA, appeared in Boston and spread elsewhere. The New England Women's Club, started in 1868 by Julia Ward Howe and others, was an early example of the women's clubs which then proliferated to the extent that a General Federation of Women's Clubs tied them together in 1890. Many women's clubs confined themselves to "literary" and social activities, but others became deeply involved in charities and reform. The New York Consumers League, formed in 1890, and the National Consumers League, formed nine years later, sought to make the buying public, chiefly women, aware of labor conditions. One of its devices was the "White List" of firms which met its minimum standards. The National Women's Trade Union League, founded in 1903, performed a similar function of bringing educated and middle-class women together with working women for the benefit of women unionists. These and the many other women's groups of the time may have aroused the fear in opponents to woman suffrage that voting women would tilt toward reform. This was the fear of the brewing and liquor interests, large business interests generally, and political machine bosses. Others, mainly in the South, expressed opposition to woman suffrage on the ground that black women would be enfranchised, or because of states'-rights views.

A JUDICIAL HARBOR FOR LAISSEZ-FAIRE Even without the support of voting women in most places, the states groped toward rudimentary measures to regulate big business and labor conditions in the public interest. By the end of the century nearly every state had provided for the regulation of railroads, if not always effectively, and had moved to supervise banks and insurance companies. North Carolina in 1899 created the first corporation commission, with jurisdiction over railroads, banks, and public utilities. Between 1887 and 1897, by one count, the states and territories passed 1,639 laws relating to conditions of work, which limited the hours of labor, provided special protection for women, limited or forbade child labor, required regular wage payments in cash, called for factory inspections, and outlawed blacklisting or the importation of "Pinkerton men." Nearly all states had boards or commissioners of labor, and some had boards of conciliation and arbitration. As one writer noted at the turn of the century, the labor laws of the time were designed "to secure the liberty of one class by curbing the license of another." Still, the effect of the effort was limited by poor enforcement and a sizable body of contrary opinion which found a special lodgment in the courts, where conservative judges in this era were busily reading laissez-faire into the Constitution.

Their chief devices were either higher-law doctrines or, more often, a revised interpretation of the Fourteenth Amendment's clauses which forbade the states to "deprive any person of life, liberty or property without due process of law" or to deny any person "the equal protection of the laws." Two significant steps of legal reasoning turned the due-process clause into a bulwark of property. First, the judges reasoned that the word "person" in the clause included corporations, which in other connections were legally artificial persons with the right to own property, buy and sell, sue and be sued like natural persons—even though, in a common expression, they had neither tail to kick nor soul to be damned. Second, the courts moved away from the old view that "due process" referred only to procedural rights and toward a doctrine of "substantive due process" which allowed court review of the substance of an action. Under this line of reasoning it was possible for legislatures by perfectly proper procedures to pass laws so extreme (in the view of the judges) as to deprive persons of property to an unreasonable degree, and thereby violate due process.

The Supreme Court first accepted the personality of the corporation in a tax case, *Santa Clara County v. Southern Pacific Railroad Company* (1886). That same year the Court in *Stone v. Farmers Loan and Trust Company* (1886) recognized the authority of Mississippi to regulate railroad rates, but declared that there might be cases in which the Court could review the rates: "Under pretense of regulating fares and freights, the State cannot require a railroad corporation to carry persons or property without reward." In *Chicago, Milwaukee and St. Paul Railway Company v. Minnesota* (1890) the justices declared unconstitutional a state law which forbade judicial review of rates set by a railroad commission. "The question of the reasonableness of a rate of charge . . . is eminently a question for judicial investigation," the Court ruled, "requiring due process of law for its determination." This was a direct reversal of the ruling in *Munn v. Illinois* (1877) that regulation was a legislative prerogative. It remained only for the Court to overturn rates set directly by a state legislature. That it did in *Smyth v. Ames* (1898), in which it struck down a Nebraska law for setting rates so low as to be, in the Court's view, unreasonable.

From the due-process clause the Court also derived a new doctrine of "liberty of contract," defined as being within the liberties protected by the due-process clause. This fine-spun theory first surfaced in *Allgeyer v. Louisiana* (1897), in which the Court struck down a Louisiana law forbidding a citizen to buy an insurance policy from a company that had not qualified to do business in the state. Liberty, the Court ruled, involved "not only the right of the citizen to be free from the mere physical restraint of his person, . . . but the term is deemed to embrace the right of the citizen to be free in the enjoyment of all his faculties," and free "to enter into all contracts" proper to carrying out such purposes. When it came to labor laws, this translated into an employee's "liberty" to contract for work under the most oppressive conditions without interference from the state. The courts continued to apply such an interpretation well into the twentieth century.

Judges in some of the lower courts found no need to spin their theories so fine. In 1886 the Pennsylvania Supreme Court, in striking down an act to protect workers against payment in commodities instead of in cash, declared it "an insulting attempt to put the laborer under a legislative tutelage, which is not only degrading to his manhood, but subversive of his rights as a citizen of the United States." The high court of West Virginia in 1889 condemned a similar law as an attempt to "foist upon the people a paternal government of the most objectionable character, because it assumes that the employer is a knave, and the laborer an imbecile." At least equally boggling in its blindness to reality was the opinion expressed by New York's Judge Robert Earl in the case of *In re Jacobs* (1885), in which he ruled against a law forbidding cigarmaking in tenements. "It cannot be perceived," Earl said, "how the cigarmaker is to be improved in his health or his morals by forcing him from his home and its hallowed associations and beneficent influences, to ply his trade elsewhere."

As the turn of the century neared, opinion in the country stood poised between such conservative rigidities and a growing sense that new occasions teach new duties. "By the last two decades of the century," wrote one observer, "many thoughtful men had begun to march under various banners declaring that somewhere and somehow the promise of the American dream had been lost—they often said 'betrayed'—and that drastic changes needed to be made to recapture it."

The last two decades of the nineteenth century had already seen a slow erosion of laissez-faire values, which had found their most secure home in the courts. From the social philosophy of the reformers, Social Gospelers, and Populists there emerged a concept of the general-welfare state which, in the words of the historian Sidney Fine, sought "to promote the general welfare not by rendering itself inconspicuous but by taking such positive action as is deemed necessary to improve the condition under which its citizens live and work." The reformers supplied no agreed-upon blueprint for a general-welfare utopia, but "simply assumed that government could promote the public interest by appropriate positive action . . . whenever the circumstances indicated that such action would further the common weal." The conflict between this notion and laissez-faire values went on into the new century, but by the mid–twentieth century, after the Progressive Movement, the New Deal, and the Fair Deal, the conflict would be "resolved in theory, in practice, and in public esteem in favor of the general-welfare state."

Further Reading

No one work synthesizes fully all aspects of Gilded Age life covered in this chapter. John A. Garraty's *The New Commonwealth, 1877–1890* (1968),° deals well with trends during the 1880s, while Robert H. Wiebe's *The Search for Order, 1877–1920* (1967),° thoroughly depicts the changes which began to transform American thought near the turn of the twentieth century. Other interpretations can be found in Howard Mumford Jones's *The Age of Energy: Varieties of American Experience* (1970) and Alan Trachtenberg's *The Incorporation of America: Culture and Society in the Gilded Age* (1982).°

Recent surveys of urbanization include Howard Chudacoff's *The Evolution of American Urban Society* (1975), Zane Miller's *The Urbanization of America* (1973), and A. Theodore Brown's *A History of Urban America* (1967). Stephen Thernstrom's *The Other Bostonians: Poverty and Progress in the American Metropolis, 1880–1970* (1973),° and Howard Chudacoff's *Mobile Americans: Residential and Social Mobility in Omaha, 1880–1920* (1972), present case studies on how some Americans fared with city life. Urban politics is treated in John M. Allswang's *Bosses, Machines, and Urban Voters* (1977), Zane Miller's *Boss Cox's Cincinnati* (1968),° and Jay Mandelbaum's *Boss Tweed's New York* (1965).° Sam Bass Warner examines how space and distance changed urban configurations in *Streetcar Suburbs: The Process of Growth in Boston, 1870–1900* (1971).° How cities dealt with growth and clutter is handled by Thomas L. Philpott in *The Slum and the Ghetto* (1978). Barbara Rosencrantz provides a kindred treatment of urban blight in *Public Health and the State* (1972). James F. Richardson's *The New York Police* (1970) examines the changing nature of crime and law enforcement.

Immigration has an extensive scholarship. Thomas Sowell presents a survey, *Ethnic America: A History* (1981).° Other general surveys include Leonard Dinnerstein and David Reimers's *Ethnic Americans: A History of Immigration and Assimilation* (1975)° and Maldwyn A. Jones's *American Immigration* (1960). Oscar Handlin's *The Uprooted* (1951)° and Philip Taylor's *The Distant Magnet: European Immigration to the U.S.A.* (1970)° are helpful in interpretating the European background which sent the immigrants over. John Higham's *Strangers in the Land: Patterns of American Nativism* (1955)° examines how old-stock residents reacted to the influx of new citizens.

More specific studies of different ethnic groups include Rowland

°These books are available in paperback editions.

Berthoff's *British Immigrants in Industrial America* (1953), John B. Duff's *The Irish in the United States* (1971), Josef Barton's *Peasants and Strangers: Italians, Rumanians, and Slovaks in an American City* (1975), Humbert Nelli's *The Italians of Chicago, 1880–1920* (1970), Irving Howe's *The World of Our Fathers: The Journey of the East European Jews to America and the Life They Made and Found* (1976),° and Stanford M. Lyman's *Chinese Americans* (1974).

Much of the recent work on education stresses how schools were designed to assimilate these new arrivals. This work includes Marvin Lazerson's *Origins of the Urban Schools* (1971), Selwyn K. Troen's *The Public and the Schools* (1975), and David Tyack's *The One Best System: A History of American Urban Education* (1974). For trends in higher education, consult Lawrence Veysey's *The Emergence of the American University* (1965) and Hugh Hawkins's *Pioneer: A History of the Johns Hopkins University* (1960) and *Between Harvard and America: The Educational Leadership of Charles W. Elliott* (1972). Burton J. Bledstein's *The Culture of Professionalism: The Middle Class and the Development of Higher Education in America* (1976)° is particularly insightful.

Sidney Fine's *Laissez-Faire and the General Welfare State* (1956)° and Morton and Lucia White's *The Intellectuals vs. the City* (1962)° survey the insights provided by the Gilded Age's leading thinkers. Richard Hofstadter's *Social Darwinism in American Thought* (1945), Robert Bannister's *Social Darwinism: Science and Myth in Anglo-American Thought* (1979), and Bruce Curtis's *William Graham Sumner* (1981) examine the impact of the theory of evolution. To trace the contours of pragmatism, consult Bruce Kuklick's *The Rise of American Philosophy* (1977).° Other intellectual trends are traced in Nathan G. Hale, Jr.'s *Freud and America: The Beginnings of Psychoanalysis in America, 1876–1917* (1971), George Dykhuizen's *The Life and Mind of John Dewey* (1973), Samuel Chugerman's *Lester F. Ward: The American Aristotle* (1936), and David Hershoff's *American Disciples of Marx: From the Age of Jackson to the Progressive Era* (1967).

Literature is treated in Jay Martin's *Harvest of Change: American Literature, 1865–1914* (1967), and Maxwell Geismer's *Rebels and Ancestors: The American Novel, 1890–1915* (1953). Larzer Ziff's *The American 1890s: The Lost Generation* (1966)° covers writers during that crucial decade. Specific studies include Justin Kaplin's *Mr. Clemens and Mark Twain* (1966),° Kenneth S. Lynn's *William Dean Howells: An American Life* (1970), and Louis D. Rubin, Jr.'s *George Washington Cable: The Life and Times of a Southern Heretic* (1969).

John L. Thomas's *Alternative America: Henry George, Edward Bellamy, Henry Demarest Lloyd, and the Adversary Tradition* (1983) and Nick Salvatore's *Eugene V. Debs: Citizen and Socialist* (1983) provide the best introductions to the social critics of the Gilded Age. Also helpful is James Weinstein's *The Decline of Socialism in America* (1967). For the Social Gospel, consult Paul A. Carter's *The Spiritual Crisis of the Gilded Age* (1971)° and Michael D. Clark's *Wordly Theologians: The Persistence of Religion in Nineteenth Century America* (1981).

William O'Neill's *Everyone Was Brave: The Rise and Fall of Feminism in America* (1969) and Eleanor Flexnor's *Century of Struggle: The Women's Rights Movement in the United States* (1959) present good introductions to the condition of women in the Gilded Age. More culturally oriented are Sheila M. Rothman's *Woman's Proper Place: A History of Changing Ideals and Practices, 1870 to the Present* (1980), and Lois Banner's *American Beauty* (1983). To gauge the impact of the increasing numbers of working women, see Carl N. Degler's *At Odds: Women and the Family in America from the Revolution to the Present* (1980),° Barbara Wertheimer's *We Were There: The Story of Working Women in America* (1977), and Susan E. Kennedy's *If All We Did Was to Weep at Home: A History of White Working-Class Women in America* (1979).

Innovations in architecture are handled in Henry Russell Hitchcock's *The Architecture of Henry H. Richardson and His Times* (1966) and Paul R. Baker's *Richard Morris Hunt* (1980). Peggy Samuels and Harold Samuels examine elements of Gilded Age art in *Frederick Remington: A Biography* (1982). An important profession is analyzed in Paul Stone's *The Social Transformation of American Medicine* (1982). George Juergens's *Joseph Pulitzer and the New York World* (1966) looks at journalistic developments. For the growth of urban leisure and sports, see Gunther Barth's *City People: The Rise of Modern City Culture in Nineteenth Century America* (1980)° and John A. Lucas and Ronald Smith's *Saga of American Sport* (1978). E. Reid Badger's *The Great American Fair: The World's Columbian Exposition and American Culture* (1979) explores the cultural implications of the Chicago World's Fair.

22

GILDED AGE POLITICS
AND AGRARIAN REVOLT

PARADOXICAL POLITICS

In 1873 Mark Twain and Charles Dudley Warner created an enduring tag for their times when they collaborated on a novel entitled *The Gilded Age.* The most unforgettable character in the book was an engaging mountebank, Col. Beriah Sellers, who always had afoot some slippery scheme to trade on political favors. Sellers had enough counterparts in the real politics of the day to enliven that story too, and their humbuggery reinforced the novelists' judgment that it was above all an age of jobbery, profiteering, and false glitter.

Perspectives on the times would eventually change, but generations of historians reinforced the two novelists' judgment. "No period so thoroughly ordinary had been known in American politics since Christopher Columbus first disturbed the balance of American society," Henry Adams wrote of the years 1870–1896. The real movers and shakers of American life were not the men who sat in the White House but the captains of industry who flung railroads across the continent and decorated its cities with their plumed smokestacks and gaudy mansions. Those presidents from Hayes to Harrison, novelist Thomas Wolfe wrote, became for later generations "the lost Americans: their gravely vacant and bewhiskered faces mixed, melted, swam together in the depths of a past intangible, immeasurable, and unknowable as the buried city of Persepolis."

Lord James Bryce, the most acute foreign observer of America in the late nineteenth century, suggested in *The American Commonwealth* (1888) that the American system, unlike the parliamentary system, tended to bring mediocre men to the top. "Since the heroes of the Revolution died with Jefferson and Adams and Madison," he wrote, "no person except General Grant has reached the [presidential] chair whose name would have been remembered had he not been President, and no President except Abraham Lincoln has displayed rare or striking qualities in the chair."

On the national issues of the day the major parties pursued for the most part a policy of evasion. Only on the tariff were there clear-cut traditions of division between protectionist Republicans and low-tariff Democrats, but there were individual exceptions even on that. On questions of the currency, regulation of big business, farm problems, civil service reform, internal improvement, and immigration, one would be hard put to distinguish between the parties. Europeans, accustomed to more ideological parties, were repeatedly perplexed at the situation until, in Lord Bryce's words, the truth began to dawn that "neither party has any principles, any distinctive tenets. Both have traditions. Both claim to have tendencies. Both have certainly war cries, organizations, interests enlisted in their support. But those interests are in the main the interests of getting or keeping the patronage of government. Tenets and policies, points of political doctrine and points of political practice, have all but vanished. They have not been thrown away but have been stripped away by Time and the progress of events, fulfilling some policies, blotting out others. All has been lost, except office or the hope of it."

What distinguished the American system was that the parties themselves comprised vast coalitions. In a country so large and diverse, James Madison had long ago argued in *The Federalist* Number 10, no one group, no one region, no one idea, no one interest could hope to constitute a majority. Such a situation protected liberty, he asserted. Any party with an expectation of governing had to include a variety of groups, interests, and ideas. The process was not unknown to European parliaments. There, splinter parties might form governing coalitions after elections. American parties simply moved the process forward one step, forming their coalitions at the party coventions in the course of choosing presidential candidates and writing platforms. The American system for electing presidents bent politics toward a two-party system.

Two things, above all, accounted for the muddled politics of this period. Americans had before them the fearsome lesson of what had happened in 1860, when parties had taken clear-cut stands on a deeply felt moral issue, with bloody consequences. But the more compelling cause of political inertia was the even division between the parties. From 1869 to 1913, from Grant to Taft, Republicans occupied the White House except during the two nonconsecutive terms of Grover Cleveland, but Republican domination was more apparent than real. In the years between 1872 and 1896 no president won office with a majority of the popular vote. In 1888 Benjamin Harrison failed to muster even a plurality over Cleveland, but carried the election anyway because his popular vote was concentrated in the states with the larger electoral votes. And while Republicans usually controlled the Senate, Democrats usually controlled the House. Only during the years 1881–1883 and 1889–1891 did a Republican president have a Republican Congress; and only between 1893 and 1895 did a Democratic president have a Democratic Congress— the only time this occurred between the Civil War and 1913, and that during a period of severe depression and turmoil.

No chief executive between Lincoln and Theodore Roosevelt could be described as a "strong" president. With the exception of Grant's their administrations were reasonably effective and honest, but none seriously challenged the prevailing view that the formulation of policy belonged to Congress. The function of the chief executive, to these presidents, was to administer the government, just as the prewar Whigs had always insisted. At the same time the almost equal strength of the parties in Congress worked against any vigorous new departures there, since most bills required bipartisan support to pass both houses. Congress thus was caught up in political maneuvers and could not come to grips with national issues.

Under such static conditions, politicians thought twice before rocking the boat. The parties became machines for seeking office and dispensing patronage. In the choice of candidates, more than ever, "availability" outweighed ability. The ideal presidential candidate had an affable personality, willingness to cooperate with the bosses, an ability to win votes from various factions, residence in a pivotal state, and a good war record. He had no views that might alienate powerful voting blocs, and few or no political enemies. Vice-presidential candidates were chosen to balance the ticket, to placate a disappointed faction, or to improve the party's chances in a key state. This process placed a premium on candidates who were relatively obscure or at least removed from national party battles capable of arousing opposition.

The Bosses of the Senate. *Joseph Keppler's 1889 cartoon bitingly portrays the alliance between big business and politics in this period.* [Library of Congress]

An alliance of business and politics, which was characteristic of the period, lent credence to the cynical maxim that the central institution of every government was the hog trough. This alliance was not necessarily corrupt, since many a politician favored business out of conviction. Nor was the public as sensitive to conflicts of interest as it would be later. So James G. Blaine of Maine, and hosts of his supporters, saw nothing wrong in his accepting stock commissions from an Arkansas railroad after helping it win a land grant from Congress. It was, they thought, a reward after the event, not a bribe in advance. John Brown Gordon of Georgia freely accepted a retainer fee of $10,000 from the Southern Pacific Railroad, a sum larger than his salary as senator, without losing his standing with his constituents. Railroad passes, free entertainment, and a host of other favors were freely given to and accepted by politicians, editors, and other leaders in positions to influence public opinion.

POLITICS AND THE VOTERS   But if many observers considered this a time of political futility in which the parties refused to face up to such "real issues" as the growth of an unregulated economy and the social injustices which resulted, it is nonetheless clear that the voters of the time thought more was at stake. Voter turnout was commonly about 70–80 per cent, even in the South, where the disfranchisement of blacks was not yet complete. (By contrast, the turnout for the 1980 presidential election was only

52.6 percent.) How was it then that leaders who failed to face up to the real issues presided over the most highly organized and politically active electorate in American history?

The answer is partly that the politicians and the voters deeply believed that they *were* dealing with crucial issues, such as the tariff, monopolies, the currency, civil service reform, and immigration. They turned out in heavy numbers for political rallies and parades. Probably more than any other generation of Americans they had the patience to follow the intricacies of lengthy debates and heavy tomes on such matters. If the major parties then failed to resolve these issues, no later generation has resolved them either, and they remain live issues, still relevant to American life a century later.

A NEW VIEW OF POLITICAL HISTORY But what motivated party loyalties and voter turnout more than anything else in these years were intense cultural conflicts among ethnic and religious groups. Recent practitioners of what has been called the "new political history" have come to this view by analyzing American politics into local, ethnic, cultural, and religious divisions. These historians approach politics less as a simple contest among economic interests, as the "progressive" historians of the earlier twentieth century saw it, than as a complex interplay of motivations, a struggle in which voters follow not simply their pocketbooks but prejudice, heritage, and convictions as well. According to Robert Kelley, one of the new political historians: "It has become clear to us . . . that the energies shaping public life are emotional as well as rational, cultural as well as economic."

Far from being like two empty bottles that differed only in their labels, as Woodrow Wilson said of the parties before the turn of the century, each party contained a different mixture of ingredients picked up in the course of its history. The Republican party, legitimate heir to the Whig tradition, attracted political insiders and active reformers. Party members were mainly Protestants of British descent or established American stock. In their own eyes, and in the eyes of many immigrants, they were prototypical Americans. Their native seat was New England, and their other strongholds were New York and the upper Middle West, both of which they had seeded with Yankee stock. Legitimate heirs to the abolitionist tradition, Republicans drew to their ranks a host of reformers and moralists, spiritual descendants of the perfectionists who populated the revivals and the reform movements of the antebellum years. The party's heritage of anti-

Catholic nativism, dating from the 1850s when the Republican party had become a haven for former Know-Nothings, would also make a comeback in the 1880s.

The Democrats, by contrast, tended to be outsiders. Since the days when Jefferson and Madison had linked up with New York's Tammany Hall, the Democrats had been a heterogeneous, often unruly coalition of unlikely allies. What they had in common was that in one way or another they differed from the Republicans. The Democratic party embraced southern whites, immigrants and Catholics of any origin, Jews, freethinkers, skeptics, and all those repelled by the "party of morality." The Democrats were the "party of personal liberty," a commitment which sometimes proved volatile. Democratic conventions tended to be more disorderly than Republican gatherings, and often the more interesting for it. There were exceptions to these broad generalizations, of course, including black Americans who though outsiders for sure, clung to the party of Lincoln, and some Protestant immigrants drawn to the Republicans by the party's image of uprightness.

The new immigration of the postbellum years, coming largely from Catholic and Jewish strongholds in eastern and southern Europe, reinforced the Democratic ranks. One result was the rebirth of nativism. In 1887 a nativist group called the American Protective Association sprang up in Clinton, Iowa, and over the next few years spread like a prairie fire through the Middle West, which became its chief stronghold. In that region especially, Republicans pressed nativist causes, calling for tighter naturalization laws, restrictions on immigration and the employment of foreigners, and greater emphasis on the teaching of the "American" language in the schools. Nativists saw as a threat those parochial schools, usually but not always Catholic, which sought to preserve Old Country cultures. German Lutherans, for instance, often maintained their own schools, and while as Protestants they gravitated to the Republicans, as Germans they were driven toward the Democrats by Republican campaigns for cultural conformity.

Prohibitionism revived along with nativism in the 1880s. Among the immigrants who crowded into the growing cities were numbers of hard-drinking Irish, beer-drinking Germans, and wine-bibbing Italians. Democratic constituents in general were more bibulous than Yankees, who increasingly saw saloons as the central social evil around which all others revolved, including vice, crime, political corruption, and neglect of families. Republicans across New England and the Middle West took up the cause of prohibition and local option, and were joined after 1869 by a Prohibition party, after 1874 by the Women's Christian Temperance Union, and after 1893 by the Anti-Saloon League. But before the turn of the century these groups attracted few Democrats to their camp.

CORRUPTION AND REFORM

CIVIL SERVICE REFORM   In the aftermath of Reconstruction, Rutherford B. Hayes admirably embodied the "party of morality." Hayes brought to the White House in 1877 a new style of uprightness that contrasted with the graft and corruption of the Grant administration. The son of an Ohio farmer, Hayes attended Kenyon College and Harvard Law School, and was admitted to the Ohio bar in 1845. He entered politics as a Whig but became one of the early Republicans, was wounded four times in the Civil War, and was promoted to major-general of volunteers. As a member of the House of Representatives for one term, from 1865 to 1867, he supported the congressional reconstruction program. Elected governor of Ohio in 1867, he served two terms and was then elected to a third nonconsecutive term in 1875, a bad year for Republicans, which marked him as presidential timber. Honest and respectable, competent and dignified, he lived in modest style. His wife startled Washington society and won the sobriquet of "Lemonade Lucy" by her refusal to serve strong drink on social occasions.

Yet Hayes's tenure was besmirched by the manner of his elec-

Rutherford B. Hayes. [Library of Congress]

tion. Snide references to him as "Old 8 to 7," the "*de facto* President," and "His Fraudulence," dogged his steps and denied him any chance at a second term, which he renounced from the beginning. Hayes's own party was split between Stalwarts and Half-Breeds, led respectively by Sen. Roscoe Conkling of New York and James G. Blaine of Maine. The difference between these Republican factions was murkier than that between the parties. The Stalwarts generally supported Grant, a Radical southern policy, and the spoils system. The Half-Breeds took a contrary view on the first two and were even vaguely touched by the sentiment for civil service reform. But for the most part the factions were loose alliances aimed at personal advancement.

Hayes himself played by the rules of the game enough to pay his political debts. All members of the Louisiana electoral returns board, which had helped elect Hayes, got jobs. But Hayes nevertheless aligned himself with the growing public discontent over the corruption and jobbery that had prevailed under Grant. American leaders were just learning about the merit system long established in the bureaucracies of France and Germany, and the new British Civil Service Act of 1870 under which jobs were filled by competitive examination. Prominent leaders such as James A. Garfield in the House and Carl Schurz in the Senate joined in the cause of civil service reform, and important journals like *Harper's Weekly* under George William Curtis and the New York *Nation* under Edwin L. Godkin endorsed the idea. A New York Civil Service Reform League appeared in 1877, and out of that grew the National Civil Service Reform League of 1881.

Before Hayes took office the most significant result of the agitation had been Grant's gesture of naming a commission to recommend measures for a merit system in the civil service. Its report was conveniently forgotten. Both Hayes and Tilden raised the issue again during the corrupt campaign of 1876, and Hayes repeated his support for reform in his inaugural address. While he failed to get legislation on the subject, he did take administrative measures for a change.

Hayes included in his cabinet such supporters of reform as Carl Schurz (Interior), John Sherman (Treasury), and William M. Evarts (State). In letters to his cabinet members and in an Executive Order of June 22, 1877, Hayes laid down his own rules for merit appointments: those already in office would be dismissed only for the good of the government and not for political reasons; party members would have no more influence in appointments than other equally respectable citizens; no assessments for political contributions would be permitted; and no office holder could manage election campaigns or political organizations, although all could vote and express opinions.

Schurz and Sherman, especially, tried to carry out the new policy. The customs houses, which fell within the Treasury Department, were notorious centers of corrupt politics, filled with political appointees with little or nothing to do but draw salaries and run political machines. Merchants sometimes found that they might gain favor by cooperating with corrupt customs officials, and might be punished for making trouble. John Sherman ordered an inquiry and laid before Hayes evidence that both Collector Chester A. Arthur and Naval Officer Alonzo Cornell were guilty of "laxity" and of using the New York Customs House for political management on behalf of Sen. Roscoe Conkling's organization. When hints went out that resignations would be welcomed, Conkling responded with an attack on reformers in a speech to the state Republican convention: "Their vocation . . . is to lament the sins of other people. Their stock in trade is rancid, canting self-righteousness. . . . When Dr. Johnson defined patriotism as the last refuge of a scoundrel, he was unconscious of the then undeveloped capabilities and uses of the word 'Reform!' " Political parties, Conkling reminded the delegates, "are not built up by deportment, or by ladies' magazines, or by gush!"

On October 15, after removing Arthur and Cornell, Hayes named replacements only to have the nominees rejected when Conkling appealed to the "courtesy of the Senate," an old custom whereby senators might control appointments in their own states. During a recess in the summer of 1878, however, Hayes appointed new replacements. When Congress reassembled, the administration put pressure on senators and, with Democratic support, carried the nominations. Even this, however, did not end the New York Customs House episode; it would flare up again under the next president.

For all his efforts to clean house, Hayes's vision of government's role remained limited. On the economic issues of the day he held to a conservative line which would guide his successors for the rest of the century. His solution to labor troubles, demonstrated in the great railway strike of 1877, was to send in troops and break the strike. His answer to demands for an expansion of the currency was to veto the Bland-Allison Act which, passed over his veto, required only a limited expansion of silver currency through the government's purchase for coinage of $2–$4 million worth of silver per month.

GARFIELD AND ARTHUR   With Hayes unavailable for a second term, the Republicans were forced to look elsewhere in 1880. The Stalwarts, led by Conkling, brought Grant forward for a third time, still a strong contender despite the tarnish of his administration's scandals. For two days the Republican convention in Chicago was deadlocked, with Grant leading but strongly challenged by Blaine and John Sherman. On the thirty-fifth ballot Wisconsin suddenly switched sixteen votes to former House Speaker (now Senator-elect) James A. Garfield, Sherman's campaign manager. Garfield rose to protest but was ruled out of order, and on the thirty-sixth ballot the convention stampeded to the dark-horse candidate, carrying him to the nomination. The Stalwarts stubbornly stood by Grant and went down, 399 to 306, but as a sop to the losing faction the convention named Chester A. Arthur of Custom House fame for vice-president.

The Democrats named Winfield Scott Hancock, a Union commander at Gettysburg, to counterbalance the Republicans' Brigadier-General Garfield and thus ward off "bloody-shirt" attacks on their party as the vehicle of Rebellion. Old Rebels, nevertheless, advised their constituents to "vote as you shot"—that is, against Republicans. In an election characterized by widespread bribery, which may have carried Indiana for Garfield, and publication of a forged letter in which Garfield allegedly championed the importation of cheap Chinese labor, the substantive highlight may have been Hancock's observation that the tariff question was a local one. Republicans ridiculed his lack of understanding, but the remark was actually a profound judgment, for tariffs were commonly produced by deals among localities, each seeking protection for its own products. The election turned out to be the closest of the century. Garfield eked out a plurality of only 39,000 votes with 48.5 per cent of the vote, but with a comfortable margin of 214 to 155 in the electoral college.

A native of Ohio, Garfield had shown the foresight to be born in a log cabin and to have a brief career on a canal towpath. Both became political assets in his rise from canal boy to president, as Horatio Alger put it in the title of a campaign biography. A graduate of Williams College, Garfield became president of Hiram College, was admitted to the bar, and won election to the Ohio Senate as a Republican in 1859. During the Civil War he distinguished himself at Shiloh and Chickamauga, served on General Rosecrans's staff, and was mustered out as a major-general when he went to Congress in 1863. Noted for his oratory and parliamentary skills, he became one of the outstanding leaders in the House and eventually its Speaker. His early appointments as president reflected the fact that he had been the candidate of a faction-ridden party. Garfield made Blaine his secretary of state, a reward for service as campaign manager in the election. The appointment of Wayne MacVeagh as attorney-general was another blow directed at the Stalwarts, since MacVeagh opposed Senator Cameron's machine in Pennsylvania—even though he was Cameron's son-in-law. But the naming of Stalwart Thomas James as postmaster-general was an important concession to the other faction.

On July 2 Garfield started on a vacation in New England to get away from the siege of office seekers. As the president passed through the Baltimore and Potomac station a deranged office seeker named Charles Guiteau shot him in the back. "I am a Stalwart," Guiteau explained to the arresting officers. "Arthur is now President of the United States," an announcement that would prove crippling to the Stalwarts. Garfield lingered for two long, hot months, his suffering eased by a contrived air conditioner—a blower rigged up by navy engineers to pass air over a vault of ice into the president's sickroom. Finally, on September 19, Garfield died of complications resulting from the shooting, having been president for a little over six months and able to transact business for less than four.

One of the chief henchmen of Stalwart leader Roscoe Conkling was now president. "Chet Arthur, President of the United States?" one of his friends exclaimed. "Good God!" Little in Arthur's past, save his record as an abolitionist lawyer who had helped secure the freedom of a fugitive slave, raised hopes that he would rise above custom-house politics. A native of Vermont, he had attended Union College, become a lawyer, and made a political career in appointive offices, most notably as New York quartermaster-general during the Civil War and collector of customs from 1871 to 1878. But Arthur demonstrated rare and striking qualities as president. He began by distancing himself from Conkling and the Stalwarts and establising a genuine independence, almost a necessity after Guiteau's announcement.

As president he vigorously prosecuted the Star Route Frauds, a kickback scheme which involved the secretary of the Republican National Committee and an assistant postmaster-general, both old political cronies of Arthur's. The president further surprised Washington in 1882 with the veto of an $18-million river and harbors bill, a "pork barrel" measure that included something for most congressional districts. He also vetoed the Chinese Exclusion Act (1882) which in his view violated the Burlingame Treaty of 1868. Congress proceeded to override both vetoes.

Most startling of all was Arthur's emergence as something of a civil service and tariff reformer. Stalwarts had every reason to expect him to oppose the merit system, but instead he allied himself with the reformers. While the assassin Guiteau had unwittingly added a certain urgency to the public support of reform, the defeat of a reform bill in 1882 sponsored by "Gentleman George" Pendleton, Democratic senator from Ohio, aroused public opinion further. The Pendleton Civil Service Act passed in January 1883, setting up a three-member Civil Service Commission independent from the regular cabinet departments, the first such federal agency established on a permanent basis. About 14 percent of all government jobs came under the category of "classified services," in which new appointments had to be made on the basis of competitive examinations. What was more, the president could enlarge the classified services at his discretion. This had important consequences over the years because after each of the next four presidential elections the "outs" emerged as victors. Each new president thus had a motive to enlarge this category because it would shield his own appointees from political removal.

The high protective tariff, a heritage of the Civil War, had by the early 1880s raised revenues to the point that the government actually enjoyed an embarrassment of riches, a surplus which drew money into the Treasury and out of circulation. Some argued that lower tariff rates would reduce prices and the cost of living, and at the same time leave more money in circulation. In 1882 Arthur named a special commission to study the problem. The appointment of John L. Hayes, secretary of the protectionist National Association of Wool Manufacturers, struck many low-tariff advocates as setting the fox to guard the henhouse. The Tariff Commission, however, brought in a recommendation for a 20–25 percent rate reduction, which gained Arthur's support, but Congress's effort to enact the proposal was marred by logrolling to further local interests, resulting in the "Mongrel Tariff" of 1883, so called because of its diverse percentage. The tariff provided for a slight rate reduction, perhaps by 5 percent, but it actually hiked the duty on some articles still imported in volume.

SCURRILOUS CAMPAIGN   When the next election came around, Arthur's record might have commended him to the voters, but it did not set well with the other leaders of his party. He had been weakened, moreover, by a political setback in his home state of New York, where his treasury secretary William J. Folger lost the 1882 governor's race to Grover Cleveland, despite Arthur's support. An even more compelling reason for Arthur's withdrawal was the fact, unknown to the public, that he had contracted Bright's disease, a fatal kidney inflamation from which he would die in 1886.

So the Republicans turned instead to the glamorous Sen. James G. Blaine of Maine, longtime leader of the Half-Breeds, and chose the Stalwart John A. Logan of Illinois as his running mate. A man with the personal magnetism a later generation would call "charisma," Blaine was the consummate politician. He never forgot a name or a face, he inspired the enthusiasm of the party faithful with his oratory, and at the same time he knew how to wheel and deal in the backrooms. He managed eloquence even when spouting the platitudes of party loyalty, waving the bloody shirt, and twisting the British lion's tail—the last of which held special appeal for the Irish, a group not normally drawn to Republican candidates.

Back in 1876 Blaine had been nominated for the presidency by Robert Ingersoll, who in an eloquent flight of oratory of his own, had announced:

> The people called for the nomination of the man who has torn from the throat of treason the tongue of slander—for the man who has snatched the mask of Democracy from the hideous face of rebellion. . . . Like an armed warrior, like a plumed knight James G. Blaine marched down the halls of American Congress and threw his shining lance full and fair against the brazen forehead of the defamers of his country and maligners of his honor.

To his followers in 1884 Blaine was still the plumed knight, but in Democratic newspapers he became the plumed knave. The "defamers of his honor" were those who found in the "Mulligan letters" evidence that Blaine was up for sale to the railroads.

During the campaign more letters surfaced with disclosures embarrassing to Blaine. For the reform element of the Republican party, this was too much, and one after another prominent leaders and supporters of the party bolted the ticket: George W. Curtis of *Harper's*, E. L. Godkin of the New York *Nation*, Carl Schurz, Charles Francis Adams, Jr., Thomas Wentworth Higginson, James Russell Lowell, Henry Ward Beecher, President Eliot of Harvard, and the New York *Times*. Party regulars scorned them as "goo-goo"—the "good-government" crowd who ignored partisan realities—and editor Charles A. Dana of the New York *Sun* jokingly called them Mugwumps, after an Algonquian word meaning a great chieftain. To regulars, in what soon became a stale joke, Mugwumps were unreliable Republicans who had their "mugs" on one side of the fence and their "wumps" on the other.

The rise of the Mugwumps, however, influenced the Democrats to nominate Stephen Grover Cleveland as a reform candidate. Cleveland experienced a rapid rise from obscurity to the White House. One of many children in the family of a small-town Presbyterian minister, he had been forced by his father's death to go to work at an early age. He got a job as clerk in a law office, read law, passed the bar examination, became an assistant state attorney-general in New York in 1863 and sheriff of Erie County in 1870. He first attracted national attention as mayor of Buffalo, elected in 1881, for battling graft and corruption. In 1882 the Democrats elected him governor, where he continued to build a reform record by fighting New York's Tammany Hall organization. Cleveland saw the corruption of government by the rich and powerful as a constant danger. As mayor and as governor he repeatedly vetoed what he considered special-privilege bills serving sordid and selfish interests.

A stocky 250-pound man with a droopy mustache, Cleveland seemed the stolid opposite of Blaine. He possessed little charisma, but impressed the public with something that was more important that year, a stubborn integrity. One supporter called him an "Ugly-honest man," and another said that "We love him for the enemies he has made." Cleveland the reformer was a godsend to Democrats who at last sighted the Promised Land, the White House. George Washington Curtis said the main issue of the campaign was not political but moral.

Then the Buffalo *Evening Telegraph* revealed some of bachelor Cleveland's earlier escapades with an attractive Buffalo widow, Maria Halperin. Mrs. Halperin had named Cleveland as the father of a child born to her in 1874, though there was no proof of paternity. Cleveland, it seemed, was only one of several likely fathers, but he took responsibility and provided for the child.

Another Voice for Cleveland. *This 1884 cartoon attacks "Grover the Good" for allegedly fathering an illegitimate child.*

The Bloody Banquet. *Republican candidate James G. Blaine is caricatured at a "royal feast" with "the money kings," while a starving family begs for morsels. [New York* World, *1884]*

When supporters asked Cleveland what to say, he answered "Tell the truth." Later he said: "The Republicans can have a monopoly of all the dirt in this campaign." Of course they did not, and the respective escapades of Blaine and Cleveland provided some of the most colorful battle cries in American political history. "Blaine, Blaine, James G. Blaine, the continental liar from the state of Maine," Democrats chanted. Republicans countered with "Ma, ma, where's my pa? Gone to the White House, ha, ha, ha!" Many voters, sorting out the scandals, seem to have made the same distinction between the public and private spheres as a voter in Chicago: "We should elect Mr. Cleveland to the public office which he is so admirably qualified to fill, and remand Mr. Blaine to the private life which he is so eminently fitted to adorn."

Near the end of the campaign Blaine and his supporters committed two fateful blunders. At New York's fashionable Delmonico's restaurant Blaine went to a private dinner with a clutch of millionaire bigwigs, including John Astor and Jay Gould, to discuss campaign finances. Cartoons and accounts of "Belshazzar's Feast" festooned the opposition press for days to come. And when a delegation of Protestant ministers visited Republican headquarters in New York, the Rev. Samuel D. Burchard referred to the Democrats as the party of "rum, Romanism, and rebellion." The judgment had a certain validity, but the tone was insolent. Blaine, who was present, let pass and perhaps failed to catch the implied insult to Catholics—a fatal oversight, since he had always cultivated Irish-American support with his anti-

British talk and public reminders that his mother was Catholic. Democrats spread word that he had let the insult pass, even that he had made it himself.

The incident may have tipped the election. The electoral vote in Cleveland's favor stood at 219 to 182, but the popular vote ran far closer; Cleveland's plurality was fewer than 30,000 votes.

CLEVELAND AND THE SPECIAL INTERESTS   For all Cleveland's hostility to the spoils system and politics as usual, he represented no sharp break with the conservative policies of his pedecessors, except in opposing governmental favors to business. "A public office is a public trust" was one of his favorite mottoes. He held to a strictly limited view of government's role in both economic and social matters, a rigid philosophy illustrated by his 1887 veto of the Texas Seed Bill, an effort to appropriate $10,000 to meet the urgent need of drought victims for seed grain. Back to Congress it went with a lecture on the need to limit the powers and functions of government—"though the people support the government the government should not support the people," Cleveland said.

For a man who took such high ground philosophically, he had a mixed record on the civil service. Cleveland had good intentions, but he also had a hungry party which had not elected a president since Buchanan in 1856. Before his inauguration Cleveland arranged to have the National Civil Service Reform League send him a letter warning that the spoils system would be a sensitive issue in the new administration. In response he repeated his support for the Pendleton Act and his intention to follow its spirit even where it did not apply; he would not remove able men on partisan grounds, he said. But he inserted one significant exception: those who had used federal jobs to forward the interests of the opposition party. In many cases, especially in the post offices, he thus had ample excuse to remove men who had practically made their offices into Republican headquarters.

Party pressures gradually forced Cleveland's hand. To a friend he remarked: "The damned everlasting clatter for office continues . . . and makes me feel like resigning and hell is to pay generally." When he left office about two-thirds of the federal officeholders were Democrats, including all internal revenue collectors and nearly all the heads of customs houses. But at the same time Cleveland had extended the classified civil service to cover about 27,000 employees, whereas about 14,000 had been covered when he came in. The result was that he satisfied neither Mugwumps nor spoilsmen, indeed he managed to antagonize both.

On other matters Cleveland's stubborn courage and concern for the public treasury led him into costly conflicts with predatory interests, conflicts which eventually cost him the White House. One such dispute arose over misue of the public domain in the West. Secretary of the Interior L. Q. C. Lamar and W. A. J. Sparks, commissioner of the General Land Office, uncovered one case after another of fraud and mismanagement: bogus surveys by govenment surveyors, public lands used fraudulently by lumbermen, mine operators, and cattlemen with the collusion of government officials, and at least 30 million acres of railroad land grants subject to forfeiture because the required lines were not built.

The administration brought suits against railroads to recover such lands, and against the Montana Improvement Company, subsidiary of the Northern Pacific Railroad, for cutting trees on public forestlands. It nullified exploitive leases of Indian lands, such as that of one cattle company which had leased 6 million acres from the Cherokees for $100,000 and subleased the land for about five times as much. Cattle barons were ordered to remove fences enclosing waterholes and grasslands on the open range. In all, during Cleveland's first term about 81 million acres of public lands were restored to the federal government.

Cleveland incurred the wrath of Union veterans by his firm stand against pension raids on the Treasury. Congress had passed the first general Civil War pension law in 1862 to provide for veterans disabled in service and for the widows, orphans, and dependents of veterans. By 1882 Cpl. James Tanner, commander of the Grand Army of the Republic, an organization of Union veterans and a powerful pressure group, was trying to get pensions paid for any disability, no matter how it was incurred. Meanwhile many veterans enjoyed such benefits by having private pension bills put through an obliging Congress. In Washington a large tribe of lawyers built careers on filing claims and pushing special laws for veterans.

Insofar as time permitted Cleveland examined such bills critically and vetoed those which seemed to him dubious. Although he signed more than any of his predecessors, running pension costs up from $56 million to $80 million, he also vetoed more. A climax came in January 1887 when Congress passed the Dependent Pension Bill, which provided funds for all ninety-day veterans dependent upon manual labor and unable to work for any reason, whether or not the reason was service conected. Cleveland sent it back with a ringing veto, declaring that the pension list would become a refuge for frauds rather than a "roll of honor." On June 5, 1887, Cleveland compounded his sins in the eyes of the old soldiers when he signed an order for the return of captured Confederate battleflags to the South. Although the order had originated in the War Department, Cleveland was the target of a stormy protest. "May God palsy the hand that wrote that order," said Commander Lucius Fairchild of the GAR. "May God palsy the brain that conceived it, and may God palsy the tongue that dictated it." Faced with such a tempest, Cleveland made the convenient discovery that he lacked authority to issue the order and revoked it after eight days. The flags finally went back with congressional approval in 1905, when Theodore Roosevelt was president.

About the middle of his term Cleveland set out after new special interests, leading in the adoption of an important new policy, railroad regulation. Since the late 1860s state after state had adopted regulatory laws, and from the early 1870s Congress had debated federal legislation to regulate the railroads. In 1886 a Supreme Court decision finally spurred action. In the case of *Wabash Railroad v. Illinois* the Court denied the state's power to regulate rates on interstate traffic. Cleveland urged in his annual message in December that since this "important field of control and regulation [has] thus been left entirely unoccupied," Congress should act.

In February Cleveland signed into law an act creating the Interstate Commerce Commission, the first such independent regulatory commission. The law empowered its five members to investigate carriers and prosecute violators. All rates had to be "reasonable and just." Railroads were forbidden to grant rebates, discriminate against persons, places, and commodities, or enter into pools (agreements to fix rates). The commission's actual powers, however, proved to be weak when first tested in the courts. If creating the ICC seemed to conflict with Cleveland's fear of big government, it accorded with his Jacksonian fear of great combinations of capital. The Interstate Commerce Act, to his mind, was a legitimate exercise of sovereign power.

Cleveland's most dramatic challenge to special interests came in his efforts to force action on tariff reform. He had entered office as the leader of the traditional low-tariff party, but his party was far from unified on the issue, and Cleveland himself confessed at first to little understanding of the tariff issue. Like most politicians of the time, he hesitated to plunge into that tangled thicket. But with greater exposure to the question and further study he decided that the rates were too high and included many inequities. Near the end of 1887 Cleveland decided on the deliberate step of dramatizing the issue by devoting his entire annual

Grover Cleveland made the issue of tariff reform central to the politics of the late 1880s. [Library of Congress]

message to the subject. He did so in full knowledge that he was focusing attention on a political minefield on the eve of an election year, against the warnings of his advisers. "What is the use of being elected if you don't stand for something?" he asked.

Cleveland's message was a classic summary and exposition of the current arguments against protection. He noted that tariff revenues had bolstered the surplus, making the Treasury "a hoarding place for money needlessly withdrawn from trade and the people's use." It pushed up prices for everybody, and while it was supposed to protect American labor against the competition of cheap foreign labor, the most recent census showed that of 17.4 million Americans gainfully employed only 2.6 million were in "such manufacturing industries as are claimed to be benefitted by a high tariff." It was evident, moreover, that while business combinations could push prices up to the artificial level set by the prices of dutied foreign goods, prices often fell below that level when domestic producers were in competition, "proof that someone is willing to accept lower prices for such commodity and that such prices are renumerative." Congress, Cleveland argued, should study the more than 4,000 articles subject to duties with an eye to cutting the cost of necessities and of the raw materials used in manufacturing. "Our progress toward a wise conclusion will not be improved by dwelling upon the theories of protection and free trade. . . . It is a condition which confronts us, not a theory." The final sentence became an epigram so infectious that for the next few years public speakers worked it nearly to death.

That did not stop Blaine and other Republicans from denouncing the message as pure "free trade," a doctrine all the more suspect because it was also British policy. The House Ways and Means Committee soon reported a bill calling for modest reductions from an average level of about 47 percent of the value of imported goods to about 40 percent. House Democrats rallied to its support, some of them under assurances that it could not become law. Passed by the House, the bill stalled in the Republican Senate and finally died a lingering death in committee. If Cleveland's talk accomplished his purpose of drawing party lines more firmly, it also confirmed the fears of his advisers. The election of 1888 for the first time in years highlighted a difference between the major parties on an issue of substance.

Cleveland was inevitably the nominee of his party. The platform endorsed "the views expressed by the President in his last message to Congress." The Republicans passed up old warhorses like Blaine and Sherman and turned to the obscure Benjamin Harrison, who had all the attributes of availability. Grandson of a former president, a flourishing lawyer in Indiana, the diminutive Harrison resided in a pivotal state, and had a good war record and little in his political record to offend any voter. He had lost a race for governor and served one term in the Senate (1881–1887). For vice-president the party named Levi P. Morton of New York. The Republican platform picked up the gauntlet thrown down by Cleveland, accepted the protective tariff as the chief issue, and promised generous pensions to veterans.

The campaign thus became the first waged mainly on the tariff issue. Sen. Matthew Quay, Harrison's campaign chairman and Republican boss of Pennsylvania, took the advice of a friend to "put the manufacturers of Pennsylvania under the fire and fry all the fat out of them." As insurance against tariff reduction, manufacturers obligingly larded the campaign fund, which was used to denounce Cleveland's un-American "free trade," his pension vetoes, and his Confederate battleflag order. In Indiana party workers were told: "Divide the floaters into blocks of five and put a trusted man in charge . . . with the necessary funds, and make him responsible that none get away, and that all vote our ticket." Democratic poll-watchers claimed that floaters got $15 to $20 each for their votes.

Personal attacks too were leveled against Cleveland. The old charges of immorality had played out. After Cleveland entered the White House he had married young Frances Folsom, who later presented him with a daughter whose name would be immortalized one day by the "Baby Ruth" candy bar. During the campaign, though, the rumor went abroad that a drunken Cleveland had taken to wife-beating. On the eve of the election Cleveland suffered a more devastating blow from the phony "Murchison letter." A California Republican named George A.

Osgoodsby had written British Minister Sir Lionel Sackville-West over the false name "Charles F. Murchison." Posing as an English immigrant he asked advice on how to vote. Sackville-West, engaged at the time in sensitive negotiations over Canadian fisheries, hinted that he should vote for Cleveland. Published on October 24, the letter aroused a storm of protest against foreign intervention and further linked Cleveland to British free-traders. Democratic explanations never caught up with the original sense of outrage.

The outcome was very close. Cleveland was vindicated in the popular vote by 5,538,000 to 5,447,000, but that was poor comfort. The distribution was such that Harrison, with the key states of Indiana and New York on his side, carried the electoral college by 233 to 168. For once the country had not only a minority president, but one who lacked even a plurality in the popular vote.

REPUBLICAN REFORM UNDER HARRISON   Harrison became a competent and earnest figurehead, overshadowed by his secretary of state, James G. Blaine. He proved something of a cold fish in personal relations. "Harrison can make a speech to ten thousand men and every man of them will go away his friend," said one observer. "Let him meet the same ten thousand in private and every one will go away his enemy." When Sen. Matthew Quay came to call with the election returns, Harrison exclaimed fervently: "Providence has given us the victory." The cynical Quay later remarked that Harrison "ought to know that Providence hadn't a damn thing to do with it" and opined that the president "would never know how close a number of men were compelled to approach a penitentiary to make him president."

Harrison had aroused the hopes of civil service reformers. "In appointments of every grade and department," he said, "fitness and not party service should be the essential and discriminating test, and fidelity and efficiency the only sure tenure of office." Nevertheless he appointed John Wanamaker, the Philadelphia merchant prince, as his postmaster-general, allegedly as a reward for a generous contribution. J. S. Clarkson, the first assistant postmaster-general, announced less than a year later: "I have changed 31,000 out of 55,000 fourth-class postmasters and I expect to change 10,000 more before I finally quit." Harrison made a few feckless efforts to resist partisan pressures, but the party leaders had their way. His most significant gesture at reform was to name young Theodore Roosevelt to the Civil Service Commission.

BILLION- DOLLARISM > HOLE

A cartoon attacking Benjamin Harrison's spending policies. He is shown pouring Cleveland's huge surplus down a hole. [W. Bencough, Democratic National Committee]

Harrison owed a heavy debt to the old-soldier vote, which he discharged by naming Cpl. James Tanner of the GAR to the office of pension commissioner. "God help the surplus," Tanner reportedly exclaimed, and proceeded to approve pensions with such abandon that Secretary of the Interior J. W. Noble removed him six months and and several million dollars later. In 1890 Congress passed, and Harrison signed, the Disability Pension Act, substantially the same measure that Cleveland had vetoed. Any ninety-day veteran unable to make a living by manual labor was granted $6 to $12 a month according to the degree of his disability. The pension rolls shot up from 490,000 in 1889 to 966,000 in 1893, and the program's costs from $89 million to $175 million. Eventually, in 1904 a presidential order placed all veterans over age sixty-two on the pension rolls, and by 1936 Civil War pensions had totaled near $8 billion, not counting the pensions paid by southern states to old Confederates, their widows and dependents.

During the first two years of Harrison's term the Republicans controlled the presidency and both houses of Congress for the only time in the twenty years between 1875 and 1895. They were positioned to have pretty much their own way, and they made the year 1890 memorable for some of the most significant legislation enacted in the entire period. In addition to the Dependent Pension Act, Congress and the president approved the Sherman Anti-Trust Act, the Sherman Silver Purchase Act, the McKinley Tariff, and the admission of the last of the "omnibus states," Idaho and Wyoming, which followed the admission of the Dakotas, Montana, and Washington in 1889.

Both parties had pledged themselves to do something about the growing power of trusts and monopolies. The Sherman Anti-Trust Act, named for Sen. John Sherman, chairman of the Senate Judiciary Committee that drafted it, sought to incorporate into federal law a long-standing principle of the common law against "restraint of trade." It forbade contracts, combinations, or conspiracies in restraint of trade or in the effort to establish monopolies in interstate or foreign commerce. A broad consensus put the law through, but its passage turned out to be largely symbolic. The common law prevailed only in state courts, and the largest corporations had grown well beyond the boundaries of a single state, and beyond the ability of state courts to control them. During the next decade successive administrations expended little effort on the act's enforcement. From 1890 to 1901 only eighteen suits were instituted, and four of those were against labor unions.

Congress meanwhile debated currency legislation against the backdrop of growing distress in the farm regions of the West and South. Hard-pressed farmers were now agitating to inflate the currency by an increased coinage of silver. Increased coinage would raise prices, making it easier for farmers to raise the money with which to pay their debts. The silverite forces were also strengthened, especially in the Senate, by members from the new omnibus states, which had silver-mining interests. The pro-silver Senate easily passed the new measure, and in the House the western silverites struck a bargain with eastern protectionists strengthening support for both an increased silver coinage and a higher tariff. The new Sherman Silver Purchase Act, passed on July 14, replaced the Bland-Allison Act of 1878; it required the Treasury to purchase 4.5 million ounces of silver each month and to issue in payment Treasury notes redeemable in either gold or silver. The act failed to satisfy the demands of the silverites, however. Although it approximately doubled the amount of silver purchased, that was still too little to have an inflationary impact on the economy. Eastern business and financial groups, on the other hand, saw a threat to the gold reserve in the growth of paper currency which holders could redeem in gold at the Treasury. The stage was set for the currency issue to eclipse all others in a panic that swept the country three years later.

Republicans took their victory over Cleveland as a mandate not just to maintain the protective tariff but to raise it. But the mandate was less than clear, in view of Cleveland's plurality, and passage of the new tariff remained doubtful until its backers struck their bargain with western silverites. Piloted through by

William McKinley, House Ways and Means chairman, and Sen. Nelson W. Aldrich, the McKinley Tariff of 1890 raised duties on manufactured goods to an average of about 49.5 percent, the highest to that time. And it included three interesting new departures. First, the protectionists reached out for farmers' votes with high duties on agricultural products. Second, they sought to lessen the tariff's impact on consumers by putting sugar, a universal necessity, on the free list—thus reducing its cost—and then compensating Louisiana and Kansas sugar growers with a bounty of two cents a pound out of the federal treasury. And third, the measure included a reciprocity section which empowered the president to hike duties on sugar, molasses, tea, coffee, and hides to pressure countries exporting those items into reducing unreasonably high duties on American goods.

The absence of a public concensus for higher tariffs became clearly visible in the 1890 elections. By the time the November congressional election returns were in it seemed apparent, at least to Democrats, that the voters had repudiated the McKinley tariff, which had become law in October, with a landslide of Democratic votes. In the new House Democrats outnumbered Republicans by 235 to 88; in the Senate the Republican majority was reduced to 8. One of the election casualties was McKinley himself, the victim of a few tricks the Democrats used to reinforce the widespread revulsion against the increased duties. In McKinley's Ohio district itinerent peddlers offered household utensils at exorbitant prices, explaining that the McKinley Tariff had caused the price increases. But there was more to the election than the tariff. Voters reacted also against the baldly partisan measures of the Harrison administration and its extravagant expenditures on pensions and other programs. Democrats raised a ruckus about the Republicans' "billion-dollar Congress," to which Speaker Thomas B. Reed responded with the question: "Isn't this a billion dollar country?" But with expenditures rising and revenues dropping, largely because the tariff was not high enough to discourage imports, the nation's surplus was shrinking at a rapid pace.

The large Democratic vote in 1890 may have also been a reaction to Republican efforts to legislate against alcohol and parochial schools. In the years from 1880 to 1890 sixteen out of twenty-one states outside the South held referenda on constitutional prohibition, and a number of state legislatures provided for votes on the issue of local option. In the referenda only six states voted dry (for prohibition), however, and one of these, Rhode Island, reversed its dry vote of 1886 three years later. With the politics of righteousness, then, Republicans were playing a losing game, arousing wets (antiprohibitionists) on the Democratic side. In 1889 Wisconsin Republicans compounded their party's problems by pushing through a law which struck at parochial schools. The law held that a school could be accredited only if it taught the basic subjects in the English language. That was the last straw: it turned hordes of threatened and outraged immigrants into Democratic activists. In 1889 and 1890 the Democrats swept state after state.

The election returns reflected something even more than a reaction against the Republican tariff, spoils politics, extravagance, and moralizing. The returns revealed a deep-seated unrest in the farming communities of the South and West that was beginning to find voice in the new People's party. In the Fifty-second Congress there would be eight Populist representatives and two Populist senators.

THE PROBLEMS OF FARMERS

ECONOMIC CONDITIONS For some time farmers had been subject to worsening economic and social conditions. The source of their problem was a long-term decline in commodity prices from 1870 to 1898, the product of domestic overproduction and growing international competition for world markets. The vast new lands brought under cultivation in America poured an ever-increasing supply of farm products into the market, driving down prices. This effect was reinforced as innovations in transportation and communications brought American farmers ever more into competition with farmers around the world, further increasing the supply of farm commodities. Considerations of abstract economic forces, however, puzzled many farmers. They would never quite understand how want could be caused by plenty. They shared the puzzlement that Kansas's Populist Gov. Lorenzo Dow Lewelling professed at a friend's argument in the 1890s that "there were hungry people . . . because there was too much bread" and "so many . . . poorly clad . . . because there was too much cloth." How could one speak of overproduction when so many remained in need? Instead there must be a screw loose somewhere in the system.

The railroads and the middlemen who handled the farmers' products became the prime villains. Farmers felt victimized by the high railroad rates which prevailed in farm regions that had no alternative forms of transportation. Individual farmers could not get the rebates the Rockefellers could extract from railroads, and could not exert the political influence wielded by the railroad lobbies. In other ways farmers found themselves with little bargaining power either as buyers or sellers. When they went to sell wheat or cotton, the buyer set the price; when they went to buy a plow point, the seller set the price.

High tariffs operated to the farmers' disadvantage because they protected manufacturers against foreign competition, allowing them to raise the prices of factory goods on which farmers depended. Farmers, however, had to sell their wheat, cotton, and other staples in the world market, where competition lowered prices. Tariffs inflicted a double blow on farmers because insofar as they hampered imports, they indirectly hampered exports by making it harder for foreign buyers to get the necessary American currency or exchange to purchase American goods.

Debt has been a perennial problem of agriculture. After the Civil War farmers became ever more enmeshed in debt, western farmers in mortgages to cover the costs of land and machinery, southern farmers in crop liens. As prices dropped, the burden of debt grew because farmers had to cultivate more wheat or cotton to raise the same amount of money; and by growing more they furthered the vicious cycle of surpluses and price declines.

AN INADEQUATE CURRENCY Currency deflation was yet another cause of declining prices. Ultimately, farm discontent became focused on the currency issue, magnifying this grievance out of proportion to all others. The basic problem with the nation's currency in the late nineteenth century was that it lacked the flexibility to grow along with America's expanding economy. From 1865 to 1890 the amount of currency in circulation decreased from about $30.20 to $27.06 per capita. Three types of currency existed in those days: greenbacks, national banknotes, and hard money (gold and silver coins or certificates). The amount of greenback money in circulation had been set at $346 million in 1878, and had remained fixed at that amount, despite agitation for more paper money by debtors (largely farmers) and expansion-minded businessmen. National banknotes, based on government bonds, actually contracted in volume as the government paid off its bonds, which it was able to do rapidly with revenues from tariffs and land sales.

Metallic currency dated from the Mint Act of 1792, which authorized free and unlimited coinage of silver and gold at a ratio of 15:1 in weight.° The phrase "free and unlimited coinage" sim-

---

°The ratio meant that the amount of precious metal in a silver dollar weighed fifteen times as much as that in a gold dollar. This reflected the relative values of silver and gold at the time.

ply meant that owners of precious metals could have any quantity of their gold or silver coined free, except for a nominal fee to cover costs. A fixed ratio of values, however, could not reflect fluctuations in the market value of the metals. When gold rose to a market value higher than that reflected in the official ratio, owners ceased to present it for coinage. The country was actually on a silver standard until 1837, when Congress changed the ratio to 16:1, which soon reversed the situation. Silver became more valuable in the market than in coinage, and the country drifted to a gold standard. This state of affairs prevailed until 1873, when Congress passed a general revision of the coinage laws and, without fanfare, dropped the then-unused provision for the coinage of silver. The action came, however, just when silver production began to increase, reducing its market value through the growth in supply. Under the old laws this would have induced owners of silver to present it at the mint for coinage. Soon advocates of currency inflation began to denounce the "crime of '73," which they had scarcely noticed at the time. Gradually a suspicion, and in some cases a belief, grew that creditor interests had conspired in 1873 to ensure a scarcity of money. But the silverites had little more legislative success than the advocates of greenback inflation. The Bland-Allison Act of 1878 and the Sherman Silver Purchase Act of 1890 provided for some silver coinage, but too little in each case to offset the overall contraction of the currency.

Aside from economic and political forces, physical problems of geography and climate conspired to torment farmers with problems of drought, flood, blizzards, soil depletion, and insects. The farmers' response to these problems was crippled by the American ideal of the individual family farm, which in fostering their social and intellectual isolation made it more difficult for them to act collectively.

AGRARIAN REVOLT

THE GRANGER MOVEMENT   When the Department of Agriculture sent Oliver H. Kelley on a tour of the postbellum South in 1866, it was the farmers' isolation which most impressed him. Resolving to do something about it, Kelley and some government clerks in 1867 founded the Patrons of Husbandry, better known as the Grange. In the next few years the Grange mushroomed, reaching a membership as high as 1.5 million by 1874. The Grange started as a social and educational response to the farmers' isolation, but as it grew it began to promote farmer-owned cooperatives for buying and selling and soon became indirectly involved in politics through independent third parties, especially in the Midwest, during the early 1870s.

The Grangers' political goal was chiefly to regulate the rates charged by railroads and warehouses. In five states they brought about the passage of "Granger Laws" which at first proved relatively ineffective, but laid a foundation for stronger legislation later. Owners subject to their regulation challenged these laws in cases which soon rose to the Supreme Court, where the plaintiffs in the "Granger Cases" claimed to have been deprived of property without due process of law. In a key case involving warehouse regulation, *Munn v. Illinois* (1877), the high court ruled that the state under its "police powers" had the right to regulate property in the interest of the public good where that property was clothed with a public interest. If regulatory power were abused, the ruling said, "the people must resort to the polls, not the courts." Later, however, the courts would severely restrict state regulatory powers.

The Granger movement gradually declined (but never disappeared) as members' energies were drawn off into cooperatives, many of which failed, and into political action. Out of the independent political movements of the time there grew in 1875 a party calling itself the Independent National party, more commonly known as the Greenback party because of its emphasis on that issue. In 1876 it nominated philanthropist Peter Cooper of New York for president, but polled only 82,000 votes for its slate. In the 1878 midterm elections it enjoyed greater success, polling over 1 million votes and electing fifteen congressmen. But in 1880 the party's fortunes declined, and it disintegrated after 1884.

FARMERS' ALLIANCES   The more direct antecedents of the People's party were the Farmers' Alliances which grew with startling speed as the Greenback agitation petered out. By 1890 there were two major groups: the northwestern Alliance, organized in 1880 by Milton George, editor of the *Western Rural* in Chicago, was never effective and by the late 1880s was mostly a paper organization; the southern Alliance, which had various official names in its brief heyday, proved the more militant, the more effective, the more radical, and ultimately the more national of the two. The southern group, which started as a frontier farmers' club in Lampasas County, Texas, in 1877, grew into the Grand State Alliance in 1879. In 1886 Dr. Charles W. Macune became its leader and dazzled members with a glittering vision of large-

After Reconstruction ended, many black families (called "Exodusters") left the South to farm in Kansas. They laid the groundwork for later organizations like the Colored Farmers Alliance. Kansas State Historical Society]

scale cooperatives, which drew new converts rapidly to the organization. By absorbing existing farm groups and organizing new locals, the Alliance swept the cotton belt and established strong positions in Kansas and the Dakotas. By 1890 it had members from New York to California numbering about 1.5 million. A parallel Colored Farmers Alliance claimed over 1 million members.

The Alliance had an elaborate social and educational program, and about 1,000 affiliated newspapers. But unlike the Grange, the Alliance proposed from the beginning an elaborate economic program. In 1890 Alliance agencies and exchanges in some eighteen states claimed a business of $10 million, but they soon went the way of the Granger cooperatives, victims of discrimination by wholesalers, manufacturers, railroads, and bankers, but above all victims of inexperienced management and overextended credit. Increasingly farmers decided that they could not lift themselves by their own bootstraps, that they needed political power to secure railroad regulation, currency inflation, fertilizer inspections, state departments of agriculture, antitrust laws, farm credit, and the other measures they sought.

In 1980 Alliance members plunged headlong into politics. In the West, where hard times had descended after the collapse of land values in 1887, farmers were ready for third-party action. In the South, however, white Alliancemen hesitated to bolt the Democratic party, seeking instead to influence or control it. Both approaches gained startling success. Independent parties under various names upset the political balance in western states, electing a governor under the banner of the People's party in Kansas, and taking control of one house of the legislature there and both houses in Nebraska. In South Dakota and Minnesota

"Sockless Jerry" Simpson, on the stump at Harper,
Kansas, 1892. [Kansas State Historical Society]

they gained a balance of power in the legislatures, while Kansas
and Nebraska sent Populists to the Senate. The Populists produced colorful leaders, especially in Kansas, where the popular
imagination was captured by: Mary Elizabeth Lease, who advised farmers "to raise less corn and more hell"; Rep. "Sockless
Jerry" Simpson, who got his nickname as a riposte to his own
charge that his Republican opponent, "Prince Hal," wore silk
stockings; and William Alfred "Whiskers" Peffer, a Topeka editor and senator.

In the South the Alliance won equal if not greater success by
forcing the Democrats to nominate candidates pledged to their
program. The southern states elected four pro-Alliance governors, seven pro-Alliance legislatures, forty-four pro-Alliance
congressmen, and several senators. Few of these officials, however, supported the subtreasury plan, which southern Alliancemen saw as the cure for their ills. Under this plan, formulated by
C. W. Macune, farmers could store their crops in government
warehouses and secure government loans for up to 80 percent of
their crops' value at 1 percent interest. Besides credit, the plan
allowed the farmer the leeway to hold his crop for a good price,
since he would not have to sell it immediately at harvest time to
pay off debts, and it promoted inflation because loans to farmers
would be made in new legal-tender notes. The plan went before
Congress in 1890 but was never adopted.

THE POPULIST PARTY In May 1891 a conference in Cincinnati
brought together delegates from farm, labor, and reform organizations to discuss strategy. The meeting endorsed a national

third party and formed a national executive committee of the People's party. Few southerners were at Cincinnati, but many endorsed the third-party idea after their failure to move the Democratic party toward the subtreasury plan. In February 1892 a larger meeting at St. Louis called for a national convention of the People's party at Omaha on July 4 to adopt a platform and choose candidates. The stirring platform, written by Ignatius Donnelly of Minnesota, typified the apocalyptic, almost paranoid, style that increasingly characterized both the farmers' movement and its opponents:

> We meet in the midst of a nation brought to the verge of moral, political, and material ruin. Corruption dominates the ballot-box, the Legislatures, the Congress, and touches even the ermine of the bench. The newspapers are largely subsidized or muzzled, public opinion silenced, business prostrated, homes covered with mortgages, labor impoverished, and the land concentrating in the hands of the capitalists. . . . A vast conspiracy against mankind has been organized. . . . If not met and overthrown at once it forebodes terrible social convulsions . . . or the establishment of an absolute despotism.

The platform itself focused on issues of finance, transportation, and land. Its financial program demanded the new legal-tender currency proposed in the subtreasury plan, or a variation on it, free and unlimited coinage of silver at the 16:1 ratio, an increase in the amount of money in circulation to $50 per capita, an income tax, and postal savings banks to protect depositors who otherwise risked disastrous losses in small-town banks vulnerable to farm depression. As to transportation, the time had come "when the railroad corporations will either own the people or the people must own the railroads." Let government therefore nationalize the railroads, and the telephone and telegraph systems as well. For land, "the heritage of the people," the Populist remedy was for the government to reclaim from railroads and other corporations lands "in excess of their actual needs," and to forbid land ownership by aliens. Finally, the platform endorsed the eight-hour day and restriction of immigration, and denounced the use of Pinkerton agents as strikebreakers. The party took these positions to win support from the urban workers, whom Populists looked upon as fellow "producers."

The party's platform turned out to be more exciting than its candidate. The front-runner for the nomination, the southern Alliance's president Leonidas L. Polk of North Carolina, suddenly fell ill and died just before the convention. The party then turned to James B. Weaver of Iowa. The choice was unfortunate, for Weaver, an able and prudent man, carried the stigma of his defeat on the Greenback ticket twelve years before. To balance Weaver, a Union general, the party named James G. Field of Virginia, a former Confederate general, for vice-president.

The third party was the startling new feature of the 1892 campaign, but for the major parties it was a repetition of 1888, with Grover Cleveland the Democratic candidate and Benjamin Harrison the Republican, and with the tariff the chief issue between them. The outcome, however, was different. Both major candidates polled over 5 million votes, but Cleveland carried a plurality of the popular votes and the electoral college. Weaver polled over 1 million votes, and carried Colorado, Kansas, Nevada, and Idaho, for a total of twenty-two electoral votes. Alabama was the banner Populist state of the South, with 36.6 percent of its vote for Weaver, even as reported by a Democratic returns board.

THE DEPRESSION OF 1893 Cleveland's second administration came to grief early. Before it ended, Cleveland had antagonized every major segment of the public: the farmers and silverties opposed his efforts to maintain the gold standard, business groups disliked his attempt to lower the tariff, and a large segment of labor was alienated when he put down the Pullman Strike. Worst of all, his second term coincided with one of the worst depressions in history, set off just before he took office by the failure of the Philadelphia and Reading Railroad and a panic on Wall Street. By 1894 many people had reached bottom. That year some 750,000 workers went out on strike, including the Pullman workers; millions found themselves unemployed; railroad construction workers, laid off in the West, began tramping east and, to the dismay of alarmists who sniffed revolution in the air, talked of marching on Washington. Few of the groups made it to the capital. One that did was the Army of the Commonweal of Christ, led by Jacob S. Coxey, an Ohio Populist, who demanded mass employment on public works. When "Coxey's Army" of about 400 finally straggled into Washington, Coxey was arrested for walking on the grass.

In this climate of anxiety the midterm elections took place. The outcome disappointed the Populists, who had expected to profit from the discontent. In North Carolina a Populist fusion with Republicans actually captured the legislature from the Democrats, after which the fusionists named to the Senate one Populist and one Republican. But it was the only southern legislature lost by the Democrats, and that only for four years. Nationally, the elections amounted to a severe setback for

Democrats, and the Republicans were the chief beneficiaries. The Populists emerged with six senators and seven representatives. They had polled 1.5 million votes for their congressional candidates and still expected the simmering discontent to carry them to power in 1896.

SILVERITES VS. GOLDBUGS The course of events, however, would dash that hope. In the mid-1890s events conspired to focus all agitations on the currency issue. One of the causes of the depression had been the failure of the British banking house of Baring Brothers, which led many British investors to unload American investments in return for gold. Soon after Cleveland's inauguration the gold reserve fell below $100 million. To plug this drain on the Treasury the president sought repeal of the Sherman Silver Purchase Act in order to stop the issuance of silver notes redeemable in gold. Cleveland won the act's repeal in 1893, but at the cost of irreparable division in his own party. To further build the gold reserve, the administration floated four bond issues in the years 1894 to 1896. The first two brought little response, but in 1895 the administration made a deal with J. P. Morgan and other financiers, who promised to get from abroad half the gold needed to buy the bonds, and to use their influence to stop demands on the Treasury. The deal worked, but it created the unfavorable image of Cleveland and the financial oligarchy working hand in glove.

Meanwhile the American Bimetallic League, heavily financed by silver miners, raised the agitation for silver coinage to a crescendo. Their greatest propaganda windfall came from the appearance in mid-1894 of William H. Harvey's book *Coin's Financial School*, which soon became a bestseller, the *Uncle Tom's Cabin* of the silver movement. In the book the youthful "Professor Coin" delivered lectures in which he resolutely confounded the "goldbugs" with his logic. The growing importance of the currency issue presented a dilemma for Populists: Should the party promote the whole spectrum of reform it advocated, or should it try to ride the silver issue into power? The latter was the practical choice, so the Populist leaders decided, over the protest of more radical members, to hold their 1896 convention last, confident that the major parties would at best straddle the silver issue and that they would then reap a harvest of bolting silverites.

THE ELECTION OF 1896 Contrary to these expectations the major parties took opposite positions on the currency issues. The Republicans, as expected, chose William McKinley on a gold-

William Jennings Bryan at the Democratic convention in 1896. [Culver Pictures]

standard platform. McKinley, a former congressman and governor of Ohio, benefited from the political steamroller organized by his campaign manager, Marcus A. Hanna. On the Democratic side, early organizing paid off for the prosilver forces, who captured the convention for their platform. William Jennings Bryan arranged to give the closing speech for the silver plank. A two-term congressman from Nebraska who had been swept out in the Democratic losses of 1894, Bryan had distinguished himself mainly with an exhausting three-hour speech he gave against repeal of the Sherman Silver Purchase Act. In the months before the convention he had traveled the South and West, speaking for free silver. His rehearsed phrases swept the convention into a frenzy:

> I come to speak to you in defense of a cause as holy as the cause of liberty—the cause of humanity. . . . We have petitioned, and our petitions have been scorned. We have entreated, and our entreaties have been disregarded. We have begged, and they have mocked when our calamity came. We beg no longer, we entreat no more; we petition no more. We defy them!

By the time he reached his peroration there was little doubt that he would get the nomination: "You shall not press down upon the brow of labor this crown of thorns. You shall not crucify mankind upon a cross of gold!"

When the Populists met in St. Louis two weeks later they faced an impossible choice. They could name their own candidate and divide the silver vote or endorse Bryan and probably lose their identity. In the end they named Bryan, but chose their own vice-presidential candidate, former Rep. Thomas E. Watson of Georgia, and invited the Democrats to drop their vice-presidential nominee, Arthur Sewall—an action which Bryan refused to countenance. Given the workings of the electoral college, the two different candidates for vice-president might have caused a split in the silverite vote had the parties insisted on separate slates. Some diehard Populists did, but in twenty-eight of the forty-four states Democrats and Populists put out fusion slates which carried candidates for elector from both parties.

The thirty-six-year-old Bryan, the "boy orator of the Platte," traveled the country and exploited his spellbinding eloquence, while McKinley conducted a "front-porch campaign," receiving selected delegations at his home in Canton, Ohio, and giving only prepared responses. At the battle's end the Democratic-Populist-Silverite candidates were overwhelmed by the well-organized and well-financed Republican campaign directed by Mark Hanna. McKinley carried the popular vote by 7.1 million to 6.5 million and the electoral college by 271 to 176. Bryan carried most of the West and the South below the border states, but the problem neither the Populists nor Bryan ever overcame was that of breaking into metropolitan centers east of the Mississippi and north of the Ohio and Potomac. In the critical midwestern battleground, from Minnesota and Iowa eastward to Ohio, Bryan carried not a single state. Despite efforts on his behalf by reformers and unionists in the Midwest and East, unorganized workers found it easier to identify with McKinley's "full dinner pail" than

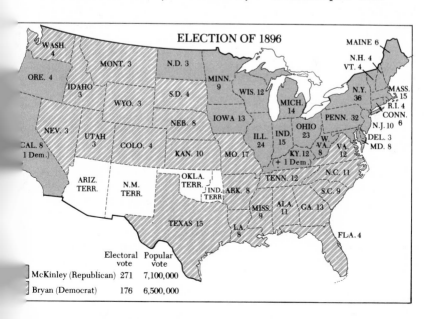

ELECTION OF 1896

	Electoral vote	Popular vote
McKinley (Republican)	271	7,100,000
Bryan (Democrat)	176	6,500,000

with Bryan's free silver. Some workers may have been intimidated by businessmen's threats to close shop if the "Demopop" heresies triumphed. Many ethnic voters, normally drawn to the Democrats, were no doubt repelled by Bryan's flamboyant evangelical style. Farmers in the Northeast, moreover, were hurting less than farmers in the wheat and cottonbelts.

A NEW ERA   It had been a climactic political struggle, falling almost precisely in the middle of what the historian Walter Nugent called the Grand Conjuncture between rural and metropolitan America, 1870–1920. And metropolitan America had won. Henry Adams, who lived through the 1890s, wrote in *The Education of Henry Adams:*

> For a hundred years . . . the American people had hesitated, vacillated, swayed forward and back, between two forces, one simply industrial [productive], the other capitalistic, centralizing and mechanical. . . . the majority at last declared itself, once and for all, in favor of the capitalistic system with all its necessary machinery. All one's friends, all one's best citizens, reformers, churches, colleges, educated classes, had joined the banks to force submission to capitalism. . . .

The first important act of the McKinley administration was to call a special session of Congress to raise the tariff again. The Dingley Tariff of 1897 became the highest to that time. By 1897 prosperity was returning, helped along by inflation of the currency, which bore out the arguments of greenbackers and silverites. But the inflation came, in one of history's many ironies, from neither greenbackers nor silver, but from a new flood of gold into the market and into the mints. During the 1880s and 1890s new discoveries of gold in the South African Rand, the Canadian Yukon, and in Alaska, aided by the development of a new cyanide process for extracting gold from its ore, led to spectacular new gold rushes. The Yukon alone, from 1897 to 1904, was estimated to have added some $100 million worth of gold to the world's store. In 1900 Congress passed a Gold Standard Act, which marked the temporary passing of the silver issue.

The old issues of tariffs and currency were now swallowed up by the Spanish-American War, which ushered in a new era. "The Spanish War finished us," said old Populist Tom Watson. "The blare of the bugle drowned the voice of the Reformer." And yet to compound the irony, most of the Populists' Omaha platform, which seemed so radical at the time, would be in effect within two decades.

FURTHER READING

Overviews of the Gilded Age deal in detail with politics. Vincent P. DeSantis's *The Shaping of Modern America, 1877–1916* (1973),° gives a clear narrative of political tangles, while Robert H. Wiebe's *The Search for Order, 1880–1920* (1967),° is more interpretive. Matthew Josephson's *The Politicos, 1865–1896* (1938),° argues the traditional view that those in power lacked principle. More comprehensive and sweeping in its coverage of change is Morton Keller's *Affairs of State: Public Life in Nineteenth Century America* (1977),° an indispensable guide to the forces which positively affected politics.

Some scholars treat the subject by focusing on party process. Leonard D. White's *The Republican Era, 1869–1901* (1958), concentrates on activities at the federal level. H. Wayne Morgan's *From Hays to McKinley: National Party Politics, 1877–1896* (1966), takes an organizational approach. Also party-specific are Robert D. Marcus's *GOP: Political Structure in the Gilded Age, 1880–1896* (1971), and Horace S. Merrill's *Bourbon Democracy in the Midwest, 1865–1896* (1967).° David J. Rothman concentrates on one legislative group in *Politics and Power: The United States Senate, 1869–1901* (1966).

Much recent scholarship concentrates on the ethnocultural thesis which stresses that community values as represented by religious affiliation separated the voters. Paul Kleppner's *The Cross of Culture: A Social Analysis of Midwestern Politics, 1850–1900* (1970), and *The Third Electoral System, 1852–1892* (1979), are salient works for this approach. Others include Samuel T. McSeveney's *The Politics of Depression: Political Behavior in the Northeast, 1893–1896* (1972), and Richard J. Jensen's *The Winning of the Midwest: Social and Political Conflicts, 1888–1896* (1971).

For reviews of the administrations of Gilded Age presidents, see William S. McFeeley's *Grant: A Biography* (1981),° Justis D. Doenecke's *The Presidencies of James A. Garfield and Chester A. Arthur* (1981), Allan Peskin's *Garfield: A Biography* (1978), Thomas C. Reeves's *Gentleman Boss: The Life of Chester Alan Arthur* (1975), and Lewis L. Gould's *The Presidency of William McKinley* (1980).

Biographies on other notables include David D. Anderson's *William Jennings Bryan* (1981), a short introduction, and David Jordan's *Roscoe Conkling of New York* (1971).

Issues and interest groups also receive special attention. Mary R. Dearing's *Veterans in Politics* (1952) details the influence of the veterans' lobby. John G. Sproat's *The Best Men: Liberal Reformers in the Gilded Age* (1968),° Gerald W. McFarland's *Mugwumps, Morals, and Politics, 1884–1920* (1975), and Ari Hoogenboom's *Outlawing the Spoils: A History of the Civil Service Reform Movement, 1865–1883* (1961), all examine the issue of government service. Tom E. Terrill's *The Tariff, Pol-*

°These books are available in paperback editions.

itics, and American Foreign Policy, 1874–1901 (1973), lends clarity to that complex issue. The finances of the Gilded Age are covered in Irwin Unger's *The Greenback Era: A Social and Political History of American Finance, 1865–1879* (1964),° Walter T. K. Nugent's *Money and American Society, 1865–1880* (1968), and Allen Weinstein's *Prelude to Populism: Origins of the Silver Issue, 1867–1878* (1970).

The study of issues and interest groups comes together in books on populism. The most comprehensive and controversial work on the subject is Lawrence Goodwyn's *Democratic Promise: The Populist Movement in America* (1976), also available in condensed form as *The Populist Moment* (1978).° Goodwyn's emphasis on the cooperative nature of agrarian protest contradicts the interpretations of John Hicks in *The Populist Revolt* (1931),° which portrays agrarians as forerunners of liberal reform, and Richard Hofstadter's *The Age of Reform* (1954),° which depicts them as reactionary. Norman Pollack's *The Populist Response to Industrial America* (1966) is more Marxist in tone.

State-level studies add to the diversity of interpretation. Among the better works are Sheldon Hackney's *From Populism to Progressivism in Alabama* (1969), William W. Rogers's *One-Galloused Revolution: Agrarianism in Alabama, 1865–1896* (1970), Walter T. K. Nugent's *The Tolerant Populists: Kansas, Populism, and Nativism* (1963), and O. Gene Clanton's *Kansas Populism: Ideas and Men* (1969).

Robert McMath's *Populist Vanguard: A History of the Southern Farmers Alliance* (1975),° J. Morgan Kousser's *The Shaping of Southern Politics: Suffrage Restriction and the Establishment of the One-Party South, 1880–1910* (1974),° and Bruce Palmer's *Man over Money: The Southern Populist Critique of American Capitalism* (1980) each deals with selected aspects of the agrarian cause.

Biographies of leading agrarians include C. Vann Woodward's *Tom Watson, Agrarian Rebel* (1973),° Stuart Noblin's *Leonidas Lafayette Polk: Agrarian Crusader* (1949), Peter Argersinger's *Populism and Politics: William Alfred Peffer and the People's Party* (1974), and Louis W. Koenig's *Bryan: A Political Biography of William Jennings Bryan* (1971).° For the role of leading populists in the election of 1896, consult Paul W. Glad's *McKinley, Bryan, and the People* (1964) and Robert F. Durden's *The Climax of Populism: The Election of 1896* (1965).°

23

THE COURSE OF EMPIRE

TOWARD THE NEW IMPERIALISM

DIPLOMACY AFTER THE CIVIL WAR   Foreign affairs remained low on the horizon of public awareness, throughout most of the late nineteenth century. The overriding concerns of the time were the development of industry, settlement of the West, and domestic politics. Compared to these, foreign relations simply were not important to the vast majority of Americans. The major issues of foreign affairs stemming from the Civil War were settled within a few years of its end, after which few conflicts or major issues arose to trouble the American people. A mood of isolation settled upon the United States, favored since the War of 1812 with what the historian C. Vann Woodward called "free security:" wide oceans as buffers on either side, the British navy situated between America and the powers of Europe, and militarily weak neighbors in the Western Hemisphere.

At the end of the Civil War Lincoln's Secretary of State William H. Seward continued to serve under President Johnson and persisted in his policy of protest and watchful waiting on the French occupation of Mexico, which had begun while the United States was distracted by its domestic conflicts. His patience paid off when the growing power in Europe of Bismarck's Prussia impelled Napoleon III to end his Mexican adventure in 1867, four years after it began, in order to bolster French defenses at home. Napoleon's puppet in Mexico, Emperor Maximilian, continued a hopeless fight, but without French troops to prop him up was soon overwhelmed and executed by Mexican forces under Benito Juarez, who became president of a restored republic in June 1867. In the same year Seward negotiated the puchase of Alaska from the Russians for $7.2 million, thus removing the most recent colonial power from the New World. "Seward's folly" of buying the Alaskan "icebox" proved in time to be the biggest bargain for the United States, economically and strategically, since the Louisiana Purchase. Seward's effort to buy the Virgin Islands from Denmark for $7.5 million met with rebuff from the Radicals in Congress, but his proclamation of annexation of the Midway Islands (1867) was carried without effective challenge.

Seward's successor under Grant, Hamilton Fish, proceeded to settle the outstanding issues in controversy with Great Britain through the 1871 Treaty of Washington. Under the treaty an arbitration panel of five nations settled the "Alabama claims" brought by the government for destruction wrought by Confederate raiders built in Britain. The panel awarded some $15 million to the United States but partially balanced that off with $5.5 million to the British for damages suffered during the Civil War. The disputed ownership of the San Juan Islands was settled when the German kaiser ruled that they lay on the American side of the main channel between Vancouver Island and the state of Washington. Finally, mutual agreement was reached on fishing rights for Americans off Canada and for Canadians south to the Thirty-ninth Parallel. With these decisions, foreign affairs receded for a time.

EXPANSION IN THE PACIFIC   Yet the spirit of Manifest Destiny remained alive, if muted. Expansionism surfaced in Grant's attempt to annex Santo Domingo in 1870, which was defeated in the Senate. Seward had articulated a vision of empire which "must continue to move on westward until the tides of the renewed and the decaying civilizations of the world meet on the shores of the Pacific Ocean." Seward, whom the historian Walter LaFeber called "the prince of players" in this drama, was followed at the State Department by a line of secretaries who never completely lost sight of this expansionist vision, including Fish, James G. Blaine, and Richard Olney.

The Pacific Ocean remained the major field of overseas activity. America's interest in the area was nearly as old as the Republic. The China trade, begun in 1784, had been a steady if minor part of the nation's foreign trade ever since, and had brought with it a variety of other contacts in the Pacific. Whalers, first active in the colonial period, pursued their prey into the Pacific. The missionary impulse had taken Americans into India and Burma as early as 1812, into Hawaii by the 1820s, and into China by the 1830s.

The urge to annex islands in the Pacific was first expressed by Commodore Perry in 1853–1854. Perry had his eye on the Bonin Islands, off the coast of Japan. He was overruled, but in the flush years of expansionism during the 1850s the United States laid claim to various small islands and coral atolls of the mid-Pacific, sometimes in conflict with the claims of other nations. Among these islands, two inhabited groups occupied especially strategic positions about twenty degrees from either side of the equator: Samoa on the south and Hawaii (the Sandwich Islands) on the north. Both had major harbors, Pago Pago and Pearl Harbor respectively, with which Americans had made contact as early as the 1820s. In the years after the Civil War American interest in these islands gradually deepened.

SAMOA In 1872 U.S. Navy Commander R. W. Meade negotiated a treaty with a Samoan chieftain giving the United States a naval station at Pago Pago. The Senate took no action on the treaty. Col. A. B. Steinberger, a special agent of Grant, then organized a government on his own initiative and installed himself as prime minister of Samoa, but was soon overthrown and deported on a British vessel. Finally, in 1878, a permanent American presence was established. The Samoans signed a treaty with the United States which granted a naval base at Pago Pago, extraterritoriality for Americans (meaning that in Samoa they remained subject only to American law), exchanged trade concessions, and called for the United States to extend its good offices in case of a dispute with another nation. The Senate ratified this accord and in the following year the German and British governments worked out similar arrangements on other islands of the Samoan group.

There things rested until civil war broke out in 1887 when the Germans backed a pretender against the native Samoan king and finally installed him under a German protectorate. The sequel to this incident was a conference in Berlin, called at the suggestion of German Chancellor Bismarck, which established a tripartite protectorate, with Germany, Great Britain, and the United States in an uneasy partnership.

HAWAII In Hawaii the Americans had more nearly a clear field. The islands, a united kingdom since 1795, had a sizable settlement of American missionaries and planters and were strategically more important to the United States. Occupation by another major power might have posed a threat to American commercial interests and even to American defense. As early as 1842 Secretary of State Daniel Webster said that the United

States would be "dissatisfied" to see any other power take possession.

In 1875 the kingdom entered a reciprocal trade agreement under which Hawaiian sugar entered the United States duty free. Hawaii also promised that none of its territory would be leased or granted to a third power. In 1884 the agreement was renewed but it was not ratified by the Senate until 1887, when it was amended to grant the United States exclusive right to a fortified naval base at Pearl Harbor, near Honolulu. These agreements resulted in a boom in sugar growing, and American settlers in Hawaii came to have a dominant position economically. The fortunes of white planters were based on cheap immigrant labor, mainly Chinese, Japanese, and Portuguese. By the 1890s the native population had been reduced to a minority by smallpox and other foreign diseases, and Orientals quickly became the most numerous group in Hawaii. In 1887 the Americans forced King Kalakaua to grant a constitutional government which they dominated.

Things changed sharply when the king's sister, Queen Liliuokalani, ascended the throne in 1891 and began efforts to restore absolute power. Shortly before that the McKinley Tariff had destroyed Hawaii's favored position in the sugar trade by putting the sugar of all countries on the free list and granting growers in the United States a two-cent bounty. The resultant discontent led the white population to stage a revolt early in 1893. A committee of public safety under Sanford B. Dole, justice of the Hawaiian Supreme Court, seized power. The American minister, John L. Stevens, brought in marines from the cruiser *Boston* to

Queen Liliuokalani. [Public Archives of Hawaii]

support the coup. Within a month a committee of the new government turned up in Washington and in February signed a treaty of annexation with Secretary of State John W. Foster.

The treaty, however, came just weeks before President Harrison left office, and Democratic senators blocked ratification. On March 9 President Cleveland withdrew the treaty and sent former Rep. James H. Blount of Georgia as a special commissioner to investigate. Blount withdrew the American marines and reported that Stevens had acted improperly. Most Hawaiians opposed annexation, Blount said. He thought that the revolution had been engineered mainly by sugar planters hoping to get the domestic sugar bounty by annexation. Cleveland therefore proposed to restore the queen in return for amnesty to the revolutionists. The provisional government refused and on July 4, 1894, proclaimed the Republic of Hawaii, which had in its constitution a standing provision for American annexation, presumably after Cleveland yielded to a president whose sensibilities were less easily offended.

STEPS TO WORLD POWER

The antebellum spirit of expansionism thus had neither died out with the 1850s nor gone completely dormant. It would return full blown in the 1890s with the addition of some new flourishes. European powers from about 1870 on set an example with a new surge of imperialism in Africa and Asia, where they acquired colonies, protectorates, and economic privileges. All of Africa except Liberia and Ethiopia fell under outside dominion. Above all, the new imperialism was economic, a quest for markets and raw materials, and to more than one American the European example seemed relevant to the American experience. The closing of the frontier, brought forcefully to public attention by the census of 1890 and by Frederick Jackson Turner's classic essay on the significance of the frontier in 1893, might well signal the end of a constantly growing market and a need to seek markets overseas, many people reasoned. Turner himself had written: "He would be a rash prophet who would assert that the expansive character of American life has now entirely ceased. Movement has been its dominant fact, and, unless this training has no effect upon a people, the American energy will continually demand a wider field for its exercise."

Most Americans shared a concern with world markets as developments in transportation and communication quickened the pace of commerce and diplomacy. From the first, exports of farm products had been the basis of American economic growth. Now the conviction grew that American manufactures had matured to the point that they could outsell foreign goods in the world market. The new conviction challenged an old Republican principle that industry must be protected against foreign competition in the domestic market. But should the expansion of markets lead to territorial expansion as well? Or to intervention in the internal affairs of other countries? On this point Americans disagreed, but a growing minority in public life were ready to entertain the idea of overseas possessions; they were led by Sen. Albert J. Beveridge of Indiana and Henry Cabot Lodge of Massachusetts, Theodore Roosevelt, and not least of all, Capt. Alfred Thayer Mahan.

NAVAL POWER   Captain Mahan, son of Dennis T. Mahan, West Point's one-time strategist of land war, became himself a leading advocate of sea power. A graduate of Annapolis, he served for years as president of the Naval War College at Newport, Rhode Island. A series of his lectures on naval history grew into a volume published in 1890, *The Influence of Sea Power upon History, 1660–1783*, in which he argued that national greatness and prosperity flowed from sea power, which had a fundamentally economic importance. To Mahan, economic development called for a big navy, a strong merchant marine, foreign commerce, colonies, and naval bases. The age of steam made coaling stations a new matter of strategic concern. Mahan expounded on America's destiny to control the Caribbean, build an isthmian canal, and spread Western civilization in the Pacific. His ideas were widely circulated in popular journals.

Even before Mahan's writings became influential a gradual expansion of the navy had gotten under way, after a season of post–Civil War neglect led the *Army and Navy Journal* in 1874 to call the American fleet a "heterogeneous collection of naval trash." In 1880 the nation had fewer than a hundred sea-going vessels, many of them rusting or rotting at the docks. By the time Cleveland entered office four new steel vessels had been authorized, and Cleveland's navy secretary, William C. Whitney, got funds in 1886 for twenty more, including the battleships *Maine* and *Texas*. By 1896 eleven battleships had been built or authorized. The depression of the 1890s was little felt at the Newport News Shipbuilding and Drydock Company and other shipyards. In 1897 Theodore Roosevelt, as assistant secretary of the navy under John D. Long in the McKinley administration, worked overtime to get the new navy in condition for a war he expected —and even wanted.

The battleship Maine, *funded in 1886, shown here entering Havana Harbor in 1898.* [National Archives]

RACIAL THOUGHT   Meanwhile certain intellectual currents of the day workd to bolster the new Manifest Destiny. The Darwinian idea of natural selection afforded a handy argument for imperialism. If natural selection worked in the biological realm, would it not apply also in human society? Among nations, as among individuals, the fittest survive and prevail. "There is apparently much truth in the belief that the wonderful progress of the United States, as well as the character of the people, are the results of natural selection," Darwin himself wrote in *The Descent of Man* (1871), "the more energetic, restless and courageous men from all parts of Europe having emigrated during the last ten or twelve generations to that great country and having there succeeded best." Darwin himself, however, cannot fairly be tagged a champion of imperialism or of racial "purity."

John Fiske, the historian and popular lecturer on Darwinism, nevertheless developed racial corollaries from Darwin's idea. In *American Political Ideas* (1885) he stressed the superior character of "Anglo-Saxon" institutions and peoples. The English "race," he argued, was destined to dominate the globe: in the institutions, traditions, language, even in the blood of the world's peoples. John W. Burgess, a historian and political scientist at Columbia University, argued similarly that the Teutonic peoples had a superior political talent and a duty to spread the blessings of their superior institutions.

Josiah Strong, a Congregational minister, added the sanction of religion. In his book *Our Country: Its Possible Future and Its Present Crisis* (1885), Strong argued that "Anglo-Saxons" embodied two great ideas: civil liberty and "a pure spiritual Christianity." The Anglo-Saxon was "divinely commissioned to be, in a pecular sense, his brother's keeper." Expansion to establish foreign missions found favor in both Protestant and Catholic churches, the chief opposition coming from minority groups like the Quakers and Unitarians.

LATIN AMERICA   By the 1890s events drew the United States more and more into the orbit of world affairs. One significant step came with the First International American Conference in Washington, which met from late 1889 through early 1890. The idea of closer commercial and cultural ties with Latin America had been for years associated with the name of James G. Blaine. Like Henry Clay, whose "American System" he admired, Blaine hoped to expand trade with Latin America and bring the American republics closer together. Named secretary of state by Garfield, late in 1881 he sent out invitations to a general peace conference of American republics to meet in November 1882. The succession of Arthur brought Blaine's resignation and the plan fell through.

Blaine's vindication awaited yet another administration. In 1888 Congress authorized President Cleveland to call a conference of American states, but when the First International American Conference met on October 2, 1889, Blaine was again secretary of state, this time under Harrison. Seventeen Latin American states sent delegates. Blaine's ultimate hope was to establish a customs union and to initiate free trade among American nations. The Latin delegates, however, were afraid of damaging their ties with Europe for the benefit of manufacturers in the United States. They resolved therefore in favor of reciprocity agreements, and over the next few years Blaine secured tariff concessions from ten Latin countries by executive agreements under the provisions of the McKinley Tariff. Though it failed to set up machinery for the arbitration of disputes, the conference did establish a permanent agency as a clearinghouse for information: the Bureau of American Republics, later the Pan-American Union, which in 1948 became the Organization of American States.

CANADA AND SOUTH AMERICA   But not all was sweetness and light in the Western Hemisphere. In the 1880s and 1890s incidents in the Bering Sea, in Chile, and in Venezuela stirred the bumptious spirit of national pride that never lay far below the surface. At issue in the Bering Sea was the practice of pelagic (oceanic) sealing by foreign nationals, mostly Canadians, in offshore waters where the difficulty of distinguishing males and females resulted in the loss of many pups when their mothers were killed. This was an issue because a caprice of fashion had put sealskin coats and muffs much in demand. In 1886 American revenue cutters began seizing Canadian ships engaged in the practice, and in 1889 Congress declared the Bering a closed sea under United States dominion. In an exchange of notes in 1890, however, British Foreign Minister Lord Salisbury refused to accept the legitimacy of Congress's claim. There was a flurry of bluster in the American press, but never much chance that the two countries would come to blows over what a Spokane Falls newspaper called "a few greasy, ill-smelling sealskins." Eventually, under an arbitration treaty of 1892, it was decided that while the Bering was an open sea, by mutual agreement pelagic sealing was forbidden within sixty miles of the Pribilof Islands. Later, in 1911, by treaty with Britain, Russia, and Japan, pelagic sealing was prohibited throughout the North Pacific and Bering Sea.

Trouble in Chile flared intensely, but passed quickly. When civil war broke out in that country in 1891, American authorities briefly detained a rebel ship carrying arms from San Diego, then found that there had been no violation of neutrality laws. This left a lingering resentment among the rebels, who soon took over Chile's government. In October 1891, when the cruiser *Baltimore* called at Valparaiso, a mob attacked sailors returning from the True Blue Saloon. Two sailors were killed and seventeen hurt in the fracas, and some were thrown into jail. For a season tempers ran hot as the countries exchanged imprecations. By January 1892 Secretary Blaine was theatening to break off relations, and President Harrison waxed bellicose in a special message to Congress. Happily, tempers cooled in Valparaiso and Chile offered an apology and an indemnity of $75,000.

Far more serious was the Venezuelan boundary dispute with British Guiana, which had simmered since colonial days but took on new urgency when gold was found in the disputed area. When Venezuela suspended diplomatic relations with Britain in 1887, the American State Department suggested arbitration, but the matter was still unsettled in 1892 when Cleveland was reelected to the White House. In 1895 Congress passed a resolution for arbitration, largely at the instigation of William L. Scruggs, who had been Harrison's minister to Venezuela. Cleveland was almost forced to "twist the lion's tail" or see his political opponents do it. He may even have found the occasion a welcome diversion from his domestic problems. His secretary of state, Richard L. Olney, got up a note dated July 20 in which he invoked the Monroe Doctrine against British interference in the affairs of the New World. Cleveland claimed to have softened the "verbiage" a bit, but still dubbed it a "20 inch gun" note.

> Today [Olney wrote] the United States is practically sovereign on this continent, and its fiat is law upon the subjects to which it confines its interposition. Why? ... It is because, in addition to all other grounds, its infinite resources combined with its isolated position render it master of the situation and practically invulnerable as against any or all other powers.

The note was calculated to provoke a quick reply, but Lord Salisbury let it lie for a maddening four months. The British government was preoccupied elsewhere and assumed the note was largely for domestic American consumption anyway. When Salisbury did respond on November 26, he rejected the demand for arbitration and noted that the Monroe Doctrine was not recognized international law, and in any case was irrelevant to a boundary dispute. Clevelend pronounced himself "mad clear through" at such a rebuff to the "friendly" suggestion of the United States. Congress, at Cleveland's request, unanimously voted for a boundary commission to run the line in spite of the British. Enthusiasm swept the country. Theodore Roosevelt vented his opinion that "this country needs a war." But cooler heads soon prevailed. The British faced more urgent problems in South Africa and a growing German navy, and through the good offices of the United States finally came around to an arbitration treaty with Venezuela, signed in 1897. By the time an international commission handed in its findings in 1899, the focus of public attention was elsewhere. The settlement turned out to be about what the British had offered in the first place.

THE SPANISH-AMERICAN WAR

"CUBA LIBRE" Until the 1890s a certain ambivalence about overseas possessions had checked America's drive to expand. Suddenly in 1898 and 1899 the inhibitions collapsed and American power thrust its way to the far reaches of the Pacific. The occasion for this explosion of imperialism lay neither in the Pacific nor in the quest for bases and trade, but to the south in Cuba. The chief motive was a sense of outrage at another country's imperialism.

After the age of filibustering in the 1850s diplomatic interest in Cuba had waned; it revived only briefly during a ten-year insurrection, from 1868 to 1878. After the insurrection was brought under control in 1878, American investments in Cuba, mainly in sugar and mining, rose to about $50 million. The United States in fact traded more with Cuba than Spain did. On February 24, 1895, insurrection broke out again. Simmering discontent with Spanish rule had been aggravated by the Wilson-Gorman Tariff of 1894, which took sugar off the free list in the midst of a depression already damaging to the market for Cuban sugar. Public feeling in the United States was with the rebels, and many Americans extended help to the Cuban Revolutionary party which organized the revolt from headquarters in New York. Its leader, José Marti, returned to the island soon after the outbreak and was killed in a skirmish with Spanish troops. Leadership then fell to Maximo Gomez, a native Santo Domingan, who had led the earlier Ten Years' War.

The insurrectionists' strategy was to wage guerrilla warfare and to damage the economic life of the island, which in turn would excite the concern of American investors. The strategy dictated hit-and-run attacks on trains, railways, and plantations. The movement found one source of income by selling "protection" against attack. Such tactics forced people either into the insurgent forces or into garrisoned towns, which in turn might be cut off from food supplies. Revolutionary propaganda of course presented the effort in a different light, and Americans were more than ready to look upon the insurrection in the light of their own War of Independence. American attentions were distracted by the Venezuelan crisis and the election of 1896, but Spanish authorities insisted that only aid from the United States kept the revolt alive.

The strategies needed to counter guerrilla warfare nearly always cast their practitioners in a bad light. In 1896 Spanish Gen. Valeriano Weyler adopted a policy of gathering Cubans behind Spanish lines, often in detention *(reconcentrado)* centers so that no one could join the insurrections by night and appear peaceful by day. In some of the centers a combination of tropical climate, poor food, and unsanitary conditions soon brought a heavy toll of disease and death. The American press promptly christened the Spanish commander "Butcher" Weyler.

Events in Cuba supplied exciting copy for the popular press. Chance had it that William Randolph Hearst's New York *Journal* and Joseph Pulitzer's New York *World* were at the time locked in a monumental struggle for circulation. "It was a battle of gigantic proportions," the journalist Walter Mills wrote, "in which the sufferings of Cuba merely chanced to furnish some of the most convenient ammunition." Another device of the circulation war was the new-fangled comic strip and one of the most popular was "The Yellow Kid," the cartoonist for which Hearst lured from Pulitzer with a high salary. Hence, by association, the unbuttoned sensationalism at which the papers vied came to be called "yellow journalism." Hearst emerged as the undisputed champion. Frederick Remington, the artist best known for his cowboy pictures, supplied Hearst's *Journal* an imaginary picture which left the impression that three Cuban women on a detained American ship had been forced to disrobe in the presence of male Spanish officers. Pulitzer was able to demonstrate the falsity of the report, but truth was a poor substitute for titillation. A Hearst reporter, by means of bribery and intrigue, spirited one Evangeline Cisneros out of a Spanish prison and away from Cuba, whereupon a member of Congress suggested hiring a thousand such reporters to liberate the whole island. The *Journal* excelled also at invective against "Weyler the brute, the devastator of haciendas, the destroyer of men."

At the outset the Cleveland administration tried to protect American rights but avoided involvement beyond an offer of mediation. Mounting public sympathy for the cause, however, manifested itself in Congress. By concurrent resolution on April 6, 1896, the two houses endorsed recognition of the Cuban belligerents and urged the president to seek a peace on the basis of Cuban independence. Cleveland, however, denied any designs against Spanish rule and offered to cooperate with Spain in bringing peace on the basis of home rule. The Spanish politely refused. Meanwhile America's revenue service and naval forces did their best to break up filibustering and gun-running expeditions launched from the Atlantic and Gulf coasts.

PRESSURE FOR WAR   The posture of neutrality changed sharply when McKinley entered office. He had been elected on a platform that endorsed independence for Cuba, as well as American control of Hawaii and of an isthmian canal. In October a new Spanish commander, Ramon Blanco, set out to liberalize the reconcentration system and in November Spain's queen regent offered Cuba autonomy in return for peace. What the Cubans might once have welcomed, however, they now rejected, insurrectionists and Spanish loyalists alike. Spain was impaled on the horns of a dilemma, unable to end the war and unready to give up Cuba.

Early in 1898 events moved rapidly to arouse opinion against Spain. On January 12 a riotous demonstration of loyalists in Havana denounced Weyler's recall and the offer of autonomy. Consul-General Fitzhugh Lee seized the occasion to request a warship nearby, perhaps at Key West, to help assure the security of American citizens and property. The battleship *Maine* showed up on January 25, but in Havana harbor, ostensibly on a courtesy call. On February 9 Hearst's New York *Journal* released the text of a letter from Spanish Minister Depuy de Lôme to a friend in Havana, stolen from the post office by a Cuban spy. In the letter de Lôme called President McKinley "weak and a bidder for the admiration of the crowd, besides being a would-be politician who tries to leave a door open behind himself while keeping on good terms with the jingoes of his party." This was hardly more extreme than what McKinley's assistant secretary of the navy Theodore Roosevelt had said about him: "no more backbone than a chocolate eclair." But that comment had remained private. De Lôme resigned to prevent further embarrassment to his government.

Six days later, on February 15, the *Maine* exploded in Havana harbor and sank with a loss of 260 men. A naval court of inquiry reported in March that an external mine had set off an explosion in the ship's magazine. Lacking evidence, the court made no effort to fix the blame, but the yellow press had no need of evidence. The outcry against Spain reached a crescendo in the words "Remember the Maine!" Never mind that one cannot imagine any advantage Spain could derive from such an act. What actually happened, whether accidentally or on purpose, remains a mystery.

Hearst's Journal *reports the sinking of the* Maine. *The uproar created by the incident and its coverage in the "yellow press" edged McKinley toward war.* [New York Historical Society]

McKinley, under the mounting pressure of public excitement, tried to maintain a steady course but requested and quickly got from Congress on March 9 a $50-million appropriation for defense. One month later the Spanish government ordered General Blanco to suspend hostilities unilaterally. On April 10 the Spanish minister gave the State Department a message that amounted to a surrender: the United States should indicate the nature and duration of the armistice; Cuba would have an autonomous government; and the two countries would submit the question of the *Maine* to arbitration. On the same day United States Minister Stewart L. Woodford cabled from Madrid an expression of hope that McKinley would get full authority from Congress to secure peace by negotiations. "I hope nothing will now be done to humiliate Spain, as I am satisfied that the present government is going, and is loyally ready to go, as fast and as far as it can." McKinley, he predicted, could win settlement by August 1 on any terms: autonomy, independence, or cession of Cuba to the United States.

The following day found McKinley sending Congress what amounted to a war message. He asked for power to use armed forces in Cuba to abate a nuisance off the United States' shores and to protect American property and trade. The Cuban situation, McKinley said, was a constant menace to the peace. Back to the president came a joint resolution of Congress, which went beyond endorsing the use of the armed forces: it declared Cuba independent an demanded withdrawal of Spanish forces. The Teller Amendment, added on the Senate floor, disclaimed any American designs on Cuban territory. McKinley signed the resolution and a copy went off to the Spanish government, with notice that McKinley would execute it unless Spain gave a complete and satisfactory response by noon, April 23. Meanwhile, on April 22 the president announced a blockade of Cuba's northern coast and the port of Santiago. Under international law this was an act of war. Rather than give in to an ultimatum, the Spanish government declared war on April 24. Congress then, determined to be first, declared war on April 25, retroactive to April 21.

Why such a rush into war after Woodford had predicted that Spain would cave in before the summer was out? Chiefly because too much momentum and popular pressure had already built up for a confidential message to change the course of events. Also, leaders of the business community, which tolerates uncertainty poorly, were demanding a quick resolution of the problem. Many lacked faith in the willingness or ability of the Spanish government to carry out a moderate policy in the face of a hostile public opinion. Still, it is fair to ask why McKinley did not take a stand for peace, knowing what he did. He might have defied Congress and public opinion, but in the end the political risk was too high. The Democrats were likely to adopt the popular cause of Cuba. The ultimate blame for war, if blame must be levied, belongs to the American people for letting themselves be whipped up into such a hostile frenzy.

DEWEY TAKES MANILA The war itself was short, lasting four months, and for America, victorious. John Hay called it "a splendid little war." The war's end was also the end of Spain's once-great New World empire, which had begun with Columbus. It marked as well the emergence of the United States as a world power. If American participation saved many lives by ending the insurrection in Cuba, it also led to American involvement in another insurrection, in the Philippines, and created a host of problems that persisted into the twentieth century.

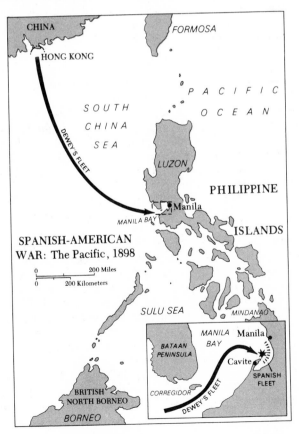

The war was barely under way before the navy produced a quick, spectacular victory in an unexpected quarter—Manila Bay. While public attention was fixed on Cuba, young Theodore Roosevelt was thinking of the Philippines. As assistant secretary of the navy, he had Commodore George Dewey appointed commander of the small Asiatic squadron, and had seen to it that ample supplies went out to the squadron at Hong Kong along with orders to engage Spain in the Philippines in case of war. President McKinley had approved those orders.

Arriving late on April 30 with four cruisers and two gunboats, Dewey proceeded on May 1 to destroy or capture all the Spanish warships in Manila Bay. The Spanish force lost 381 men killed, while Dewey's squadron suffered casualties of 8 wounded. Dewey, without a force of occupation, was now in awkward possession of Manila Bay. Promised reinforcements, he stayed while foreign warships, including a German force equal if not superior to Dewey's, hung about the scene like watchful vultures. Land reinforcements finally arrived, and with the help of Filipino insurrectionists under Emilio Aguinaldo, Dewey's forces entered Manila on August 13.

THE CUBAN CAMPAIGN While these events transpired halfway around the world, the war reached a quick climax closer to home, which was surprising because American preparation for this war was spotty. The navy was fit, but the army could muster only an ill-assorted guard of 28,000 regulars and about 100,000 militiamen. Altogether during the war about 200,000 more militiamen were recruited, chiefly as state volunteers. The armed forces suffered badly from both inexperience and maladministration, with the result that more died from disease than from enemy action. The United States' salvation was that Spanish forces were even worse off, their morale infinitely so.

Events pushed the United States into a Cuban campaign sooner than at first planned. On April 29 Spanish Adm. Pascual Cervera left the Cape Verde Islands with four cruisers and three destroyers, turning up finally in Santiago de Cuba where the U.S. Navy put the Spanish fleet under blockade. Adm. William T. Sampson soon arrived to assume command, and found a situation in need of land forces. The navy could not venture too close to shore, land troops might force Cervera to flee bombardment from land batteries and risk battle at sea.

So it fell out that land and sea battles around Santiago early in July broke Spanish resistance and ended the war within another month. A force of some 17,000 troops hastily assembled at

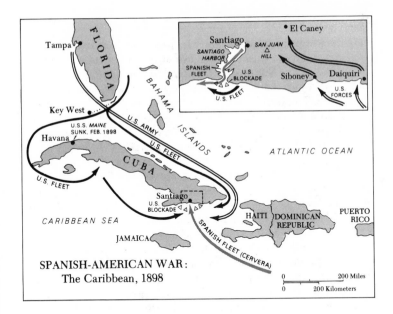

SPANISH-AMERICAN WAR:
The Caribbean, 1898

Tampa under the command of General Shafter. One significant element of that force was Col. Leonard Wood's First Volunteer Cavalry, better known as the "Rough Riders" and best remembered because Lt.-Col. Theodore Roosevelt was second in command. Eager to get "in on the fun," Roosevelt had quit the Navy Department to join a colorful volunteer regiment of eastern dudes and southwestern deadshots. At Tampa Roosevelt found three regiments assigned to a ship that could hold but one, whereupon he double-timed the Rough Riders on board. "There was a great deal of expostulation," he wrote later, "but we had possession." There they sat for six days in a stream of sewage. Their landing at Daiquiri was an equally mad scramble. The horses went somewhere else leaving the horseless Rough Riders "Wood's Weary Walkers." The disorganized army might have been defeated by a determined attack at that point.

The major land action of the campaign occurred on July 1. About 7,000 Americans took the fortified village of El Caney from about 600 of the enemy garrison. While a much larger force attacked San Juan Hill, a smaller unit, including the dismounted Rough Riders, together with black soldiers from the Ninth and Tenth Cavalry seized the enemy position atop nearby Kettle Hill. The two battles put American forces atop heights from which to the west and south they could bring Santiago and the Spanish fleet under seige. On July 3 Admiral Cervera made a gallant run for it, but his decrepit ships were little more than sitting ducks for the newer American fleet, which included five battleships and two cruisers. The casualties were as one-sided as at Manila: 474 Spanish were killed and wounded and 1,750 were taken prisoner, while only one American was killed and one wounded. The timely battle afforded Fourth of July orators the rarest opportunity they had had since the twin Union victories of Vicksburg and Gettysburg thirty-five years before. Santiago surrendered with a garrison of 24,000 on July 17. On July 25 a force under Gen. Nelson A. Miles moved into Puerto Rico against minor resistance. What was to have been the first action of the war became, in the words of Finley Peter Dunne's Mr. Dooley, fictional Irish bartender and commentator on the passing scene, General Miles's "gran' picnic and moonlight excursion."

The day after Miles landed the Spanish government sued for peace through the French ambassador in Washington. After discussions lasting two weeks, an armistice was signed on August 12, less than four months after the war's start and the day before Americans entered Manila. The peace protocol specified that Spain should give up Cuba, and that the United States should annex Puerto Rico and one island in the Ladrones (later called the Marianas), and should occupy the city, bay, and harbor of Manila pending disposition of the Philippines. Among more than 274,000 Americans who served during the war and the ensuing demobilization, 5,462 died, but only 379 in battle. The total wounded numbered 1,704.

THE DEBATE OVER ANNEXATION On October 1, a delegation headed by Secretary of State William R. Day opened negotiations that led to the Treaty of Paris, signed on December 10. Most of the major points had been settled in the peace protocol, but Guam was now designated as the island in the Ladrones to be annexed. Two fundamental questions remained: the Cuban debt and the Philippines. The United States simply refused to assume the Cuban government's debt of $400 million, incurred in the first place largely to subdue the insurrection. The Philippines posed a harder question, indeed one of the biggest decisions to face United States foreign policy to that time, and one that was sprung upon the country without preparation. At first, Mr. Dooley remarked, the American people "did not know whether the Philippines were islands or canned goods." McKinley, who claimed that at first he himself could not locate them within two thousand miles, gave ambiguous signals to the peace commission. The commission itself was divided.

There had been no demand for annexation before the war, but

Dewey's victory quickly kindled expansionist fever. Business-men began thinking of the commercial possibilities not so much in the islands as in the nearby continent of Asia, such as oil for the lamps of China and textiles for its teeming millions. Missionary societies saw the chance to save the "little brown brother." The Philippines promised to provide a useful base for all such activities. It was neither the first nor the last time that Americans would get caught up in fantasies of saving Asia or getting rich there. McKinley pondered the alternatives and later explained his reasoning to a group of Methodists:

> And one night late it came to me this way—I don't know how it was, but it came: (1) that we could not give them back to Spain—that would be cowardly and dishonorable; (2) that we could not turn them over to France or Germany—our commercial rivals in the Orient—that would be bad business and discreditable; (3) that we could not leave them to themselves—they were unfit for self-government—and they would soon have anarchy and misrule over there worse than Spain's was; and (4) that there was nothing left for us to do but to take them all, and to educate the Filipinos, and uplift and civilize and Christianize them, and by God's grace do the very best we could by them, as our fellowmen for whom Christ also died. And then I went to bed, and went to sleep and slept soundly.

In one brief statement he had summarized the motivating ideas of imperialism: (1) national honor, (2) commerce, (3) racial superiority, and (4) altruism. So despite the fact that these candidates for conversion were already largely Catholic, the word went forth to take the Philippines. Spanish negotiations raised the delicate point that American forces had no claim by right of conquest, and had even taken Manila after the armistice. American negotiators finally offered the Spanish compensation of $20 million.

The treaty then added to American territory Puerto Rico, Guam, and the Philippines. Meanwhile Americans had taken other giant steps in the Pacific. Hawaiian annexation, promised in McKinley's platform, failed to get a two-thirds majority in the Senate, but the war demonstrated the islands' strategic importance all the more. The administration therefore moved to annex Hawaii, like Texas, by joint resolution. The resolution passed on July 7, 1898, in the midst of the war. Within a year of the peace treaty, in 1899, after another outbreak of fighting over the royal succession in Samoa, Germany and the United States agreed to partition the Samoan Islands. The United States annexed Tutuila and the other easternmost islands; Germany took the rest, including the largest island, Upolu. Britain ceded its claims in Samoa in return for German concessions in the Pacific (the Tongas and the Solomons) and in Africa. Meanwhile the United States laid claim to Wake Island (1898), which would be a vital link in a future trans-Pacific cable line.

The Treaty of Paris had yet to be ratified in the Senate, where most Democrats and Populists, and some Republicans, opposed it. Anti-imperialists argued that acquisition of the Philippines would undermine American democracy. They appealed to traditional isolationism, American principles of self-government, the inconsistency of liberating Cuba and annexing the Philippines, the involvement in foreign entanglements that would undermine the logic of the Monroe Doctrine, and the danger that the Philippines would become an Achilles heel, expensive if not impossible to defend. The prospect of incorporating so many alien peoples into American life was not the least of some people's worries. "Bananas and self-government cannot grow on the same piece of land," Senator Pettigrew said.

The opposition may have been strong enough to kill the treaty had not William Jennings Bryan influenced the vote for approval. Ending the war, he argued, would open the way for the future independence of Cuba and the Philippines. Finally, ratification came on February 6, 1899, by a vote of 57 to 27. On February 14 the deciding vote of Vice-President Garret A. Hobart defeated a resolution for Philippine independence. That same month in *McClure's* magazine Rudyard Kipling's poem, "The White Man's Burden," called the American people to a new duty:

> Take up the White Man's burden—
>   Send forth the best ye breed—
> Go, bind your sons to exile
>   To serve your captive's need;
> To wait in heavy harness
>   On fluttered folk and wild—
> Your new-caught sullen peoples,
>   Half devil and half child.

By this time Americans had already clashed with Filipino insurrectionists near Manila. The Filipino leader, Emilio Aguinaldo, was in exile until Commodore Dewey brought him back to Luzon to make trouble for the Spanish. Since Aguinaldo's forces were more or less in control of the islands outside of Manila, what followed was largely an American war of conquest which lasted more than two years. Organized Filipino resistance was broken by the end of 1899, but even after the capture of Aguinaldo in

Philippine insurrectionists, led by Emilio Aguinaldo. [Library of Congress]

March 1901 sporadic guerrilla action lasted until mid-1902. It was a sordid little war, marked by massacre and torture on both sides.

Against the backdrop of this agony the great debate over imperialism continued. The treaty debates inspired a number of anti-imperialist groups which united in October 1899 as the American Anti-Imperialist League. The league attracted members representing many shades of opinion; the main thing they had in common was that most belonged to an older generation. George S. Boutwell, the old Stalwart from Massachusetts, was president, but the group included as well Democrat "Pitchfork Ben" Tillman of South Carolina. Andrew Carnegie footed the bills, but on imperialism at least Samuel Gompers was in agreement with him. The group included such prominent figures as Sens. George F. Hoar and George F. Edmunds, Carl Schurz, Charles Francis Adams, Jr., House Speaker Thomas B. Reed, and John Sherman. Presidents Charles Eliot of Harvard and David Staff Jordan of Stanford supported the group, along with social reformer Jane Addams and editor E. L. Godkin of the *Nation.* The drive for power, said the philosopher William James, had caused the nation to "puke up its ancient soul." Mark Twain addressed a letter "To the Person Sitting in Darkness" (McKinley) suggesting that, given current policies, the flag should have "the white stripes painted black and the stars painted by the skull and cross bones."

ROOSEVELT'S RISE   In the fall elections of 1898 Republicans benefited from the euphoria of victory and increased their majority in

Congress. That hardly amounted to a mandate for imperialism, however, since the election preceded most of the debates on the issue. In 1900 the Democrats turned once again to Bryan, who sought to make imperialism the "paramount issue" of the campaign. The Democratic platform condemned the Philippine involvement as "an unnecessary war" which had "placed the United States, previously known and applauded throughout the world as the champion of freedom, in the false and un-American position of crushing with military force the efforts of our former allies to achieve liberty and self-government."

The Republicans welcomed the issue. They renominated McKinley, and to fill the vacancy left by the death of Vice-President Hobart they turned to Theodore Roosevelt, who after his role in both the Philippine and Cuban action was virtually "Mr. Imperialism." Somehow, whether by luck or design, Roosevelt always had correspondents nearby to report on his actions. And lest the public forget, he had hastened into print with his own account of the Rough Rider—a book the wry Mr. Dooley said should have been entitled "Alone in Cuba." After his triumphant return as a war hero Roosevelt had been elected governor of New York in the fall of 1898. Now he profited from support in the West as well as the East, and perhaps as well from the eagerness of New York's Boss Platt to kick the independent Roosevelt upstairs into the harmless post of vice-president.

"Don't haul down the flag!" was a Republican slogan. The question, Bryan retorted, was "Who will haul down the President?" The trouble with Bryan's idea of a solemn referendum on imperialism was the near impossibility of making any presiden-

This 1900 cartoon shows the Republican vice-presidential candidate, Theodore Roosevelt, overshadowing his running mate, President McKinley. [Horace Taylor, January 1, 1900]

tial contest so simple. Bryan himself complicated things by insisting once again on free silver, and the tariff became an issue again too. The Republican's biggest advantage was probably the return to prosperity, which they were fully ready to take credit for. So those who opposed imperialism but also opposed free silver or tariff reduction faced a bewildering choice. One voter was said to have reasoned finally: "It is a choice between evils, and I am going to shut my eyes, hold my nose, vote, go home and disinfect myself."

The outcome was a victory for McKinley greater than his last, by 7.2 million to 6.4 million in the popular vote and by 292 to 155 in the electoral vote. If there had been no clear-cut referendum on annexations, the question was settled nonetheless, although it would take yet another year and a half to subdue the Filipino rebels. The job would be finished, however, under the direction of another president.

On September 6, 1901, while McKinley attended a reception at the Pan-American Exposition in Buffalo, a fanatical anarchist named Leon Czolgosz approached him with a gun concealed in a bandaged hand and fired at point-blank range. McKinley died six days later and Theodore Roosevelt was suddenly elevated to the White House. "Now look," Mark Hanna erupted, "that damned cowboy is President of the United States!" Six weeks short of his forty-third birthday, Roosevelt was the youngest man ever to reach the office, but he brought to it more experience in public affairs than most and perhaps more vitality than any.

Descended from a line of well-to-do New Yorkers and from the Bullochs of Georgia, son of a wealthy merchant, he grew up in surroundings of comfort and culture, visited Europe as a child, spoke German fluently, and finished Harvard in 1880. A sickly, asthmatic, astigmatic child, he built himself up by force of will into a physical and intellectual athlete, a lifelong preacher and practitioner of the "strenuous life," ready, willing, and able to express opinions on any and all subjects.

After Harvard, Roosevelt read law briefly and within two years of graduation won election to the New York legislature and published *The Naval War of 1812*, the first of a number of historical, biographical, and other writings to flow from his pen. After the untimely death of his first wife he moved west to take up the cattle business on the Dakota frontier. His western career was brief, but he never quite got over being a cowboy. Back in New York he ran for mayor, and later served as civil service commissioner, New York City police commissioner, assistant secretary of the navy, colonel of the "Rough Riders," and governor of New York.

TR on the stump.
[Library of Congress]

Teddy Roosevelt was an American original, the embodiment of many a Boy Scout's fantasies. His glittering spectacles and glistening teeth, along with his bouncing ebullience, were a godsend to the cartoonists, who added another trademark when he pronounced the adage: "Speak softly, and carry a big stick." Along with his boundless energy went an unshakable conviction of righteousness and a tendency to cast every issue in moral terms. But appearances were deceiving. The boundless energy left a false impression of impulsiveness and the talk of morality cloaked a cautious pragmatism. Roosevelt could get carried away on occasion, but as he said of his foreign policy steps, this was likely to happen only when "I am assured that I shall be able eventually to carry out my will by force."

ORGANIZING THE NEW ACQUISITIONS   Soon it would be Roosevelt, one of the chief proponents of the American Empire, who would round out its organization. In the Philippines McKinley had already moved toward setting up a civil government. The commission of five he sent to study the situation in the Philippines suggested delay because of unsettled conditions. In 1900 another commission went out under Federal Circuit Judge William Howard Taft with instructions to set up a civil government. Unlike some of the Americans on the scene, Taft seemed genuinely to like the Filipinos and gradually established a rapport with his "little brown brothers." He encouraged them to participate, and eventually to sit on the commission itself.

On July 4, 1901, military government ended and under an act of Congress Taft became the civil governor with appointed provincial governors under his authority. The five-man Philippine Commission continued to function, with three Filipino members added. The Philippine Government Act, passed by Congress on July 1, 1902, made the Philippine Islands an "unorganized territory" and made the inhabitants citizens of the Philippines. When the first elective assembly met in 1907 the commission became the upper house of the legislature—much as the governor's council had been in colonial America. In 1916 the Jones Act made both houses elective and affirmed America's intention to grant the Philippines independence at an indefinite date. Finally, the Tydings-McDuffie Act of 1934 offered independence after a tutelary period of ten more years. A constitution was drafted and ratified, and on September 17 Manuel Quezon was elected the first president of the Philippines. Independence, delayed by World War II, finally took effect on July 4, 1946.

Puerto Rico had been acquired from Spain ostensibly in lieu of a Spanish indemnity, but also as an American outpost on the approaches to the Caribbean and any future isthmian canal. On April 12, 1900, the Foraker Act established a civil government on the island. This act would resemble the one passed two years later for the Philippines. The president appointed a governor and eleven members of an executive council, and an elected house of Delegates made up the lower house of the legislature. Residents of the island were citizens of Puerto Rico but not of the United States until 1917 when the Jones Act granted United States citizenship and made both houses of the legislature elective. In 1947 the governor also became elective, and in 1952 Puerto Rico became a commonwealth with its own constitution and elected officials, a unique status. Like a state, Puerto Rico is free to change its constitution insofar as it does not conflict with the United States Constitution.

The Foraker Act of 1900 also levied a temporary duty on imports from Puerto Rico. The tariff was challenged in the federal courts on the grounds that the island had become part of the United States. In *Downes v. Bidwell* the Supreme Court upheld the tariff. In this and other "Insular Cases" federal judges faced a question which went to the fundamental nature of the American Union, and to the civil and political rights of the people in America's new possessions. In public discussions of the day the issue was summed up in the question: Does the constitution follow the flag? The Court ruled in effect that it did not unless Congress extended it. A concurring opinion by Justice Edward D. White advanced the doctrine of "incorporation." Always before, territories treated as an integral part of the United States had been "incorporated" either by treaty or by act of Congress. Puerto Rico had not, the Court ruled. White suggested "that there may be a distinction between certain natural rights enforced in the Constitution . . . and what may be termed artificial or remedial rights."

Justice John Marshall Harlan confessed that "this idea of 'incorporation' has some occult meaning which my mind does not apprehend." In rapid order, nevertheless, it became an operative doctrine in other cases. The effect was that none of the overseas possessions was declared by the courts "incorporated," not even Hawaii under the Organic Act of 1900, which established a territory in the manner of those on the mainland. Only Alaska was ruled incorporated, although it did not have a territorial government until 1912. In short, outside continental North America Congress could deal with territorial possessions pretty much as it saw fit, except with respect to such fundamental rights as free speech and religion, due process of law, and equal protection of the law.

American authorities soon learned that "Cuba libre" posed problems at least as irksome as those in the new possessions. Cuba's insurgent government was weak and its economy in a state of collapse. Bad relations between American soldiers and Cubans set in almost immediately. General Shafter would not even let the rebels have a hand in the formal surrender of Santiago, and when McKinley set up a military government for the island late in 1898, it was at odds with rebel leaders almost immediately.

Many Europeans expected annexation, and Gen. Leonard Wood, who became Cuba's military governor in December 1899, thought this the best solution. But the United States finally did fulfill the promise of independence for Cuba after the military regime had restored order, gotten schools under way, and improved sanitary conditions. The problem of disease in Cuba provided a focus for the work of Dr. Walter Reed, who made an outstanding contribution to the health of people in warm climates around the world. Named head of the Army Yellow Fever Commission in 1900, he directed experiments with volunteers which proved the theory of Cuban physician Dr. Carlos Finlay that yellow fever was carried by stegomyia mosquitoes. This led the way to effective control of the disease.

In 1900, at President McKinley's order, General Wood called an election for a Cuban constitutional convention. The convention met in November 1900 and drafted a basic law modeled on that of the United States. The Platt Amendment to the Army Appropriation Bill passed by Congress in March 1901, however, sharply restricted the independence of the new government. The amendment required Cuba never to impair its independence by treaty with a third power, to maintain its debt within the government's power to repay out of ordinary revenues, and to acknowledge the right of the United States to intervene for the preservation of Cuban independence and the maintenance of "a government adequate for the protection of life, property, and individual liberty." Finally, Cuba was called upon to sell or lease to the United States lands to be used for coaling or naval stations—a proviso which eventuated in an American naval base at Guantanamo Bay. Under pressure, on June 12, 1901, the Cuban delegates added the Platt Amendment as an appendix to their own constitution. The new Cuban government, established May 20, 1902, then incorporated its provisions in a treaty with the United States signed a year later. As early as August 1906 an insurrection arose against the new government, and President Theodore Roosevelt responded by sending Secretary of War William Howard Taft to "sit on the lid"—weighing in at more than 300 pounds, he was not a bad choice for the job. Backed up by American armed forces Taft assumed full governmental authority, as he had in the Philippines, and the American army stayed until 1909 when a new president was peacefully elected. Further interventions would follow for more than two decades: in 1912 under President Taft, in 1917 under Woodrow Wilson, and in 1933 when President Franklin D. Roosevelt dispatched warships to Cuba. In 1934, however, as part of his "Good Neighbor Policy," Roosevelt negotiated a new treaty which abrogated the Platt Amendment.

IMPERIAL RIVALRIES IN THE FAR EAST

CHINA AND THE "OPEN DOOR" During the 1890s not only the United States but also Japan emerged as a world power. Commodore Perry's voyage of 1853–1854 had opened Japan to Western ways and the country began modernization in earnest after the 1860s, when the Meiji Restoration overthrew the old shogunate. Flexing its new muscles, Japan engaged the moribund Chinese Empire in the Sino-Japanese War (1894–1895) and as a result picked up the Pescadores Islands and the island of Taiwan (renamed Formosa). China's weakness, demonstrated in the war, brought the great powers into a scramble for leaseholds and "spheres of influence" on that remaining frontier of imperialist expansion. Russia secured the privilege of building a railroad across Manchuria and established itself in Port Arthur and the

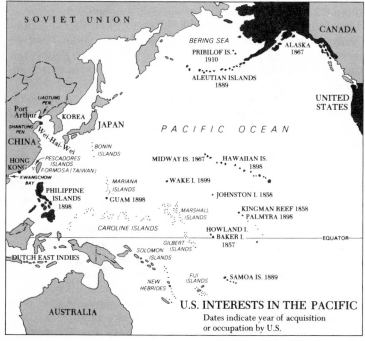

PACIFIC OCEAN

BERING SEA

PRIBILOF IS.
1910

ALASKA
1867

ALEUTIAN ISLANDS
1889

SOVIET UNION

CANADA

UNITED
STATES

LIAOTUNG
PEN.

Port
Arthur

KOREA

JAPAN

SHANTUNG
PEN.

CHINA

Wei-Hai-Wei

BONIN
ISLANDS

MIDWAY IS. 1867

HAWAIIAN IS.
1898

HONG
KONG

PESCADORES
ISLANDS

FORMOSA (TAIWAN)

MARIANA
ISLANDS

WAKE I. 1899

KWANGCHOW
BAY

PHILIPPINE
ISLANDS
1898

GUAM 1898

JOHNSTON I. 1858

MARSHALL
ISLANDS

KINGMAN REEF 1858
PALMYRA 1898

CAROLINE ISLANDS

HOWLAND I.
BAKER I.
1857

EQUATOR

DUTCH EAST INDIES

GILBERT
SOLOMON ISLANDS
ISLANDS

NEW
HEBRIDES

FIJI
ISLANDS

SAMOA IS. 1889

AUSTRALIA

U.S. INTERESTS IN THE PACIFIC
Dates indicate year of acquisition
or occupation by U.S.

Liaotung Peninsula. The Germans moved into Shantung, the French into Kwangchow Bay, the British into Wei-hai-wei.

The bright prospect of American trade with China dimmed with the possibility that the great powers would throw up tariff barriers in their own spheres of influence. The British, ensconced at Hong Kong since 1840, had more to lose though, for they already had far and away the largest foreign trade with China. Just before the Spanish-American War, in March 1898, British Minister Sir Julian Pauncefote suggested joint action with the United States to preserve the integrity of China, and renewed the proposal early in 1899. Both times it was rejected by the Senate because it risked an entangling alliance.

In its origins and content, what soon came to be known as the Open Door Policy was reminiscent of the Monroe Doctrine. In both cases the United States proclaimed unilaterally a hands-off policy which the British had earlier proposed as a joint statement. The policy outlined in Secretary of State John Hay's Open Door Note, dispatched on September 6, 1899, to London, Berlin, and St. Petersburg, and a little later to Tokyo, Rome, and Paris, proposed to keep China open to trade with all countries on an equal basis. More specifically it called upon foreign powers, within their spheres of influence: (1) not to interfere with any treaty port (a port open to all by treaty) or any vested interest, (2) to permit Chinese authorities to collect tariffs on an equal basis, and (3) to show no favors to their own nationals in the matter of harbor dues or railroad charges. Hay's request that each of the powers accept these principles was, the diplomat George Kennan later wrote, like asking everyone who believes in truth to stand: the liars would be the first on their feet. As it turned out, none except Britain accepted Hay's principles, but none rejected them either. The rest gave equivocal answers, usually conditioned on the action of the others. On March 20 Hay blandly announced that all powers had accepted the policy. None stood to deny it.

Soon after that a new crisis arose. In June 1900 a group of Chinese nationalists known to the Western world as Boxers ("Fists of Righteous Harmony") rose in rebellion against foreign encroachments on China laying siege to foreign embassies in Peking. An international expedition of British, German, Russian, Japanese, and American forces was quickly mounted to relieve the embassy compound. Hay, fearful that the intervention might become an excuse to dismember China, seized the chance to further refine the Open Door Policy. The United States, he said in a circular letter of July 3, 1900, sought a solution which would "preserve Chinese territorial and administrative integrity" as well as "equal and impartial trade with all parts of the Chinese Empire."

On August 14 the expedition reached Peking and broke the

This Puck *cartoon shows "Civilization" accusing the Chinese government of complicity in the Boxer Rebellion. [Library of Congress]*

Boxer Rebellion. The occupying powers then agreed to settle for an indemnity from China of approximately $333 million. Of this total the United States got $25 million, of which nearly $11 million was refunded once all claims were paid. Most of this the Chinese government put into a fund to support Chinese students in American colleges.

The Open Door Policy, if rooted in the self-interest of American businessmen eager to exploit the markets of China, also tapped the deep-seated sympathies of those who opposed imperialism, especially as it endorsed China's territorial integrity. But it had little more legal standing than a pious affirmation. When the Japanese, concerned about Russian pressure in Manchuria, asked Hay how he intended to enforce the policy, Hay replied that the United States was "not prepared . . . to enforce these views on the east by any demonstration which could present a character of hostility to any other power." So it would remain for forty years, until American insistence upon the integrity of China would bring war with Japan in 1941.

THE RUSSO-JAPANESE WAR   For the time being, however, Hay's policy was hailed as a brilliant success. It worked after a fashion, but less because of its moral authority than because the powers meddling in China tended to balance each other off. The balance was upset, however, when rivalries between Russia and Japan flared into a fight over the prostrate forms of China and Korea. Russian encroachments had brought about a fifteen-year defensive treaty with China in 1896, in which China conceded to Russia the right to build the Chinese Eastern Railway across Manchuria, providing a shorter route to Vladivostok. In 1898 Russia secured a leasehold at Port Arthur on the Liaotung Peninsula with the right to build a rail line southward from Harbin, Manchuria. Russian ambitions soon extended to Korea, in which Japan too was interested, prompting Japan to make a defensive alliance in 1902 with Great Britain, which feared Russian threats to her interests in Asia and the Mediterranean.

On February 8, 1904, war broke out when the Japanese launched a surprise attack on Port Arthur, devastated the Russian fleet, occupied Korea, and drove the Russians back into Manchuria. But neither side could score a knockout blow, and neither relished a long stalemate. When the Japanese signaled President Roosevelt that they would welcome help in a settlement, the president agreed to sponsor a peace conference in Portsmouth, New Hampshire. In the Treaty of Portsmouth, signed on September 5, 1905, the concessions all went to the

Japanese. Russia acknowledged Japan's "predominant political military, and economic interests in Korea" (Japan would annex the kingdom in 1910), and ceded to Japan the leasehold at Port Arthur, railroad rights, and the southern half of Sakhalin Island. Both powers agreed to evacuate Manchuria.

AMERICA'S RELATIONS WITH JAPAN   American sentiment at first favored the Japanese as a counterweight to Russian aggression, but Japan's show of strength in the war raised doubts about the security of the Philippines. During the Portsmouth talks Roosevelt sent William Howard Taft to meet with the Japanese foreign minister in Tokyo and the two men arrived at the Taft-Katsura Agreement of July 29, 1905, in which the United States accepted Japanese control of Korea and Japan disavowed any designs on the Philippines. The understanding was reinforced by the Root-Takahira Agreement on November 30, 1908, negotiated by Secretary of State Elihu Root and the Japanese ambassador, in which both sides endorsed the status quo, promised to respect the other's possessions, and reinforced the Open Door Policy by supporting "the independence and integrity of China" and "the principle of equal opportunity for commerce and industry in China."

Behind the diplomatic facade of goodwill, however, lay mutual distrust. At Portsmouth the Japanese had hoped to get financial indemnities from Russia; they blamed their failure on the United States, and especially President Roosevelt, who had indeed opposed indemnities. For many Americans the Russian threat in East Asia now gave way to the "yellow peril" of Japan.[*] Racial animosities on the West Coast helped sour relations with Japan. In October 1906 the San Francisco school board ordered students of Chinese, Japanese, and Korean descent to attend a separate public school. The Japanese government sharply protested this show of prejudice, and President Roosevelt managed to talk the school board into changing its mind after making sure that Japanese authorities would not issue passports to "laborers" except former residents of the United States, the parents, wives, or children of residents, or those who already possessed interest in an American farming enterprise. This "Gentlemen's Agreement" of 1907, the precise terms of which have never been revealed, halted the influx of Japanese immigrants and brought some respite in racial agitations in California.

[*]The term "yellow peril" was apparently coined by Kaiser Wilhelm II of Germany.

TR's FOREIGN POLICY

BUILDING THE PANAMA CANAL   After the Spanish-American War the United States became more deeply involved in the Caribbean area. One issue overshadowed every other in the region: the Panama Canal. The narrow isthmus of Panama had excited dreams of an interoceanic canal ever since Balboa's crossing in 1513. Admiral Mahan regarded a canal as important to American commerce and naval power, a point dramatized in 1898 by the long voyage of the battleship *Oregon* around South America's Cape Horn to join the fleet off Cuba.

Transit across the isthmus had first become a strong concern of the United States in the 1840s when it became an important route to the California gold fields. Two treaties dating from that period loomed years later as obstacles to construction of a canal. The Bidlack Treaty (1848) with Colombia (then New Granada) guaranteed both Colombia's sovereignty over Panama and the neutrality of the isthmus, so that "free transit . . . not be embarrassed in any future time." In the Clayton-Bulwer Treaty (1850)

U.S. INTERESTS IN THE CARIBBEAN

the British agreed to acquire no more Central America territory, and the United States joined them in agreeing to build or fortify a canal only by mutual consent.

After the Spanish-American War, Secretary Hay commenced talks with the British ambassador to estsablish such consent. The outcome was the Hay-Pauncefote Treaty of February 1900, but the Senate rejected it on the grounds that it forbade fortification of the canal and required that the canal be neutral even in time of war. By then a bill was already pending in Congress for a Nicaraguan canal and the British apparently decided to accept the inevitable. In November 1901 the Senate ratified a second Hay-Pauncefote Treaty which simply omitted reference to the former limitations.

Other obstacles remained, however. From 1881 to 1887 a French company (Compagnie Universelle du Canal Interocéanique) under Ferdinand de Lesseps, who had engineered the Suez Canal in 1877, had spent nearly $300 million and some 20,000 lives to dig less than a third of the canal through Panama. The company now wanted $109 million for its holdings. Consequently an Isthmian Canal Commission, appointed by McKinley, reported in 1901 that a Nicaraguan route would be cheaper. When the House of Representatives quickly passed an act for construction there, the Panama Company lowered its price to $40 million and the Canal Commission made Panama its first choice.

Meanwhile Secretary Hay had opened negotiations with Ambassador Thomas Herrán of Colombia. In return for a Canal Zone six miles wide, the United States agreed to pay $10 million in cash and a rental fee of $250,000 a year. The United States Senate ratified the Hay-Herrán Treaty in 1903, but the Colombian Senate held out for $25 million in cash. At this action of those "foolish and homicidal corruptionists at Bogotá," Theodore Roosevelt, by then president, flew into a rage punctuated by references to "dagoes" and "contemptible little creatures." Meanwhile in Panama, an isolated province long at odds with the remote Colombian authorities in Bogotá, feeling was heightened by Colombia's rejection of the treaty. One Manuel Amador, an employee of the French canal company, then hatched a plot in close collusion with the company's representatives Philippe Bunau-Varilla and William Nelson Cromwell. Bunau-Varilla paid visits to Roosevelt and Hay and, apparently with inside information, informed the conspirators that the U.S.S. *Nashville* would call at Colón in Panama on November 2.

With an army of some 500, reinforced by Colón's fire department, Amador staged a revolt the next day. Colombian troops,

A *New York* Times *cartoon suggests that Bunau-Varilla
and TR were behind Panama's revolt against Colombia.
Their aim: to secure American rights to build a Panama-
nian canal.* [Drake in the New York Times]

who could scarcely penetrate the overland jungle, found American ships athwart the sea lanes. On November 13 the Roosevelt
administration received its first ambassador from Panama, whose
name happened to be Philippe Bunau-Varilla, and on November
18 signed a treaty which extended the Canal Zone from six to ten
miles in width. For $10 million down and $250,000 a year the
United States got "in perpetuity the use, occupation and control" of the zone. Just who got the $40 million paid to the French
canal company remains unknown. Attorney-General Philander
C. Knox, asked to supply a legal opinion upholding Roosevelt's
actions, responded wryly: "No, Mr. President, if I were you I
would not have any taint of legality about it."

In 1904 Congress created a new Isthmian Canal Commission
to direct construction. Despite sanitary problems, the biggest
obstacle at first, Roosevelt instructed the commission to make
the "dirt fly." Speaking to an audience at the University of California in 1911, he said: "If I had followed traditional, conservative methods I would have submitted a dignified State paper of
probably 200 pages to Congress and the debates on it would
have been going on yet; but I took the Canal Zone and let Congress debate; and while the debate goes on the Canal does also."

And so did a rankling resentment in Colombia. By needlessly
offending Latin American sensibilities, Roosevelt had committed
one of the greatest blunders in American foreign policy. Colombia eventually got its $25 million from the Harding administra-
tion, but only once America's interest in Colombia oil had
lubricated the wheels of diplomacy. There was no apology, but
the payment was made to remove "all misunderstandings grow-

ing out of the political events in Panama, November, 1903." Meanwhile the canal had opened on August 15, 1914, less than two weeks after the outbreak of World War I in Europe.

THE ROOSEVELT COROLLARY   Even without the canal, the United States would have been concerned with the stability of the Caribbean area, and particularly with the activities of any hostile power. A prime excuse for intervention in those days was to force the collection of debts owed to foreign nationals. In 1904 a crisis over the debts of the Dominican Republic gave Roosevelt an opportunity to formulate American policy. In his annual address to Congress in 1904 he set forth what came to be known as the Roosevelt Corollary to the Monroe Doctrine: the principle, in short, was that since the Monroe Doctrine enjoined intervention in the region by Europeans, the United States was justified in intervening first to forestall the actions of outsiders.

In the president's words the Roosevelt Corollary held that: "Chronic wrongdoing . . . may in America, as elsewhere, ultimately require intervention by some civilized nation, and in the Western Hemisphere the adherence of the United States to the Monroe Doctrine may force the United States, however reluctantly, in flagrant cases of such wrongdoing or impotence, to the exercise of an international police power." As put into practice by mutual agreement with the Dominican Republic in 1905, the Roosevelt Corollary called for the United States to install and protect a collector of customs who would apply 55 percent of his revenues to debt payments.

The World's Constable. *TR, shown here as the world's policeman, wields the "big stick" symbolizing his approach to diplomacy. [Library of Congress]*

DOLLAR DIPLOMACY   The principle, applied peaceably in 1905, became the basis for more forcible interventions later. During President Taft's term (1909–1913) refinements of the policy earned from its opponents the less exalted—if fairly descriptive —title of "dollar diplomacy." The policy so tagged had its origin in China in 1909, when President Taft personally cabled the Chinese government on behalf of American financiers interested in an international consortium to finance railroad lines in the Yangtze Valley. Philander C. Knox, by then secretary of state, wrote that the government regarded such cooperation "as best calculated to maintain the Open Door and the integrity of China." In 1911 the Americans were let in on the deal with British, French, and German capitalists, and in 1912 entered an even larger scheme to make a gigantic loan to the new Chinese Republic. Both schemes were repudiated, however, when Woodrow Wilson became president in 1913, and the American investors, lacking support from the government, withdrew.

In Latin America "dollar diplomacy" worked differently and with somewhat more success. The idea was to encourage American bankers to help prop up the finances of shaky governments in the Caribbean region. In 1910 Knox got several lenders to invest in the national bank of Haiti. In 1911 he signed treaties with Nicaragua and Honduras providing them with private loans to bolster their treasuries and ensuring payment by installing American collectors of customs. The Senate refused to go along with the treaties, but the administration continued its private appeals for American bankers to assume debts in the region.

In 1912, however, when the Nicaraguan president asked for help in putting down disorders, American marines entered the country. An American collector of customs was then installed and the government placed on a monthly allowance doled out by a commission of two Americans and one Nicaraguan. American forces stayed until 1925, then returned in 1926 to stay until 1933. Similar forcible interventions occurred in Haiti in 1915 and the Dominican Republic in 1916.

THE UNITED STATES AND EUROPE   During the years of expansionism the United States was looking mainly westward and southward. Toward Europe's affairs the fixed policy was, as Admiral Mahan affirmed it should be, abstention. Differences between the United States and European powers usually had to do with possessions in the Western Hemisphere, and one such matter came to a head during Roosevelt's presidency: the Alaskan boundary dispute. Years before the American purchase in 1867 an Anglo-

Russian Treaty of 1825 had given the boundary of the Alaska panhandle a geographically impossible definition. Nobody cared much until 1896, when gold was discovered in the Canadian Klondike to which the panhandle offered the readiest access. The Canadians then pressed an extreme claim whereby they would control the heads of the major inlets.

In 1899 Secretary Hay proposed a commission of six, three chosen by each side, to draw the line. A renewal of the offer in 1902 led to a treaty early the next year. The "impartial jurists" named for the panel by Roosevelt included Secretary of War Elihu Root, Roosevelt's close friend Henry Cabot Lodge, and George Turner, a former senator from Washington, a state with an intense interest in the boundary. Roosevelt also got word indirectly to the British leaders that if the commission decided wrongly, he planned to run the line by force, if need be. As it turned out only the two Canadian members of the board held out for their extreme claim. The one British member voted with the Americans for a line that would give the United States control of the major inlets. It was the third major understanding between the two powers in a dozen years (the fur seal and Venezuelan settlements were the others) and it opened the way to a growing rapprochement in Anglo-American relations.

To Roosevelt, however, total abstention from European affairs was an improper stance for a newly arrived world power. While he was moving toward mediation of the Russo-Japanese War in 1905, another dangerous crisis began heating up in Morocco. There, on March 31, 1905, German Kaiser Wilhelm II stepped ashore at Tangier and gave a saber-rattling speech defending the independence of the sultan. This was a deliberate response to growing French influence there, and particularly to the Franco-British Entente of 1904, under which Britain recognized French dominance in Morocco in return for French recognition of British dominance in Egypt. The kaiser's speech aroused a diplomatic storm of dangerous proportions. Roosevelt felt that the United States had something at stake in preventing the outbreak of a major war. At the kaiser's behest he talked the French and British into attending an international conference at Algeciras, Spain, with American delegates present. Roosevelt then maneuvered the Germans into accepting his lead.

The Act of Algeciras, signed on April 7, 1906, affirmed the independence of Morocco and guaranteed an open door for trade there, but provided for the training and control of Moroccan police by France and Spain. The United States Senate ratified the agreement, but only with the provison that it was not to be construed as a departure from America's traditional policy of noninvolvement in European affairs. It was, of course, and one that may well have prevented a general war, or at least postponed it until 1914. Roosevelt received the Nobel Peace Prize in 1906 for his work at Portsmouth and Algeciras. For all his bellicosity on other occasions, he had earned it.

Before Roosevelt left the White House he celebrated America's rise to world power with one great flourish. In December 1907 he sent the United States Navy, by then second only to the British, on a grand tour around the world, their commander announcing he was ready for "a feast, a frolic, or a fight." He got mostly the first two, and none of the last. At every port of call the "Great White Fleet" set off rousing celebrations, down the Atlantic coast of South America, up the west coast, out to Hawaii, and down under to New Zealand and Australia. It was the first such show of American naval might in the Pacific, and many feared the reaction of the Japanese, for whose benefit Roosevelt had in fact staged the show. They need not have worried, for in Japan the flotilla got the greatest welcome of all. Thousands of schoolchildren turned out waving tiny American flags and singing "The Star Spangled Banner" in English. The triumphal procession continued home by way of the Mediterranean, and steamed back into American waters in February 1909, just in time to close out Roosevelt's presidency on a note of success.

But it was a success that would have mixed consequences. As one close student of Roosevelt's role in America's rise to world power wrote: "One comes away from the study with admiration for Roosevelt's ability, his energy, and his devotion to his country's interests as he saw them but with a sense of tragedy that his abilities were turned toward imperialism and an urge for power, which were to have consequences so serious for the future." Roosevelt had influenced the United States "in a direction that . . . was to bring her face to face with grave dangers" before the mid–twentieth century.

FURTHER READING

Two recent surveys trace Gilded Age diplomacy and lend a balanced treatment to current interpretations: consult Charles S. Campbell's *The Transformation of American Foreign Relations, 1865–1900* (1976),° and Robert L. Beisner's shorter *From the Old Diplomacy to the*

°These books are available in paperback editions.

New, 1865–1900 (1975).° Ernest R. May's *Imperial Democracy: The Emergence of America as a Great Power* (1961)° is more traditional. Relevant chapters in Lloyd C. Gardner, Walter LaFeber, and Thomas McCormick's *The Creation of the American Empire* (1973)° give condensed treatment to revisionist interpretations. William Appleman Williams's *The Tragedy of American Diplomacy* (1972)° advances most clearly the economic interpretation. Marilyn B. Young (ed.), *American Expansion: The Critical Issues* (1973), reviews the scholarly debate over imperialistic motives.

Particularly useful as background for the events of the 1890s are Walter LaFeber's *The New Empire: An Interpretation of American Expansion, 1860–1898* (1963), and Milton Plesur's *America's Outward Thrust: Approaches to Foreign Affairs, 1865–1890* (1971).° Also useful is David Pletcher's *The Awkward Years: America's Foreign Relations under Garfield and Arthur* (1962). To elaborate on the influence of A. T. Mahan, consult Peter Karster's *The Naval Aristocracy* (1972). Richard Hofstadter's *Social Darwinism in American Thought* (1949) details the intellectual justifications for expansion.

An early dispute over American policy in the Pacific is covered in Thomas J. Osborne's *"Empire Can Wait": American Opposition to Hawaiian Annexation, 1893–1898* (1981), and William A. Russ, Jr.'s *The Hawaiian Republic, 1894–98, and Its Struggle to Win Annexation* (1961).

David Healy's *United States Expansion: The Imperialist Urge in the 1890s* (1970) provides a survey of that decade, while David F. Transk's lengthy *The War with Spain* (1981) is the comprehensive volume on that conflict. Other accounts include H. Wayne Morgan's concise *America's Road to Empire: The War with Spain and Overseas Expansion* (1965)° and Frank Friedel's *The Splendid Little War* (1958). More detailed and revisionist is Philip S. Foner's *The Spanish-Cuban American War and the Birth of American Imperialism* (2 vols.; 1972). A special angle is taken in Charles H. Brown's *The Correspondents' War: Journalists in the Spanish-American War* (1967). For the role played by political leadership, see Lewis L. Gould's *The Presidency of William McKinley* (1980). Richard Challener's *Admirals, Generals, and American Foreign Policy, 1889–1914* (1973), stresses the influence of the military in the war, while Graham A. Cosmos's *An Army for Empire: The United States Army in the Spanish-American War* (1971) concentrates on infantry operations in Cuba.

The effects of victory in the Pacific are gauged by James Thomson, Jr., Peter Stanley, and John C. Perry in *Sentimental Imperialists: The American Experience in East Asia* (1981).° More specific are Stuart C. Miller's *"Benevolent Assimilation": American Conquest of the Philippines, 1899–1903* (1982), and Peter Stanley's *A Nation in the Making: The Philippines and the United States* (1974). Also useful is Glenn May's *Social Engineering in the Philippines* (1980). For the debate over annexation, see Robert L. Beisner's *Twelve against Empire: The Anti-Imperialists, 1898–1900* (1968), and E. Berkeley Tompkins's *Anti-Imperialism in the United States: The Great Debate, 1890–1920* (1970).

A good introducton to American interest in China is Robert McClellan's *The Heathen Chinese: A Study of American Attitudes toward China* (1971). More expansive is Marilyn B. Young's *The Rhetoric for Empire: America's China Policy, 1893–1901* (1968). Two interpretations of the Open Door are Thomas McCormick's *China Market: America's Quest for Informal Empire, 1893–1901* (1967),° and Paul A. Varg's *The Making of a Myth: The United States and China, 1899–1922* (1968). For the immediate consequences of the Open Door, see Warren Cohen's *America's Response to China* (1971) and Jerry Israel's *Progressivism and the Open Door: America and China, 1905–1921* (1971). Kenton J. Clymer's *John Hay: The Gentleman as Diplomat* (1975) examines the role of this key secretary of state in forming policy.

Works which deal with the role of Theodore Roosevelt in foreign policy both before and during his time as president include Howard K. Beale's *Theodore Roosevelt and the Rise of America to World Power* (1956), Raymond A. Esthus's *Theodore Roosevelt and the International Rivalries* (1970), and Edmund Morris's *The Rise of Theodore Roosevelt* (1979).° Roosevelt's influence also shows through in Robert A. Hart's *The Great White Fleet: Its Voyage around the World* (1965) and Robert C. Hildebrand's *Power and the People: Executive Management of Public Opinion in Foreign Affairs, 1897–1921* (1981).

David McCollough's *Path between the Seas: The Creation of the Panama Canal, 1870–1914* (1977),° presents the fullest account of how the United States secured the canal. Walter LaFeber's *The Panama Canal: The Crisis in Historical Perspective* (1970)° gives a revisionist interpretation of American policy on the canal. Dwight C. Miner's *Fight for the Panama Canal* (1966) covers the political intrigues involved. Policy subsequent to Roosevelt is the subject of Walter V. Scholes and Marive V. Scholes's *The Foreign Policies of the Taft Administration* (1970) and Dana G. Muroe's *Intervention and Dollar Diplomacy in the Caribbean, 1900–1921* (1964).

24

PROGRESSIVISM: ROOSEVELT, TAFT, AND WILSON

ELEMENTS OF REFORM

Theodore Roosevelt was an ambitious man whose eagerness to leave his mark moved easily from the world arena to his own country. But Roosevelt was more calculating in domestic politics than in foreign affairs and more inclined to follow the dictates of experience. He recognized that 1901 was no time for a "big stick" domestic policy.

The prudence Roosevelt displayed in making domestic policy, if uncharacteristic of the man, was a necessity of the time. Roosevelt's emergence as a national leader coincided roughly with the onset of progressivism, a reform movement so broad-gauged it almost defied definition.

The Progressives saw themselves as engaged in a democratic reform movement against the abuses of Gilded Age bosses and robber barons. Its goals were greater democracy, good government, the regulation of business, social justice, and public service. But the Kansas editor William Allen White hinted at a paradox in the movement when he called progressivism just populism that had "shaved its whiskers, washed its shirt, put on a derby, and moved up into the middle class." As White suggested, urban business and professional leaders brought to progressivism a certain respectability that populism had lacked. They also brought a more businesslike, efficient approach to reform. While progressivism still had about it the glorious glow of agrarian democracy and its antitrust traditions, newer themes of efficiency soon gained ascendancy. Even farm groups abandoned the mass movement for more bureaucratic forms of organization. In so doing, they and other Progressives may have been trying to find identity, no longer derived from the local community, in business and professional groups.

Another paradox in the movement was that it contained an element of conservatism. In some cases the regulation of business turned out actually to be regulation *by* businessmen, who preferred stability to the chaos and uncertainty of unrestrained competition. It should be clear, then, that when we speak of a Progressive movement, we refer to the common spirit of an age rather than to an organized group or party. Much like the reform spirit of the 1830s and 1840s, once called Jacksonian Democracy, progressivism was diverse in both origins and tendencies. Few people adhered to all progressive causes. Most, like Theodore Roosevelt, were selective.

ANTECEDENTS TO PROGRESSIVISM   Populism was indisputably one of the harbingers of progressivism. The program the Populists set forth in their platform of 1892 outlined many reforms that would be accomplished in the progressive era. Many old populists, in addition, believed that their movement achieved vindication in the progressive era. William Allen White wrote that populism "was the beginning of a movement that in another decade was to change the politics of the nation: indeed it was a symptom of a world wide drift to liberalism, which reached its peak in Christendom twenty-five years later."

After the collapse of the farmers' movement the focus of the reform spirit shifted to cities, where middle-class reformers had for years attacked the problems of political bossism and urban development. The Mugwumps, those gentlemen reformers who had fought the spoils system and promoted a civil service based on merit, supplied the Progressive movement with an important element of its thinking, the good-government ideal. Over the years their ranks had been supplemented and the good-government outlook broadened by leaders who confronted such new urban problems as crime, vice, and the efficient provision of gas, electricity, water, sewers, mass transit, and garbage collection.

Finally, a minor but significant force in fostering the spirit of progressivism was the growing familiarity of socialist doctrines and their critiques of living and working conditions. The Socialist party of the time can be considered the left wing of progressivism. Still, most Progressives found socialist remedies unacceptable, and the Progressive reform impulse grew in part from a desire to counter the growing influence of socialist doctrines. More important in spurring Progressive reform, however, were those social critics who over the years had attacked the social evils of American life. Chief among these were thinkers such as Lester F. Ward, Henry George, Henry Demarest Lloyd, Jacob Riis, and Thorstein Veblen.

THE MUCKRAKERS   In the early twentieth century the exposure of social evils became a profitable enterprise. The writers who thrived on exposing scandal got their name when Theodore Roosevelt compared them to a character in John Bunyan's *Pilgrim's Progress:* "A man that could look no way but downwards with a muckrake in his hands." The "muckrakers" (and TR was no mean muckraker himself) "are often indispensable to ... society," Roosevelt said, "but only if they know when to stop raking the muck."

Henry Demarest Lloyd is sometimes cited as the first of the muckrakers for his critical examination of the Standard Oil Company and other monopolies, *Wealth against Commonwealth* (1894). Lloyd exposed the growth of corporate giants responsible to none but themselves, able to corrupt if not control governments. Another early muckraker was Jacob August Riis, a Danish immigrant who as an influential New York journalist exposed slum conditions in *How the Other Half Lives* (1890) and *The Battle with the Slum* (1902). The chief outlets for these social critics were the cheap popular magazines which began to flourish in the 1890s, such as *The Arena* and *McClure's Magazine,* founded in 1893 by Samuel S. McClure, an Irish immigrant who had begun the first newspaper syndicate in the country.

The golden age of muckraking is sometimes dated from October 1902 when *McClure's* began to run articles by the reporter Lincoln Steffens on municipal corruption, later collected into a book: *The Shame of the Cities* (1904). *McClure's* also ran Ida M. Tarbell's *History of the Standard Oil Company* (1904). McClure had set her to research on the project more than three years before. The result was a more detailed treatment than the earlier book by Lloyd, but all the more damaging in its detail. Other outstanding books which began as magazine articles included Thomas Lawson's *Frenzied Finance* (1904), on stock-market manipulation; Charles Edward Russell's *The Greatest Trust in the World* (1905), on the meat industry; David Graham Phillip's *The Treason of the Senate* (1906), on the influence of special interests; Burton J. Hendrick's *The Story of Life Insurance* (1907); and Ray Stannard Baker's *Following the Color Line* (1908). The inexhaustible market for scandal even absorbed such tomes as Gustavus Myers's *History of the Great American Fortunes* (3 vols., 1910).

Without the muckrakers, progressivism surely would never have achieved the popular support it had. In feeding the public's appetite for facts about their new urban industrial society, the muckrakers demonstrated one of the salient features of the Progressive movement, and one of its central failures. The Progressives were stronger on diagnosis than on remedy, thereby reflecting a naïve faith in the power of democracy. Let the people know, expose corruption, and bring government close to the people, went the rationale, and the correction of evils would follow automatically. The cure for the ills of democracy was more democracy.

THE FEATURES OF PROGRESSIVISM

DEMOCRACY   The most important reform with which the Progressives tried to democratize government was the direct primary or the nomination of candidates by the vote of party members. Under the existing convention system, the reasoning went, only a small proportion of the voters attended the local caucuses or precinct meetings which sent delegates to county, and in turn to state and national, conventions. While the system allowed seasoned leaders to sift the candidates, it also lent itself to domination by political professionals who were organized to turn out early and stay late. Direct primaries at the local level had been held sporadically since the 1870s, but after South Carolina adopted the first statewide primary in 1896 the movement spread within two decades to nearly every state.

The primary was but one expression of a broad movement for direct democracy. In 1898 South Dakota became the first state to adopt the initiative and referendum, procedures which allowed voters to enact laws directly. If a designated number of voters petitioned to have a measure put on the ballot (the initiative), the electorate could then vote it up or down (the referendum). Oregon, largely through the influence of William S. U'Ren, a blacksmith turned editor and lawyer, adopted a whole spectrum of reform measures including a voter registration law (1899); the initiative and referendum (1902); the direct primary (1904); a sweeping corrupt-practices act (1908); and the recall (1910), whereby public officials could be removed by petition and vote. Within a decade nearly twenty states had adopted the initiative and referendum and nearly a dozen the recall.

Most states came to use the party primary even in the choice of United States senators. Nevada was first, in 1899, to let voters express a choice which state legislators of their party were expected to follow in choosing senators. The popular election of senators required a constitutional amendment, and the House of Representatives four times adopted such an amendment (in 1894, 1898, 1900, and 1902) only to see it defeated in the Senate, which came under increasing attack as a "millionaire's club." By 1912 thirty states had provided preferential primaries. The Senate in that year finally accepted the inevitable and agreed to the Seventeenth Amendment, authorizing popular election of senators. The amendment was ratified in 1913.

EFFICIENCY A second major theme of progressivism was the "gospel of efficiency," which found a home in both private and public bureaucracies. In the business world during those years Frederick W. Taylor, the original "efficiency expert," was developing the techniques he summed up in his book *The Principles of Scientific Management* (1911): efficient management of time and costs, the proper routing and scheduling of work, standardization of tools and equipment, and the like. In government, efficiency demanded the reorganization of agencies to prevent overlapping, to establish clear lines of authority, and to fix responsibility. One long-held theory had it that the greater the number of offices chosen by popular vote the greater the degree of democracy, but Progressives considered this inefficient. They believed that voters could make wiser choices if they had a shorter ballot and chose fewer officials in whom power and responsibility were clearly lodged. Many states and localities worked at rationalizing their finances by equalizing tax assessments, and during the first decades of the twentieth century by adopting budget systems. The federal government finally got around to a budget system with passage of the Budget and Accounting Act in 1921.

Two new ideas for making municipal government more efficient gained headway in the first decade of the new century. The commission system, first adopted by Galveston, Texas, in 1901, when local government there collapsed in the aftermath of a hurricane and tidal wave, placed ultimate authority in a board composed of elected administrative heads of city departments— commissioners of sanitation, police, utilities, and so on. The more durable idea, however, was the city-manager plan, under which a professional administrator ran the government in accordance with policies set by the elected council and mayor. Staunton, Virginia, first adopted the plan in 1908. By 1914 the

National Association of City Managers heralded the arrival of a new profession.

When America was a preindustrial society, Andrew Jackson's notion that any reasonably intelligent citizen could perform the duties of any public office may have been true. In the more complex age of the early twentieth century it was apparent that many functions of government and business had come to require expert specialists. This principle was promoted by progressive Gov. Robert M. La Follette of Wisconsin (1901–1906), who established a Legislative Reference Bureau to provide research, advice, and help in the drafting of legislation. The "Wisconsin Idea" of efficient government was widely publicized and copied. La Follette also worked for such reforms as the primary, stronger railroad regulation, the conservation of natural resources, and workmen's compensation. Counterparts to La Follette appeared as progressive governors in other states. In 1905 Joseph W. Folk was elected governor of Missouri after prosecuting and convicting a ring of boodlers (corruptionists) in St. Louis. As counsel to a legislative committee in New York, Charles Evans Hughes became a national figure by uncovering spectacular insurance frauds and won the governorship in 1906. In Georgia and Alabama that year Hoke Smith and Braxton Bragg Comer won governorships by promising to regulate the railroads. Hiram Johnson of California, after getting in 1908 a conviction of Abe Ruef, the grafting boss of San Francisco, won the governorship in 1910 on the promise of reining in the Southern Pacific Railroad.

REGULATION Of all the problems facing American society, one engaged a greater diversity of reformers, and elicited more— and more controversial—solutions than any other: the regulation of giant corporations, which became a third major theme of progressivism. Concern over the concentration of economic power had brought bipartisan support to the passage of the Sherman Anti-Trust Act in 1890, but in its effects the act had turned out to be more symbolic than effective.

The problem of economic power and its abuse offered a dilemma for Progressives. Four broad solutions were available, but of these, two were extremes which had limited support: letting business work out its own destiny under a policy of laissez-faire, or adopting a socialist program of public ownership. At the municipal level, however, the socialist alternative was rather widely adopted in public utilities and transportation—so-called gas and water socialism—but otherwise was not seriously considered as a general policy. The other choices were either to adopt a policy of trust-busting in the belief that restoring old-fashioned competition would best prevent economic abuses, or to accept big business in the belief that it brought economies of scale, but to regulate it to prevent abuses.

Efforts to restore the competition of small firms proved unworkable, partly because breaking up large combinations was complex and difficult. The trend over the years was toward regulation of big business. To some extent regulation and "stabilization" won acceptance among businessmen who, whatever respect they paid to competition in the abstract, preferred not to face it in person. In the long run, although it was not at first apparent, regulation posed the problem raised in the old maxim: Who will guard the guards? Regulatory agencies often came under the influence or control of those they were supposed to regulate. Railroad men, for instance, generally had more intimate knowledge of the intricate details involved in their business, giving them the advantage over the outsiders who might be appointed to the Interstate Commerce Commission.

SOCIAL JUSTICE   A fourth important feature of the progressive spirit was the impulse toward social justice, which motivated diverse actions from private charities to campaigns against child labor and liquor. The settlement house movement of the late nineteenth century had spawned a corps of social workers and genteel reformers devoted to the uplift of slum dwellers. But with time it became apparent that social evils extended beyond the reach of private charities and demanded the power of the state. Progressives found that old codes of private ethics and accountability scarcely applied to a complex industrial order. In his book *Sin and Society* (1907) the sociologist E. A. Ross observed: "Unlike the old time villain, the latter-day malefactor does not wear a slouch hat and a comforter, breathe forth curses and an odor of gin, go about his nefarious work with clenched teeth and an evil scowl. . . . The modern high-powered dealer of woe wears immaculate linen, carries a silk hat and a lighted cigar, sins with calm countenance and a serene soul, leagues or months from the evil he causes. Upon his gentlemanly presence the eventual blood and tears do not obtrude themselves."

Labor legislation was perhaps the most significant reform to emerge from the drive for social justice. The National Child Labor Committee, organized in 1904, led a movement for laws banning the still widespread employment of young children. Through propaganda, the organization of state and local committees, and a telling documentation of the evils of child labor by

Girl at work in a North Carolina textile mill, 1908. Photograph by Lewis Hine. [Library of Congress]

the photographer Lewis W. Hine, the committee within ten years brought about legislation in most states banning the labor of underage children (the minimum age varied from twelve to sixteen) and limiting the hours of older children. Many states also outlawed night work and labor in dangerous occupations for both women and children. But numerous exemptions and inadequate enforcement often virtually nullified the laws.

The Supreme Court pursued a curiously erratic course in ruling on state labor laws. In *Holden v. Hardy* (1898) it upheld a Utah law limiting the working day in mining and smelting to eight hours as a proper exercise of the state police power to protect the health and safety of workers. The Court even referred to the unequal bargaining power of workers and employers as a justification for state action. In *Lochner v. New York* (1905), however, the Court voided a ten-hour day because it violated workers' "liberty of contract" to accept any terms they chose. Justice Oliver Wendell Holmes, Jr., dissented sharply. "The 14th Amendment does not enact Mr. Herbert Spencer's *Social Statics*," he said, meaning it did not enact Spencer's laissez-faire dogmas. Then in *Muller v. Oregon* (1908) the high court upheld a ten-hour law for women largely on the basis of sociological data which Louis D. Brandeis presented regarding the effects of long hours on the health and morals of women. In *Bunting v. Oregon* (1917) the Court accepted a ten-hour day for both men and women, but held out for twenty more years against state minimum-wage laws.

Legislation to protect workers against accidents gained impetus from disasters like the 1911 fire at the Triangle Shirtwaist Company in New York in which 146 people, mostly women, died for want of adequate exits. They either were trapped on the three upper floors of a ten-story building or plunged to the street below. Stricter building codes and factory inspection acts followed. One of the most important advances along these lines was the series of workmen's compensation laws enacted after Maryland led the way in 1902. Accident insurance systems replaced the old common-law principle that an injured worker was entitled to compensation only if he could prove employer negligence, a costly and capricious procedure from which the worker was likely to win nothing, or as often happened, excessive awards from overly sympathetic juries.

For many the cause of prohibition absorbed the yearnings for reform. Opposition to strong drink was an ideal cause in which to merge the older private ethics and the new social ethics. Given the moral disrepute of saloons, prohibitionists could equate the "liquor traffic" with progressive suspicion of bossism and "special interests." When reform pressures mounted, prohibition offered an easy outlet, bypassing the complexities of corporate regulation.

The battle against booze dated far back into the nineteenth century. The Women's Christian Temperance Union had promoted the cause since 1874 and a Prohibition party had entered the field in 1876. But the most successful political action followed the formation in 1893 of the Anti-Saloon League, an organization which pioneered the tactics of the single-issue pressure group. By singleness of purpose it forced the prohibition issue into the forefront of state and local elections. At its "Jubilee Convention" in 1913 the Anti-Saloon League endorsed a prohibition amendment to the Constitution, adopted by Congress that year. By the time it was ratified six years later, state and local action already had dried up areas occupied by nearly three-fourths of the nation's population.

ACTIVE GOVERNMENT   A fifth feature of progressivism, and perhaps the most significant of all in its long-term impact, was its emphasis on the public-service functions of government. Governments were now called upon to extend a broad range of direct services: schools, good roads (a movement propelled first by cyclists and then by automobilists), conservation, public health and welfare, care of the handicapped, farm loans, and farm demonstration agents, among other things.

The good-roads movement, the automobile-age equivalent of the nineteenth-century railroad movement, went forward first by means of conventions, associations, and heroic caravans in dusters and goggles, and finally triumphed through broad-gauged planning of integrated networks with the Federal Highways Acts of 1916 and 1921 and the development of state systems. A bewildering profusion of local associations followed the founding of the magazine *Good Roads* (1892), the National Good Roads Association (1900), and the American Automobile Association (1902). In the first flush of excitement over the liberation brought by the automobile, few foresaw the dependence it would later entail or the devastating effect it would eventually have on rail transit. Good roads were in fact often promoted at first as feeders to the existing rail network.

ROOSEVELT'S PROGRESSIVISM

Theodore Roosevelt's version of Progressive reform was a cautious one. As a reformer he best displayed his political skills. He cultivated party leaders in Congress, and steered away from such political meat-grinders as the tariff and banking issues. And when he did approach the explosive issue of the trusts, he always took care to reassure the business community. For him, politics was the art of the possible. Unlike the more advanced progressives and the doctrinaire "lunatic fringe," as he called them, he would take half a loaf rather than none at all. Roosevelt acted in large part out of the conviction that reform was needed to keep things on an even keel. Control should rest in the hands of sensible Republicans, and not with irresponsible Democrats or, worse, the growing socialist movement.

EXECUTIVE ACTION   At the outset of his presidency in 1901 Roosevelt took up McKinley's policies and promised to sustain them. He touched base with McKinley's friend and manager Mark Hanna, and worked with Republican leaders in Congress, against whom the minority of new Progressives was as yet powerless. Republican Speaker Joe Cannon, who now wielded the dictatorial powers once held by "Czar" Reed, was able to announce on one occasion to a helpless House, "We will now perpetrate the following outrage."

Roosevelt, it turned out, would accomplish more by vigorous executive action than by passing legislation, and in the exercise of executive power he was not inhibited by points of legal detail.

The president, he argued, might do anything not expressly forbidden by the Constitution. The Constitution, he said later, "must be interpreted, not as a straight jacket, not as laying the hand of death upon our development, but as an instrument designed for the life and healthy growth of the Nation." He was even credited with asking: "What's the Constitution between friends?" but that query seems to have been apocryphal.

Caution suffused Roosevelt's first annual message, delivered in December 1901, but he felt impelled to take up the trust problem in the belief that it might be more risky to ignore it. The message carefully balanced arguments on both sides of the question. "The mechanism of modern business is so delicate," he warned, "that extreme care must be taken not to interfere with it in a spirit of rashness or ignorance." A widespread belief nevertheless held the great corporations "in certain of their features and tendencies hurtful to the general welfare." The president endorsed the "sincere conviction that combination and concentration should be, not prohibited, but supervised and within reasonable limits controlled. . . ." The first essential was "knowledge of the facts—publicity . . . the only sure remedy we can now invoke." Later would follow regulatory legislation, perhaps based on the experience of the Interstate Commerce Commission (ICC).

Finley Peter Dunne's Mr. Dooley summarized the essence of Roosevelt's message this way: "Th' trusts, says he, are heejoous monsthers built up be the enlightened intherprise iv th' men that have done so much to advance progress in our beloved country, he says. On wan hand I wud stamp thim undher fut; on th' other hand not so fast." The result, in fact, was not so fast. But in August 1902 Roosevelt carried the trust issue to the people on a tour of New England and the Midwest. He endorsed a "square deal" for all, calling for enforcement of existing antitrust laws and stricter controls on big business.

From the outset, however, Roosevelt believed that wholesale trust-busting was too much like trying to unscramble eggs. Effective regulation, he believed, was better than a futile effort to restore small business, which might be achieved only at a cost to the efficiencies of scale gained in larger operations. Roosevelt nevertheless soon acquired a reputation as a "trustbuster."

Because Congress boggled at regulatory legislation, Roosevelt sought to force the issue by a more vigorous prosecution of the Sherman Anti-Trust Act. He chose his target carefully. In the case against the Sugar Trust (*United States v. E. C. Knight and Company*, 1895) the Supreme Court had declared manufacturing a strictly intrastate activity. Railroads, however, were beyond question engaged in interstate commerce and thus subject to federal authority. In February 1902 Roosevelt ordered Attorney-General Philander C. Knox to move against the Northern Securities Company, a firm vulnerable to both the law and public opinion. That company, formed the previous year, had taken shape during a gigantic battle in the New York Stock Exchange between E. H. Harriman of the Union Pacific and James J. Hill and J. P. Morgan of the Great Northern and Northern Pacific. The stock battle raised the threat of a panic, and led to a settlement in which the chief contenders made peace. They formed Northern Securities as a holding company to control the Great Northern and Northern Pacific.

At about the time Roosevelt ordered suit against Northern Securities in 1902, he balanced his action with a speech at the South Carolina and West Indian Exposition in Charleston denouncing demagogues who raved "against the wealth which is simply the form of embodied thrift, foresight, and intelligence." But when J. P. Morgan invited Roosevelt to "send your man to my man and they can fix it up," the president refused. Hill complained: "It seems hard that we should be compelled to fight for our lives against the political adventurers who have never done anything but pose and draw a salary. . . ." Knox pressed the case and in 1904 the Supreme Court ordered the combination dissolved. "What has been the result?" Hill asked. "To the owners . . . merely the inconvenience of holding two certificates of stock of different colors instead of one. To the public, no difference at all except that it has missed the advantages which the simpler and more businesslike plan would have secured."

THE COAL STRIKE   Support for Roosevelt's use of the "big stick" against corporations was strengthened by the stubbornness of mine owners in the anthracite coal strike of 1902. On May 12 the United Mine Workers (UMW), led by John Mitchell, walked out demanding a 20 percent wage increase, a reduction in hours from ten to nine, and union recognition. The mine operators, having granted a 10 percent raise two years before, dug in their heels against further concessions, and shut down in preparation for a long struggle to starve out the miners. Their spokesman, George F. Baer, president of the Reading Railroad, helped the union cause more than his own with an arrogant pronouncement: "The rights and interests of the laboring man will be protected and cared for," he said, "not by the labor agitators, but by the Christian men to whom God in his infinite wisdom has given control of the property interests of the country."

The prospect of a coal shortage seemed real. Roosevelt called a conference at the White House on October 3 and the operators came but refused even to speak to the UMW leaders. The enraged president confessed a temptation to throw Baer bodily through a window of the White House. When the conference ended in an impasse, Roosevelt threatened to take over the mines and run them with the army. It would have been an act of dubious legality, but the owners feared that TR might actually do it and that public opinion would support him.

The coal strike ended in October with an agreement to submit the issues to an arbitration commission named by the president. After a last-minute flurry over the operators' refusal to accept a union man on the panel, the president blithely reclassified the head of the railway conductors' union, E. E. Clark, as an "eminent sociologist." The agreement enhanced the prestige of both Roosevelt and union leader Mitchell, although it produced only a partial victory for the miners. By the arbitrators' decision of March 21, 1903, the miners won only a 10 percent wage increase and a nine-hour day, but no union recognition.

TOWARD A SECOND TERM   Roosevelt continued to use his executive powers to enforce the Sherman Act, but he avoided conflict in Congress by drawing back from further antitrust legislation. Altogether his administration brought about twenty-five antitrust suits, the most notable victory coming in *Swift and Company v. United States* (1905), a decision against the "beef trust" through which most of the packers had avoided competitive bidding in

No Lack of Big Game. *A 1905 cartoon shows TR going after the trusts.* [Library of Congress]

NO LACK OF BIG GAME
The President Seems to Have Scared Up Quite a Bunch of Octopi.

the purchase of livestock. In this decision the Supreme Court put forth the "stream of commerce" doctrine which overturned its previous holding that manufacturing was strictly intrastate. Since both livestock and the meat products of the packers moved in the stream of interstate commerce, the Court reasoned, they were subject to federal regulation. This interpretation of the interstate commerce power would be broadened in later years until few enterprises would remain beyond the reach of federal regulation.

In 1903 Congress came around to legislation that somewhat strengthened both antitrust enforcement and governmental regulation. Within one week in February of that year, Congress approved three important measures: the Expedition Act, whereby circuit courts had to give priority to antitrust suits upon request of the attorney-general; an act creating the Department of Commerce and Labor, including the Bureau of Corporations; and the Elkins Act, which made it illegal to take as well as to give rebates.

The new Bureau of Corporations had no direct regulatory powers, but it did have a mandate to study and report on the activities of interstate corporations. Headed by James R. Garfield, son of the former president, the bureau followed a policy of concord rather than conflict. Its findings could lead to antitrust suits, but its purpose was rather to help corporations correct malpractices and avoid the need for lawsuits. Many companies, among them United States Steel and International Harvester, worked closely with Garfield, but others held back. When Standard Oil refused to turn over records, the government brought an antitrust suit which resulted in its dissolution in 1911. The American Tobacco Company was dissolved at the same time. This approach fell short of the direct regulation which Roosevelt preferred, but without a congressional will to pass such laws, little more was possible. Trusts which cooperated were left alone; others had to run the gauntlet of antitrust suits.

Roosevelt's policies built a coalition of progressive- and conservative-minded voters which assured his election in his own right in 1904. He had skillfully used patronage, and his progressive policies, achieved mainly by executive action, had not challenged congressional conservatives. Nor did Roosevelt try to take on the Old Guard at the Chicago convention in June. He accepted a harmless platform which dwelt on past achievements, and the convention chose him by acclamation. The Democrats, having lost with Bryan twice, turned to Alton B. Parker who, as chief justice of New York, had upheld labor's right to the closed shop and the state's right to limit hours of work. Despite his liberal record party leaders presented him as a safe conservative, and his acceptance of the gold standard as "firmly and irrevocably established" bolstered such a view. The effort to present a candidate more conservative than Roosevelt proved a futile gesture for the party which had twice nominated Bryan. Despite Roosevelt's trust-busting proclivities, most businessmen, according to the New York *Sun*, preferred the "impulsive candidate of the party of conservatism to the conservative candidate of the party which the business interests regard as permanently and dangerously impulsive." Even J. P. Morgan and E. H. Harriman contributed handsomely to Roosevelt's campaign chest. Parker made little headway with his charge that businessmen expected favors in return.

An invincible popularity plus the sheer force of personality swept Roosevelt to an impressive victory by a popular margin of 7.6 million to 5.1 million. Parker carried only the Solid South of the former Confederacy and two border states: Kentucky and Maryland. It was a great personal triumph for Roosevelt. Amid the excitement of election night he announced that he would not run again, a statement he later had reason to regret.

LEGISLATIVE LEADERSHIP   Elected in his own right, Roosevelt approached his second term with heightened confidence and a stronger commitment to progressive reform. In December 1905 he devoted most of his annual message to the regulation and control of business. He took aim at the railroads first, and it was with reference to railroads that his demands most nearly approached success. The Elkins Act of 1903, finally outlawing rebates, had been a minor step. Railroad men themselves welcomed it as an escape from shippers clamoring for special favors. But the new Hepburn proposal was something else again, for it would both extend the authority of the ICC and give it effective control over rates for the first time.

Roosevelt had to mobilize all the pressure and influence at his disposal to push through the bill introduced by Rep. Peter Hepburn of Iowa. Nelson Aldrich, leader of the Senate conservatives, sought to embarrass the president by making the Democrat "Pitchfork Ben" Tillman floor manager for the bill, but Roosevelt and the South Carolinian put aside partisan differences to get it passed. Enacted on June 29, 1906, the Hepburn Act for the first time gave the ICC power to set maximum rates. The commission no longer had to go to court to enforce its decisions. While the carriers could challenge the rates in court, the burden of proof now rested on them rather than on the ICC. As part of the compromise required to pass the law, however, new rates under challenge would be suspended pending decision of the courts. In other ways too the Hepburn Act enlarged the mandate of the ICC. Its reach now extended beyond railroads to pipelines, express companies, sleeping-car companies, bridges, and ferries, and it could prescribe a uniform system of bookkeeping to provide uniform statistics. In addition, the act forbade carriers to grant free passes except to their own employees, or to carry commodities they had produced themselves, such as coal or timber, except for their own use.

For more dedicated progressives like Senator La Follette, the Hepburn Act was but half a loaf. They would have preferred that ICC rates continue in effect while appeals were pending, and to have the ICC estimate the overall value of the roads as a basis for rate-fixing. Before many years, though, they would get both of these.

Railroads took priority, but a growing movement for the regulation of meat-packers, food processors, and makers of drugs and patent medicines reached fruition, as it happened, on the very day after passage of the Hepburn Act. Discontent with abuses in these fields had grown rapidly as a result of the muckrakers' reports. Dr. W. H. Wiley, chief chemist of the Agriculture Department, and Dr. E. F. Ladd, food commissioner of North Dakota, supplied telling evidence of harmful preservatives and adulterants in the preparation of "embalmed meat" and other food products. Edward Bok and Mark Sullivan in the *Ladies Home Journal,* and Samuel Hopkins Adams in *Colliers,* provided evidence of false claims and dangerous ingredients in patent medicines, what Adams called "The Great American Fraud." One of the more notorious nostrums, Lydia Pinkham's Vegetable Compound, was advertised to work wonders in the relief of "female complaints"; it was no wonder, for the compound was 18 percent alcohol.

But perhaps the most telling blow against such abuses was struck by Upton Sinclair's novel *The Jungle* (1906). Sinclair meant the book to be a tract for socialism, but its main impact came from its portrayal of filthy conditions in Chicago's meat-packing industry: "It was too dark in these storage places to see well, but a man could run his hand over these piles of meat and sweep off handfuls of the dried dung of rats. These rats were nuisances, and the packers would put poisoned bread out for them, they would die, and then rats, bread, and meat would go into the hoppers together." Roosevelt, an omnivorous reader, read *The Jungle*—and reacted quickly. He sent two agents to Chicago and their report confirmed all that Sinclair had said: "We saw meat

A Modern First Class Pork Packing & Canning Establishment. *Upton Sinclair's exposé of the filthy conditions in meat-packing plants belied the pristine surroundings pictured here.* [Chicago Historical Society]

shovelled from filthy wooden floors, piled on tables rarely washed, pushed from room to room in rotten box carts, in all of which processes it was in the way of gathering dirt, splinters, floor filth, and the expectoration of tuberculous and other diseased workers."

The Meat Inspection Act of June 30, 1906, required federal inspection of meats destined for interstate commerce and empowered officials in the Agriculture Department to impose standards of sanitation. The Pure Food and Drug Act, enacted the same day, placed restrictions on the makers of prepared foods and patent medicines, and forbade the manufacture, sale, or transportation of adulterated, misbranded, or harmful foods, drugs, and liquors.

Thus during one week of February 1903, and during two days of June 1906, Theodore Roosevelt's campaign for regulatory legislation reached its chief goals: in 1903 the Expedition Act, the Elkins Act, and the establishment of the Department of Commerce and Labor with its Bureau of Corporations; in 1906 the Hepburn Act, the Meat Inspection Act, and the Pure Food and Drug Act. If in later years these would seem modest achievements for all of Roosevelt's bluster, they had moved the federal government a great distance from the laissez-faire policies which had prevailed before the turn of the century.

CONSERVATION   One of the most enduring legacies of the Roosevelt years was the push he gave to the conservation movement.

Concern for protecting the environment grew with the rising awareness that the frontier was being exhausted by the end of the nineteenth century. A large section of Roosevelt's first annual message was devoted to the subject. As early as 1872 Yellowstone National Park had been set aside as a public reserve (the National Park Service would be created in 1916 after other parks had been added). In 1881 Congress had created a Division of Forestry in the Department of Agriculture, and Roosevelt's appointment of Gifford Pinchot, one of the country's first scientific foresters, as chief brought vigorous administration of forests on public lands. After 1891 the Forest Reserve Act had permitted the president to exclude certain timberlands from settlement. When Roosevelt took office approximately 46 million acres had been set aside; by the end of his presidency some 172 million acres had been withdrawn, including acreage important mainly for coal, phosphates, and waterpower.

Forestry Chief Pinchot worked vigorously, with TR's full support, to develop programs and public interest in conservation. In 1903 a Public Lands Commission called for a review of the nation's resources by the Geological Survey. In 1907 an Inland Waterways Commission proposed regional development with an eye to reviving steamboats on the rivers. Congressional resistance to this and other proposals led Pinchot and Roosevelt to publicize the cause through a White House Conference on Conservation in 1908, and later that year by setting up a National Conservation Commission which proposed a thorough survey of resources in minerals, water, forests, and soil. Within eighteen months some forty-one state conservation commissions sprang up, and a number of private groups took up the cause. The movement remained divided, however, between those who wanted to conserve resources for continuous human use and those who wanted to set aside wilderness areas. Pinchot, for instance, won the enmity of naturalist John Muir in 1906 when he endorsed a water reservoir in the wild Hetch Hetchy Valley of Yosemite National Park to supply the needs of San Francisco.

FROM ROOSEVELT TO TAFT

Unlike most presidents, Roosevelt was strong enough to handpick a successor to carry out "the policies." He decided that the heir to the White House should be Secretary of War William Howard Taft, and the Republican convention ratified the choice on its first ballot in 1908. The Democrats, whose conservative strategy had backfired in 1904, decided to give William Jennings

Bryan one more chance at the highest office. Still vigorous at forty-eight, Bryan retained a faithful following. But once again it was not enough. The Republican platform declared its support of Roosevelt's policies, including conservation and further strengthening of the ICC. On the tariff and the use of labor injunctions the platform made vague references to revision but without any specifics. The Democratic platform hardly differed on regulation, but endorsed a lower tariff and an AFL-supported plank opposing court injunctions against labor actions. Bryan himself went beyond support of regulation by calling for federal incorporation of interstate business and even government ownership of railroads, "not as an immediate issue, but as an ultimate solution." In the end the voters opted for Roosevelt's chosen successor, leaving Bryan only the southern states plus Nebraska, Colorado, and Nevada. Taft swept the electoral college by 321 to 162.

Once out of office, still only fifty, Roosevelt left on a big-game hunt in Africa, followed by a triumphant procession through Europe. The new president he left behind was an entirely different kind of political animal, in fact hardly a political animal at all. Offspring of a family long prominent in Cincinnati—his father Alphonso had been Grant's attorney-general—Taft had progressed through appointive offices, from judge in Ohio to solicitor in the Justice Department, federal judge, commissioner and governor-general in the Philippines, and secretary of war. The presidency was the only elective office he ever held. Later he would be chief justice (1921–1930), a job more suited to his temperament. Weighing in at some 300 pounds, Taft was more

William Howard Taft, on the golf course. [Culver Picture Service]

attuned to the sedentary reflections of the bench than to the active give and take of the political arena. "I don't like politics," he wrote once. "I don't like the limelight." The political animal in the family was his wife, who had wanted the White House more than he. One of the major tragedies of Taft's presidency was that Helen Taft fell seriously ill soon after they entered the White House, and for most of his term remained unable to serve as his political adviser.

TARIFF REFORM   Contrary to Republican tradition, Taft preferred a lower tariff. This he made the first important issue of his presidency. Once a student of William Graham Sumner at Yale, Taft had absorbed the laissez-faire views of his mentor and had since differed with orthodox Republican protectionism. Early in the campaign, and contrary to TR's advice, he had clarified the vague tariff plank in the platform by affirming that it meant revision downward. In keeping with the platform pledge for a special session, Taft called Congress to meet on March 15, 1909, eleven days after his inauguration. But if, in pressing an issue that TR had skirted, Taft seemed the bolder of the two, he proved the less adroit.

A bill sponsored by Sereno E. Payne of New York passed the House with surprising ease. It lowered rates less than Taft would have preferred but made some important reductions and enlarged the free list. But the chairman of the Senate Finance Committee, Nelson W. Aldrich, guided through a bill drastically revised by more than 800 changes. Many of these were "jokers" which concealed increases by changing specific duties to *ad valorem* duties (in proportion to value) or the other way around. Finley Peter Dunne's Mr. Dooley ridiculed the free list which, he said, included such important things as divvy-divvy, spunk, silkworm eggs, stilts, skeletons, and leeches. "The new tariff bill," he said, "puts these familyar commodyties within the reach iv all." What finally came out of a conference committee was a measure close to the Senate version, although Taft did get some reductions on important items: hides, iron ore, coal, oil, cottons, boots, and shoes.

In response to the higher rates in Aldrich's bills, a group of midwestern Republicans took the Senate floor to fight what they considered a corrupt throwback to the days when the Republican party had served big business unquestioningly. In all, ten progressive Republicans joined the Democrats in an unsuccessful effort to defeat the bill. Taft at first agreed with them; then, fearful of a party split, backed the majority and agreed to an imperfect bill. He lacked TR's love of a grand battle as well as his gift for working both sides of the street. Temperamentally conservative, inhibited by scruples about interfering too much with the legislative process, he drifted into the orbit of the Republican Old Guard and quickly alienated the progressive wing of his party, whom he tagged "assistant Democrats." Aware of rising discontent in the corn and wheat belts, Taft embarked in late summer on a speaking tour of the West only to make things worse when he pointedly ignored insurgent senators and pronounced the Payne-Aldrich Act the best tariff bill the Republican party had ever passed.

BALLINGER AND PINCHOT   In 1910 Taft's policies drove the wedge deeper between the Republican factions. The Ballinger-Pinchot controversy made Taft appear to be a less reliable custodian of TR's conservation policies than he actually was. Taft's secretary of the interior, Richard A. Ballinger of Seattle, was well aware that many westerners opposed conservation programs on the grounds that they held back full development of the region. The strongest conservation leaders were often easterners like TR and Gifford Pinchot of Pennsylvania. Ballinger threw open to use more than a million acres of waterpower sites which Roosevelt had withdrawn in the guise of ranger stations. Ballinger's reasoning was that the withdrawal had "gone far beyond legal limitations," and Taft agreed. At about the same time Ballinger turned over certain coal lands in Alaska to a group of Seattle men, some of whom he had represented as a lawyer. Apparently without Ballinger's knowledge, this group had already agreed to sell part of the lands to a Morgan-Guggenheim syndicate.

This was too much for Louis R. Glavis, an investigator with the General Land Office, who went to Chief of Forestry Pinchot with evidence of the collusion. Pinchot in turn called it to the attention of Taft, who then fired Glavis for his pains. When Pinchot went public with the controversy, he in turn was fired for insubordination early in 1910. A joint congressional investigation of Ballinger exonerated him from all charges of fraud or corruption, but progressive suspicions created such pressures that he resigned in 1911.

Taft acted on the strictly legal view which his training had taught him to value, but circumstances tarnished his image in the public mind. "In the end," one historian has written, "the Ballinger-Pinchot affair had more impact on politics than it did on conservation." Taft had been elected to carry out the Roosevelt policies, his opponents said, and he was carrying them out—"on a stretcher." Pinchot was soon off to Africa carrying the word to Roosevelt.

Meanwhile, in the House of Representatives rebellion had broken out among the more progressive Republicans. When the regular session opened in March 1910 the insurgents joined Democrats in voting to investigate Ballinger. Flushed with that victory, they resolved to clip the wings of Speaker Joseph G. Cannon (R-Ill.), a conservative who held almost a stranglehold on procedures by his power to appoint all committees and their chairmen, and especially by his control of the Rules Committee, of which he was a member. A Democratic-insurgent coalition overrode a ruling from the Speaker and proceeded to adopt new rules offered by George W. Norris (R-Neb.) which enlarged the Rules Committee from five to fifteen members, made them elective by the House, and excluded the Speaker as a member. About forty Republicans joined the Democratic minority in the move. In the next Congress the rules would be further changed to make all committees elective.

In all these matters, events had conspired to cast Taft in a conservative role at a time when progressive sentiment was riding high in the countryside. The result was a severe rebuke to the president in the congressional elections of 1910, first by the widespread defeat of pro-Taft candidates in the Republican primaries, then by the election of a Democratic majority in the House and of enough Democrats in the Senate that insurgent Republicans could wield the balance of power.

TAFT AND ROOSEVELT   In June 1910 Roosevelt had returned from his travels abroad. He had been reading new accounts and letters about the Taft "betrayal," but unlike some of his supporters, he refused to break with his successor. With rather severe politeness, however, Roosevelt refused an invitation to visit the White House. But, he wrote Taft: "I shall keep my mind open as I keep my mouth shut." Neither was easy for Roosevelt, who was beset by followers urging him to action. Soon he was rallying support for gubernatorial candidate Henry L. Stimson in New York, and then he was off on a speaking tour of the West in advance of the congressional elections. At Osawatomie, Kansas, on August 31, 1910, he gave a catchy name to his principles, the "New Nationalism," and issued a stirring call for stronger regulatory power and new measures of direct democracy. Most offensive to conservatives, perhaps, was his support for the recall of judicial decisions by popular vote.

Relations between Roosevelt and Taft remained tense, but it

was another year before they came to an open break. It happened in the fall of 1911 when the Taft administration announced an antitrust suit against United States Steel, citing specifically as cause the company's acquisition of Tennessee Coal and Iron Company in 1907, a move to which TR had given tacit approval in the belief it would avert a panic. In mid-November Roosevelt published a sharp attack on Taft's "archaic" attempt to restore competition. The only sensible response to the problem, he argued, was to accept business combinations in modern circumstances but to enlarge the government's power to regulate them. His entry into the next presidential campaign was now only a matter of time.

Not all progressive Republicans wanted TR back in the White House. A sizable number proposed to back Senator La Follette in 1912, but some of La Follette's supporters were ready to switch if TR entered the race. An opening came on February 2, 1912, when La Follette betrayed signs of nervous exhaustion in a rambling speech at a publishers' dinner in Philadelphia. As his following began to drop away, a group of seven Republican governors met in Chicago on February 10 and called on Roosevelt to become a candidate. On February 24 Roosevelt threw his hat in the ring. "I hope that so far as possible the people may be given the chance, through direct primaries," Roosevelt wrote the governors, "to express their preference. . . ."

The rebuke implicit in Roosevelt's decision to run against Taft, his chosen successor, was in many ways undeserved. During Taft's first year in office one political tempest after another left his image irreparably damaged. The three years of solid achievement that followed came too late to restore its luster or to reunite his divided party. Taft had at least attempted tariff reform, which TR had never dared. He replaced Ballinger with Walter Fisher of Chicago and Pinchot with Henry S. Graves, former head of the Yale Forestry School, both men of impeccable credentials in conservation matters. He won from Congress the power to protect public lands for any reason, and was the first president to withdraw oil lands from use. Under the Appalachian Forest Reserve Act (1911) he enlarged the national forests by purchase of lands in the East. In the end his administration withdrew more public lands in four years than TR's had in nearly eight, and brought more antitrust suits, by a score of eighty to twenty-five.

In 1910, with Taft's support, Congress passed the Mann-Elkins Act, which empowered the ICC for the first time to initiate rate changes, extended regulation to telephone and telegraph companies, and set up a Commerce Court to expedite appeals from the ICC rulings. Taft's reform record was further extended by passage of a postal-savings law (1910) and a parcel-post law (1913), the establishment of the Bureau of Mines and the Federal Children's Bureau (1912), and the provision of statehood for Arizona and New Mexico and territorial government for Alaska (1912). The Sixteenth Amendment (1913), authorizing a federal income tax, was ratified with Taft's support before he left office, and the Seventeenth Amendment (1913), providing for the popular election of senators, was ratified soon after he left office.

Despite this record, Roosevelt now hastened Taft's demise. In all but two of the thirteen states which held presidential primaries, Roosevelt won, even in Taft's Ohio. But the groundswell of popular support was no match for Taft's decisive position as president and party leader. In state conventions the party regulars held the line, so that Roosevelt entered the Republican national convention about 100 votes short of victory. The regulars' control of the convention machinery, operating under established rules, ensured their triumph and the Taft forces proceeded to nominate their man by the same "steamroller" tactics that had nominated Roosevelt in 1904. Outraged at such "naked theft," the Roosevelt delegates assembled in a rump convention. "If you wish me to make the fight I will make it," Roosevelt told the delegates, who then issued a call for a Progressive party convention, which assembled in Chicago on August 5. TR appeared, feeling "fit as a bull moose." He was "stripped to the buff and ready for the fight," he said. "We stand at Armageddon and we battle for the Lord." But the convention was filled with advanced

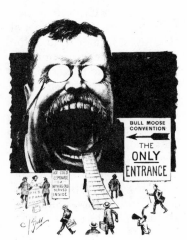

A skeptical view of TR, the Bull Moose candidate in 1912. [Library of Congress]

thinkers, social workers like Jane Addams of Hull House and the New Jersey business progressive George L. Record, and few professional politicians turned up. Progressive Republicans decided to preserve their party credentials and fight another day. For the time being, with the disruption of the Republican party, the progressive torch was about to be passed on to the Democrats.

WILSON'S PROGRESSIVISM

WILSON'S RISE   The emergence of Thomas Woodrow Wilson as the Democratic nominee climaxed a political rise even more rapid than that of Cleveland. In 1910, before his nomination and election as governor of New Jersey, Wilson had been president of Princeton University, but had never run for public office. Born in Staunton, Virginia, in 1856, Wilson had grown up the son of a Presbyterian minister in Georgia and the Carolinas during the Civil War and Reconstruction. He attended Davidson College for one year, finished his undergraduate career at Princeton in 1879, and after law school at the University of Virginia he tried a brief and profitless law practice in Atlanta. From there he went to the new Johns Hopkins University in Baltimore, where he found his calling in the study of history and political science under Herbert Baxter Adams.

Wilson's dissertation, *Congressional Government*, published in 1885, outlined the operation of the committee system, until then little understood except among politicians, and the view, later elaborated in *Constitutional Government in the United States* (1908), that the president, like the British prime minister, should be the leader of party government, as active in directing legislation as in the administration and enforcement of laws. In calling for a strong presidency he expressed views closer to those of Roosevelt than those of Taft, but over the years more typical of Democratic than of Republican presidents.

After Johns Hopkins, Wilson taught at Bryn Mawr, moved to Princeton in 1890, and twelve years later became its president. In that position he showed the first evidence of reform views and a tenacity buttressed by his Presbyterian sense of righteousness. At Princeton he started a preceptorial system to supplement lectures, but met defeat when he tried to democratize student life by banning the exclusive dining clubs and putting the graduate school at the center of the campus as a leaven for undergraduate programs. When these plans were blocked by the opposition of alumni and the dean of the graduate school, Wilson faced a choice of giving up or leaving.

Woodrow Wilson. [National Archives]

At this juncture James Smith, the Democratic boss of New Jersey, offered Wilson his support for the 1910 gubernatorial nomination, and Wilson accepted. Smith sought a respectable candidate to ward off progressive challengers. He discovered, too late, that the supposedly innocent schoolmaster actually had a will of iron. Elected as a reform candidate, Wilson proceeded to push progressive measures through the legislature. Wilson, for instance, insisted that the legislature honor the senatorial nomination won by James E. Martine in the Democratic primary—despite Smith's desire for the job. The legislature heeded Wilson. Under pressure from the governor the lawmakers also enacted a workmen's compensation law, a corrupt-practices law, measures to regulate public utilities, and ballot reforms. Such strong leadership in a state known as the "home of the trusts" for its lenient corporation laws brought Wilson to national attention.

THE ELECTION OF 1912 In the spring of 1911 a group of southerners resident in New York opened a Wilson presidential campaign headquarters, and Wilson set forth on strenuous tours into all regions of the country, denouncing special privilege and political bossism. But by convention time, despite a fast start, the Wilson campaign seemed headed for defeat by Speaker Bennett Champ Clark of Missouri, who garnered supporters among Bryanites, the Hearst newspapers, and party hacks. Clark had enough for a majority in the early ballots, but the Wilson forces combined with supporters of Oscar Underwood of Alabama to prevent a two-thirds majority. On the fourteenth ballot Bryan came over to Wilson. When Roger Sullivan, Democratic boss of Illinois, deserted Clark on the forty-second ballot and the Underwood delegates went over to Wilson on the forty-sixth, he swept to the nomination.

It quickly became clear that in a three-man race Taft was out of the running. "There are so many people in the country who don't like me," he lamented. The campaign settled down to a running debate over the competing ideologies of the two front-runners: Roosevelt's "New Natonalism" and Wilson's "New Freedom." The inchoate ideas that Roosevelt fashioned into his New Nationalism had first been presented systematically in *The Promise of American Life* (1909), a treatise by Herbert Croly, a then-obscure New York journalist. Its central point was often summarized in a useful catch-phrase: Hamiltonian means to achieve Jeffersonian ends, meaning that Hamilton's program of governmental intervention, once indentified with the business interests, should be used to achieve democratic and egalitarian Jeffersonian goals. The times required progressives to give up Jeffersonian prejudices against big government and use a strong central government to achieve democratic ends in the interest of the people.

The old nationalism had been used "by the sinister . . . special interests," TR said. The New Nationalism would enable government to achieve social justice, and more specifically to effect such reforms as graduated income and inheritance taxes, workmen's compensation, regulation of the labor of women and children, and a stronger Bureau of Corporations. These and more went into the platform of the Progressive party, which called for a federal trade commission with sweeping authority over business and a tariff commission to set rates on a "scientific basis." The Progressive platform, the historian Arthur Link has written, "provided the basis for the future development of the progressive movement in the United States after 1912, just as the Populist platform of 1892 had earlier provided a foundation for the first phase of American progressivism."

Before the end of his administration, Wilson would be swept into the current of the new nationalism too. But for now he spoke for the decentralizing antitrust traditions of his party. Before the start of the campaign Wilson conferred with Louis D. Brandeis, a progressive lawyer from Boston who focused Wilson's thought much as Croly had focused Roosevelt's. The central idea of the New Freedom was that government should "so restrict the wrong use of competition that the right use of competition will

Wilson's view of Roosevelt's New Nationalism.
Wilson argued that TR's program of monopoly
regulation played into the hands of the big trusts.
[Library of Congress]

destroy monopoly." This was the dream of restoring an economy
of small-scale competitive units, and Roosevelt dismissed it as illusory.

The Republican schism opened the way for Woodrow Wilson
to win by 435 electoral votes to 88 for Roosevelt and 8 for Taft.
But in popular votes Wilson had only 42 percent of the total. It
was the victory of a minority over a divided opposition. The
election of 1912 assumes significance in several ways. First, it
was a high-water mark for progressivism. The election was the
first to feature presidential primaries. The two leading candidates debated the basic issues of progressivism in a campaign
unique for its focus on vital alternatives and for its high philosophical tone. Taft too, despite his temperament and associations, showed his own progressive instincts. And the Socialist
party, the left wing of progressivism, polled over 900,000 votes
for Eugene V. Debs, about 6 percent of the total vote, its highest
proportion ever.

Second, the election brought the Democrats back into effective national power for the first time since the Civil War. For two
years during the second Cleveland administration, 1893–1895,

they had held the White House and majorities in both houses of Congress, but they quickly fell out of power during the most severe depression in American history to that time.

Third, the election of Wilson brought southerners back into the orbit of national and international affairs in a significant way for the first time since the Civil War. In Washington, one reporter said, "you feel it in the air . . . you listen to evidence of it in the mellow accent with which the South makes our English a musical tongue." Wilson himself once said that "the only place in the world where nothing has to be explained to me is the South." Five of his ten cabinet members were born in the South, three still resided there, and William Jennings Bryan, the secretary of state, was an idol of the southern masses. At the president's right hand, and one of the most influential members of the Wilson circle, at least until 1919, was Col. Edward M. House of Texas. On Capitol Hill southerners, by virtue of their seniority, held the lion's share of committee chairmanships. As a result much of the progressive legislation of the Wilson era would bear the names of the southerners who guided it through Congress.

Fourth and finally, the election of 1912 had begun to alter the character of the Republican party. Even though most party pro-

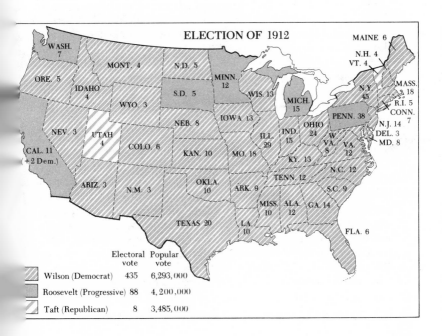

ELECTION OF 1912

	Electoral vote	Popular vote
Wilson (Democrat)	435	6,293,000
Roosevelt (Progressive)	88	4,200,000
Taft (Republican)	8	3,485,000

fessionals remained, the defection of the Bull Moose Progressives had weakened the party's progressive wing. The leader of the Republican party which would return to power in the 1920s would be more conservative in tone and temperament.

WILSONIAN REFORM   Inauguration day of 1913 was "one of the most perfect March days Washington had ever known," a happy omen it seemed as the former Confederate, Chief Justice Edward Douglass White of Louisiana, gave the oath. Wilson's address voiced in eloquent tones the ideals of social justice that animated many progressives. "We have been proud of our industrial achievements," he said, "but we have not hitherto stopped thoughtfully enough to count the human cost . . . the fearful physical and spiritual cost to the men and women and children upon whom the dead weight and burden of it all has fallen pitilessly the years through." He promised specifically a lower tariff and a new banking system. "This is not a day of triumph; it is a day of dedication. Here muster, not the forces of party, but the forces of humanity."

Wilson offered his party its first chance since the Civil War to make a record of achievement. Democrats were bound to him by their need to disprove the slur voiced by Republican Rep. Nicholas Longworth that they were "the organized incapacity of the country." They were bound even more by Wilson's determination to be their leader. If Roosevelt had been a strong president by force of personality, Wilson became a strong president by force of conviction. The president, he wrote in *Constitutional Government*, "is . . . the political leader of the nation, or has it in his choice to be. The nation as a whole has chosen him, and is conscious that it has no other political spokesman. His is the only national voice in affairs."

Wilson courted popular support, but he also courted members of Congress through personal contacts, invitations to the White House, and visits to the Capitol. He used the patronage power to reward friends and punish enemies. He might have acted through a progressive coalition, but chose instead to rely on party loyalty. "I'd rather trust a machine Senator when he is committed to your program," he told Navy Secretary Josephus Daniels, "than a talking Liberal who can never quite go along with others because of his admiration of his own patented plan of reform." Wilson therefore made use of the party caucus, in which disagreements among Democrats were settled, and often directed caucus strategy.

Wilson's leadership got its first big test on the issue of tariff reform. Wilson summoned Congress into special session on April 7, 1913, and the day after it convened he went before it in person —the first president to do so since John Adams. (Roosevelt was said to have asked, "Why didn't I think of that?") "The object of the tariff duties henceforth laid must be effective competition," Wilson said, "the whetting of American wits by contest with the wits of the rest of the world." Congress now acted vigorously on tariff reductions. In the House, where Oscar Underwood's Ways and Means Committee had been working since January, the outcome was never in doubt. Only four Democrats bolted the party line as the bill passed the House easily.

The crunch came in the Senate, the traditional graveyard of tariff reform. Swarms of lobbyists got so thick in Washington, Wilson said, that "a brick couldn't be thrown without hitting one of them." But Wilson turned the tables with a public statement that focused the spotlight on the "industrious and insidious" tariff lobby. "It is of serious interest to the country," he said, "that the people at large should have no lobby and be voiceless in these matters, while great bodies of astute men seek to create an artificial opinion and to overcome the interests of the public for their private profit." In the end the two "sugar senators" from Louisiana were the only Democrats to vote against the bill, which received the president's signature on October 3.

The Underwood-Simmons Tariff of 1913, based throughout on *ad valorem* duties, reduced import duties on 958 items, raised them on only 86, and left 307 the same, with the effect of lowering the overall average duty from about 37 to about 29 percent. A free list of some 300 items, about 100 of them new to the list, included important consumer goods and raw materials: sugar, wool, iron ore, steel rails, agricultural implements, cement, coal, wood and woodpulp, and many farm products.

The act lowered tariffs but raised internal revenues with the first income tax levied under the newly ratified Sixteenth Amendment: 1 percent on incomes over $3,000 ($4,000 for married couples) and a surtax graduated from 1 percent on incomes of about $20,000 to 6 percent on incomes above $500,000. The highest total tax thus would be 7 percent. Opponents objected that the tax was class legislation and a sectional raid on eastern wealth, but Cordell Hull (D-Tenn.), who guided it through the House, disclaimed any purpose of sharing the wealth and justified the tax on the principle that eastern profits derived from all parts of the country.

Before the new tariff had cleared the Senate, the administration proposed the first major banking and currency reform since the Civil War. The need for a change had been acknowledged since the brief panic of 1907, which threatened to bring on widespread bank failures. The panic had occasioned the appointment of a National Monetary Commission headed by Sen. Nelson W. Aldrich, which in 1912 recommended creation of a National Reserve Association with fifteen branches. The plan aimed to strengthen the banking system by pooling bank reserves and maintaining a flexible currency.

But to progressive Democrats it seemed a plan to revive the second Bank of the United States, which Jackson had destroyed, and to extend the Wall Street "Money Trust's" control of business and finance, which a House committee under A. P. Pujo (D-La.) began to expose in the fall of 1912. Dominant figures in framing the Democrats' counterproposal were Rep. Carter Glass, a pugnacious redhead from Virginia, and the economist H. Parker Willis. Glass's chief contribution was a provision, which appealed to traditional Democratic fears of centralization, for regional reserve banks to be owned by member banks. Wilson, however, insisted on a central board of governors, comprising only a minority of bankers, as the capstone of the system.

A group of radical agrarians, with support from William Jennings Bryan, insisted that the entire system, including the banks and the governing board, should be under governmental control. They won a compromise arrangement excluding bankers' representatives from the central board, making Federal Reserve Notes obligations of the federal government, and providing short-term, ninety-day farm loans as well as business loans. The Glass-Owen Federal Reserve Act, signed into law two days before Christmas 1913, created a new banking system along regional lines, with twelve Federal Reserve Banks, each owned by member banks in its district. All national banks became members; state banks and trust companies could join if they wished. Each member bank had to subscribe 6 percent of its capital to the Federal Reserve Bank and deposit a portion of its reserve there, the amount depending on the size of the community.

These "bankers' banks" dealt chiefly with their members and not at all with individuals. Along with other banking functions, the chief service to member banks was to rediscount their loans, that is, to take them over in exchange for Federal Reserve Notes, which member banks might then use to make further loans. The Federal Reserve Notes in turn were based 40 percent on government gold and 60 percent on commercial and agricultural paper (the promissory notes signed by borrowers). This arrangement made it possible to expand both the money supply and bank

Reading the Death Warrant. *Wilson's plan for banking and currency reform spells the death of the "Money Trust" according to this New York World* cartoon. *[C. R. Macauley]*

credit in times of high business activity, or as the level of borrowing increased. A Federal Reserve Board with seven members (eight after 1922) named three of the nine members on each Reserve Bank's board (member banks chose the remaining six) and exercised general supervision, including review of the rediscount rates. These rates might be raised to fight inflation by tightening credit or lowered to stimulate business by making credit more easily available.

This new system corrected three great defects in the previous arrangements. Now reserves could be pooled, affording greater security; both the currency and bank credit became more elastic; and the concentration of reserves in New York was lessened. The system represented a new departure in active governmental intervention and control in one of the most sensitive segments of the economy.

The next major issue confronting Wilson, after tariffs and banking, concerned the antitrust laws. In his campaign Wilson had made trust-busting the central focus of the New Freedom, and information gathered by the Pujo Committee showed that the concentration of economic power had continued to grow despite the Sherman Act and the Bureau of Corporations. Wilson's solution to the problem was revision of the Sherman Act to define more explicitly what counted as "restraint of trade."

During the summer of 1914, while Congress took up several bills, Wilson suddenly reversed himself and, influenced by attorneys Brandeis and George Rublee, decided to make a strong Federal Trade Commission the cornerstone of his antitrust program.

Created by an act of September 1914, the five-member commission replaced Roosevelt's Bureau of Corporations and assumed new powers to define "unfair trade practices" and to issue "cease and desist" orders when it found evidence of unfair competition.

Having embraced the Brandeis principle of "controlled competition," Wilson seemed to lose interest in the antitrust bill drafted by Henry D. Clayton (D-Ala.) of the House Judiciary Committee, which followed the president's original idea of defining specific acts in restraint of trade. The Clayton Antitrust Act, passed in October 1914, outlawed such practices as price discrimination (charging different customers different prices for the same goods), "tying" agreements which limited the right of dealers to handle the products of competing manufacturers, interlocking directorates connecting corporations with a capital of more than $1 million (or banks with more than $5 million), and corporations' acquisition of stock in competing corporations. In every case, however, conservative forces in the Senate qualified these provisions by tacking on the weakening phrase "where the effect may be to substantially lessen competition" or words of similar effect. In accordance with the president's recommendation, however, corporate officials were made individually responsible for any violations. Victims of price discrimination and tying agreements could sue for compensation three times the amount of damages suffered.

Agrarian radicals, in alliance with organized labor, won a stipulation which supposedly exempted farm labor organizations from the antitrust laws, but actually only declared them not to be, per se, unlawful combinations in restraint of trade. Injunctions in labor disputes, moreover, were not to be handed down by federal courts unless "necessary to prevent irreparable injury to property." Hailed by Samuel Gompers as labor's "Magna Carta," these provisions were little more than pious affirmations, as later court decisions would demonstrate. Wilson himself remarked that the act did little more than affirm the right of unions to exist by forbidding their dissolution for being in restraint of trade.

Administration of the antitrust laws generally proved disappointing to the more vehement progressives under Wilson. In the wake of a business setback late in 1913 Wilson set out to reassure business that his purposes were friendly. As Secretary of Commerce William C. Redfield put it later, Wilson hoped to "create in the Federal Trade Commission a counsellor and friend to the business world." Its first chairman, Joseph E. Davies of

Wisconsin, lacked forcefulness, and under Edward N. Hurley, a Chicago industrialist who succeeded Davies in June 1916, the FTC practically abandoned its function of watchdog. Under Attorney-General McReynolds the Justice Department offered help and advice to businessmen interested in arranging matters so as to avoid antitrust prosecutions. The appointment of conservative men to the Interstate Commerce Commission and the Federal Reserve won plaudits from the business world and profoundly disappointed progressives.

The fact was that Wilson had never been a strong progressive of the social-justice persuasion. He had carried out promises to lower the tariff, reorganize the banking system, and strengthen the antitrust laws. Swept along by the course of events, and the pressures of more far-reaching progressives, he was pushed farther than he intended to go on some points. The New Freedom was now complete, he wrote Treasury Secretary McAdoo late in 1914; the future would be "a time of healing because a time of just dealing." Although Wilson endorsed state action for women's suffrage, he declined to endorse a suffrage amendment because his party platform had not. He had cultivated the support of black voters, but let members of his cabinet extend Jim Crow practices in the federal government and froze out all but a few black appointees. He withheld support from federal child labor legislation because he regarded it a state matter. He opposed a bill for federal support of rural credits on the ground that it was "unwise and unjustifiable to extend the credit of the government to a single class of the community." Not until the second anniversary of his inauguration (March 4, 1915) did Wilson sign an important piece of social-justice legislation, the La Follette Seamen's Act. The product of stubborn agitation by Andrew Furuseth, eloquent president of the Seamen's Union, the act strengthened safety requirements, reduced the power of captains, set minimum food standards, and required regular wage payments. Seaman who jumped ship before their contracts expired, moreover, were relieved of the charge of desertion.

PROGRESSIVE RESURGENCE   It was the need to weld a winning coalition in 1916 that pushed Wilson back on the road of reform. Progressive Democrats were restless, and after war broke out in Europe in August 1914, further divisions arose over defense and foreign policy. At the same time the Republicans were repairing their own rift, as the Progressive party showed little staying power in the midterm elections and Roosevelt showed little will to preserve it. It was plain to most observers that Wilson could shape a majority only by courting progressives of all parties. In January 1916 Wilson scored points with them when he nominated Louis D. Brandeis to the Supreme Court. Conservatives waged a vigorous battle against Brandeis, but Senate progressives rallied to win confirmation of the social-justice champion, the first Jewish member of the Supreme Court.

Meanwhile Wilson began to embrace a broad program of farm and labor reforms. On farm credit, after having first opposed it he reversed himself abruptly, supporting early in 1916 a proposal to set up land banks to sponsor long-term farm loans. With this boost the Federal Farm Loan Act became law on July 17. Under the control of a Federal Farm Loan Board, twelve Federal Land Banks, each with a minimum capital of $750,000, paralleled the Federal Reserve Banks and offered farmers loans of five to forty years' duration at low interest rates.

Thus the dream of cheap rural credits, sponsored by a generation of Alliancemen and Populists, came to fruition. Democrats never embraced the Populist subtreasury plan, but made a small step in that direction with the Warehouse Act of 1916. This measure authorized federal licensing of private warehouses; federal backing made their receipts for stored produce more acceptable as collateral for short-term bank loans. Other concessions to farm demands came more readily in the Smith-Lever Act of 1914 and the Smith-Hughes Act of 1917, both of which passed with little controversy. The first, sponsored by Sen. Hoke Smith (D-Ga.) and Rep. A. F. Lever (D-S.C.), provided federal grants-in-aid for farm demonstration agents under the supervision of land-grant colleges. The measure made permanent a program that had started in Texas in 1903 and that had already spread to many localities with help from the Agriculture Department and the General Education Board. In 1923 the county farm agents were organized into an Extension Service supervised by state land-grant colleges. The second measure, sponsored by Smith and Rep. Dudley M. Hughes (D-Ga.), extended agricultural and mechanical education to high schools through grants-in-aid.

Farmers with automobiles had more than a passing interest as well in the Federal Highways Act of 1916, which provided dollar-matching contributions to states with highway departments that met certain federal standards. The measure authorized distribution of $75 million over five years, and marked a sharp departure from Jacksonian opposition to internal improvements at federal expense, just as the Federal Reserve System departed from Jacksonian banking principles. Although the argument that highways were one of the nation's defense needs weakened constitutional scruples against the act, it still restricted support to "post roads." A renewal act in 1921 would mark the beginning of a systematic network of numbered United States highways.

The progressive resurgence of 1916 broke the logjam on labor reforms as well. With newfound support from the administration, the Kern-McGillicuddy Bill, a workmen's compensation measure for federal employees, passed in August. Advocates of child-labor legislation persuaded Wilson that social-justice progressives would regard his stand on the issue as an important test of his humanitarian concerns, and Wilson overcame doubts of its constitutionality to support and sign the Keating-Owen Child Labor Act, which excluded from interstate commerce goods manufactured by children under fourteen. Both the Keating-Owen Act and a later act of 1919 to achieve the same purpose with a prohibitory tax were ruled unconstitutional by the Supreme Court on the grounds that regulation of interstate commerce could not extend to the conditions of labor. Effective action against the social evil of child labor had to await the New Deal, although it seems likely that discussion of the issue contributed to the sharp reduction in the number of underage workers during the next few years. Another important accomplishment was the eight-hour day for railroad workers, a measure that the Supreme Court upheld. The Adamson Act of 1916 was brought about by a threatened strike of railroad brotherhoods demanding the eight-hour day and other concessions. Wilson, who objected to some of the union demands, nevertheless went before Congress to request action on the hours limitation. The resulting Adamson Act required an eight-hour day, beginning January 1, 1917, with time and a half for overtime, and appointed a commission to study the problem of railroad labor.

In Wilson's first term progressivism reached its zenith. A creative time, the age of progressivism set at the beginning of the twentieth century a framework within which American politics and society would still function, by and large, near the end of the century. Progressivism had conquered the old dictum that the government is best which governs least, whatever political rhetoric might be heard to the contrary, and left the more extreme doctrines of limited government as dead as Herbert Spencer. Progressivism, an amalgam of agrarian, business, governmental, and social reform, amounted in the end to a movement for positive government. From two decades of ferment (three, if the Populist years be counted) the great fundamental contribution of progressive politics was the firm establishment and general acceptance of the public-service concept of the state.

THE LIMITS OF PROGRESSIVISM

The Progressive period was an optimistic age in which reformers of various hues were persuaded, in Walter Lippmann's terms, that drift would give way to mastery over social ills and that no problem lay beyond solution. But like all great historic movements, progressivism had elements of paradox and irony. Despite its talk of democracy, it was the age of disfranchisement for southern blacks—an action seen by many whites as progressive. The initiative and referendum, supposed democratic reforms, proved subject to manipulation by well-financed publicity campaigns. And much of the public policy of the time came to be formulated by experts and members of appointed boards, not by broad segments of the population. There is a fine irony indeed in the fact that the drive to increase the political role of ordinary people moved parallel with efforts to strengthen executive leadership and exalt expertise. This age of efficiency and bureaucracy, in business as well as government, brought into being a society in which more and more of the decisions affecting people's lives were made by faceless policy-makers.

Progressivism was largely a middle-class movement in which the poor and unorganized had little influence. The supreme irony was that a movement so dedicated to the rhetoric of democracy should experience so steady a decline in voter participation. In 1912, the year of the Bull Moose campaign, voting dropped off by between 6 and 7 percent. The new politics of issues and charismatic leaders proved to be less effective in turning out voters than party organizations and bosses had been. And by 1916 the optimism of an age that looked to infinite progress was already confronted by a vast slaughter. Europe had already stumbled into war, and America would soon be drawn in. The twentieth century, which dawned with such bright hopes, held in store episodes of horror unparalleled in history.

FURTHER READING

A good introduction to the issues which faced the Progressives can be found in William L. O'Neill's *The Progressive Years: America Comes of Age* (1975).° Otis L. Graham, Jr.'s *The Great Campaigns: Reform and War in America, 1900–1928* (1971), reviews the scholarly interpretations and carries the Progressive impulse in its altered forms up to the

°These books are available in paperback editions.

depression. George E. Mowry's *The Era of Theodore Roosevelt* (1958)°
and Arthur S. Link's *Woodrow Wilson and the Progressive Era* (1954)°
block out the periods of reform according to which party held power.
Lewis L. Gould's *Reform and Regulation: American Politics, 1900–1916*
(1978), is a more recent review of scholarship on the entire period.

Progressivism has been interpreted in many ways. Lewis L. Gould
(ed.), *The Progressive Era* (1973),° and David M. Kennedy (ed.), *Progressivism: The Critical Issues* (1971),° each provides a variety of short essays
on the subject. Robert H. Wiebe's *The Search for Order, 1877–1920*
(1966),° presents the organizational model for reform. Richard Hofstadter's *The Age of Reform: From Bryan to FDR* (1955)° examines the
consensus at the basis of reform. Christopher Lasch counters that view in
The New Radicalism in America, 1889–1963 (1965),° and John P. Diggins
supports the Lasch view in *The American Left in the Twentieth Century*
(1973).° Gabriel Kolko sees reform as another means of social control in
The Triumph of Conservatism (1963).° John D. Buenker's *Urban Liberalism and Progressive Reform* (1973)° stresses the role played by immigrant voters in supporting reformers. Other interpretative works
include Samuel P. Hayes's *The Response to Industrialism, 1885–1914*
(1957),° James Weinstein's *The Corporate Ideal in the Welfare State,
1900–1918* (1968),° Arthur Ekrich's *Progressivism in Practice* (1974),
and Jean Quandt's *From the Small Town to the Great Community: The Social Thought of Progressive Intellectuals* (1970).

Scholars disagree not only about the goals of the Progressives but
about just who the Progressives were. George E. Mowry's *The California
Progressives* (1951)° and Richard Hofstadter's *The Age of Reform*
(1955)° argue that the reform impulse originated out of old-stock voter
anxieties over the new immigration. David P. Thelen, among others,
argues in *The New Citizenship: Origins of Progressivism in Wisconsin,
1885–1900* (1972), that reform groups were diverse coalitions interested in efficiency. Sheldon Hackney's *Populism to Progressivism in Alabama* (1969) sees the two reform groups as coming from different classes
in society. Jack T. Kirby's *Darkness at the Dawning: Race and Reform in
the Progressive South* (1972) documents how blacks were excluded from
certain areas of "progress." Robert H. Wiebe's *Businessmen and Reform*
(1962) locates the reform impulse in the hands of an emerging economic
interest group.

Biographers of the three progressive presidents elaborate on the
complexity of reform. Edmund E. Morris's *The Rise of Theodore Roose-
velt* (1979),° a favorable account, can be balanced with G. Wallace
Chessman's *Theodore Roosevelt and the Politics of Power* (1968) and
William H. Harbaugh's *Power and Responsibility: The Life and Times of
Theodore Roosevelt* (1961).° Also helpful is John M. Blum's *The Republi-
can Roosevelt* (1954).° Taft receives sympathetic treatment in Paolo E.
Colletta's *The Presidency of William Howard Taft* (1973) and more criti-
cal assessment in Donald E. Anderson's *William Howard Taft* (1973).
For Wilson, begin with the multivolume biography (1947–1965) by Ar-
thur S. Link, particularly *The New Freedom* (1956). Other treatments of
Wilson's domestic policies are John M. Blum's *Woodrow Wilson and the*

Politics of Morality (1956)° and John A. Garraty's *Woodrow Wilson* (1956).°

Different scholarly approaches detail the impact of reform at the urban level. A survey of a state's efforts to cope with urban problems is Richard N. Abrams's *Conservatism in a Progressive Era: Massachusetts Politics, 1900–1912* (1964). Roy Lubove's *The Progressives and the Slums* (1962), Jack Hall's *Juvenile Reform in the Progressive Era* (1971), and Allen Davis's *Spearheads for Reform: The Social Settlements and the Progressive Movement, 1890–1919* (1967),° all examine the problem of urban decay. Steven A. Reiss's *Touching Base: Professional Baseball and American Culture in the Progressive Era* (1980) and Dominick Cavallo's *Muscles and Morals: Organized Playgrounds and Urban Reform, 1880–1920* (1981), link athletics to new forms of organization and socialization. Health issues are covered in David M. Kennedy's *Birth Control in America: The Career of Margaret Sanger* (1970),° David J. Rothman's *Conscience and Convenience: The Asylum and Its Alternatives in Progressive America* (1980),° and John Ettling's *The Germ of Laziness: Rockefeller Philanthropy and Public Health in the New South* (1981).

Other aspects of the progressive impulse receive focus in James H. Timberlake's *Prohibition and the Progressive Movement, 1900–1920* (1963),° Samuel Haber's *Efficiency and Uplift: Scientific Management in the Progressive Era* (1964), David M. Chalmers's *The Social and Political Ideas of the Muckrakers* (1964),° and Harold S. Wilson's *McClure's Magazine and the Muckrakers* (1970). Samuel P. Hayes's *Conservation and the Gospel of Efficiency: The Progressive Conservation Movement, 1890–1920* (1959),° James L. Penick's *Progressive Politics and Conservation: The Ballinger-Pinchot Affair* (1968), and Harold T. Pinkett's *Gifford Pinchot: Private and Public Forester* (1970) cover that controversy.

Labor studies include Stephen Meyer III's *The Five Dollar Day: Labor Management and Social Control in the Ford Motor Company, 1908–1921* (1981), Peter R. Shergold's *Working Class Life: The "American Standard" in Comparative Perspective, 1899–1913* (1982), and Tamara K. Hareven's *Family Time and Industrial Time: The Relationship between the Family and Work in a New England Industrial Community* (1982).°

Biographies of public figures during the Progressive Era include Richard Lovitt's *George W. Norris: The Making of a Progressive* (1963), Louis R. Harlan's *Booker T. Washington: The Wizard of Tuskegee, 1901–1915* (1982),° Michael E. Parrish's *Felix Frankfurter and His Times: The Reform Years* (1982), George H. Nash's *The Life of Herbert Hoover: The Engineer, 1874–1914* (1983), David P. Thelen's *Robert M. La Follette and the Insurgent Spirit* (1976),° John Braeman's *Alfred J. Beveridge* (1971), and R. F. Wessner's *Charles Evans Hughes: Politics and Reform in New York, 1905–1910* (1967).

25

WILSON AND THE
GREAT WAR

WILSON AND FOREIGN AFFAIRS

When Woodrow Wilson was sworn in as the president of the United States in March 1913 the former historian brought to the office little background in the study of diplomacy and none at all in its practice. Wilson tacitly admitted this when he remarked just before taking office, "It would be an irony of fate if my administration had to deal chiefly with foreign affairs." But events in Europe were to make the irony all too real. From the summer of 1914, when the guns of August heralded a World War, foreign relations increasingly overshadowed all else, including Wilson's domestic program, the New Freedom.

AN IDEALIST'S DIPLOMACY   Although lacking in international experience, Wilson did not lack ideas or convictions in this area. The product of a Calvinist past, Wilson brought to diplomacy a version of progressivism more than a little touched with Calvinist righteousness. Both Wilson and his secretary of state, William Jennings Bryan, believed that America had been called to advance democracy and moral progress in the world. If they did not always follow principle at the expense of national self-interest, they did in many respects try to develop a diplomatic policy based on idealism.

The teetotaling Bryan, undismayed by ridicule of his "grape juice diplomacy," during 1913–1914 negotiated some thirty "cooling-off" treaties under which participating nations pledged themselves not to go to war over any disagreement for a period of twelve months pending arbitration by an international panel. Arbitration treaties were in fact not an invention of Bryan's, although the "cooling-off" feature gave them a new twist. In any case the treaties were of little consequence, soon forgotten in the revolutionary sweep of world events that would make the twentieth century the bloodiest in recorded history.

One of the first applications of Wilsonian idealism to foreign policy came when the president renounced dollar diplomacy. The government, he said, was not supporting any "special groups or interests." As good as his word, on March 18, 1913, he withdrew governmental support of the Six-Power Consortium then preparing to float a large loan to China. Such a monopolistic grant, he said, would compromise China's integrity and possibly involve the United States in a future intervention. Without governmental backing, American bankers withdrew.

INTERVENTION IN MEXICO Closer to home Wilson found it harder to take such high ground. Nor did the logic of his "missionary diplomacy" always imply nonintervention. Mexico, which had been in the throes of revolution for nearly three years, presented a thorny problem. For most of the thirty-five years from 1876 to 1911 President Porfirio Diaz had dominated Mexico. As military dictator he had suppressed opposition and showered favors on his followers and on foreign investors, who piled up holdings in Mexican mines, petroleum, railroads, and agriculture. But eventually the dictator's hold slipped, and in 1910 popular resentment boiled over in revolt. In May 1911 revolutionary armies occupied Mexico City and Diaz fled.

The leader of the rebellion, Francisco I. Madero, proved unable to manage the tough customers drawn by the scramble for power. In February 1913 Gen. Victoriano Huerta assumed power and Madero was murdered soon afterward. Confronted with this turn to rule by a military dictator, Wilson enunciated a new doctrine of nonrecognition: "We hold, as I am sure all thoughtful leaders of republican government everywhere hold, that just government rests upon the consent of the governed," he said. Recognition, formerly extended routinely to governments which exercised *de facto* power, now might depend on judgments of their legality: an immoral government presumably would not pass muster.

Huerta's hold on power was still unsure, and for a while Wilson resisted the impulse to intervene. In October 1913 he sought to quiet fears of intervention with a statement that the United States "will never again seek one additional foot of territory by conquest." Nevertheless he obliquely expressed sympathy with the revolutionary movement and began to put diplomatic pressure on Huerta. "I am going to teach the South American republics to elect good men," he told a visiting British diplomat. Early in 1914 he removed an embargo on arms to Mexico in order to help the resurgent revolutionaries under Venustiano Carranza of the Constitutionalist party, and stationed warships off Vera Cruz to halt arms shipments to Huerta.

On April 9, 1914, several American sailors, gathering supplies in Tampico, strayed into a restricted area and were arrested. The local commander, a Huertista, quickly released them and sent an apology to Adm. Henry T. Mayo, the American naval commander. There the incident might have ended, but Mayo demanded a salute to the American flag. Wilson backed him up and got from Congress authority to use force to bring Huerta to terms. Before the Tampico incident could be resolved, Wilson authorized a naval force to enter Vera Cruz and stop the imminent landing of an arms shipment. American marines and sailors went ashore on April 21, 1914, and occupied the town at a cost of 19 killed and 47 wounded. The Mexicans lost at least 200 killed and 300 wounded.

In Mexico the occupation aroused the opposition of all factions, and Huerta tried to rally support against foreign invasion. At this juncture Wilson accepted an offer of mediation by the ABC powers (Argentina, Brazil, and Chile), which in June proposed withdrawal of United States forces, the removal of Huerta, and installation of a provisional government sympathetic to reform. Huerta refused, but the moral effect of the proposal, his isolation abroad, and the growing strength of his foes forced him to leave office in July. In August the Carranzistas entered Mexico City, and in November the Americans left Vera Cruz. Finally, in October 1915 the United States and several Latin American governments recognized Carranza as president of Mexico.

Still, the troubles south of the border continued. The disorders had spawned independent bands of freebooters, Pancho Villa's among the wildest. All through 1915 fighting between the forces of Villa and Carranza swayed back and forth. In January 1916 Villa seized a train at Santa Ysabel and murdered eighteen American mining engineers in a deliberate attempt to provoke American intervention, discredit Carranza, and build himself up as an opponent of the "Gringos." That failing, he crossed the border on raids into Texas and New Mexico. On March 9 he entered Columbus, New Mexico, burned the town, and killed seventeen Americans.

Wilson then had to abandon his policy of "watchful waiting." With the reluctant consent of Carranza, he sent Gen. John J.

Pancho Villa (center) and his generals. [National Archives]

Pershing across the border with a force of some 15,000 men and mobilized 150,000 National Guardsmen along the frontier. For nearly a year Pershing went on a wild-goose chase after Villa through northern Mexico and, missing his catch, was ordered home in January 1917. Carranza then pressed his own war against the bandits and put through a new liberal constitution in 1917. Mexico was by then well on the way to a more orderly government.

PROBLEMS IN THE CARIBBEAN   In the Caribbean Wilson found it as hard to act on his ideals as in Mexico. Despite Wilson's stand against dollar diplomacy, American marines who had entered Nicaragua in 1912 stayed there to prevent renewed civil war. In July 1915 American marines landed in Haiti after two successive revolutions and subsequent disorders. Later that year a new Haitian government imposed by the American military signed a treaty which placed the United States in control of customs collections. The American forces stayed until 1934. Disorders in the Dominican Republic brought American marines to the country in 1916; they remained until 1924.

THE GREAT WAR AND AMERICA

Such problems in Latin America and the Caribbean loomed larger than the gathering storm in Europe. When the thunderbolt of war struck Europe in the summer of 1914 it came to most Americans, one North Carolinian wrote, "as lightning out of a clear sky." Whatever the troubles in Mexico, whatever disorders and interventions agitated other countries, it seemed unreal that civilized Europe could descend into such an orgy of destruction. Since the fall of Napoleon in 1815, Europe had known local wars but only as interruptions of a general peace that contributed to a century of unprecedented material progress. But the assassination in Sarajevo of Austrian Archduke Franz Ferdinand by a Serbian nationalist, Austria-Hungary's determination to punish Serbia, and Russia's mobilization in sympathy with her Slavic brothers in Serbia suddenly triggered a European system of alliances: the Triple Alliance or Central Powers (Germany, Austria-Hungary, and Italy) and the Triple Entente (France, Great Britain, and Russia). When Russia refused to stop its mobilization, Germany declared war on Russia on August 1, 1914, and on Russia's ally France two days later. Germany then invaded Belgium to get at France, which brought Great Britain into the war on August 4. Japan, eager to seize German holdings in the Pacific, declared war on August 23 and Turkey entered on the side of the Central Powers a week later. Italy stayed out, however, and struck a bargain under which she joined the Allies in 1915.

EUROPE AT WAR

Central Powers (Triple Alliance)

Allied Powers (Triple Entente)

Neutral countries

AMERICA'S INITIAL REACTIONS   The initial reaction of shock in the
United States was followed by gratitude that an ocean stood between America and the battlefields. "Our isolated position and
freedom from entangling alliances," said the *Literary Digest,*
"inspire our press with cheering assurance that we are in no peril
of being drawn into the European quarrel." Beginning on August
4 President Wilson issued routine declarations of neutrality. On
August 19 he urged the American people to be "impartial in
thought as well as action."

That was more easily said than done, not least for Wilson himself. Americans might want to stay out, but most of them cared
which side won. In the 1910 population of 92 million, more than
32 million were "hyphenated Americans," first- or second-gen-
eration immigrants who retained ties to their old countries.
Among the more than 13 million from the countries at war, by far
the largest group were 8 million German-Americans. And 4 million Irish-Americans harbored a deep-rooted enmity to Britain,
further heightened by British suppression of the Irish Easter Rebellion of 1916. These groups instinctively leaned toward the
Central Powers.

But old-line Americans, largely of British origin, were sympathetic to the Allies. If, as has been said, Britain and the United
States were divided by a common language, they were united by
ties of culture and tradition. Since the British had yielded on the
Venezuelan and Alaskan boundary disputes, a grand rapprochement in sympathy and good relations had occurred. Americans
identified also with France, which had contributed to American
culture and ideas, and to independence itself. Britain and
France, if not their ally Russia, seemed the custodians of liberal
democracy, while Germany more and more seemed the embodiment of autocracy and militarism. If not a direct threat to the
United States, Germany would pose at least a potential threat if it
destroyed the balance of power in Europe. High officers of the
United States government were pro-British in thought from the
outset. Robert Lansing, first counselor of the State Department,
Walter Hines Page, ambassador to London, and Col. Edward
House, Wilson's close adviser, saw in German militarism a potential danger to America.

Just what effects the propaganda of the warring powers had is
unclear. The Germans and the British were particularly active,
but German propaganda, which played on American dislike of
Russian autocracy and Russian anti-Semitism, fell mainly upon
barren ground. Only German- and Irish-Americans responded to
a "hate England" theme. From the outset the British had one su-

Most Americans leaned toward the Allies, but all were shocked at the outbreak of the Great War. In this cartoon, the Samson-like War pulls down the temple of Civilization. [Harding in the Brooklyn Eagle]

preme advantage in this area. Once they had cut the direct cable from Germany early in the war, nearly all news from the battle fronts had to clear through London. Wellington House, the British propaganda agency, used the services of Viscount James Bryce, a close student of the American scene, among others, and reports of German atrocities endorsed by Bryce were convincing to Americans. Some of these stories later proved to be highly embellished, but there were real atrocities enough in the German occupation of Belgium to affront American feelings. Most Americans already knew pretty well which way they were leaning.

A STRAINED NEUTRALITY At first the war brought a slump in American exports and the threat of a depression, but by the spring of 1915 the Allies' demand for supplies generated a wartime boom. The Allies at first financed their purchases by disposing of American securities, but ultimately they needed loans. Early in the war Secretary Bryan informed J. P. Morgan that loans to any warring nation were "inconsistent with the true spirit of neutrality." Money, he warned, "is the worst of all contrabands because it commands everything else." Still, by October 1914 Wilson quietly began approving short-term credits to sustain trade with the Allies. When in September 1915 it became apparent that the Allies could no longer carry on without long-term credit, the administration raised all restrictions and Morgan soon extended a loan of $500 million to England and France. American investors would advance over $2 billion to the Allies before the United States entered the war, and only $27 million to Germany.

The administration nevertheless clung to the fond hope of

neutrality through two and a half years of warfare in Europe and tried to uphold the traditions of "freedom of the seas" which had guided American policy since the Napoleonic Wars. As the German drive through Belgium and toward Paris finally ground down into the stalemate of trench warfare, trade on the high seas assumed a new importance. In a war of attrition survival depended on access to supplies, and in such a war British naval power counted for a great deal. With the German fleet outclassed and bottled up almost from the outset, the war in many ways assumed the pattern that had once led America into war with Britain in 1812. Indeed, as British Orders in Council (familiar from a century before) restricted trade with central Europe, they once again raised some of the old issues. Wilson remarked that only two Princeton men had been president, and that both he and Madison faced similar problems of "freedom of the seas."

On August 6, 1914, Secretary Bryan called upon the belligerents to accept the Declaration of London, drafted and signed in 1909 by leading powers but never ratified by the British. That document, the culmination of nineteenth-century liberal thought on the rules of warfare, reduced the list of contraband items and specified that a blockade was legal only when effective just outside enemy ports. The Central Powers promptly accepted. The British almost as promptly refused, lest they lose some of their advantage in sea power. Beginning with an Order in Council of August 20, 1914, Britain gradually extended the list of contraband goods to include all sorts of things formerly excluded, such as food, cotton, wood, and certain ores. Wilson protested, but Ambassador Page, personally pro-British, assured Foreign Minister Sir Edward Grey that the two could find ways of getting around the problem. The British consequently gave little serious heed to further protests.

In November 1914 the British declared the whole North Sea a war zone, sowed it with mines, and ordered neutral ships to enter only by the straits of Dover, where they could be easily searched. In March 1915 they further announced that they would detain and carry into port ships carrying goods of presumed enemy destination, ownership, or origin. Previous rules had required search on the high seas and this, combined with Britain's new policy, caused extended delays, sometimes running into months. The same order also directed British ships to stop vessels carrying German goods via neutral ports. When the State Department protested, Earl Grey reminded the Americans that this was the same doctrine of continuous voyage on which the United States had acted in the 1860s to keep British goods out of the Confederacy.

NEUTRAL RIGHTS AND SUBMARINES   British actions, including black-listing of companies that traded with the enemy and censorship of the mails, raised some old issues of neutral rights, but the German reaction introduced an entirely new question. With the German fleet bottled up, only German submarines could venture out to harass the enemy. On February 4, 1915, in response to the "illegal" British blockade, the German government proclaimed a war zone around the British Isles. Enemy merchant ships in those waters were liable to sinking, the Germans declared, "although it may not always be possible to save crews and passengers." Since the British sometimes flew neutral flags as a ruse, neutral ships in the zone would also be in danger. U-boat (*Unterseeboot*) warfare violated the established procedure of stopping enemy vessels on the high seas and providing for the safety of passengers and crews, since the chief advantage was in surprise.

The United States pronounced the German policy "an indefensible violation of neutral rights" and warned that Germany would be held to "strict accountability" for any destruction of American lives and property. If the meaning of the phrase was unclear, the stern tone of the note was unmistakable. The administration asked the British to give up flying neutral flags and its blockade of foodstuffs in return for German renunciation of submarine warfare, but nothing came of the effort. On March 28, 1915, one American drowned when the Germans sank the British steamer *Falaba* in the Irish Sea. On May 1 the American tanker *Gulflight* went down with a loss of two lives. The adminis-

Cunard announces the sailing of the Lusitania. The German Embassy warns travelers that British ships sailing in the war zone are "liable to destruction." [New York Public Library]

tration was divided on the proper course of action. Bryan wanted to say that American citizens entered the war zone at their own risk; his counselor, Robert Lansing, and Colonel House wanted to imply a possible break in diplomatic relations with Germany. Then, as Wilson pondered the alternatives, the sinking of the British Cunard liner *Lusitania* provoked a crisis.

On May 7, 1915, the captain of the German U-20 sighted a four-stack liner moving slowly through the Irish Sea and fired a torpedo. It hit the mark, and the ship exploded and sank within eighteen minutes. Only as it tipped into the waves was he able to make out the name *Lusitania* on the stern. Before the ship left New York bound for Liverpool the German Embassy had published warnings in the American press against travel to the war zone, but among the 1,198 persons lost were 128 Americans.

The American public was outraged. It was an act of piracy, Theodore Roosevelt declared. In an effort to quiet the uproar Wilson, speaking to newly naturalized citizens in Philadelphia, said: "There is such a thing as a man being too proud to fight. There is such a thing as a nation being so right that it does not need to convince others by force that it is right." Wilson's previous demand for "strict accountability," however, forced him to make a strong response. On May 13 Bryan reluctantly signed a note demanding that the Germans abandon unrestricted submarine warfare, disavow the sinking, and pay reparations. The Germans responded that the ship had been armed (which it was not) and carried a cargo of small arms and ammunition (which it did). A second note on June 9 repeated American demands in stronger terms. The United States, Wilson asserted, was "contending for nothing less high and sacred than the rights of humanity." Bryan, unwilling to risk war on the issue, resigned in protest and joined the peace movement as a private citizen. His successor, Robert Lansing, signed the note. A third note on July 21 warned that repetition of such sinkings would be regarded as "deliberately unfriendly."

Before the lengthy exchange ended in February 1916, other events took the spotlight and aroused further hostility to the Central Powers. In New York a German agent, Dr. Heinrich Albert, absent-mindedly left his briefcase on a subway where an alert American agent picked it up. On August 15, 1915, the New York *World* began to publish letters revealing Albert's subversive activities, which included subsidizing pro-German speakers and efforts to buy up munitions plants. More damaging were papers which fell into British hands, revealing that Austrian Ambassador Dr. Constantin Dumba was attempting to foment strikes in war industries, and finally, that German attachés Franz von Papen and Karl Boy-ed were fomenting sabotage.

In response to the uproar over the *Lusitania*, the German government had secretly ordered U-boat captains to avoid sinking large passenger vessels. When, despite the order, two American lives were lost in the sinking of the British liner *Arabic*, bound for New York, German Ambassador Count von Bernstorff demanded and got from Berlin an offer of indemnity and a public assurance which he delivered on September 1, 1915: "Liners will not be sunk by our submarines without warning and without safety of the lives of non-combatants, provided that the liners do not try to escape or offer resistance." With this "Arabic pledge" Wilson's resolute stand seemed to have resulted in a victory for his policy.

During the fall of 1915 Wilson's trusted advisor Edward M. House proposed to renew a mediation effort he had explored on a visit to London, Paris, and Berlin the previous spring—before the *Lusitania* sinking. In January and February 1916 House visited those capitals again, but found neither side ready to begin serious negotiations. The French and British would soon be engaged in destructive battles, the French at Verdun and the British at the Somme, and both were determined to fight until they could bargain from strength.

Peace advocates in Congress now rose up to challenge the administration's policy on neutral rights. In February 1916 Rep. Jeff McLemore (D-Tex.) and Sen. Thomas P. Gore (D-Okla.) introduced similar resolutions warning Americans against traveling on armed belligerent vessels. Such surrender to the German threat, Wilson asserted, would be a "deliberate abdication of our hitherto proud position as spokesmen, even amidst the turmoil of war, for the law and the right." Once accept a single abatement of right and "the whole fine fabric of international law might crumble under our hands piece by piece." The administration worked desperately to bring Democratic congressmen in line, and with the help of some Republicans managed to defeat both resolutions by a solid margin. On March 24, 1916, a U-boat torpedoed the French steamer *Sussex* with injury to two Americans. This time Wilson threatened to break off relations with Germany, but got a renewed pledge that U-boats would not torpedo merchant and passenger ships.

THE DEBATE OVER PREPAREDNESS The *Lusitania* incident, and more generally the quarrels over neutral commerce, contributed to a growing demand for a stronger army and navy. Even before the end of 1914 spokesmen for preparedness included Elihu Root,

Lansing, Roosevelt, Sen. Henry Cabot Lodge, and editors George Harvey of the *North American Review* and Lyman Abbott of the *Outlook*. On December 1, 1914, the champions of preparedness organized the National Security League to promote their cause. After the *Lusitania* sinking the outcry from such people grew into a clamor. Although Wilson did not announce his intentions until November 4, 1915, war preparation plans were public knowledge the previous July, when Wilson asked the War and Navy Departments to draft proposals. In his annual message in December Wilson alerted Congress to forthcoming requests.

The response was far from unanimous. Progressives and pacifists, and a broad-based antiwar sentiment running through the rural South and West, awakened the traditional American suspicion of military establishments, especially standing armies, which dated back to the colonial period. The new Democratic leader in the house, Claude Kitchin of North Carolina, opposed "the big Navy and big Army program of the jingoes and war traffickers." In the East, leaders of the peace movement organized a League to Limit Armament. Jane Addams and suffragist Carrie Chapman Catt organized a Women's Peace party. Bryan, La Follette, and other leaders lent their voices to the peace movement.

Secretary of War Lindley M. Garrison's plan to enlarge the regular army and create a national reserve force of 400,000 ran into stubborn opposition in the House Military Affairs Committee. Wilson was forced to accept a compromise between advocates of an expanded force under federal control and advocates of a traditional citizen army. The measure finally passed after Secretary Garrison gave up his office to Newton D. Baker, the mayor of Cleveland, a step which reassured progressives. The National Defense Act of June 3, 1916, expanded the regular army from 90,000 to 175,000 and permitted gradual enlargement to 223,000. It also authorized a National Guard of 440,000, made provision for their training, and gave federal funds for summer training camps for civilians. In August the Army Appropriation Act provided for a Council of National Defense to include six cabinet members, and a civilian National Defense Advisory Commission.

The bill for an increased navy had less trouble because of the general feeling expressed by Secretary Josephus Daniels that there was "no danger of militarism from a relatively strong navy such as would come from a big standing army." The Naval Construction Act of August 15 authorized between $500 million and $600 million for a three-year program of enlargement, and another act on September 7 created the United States Shipping Board, empowered to spend up to $50 million for the building or purchase of merchant vessels suitable for use as naval auxiliaries.

Forced to relent on preparedness, progressive opponents of the action like Claude Kitchin and Sen. George Norris determined that the financial burden should rest on the wealthy people they held responsible for the effort. The income tax became their weapon. Supported by a groundswell of popular support, they wrote into the Revenue Act of 1916 changes which doubled the basic income tax from 1 to 2 percent, lifted the surtax to a maximum of 13 percent (a total of 15 percent) on incomes over $2 million, added an estate tax graduated up to a maximum of 10 percent, levied a 12½ percent tax on gross receipts of munitions makers, and added a new tax on corporation capital, surplus, and undistributed profits. The new taxes on wealth amounted to the most clear-cut victory of radical progressives in the entire Wilson period, a victory further consolidated and advanced after war came. It was the capstone to the edifice of progressive legislation which Wilson supported in preparation for the election of 1916.

THE ELECTION OF 1916   Republicans started that year hoping to regain their normal majority, and Roosevelt started out hoping to be their leader again. But he had committed the deadly sin of bolting his party and, what was more, expressed a bellicosity on war issues that would scare off voters. Needing somebody who would draw Bull Moose Progressives back into the fold, the regulars turned to Justice Charles Evans Hughes, who had made a progressive record in New York where he was governor from 1907 to 1910. On the Supreme Court since then, he had neither taken a stand in 1912 nor spoken out on foreign policy. To round out the ticket the party named Roosevelt's vice-president, Charles W. Fairbanks (Ind.), once again. The remnants of the Progressive party gathered in Chicago at the same time as the Republicans. Roosevelt had held out the vain hope of getting both nominations, but he now declined to lead a moribund party. Two weeks later the Progressive National Committee disbanded the party and endorsed Hughes; a minority, including their vice-presidential nominee, John M. Parker (La.), came out for Wilson.

The Democrats, as expected, chose Wilson and Marshall once again, and in their platform endorsed a program of social legislation, neutrality, and reasonable preparedness. The party further commended women's suffrage to the states, denounced groups that placed the interests of other countries above those of the United States, and pledged support for a postwar League of Nations to enforce peace with collective security measures against aggressors. The Democrats found their most popular issue, however, when former New York Gov. Martin H. Glynn in the keynote speech got an unexpected response to his recital of historic cases in which the United States had refused under provocation to go to war. As he mentioned successive examples, the crowd chanted "What did we do? What did we do?" and Glynn responded: "We didn't go to war! We didn't go to war!" The peace theme, refined into the slogan "He kept us out of war," became the rallying cry of the campaign, one that had the merit of taking credit without making any promises for the future.

Rooseveltians found themselves drawn in large numbers to Wilson who, according to Walter Lippmann, "is temporarily at least creating, out of the reactionary, parochial fragments of the Democracy, the only party which at this moment is national in scope, liberal in purpose, and effective in action." The impression of Democratic purpose and effectiveness was heightened by Republican feuding and ineptitude. On foreign policy Hughes worked both sides of the street. While trying to keep the votes of German-Americans and other "hyphenates," Hughes refused to disavow Roosevelt, who was going about the country denouncing the kaiser. On social reform issues Wilson was far ahead of Hughes, and Hughes found himself often the captive of old-line Republican bosses more eager to punish Bull Moose Progressives by excluding them than to win the election for Hughes.

In the end Wilson's twin rallying cries of peace and progressivism, a unique combination of issues forged in the legislative and diplomatic crucibles of 1916, brought victory.

Peace with Honor. *Wilson's neutral policies proved popular in the 1916 campaign. [United Press International]*

Early returns showed a Republican sweep in the East and Midwest, signaling a victory for Hughes, but the outcome remained in doubt until word came that Wilson had carried California by 3,772 votes, where one incident may have decided the outcome. While visiting California Hughes unintentionally snubbed the popular Gov. Hiram Johnson who, without Hughes's knowledge, was in the same hotel. The final vote showed a Democratic sweep of the Far West and South, enough for victory in the electoral college by 277 to 254, and in the popular vote by 9 million to 8.5 million. "It is the combination which made Jefferson and Jackson," the historian William E. Dodd exulted. "It is the South and the West united; the farmers, small businessmen and perhaps a large sprinkle of Union labor against the larger industrial, transportation and commercial interests." Dodd might have added that Wilson also carried many social-justice Progressives who had previously supported the Bull Moose campaign.

LAST EFFORTS FOR PEACE   Late in the 1916 contest Wilson expressed a belief that this was the last world war the United States could keep out of, although as a historian he should have known that America had been drawn into every general European war since colonization began. Relations with Britain in 1916 had become almost as troubled as relations with Germany. The British dragged their heels on Colonel House's mediation offer; they put down the Irish Easter Rebellion so severely that they offended American opinion in general; they stepped up their economic warfare, and blacklisted firms suspected of dealing with the Central Powers. Immediately after the election Wilson began to plan another peace move, but before he was ready the German government announced on December 12 its readiness to begin discussion of peace terms.

Six days later Wilson sent identical notes to the belligerent powers, asking each to state its war aims. The Germans responded promptly that they would state theirs only to a conference of the belligerents at a neutral site. In January 1917 the Allies made it plain that they intended to exact reparations, break up the Austro-Hungarian and Ottoman Empires, and destroy German power. Wilson then decided to make one more appeal, in the hope that public opinion would force the hands of the warring governments. Speaking before the Senate on January 22, 1917, he asserted the right of the United States to a share in laying the foundations for a lasting peace, which would have to be a "peace without victory" for only a "peace among equals" could endure. The peace must be based on the principles of government by the consent of the governed, freedom of the seas, and disarmament, and must be enforced by an international league for peace established to make another such catastrophe impossible. "I would fain believe," the president ended, "that I am speaking for the silent mass of mankind everywhere who have as yet had no place or opportunity to speak their real hearts out concerning the death and ruin they see to have come already upon the persons and homes they hold most dear."

Although Wilson did not know it, he was already too late. Exactly two weeks before he spoke, German leaders had decided to wage unrestricted submarine warfare. They took the calculated risk of provoking American anger in the hope of scoring a quick knockout. On January 31 the new policy was announced, effective the next day. All vessels in the war zone, belligerent or neutral, would be sunk without warning, with the exception that one American passenger ship could approach Falmouth weekly, provided it were painted with red and white stripes and carried a checkered flag, but no contraband. "Freedom of the seas," said the Brooklyn *Eagle*, "will now be enjoyed by icebergs and fish."

On February 3, 1917, Wilson told a joint session of Congress that the United States had broken diplomatic relations with the German government. He added that he still did not believe the Germans would do what they said they felt at liberty to do—only overt acts would persuade him that they actually intended to sink neutral ships. In case of such acts, he would take measures to protect American seamen and citizens. On February 26 Wilson went before another joint session to ask for authority to arm American merchant ships and "to employ any other instrumentalities or methods that may be necessary and adequate to protect our ships and our people." There was little quarrel with arming merchantmen, but bitter opposition to Wilson's vague reference to "any other instrumentalities or methods." A group of eleven or twelve die-hard noninterventionists including Senators La Follette and Norris filibustered the measure until the regular session expired on March 4. Thus, in Wilson's words: "A little group of willful men, representing no opinion but their own, have rendered the great Government of the United States helpless and contemptible." On March 12 the State Department announced that a forgotten law of 1792 allowed the arming of merchant ships regardless of congressional inaction.

In the midst of the debate, on March 1, news of the Zimmerman Note broke in the American press. Word had reached Wilson four days earlier from Ambassador Page in London that the British had intercepted and decoded an important message from

German Foreign Secretary Alfred Zimmerman to his ambassador in Mexico. The note instructed the envoy to offer an alliance and financial aid to Mexico in case of war between the United States and Germany. In return for diversionary action against the United States, Mexico would recover "the lost territory in Texas, New Mexico, and Arizona." Carranza, moreover, should invite Japan to swap sides and join the coalition. All this was contingent on war with the United States, but an electrified public read in it an aggressive intent. Then, later in March a revolution overthrew Russia's czarist government and established the provisional government of a Russian Republic. The fall of the czarist autocracy allowed Americans the illusion that all the major Allied powers were now fighting for constitutional democracy. Not until November 1917 was this illusion shattered when the Bolsheviks seized power in Russia.

AMERICA'S ENTRY

The overt acts Wilson awaited came in March when German submarines sank five American merchant vessels. On March 20 Wilson's cabinet unanimously endorsed a declaration of war and the following day the president called a special session of Congress. When it met on April 2, Wilson asked Congress to recognize the war that Imperial Germany was already waging against the United States, then turned to a discussion of the issues. The German government had revealed itself as a natural foe of liberty, and therefore "The world must be made safe for democracy. Its peace must be planted upon the tested foundations of political liberty." The war resolution passed the Senate by a vote of 82 to 6 on April 4. The House concurred, 373 to 50, and Wilson signed the measure on April 6. It was Good Friday.

How had it come to this, less than three years after Wilson's proclamation of neutrality? Prominent among the various explanations of America's entrance into the war are the effects of British propaganda, and America's deep involvement in trade with the Allies, which some observers then and later credited to the intrigues of war profiteers and munitions makers. Some Americans thought German domination of Europe would be a threat to American security, especially if it meant the destruction or capture of the British navy. But whatever the influence of such factors, they likely would not have been decisive without the issue of submarine warfare. This issue need not have become decisive, since such neutrals as Norway, Sweden, and Denmark took relatively heavier losses and yet stayed out of the war. But once Wilson had taken a stand for the traditional rights of neutrals and noncombatants, he was to some extent at the mercy of decisions by the German high command and was led step by step into a war over what to a later generation would seem a rather quaint, if noble, set of principles.

AMERICA'S EARLY ROLE Having entered the war, the scope of America's role remained unclear. Few on either side of the Atlantic expected more from the United States than a token military effort. Despite Congress's preparedness measures the army remained small and rudimentary. The navy also was largely undeveloped. A few days before the declaration of war, however, Rear Adm. William S. Sims was given command of American ships in European waters, and he then systematically built up the United States Navy. He brought the first contingent of six American destroyers to Queenstown, Ireland, on May 4, and more came later. The Americans, in addition, made two important contributions to Allied naval strategy. Previously, merchant ships had survived through speed and evasive action. Sims persuaded the Allies to adopt a convoy system of escorting merchant ships in groups, and the result was a decrease in Allied shipping losses from 881,000 tons in April 1917 to 289,000 in November of the same year. Later the United States Navy conceived and laid a gigantic minefield across the North Sea which practically eliminated the U-boats' access to the North Atlantic.

Within a month of the declaration of war, British and French missions arrived in the United States. First they requested money with which to buy supplies, a request Congress had already anticipated in the Liberty Loan Act of April 24, which added $5 billion to the national debt in "Liberty Bonds." Of this amount, $3 billion could be loaned to the Allied powers. The United States was also willing to furnish naval support, credits, supplies, and munitions, but to raise and train a large army, equip it, and send it across a submarine-infested ocean seemed out of the question. Marshal Joffre, who came with the French mission, nevertheless insisted that the United States send a token force to bolster morale, and on June 26, 1917, the first contingent of Americans, about 14,500 men commanded by Gen. John J. Pershing, began to disembark at St. Nazaire. Pershing and his troops were able to fight their way to Paris by July 4. On the scene, Pershing soon decided that the war-weary Allies would be unable to mount an offensive by themselves. He advised the War Department that plans should be made to send a million American troops by the following spring. It was done.

Fresh recruits sign up for the Marines, 1917. [Library of Congress]

When the United States entered the war the combined strength of the regular army and National Guard was only 378,619; at the end it would be 4.8 million. The need for such large numbers of troops converted Wilson to the idea of conscription. Under the Selective Service Act of May 18, 1917, all men aged twenty-one to thirty (later, from eighteen to forty-five) had to register for service. Registrants went into five classes, the first being able-bodied unmarried men without dependents. From this group alone came all the 2.8 million ultimately drafted. All told, about 2 million Americans crossed the Atlantic and about 1.4 million saw some action. Training of the soldiers went on in some thirty-two camps located mostly in the South for reasons of climate. The example of the Spanish-American War was well learned: the camps were for the most part sanitary and equipped with modern plumbing, hospitals, and recreation centers.

MOBILIZING A NATION The war required of all belligerent nations complete economic mobilization on the home front. "In the sense in which we have been wont to think of armies," Wilson said, "there are no armies in this struggle; there are entire nations armed." Germany especially had perfected this kind of mobilization under a system that came to be known as War Socialism. A group of War Companies fixed prices, allocated materials, set priorities, and dictated what should be produced throughout the economy. In the United States, war brought more regulation of industry than most progressives had dreamed of.

The Army Appropriation Act of August 1916 had created a Council of National Defense, which in turn led to the creation of more new wartime agencies. The United States Shipping Board, started in 1916, operated the Emergency Fleet Corporation, which by the fall of 1918 had more than forty steel and ninety wooden ships coming off the ways monthly. The Lever Food and Fuel Control Act of August 1917 created a Food Administration, headed by Herbert Hoover, a future president, and a Fuel Administration, under Harry A. Garfield, son of a former president. Both had begun as committees under the Council of National Defense. Hoover, a mining engineer and former head of the Commission for Relief in Belgium, had the responsibility of raising production while reducing civilian use of foodstuffs. "Food will win the war" was the slogan. Hoover had coercive authority, but preferred to use voluntary methods and directed a propaganda campaign which "Hooverized" the country with "Wheatless Mondays," "Meatless Tuesdays," "Porkless Thursdays," the planting of victory gardens, and the use of leftovers.

Garfield's Fuel Administration introduced the country to Daylight Saving Time and "heatless Mondays." His greatest crisis came in January 1918 when a severe winter caused a coal shortage that held up the departure of munitions ships and shut down all factories east of the Mississippi for five days. The Railroad Administration, created in December 1917 and headed by Treasury Secretary William G. McAdoo, operated the nation's roads as a single unitary system, giving priority to military traffic. The War Trade Board, run by Vance McCormick, a publisher in Harrisburg, Pennsylvania, sought to reduce nonessential imports and exports in order to free shipping for the war effort, and tried to keep American goods from finding their way into Germany. The Trading with the Enemy Act of October 1917 also granted the president the right to seize and administer enemy property in the United States.

In July 1917 the Council for National Defense established the War Industries Board (WIB), which would become the most important of all the mobilization agencies. For nearly a year, however, this body floundered in confusion. The solution came on March 4, 1918, when Wilson summoned Bernard Baruch, a brilliant Wall Street speculator, to head the board, giving him a virtual dictatorship over the economy. Under Baruch the purchasing bureaus of the United States and Allied governments submitted their needs to the board, which set priorities and planned production. The board could allocate raw materials, tell manufacturers what to produce, order construction of new plants, and with the approval of the president, fix prices. For the sake of greater efficiency the WIB standardized product styles and designs.

The National War Labor Board (WLB), set up in April 1918 under former President Taft and the labor lawyer Frank P. Walsh, encouraged conciliation and mediated labor disputes that could not be settled otherwise. Where settlement proved impossible the government resorted to coercion. When the Smith and Wesson Arms Company of Springfield, Massachusetts, rejected a WLB decision, the War Department took over the plant. Munitions workers who struck in defiance of the board were threatened with loss of their draft exemptions. AFL President Samuel Gompers built goodwill with a policy of limiting labor disputes. A separate War Labor Policies Board, under a young lawyer, Felix Frankfurter, standardized policies regarding wages, hours, and working conditions in the war industries.

With the high wartime demand for labor and the movement of many men from the labor force into the armed services, labor was in a position to score solid advances in employment and wages, despite the rise in prices. A newly created United States Employment Service placed some 4 million workers in war-related jobs. Labor unions benefited from expanded employment, the increased demand for labor, government policies favorable to collective bargaining, and the goodwill built by Gompers. From 1913 to 1918 the AFL increased its membership by 37 percent.

The war mobilized more than economic life: the progressive gospel of efficiency suggested mobilizing public opinion as well. On April 14, 1917, eight days after the declaration of war, an ex-

A poster calling for cooperation between American "wage-payers" and "wage-earners" to defeat the "common foe—Autocracy." [Wisconsin Historical Society]

ecutive order established the Committee on Public Information, composed of the secretaries of state, war, and the navy. Its executive head, George Creel, a Denver newsman, sold Wilson on the idea that the best approach to influencing public opinion was "expression, not repression"—propaganda instead of censorship. Creel's purpose was to organize a propaganda machine that would carry word of the Allies' war aims to the people, and above all to the enemy, where it might encourage the forces of moderation.

To sell the war Creel gathered a remarkable group of journalists, photographers, artists, entertainers, and others useful to his purpose. Charles Dana Gibson, James Montgomery Flagg, and other artists contributed posters. Historians under the direction of Guy Stanton Ford turned out little "Red, White, and Blue Books" with such titles as *How the War Came to America, German War Practices,* and *Conquest and Kultur.* A film division produced such pictures as *The Beast of Berlin,* starring, as the spike-helmeted embodiment of Prussian villainy, Erich von Stroheim. Hardly any public group escaped a harangue by one of the 75,000 Four-Minute Men, organized to give short speeches on Liberty Bonds, the need to conserve food and fuel, and other timely topics. Creel took special pains to get propaganda into Germany, where it was more likely to accentuate the size of the American war effort, Wilson's idealism, and offers of an easy peace if the German people would rebel against their government.

CIVIL LIBERTIES   The ultimate irony in Creel's "expression, not repression," however, was that the one led to the other. By arousing public opinion to such a pitch of excitement, the war effort channeled the crusading zeal of progressivism into grotesque campaigns of "Americanism" and witch-hunting. Wilson had foreseen such consequences. "Once lead this people into war," he told Frank Cobb, the editor of the New York *World,* "and they'll forget there even was such a thing as tolerance." Popular prejudice equated anything German with disloyalty. Schools dropped courses in the German language, violinist Fritz Kreisler was prevented from giving concerts, and patriots translated sauerkraut into "liberty cabbage," German measles into "liberty measles," and dachshunds into "liberty pups." In New Orleans Berlin Street became General Pershing Street.

While mobs hunted spies and chased rumors, the federal government stalked bigger game, with results often as absurd. Under the Espionage and Sedition Acts, criticism of government leaders and war policies was in effect outlawed. The Espionage Act of June 15, 1917, set penalties of up to $10,000 and twenty years in prison for those who gave aid to the enemy, who incited or tried to incite insubordination, disloyalty, or refusal of duty in the armed services, or who circulated false reports and statements with intent to interfere with the war effort. The postmaster-general could bar from the mails anything which violated the act or which advocated treason, insurrection, or forcible resistance to any United States law. The Sedition Act of May 16, 1918, extended the penalties to those who did or said anything to obstruct the sale of Liberty Bonds or advocate cutbacks in production, and—just in case something had been overlooked—for saying, writing, or printing anything "disloyal, profane, scurrilous, or abusive" about the American form of government, the Constitution, or the armed forces.

The penalties applied under these acts by the Democratic successors of Jefferson exceeded in both absurdity and severity anything done under the infamous Alien and Sedition Acts of John Adams. Under those acts of 1798, 25 prosecutions had resulted in 10 convictions; under Wilson's Espionage and Sedition Acts more than 1,500 prosecutions resulted in more than 1,000 convictions. According to one professor of law: "It became criminal to advocate heavier taxation instead of bond issues, to state that conscription was unconstitutional though the Supreme Court had not yet held it valid, to say that the sinking of merchant vessels was legal, to urge that a referendum should have preceded our declaration of war, to say that war was contrary to the teachings of Christ." One patriotic film producer drew a ten-year sentence for making a film on the American Revolution, *The Spirit of Seventy-six*, because it risked stirring sentiment against the British!

The impact of the acts fell with most severity upon Socialists and other radicals. Victor Berger, Socialist congressman from Milwaukee, got a twenty-year sentence for editorials in the Milwaukee *Leader* which called the war a capitalist conspiracy. Eugene V. Debs, who had polled over 900,000 votes for president in 1912, got twenty years for statements that had a "tendency" to bring about resistance to the draft. In 1920, still in jail, he polled nearly 1 million votes for president. In Chicago over 100 leaders of the Industrial Workers of the World went on trial before Judge Kenesaw Mountain Landis for opposing the war effort. All were found guilty. The IWW never fully recovered from the blow.

In two important decisions just after the war the Supreme

Court upheld the Espionage and Sedition Acts. *Schenck v. United States* (1919) upheld the conviction of a man for circulating anti-draft leaflets among members of the armed forces. In this case Justice Holmes said: "Free speech would not protect a man in falsely shouting fire in a theater, and causing a panic." The act applied where there was "a clear and present danger" that speech in wartime might create evils Congress had a right to prevent. In *Abrams v. United States* (1919) the Court upheld conviction of a man who circulated pamphlets opposing intervention in Russia. Here Holmes and Brandeis dissented. The "surreptitious publishing of a silly leaflet by an unknown man," they argued, posed no real danger to government policy.

"THE DECISIVE POWER"

American troops took little more than a token role in the fighting until the end of 1917. American units were parceled out in quiet sectors mainly to show the flag and bolster the morale of British and French soldiers. All through 1917 the Allies remained on the defensive and late in the year their situation turned desperate. In October the Italian lines collapsed at Caporetto and the Austrians swarmed into the plain of Friuli. With the help of Allied forces from France the Italians finally held along the Piave. In November the Bolshevik Revolution overthrew the infant Russian Republic, and the new Soviet government dropped out of the war.

ALLIED VICTORIES   With the Central Powers now free to concentrate their forces on the Western Front, the American war effort became a "race for France" to restore the balance of strength. By May 1918 Pershing had his 1 million men, and by November 2 million were "over there." The Allied lines held, and with the arrival of fresh troops the Allies' growing numerical majority finally turned the tide. "America," wrote German Commander-in-Chief von Ludendorff, "thus became the decisive power in the war." Meanwhile, on March 21 the Germans had begun their great offensive to end the war before the Americans arrived in force. On the Somme they broke through at the juncture of British and French sectors and penetrated about thirty-five miles, nearly to the rail and supply center at Amiens. Farther north, the Germans struck on April 9 in Flanders, where the Allies still held a corner of Belgium, broke through at Lille, and pushed the British back along a front from Ypres to Armentières. At this critical

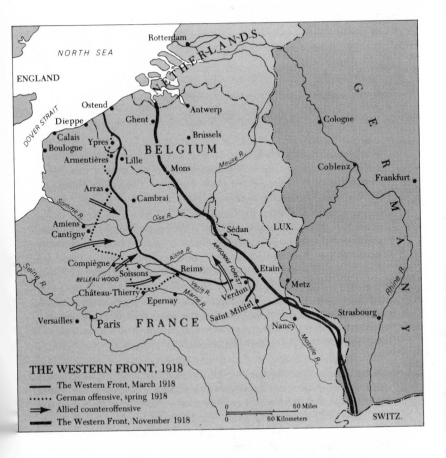

THE WESTERN FRONT, 1918
—— The Western Front, March 1918
••••• German offensive, spring 1918
——→ Allied counteroffensive
—— The Western Front, November 1918

point, on April 14 the Allies made French Gen. Ferdinand Foch the supreme commander of all Allied forces.

On May 27 the Germans began their next drive along the Aisne River, took Soissons, and pushed on to the Marne along a forty-mile front. To that time only token American forces had joined the defensive effort, but now the fresh American troops for the first time made a difference. In a counterattack American forces took Cantigny on May 28 and held it. A week later, on June 2–3, a marine brigade of the Second Division with the help of French colonials blocked the Germans at Château-Thierry and threw them back across the Marne. On June 5 the Second Division took the offensive at Bellau Wood and in three weeks cleared out the Germans and pushed them back. Though these actions had limited military significance, their effect on morale was immense. Each was a solid American success, and together they reinforced Pershing's demand for a separate American army.

Before that could come to pass, the turning point in the campaign came on July 15 in the Second Battle of the Marne. On both sides of Rheims, the eastern end of a great bulge toward Paris, the Germans commenced their push against the French lines. Their heaviest attack came at Château-Thierry where the American and French forces held off the threat to the French capital. Elsewhere the Germans made slight gains, but little progress. Within three days they had shot their bolt, and the Allies went on the offensive to wipe out German troops on the Marne, a job completed by August 6.

Soon the British along the Somme River and the French along the Oise-Aisne began to roll the German front back toward and into Belgium. American forces helped on both fronts. Then on August 10 the First U.S. Army was organized with the consent of General Foch and assigned the task of liquidating the Germans at St. Mihiel, southeast of Verdun. There, on September 12, an army of more than 500,000 staged the first strictly American offensive of the war. Within twenty-four hours the Germans had been cut off. Pershing wanted to push on from there to the fortress city of Metz, a German supply center, but Foch wanted to use the First Army to the west of Verdun, between the Marne and the Argonne Forest. The Meuse-Argonne offensive, begun September 26, employed every available American division in a drive toward Sedan and its railroad to Metz. The largest American action of the war, it involved some 1.2 million American troops and cost 117,000 American casualties. Through October and early November the battle raged. By the first week of November the Americans were at the outskirts of Sedan and had cut the railroad from Metz. All along the front from Sedan to Flanders the Germans were in retreat.

THE FOURTEEN POINTS   The approaching end of the war brought to the point of decision the question of war aims. Neither the Allies nor the Central Powers, despite Wilson's prodding, had stated frankly and openly what they hoped to gain. Wilson insisted throughout that the Americans had no selfish ends. "We desire no conquest, no dominion," he said in his war message. "We seek no indemnities for ourselves, no material compensation for the sacrifices we shall freely make. We are but one of the champions of the rights of mankind." Unfortunately for his purpose, after the Bolsheviks seized power in November 1917 they captured and published copies of secret treaties in which the Allies had promised territorial gains in order to win Italy, Rumania, and Greece to their side. When an Interallied Conference in Paris late in 1917 failed to agree on a statement of aims, Colonel House advised Wilson to formulate his own.

During 1917 House had been drawing together an informal panel of American experts called "The Inquiry" to formulate plans for peace. With advice from these experts, Wilson drew up a statement which would become the famous Fourteen Points. These he delivered to a joint session of Congress on January 8, 1918, "as the only possible program" for peace. The first five points in general terms called for open diplomacy, freedom of the seas, removal of trade barriers, reduction of armaments, and an impartial adjustment of colonial claims based on the interests of the populations involved. Most of the remainder called on the Central Powers to evacuate occupied lands and endorsed self-determination for various nationalities. Point 13 endorsed an independent Poland with access to the sea. Point 14, the capstone in Wilson's thinking, championed a general association of nations to secure guarantees of independence and territorial integrity to all countries, great and small.

The Fourteen Points set forth a firm commitment in which Wilson persisted, but they also served the purposes of psychological warfare. One of their aims was to keep Russia in the war by a more liberal statement of purposes—a vain hope, as it turned out. Another was to reassure the Allied peoples that they were involved in a noble cause. A third was to drive a wedge between the governments of the Central Powers and their people by the offer of a reasonable peace. Wilson's promise of "autonomous development" for the subject nationalists of Austria-Hungary (Point 10) might have weakened the unity of the polyglot Habsburg Empire, though it was no part of his purpose to break up the empire. But the chaos into which central Europe descended in 1918, and the national aspirations of the empire's peoples, took matters out of his hands.

On September 29, 1918, German Commander-in-Chief Erich von Ludendorff advised his government to seek the best peace terms possible. On October 3, a new chancellor, Prince Max of Baden, made the first German overtures for peace on the basis of the Fourteen Points. A month of diplomatic fencing followed between Colonel House and Allied representatives. Finally, a threat by House to pursue separate negotiations led the Allies to accept the Fourteen Points as a basis of peace, but with two significant reservations: they reserved the right to discuss freedom of the seas further, and they demanded reparations for war damages.

Meanwhile the German home front was being torn apart by a

naval mutiny at Kiel, a revolution in Bavaria, and disturbances elsewhere. Germany's allies had dropped out of the war: Bulgaria on September 29, Turkey on October 30, and Austria-Hungary on November 3. On November 8 a German delegation crossed the lines to meet with General Foch at Compiègne; the next day the kaiser abdicated and a German Republic was proclaimed. On November 11, at 5:00 A.M., an armistice was signed. Six hours later, at the eleventh hour of the eleventh day of the eleventh month, the guns fell silent. Under the Armistice the Germans had to evacuate occupied territories, pull back behind the Rhine, and surrender their submarines, railroad equipment, and other materials. The naval blockade would continue until a final peace settlement was reached, and the Germans were assured that the Fourteen Points would be the basis for the peace conference.

THE FIGHT FOR THE PEACE

WILSON'S ROLE Wilson now made a fateful decision to attend in person the peace conference which convened in Paris on January 18, 1919. It shattered precedent for a president to leave the country for so long a time, but it dramatized all the more Wilson's desire to ensure his goal of a lasting peace. From one viewpoint it was a shrewd move, for his prestige and determination made a difference in Paris. But he lost touch with developments at home. His progressive coalition was already unraveling under the pressures of wartime discontent. Western farmers complained about the government's control of wheat prices while southern cotton rode the wartime inflation. Eastern businessmen chafed at revenue policies designed, according to the New York *Sun,* "to pay for the war out of taxes raised north of the Mason and Dixon Line." Labor, despite manifest gains, was unhappy with inflation and the problems of reconversion to a peacetime economy.

In the midterm elections of 1918, Wilson made matters worse with a partisan appeal for a Democratic Congress to ensure support of his foreign policies. Republicans, who for the most part had supported war measures, took affront. In elections held on November 5, a week before the Armistice, the Democrats lost control of both houses of Congress. Wilson thus lost face at home just as he prepared to go abroad. With an opposition majority in the new Congress, he further weakened his standing by failure to involve a single prominent Republican in the negotiations. The

United States Peace Commission, in addition to Wilson, consisted of Colonel House, Secretary Lansing, Gen. Tasker Bliss, and Henry White, a career diplomat and a nominal Republican.

When Wilson reached Europe in December, riotous demonstrations of affection greeted him on his tour of England, France, and Italy. The cheering millions had found a symbol of hope and a spokesman for humanity. Their heartfelt support no doubt strengthened his hand at the conference. But in Paris Wilson had to deal with some tough-minded statesmen. The conference comprised a body of delegates from all countries that had declared war or broken diplomatic relations with Germany. It was dominated at first by the Council of Ten (two each from Japan, Britain, France, Italy, and the United States), but ended with major decisions controlled by the Big Four: the prime ministers of Britain, France, and Italy, and the president of the United States. Japan restricted its interests to Asia and the Pacific. French Premier Georges Clemenceau, as John Maynard Keynes put it, had but one illusion—France—and insisted on stern measures to weaken Germany and ensure French security. Lloyd George of England was a gifted politician fresh from electoral victory on the slogan "Hang the Kaiser." Vittorio Orlando of Italy was there to pick up the spoils promised in the secret Treaty of London (1915) and, if possible, also the Adriatic port of Fiume.

"Vive Wilson." Paris welcomes the American president as a hero. [National Archives]

THE LEAGUE OF NATIONS   Wilson carried the point that his cherished League of Nations must come first, in the conference and in the treaty provisions. Whatever compromises he might have to make, whatever mistakes might result, Wilson believed that a permanent agency of peace would assure international stability. Wilson presided over the commission set up to work out a charter for the League.

The security-conscious French advanced a plan for an international general staff and a League army to enforce the peace. Wilson knew that Senate ratification would be foredoomed by such a provision, and with the help of Lloyd George he squelched the plan. Article X of the covenant, which Wilson called "the heart of the League," pledged members to consult on military and economic sanctions against aggressors. The use of arms would be a last (and an improvised) resort. The League, it was assumed, would exercise enormous moral influence, but when push came to shove it would have little force at its disposal. The League structure allowed each member an equal voice in the Assembly; the Big Five (Britain, France, Italy, Japan, and the United States) and four other nations would make up the Council; the administrative staff in Geneva would make up the Secretariat; and finally, a Permanent Court of International Justice (set up in 1921 and usually called the World Court) could "hear and determine any dispute of an international character." All treaties had to be registered with the Secretariat to be valid.

On February 14 Wilson reported the finished draft to the plenary session of the conference and departed the next day for a month-long visit home to see after routine business and talk up the League. Already he faced rumblings of opposition, and shortly before his return to Paris, Sen. Henry Cabot Lodge brought forward a statement that the League covenant was unacceptable "in the form now proposed." The Round Robin, as Lodge's statement of March 4 was called, bore the signatures of thirty-nine Republican senators or senators-elect, more than enough to block ratification. That evening Wilson confidently retorted: "When the treaty comes back, gentlemen on this side will find the covenant not only in it, but so many threads of the treaty tied to the covenant that you cannot dissect the covenant from the treaty without destroying the whole vital structure."

TERRITORY AND REPARATIONS   Yet, back in Paris, Wilson found it politic to seek amendments to meet the objections at home. These provided that any member nation could withdraw from the League on two years' notice, that none could be required to take a mandate to administer former enemy possessions now under League supervision, that domestic affairs remained outside League jurisdiction, and that regional understandings like the Monroe Doctrine would remain undisturbed. All these went pretty much without saying, but the French exploited Wilson's discomfort to press for harsh measures: territorial concessions and reparations from Germany to keep her weak for years to come. Wilson clashed sharply with Clemenceau, and after the president threatened to leave the conference they settled on French recovery of Alsace-Lorraine (lost in 1870), a demilitarized Rhineland (up to fifty kilometers beyond the river), French occupation of this zone for fifteen years, and League administration of the Saar Basin. France could use Saar coal mines for fifteen years, after which a plebiscite would determine the region's status.

In other territorial matters Wilson had to compromise his principle of national self-determination. There was in fact no way to make boundaries correspond to ethnic divisions. The folk wanderings of centuries had left mixed populations scattered through central Europe. In some areas, moreover, national self-determination yielded to other interests: the Polish Corridor, for instance, gave Poland its much-needed outlet to the sea through German territory, and the South Tyrol, home for some 200,000 German-speaking Austrians, gave Italy a more defensible frontier at the Brenner Pass. One part of the Austro-Hungarian Empire became Czechoslovakia, which included the German-speaking Sudetenland, an area favored with good defenses. Another part of the empire united with Serbia to create the kingdom of Yugoslavia. Still other substantial parts passed to Poland (Galicia), Rumania (Transylvania), and Italy (Trentino and Trieste). Fiume on the Adriatic, claimed also by Yugoslavia, had not been promised to Italy, but it had been occupied by freebooters led by the poet Gabrial d'Annunzio, a romantic Italian nationalist. The conference finally left the matter for future settlement. In 1921 Italy and Yugoslavia divided the adjacent lands and made Fiume a free city, but in 1924 Yugoslavia accepted Italian annexation.

Where political decisions did not override considerations of nationality the Big Four could more easily follow recommendations from the committees of experts who made exhaustive studies of history, geography, and populations. Because of Colonel House's body of experts, The Inquiry, the American delegation was probably better informed than other delegations. In a few cases issues in doubt were decided by plebiscites of the people

EUROPE AFTER VERSAILLES

- .... 1914 boundaries
- New nations
- Plebiscite areas
- Occupied area

themselves. All in all, despite some aberrations, the new boundaries more nearly followed the ethnic divisions of Europe than the prewar lines.

The discussion of reparations began after the French felt they had already given up a great deal in territorial matters. Britain and France both sought reparations, and the French wanted enough to cripple Germany. Discussions of the issue were among the longest and most bitter at the conference. Despite a pre-Armistice agreement that Germany would be liable only for civilian damages, Clemenceau and Lloyd George proposed reparations for the entire cost of the war. On this point Wilson made perhaps his most fateful concessions. He accepted in the treaty a clause by which Germany confessed responsibility for the war and thus for its entire costs. The "war guilt" clause was an offense to all Germans and a source of persistent bitterness. A down payment of $5 million was to be extracted from Germany immediately; in 1921 a Reparations Commission estimated that Germany owed $33 billion in all.

On May 7 the victorious powers presented the treaty to the German delegates, who returned three weeks later with 443 pages of criticism protesting that the terms violated the Armistice agreement to abide by the Fourteen Points. A few small changes were made, but when the Germans still refused to sign Marshal Foch prepared to move across the Rhine. On June 28 they gave in and signed the treaty in the Hall of Mirrors at Versailles, where France had capitulated to Bismarck and Kaiser Wilhelm I in 1871. Treaties with the lesser powers followed the arrangements already made. Each, like the Versailles Treaty, bore the name of the palace near Paris were it was signed: St. Germain (with Austria), Trianon (with Hungary), Neuilly (with Bulgaria), and Sèvres (with Turkey).

WILSON'S LOSS AT HOME Wilson returned home with the Versailles Treaty on July 8. Two days later he called on the Senate to accept "this great duty." The force of Wilson's idealism struck deep, and he returned amid a great clamor of popular support. A third of the state legislatures had endorsed the League, as had thirty-three of forty-eight governors. Sen. Henry Cabot Lodge, chairman of the Senate Foreign Relations Committee, later said: "What I may call the vocal classes of the community . . . were friendly to the League as it stood and were advocating it."

But Lodge, a partisan Republican who nourished an intense dislike for Wilson, was now sharpening his knives. He, like other senators, knew all too well the fickle nature of popular acclaim. He knew also the undercurrents already stirring up opposition to the treaty: the resentment of German, Italian, and Irish "hyphenates," the disappointment of liberals at Wilson's compromises, the postwar letdown, the distractions of demobilization and resulting domestic problems, and the revival of isolationism. In the Senate a group of "irreconcilables," fourteen Republicans

Sen. Henry Cabot Lodge, leader of the opposition to the League. [Library of Congress]

and two Democrats, were unwilling to allow America entrance to the League on any terms. They were mainly western or midwestern progressives who stood on principle. The irreconcilables would be useful to Lodge's purpose, but he belonged to a larger group of "reservationists" who were ready to go partway with Wilson, but insisted on limiting American participation in the League and its actions. Wilson of course said that he had already amended the covenant to these ends, pointing out that with a veto in the League Council the United States could not be obligated to do anything against its will.

Lodge resorted to delays. First he arranged a reading of the entire treaty to a nearly empty committee room—the 264 pages consumed two weeks—then held lengthy hearings in which every critic could get in his licks. Lodge, who set more store by the old balance of power than by the new idea of collective security, brought forward a set of amendments, or reservations. Wilson responded by agreeing to interpretive reservations, but to nothing that would reopen the negotiations. He especially opposed weakening Article X, which provided for collective action against aggression.

By September, with momentum for the treaty slackening, Wilson decided to go to the people and, as he put it, "purify the wells of public opinion." Bold appeals to public opinion had helped get the New Freedom through Congress—why not the treaty? Against the advice of doctors and friends he set forth on a swing through the Midwest to the West Coast, pounding out speeches on his typewriter between stops. In all he traveled 8,000 miles in twenty-two days, gave thirty-two major addresses and eight minor ones, refuted his opponents, and voiced warnings. "Everywhere we go, the train when it stops is surrounded with little children . . ." he said in Tacoma, Washington. "These glad youngsters with flags in their hands—I pray God that they may never have to carry that flag upon the battlefield!"

For a while he seemed to be regaining the initiative, but then his body rebelled. His six years as president, during which he wrestled with major issues of war and peace, had depleted his resources. After a speech at Pueblo, Colorado, on September 25, the signs of exhaustion were so clear that his doctor canceled the tour and hurried the president's train back to Washington. On October 2 Wilson suffered a severe stroke and paralysis on his left side, leaving him helpless for weeks. He never recovered completely. For more than seven months he did not meet the cabinet, and was kept isolated from all but the most essential business by a protective wife. The illness intensified his traits of stubbornness and hostility. He might have done better to stay in the White House and secure the best compromise possible, but now he refused to yield anything. Wilson ended up committing what the historian Thomas A. Bailey called the supreme infanticide, the destruction of his own brainchild.

Between November 7 and 19 the Senate adopted fourteen reservations presented by Lodge, most having to do with the League. Wilson especially opposed the reservation to Article X which, he said, "does not provide for ratification but, rather, for the nullification of the treaty." As a result the Wilsonians found themselves thrown into an unlikely combination with irreconcilables who opposed the treaty under any circumstances. The Senate vote was 39 for and 55 against. On the question of taking the treaty without reservations, irreconcilables and reservationists combined to defeat ratification again, with 38 for and 53 against. The American public, however, would not permit the treaty to be laid aside because senators professing support could not reach agreement on a few reservations. In the face of public reaction the Senate voted to reconsider. But Wilson remained adamant: "Either we should enter the league fearlessly, accepting with responsibility and not fearing the role of leadership which we now enjoy, contributing our efforts toward establishing a just and permanent peace, or we should retire as gracefully as possible from the great concert of powers by which the world was saved." On March 19, 1920, twenty-one Democrats deserted Wilson and joined the reservationists, but the treaty once again fell short of a two-thirds majority by a vote of 49 yeas and 35 nays. The real winners were the smallest of the three groups in the Senate, neither the Wilsonians nor the reservationists but the irreconcilables.

Three Senators Refuse the Lady a Seat. *Americans reacted against the Senate's defeat of the Versailles peace treaty.* [Library of Congress]

Wilson still nourished the hope that he could make the next presidential election a "solemn referendum" on the League of Nations. He deluded himself, as Bryan had in 1900, for presidential elections are touched by many issues. When Congress declared the war at an end by joint resolution on May 20, 1920, Wilson vetoed the action; it was not until after he left office, on July 2, 1921, that a joint resolution ended the state of war with Germany and Austria-Hungary. Peace treaties with Germany, Austria, and Hungary were ratified October 18, 1921, but by then Warren Gamaliel Harding was president of the United States.

Lurching from War to Peace

The Versailles Treaty, for all the time it took in the Senate, was but one issue competing for public attention in the turbulent year after the war. But on the domestic scene Wilson's leadership was missing. He had been preoccupied by the war and the League, and once broken by his illness became strangely grim and peevish. His administration floundered through its last two years.

Demobilization proceeded without plan, indeed without much sense that a plan was needed once the war was over. The War Industries Board closed shop on January 1, 1919, and vanished so quickly that Bernard Baruch paid out of his pocket travel expenses home for some of his aides. The sudden cancellation of war contracts left workers and businessmen to cope with reconversion on their own. By April 1919 the armed forces were discharging about 4,000 men daily, and within a year the process was nearly complete.

THE ECONOMIC TRANSITION Events once again bore out the adage that there seems to be a special providence for fools, drunkards, and the United States of America. An unforeseen postwar boom eased the country over the difficult economic transition from war to peace. The boom fed on markets renewed by pent-up demand and wartime savings, and on overseas trade left open because German and British shippers had been weakened by wartime damage. Both farmers and businessmen benefited. The $2-billion cotton crop, which resulted from a happy mix of high prices and high production in 1919, was the most valuable ever. Reports from the southern countryside marveled at the unaccustomed wealth to be found among tenants and sharecroppers, but this was soon ended by a drop in farm prices in 1920 and a general business slump in 1921.

Government quickly extracted itself from "war socialism" in communications and transport. Telegraph, telephone, cable, and radio facilities were back in private hands by August 1919. On Christmas Eve 1919 Wilson announced that the railroads would go back to their owners on March 1, and Congress responded quickly. The Esch-Cummins Transportation Act of February 28, 1920, undertook to retain some of the advantages of unified operation. Unlike previous railroad laws, it gave up the pretense of enforcing competition and instead encouraged consolidation. The ICC, now enlarged from nine to eleven members, was authorized to work out plans to eliminate wasteful competition. It acquired in addition powers over the issuance of securities, the construction or abandonment of track, and the fixing of minimum as well as maximum rates. The commission was to evaluate all railroad property and thereby fix a fair rate of return to stockholders and fair rates for freight and passengers. Transferring the nation's great merchant fleet from public management to private management was less successful. Demand for the merchant fleet did not revive after the war. As a result, many of the ships were left to rot or rust.

The problems of postwar readjustment were worsened by general labor unrest. Prices rose along with employment after the war, and discontented workers, released from wartime constraints, were more willing to strike for their demands. In 1919, more than 4 million workers went out in thousands of disputes. Some workers in the East won their strike demands early in the year, but after a general strike in Seattle public opinion began to turn hostile. Seattle Mayor Ole Hansen denounced the general walkout of 60,000 workers as evidence of Bolshevik influence. The strike lasted only five days, but public alarm at the affair damaged the cause of unions across the country.

An AFL campaign to organize steelworkers suffered from charges of radicalism against its leader, William Z. Foster, a former Bryanite who joined the Socialists in 1900 and later emerged as a Communist. Attention to Foster's radicalism obscured the squalid conditions which had marked the steel industry since the Homestead strike of 1892. The twelve-hour day, often combined with a seven-day week, was common for steelworkers. On September 22, 1919, after U.S. Steel refused to talk, about 340,000 men walked out, mainly in the Chicago-Gary and western Pennsylvania areas. But the union succumbed to a back-to-work movement and gave up the strike four months later. When information about conditions became widely known, public opinion turned in favor of the steelworkers, but too late: the strike was over.

The most celebrated postwar labor dispute was the Boston Police Strike. If less significant than the steel strike in the numbers involved, it inadvertently launched a presidential career. When a local society of police, the Boston Social Club, applied to the AFL for a union charter, the Boston police commissioner dismissed eight members. A citizens' committee named by the mayor to investigate suggested arbitration and reinstatement of the fired officers, but the commissioner responded by firing nineteen more. On September 9, 1919, most of Boston's police force went out on strike. Gov. Calvin Coolidge mobilized the National Guard to keep order, and after four days the strikers were ready to return, but the commissioner refused to take them. When Samuel Gompers appealed that they be reinstated, Coolidge responded in words that suddenly turned him into a national figure: "There is no right to strike against the public safety by anybody, anywhere, any time."

RACIAL FRICTION   The summer of 1919 also brought a season of race riots, both North and South. Within a few weeks of the Armistice rumors began to circulate about black soldiers who had been "French-women ruined" or who had fallen under Bolshevik influence. What black leader James Weldon Johnson called "The Red Summer" ("Red" here signified blood) began in July, when whites invaded the black section of Longview, Texas, in search of a teacher who had allegedly accused a white woman of a liaison with a black man. They burned a number of shops and homes and ran several blacks out of town. A week later in Washington reports of black attacks on white women aroused white mobs and for four days gangs of white and black rioters waged race war in the streets until soldiers and driving rains ended the fighting. These were but preliminaries to the Chicago riot of late July in which 38 people were killed and 537 injured. The climactic disorders of the summer occurred in the rural area around Elaine, Arkansas, where black tenant farmers tried to organize a union. According to official reports 5 whites and 25 blacks died, but whites told one reporter in the area that more than 100 blacks died. Altogether twenty-five race riots took place in 1919, and more were threatened.

THE RED SCARE   Public reaction to the wave of strikes and riots was influenced by the impact of the Bolshevik Revolution. A mi-

Red Scare. A 1920 cartoon reflects popular alarm at the "Red menace" in America. [New York Public Library]

WHOSE COUNTRY IS THIS, ANYHOW?

nority of radicals thought America's domestic turbulence, like that in Russia, was the first scene in a drama of revolution. A much larger public was persuaded that they might be right. After all, a tiny faction in Russia had exploited confusion to impose its will. In 1919 the Socialist party, already depleted by wartime persecution, suffered the further defection of radicals inspired by the Russian example. Left-wing members formed the Communist and the short-lived Communist Labor parties. Wartime hysteria against all things German was readily transformed into a postwar Red Scare.

Fears of revolution might have remained latent except for the actions of a lunatic fringe. In April 1919 the post office intercepted in all nearly forty bombs addressed to various prominent citizens. One slipped through and blew off the hands of Georgia Sen. Thomas R. Hardwick's maid. In June another destroyed the front of Attorney-General A. Mitchell Palmer's home in Washington. Assistant Navy Secretary Franklin D. Roosevelt and his wife, who had just entered their house across the street, had a narrow escape. The random violence of these criminals formed no part of Bolshevik tactics, but many Americans saw Red on all sides and condoned attacks on all kinds of minorities in retaliation.

Soon the government itself was promoting witch-hunts. Attorney-General Palmer, a Pennsylvania Quaker and once a progressive congressman with prolabor leanings, harbored an entrenched distrust of aliens and a strong desire for the presidency. In June 1919 the Justice Department decided to deport radical aliens, and Palmer set up as the head of the new General Intelligence Division the young J. Edgar Hoover, who began to collect an index file on radicals. Raids began on November 7, 1919, when agents swooped down on the Union of Russian Workers in twelve cities. On December 22 the transport ship *Buford*, dubbed the "Soviet Ark," left New York for Russia with 249 people, including assorted anarchists, criminals, and public charges. All were deported without the benefit of a court hearing. On January 2, 1920, a series of raids by police in dozens of cities swept up some 6,000 suspects, often taken from their homes without search warrants, of whom about half were kept in custody. That same month the New York legislature expelled five duly elected Socialist members.

Basking in popular approval, Palmer continued to warn of the Red menace, but like other fads and alarms, the mood passed. Widespread disruptions predicted for May 1 never took place. Acting Secretary of Labor Louis F. Post began to scrutinize arrest warrants that required his approval. By the summer of 1920 the Red Scare had begun to evaporate. Communist revolutions in Europe died out, leaving Bolshevism isolated in Russia; bombings tapered off; the strike wave and race riots receded. Congress refused to pass peacetime sedition bills, although thirty-two states enacted criminal laws which made it illegal to join groups that called for the overthrow of the government by force. The attorney-general and his mimics began to seem more threatening to civil liberties than a handful of radicals. By September 1920, when a bomb explosion at the corner of Broad and Wall Streets in New York killed thirty-three people, Americans were ready to take it for what it was, the work of a crazed mind and not the start of a revolution. The Red Scare nevertheless left a lasting mark on American life. Part of its legacy was the continuing crusade for "100 percent Americanism" and restrictions on immigration. It left a stigma on labor unions and contributed to the anti-union open-shop campaign—the "American Plan," its sponsors called it. But for many Americans the chief residue of the Great War and its disordered aftermath was the profound disillusionment which pervaded American thought in the postwar decades.

FURTHER READING

Different interpretations of why the United States entered the First World War appear in George F. Kennan's *American Diplomacy, 1900–1950* (1951), and William Appleman Williams's *The Tragedy of American Diplomacy* (1959). Also valuable are Foster R. Dulles's *America's Rise to World Power, 1898–1954* (1955), John A. S. Grenville and

George B. Young's *Politics, Strategy, and American Diplomacy, 1873–1917* (1966), and Lloyd C. Gardner, Walter LaFeber, and Thomas McCormick's *The Creation of the American Empire* (1973). Otis L. Graham, Jr.'s *The Great Campaigns: Reform and War in America, 1900–1928* (1971), shows the link between progressive reform and the impulse for war. Good for background about American relations with the British is Bradford Perkins's *The Great Rapprochement: England and the United States, 1895–1914* (1968).

A number of scholars concentrate on the neutrality issue. Arthur S. Link, Woodrow Wilson's biographer, is sympathetic to the ideals of the president in *Wilson the Diplomatist* (1957) and *Woodrow Wilson: War, Revolution, and Peace* (1979). Other, more critical, efforts are Ernest R. May's *The World War and American Isolation, 1914–1917* (1959), John M. Cooper, Jr.'s *The Vanity of Power: American Isolation and the First World War, 1914–1917* (1969), Carl P. Parrini's *Heir to Empire: United States Economic Diplomacy, 1916–1923* (1969), and Ross Gregory's *The Origins of American Intervention in the First World War* (1971). John W. Coogan's *The End of Neutrality: The United States, Britain, and Maritime Rights, 1899–1915* (1981), argues that the issue of maritime rights was resolved before the war.

Other scholars have attempted to understand Wilsonian diplomacy by examining the president's actions in the Caribbean. For the Mexican intervention, consult P. Edward Haley's *Revolution and Intervention: The Diplomacy of Taft and Wilson with Mexico, 1910–1917* (1970), and Robert E. Quirk's *An Affair of Honor: Woodrow Wilson and the Occupation of Vera Cruz* (1962).° Frederick Katz's *The Secret War in Mexico: Europe, the United States, and the Mexican Revolution* (1981) gives an international perspective to the conflict. To gain a comparative perspective, see Hans R. Schmidt's *The United States Occupation of Haiti, 1915–1934* (1971).

Daniel M. Smith's *The Great Departure: The United States in World War I, 1914–1920* (1965), briefly surveys the war's impact both at home and abroad, while Frederick L. Paxton's *American Democracy and the World War* (3 vols.; 1936–1948) provides a lengthier treatment. Russell F. Weigley's *The American Way of War: A History of United States Military Strategy and Policy* (1973) has good interpretive chapters on the Expeditionary Force. Edward M. Coffman's *The War to End Wars: The American Military Experience in World War I* (1968) is a detailed presentation of America's military involvement.

David M. Kennedy's *Over Here: The First World War and American Society* (1980)° is an important recent survey of the impact of the war on the home front. Other studies of mobilization include Charles Gilbert's *American Financing of World War I* (1970), Robert Cuff's *The War Industries Board: Business-Government Relations during World War I* (1973), and Maurine Wiener Greenwald's *Women, War, and Work: The Impact of World War I on Women Workers in the United States* (1980).

William Preston, Jr., fits opposition to the war into a general pattern

°These books are available in paperback editions.

of dissent in *Aliens and Dissenters: Federal Suppression of Radicals, 1903–1933* (1953). More specific for the war period are Frederick C. Luebke's *Bonds of Loyalty: German-Americans and World War I* (1974) and Paul L. Murphy's *The Meaning of Freedom of Speech: First Amendment Freedoms from Wilson to FDR* (1972).

The tensions of the immediate postwar years are chronicled in Robert K. Murray's *Red Scare: A Study of National Hysteria, 1919–1920* (1955), and William Tuttle, Jr.'s *Race Riot: Chicago and the Red Summer of 1919* (1970). Other perspectives on these tensions can be found in Stanley Coben's *A. Mitchell Palmer: Politician* (1963) and A. E. Barbeau and Florette Henri's *The Unknown Soldiers: Black American Troops in World War I* (1974). Labor tensions are examined in Robert L. Friedheim's *The Seattle General Strike* (1964), David E. Brody's *Labor in Crisis: The Steel Strike of 1919* (1965), and Francis Russell's *A City in Terror: 1919, the Boston Police Strike* (1975).

How American diplomacy fared in the making of peace received considerable attention. In addition to the Link books on Wilson, the role of the president is treated in Arno J. Mayer's *Politics and Diplomacy in Peacemaking: Containment and Counterrevolution at Versailles, 1918–1919* (1967), and N. Gordan Levin, Jr.'s *Woodrow Wilson and World Politics: America's Response to War and Revolution* (1968).° The treaty controversy is handled in Thomas A. Bailey's *Woodrow Wilson and the Lost Peace* (1944) and *Woodrow Wilson and the Great Betrayal* (1945). Another perspective can be found in John A. Garraty's *Henry Cabot Lodge* (1953) and Ralph A. Stone's *The Irreconcilables: The Fight against the League of Nations* (1970). Peter G. Filene in *Americans and the Soviet Experiment* (1967) and Betty M. Unterberger in *America's Siberian Expedition* (1956) investigate American response to the Bolshevik takeover.

26

THE MODERN TEMPER

REACTION IN THE TWENTIES

On August 5, 1914, the day after Britain entered the Great War, the American novelist Henry James wrote to a friend: "The plunge of civilization into this abyss of blood and darkness . . . so gives away the whole long age during which we have supposed the world to be . . . gradually bettering, that to have to take it all now for what the treacherous years were all the while really making for and *meaning* is too tragic for any words." The war, as James foresaw, dealt a shattering blow to what another author called "the prevailing Meliorist myth," that civilization was progressing, moving forward, a myth which had dominated the public consciousness for a century and which had been so powerful a stimulant to progressivism. The fighting imprinted on modern memory scenes of carnage worse than those once supposedly consigned to a barbaric past. The postwar disillusionment hastened a growing challenge in modern thought to all the old values. Ernest Hemingway wrote in his war novel *A Farewell to Arms* (1929) that "abstract words such as glory, honor, courage or hallow were obscene beside the concrete names of villages, the number of roads, the names of rivers, the numbers of regiments and dates." Young men had simply gone off to die for a European civilization that was, in the words of the poet Ezra Pound, "an old bitch gone in the teeth, . . . a botched civilization."

To many others, watching the postwar wave of strikes, bombings, red scares, and race riots, it seemed that America had entered a frightening new terrain of diversity and change in which there lurked a thousand threats to the older orthodoxies. And those threats centered in the polyglot cities teeming with immigrants and foreign ideas. The defensive mood of the 1920s fed on a growing tendency to connect American nationalism with nativism, Anglo-Saxon racism, and militant Protestantism.

NATIVISM   The foreign connections of so many radicals strengthened the sense that sedition was chiefly foreign-made. That it went hand in hand with crime seemed confirmed by the most celebrated case of the times, which involved two Italian-born anarchists, Nicola Sacco and Bartolomeo Vanzetti. Arrested on May 5, 1920, for a payroll robbery and murder in South Braintree, Massachusetts, they were brought for trial before Judge Webster Thayer, who privately referred to the defendants as "those anarchist bastards." In the courtroom, wrote Felix Frankfurter of the Harvard Law School, Thayer allowed the prosecutor to exploit the Communist hysteria and "thus to divert and pervert the jury's mind." The question of the two men's guilt remains in doubt, though not the bias of the court, and the belief persists that they were sentenced for their beliefs and their ethnic origins rather than for any crime they had committed. The case became a great radical and liberal cause célèbre of the 1920s, but despite pleas for mercy and public demonstrations around the world on behalf of the two men, they went to the electric chair on August 23, 1927, their last appeals denied.

The surging postwar nativism brought an end to three centuries of immigration that dated from the first European settlements. The push to restrict immigration was reinforced by a pseudo-scientific racism which found expression in two widely read books: Madison Grant's *The Passing of the Great Race* (1916)—the great race being the Nordics of northern Europe, threatened by the Slavic and Latin people of eastern and southern Europe—and Lothrop Stoddard's *The Rising Tide of Color* (1920). The flow of immigrants, slowed by the war, rose again at its end. From June 1920 to June 1921 more than 800,000 per-

Sacco (middle) and Vanzetti (right) in court. [Brown Brothers]

sons entered the country, 65 percent of them from southern and eastern Europe; and more were on the way. An alarmed Congress passed the Emergency Immigration Act of 1921, which restricted new arrivals each year to 3 percent of the foreign-born of any nationality as shown in the 1910 census. A new quota law in 1924 reduced the number to 2 percent based on the 1890 census, which included fewer of the "new" immigrants. This law set a permanent limitation, which became effective in 1929, of slighty over 150,000 per year based on the "national origins" of the American people as of 1920. Since national origins could not be determined with precision, officials were called upon to use available statistics on migration, natural increase, and "such other data as may be found reliable." However inexact the quotas, the purpose clearly was to tilt the balance in favor of the old immigration from northern and western Europe, which was assigned about 85 percent of the total. The law completely excluded people from East Asia—a gratuitous insult to the Japanese, who were already kept out by their "Gentlemen's Agreement" with Theodore Roosevelt.

On the other hand the law left the gate open to new arrivals from Western Hemisphere countries, so that an ironic consequence was a great increase in the United States' Hispanic Catholic population. The legal arrivals from Mexico peaked at 89,000 in 1924. Lower figures after that date merely reflect policies of the Mexican government to clamp down on the outflow of labor and stronger American enforcement of old regulations like the 1882 exclusion of those immigrants likely to become public charges. Uncounted illegal immigrants continued to come, however, in response to southwestern agriculture's demand for "stoop" labor. People of Latin American descent (chiefly Mexicans, Puerto Ricans, and Cubans) became the fastest growing ethnic minority in the country.

THE KLAN During the postwar years the nativist tradition adopted a new form, a revived Ku Klux Klan modeled on the group founded during Reconstruction, but in a striking departure from its predecessor, devoted to "100 percent Americanism" and restricted in membership to native-born white Protestants. America was no melting pot, its founder William J. Simmons warned: "It is a garbage can! . . . When the hordes of aliens walk to the ballot box and their votes outnumber yours, then that alien horde has got you by the throat." A habitual joiner and promoter of fraternal orders, Simmons had gathered a hooded group atop Stone Mountain near Atlanta on Thanksgiving night, 1915. There, "bathed in the sacred glow of the fiery cross, the invisible empire was called from its slumber of half a century to take up a new task." It was a "living memorial" to the earlier Klan, but also something of a fraternal order with an elaborate ceremonial and secret passwords, all of which the founder took care to copyright in his name—thereby making the "secrets" available through copies in the Library of Congress.

The KKK had little success before 1920, when Simmons made a fateful alliance with Edward Young Clarke and Mrs. Elizabeth Tyler, two promoters who had honed their skills in the Red Cross and other wartime drives. Granted exclusive rights to publicize and propagate the Klan, the two got $8 out of each $10 Klecktoken (initiation fee), from which they paid all promotional expenses. By shrewd exploitation of ballyhoo, they transformed bigotry into big business. In the "idea of selling people their own prejudices," a sardonic editor remarked in Charleston, South Carolina, Simmons had displayed a genius "almost equal to the old bunco game of selling a hick the Capitol." The Klan always had about it a taint of racketeering—and its promoters also developed a profitable business in bedsheets on the side.

In 1921 a sensational exposé by the New York *World* and a congressional investigation only publicized the Klan further. In living testimony to the cynical adage that there is no such thing as bad publicity, the Klan thrived on the exposure. In going nativist, the Klan had gone national and was no longer restricted to the South. Its appeal reached areas as widely scattered as Oregon and Maine. It flourished mainly among the uprooted and insecure newcomers to the cities and towns. The robes, the flaming crosses, the eerie processionals, the kneeling recruits, the occult liturgies—all tapped a deep American urge toward mystery and brought drama into the dreary routine of a thousand communities.

A Klan rally on a baseball field in Beckley, West Virginia, 1923. [Library of Congress]

At the same time it was paradoxically a reflex against the strange and exotic, against shifting moral standards, the declining influence of churches, the broadmindedness of cities and colleges. It represented a degradation of the hopes aroused by progressivism and the war. In the Southwest it became more than anything else a moral crusade. "It is going to drive the bootleggers forever out of this land," declared a Texan. "It is going to bring clean moving pictures . . . clean literature . . . break up roadside parking . . . enforce the laws . . . protect homes." All these things it set out to achieve by nightriding and floggings. Enemies of the Klan, said a Kentucky Klansman, were uncertain who its members were, or how many. "It is the invisible something that gets their goat."

Simmons, always something of a dreamer, betrayed a fatal inability to control the tough customers attracted to the Klan by the scramble for power and booty. In 1922 a palace revolution toppled Simmons who, threatened with violence, sold his copyright on the Klan and abdicated to a new Imperial Wizard, Hiram Wesley Evans, a dentist from Dallas. The hooded order became a political power in thousands of communities. Officeholders either cultivated the Klan or were struck dumb on the subject. But the Klan never achieved much politically beyond securing the dismissal of a Catholic here and there or afflicting officials with blindness to floggings. Diligent research has uncovered only one Klan-inspired law, an Oregon act requiring Catholic children to attend public schools—and it was found unconstitutional. The order had neither a political program nor a dynamic leadership. Unlike kindred movements in postwar Europe, it conjured up no Mussolini, no Hitler.

Estimates of its peak membership, probably inflated, range from 3 million to 8 million, but the Klan's influence decayed as quickly as its numbers grew. For one thing, the Klan suffered from a decline in nativist excitement after passage of the 1924 immigration law. For another, it suffered recurrent factional quarrels and schisms. And its moral pretensions were tarnished by the violence it perpetrated, by charges of dubious relations between the promoters Clark and Tyler, and above all by a sordid scandal involving the Indiana Klan leader. Grand Dragon David C. Stevenson organized a political machine which for a while dominated the state through control of the Republican party, but the whole thing collapsed in 1925 after he forced a State House secretary aboard a train and fatally assaulted her. Convicted of second-degree murder, Stevenson got a life sentence. When the governor (elected as his stooge) refused to pardon him, Stevenson drew from a "little black box" the evidence that sent a congressman and several other officials to jail. The governor barely escaped a bribery charge. The "best people" of many towns had joined what they thought was an agency of reform, but drifted away as the Klan became a cloak for outrage; in that respect, at least, the organization repeated the history of its ancestor.

FUNDAMENTALISM   While the Klan saw a threat mainly in the alien menace, many adherents of the old-time religion saw threats from modernism in the churches: new ideas that the Bible should be studied in the light of modern scholarship (the "higher criticism") or that it could be reconciled with evolution. With the dawning knowledge that such notions had infected schools and even pulpits, orthodoxy took on a new militancy in fundamentalism. The movement had acquired a name and definition from a series of pamphlets, *The Fundamentals* (1910), published in Los Angeles. Armed with the "Five Points" fundamental to the faith —an inerrant Bible, the Virgin Birth, the Vicarious Atonement, the Resurrection, and the Second Coming of Christ—the fundamentalists were distinguished less by their belief in a faith which many others shared than by their posture of hostility toward any other belief.

Among the movement's leaders only William Jennings Bryan had the following and the eloquence to make the movement a popular crusade. In 1921 he sparked a drive for laws to prohibit the teaching of evolution. Bryan denounced Darwin with the same zeal he had once directed against the goldbugs. Many old-time admirers thought he had gone over to the forces of reaction, but to Bryan's mind the old reformer still spoke through the new fundamentalist. "Evolution," he said, "by denying the need or possibility of spiritual regeneration, discourages all reforms, for reform is always based upon the regeneration of the individual." Antievolution bills began to turn up in the hoppers of legislatures in the Midwest and South, but the only victories came to the South—and there were few of those. Some officials took direct action without legislation. Gov. Miriam "Ma" Ferguson of Texas ordered elimination from state schools of textbooks upholding Darwinism. "I am a Christian mother . . ." she declared, "and I am not going to let that kind of rot go into Texas schoolbooks."

The climax came in Tennessee, where in 1925 an obscure legislator, John Washington Butler, introduced a bill to outlaw the teaching of evolution in public schools and colleges. The bill passed by overwhelming majorities and the governor, unwilling to endanger a pending school program, signed with the observa-

Ballyhoo surrounding "the monkey trial" in Dayton, Tennessee. William Jennings Bryan and the Rev. T. T. Martin were leaders of the fundamentalist crusade. [Library of Congress]

tion that it would probably never be applied. He reckoned without the civic boosters of Dayton, Tennessee, who inveigled a young high school teacher, John T. Scopes, into accepting an offer of the American Civil Liberties Union to defend a test case —chiefly to put their town on the map. They succeeded beyond their wildest hopes: the publicity was worldwide, and enduring. Before the opening day of the "monkey trial" on July 13, 1925, the streets of Dayton swarmed with sundry oddments of humanity drawn to the carnival: publicity hounds, curiosity-seekers, professional evangelists and professional atheists, a blind mountaineer who proclaimed himself the world's greatest authority on the Bible, hot-dog and soda-pop hucksters, and a miscellany of reporters.

The two stars of the show—Bryan, who had offered his services to the prosecution, and Clarence Darrow, renowned trial lawyer of Chicago and self-confessed agnostic—united at least in their determination to make the trial an exercise in public education. When Judge John T. Raulston ruled out scientific testimony, however, the defense called Bryan as an expert witness on biblical interpretation. In his colloquy with Darrow, he repeatedly entrapped himself in literal-minded interpretations and indeed his ignorance of biblical history and scholarship. He stated a belief that a "great fish" actually swallowed Jonah, that Joshua literally made the sun stand still, that the world was created in 4004 B.C.—all, according to Darrow, "fool ideas that no intelligent Christian on earth believes."

But the only issue before the court, the judge ruled, was whether or not Scopes had taught evolution, and no one denied that he had. He was found guilty, but the Tennessee Supreme Court, while upholding the act, overruled the $100 fine on a legal technicality. The chief prosecutor accepted the higher court's advice against "prolonging the life of this bizarre case" and dropped the issue. With more prescience than he knew, Bryan had described the trial as a "duel to the death." A few days after it closed he died suddenly of a heart condition aggravated by heat and fatigue.

After Dayton the rest was anticlimactic. No other leader could assume Bryan's mantle, but in Mississippi the Bible Crusaders, led by the Rev. T. T. Martin, author of *Hell and the High Schools*, descended on the state legislature and got another antievolution law in 1926. One final fundamentalist victory came in Arkansas by the use of two progressive reforms, the initiative and the referendum, in 1928. With that, the fundamentalists had spent their fury. Their very victories were self-defeating, for they served to publicize what they opposed as heresy. The states that went through the fiercest controversies became prime markets for books on evolution, and the movement roused a liberal defense of academic freedom. Fundamentalists, usually defeated, suffered the complacent scorn of those people the sociologist Howard Odum called the "learned ignoranti," whose contempt for the beliefs of plain folk mirrored the intolerance of fundamentalists and whose own belief in science mirrored the fundamentalists' belief in the "Five Points."

PROHIBITION Prohibition offered another example of reforming zeal channeled into a drive for moral righteousness and conformity. Around the turn of the century the leading temperance organizations, the Women's Christian Temperance Union and the Anti-Saloon League, had converted from efforts to change individuals to a campaign for legal prohibition. Building upon the general moral disrepute of saloons, they were able to equate the "liquor traffic" with the trusts and "special interests." For the churches, prohibition could easily become, as one historian put it, "a surrogate for the Social Gospel." At the same time, contrary to certain oldtime folk beliefs that alcohol was beneficial, medical and scientific opinion now showed that it did more harm than good. By the 1910s the Anti-Saloon League had become one of the most effective pressure groups in American history, mobilizing Protestant churches behind its single-minded battle to elect "dry" candidates.

"Close the Saloons." A Prohibition poster of the 1920s. [American Heritage Society]

At its "Jubilee Convention" in November 1913 the league endorsed a national prohibition amendment to the Constitution. That December some 4,000 White Ribboners marched on the Capitol to present resolutions for a constitutional amendment. The 1916 elections finally produced two-thirds majorities for prohibition in both houses of Congress. Soon the wartime spirit of sacrifice, the need to use grain for food, and wartime hostility to German-American brewers transformed the cause virtually into a test of patriotism. On December 18, 1927, Congress passed and sent to the states the Eighteenth Amendment which, one year after ratification on January 16, 1919, banned the manufacture, sale, or transport of intoxicating liquors.

By then, however, about three-fourths of the American people already lived in states and counties that were legally dry. The wartime Lever Food and Fuel Control Act, moreover, had banned the use of grain for distilling and brewing. In 1919 the Volstead Act extended the ban and defined as "intoxicating" all beverages containing more than 0.5 percent alcohol, which became illegal once the Eighteenth Amendment went into effect on January 16 ,1920. On that date the corpse of John Barleycorn arrived in Norfolk, Virginia, on a special train. While his Satanic Majesty trailed along in deep mourning and anguish, twenty pallbearers carried an enormous coffin to a tabernacle where evangelist Billy Sunday preached the funeral oration to more than 10,000 people.

But John Barleycorn, like the labor hero Joe Hill, never died. The Eighteenth Amendment had been effective less than eight months when authorities found a still with a daily capacity of 130 gallons near Austin, Texas, on a farm belonging to Morris Shep-pard, the "Father of National Prohibition." Congress never sup-plied adequate enforcement, if such were indeed possible given the public thirst, the spotty support of local officials, and the profits to be made in bootlegging. With 1,520 agents in the Pro-hibition Bureau in 1920 and 2,836 ten years later, the govern-ment could hardly plug up all the leaks in the coastline and the borders. Rumrunning into Florida provided the Bahamas enough revenue to get out of debt. In Detroit, just across the river from Ontario, the liquor industry was second in size only to automo-biles. From Vancouver Island in the Northwest ships left with booze consigned to Mexico and returned empty within twenty-four hours—most likely not having gotten much beyond Seattle!

Imported liquors tended to be the real thing, but a lucrative trade developed in denatured grain alcohol, which could be re-distilled or "cooked" to make it potable and treated with flavor-ing and artificial coloring to impress desperate palates as facsimiles of bourbon, rye, or gin. But as "forbidden fruit," even fake liquor was all the more enticing and arrests for public drunk-enness went up sharply. Speakeasies, hip flasks, and cocktail par-ties were among the social innovations of the prohibition era, along with increased drinking by women.

It would be too much to say that prohibition gave rise to orga-nized crime, for organized vice, gambling, and extortion had long been practiced, and often tied in with the saloons. But pro-hibition supplied criminals an enormous new source of income, while the automobile and the submachine gun provided greater mobility and firepower. Gangland leaders showed remarkable gifts for exploiting loopholes in the law, when they did not sim-ply buy up policemen and politicians. George Remus, a crime boss who operated in the Midwest, bought a chain of drugstores so he could order medicinal liquors and then hijack his own trucks as they transported the goods.

But the most celebrated gangster and racketeer (a word coined in the 1920s) was "Scarface" Al Capone, who moved from New York to Chicago in 1920 and within a few years be-came the city's leading bootlegger, and gambling and vice lord. By 1927 he had an income of $60 million a year and a private army of gunmen. He asked once: "What's Al Capone done, then? He's supplied a legitimate demand. Some call it bootlegging. Some call it racketeering. I call it business. They say I violate the prohibition law. Who doesn't?" The widespread toleration of such "business" by its customers began to wear thin, however, in the face of the St. Valentine's Day Massacre in 1929, in which seven members of Chicago's Dion O'Banion gang were gunned

"Scarface" Al Capone.
[Brown Brothers]

down by members of a rival gang dressed as policemen. No indictments were ever made. Law-enforcement officials were unable to pin anything on Capone until a Treasury agent infiltrated his gang and got evidence to nail him in 1929 for income-tax evasion.

It came as no great surprise in 1931 when a commission under former Attorney-General George W. Wickersham reported evidence that enforcement of prohibition had broken down. Of the commission's eleven members only five approved continued efforts to enforce prohibition without change, four favored modifications, and two personally favored repeal. Still, the commission as a whole voted for further trial, and President Hoover chose to stand by what he called the "experiment, noble in motive and far-reaching in purpose."

THE ROARING TWENTIES

In many ways the defensive temper of the 1920s and the repressive movements to which it gave rise seem the dominant trends of the times, but they arose in part as reactions to a social and intellectual revolution that seemed about to sweep America away from its old moorings. In various labels given to the times, it was an era of excess, the jazz age, the era of wonderful nonsense, the roaring twenties, the ballyhoo years, the aspirin age. During those years a new America confronted an old America, and cultural conflict reached new levels of tension.

The smart set of the sophisticated metropolis developed an active disdain for the old-fashioned rural–small-town values of the hinterlands. In Sinclair Lewis's novel *Main Street* (1920), for instance, one encountered the stifling, mean, and cramped life out there on the prairie, a theme continued in his *Babbitt* (1922). In *Look Homeward, Angel* (1929), Thomas Wolfe scandalized his native Asheville, North Carolina, with his unrelenting drive to escape the encircling hills for the "billion-footed city." The banality of small-town life became a pervasive theme in the literature of the time and the popular outlook of city folk. Writing for the *Smart Set* and *American Mercury,* H. L. Mencken was the most merciless in his attacks on the American "booboisie." The daily panorama of America, he wrote, has become "so inordinately gross and preposterous . . . that only a man who was born with a petrified diaphragm can fail to laugh himself to sleep every night, and to awake every morning with all the eager, unflagging expectation of a Sunday-school superintendent touring the Paris peep-shows." The hinterlands responded with counterimages of alien cities infested with vice, crime, corruption, and foreigners. The tension erupted into the national political arena on several occasions, and rather than let the growing cities register their increase in Congress, traditionalists managed (for the only time in American history) to block any reapportionment of the House of Representatives after the census of 1920.

THE NEW MORALITY   Much of the shock to oldtimers came from the revolution in manners and morals, evidenced first among young people, and especially in the college campuses, where H. L. Mencken had become a hero. Folkways seemed to be changing faster than William Graham Sumner would ever have believed possible. In *This Side of Paradise* (1920), a novel of student life at Princeton, F. Scott Fitzgerald wrote of "the great current American phenomenon, the 'petting party.' " None of the Victorian mothers, he said, "had any idea how casually their daughters were accustomed to be kissed." One of the old muckrakers, Samuel Hopkins Adams, published a novel under the pen name of Warner Fabian, *Flaming Youth* (1923), which gave an enduring tag to the phenomenon. From such novels and from current magazine pieces the heartland learned about the "accent on youth," wild parties, bathtub gin, promiscuity, the new uses to which automobiles were put on secluded lovers' lanes, speakeasies, roadhouses, and "shimmy dancers" imitating Gilda Gray, who titillated the boys by shaking her chemise.

If flaming youth generated perhaps more smoke than fire, taboos were nonetheless loosening and remained loosened in the 1930s. Some young women abandoned corsets because, as one said: "The men won't dance with you if you wear corsets." By the mid-1920s women's fashion called for a cloche hat that fit tightly over bobbed hair, thin dresses with short sleeves, tightly strapped bust, waistlines where hips used to be, and hemlines that rose to alarming heights. On the feet, at least in John Held's cartoons in the old *Life*, fashionable women wore unfastened galoshes, and hence were called "flappers." Ironically, the more boyish the look, the more the flapper painted her face. Cosmetics joined other growth industries of the decade.

Whatever people did, however few flappers went "all the way," sex came to be discussed with a frankness once unheard of. One father, Frederick Lewis Allen reported, said his daughter "would talk about anything; in fact, she hardly ever talked about anything else." Much of the talk derived from a spreading awareness of Dr. Sigmund Freud, the Viennese father of psychoanalysis. When Freud visited Clark University in 1909, he was surprised to find himself so well known "even in prudish America." The following year appeared the first English translation of his *Three Contributions to a Theory of Sex*. By the 1920s and 1930s his ideas had begun to percolate into the popular awareness, and the talk spread in society and literature about libido, inhibitions, Oedipus complexes, transference, sublimation, and repression.

An obsession with sex permeated much of the literature and popular media of the day. James Branch Cabell, who became famous when his novel *Jurgen* (1919) was banned in Boston, exploited his "phallic candour" in a string of novels, while Eugene O'Neill used Freudian themes onstage in *Desire under the Elms* (1924), *Mourning Becomes Electra* (1931), and other plays. Sex became the stock-in-trade of a prosperous tabloid press, and a new form of literature, the confession magazine, featured lurid

Sweet Sexteen. *One of cartoonist John Held's "flappers" reading up on her Freud.* [Life *magazine*]

stories about women who had gone wrong. Pulp magazines like *Spicy Stories, Paris Nights,* or *Flapper Experiences* aroused interest and sales. In motion pictures "America's Sweetheart," the maidenly Mary Pickford, yielded stardom to the "vamp," Theda Bara, and the "It" girl, Clara Bow, followed in the 1930s by Jean Harlow, the movies' first "platinum blonde." A rising protest over such movie fare as *Up in Mable's Room, Sinners in Silk,* and *Her Purchase Price* impelled the movie industry to follow the example of organized baseball, which had made Judge Kenesaw Mountain Landis its commissioner or "czar" after Chicago White Sox players were charged with selling out their team in the 1919 World Series. In 1922 Postmaster-General Will H. Hays became the "Judge Landis of the Movies."

By 1930 the thrill of rebellion was waning; the revolution against Victorian codes had run its course. Its extreme expressions in time aroused doubts that the indulgence of lust equaled liberation. Frederick Lewis Allen wrote of a fictional "Mrs.Y, who had so stoutly believed in her right to sleep where she pleased and had been sure that she didn't care with whom Mr. Y slept, had found she couldn't take it after all and had marched off to Reno"—a discovery more than one generation had to make for itself. Women's styles never went back to the layered look of an earlier day, but they did once again acknowledge and exploit the difference between the sexes. Still, some new folkways had come to stay. In "Middletown" (Muncie, Indiana), where Robert and Helen Lynd had researched a classic community study in the mid-1920s, a young man told them on their return in 1935 that young people had "been getting more and more knowing and bold. The fellows regard necking as a taken-for-granted part of a date." In the late 1930s a survey disclosed that among college women almost one-half (47 percent) had yielded their virginity before marriage, but of these three-quarters had had sexual relations only with their future spouses. Most of them no doubt would have been shocked to discover that colonial Puritans accepted that much, if reluctantly.

The most pervasive change brought by the new moral code was in its views of marriage. The old Victorian code had made the husband head and master of the family, responsible for its support, while limiting the wife's "sphere" to the care of the home and the children, and the nurturing and gentling of the male animal. Children learned respect for parental authority. By the 1930s a code exalting romantic love and companionship as the basis for marriage had gained ascendancy. The sociologist Ernest R. Groves, in *The American Family* (1934), announced that the "breaking of the former taboo on sex has made possible for younger men and women a healthier attitude toward marital relationship" and a greater chance for mutual happiness. More important than breaking taboos may have been the social and economic evolution of a century which had taken away functions the family once had and delivered them to the factory, the school, and other institutions. Much alarm was expressed in the 1920s at the rising divorce rate. The rate declined briefly with the onset of the Great Depression in 1929, but picked up again during the later 1930s and 1940s. The divorce rate reflected perhaps less an increase in unsatisfactory marriages than a greater willingness and ability to abandon an intolerable situation.

THE WOMEN'S MOVEMENT   Equal suffrage for women arrived in 1920. It had been an unconscionably long time in coming. A span of seventy-two years separated the Seneca Falls Declaration of 1848, which marked the start of the political movement for women's rights, from ratification of the Nineteenth Amendment, which secured women the vote. The suffrage movement, which had been in the doldrums since 1896, sprang back to life in the second decade of the new century. In 1912 Alice Paul, a Quaker and social worker, returned from an apprenticeship with the militant suffragists of England, and became chairman of the National American Woman Suffrage Association's Congressional Committee. The day before Wilson's inauguration in 1913, when Washington was full of visitors, she organized a march to promote the suffrage amendment. When unruly crowds nearly broke up the parade, the resultant publicity revitalized the suffrage campaign. Paul's militant tactics and single-minded focus on the federal amendment, however, increasingly drove a wedge between her and the larger national group. The Congressional Union, formed by her committee in 1913, became a separate organization in 1915 and changed its name to the Woman's party in 1916. This group copied the British suffragists in holding the party in power responsible for failure to act, a reasonable stance under a parliamentary system but one which led them to oppose every Democrat, which the mainline suffragists found self-defeating in America. Alice Paul nevertheless knew how to get publicity for the cause. By 1917 she and her followers were engaged in picketing the White House and deliberately provoking arrests, after which they went on hunger strikes in prison. The authorities obligingly cooperated in making martyrs by the hundreds.

Women suffragists picketing the White House in 1917. Their sign points up the irony of Wilson's aim to make the world safe for democracy. [Library of Congress]

Meanwhile, Carrie Chapman Catt became head of the National Suffrage Association once again in 1915 and revived it through her gift for organization. She brought with her a legacy of about $1 million from Mrs. Frank Leslie, publisher of *Leslie's Weekly,* dedicated "to the furtherance of the cause of woman suffrage." The money became available in 1917 and contributed to organizing the final campaigns for voting rights. For several years President Wilson evaded the issue of an amendment, but he voted for suffrage in a New Jersey referendum and supported a plank in the 1916 Democratic platform endorsing state action for woman suffrage, addressed the National Suffrage Organization that year, and thereafter worked closely with its leaders.

Finally, in 1918, after the House had passed the "Anthony Amendment," Wilson went before the Senate on September 30 to plead for its passage there. The Senate fell short of the two-thirds majority by two votes, but the attention centered on the issue helped defeat two antisuffrage senators. On June 4, 1919, the Senate finally adopted the amendment by a bare two-thirds majority. Ratification of the Nineteenth Amendment took another agonizing fourteen months. The Tennessee legislature had the distinction of completing the ratification, on August 21, 1920. It was one of the climactic achievements of the progressive era.

Even before ratification the suffrage organization began transforming itself into the League of Women Voters, founded in 1919, and women thereafter entered politics in growing numbers. But, it was often noted, this did not usher in a political millennium or any sudden release of women from all the trammels of custom and law. What was more, the suffrage victory left the broader feminist movement prey to a letdown that lasted for a generation. A few years after the triumph Carrie Chapman Catt wrote that suffragists were disappointed "because they miss the exaltation, the thrill of expectancy, the vision which stimulated them in the suffrage campaign. They find none of these appeals to their aspiration in the party of their choice."

One group, however, wanted to advance equality yet further. Alice Paul and the Woman's party set a new feminist goal, first introduced in Congress in 1923: an Equal Rights Amendment which would eliminate any remaining legal distinctions between the sexes—including the special legislation for the protection of working women put on the books in the previous fifty or so years. Feminists who had been caught up in the social-justice movement considered this a sacrifice of gains painfully accomplished. If would be another fifty years before Alice Paul would see Congress adopt her amendment in 1972; she did not live, however, to see it fall short of ratification.

The sharp increase in the number of women in the workforce during World War I proved ephemeral, but in the longer view a steady increase in the numbers of employed women occurred in the 1920s and, surprisingly, continued through the depression decade of the 1930s. Still, this phenomenon represented more evolution than revolution. The greatest breakthroughs had come in the nineteenth century, and by 1900 women had at least a token foothold in most of the gainful occupations. By 1910 they made up almost a quarter of all nonagricultural workers, and in 1920 were found in all but 35 of the 572 job categories listed by the census. The continued entry of women into the workforce brought their numbers up from 8.2 million in the 1920 census to 10.4 million in 1930, and 13 million in 1940. Still these women remained concentrated in traditional occupations: domestics, office workers, teachers, clerks, salespeople, dressmakers, milliners, and seamstresses. In manufacturing they were found mainly in related work, such as textiles or garment making. On the eve of World War II women's work was little more diversified than it had been at the turn of the century, but by 1940 it was on the eve of a great transformation.

THE "NEW NEGRO" The discriminations that have befallen blacks and women have many parallels, and the loosening of restraints for both have often gone together. The most significant development in black life during these years was the Great Migration, which one historian pronounced "the greatest watershed in American Negro history" after emancipation. The movement of blacks northward got under way in 1915–1916 when war industries were depleting the ranks of common labor at a time when the war prevented replacement by foreign immigrants; legal restrictions on immigration continued the movement in the 1920s. Altogether, between 1910 and 1920 the Southeast lost some 323,000 blacks, or 4.9 percent of the native black population, and by 1930 had lost another 615,000, or 8.2 percent of the native black population in 1920. With the migration a slow but steady growth in black political influence set in, for not only were blacks freer to speak and act in a northern setting; they gained political leverage by concentrating in large cities located in states with many electoral votes.

Along with political activity came a bristling spirit of protest among blacks, a spirit which received cultural expression in a literary and artistic movement tagged the "Harlem Renaissance." Claude McKay, a Jamaican immigrant, was the first significant writer of the movement which was a rediscovery of black folk culture and an emancipation from the genteel tradition. Poems collected in McKay's *Harlem Shadows* (1922) expressed defiance in such titles as "If We Must Die" and "To the White Fiends." Other emergent writers included the versatile and prolific Langston Hughes, poet, novelist, and columnist; Zora Neal Hurston, folklorist and novelist; Countée Cullen, poet and novelist; and James Weldon Johnson, who pictured the Negro mecca in *Black Manhattan.* Perhaps the greatest single creation of the

Major figures of the Harlem Renaissance. From left, Langston Hughes, Charles Johnson, and the historian E. Franklin Frazier. [Schomberg Collection, New York Public Library]

time was Jean Toomer's novel *Cane,* which pictured the lives of simple blacks in Georgia's black belt and the sophisticated inhabitants of Washington's brown belt. White writers like Eugene O'Neill, DuBose Heyward, Julia Peterkin, and Sherwood Anderson also took up the theme of what Alain Locke in 1925 called "The New Negro," but more often than not they merely abandoned the old stereotype of the "darkie" for a new stereotype of the exotic primitive, a caricature the more fully alive for its want of inhibitions.

In its extreme expression the spirit of the New Negro found outlet in what came to be called "Negro nationalism," which exalted blackness, black cultural expression, and black exclusiveness. The leading spokesman for such views was Marcus Garvey, who in 1916 brought to New York the United Negro Improvement Association (UNIA), which he had started in his native Jamaica two years before. His organization grew rapidly under the strains of the postwar years. Racial bias, he said, was so ingrained in whites that it was futile to appeal to their sense of justice. The only hope for blacks was to flee America and build a Negro republic in Africa. Garvey began to organize ancillary groups such as the Universal African Legion, the Universal Black Cross Nurses, and the Black Star Steamship Line. Much of their appeal paralleled that of fraternal groups which enjoyed parading in uniform. Garvey quickly enlisted half a million members and claimed as many as 6 million by 1923. At that point he was charged with fraudulent use of the mails in raising funds for his steamship line. Found guilty, he went to the Atlanta penitentiary in 1925, where he remained until President Coolidge pardoned and deported him to Jamaica in 1927. Garvey, one biographer concluded, had suffered from a lack of business experience rather than from an intent to defraud. He died in obscurity in London in 1940, but the memory of his movement kept alive an undercurrent of Negro nationalism which would reemerge later under the slogan of "black power."

The year in which the Great Migration began, 1915, marked another milestone with the passing of Booker T. Washington. His position of race leadership was taken up not by a single spokesman but more and more by an organization, the National Association for the Advancement of Colored People (NAACP). It had started with writer William English Walling's call in *The Independent* for a revival of the abolitionist spirit in response to a 1908 race riot in Springfield, Illinois, Lincoln's hometown. Plans laid at a meeting in May 1909 led to a formal organization in 1910. Two participants supplied a direct link to the abolitionists: Oswald Garrison Villard, who was the grandson of William Lloyd Garrison, wrote the call for the 1909 meeting, and Moorefield Storey, in his youth the secretary to the abolitionist Charles Sumner, became the organization's first president. Black participants came mainly from a group associated with W. E. B. Du Bois since 1905 called the Niagara Movement, which had met each year at a place associated with antislavery (Niagara Falls, Oberlin, Boston, Harper's Ferry) and issued a defiant statement against discrimination. Du Bois became the NAACP's director of publicity and research, and editor of its journal, *The Crisis*.

Although most progressives were not in harmony with the NAACP, the new group took seriously the progressive idea that the solution to social problems began with informing the people, and it planned an active press bureau to accomplish this. Its main strategy, however, came over the years to be legal action aimed at warming the Fourteenth and Fifteenth Amendments back to life. One early victory came with *Guinn v. United States* (1915), in which, after the NAACP submitted a friend of the court brief, the Supreme Court struck down Oklahoma's grandfather clause, used in the state to deprive blacks of the vote. In *Buchanan v. Worley* (1917) the Court invalidated a residential segregation ordinance in Louisville, and in *Moore v. Dempsey* (1923) ruled that trials of blacks after the Elaine, Arkansas, riots in 1919 violated due process because they took place in an atmosphere of mob hysteria.

Meanwhile, in 1919 the NAACP launched a campaign against lynching with a statistical survey of the practice and a conference. Rep. L. C. Dyer of St. Louis introduced an antilynching bill to make mob murder a federal offense. The bill passed the House in 1922, but lost to a filibuster by southern senators. The bill stayed before the House until 1925, and NAACP Field Secretary James Weldon Johnson believed the continued agitation of the issue did more than the bill's passage would have to reduce lynchings, which fell off to a third of what they had been the previous decade.

The emergent black political renaissance found expression in two events: Oscar DePriest's election from a Chicago district in 1928 as the first black congressman since 1901, the first ever from the North; and the fight against the confirmation of Judge John J. Parker for the Supreme Court in 1930. When President Hoover submitted Parker's name the NAACP found that as the 1920 Republican candidate for governor of North Carolina Parker had pronounced Negro suffrage "a source of evil and danger." The NAACP conducted its campaign, Du Bois said, "with a snap, determination, and intelligence never surpassed in colored America." Parker lost by the close vote of 41 to 39 to a convergence of unlikely allies: the AFL, unhappy at a Parker labor decision, insurgents who found him too conservative, and southern Democrats opposed to a southern Republican. His defeat nevertheless represented the first instance of significant black impact on Congress since Reconstruction.

In 1930 the NAACP began laying plans for a legal assault on segregation in American life. The administration of Franklin D. Roosevelt saw the political influence of blacks grow further after 1933. Like Wilson, Roosevelt did not give a high priority to Negro affairs, but he tolerated people in his administration who did. By 1936 there was a "Black Cabinet" of some thirty to forty advisors in government departments and agencies, and black voters were fast transferring their political loyalty from Republicans to Democrats.

During the 1930s the NAACP's legal campaign gathered momentum. A major setback occurred in *Grovey v. Townsend* (1935), which upheld the Texas Democrats' white primary as the practice of a voluntary association and thus not state action. But the *Grovey* decision held up for only nine years and marked the end of major decisions that for half a century had narrowed application of the Reconstruction Amendments. A trend in the other direction had already set in. Two important precedents arose from the celebrated Scottsboro case of 1931, in which nine black youths were convicted of raping two white women while riding a freight train in Alabama. The first verdict failed, the high court ruled in *Powell v. Alabama* (1932), for want of due process because the judge's appointing "all of the members of the bar" to defend the accused was "little more than an expensive gesture imposing no substantial or definite obligation upon anyone." Another verdict fell to a judgment in *Norris v. Alabama* (1935) that the systematic exclusion of Negroes from Alabama juries had denied the defendants equal protection of the law—a principle that had significant and widespread impact on state courts.

The Culture of Modernism

SCIENCE AND SOCIAL THOUGHT As the twentieth century advanced, the easy faith in progress and reform expressed by social gospelers and other liberals fell victim to a series of frustrations and disasters: the Great War, failure of the League of Nations, the failure of prohibition, the Great Depression, the rise of Communist and fascist dictators, continuing world crises. New currents in science and social thought also brought shocks to the easy faith in a rational or melioristic universe. Darwin's biology portrayed man as more akin to apes than to angels. Darwin's contemporary Karl Marx influenced even people who rejected his Communist doctrine but saw relevance in his emphasis on the material, economic basis of society. In capitalist society, Marx argued, freedom was an illusion: people were actually driven by impersonal economic forces. In Freud's psychology people were also driven, but by needs arising from the depths of the unconscious. If Darwin, Marx, and Freud suggested that rational man was not the master of his fate, startling new findings in physics further shook the verities underlying American life and thought in the progressive period.

Modern times began, one writer has asserted, on May 29, 1919, when photographs taken during a solar eclipse confirmed Albert Einstein's theory of relativity by showing that the sun's gravitational pull actually bent rays of light from distant stars. The new findings in physics altered the image of the cosmos in ways that seemed almost a calculated assault on common sense. The conventional wisdom since Sir Isaac Newton held the universe to be governed by laws which the scientific method could ultimately uncover. The world was a machine, a scientific writer of the early twentieth century said. "In its motions there is no uncertainty, no mystery." A world of such certain order bolstered hopes of infinite progress in human knowledge, and good Victorians of the nineteenth century could readily accommodate even Darwinism to their optimistic outlook.

This world of order and certainty came apart when Albert Einstein, a young German physicist working in the Swiss patent office, puzzled over recent experiments and reasoned that space, time, and mass were not absolutes but relative to the location and motion of the observer. In 1905 he published a paper, "On the Electrodynamics of Moving Bodies," which became known as the special theory of relativity. Ten years later he elaborated his general theory of relativity, which covered gravitational fields and challenged the Newtonian cosmos. Newton's mechanics, according to Einstein, worked well enough at relatively slow speeds, but the more nearly one approached the velocity of light (about 186,000 miles per second) the more all measuring devices would change accordingly, so that yardsticks would become shorter, clocks and heartbeats would slow down. An observer on another planet moving at a different speed would see a quite different universe from the one we see. Even more incredibly, a

Albert Einstein. [United Press International]

person traveling on a spaceship at immense velocity, and unaware that for him time had slowed relative to earth time, might return to find that centuries had passed in his absence.

Certainty dissolved the farther one reached out into the universe. The same thing happened the farther one reached down into the minute world of the atom. The discovery of radioactivity in the 1890s showed that atoms were not irreducible units of matter but that some of them emitted particles of energy. What this meant, Einstein noted, was that mass and energy were not separate phenomena but interchangeable. In 1907 Einstein quantified this relationship in the famous and deceptively simple formula $E = mc^2$, energy equals mass times the speed of light squared. Meanwhile the researches of Max Planck in Berlin had led Planck to find that electromagnetic emissions of energy, whether as electricity or light, came in little bundles which he called quanta. The development of quantum theory suggested that atoms were far more complex than once believed and, as German physicist Werner Heisenberg stated in his principle of uncertainty in 1927, ultimately indescribable. One could never know both the position and the velocity of an electron, Heisenberg concluded, because the very process of observation would inevitably have an impact on the behavior of the particle, altering its position and velocity.

Heisenberg's thesis meant that beyond a certain point things could not possibly be measured, so that human knowledge had limits. "The physicist thus finds himself in a world from which the bottom has dropped clean out," a Harvard mathematician wrote in 1929. He had to "give up his most cherished convictions and faith. The world is not a world of reason, understandable by the intellect of man, but as we penetrate ever deeper, the very law of cause and effect, which we had thought to be a formula to which we could force God Himself to subscribe, ceases to have any meaning." Hard for the public to grasp, such findings proved too much even for Einstein, who spent much of the rest of his life in quest of an explanation through a unified field theory which would combine electromagnetism and gravitation in one system and unify the relativity and quantum theories. "I shall never believe that God plays dice with the world," Einstein said.

Though few people understood it, Einstein's theory especially captured the imagination of a public whose common experience told them that observers differently placed got a different view of things. Just as Enlightenment thinkers drew on Newton's laws of gravitation two centuries before to formulate their views on the laws governing society, the ideas of relativity and uncertainty in the twentieth century carried over into denials of absolute values in any sphere of society, and thus undermined the concepts of personal responsibility and absolute standards. Anthropologists aided the process by transforming the word "culture," which had before meant refinement, into a term for the whole system of ideas, folkways, and institutions within which any group lived. Even the most primitive groups had cultures and, all things being relative, one culture had no place imposing its value judgments on another. Two students of Columbia University anthropologist Franz Boas, Ruth Benedict and Margaret Mead, were especially effective in spreading this viewpoint. Benedict's *Patterns of Culture* (1934), a steady seller, introduced millions to the different values of unusual cultures from the North American Indians to the Melanesians, and Mead's *Coming of Age in Samoa* (1928) celebrated the healthfulness of the uninhibited sex she observed there. The uncertainty principle got an ironic twist in Mead's case, however, when over fifty years later another anthropologist insisted that she was the victim of a gigantic put-on by Samoans who told her what they thought she wanted to hear.

MODERNIST LITERATURE The cluster of scientific ideas associated with Darwin and Einstein inspired a revolution in the minds of intellectuals and creative artists which they expressed in a new modernism. Some observers now count this new intellectual current as ranking with the Enlightenment, romanticism, or Victorianism in its sweep and significance. The historian Daniel J. Singal has identified certain major features of the modernist movement. First, it undertook "to plumb the nether regions of the psyche," to explore the irrational as an essential part of human nature. Second, it viewed the universe as turbulent and

Louis Armstrong's Hot Five. Jazz emerged during this period as an especially American expression of the modernist spirit. Black artists bent musical conventions to give fuller reign to improvisation. [United Press International]

unpredictable, and presented uncertainty as a desirable condition. Third, it displaced the Victorian ideals of "bliss" and "peace" with a positive view of conflict. Finally, the modernist displayed "a critical temperament uninhibited by considerations of formal manners," for rules of gentility had to yield to the urge to make contact with "reality," no matter how distasteful. In the various arts related technical features appeared: abstract painting which represented an inner mood rather than an image of an object, atonal music, free verse in poetry, stream-of-consciousness narrative, and interior monologues in stories and novels. Writers dramatized our separation from the past. They showed an intense concern with new forms in language in an effort to avoid outmoded forms and structures and to violate expectations and shock their audiences.

The search for the new centered in America's first major artistic bohemias: Chicago, where cheap housing built for visitors to the Columbian Exposition offered a haven on the South Side; and New York, where the area in lower Manhattan soon known as Greenwich Village offered a lure for aspiring artists, and radicals —and their camp followers. In the words of the radical writer John Reed, the Village featured "inglorious Miltons by the score, and Rodins, one to every floor." As early as 1909 the photographer Alfred Stieglitz hung Matisse paintings in his Photo-Secession gallery on Fifth Avenue. At Mabel Dodge's Fifth Avenue salon intellectuals rubbed shoulders with IWW leader Big Bill Haywood and discussed the new ideas. In 1913 the Armory Show in New York, which went then to Chicago, Philadelphia, and Boston, shocked traditionalists with its display of the latest in experimental and nonrepresentational art: post-impressionists, Fauvists, expressionists, primitives, and cubists. ablo Picasso's work made its American debut there. Mabel Dodge thought the show the most important event in America since 1776. It aroused a portion of shocked indignation and not a little good-natured ridicule, but it was a huge success. Audiences flocked to the show and buyers afterward snapped up the pieces for sale.

Suddenly everything was new: the "New Freedom," the "New Nationalism," the new poetry, the new art, the new ethics, the new marriage. In 1913 James Harvey Robinson of Columbia announced in *The New History* a purpose of making history a pragmatic science oriented toward explaining the present, and in the same year his colleague Charles A. Beard sent out shock waves with *An Economic Interpretation of the Constitution.* Late in 1912 Max Eastman had taken over the socialistic *Masses* and turned it into a lively magazine; in 1914 Herbert Croly established the less radical *New Republic.* Literary magazines mushroomed: the *Seven Arts, Dial,* the *Little Review,* the *Bohemian,* the *Criterion,* and many others.

"The fiddles are tuning as it were all over America," the Irish poet John Butler Yeats wrote. In Chicago, Harriet Monroe provided a sounding board in *Poetry: A Magazine of Verse.* A poet of some local renown, author of the official ode for the Columbian Exposition, and already past fifty when she started *Poetry* in 1912, she found her vocation as patron to a renaissance. Within a few years she had brought to light a dozen and more major figures: Carl Sandburg, celebrator of Chicago, "Stormy, husky, brawling, City of the Big Shoulders"; Vachel Lindsay, vagabond poet who sought to restore the "primitive singing voice" in poems like "General Booth Enters Heaven" and "The Congo"; the lyricists Sara Teasdale, Elinor Wylie, and Edna St. Vincent Millay; Robinson Jeffers, poet of tragic despair; the imagists Amy Lowell, Conrad Aiken, and William Carlos Williams. To her eternal regret Harriet Monroe "missed" Edgar Lee Masters, a lawyer resident in Chicago and author of *Spoon River Anthology* (1915), his poetic epitaphs for middle western types. She also missed Sherwood Anderson, whose stories of midwestern characters in *Winesburg, Ohio* (1919), offered a prose parallel to *Spoon River.*

The chief American prophets of modernism were in neither Chicago nor New York, but emigrés in Europe: Ezra Pound and T. S. Eliot in London, and Gertrude Stein in Paris, all deeply concerned with creating new and often difficult styles of expression. Pound, as foreign editor for *Poetry*, became the conduit through which many American poets achieved publication in America and Britain. At the same time he became the leader of the imagist movement, a revolt against the ornamental verbosity of Victorian poetry in favor of the concrete image, exclusion of "superfluous words," and the rhythm of the "musical phrase" rather than the "sequence of a metronome." In the course of a long life, Pound was to embrace a number of causes, continue his expatriation in Paris and Italy, encourage new writers, seek new poetic techniques, and compose as his lifetime project an endless series of difficult and obscure *Cantos*.

Pound's supreme protégé was T. S. Eliot, who in 1915 contributed to *Poetry* his first major poem, "The Love Song of J. Alfred Prufrock," the musings of an ineffectual man who "after tea and cakes and ices" could never find "the strength to force the moment to its crisis." Eliot's "The Waste Land" (1922) made few concessions to readers in its arcane allusions, its juxtaposition of unexpected metaphors, its deep sense of postwar disillusionment and melancholy, and its suggestion of a burnt-out civilization; but it became for a generation almost the touchstone of the modern temper along with the Irishman James Joyce's stream-of-consciousness novel *Ulysses*, published the same year. As poet and critic in *The Criterion*, which he founded in 1922, Eliot became the arbiter of modernist taste in Anglo-American literature.

Gertrude Stein, in voluntary exile since 1903, was with her brother Leo an early champion of modern art and a collector of early Cézannes, Matisses, and Picassos. Long regarded as no more than the literary eccentric who wrote "Rose is a rose is a rose is a rose" and "Pigeons on the grass alas," she came later to be recognized as one of the chief originators and propagators of modernist style, beginning with *Three Lives* (1906). Included in this work is the classic "Melanctha," perhaps the first story by a white author to treat a black character as something other than a stereotype. Having studied psychology under William James, Stein sought to develop in writing the equivalent of nonrepresentational painting; her work captured interior moods in such books as *The Making of Americans* (1911, published 1925) and *Tender Buttons* (1914).

But she was long known chiefly through her influence on such 1920s expatriates as Sherwood Anderson and Ernest Hemingway, whom she told: "All of you young people who served in the war, you are the lost generation." The earliest chronicler of that generation, F. Scott Fitzgerald, blazed up brilliantly and then quickly flickered out, like all the tinseled, blithesome, sad young people of his novels. Successful and famous at age twenty-four with *This Side of Paradise* (1920), along with his wife Zelda he lived in and wrote up the "greatest, gaudiest spree in history," and then both had their crack-up in the Great Depression. What gave depth to the best of his work was what a character in *The Great Gatsby* (1925), his finest novel, called "a sense of the fundamental decencies" amid all the surface gaiety—and almost always a sense of impending doom.

Hemingway's first novel, *The Sun Also Rises* (1926), pictures an even more desperate search for life by the expatriate crowd, chasing about frantically from the bistros of Paris to the bullrings of Spain. Young Jake Barnes, emasculated by a war wound, cannot marry his love, Lady Brett Ashley. "Oh, Jake," she says in the poignant ending, "we could have had such a damned good time together." "Yes," he replied. "Isn't it pretty to think so?" Hemingway's second novel, *A Farewell to Arms* (1929), is another tale of lost love. Based on Hemingway's experience in the ambulance corps in northern Italy, where he had caught shrapnel in both legs during the retreat from Caporetto, it pursues the love affair of a driver and a nurse who abandon the war for Switzerland, where the young woman dies in childbirth.

Already in these novels are found the lively, even frenetic action, and the cult of athletic masculinity (epitomized by the bullfighter), which became the stuff of the public image which Hemingway cultivated for himself and the hallmark of such novels as *Death in the Afternoon* (1932), *To Have and Have Not* (1937), *For Whom the Bell Tolls* (1940), and *The Old Man and the Sea* (1952). Hundreds of writers tried to imitate Hemingway's terse style, but few had his gift, which lay less in what he had to say than in the way he said it. The critic Alfred Kazin passed judgment in one short sentence: "He brought a major art to a minor vision of life."

THE RETURN OF SOCIAL SIGNIFICANCE   In view of the studied alienation of writers caught in the materialistic world of the 1920s, one might have expected the onset of the Great Depression in 1929 to deepen the despair. Instead it brought a renewed sense of commitment and affirmation, as if people could no longer afford the art-for-art's-sake affectations of the 1920s. The surprisingly popular musical show *Pins and Needles* (1936), put on by members of the International Ladies' Garment Workers Union, caught the new feeling of dedication in one of its numbers: "Sing Me a Song with Social Significance."

In the early 1930s the commitment sometimes took the form of allegiance to revolution. For a time leftist politics and rhetoric made significant inroads in literary circles. By the summer of 1932 even the "golden boy" of the lost generation, F. Scott Fitzgerald, was saying that "to bring on the revolution, it may be necessary to work within the Communist party." In September 1932 fifty-three artists and intellectuals signed an open letter endorsing William Z. Foster, the Communist party candidate for president, and many writers flocked into the party's John Reed Clubs, named for the American journalist who had observed and written about the Bolshevik revolution.

Until 1935, following the line laid down by the Soviet dictator Joseph Stalin, the Communist party refused to collaborate with other groups. In 1935 the party line switched to endorse a broad "popular front" with democratic and socialistic groups opposed to fascism. In 1935 the John Reed clubs gave way to the more broadly based League of American Writers, which held an annual American Writers' Congress for several years. It paralleled other popular-front groups like the American Youth Congress, the American Negro Congress, and the American League for Peace and Democracy. It drew into its activities, among others, Hemingway, Erskine Caldwell, Waldo Frank, Archibald MacLeish, Richard Wright, John Dos Passos, Theodore Dreiser, John Steinbeck, and Langston Hughes. But few remained for long. Writers being a notoriously independent lot, they rebelled at demands to hew to a shifting line. Over the years a series of shocks persuaded most of them that Joseph Stalin practiced tyranny and terror more efficient and more bloody than anything under the czars. The climactic events were the staged treason trials of Stalin's former comrades in 1936 and Stalin's Non-Aggression Pact with Hitler in 1939 which opened the way for World War II in Europe.

In the heyday of the "Red Decade" there was much talk of a proletarian literature, but the only product of lasting significance to come out of the leftist cultural movement was the *Partisan Review*, founded in 1934 as the organ of New York's John Reed Club and, after a brief hiatus in 1936–1937, revived as an anti-Stalinist literary journal. Among the writers who sang songs with social significance at least three novelists deserve special notice: John Dos Passos, John Steinbeck, and Richard Wright.

After Harvard and a stint as an ambulance driver in France and Italy during the Great War, Dos Passos first got wide notice with *Three Soldiers* (1921), an exposé of the sordid and brutal nature of war. *Manhattan Transfer* (1925) presented a similar picture of modern urban society and began to use the kaleidoscopic techniques of his great trilogy *U.S.A.* (1930–1936), which undertook no less than a panorama of American society from 1900 to 1936. In its three parts—*The Forty-second Parallel, 1919,* and *The Big Money*—the sprawling story line served mainly as a device to place its eleven major characters at crucial junctures of the national experience. Three structural devices lent a special flavor to the book. One, the "Newsreel," presented a collage of newspaper stories and headlines, popular songs, and quotations from public figures to evoke a feeling of the times. The second, the "Camera Eye," gave brief impressionistic sketches of responses to the issues and scenes of the times. Third was the series of biographies of public figures such as Isadora Duncan, Robert La Follette, Thomas A. Edison, and many others. The trilogy ends by contrasting a hungry, dirty hitchhiker by a roadside to a wealthy, well-fed executive passing overhead on a transcontinental plane. The scene underscored the radical vision of the trilogy that America had become divided into "two nations." A lengthy flirtation with Communist causes in the 1920s and early 1930s ended in disillusionment at the Communists' use of violence against Socialist opponents who preferred democratic methods. After the mid-1930s his viewpoint moved away from Marxism and ever more toward affirmations of patriotism, but his creative powers never again equaled those which produced *U.S.A.*

The single piece of fiction that best captured the ordeal of the depression, John Steinbeck's *The Grapes of Wrath* (1939), was also the most memorable "proletarian" novel of the times because it escaped political formula to treat workers as people. Steinbeck had taken the trouble to travel with displaced "Okies" driven from the Oklahoma Dust Bowl by bankers and farm combines to pursue the illusion of jobs in the fields of California's Central Valley. The story focused on the Joad family as they made their painful journey from Oklahoma west along U.S. 66, enticed by job ads aimed really at producing a labor surplus and depressed wages. Met chiefly with contempt and rejection, caught up in labor agitations, Ma Joad strove to keep hope alive and at the end, even as the family was breaking up under the pressure, she grasped at a broader loyalty: "Use'ta be the fambly was fust. It ain't so now. It's anybody. Worse off we get, the more we got to do." The novel was more than a period piece about the depression. As one critic observed: "It is an allegory that is applicable wherever prejudice and a sense of self-importance inhibit co-operation."

Steinbeck produced a bountiful harvest of writing, most suc-

Migrant Mother, *photograph by Dorothea Lange, 1936. This care-worn but proud migrant mother appears the real-life counterpart to Steinbeck's Ma Joad. [Library of Congress, FSA Collection]*

cessfully when he dealt with his native California, as in "The Red Pony" (1933, 1938), the story of a boy's maturing through experience of the tragic nature of life, or *Tortilla Flat* (1935) and *Cannery Row* (1935), which celebrated the vagabond lives of the mixed-blood *paisanos* and dockside bums of Monterey. Fame arrived for Steinbeck with *In Dubious Battle* (1936), about a strike of fruit pickers exploited both by the bosses for profit and by their Communist leader for the sake of power, and with *Of Mice and Men* (1937), about the tragedy of two ranchhands. He continued writing into the 1960s, but *The Grapes of Wrath* remained his masterpiece.

Among black novelists the supreme genius was Richard Wright. Born on a plantation near Natchez, Mississippi, the son of a matriarch whose husband deserted the family, Wright grew up in the course of moving from town to town, ended his formal schooling with the ninth grade (as valedictorian of his class), worked in Memphis, and greedily devoured books he borrowed on a white friend's library card, all the while saving up to go north. In Chicago, where he arrived on the eve of the depression, the Federal Writers' Project gave him a chance to perfect his talent, and his period as a Communist from 1934 to 1944 gave him an intellectual framework, Marxism, which did not, however, overpower his fierce independence. His first book, *Uncle Tom's Children* (1938), a collection of four novellas, and his autobiographical *Black Boy* (1945) revealed in their very rebellion against racial injustice his ties to the South, for, he wrote, "there had been slowly instilled into my personality and consciousness, black though I was, the culture of the South."

Native Son (1940), Wright's masterpiece, was set in the Chicago he had come to know before moving on to New York. It was the story of Bigger Thomas, a product of the black ghetto, a man hemmed in and finally impelled to murder by forces beyond his control. "They wouldn't let me live and I killed," he said unrepentently at the end. Somehow Wright managed to sublimate into literary power his bitterness and rage at what he called "The Ethics of Living Jim Crow," an art he never quite mastered. In the black experience, he wrote, America had "a past tragic enough to appease the spiritual hunger of even a James; and . . . in the oppression of the Negro a shadow athwart our national life dense and heavy enough to satisfy even the gloomy broodings of a Hawthorne."

THE SOUTHERN RENAISSANCE   In different ways southern whites had shared that tragic past. Out of the memory and the consciousness of change the writers among them nurtured a renaissance that burgeoned into one of the most notable literary growths since the flowering of New England a century before. There was little reason to expect it in 1920 when H. L. Mencken published in his *Prejudices: Second Series* his essay "The Sahara of the Bozart," which described the southern cultural landscape as a barren wasteland: "One thinks of the interstellar spaces, of the colossal reaches of the now mythical ether. . . . It would be impossible in all history to match so complete a drying-up of civilization." Among the writers Mencken missed was Ellen Glasgow, of Richmond, Virginia, who in the Victorian twilight at the turn of the century had begun a lonely revolt against the "twin conventions of prudery and platitude" in her "Novels of the Commonwealth," a realistic social history of Virginia from the Civil War. *Barren Ground* (1925), about a heroic female figure of endurance, brought her recognition that was long overdue.

What Mencken's essay had also missed was that the South had reached a historical watershed, that it stood between two worlds: the dying world of tradition and the modern, commercial world struggling to be born. The resultant conflict of values, felt more intensely in the South than in the North, aroused the Ku Klux Klan and fundamentalist furies, but had quite another effect on the South's young writers. Allen Tate, a talented young poet, novelist, and critic, saw in the South the "curious burst of intelligence that you get at a crossing of the ways, not unlike, on an infinitesimal scale, the outburst of poetic genius at the end of the sixteenth century when commercial England began to crush feudal England."

That Mencken had touched a sensitive nerve was apparent from the frequent references to him in the literary groups and little magazines that sprang to life in his Sahara. The Poetry Society of South Carolina noted in its first *Year Book* (1921) that the desert had already sprouted oases where the fig trees were not entirely barren. In New Orleans *The Double Dealer* (1921–1926) became the focus of a literary bohemia which for a time included Sherwood Anderson and William Faulkner. In Nashville *The Fugitive: A Journal of Poetry* (1922–1925) announced the arrival of the most influential group in American letters since the New England transcendentalists.

The Fugitive poets began as a group of student intellectuals at Vanderbilt University who first gathered for discussions in 1915, then regrouped after the war with young Prof. John Crowe Ransom as their dean and mentor. Four of the group eventually stood out in their commitment to literature as a profession: Ransom, Donald Davidson, Allen Tate, and Robert Penn Warren. The Fugitives admired T. S. Eliot and were committed to the new doctrines of modernism in literature. They cultivated a style distinguished by attention to form and language, by complexity and allusion that yielded only to the closest study. They began in revolt against the twin images of southern sentimentalists and commercial boosters. *"The Fugitive,"* Ransom wrote, "flees from nothing faster than from the high-caste Brahmins of the Old South."

It dawned on them that they had protested too much, however, when reporters drawn to the Scopes trial vied with Mencken in mocking the Bible Belt and the benighted South. In reaction the Fugitives began to seek a usable past in the southern agrarian tradition. They brought others into the project, and their manifesto, *I'll Take My Stand* (1930), by twelve southerners, appeared fortuitously just when industrial capitalism seemed on the verge of collapse. In reaction against images of the New South and the Benighted South, the Vanderbilt agrarians championed, in Donald Davidson's words, a "traditional society . . . that is stable, religious, more rural than urban, and politically conservative," a society in which human needs were supplied by "Family, bloodkinship, clanship, folkways, custom, community. . . ." In the end their agrarianism proved less important as a social-economic force than as a context for creative literature. Yet their image of the agrarian South, as Louis Rubin later wrote, provided "a rich, complex metaphor through which they presented a critique of the modern world." Their critique of the frenzy of modernism "has since been echoed by commentator after commentator."

While agrarianism quickened a generation of southern writers with its vision of southern tradition beset by change, southern regionalism quickened a generation of social scientists with its vision of the "Problem South." The school of southern regionalism was based in the University of North Carolina at Chapel Hill and was led chiefly by the sociologists Howard W. Odum and Rupert B. Vance. They inspired no single manifesto but their most important works were Vance's *Human Geography of the South* (1932) and Odum's *Southern Regions of the United States* (1936). Odum proposed to overcome the divisiveness of traditional sectionalism by presenting regional diversity as a national strength. He explored the social problems plaguing the South, and argued that rational planning would aid the "Problem South" and develop its rich potential.

With remarkable speed after 1920 Mencken's cultural Sahara turned into a forest populated with nests of singing birds. "One may reasonably argue," wrote the critic Howard Mumford Jones in 1930, "that the South is the literary land of promise today." Just the previous year two vital figures had emerged: Thomas Wolfe, with *Look Homeward, Angel*, and William Faulkner, with *Sartoris* and *The Sound and the Fury.* Fame rushed in first on Wolfe and his native Asheville, North Carolina, which became in the last golden October of the 1920s a classic example of the scandalized community. "Against the Victorian morality and the Bourbon aristocracy of the South," Wolfe had "turned in all his fury," his former classmate, Jonathan Daniels, wrote. The reaction was not an uncommon response to the works of the southern renaissance, created by authors who had outgrown their hometowns and looked back from new perspectives acquired in travel and education.

For all his gargantuan lust for experience and knowledge, his demonic drive to escape the encircling hills for the "fabled" world outside, his agonized search for some "lost lane-end into heaven," Wolfe never completely severed his roots in the South. *Look Homeward, Angel*, his first novel, remained his most successful; it was the lyrical and searching biography of Eugene Gant's (actually Wolfe's) youth in Altamont (Asheville) and his college days in Pulpit Hill (Chapel Hill). It established him as "the giant among American writers of sensitive youth fiction." Three later books, two edited posthumously from a mountain of manuscript after his untimely death at age thirty-seven, traced his further wanderings as Eugene Gant in *Of Time and the River* (1935), and as George Webber in *The Web and the Rock* (1939) and *You Can't Go Home Again* (1940).

William Faulkner himself ranked Wolfe first among contemporary novelists because he "made the best failure. . . . My admiration for Wolfe is that he tried to get it all said; he was willing to throw away style, coherence, all the rules of preciseness, to try to put all the experience of the human heart on the head of a pin, as

William Faulkner. [University of Virginia]

it were." Faulkner's own achievement, more than Wolfe's, was rooted in the world that produced him. Born near Oxford, Lafayette County, Mississippi, he grew up there and transmuted his hometown into Jefferson, Yoknapatawpha County, in his fiction. After a brief stint with the Royal Canadian Air Force he passed the postwar decade in what seemed to fellow townsmen an aimless drifting. He briefly attended classes at the University of Mississippi, worked at odd jobs, and went to New Orleans where he wrote *Soldiers' Pay* (1926), a caricature of the New Orleans bohemians yachting on Lake Pontchartrain. Between books he shipped out briefly for Europe, and after knocking around the Gulf Coast, returned to Oxford.

There, in writing *Sartoris* (1929), he began to discover that his "own little postage stamp of native soil was worth writing about" and that he "would never live long enough to exhaust it." In this book a postwar wasteland stood out the more starkly against a legend of past glory in the Sartoris family. Young Bayard Sartoris, denied the romantic end that befell his twin brother, who had been shot down over France, pursued a kind of gallant death wish by automobile and airplane until he found release in a plane crash. With *Sartoris* and the creation of his mythical land of Yoknapatawpha, Faulkner kindled a blaze of creative energy. Next, as he put it, he wrote his gut into *The Sound and the Fury*, again the story of a demoralized family. It was one of the triumphs of the modernist style, but early readers, taking their cue from the title instead of the critics, found it signified nothing.

Faulkner's creative frenzy continued through the writing of *As I Lay Dying* (1930) and *Light in August* (1932). He began to fill in the early history of Yoknapatawpha with *Absalom! Absalom!* (1936), a story which unfolded slowly as Quentin Compson, in midnight conversations with his Canadian roommate at Harvard, attempted to reconstruct the story of Sutpen Hundred from bits and pieces of information he had picked up. The process, familiar to historians, was disconcerting to readers looking for the completed narrative. Faulkner rounded out further the history of Yoknapatawpha and the conflict between tradition and the modern world. *The Hamlet* (1940), *The Town* (1957), and *The Mansion* (1950) followed the rise of Flem Snopes and his myriad relatives, who lacked an ethical code and aimed to displace the old families who still clung to shopworn tradition.

Most critics at first missed what Faulkner was attempting. Some viewed him as an exemplar of what Ellen Glasgow called "Southern Gothic," the leader in a "cult of cruelty." Others found disturbing his obscurity, the slow unfolding of meaning, convoluted syntax, and runaway rhetoric of his novels. *Absalom! Absalom!*, one critic complained, used the "non-Stop or Life Sentence," a method of "Anti-Narrative, a set of complex devices used to keep the story from getting told." But that, of course, was Faulkner's point—to vary the usual strategies of rhetoric so that new insights overtook the reader by surprise. Not until the mid–twentieth century did critics generally begin to grasp that Faulkner, in composing his mythical history of Yoknapatawpha, had become also—certainly among Americans—the most skillful creator of modernist styles in the novel during the first half of the twentieth century.

DOCUMENTARY EXPRESSION IN THE THIRTIES   Somewhere between belles lettres and academic treatise fell a literature of social exploration and descriptive journalism that formed the southern expression of what Alfred Kazin called the "now innocent, now calculating, now purely rhetorical, but always significant experience in national self-discovery that occurred in the 1930s." The New Deal, through the Works Progress Administration's Federal Writers' Project, among other things contributed to the collection of a "vast granary of facts" in fifty-one state and territorial guidebooks, catalogs of archives, collections of folklore and folksongs, and even records of tombstone inscriptions. The Writers' Project pioneered in the oral history of the "inarticulate." In *These Are Our Lives* (1939), the Writers' Project in North Carolina, Tennessee, and Georgia gathered case histories of workers, sharecroppers, and Negroes in a form that Charles A. Beard called "literature more powerful than anything I have read in fiction, not excluding Zola's most vehement passages." *Lay My Burden Down* (1944) presented the life stories of former slaves as recorded by Writers' Project interviewers.

Two women at a convention of former slaves. The period saw Americans reflecting on their culture and history. [Library of Congress]

A new genre of documentary literature teamed social reporters with photographers: Erskine Caldwell and Margaret Bourke-White, *You Have Seen Their Faces* (1937) and *Say, Is This the USA?* (1941); Dorthea Lange and Paul S. Taylor, *An American Exodus* (1939); and James Agee and Walker Evans, *Let Us Now Praise Famous Men* (1941). The last of these, a sensitive and effective evocation of tenant life in Alabama, got little notice at the time but gradually came to be recognized as a unique masterpiece of documentation and art. Under the direction of Roy Stryker the Farm Security Administration built up an enormous photographic documentation of everyday life in America, making familiar in the credits such names as Dorothea Lange and Ben Shahn. Pare Lorenz pioneered the motion picture documentary in *The Plow That Broke the Plains* and *The River*.

In the 1930s America experienced what *Fortune* magazine called "a sort of cultural revolution," largely through the WPA projects in writing, arts, music, theater, and historical research. Americans learned that, like it or not, they had a culture and had had one all along—it had simply been overlooked. Now Americans tried to make up for lost time by tracking the culture down, recording, restoring, and celebrating it. They became intrigued with American art of all kinds, and particularly that least influenced by Europe: primitive, folk, or as it was called most often, "popular" art. American artists, such as Grant Wood and other regionalists, turned their attention to their homeland.

America's "cultural nationalism" in the 1930s would have been "thin and elitist" without the WPA, the historian William Stott wrote, but the "cultural revolution would have happened without the WPA arts projects or indeed any governmental impetus. Its causes—the Depression, America's isolation in a menacing world, the Russian and German examples—were more compelling than any Washington could legislate." And so the two decades of the 1920s and 1930s, times of unusually creative vitality, ended with Americans engaged in the rediscovery of America.

FURTHER READING

The standard surveys of the interwar period cover many of the trends discussed in the chapter. Start with William Leuchtenberg's *The Perils of Prosperity, 1914–1932* (1958).° Still appealing is Frederick Lewis Allen's longtime favorite, *Only Yesterday* (1931).° Allen covers some cultural developments for the 1930s in *Since Yesterday* (1939).° Also helpful are the chapters on the 1920s in Otis L. Graham, Jr.'s *The Great Campaigns: War and Reform in America, 1900–1928* (1971),° and George E. Mowry and Blaine Brownell's *The Urban Nation, 1920–1980* (1980).° The best single introduction to the culture of the 1920s is Loren Baritz's *The Culture of the Twenties* (1969).° A good accompaniment is Richard H. Pells's *Radical Visions and American Dreams: Culture and Social Thought in the Depression Years* (1973).°

Don S. Kirschner's *City and Country: Rural Responses to Urbanization in the 1920s* (1970) highlights many of the cultural tensions which plagued the decade, and John Higham's *Strangers in the Land: Patterns of American Nativism, 1860–1925* (1955),° handles immigration restrictions. For analysis of the more extreme nativist measures, see David Chalmers's *Hooded Americanism: The History of the Ku Klux Klan* (1965)° and Kenneth T. Jackson's *The Ku Klux Klan in the Cities, 1915–1930* (1967). Religious trends are handled in George M. Marsden's *Fundamentalism and American Culture* (1980) and Normal Furniss's *The Fundamentalist Controversy* (1954). Lawrence Levine's *Defender of the Faith: William Jennings Bryan, the Last Decade, 1915–1925* (1965), and Ray Ginger's *Six Days or Forever? Tennessee v. John Scopes* (1958)° cover the antievolution fight in Dayton, while Willard B. Gatewood's *Preachers, Pedagogues, and Politicians* (1966) examines the same controversy in North Carolina. Two contrasting views of prohibition are in Andrew Sinclair's *Prohibition: The Era of Excess* (1962)° and Norm Clark's *Deliver Us from Evil* (1976).° Humbert S. Nelli's *The Business of Crime* (1976) examines those who profited from bootlegging, including Al Capone, while Edward M. Morgan's *The Legacy of Sacco and Venzetti* (1948) chronicles the fate of those accused radicals.

Other social groups also receive scholarly treatment. For blacks, see Charles Kellogg's *NAACP* (1967), for his analysis of the pioneering court cases. Gilbert Osofsky's *Harlem: The Making of a Ghetto, 1890–1930*

°These books are available in paperback editions.

(1966),° Nathan J. Huggins's *Harlem Renaissance* (1972),° and Jervis Anderson's *This Was Harlem: A Cultural Portrait, 1900–1950* (1981),° cover the impact of the Great Migration. For political implications, see Theodore G. Vincent's *Black Power and the Garvey Movement* (1971) and Randall Burkett's *Garveyism as a Religious Movement* (1978). Also valuable are the relevant sections of James Bouchat's *Alley Life in Washington: Family, Community, Religion, and Folk Life in the City, 1850–1980* (1980).

The impact of transportation is gauged in John Roe's *The Road and the Car in American Life* (1971) and Reynold M. Wik's *Henry Ford and Grassroots America* (1973).° Stuart Erven looks at the effect of mass advertising in *Captains of Consciousness* (1976). Motion pictures are the subject of Robert Sklar's *Movie-Made America* (1975) and Larry May's *Screening out the Past* (1980).

Woman's suffrage is treated extensively in J. Stanley Lemon's *The Woman Citizen: Social Feminism in the 1920s* (1973) and Susan D. Becker's *The Origins of the Equal Rights Amendment: American Feminism between the Wars* (1981). Lois Banner's *American Beauty* (1983) and Elaine Tyler May's *Great Expectations: Marriage and Divorce in Post-Victorian America* (1980) trace changing attitudes about the role of women. Paula S. Fass's *The Damned and the Beautiful: American Youth in the 1920s* (1977)° traces the social attitudes of youth in general.

Much of the theoretical basis for the chapter's discussion of "modernism" comes from Daniel J. Singal's *The War Within: From Victorian to Modernist Thought in the South, 1919–1945* (1982).° Also valuable are Mortin G. White's *Social Thought in America: The Revolt against Formalism* (1957), Arthur A. Ekrich's *Ideologies and Utopias: The Impact of the New Deal on American Thought* (1969), and Edward A. Purcell, Jr.'s *The Crisis of Democratic Theory: Scientific Naturalism and the Problem of Values* (1973). A good introduction to the impact of Darwin is Cynthia E. Russett's *Darwin in America* (1976). For Einstein, see Cornelius Lanczos's *The Einstein Decade, 1905–1915* (1974). Nathan G. Hale, Jr.'s *Freud and America* (1971) examines the impact of psychoanalysis. For a critique of left-wing American thought, see William L. O'Neill's *A Better World: The Great Schism, Stalinism and American Intellectuals* (1982).

Alfred Kazin's *On Native Grounds* (1942)° is a good introduction to the literature of the period. Also valuable is Frederick J. Hoffman's *The Twenties: American Writing in the Postwar Decade* (1962). Studies on individual authors include Eugene Levy's *James Weldon Johnson* (1973),° Hendy D. Piper's *F. Scott Fitzgerald: A Critical Portrait* (1972), Carlos H. Baker's *Hemingway: The Writer as Artist* (1956),° Mark Schorer's *Sinclair Lewis* (1961), Cleanth Brooks's *William Faulkner: The Yoknapatawpha Country* (1963),° C. Hugh Holman's *The Loneliness at the Core: Studies in Thomas Wolfe* (1975), and Townsend Ludington's *John Dos Passos: A Twentieth Century Odyssey* (1980). For the influence of Mencken, see Fred C. Hobson's *Serpent in Eden: H. L. Mencken and the South* (1974).° Louis D. Rubin examines the Fugitives of Vanderbilt in *The Wary Fugitives* (1978).°

27

TO NORMALCY—AND BACK

Progressivism Dissolved and Transformed

The progressive coalition which had reelected Woodrow Wilson in 1916 proved to be a fragile, temporary thing, and by 1920 it had dissolved. It came apart because radicals and other opponents of the war grew disaffected with America's entrance into the conflict and by the war's aftermath, because organized labor was unhappy with the administration's unsympathetic attitude toward the strikes of 1919–1920, and because farmers of the Plains and West thought that wartime price controls had discriminated against them. Intellectuals and elements of the middle class also drifted away from their former support of progressivism. The intellectuals became disillusioned with democracy because of popular support for prohibition and the antievolution movements. The larger middle class became preoccupied with building a new business civilization "based not upon monopoly and restriction," in the words of the historian Arthur Link, "but upon a whole new set of business values—mass production and consumption, short hours and high wages, full employment, welfare capitalism." Progressivism's final triumphs at the national level were already pretty much foregone conclusions before the war's end: the Eighteenth Amendment, ratified in 1919, which imposed national prohibition, and the Nineteenth Amendment, ratified in 1920, which extended women's suffrage to the entire country.

Progressivism, however, did not disappear in the 1920s. Progressives dominated Congress during much of the decade even while the White House was in conservative hands. The progressive impulse for "good government" and public services remained strong, especially at the state and local levels, where movements for good roads, education, public health, and social welfare all gained momentum during the decade. The progressive impulse for reform, however, was transformed into the drive for moral righteousness and conformity animating the Ku Klux Klan and the fundamentalist movement. Prohibition, at first a direct outgrowth of the reform spirit, came to be increasingly associated with the narrow intolerance of the times.

"Normalcy"

HARDING'S ELECTION   Amid the postwar tumult another presidential season approached. The country was now weary of crusades and no leader was likely to sound the trumpet of reform. Wilson was ill, Theodore Roosevelt had died in 1919, and World War I had produced no military hero of presidential stature. Herbert Hoover, still in his mid-forties, came out of the war with a brilliant record as director of food policies and war relief, but he was not in the race. Even his party affiliation was unknown until, after sweeping the Democratic presidential preference primary in Michigan, he announced that he would refuse a Democratic nomination.

When the Republicans met in Chicago in June 1920 the Old Guard was ready to reclaim its heritage. The regulars found their man in Ohio's Sen. Warren Gamaliel Harding, who had set the tone of his campaign in May, when he told a Boston audience: "America's present need is not heroics, but healing; not nostrums, but normalcy; not revolution, but restoration; not agitation, but adjustment; not surgery, but serenity; not the dramatic, but the dispassionate; not experiment, but equipoise; not submergence in internationality, but sustainment in triumphant nationality." His speeches, said Wilson's treasury secretary, William G. McAdoo, were "an army of pompous phrases moving over the landscape in search of an idea."

Still, Harding caught the mood of the times, a longing for "normalcy" which was unfriendly to ideas. The Republican convention, as Harding's campaign manager, Harry Daugherty, had predicted, reached a deadlock which was broken when a group of tired men sat down in a "smoke filled room" and chose its candidate. Harding fit the bill because, though he might not set the pulses pounding, nobody was mad at him. He had all the classic attributes of availability. The vice-presidential choice fell on Calvin Coolidge, who had caught the public fancy with his pronouncement opposing the Boston Police Strike.

The Democrats met at San Francisco later in June in the first convention west of the Rockies. Their choice lay among three leading candidates: A. Mitchell Palmer, whose Red Scare had peaked too soon; William Gibbs McAdoo, Wilson's son-in-law, who was hobbled by Wilson's stubborn hope that the Democrats would again turn to him; and James Cox, former newsman and former governor of Ohio, who won the nomination on the forty-fourth ballot. For vice-president the convention named Franklin D. Roosevelt, who as assistant secretary of the navy occupied the same position his Republican cousin had held before him. Wilsonians tried to make the vote the "solemn referendum" their leader wanted, but the platform, while broadly endorsing the New Freedom, did not fully endorse the League of Nations. Cox waged an active campaign while the Republicans kept Harding home to conduct a front-porch campaign in the McKinley style —they even redid Harding's porch to look like McKinley's. The Republican platform was a masterpiece of evasion which pledged the party to "agreement among the nations to preserve the peace of the world" but "without the compromise of national independence." The phrasing satisfied both reservationists and irreconcilables. Harding himself scaled the clouded heights of obfuscation on the issue, denouncing Wilson's covenant but talking vaguely about a real "association of nations."

The issue was too foggy for a "solemn referendum." Besides, the Democrats' fate was sealed by the breakup of the Wilsonian coalition. In the words of William Allen White, Americans in 1920 were "tired of issues, sick at heart of ideals, and weary of being noble." Wilson therefore became the Republicans' target rather than Cox, who remained a nonentity, and the country voted overwhelmingly for a "return to normalcy." Harding got 16 million votes, about 61 percent of the total, to 9 million for Cox. Harding's electoral margin was 404 to 127. Cox carried no state outside the Solid South, even there losing Tennessee. In the minority again, the Democrats had returned to normalcy too.

EARLY APPOINTMENTS AND POLICY Harding in office had much in common with Ulysses Grant. His cabinet, like Grant's, mixed some of the "best minds" in the party, whom he had promised to seek out, with some of the worst, cronies who sought him out. Charles Evans Hughes, like Grant's Hamilton Fish, became a distinguished secretary of state. Herbert Hoover in the Commerce Department, Andrew W. Mellon in Treasury, and Henry A. Wallace in Agriculture were men who functioned efficiently and made policy on their own. Of the others, Secretary of the Interior Albert B. Fall landed in prison and Attorney-General Harry

M. Daugherty only narrowly escaped. Many lesser offices went to members of the soon notorious "Ohio Gang," headed by Daugherty, a group with which Harding met in a "Little House on H Street" to get away from the pressures of the White House.

Until he became president, politics had been a joy for Harding. He was the party hack par excellence, "bloviating" (a verb of his own making, which meant speaking with gaseous eloquence) on the stump, jollying it up in the clubhouse and cloakroom, hobnobbing with the great and near-great in Washington. As president, Harding was very simply in over his head, and self-doubt overwhelmed him. "I don't think I'm big enough for the Presidency," he confided to a friend. Woodrow Wilson had said once that it seemed impossible to get an explanation to lodge in Senator Harding's head, and President Harding later confessed as much to his secretary: "I don't know what to do or where to turn in this taxation matter. Somewhere there must be a book that tells all about it. . . . There must be a man in the country somewhere who could weigh both sides and know the truth. . . . But I don't know where to find him. . . . My God, this is a hell of a place for a man like me to be." How much better to get away with the "Ohio Gang," who shared his taste for whiskey, poker, and women. Alice Roosevelt Longworth, Theodore Roosevelt's oldest daughter, witnessed one poker session in the president's study. "Harding wasn't a bad man," she said later. "He was just a slob."

Harding and his friends set a pro-business tone such as had been absent from the White House since McKinley. Big business, whipping-boy of the progressives, had won respectability and acceptance by expanding production during the war and by

Warren Harding "bloviating" on the stump. [Ohio Historical Society]

building a New Era of prosperity after the postwar slump in 1921. Secretary of the Treasury Mellon pushed vigorously and persistently a Republican policy of economy and tax reduction. To get a better handle on expenditures he persuaded a lukewarm Congress to pass the Budget and Accounting Act of 1921, which embodied an idea advanced ten years before by Taft's Commission on Efficiency and Economy. The act created a new Bureau of the Budget, headed by a Chicago banker Charles G. Dawes, to prepare a unified budget, and a General Accounting Office, headed by a comptroller general to audit the accounts. General tax reductions from the wartime level seemed called for, but Mellon insisted that they should go mainly to the rich, on the Hamiltonian principle that wealth in the hands of the few would augment the general welfare through investment in gainful enterprise. Mellon's admirers tagged him "the greatest Secretary of the Treasury since Alexander Hamilton."

A group of western Republicans and southern Democrats fought a dogged battle to preserve the progressive principle built into wartime taxes, but Mellon, in office through the 1920s, eventually carried his points. In 1921 at his behest Congress repealed the wartime excess-profits tax, but balked at the request to lower the maximum rate on personal income from 65 to 32 percent that year and 25 percent thereafter. Instead the lawmakers held the maximum rate at 50 percent, and raised the corporate tax from 10 to $12\frac{1}{2}$ percent while granting some relief to lower income groups with higher exemptions for heads of family and dependents. Subsequent revenue acts lowered the maximum rate to 40 percent in 1924 and 20 percent in 1926. The act of 1926 extended further benefits to high-income groups by lowering estate taxes and repealing the gift tax. In the end, however, the progressive principle was at least in part retained, since the graduated tax was never rolled back to the prewar level of 7 percent. Unfortunately, much of the money released to wealthy people by these acts seems to have augmented the speculative excess of the late 1920s as much as it augmented gainful enterprise. Mellon, however, did balance the federal budget for a time. Governmental expenditures fell from $6.4 billion in 1920 to $3.4 billion in 1922, and to a low of $3 billion in 1927. The national debt went down from $25.5 billion in 1919 to $16.9 billion in 1929.

Mellon favored the time-honored Republican policy of high tariffs, and innovations in the chemical and metal industries revived the argument for protection of infant industries. The Emergency Tariff Act of 1921, which reflected a new protectionism in the depressed farm belts of the West, levied high duties on farm products but had little effect since few major cash crops competed with foreign goods in the home market. The Fordney-McCumber Tariff of 1922 increased rates severely on chemical and metal products as a safeguard against the revival of German industries which had previously commanded the field. In general it restored to industry the protection which had prevailed before the Underwood-Simmons Tariff of 1913. To please the farmers the new act further extended the duties on farm products.

Higher tariffs, however, had ramifications which had never prevailed before and which were not quickly perceived. During the war the United States had been transformed from a debtor to a creditor nation. In former years foreign capital had flowed into the United States, playing an important role in the economic expansion of the nineteenth century. But the private and public credits given the Allies during the war had reversed the pattern. Mellon insisted that the European powers must repay all that they had borrowed, and Coolidge is supposed to have said, "Well, they hired the money, didn't they?" Both, however, were unmindful that the tariff walls erected around the country made it all the harder for other nations to sell in the United States and thus acquire the dollars or credits with which to repay their war debts. For nearly a decade further extensions of American loans and investments sent more dollars abroad, postponing the reckoning.

Neither Harding nor his successor Coolidge could dissolve the regulatory agencies, but by naming commissioners who were less than sympathetic to regulation they rendered these agencies ineffective. Harding named conservative advocates of big business to the Interstate Commerce Commission, the Federal Reserve Board, and the Federal Trade Commission. In 1925 Coolidge made William E. Humprey, former congressman from Washington, chairman of the FTC. The commission, Humphrey asserted, would not be used "as a publicity bureau to spread socialistic propaganda." He and his colleagues, in a departure from Wilson's principle of "pitiless publicity," decided to withhold publicity on all cases until they were settled. While this was defensible, the commission also skirted the edge of legality in giving its support to agreements which allowed trade associations to avoid certain kinds of competition. Sometimes these included secret clauses forbidding price cutting. "Congress," said the chairman, ". . . satisfied its dogmatic tendencies by ordering all sorts of investigations—which come to nothing." Sen. George Norris characterized the new appointments as "the nullification of federal law by a process of boring from within."

Bargain Day in Washington. *The Harding administration, according to this cartoon, put the government up for sale. [Library of Congress]*

A CORRUPT ADMINISTRATION   These conservatives were at least operating out of conviction. The "Ohio Gang," however, used White House connections to line their own pockets. In 1923 Harding learned that Charles R. Forbes of the Veterans Bureau was systematically looting medical and hospital supplies. Forbes fled to Europe and resigned. His general counsel, Charles Cramer, committed suicide in Harding's old house in Washington. Not long afterward Jesse Smith, a close crony of Attorney-General Daugherty, also shot himself. Smith, who held no appointment, had set up an office in the Justice Department from which he peddled influence for a fee. Daugherty himself was implicated in the fraudulent handling of German assets seized after the war. When this was discovered, he refused to testify on the ground that he might incriminate himself. Twice brought to court, he was never indicted for want of evidence, possibly because he had destroyed pertinent records. These were but the most visible among many scandals that touched the Justice Department, the Prohibition Bureau, and other agencies under Harding.

But one major scandal rose above all these petty peculations. Teapot Dome, like the Watergate Apartments fifty years later, became the catchword for an epoch of corruption. An oil deposit under the sandstone Teapot Rock in Wyoming, Teapot Dome had been set aside as a naval reserve, along with the Elk Hills deposit in California. Early in Harding's term Navy Secretary Edwin N. Denby transferred them to the control of the Interior Department under Albert B. Fall. The move seemed at the time a sensible attempt to unify control over public reserves, and

Denby regarded it so. But once Fall had control, he signed contracts letting private interests exploit the deposits: Harry Sinclair's Mammoth Oil Company at Teapot Dome and Edward L. Doheny's Pan-American Petroleum and Transport Company at Elk Hills. Fall argued that these contracts were in the government's interest. It was harder for Fall to explain, however, why he acted in secret, without allowing competitive bids.

Suspicion grew when Fall's standard of living suddenly rose. It turned out that he had taken loans of about $100,000 (which came in "a little black bag") from Sinclair and $300,000 from Doheny. As the scandal unraveled, Fall emerged as a figure of tragic weakness. Once wealthy, he had lost extensive mine holdings in the Mexican Revolution, which left him with little more than an expensive dream ranch in New Mexico. Desperate for money, he took loans extended by two old friends—he and Doheny had once worked together in the mines. For the rest of his life Fall insisted that the loans were unrelated to the leases, and that he had contrived a good deal for the government, but at best the circumstances revealed a fatal blindness to his impropriety.

The question of bribery aside, his actions activated the hostility of conservationists. Fall, like Ballinger before him, had regarded conservation as the doctrine of easterners indifferent to jobs and development in the West. After Senator La Follette demanded a senatorial investigation, a committee under Thomas J. Walsh of Montana laid out the whole mess during 1924 to the accompaniment of public outrage.

Harding himself was spared the humiliation of public disgrace. How much he knew is still not clear, but he knew enough to become visibly troubled. "My God, this is a hell of a job!" he confided to the editor William Allen White. "I have no trouble with my enemies, I can take care of my enemies all right. But my damn friends, my God-damn friends, White, they're the ones that keep me walking the floor nights!" In June 1923 Harding left on what would be his last journey, a western speaking tour and a trip to Alaska. Sailing to Alaska, he fell into conversation with Commerce Secretary Herbert Hoover: "If you knew of a great scandal in our administration," he asked, "would you for the good of the country and the party expose it publicly or would you bury it?" Hoover replied quickly: "Publish it, and at least get credit for integrity on your side." But little time was left to Harding. Back in Seattle he fell ill with what was diagnosed first as ptomaine poisoning, but was actually a heart attack. He recovered briefly, then died in a San Francisco hotel of either coronary or cerebral thrombosis.

Not since the death of Lincoln had there been such an outpouring of grief for a "beloved President," for the kindly, ordinary man with the face of a Roman senator, the man who found it in his heart (as Wilson had not) to pardon Eugene Debs and receive him at the White House, and to pressure the steel magnates into giving up their barbarous seven-day week. As the black-streamered funeral train moved toward Washington, then back to Ohio, millions stood by the tracks to honor their lost leader. Eventually, however, grief yielded to scorn and contempt. For nearly a decade the revelations of scandal were paraded before committees and then courts. Harding's long affair with Nan Britton came to light, first the birth of their illegitimate child and later their pathetic couplings among the overshoes in a White House closet. Shortly before the centennial of his birth, Harding's love letters to another man's wife surfaced. For years his friends tried in vain to get his successors to dedicate to him a marble memorial in Marion, Ohio. Finally, in the spring of 1931 Herbert Hoover came to honor "a man whose soul was seared by a great disillusionment."

"SILENT CAL" Some kind of charmed existence seemed to put Calvin Coolidge in the right place at the right time. The news of Harding's death came when he was visiting his father in the mountain village of Plymouth, Vermont, his birthplace. There at 2:47 on the morning of August 3, 1923, by the light of a kerosene lamp, Col. John Coolidge administered the oath of office to his son in a commonplace room which doubled as living room and office. A day later the new president would have been visiting the baronial estate of Guy Currier at Peterboro. The atmosphere there might better have symbolized the era of business prosperity over which Coolidge would preside, but the rustic simplicity of Plymouth, the very name itself, evoked just the image of roots and solid integrity that the country would long for amid the coming disclosures of corruption. The new first lady, Grace Coolidge, was as unpretentious as her husband, and Alice Roosevelt Longworth found the new atmosphere of the White House "as different as a New England front parlor is from the back room in a speakeasy."

Americans took to their hearts the unflappability of "Silent Cal," his gargantuan midday naps, and the pictures of him fishing, pitching hay, and wearing Indian bonnets while primly clad in business suit and necktie. His taciturn nature became the subject of affectionate humor, often no doubt apocryphal, as in the story of a dinner guest who told Coolidge of a bet that she could make him say three words. "You lose," he replied. "Mr. Coo-

Calvin Coolidge dresses up for the photographers. [Brown Brothers]

lidge's genius for inactivity is developed to a very high point," the journalist Walter Lippmann wrote. "It is a grim, determined, alert inactivity, which keeps Mr. Coolidge occupied constantly." That too suited the mood of the country, which chuckled over the story of the president's awakening from his daily nap and slyly asking: "Is the country still there?" The Coolidge luck held out for the duration of his term. After him, and in at least some measure because of him, the luck of the whole nation ran out.

The change in the White House was more a matter of style than substance. Like Harding, Coolidge embraced the orthodox creed of business. "The business of America is business," he intoned. "The man who works there worships there." It was the business philosophy of the 1880s, absorbed at Amherst where he was taught to associate "the rich, the wise, and the good." At White House functions the rich nearly monopolized the guest lists.

THE 1924 ELECTION   Coolidge was also married to politics, and proved better at it than Harding. He distanced himself from the Harding scandals, and put in charge of the prosecutions two lawyers of undoubted integrity. Yet he kept Daugherty as attorney-general until growing evidence of Daugherty's complicity led to his removal in March 1924. In his place Coolidge named the former dean of the Columbia Law School, Harlan Fiske Stone, once a fellow student at Amherst. Coolidge quietly took control of the Republican party machinery and seized the initiative in the campaign for nomination, which he won with only token opposition. For vice-president the convention chose Charles G.

Dawes, former director of the budget, now fresh from a successful settlement of the German reparations issue.

The Coolidge luck held as the Democrats fell victim to internal dissensions. The source of the party's trouble was its uneasy alliance of incongruous elements which lent much truth to Will Rogers's classic statement: "I am a member of no organized political party. I am a Democrat." A deep alienation was growing up between the metropolis of the Roaring Twenties and the more traditional hinterland, a gap that the Democratic party could not bridge.

The rival candidacies of William Gibbs McAdoo and Alfred E. Smith magnified the divisions in the party. A spate of Republican scandals should have helped a progressive Democrat, but McAdoo, who as a lawyer had represented Edward L. Doheny, was tainted. Oscar Underwood of Alabama, hoping to benefit from party divisions, urged the Democrats to revive a plank from the 1856 platform that had condemned Know-Nothing bigotry. By convention time all the major candidates supported the plank, but the Underwood and Smith forces made the issue one of condemning the Ku Klux Klan by name, a move defeated on a very close vote. The quarrel over this led to the symbolic spectacle of the aging William Jennings Bryan goaded and heckled by Tammany gallants in the galleries of Madison Square Garden. McAdoo and Smith canceled each other out, and it took 103 ballots to bestow the tarnished nomination on John W. Davis, a Wall Street lawyer from West Virginia who could hardly outdo Coolidge in conservatism. For a token balance the convention chose Nebraska Gov. Charles W. Bryan, brother of William Jennings, as its vice-presidential nominee.

Meanwhile a new farmer-labor coalition was mobilizing a third-party effort. In 1922 the railroad unions, smarting from administration opposition, sponsored a Conference for Progressive Political Action which got the support of many farmers who were suffering from price declines at the time. Active on a nonpartisan basis, in 1922 the group had helped defeat a number of Old Guard Republicans. In Minnesota a new Farmer-Labor party during 1922 and 1923 elected two United States senators, a congressman, and some lesser officeholders. Meeting in Cleveland on July 4, 1924, the conference reorganized as the Progressive party and nominated Robert M. La Follette for president and Sen. Burton K. Wheeler (Mont.) for vice-president. La Follette also won the support of Minnesota's Farmer-Labor party, the Socialist party, and the American Federation of Labor.

In the campaign Coolidge chose to focus on La Follette, whom he called a dangerous radical who would turn America into a "communistic and socialistic state." The country preferred to "keep cool with Coolidge," who swept both the popular and electoral votes by decisive majorities. Davis took only the Solid South, and La Follette carried only his native Wisconsin. The popular vote went 15.7 million for Coolidge, 8.4 million for Davis, and 4.8 million for La Follette—the largest popular vote ever polled by a third-party candidate. The electoral result was 382 to 136 to 13.

THE NEW ERA

Businessmen interpreted the Coolidge victory as a vindication of their leadership, and Coolidge saw in the surging prosperity of the time a confirmation of his philosophy. In fact the prosperity and technological achievements of the time had much to do with Coolidge's victory over the Democrats and Progressives. Those in the large middle class who before had formed an important part of the Progressive coalition were now absorbed instead in the new world created by advances in communications, transportation, and business organization.

The gross national product had reached a peak of $88.9 billion in 1920; after a slump to $74 billion in 1921 and 1922, the GNP grew steadily to $104.4 billion in 1929. Per-capita income went from $672 in 1922 to $857 in 1929. A larger public than ever before had the money and leisure to taste of the affluent society, and a growing advertising industry fueled its appetites. By the mid-1920s advertising had grown into both a major industry, with a volume of $3.5 billion, and a major institution of social control. Oldtime values of thrift and saving gave way to a new economic ethic which made spending a virtue. The innovation of installment buying made increased consumption feasible for many.

MOVIES, RADIO, AND THE ECONOMY Consumer-goods industries fueled much of the boom from 1922 to 1929. Moderately priced creature comforts, including such items as hand cameras, wristwatches, cigarette lighters, vacuum cleaners, washing machines, and linoleum, became increasingly available. Inventions in communications and transportation, such as motion pictures, radio, telephones, and automobiles, not only fueled the boom but brought transformations in society.

In the 1890s a quick sequence of inventions had made it possible for a New York audience to see the first picture show in 1896. The first full-length story depicted in a movie was *The Great Train Robbery* in 1903. By 1905 the first movie house opened in Philadelphia, and within three years there were nearly 10,000. By the teens Hollywood had become the center of movie production, grinding out serials, features, westerns, and the timeless two-reel comedies of Mack Sennett's Keystone Studios, where a raft of slapstick comedians, most notably Charlie Chaplin, perfected their art into a form of social criticism. The twelve-reel *Birth of a Nation,* directed in 1915 by D. W. Griffith, became a triumph of cinematic art which marked the arrival of the modern motion picture and at the same time perpetuated a grossly distorted image of Reconstruction. Based on Thomas Dixon's novel *The Clansman,* the movie was replete with stereotypes of villainous Radicals, sinister mulattoes, blameless southerners, and faithful "darkies." The film grossed $18 million and revealed the industry's enormous potential. By the mid-1930s every large American city and most small towns had theaters, and movies replaced oratory as the chief mass entertainment of Americans. A further advancement in technology came with the "talkies." The first movie with sound accompaniment was Warner Brothers' *Don Juan* (1926), but the success of talking pictures was established by Warners' *The Jazz Singer* (1927), starring Al Jolson.

Charlie Chaplin in The Kid, *1921. [Museum of Modern Art / Film Stills Archive]*

A farm family gathered around the radio, Hood River County, Oregon, July 1925. [National Archives]

Radio broadcasting had an even more spectacular growth. Except for experimental broadcasts, radio served only the function of communication until 1920. In August of that year WWJ in Detroit began transmitting news bulletins from the Detroit *Daily News*, and in November KDKA in Pittsburgh, owned by the Westinghouse Company, began regular programs. The first radio commercial was aired by WEAF in New York, in 1922. By the end of that year there were 508 stations and some 3 million receivers in action. In 1926 the National Broadcasting Company, a subsidiary of RCA, began linking stations into a network; the Columbia Broadcasting System entered the field the next year. In 1927 a Federal Radio Commission was established to regulate the industry; in 1934 it became the Federal Communications Commission, with authority over other forms of communication as well.

AIRPLANES, AUTOMOBILES, AND THE ECONOMY   Advances in transportation were startling in this period. Wilbur and Orville Wright of Dayton, Ohio, built and flew the first airplane at Kitty Hawk, North Carolina, on December 17, 1903, but the use of planes advanced slowly until the outbreak of war in 1914, after which the Europeans rapidly developed the plane as a military weapon. When the United States entered the war it still had no combat planes—American pilots did battle in craft of British or French make. An American aircraft industry developed during the war but foundered in the postwar demobilization. Under the

Orville Wright pilots the first flight of a power-driven airplane, while Wilbur runs alongside. [National Archives]

Kelly Act of 1925, however, the government began to subsidize the industry through airmail contracts. This encouragement was greatly strengthened by the Air Commerce Act of 1926, which started a program of federal aid to air transport and navigation, including aid in establishing airports.

A psychological boost to aviation came in May 1927 with the solo flight of Charles A. Lindbergh, Jr., from New York to Paris in thirty-three hours and thirty minutes. The drama of the deed, which won him a prize of $25,000, was heightened by the fact that he was flying blind through a fog for part of the way and at times dropped to within ten feet of the water before sighting the Irish coast and regaining his bearings. The parade down Broadway in his honor surpassed even the celebration of the Armistice. The New York City Department of Sanitation estimated that 1,800 tons of ticker tape and shredded paper fell on Lindbergh's parade while only 155 tons showered the Armistice celebration.

By 1930 the industry had forty-three airlines which carried 385,000 passengers over routes of 30,000 miles. Another great impetus came after 1936 when the slow Ford trimotor plane was displaced by the more efficient twin-engine Douglas DC-3 as the chief carrier. In 1940, nineteen airlines carried 2.8 million passengers over routes of 43,000 miles.

By far the most significant development of the time, economic and social, was the automobile. The first motor car had been manufactured for sale in 1895, but in 1900 the census did not even give the industry a separate listing. The founding of the Ford Motor Company in 1903 revolutionized the industry. Ford's reliable Model T (the celebrated "tin lizzie") came out in 1908 at a price of $850 (in 1924 it would sell for $290). In 1916 for the first time the number of cars manufactured passed 1 million; by 1920 more than 8 million were registered, and in 1929 more than 23 million. The production of automobiles consumed large parts of the nation's steel, rubber, glass, and textile output, among other materials. It gave rise to a gigantic market for oil products just as the Spindletop gusher (1901) in Texas heralded the opening of vast southwestern oilfields. It quickened the movement for good roads, financed in large part from a gasoline tax, speeded transportation, encouraged the sprawl of suburbs, and sparked real-estate booms in California and Florida. The car provided liberation for "flaming youth."

The good-roads movement became the automobile-age equivalent of the nineteenth-century railroad movement. Through it the automobile industry received indirect subsidies greater than all government aid to railroads, which had now begun their decline. Road building ranked first or second in state budgets by the end of the 1920s, and the legislative lobbies of road builders and truckers supplanted those of the railroads in influence.

By virtue of its size and importance the automobile industry became the salient example of mass production. When Ford brought out the Model T in 1908, demand ran far ahead of production. Ford and his partner James Couzens then called in a factory expert named Walter E. Flanders as a production manager. By rearranging the plant and putting in new equipment, Flanders met his goal of producing 10,000 cars in twelve months (with two days to spare), earning his bonus of $20,000. The next year Ford's new Highland Park plant was planned with job analysis in mind. In 1910 gravity slides were installed to move parts

Ford Motor Company's Highland Park Plant, 1913. Gravity slides and chain conveyors aided the mass production of automobiles.
[The Henry Ford Museum]

from one workbench to the next, and by the end of 1913 the system was complete, with endless chain conveyors pulling the parts along feeder lines and the chassis down the final-assembly line.

Flanders, the creator of this modern miracle, was in turn a disciple of Frederick W. Taylor (1856–1915), the original "efficiency expert." In the 1880s, working as a foreman for the Midvale Steel Company, Taylor decided that the prevailing practice of having foremen pressure workers for greater output merely resulted in conflict: "Throughout American industry, management's concept of a proper day's work was what the foreman could drive workers to do and the workers' conception was how little they could do and hold their jobs." By the 1890s Taylor's ideas had drawn attention and he had set up shop as a consulting engineer in Philadelphia. In 1895 he outlined his ideas in a paper, "A Piece Rate System," read to the American Society of Mechanical Engineers. The basic principle was to use the carrot instead of the stick, to determine the maximum speed at which work could be done and then offer the incentive of higher piece rates to workers who could attain larger output. His book *The Principles of Scientific Management* (1911) summed up his ideas, which stressed proper organization, improvement of factory arrangement, the use of standardized tools and equipment, proper routing and scheduling of work, and the development of planning departments. "Taylorization" caught on widely in the business world and efficiency experts became a normal part of the business scene. Labor tended to view them with skepticism, and in some cases careless or deliberate planning resulted only in ruthless speedups and more of the conflict that Taylor himself deplored. In the 1920s southern textile workers took to calling such bastard efficiency programs the "stretchout."

STABILIZING THE ECONOMY   The drive for efficiency manifest once in the progressive impulse was now powering the wheels of mass production and consumption, and had become a cardinal belief of Republican leaders. Herbert Hoover, who served as secretary of commerce through the Harding-Coolidge years, was himself an engineer who had made a fortune in far-flung mining operations in Australia, China, Russia, and elsewhere. Out of his experiences in business and his management of Belgian relief, the Food Administration, and other wartime activities, Hoover had developed a philosophy which he set forth in his book *American Individualism* (1922). The idea might best be called "cooperative individualism," or in one of his favorite terms, "associationalism." The principle also owed something to his Quaker upbringing, which taught him the Friends' combination of the work ethic and mutual help. When he applied it to the relations of government and business, Hoover prescribed a kind of middle way between the regulatory and trust-busting traditions, a way of voluntary cooperation.

As secretary of commerce, Hoover was a human dynamo who made the trifling Commerce Department into the most dynamic agency of two listless administrations. During a period of governmental retrenchment he was engaged in expansion. Through an enlarged Bureau of Foreign and Domestic Commerce he sought out new opportunities and markets for business. A Division of Simplified Practice in the Bureau of Standards sponsored more than a thousand conferences on design, production, and distribution, and carried forward the wartime move toward standardization of everything from automobile tires and paving bricks to bedsprings and toilet paper, and reduced in number the different kinds of bolts, nuts, and screws. "When I go to ride in an automobile," Hoover told the author Sherwood Anderson, "it does not matter to me that there are a million automobiles on the road just like mine. I am going somewhere and I want to get there in what comfort I can and at the lowest cost." In 1926 Hoover created a Bureau of Aviation and the next year set out to bring order into the new field of radio with the Federal Radio Commission.

Through conferences and organized public relations, techniques that he had used as food administrator, Hoover promoted his ideas. Most of all he endorsed the burgeoning trade-association movement. The organization of trade associations in business became his favorite instrument for "stabilization" to avoid the waste inherent in competition. Through such associations businessmen in a given field would gather and disseminate information on everything: sales, purchases, shipments, production, and prices. This information allowed them to lay plans with more confidence, the advantages of which included predictable costs, prices, and markets, as well as more stable employment and wages. Sometimes abuses crept in as trade associations skirted the edge of legality by price-fixing and other monopoly practices, but the Supreme Court in 1925 held the practice of sharing information as such to be within the law.

As to the great business combinations themselves, the Supreme Court held to the "rule of reason" it had pronounced in dissolving the Standard Oil Company in 1911. In 1920 the Court found the United States Steel Company an acceptable combination under that rule. After that, wrote two constitutional historians, "almost any monopoly could put up a plausible argument for its social responsibility and thus claim to be a 'reasonable' combination."

THE BUSINESS OF FARMING Agriculture remained a weak point in the economy, in many ways as weak as its position in the 1890s, when cities flourished and agriculture languished. Briefly after the war the farmers' hopes soared on wings of prosperity. The wartime boom lasted into 1920, and then prices collapsed. Wheat went in eighteen months from $2.50 a bushel to less than $1; cotton from 35¢ per pound to 13¢. Low prices persisted into 1923, especially in the wheat and corn belts, and after that improvement was spotty. A bumper cotton crop in 1926 resulted only in a price collapse and an early taste of depression in much of the South, where foreclosures and bankruptcies spread.

Yet in many ways farmers shared the business outlook of the New Era. Farms, like corporations, were getting larger, more efficient, and more mechanized. By 1930 about 13 percent of all farmers had tractors, and the proportion was even higher on the western Plains. After 1925 the introduction of the smaller Farmall tractor encouraged greater use of the machine on the smaller farms and hilly lands of the Southeast. Better plows, drills, cultivators, planters, and other machines were part of the mechanization process which accompanied improved crops, fertilizers, and animal breeding.

Farm organizations of the 1920s moved away from the alliance with urban labor that marked the Populist era and toward a new view of farmers as businessmen. During the postwar farm depression the idea of marketing cooperatives became the farmer's equivalent of the businessman's trade-association movement. The great promoter of the cooperative movement was a young spellbinder, Aaron Sapiro, a California lawyer who had risen from poverty to success as organizer of marketing associations in raisins, eggs, and other specialties. Much in demand as a speaker in the early 1920s, he infected farm groups with his own zeal for regional commodity-marketing associations; ironclad contracts with producers ("horse-high, bull-strong, and pig-tight") to deliver their crops over a period of years; and "orderly marketing," which required standards and grades, efficient handling and advertising, and a businesslike setup with professional technicians and executives. His program, Sapiro said, "turned the interest of the average farmer from a wild sort of indefinite political hankering to some real intelligent attention to the economic phases of his problem."

While industry boomed, agriculture remained weak in the 1920s. [Library of Congress]

Among the various farm groups, one did carry into the twentieth century the oldtime gospel of Populism. The Farmers' Union, founded in Texas in 1902 by former Allianceman Newt Gresham, had a mercurial growth in the Southeast much like the Alliance's, but emerged in the 1920s mainly as a western wheatbelt group. It was soon overshadowed by the American Farm Bureau Federation, a new group representing the "businesslike" attitude of commercial agriculture in the New Era. Founded in 1920 at a meeting in Chicago, the Farm Bureau was an unexpected outgrowth of the farm demonstration movement. It grew from committees (usually called "bureaus") formed to support county agents and from state federations of those committees. Its philosophy stemmed in part from association with business leaders who supported the bureaus, but in larger part from the predominance of the larger commercial farmers in its membership, a situation that in turn reflected the county agents' practice of working with the more successful farmers in order to make a better showing in their demonstrations. Farm Bureau strength in the Midwest and South represented what by the 1920s was being called a "marriage of cotton and corn."

But if concern with marketing co-ops and other businesslike approaches drew farmers ever farther away from Populism, it was still inevitable that farm problems should invite political solutions. The most effective political response to the crisis of the early 1920s was the formation of the Farm Bloc, a coalition of western Republicans and southern Democrats that put through an impressive, if fairly moderate, program of legislation over a period of three years. The Farm Bloc originated in 1921 in the office of Gray Silver, Washington agent of the Farm Bureau, and eventually mustered some twenty-five senators and about a hundred representatives, led by Arthur Capper of Kansas and L. J. Dickinson of Iowa respectively.

From 1921 to 1923 the Farm Bloc added important legislative achievements to the agrarian program of the Wilson period. It supported a three-year extension of the War Finance Corporation to assist cooperative, storage, and export operations. It pushed passage of the Packers and Stockyards Act (1921) and the Capper-Tincher Grain Futures Act (1922) which sought to prevent collusion designed to keep farm prices down. In addition the Capper-Volstead Cooperative Marketing Act (1922) exempted farm cooperatives from antitrust laws, and the Intermediate Credit Act (1923) set up twelve intermediate credit banks on the model of the Federal Land Banks. The new banks filled the gap of six months to three years between the terms of short-term loans under the Federal Reserve System and long-term loans by the Land Banks, and could lend to cooperative producing and marketing associations.

Meanwhile a new panacea appeared on the horizon. In the spring of 1924 Sen. Charles L. McNary of Oregon and Rep. Gilbert N. Haugen of Iowa introduced the first McNary-Haugen bill. The bill embodied a plan worked out by George N. Peek and Hugh S. Johnson, both of the Moline Plow Company, to secure "equality for agriculture in the benefits of the protective tariff." Complex as it would have been in operation, it was simple in conception: in short, a plan to dump surpluses on the world market in order to raise prices in the home market. The goal was to achieve "parity"—that is, to raise domestic farm prices to a point where they would have the same purchasing power relative to other prices they had had between 1909 and 1914, a time viewed in retrospect as a golden age of American agriculture.

The first bill failed of passage in 1924, but a McNary-Haugen bill passed both houses of Congress in 1927, only to be vetoed by President Coolidge. The process was repeated in 1928. Coolidge pronounced the measure an unsound effort at price-fixing, un-American and unconstitutional to boot. In a broader sense, however, McNary-Haugenism did not fail. The debates made the farm problem into an issue of national policy and defined it as a problem of surpluses. The evolution of the McNary-Haugen plan, moreover, revived the idea of an alliance between the South and West, a coalition which became in the next decade a dominant influence on national farm policy. That policy would follow a different procedure, but its chief focus would be on surpluses, its goal would be "parity," and George N. Peek would preside over its management.

SETBACKS FOR UNIONS   Urban workers shared more than farmers in the affluence of the times. Annual per-capita earnings rose between 1921 and 1928 from an average of $1,171 to $1,408. Without a matching rise in living cost, this meant a gain of about 20 percent in real wages. The benefits of this rise, however, were distributed unevenly. Miners and textile workers suffered a decline in real wages. In these and other trades technological unemployment followed the introduction of new methods and machines, although technology created as well as destroyed jobs. "A workman is far better paid in America than anywhere else in the world," French visitor Andrae Siegfried wrote in 1927, "and his standard of living is enormously higher. The difference, which was noticeable before the War, has been greatly accentuated since, and is now the chief contrast between the old and the new continents. . . ."

Organized labor, however, did no better than organized agriculture in the 1920s. In fact unions suffered a setback after the growth years of the war. The Red Scare and strikes of 1919 left the uneasy impression that unions and subversion were linked, an idea which the enemies of unions promoted. The brief postwar depression of 1921 further weakened the unions, and they felt the severe impact of open-shop associations which proliferated across the country after the war, led by chambers of commerce and other business groups. In January 1921 the local groups came together at a meeting in Chicago where the open shop was officially designated the "American Plan" of employment. While the open shop in theory implied only the employer's right to hire whom he pleased, in practice it meant discrimination against unionists and refusal to recognize unions even in shops where most of the workers belonged.

Nor were employers always above the use of strong-arm methods, such as requiring "yellow-dog" contracts which forced workers to agree to stay out of unions, using labor spies, exchanging blacklists, and resorting to intimidation and coercion. Some employers tried to kill the unions with kindness. They introduced programs of "industrial democracy" guided by company unions or various schemes of "welfare capitalism" such as profit-sharing, bonuses, pensions, health programs, recreational activities, and the like. The benefits of such programs were often very real.

The mood of the times generally impelled governments as well as business into hostility toward unions. When in 1914 the Clayton Anti-Trust Act pronounced labor not an item of commerce, it was hailed as "Labor's Magna Charta." But this turned out to make little difference in the courts' willingness to issue labor injunctions. During the 1920s the high court ruled that the act might limit injunctions against individual workers, but not against certain union activities. In *Duplex Printing Press Company v. Deering* (1921) the court upheld an injunction against a secondary boycott (a boycott of one company's product by another company). A more telling blow was struck by an injunction against the railway shopmen's strike of 1922. The Railway Labor Board in 1920 had approved a postwar wage cut of 12 percent; when it approved another such cut two years later, the shopmen walked out. On September 1, 1922, Attorney-General Daugherty secured a sweeping injunction against picketing, strike meetings, statements to the public, expenditure of union funds for strike purposes, or the use of any means of communication by union leaders. "So long as I can speak for the government of the United States," said Daugherty, "I will use the power of the government . . . to prevent the labor unions of the country from destroying the open shop." The strike collapsed under the impact of the injunction, and while the union got contracts from friendly railroads for about 225,000 workers, some 175,000 were forced into company unions.

The combined result of prosperity, propaganda, welfare capitalism, and active hostility was a decline in union membership from about 5 million in 1920 to 3.5 million in 1929. In 1924 Samuel Gompers, founder and longtime president of the AFL, died; William Green of the mine workers, who took his place, embodied the conservative, even timid, attitude of unions during the period. The one outstanding exception to the anti-union policies of the decade was passage of the Railway Labor Act in 1926, which abolished the Railway Labor Board and substituted a new Board of Mediation. The act also provided for the formation of railway unions "without interference, influence, or coercion," a statement of policy not extended to other workers until the 1930s.

President Hoover, the Engineer

HOOVER VS. SMITH On August 2, 1927, while on vacation in the Black Hills of South Dakota, President Coolidge passed out to reporters slips of paper with the statement: "I do not choose to run for President in 1928." Exactly what he meant puzzled observers then and has since. Apparently he at least half hoped for a convention draft, but his statement cleared the way for Herbert Hoover to mount an active campaign. Well before the June Re-

Herbert Hoover on the campaign trail in 1928. [Library of Congress]

publican convention in Kansas City, Hoover was too far in the lead to be stopped by a clutch of favorite sons. For vice-president the party named one of the faithful, Sen. Charles Curtis of Kansas. The platform took credit for prosperity, economy ("raised to a principle of government"), debt and tax reduction, and the protective tariff ("as vital to American agriculture as it is to manufacturing"). It rejected the McNary-Haugen program, but promised a farm board to promote orderly marketing as a way to manage surpluses.

The Democratic nomination was as quickly decided in Houston later in June. Gov. Alfred E. Smith of New York, pronounced the "Happy Warrior" in Franklin D. Roosevelt's nominating speech, faced no effective opposition. The Democrats balanced their ticket by naming Sen. Joseph T. Robinson of Arkansas for vice-president. Their farm plank, while not endorsing McNary-Haugen, did pledge "economic equality of agriculture with other industries." Like the Republicans, the Democrats pledged enforcement of the Volstead Prohibition Act, and aside from calling for stricter regulation of waterpower resources, promised nothing that departed from the conservative position of the Republicans.

The Democratic party had had its fill of factionalism in 1924, and all remained fairly harmonious until the Happy Warrior gave the occasion, if not the cause, for revolt by stating in his acceptance speech a personal desire to liberalize the Volstead Act, and then by selecting for national party chairman John J. Raskob, who was Catholic, wet, a General Motors executive, and at least until recently a Republican. Hoover by contrast had pronounced prohibition "a great social and economic experiment, noble in motive and far-reaching in purpose," and called for a study of enforcement. The two candidates projected sharply different images which obscured the essential likeness of their programs. Hoover was the Quaker son of middle America, the successful businessman, the architect of Republican prosperity, while Smith was the prototype of those things rural–small-town America distrusted: the son of Irish immigrants, Catholic, wet, and a Tammanyite whose East Side twang as he spoke on the "raddio" offended the ears of the hinterland. Outside the large cities all those things were handicaps he could scarcely surmount for all his affability and wit.

In the election Hoover won in the third consecutive Republican landslide, with 21 million popular votes to Smith's 15 million, and an even more top-heavy electoral majority of 444 to 87. Hoover even cracked the Solid South, leaving Smith only a hard core of six Deep South states plus Massachusetts and Rhode Island. The election was above all a vindication of Republican prosperity. As the historian William Leuchtenburg wrote: "If Smith had been Protestant, dry, and born in a log cabin of good yeoman stock, he would still have been defeated." But the shattering defeat of the Democrats concealed a portentous realignment in the making. Smith had nearly doubled the vote for Davis, the Democratic candidate of four years before. Smith's image, though a handicap in the hinterlands, swung big cities back into the Democratic column. In the farm states of the West there were signs that some disgruntled farmers had switched over to the Democrats. A coalition of urban workers and unhappy farmers was in the making.

HOOVER IN CONTROL The year 1929, a fateful milestone in history, dawned with high hopes. Business seemed good, incomes were rising, and the chief author of Republican prosperity was about to enter the White House. "I have no fears for the future of our country," Hoover told the audience at his inauguration. "It is bright with hope." For Hoover the presidency crowned a career of steady ascent, first in mining, then in public service. Hoover's image combined the benevolence fitting for a director of wartime relief and the efficiency of a businessman and administrator. More than most presidents, he had articulated a philosophy of public affairs, to which in his last speech of the 1928 campaign he gave the misleading tag of "rugged individualism." But since he found initiative and enterprise best served by "orderly liberty" and by cooperation, his notion of individualism was less rugged than the slogan suggested.

Hoover approached his new duties much as he might have set about reshaping a mining venture during his days as a consulting engineer. He assigned specific duties to each member of the staff. He promoted voluntary cooperation through "publicity conferences," much as he had done at the Commerce Department. His passion for facts and figures resulted in several major studies of American life at the time: by the Wickersham Commission on Crime and Law Enforcement, and by the Committees on Recent Social Trends, on Recent Economic Change, and on Child Health and Protection—the last a lifetime concern of a man who had himself been orphaned.

Forgotten in the rush of later events would be Hoover's credentials as progressive and humanitarian. Over the objection of Treasury Secretary Mellon, he ordered that publicity be given to large refunds on income, estate, and gift taxes, and announced a plan for tax reductions in the low-income brackets. He took action against corrupt patronage practices, and refused to countenance "red hunts" or interference with peaceful picketing of the White House. He defended his wife's right to entertain the wife of Oscar DePriest, the first black congressman since 1901 and the first ever from the North, sought more money for all-black Howard University, and proposed that the new federal parole board reflect the number of blacks and women in prison. He went along, however, with his party's "lily-white" strategy of ignoring or excluding blacks in most southern states.

His program to stabilize business carried over into his program for agriculture, the most visibly weak sector of the economy. To treat the malady of glutted markets he had two main remedies: federal help for cooperative marketing and higher tariffs on farm products. He pushed through a special session of Congress in June 1929 the Agricultural Marketing Act, which gave support to farm cooperatives by setting up a Federal Farm Board of nine members with a revolving loan fund of $500 million to help cooperatives market the major commodities. The act provided also, at the demand of the farm bloc, a program in which the Farm Board could set up "stabilization corporations" empowered to buy surpluses off the market. Unluckily for any chance of success the plan might have had, it got under way almost simultaneously with the onset of the depression that fall.

Farmers gained even less from tariff revision. What Hoover got after fourteen months of struggle with competing local interest was a general upward revision on manufactures as well as farm goods. The Hawley-Smoot Tariff of June 1930 carried duties to an all-time high. Average *ad valorem* rates went from about 32 to 40 percent, but on actual dutiable imports the average rate was 52.8 percent for the years 1930–1933. Rates went up on some 70 farm products and more than 900 manufactured items. More than 1,000 economists petitioned Hoover to veto the bill

because, they said, it would raise prices to consumers, damage
the export trade, and thus hurt farmers, promote inefficiency,
and provoke foreign reprisals. Events proved them right, but Hoover felt that he had to go along with his party in an election year.

THE ECONOMY OUT OF CONTROL   The tariff did nothing to check a
deepening crisis of confidence in the economy. After the slump
of 1921 the idea grew that with recovery business had entered a
New Era of permanent growth. But real growth propelled an expansive ballyhoo, and a growing contagion of get-rich-quick
schemes. Speculative mania fueled the Florida real-estate boom
which got under way when the combination of Coolidge prosperity and Ford's "tin lizzies" gave people extra money and
made Florida an accessible playground. By 1925 Miami had become a scene of frantic excitement. In the fun-fair of fast turnover the reckless speculator was, if anything, more likely to gain
than the prudent investor, and the "binder boys" perfected to a
fine art the practice of making money at little or no risk. The
principle was to pay a small "binder" fee for an option to buy on
promise of a later down payment, then reap a profit by selling
binders which might pass through a dozen hands and might or
might not convey title. It was the latest in a series of speculative
bubbles that had been bursting on the American scene since the
British South Sea Bubble of the eighteenth century. By
mid-1926, when there were no more "bigger fools" left to whom
one could "pass the baby," the Florida bubble burst.

For the losers it was a sobering lesson, but it proved to be but a
tryout for the Great Bull Market in stocks. Until 1927 stock
values had gone up with profits, but then they began to soar on
wings of speculation. Mellon's tax reductions had released
money which, with the help of aggressive brokerage houses,
found its way to Wall Street. Instead of trading binders on real
estate, one could buy stock on margin—that is, make a small
down payment and borrow the rest from a broker who held the
stock as security against a down market. Brokers' loans rose
steadily from about $3.5 million in June 1927 to $8 million in
September 1929.

Gamblers in the market ignored warning signs. By 1927 residential construction and automobile sales were catching up to
demand, business inventories rose, and the rate of consumer
spending slowed. By mid-1929 production, employment, and
other signs of economic activity were declining. Still the market
rose. Among the blue chips, American Telephone and Telegraph
went from 179½ in March 1928 to 304 on September 3, 1929,
which was when the market peaked. Glamor stocks moved much

faster: Radio Corporation of America, for example, rose from under 100 to over 500 during the same period.

By 1929 the market was functioning in a fantasy world. Conservative financiers and brokers who counseled caution found their feeble admonitions lost in the hubbub of the market. The president worried too, and urged stock exchange and Federal Reserve officers to discourage speculation. In August the Federal Reserve Board raised the rate on loans to member banks (the rediscount rate) to 6 percent, but with no effect. On September 4, stock prices wavered, and the day after that they dropped. Investment advisor Roger Babson recalled the Florida boom and said on September 5: "Sooner or later a crash is coming, and it may be terrific." What was promptly dubbed the Babson Break opened a season of fluctuations. The Great Bull Market staggered on into October, trending downward but with enough good days to keep hope alive. On October 22 Charles E. Mitchell, president of the National City Bank, returning from Europe, told reporters: "I know of nothing fundamentally wrong with the stock market or with the underlying business and credit structure."

THE CRASH AND ITS CAUSES   The next day prices crumbled, and the day after that a wild scramble to unload stocks lasted until word arrived that leading bankers had formed a pool to stabilize prices. Prices steadied for the rest of the week, but after a weekend to think the situation over, stockholders began to unload on Monday. The New York *Times* index of industrials went down 49 points. On Tuesday, October 29, the most devastating single day in the market's history, the index dropped another 43 points. The market reported sales of 16.4 million shares (at the time 3

Wall Street on October 29, 1929. Confusion prevailed on the street and in the markets. [Culver Picture Service]

million shares traded was a busy day) and some issues went begging for buyers. The plunge in prices fed on itself as brokers sold the shares they held for buyers who failed to meet their obligations. During October stocks on the New York Exchange fell in value by 37 percent.

The first impulse of business and government leaders was to express hope. According to President Hoover, "the fundamental business of the country" was sound. John D. Rockefeller issued his first public statement in decades: ". . . my son and I have for some days been purchasing sound common stocks." The comedian Eddie Cantor retorted: "Sure, who else has any money left?" Some speculators who got out of the market went back in for bargains but found themselves caught in a slow, tedious erosion of values. By March 1, 1933, the value of stocks on the New York Exchange was less than a fifth of the value at the market's peak. The New York *Times* stock average, which stood at 452 on September 3, 1929, bottomed at 52 in July 1932.

Caution became the watchword for consumers and businessmen. Buyers held out for lower prices, orders fell off, wages fell or ceased altogether, and the decline in purchasing power brought further cutbacks in business. From 1929 to 1932 Americans' personal incomes declined by more than half, from $82 million to $40 million. Unemployment continued to rise. Farmers, already in trouble, faced catastrophe.

The crash had revealed the fundamental business of the country to be unsound. Most harmful was the ability of business to maintain prices and take profits while holding down wages and the cost of raw materials, with the result that about one-third of the personal income went to only 5 percent of the population. By plowing profits back into expansion, business brought on a growing imbalance between rising productivity and declining purchasing power. As the demand for goods declined, the rate of investment in new plant began to decline. For a time the softness of purchasing power was concealed by greater use of installment buying, and the deflationary effects of high tariffs were concealed by the volume of loans and investments abroad which supported foreign demand for American goods. But the flow of American capital abroad began to dry up when the stock market began to look more attractive. Swollen profits and dividends, together with the Mellon tax policies, enticed the rich into market speculation. When trouble came, the bloated corporate structure collapsed.

Governmental policies also contributed to the debacle. Mellon's tax reductions brought oversaving, which helped diminish demand. The growing money supply fed the fever of speculation.

Hostility toward labor unions discouraged collective bargaining and may have worsened the prevalent imbalances in income. High tariffs discouraged foreign trade. Lax enforcement of anti-trust laws encouraged concentration, monopoly, and high prices.

HOOVER'S EFFORTS AT RECOVERY   Not only did the policies of public officials help bring on economic collapse, but few public leaders acknowledged the crisis: all that was needed, they thought, was a slight correction of the market. Those who held to the dogma of laissez-faire thought the economy would cure itself. The best policy, Secretary Mellon advised, would be to "liquidate labor, liquidate stocks, liquidate the farmers, liquidate real estate." Hoover himself had little patience with speculators, but he was unwilling now to sit by and let events take their course. Hoover in fact did more than any president had ever done before in such dire economic circumstances. Still, his own philosophy, now hardened into dogma, set limits to governmental action, and he was unready to set it aside even to meet an emergency.

As food administrator and promoter of voluntary associations Hoover had insisted on strong public relations departments. He believed also that the nation's fundamental business structure was sound and that the country's main need was confidence. In speech after speech Hoover exhorted the public to keep up hope, and summoned businessmen and labor leaders for talks at the White House. Hoover asked businessmen to keep the mills and shops open, maintain wage rates, and spread the work to avoid layoffs—in short to let the first shock fall on corporate

An incredulous citizen watches as Hoover fills the Christmas stocking with business confidence. It proved cold comfort. [Library of Congress]

profits rather than on purchasing power. In return union leaders, who had little choice, agreed to refrain from wage demands and strikes. As it happened, however, words were not enough, and the prediction that good times were just around the corner (actually made by Vice-President Charles Curtis though attributed to Hoover) eventually became a sardonic joke.

Hoover did more than try to reassure the American public. He hurried the building of public works in order to provide jobs, but state and local cutbacks more than offset federal spending. At Hoover's demand the Federal Reserve returned to an easier credit policy, and Congress passed a modest tax reduction to put more purchasing power in people's pockets. The Federal Farm Board stepped up its loans and its purchases on farm surpluses only to face bumper crops in 1930 despite droughts in the Middle West and Southwest. The high Hawley-Smoot Tariff, proposed at first to help farmers, brought reprisals abroad, devastating foreign trade.

As always, depression hurt the party in power. At the Democratic National Committee, publicity director Charles Michelson exploited Hoover's predicament for all it was worth, and more. But Michelson's role in building the depression image of Hoover has been overblown. In 1930, the Second Year of the Abolition of Poverty (as one newsman put it), the floundering president was easy game. During the war, "to Hooverize" had signified patriotic sacrifice; now the president's name signified distress. Near the city dumps, along the railroad tracks, the dispossessed huddled in shacks of tarpaper and galvanized iron, old packing boxes, abandoned cars. These squalid settlements became "Hoovervilles." A "Hoover blanket" was a newspaper; a "Hoover flat," an empty pocket turned inside out; "Hoover wagons" were cars pulled by mules; "Hoover hogs" were jackrabbits. In November 1930 the Democrats gained their first national victory since 1916, winning a majority in the House and enough gains in the Senate to control it in coalition with western agrarians.

One irony of the time was that the great humanitarian of wartime relief was recast as the stubborn opponent of depression relief. But Hoover was still doing business at the same old stand: his answer remained voluntarism. When Col. Arthur H. Woods, head of the Emergency Committee for Employment, strongly recommended a governmental program of $840 million for road building and other public works, the president turned it down. His annual message to Congress in December 1930 demanded that each community and state undertake the relief of distress "with that sturdiness and independence which built a great Nation." Edmund Wilson, then early in his career as a literary critic, found it "a reassuring thought, in the cold weather, that the emaciated men in the bread lines, the men and women beggars in the streets, and the children dependent on them, are all having their fibre hardened."

In the first half of 1931 economic indicators rose, renewing hope for an upswing. Then, as recovery beckoned, another shock fell. In May 1931 the failure of Austria's largest bank, the Credit Anstalt, triggered panic in central Europe. On June 20, to halt the domino effect of spreading defaults, President Hoover proposed a one-year moratorium on both reparations and war-debt payments. The moratorium, as it happened, became permanent simply by process of default. In July the major European nations accepted the moratorium and later also a temporary "standstill" on settlement of private obligations between banks. The general shortage of exchange drove Europeans to withdraw their gold from American banks and dump their American securities. One after another European country abandoned the gold standard and devalued its currency. In September even the Bank of England went off the gold standard. The United States meanwhile slid into the third bitter winter of depression.

CONGRESSIONAL INITIATIVES   With a new Congress in session, demands for federal action impelled Hoover to stretch his philosophy to its limits. He was ready now to use governmental resources at least to shore up the financial institutions of the country. Eugene Meyer, Jr., former head of the War Finance Corporation, prompted Hoover to bring back the agency for a new purpose. In January 1932 the new Congress set up the Reconstruction Finance Corporation (RFC) with $500 million (and authority to borrow $2 billion more) for emergency loans to banks, life insurance companies, building and loan societies, farm mortgage associations, and railroads. Under former Vice-President Charles G. Dawes, it authorized $1.2 billion in loans within six months. The RFC staved off bankruptcies, but Hoover's critics found in it favoritism to business, the most damaging instance of which was a $90-million loan to Dawes's Chicago bank, made soon after he left the RFC in June 1932. The RFC nevertheless remained a key agency through the New Deal and World War II.

Further help to the financial structure came with the Glass-Steagall Act of February 1932, which broadened the definition of commercial loans which the Federal Reserve would support.

The new arrangement also released about $750 million in gold formerly used to back Federal Reserve Notes, countering the effect of foreign withdrawals and domestic hoarding of gold at the same time that it enlarged the supply of credit. For homeowners the Federal Home Loan Bank Act of July 1932 created with Hoover's blessing a series of discount banks for home mortgages. They provided for savings and loan and other mortgage agencies a service much like that the Federal Reserve System provided to commercial banks.

All these measures reflected a dubious "trickle-down" theory, Hoover's critics said. If government could help banks and railroads, asked New York's Sen. Robert G. Wagner, "is there any reason why we should not likewise extend a helping hand to that forlorn American, in every village and every city of the United States, who has been without wages since 1929?" By 1932 members of Congress were filling the hoppers with bills for federal relief. At that point Hoover might have pleaded "dire necessity" and, backed by his reputation in the field, taken the leadership of the relief movement and salvaged his political fortunes.

Instead he held back and only grudgingly edged toward federal relief. House Speaker John Nance Garner of Texas, with his own eye cocked to the White House, proposed a $1-billion bond issued for federal public works, another $1 billion for RFC loans to state and local public works, and $100 million for distribution to the needy. Senator Wagner proposed even more, but a compromise bill that came out of conference committee met a presidential veto. Then on July 21, 1932, Hoover signed the Emergency Relief and Construction Act, which avoided a direct federal dole but gave the RFC $300 million for relief loans to the states, authorized loans of up to $1.5 billion for state and local public works, and appropriated $322 million for federal public works.

Relief for farmers had long since been abandoned. The Grain and Cotton Stabilization Corporations set up under the Farm Board had lost $345 million in futile efforts to buy up surpluses. In mid-1931 they quit buying altogether and helplessly watched prices slide. In 1919 wheat had fetched $2.16 a bushel; by 1932 it had sunk to 38¢. Cotton reached a high of 41.75¢ a pound in 1919; before the 1932 harvest it went to 4.6¢. Other farm prices declined comparably. Net cash income for farmers slid from $12 billion in 1929 to $5.3 billion in 1932. Between 1930 and 1934 nearly a million farms passed from their owners to the mortgage holders.

FARMERS AND VETERANS IN PROTEST   Faced with the loss of everything, farmers began to defy the law. Angry mobs stopped foreclosures and threatened to lynch the judges sanctioning them. In Nebraska farmers burned corn to keep warm. In Iowa, Milo Reno, once head of the state's Farmers Union, formed the militant Farmers' Holiday Association which called a farmers' strike and forcibly blocked deliveries of produce. Dairymen dumped milk into roadside ditches. On the whole, like voluntary efforts to reduce acreage, the strikes failed, but they vividly dramatized the farmer's mood.

In the midst of the crisis there was desperate if nebulous talk of revolution. "Folks are restless," Mississippi's Gov. Theodore Bilbo told reporters in 1931. "Communism is gaining a foothold. . . . In fact, I'm getting a little pink myself." Bilbo was doing his usual put-on, but across the country the once-obscure Communist party began to draw crowds to its rallies and willing collaborators into its Unemployed Councils and "hunger marches." In Alabama it formed a Share Croppers Union and reaped a propaganda windfall when the party went to the defense of the Scottsboro Boys, nine black itinerants accused on flimsy evidence of raping two white girls atop a gondola car of gravel in northern Alabama. Around Harlan, Kentucky, desperate coal miners embraced the Communist-run National Mine Workers' Union, which fell victim to guns and whips and ultimately to the rock-ribbed faith of miners who heard leaders "denounce our government and our flag and our religion." For all the sound and fury, few were converted to the Communist view. Party membership never rose much above 100,000.

Visions of disorder took shape when unemployed veterans converged on Washington in the spring of 1932. The "Bonus Expeditionary Force" budded first in the brain of Walter W. Waters in Portland, Oregon, but after his first contingent of 330 arrived late in May, the number grew quickly to more than 15,000. Their purpose was to get immediate payment of the bonus which Congress had voted in 1924. It took the form of endowment life insurance payable in 1945—or earlier to the heirs of veterans who died before that date. In 1931, over Hoover's veto, Congress had authorized loans of up to 50 percent of the value of each insurance certificate, but the veterans now wanted everything in cash. The House approved a bonus bill introduced by Wright Patman of Texas, but when the Senate voted it down in June most of the veterans went home. The rest, having no place to go, camped in vacant government buildings and in a shantytown on Anacostia Flats, within sight of the Capitol.

Hunger marchers demonstrating in Washington, D.C., for unemployment insurance, December 1931. [Library of Congress]

The chief of the Washington police, once the youngest brigadier-general of the American Expeditionary Force (the name given to American forces in Europe during the war), gave them a friendly welcome and won their trust. But a fearful White House fretted. Eager to disperse them, Hoover got Congress to vote funds, in the form of loans against the bonus certificates, to buy their tickets home. More left, but others stayed even after Congress adjourned, hoping at least to meet with the president. Late in July the administration ordered the government buildings cleared. In the ensuing melee, one policeman panicked, fired into the crowd, and killed two veterans. This "riot" afforded the excuse that Secretary of War Patrick J. Hurley had been seeking, and the president acceded to his request to move in about 700 soldiers under Gen. Douglas MacArthur, aided by junior officers Dwight D. Eisenhower and George S. Patton, Jr. The soldiers easily drove out the unarmed veterans and their families and burned the shacks. Among the evicted was Joe Angelo of New Jersey, who had received the Distinguished Service Cross for a wartime exploit that saved the life of George Patton. The one fatality—from tear gas—was eleven-week-old Bernard Myers, born at Anacostia.

General MacArthur said the "mob," animated by "the essence of revolution," was about to seize control of the government. The administration insisted that the Bonus Army consisted mainly of Communists and criminals, but neither a grand jury nor the Veterans Administration could find evidence to support the charge. One observer wrote before the incident: "There is about the lot of them an atmosphere of hopelessness, of utter despair, though not of desperation. . . . they have no enthusiasm whatever and no stomach for fighting."

Their mood, and the mood of the country, was much like that of Hoover himself. He worked hard, but took no joy from his labors. "I am so tired," he sometimes said, "that every bone in my body aches." He was, as William Allen White said, "constitutionally gloomy, a congenital pessimist who always saw the doleful side of any situation." A private meeting with Hoover, Secretary of State Stimson said, was "like sitting in a bath of ink." News conferences became more strained and less frequent. When friends urged him to seize the leadership he said, "I can't be a Theodore Roosevelt," or "I have no Wilsonian qualities." The gloom, the sense of futility, communicated itself to the country. In a mood more despairing than rebellious, people waited to see what another presidential campaign would bring forth.

FURTHER READING

The most recent synthesis of events following the First World War is Ellis W. Hawley's *The Great War and the Search for a Modern Order: A History of the American People and Their Institutions, 1917–1933* (1979). A more traditional narrative is John D. Hicks's *Republican Ascendancy, 1921–1933* (1960). Two short introductions to the period are William E. Leuchtenberg's *The Perils of Prosperity, 1914–1932* (1958),° and Paul A. Carter's *The Twenties in America* (1968). The chapter on the 1920s in Blaine Brownell and George E. Mowry's *The Urban Nation, 1920–1960* (1965),° explains the influence of the twenties on later events.

Presidential politics has attracted many scholars. Introductions to Harding include Francis Russell's *The Shadow of Blooming Grove: Warren G. Harding in His Times* (1968), Robert K. Murray's *The Harding Era: Warren G. Harding and His Administration* (1969), and Andrew Sinclair's *The Available Man: The Life behind the Masks of Warren Gamaliel Harding* (1965). For Coolidge, see Donald R. McCoy's *Calvin Coolidge: The Silent President* (1967) and William Allen White's *A Puritan in Babylon* (1940). Studies on Hoover include Joan Hoff Wilson's *Herbert Hoover: Forgotten Progressive* (1975), David Burner's *Herbert Hoover: The Public Life* (1978), and George Nash's *The Life of Herbert Hoover—The Engineer* (vol. 1, 1983).

Studies of other prominent 1920s figures include Oscar Handlin's *Al Smith and His America* (1958), William Harbaugh's *Lawyer's Lawyer: The Life of John W. Davis* (1973), LeRoy Ashby's *The Spearless Leader: Senator Borah and the Progressive Movement in the 1920s* (1972), and David P. Thelen's *Robert M. La Follette and the Insurgent Spirit* (1978).

°These books are available in paperback editions.

Other works on politics include Burl Noggle's *Teapot Dome: Oil and Politics in the 1920s* (1962),° David Burner's *The Politics of Provincialism: The Democratic Party in Transition, 1918–1932* (1967), and James Gilbert's *Designing the Industrial State: The Intellectual Pursuit of Collectivism in America, 1880–1940* (1972). Alan Lichtman's *Prejudice and the Old Politics* (1978) and George B. Tindall's *The Emergence of the New South, 1914–1945* (1967),° cover the election of 1928. John D. Hicks and Theodore Saloutos's *Twentieth Century Populists: Agricultural Discontent in the Midwest, 1900–1939* (1964), and Gilbert Fite's *George Peek and the Fight for Farm Parity* (1954) discuss the Farm Bloc. William Chafe's *The American Woman: Her Changing Social, Economic, and Political Roles* (1970)° is a good introduction to the achievement of suffrage.

An overview of the depression is found in C. P. Kinderberger's *The World in Depression* (1973). A review of the economics of the 1920s is given in George Soule's *Prosperity Decade* (1947) and John Kenneth Galbraith's *Money: Whence It Came, Where It Went* (1975). Galbraith also details the fall of the stock market in *The Great Crash of 1929* (1955).° Another interpretation is given in Peter Temin's *Did Monetary Forces Cause the Great Depression?* (1976).° Albert Romesco's *The Poverty of Abundance: Hoover, the Nation, and the Great Depression* (1965), Jordan A. Schwartz's *Interregnum of Despair: Hoover's Congress and the Depression* (1970), Roger Daniels's *The Bonus March* (1971), and Donald Lisio's *The President and Protest* (1974) all explore what Hoover did and did not do during the crisis. John A. Garraty's *Unemployment in History: Economic Thought and Public Policy* (1979) explores what the nation thought about its plight.

28

FRANKLIN D. ROOSEVELT
AND THE NEW DEAL

FROM HOOVERISM TO THE NEW DEAL

FDR'S ELECTION On June 14, 1932, while the Bonus Army was still encamped in Washington, Republicans gathered in Chicago to renominate Hoover and Curtis. The proceedings were apathetic and dreary, enlivened only by debate over a prohibition plank, the final version of which straddled the issue. The delegates went through the motions in a mood of defeat. The Democrats, in contrast, converged on Chicago late in June confident that they would nominate the next president. New York Gov. Franklin D. Roosevelt was already the front-runner with most of the delegates lined up, but he still faced an uphill battle for a two-thirds majority. Al Smith, long a favorite of the party machines, felt entitled to one more chance at the White House. But Smith's time had passed; he could not even control his own state's delegation. Among the favorite sons only House Speaker John Nance Garner of Texas had any serious chance. After a Garner delegation won the California primary, the Texan was in a position to deadlock the convention, but the memory of the 1924 deadlock remained strong. When Rep. Sam Rayburn described the line-up on the telephone, Garner replied: "All right, release my delegates. . . . Hell, I'll do anything to see the Democrats win one more national election." Thus Roosevelt went over the top on the fourth ballot; Garner's reward was the vice-presidency, an office he later pronounced "not worth a pitcher of warm spit."

In a bold gesture, Roosevelt flew to Chicago and appeared before the convention in person to accept the nomination instead of awaiting formal notification. "Let it . . . be symbolic that . . . I broke traditions," he told the delegates. "Republican leaders not only have failed in material things, they have failed in national vision, because in disaster they have held out no hope. . . . I pledge you, I pledge myself to a new deal for the American people." What the New Deal would be Roosevelt himself had little idea as yet, but unlike Hoover, he was flexible and willing to experiment. What was more, his ebullient personality communicated joy and hope. His campaign song was "Happy Days Are Here Again."

Roosevelt was strengthened also by his background and experience. Born to a comfortable fortune in 1882, he had the advantage of a proper education at Groton School and Harvard, topped off by the Columbia Law School. Although raised a Democrat, he admired his distant cousin Theodore and up to a point his career retraced the same path. Elected to the New York state legislature in 1910, he caught the public eye by opposing Tammany's candidate for the United States Senate. In 1912 he backed Wilson, and for both of Wilson's terms was his assistant secretary of the navy. Then in 1920, largely on the strength of his name, he became Cox's running mate. In defeat the parallel with Theodore ended, and the following year his career seemed cut short by an attack of poliomyelitis which left him permanently crippled, unable to stand or walk without braces. But the struggle for recovery transformed the once supercilious young aristocrat into one of the most outgoing political figures of the century. Justice Oliver Wendell Holmes, Jr., later summed up his qualities this way: "A second-class intellect—but a first-class temperament."

For seven years he fought his way back to health and in 1928 emerged again on the national scene to nominate Al Smith in Houston. At Smith's urging he ran for governor of New York to strengthen the ticket and won while Smith was losing the state. Reelected by a whopping majority of 700,000 in 1930, he became a shining beacon for 1932.

Partly to dispel doubts about his health, Roosevelt set forth on a grueling campaign tour. His other purposes were to pin responsibility for the depression on Hoover and the Republicans, and to define the New Deal. Always deft at picking other men's brains, he relied mainly on a panel of advisors from Columbia University: Raymond Moley, G. Rexford Tugwell, and A. A. Berle, Jr. In turn this Brain Trust, as newsmen quickly dubbed it, tapped other sources in preparing drafts for major speeches. Roosevelt

Gov. Franklin D. Roosevelt, the Democratic nominee, campaigning in Topeka, Kansas. Roosevelt's confidence inspired voters. [Wide World Photos]

of course tempered their ideas to political realities, often fuzzing them over to avoid offending any large bloc of voters, and usually hedged his bets by offering alternative courses of action.

Like Hoover, Roosevelt made the requisite promise to balance the budget, but he left open the loophole that he would incur deficits to prevent starvation and dire want. On the tariff he was evasive. On farm policy he offered several options pleasing to farmers and ambiguous enough not to alarm city-dwellers. He did come out unequivocally for strict regulation of utilities and for at least some development of public power, and he consistently stood by his party's pledge to repeal the Prohibition Amendment. At the Commonwealth Club in San Francisco the candidate gazed into a clouded crystal ball and announced that economic expansion, like Frederick Jackson Turner's frontier, had come to an end. Such opinions prevailed widely at the time. A mature economy would require national planning, Roosevelt said. "The country needs, and, unless I mistake its temper, the country demands bold, persistent experimentation. . . . Above all, try something."

What came across to voters, however, was less the content of his speeches than the confidence of the man. His most banal utterances seemed somehow significant. Hoover by contrast had no confidence. He could turn a neat phrase, but many elegant passages suffered from the pedestrian manner of his delivery. Democrats, he argued, ignored the international causes of the depression. They were taking a reckless course. Roosevelt's evasive stand on the tariff, he said, made the Democratic candidate look like a chameleon on plaid. Roosevelt's policies, he warned,

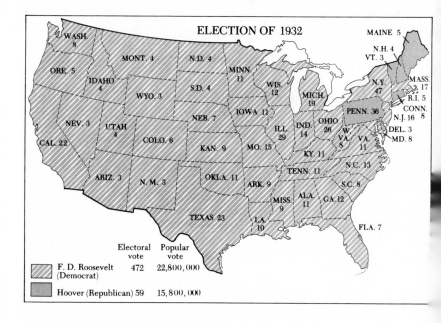

ELECTION OF 1932

WASH. 8
ORE. 5
MONT. 4
N.D. 4
MINN. 11
IDAHO 4
S.D. 4
WIS. 12
WYO. 3
MICH. 19
IOWA 11
NEB. 7
ILL. 29
IND. 14
OHIO 26
NEV. 3
UTAH 4
COLO. 6
KAN. 9
MO. 15
KY. 11
CAL. 22
ARIZ. 3
N.M. 3
OKLA. 11
ARK. 9
TENN. 11
N.C. 13
S.C. 8
MISS. 9
ALA. 11
GA. 12
TEXAS 23
LA. 10
FLA. 7
MAINE 5
N.H. 4
VT. 3
N.Y. 47
MASS. 17
R.I. 5
CONN. 8
PENN. 36
N.J. 16
DEL. 3
W. VA. 8
VA. 11
MD. 8

	Electoral vote	Popular vote
F. D. Roosevelt (Democrat)	472	22,800,000
Hoover (Republican)	59	15,800,000

"would destroy the very foundations of our American system." Pursue them, and "grass will grow in the streets of a hundred cities, a thousand towns." But few were listening. Amid the persistent depression the country wanted a new course, a new leadership, a new deal.

Many thoughtful observers were disappointed in both candidates. They agreed with Walter Lippmann's earlier judgment that Roosevelt was "a pleasant man, who, without any important qualifications for the office, would very much like to be President." Those who believed only a radical departure would suffice went over to Socialist Norman Thomas, who polled 882,000 votes, and some went on to Communist William Z. Foster, who got 103,000. The wonder is that a desperate people did not turn in greater numbers to radical candidates. Instead they swept Roosevelt into office by 22.8 million votes to Hoover's 15.8 million. Hoover carried only four states in New England plus Pennsylvania and Delaware, losing in the electoral college by 472 to 59.

THE INAUGURATION   For the last time the country waited four long months, until March 4, for a new president and Congress to take office. The Twentieth Amendment, ratified on February 6, 1933, provided that the president would take office thereafter on January 20 and the newly elected Congress on January 3. Before the end of November the president-elect went to the White House for an inconclusive conference. Hoover proposed a joint effort, but only on his own terms, so Roosevelt, like Lincoln, warily avoided commitment until power was his own. With policy abandoned to drift, the bleak winter of 1932–1933 became what one historian called "the interregnum of despair." Amid spreading destitution and misery, unemployment continued to rise and panic struck the banking system. Depositors increasingly played it safe by taking their cash out and squirreling it away. In Michigan, where automobile production was severely curtailed, the threat of runs on the banks impelled the governor to extend the Lincoln's Birthday closing indefinitely. As panic spread, governors of other states also found excuses for banking holidays. When the Hoover administration ended, four-fifths of the nation's banks were closed and the country was on the brink of economic paralysis.

A profound crisis of confidence prevailed when Roosevelt took the oath of office on March 4, 1933, but it was tempered by a mood of expectancy. The new president exploited both with a spirit of assurance that conveyed a new sense of vigor and action. First, he asserted a "firm belief that the only thing we have to fear is fear itself—nameless, unreasoning, unjustified terror which paralyzes needed efforts to convert retreat into advance." Roosevelt promised to fill the vacuum of leadership: "The money changers have fled from their high seats in the temple of our civilization. We may now restore that temple to the ancient truths." He would not merely exhort, he promised: "This nation asks for action, and action now!" He warned that emergency measures might call for a temporary departure from the normal balance of executive and legislative authority. If need be, he said, "I shall not evade the clear course of duty. . . . I shall ask the Congress for the remaining instrument to meet the crisis—broad executive power to wage a war against the emergency as great as the power that would be given me if we were in fact invaded by a foreign foe." It was a measure of the country's mood that this call received the loudest applause.

Roosevelt was not the first to resort to what the historian William Leuchtenburg has called "the analogue of war." Time and again the nation's mobilization for World War I was held up as a model for action in the new crisis. The Reconstruction Finance Corporation, started under Hoover but sometimes called the first New Deal agency, was but the War Finance Corporation reborn. Many of Roosevelt's appointees had been involved in the mobilization. George Peek and Hugh S. Johnson, for instance, had once worked for the War Industries Board; soon they would head the New Deal farm and industrial recovery programs.

STRENGTHENING THE MONETARY SYSTEM   The first order of business for the new administration was to unclog the channels of finance. On his second day in office, Roosevelt called Congress to meet in special session on March 9, and then declared a four-day banking holiday, invoking powers under the Trading with the Enemy Act of 1917. It took Congress only seven hours to pass the Emergency Banking Relief Act, which permitted sound banks to reopen under license from the Treasury and provided managers for those that were still in trouble. On March 12, in the first of his radio "fireside chats," the president told his audience it was safer to "keep your money in a reopened bank than under the mattress." The following day, deposits in reopened banks exceeded withdrawals, and by March 15 banks controlling nine-tenths of the nation's banking resources were once again open. The crisis had ended and the new administration was ready to get on with its broader program.

In rapid order Roosevelt undertook to meet two specific pledges in the Democratic platform. At his behest, on March 20 Congress passed an Economy Act granting the executive the power to cut salaries, reduce payments to veterans for non-service-connected disabilities, and reorganize agencies in the interest of economy. On March 22 the Beer-Wine Revenue Act amended the Volstead Act to permit sale of beverages with an alcoholic content of 3.2 percent. The Twenty-first Amendment, already submitted by Congress to the states on February 20, would be declared ratified on December 5, thus ending the "noble experiment" that was prohibition.

The measures of March were but the beginning. During the session from March 9 to June 16, the so-called Hundred Days, Congress received and enacted fifteen major proposals from the president, leaving a record unlike anything seen before in American history:

March 9	The Emergency Banking Act
March 20	The Economy Act
March 31	Establishment of the Civilian Conservation Corps
April 19	Abandonment of the gold standard
May 12	The Federal Emergency Relief Act
May 12	The Agricultural Adjustment Act, including the Thomas amendment which gave the president powers to expand the money supply
May 12	The Emergency Farm Mortgage Act, providing for the refinancing of farm mortgages

May 18 The Tennessee Valley Authority Act, providing for the unified development of the Tennessee Valley

May 27 The Truth-in-Securities Act, requiring full disclosure in the issue of new securities

June 5 The Gold Repeal Joint Resolution, which abrogated the gold clause in public and private contracts

June 13 The Home Owners' Loan Act, setting up the Home Owners' Loan Corporation to refinance home mortgages

June 16 The National Industrial Recovery Act, providing for a system of industrial self-regulation under federal supervision and for a $3.3-billion public works program

June 16 The Glass-Steagall Banking Act, separating commercial and investment banking and establishing the Federal Deposit Insurance Corporation

June 16 The Farm Credit Act, which reorganized the agricultural credit system

June 16 The Railroad Coordination Act, setting up a federal coordinator of transportation

With the banking crisis over, there still remained an acute debt problem for farmers and homeowners, and a lingering distrust of the banks which might yet be aroused again. On March 27, by executive decree, Roosevelt reorganized all farm credit agencies into the Farm Credit Administration (FCA). By the Emergency Farm Mortgage Act (May 12) and the Farm Credit Act (June 16) Congress confirmed that action and authorized extensive refinancing of farm mortgages at lower interest rates. Within seven months the FCA loaned farmers more than $100 million, nearly four times as much as all the land-bank loans made the previous year. The Home Owners' Loan Act (June 13) provided a similar service to city-dwellers through the new Home Owners' Loan Corporation (HOLC)—something which, incidentally, Hoover had vainly urged on Congress in 1931. The Glass-Steagall Banking Act (June 16) further shored up confidence in the banking system. It created the Federal Deposit Insurance Corporation (FDIC) to guarantee bank deposits of up to $5,000. To prevent speculative abuses, it separated investment and commercial banking corporations and extended the Federal Reserve's regulatory power over credit. The Federal Securities Act (May 27) required the full disclosure of information about new stock and bond issues, at first by registration with the Federal Trade Commission, later with the Securities and Exchange Commission (SEC), which was created on June 6, 1934, to regulate the stock and bond markets.

Throughout 1933 Roosevelt tinkered with devaluation of the currency as a way to raise prices and thus ease the debt burden.

Just Another Hole, *a skeptical view of FDR's attempts to boost the economy by devaluing the currency, thereby raising prices. [Lute Pease, Newark Evening News]*

Having already placed an embargo on the withdrawal of gold deposits at the outset of his administration, on April 5 he used powers granted by the Emergency Banking Act to order all gold turned in to the Federal Reserve Banks, except small amounts for industrial, professional, or artistic uses. On April 19 the government officially abandoned the gold standard: the consequent decline in the value of the dollar increased the prices of commodities and stocks at home. The Gold Repeal Joint Resolution (June 5) canceled the gold clause in federal and private obligations, made all contracts payable in legal tender, and thus completed the abandonment of the gold standard. The experiment ended when Congress passed the Gold Reserve Act of January 30, 1934, which authorized the president to impound all gold in the Federal Reserve Banks and reduce the theoretical gold value of the dollar. By executive order he set the price of an ounce of gold at $35, which reduced the dollar's gold content as compared to its gold content the previous October. It was done, Roosevelt said, "to make possible the payment of . . . debts at more nearly the price level at which they had been incurred." Prices did rise, and the high price set on gold drew most of the world's supply to the United States, where it was buried in the vaults at Fort Knox, Kentucky.

Another time-honored inflationary device was the coinage of silver, and for a time the ghost of William Jennings Bryan stalked the halls of Congress. A silver bloc, led by Elbert Thomas of Oklahoma, pursued the goal of "reflation" by authorizing free coinage of silver. In May 1933 the silverites got a compromise amendment to the farm bill giving the president discretionary authority to reduce further the gold content of the dollar and to purchase silver for coinage. The president used the first but refused to act on the second. Eventually, however, he yielded to pressure from the farm and Rocky Mountain states and accepted the Silver Purchase Act, passed on June 19, 1934. Under this measure the Treasury was in effect required to buy the entire output of American silver mines. By presidential order of August 9, 1934, the government bought the silver with certificates at the rate of $1.29 an ounce, thereby making twenty-seven ounces of silver equal in value to one ounce of gold (a 27:1 ratio). Since the total stock of silver was by then too small to have much inflationary effect, the result was mainly to memorialize Bryan and to subsidize the silver mines.

RELIEF MEASURES   In 1933 the relief of personal distress was an urgent priority, as it would remain until World War II. A first step toward such relief came with the creation in March of the Civilian Conservation Corps (CCC), which was designed to give work relief to young men aged eighteen to twenty-five, and incidentally to remove them from the job market. Beginning on a cold, rainy day in April 1933 when a caravan of motor trucks set out from Washington to put up the first CCC camp in Virginia's George Washington National Forest, nearly 3 million young men took to the woods to work at a variety of jobs in forests, parks, recreational areas, and soil conservation projects at a nominal pay of $30 a month. Directed by army officers and foresters, they worked under a semi-military discipline and provided perhaps the most direct analogue of war in the whole New Deal.

The Federal Emergency Relief Administration (FERA), created on May 12, 1933, with an authorization of $500 million, addressed the broader problems of human distress. Harry L. Hopkins, an indefatigable social worker who had directed Roosevelt's state relief program in New York, pushed the program

October 17, 1934. The depression was more than the collapse of prices and markets, and New Deal relief efforts recognized this. [Library of Congress]

with a seemingly boundless nervous energy, all the while giving off (in the words of one observer) "a suggestion of quick cigarettes, thinning hair, dandruff, brief sarcasm, fraying suits of clothes, and a wholly understandable preoccupation." The FERA continued and expanded the assistance that had begun under Hoover's RFC, but with a difference. Federal monies flowed to the states in grants rather than "loans." While FERA continued to channel aid through state agencies to relief clients mainly in direct payments, Hopkins enlarged its scope by gradually developing work programs for education, student aid, rural rehabilitation, and transient relief. He pushed an "immediate work instead of dole" approach on local officials, but they preferred the dole as an easier and quicker way to reach the needy.

The first large-scale experiment with work relief came with formation of the Civil Works Administration (CWA) during the winter of 1933–1934, when it had become apparent that even the largesse of the FERA would not prevent widespread privation. Created in November 1933, the CWA provided jobs and wages to those able to work. It was conceived and implemented in haste, and many of its projects were "make-work" jobs such as leaf-raking and ditch-digging; but it spent over $900 million (mostly in wages) for a variety of useful projects, from highway repairs to teaching jobs that helped keep the schools open. The CWA, unlike the FERA, was a federal operation from top to bottom. The CWA was abandoned in the spring of 1934, having served its purpose of helping people weather the winter; but Roosevelt and Hopkins continued to believe that work-relief was preferable to the "dole," which they believed to have a debilitating effect psychologically on recipients.

Recovery through Regulation

Beyond rescuing the banks and providing relief lay the long-term goals of recovery for agriculture and business. Members of Roosevelt's Brain Trust and others who influenced policies during the "hundred days" were heirs largely to an earlier Roosevelt's New Nationalism, whether avowedly so or not. They held the trend toward economic concentration to be inevitable. They also believed that the mistakes of the 1920s showed that the only way to operate an integrated economy at capacity and in the public interest was through regulation and organized central planning, not through trust-busting. The success of centralized planning during World War I reinforced such ideas. New farm and recovery programs sprang from their beliefs.

AGRICULTURAL RECOVERY: THE AAA   Early on, the Department of Agriculture produced an omnibus farm bill in consultation with farm leaders, and on March 16 the president urgently submitted it to Congress. The Agricultural Adjustment Act, signed into law on May 12, contained nearly every major device applicable to farm relief including authority to dump surpluses abroad, but only some of its provisions were implemented. The core of the act was a plan to compensate farmers for voluntary cutbacks in production. The goal was to restore farm prices to "parity," or the same level they had reached during the farmers' golden age of 1909–1914 (1919–1929 for tobacco). The act covered seven "basic commodities," a number later enlarged, and the money for benefit payments came from a processing tax levied on each —at the cotton gin, for example, or the flour mill.

By the time Congress acted, the growing season was already advanced. "Wherever we turn," said George N. Peek, first head of the Agricultural Adjustment Administration (AAA), ". . . we have in prospect a race with the sun." The most urgent problem was the prospect of another bumper cotton crop, and the AAA reluctantly resolved to sponsor a plow-under program. Using county demonstration agents the AAA signed up bewildered farmers. Trouble came sometimes from balky mules, trained to avoid trampling the crop, and occasionally from stubborn tenants who, like the oldtime Populists, could not understand how prosperity could come from creating an artificial scarcity. To destroy a growing crop was a "shocking commentary on our civilization," Agriculture Secretary Henry A. Wallace lamented. "I could tolerate it only as a cleaning up of the wreckage from the old days of unbalanced production." Even more troubling was the spectacle of some 6 million little pink pigs slaughtered "before they could reach the full hogness of their hogdom." It could be justified, Wallace said, only as a means of helping farmers to do with pigs what steelmakers did with pig iron—cut production to fit the market.

It worked temporarily. Cotton farmers got about $112 million in benefit payments, and the crop was reduced by about 4 million bales below the estimate. Cotton prices rose above 11¢ per pound in July (parity was 12.7¢), but sagged again as the crop came in. In an effort to take up the slack, in October 1933 the president set up the Commodity Credit Corporation (another CCC!) which extended loans first on cotton and later on other crops kept in storage and off the market. In principle, if not in form, it was a revival of the old Farmers' Alliance–Populist subtreasury plan. With loans averaging 10¢ per pound on the 1933 crop and 12¢ per pound in 1934, it pegged the prices at those levels because no farmer had to sell for less. But the carry-over from the crops of previous years still weighed the prices down. Another drastic step was taken on April 21, 1934, with passage of the Bankhead Cotton Control Act, which set marketing quotas at 10 million bales in 1934 and 10.5 million in 1935; farmers who tried to sell more than their share of the quota would be stopped by a prohibitive tax. The Kerr-Smith Tobacco Control Act of 1934 applied similar quotas to tobacco.

In 1933 widespread drought in the wheat belt reduced production and removed any need to plow up growing wheat, but benefit payments went to farmers who agreed to cut their wheat acreage in 1934 and 1935. Crop reductions were also brought about in corn, rice, and dairy products. Through a variety of causes—acreage reduction, drought, benefit payments, and currency devaluation—farm income increased from $5.5 billion in 1932 to nearly $8.7 billion in 1935.

Then on January 6, 1936, in the Hoosac Mills Case *(United States v. Butler)* the Supreme Court, by a vote of 6 to 3, held the AAA's processing tax unconstitutional because farm production was intrastate and thus beyond the reach of the power to regulate interstate commerce. In a sharp dissent, Justice Harlan Fiske Stone protested that "the present levy is held invalid, not for any want of power in Congress to lay such a tax" and argued that it came "within the specifically granted power to levy taxes to 'provide for the general welfare.' " But the decision stood. The administration hastily devised a new plan in the Soil Conservation and Domestic Allotment Act, which it pushed through Congress in six weeks. The new act, which became law on February 29, 1936, omitted processing taxes and acreage quotas, but provided benefit payments for soil conservation practices which took land out of soil-depleting staple crops—thus indirectly achieving crop reduction. Since the money came out of general funds and not from taxes, this approach was not vulnerable to suit. The act boosted a developing conservation movement directed by the Soil Conservation Service, which had been created in 1935.

The act was an almost unqualified success as an engineering and educational project because it went far to heal the scars of erosion and the plague of dust storms. But soil conservation nevertheless failed as a device for limiting production. With their worst lands taken out of production, farmers cultivated their fertile acres more intensively. In response, Congress passed the second Agricultural Adjustment Act (February 16, 1938), which reestablished the earlier programs but left out the processing taxes. Benefit payments would come from general funds. By the time the second AAA reached a test in the Supreme Court, changes in the Court's personnel had changed its outlook. This time the law was upheld as a legitimate exercise of the inter-state-commerce power. Agriculture, like manufacturing, was now held to be in the stream of commerce.

INDUSTRIAL RECOVERY: THE NRA   For industry, the counterpart to the AAA was the National Recovery Administration (NRA), and the counterpart to AAA chief George Peek was NRA chief Hugh S. Johnson, Peek's former associate at the Moline Plow Company. The recovery act was hastened into being when Senate passage of a bill limiting the workweek to thirty hours, introduced by Sen. Hugo Black (D-Ala.), indicated a mood of impatience with continued unemployment, which the thirty-hour week was supposed to relieve. The administration quickly planned and submitted a more comprehensive bill that emerged on June 16, 1933, as the National Industrial Recovery Act (NIRA), the two major parts of which dealt with recovery and public works. The latter part, Title II, created the Public Works Administration (PWA) with $3.3 billion for public buildings, highway programs, flood control, and other improvements. The purpose was to "prime the pump" of business with new expenditures and provide jobs for the unemployed. Under the direction of Interior Secretary Harold L. Ickes, the PWA indirectly served the purpose of work relief, although Ickes directed it toward well-planned permanent improvements rather than the provision of hasty make-work.

The purposes of the NRA, briefly stated, were twofold: first, to stabilize business with codes of "fair" competitive practice, and second, to generate more purchasing power by providing jobs, defining labor standards, and raising wages. Three related streams of thought merged in the creation of the NRA. One was Theodore Roosevelt's New Nationalism. The second was the idea that the New Deal was the analogue of war, that it could repeat the miracles wrought by the War Industries Board. Another source for the NRA was the trade-association movement, championed by Hoover in the 1920s and carried beyond his ideas of voluntary association now by force of law. The NRA also enlisted trade union hopes for protection of basic hour and wage standards and liberal hopes for comprehensive planning.

In each major industry, committees representing management, labor, and government drew up the codes of fair practice. General Johnson turned to existing trade associations for help in drafting them. A plan submitted by the Cotton Textile Institute, for instance, became the basis for Code No. 1, which imposed restraints on plant expansion, limited operations to eighty hours a week, and required reports on operations every four weeks. The labor standards featured in every code set a forty-hour week and minimum weekly wages of $13 ($12 in the South, where living standards were considered lower) which more than doubled earnings in some cases. Announcement of a proviso against child labor under the age of sixteen set off roars of applause in the hearing room. It did "in a few minutes what neither law nor constitutional amendment had been able to do in forty years," Johnson said.

As the drafting of other codes began to drag, Johnson proposed a "blanket code" pledging employers generally to observe the same labor standards as applied to cotton textiles. In mid-July he launched a crusade to whip up popular support for the NRA and its symbol of compliance, the "Blue Eagle," which had been modeled on an Indian thunderbird and embellished with the motto "We do our part." The eagle was displayed in show windows and stamped on products. It was a gamble, but the public responded. The climax to Johnson's effort came early in September when a Blue Eagle parade down New York's Fifth Avenue drew a quarter of a million marchers. Some 2 million employers signed the pledge, and the impact of the campaign broke the logjam in code making.

For a time it worked, perhaps because a new air of confidence

That Ought to Jolt Him. *The NRA eagle jolts the depression with jobs and wages, 1933.* *[Library of Congress]*

had overcome the depression blues and the downward spiral of wages and prices had ended. But as soon as recovery began, the honeymoon was over. The daily annoyances of code enforcement inspired growing hostility among businessmen. Charges mounted that the larger companies dominated the code authorities, that allocations froze the existing industrial structure and limited production, and that price-fixing robbed small producers of the chance to compete. In 1934 an investigating committee under Clarence Darrow, the noted lawyer, substantiated at least some of the charges. Limiting production, moreover, had discouraged investment. By 1935 the NRA had developed more critics than friends. When it died in May 1935, struck down by the Supreme Court as unconstitutional, few paused to mourn.

The NRA experiment was generally put down as a failure, but it left an enduring mark. With dramatic suddenness, the codes had set new standards, such as the forty-hour week and the end of child labor, from which it was hard to retreat. The NRA's endorsement of collective bargaining spurred the growth of unions. The codes, moreover, advanced trends toward stabilization and rationalization that were becoming the standard practice of business at large and that, despite misgivings about the concentration of power, would be further promoted by trade associations and by outright integration.

REGIONAL PLANNING: THE TVA   But the eclectic philosophy of the New Deal embraced more than the restrictive approaches of the NRA. The creation of the Tennessee Valley Authority (TVA) was a truly bold venture. Among the measures of the Hundred Days, most of which were efforts to salvage the wreckage of depression, TVA became a massive monument of growth, a living rebuttal to the idea that the economy had reached its full measure of mature development. It was the product neither of a single imagination nor of a single concept, but of an unfolding progression of purposes. In 1916, when the government started power and nitrate plants at Muscle Shoals, Alabama, strengthening national defense was the aim. New objectives unfolded in succession: the plants could produce nitrate fertilizers as well as nitrate explosives, general industrial development, and cheap public power to be used as a "yardstick" for private utility rates. Waterpower development pointed in turn to navigation, the control of stream flow for both power and flood control, and to conservation of soil and forests to prevent silting. The chain of connections led ultimately to the concept of overall planning for an entire watershed, which included a total drainage area of 41,000 square miles overlapping seven states, four-fifths the size of England.

Through the 1920s Nebraska Sen. George W. Norris had fought conservative administrations in an effort to sell the Alabama project, but never got sufficient support for the objective of providing public power. In 1932, however, he backed Roosevelt, and then won the new president's support for a vast enlargement of the Muscle Shoals project.

Muscle Shoals, Roosevelt said, "gives us the opportunity . . . of setting an example of planning, not just for ourselves but for generations to come, tying in industry and agriculture and forestry and flood prevention . . . over a distance of a thousand miles." On May 18, 1933, Congress created the TVA as a multipurpose public corporation. Mobilizing local support under TVA Director David E. Lilienthal's slogan of "grass-roots democracy," the TVA won almost universal loyalty among the people of the region. By 1936 the TVA board had six dams completed or under way, and a masterplan to build nine high dams on the main river, which would create the "Great Lakes of the South," and other dams on the tributaries. The agency, moreover, opened the

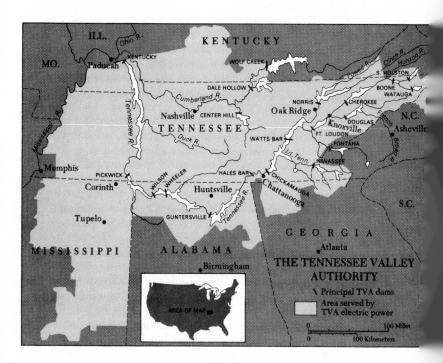

THE TENNESSEE VALLEY
AUTHORITY

⟍ Principal TVA dams
▢ Area served by
TVA electric power

0   100 Miles
0   100 Kilometers

rivers for navigation, fostered soil conservation and forestry, experimented with fertilizers, drew new industry to the region, and sent cheap power pulsating through the valley. Cheap public power, Lilienthal's main passion, became more and more TVA's reason for being—a purpose that would become all the more important during World War II. TVA's success at generating greater power consumption and lower rates awakened private utilities to the mass consumer markets. Cheap power transported farmers of the valley from the age of kerosene to the age of electricity. "The women went around turning the switches on and off," said a Farm Bureau man who witnessed the transition. "The light and wonder in their eyes was brighter than that from the lamps." TVA's first rural cooperative, set up at Corinth, Mississippi, in 1934, pointed the way to the electrification of the nation's farms in the decade that followed. The Rural Electrification Administration (REA), formed as a relief agency by presidential order in 1935, achieved a permanent statutory basis in 1936. By 1940 it had extended loans of more than \$321 million to rural cooperatives.

LAUNCHING THE SECOND NEW DEAL

During Roosevelt's first year in office his programs and his personal charms aroused massive support. The president's travels and speeches, his twice-weekly press conferences, and his "fireside chats" over the radio generated vitality from a once-remote White House. In the congressional elections of 1934 the Democrats actually increased their strength in both House and Senate, an almost unprecedented midterm victory for the party in power. When it was over only seven Republican governors remained in office throughout the country.

Criticism of the New Deal was muted or reduced to helpless carping. But as the sense of crisis passed, the spirit of unity relaxed. In August 1934 a group of conservative businessmen and politicians, including Al Smith and John W. Davis, two previous Democratic presidential candidates, formed the American Liberty League to oppose New Deal measures and to "teach the necessity of respect for the rights of person and property."

THUNDER ON THE LEFT   But if there was any real threat to Roosevelt in those years, it came from the hucksters of social nostrums, old and new. The most flamboyant of the group, by far, was Louisiana's "Kingfish," Sen. Huey P. Long, Jr. First as governor, then as political boss of the state, he had delivered to its citizens

The "Kingfish," Huey Long of Louisiana. [Keystone Photos]

tax favors, roads, schools, free textbooks, charity hospitals, and generally better public services, all at the cost of corruption and personal dictatorship. Louisiana, however, became only the base from which he ventured out to conquer other worlds. The vehicle was Long's Share Our Wealth program, first unveiled in 1932 and refined over the next three years. In one version Long proposed to liquidate large personal fortunes, guarantee every family an allowance of $5,000, every worker an annual income of $2,500, grant pensions to the aged, reduce the hours of labor, pay veterans' bonuses, and assure a college education for every qualified student. His book *Every Man a King* (1933) held out the promise of economic security for all. Whether he had a workable plan or not, his scheme dramatized a fundamental issue in a society that had solved the problem of production but not that of distribution, an issue few politicians were so imprudent as to tackle directly. By early 1935 Huey Long was claiming 27,431 Share Our Wealth Clubs and a file of 7.5 million names.

Another scheme came from a California doctor, Francis E. Townsend. Outraged by the sight of three haggard old women raking through garbage cans in Long Beach, Townsend proposed pensions for the aged. In January 1934 he and Robert Clements, a real-estate promoter, founded Old Age Revolving Pensions, Limited, to promote the Townsend Plan of paying $200 a month to every citizen over sixty who retired from employment and promised to spend the money within the month. The plan had the lure of providing both security for the aged and job openings for the young. As the Townsend Clubs grew, critics noted that the cost would be more than half the national income. "I'm not in the least interested in the cost of the plan," Townsend blandly told a House committee.

A third huckster of panaceas, Father Charles E. Coughlin, the "radio priest" of the Shrine of the Little Flower in Royal Oak, Michigan, founded the National Union for Social Justice in 1934. In broadcasts over the CBS network, he specialized in schemes for the coinage of silver and attacks on bankers which carried growing overtones of anti-Semitism.

Coughlin, Townsend, and Long drew support largely from a lower middle class squeezed by the depression. Of the three, Long had the widest following. A canvass by the Democratic National Committee showed that he could draw 5–6 million votes as a third-party candidate for president, perhaps enough to undermine Roosevelt's chances of reelection.

A new militancy and new drives to organize labor added to the "thunder on the left." Beset by pressures from both ends of the political spectrum, Roosevelt drifted through months of hesitation before deciding to "steal the thunder" from the left with new programs of reform and social security. Political pressures impelled Roosevelt, but so did the growing influence of Justice Brandeis, Felix Frankfurter, and the Frankfurter protégés (the "little hot dogs") Thomas G. Corcoran, a presidential assistant, and Benjamin V. Cohen at Interior. These men urged Roosevelt to be less cozy with big business and to push for restored competition and heavy taxes on large corporations.

LIGHTNING FROM THE COURT   What finally galvanized the president into action was the behavior of the Supreme Court. Early in 1935 the Court for the first time struck down a piece of New Deal legislation, a provision of the National Industrial Recovery Act forbidding interstate shipment of "hot oil"—oil produced in excess of quotas set by the states. A few weeks later the gold resolution of 1933, which abandoned the gold standard, was barely upheld on a close vote of 5 to 4. Then on May 27, 1935, the Court in three decisions annulled a farm mortgage relief act, found that the president had used his removal power wrongfully, and killed the National Industrial Recovery Act by unanimous vote.

In *Schechter Poultry Corporation v. United States,* quickly tagged the "sick chicken" case, the defendants, who sold to kosher retailers, had been convicted of selling an "unfit chicken" and violating other code provisions as well. The high court ruled that Congress had delegated too much power to the executive when it granted the code-making authority and had exceeded its power under the commerce clause. Chief Justice Hughes's opinion held that the poultry in question had "come to permanent rest within the state," although it had been moved across state lines. In a press conference soon afterward, Roosevelt said: "We have been relegated to the horse-and-buggy definition of interstate commerce." The same line of reasoning, he warned, might endanger much of the New Deal program.

LEGISLATIVE ACHIEVEMENTS In June Roosevelt ended the stalemate in Congress and launched the so-called Second New Deal with demands for "must" legislation, most of which was already pending. Congress passed these measures with a rush:

July 5	The Wagner National Labor Relations Act, guaranteeing the right of labor to organize and bargain collectively
August 14	The Social Security Act, providing unemployment and old-age insurance and public welfare programs
August 23	The Banking Act of 1935, strengthening the Federal Reserve System
August 28	The Wheeler-Rayburn Public Utility Holding Company Act, preventing the pyramiding of holding companies
August 30	The Revenue Act of 1935, the "Soak the Rich" tax
August 30	The Guffey-Snyder Coal Act, setting up the "little NRA"

The National Labor Relations Act, often called the Wagner Act, gave workers the right to bargain through unions of their own choice and prohibited employers from interfering with union activities. A National Labor Relations Board of five members could supervise plant elections and certify unions as bargaining agents where a majority of the workers approved. The board could also investigate the actions of employers and issue "cease and desist" orders against specified unfair practices. Under the protection of the law, union activities quickly intensified.

The Wagner Act salvaged the labor guarantees of Section 7a of the National Industrial Recovery Act, while other measures revived other parts of the NIRA. The Public Contracts Act applied NRA wage and hour standards to work under government contracts. The Guffey-Snyder Coal Act established for the coal industry alone a "little NRA," but it too fell before the Supreme Court in 1936 and never became operative. The Guffey-Vinson Coal Act of 1937 set up a Bituminous Coal Commission which enforced minimum prices and certain fair-marketing rules, but that act expired in 1943. The oil code gave way in August 1935 to an interstate compact among seventeen oil states by which they agreed to standard practices regulated by the states.

The Social Security Act of 1935, Roosevelt said, was the New Deal's "cornerstone" and "supreme achievement." In common parlance "social security" came to mean the national Old-Age and Survivors' Insurance, under which workers and employers contributed payroll taxes to cover annuities paid to those who retired after age sixty-five. But that was only one of the act's three major provisions. The act also set up a shared federal-state plan of unemployment insurance and committed the national government to a broad range of welfare activities. The principle was that "unemployables"—people who were unable to work—would remain a state responsibility while the national government would provide work relief for the able-bodied. To that end the law inaugurated grants-in-aid for three public assistance programs—old age assistance, aid for dependent children, aid for the blind—and further aid for maternal, child welfare, and public health services. Congress had already passed in April a $4.8-billion bill providing work relief for jobless workers. To manage these programs, the Works Progress Administration (WPA), headed by Harry L. Hopkins, replaced the Federal Emergency Relief Administration. The act did not provide a dole which, Roosevelt told Congress, had been "a narcotic, a subtle destroyer of the human spirit. . . ."

"Yes, You Remembered Me"

The social legislation of the Second New Deal prompted this cartoon of FDR as the friend of "The Forgotten Man." [Library of Congress]

Hopkins favored the lighter public works which would provide jobs quickly, with the consequence that some jobs appeared to be make-work or mere "leaning on shovels." But before its death in World War II the WPA left permanent monuments on the landscape in the form of buildings, bridges, hard-surfaced roads, airports, and schools. The WPA employed a wide range of talents, often saving them from atrophy, in the Federal Theater Project, the Federal Art Project, and the Federal Writers' Project. The National Youth Administration, under WPA, gave part-time employment to students, set up technical training programs, and provided aid to jobless youth. Although WPA took care of only about 3 million out of some 10 million jobless at any one time, in all it tided some 9 million clients over desperate times before it expired in 1943.

The Banking Act of 1935 strengthened the control of the Federal Reserve Board over rediscount rates and reserve requirements, and diminished the power of private bankers in the money market. It accomplished this by concentrating in the board's hands all open-market operations—that is, the buying or selling of government securities to increase (by buying) or decrease (by selling) the money supply. The act greatly strengthened the board's control of the whole monetary system.

The Public Utility Holding Company Act struck at financial corruption in the public utility industry. Like railroads in the 1800s, utilities in their early stages of growth had spawned buccaneers interested more in manipulation than in good business. The act passed despite the high-pressure lobbying tactics of the utilities which, Rep. Sam Rayburn said later, could "produce more noise and fewer votes than any crowd I ever saw."

The final measure endorsed by Roosevelt and the last of the major laws passed during this period was the Revenue Act of 1935, sometimes called the Wealth Tax Act, but popularly known as the "Soak-the-Rich" tax. In asking for the law, Roosevelt told Congress: "Our revenue laws have operated in many ways to the unfair advantage of the few, and they have done little to prevent an unjust concentration of wealth and economic power." The Revenue Act raised surtax rates on incomes above $50,000, and steeply graduated taxes on incomes above $5 million to a maximum of 75 percent on incomes above $5 million. Estate and gift taxes went up, as did the corporate tax on all but small corporations—those with less than $50,000 income. Congress even added to Roosevelt's recommendations an "excess profits" levy on corporate earnings above 10 percent.

The Philadelphia *Inquirer* accused the president of "a bald political stroke . . . to lure hosannas from the something-for-nothing followers of Huey Long, 'Doc' Townsend . . . and the whole tribe of false prophets." By "soaking" the rich and enacting Social Security he did indeed steal much of the thunder from the left, although the results fell short of the promise. The new tax law failed to increase revenue significantly, nor did it result in a redistribution of income: the wealthiest 1 percent of the nation in fact slightly increased its share of the wealth after the tax took effect. At the same time the hoopla over "soaking the rich" obscured the more significant impact of both the Social Security payroll tax, which was regressive—that is, it fell more heavily on lower incomes—and the policy of returning indigents to the care of the states. Most states, insofar as they assumed this burden, raised the needed revenue with sales taxes, which were also regressive. Such taxes impeded recovery by reducing total purchasing power.

The viewpoint of the time was that Roosevelt had moved in a radical direction. But the extent of the new departure taken by the Second New Deal is easy to exaggerate. Such measures as work relief, Social Security, utility regulation, and progressive income taxes had long been in the works in Congress. The president himself had little use for theoretical speculation. He was still pursuing the bold experiments he promised before the election. "Roosevelt's program," the historian William E. Leuchtenburg has written, "rested on the assumption that a just society could be secured by imposing a welfare state on a capitalist foundation."

THE ELECTION OF 1936 Whatever economic or philosophical judgment might be passed on the New Deal program, Roosevelt's political instincts were acute. Businessmen fumed over his tax and spending policies. The wealthy resented their loss of status and the growing power of government and labor. They vented an intemperate rage against Roosevelt, whom they called "a traitor to his own class," and against all the works of the New Deal. So many landmarks of a once stable and secure world now seemed threatened, from the gold standard itself to a man's right to run his business as he saw fit. Hoover called the New Deal an attack on "the whole philosophy of individual liberty." Visitors at the home of J. P. Morgan, Jr., were cautioned not to mention Roosevelt's name lest it raise his blood pressure. But the conservative coalition of business and wealth, by its incoherent rage, made a perfect foil for the confident president.

The popularity of the president and his policies impelled the

Come along, we're going to the Trans-Lux to hiss Roosevelt. *Peter Arno's 1936 cartoon satirizes the resentment felt by many of the wealthy for Roosevelt.* [© The New Yorker]

Republican convention in 1936 to avoid candidates too closely identified with the "hate-Roosevelt" contingent. The party chose Gov. Alfred M. Landon of Kansas, a former Bull Moose Progressive, who had fought the Ku Klux Klan, supported civil liberties, and favored regulation of business. While conservative in matters of finance, Landon had endorsed many programs of the New Deal. The most progressive Republican candidate in years, he was probably more liberal than most of his backers, and clearly more so than the party's platform, which accused the New Deal of usurping power. For vice-president the party nominated the more conservative Frank Knox, a newspaper publisher, former Bull Mooser, and one of the original Rough Riders.

Landon started the campaign on a moderate note, arguing that a Republican president could achieve the objectives of the New Deal more efficiently and thriftily. But as the campaign progressed, his statements became more and more conservative. Before the end, Republican party leaders even tried to make an issue of the Social Security program, which they denounced as dangerous "regimentation." The Social Security Act, said Knox, "puts half the working people of America under federal control." Republican Chairman John D. M. Hamilton warned that every worker would have to wear metal dogtags bearing his Social Security number.

Such appeals carried little weight. The chief hope of the Republicans was that the followers of Coughlin, Townsend, and other dissidents would combine to draw enough votes away from Roosevelt to throw the election to them. But that possibility faded when an assassin gunned down Huey Long. Coughlin,

Townsend, and a remnant of the Long movement did support Rep. William Lemke of North Dakota on a Union party ticket, but it was a forlorn and foredoomed effort that polled only 882,000 votes.

In 1936 Roosevelt was able to forge a new electoral coalition which would affect national politics for years to come. While holding the support of most traditional Democrats North and South, FDR made strong gains among beneficiaries of the farm program in the West. In the northern cities he held on to the strong support of ethnic groups helped by New Deal welfare measures and afforded greater recognition in appointments. Middle-class voters, whose property had been saved by New Deal measures, flocked to Roosevelt's support, along with intellectuals stirred by the ferment of new ideas in government. The revived labor movement threw its support to Roosevelt, and Socialist voters deserted Norman Thomas for the New Deal coalition. In the most profound new departure of all, black voters for the first time cast the majority of their ballots for a Democratic president. "My friends, go home and turn Lincoln's picture to the wall," Robert L. Vann of the Pittsburgh *Courier* told black Republicans. "That debt has been paid in full." In perhaps the most seismic and enduring change in the political landscape during the 1930s, a majority of politically active blacks moved away from their traditional adherence to the Republican party.

Roosevelt campaigned with tremendous buoyancy. In his acceptance speech to the Democratic convention in Philadelphia he dropped efforts to reassure businessmen. As the Americans of 1776 had sought freedom from political autocracy, he said, the Americans of 1936 sought freedom from the "economic royalists" who had created "a new despotism." "They complain that we seek to overthrow the institutions of America. What they really complain of is that we seek to take away their power." The campaign closed on an even more strident note, when Roosevelt spoke at Madison Square Garden: "I should like to have it said of my first Administration that in it the forces of selfishness and of lust for power met their match. I should like to have it said of my second administration that in it these forces met their master."

On November 3 the election went as Democratic Chairman James A. Farley had predicted. Roosevelt carried every state except Maine and Vermont with a popular vote of 27.7 million to Landon's 16.7 million, and won what was the closest to a unanimous electoral vote since Monroe's victory in 1820, by 523 to 8. Democrats would dominate Republicans in the new Congress, by 77 to 19 in the Senate and 328 to 107 in the House. The editor William Allen White of Emporia, Kansas, wrote: "The water of liberalism has been dammed up for forty years by the two major parties. The dam is out. Landon went down the creek in a torrent." Roosevelt himself said he felt as if he had experienced "baptism by total immersion."

SECOND-TERM SETBACKS AND INITIATIVES

But as Jefferson and Jackson found (and Lyndon Johnson and Richard Nixon also discovered), some malevolent fate often seems to have it in for presidents who win such victories, and Roosevelt found himself deluged in a sea of troubles over the next year. Roosevelt's Second Inaugural Address, given on January 20, 1937, suggested that he was ready to move toward even further reform. The challenge of American democracy, he said, was that millions of citizens "at this very moment are denied the greater part of what the very lowest standards of today call the necessities of life. . . . I see one-third of a nation ill-housed, ill-clad, ill-nourished." The election of 1936 had been a mandate for extensive reform, he argued; and the overwhelming Democratic majorities in Congress ensured passage. But one major roadblock stood in the way: the Supreme Court.

THE COURT-PACKING PLAN   By the end of the 1936 term the Court had ruled against New Deal laws in seven of the nine major cases it reviewed. Having struck down both major accomplishments of the First New Deal, the AAA and the NRA, the Court moved on in 1936 to rule against the Guffey Coal Act. In the spring of 1936 it denied that states had the power to fix minimum wages. Since it had already ruled, in 1923, that the federal government had no such power, it had left, as Roosevelt protested, a " 'no-man's land,' where no Government—State or Federal" could act. Suits against the Social Security and Wagner Labor Relations Acts now pended. Given the established trend of rulings, often by margins of 5 to 4 or 6 to 3, the Second New Deal seemed in danger of being nullified like the first.

For that reason, Roosevelt and Attorney-General Homer Cummings decided to do something about the Court. Avenues of action included seeking a constitutional amendment, or having Congress limit the cases subject to the Court's review. Roosevelt and Cummings took neither of these courses, deciding finally to change the Court by enlarging it, a move for which there was ample precedent and power. Congress, not the Constitution, determined the size of the Court, which at different times had numbered six, seven, nine, and ten justices, and in 1937 numbered nine. On February 5 Roosevelt sent his plan to Congress, without having consulted congressional leaders or more than a few within his administration. He wanted to create up to fifty new federal judges, including six new Supreme Court justices, and to diminish the power of the judges who had served ten or more years or reached the age of seventy.

The "court-packing" maneuver, as opponents quickly tagged it, handed a viable issue to men who previousy had shunned a fight with Roosevelt. The plan was a shade too contrived. In implying that some judges were impaired by senility, it affronted the elder statesmen of Congress, and especially Louis D. Brandeis, who was both the oldest and the most liberal of the justices. It ran headlong into a deep-rooted veneration of the courts and aroused fears that another president might use the precedent for quite different purposes. Sen. Carter Glass of Virginia feared "the reversal of those decisions of the Court that saved the civilization of the South," by which he meant decisions upholding white supremacy. The newsman Oswald Garrison Villard warned, on the other hand, that "a future Woodrow Wilson could pack the Supreme Court so that no Negro could get within a thousand miles of justice. . . ." In the Senate the Republicans shrewdly stood aside while the Democrats plunged into a family squabble.

As it turned out, no direct vote ever tested senatorial convictions on the matter. Unforeseen events blunted Roosevelt's drive to change the Court. A sequence of Court decisions that spring reversed previous judgments in order to uphold a Washington state minimum-wage law, the Wagner Act, and the Social Security Act. Chief Justice Charles Evans Hughes testified that the Court had kept up with its docket. Conservative Justice Willis Van Devanter resigned, and Roosevelt named to the vacancy one of the most consistent New Dealers, Sen. Hugo Black of Alabama. In mid-July the sudden death of Senate Majority Leader Joseph T. Robinson redirected attention to the divisive struggle for leadership, and the court bill went back to the Judiciary Committee, which had reported it unfavorably in the first place.

Finally, in August, Vice-President Garner arranged a settlement providing reforms in court procedures and more generous retirement provisions, but adding no new judges. Roosevelt later claimed he had lost the battle but won the war. The Court had reversed itself on important New Deal legislation, and Roosevelt was able to appoint justices in harmony with the New Deal. But

ALL I SAID
WAS 'GIMME
SIX MORE
JUSTICES!"

Roosevelt's "court-packing" scheme aroused strong opposition from fellow Democrats. The Democratic donkey here kicks up a storm. [Library of Congress]

it was a pyrrhic victory which sowed dissension in his party and blighted Roosevelt's own prestige. For the first time Democrats in large numbers deserted the "champ," and the opposition found an issue on which it could openly take the field. During the first eight months of 1937 the momentum of Roosevelt's great 1936 victory was lost.

A NEW DIRECTION FOR LABOR   Rebellions erupted on other fronts even while the Court bill pended. Under the impetus of the New Deal the moribund labor movement stirred anew. When Section 7a of the National Industrial Recovery Act demanded in every industry code a statement of the workers' right to organize, alert unionists quickly translated it to mean "The President wants you to join the union." John L. Lewis of the United Mine Workers was among the first to exploit the spirit of the Blue Eagle. Leading a union decimated by depression, he rebuilt it from 150,000 members to 500,000 within a year. Spurred by the mine workers' example, Sidney Hillman of the Amalgamated Clothing Workers and David Dubinsky of the International Ladies Garment Workers joined Lewis in promoting a campaign to organize workers in the mass-production industries. As leaders of some of the few industrial unions in the AFL, they found the craft unions to be obstacles to organizing the basic industries.

In 1934 they persuaded the AFL and its president William Green to charter industrial unions in the unorganized industries. But Green and other craft unionists saw these "federal" unions as temporary pools from which to draw members into the crafts. Lewis and the industrial unionists saw them as a chance to organize on a massive scale. In 1935, with passage of the Wagner Act, action began in earnest. The industrial unionists formed a Committee for Industrial Organization (CIO) and craft unionists began to fear submergence by the mass unions. Jurisdictional disputes divided them, and in 1936 the AFL expelled the CIO unions, which then formed a permanent structure called after 1938 the Congress of Industrial Organizations. The rivalry spurred both groups to greater efforts.

The CIO's major organizing drives in automobiles and steel began in 1936, but until the Supreme Court upheld the Wagner Act in 1937 there was little compliance with unions on the part of industry. There was instead widespread use by industry of blacklisting, private detectives, labor spies, vigilante groups, and intimidation. Early in 1937 automobile workers spontaneously adopted a new technique, the "sit-down strike," in which workers refused to leave the shop until the employers granted collective bargaining. Many employers and much of the public saw in such revolutionary tactics a threat to property rights, an alarming gesture of contempt for authority, and further evidence of the New Deal's evil influence. Union leaders, fearing a backlash of public opinion, frowned on the tactic, but it brought the first union victory in a major industry. In February 1937 General Motors recognized the United Automobile Workers as bargaining agent for its employees. The following month, United States Steel capitulated to the Steel Workers Organizing Committee (later the United Steelworkers of America), granting it recognition, a 10 percent wage hike, and a forty-hour week.

Having captured two giants of heavy industry, the CIO went on in the next few years to organize much of industrial America: rubber, oil, electronics, and a good part of the textile industry, in which unionists had to fight protracted struggles to organize scattered plants. The laggard pace in textiles denied the CIO a major victory in the South comparable to its swift conquest of autos and steel, but even there a labor movement appeared that was at last something more than a vehicle for sporadic revolt. Some of the giants of heavy industry held out for yet a few years. The "Little Steel" companies, led by Tom Girdler of Republic Steel, and the Big Four meat-packers remained adamant, but all had capitulated by the end of 1941. Violence punctuated these struggles, most vividly at Girdler's Republic Steel plant in Chicago where police killed ten strikers on Memorial Day in 1937. Company guards brutally beat up Walter Reuther and other organizers at Henry Ford's River Rouge plant in Detroit. In Harlan County, Kentucky, deputized company hoodlums conducted a reign of terror until the NLRB forced operators to bargain with the United Mine Workers late in 1938.

Union organizing drives were helped by the sympathy or at least neutrality of public officials. In Michigan, for instance, Gov. Frank Murphy refused to use troops against sit-down strikers. The Wagner Act put the power of the federal government behind the principle of unionization. In the Congress, a Senate subcommittee under Robert M. La Folette, Jr., exposed practices of violence against unions, while President Roosevelt, though opposed to the tactic, refused to use force against sitdowners. The unions, he said, would soon learn that they could not continue to use a "damned unpopular" tactic. Roosevelt himself had come late to the support of unions and sometimes took exception to their behavior. In the fall of 1937 he became so irritated with the warfare between Lewis and Girdler that he pronounced "a plague on both your houses." The grandiloquent Lewis responded: "It ill behooves one who has supped at labor's table and who has been sheltered in labor's house to curse with equal fervor and fine impartiality both labor and its adversaries when they become locked in a deadly embrace." In 1940 an angry Lewis would back the Republican presidential candidate, but he would be unable to carry labor with him. As workers became more organized, they became more identified with the Democratic party.

A SLUMPING ECONOMY   Beset by the divisive effects of the Court fight and the sit-down strikes, the New Deal in the fall of 1937 also faced a renewed depression. The years 1935 and 1936 had been marked by steady economic improvement. By the spring of 1937 output had moved above the 1929 level. Then in August the economy suddenly cracked, and in the following months it slid into a deep business slump, which the press called a "recession" to distinguish it from the "depression." Actually the collapse was sharper than that in 1929. The Dow-Jones stock averages fell from 190 in August to 115 in October. The New York *Times* business index in the same period went from 110 to 85, back to the level of 1935. By the end of the year 2 million people had been thrown out of work; scenes of the earlier depression reappeared.

The prosperity of early 1937 had been achieved largely through governmental spending. On top of relief and public-works outlays, Congress in 1936 had provided for cash payments of veterans' bonuses upon demand. But in June 1937 Roosevelt, worried about deficits and inflation, ordered sharp cuts in spending. At the same time the Treasury began to diminish disposable income by collecting $2 billion in Social Security taxes.

In 1937, the "American Way" remained out of reach for many. [Photograph by Margaret Bourke-White, Life magazine, © 1965, Time, Inc.]

Private spending could not fill the gap left by reductions in government spending, and business still lacked the faith to risk large investments. The result was the slump of 1937.

The recession brought to a head a fierce debate within the administration. One group, led by Treasury Secretary Henry Morgenthau, Jr., favored less spending and a balanced budget. The slow pace of recovery, Morgenthau thought, resulted from the reluctance of business to invest, and that in turn from fear that federal spending would bring inflation and heavy taxes. The other group, which included Harry Hopkins and Harold Ickes, argued for renewed spending. The recession, they noted, had come just when the budget was brought into balance. "The Government," said another supporter of this view, "must be the compensatory agent in this economy; it must unbalance its budget during the deflation and create surpluses in periods of great business activity."

This view echoed that of the English economist John Maynard Keynes, who had given extended development to the idea in his book *The General Theory of Employment, Interest and Money* (1936). Keynesian economics offered a convenient theoretical justification for what New Dealers had already done in pragmatic response to existing conditions. Many, if not most, of the liberals attracted by Keynesian fiscal policies also subscribed to Brandeisian opposition to monopoly, which held that competition provided the best condition for a thriving economy. "Administered" prices, they argued, held back recovery. When demand slackened, large-scale industries could maintain their prices while cutting production and employment. This camp called for antitrust investigations and action. Their views marked a sharp break with the early New Deal's emphasis on regulation.

ECONOMIC POLICY AND REFORM Roosevelt waited as the rival theorists sought his approval. "As I see it," Morgenthau remarked, "what you are doing now is treading water . . . to wait to see what happens this spring." Roosevelt responded: "Absolutely." When spring failed to bring recovery, Roosevelt endorsed the ideas of the spenders and antitrusters. On April 14, 1938, he asked Congress to adopt a large-scale spending program, and Congress voted $33 billion mainly for public works by the PWA and the WPA, with lesser amounts for other programs. In a short time the increase in spending reversed the economy's decline, but the recession and Roosevelt's reluctance to adopt the massive spending called for in Keynesian theory forestalled the achievement of full recovery by the end of the decade. Only during World War II would full production and full employment be achieved.

On April 29, two weeks after his spending message, Roosevelt asked Congress to look into the concentration of economic power. Congress responded by setting up the Temporary National Economic Committee, which drew half its members from Congress and half from federal agencies, with Sen. Joseph O'Mahoney of Wyoming as chairman. It was the first major inquiry of the sort since the Pujo committee reported on the money trust in 1912. Over a period of three years the TNEC produced thirty-nine volumes of testimony and forty-three monographs, a treasure trove of information on the economy. Meanwhile Thurman Arnold, named chief of the Justice Department's Antitrust Division in 1938, swung into action. Within five years he filed almost as many antitrust suits as had been brought previously since passage of the Sherman Act in 1890, but neither he nor the TNEC was able to accomplish much of substance before national defense took precedence. Like earlier antitrust efforts, this one turned out to be largely ceremonial.

The Court fight, the sit-down strikes, and the recession in 1937 all undercut Roosevelt's prestige and dissipated the mandate of the 1936 elections. When the 1937 session ended, the only major new reforms enacted for the benefit of the "ill-housed, ill-fed, and ill-clad" were the Wagner-Steagall National

Housing Act and the Bankhead-Jones Farm Tenant Act. In 1938 came three more major reforms, the last of the New Deal era: the second Agricultural Adjustment Act, the Food, Drug and Cosmetic Act, and the Fair Labor Standards Act.

The Housing Act set up the United States Housing Authority (USHA) in the Department of the Interior, which extended long-term loans to local agencies willing to assume part of the cost for slum clearance and public housing. The agency also subsidized low rents. Later, during World War II, it financed housing in connection with defense projects.

The Farm Tenant Act addressed the problem of rural poverty, which in some ways the New Deal's larger farm program had aggravated. Tenants were supposed to be kept on in spite of government-sponsored cutbacks in production, but landlords often made the most of cutbacks by evicting workers and withholding their shares of benefit payments. Social scientists and journalists called attention to the problem, and in northeastern Arkansas tenant farmers themselves found voice when they organized the Southern Tenant Farmers' Union (STFU) in 1934. The union, however, was never able to function effectively in collective bargaining with what one of its founders, H. L. Mitchell, called "an industry that is disorganized, pauperized and kept alive only by government subsidy." But the union did focus public attention on the problem. Some programs offered loans and grants to keep farmers off the relief rolls, and several cooperative farming communities grew up with New Deal support. These scattered efforts were regrouped into the Resettlement Administration (RA), created by executive order in 1935.

Then, on the recommendation of a President's Committee on Farm Tenancy, Congress in 1937 passed the Tenant Act, administered by a new agency, the Farm Security Administration (FSA). The program made available rehabilitation loans to shore up marginal farmers and prevent their sinking into tenancy. It also made loans to tenants for purchase of their own farms. But the idea of small homesteads by the late 1930s was, as the STFU warned, "an economic anachronism, doomed to failure." American mythology still exalted the family farm, but in reality the ever-larger agricultural unit predominated. In the end the FSA proved to be little more than another relief operation which tided a few farmers over difficult times. A more effective answer to the problem, sadly, awaited mobilization for war, which took many tenants off into the military services or defense industries, broadened their horizons, and taught them new skills.

The Agricultural Adjustment Act of 1938 was a response to renewed crop surpluses and price declines during the recession. It reenacted the basic devices of the earlier AAA, with some new twists. Before government could apply marketing quotas to a given crop, for instance, it had to hold a plebiscite among the growers and win a two-thirds majority. The new Food, Drug and Cosmetic Act broadened the coverage of the 1906 Pure Food and Drug Act and forbade the use of false or misleading advertising. Enforcement of the advertising provision became the responsibility of the Federal Trade Commission. The Fair Labor Standards Act applied to enterprises which operated in or affected interstate commerce. It set a minimum wage of 40¢ an hour and a maximum workweek of forty hours, to be put into effect over several years. The act also prohibited child labor under the age of sixteen, and in hazardous occupations under eighteen.

THE LEGACY OF THE NEW DEAL

SETBACKS FOR THE PRESIDENT   As the New Deal turned its focus less on recovery and more on reform, an effective opposition emerged within the president's party, especially in the southern wing. Local power elites in the South felt that the New Deal jeopardized their position. They felt threatened too when in 1936 the Democratic convention eliminated the two-thirds rule for nominations, thereby removing the South's veto power, and seated Negro delegates. Southern Democrats were at best uneasy bedfellows with organized labor and blacks. Consequently some of them drifted toward coalition with conservative Republicans. By the end of 1937 a conservative bloc, if unorganized and mutable, had appeared.

In 1938 the conservative opposition stymied an executive reorganization bill amid cries that it would lead to dictatorship. They also secured drastic cuts in the undistributed-profits and capital-gains taxes to help restore business "confidence." The House set up a Committee on Un-American Activities chaired by Martin Dies of Texas who took to the warpath against Communists. Soon he began to brand New Dealers as Red Dupes. "Stalin baited his hook with a 'progressive' worm," Dies wrote in 1940, "and New Deal suckers swallowed bait, hook, line, and sinker."

As the political season of 1938 advanced Roosevelt unfolded a new idea as momentous as the Court plan—a proposal to reshape the Democratic party in the image of the New Deal. On June 24 he announced his purpose to intervene in Democratic primaries as the party leader, "charged with the responsibility of carrying out the definitely liberal declaration of principles set forth in the 1936 Democratic platform." The effort ended in a standoff. The administration ousted only one of its opponents, John O'Connor of New York, chairman of the House Rules Committee; the opposition displaced Sen. James Pope of Idaho. Administration defeats in efforts to unseat Sen. Walter George of Georgia, "Cotton Ed" Smith of South Carolina, and Millard Tydings of Maryland broke the spell of presidential invincibility, or what was left of it. As in the Court fight, Roosevelt had risked his prestige while handing his adversaries persuasive issues. His opponents tagged his intervention in the primaries an attempted "purge"; the word evoked visions of Adolf Hitler and Josef Stalin, tyrants who had purged their Nazi and Communist parties in blood.

The elections of November 1938 handed the administration another setback, a result partly of the friction among Democrats. Their majority in the House fell from 229 to 93, in the Senate from 56 to 42. The margins remained large, but the president headed a restive and divided party. In his State of the Union message in January 1939 Roosevelt for the first time proposed no new reforms, but spoke of the need "to invigorate the process of recovery, in order to *preserve* our reforms." In 1939 the administration won an extension of Social Security and finally put through its reorganization plan. Under the Administrative Reorganization Act the president could "reduce, coordinate, consolidate, and reorganize" the agencies of government. Plans proposed by the president became effective in sixty days unless disapproved by concurrent resolution of Congress.

But the opposition was now able to cut relief expenditures, eliminate the Federal Theater Project, reject Roosevelt appointments, and abolish the undistributed-profits tax. The House set up an investigation of the NLRB under the hostile Howard W. Smith of Virginia, and attempted to narrow the scope of the wage-hour law. The conservative coalition and the administration had reached a standoff.

EMERGENCE OF THE BROKER STATE   The New Deal had lost momentum, but it had wrought some enduring changes. By the end of the 1930s the power of the national government was vastly enlarged over what it had been in 1932. Government had taken on the duty of ensuring the economic and social stability of the country. It had established minimum standards for labor conditions and public welfare. It had helped middle-class Americans hold on to their savings, their homes, and their farms. The protection afforded by deposit insurance, unemployment pay, and Social Security pensions would come to be universally accepted as a safeguard against such disasters as the depression.

Roosevelt had steered a course between the extremes of laissez-faire and socialism. The first New Deal had experimented for a time with a managed economy under the NRA, but had abandoned that experiment for a turn toward enforcing competition and priming the economy with government spendings. The effect of heavy governmental expenditures, which finally produced full employment during World War II, seemed to confirm the arguments of Keynesians.

But the old progressive formulation of regulation versus trust-busting had finally been superseded by the rise of the "broker state," a government which mediated among major interest groups. Government's role was to act as an honest broker protecting a variety of interests, not just business but workers, farmers, consumers, small business, and the unemployed.

Roosevelt himself, impatient with theory, was a pragmatist in developing policy: he kept what worked and discarded what did not. The result was, paradoxically, both profoundly revolutionary and profoundly conservative. The New Deal left America greatly changed in many ways, its economy more socialized than before. At the same time it left the basic capitalistic structure of the economic system in place. "For a permanent correction of grave weaknesses in our economic system," Roosevelt said, "we have relied on new applications of old democratic processes."

FURTHER READING

A sound introduction to the decade of the New Deal is in William E. Leuchtenberg's *Franklin D. Roosevelt and the New Deal, 1932–1940* (1963).° Arthur S. Schlesinger, Jr., provides a more detailed account in *The Age of Roosevelt* (3 vols.; 1957–1960). A more critical interpretation of the same policies can be found in Paul Conkin's *The New Deal* (1968).° Valuable for a balance of interpretation is Otis L. Graham, Jr.'s *The New Deal: The Critical Issues* (1971). Also helpful is Frank Friedel's *Launching the New Deal* (1973), particularly for its coverage of the One Hundred Days.

Susan Estabrook Kennedy's *The Banking Crisis of 1933* (1973) details the effects of the Banking Holiday and subsequent reforms. James T. Patterson's *The New Deal and the States* (1969) examines how initial welfare aid was channeled into local agencies. Van L. Perkins looks at

°These books are available in paperback editions.

farming in *Crisis in Agriculture* (1969), and Sidney Baldwin explores the plight of tenant farmers in *Poverty and Politics: The Rise and Decline of the Farm Security Administration* (1968). Michael Parrish's *Security Regulation and the New Deal* (1970) and Ellis Hawley's *The New Deal and the Problem of Monopoly* (1966) analyze government attempts to forestall another market crash. Robert F. Himmelberg's *The Origins of the National Recovery Act* (1976) and Bernard Pellush's *The Failure of the NRA* (1977) study government relations with business. John Salmond's *The Civilian Conservation Corps* (1967) is insightful. Social Security is covered in Roy Lubove's *The Struggle for Social Security, 1900–1937* (1968). For ideas of leading New Dealers, see Elliot Rosen's *Hoover, Roosevelt, and the Brains Trust* (1977), Otis L. Graham, Jr.'s *Toward a Planned Society: From Roosevelt to Nixon* (1976), and Marion Clawson's *New Deal Planning: The National Resources Planning Board* (1981). The bureaucratic side of reform is handled in Richard Polenberg's *Reorganizing Roosevelt's Government: The Controversy over Executive Reorganization, 1936–1939* (1966).

The New Deal can also be understood by studying its chief proponents. Frank Freidel's *Franklin D. Roosevelt* (4 vols.; 1952–1973) and Arthur Schlesinger's aforementioned *The Age of Roosevelt* are multivolume, detailed works. James MacGregor Burns's *Roosevelt: The Lion and the Fox* (1956)° is an astute political analysis. More personal is Joseph P. Lash's *Eleanor and Franklin: The Story of Their Relationship Based on Eleanor Roosevelt's Private Papers* (1971).° Some of Roosevelt's New Deal lieutenants have compiled memoirs about the decade. Among the better are Raymond Moley's *After Seven Years* (1937), Frances Perkins's *The Roosevelt I Knew* (1946), and Rexford G. Tugwell's *The Democratic Roosevelt* (1957). Studies about leading New Deal lieutenants include Paul A. Kurzman's *Harry Hopkins and the New Deal* (1974), George Martin's *Madam Secretary: Frances Perkins* (1976), and Linda J. Lear's *Harold L. Ickes: The Aggressive Progressive, 1874–1933* (1981). Peter H. Juno's *The New Deal Lawyers* (1982) studies those lieutenants as a social group. An interesting contrast is found in a study of how old Progressives reacted to New Deal reform; see Otis L. Graham, Jr.'s *Encore for Reform* (1967).

For scholarship about the various groups involved in the New Deal, consult Raymond Walters's *Negroes and the Great Depression* (1970), Harvard Sitkoff's *A New Deal for Blacks* (1978),° James T. Patterson's *Congressional Conservatism and the New Deal* (1967), and John M. Allswang's *A House of All People: Ethnic Politics in Chicago, 1890–1936* (1971). Works on the critics of the New Deal include T. Harry Williams's *Huey Long* (1969),° Abraham Holzman's *The Townsend Movement* (1963), Charles J. Tull's *Father Coughlin and the New Deal* (1965), and Alan Brinkley's *Voices of Protest: Huey Long, Father Coughlin, and the Great Depression* (1982).° For radical leftist reactions to reform, see Irving Howe's *The American Communist Party* (1957) and David Shannon's *The Socialist Party of America* (1955).

One particular interest group which was both supportive and critical of New Deal policies was organized labor, treated in books such as Irving Bernstein's *Turbulent Years: A History of the American Worker, 1933–1941* (1970), Sidney Fine's *Sitdown: The General Motors Strike of 1936–1937* (1969), Melvyn Dubofky and Warren Van Tine's *John L. Lewis: A Biography* (1977), and Jerold S. Auerbach's *Labor and Liberty: The La Follette Committee and the New Deal* (1966).

One region of the nation—the South—particularly concerned the New Dealers. The fullest introduction to the New Deal in the South remains the relevant chapters in George B. Tindall's *The Emergence of the New South, 1914–1945* (1967).° How the president dealt with the South is handled in Frank Friedel's *Franklin D. Roosevelt and the South* (1965). A more critical view of the New Deal's limitations is found in Paul Mertz's *The New Deal and Southern Rural Poverty* (1978). How southern farmers fared is examined in David E. Conrad's *The Forgotten Farmers: The Story of the Sharecroppers in the New Deal* (1972), Donald Grubb's *Cry from the Cotton: The Southern Tenant Farmers Union and the New Deal* (1971), and Pete Daniel's *The Shadow of Slavery: Peonage in the South, 1901–1969* (1972).° Thomas McCraw's *TVA and the Power Fight* (1971) and Phillip J. Funigiello's *Toward a National Power Policy: The New Deal and Electric Utility Industry, 1933–1941* (1973), detail federal efforts in public power regulation. Dan T. Carter provides an insightful analysis of the influence of the 1930s reforms on race relations in *Scottsboro: A Tragedy of the American South* (1969).°

For the cultural impact of the New Deal, consult Charles C. Alexander's *Nationalism in American Thought, 1930–1945* (1969), Richard H. Pells's *Radical Visions and American Dreams: Cultural and Social Thought in the Depression Years* (1973), Jane DeHart Mathews's *The Federal Theatre, 1935–1939* (1967), and Richard D. McKinzie's *The New Deal for Artists* (1973).

29 &

FROM ISOLATION TO
GLOBAL WAR

Postwar Isolationism

THE LEAGUE AND THE U.S.   In the late 1930s, as the winds of war
swept Asia and Europe, the focus of American politics moved
abruptly from domestic to foreign affairs. Another Democratic
president had to shift attention from reform to preparedness and
war. But between Wilson and Roosevelt lay two decades of isolation from foreign connections. The postwar mood of 1920 set the
pattern. The voters expressed their yearning for normalcy, and
President-elect Harding lost little time in indulging it by disposing of the League of Nations. "You just didn't want a surrender
of the United States . . ." he told the people in his victory speech.
"That's why you didn't care for the League, which is now de-
ceased." The spirit of isolation found other expressions as well:
the higher tariff walls, the Red Scare, the rage for "100 percent
Americanism," and tight immigration laws by which a nation of
immigrants all but shut the door to any more newcomers.

The United States may have felt the urge to leave a wicked
world to its own devices, but it could hardly stop the world and
get off. American business, despite the tariff walls, now had
worldwide connections. American investments and loans abroad
put in circulation the dollars that purchased American exports.
Overseas possessions, moreover, directly involved the country in
world affairs, especially in the Pacific. Even the League of Nations was too great a fact entirely to ignore, although messages
from the League at first went unanswered by American diplo-

mats. As late as 1922 Joseph C. Grew, then American ambassador to Switzerland, confessed anxiety that a reporter who saw him waiting for a friend outside League headquarters in Geneva might reveal the indiscretion. Before that year was out, however, the United States had "unofficial observers" at the League, and after 1924 gradually entered into joint efforts on such matters as the international trade in drugs and arms, the traffic in women and children, and a variety of economic, cultural, and technical conferences.

Americans had mixed feelings about adherence to the World Court. The Permanent Court of International Justice, established by the League at The Hague in 1922, was open to any country, whether a member of the League or not. The idea of bringing foreign disputes before a panel of jurists appealed to legal-minded Americans; the United States had in fact urged the idea at the Hague Peace Conferences of 1899 and 1907. Still, it smacked too much of extranational authority for isolationists, even though its jurisdiction was always optional. Repeated efforts to join the World Court therefore met with rebuff from the Senate. Franklin D. Roosevelt pressed the issue in 1935, and the Senate voted 52 to 36 in favor, but fell short of a two-thirds majority. American judges served on the Court panel, but the United States stayed out.

WAR DEBTS AND REPARATIONS Probably nothing did more to heighten American isolationism—or anti-American feeling in Europe—than the war-debt tangle. When in 1917 the Allies had begun to exhaust private credit in the United States, the government then advanced them funds first for the war effort and then for postwar reconstruction. A World War Foreign Debt Commission, created by Congress in 1922, renegotiated the Allied debt to America to a total of about $11.5 billion. Adding the interest payable over sixty-two years to this principal, the Allied debt came to something over $22 billion.

To Americans at large it all seemed a simple matter of obligation, but Europeans commonly had a different perception. In the first place, Americans who thought their loan money had flowed to Europe were wrong: most of it went toward purchases in the United States, which fueled the wartime boom. Then, too, the Allies held off the enemy at great cost of blood and treasure while the United States was raising an army. American states, the British noted, had been known to repudiate debts to British investors; and the French pointed out that they had never been repaid for help in the American Revolution. But most difficult were the practical problems of repayment. To get dollar exchange,

The War Debt Controversy. *The ghost of a French soldier asks America, "In your accounting, have you included my blood and that of my brother soldiers?"* [Library of Congress]

European debtors had to sell their goods to the United States, but tariff walls went higher in 1921 and 1922, and again in 1930, making debt payment problematic. Payment in gold would have undermined the European currencies. When the United States refused to relent, French newspapers rechristened Uncle Sam "l'Oncle Shylock."

The French and British insisted that they could pay America only as they collected reparations from Germany. Twice during the 1920s the resulting strain on Germany brought the structure of international payments to the verge of collapse, and both times the Reparations Commission called in private American bankers to work out rescue plans.

The whole structure finally did collapse during the Great Depression. In 1931 President Hoover negotiated a moratorium on both German reparations and Allied payment of war debts, thereby indirectly accepting the connection between the two. The purpose, among other things, was to shore up American private loans of several billion dollars in Germany, which for the time had kept the international credit structure intact. Once the United States had accepted the connection between reparations and war debt, the Allies virtually cancelled German reparations, reducing them in the Lausanne Agreement of 1932 to only $750 million, which was never paid. At the end of 1932, after Hoover's debt moratorium ended, most of the European countries defaulted on their war debts to the United States; by 1934 all but Finland had defaulted. In retaliation, Congress passed the Johnson Debt Default Act of 1934, which prohibited private loans to any such government.

ATTEMPTS AT DISARMAMENT Yet, for all the isolationist sentiment of the time, Wilsonian idealism had struck a responsive chord in the American people. A lingering doubt, tinged with guilt, haunted Americans about their rejection of the League. Before long the Harding people hit upon a happy substitute—disarmament. The conviction had grown after World War I that large armaments had been the war's cause, and that arms limitation would bring peace. The United States had no intention of maintaining a large army, but under the building program begun in 1916 the United States constructed a navy second only to that of Britain. Neither the British nor the Americans had much stomach for the cost of a naval armaments race with the other, but both shared a common concern with the alarming growth of Japanese power.

During and after the war Japanese-American relations grew increasingly strained. The United States objected to continued Japanese encroachments in Asia. In 1902 Japan had made a defensive alliance with Great Britain, directed then at Russia but invoked in 1914 against Germany in order to pick up German concessions and territories in the Far East. The Japanese quickly took the Shantung Peninsula and the islands of Micronesia, which Germany had purchased not long before from Spain. The Paris Peace Conference reluctantly confirmed Japanese seizure of the Shantung Peninsula, and the League of Nations authorized a Japanese mandate of Micronesia north of the equator. Occupation of Micronesia put the Japanese squarely athwart eastern approaches to the Philippines.

During the war the Japanese had seized the chance for further moves against China. In 1915 the cabinet at Tokyo issued what came to be known as the Twenty-one Demands, which would have brought China virtually under Japanese control. The United States protested, and fortunately the Japanese decided not to force their most rigorous demands. In 1917, after the United States entered the war, Viscount Kikujiro Ishii visited Washington to secure American recognition of Japan's position in Asia, dropping hints that Germany had several times tried to get Japan to quit the war. To forestall such a result, Secretary of State Lansing entered an ambiguous agreement that "territorial propinquity creates special relations between countries" and therefore "Japan has special interests [translated by the Japanese as 'paramount interests'] in China." Americans were unhappy with the Lansing-Ishii Agreement, but it was feared that this was the only way to keep Japan in the war.

To deal with the growing strains, late in 1920 Sen. William E. Borah (R-Ida.), an irreconcilable on the Versailles Treaty, sponsored a resolution for a conference on arms reductions. President Harding then invited nine principal powers to a conference on arms and also on Pacific and East Asian affairs. The Washington Armaments Conference met on November 11, 1921, in time for the delegates to attend the interment of the Unknown Soldier at Arlington National Cemetery.

President Harding delivered a formal address to open the conference. Then American Secretary of State Charles Evans Hughes, in what was expected to be a perfunctory greeting, suddenly announced that "the way to disarm is to disarm." The only way out of an armaments race, he said, "is to end it now." He proceeded to offer concrete suggestions which ultimately became the basis of agreement. It was one of the most dramatic moments in American diplomatic history. In less than fifteen minutes, one electrified reporter said, Hughes had destroyed more tonnage "than all the admirals of the world have sunk in a cycle of centuries."

The upshot was that delegates from the United States, Britain, Japan, France, and Italy reached agreement on a Five-Power Naval Treaty incorporating Hughes's plan for tonnage limits and a naval holiday of ten years during which no capital ships (battleships and aircraft carriers) would be built. These powers also agreed to refrain from further fortification of their Pacific possessions: Japan in all areas except those adjacent to the homeland; Britain and the United States in areas east of Singapore and west of Hawaii, as far north as the Aleutians. The result was to expose Hong Kong and the Philippines in the event of war, but Hong Kong was clearly indefensible and the Philippines only slightly less so given the Japanese presence in Micronesia. The agreement in effect partitioned the world: United States naval power became supreme in the Western Hemisphere, Japanese power in the western Pacific, British power from the North Sea to Singapore.

Two other major agreements came out of the Washington Conference. With the Four-Power Treaty, the United States, Britain, Japan, and France agreed to respect each other's possessions in the Pacific, and to refer any disputes or any outside threat to consultation. In return for this guarantee Britain and Japan abrogated their alliance dating from 1902. The Nine-Power Treaty for the first time formally pledged the signers to support the Open Door and the territorial integrity of China. The powers, in addition to those signing the Five-Power Treaty, were China, Belgium, Portugal, and the Netherlands.

With these agreements in hand within a year of Harding's inauguration, his people could boast of a brilliant diplomatic stroke which relieved American taxpayers of the need to pay for an enlarged navy, and which anticipated potential conflicts in the Pacific. Having learned from one of Wilson's errors, Hoover named to the delegation two senators, one from each party: Henry Cabot Lodge and Oscar W. Underwood. A grateful Senate approved the naval treaty with one dissenting vote. The Four-Power Treaty aroused real opposition, but finally passed with the support of Democrats after the Senate tacked on a reservation that "there is no commitment to armed force, no alliance, no obligation to join in any defense."

There was the rub. Though the agreements tapped a deep urge toward peacemaking, they were uniformly without obligation and without teeth. The signers of the Four-Power Treaty agreed only to consult, not to help each other, a point that was clear even before the Senate tacked on its reservation. The formal endorsement of the Open Door in the Nine-Power Treaty was just as ineffective, and the American people remained unwilling as yet to uphold the principle with anything but pious affirmation. The naval disarmament treaty set limits only on capital ships; the race to build cruisers, destroyers, submarines, and other smaller craft continued. In 1930 a London Naval Conference attempted to set tonnage limits on smaller craft, but failed when Japan withdrew from the agreement four years later. Thus twelve years after the Washington Conference the dream of naval disarmament died.

During and after the "war to end war" the ideal of abolishing war caught the American imagination. Peace societies thrived and spawned innumerable programs, foremost among them the Carnegie Endowment for International Peace, founded in 1910. In 1921 a wealthy Chicagoan named Salmon Levinson founded the American Committee for the Outlawry of War. "We can outlaw this war system just as we outlawed slavery and the saloon," said Colonel Robins, active in many reform causes and one of the more enthusiastic converts.

THE KELLOGG-BRIAND PACT   The glorious vision of abolishing war at the stroke of a pen culminated in the signing of the Kellogg-Briand Pact in 1928. This unique treaty started with an initiative from French Foreign Minister Aristide Briand, who had busied himself winning allies against a possible resurgence of German power. In 1927 Briand proposed to Secretary of State Frank B. Kellogg not an alliance but an agreement that the two countries would never go to war with each other. This innocent-seeming proposal was actually a clever ploy to draw the United States into the French security system by the back door. In any future war, for instance, such a pact would inhibit the United States from re-

*Plans for international disarmament, popular in the
1920s, proved impractical. [New York Public Library]*

prisals against any French intrusions on neutral rights. Kellogg
gave the idea a cool reception, and was outraged to discover that
Briand had urged leaders of the American peace movements to
put pressure on the government to sign.

Finally Kellogg turned the tables on Briand. He countered
with a scheme to have all nations brought into the pact, an idea
all the more acceptable to the peace movements. Caught in a
trap of his own making, the French foreign minister finally relented. The Pact of Paris (its official name), signed on August 27,
1928, solemnly declared that the signatories "condemn recourse
to war . . . and renounce it as an instrument of national policy."
Eventually sixty-two powers adhered to the pact, but all explicitly or tacitly reserved "self-defense" as an escape hatch. The
United States Senate included a reservation declaring the
Monroe Doctrine necessary to self-defense, and then ratified the
agreement by a vote of 85 to 1. Carter Glass of Virginia, who
voted for "this worthless, but perfectly harmless peace treaty,"
wrote a friend later that he feared it would "confuse the minds of
many good people who think that peace may be secured by polite professions of neighborly and brotherly love."

His judgment aptly described the euphoric assumptions of
many Americans at the time. The treaty proved to be the grand-
est illusion in an age of illusions. Its "only discernible influence,"
the historian Robert H. Ferrell wrote, "was to inaugurate a fashion whereby wars would be fought under justification of national
defense and without formal declaration of hostilities." Such a
war broke out just a year later in Manchuria, where Russian
forces quickly put down a Chinese effort to regain control of the
Chinese Eastern Railway. When Hoover's secretary of state,
Henry L. Stimson, called the Soviet Union's attention to the Pact
of Paris, Soviet Foreign Minister Litvinov called attention to the

fact that the United States had not yet recognized the Soviet government, and scorned the presumption of Stimson's communication.

THE "GOOD NEIGHBOR" POLICY   In Latin America the spirit of peace and noninvolvement helped allay resentments against the Colossus of the North, which had freely intervened in the Caribbean during the first two decades of the century. The Harding administration agreed in 1921 to pay the republic of Colombia the $25 million they had once demanded for canal rights. In 1924 American forces left the Dominican Republic, occupied since 1916, although United States officials continued to collect customs duties there until 1941.

The marines left Nicaragua in 1925, but returned a year later with the outbreak of disorders and civil war. There in 1927, Coolidge's personal representative Henry L. Stimson brought both parties into an agreement for American-supervised elections, but one rebel leader, César Augusto Sandino, held out and the marines stayed until 1933. The unhappy legacies of this intervention were enmity toward the United States and a Nicaraguan National Guard, created to keep order after the marines left, but used in 1936 to set up the dictatorship of Anastasio Somoza. These legacies continue to have their effects down to the present day.

The troubles in Nicaragua increased strains in relations with Mexico. Relations were already troubled by repeated Mexican threats to expropriate American oil properties under the Constitution of 1917, which nationalized all mineral and oil resources in the country. In 1927, however, Coolidge sent his Amherst classmate Dwight L. Morrow as ambassador, and Morrow so mollified the Mexicans by his gestures of friendship that a year later he was able to get an agreement protecting American rights acquired before 1917. Expropriation did in fact occur in 1938, but the Mexican government then agreed to reimburse American owners.

In 1928, with problems apparently clearing in Mexico and Nicaragua, President Coolidge traveled to Havana to open the Pan-American Conference, sixth in a series that dated from Blaine's first conference in 1889–1890. It was an unusual gesture of friendship, and so was the choice of Charles Evans Hughes, the former secretary of state, to head the American delegation. Hughes announced United States' withdrawal from Nicaragua and Haiti as soon as possible, although he did block a resolution declaring that "no state has the right to intervene in the affairs of another."

At the end of 1928 President-elect Hoover began a tour of ten Latin American nations. Once in office he reversed Wilson's policy of refusing to recognize "bad" regimes and reverted to the older policy of recognizing governments in power. In 1930 he gained more goodwill points by permitting publication of a 236-page memorandum drawn up in 1928 by Undersecretary of State J. Ruben Clark. The Clark Memorandum denied that the Monroe Doctrine justified American intervention in Latin America. It stopped short of repudiating intervention on any grounds, but that fine point hardly blunted the celebration in Latin America. Although Hoover never endorsed the Clark Memorandum, he never intervened in the area. Before he left office, steps had already been taken to withdraw American forces from Nicaragua and Haiti.

Franklin D. Roosevelt likewise embraced "the policy of the good neighbor" and soon advanced it in practice. In December 1933 at the seventh Pan-American Conference in Montevideo, Uruguay, Secretary of State Cordell Hull supported a resolution saying "No state has the right to intervene in the international or external affairs of another." Under Roosevelt the marines completed their withdrawals from Nicaragua and Haiti, and in 1934 the president negotiated with Cuba a treaty which abrogated the Platt Amendment and thus ended the last formal claim to a right of intervention in Latin America. Roosevelt reinforced hemispheric goodwill in 1936, when he opened the Pan-American Conference in Buenos Aires with a speech declaring that outside aggressors "will find a Hemisphere wholly prepared to consult together for our mutual safety and our mutual good."

War Clouds

JAPANESE INCURSIONS IN CHINA   The lessening of irritants in the Western Hemisphere proved an exception in an otherwise dismal world scene, as war clouds deepened over Europe and Asia. Actual conflict came first in Asia, where unsettled conditions in China had invited foreign encroachments since before the turn of the century. The tottering Manchu dynasty had collapsed in 1911 and the series of governments that followed in Peiping exercised only nominal authority over local warlords. Finally the Kuomintang (or National Party) under Dr. Sun Yat-sen and, later, Chiang Kai-shek, extended its power from a southern base around Canton to take Peiping in 1928 and set up a new capital in Nanking. But when the new government tried to extend its power in Manchuria it ran into the vested interest of the Russians and Japanese there. Its effort to take over the Chinese Eastern Railway in 1929 led to a short undeclared war with Russia and humiliation for the Kuomintang. More important, Chinese nationalist aspirations convinced the Japanese that their own extensive rights in Manchuria, including the South Manchurian Railway, were in danger.

The Japanese army at the time had a nationalist movement of its own, led by a strong cadre of young officers devoted to the vague idea of a "Showa restoration" (Showa being the reign name of Emperor Hirohito) which would overturn corrupt politicians and bring about a moral regeneration for Japan. Economic pressures strengthened this nationalist movement, for Japan was suffering from the Great Depression and Chinese boycotts of Japanese goods. Manchuria offered both a tempting target and a promising market. Japanese occupation of Manchuria began with the Mukden Incident of September 18, 1931, an explosion which destroyed a section of track near that city. The Japanese "Kwantung Army," based in Manchuria to guard the railway, blamed the incident on the Chinese and used it as a pretext to begin its occupation, which it extended during the winter of 1931–1932 to all of Manchuria, including the Russian sphere of influence. In 1932 the Japanese converted Manchuria into the puppet empire of "Manchukuo" and resurrected the former boy emperor of China, deposed in 1911, to head the new state. The Manchuria Incident, as the Japanese called their undeclared war, was a flagrant breach of the Nine-Power Treaty, the Kellogg-Briand Pact, and Japan's pledges as a member of the League of Nations. But when China asked the League and the United States for help, neither was ready to take effective action. President Hoover was unwilling to invoke either military or economic sanctions. Secretary of State Stimson, who would have preferred to do more, issued a statement in January 1932 warning that the United States refused to recognize any treaty, agreement, or situation which violated American treaty rights, the Open Door, or the territorial integrity of China, or any situation brought about by violation of the Kellogg-Briand Pact. This statement, later known as the Stimson Doctrine, had no effect on Japanese action, for later in the same month the Japanese navy attacked and briefly occupied Shanghai.

Indiscriminate bombing of Shanghai's civilian population aroused indignation, but no further Western action. When the League of Nations condemned Japanese aggression in February 1933, Japan's response was to withdraw from the League and keep the islands of Micronesia as a souvenir. During the spring of

Japan's seizure of Manchuria in 1931 prompted this American condemnation. [Granger Collection]

1933 hostilities in Manchuria gradually subsided and ended with a truce on May 31, 1933. Then an uneasy peace settled upon East Asia for four years, during which the leaders of Japan's military further extended their political sway.

ITALY AND GERMANY The rise of the Japanese militarists paralleled the rise of warlike dictators in Italy and Germany. In 1922 Benito Mussolini had seized power in Italy. A one-time Socialist leader, Mussolini had broken with the party over its antiwar stand, and after returning from World War I as a wounded veteran, had organized the Fascist movement, which was based on a composite faith in nationalism and socialism. The movement's name came from the ancient Roman *fasces*, a symbol of authority consisting of a bundle of sticks bound around an axe. The program, and above all Mussolini's promise to restore order in a country fragmented by dissension, enjoyed a wide appeal. Once in power, Mussolini largely abandoned the socialist part of his platform and gradually suppressed the opposition. By 1925 he wielded dictatorial power as Il Duce (the leader) in a one-party state.

To most Americans there was always something ludicrous about the magniloquent Mussolini posing jut-jawed on the balcony of the Palazzo Venezia. Italy afforded but a limited power base in the total European picture. But Germany was another matter, and Americans were not amused, even at the beginning, by Il Duce's counterpart, Adolf Hitler, despite his Charlie Chaplin moustache. Hitler's National Socialist (Nazi) party duplicated the major features of Italian Fascism, including the ancient Roman salute. Hitler, having failed to duplicate Mussolini's success in a premature *Putsch* in 1923, did manage to win a foothold for his party in the German Reichstag (parliament). The impo-

Mussolini and Hitler. [Wide World Photos]

tence of the Weimar Republic in the face of world depression finally offered his opening. Made chancellor on January 30, 1933, he moved swiftly to intimidate the opposition, won dictatorial powers from a subservient Reichstag on March 24, and after the death of President Hindenburg in 1934 assumed the title of Reichsführer (national leader) with absolute powers. The Nazi police state cranked up the engines of tyranny, persecuting Jews, whom Hitler blamed for all Germany's troubles, and rearming in defiance of the Versailles Treaty. Hitler flouted international agreements, pulled Germany out of the League of Nations in October 1933, and frankly proclaimed that he meant to extend control over all German-speaking peoples. Despite one provocation after another the European democracies seemed to lack the will to resist.

THE MOOD IN AMERICA Americans, absorbed by the problems of the depression, chose to retreat all the more into isolationism during the early 1930s. In the campaign of 1932 Roosevelt had found it prudent to renounce his Wilsonian past and state that he now opposed joining the League of Nations. Once in office he rejected an early chance to deal with economic problems on an international basis. Hoover, convinced that the depression called for world action, had pledged the United States to participate in the London Economic Conference on reparations. The conference of sixty-four nations was to deal with the related issues of currency stabilization, world trade, and war debts. But when a group of gold-bloc nations (led by France) insisted on a return to the gold standard, Roosevelt demurred and the conference ended in futility. The president wanted to be free to experiment with currency manipulation as a device to fight the depression. Roosevelt's action dealt a severe blow to international cooperation. The epilogue was Europe's final default on the war debts, and further American drift toward isolation.

The chief exception to the administration's isolationism was Secretary of State Cordell Hull's grand scheme of reciprocal trade agreements. Hull, a former Tennessee judge and congressman, held to the firm conviction that to release the fetters on world trade would advance understanding and peace. His economic thinking, said one historian, was "a blend of Adam Smith and the cotton South." In 1934 the administration threw its support behind Hull's pet project, and over the objections of business interests and Republicans Congress adopted the Trade Agreements Act, which authorized the president to lower tariff rates as much as 50 percent for countries which made similar concessions on American products. Agreements were made with fourteen countries by the end of 1935, and twenty-nine by 1945. The economic results are hard to measure, since the following years were so troubled.

Another scheme for building foreign markets, diplomatic recognition of Soviet Russia, won more support in business quarters than had the reciprocity plan. The vast expanse of Russia stirred fantasies of a trade boom, much as China had at the turn of the century. By 1933 the reasons for American refusal to recognize the Bolshevik regime had grown stale. Japanese expansionism in Asia, moreover, gave Russia and the United States a common concern. Given an opening by the shift of opinion, Roosevelt invited Maxim Litvinov, Soviet commissar for foreign affairs, to visit Washington. After nine days of talks, a formal exchange of notes on November 16, 1933, signaled the renewal of diplomatic relations. Litvinov promised that his country would abstain from propaganda in the United States, extend religious freedom to Americans in the USSR, and reopen the question of czarist debts.

THE EXPANDING AXIS   But a catastrophic chain of events in Asia and Europe sent the world hurtling toward disaster. In 1934 Japan renounced the Five-Power Naval Treaty. In 1935 Mussolini commenced an Italian conquest of Ethiopia. The same year a referendum in the Saar Basin, held in accordance with the Versailles Treaty, delivered that coal-rich region into the hands of Hitler. In 1936 Hitler reoccupied the Rhineland with armed forces, in violation of the Versailles Treaty but without any forceful response from the French. (It is now known that such a response would have forced him to break down.) The year 1936 also brought the Spanish Civil War, which began with an uprising of the Spanish armed forces in Morocco, led by Gen. Francisco Franco. In three years Franco had established a fascist dictatorship with help from Hitler and Mussolini while the democracies stood by and left the Spanish Republic to its fate. On July 7, 1937, Japanese and Chinese troops came into conflict at the Marco Polo Bridge near Peiping. The incident quickly developed into a full-scale war which the Japanese persisted in calling the "China Incident." It was the beginning of World War II in Asia, two years before war came to Europe. That same year Japan joined Germany and Italy in the "Anti-Comintern Pact," allegedly directed at the Communist threat, thus establishing the Rome-Berlin-Tokyo "Axis."

By 1938 the peace of Europe trembled in the balance. Having rebuilt German military force, Hitler forced the *Anschluss* (union) of Austria with Germany in March 1938, and six months

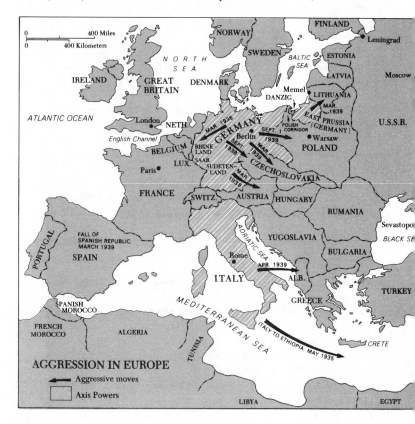

AGGRESSION IN EUROPE
← Aggressive moves
☐ Axis Powers

The swastika, symbol of Nazi Germany, about to crush Poland. [D. R. Fitzpatrick, St. Louis Post Dispatch]

later took the Sudeten territory from Czechoslovakia after signing an agreement at Munich under which Britain and France abandoned a country that had probably the second-best army in central Europe. The mountainous Sudetenland, largely German in population, was vital to the defense of Czechoslovakia. Having said this was his last territorial demand, Hitler in March 1939 occupied the remainder of Czechoslovakia. In quick succession the Spanish Republic finally collapsed on March 28 and Mussolini seized the kingdom of Albania on April 7. Finally, during the summer Hitler heated up a "war of nerves" over control of the free city of Danzig and the Polish Corridor, and on September 1 launched his conquest of Poland. A few days before, he had reached a nonaggression pact with Russia. Having deserted Czechoslovakia, Britain and France now honored their commitment to go to war if Poland were invaded.

DEGREES OF NEUTRALITY During these years of deepening crisis, the Western democracies remained infirm of purpose, hoping in vain that each concession would appease the appetites of fascist dictators. The response of the United States was to retreat more deeply into isolation. The prevailing mood was reinforced by a Senate inquiry into the role of bankers and munitions makers in World War I. Under Sen. Gerald P. Nye of North Dakota, a progressive Republican, the committee sat from 1934 to 1937, and after hauling to the witness stand J. P. Morgan, Jr., and the du Pont brothers, among others, reached the foregone conclusion that bankers and munitions makers had made scandalous profits from the war. Although Nye never showed that greed for profit had actually impelled Wilson into war, millions of Americans became convinced that Uncle Sam had been duped by the "merchants of death."

Historians then rehashing the European origins of World War I challenged the idea of German war guilt; some condemned America's entry into the war. In one of the bestsellers of the time, *The Road to War: America, 1914–1917* (1935), Walter Millis, a freelance journalist and historian, argued that a combination of British propaganda, economic involvement with the Allies, and Wilson's uneven response to British and German violations of neutrality had sucked the United States into a war it should have kept out of. In 1934 Charles Warren, assistant attorney-general under Wilson, wrote in the journal *Foreign Affairs* that modern warfare had rendered obsolete old notions of freedom of the seas. If the United States wanted to remain neutral in the current crisis, therefore, it would have to keep Americans out of war zones, keep belligerent vessels out of American ports, embargo arms shipments, and set quotes on the export of contraband. Such ideas became official policy as war enveloped Asia and Europe.

Like generals who are said to be always preparing for the last war, Congress occupied itself with keeping out of the last war. Neutrality laws of the 1930s moved the United States back toward Jefferson's embargo policies and complete isolation from the quarrels of Europe. Americans wanted to keep out of war, but their sympathies were more strongly than ever with the Western democracies, and the triumph of fascist aggression aroused growing fears for national security.

On August 31, 1935, President Roosevelt signed the first in a series of neutrality acts, one which anticipated Italy's invasion of Ethiopia. The Neutrality Act of 1935 forbade the sale of arms and munitions to all belligerents whenever the president proclaimed that a state of war existed. Americans who traveled on belligerent ships thereafter did so at their own risk. Roosevelt would have preferred discretionary authority to levy an embargo only against aggressors, but reluctantly accepted the act because it would be effective only six months, and for the time being "meets the need of the existing situation." That is, it would actually be enforced against Italy in its war with Ethiopia. When he signed the act on August 31, Roosevelt nevertheless urged reconsideration of the arms embargo on all belligerents: "History is filled with situations that call for some flexibility of action. It is conceivable that situations may arise in which the wholly inflexible provisions . . . of this act . . . might drag us into war instead of keeping us out."

On October 3, 1935, Italy invaded Ethiopia and the president invoked the act. One shortcoming in its provisions became apparent right away: the key problem was neither arms traffic nor passenger travel, but trade in contraband not covered by the Neutrality Act. Secretary of State Hull warned, however, that anybody trading with the belligerents, meaning in effect Italy since there was little trade with Ethiopia, did so at his own risk. He asked, moreover, for a "moral embargo" on oil and other products. Sanctions imposed under the Neutrality Act had no deterrent effect on Mussolini or his suppliers. In the summer of 1936 Il Duce completed his conquest of Ethiopia.

When Congress reconvened in January 1936, it fell into a three-cornered debate among the advocates of mandatory embargoes, flexible embargoes aimed at aggressors, and traditional neutrality. After six weeks Congress simply extended the arms embargo and added a provision forbidding loans to belligerents. Then in July 1936, while Italian troops mopped up the last resistance in Ethiopia, the Spanish Army revolted in Morocco. Ironically, Roosevelt now became more isolationist than some of the isolationists. Although the Spanish Civil War involved a fascist uprising against a recognized, democratic government, Roosevelt accepted the French and British position that only nonintervention would localize the fight. There existed, moreover, a strong bloc of pro-Franco Catholics in America who feared that the Spanish Republic was a threat to the church. They feared Communist influence in the Spanish government; intrigues by Spanish Communists did prove divisive and the Soviet Union in fact did supply aid to the Republic, but nothing like the quantity of German and Italian aid to Franco.

Roosevelt asked for another "moral embargo" on the arms trade, and asked Congress to extend the neutrality laws to cover civil wars. Congress did so in January 1937 with only one dissenting vote—although many, including Senator Nye, had second thoughts later about leaving the Spanish Republic thus to its fate. The Western democracies then stood witness while German and Italian soldiers, planes, and armaments supported Franco's overthrow of Spanish democracy, which was completed in 1939.

In the spring of 1937 isolationism reached a peak. The Gallup poll found that 94 percent of its respondents preferred efforts to keep out of war over efforts to prevent war. That same spring Congress passed yet another neutrality law, which continued restraints on arms sales and loans, forbade Americans to travel on belligerent ships, and forbade the arming of American merchant ships trading with belligerents. The president also got discre-

"Come on in. I'll treat you right. I used to know your daddy." *This Pulitzer Prize–winning cartoon by Clarence Bachelor reflects American isolationism of the 1930s.* [New York News]

tionary authority to require that goods other than arms or munitions exported to belligerents be placed on a cash-and-carry basis. This was an ingenious scheme to preserve a profitable trade without running the risk of war.

The new law had its first test on July 7, 1937, when Japanese and Chinese forces clashed at the Marco Polo Bridge west of Peiping. Since neither side declared war, Roosevelt was able to use his discretion about invoking the neutrality law. He decided to wait, and in fact never invoked it. This was because its net effect would have favored the Japanese, since China had greater need of arms but few means to get supplies past the Japanese Navy. A flourishing trade in munitions to China flowed around the world as ships carried arms across the Atlantic to England, where they were reloaded on British ships bound for Hong Kong. Roosevelt, by inaction, had challenged strict isolationism.

He soon ventured a step further. On October 5, 1937, Roosevelt delivered a forthright denunciation of the "reign of terror and international lawlessness" in which 10 percent of the world's population threatened the peace of the other 90 percent. "When an epidemic of physical disease starts to spread, the community approves and joins in a quarantine of the patients in order to protect the health of the community. . . ." There should also be a quarantine against nations "creating a state of international anarchy and instability from which there is no escape through mere isolation or neutrality." On the whole, public reaction to the speech was mixed. The president quickly backed off from its implications and refused to spell out any specific program. The day after his address, the League of Nations condemned Japanese aggression and called for a conference of the

Nine-Power Treaty signatories. The meeting, held at Brussels in November 1937, did nothing but reaffirm the principle of the Open Door Policy and then adjourn.

Three weeks after the Brussels Conference, on December 12, 1937, Japanese planes bombed and sank the American gunboat *Panay,* which had been lying at anchor in the Yangtze River and prominently flying the American flag, and then attacked three Standard Oil tankers. Two members of the *Panay* crew and an Italian journalist died; thirty more were injured. Though the Japanese government was quick to apologize and pay the reparations demanded—nearly $2¼ million—the incident reinforced American animosity toward Japan. The private boycott of Japanese goods spread, but isolationist sentiment continued strong, as was vividly demonstrated by support for the Ludlow Amendment in Congress. The proposed constitutional amendment would have required a referendum for a declaration of war except in case of attack on American territory. Only by the most severe pressure from the White House, and a vote of 209 to 188, was consideration of the measure stopped in January 1938.

Still, the continuing Japanese war against China brought public outrage and protests from Secretary Hull. On July 1, 1938, after nearly a year of war in China, the government notified domestic aircraft manufacturers and exporters that it opposed sales to those guilty of attacks on civilian populations. To have imposed an outright embargo would have violated a commercial treaty of 1911 with Japan, but after another year, on July 26, 1939, the United States gave six-months' notice of the termination of the treaty—thus clearing the way for an embargo on war materials.

By then Hitler had brought Europe into war. After the German occupation of Czechoslovakia, Roosevelt no longer pretended impartiality in the impending struggle. He urged Congress to repeal the embargo and permit the United States to sell arms on a cash-and-carry basis to Britain and France, but to no avail. "You haven't got the votes," Vice-President Garner told him, "and that's all there is to it." When the German attack on Poland came on September 1, 1939, Roosevelt proclaimed neutrality, but in a radio talk said that he did not, like Wilson, ask Americans to remain neutral in thought because "even a neutral has a right to take account of the facts."

Congress, summoned into special session on September 21, was asked once again to amend the Neutrality Act. "I regret the Congress passed the Act," the president said. "I regret equally that I signed the Act." This time he got what he wanted by winning the support of conservative Democrats who had opposed his domestic policies. Under the Neutrality Act of 1939 the Allies could come, buy for cash, and take away arms or anything else they wanted. American ships, on the other hand, were excluded from belligerent ports and from specified war zones. Roosevelt then designated as a war zone the Baltic Sea and the waters around Great Britain and Ireland from Norway south to the coast of Spain. One ironic effect of this move was to relieve Hitler of any inhibitions against using unrestricted submarine warfare to blockade Britain.

American attitudes continued to vacillate. As the war crisis developed, an isolationist policy of hands-off prevailed. Once the great democracies of western Europe faced war, American public opinion, appalled at Hitler's tyranny, came to support measures short of war to help their cause. "What the majority of the American people want," the editor Freda Kirchwey wrote in the *Nation,* "is to be as unneutral as possible without getting into war." On October 3, while Congress debated repeal of the arms embargo, the foreign ministers of the American republics adopted the Declaration of Panama, which created a "chastity belt" around the Americas, south of Canada, a zone 300 to 1,000 miles wide in which belligerents were warned not to pursue naval action. For a time it seemed possible that the Western Hemisphere could remain insulated from the war. After Hitler overran Poland in less than a month, the war settled into an unreal stalemate that began to be called the "Phony War." What lay ahead, it seemed, was a long war of attrition in which Britain and France would have the resources to outlast Hitler. The illusion lasted through the winter.

The Storm in Europe

BLITZKRIEG In the spring of 1940 the winter's long *Sitzkrieg* suddenly erupted into *Blitzkrieg*—lightning war. At dawn on April 9, without warning, Nazi troops entered Denmark and disembarked along the Norwegian coast. Denmark fell in a day, Norway within a few weeks. On May 10 Hitler released his dive bombers and panzer tank divisions on neutral Belgium and the Netherlands. On May 21 German forces moving down the valley of the Somme reached the English Channel, cutting off a British force sent to help the Belgians and French. A desperate evacuation from the beaches at Dunkirk enlisted every available boat from warship to tug. Some 338,000 men, including a few French, escaped to England. Having outflanked the forts on

France's defense perimeter, the Maginot Line, the German forces rushed ahead, cutting the French armies to pieces and spreading panic by strafing refugees in a deliberate policy of terror. On June 10 Mussolini entered the war. "I need only a few thousand dead to enable me to take my seat . . . at the peace table," Il Duce said. Speaking at the University of Virginia the same day, Roosevelt grimly ad libbed: "The hand that held the dagger has plunged it into the back of France." On June 14 the swastika flew over Paris. On June 22 French delegates, in the presence of Hitler, submitted to his terms in the same railroad car at Compiègne in which German delegates had signed the Armistice of 1918.

AMERICA'S GROWING INVOLVEMENT   Britain stood alone, but in Parliament Prime Minister Winston Churchill, who had replaced Chamberlain amid the *Blitzkrieg*, breathed defiance. "We shall go on to the end," he said; "we shall never surrender." Even if the home islands should fall, the Empire "would carry on the struggle, until, in God's good time, the New World with all its power and might, steps forth to the rescue and liberation of the Old." Despite the grim resolution of the British, America seemed suddenly vulnerable as Hitler turned his air force against Britain. President Roosevelt, who in his annual budget had requested $1.9 billion for defense, now asked for more, and called for the production of 50,000 combat planes a year. By October 1940 Congress had voted more than $17 billion for defense. In response to Churchill's appeal for military supplies, the War and Navy Departments began releasing stocks of arms, planes, and munitions to the British. They resorted to a World War I law which permitted the government to trade in equipment for newer models—the manufacturers could then send the trade-ins to Britain on a cash-and-carry basis.

America continued to prepare its defense. On June 15, 1940, the president set up the National Defense Research Committee under Dr. Vannevar Bush of the Carnegie Institution to coordinate military research, including a secret look into the possibility of developing an atomic bomb, suggested the previous fall by Albert Einstein and other scientists. To bolster national unity, on June 19 Roosevelt named two Republicans to the defense posts in his cabinet: Henry L. Stimson as secretary of war and Frank Knox as secretay of the navy. On July 20 Roosevelt signed a bill authorizing a two-ocean navy at a cost of $4 billion, and on July 30 delegates to the Pan-American Conference approved the Declaration of Havana, under which the republics might take over and administer European possessions that were in danger of falling into unfriendly hands. In August the United States and Canada set up a Permanent Joint Board on Defense. At the end of the month units of the National Guard began to be inducted into federal service.

The summer of 1940 brought the desperate Battle of Britain, in which the Royal Air Force, with the benefit of the new technology of radar finding, outfought the numerically superior German Luftwaffe and finally forced the Germans to give up plans to invade. Submarine warfare meanwhile strained the resources of the battered Royal Navy. To relieve the pressure, Churchill urgently requested the transfer of American destroyers. Secret negotiations led to an executive agreement on September 2, under which fifty "overaged" destroyers went to the British in return for ninety-nine-year leases on naval and air bases in Newfoundland, Bermuda, the Bahamas, Jamaica, St. Lucia, Trinidad, Antigua, and British Guiana. It was, Roosevelt declared expansively, "the most important action in the reinforcement of our national defense that has been taken since the Louisiana Purchase." Two weeks later, on September 16, 1940, Congress adopted the first peacetime conscription in American history. The Burke-Wadsworth Act called for the registration of all men aged twenty-one to thirty-five for a year's military service within the United States.

The new state of affairs prompted vigorous debate between "internationalists" who believed national security demanded aid to Britain and isolationists who charged that Roosevelt was drawing the United States into a needless war. In May 1940 the nonpartisan Committee to Defend America by Aiding the Allies was organized with the Kansas journalist William Allen White as chairman. It drew its strongest support from the East and West Coasts and the South, and included among its members General Pershing, Harold Ickes, Harry Hopkins, and Henry Stimson. In June, moreover, thirty men known as the Century Group, after the New York club where they met, urged immediate declaration of war on Germany. One of them was Walter Millis, whose book on World War I had done so much five years earlier to bolster isolationism.

In July 1940, on the other hand, isolationists formed the America First Committee. The organizer was a Yale law student, R. Douglas Stuart, Jr., whose father was president of the Quaker Oats Company. The group included midwestern businessmen like Gen. Robert Wood of Sears, Roebuck, and Jay Hormel, the meat-packer, as well as the historian Charles A. Beard, Herbert Hoover, and Charles A. Lindbergh. Before the end of 1941 the committee had about 450 chapters around the country, but probably two-thirds of its members lived within a 300-mile radius of Chicago. The isolationists argued that the war involved, in Senator Borah's words, "nothing more than another chapter in the bloody volume of European power politics," and that a Nazi victory, while distasteful, would pose no threat to national security.

A THIRD TERM FOR FDR   In the midst of these developments the quadrennial presidential campaign came due. Isolationist sentiment was strongest in the Republican party and both the leading Republican candidates were noninterventionists, but neither loomed as a man of sufficient stature to challenge the "champ," assuming Roosevelt decided to run again. Sen. Robert A. Taft of Ohio, son of the former president, lacked popular appeal, and New York District Attorney Thomas E. Dewey, who had won fame as a "racket buster," at thirty-eight seemed young and unseasoned. This left an opening for an inspired group of political amateurs to promote the dark-horse candidacy of Wendell L. Willkie. Willkie seemed at first an unlikely choice: a former Democrat who had voted for Roosevelt in 1932, a utility president who had fought TVA, but in origins a Hoosier farm boy whose disheveled charm inspired strong loyalty. He was "a simple, barefoot Wall Street lawyer," in the devastating phrase of Interior Secretary Harold L. Ickes. Unlike the front-runners, he openly supported aid to the Allies, and the Nazi *Blitzkrieg* had brought many other Republicans to the same viewpoint. As late

GOP presidential nominee Wendell L. Willkie parading through Elwood, Indiana, 1940. [Wide World Photos]

as April Willkie did not have a single delegate, but when the Republicans met at Philadelphia on June 28, six days after the French surrender, the convention was stampeded by the cry of "We Want Willkie" from the galleries. Sen. Charles L. McNary of Oregon was the choice for vice-president.

The Nazi victory also ensured another nomination for Roosevelt. The president cultivated party unity behind his foreign policy and kept a sphinx-like silence about his intentions. Amid the uncertainty no other hopefuls rose high enough to challenge him. The world crisis reconciled southern conservatives to the man whose foreign policy at least they supported. At the July convention in Chicago Roosevelt won nomination for a third term with only token opposition from Farley and Garner. The vice-presidential nod went to Agriculture Secretary Henry A. Wallace. A former Republican with a reputation more for mysticism than for politics, Wallace was anathema to the professionals, but they swallowed hard and took him.

Through the summer Roosevelt assumed the role of a man above the political fray, busy rather with urgent matters of defense and diplomacy: Pan-American agreements for mutual defense, the destroyer-bases deal, and visits to defense facilities which took the place of campaign trips. Willkie inspired a more intense personal devotion than any Republican candidate since Theodore Roosevelt, but he had trouble positioning himself since there was little on which he disagreed with Roosevelt. The New Deal programs were too popular, in any case, to oppose head-on.

Like Landon, Willkie was reduced to attacks on New Deal red tape, and promises to run the programs better. A widespread reluctance to violate the tradition against a presidential third term strengthened his argument that new blood was needed in the White House. In the end, however, he switched to an attack on Roosevelt's conduct of foreign policy. In October he warned: "If you re-elect him you may expect war in April, 1941." To this Roosevelt responded, "I have said this before, but I shall say it again and again and again: Your boys are not going to be sent into any foreign wars." Three days before the election he declared in Buffalo: "Your President says this country is not going to war." Neither man distinguished himself with such hollow statements, since both knew the risks of all-out aid to Britain, which both supported.

Roosevelt won the election by a comfortable margin of 27 million votes to Willkie's 22 million, and a wider margin of 449 to 82 in the electoral college. The popular vote was closer than any presidential vote since 1916. Given the dangerous world situation a majority of the voters agreed with the Democrats' slogan: "Don't switch horses in the middle of the stream."

THE ARSENAL OF DEMOCRACY Bolstered by the mandate for an unprecedented third term, Roosevelt moved quickly for greater measures of aid to Britain. Since the outbreak of war Roosevelt had corresponded with Winston Churchill, who as first lord of the Admiralty used the signature "Navy Person"; as prime minister he became "Former Naval Person." Soon after the election Churchill informed Roosevelt that British credit was fast running out. Since direct American loans would arouse memories of earlier war-debt defaults—the Johnson Act of 1934 forbade such loans anyway—the president created an ingenious device to bypass that issue and yet supply British needs, the "lend-lease" program.

In a fireside chat on December 29, 1940, he told the nation that it must become "the great arsenal of democracy" because of the threat of Britain's fall. In his annual message to Congress on January 6, 1941, he warned that only the British navy stood between America and the peril of attack. Greater efforts to bolster British defenses were therefore in order: "They do not need manpower. They do need billions of dollars worth of the weapons of defense." At the end of the speech he enunciated the Four Freedoms for which the democracies fought: freedom of speech, freedom of worship, freedom from want, and freedom from fear. The Lend-Lease Bill, introduced in Congress on January 10, authorized the president to sell, transfer, exchange, lend, lease, or otherwise dispose of arms and other equipment and supplies to "any country whose defense the President deems vital to the defense of the United States."

For two months a bitter debate over the bill raged in Congress and the country. Isolationists saw it as the point of no return. "The lend-lease-give program," said Sen. Burton K. Wheeler, "is the New Deal's triple A foreign policy; it will plow under every fourth American boy." Roosevelt pronounced this "the rottenest thing that has been said in public life in my generation." Administration supporters denied that lend-lease would lead to war, but it did manifestly increase the risk. On March 11, 1941, as "An Act to Promote the Defense of the United States," lend-lease became law. The next day the president asked that the program be funded with an appropriation of $7 billion, the largest single appropriation in American history to that time, more than ninety times the national debt refunded by Alexander Ham-

Women Pray for Defeat of Lend-Lease Bill. *These women shared Senator Wheeler's fear that lend-lease would "plow under every fourth American boy." [Wide World Photos]*

ilton in 1790. Congress complied, and Britain and China became the first beneficiaries.

While the nation debated, the war was spreading. In October 1940 when the presidential campaign approached its climax, Mussolini launched attacks on Greece and, from Italian Libya, on the British in Egypt. But he had bitten off more than he could chew, and his forces had to fall back in both cases. In the spring of 1941 Hitler came to his aid. German forces under Gen. Erwin Rommel joined the Italians in Libya, forcing the British, whose resources had been drained to help Greece, to withdraw into Egypt.

In April lightning attacks by Nazi panzer divisions overwhelmed Yugoslavia and Greece, and by the end of May airborne forces subdued the Greek island of Crete, putting Hitler in a position to menace the entire Middle East. With Hungary, Rumania, and Bulgaria forced into the Axis fold, Hitler controlled nearly all of Europe. Then, on June 22, 1941, he suddenly fell upon Russia. Frustrated in the purpose of subduing Britain, he thought to eliminate the potential threat on his rear with another lightning stroke. The Russian plains offered an ideal theater for *Blitzkrieg*, or so it seemed, and Russian resources were a seductive lure. With Rumanian and Finnish allies, the Nazis moved on a 2,000-mile front from the Arctic to the Black Sea with seeming invincibility until, after four months, the Russian soldiers rallied in front of Leningrad, Moscow, and Sevastopol. During the winter of 1941–1942 Hitler began to learn the bitter lesson the Russians taught Napoleon in 1812.

Winston Churchill had already decided to offer British support to Russia in case of such an attack. "If Hitler invaded Hell," he said, "I would make at least a favorable reference to the Devil in the House of Commons." Roosevelt adopted the same policy, offering American aid two days after the attack. Stalinist Russia, so long as it held out, ensured the survival of Britain. American aid was now indispensable to Europe's defense, and the logic of lend-lease led on to deeper American involvement. In order to deliver aid to Britain, goods had to be maneuvered through the U-boat "wolf packs" in the North Atlantic. So on April 11, 1941, Roosevelt informed Churchill that the United States Navy would extend its patrol areas in the North Atlantic out to 26° West Longitude, nearly all the way to Iceland.

In August 1941 Roosevelt and Churchill held a secret rendezvous in Placentia Bay, Newfoundland, alternately aboard the American cruiser *Augusta* and the British battleship *Prince of Wales*. There they drew up a statement of principles that came to be known as the Atlantic Charter, issued as a press release on August 14. In effect the "common principles" upon which the parties based "their hopes for a better future for the world" amounted to a joint statement of war aims, its eight points a mixture of the idealistic goals of the New Deal and Wilson's Fourteen Points. It called for the self-determination of all peoples, equal access to raw materials, economic cooperation, freedom of the seas, and a new system of general security. In September it was announced that fifteen anti-Axis nations, including the Soviet Union, had endorsed the statement.

Thus Roosevelt had led the United States into a joint statement of war aims with the anti-Axis powers. It was not long before shooting incidents involved Americans in the North Atlantic. As early as May 21, 1941, in fact, a German U-boat had sunk the American merchantman *Robin Moor* off the coast of Brazil, in retaliation for which Roosevelt froze all German and Italian assets in the United States, as well as those of Axis-controlled countries, and closed down German and Italian consulates. On September 4 came the first attack on an American warship, when a German submarine fired two torpedoes at the destroyer *Greer*. The president announced a week later orders to "shoot on sight" any German or Italian raiders ("rattlesnakes of the Atlantic") which ventured into American defensive waters. Five days later the United States Navy announced convoying all the way to Iceland. Then on October 17, while the destroyer *Kearny* was attacking German submarines, it sustained severe damage and loss of eleven lives from a German torpedo.

In his Navy Day speech of October 27 Roosevelt asserted that

"America has been attacked" and that "the shooting has started." Three days later, on the night of October 30, a submarine torpedoed and sank the destroyer *Reuben James*, with a loss of ninety-six officers and men, while it was on convoy duty west of Iceland. This act hastened Congress into making changes in the neutrality act already requested by the president. On November 17 the legislation was in effect repealed when the bans on arming merchant vessels and allowing them to enter combat zones and belligerent ports were removed. Step by step the United States had given up neutrality and embarked on naval warfare against Germany. Still, the American people hoped to avoid taking the final step into all-out war. The decision for war, when it came, came in an unexpected quarter—the Pacific.

THE STORM IN THE PACIFIC

JAPANESE AGGRESSION After the Nazi victories in the spring of 1940, relations with Japan also took a turn for the worse. Japanese militarists, bogged down in the vastness of China, now eyed new temptations: French Indochina, the Dutch East Indies, British Malaya, and Burma. Here they could cut off one of China's last links to the west, the Burma Road. What was more, they could incorporate into their "Greater East Asia Co-Prosperity Sphere" the oil, rubber, and other strategic materials which the crowded homeland lacked. As it was, they depended on the United States for important supplies, including 80 percent of their oil. During the summer of 1940 Japan forced the helpless French government at Vichy to permit the construction of Japanese airfields in northern Indochina and to cut off the railroad into South China. The United States responded with a loan to China and the Export Control Act of July 2, 1940, which authorized the president to restrict the export of arms and other strategic materials to Japan. Gradually Roosevelt extended embargoes on aviation gas, scrap iron, and other supplies.

On September 27, 1940, the Tokyo government signed a Tripartite Pact with Germany and Italy, by which each pledged to declare war on any nation which attacked any of them. The pact could have been directed against either the United States or Russia. The Germans hoped to persuade Japan to enter Siberia when their forces entered Russia from the west. The Soviet presence in Siberia did inhibit the Japanese impulse to move southward, but on April 13, 1941, while the Nazis were sweeping through the Balkans, Japan signed a nonaggression pact with

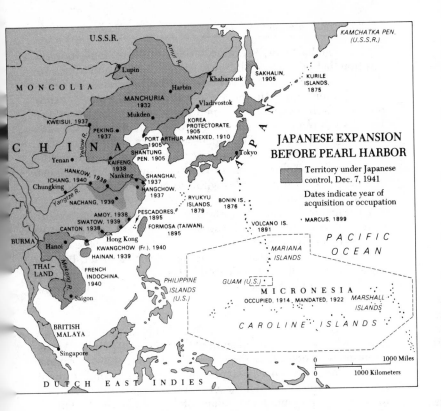

Russia and, once the Nazis invaded Russia in June, the Japanese were freed of any threat from the north.

Their first move southward came on July 25, 1941, when Japan announced that it was assuming a protectorate over all of French Indochina. Roosevelt took three steps in response on the next day: he froze all Japanese assets in the United States; he restricted exports of oil to Japan; and he took the armed forces of the Philippines into the Army of the United States and put their commander, Gen. Douglas MacArthur, in charge of all United States forces in the Far East. By September the oil restrictions had tightened into an embargo. The commander of the Japanese navy estimated that their oil reserves would last two years at most, eighteen months in case of an expanded war. Forced by the embargo to secure other oil supplies, the Japanese army and navy began to lay plans for attacks on the Dutch and British colonies to the south.

Actions by both sides put the United States and Japan on the way to a war which neither wanted. In his regular talks with the

Japanese ambassador, Secretary of State Cordell Hull took the position that Japanese withdrawal from Indochina and China was the price of renewed trade. Though the United States was under no obligation to fuel the Japanese war machine, a more flexible position might have strengthened the moderates in Japan. The Japanese were not then pursuing a concerted plan of aggression comparable to Hitler's. The Japanese military had stumbled crazily from one aggression to another without approval from the government in Tokyo. Premier Konoye, however, while known as a man of liberal principles who preferred peace, caved in to pressures from the warlords.

The Japanese warlords, for their part, seriously misjudged the United States. The desperate wish of Americans to stay out of war might still have enabled the Japanese to conquer the British and Dutch colonies before an American decision to act. But the warlords decided that they dared not leave the American navy intact and the Philippines untouched on the flank of their new lifeline to the south.

TRAGEDY AT PEARL HARBOR   Thus a tragedy began to unfold with a fatal certainty mostly out of sight of the American people, whose attention was focused on the war in the Atlantic. Late in August Prince Konoye proposed a personal meeting with President Roosevelt. Hull smelled a rat. On his advice, Roosevelt refused to go unless agreement on fundamentals could be reached in advance. Soon afterward, on September 6, an imperial conference approved preparations for an attack and gave Premier Konoye six more weeks to reach a settlement. The Japanese emperor's clear displeasure with the risks of an attack afforded the premier one last chance to pursue a compromise, but the stumbling block was still the presence of Japanese troops in China. In October he urged War Minister Hideki Tojo (nicknamed "The Razor") to consider withdrawal while saving face by keeping some troops in North China. Tojo retorted that at times one must have the courage to take the plunge—or as he put it, to jump off Kiyomizu (a mountainside Buddhist temple in Kyoto). Faced with this rebuff, and Tojo's threat to resign and bring down the cabinet, Konoye himself resigned on October 15; Tojo became premier the next day. The war party was now in complete control.

On the very day that Tojo became premier a special envoy, Saburo Kurusu, conferred with Hull and Roosevelt in Washington. His arrival was largely a cover for Japan's war plans, although neither he nor Ambassador Nomura knew that. On November 20 they presented Tojo's final proposal. Japan would occupy no more territory if the United States would cut off aid to China, restore trade, and help Japan get supplies from the Dutch Indies. In that case Japan would pull out of southern Indochina immediately and abandon the remainder once peace had been established with China—presumably on Japanese terms. Tojo expected the United States to refuse such demands. On November 26 Hull repeated the demand that Japan withdraw altogether from China. That same day a Japanese naval force left its rendezvous at Hitokappu Bay on one of the remote Kurile Islands. Six carriers, two battleships, and an escort of cruisers, destroyers, and submarines headed silently across the North Pacific, through rough waters deserted by shipping in the late fall, toward Pearl Harbor.

Washington already knew that war was imminent. Reports of troop transports moving south from Formosa prompted Washington to send war warnings to Pearl Harbor and Manila, and to the British government. The massive movements southward clearly signaled attacks on the British and the Dutch. American leaders had every reason to expect war in the southwest Pacific, but none expected that Japan would commit most of its carriers to another attack 5,000 miles away at Pearl Harbor.

On the morning of December 7, 1941, American cryptanalysts decoded the last part of a fourteen-part Japanese message breaking off the negotiations. Nomura was instructed to deliver the message at 1:00 P.M. (7:00 A.M. in Honolulu), about a half hour before the blow fell, but delays in decoding the message held up delivery until more than an hour later than scheduled. Gen. George Marshall and Adm. Harold R. Stark sent out an alert at noon that something was about to happen, but the message, which went by commercial wire because radio contacts were broken, arrived in Hawaii eight and a half hours later.

It was still a somnolent Sunday morning when the first Japanese planes roared down the west coast and the central valley of Oahu to begin their assault. At 7:53 A.M. the flight commander, Mitsuo Fuchida, rounded Barber's Point and sounded the cry "Tora! Tora! Tora!" ("Tiger! Tiger! Tiger!"), the signal that the attackers had taken the American Pacific fleet by surprise. For nearly two hours the Japanese planes kept up their attack on an unready Pacific fleet. Of the eight battleships in Pearl Harbor, three were sunk, one grounded, one capsized, and the others badly battered. Altogether nineteen ships were sunk or disabled. At the adjoining Hickam Field and other airfields on the island the Japanese found planes parked wing to wing, and destroyed in all about 150 of them. Few were able to get airborne, and Japa-

Pearl Harbor. The view from this attacking Japanese airplane shows American ships in vulnerable positions. [National Archives]

nese losses numbered fewer than thirty planes. Before it was over the raid had killed more than 2,400 American servicemen and civilians, and wounded 1,178 more. The surprise attack fulfilled the wildest dreams of its planners, but it fell short of total success in two ways. The Japanese ignored shore installations and oil tanks, without which the surviving ships might have been forced back to the West Coast, and they missed the American aircraft carriers which were out on mission at the time. In the naval war to come, these carriers would be decisive.

Later the same day (December 8 in the western Pacific) Japanese forces began assaults on the Philippines, Guam, and Midway, and on the British forces in Hong Kong and the Malay Peninsula. With one stroke the Japanese had silenced America's debate on neutrality, and a suddenly unified nation prepared for the struggle. The next day President Roosevelt delivered his war message to Congress:

> Yesterday, December 7, 1941—a date which will live in infamy—the United States of America was suddenly and deliberately attacked by naval and air forces of the Empire of Japan. . . .
>
> The facts of yesterday speak for themselves. The people of the United States have already formed their opinions and well understand the implications to the very life and safety of our Nation. . . .

Congress voted for the war resolution unanimously, with the sole exception of Rep. Jeanette Rankin, who was unable in conscience to vote for war in 1917 or 1941. For several days it was uncertain whether war with the other Axis powers would follow. The defensive Tripartite Pact carried no obligation for them to enter, but Hitler, impatient with American aid to Britain, willingly joined his Oriental allies. On December 11 Germany and Italy declared war on the United States. The separate wars in Asia and Europe had become one global war.

FURTHER READING

Selig Adler's *The Uncertain Giant: American Foreign Policy between the Wars* (1966) provides a detailed narrative of the events covered in this chapter. For a focus on the 1920s, see L. Ethan Ellis's *Republican Foreign Policy, 1921–1933* (1968). John E. Wiltz's *From Isolation to War, 1931–1941* (1968), and Robert Dallek's *Franklin D. Roosevelt and American Foreign Policy, 1932–1945* (1979),° cover the 1930s. A number of revisionists stress the economic bases of foreign policy: see William Appleman Williams's *The Tragedy of American Diplomacy* (1962), Joan Hoff Wilson's *American Business and Foreign Policy, 1920–1931* (1971), and Michael J. Hogan's *Informal Entente: The Private Structure of Cooperation in Anglo-American Economic Diplomacy, 1918–1929* (1977).

Other scholars have concentrated on specific policies of the 1920s. Thomas H. Buckley's *The United States and the Washington Conference, 1921–1922* (1970), and Raymond G. O'Connor's *Perilous Equilibrium: The United States and the London Naval Conference* (1962) examine disarmament. Keith Nelson's *Victors Divided: America and the Allies in Germany, 1918–1923* (1975), deals with the reparations issue. For a study of the Kellog-Briand pact, see Robert H. Ferrell's *Peace in Their Time: The Origins of the Kellog-Briand Pact* (1962).°

For American relations in the Pacific during the period, see Warren I. Cohen's *America's Response to China: An Interpretative History of Sino-American Relations* (1971) and Akira Iriye's *After Imperialism: The Search for a New Order in the Far East, 1921–1933* (1965).

For relations with countries south of the border, see David Green's *The Containment of Latin America* (1971), Bryce Wood's *The Making of the Good Neighbor Policy* (1961), and Alexander DeConde's *Herbert Hoover's Latin American Policy* (1951). Diplomacy in Europe is examined in Arnold A. Offner's *American Appeasement: United States Foreign Policy and Germany, 1933–1938* (1969), Brice Harris, Jr.'s *The United States and the Italo-Ethiopian Crisis* (1964), and Allen Guttman's *The Wound in the Heart: America and the Spanish Civil War* (1962).

For the eventual entry of the United States into World War II, see the two volumes of *The World Crisis and American Foreign Policy* by William L. Langer: *The Challenge to Isolationism, 1937–1940* (1952), and *The Undeclared War, 1940–1941* (1953). Other interpretations of Roosevelt

°These books are available in paperback editions.

and diplomacy include Robert A. Divine's *Roosevelt and World War II* (1969),° James MacGregor Burns's *Roosevelt: The Soldier of Freedom* (1970), and Lloyd C. Gardner's *Economic Aspects of New Deal Diplomacy* (1964). Other scholars concentrate on American relations with Great Britain: see David Reynolds's *The Creation of the Anglo-American Alliance, 1937–1941: A Study in Competitive Cooperation* (1981), C. A. McDonald's *The United States, Britain, and Appeasement, 1936–1939* (1981), and Joseph P. Lash's *Roosevelt and Churchill* (1976).°

How some dissenting Americans reacted to the Roosevelt policies is traced by Wayne S. Cole in *Gerald P. Nye and American Foreign Relations* (1962) and *America First: The Battle against Intervention, 1940–1941* (1967). Also helpful is Ellsworth Barnard's *Wendell Willkie: Fighter for Freedom* (1966). An unusual approach to the impact of foreign policy is found in David H. Culbert's *News for Everyman: Radio and Foreign Affairs in Thirties America* (1976). For Lend-Lease and the domestic reaction, see Warren F. Kimball's *The Most Unsordid Act: Lend-Lease, 1939–1941* (1969).

Two introductions to Pearl Harbor are Roberta Wohlstetter's *Pearl Harbor, Warning and Decision* (1962) and Gordon W. Prange's *At Dawn We Slept: The Untold Story of Pearl Harbor* (1981).° The Japanese perspective is given in Robert J. Burtow's *Tojo and the Coming of the War* (1961). Bruce M. Russell's *No Clear and Present Danger: A Skeptical View of United States Entry into World War II* (1972) provides a critical account.

30 &

THE WORLD AT WAR

AMERICA'S EARLY BATTLES

SETBACKS IN THE PACIFIC For months after Pearl Harbor the news from the Pacific was "all bad," as President Roosevelt frankly confessed. On the first day of the war American planes in the Philippines were caught lined up at Clark Field near Manila despite ten hours' notice of the attack on Pearl Harbor—an event that defies plausible explanation. That same day enemy planes sank the British battle cruiser *Repulse* and the battleship *Prince of Wales* near Singapore while Japanese land forces entered Malaya and Thailand. Thailand prudently surrendered, becoming a passive ally of the Japanese. In quick sequence these Allied outposts fell to the enemy before the end of December: Guam, Wake Island, the Gilbert Islands, and Hong Kong. Rabaul in New Britain fell in January 1942, Singapore and Java in February. Adm. Thomas C. Hart's tiny Asiatic Fleet, with British and Dutch help, fought holding actions in the Dutch East Indies through January and February, all of them defeats climaxed by the disastrous Battle of the Java Sea (February 27 to March 1). The fall of Rangoon on March 9 cut off the Burma Road, the main link to Nationalist China.

In the Philippines, where General MacArthur abandoned Manila on December 27, the main American forces, outmanned and outgunned, held out on Bataan Peninsula until April 9, and then on "The Rock," the fortified island of Corregidor. MacArthur slipped away in March, when he was ordered out to Australia to take command of Allied forces in the Southwest Pacific. By May 6, when American forces surrendered Corregidor, Japan controlled a new empire that stretched from Burma eastward through the Dutch Indies and on out to Wake Island and the Gilberts.

If the Japanese had been willing to quit while they were ahead, they might have consolidated an almost impregnable empire with the resources they had seized. But the Japanese navy succumbed to what one of its admirals later called "victory disease." Though the Supreme Command decided to stop at the gates of India, behind the mountain barriers of Burma, it resolved to push on into the South Pacific, isolate Australia, and strike again at Hawaii. Their aim was to draw out and destroy the American navy before the productive power of the United States could be brought to bear on the war effort.

A Japanese mistake and a stroke of American luck, however, enabled the United States Navy to frustrate the plan. Japan's failure to destroy the shore facilities at Pearl Harbor left the base relatively intact, and most of the ships damaged on December 7 lived to fight another day. The aircraft carriers at sea during the attack spent several months harassing Japanese outposts in the Gilberts and Marshalls. Their most spectacular exploit, an air raid on Tokyo itself launched on April 18, 1942, was delivered by Col. James H. Doolittle's B-25 bombers which took off from the carrier *Hornet* and, unable to land on its deck, proceeded to China. The raid caused only token damage, but did much to lift American morale amid a series of defeats elsewhere.

Japanese advances were finally halted in two decisive naval battles, the first of which started the day after Corregidor fell. The Battle of the Coral Sea (May 7–8, 1942) stopped a fleet convoying Japanese troop transports toward Port Moresby, on the southern coast of New Guinea. Planes from the *Lexington* and *Yorktown* sank one Japanese carrier, damaged another, and destroyed smaller ships. American losses were greater, and included the carrier *Lexington*, but the Japanese transports had to turn back. Port Moresby was secured, thwarting the Japanese advance on Australia.

MIDWAY: A TURNING POINT Less than a month after the Coral Sea engagement Adm. Isoruku Yamamoto, the Japanese naval commander, decided to force a showdown in the central Pacific. With nearly every capital ship under his personal command, he headed for Midway Island, from which he hoped to render Pearl Harbor helpless. This time it was the Japanese who were the victims of surprise. American cryptanalysts had by then broken their naval code, and Adm. Chester Nimitz, commander of the central Pacific, knew what was up. He reinforced Midway with planes and the carriers *Enterprise, Hornet,* and *Yorktown.*

The first Japanese foray against Midway, on June 4, severely damaged the island, but at the cost of about a third of the Japanese planes. Before another attack could be mounted, American torpedo planes and dive bombers had caught three of the four Japanese carriers in the process of servicing their planes. The first wave of slow American torpedo bombers was almost all shot down, but dive bombers disabled the carriers *Akagi*, *Kaga*, and *Soryu*, and left them to sink. The fourth, the *Hiryu*, managed to send up planes which disabled the *Yorktown*, but American planes found and sank the *Hiryu* that afternoon. A Japanese submarine later sank the *Yorktown*. The only other major American loss was a destroyer. Yamamoto had to retreat, and the Japanese navy, having lost its four best aircraft carriers, all veterans of Pearl Harbor, was forced into retreat less than six months after the attack on Hawaii. The Japanese scored one dubious success, a diversionary action which captured the Aleutian Islands of Attu and Kiska in a vain effort to draw the navy off from Midway. The Japanese defeat was the turning point of the Pacific war, a loss they were never able to make up.

SETBACKS IN THE ATLANTIC Early setbacks in the Pacific were matched by setbacks in the Atlantic. Since the *Blitzkrieg* of 1940 German submarine "wolf-packs" had issued out of bombproof pens on the French coast, wreaking havoc in the North Atlantic. In January 1942, after an ominous lull, German submarines suddenly appeared off American shores and began to sink coastal shipping, much of it tankers. Fourteen ships went down off the United States coast that month, and twelve in Canadian waters. By February nineteen had been sunk in the Caribbean and Gulf of Mexico. Until April and May, when coastal cities were blacked out, passing freighters and tankers were like sitting ducks, silhouetted against the horizon. From January through June 1942 nearly 400 ships were lost in American waters before effective countermeasures brought the problem under control. Adm. Ernest J. King, who became the commander of the United States Navy on December 20, 1941, hastened the building of small escort vessels, meanwhile pressing into patrol service all kinds of surface craft and planes, some of them civilian. During the second half of 1942 he brought the losses down to a negligible number.

MOBILIZATION AT HOME

The Pearl Harbor attack ended not only the long debate between isolation and intervention but also the long depression decade of the 1930s, and with the same finality with which the market crash of 1929 ended the prosperity decade of the 1920s. There was no doubt that the war effort would require all of America's huge productive capacity and full employment of the workforce. Soon after Pearl Harbor, Winston Churchill recalled that, thirty years before, Edward Grey had compared the United States to a gigantic boiler: "Once the fire is lighted under it, there is no limit to the power it can generate."

Mobilization was in fact already farther along than preparedness had been in 1916–1917. Selective services had been in effect for more than a year, and the army had grown to more than 1.4 million men by June 30, 1941. Congress quickly repealed the ban on sending draftees outside the Western Hemisphere and extended their service to six months after the end of the war. Men between eighteen and forty-five became subject to service. Altogether more than 15 million men and women served in the armed forces.

ECONOMIC CONVERSION The economy too was already partially mobilized by lend-lease and defense efforts. As early as May 1939 the president had named a War Resources Board to study supply needs. In May 1940, while *Blitzkrieg* enveloped France, Roosevelt revived the National Defense Advisory Commission, from which evolved multiple bureaus of war production and controls. The War Powers Act of December 18, 1941, gave the president a mandate to reshuffle government agencies, and a Second War Powers Act, of March 1942, empowered the government to allot materials and facilities as needed for defense, with penalties for those who failed to comply.

The War Production Board (WPB), created in January 1942 under Donald Nelson of Sears, Roebuck, became the new counterpart to Bernard Baruch's War Industries Board in directing industrial conversion to war production. Auto makers switched to producing tanks, makers of shirts switched to mosquito netting, model train plants to hardware, and the makers of refrigerators, stoves, and cash registers to munitions. The Reconstruction Finance Corporation, a depression agency, now financed war plants. For a year the War Production Board oversaw a wild scramble of manufacturers for available supplies. As War Secretary Stimson put it, it was "like . . . hungry dogs quarreling over a very inadequate bone" until the WPB instituted its Controlled Materials Plan, which allocated scarce items to claimants according to its best judgment of need.

Some shortages called for more heroic efforts. The government named special administrators, or "czars," to promote production of rubber and oil. Rubber Director William Jeffers,

At the Kaiser shipyard in Vancouver, Washington, a merchant ship was launched every ten days, 1942. [National Archives]

president of Union Pacific Railroad, pushed construction of synthetic rubber plants, which by 1944 produced 800,000 tons, or 87 percent of the country's requirements. Tire rationing began in December 1941, and gasoline rationing at the end of 1942. Since German sinkings of coastal tankers placed an unusual burden on railways in getting oil to the East Coast, Petroleum Administrator Harold Ickes hastened construction of the "Big Inch" pipeline, which was twenty-four inches in diameter and ran 1,250 miles from the Texas oilfields to the New York–Philadelphia region. Begun in the summer of 1942, it was finished a year later. Through the Office of Scientific Research and Development Dr. Vannevar Bush mobilized thousands of "scientists against time" to create and modify radar, sonar, the proximity fuse, the bazooka, means to isolate blood plasma, and myriads of other innovations.

The pressure of wartime needs and the stimulus of government spending sent the gross national product soaring from $100.6 billion in 1940 to $213.6 billion in 1945. Government expenditures during the war years rose from $20 billion in calendar year 1941 to $97.2 billion in 1944. From July 1, 1940, to June 30, 1946, expenditures totaled $337 billion, of which $304 billion went to the war effort. The figure for total expenditures was twice as great as the total of all previous federal spending in the history of the republic, and about 10 times what America spent in World War I, and 100 times the expenditures during the Civil War.

FINANCING THE WAR   To cover the war's huge cost the president preferred taxes to borrowing. "I would rather pay one hundred percent of taxes now than push the burden of this war onto the shoulders of my grandchildren," he said in December 1942. Taxes also had the merit of relieving upward pressures on prices. The wartime Congress, however, dominated by conservatives, feared taxes more than deficits and refused to go more than half-way with Roosevelt's fiscal prudence. The Revenue Act of 1942 provided for only about $7 billion in increased revenue, less than half that recommended by the Treasury. It also greatly broadened the tax structure by lowering exemptions from $750 to $500 for single persons, and from $1,500 to $1,200 for married persons. Whereas in 1939 only about 4 million people filed returns, the new act, in the words of a tax historian, "made the Federal income tax a genuine mass tax." By 1943 the idea was gaining ground of putting all tax collections on a current basis through regular payroll deductions, which would further fight inflation. Before the year was out the plan had been adopted.

In February 1944 a rebellion against an administration request for a tax increase to combat inflation and finance the war led Roosevelt to veto a tax bill. It was "a tax relief bill . . . not for the needy, but for the greedy," the president said. Sen. Alben Barkley angrily resigned as Senate majority leader, only to be reelected unanimously, and both houses promptly overrode the veto by large votes. Still, a few months later an act for the next fiscal year reduced the basic tax rate from 6 to 3 percent while raising surtaxes to 91 percent in the highest bracket.

The result was that the government covered about 45 percent of its 1939–1946 costs with tax revenues. Roosevelt would have preferred to cover more, but the figure compared favorably with 30 percent for World War I and 23 percent for the Civil War. To cover the rest of its costs the government borrowed from the public. War-bond drives, including a Victory Drive in 1945, induced citizens to put aside more than $150 billion in bonds rather than use it to bid up prices. Financial institutions picked up most of the rest of the government's debt. In all, by the end of the war the national debt had grown to about $260 billion, about

Mobilization for war deflected many New Deal efforts. [Library of Congress]

six times its size at the time of Pearl Harbor. One of its effects was to make converts to the Keynesian argument that government spending would end the depression.

The basic economic problem was no longer finding jobs but finding workers for the booming shipyards, aircraft factories, and powder mills. Millions of people were brought fully into the economic system who before had lived on its margin, which leveled out somewhat the economic pyramid. Between 1939 and 1944 the share of the income going to the wealthiest 5 percent declined from 23.7 to 16.8 percent. Stubborn poverty did not disappear, but for most of those who stayed home the war spelled neither hardship nor suffering but better life than ever before, despite shortages and rationing.

ECONOMIC CONTROLS   Increased incomes and spending during the war conjured up the spectre of inflation. Some of the available money went into taxes and war bonds, but even so, more was sent chasing after civilian goods just as production was converting to war needs. Such consumer durables as cars, washing machines, and nondefense housing in fact ceased to be made at all. It was apparent that only strict restraints would keep prices from soaring out of sight. The administration, having set out in 1933 to raise prices, now reversed its ground and set out to hold them down. In April 1941 Roosevelt had created the Office of Price Administration (OPA) under Leon Henderson, a New Deal economist. By July 1941 Roosevelt was seeking statutory price controls and finally, in January 1942, Congress authorized the OPA for the first time to set price ceilings. While some increases were deemed necessary as incentives to production, the General Maximum Price Regulation of April 1942 froze prices at the highest level they had reached in March 1942. With prices frozen, goods had to be allocated through rationing, which began with auto tires in December 1941 and was gradually extended to other goods in short supply, with coupons doled out for sugar, coffee, gasoline, and meats.

Wages and farm prices were not controlled, however, and this complicated things. War prosperity offered farmers a chance to redress the balance from two decades of distress, and farm-state congressmen fought to raise both floors and ceilings on farm prices. Price supports continued for basic crops, and the Emergency Price Control Act limited farm-price ceilings to no less than 110 percent of parity. Some farm prices rose to 150 percent of parity. Higher food prices reinforced worker demands for higher wages, and the War Labor Board tried to hold the line with the Little Steel formula of July 1942, which permitted wage increases in line with the 15 percent increase in the cost of living since January 1941. The WLB, however, had jurisdiction only over wage increases resulting from labor disputes.

Under the Stabilization Act of October 1942 the president got new authority to control wages and farm prices, which he took back to simple parity. At the same time he set up the Office of Economic Stabilization under James F. Byrnes, who left his seat on the Supreme Court to coordinate the effort. Stabilization proved to be one of the most complex jobs of the war effort, subject to constant sniping by special interests. By December 1942 Leon Henderson had offended so many congressmen by his zeal to keep prices down that he was forced to resign. Chester Bowles, who replaced him at the OPA, proved equal to the challenge.

Both business and workers chafed at the wage and price controls. On occasion the government was forced to seize industries threatened by strike. The coal mines and railroads both came under government operation for a short time in 1943, and in 1944 the government briefly took over Montgomery-Ward Company. Soldiers had to carry its chairman bodily out of his office when he stubbornly defied orders of the War Labor Board. Despite these problems, stabilization was on the whole a success story. Roosevelt's "hold-the-line" order of April 8, 1943, freezing prices, wages, and salaries, finally brought the price level to a plateau for the rest of the war. By the end of the war consumer prices had risen about 31 percent, a far better record than the wartime rise of 62 percent before the Armistice of 1918.

SOCIAL EFFECTS: WOMEN   The war became an important watershed in the changing status of women. The proportion of women

A Women's Army Corps poster. [State Historical Society of Wisconsin]

Women at work on the noses of fighter planes at Douglas Aircraft, 1943.
"Stars over Berlin and Tokyo will soon replace these factory lights
reflected" on the plane noses. [National Archives]

working had barely altered from 1910 to 1940, but at a time
when millions of men were going into military service the demand for labor shook up old prejudices about sex roles in the
workplace—and in the military. Nearly 200,000 women went
into the Women's Army Corps (WAC) and the navy's equivalent,
Women Accepted for Volunteer Emergency Service (WAVES).
Lesser numbers joined the Marine Corps, the Coast Guard, and
the Women's Auxiliary Ferrying Squadron (WAFS) of the Army
Air Force. By the end of the war over 6 million women had entered the workforce, an increase in general of over 50 percent
and in manufacturing alone of some 110 percent. Old barriers
fell overnight as women entered employment of all sorts, becoming toolmakers, machinists, crane operators, lumberjacks,
stevedores, blacksmiths, and railroad track workers. Such arduous occupations were no longer reserved for men.

By 1944 women made up 14 percent of all workers in shipbuilding and 40 percent in aircraft plants. Rosie the Riveter
symbolized women in war work, and her real counterparts
performed so well in jobs once thought unsuited for women that
attitudes about the abilities of women were permanently altered.
One striking feature of the new scene was the larger proportion
of older, married women in the workforce. In 1940 about 15.2
percent of married women went into gainful employment; by
1945 it was 24 percent. In the workforce as a whole, married
women for the first time outnumbered single women. Attitudes
sharply changed from those of the depression days, when over

80 percent of Americans opposed work by married women; by 1942 a poll showed 60 percent in favor of hiring married women in war industries. Defense jobs, however, were the ones most vulnerable to postwar cuts.

SOCIAL EFFECTS: BLACKS Potentially the most inflammable issue ignited by the war was that of black participation in the defense effort. From the start black leaders demanded full recognition in the armed forces and defense industries. Eventually about a million Negroes served in the armed forces, in every branch and every theater. But they served usually in segregated units which mirrored the society from which they came. Every army camp had its little Harlem, its separate facilities, its periodic racial "incidents." The most important departure was a 1940 decision to give up segregation in officer candidate schools, except those for air force cadets. A separate flight school at Tuskegee, Alabama, trained about 600 Negro pilots, many of who saw action over Europe.

War industries were even less accessible to black influence and pressure, although government policy theoretically opposed discrimination. In February 1941 A. Philip Randolph, head of the Brotherhood of Sleeping Car Porters, organized a March on Washington Movement to demand an end to discrimination in defense industries. As the movement grew, its leaders promised to mobilize 100,000 marchers. The administration, alarmed at the prospect of a mass descent on Washington, struck a bargain. The Randolph group called off its march in return for Executive Order 8802, which forbade discrimination in defense work and training programs by requiring a nondiscrimination clause in defense contracts, and set up the Committee on Fair Employment Practices (FEPC). The FEPC's authority was chiefly moral, since

A unit of black soldiers about to conduct religious services, [Photoworld/FPG]

it had no power to enforce directives. It nevertheless offered willing employers the chance to say they were following government policy in giving jobs to black citizens, and no doubt persuaded others to go along. About 2 million blacks were working in war plants by the end of 1944. The demand for black labor revived migration out of the South, which had lagged during the depression, and large numbers of blacks now headed for the Far West as well as the North. States with the largest proportionate gains of black population in the 1940s were, in order, California, Michigan, Oregon, Washington, Utah, Colorado, Wisconsin, Illinois, and New York.

Blacks quickly broadened their drive for wartime participation into a more inclusive social and political front. Early in 1942 the Pittsburgh *Courier* endorsed the "Double V," which stood for victory at home and abroad. The slogan became immensely popular in black communities, and reflected a growing urge to rid the world not just of Hitler but of Hitlerism, as one editor put it. Blacks began to challenge more openly all kinds of discrimination, including racial segregation itself. "It was as if some universal message had come through to the great mass of Negroes," the sociologist Howard Odum wrote in 1943, "urging them to dream new dreams and to protest against the old order." Confirmation of his observation came in *What the Negro Wants* (1944), a symposium to which the University of North Carolina Press invited fourteen blacks of various viewpoints to contribute. The editor and black historian Rayford W. Logan noted "surprising unanimity" among the contributors, all of whom "want Negroes eventually to enjoy the same rights, opportunities and privileges that are vouchsafed to all other Americans." A foundation was being laid for a great expansion of civil-rights efforts after the war. Membership in the NAACP grew during the war from 50,000 to 450,000. Blacks could look forward to greater political participation after the Supreme Court, in *Smith v. Allwright* (1944), struck down Texas's white primary on the grounds that Democratic primaries were part of the election process and thus subject to the Fifteenth Amendment.

The growing militancy of blacks of course aroused antagonism from some whites. Racial violence this time did not approach the level of that in World War I, but growing tensions on a hot summer afternoon in Detroit sparked incidents on crowded Belle Isle, an offshore park in the Detroit River. Fighting raged through June 20–21, 1943, until federal troops arrived on the second evening to stop it. Twenty-five blacks and nine whites had been killed.

The first day of evacuation from the Japanese quarters in San Francisco, April 1942. Photo by Dorothea Lange. [National Archives]

SOCIAL EFFECTS: JAPANESE-AMERICANS   The record on civil liberties during World War II was on the whole better than that during World War I, if only because there was virtually no opposition to the war effort after the attack on Pearl Harbor. Neither German-Americans nor Italian-Americans faced the harassments meted out to their counterparts in the previous war; few had much sympathy for Hitler or Mussolini. The shameful exception to an otherwise improved record was the treatment given to more than 100,000 Americans of Japanese descent who were forcibly removed from homes and businesses on the West Coast to "War Relocation Camps" in the interior. They were not disloyal, but victims of fear and racial prejudice. In 1983, more than forty years later, the federal government agreed with this view, and proposed granting those Nisei still living $20,000 each in compensation.

In Hawaii, a far more sensitive area, the Japanese formed the largest single ethnic group in a mixed population. These Japanese were plagued by rumors of sabotage at Pearl Harbor and on the mainland, all unfounded. In fact Japanese Hawaiians and mainlanders made up two of the most celebrated infantry units in the war, fighting with distinction on the Italian front. Other thousands of Nisei served as interpreters and translators, the "eyes and ears" of the American armed forces in the Pacific.

DOMESTIC CONSERVATISM   In domestic politics the wartime period was marked by a growing conservatism. Discontent with price controls, labor shortages, rationing, and a hundred other petty vexations spread. In 1942 the congressional elections registered a national swing against the New Deal. Republicans gained forty-six seats in the House and nine in the Senate, chiefly in the Middle States farm areas. Democratic losses outside the South strengthened the southern delegation's position within the party, and the delegation itself reflected conservative victories in southern primaries. A coalition of conservatives proceeded to eviscerate "nonessential" New Deal agencies. In 1943 Congress abolished the Work Projects Administration, the National Youth Administration, and the Civilian Conservation Corps, began to dismantle the Farm Security Administration, and liquidated the National Resources Planning Board by refusing it funds.

Organized labor, despite substantial gains during the war, was vulnerable to the conservative trend. In the spring of 1943, when John L. Lewis led the coal miners out on strike, widespread resentment led Congress to pass the Smith-Connally War Labor Disputes Act, which authorized the government to seize plants useful to the war, required prestrike plebiscites, and forbade unions to make political contributions. The intended effect of the act was somewhat blunted by the tendency of unionists to vote routinely for strikes as a bargaining ploy. In 1943 a dozen states adopted laws variously restricting picketing and other union activities, and in 1944 Arkansas and Florida by constitutional amendment set in motion a wave of "right-to-work" legislation which outlawed the closed shop and other union security devices.

Congress generally cooperated with the administration's war effort. The Senate War Investigating Committee under Harry S Truman of Missouri devoted itself to rooting out waste and inefficiency in the war effort. Unity on foreign relations persisted through the war, and in 1943 both houses of Congress passed resolutions in favor of an international peacekeeping organization after the war.

THE ALLIED DRIVE TOWARD BERLIN

By mid-1942 the "home front" began to get news from the war fronts that some of the lines were holding at last. Japanese naval losses at the Coral Sea and Midway had secured Australia and Hawaii. By midyear Admiral King's motley fleet of air and sea subchasers was ending six months of happy hunting for U-boats off the Atlantic coast. This was all the more important because war plans called for the defeat of Germany first.

WAR AIMS AND STRATEGY There were many reasons for the priority of defeating Hitler. Nazi forces in western Europe and the Atlantic posed a more direct threat to the Western Hemisphere;

German war potential was greater and German science was more likely to come up with some devastating new weapon. Lose in the Atlantic, Gen. George Marshall said, and you lose everywhere. Hitler's attack on Russia in June 1941 strengthened the argument. Once defeat Germany, strongest of the Axis powers, and Japan would face overwhelming force. Despite the understanding, Japanese attacks involved Americans directly in the Pacific war from the start, and as a consequence, during the first year of fighting more Americans went to the Pacific than across the Atlantic.

The Pearl Harbor attack brought Prime Minister Churchill quickly to Washington for lengthy talks about a common war plan. Out of these exchanges came several major and a number of minor decisions, including the one, urged by General Marshall, to name a supreme commander in each major theater of war. Each commander would be subject to orders from the British-American Combined Chiefs of Staff with headquarters in Washington. Marshall, Adm. Ernest J. King, and Army Air Force Gen. H. H. "Hap" Arnold thereafter met periodically with their British counterparts to review strategy. Other joint boards allotted munitions, raw materials, and shipping. American and British war plans thereafter proceeded in close concert, and often launched joint operations, especially against Germany. No such concert was ever effected with Russia, which fought its own war on the eastern front, separate except for the coordinated timing of some major offensives. In Washington on January 1, 1942, representatives of twenty-six governments then at war with the Axis signed the Declaration of the United Nations, affirming the Principles of the Atlantic Charter, pledging their full resources to the war, and promising not to make separate peace with the common enemies. Finally, in the course of their talks the British and American leaders reaffirmed the priority of war against Germany.

Agreement on war aims, however, was not agreement on strategy. Roosevelt and Winston Churchill, meeting at the White House again in June 1942, could not agree on where to hit first. American military planners wanted to strike directly across the English Channel before the end of 1942, secure a beachhead, and move against Germany in 1943. The British preferred to keep the Germans off balance with hit-and-run raids and air attacks, while continuing to build up their forces. With vivid memories of the last war, the British feared a mass bloodletting in trench warfare if they struck prematurely. When General Marshall argued in London for an early assault on the score of German strength, Lord Cherwell told him: "It's no use—you are arguing against the casualties on the Somme." The Russians, bearing the brunt of the German attack in the East, insisted that the Western Allies must do something to relieve the pressure. Finally, the Americans accepted Churchill's proposal to invade French North Africa.

THE NORTH AFRICA CAMPAIGN   It was not only the Russians who needed a diversion, but British forces defending Egypt against invaders from Libya. If German Gen. Erwin Rommel's Afrika Korps took Alexandria and Suez, little more than distance would stand between them and India, where they could link up with the Japanese. Late in October 1942 Gen. Sir Bernard Montgomery began a counterattack on Rommel at El-Alamein. On November 8, 1942, Anglo-American forces under the command of Gen. Dwight D. Eisenhower landed at Casablanca in Morocco and at Oran and Algiers in Algeria. Completely surprised, French forces under the Vichy government (which collaborated with the Germans) had little will to resist. Hitler therefore occupied the whole of France and sent German forces into French Tunisia. By chance Adm. Jean-François Darlan, second to Marshal Petain in the collaborationist Vichy government, was visiting in Algiers and was persuaded to order a cease-fire on November 11.

Since Darlan seemed the man the French forces would most likely obey, a deal was struck to make him the leader of the French in the North African colonies. A military expedient which probably saved thousands of Allied lives, this deal with a former Nazi collaborator was widely criticized in America and Britain until the assassination of Darlan on Christmas Eve relieved the Allies of the embarrassment. Gen. Henri Giraud, who had escaped a Nazi prison, took his place. Still, Gen. Charles De Gaulle, leader of the "Free French" who had escaped to England, had little influence in North Africa. Not until October 1944 did the United States formally recognize him as leader of the French nation.

Farther east the tide had turned and General Montgomery was pushing Rommel back across Libya, but green American forces were held in stalemate by seasoned Nazis pouring into Tunisia. Before spring, however, Montgomery had taken Libya and the Germans were caught in a gigantic pincers. By April Montgomery had linked up with American forces and one month later, on May 7, 1943, Bizerte fell to the Americans and Tunis to the British. The remaining Germans made a last stand on Cape Bon. Hammered from all sides, unable to retreat across the Mediterra-

WAR IN EUROPE AND AFRICA,
1942-1945

Axis Powers at outbreak of war

Maximum extent of Axis military power

Allies

Neutral countries

← Allied offensives

--- Heaviest Allied aerial bombing

.... Inside limit of German U-boat operati

nean, an army of 275,000 surrendered on May 13, 1943, leaving all of North Africa in Allied hands.

While the battle of Tunisia was still shaping up, in January 1943 Roosevelt and Churchill and the Combined Chiefs of Staff met at Casablanca to plan the future. Stalin declined to leave Russia for the meeting but continued to press for a second front in Europe. For the time, however, the decision was reached to postpone the cross-Channel invasion further, and to carry out Churchill's scheme to attack what he called the "soft underbelly of the Axis" by invading Sicily. Admiral Nimitz and General MacArthur were authorized meanwhile to start an offensive in the Pacific islands. Top priority, however, went to an antisubmarine campaign in the Atlantic. Before leaving Casablanca, Roosevelt announced, with Churchill's endorsement, that the war would end only with the "unconditional surrender" of all enemies. An echo of Ulysses Grant's ultimatum at Fort Donelson, the formula was designed to reassure Stalin and to quiet suspicions aroused by the Darlan deal that the Western Allies might negotiate separately with the enemy. The announcement owed a good bit also to the determination that, as Roosevelt put it, "every person in Germany should realize that this time Germany is a defeated nation." This dictum was later criticized for having stiffened enemy resistance, but probably had little effect: in fact neither the Italian nor Japanese surrender would be totally unconditional.

THE BATTLE OF THE ATLANTIC   While the battles raged in North Africa the more crucial Battle of the Atlantic reached its climax on the high seas. Several factors brought success to the Allied effort. Patrols by land-based planes covered much of the Atlantic from airfields in Britain and the Western Hemisphere, and in 1943 Portugal permitted American planes to operate from the Azores, thereby closing the last gap in coverage in the North Atlantic. Scientists perfected a variety of new detection devices: radar, which the British had already used to advantage in the air Battle of Britain, bounced radio waves off objects above the surface and registered their positions on a screen; sonar gear detected sound waves from submerged U-boats, and sonobuoys, dropped from planes, radioed back their findings; advanced magnetic equipment enabled aircraft to detect objects under water. New escort carriers ("baby flat-tops") and improvements in depth charges added to the effectiveness of convoys.

By April 1943 there were in the western half of the North Atlantic at any time an average of 31 convoys with 145 escorts and 673 merchant ships, as well as 120 other ships traveling alone and a number of heavily escorted troopships. None of the troopships going to Britain or the Mediterranean was lost, although submarines sank three en route to Greenland and Iceland. The U-boats kept up the Battle of the Atlantic until the war's end; when Germany finally collapsed at least forty-nine were still at sea. But Adm. Karl Doenitz, their commander, later admitted that the Battle of the Atlantic was lost by the end of May 1943. In his memoirs he credited the difference largely to radar. What he did not know then was that the Allies had a secret weapon. By early 1943 their cryptanalysts were routinely reading messages from Doenitz and telling their sub-hunters where to look for the German prey.

SICILY AND ITALY   The North African campaign won, the Allies got ready to attack Sicily, and decided at Casablanca. On July 10 about 250,000 British and American troops landed on Sicily, the largest single amphibious action in the war to that time, scoring a complete surprise. Gen. George Patton's American Seventh Army landed on the southwest coast, and after a fierce battle at the beachhead, moved swiftly across the island to take Palermo twelve days later. Montgomery's British Eighth Army encountered more stubborn resistance near Syracuse, but the entire island was in Allied hands by August 17, although some 40,000 Germans escaped to the mainland.

The collapse in Sicily ended Mussolini's twenty years of Fascist rule. Italians never had much heart for the war into which he had dragged them. On July 25, 1943, King Victor Emmanuel III notified the dictator of his dismissal as premier. A new regime under the elderly Marshal Pietro Badoglio, former chief of the general staff, startled the Allies when it offered not only to surrender but to switch sides in the war. Unfortunately, mutual suspicions prolonged talks until September 3, while the Germans poured reinforcements into Italy and seized key points. In the confusion the Italian army disintegrated, although most of the navy escaped to Allied ports. A few army units later joined the Allied effort, and a good many of the soldiers joined bands of partisans who fought behind the German lines. Mussolini, plucked from imprisonment by a German airborne raid, became head of a shadowy puppet government in northern Italy.

Landings on the mainland therefore did not turn into a walk-over. British forces invading the foot of the peninsula in early September landed unopposed, but the main landing at Salerno on September 9 encountered heavy resistance. In hope of scoring a surprise, the invaders omitted preliminary bombardment, leaving intact the German defenses. The American Fifth Army under Gen. Mark Clark, with British troops in the assault force, nevertheless secured beachheads within a week and by October 1 were in Naples. The Germans had reduced much of the city to rubble, but the bay and port facilities were soon cleared and back in operation. Before the end of September British forces had crossed the peninsula to Foggia, on the Adriatic. From there Allied fighters could cover the front and bombers could raid Nazi facilities in the Balkans as far as the Ploesti oilfields in Rumania.

Rome was the next objective, but mountainous country stood in the way. Fighting stalled in the Appenines where the German Gustav Line held the Allies through the winter of 1943–1944 in some of the most miserable, mud-soaked, and frostbitten fighting of the war. Cartoonist Bill Mauldin's Willie and Joe, in the GI newspaper *Yank*, slogged their way to fame in the Italian campaign as typical dogface infantrymen who distilled a saving humor out of their plight. On January 22, 1944, the Allies attempted an end-run by landing at Anzio, behind the German lines near Rome. This time they surprised the enemy, but failed to move quickly enough to the commanding Alban Heights. At Anzio they held on only by dogged determination until a series of savage attacks broke the Gustav Line in mid-May 1944 and lifted the siege. On June 4, 1944, Mark Clark's Fifth Army was in Rome, which fortunately had escaped the destruction visited on Naples, or on the Benedictine abbey at Monte Cassino. The capture of Rome provided only a brief moment of glory, for the long-awaited cross-Channel landing in France came two days later. Italy, always a secondary front, faded from the limelight of world attention as the GIs labored 150 miles northward to the Gothic Line, where the Germans staged a last-ditch defense for yet another bleak winter.

STRATEGIC BOMBING OF EUROPE   Behind the long-postponed landings on the Normandy beaches lay months of preparation. While waiting, the United States Army Air Force and the Royal Air Force (RAF) carried the battle into Hitler's "Fortress Europe." In April 1942 advance units of the Eighth Air Force embarked for Britain by sea, and soon afterward planes began to be ferried across the North Atlantic by air. On July 4, 1942, six American crews took part in a raid on airfields in Holland; on August 17, 1942, heavy bombers staged the first all-American raid on freight yards in Rouen, France, and in October began hitting submarine pens in the Bay of Biscay. Late in January 1943 came the first American raid on Germany itself, on the port of Wilhelmshaven.

By 1943 American strategic bombers were full-fledged partners of the RAF in the effort to pound Germany into submission. The RAF, to cut losses during the hard days after the fall of

Mauldin's Willie and Joe. [Bill Mauldin and Wil-Jo Associates, Inc.]

"Joe, yestiddy ya saved my life an' I swore I'd pay ya back. Here's my last pair of dry socks."

France, had confined itself mostly to night raids, and continued now to specialize in nocturnal attacks. The Americans believed that they could be more effective with high-level daylight precision bombing. Between them the AAF and RAF kept German defenders on the watch day and night.

Yet despite the widespread damage it caused, the strategic air offensive ultimately failed to cut severely into German production or, as later studies found, to break civilian morale. German production in fact increased until the last few weeks of the war. Heavy Allied losses persisted through 1943. In six days of October, raids deep inside the continent, climaxed by an attack on ball-bearing works at Schweinfurt, resulted in the loss of 148 bombers, mainly from German fighters. By the end of 1943, however, jettisonable gas tanks permitted escort fighters to go as far as Berlin and back. In the "Big Week" of February 20–25, 1944, 3,300 heavy bombers of the Eighth Air Force, and 500 from the Fifteenth Air Force in Italy, focused their attack on aircraft plants. Badly damaged, the German aircraft industry continued to turn out planes to the end, but heavy losses of both planes and pilots forced the German Luftwaffe to conserve its strength and cease challenging every Allied mission.

Berlin, the air strategists assumed, was one target the German fighters would have to protect. But in March the capital became the object of repeated Allied raids, and the resultant losses left German fighters ever more reluctant to rise to the bait. The horror at enemy attacks on civilians earlier in the war proved no barrier to a response in kind. Germany, Churchill said, was reaping the whirlwind. With air supremacy assured, the Allies were free to concentrate on their primary urban and industrial targets, and when the time came, to provide cover for the Normandy landings. On April 14, 1944, General Eisenhower assumed control of the Strategic Air Forces for use in the Normandy landings, less than two months away. On D-Day he told the troops: "If you see fighting aircraft over you, they will be ours."

THE TEHERAN MEETING   By the summer of 1943 the growing American presence in Britain, combined with successes in the Battle of the Atlantic and the strategic bombing, finally brought Churchill around on the cross-Channel invasion. Late in the fall he and Roosevelt finally had their first joint meeting with Josef Stalin in Teheran, Iran. A preliminary meeting of foreign ministers was held in Moscow during late October 1943, with Secretary of State Hull and Foreign Ministers Anthony Eden and V. M. Molotov. On one point they could not reach agreement: the Russians refused to recognize the Polish government-in-exile at London. But when Hull and Eden gave assurance that a cross-Channel invasion was coming, the Russians in return promised to enter the war against Japan after Germany's defeat. The ministers also agreed to begin plans for an international organization, and at Eden's suggestion they set up a European Advisory Commission in London to lay plans for postwar Germany. It was this body that later fixed the zones of occupation.

On the way to the Teheran meeting with Stalin, Churchill and Roosevelt met in Cairo with Generalissimo Chiang Kai-shek from November 22 to 26. The resultant Declaration of Cairo

Premier Stalin (left), President Roosevelt, and Prime Minister Churchill at the Teheran conference, November 1943. [Library of Congress]

(December 1, 1943) affirmed that war against Japan would continue until Japan's unconditional surrender, that all Chinese territories taken by Japan would be restored to China—including Formosa and the Pescadores—that Japan would lose the Pacific islands acquired after 1941, and that "in due course Korea shall become free and independent."

During November 28 to December 1 the Big Three leaders conferred in Teheran. Their chief subject was the planned invasion of France and a Russian offensive timed to coincide with it. Stalin repeated his promise to enter the war against Japan, and the three leaders reaffirmed the foreign ministers' decision in favor of planning an international organization. At further discussions in Cairo (December 4–6) Roosevelt and Churchill decided to put General Eisenhower in command of the cross-Channel invasion.

D-DAY AND AFTER   In January 1944 General Eisenhower arrived in London to take command at Supreme Headquarters, Allied Expeditionary Forces (SHAEF). Already battle-tested in North Africa and the Mediterranean, he now faced the supreme test of Operation "Overlord," the cross-Channel assault on Hitler's "Atlantic Wall." In April and May while the vast invasion forces made final preparations, the Allied air forces disrupted the transportation network of northern France, smashing railroads, bridges, and rolling stock. By early June all was ready, and after postponement for one day because of weather, D-Day fell on June 6, 1944.

The invasion hit not across the narrow stretch from Dover to Calais, where the elaborate activity of Gen. George Patton's Third Army had led the Germans to expect it, but along sixty

Gen. Dwight D. Eisenhower instructing paratroopers just before they board their airplanes to begin the D-Day assault. [Library of Congress]

The Allied beachhead in Normandy. [Maritime Administration]

miles of beach in Normandy. Airborne forces dropped behind the beaches during the night while planes and battleships pounded the coastal defenses. At dawn the invasion fleet of some 4,000 ships began to pour out their cargoes of troops and supplies on the shore. On Utah Beach, at the base of the Cotentin Peninsula, the American invaders made it in against relatively light opposition, but farther east, on a four-mile segment designated Omaha Beach, bombardment had failed to take out German defenders and the Americans were caught by heavily mined water. They then had to make it across a fifty-yard beach exposed to crossfire from concrete pillboxes before they could huddle under a sea wall and begin to root out the defenders. Still farther east, British forces had less difficulty on Gold, Juno, and Sword beaches, but found themselves subjected to bitter counterattack by German forces determined to hold Caen Beach.

Within two weeks the Allies had landed a million men and seized a beachhead sixty miles wide and five to fifteen miles deep. Before the end of June they had swept up the peninsula to the port of Cherbourg, only to find the harbor so completely blocked that it took two months to clear. But they continued to pour men and matériel onto the beaches, and contrived manmade harbors by scuttling old ships to create breakwaters. On into July the Allies edged inland through the Norman marshes and hedgerows. On July 19, 1944, Gen. Omar Bradley's troops took St. Lo, a transportation hub for roads and railroads into the heart of France. Marshals Gerd von Rundstedt, the German commander, and Erwin Rommel, now in charge of Army Group B, advised withdrawal to defenses behind the Seine, but an enraged Hitler removed both men and issued disastrous orders to contest every inch of land. Rommel, convinced that all was lost, began to intrigue for a separate peace until he was arrested and granted the option of suicide. Other like-minded officers, convinced that the war was hopeless, tried to kill Hitler at his headquarters on July 20, but the Führer survived the bomb blast and hundreds of conspirators and suspects were tortured to death.

Meanwhile, the Führer's tactics brought calamity to the German forces in western France. On July 25 Gen. Omar Bradley's First Army broke through west of St. Lo and, soon augmented by George Patton's Third Army, the American forces broke out westward into Brittany and eastward toward Paris. Patton moved east and north to link up with British forces coming south from Caen, and the two caught the German Seventh and Fifth Panzer Armies in a trap. Only remnants managed to escape through the Falaise Gap before the pincers closed on August 19. Meanwhile on August 15 a joint American-French invasion force landed on the French Mediterranean coast, took Marseille and Toulon in a walkover, and raced up the Rhône Valley. German resistance in France collapsed. A Free French division under Gen. Jacques Le Clerc, aided by American forces, had the honor of liberating Paris on August 25. German forces retired pell-mell toward the prewar Siegfried Line or Westwall at the German border, and in a rush by mid-September most of France and Belgium were cleared of enemy forces. By this time the Americans were in Aachen, the old seat of Charlemagne's empire, the first German town to fall.

SLOWING MOMENTUM Things had moved so much faster than expected, in fact, that the Allies were running out of gas. Neither their plans nor their supply system could keep up with the movement. General Montgomery, whose British and Canadian forces had been the pivot of the Allied sweep, had moved forward into Belgium, where they took Antwerp. From there, he argued, a quick fatal thrust toward Berlin could end things. On the right flank, General Patton was just as sure he could take the American Third Army all the way. Eisenhower reasoned, however, that prudence demanded getting his supply lines in order first, which required clearing stubborn Germans out of the Scheldt estuary and opening a supply channel to Antwerp—a long, hard battle which lasted until the end of November. Before giving up his original plan, however, Montgomery tried one sharp thrust at Arnhem to make a bridgehead across the Rhine. His force proved inadequate, with the consequence that airborne forces dropped behind the German lines were cut off and decimated. Another winter of fighting would remain before the German collapse.

LEAPFROGGING TO TOKYO

Even in the Pacific, relegated to lower priority, Allied forces had brought the war within reach of the enemy homeland by the end of 1944. The war's first American offensive in fact had been in the southwest Pacific. There the Japanese, stopped at Coral Sea and Midway, had thrust into the southern Solomons, and were building an airstrip on Guadalcanal from which they could attack transportation routes to Australia. On August 7, 1942, two months before the North Africa landings, the First Marine Division under Gen. Alexander A. Vandegrift landed on Guadalcanal and seized the airstrip while other marines secured nearby Tulagi and its port.

These quick victories, however, provoked a savage Japanese response. Reinforcements poured in via the "Tokyo Express" down the central channel, the Solomons "Slot," and the opposing navies challenged each other in a confusing series of battles that battered both so badly the sailors named the Savo Island Sound "Iron Bottom Bay." But while the Americans had lost heavily, they delivered such punishment to Japanese carrier groups, already battered at Midway, that the Japanese navy remained on the defensive for the rest of the war. The marines, helped by reinforcements, finally cleared the steaming jungles of Japanese. By February 1943 only stragglers were left.

MACARTHUR IN NEW GUINEA Meanwhile American and Australian forces under General MacArthur had begun to push the Japanese out of their advanced positions on the north coast of New Guinea. These battles, fought through some of the hottest, most humid and mosquito-infested swamps in the world, bought advances at a heavy cost, but by the end of January 1943 the eastern tip of New Guinea up to Huon Gulf was secured.

At this stage came a critical decision on strategy. MacArthur proposed to advance westward along the northern coast of New Guinea toward the Philippines and ultimately Tokyo. Admiral Nimitz, with headquarters at Pearl Harbor, argued for a sweep through the islands of the central Pacific ultimately toward Formosa and China. In March 1943 the Combined Chiefs of Staff, meeting in Washington, agreed to MacArthur's plan and allotted resources for the purpose. Soon afterward they agreed that Nimitz should undertake his sweep too, for the central Pacific island complex would expose MacArthur's northern flank to a constant threat if it were left in Japanese hands.

A new tactic expedited the movement. During the air Battle of the Bismarck Sea (March 2–3, 1943) Gen. George Kennedy's bombers sank eight Japanese troopships and ten warships bringing reinforcements. Thereafter the Japanese dared not risk sending transports to points under siege, making it possible to use the tactic of bypassing Japanese strongholds, neutralizing them with air and sea power, and moving on, leaving them to die on the vine. Adm. Theodore S. Wilkinson called it "leapfrogging," or in a new twist on baseball language, "hitting 'em where they ain't." Premier Tojo later acknowledged the strategy as a major cause of Allied victory. Meanwhile, in mid-April, before the offensive got under way, fighters from Henderson Field on Guadalcanal shot down a plane which American codebreakers knew was carrying Admiral Yamamoto into Bougainville. The death of Japan's naval commander, the planner of the Pearl Harbor attack, was a shattering blow to Japanese morale.

The first strong point left stranded by the leapfrog strategy was Rabaul, New Britain, bastion of the "Bismarck Barrier" which threatened the flank of MacArthur's advance across New Guinea. The offensive got under way first with sharp amphibious and naval thrusts to secure the northern Solomons. After successful naval actions in the Solomons Slot (in one of which *PT 109*, Lt. John Fitzgerald Kennedy's torpedo boat, went down) American forces controlled the waters in the area. On November 1 an amphibious force landed on an undefended coast of Bougainville in the northern Solomons and carved out a beachhead from which fighters and bombers brought Rabaul under daily attack. A Japanese fleet that moved to challenge the operation was decisively beaten in the Battle of Empress Augusta Bay on November 2, 1943. In New Guinea, MacArthur's forces moved into command of the coast opposite Cape Gloucester, New Britain. Occupation of Arawe and Cape Gloucester in December secured the passageway to the north coast of New Guinea and the western Pacific. When the Admiralty Islands were taken in March 1944, the isolation of Rabaul was complete and nearly 100,000 Japanese were stranded. Thus by early 1944 the Bismarcks Barrier was broken.

NIMITZ IN THE CENTRAL PACIFIC   Admiral Nimitz's parallel advance through the central Pacific had as its first target two tiny atolls in the Gilberts: Makin and Tarawa. After advance bombing raids by the Seventh Air Force, mounted from Canton and Funa Futi in the Phoenix and Ellice Islands, a fleet of 200 ships delivered infantry and marines ashore at dawn on November 20, 1943.

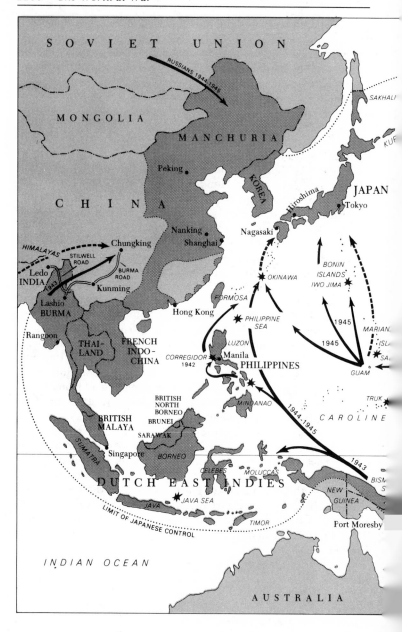

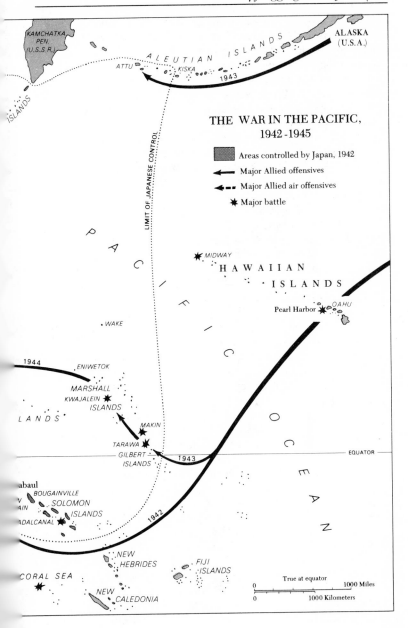

THE WAR IN THE PACIFIC,
1942-1945

Areas controlled by Japan, 1942
Major Allied offensives
Major Allied air offensives
Major battle

Makin, where the Japanese had only a small force, was soon cleared; after three days Gen. Ralph Smith radioed the terse message, "Makin taken." Tarawa, with its concrete bunkers behind a long coral reef and beach obstructions of wire and logs, was one of the most heavily protected islands in the Pacific. There nearly 1,000 American soldiers, sailors, and marines lost their lives rooting out a determined resistance by 4,000 Japanese who refused to surrender. The Gilberts provided costly lessons in amphibious operations, one of which was to confirm the value of bypassing strong points. The islands also provided airfields from which the Seventh Air Force began softening up strong points in the Marshall Islands. Japanese planes completely abandoned the region.

Invasion of the Marshalls, the next step "up the ladder" to Tokyo, began on January 31, 1944, at Kwajalein and Eniwetok, both of which were soon taken. During these operations a carrier raid wrought heavy destruction on enemy ships and aircraft at Truk, the Japanese "Pearl Harbor" in the Carolines. Then Truk, like Rabaul, was bypassed. The Americans took Saipan in the Marianas on June 15, which brought the new American B-29 bombers within striking distance of Japan itself. The Japanese navy therefore had to resist with all it had, which was not enough despite its crash program to build new carriers.

In the Battle of the Philippine Sea, the grand "Marianas Turkey Shoot" fought mostly in the air on June 19 and 20, 1944, the Japanese lost three more carriers, two submarines, and over 300 planes, at the cost of only 17 American planes. The battle secured the Marianas, and soon B-29s were winging their way to the first systematic bombings of the Japanese homeland. Defeat in the Marianas finally brought home to General Tojo the realization that the war was lost. On July 18, 1944, he and his entire cabinet resigned, and Gen. Kunikai Koiso became the new premier.

THE BATTLE OF LEYTE GULF With New Guinea and the Marianas all but conquered, President Roosevelt met with General MacArthur and Admiral Nimitz in Honolulu on July 27–28, 1944, to decide the next major step. Previous plans had marked China as the essential springboard for invading Japan, but a Japanese offensive in April 1944 had taken most of the south China airfields from which American air power had operated. This strengthened MacArthur's standing opinion that the Philippines would provide a safer staging area than Formosa. Sentimental and political considerations, as well as military, tipped the decision his way. After securing his flanks with the capture of Morotai in the Moluccas and Peleliu in the Palaus—the latter was the scene of some of the bloodiest fighting of the war, ground out in heat up to 115°—MacArthur made his move into the Philippines on October 20, landing first on the island of Leyte. Wading ashore behind the first landings, he issued an announcement: "People of the Philippines: I have returned. . . . Rally to me. . . . Let no heart be faint."

The Japanese, knowing that loss of the Philippines would cut them off from the oil and other essential resources of the East Indies, brought in fleets from three directions. The three encounters that resulted on October 25, 1944, came to be known collectively as the Battle of Leyte Gulf. Just after midnight the southern force made premature contact with American PT-boats, and then with destroyers, cruisers, and battleships. After an old-fashioned naval battle, only two Japanese ships were left to retire, with carrier planes in hot pursuit. The northern force from Formosa, designed to decoy the American fleet from the scene, worked all too well. Admiral Halsey, commanding the Third Fleet, headed north to sink the approaching carriers.

After dawn the major Japanese force, although hit by American submarines and planes, threaded through San Bernadino Straight and, off Samar Island, ran into American forces. Inadequately protected by three destroyers and four destroyer escorts, Rear Adm. Clifton Sprague put up a desperate fight against superior firepower. Two destroyers and one escort went down, but Sprague's forces disabled a Japanese cruiser and so upset the enemy battle line that a confused Admiral Kurita broke off back to San Bernadino Straight. He later claimed that an intercepted message persuaded him that massive American reinforcements were on the way.

The third major engagement took place off Cape Engano, Luzon, where Admiral Halsey closed on the northern force with overwhelming superiority. American planes sank four Japanese carriers and a destroyer before the fleet broke off to chase Admiral Kurita, but too late. In one day the Battle of Leyte Gulf had grown into the largest naval engagement in history. The Japanese had lost most of their remaining sea power and the ability to protect the Philippines. The battle brought the first of the suicide attacks by Japanese pilots who crash-dived into Sprague's baby carriers, sinking one and seriously damaging others. The "Kamikaze" units, named for the "Divine Wind" that saved Japan from Mongol invasion in 1281, were able to inflict severe damage on the American navy until the end of the war.

A New Age Is Born

ROOSEVELT'S FOURTH TERM   In 1944, war or no war, the calendar dictated another presidential election. This time the Republicans turned to the former crime-fighter and New York governor, Thomas E. Dewey, as their candidate. They balanced the moderately progressive Dewey with conservative John W. Bricker of Ohio as their vice-presidential nominee. Once again no Democratic challenger rose high enough to contest Roosevelt, but a fight did develop over the second spot on the ticket. Vice-President Wallace had earned the enmity of both southern conservatives and northern city bosses who feared his ties with labor, but Roosevelt finally rejected James F. Byrnes, the favorite of these groups. The outcome was the compromise choice of Missouri Sen. Harry S Truman.

Dewey ran under the same handicap as Landon and Willkie before him. He did not propose to dismantle Roosevelt's programs, but argued that it was time for younger men to replace the tired old leaders of the New Deal. Roosevelt betrayed decided signs of illness and exhaustion, but nevertheless carried the battle to the enemy. His most memorable thrust was at a Teamsters Union dinner in Washington, where FDR responded in mock outrage to stories that he had sent a destroyer to the Aleutians to pick up his Scottie, Fala. The president did not resent the attacks, he said, but as for Fala, "his Scotch soul was furious. He has not been the same dog since." On November 7, 1945, Roosevelt was once again elected, this time by a popular margin of 25.6 million to 22 million and an electoral vote of 432 to 99.

CONVERGING FRONTS   After their quick sweep across France, the Allies lost momentum in the fall of 1944 and settled down to slugging at the frontiers of Germany. Along this line the armies fought it out all winter. Bradley's Ninth Army joined the First to capture the Roer River dams by early December. Patton's Third Army, farther south, captured the Lorraine fortress city of Metz and pushed into the Saar while General Devers's Sixth Army Group took Strasbourg in Alsace and moved up the Rhine.

Then the Germans sprang a surprise in the rugged Ardennes Forest, where the Allied line was thinnest. Hitting on December 16, 1944, under clouds which prevented air reconnaissance, they advanced along a fifty-mile front in Belgium and Luxembourg. In ten days they penetrated nearly to the Meuse River on their way to Antwerp, which had been recently captured by the

Canadians, but they stalled at Bastogne. Reinforced by the Allies just before it was surrounded, Bastogne held for six days against all the Germans could bring against it. On December 22 Gen. "Tony" McAuliffe of the 101st Airborne gave his memorable answer to the demand for surrender: "Nuts." His situation remained desperate until the next day when the clouds lifted, allowing Allied airpower to hit the Germans and drop in supplies. On December 26 the Fourth Armored Division broke through to the relief of Bastogne, but it would be mid-January 1945 before the previous lines were restored.

Germany's sudden thrust upset Eisenhower's timetable, but the outcome shook German power and morale. Their effort had weakened the eastern front, and in January the Russians began their final offensive. The western offensives started in February. Advancing all along the front, the Allies by early March had reached the banks of the Rhine nearly all the way from Holland to Switzerland. On March 6 they took Cologne, and the next day, by remarkable luck, the Allies seized the bridge at Remagen before the Germans could blow it up. Troops poured across the Rhine there and soon afterward at other points.

The Allies then encircled the Ruhr Valley, center of Germany's heavy industry. Hodges's First Army on the south and Simpson's Ninth on the north in quick sweeps closed the pincers on some 400,000 German soldiers in the region and pounded them into submission. By mid-April resistance there was over. Meanwhile the Russian offensive had also reached Germany itself, after taking Warsaw on January 17 and Vienna on April 13.

YALTA AND THE POSTWAR WORLD   As the final offensives got under way, the Yalta Conference (February 4–11, 1945) brought the Big Three leaders together again in a czar's palace at the Crimean resort. While the focus at Teheran in 1943 had been on wartime strategy, it was now on the shape of the postwar world. Two aims loomed large in Roosevelt's thinking. One was the need to ensure that the Soviet Union join the war against Japan. The other was based on the lessons he drew from the previous World War. Just as the Neutrality Acts of the 1930s were designed with lessons from the previous war in mind, thoughts about the future were now influenced by memories of the interwar years. Americans, the historian Ernest May has written, visualized World War II as parallel to World War I. "They expected its aftermath to be in most respects the same. And they defined statesmanship as doing those things which might have been done to prevent World War II from occurring." Chief among the mis-

The first session of the Yalta Conference, convened in February 1945 to shape the postwar world. Stalin (left), FDR (upper right), and Churchill (lower right) confer. [National Archives]

takes to be remedied this time were the failure of the United States to join the League of Nations and the failure of the Allies to maintain a united front against the German aggressors.

The Yalta meeting began by calling for a conference on world organization to be held in the United States, beginning on April 25, 1945. The Yalta conferees decided also that Russia would have three votes in the organization's General Assembly and that substantive decisions in the Security Council would require the acquiescence of its five permanent members: the United States, Britain, Russia, France, and China.

GERMANY AND EASTERN EUROPE   With Hitler's "Thousand-Year Reich" stumbling to its doom, arrangements for the postwar governance of Germany had to be made. The war map dictated the basic pattern of occupation zones: Russia would control the east and the Western Allies would control the rich industrial areas of the west. Berlin, isolated within the Russian zone, would be subject to joint occupation. At the behest of Churchill and Roosevelt, liberated France got a zone along its border and also in Berlin. Similar arrangements were made for Austria, with Vienna like Berlin under joint occupation within the Russian zone. Russian demands for reparations of $20 billion, half of which would go to Russia, were referred to a Reparations Commission in Moscow. The commission never reached agreement, although the Russians made off with untold amounts of machinery and equipment from their occupation zone.

With respect to eastern Europe, where Russian forces were

advancing on a broad front, there was little the Western Allies could do to influence events. Roosevelt was inhibited by his wish to win Russian cooperation in the fight against Japan and in the effort to build the proposed United Nations organization. Poland became the main focus of Western concern. Britain and France had gone to war in 1939 to defend Poland and now, six years later, the course of the war had left Poland's fate in the hands of the Russians. Events had long foreshadowed the outcome. Controversy over the Katyn Forest massacre of 1940, in which the Russians had gunned down over 14,000 Polish officers, led the Russians in 1943 to break relations with the Polish government-in-exile in London. When Russian forces reentered Poland in 1944, the Soviets placed civil administration under a Committee of National Liberation in Lublin, a puppet regime representing few Poles. When Soviet troops reached the gates of Warsaw, the underground resistance in the city rose against the Nazi occupiers. The underground, however, held allegiance to the London government-in-exile. The Russians then stopped their offensive for two months while the Nazis wiped out thousands of Poles, potential rivals to the Lublin puppet government.

That optimism about postwar cooperation could survive such events was a triumph of hope over experience. The attitude was remotely reminiscent of 1919, when Wilson made concessions to win approval of the League of Nations in the hope that the League could later remedy any injustices which had crept into the peace settlement. But in any case the Western Allies could do no more than acquiesce or stall. On the Soviet proposal to expand the Lublin Committee into a provisional government together with representatives of the London Poles, they acquiesced. On the issue of Poland's boundaries, they stalled. The Russians proposed to keep eastern Poland, offering land taken from Germany as compensation. Roosevelt and Churchill accepted the proposal, but considered the western boundary at the Oder–Western Neisse Rivers only provisional. The peace conference at which the western boundary of Poland was to be settled never took place because of later disagreements. The presence of the London Poles in the provisional government only lent a tone of legitimacy to a regime dominated by the Communists, who soon ousted their rivals.

The Big Three promised to sponsor free elections, democratic governments, and constitutional safeguards of freedom throughout the rest of Europe. The Yalta Declaration of Liberated Europe reaffirmed faith in the principles of the Atlantic Charter and the United Nations, but in the end it made little difference. It may have postponed Communist takeovers in eastern Europe for a few years, but before long Communist members of coalition governments had their hands on the levers of power and ousted the opposition. Aside from Czechoslovakia, though, the countries of eastern Europe lacked strong democratic traditions in any case. And Russia, twice invaded by Germany in the twentieth century, had good reason for wanting buffer states between it and the Germans.

YALTA'S LEGACY   The Yalta agreements were later attacked for giving eastern Europe over to Soviet domination. But the course of the war shaped the actions at Yalta. By suppressing opposition, moreover, the Soviets were not acting under the Yalta accords, but in violation of them.

Perhaps the most bitterly criticized of the Yalta understandings was a secret agreement on the Far East, not made public until after the war. As the Big Three met, fighting still raged in the Philippines and Burma. The Joint Chiefs of Staff still estimated that Japan could hold out for eighteen months after the defeat of Germany. Costly campaigns lay ahead and the atomic bomb was still an expensive gamble on the unknown. Roosevelt accepted Stalin's demands on postwar arrangements in the Far East, subject technically to later agreement by Chiang Kai-shek. Stalin wanted continued Russian control of Outer Mongolia through its puppet People's Republic there, acquisition of the Kurile Islands from Japan, and recovery of rights and territory lost after the Russo-Japanese War in 1905, which included the southern half of Sakhalin Island, control of Port Arthur (Dairen), and joint Soviet-Chinese operation of the major railroads in Manchuria. Stalin in return promised to enter the war against Japan two or three months after the German defeat, to recognize Chinese sovereignty over Manchuria, and to conclude a treaty of friendship and alliance with the Chinese Nationalists. Later Roosevelt's concessions would appear in a different light, but given their geographical advantages in Asia as in eastern Europe, the Soviets were in a position to get what they wanted in any case.

THE THIRD REICH COLLAPSES   The collapse of Nazi resistance was imminent, but President Roosevelt did not live to join the celebrations. All through 1944 his health had been declining, and photographs from early 1945 revealed a very sick man. Roosevelt had always before been able to recharge his batteries with brief rests, and in the spring of 1945 he went to his second home in Warm Springs, Georgia, to rest up for the Charter Conference of the United Nations at San Francisco. On April 12, 1945, while he was drafting a Jefferson Day speech, a cerebral hemorrhage brought sudden death. The last words he wrote into the speech were: "The only limit to our realization of tomorrow will be our doubts of today. Let us move forward with strong and active faith."

The collapse of Hitler's Germany came less than a month later. The Allied armies rolled up almost unopposed to the Elbe River, where they met advanced detachments of Russians at Torgau on April 25. Three days later Italian partisans caught and killed Mussolini and his mistress as they tried to flee. In Berlin, which was under siege by the Russians, Hitler married his mistress, Eva Braun, in an underground bunker on the last day of April just before killing her and himself in a suicide pact. On May 2 Berlin fell to the Russians. That same day German forces in Italy surrendered. Adm. Karl Doenitz, Hitler's designated successor, desperately tried to surrender to the Western Allies, but Eisenhower declined to act except in concert with the Russians. Finally, on May 7 Marshal Alfred Jodl signed an unconditional surrender in Allied headquarters at Rheims. So ended the Thousand-Year Reich, little more than twelve years after its Führer came to power.

Massive celebrations of victory in Europe on V-E Day, May 8, 1945, were tempered by the tragedies that had engulfed the world: mourning for the lost president and the death and mutilation of untold millions. Most shocking was the discovery of the Nazi Holocaust, scarcely believable until the Allied armies came upon the death camps in which the Nazis had sought to apply their "final solution" to the Jewish "problem": the wholesale extermination of some 6 million Jews along with more than 1 million others who had incurred the Nazi contempt and displeasure for one reason or another. The sobering thought that the defeat of Japan remained to be accomplished cast a further pall over the celebrations.

A GRINDING WAR American forces continued to penetrate and disrupt the Japanese Empire in the early months of 1945, but at heavy cost. Stubborn opposition by the Japanese slowed the reconquest of the Philippines. Japanese forces in Manila held out until March 4. By July 1 the Sixth Army had those parts of Luzon it most needed, but about 50,000 Japanese continued to fight until the end of the war. While fighting went on in the Philippines, on February 19, 1945, marine assault forces invaded Iwo Jima, a speck of volcanic rock in the Bonin group, 750 miles from Tokyo. It was needed to provide fighter escort for bombers over

Japan and a landing strip for disabled B-29s. Nearly six weeks were required to secure an island five miles square from defenders hiding in an underground labyrinth. The cost was more than 20,000 American casualties and nearly 7,000 dead.

The fight for Okinawa, beginning on Easter Sunday, April 1, was even bloodier. The largest island in the Ryukyu chain, Okinawa was large enough to afford a staging area for invasion. It was the largest amphibious operation of the Pacific war, involving some 300,000 line and service troops. From a beachhead on the northern coast the invaders fought their way south through rugged terrain. Desperate Japanese counterattacks inflicted heavy losses on land, by air, and by sea. Kamikaze planes came in by the hundreds. Finally, the battleship *Yamato,* a survivor of Leyte Gulf, left Kyushu with nine other ships—the remnant of a once-great navy—with fuel only for a one-way trip, all that was available. American seaplanes intercepted the pathetic armada, sank the *Yamato* and two other warships, and badly damaged the rest. It was the end of the Japanese navy, but the fight for Okinawa raged until late June, when the bloody attrition destroyed any further Japanese ability to resist. The fighting brought nearly 50,000 American casualties; the dead included their commander, Gen. Simon B. Buckner, Jr., and one of the GIs' favorite correspondents, Ernie Pyle. The Japanese lost an estimated 140,000 dead, but more than 10,000 surrendered. Casualties included about 42,000 Okinawans.

The campaign was significant mainly for wearing down the remaining defenses of the Japanese. Now American ships could roam the coastline of Japan, shelling targets ashore. American planes bombed at will and mined the waters of the Inland Sea. Tokyo, Nagoya, and other major cities were devastated by firestorms from incendiary bombs, made all the worse by the prevalence of wooden structures in earthquake-prone Japan. Still, it seemed that ahead lay further beachheads and more bitter fighting against the same suicidal fury that had made Okinawa so costly a conquest. But as the irony of timing would have it, Okinawa was never needed as a staging area. When the Americans invaded Okinawa the emperor named a new premier, and when resistance on the island collapsed he instructed the new premier to seek peace terms. Washington had picked this up by decoding Japanese messages, which suggested either an effort to avoid unconditional surrender or perhaps just a stall.

THE ATOMIC BOMB By this time, however, a new force had changed all strategic calculations: President Truman had just got word of the first atomic explosion, the result of several years of

intensive work. The strands of scientific development that led to
the bomb ironically ran back to Germany. Except for the Nazi
bigotry that drove scientists into exile, Germany might well have
developed the atomic bomb first. Early in 1939 a German scientific journal revealed that the uranium atom had been split at the
Kaiser Wilhelm Institute in Berlin; experiments in Denmark and
the United States soon confirmed the finding. On October 11,
1939, President Roosevelt learned of the matter when an emissary, Dr. Alexander Sachs, delivered a letter from Albert Einstein and a memorandum from Dr. Leo Szilard, explaining the
potential of nuclear fission and warning that the Germans might
steal the march. Roosevelt quickly set up a committee to coordinate information in the field, and in 1940 some army and navy
funds were diverted into research which grew ultimately into the
$2 billion top-secret Manhattan Project.

On August 13, 1942, the Army Engineers set up the Manhattan Engineering District under Brig.-Gen. Leslie R. Groves to
direct development and production of the bomb. On December
2, 1942, Dr. Enrico Fermi and other scientists achieved the first
atomic chain reaction in a squash court at the University of Chicago's Stagg Field, removing any remaining doubts of the bomb's
feasibility. Gigantic plants sprang up at Oak Ridge, Tennessee,
and Hanford, Washington, to make plutonium, while a group of
physicists under Dr. J. Robert Oppenheimer worked out the scientific and technical problems of bomb construction in a laboratory at Los Alamos, New Mexico. On July 16, 1945, the first
atomic fireball rose from the New Mexico desert. The awestruck
Oppenheimer said later that in the observation bunker "A few

*"I am become death, the shatterer of
worlds." [Library of Congress]*

people laughed, a few people cried, most people were silent. There floated through my mind a line from the Bhagavad-Gita in which Krishna is trying to persuade the prince that he should do his duty: 'I am become death, the shatterer of worlds.' " Colleagues crowded forward with their congratulations: "Oppie," said one, "now we're all sons of bitches."

The question of how to use this awful weapon had already come before a committee of officials and scientists. Some of the scientists, awed at the ghastly prospect, favored a demonstration in a remote area, but the decision went for military use because only two bombs were available, and even those might misfire. More consideration was given to the choice of targets. Four cities had been reserved from conventional bombing as potential targets. After Secretary Stimson eliminated Kyoto, the ancient capital and center of many national and religious treasures, priority went to Hiroshima, center of war industries, headquarters of the Second General Army, and command center for the homeland's defenses.

On July 25, 1945, President Truman, then at the Big Three Conference in Potsdam, Germany, ordered the bomb dropped if Japan did not surrender before August 3. The next day the heads of the American, British, and Chinese governments issued the Potsdam Declaration demanding that Japan surrender or face "prompt and utter destruction." The deadline passed, and at 9:15 A.M. on August 6, 1945, a B-29 out of Tinian, the *Enola Gay*, with a crew commanded by Col. Paul W. Tibbetts, dropped the bomb over Hiroshima. A sudden flash wiped out four square miles of the city, wrecked the defense headquarters, wiped out most of the Second General Army, and killed in all more than 60,000 people. Dazed survivors wandered the streets, so painfully burned that their skin began to peel in large strips. In one of history's most pungent ironies, Capt. Mitsuo Fuchida, flight commander of the Pearl Harbor attack, flew into Hiroshima Airport that morning and found himself facing "a procession of people who seemed to have come out of Hell." Even those who appeared unhurt began mysteriously to sicken and die, the first victims of a deadly radiation which blighted lives for years to come. In the United States, Americans greeted the first news with elation: it promised a quick end to the long nightmare of war. Only later would the awareness dawn that it marked the start of a more enduring nightmare, the atomic age.

Three days later Russia hastened to enter the war, and a few hours after that, about noon on August 9, the second bomb exploded over the port city of Nagasaki, legendary home of Ma-

Nagasaki, blasted by the atomic bomb. [George Silk, Life magazine, © 1971 Time Inc.]

dame Butterfly and once the isolated kingdom's only window to the world, killing 36,000 more. That night the emperor urged his cabinet to accept the inevitable and surrender on the sole condition that he remain as sovereign. The next day the United States government, to facilitate surrender and an orderly transition, announced its willingness to let him keep the throne, but under the authority of an Allied supreme commander. Frantic exchanges ended with Japanese acceptance on August 14, 1945, when the emperor himself broke precedent to record a radio message announcing the surrender to his people. Even then a last-ditch palace revolt had to be squashed. After preliminary arrangements by Japanese emissaries in Manila, an American advance party arrived at Atsugi airfield on August 28 and General MacArthur came in two days later to take up residence at the New Grand Hotel. On September 2, 1945, he and other allied representatives accepted Japan's formal surrender on board the battleship *Missouri*. MacArthur then settled in at his headquarters in the Dai Ichi, "Building One," facing the Imperial Palace across the street, behind its moat. Just seventy-seven years after the Meiji Restoration had overthrown the last Tokugawa shogun, Japan had a new American shogun.

THE FINAL LEDGER   Thus ended the most deadly conflict in human history. No effort to tabulate a ledger of death and destruction can ever take the full measure of the war's suffering, nor hope to be more than an informed guess as to the numbers involved. One estimate has it that 70 million in all fought in the war, at a cost in human lives of 17 million military dead and more than 18 million civilian dead. Material costs were also enormous, perhaps $1 trillion in military expenditures and twice that in property losses. The Soviet Union suffered the greatest losses of all, over 6 million military deaths, over 10 million civilians dead, and at least 25 million left homeless. World War II was more costly for the United States than any other of the country's foreign wars: 294,000 battle deaths and 114,000 other deaths. But in proportion to population, the United States suffered a far smaller loss than any of the major allies or enemies, and American territory escaped the devastation visited on so many other parts of the world.

The war's end opened a new era for the United States. It accelerated the growth of American power while devastating all other world powers, leaving the United States economically and militarily the strongest nation on earth. But Russia, despite its human and material losses, emerged from the war with much new territory and enhanced influence, making it the greatest power on the whole Eurasian land mass. Just a little over a century after Alexis de Tocqueville predicted that western Europe would come to be overshadowed by the power of the United States and Russia, his prophecy had come to pass.

Further Reading

Two surveys which detail American involvement in the global conflict are John Morton Blum's *V Was for Victory: Politics and American Culture during World War II* (1976)° and Martha Hoyle's *A World in Flames: A History of World War II* (1970). Albert R. Buchanan's *The United States and World War II* (2 vols.; 1962) is more thorough, particularly on the military aspects of the struggle.

Russell F. Weigley's *The American Way of War: A History of United States Military Strategy and Policy* (1973) provides a scholarly assessment of why the war was fought as it was. Gordon Wright's *The Ordeal of Total War, 1939–1945* (1968), surveys the conflict in Europe, while Charles B. McDonald's *The Mighty Endeavor: American Armed Forces in the European Theatre in World War II* (1969) concentrates on American involvement there. Another perspective on the European conflict can be found in the memoirs of Dwight D. Eisenhower, *Crusade in Europe*

°These books are available in paperback editions.

(1948). Stephen Ambrose's *The Supreme Commander: The War Years of General Dwight D. Eisenhower* (1970) takes a look at Eisenhower's contribution. Books on specific campaigns in Europe include Trumball Higgins's *Soft Underbelly: The Anglo-American Controversy and the Italian Campaign, 1939–1945* (1968), Cornelius Ryan's *The Longest Day* (1959),° on the D-Day operation, and his *The Last Battle* (1966) and John Toland's *The Last Hundred Days* (1966), both on the last days of the Nazi resistance. Two other views of the European conflict can be found in the memoirs of Omar Bradley, *A General's Life: An Autobiography* (1983), and Forrest C. Pogue's *George C. Marshall* (3 vols.; 1963–1973). The Pacific theater is reviewed in Samuel E. Morison's *Strategy and Compromise: The Two-Ocean War* (1963), which covers naval operations, and D. Clayton James's *The Years of MacArthur* (1970, 1975), which concentrates on land strategy. Other perspectives on the war in the Far East are considered by Barbara Tuchman in *Stilwell and the American Experience in China, 1911–1945* (1971), John Toland's *The Rising Sun: The Decline and Fall of the Japanese Empire* (1970),° and Edwin P. Hoyt's *How They Won in the Pacific: Nimitz and His Admirals* (1970).

Overviews of the war on the home front include Gerald D. Nash's *The Great Depression and World War II: Organizing America* (1979), Richard Polenberg's *The War and Society* (1972), Richard Lingeman's *Don't You Know There's a War On* (1970), and the aforementioned Blum volume. The economic measures taken to undergird the war effort are viewed in Eliot Janeway's *Struggle for Survival* (1951), Chester Bowles's *Promise to Keep* (1971), Lester V. Chandler's *Inflation in the United States, 1940–1948* (1951), and John Kenneth Galbraith's *A Life in Our Times* (1982). Carl Degler treats the new working environment for women in *At Odds: Women and the Family in America from the Revolution to the Present* (1980).° Neil Wynn looks at the participation of blacks in *The Afro-American and the Second World War* (1976). The story of the oppression of Japanese-Americans is told by Roger Daniels in *Concentration Camps USA: Japanese Americans and World War II* (1971) and by Audie Girdner and Anne Loftis in *The Great Betrayal: The Evacuation of the Japanese-Americans during World War II* (1969).

Sound introductions to American diplomacy during the conflict can be found in Gaddis Smith's *American Diplomacy during the Second World War, 1941–1945* (1965), and Robert Beitzell's *The Uneasy Alliance: America, Britain, and Russia, 1941–1943* (1972). Gabriel Kolko's *The Politics of War: The World and United States Foreign Policy, 1943–1945* (1968) is a revisionist view. To understand the role Roosevelt played in policy-making, consult Raymond G. O'Connor's *Diplomacy for Victory: Franklin D. Roosevelt and Unconditional Surrender* (1971), Joseph P. Lash's *Roosevelt and Churchill* (1976), James MacGregor Burns's *Roosevelt: The Soldier of Freedom* (1970), and Robert A. Divine's *Roosevelt and World War II* (1969).° Diane Shaver Clemens is critical of Roosevelt in *Yalta* (1970).

An introduction to the issues and events which led to the deployment of atomic weapons is traced by Herbert Feis in *The Atomic Bomb and the End of World War II* (1966). Also helpful are Greg Herken's *The Winning Weapon* (1980),° Martin Sherwin's *A World Destroyed: The Atomic Bomb and the Grand Alliance* (1975), and Neill Davis's *Lawrence and Oppenheimer* (1968). Gar Alperovitz's *Atomic Diplomacy: Hiroshima and Potsdam* (1965), Michael Sherry's *Preparing for the Next War: American Plans for Postwar Defense, 1941–1945* (1977), and Richard G. Hewlett and Oscar E. Anderson's *A History of the United States Atomic Energy Commission: The New World, 1939–1946* (1962) and *Atomic Shield, 1947–1952* (1969), detail how the bomb helped shape American postwar policy.

Ruth B. Russell's *A History of the United Nations Charter* (1958) and Robert A. Divine's *Second Chance: The Triumph of Internationalism during World War II* (1967) chronicle America's emergence as a postwar world leader. Martin Gilbert's *Auschwitz and the Allies* (1981)° explains how the Holocaust shaped postwar attitudes.

31

THE FAIR DEAL
AND CONTAINMENT

DEMOBILIZATION UNDER TRUMAN

TRUMAN'S UNEASY START   "Who the hell is Harry Truman?" Admiral Leahy, the president's chief-of-staff asked Roosevelt in the summer of 1944. The question unwittingly echoed a campaign slogan of exactly a century before: "Who is James K. Polk?" The question was on more lips when, after less than twelve weeks as vice-president, Harry Truman took the presidential oath on April 12, 1945. It may have recurred two days later, when he impulsively began his first speech to Congress and House Speaker Sam Rayburn interrupted sotto voce: "Just a minute. Let me present you, will you, Harry?" Clearly he was not Franklin Roosevelt, and that was one of the burdens he would bear. "With Roosevelt you'd have known he was President even if you hadn't been told," the journalist Merle Miller wrote years later. "He looked imperial, and he acted that way, and he talked that way. Harry Truman, for God's sake, looked and acted and talked like—well, like a failed haberdasher"—which he was.

In their origins Roosevelt and Truman came from different worlds. For Truman there had been no inherited wealth, no early contact with the great and near-great, no European travel, no Groton, no Harvard—indeed, no college at all. Born in 1884 in the western Missouri town of Lamar, Truman had pioneer grandparents from Kentucky and a Southern Baptist background. He grew up in Independence, once the staging area for the Oregon and Santa Fe Trails, but by the time of his youth an unglamorous satellite to Kansas City. Too nearsighted to join in the activities of other boys, Truman became bookish, introverted, and withdrawn. But after high school he moved to his grandfather's farm near Grandview, worked at a variety of jobs, became active in the National Guard, Masons, Democratic party, and other groups, grew into an outgoing young man, and learned the salty language that seasoned his speech in later years.

During World War I he served in France as captain of an artillery company. Afterward he and a partner went into the haberdashery business, but the business failed in the recession of 1922 and Truman after that became a professional politician under the tutelage of Kansas City boss Tom Pendergast. Elected county judge in 1922, he was defeated in 1924 and elected once again in 1926. In 1934 Missouri sent him to the United States Senate, where he remained fairly obscure until he became chairman of the committee to investigate war mobilization.

Something about Harry Truman evoked the spirit of Andrew Jackson: his decisiveness, his feisty character, his pungent language, his truculent prickliness, his family loyalty. But that was a side of the man that the American people came to know only as he settled into the job. On his first full day as president, he was still awestruck. "Boys, if you ever pray, pray for me now," he told a group of reporters. "I don't know whether you fellows ever had a load of hay fall on you, but when they told me yesterday what had happened, I felt like the moon, the stars and all the planets had fallen on me."

Truman's accession heartened the conservatives who had helped engineer his nomination. Six weeks after Roosevelt's death the Speaker of Mississippi's House of Representatives said Truman had "begun well and is making rapid progress towards returning this country to Fundamental Americanism." But as the newsman and then presidential assistant Jonathan Daniels put it, the men who put Truman in "knew what they wanted but did not know what they were getting." What they were getting was a man who favored much of the New Deal and was even prepared to extend it, but at the same time was uneasy with many New Dealers. "He was not of their clan and kidney," newsman Cabell Phillips put it. Within ninety days he had replaced much of the Roosevelt cabinet with his own choices. These included fewer Missourians and "cronies" than his detractors claimed, but on the whole they were more conservative in outlook and included enough mediocrities to lend credence to the criticism. Truman suffered the further handicap of seeming to be a caretaker for the remainder of Roosevelt's time. Few, including Truman himself at first, expected him to serve another term.

Truman's domestic policies remained unformulated while he wrestled with problems of war and peace. He gave one significant clue, however, on September 6, 1945, four days after the Japanese surrender, when he sent Congress a comprehensive peacetime program which in effect proposed to continue and enlarge the New Deal. Its twenty-one points included expansion of unemployment insurance, extension of the Employment Service, a higher minimum wage, a permanent Fair Employment Practices Commission, slum clearance and low-rent housing, regional development of the nation's river valleys, and a public works program. "Not even President Roosevelt asked for so much at one sitting," said House Republican leader Joseph Martin. "It's just a plain case of out-dealing the New Deal." Beset by other problems, Truman was unable to set priorities on his demands. The result was a domestic cold war between the president and a Congress which was dominated, as it had been since 1938, by a conservative coalition. Indeed, like Cleveland in the 1890s, Truman managed for a time to offend businessmen, farmers, and workers alike.

CONVERTING TO PEACE The raucous celebrations that greeted Japan's surrender signaled the habitual American response to victory: a rapid demobilization and a return to more congenial pursuits. Given the character and experience of the American

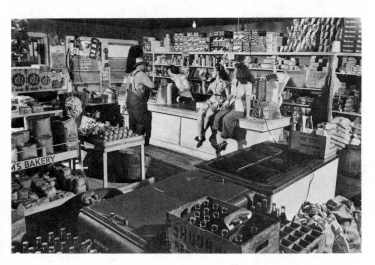

The Eldridge General Store, Fayette County, Illinois. Postwar America quickly demobilized, turning its attention to the pursuit of abundance. [University of Louisville Photographic Archives]

people, any other outcome would have been unlikely. The president and Congress were besieged by demands for bringing the boys home. By midsummer 1946 the wartime army and navy had been reduced to 1.5 million and 700,000 respectively. By 1947 the total armed forces were down to 1.5 million and Congress had decreed further cuts, reducing their number to little more than 1 million. In his memoirs Truman termed this "the most remarkable demobilization in the history of the world, or 'disintegration' if you want to call it that." It was in fact the same pattern that had prevailed since the days of the colonial wars, and it went on for several years despite mounting tensions. By early 1950 the army had fallen to 600,000 men in ten active divisions.

The veterans returned to schools, new jobs, wives, and babies. Population growth, which had dropped off sharply in the depression decade, now soared: the population increase of 8.9 million during the 1930s exploded to a growth of 19 million in the 1940s. The birth rate per 1,000 of total population grew from 19.4 in 1940 to above 24 per annum by 1946, and did not begin to show a decline until the 1960s. Americans born during this postwar period composed what came to be known as the baby-boom generation.

The end of the war, with its sudden demobilization and recon-

The electronic numerical integrator and computer, or ENIAC, 1946. Developed for the Army Ordnance Department by Dr. J. Presper Eckert, Jr., the ENIAC and its progeny would have profound consequences for the later twentieth-century world. [Library of Congress]

version to a peacetime economy, brought sharp dislocations but not the postwar depression that many feared. The economic impact of demobilization was cushioned by numerous shock-absorbers: unemployment pay and other Social Security benefits; the Servicemen's Readjustment Act of 1944, known as the "GI Bill of Rights," under which more than $13 billion was spent for veterans on education, vocational training, medical treatment, unemployment insurance, and loans for building homes or going into business; and most important, the pent-up demand for consumer goods that was fueled by wartime incomes. Instead of sinking into depression, businesses seized upon options to buy up properties from the Defense Plant Corporation and began a spurt of private investment in new plant and equipment. Gross national product first exceeded the 1929 level in 1940, when it reached $100.6 billion, but by annual increases (except in 1946) it had grown to $347 billion by 1952, Truman's last full year in office.

CONTROLLING INFLATION The problem Truman faced was not depression but inflation, one problem which President Roosevelt had not encountered. The historian Barton Bernstein summed up the political burden imposed by this difference: "Whereas the politics of depression generally allowed the Roosevelt administration, by bestowing benefits, to court interest groups and contribute to an economic upturn, the politics of inflation required a responsible government like Truman's to curb wages, prices, and profits and to deny the growing expectations of rival groups." The political problems inherent in fighting inflation were worsened by Truman's early inexperience and uncertainty.

Released from wartime restraints, the demands of businessmen and workers alike conspired to frustrate efforts at controlling rising prices. Truman endorsed demands for wage increases and argued that they were needed to cushion the shock of conversion and to sustain purchasing power. He felt that there was "room in the existing price structure" for business to grant such increases, a point management refused to concede. Within six weeks of war's end, corporations confronted a wave of union demands. In November 1945 Truman, like Wilson in 1919, called a labor-management conference to formulate a labor policy; it had as little result as the one in 1919.

A series of strikes followed. The United Automobile Workers walked out on General Motors, with Walter Reuther, head of the union's General Motors division, arguing that the company could afford a 30 percent pay raise without raising car prices. (The company denied this claim.) A strike in the steel industry finally gave rise to a formula for settling most of the disputes. President Truman suggested a pay raise of 18½¢ per hour, which the Steel Workers accepted but United States Steel refused. To break the logjam the administration in February agreed to let the company increase its prices. That pattern then became the basis for settlements in other industries, and also set a dangerous precedent of price-wage spirals that would plague consumers in the postwar world.

Major disputes soon developed in the coal and railroad industries. John L. Lewis of the United Mine Workers wanted more than the 18½¢-per-hour wage increase. He demanded also improved safety regulations and a union health and welfare fund financed by a royalty on coal. Mine owners refused the demands, and a strike followed. The government responded by using wartime powers to seize the mines. Interior Secretary Julius A. Krug then accepted nearly all the union's demands. In the rail dispute the unions and management reached an agreement, but two brotherhoods, the trainmen and locomotive engineers, held out for rule changes as well as higher wages. Truman seized the roads in May and won a five-day postponement of a strike. But when the brotherhoods' leaders refused to budge further, the president went before Congress in a burst of fury against their "obstinate arrogance" and demanded authority to draft strikers into the armed forces. In the midst of the speech he was informed that the strike had been settled, but after telling a jubilant Congress, he went on with his message. The House passed a bill including the president's demands, but with the strike settled, it died in the Senate.

Into 1946 the wartime Office of Price Administration managed to maintain some restraint on price increases while gradually ending the rationing of most goods, and Truman asked for a one-year renewal of its powers. But during the late winter and spring of 1946 the business community mounted a massive campaign against price controls and other restraints. Just a week before controls were to expire at the end of June, Congress passed a bill to continue the OPA but with such cumbersome new procedures as to cripple the agency. Truman vetoed the bill, allowing the controls to end. Congress finally extended the controls on July 25, but by then the cost of living had already gone up by 6 percent. When in August the OPA restored controls on meat prices, farmers responded by withholding beef from the market until they succeeded in forcing a reversal on October 15. After the congressional elections of 1946 Truman gave up the battle altogether, ending all controls except those on rents, sugar, and rice.

PARTISAN COOPERATION AND CONFLICT   But the legislative history of 1946 was not all deadlock and frustration. Out of the turmoil Congress and the administration extracted two signal new departures, the Employment Act of 1946 and the creation of the Atomic Energy Commission. A program of "full employment" had been a Democratic promise in the campaign of 1944, a pledge reaffirmed by Truman in 1945. The administration then backed an employment bill which proposed that the government make an annual estimate of the investment and production necessary to ensure full employment, and key its spending to that estimate in order to raise production to the full-employment level. Conservatives objected to what they regarded as carte blanche for defecit spending, and proposed a nonpartisan commission to advise the president on the status of the economy. Compromise resulted in the Employment Act of February 1946, dropping the commitment to full employment and instead setting up a three-member Council of Economic Advisers to make continuing appraisals of the economy and advise the president in an annual economic report. A new congressional Joint Committee on the Economic Report would make proposals for implementing the program.

With regard to the new force that atomic scientists had released upon the world, there was little question that the public welfare required the control of atomic energy through a governmental monopoly. Disagreements over the degree of military versus civilian control were resolved when Congress, in August 1946, created the civilian Atomic Energy Commission. The president alone was given power to order the use of atomic weapons in warfare. Subject to "the paramount objective of assuring the common defense and security," the act declared a policy of peaceful development "so far as practicable . . . toward improving the public welfare, increasing the standard of living, strengthening free competition in private enterprise, and promoting world peace." Technical problems and high costs, however, would delay for two decades the construction of nuclear powerplants, and even yet questions of feasibility, security, and public safety from radioactive pollution are unresolved.

As congressional elections approached in the fall of 1946, discontent ran high, most of it directed against the administration. Truman caught the blame for labor problems from both sides. A speaker at the CIO national convention tagged Truman "the No.

1 strikebreaker," while much of the public, angry at striking unions, laid the blame for strikes at the White House door. In September 1946 Truman fired Henry Wallace as secretary of commerce in a disagreement over foreign policy, thus offending the Democratic left. At the same time the administration was plagued by Republican charges that Communists had infiltrated the government. Coastal states were unhappy over his claim that federal authority governed use of the continental shelf, as were oil companies which preferred to deal with the states on offshore drilling rights. Republicans had a field day coining slogans. "To err is Truman" was credited to Martha Taft, wife of Sen. Robert Taft. But most effective was the simple "Had enough?" attributed to a Boston ad agency: their message was that the Democrats had simply been in too long. Then in August came the cattlemen's embargo on meat. "This is going to be a damn *beefsteak* election," said House Speaker Sam Rayburn. Truman's removal of price controls on meat only worsened his image of vacillation. In the end, Republicans won majorities in both houses of Congress for the first time since 1928.

Given the head of steam built up against organized labor, the new Congress was sure to take up restrictive legislation, and seventeen such bills were indeed introduced on the first day of the new session. The feeling of many that labor "bosses" had grown too strong encouraged moves to restrict their actions, just as business abuses against labor were restricted under the Wagner Act of 1935. The result was the Taft-Hartley Act of 1947, which banned any closed shop (in which nonunion workers could not be hired) but permitted a union shop (in which workers newly hired were required to join the union), unless banned by state law. It included provisions against "unfair" union pactices such as secondary boycotts, jurisdictional strikes (by one union to exclude another from a given company or field), "featherbedding" (pay for work not done), refusal to bargain in good faith, and contributing to campaigns. Unions' political action committees were allowed to function, but on a voluntary basis only, and union leaders had to take oaths that they were not members of the Communist party. Employers were permitted to sue unions for breaking contracts, to petition the NLRB for votes for or against the use of specific unions as collective-bargaining agents, and to speak freely during union campaigns. The act forbade strikes by federal employees, and imposed a "cooling-off" period of eighty days on any strike which the president found to be dangerous to the national health or safety.

Truman's veto of the bill, which unions called the "slave-labor act," restored his credit with labor, and many unionists who had gone over to the Republicans in 1946 returned to the Democratic fold. But the bill was passed over Truman's veto, and as it turned out, had a less than ruinous effect on unions. Its most severe impact probably was on the CIO's "Operation Dixie," a drive to win for unions a more secure foothold in the South. By 1954 fifteen states, mainly in the South, had used the Taft-Hartley Act's authority to enact "right-to-work" laws forbidding the union shop and other union security devices.

Truman clashed with the Republicans on other domestic issues as well, including tax reduction passed by Congress but successfully vetoed twice by Truman on the principle that in times of high production and employment the federal debt should be reduced. In 1948, however, Congress finally managed to override his veto of a $5-billion tax cut at a time when government debt still ran high. The controversy over the tax cut highlighted a soft point in Keynesian economics. In times of depression there was strong political support for increasing governmental expenditures, but in prosperous times support was weak for the taxes needed to reduce the deficits created by government spending. Truman paid the political price for this weakness in economic theory.

The conflicts between Truman and Congress which were so visible in the 1948 campaign obscured the high degree of bipartisan cooperation marking matters of governmental reorganization and foreign policy. After a postwar congressional investigation into the Pearl Harbor disaster made plain a fatal lack of coordination among the armed forces and intelligence services, a bipartisan majority in Congress set out to correct this problem by passing the National Security Act in July 1947. The act created a National Military Establishment, headed by a secretary of defense with subcabinet departments of army, navy, and air force, and a new National Security Council (NSC) which included the president, heads of the defense departments, the secretary of state, and the head of the National Security Resources Board (later the Office of Defense Mobilization). The act made permanent the Joint Chiefs of Staff, which had been a wartime innovation, and established the Central Intelligence Agency (CIA), descended from the wartime Office of Strategic Services (OSS), to coordinate intelligence. There was at the time no intention to have the CIA engage in covert actions as the OSS had done in the war, nor any purpose that it engage in domestic activities. But the act included two gigantic loopholes which would in time allow the CIA to engage in both: authority to perform "such other functions and duties related to intelligence" as the NSC might direct, and responsibility for "protecting intelligence sources and methods."

Congress also adopted President Truman's proposal for a change in the presidential succession. The existing law of 1886 put the secretary of state next in line after the vice-president, to be followed by other cabinet members according to rank, determined by the order in which their offices had been created. The Presidential Succession Act of 1947 inserted the Speaker of the House and the president pro tempore of the Senate ahead of the secretary of state, on the principle that the presidency should first go to elected rather than appointed officers. Congress itself took the initiative in adopting the Twenty-second Amendment, ratified in 1951, which limited presidents after Truman to two terms. Under the Legislative Reorganization Act of 1946 Congress also recast its own organization, reducing the number of standing committees in each house and requiring lobbyists to register and report their expenses.

Finally, President Truman promoted friendly partisan relations by bringing former President Hoover out of retirement to investigate programs of overseas relief, and then in 1947 to head a Commission on Organization of the Executive Branch. The Hoover Commission's 1949 reports led to extensive changes in governmental structure, most of them adopted under the Reorganization Act of 1949, which permitted the president to make organizational changes subject to a veto by either house. Of thirty-six plans submitted by Truman, Congress rejected only the creation of a new Department of Welfare.

The Cold War

BUILDING THE U.N. During World War II no one spouted slogans about making the world safe for democracy or that this was a war to end all wars. At the same time many came to reject isolationism and the disillusionment of an earlier time. As it turned out, however, the hope that the wartime concert of the United Nations would carry over into the postwar world proved but another great illusion. The pragmatic Roosevelt shared no such illusion. To the contrary, the historian Robert Dallek has argued: "His desire for a new world league . . . rested less on a faith in Wilsonian collective security than on the belief that it was a necessary vehicle for permanently involving the United States in world affairs." He expected that the Great Powers in the postwar world would have spheres of influence, but felt he had to obscure such *Realpolitik* with an organization "which would satisfy widespread demand in the United States for new idealistic or universalist arrangements for assuring the peace."

In the 1941 Atlantic Charter, Roosevelt and Churchill had looked forward to a "permanent system of general security." Its name derived later from the declaration of the "United Nations," signed at Washington on January 1, 1942, by twenty-six countries at war with the Axis powers. In the autumn of 1943 both houses of Congress passed a resolution introduced by William Fulbright of Arkansas favoring "international machinery with power adequate to establish and to maintain a just and lasting peace." That same autumn the foreign ministers of the "Big Four" (the United States, Russia, Britain, and China) issued the Declaration of Moscow calling for an international organization, and in the 1944 elections the platforms of both major parties endorsed the principle.

On April 25, 1945, two weeks after Roosevelt's death and two weeks before the German surrender, delegates from fifty nations at war with the Axis met in San Francisco's Opera House to draw up the charter of the United Nations. These fifty were joined by Poland as charter members, with the provision that additional members could be admitted by a two-thirds vote of the General Assembly. This body, one of the two major agencies set up by the charter, included delegates from all member nations and was to meet annually in regular session to approve the budget, receive annual reports from U.N. agencies, and choose members of the Security Council and other bodies. The Security Council, the other major charter agency, would remain in permanent session and had "primary responsibility for the maintenance of international peace and security." Its eleven members included six elected for two-year terms and five permanent members: the United States, Russia, Britain, France, and China. Each permanent member had a veto on any question of substance, though not of procedure. The Security Council might investigate any dispute, recommend settlement or reference to the International Court, and take measures including a resort to military force.

Four other agencies rounded out the structure: an International Court of Justice at The Hague; a Secretariat to administer the U.N.; a Trusteeship Council to oversee administration of former Italian and Japanese colonies and the former mandates of the League of Nations; and an Economic and Social Council which might conduct studies, make recommendations, and draw agreements to bring into relationship with the U.N. existing international bodies such as the Food and Agricultural Organization, the United Nations Relief and Rehabilitation Administration (established in 1943), the International Monetary Fund, the International Bank for Reconstruction and Development (the World Bank), and the International Labor Office. All but the last of these had been created by negotiations during the war to provide relief and to ensure the stability of international finances after the war.

The United States Senate, in sharp contrast to the reception it gave the League of Nations, ratified the U.N. charter by a vote of 89 to 2 after only six days of discussion. The organization held its first meeting at London in 1946, and the next year moved to temporary quarters at Lake Success, New York, pending completion of its permanent home in New York City.

TRYING WAR CRIMINALS   There was also a consensus that those responsible for the atrocities of World War II should face trial and punishment. The Potsdam Conference, among other things, gave final approval to the principle of war-crimes trials, for which a commission in London had been preparing since 1943. Both German and Japanese officials went on trial for crimes against peace, against humanity, and against the established rules of war. At Nuremberg, Germany, site of the annual Nazi party rallies, twenty-two major German offenders faced an International Military Tribunal. After a ten-month trial filled with massive documentation of Nazi atrocities, the court sentenced twelve to death, three to life imprisonment, and four to shorter terms. In Tokyo, a similar tribunal put twenty-five Japanese leaders on trial from May to November 1946, and pronounced sentences of

The Nuremberg Trials. *At far left sit the high-ranking Nazis on trial, including Albert Speer (second row, third from right) and, in dark glasses, Hans Frank. [Signal Corps Photo]*

death on seven (including General Tojo), life imprisonment on sixteen, and committed two for a term of years. Other international tribunals tried thousands of others, while many accused war criminals were remanded to the courts of the countries in which they had committed their crimes. Altogether well over 2,000 war-crimes trials are estimated to have taken place, not counting those in Russia and the East Bloc countries.

Critics argued that the trials set an unfortunate precedent of victors' taking revenge on the defeated. They argued as well that the convictions were condemnations *ex post facto*, for crimes against which no law existed at the time they were committed. Supporters responded by pointing to the Pact of Paris outlawing war, to the Geneva Convention for care of the sick and wounded prisoners, the Hague declarations on the rules of war, and the fact that crimes against humanity such as murder, rape, and pillage were already crimes under the laws of the countries where they occurred.

DIFFERENCES WITH THE SOVIETS There were signs of trouble in the grand alliance as early as the spring of 1945 as Russia moved to set up compliant governments in eastern Europe, violating the Yalta promises of democratic elections. On February 1 the Polish Committee of National Liberation, a puppet group already claiming the status of provisional government, moved from Lublin to Warsaw. In March the Soviets installed a puppet premier in Rumania. Protests at such actions led to Russian counterprotests that the British and Americans were negotiating German surrender in Italy "behind the back of the Soviet Union" and that German forces were being concentrated against Russia. A few days before his death, Roosevelt responded to Stalin: "I cannot avoid a feeling of resentment toward your informers . . . for such vile misrepresentations."

Such was the atmosphere when Truman entered the White House. A few days before the San Francisco conference, Truman gave Soviet Foreign Minister Molotov a dressing down in Washington on the Polish situation. "I have never been talked to like that in my life," Molotov said. "Carry out your agreements," Truman snapped, "and you won't get talked to like that." On May 12, 1945, four days after victory in Europe, Winston Churchill sent a telegram to Truman: "What is to happen about Europe? An iron curtain is drawn down upon [the Russian] front. We do not know what is going on behind. . . . Surely it is vital now to come to an understanding with Russia, or see where we are with her, before we weaken our armies mortally. . . ." Nevertheless, as a gesture of goodwill, and over Churchill's protest, the

American forces withdrew from the occupation zone assigned to Russia at Yalta. Americans were still hopeful that the Yalta agreements would be carried out, at least after a fashion, and even more hopeful for Russian help against Japan.

Although the Russians admitted British and American observers to their sectors of eastern Europe, there was little the Western powers could do to prevent Russian hegemony even if they had not let their military powers dwindle. The presence of Soviet armed forces frustrated the efforts of non-Communists to gain political influence. Coalition governments appeared temporarily as an immediate postwar expedient, but the Communists followed a long-range strategy of ensconcing themselves in the interior ministries in order to control the police. Opposition political leaders found themselves under accusation, "confessions" were extorted, and the leaders of the opposition were either exiled, silenced, executed, or consigned to prison.

Secretary of State James F. Byrnes, who had replaced Edward Stettinius on June 30, 1945, struggled on through 1946 with the problems of postwar settlements. As early as September 1945 the first meeting of the Council of Foreign Ministers broke up because of Byrnes's fruitless demand that the governments of Rumania and Bulgaria be broadened. A series of almost interminable meetings of the Council of Foreign Ministers wrangled over border lines and reparation from Hitler's satellites, finally producing treaties for Italy, Hungary, Rumania, Bulgaria, and Finland. The treaties, signed on February 10, 1947, in effect confirmed Russian control over eastern Europe, which in Russian eyes seemed but a parallel to American control in Japan and Western control over most of Germany and all of Italy. The Yalta guarantees of democracy in eastern Europe had turned out much like the Open Door Policy in China, little more than pious cant subordinate to the pressures of *Realpolitik.* Byrnes's impulse to brandish the atomic bomb only added to the irritations, intimidating no one.

The United States, together with Britain and Canada (partners in developing the atomic bomb), had exclusive possession of atomic weapons at the time, but in 1946 proposed to internationalize the control of atomic energy through a plan presented to the U.N. Atomic Energy Commission. Under the plan, drawn up chiefly by Dean Acheson and David E. Lilienthal, an International Atomic Development Authority would have a monopoly of atomic explosives and atomic energy. The Russians, fearing Western domination of the agency, proposed instead simply to outlaw the manufacture and use of atomic bombs, with enforcement vested in the Security Council and thus subject to a veto. Later they conceded the right of international inspection, but still refused to give up the veto, and the American government rejected the arrangement, which it considered a compromise of international control. The plan was a failure, another manifestation of the inability to find any common ground for agreement on far-reaching issues.

CONTAINMENT By the beginning of 1947 relations with the Soviet Union had become very troubled. A year before, Stalin had already pronounced international peace impossible "under the present capitalist development of the world economy." His statement impelled George F. Kennan, counselor of the American Embassy in Moscow, to send an 8,000-word dispatch in which he sketched the roots of Russian policy and warned that the Soviet Union was "committed fanatically to the belief that with the U.S. there can be no permanent *modus vivendi*, that it is desirable and necessary that the internal harmony of our society be disrupted, our traditional way of life be destroyed, the international authority of our state be broken, if Soviet power is to be secure."

More than a year later, by then back at the State Department in Washington, Kennan spelled out his ideas for a proper response to the Soviets in a July 1947 article published anonymously in *Foreign Affairs*. "It is clear," he wrote, "that the main element of any United States policy toward the Soviet Union must be that of a long-term, patient but firm and vigilant containment of Russian expansive tendencies. . . . such a policy has nothing to do with outward histrionics: with threats or blustering or superfluous gestures of outward 'toughness.' " Americans, he argued, could hope for a long-term moderation of Soviet ideology and policy, so that in time tensions with the West would lessen. There was a strong possibility "that Soviet power, like the capitalist world of its conception, bears within it the seeds of its own decay, and that the sprouting of those seeds is well advanced."

Kennan's statement on containment supplied the rationale for the radical new departure in American foreign policy which America's political leaders had already decided to take. Behind this shift in policy lay a growing fear that Russian aims reached beyond eastern Europe, posing dangers in the eastern Mediterranean, the Middle East, and western Europe itself. The first major postwar crisis occurred in Iran, which borders the Soviet Union on the south and provided important trade routes to the

USSR. Soviet troops had been stationed in northern Iran while British-American troops were in the south, and all were supposed to pull out six months after the war. But the Soviets remained beyond the deadline of March 2, 1946, all the while stirring revolts in the northern provinces. The crisis finally blew over when a Soviet-Iranian agreement brought Russian withdrawal in early May.

Meanwhile the USSR was looking for a breakthrough into the Mediterranean, long important to Russia for purposes of trade and defense. After the war the USSR began to press Turkey for territorial concessions and the right to build naval bases on the Bosporus, an important gateway between the Black Sea and the Mediterranean. In August 1946 civil war broke out in Greece between a government backed by the British and a Communist-led faction, the EAM, which held the northern part of Greece and drew supplies from Yugoslavia, Bulgaria, and Albania. In February 1947 the British ambassador informed the American government that the British could no longer bear the economic and military burden of aiding Greece. When Truman conferred with congressional leaders on the situation, Arthur H. Vandenberg, chairman of the Senate Foreign Relations Committee, advised: "Scare the hell out of the American people." On March 12, 1947, President Truman appeared before Congress to ask $400 million for economic aid to both Greece and Turkey, and power to send American personnel to train their soldiers.

THE TRUMAN DOCTRINE AND THE MARSHALL PLAN   In his speech Truman stated what quickly came to be known as the Truman Doctrine, which was so far-reaching because it justified aid to Greece and Turkey in terms more active than Kennan's idea of containment and more general than this specific case warranted. "I believe," Truman declared, "that it must be the policy of the United States to support free peoples who are resisting attempted subjugation by armed minorities or by outside pressures." In May 1947, with the support of Senator Vandenberg, Congress passed the Greek-Turkish aid bill, and by 1950 had spent $659 million on the program. Turkey achieved economic stability, and Greece defeated the Communist insurrection in October 1949, partly because President Tito of Yugoslavia had broken with the Russians in the summer of 1948 and ceased to aid the EAM in mid-1949.

The Truman Doctrine was the beginning, or at least the open acknowledgment, of a contest which Bernard Baruch named in April 1947 in a speech to the legislature of his native South Car-

The Taskmaster. *Postwar Europe was a land of devastation. [Jacob Burck in the Chicago Sun-Times]*

olina: "Let us not be deceived—today we are in the midst of a cold war." Signs were growing that Greece and Turkey were but the front lines of a struggle that would involve western Europe as well. There wartime damage and dislocation had devastated factory production, and severe drought in 1947, followed by a severe winter, destroyed crops. Europe had become, in Winston Churchill's words, "a rubble heap, a charnel house, a breeding ground of pestilence and hate." Amid the chaos the Communist parties of France and Italy were flourishing, having gained credibility by working in the wartime resistance. Aid from the United Nations had staved off starvation, but had provided little basis for economic recovery.

In the spring of 1947 William L. Clayton, the State Department's chief advisor on economic affairs, reported to George C. Marshall, who had replaced Byrnes as secretary of state in January, that the United States had underestimated the extent of wartime damage in Europe. Only a program of massive aid could rescue western Europe from disaster. Late in May the Policy Planning Staff, under George Kennan, brought forth a plan which Secretary Marshall presented at the Harvard Commencement on June 5. Taking Kennan's lead, Marshall avoided the ideological overtones of the Truman Doctrine. "Our policy," Marshall said, "is directed not against country or doctrine, but against hunger, poverty, desperation, and chaos." Marshall offered aid to all European countries, including Russia, and called upon them to take the lead in judging their own needs. On June 27 the foreign ministers of France, Britain, and Russia met in London to discuss Marshall's overture. Molotov arrived with eighty advisors, but during the talks got word from Moscow to withdraw from this "imperialist" scheme. Two weeks later a meeting of delegates from western Europe formed a Committee of European Economic Cooperation (CEEC), which had a plan ready by September.

In December Truman submitted his proposal for the European Recovery Program to Congress. Two months later, a Communist coup d'état in Czechoslovakia ended the last remaining coalition government in eastern Europe. Coming just ten years after Munich, the seizure of power in Prague assured congressional passage of the Marshall Plan. From 1948 until 1951 the Economic Cooperation Administration (ECA), which managed the Marshall Plan, poured about $12 billion into European recovery through the CEEC.

DIVIDING GERMANY   The breakdown of the wartime alliance left the problem of postwar Germany unsettled. The German economy had stagnated, requiring the American army to carry a staggering burden of relief. In September 1946 Secretary Byrnes had said in a speech at Stuttgart that the zonal boundaries should not be regarded "as self-contained economic and political units," and in December of that year the Americans and British united their zones economically. Slowly, zones of occupation evolved into functioning governments. In February 1948 the British and Americans united their zones into what came to be called "Bizonia," which the French joined to create "Trizonia" in June. The West Germans were then invited to organize state governments and elect delegates to a federal constitutional convention.

Soviet reactions to the Marshall Plan and the unification of West Germany were sharp, and they were quickly focused on Berlin. In April 1948 the Russians began to restrict the flow of traffic into West Berlin; on June 23 they stopped all traffic. The blockade was designed to leave the allies no choice but to give up either Berlin or the plan to unify West Germany. But Gen. Lucius D. Clay, American commander in Germany, proposed to stand firm. "When Berlin falls, Western Germany will be next," he told the Pentagon. "If we mean . . . to hold Europe against communism, we must not budge."

Truman agreed, and after considering the use of armed convoys to supply West Berlin, opted for a massive airlift. At the time this seemed an enormous and perhaps impossible task, requiring, according to General Clay's estimate, 4,500 tons of supplies a day. But by quick work the allied air forces brought in planes from around the world and by October 1948 were flying in nearly 5,000 tons of food and equipment a day. Altogether, from June 1948 to mid-May 1949, the Berlin Airlift carried in

OCCUPATION OF GERMANY AND AUSTRIA

French zone   British zone   U.S. zone   Soviet zone

more than 1.5 million tons of supplies, or above a half ton for each of the 2.5 million West Berliners. Gen. Frank L. Howley, American commandant in Berlin, meanwhile got in a few licks at his Russian counterpart by cutting off a gas main that ran through the American sector to Marshal Vasily Sokolovsky's house, forcing him to move. When Sokolovsky's aides tried to truck his furniture through the American zone, Howley seized the furniture.

Finally, on May 12, 1949, after extended talks, the Russians lifted the blockade in return for a meeting of the Council of Foreign Ministers in Paris. This was purely a face-saving gesture, and the meeting resulted in no important decision on Germany. That same May, West Germany adopted a constitution, and before the end of the year the German Federal Republic had a government functioning under Christian Democratic Chancellor Konrad Adenauer. At the end of May 1949 a German "Democratic" Republic arose in the eastern zone, making the division of Germany a permanent fact. West Germany gradually acquired more authority, until the Western powers recognized its full sovereignty in 1955.

BUILDING NATO   As relations between the Soviets and western Europe chilled, transatlantic unity ripened into an outright military alliance. By March 1948, Britain, France, and the "Benelux" countries (Belgium, the Netherlands, and Luxembourg) had signed a fifty-year treaty of alliance and economic cooperation, the Brussels Pact. That June the Senate passed a resolution introduced by Senator Vandenberg authorizing the administration to develop a collective defense pact under Article 51 of the U.N. Charter. Negotiations for an Atlantic alliance got under way in July. On April 4, 1949, the North Atlantic Treaty was signed at Washington by representatives of twelve nations: the five Brussels Pact countries plus the United States, Canada, Denmark, Iceland, Italy, Norway, and Portugal. Greece and Turkey joined the alliance in 1952. The treaty pledged that an attack against any one of the signers would be considered an attack against all, and provided for a council of the North Atlantic Treaty Organization (NATO) which could establish other necessary agencies. In September 1950 the council decided to create an integrated defense force for western Europe and later named General Eisenhower to head the Supreme Headquarters of the Allied Powers in Europe (SHAPE). In 1955 the Warsaw Treaty Organization appeared as the eastern European counterpart to NATO. Senate ratification of the North Atlantic Treaty by a vote of 82 to 13 suggested that the isolationism of the prewar period no longer exerted a hold on the American people.

One other foreign-policy decision with long-term consequences came during the eventful year 1948. Palestine, as the

NATO, a hopeful sign for the West. [*The Hartford* Courant]

biblical Holy Land had come to be known, had been long occupied by Arabs, and was under Turkish suzerainty until the League of Nations made it a British mandate after World War I. Over the early years of the twentieth century many Zionists, who advocated a Jewish state in the region, had migrated there. Still more came after the British entered, and a greatly increased number came (illegally, under British rule) after World War II. Offered tenuous promises by the British of a national homeland, the Jewish inhabitants demanded their own state. Late in 1947 the U.N. General Assembly voted to partition Palestine into Jewish and Arab states, but this met with fierce Arab opposition. Finally, the British mandate expired without firm action by the U.N. to enforce its decision, and on May 14, 1948, Jewish leaders proclaimed the independence of the state of Israel. President Truman, who had been in close touch with Jewish leaders, ordered recognition of the new state within minutes—the United States became the first nation so to act. The neighboring Arab states reacted by going to war against Israel, which, however, held its own. U.N. mediators gradually worked out truce agreements with Israel's Arab neighbors and an uneasy peace was restored by May 11, 1949, when Israel was admitted as a member of the United Nations. But the hard feelings and intermittent warfare between Israel and the Arab states have festered ever since, complicating American foreign policy, which has tried to maintain friendship with both sides.

HARRY GIVES 'EM HELL

SHAPING THE FAIR DEAL   The determination Truman projected in foreign affairs had not yet altered his image on the domestic front. By early 1948, after three years in the White House, Truman had yet to shake the impression that he was not up to the job. The columnists Joseph and Stuart Alsop wrote before the Democratic convention that Truman would be running "the loneliest campaign in recent history." Rather than go with a loser, New Deal stalwarts and party regulars tried to draft General Eisenhower or Justice William O. Douglas, but in vain. The Democratic party seemed about to fragment: southern conservatives took umbrage at Truman's outspoken support of civil rights, while the left flared up in 1946 over his firing Secretary of Commerce Henry A. Wallace after a speech critical of the administration's policy. "Getting tough," Wallace had argued, "never brought anything real and lasting—whether for school yard bullies or world powers. The tougher we get, the tougher the Russians will get." The left itself was splitting between the Progressive Citizens of America (PCA), formed in December 1946, which gave ear to Wallace, and the Americans for Democratic Action (ADA), formed in January 1947, which also criticized Truman but took a firm anti-Communist stance.

Unknown to all these groups, Truman had a game plan for 1948; it had been outlined in a forty-three-page memorandum written by his aide, Clark Clifford, a young lawyer from St. Louis. Much of what later seemed desperate impulse actually followed Clifford's design, which urged an aggressive effort to shore up the New Deal coalition. Truman needed the midwestern and western farm belts, and happily had fairly strong support among farmers. In metropolitan areas the trick was to carry the labor and the black vote, which Truman wooed by working closely with unions and liberals, and pressing the cause of civil rights. The Solid South, Clifford predicted, could be counted on to stay in the Democratic column. The Republicans would choose Thomas E. Dewey again, and Wallace, running on a third-party Progressive ticket, would be badly compromised by Communist support. With the South and West, Truman could afford to lose some New Deal strongholds in the East and still win. On nearly every point, Clifford called the turn. He erred chiefly in underrating the rebellion that took four Deep South states out of Truman's camp.

The grand new departure in Clifford's design was its forthright emphasis on civil rights—a politically advantageous issue now that so many blacks had migrated to northern cities in states with large electoral votes. Truman's motivations in embracing the issue were complex. When in 1946 he appointed the President's Committee on Civil Rights, a panel of distinguished citizens, black and white, North and South, he acted not only in response to the pressures of black organizations, but apparently also out of outrage at several recent attacks on blacks. The committee's report, *To Secure These Rights* (1947), touched on virtually every category of racial discrimination and called for the "elimination of segregation based on race, color, creed, or national origin, from American life."

Like other presidents, Truman used his State of the Union message in January 1948 to set the agenda for an election year. The speech offered something to nearly every group the Democrats hoped to win over. The first goal, Truman said, was "to secure fully the essential human rights of our citizens" and promised a special message later on civil rights. "To protect human resources," Truman asked for federal aid to education, increased and extended unemployment and retirement benefits, a comprehensive system of health insurance, more federal support for housing, and extension of rent controls. He continued to pile on the demands: for reclamation projects, more rural electrification, a higher minimum wage, laws to admit thousands of displaced persons to the United States, money for the Marshall Plan, a "cost of living" tax credit, and much more. As Senator Taft put it, the speech "raised all the ghosts of the old New Deal with new trappings that Tugwell and Harry Hopkins never thought of." On February 2 Congress received Truman's message on civil rights, which called for a broad range of actions, none of which he seriously hoped to get out of Congress. On July 26, however, he did ban racial discrimination in hiring federal employees, and four days later ordered an end to segregation in the armed forces.

THE 1948 ELECTION The Republican Congress for the most part spurned the Truman program, which it would later regret. Republican presidential hopefuls, scenting victory in November, entered a scramble for the nomination: Senator Taft, former Minnesota Gov. Harold E. Stassen, California Gov. Earl Warren, Governor Dewey, and an array of favorite sons. At the Philadelphia convention in June Dewey won the nomination on the third ballot and designated Governor Warren as his running mate. The platform endorsed most of the New Deal reforms as an accomplished fact and approved the administration's bipartisan foreign policy, but as Landon had in 1936, promised to run things more efficiently.

In July a glum Democratic convention gathered in Philadelphia, expecting to do little more than go through the motions, only to find itself doubly surprised: first by the battle over the civil rights plank, and then by Truman's acceptance speech. To keep from stirring southern hostility any further, the administration sought a platform plank that opposed discrimination only in general terms. ADA leaders, however, sponsored a plank which called on Congress for specific action and commended Truman "for his courageous stand on the issue of civil rights." Speaking last in favor of the change, Minneapolis Mayor Hubert H. Humphrey electrified the delegates and set off a ten-minute demonstration: "The time has arrived for the Democratic party to get out of the shadow of states' rights and walk forthrightly into the bright sunshine of human rights." Segregationist delegates from Alabama and Mississippi walked, instead, out of the convention.

After the convention had nominated Truman, and as his running mate, Sen. Alben Barkley, the president appeared on the rostrum during the wee hours of the morning to give his acceptance speech. It was a new Truman, showing a new fighting style in his speeches. To overcome Truman's tendency to read speeches in a flat drone, his staff encouraged him to talk off-the-cuff from a brief outline. "Senator Barkley and I will win this election and make the Republicans like it," he said, "don't you forget it!" Near the end he sprang a bombshell. On July 26, known in Missouri as "Turnip Day," he would call Congress back into session "to get the laws the people need," many of which the Republican platform had endorsed.

On July 17 a group of rebellious southerners met in Birmingham and nominated South Carolina Gov. J. Strom Thurmond on a States' Rights Democratic ticket, quickly dubbed the "Dixiecrat" ticket by a headline writer on the Charlotte *News.* The Dixiecrats' dream was to draw enough electoral votes to preclude a majority for either major party, throwing the election into the House where they might strike a sectional bargain like that of 1877. A few days later, on July 23, the left wing of the Democratic party gathered in Philadelphia to name Henry A. Wallace on a Progressive party ticket. These splits in the Democratic ranks seemed to spell the final blow to Truman. The special session of Congress petered out in futility.

But Truman, undaunted, set out on a 31,000-mile "whistle stop" train tour during which he castigated the "do-nothing" Eightieth Congress to the accompaniment of cries from his audiences: "Pour it on, Harry!" and "Give 'em hell, Harry." And Harry would respond: "I don't give 'em hell. I just tell the truth and they think it's hell." Dewey, in contrast, ran a restrained campaign, designed to avoid rocking the boat. By so doing he

Students parade for Strom Thurmond at the States' Rights Convention in Birmingham, Alabama, July 1948. [United Press International]

The Man Who "Done
His Damndest."
*Truman's victory was a
huge upset. [United Press
International]*

may have snatched defeat from the jaws of victory. In trying to
look "presidential," the dapper Dewey came across, in Alice
Roosevelt Longworth's deadly simile, looking like the groom on
the wedding cake. He deliberately studded his speeches with
high-toned platitudes hailing the "creative genius" of a free people, damning the "prophets of gloom," and staying for the most
part on what a reporter called "a high road of rich baritone homi-
lies." In Phoenix he disclosed that "America's future—like
yours in Arizona—is still ahead of us."

   To the end the polls and the pundits predicted a sure win for
Dewey, and most speculation centered on his cabinet choices.
But on election day Truman chalked up the biggest upset in
American history, taking 24.2 million votes (49.5 percent) to
Dewey's 22 million (45.1 percent) and winning a thumping 303
to 189 margin in the electoral college. Thurmond and Wallace
each got more than a million votes, but the revolt of right and left
worked to Truman's advantage. The Dixiecrat rebellion reassured black voters who had questioned the Democrats' commitment to civil rights, while the Progressive movement made it
hard to tag Truman as "soft on Communism." Thurmond carried
the four Deep South states in which his name was accompanied
on the ballot by the Democratic party symbol (in Alabama one
could not vote for Truman) and walked off with 39 electoral
votes, including one from a Tennessee elector who repudiated
his state's decision for Truman. Thurmond's success started a
momentous disruption of the Democratic Solid South, which in a
series of elections now divided its vote. But Truman's victory also
carried Democratic majorities into Congress, where the new
group of senators included Hubert Humphrey, Tennessee's
Estes Kefauver, and by eighty-seven votes, "Landslide Lyndon"
B. Johnson of Texas.

   The outcome seemed a vindication for the New Deal and a

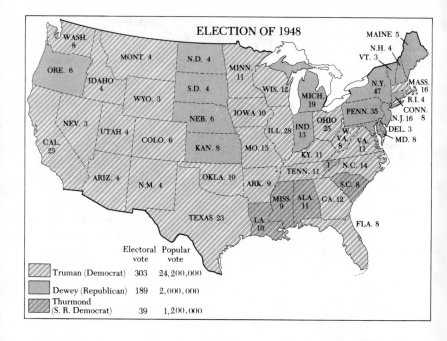

ELECTION OF 1948

	Electoral vote	Popular vote
Truman (Democrat)	303	24,200,000
Dewey (Republican)	189	2,000,000
Thurmond (S. R. Democrat)	39	1,200,000

mandate for liberalism and Truman so regarded it. "We have rejected the discredited theory that the fortunes of the nation should be in the hands of a privileged few," he said in January 1949. His State of the Union message repeated substantially the agenda he had set forth a year previously. "Every segment of our population and every individual," he said, "has a right to expect from his government a fair deal." Whether consciously or not he had invented a tag, the "Fair Deal," to set off his program from the New Deal.

The president won some of his Fair Deal proposals, but they were mainly extensions or enlargements of New Deal programs already in place: a higher minimum wage, bringing more people under Social Security, extension of rent controls, farm price supports at 90 percent of parity, a sizable slum-clearance and public housing program, and more money for the Reclamation Bureau, the TVA, rural electrification, and farm housing. Despite Democratic majorities, however, the conservative coalition was able to resist any drastic new departures in domestic policy. Congress gave the cold shoulder to civil rights bills, national health insurance, federal aid to education, and Agriculture Secretary Charles F. Brannan's plan to provide subsidies that would hold up farm incomes rather than farm prices. Congress also turned down Truman's demand for repeal of the Taft-Hartley Act.

THE COLD WAR HEATS UP

Global concerns, never far from center stage in the postwar world, plagued Truman's second term as they had his first. In his inaugural address Truman called for foreign policy to rest on four pillars: the United Nations, the Marshall Plan, NATO, and a "bold new plan" for technical assistance to underdeveloped parts of the world, a sort of global Marshall Plan which came to be known simply as "Point Four." Under the Technical Cooperation Administration, this program to aid the postwar world began in 1950 with a modest outlay of $35 million.

"LOSING" CHINA AND THE BOMB   One of the most intractable problems, the China tangle, was fast coming unraveled in 1949. The Chinese Nationalists (Kuomintang) of Chiang Kai-shek had at first accepted the help of Communists, but expelled them from their ranks in 1927. When a new leader, Mao Tse-tung, began to rebuild the Communist party by organizing the peasants instead of urban workers, the Nationalists drove him out of Kiangsi province in the south. After an arduous trek, which the Communists later romanticized as the "Long March" of 1934–1935, they entrenched themselves in northern China at Yenan in Shensi province. The outbreak of war with Japan in 1937 relieved them of pressure from the Nationalists, and at the same time enabled them to assume a patriotic stance by fighting the Japanese. During the war Roosevelt, and apparently Stalin as well, believed that the Nationalists would organize China after the war.

The commanders of American forces in China long found Chiang hard to get on with and were driven to the same conclusion as many foreign service officers: that Chiang's government was hopelessly corrupt, tyrannical, and inefficient. After the war, American forces nevertheless ferried Nationalist armies back into the eastern and northern provinces as the Japanese withdrew, and themselves temporarily occupied some of the major coastal cities in China. United States' policy during and immediately after the war was to promote peace and coalition between the factions in China, but sporadic civil war broke out late in 1945.

It soon became a losing fight for the Nationalists, as the Communists radicalized the land-hungry peasantry. In October 1948 the Communists took Mukden; three months later they were in Peking and Tientsin, beginning another long march southward. By December 1949 they had taken Canton and the Nationalist

Gen. Mao Tse-tung
reviews troops of the
Chinese Communist
Army, 1949. [Photo-
world]

government had fled to the island of Formosa, which it renamed
Taiwan.

From 1945 through 1949 the United States had funneled
some $2 billion in aid to the Nationalists, to no avail. Administra-
tion critics asked bitterly: "Who lost China?" and a State Department white paper put the blame on Chiang for his failure to hold
the support of the Chinese people. In fact it is hard to imagine
how the United States government could have prevented the
outcome short of military intervention, which would have been
very risky and unpopular. The United States continued to recognize the Nationalist government on Taiwan as the rightful government of China, delaying formal relations with Red China for
thirty years until 1979. Seeking to shore up friendly regimes
in Asia, in February 1950 the United States recognized the
French-supported regime of Emperor Bao Dai in Vietnam and
shortly afterward extended aid to the French in their battle
against Ho Chi Minh's guerrillas there.

As China fell to the Communists, American intelligence in
September 1949 found an unusual radioactivity in the air, evidence that the Soviets had set off an atomic bomb. The American
nuclear monopoly had lasted just four years, but under the um-
brella of security that it seemed to offer, the wartime military establishment had been allowed to dwindle. In a crisis, this left
American leaders the choice of doing nothing or cremating millions of people. The discovery of the Russian bomb set off an intense reappraisal of the strategic balance in the world, causing
Truman in 1950 to end a dispute among his scientific advisors by
ordering the construction of a hydrogen bomb, a weapon far
more frightful than the Hiroshima bomb, lest the Russians make
one first. The discovery also led the National Security Council to
give the president a top-secret document, NSC-68, which called
for rebuilding conventional military forces to provide options

other than nuclear war. This represented a major departure from America's time-honored aversion to keeping large standing armies in peacetime, and was a very expensive proposition. But the American public was growing more accustomed to the nation's world role, and the invasion of South Korea by Communist forces from the north then clinched the issue.

WAR IN KOREA   The division of Korea at the end of World War II, like the division of Germany, began as a temporary expedient and ended as a permanent fact. In the hectic days of August 1945 a State-War-Navy Coordinating Committee adopted a hasty proposal to divide Korea at the Thirty-eighth Parallel. The Soviets accepted to the surprise of Dean Rusk and others involved. Since they bordered on Korea, the Russians could quickly have occupied the whole country. With the onset of the Cold War, it became clear that agreement on unification was no more likely in Korea than in Germany, and by the end of 1948 separate regimes had appeared in the two sectors and occupation forces had withdrawn. American leaders then inadvertently may have given false impressions to the Communists. General MacArthur during 1949 and Secretary of State Dean Acheson in January 1950 omitted both Korea and Formosa (Taiwan) from an America defense perimeter which included the Philippines, the Ryukyu Islands, and Japan. The weakened state of the American military may have contributed to the impression that South Korea was vulnerable.

For whatever reasons, North Korean forces crossed the boundary on June 24, 1950, and swept quickly down the peninsula. President Truman responded decisively. Korea might have been outside America's defense perimeter, but its southern tip was dangerously close to Japan. Besides, American foreign policy was still much subject to what might be called the "Munich syndrome," or what General MacArthur called "history's clear lesson . . . that appeasement but begets new and bloodier war." Failure to act, Truman reasoned, would embolden Communist leaders "to override nations closer to our own shores."

An emergency meeting of the U.N. Security Council quickly censured the North Korean "breach of peace." The Soviet delegate, who held a veto power, was at the time boycotting the council because it would not seat Red China in place of Nationalist China. On June 27, its first resolution having been ignored, the Security Council called on U.N. members to "furnish such assistance to the Republic of Korea as may be necessary to repel the armed attack and to restore international peace and security

THE KOREAN WAR, 1950

CHINA
MANCHURIA

Vladivostok
U.S.S.R.

Yalu R.
Chosan

NORTH KOREA

SEA OF JAPAN

Pyongyang

NORTH KOREAN OFFENSIVE, JUNE-SEPT. 1950

38°

Inchon • Seoul

SOUTH KOREA

YELLOW SEA

U.N. POSITION SEPT. 1950

Pusan

KOREA STRAIT

0   100 Miles
0   100 Kilometers

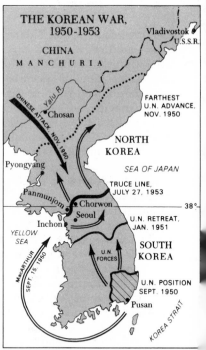

THE KOREAN WAR, 1950-1953

CHINA
MANCHURIA

Vladivostok
U.S.S.R.

Yalu R.
Chosan

CHINESE ATTACK NOV. 1950

FARTHEST U.N. ADVANCE, NOV. 1950

NORTH KOREA

SEA OF JAPAN

Pyongyang

Panmunjom

TRUCE LINE, JULY 27, 1953

Chorwon
Seoul

38°

Inchon

U.N. RETREAT, JAN. 1951

YELLOW SEA

U.N. FORCES

SOUTH KOREA

MacARTHUR SEPT. 15, 1950

U.N. POSITION SEPT. 1950

Pusan

KOREA STRAIT

in the area." Truman then ordered American air, naval, and ground forces into action. In all, some fourteen other U.N. members sent in military units, the largest from Britain and Turkey, and five sent medical units. Later, when the U.N. voted a unified command, General MacArthur was designated to take charge. The war remained chiefly an American affair, and one that set a precedent of profound consequence: war by order of the president rather than by vote of Congress. It had the sanction of the U.N. Security Council, to be sure, and could be considered a "police action," not a war. And other presidents had ordered American troops into action without a declaration of war, but never on such a scale.

For three months things went badly indeed for the Republic of Korea (ROK) and U.N. forces. By September they were barely hanging on to the Pusan perimeter in the southeast corner of Korea. Then, in a brilliant ploy, on September 15 MacArthur landed a new force to the North Korean rear at Inchon, port city of Seoul. Synchronized with a breakout from Pusan, the sudden blow stampeded the enemy back across the border. At this point George Kennan argued that the U.N. forces should stop at the

Thirty-eighth Parallel and negotiate, but a decision was taken on MacArthur's assurance to push on and seek to reunify Korea. The Russian delegate was back in the Security Council, wielding his veto, so on October 7 the United States got approval for this course from the U.N. General Assembly, where the veto did not apply. United States forces had already crossed the boundary by October 1, and now continued northward against minimal resistance. President Truman, concerned over broad hints of intervention by Red China, flew out to Wake Island for a conference with General MacArthur on October 15. There the general discounted chances that the Red Army would act, but if it did, he predicted "there would be the greatest slaughter."

That same day Peking announced that China "cannot stand idly by." But by October 20 U.N. forces had entered Pyongyang, the North Korean capital, and on October 26 the most advanced units had reached Chosan on the Yalu River border with China. MacArthur now predicted total victory by Christmas, but on the night of November 25 Chinese "volunteers" counterattacked, and massive "human wave" attacks, with the support of tanks and planes, turned the tables on the U.N. forces, sending them into a desperate retreat just at the onset of winter. It had become "an entirely new war," MacArthur said. Soon he was putting out word that the fault for the war's continuance lay with the administration for requiring that he conduct a limited war. He proposed raids on China's "privileged sanctuary" in Manchuria, a blockade of China, and an invasion of the mainland by the Taiwan Nationalists, but Truman resisted. MacArthur seemed to have forgotten altogether his one-time reluctance to bog the country down in a major war on the Asian mainland.

The landing at Inchon, September 1950. [Hank Walker, Life *magazine, © 1978 Time Inc.]*

Truman stood firmly against leading the United States into the "gigantic booby trap" of war with China, and the U.N. forces soon rallied. By January 1951 U.N. troops under Gen. Matthew Ridgway finally secured their lines below Seoul, and then launched a counterattack that carried them back across the Thirty-eighth Parallel in March. When Truman seized the chance and offered negotiations to restore the boundary, Mac-Arthur undermined the move by issuing an ultimatum for China to make peace or be attacked. Truman decided then that Mac-Arthur would have to go. On April 5, on the floor of the House, Republican Minority Leader Joseph Martin read a letter in which MacArthur criticized the president and said that "there is no substitute for victory." Such an act of open insubordination left the commander-in-chief no choice but to accept MacArthur's policy or fire him. Civilian control of the military was at stake, Truman later said, and he did not let it remain at stake very long. The Joint Chiefs of Staff all backed the decision, and on April 11, 1951, the president removed MacArthur from all his commands and replaced him with Matthew B. Ridgway.

Truman's action set off an immediate uproar in the country, and a tumultuous reception greeted MacArthur upon his return home for the first time since 1937. MacArthur's speech to a joint session of Congress provided the climactic event. "Once war is forced upon us," he said, "there is no alternative than to apply every available means to bring it to a swift end. War's very object is victory. . . . Why, my soldiers asked of me, surrender military advantages to an enemy in the field? I could not answer them." MacArthur ended the speech in memorable fashion. He recalled a barracks ballad of his youth "which proclaimed most proudly that old soldiers never die, they just fade away." And like the old soldiers of that ballad, he said, "I now close my military career and just fade away, an old soldier who tried to do his duty as God gave him the light to see that duty." A Senate investigation, with Richard Russell of Georgia in the chair, brought out the administration's arguments, best summarized by Gen. Omar Bradley, chairman of the Joint Chiefs of Staff. "Taking on Red China," he said, would lead only "to a larger deadlock at greater expense." The MacArthur strategy "would involve us in the wrong war at the wrong place at the wrong time and with the wrong enemy." Americans, nurtured on classic western showdowns in which good always triumphed over evil, found the logic of limited war hard to take, but also found Bradley's logic persuasive.

On June 24, 1951, the Soviet representative at the United Nations proposed a cease-fire and armistice along the Thirty-eighth

Parallel; Secretary of State Acheson accepted in principle a few days later with the consent of the U.N. China and North Korea responded favorably—at the time General Ridgway's "meat-grinder offensive" was inflicting severe losses—and truce talks started on July 10, 1951, only to drag out for another two years while the fighting continued. The chief snags were prisoner exchanges and the insistence of South Korea's President Syngman Rhee on unification. By the time a truce was finally reached on July 26, 1953, Truman had relinquished the White House to Dwight D. Eisenhower. The truce line followed the front at that time, mostly a little north of the Thirty-eighth Parallel, with a demilitarized zone of four kilometers separating the forces; repatriation of prisoners would be voluntary, supervised by a neutral commission. No final peace conference ever took place, and Korea, like Germany, remained divided. The war had cost the United States more than 33,000 battle deaths and 103,000 wounded and missing. South Korean casualties, all told, were about 1 million, and North Korean and Chinese casualties an estimated 1.5 million.

ANOTHER RED SCARE   In calculating the costs of the Korean War one must add in the far-reaching consequences of the Second Red Scare, which had grown since 1945 as the domestic counterpart to the Cold War abroad and reached a crescendo during the Korean conflict. Since 1938, a House Committee on Un-American Activities had kept up a drumfire of accusations about subversives in government. In 1945 government agents found that secret American documents had turned up in the offices of a Communist-sponsored magazine, and in 1946 more dramatic revelations came from a Canadian royal commission which uncovered several spy rings in the Canadian bureaucracy. On March 21, 1947, just nine days after he announced the Truman Doctrine, the president signed an executive order setting up procedures for an employee loyalty program in the federal government. Every person entering the civil employ of the government would be subject to an investigation. By early 1951 the Civil Service Commission had cleared over 3 million people, while over 2,000 had resigned and 212 had been dismissed for doubtful loyalty, but no espionage ring was uncovered. The program covered all government employees, not just those in sensitive positions.

The Truman program was designed partly if not mainly to protect the president's political flank, but it failed of that purpose, mainly because of disclosures of earlier Communist penetrations into government that were few in number but sensational in character. The loyalty review program may in fact have heightened the politically explosive hysteria over Communist infiltration.

Perhaps the single case most damaging to the administration involved Alger Hiss, president of the Carnegie Endowment for International Peace, who had served in several government departments, and while in the State Department had been secretary-general of the United Nations charter conference. Whittaker Chambers, a former Soviet agent and later an editor of *Time* magazine, told the House Un-American Activities Committee in 1948 that Hiss had given him a number of secret documents ten years earlier, when Chambers worked for the Soviets. Hiss sued for libel, and Chambers produced microfilms of the State Department documents Hiss had passed on to him. Before a federal grand jury Hiss denied the accusation, whereupon he was indicted for perjury and, after one mistrial, convicted in January 1950. The charge was perjury, but he was convicted of lying about espionage—for which he could not be tried because the statute of limitations on the crime had expired. Most damaging to the administration was the fact that President Truman, taking at face value the many testimonials to Hiss's integrity, called the charges against him a "red herring." Secretary of State Dean Acheson compounded the damage when, meaning to express compassion, he said: "I do not intend to turn my back on Alger Hiss." The Hiss affair had another political consequence: it raised to national prominence a young California congressman, Richard M. Nixon, who doggedly insisted on pursuing the case and then exploited the anti-Communist cause to win election to the Senate in 1950.

More cases surfaced. In 1949, the government brought about the conviction of eleven top Communist party leaders under the Smith Act of 1940, which outlawed any conspiracy to advocate the overthrow of the government. The Supreme Court upheld the law under the doctrine of a "clear and present danger," which overrode the right to free speech. In 1950, the government disclosed the existence of a British-American spy network which had fed information about the development of the atomic bomb to Russia. These disclosures led to the arrest of, among others, Klaus Fuchs in Britain and Julius and Ethel Rosenberg in the United States. The Rosenbergs, convicted of espionage in wartime, were executed in 1953. The importance of the secrets they transmitted is doubtful. In a time of less excitement their sentence might well have been commuted.

MCCARTHY'S WITCH-HUNT   Such revelations encouraged politicians to exploit public fears. If a man of such respectability as Hiss were guilty, many wondered, who then could be trusted? The United States, which bestrode the world like a colossus in 1945, had since "lost" eastern Europe and Asia, and "lost" its atomic secrets to Russia. (Physicists, however, insisted that there was nothing secret about the basic principles underlying the bomb.) Early in 1950 the hitherto obscure Sen. Joseph R. McCarthy suddenly surfaced as the shrewdest and most ruthless exploiter of such anxieties. Seeking a way to augment his chances of reelection in 1952, he took up the cause, or at least the pose, of anticommunism. He began with a speech at Wheeling, West Virginia, on February 9, 1950, in which he said that the State Department was infested with Communists and that he held in his hand a list of their names. Later there was confusion as to whether he had said 205, 81, 57, or "a lot" of names, and even whether the sheet of paper carried a list. But such confusion always pursued McCarthy's charges.

Challenged to provide names, he finally pointed to Owen Lattimore of the Johns Hopkins University, an Asian expert, as head of "the espionage ring in the State Department." A special committee under Sen. Millard Tydings looked into the matter and pronounced McCarthy's charges "a fraud and a hoax." McCarthy then turned, in what became his common tactic, to other charges, other names. Whenever his charges were refuted, he loosed a scattershot of new charges. In his hit-and-run tactics, McCarthy displayed the instincts of Shakespeare's Iago, planting suspicions without proof and growing ever more impudent. "He lied with wild abandon," the commentator Richard Rovere wrote; "he lied without evident fear; . . . he lied vividly and with bold imagination; he lied, often, with very little pretense of telling the truth."

McCarthy never uncovered a single Communist agent in gov-

Sen. Joseph McCarthy. [United Press International]

ernment. But with the United States at war with Korean Communists in mid-1950, he continued to mobilize true believers. In the elections of 1950 he intervened in Maryland and helped defeat the conservative Senator Tydings with trumped-up charges that Tydings was pro-Communist. Republicans, even for a time a man of such probity as Robert Taft, encouraged him to keep up the game. By 1951 he was riding so high as to list Gens. George C. Marshall and Dwight D. Eisenhower among the disloyal. He kept up his campaign without successful challenge until the end of the Korean War. But all his discoveries, according to Richard Rovere, added up to "nothing more exciting than a Major Peress [a "pink" army dentist], a citation of Corliss Lamont [a Soviet apologist] in a bibliography, a girl who had heard talk on unwedded bliss in a propaganda agency, a novel by a Communist on a library shelf, and an ex-Communist here and there in some minor agency. He did no better than that."

Under the influence of anti-Communist hysteria the Congress in 1950 passed the McCarran Internal Security Act over President Truman's veto. The act made it unlawful "to combine, conspire, or agree with any other person to perform any act which would substantially contribute to . . . the establishment of a totalitarian dictatorship." Communist and Communist-front organizations had to register with the attorney-general. Aliens who had belonged to totalitarian parties were barred from admission to the United States, a provision that discouraged any temptation for Communists to defect to the United States. Enforcement was placed under a Subversive Activities Control Board.

The McCarran Act, Truman said in his veto message, would "put the Government into the business of thought control." He might in fact have said as much about the Smith Act of 1940, or even his own program of loyalty investigations. In the mid-1950s, looking back over the recent era of hysteria, John Lord O'Brian, once an advisor to Hoover's attorney-general, said, "in reality we have been establishing something like a new system of preventive law applicable to the field of ideas and essentially different from traditional American procedures."

During the late summer of 1951, while the off-and-on peace negotiations continued in Korea, the United States buttressed its defense perimeter through treaties with offshore allies which, just six years after the end of the war, now included Japan. On September 8, 1951, in the San Francisco Opera House, the United States and forty-eight other nations—the USSR declined to participate—signed a peace treaty with Japan, which recognized restoration of Japan's sovereignty but stripped the empire of all claims to Korea, Formosa, the Pescadores, the Kuriles, Sakhalin, and the Pacific islands formerly held under League of Nations mandate. These, along with the Ryukyu and Bonin Islands, now passed to a U.N. trusteeship under the United States. By another treaty signed with Japan that same day, the United States was permitted to maintain armed forces in the defeated country. Just a week earlier, on September 1, as the delegates gathered for the peace conference, the United States, Australia, and New Zealand entered a Tripartite Security Treaty which provided for mutual defense. Two days before that, on August 30, the presidents of the United States and the Philippines signed a similar agreement in Washington.

ASSESSING THE COLD WAR   In retrospect the onset of the Cold War takes on an appearance of terrible inevitability. American and Soviet misunderstanding of each other's motives was virtually unavoidable. America's preference for international principles, such as self-determination and democracy, conflicted with Stalin's preference for international spheres of influence. Russia, after all, had been invaded by Germany twice in the first half of the twentieth century, and Soviet leaders wanted tame buffer states on their borders for protection. The people of eastern Europe, as usual, were caught in the middle. But the Communists themselves held to a universal principle: world revolution. And since the time of President Monroe, Americans had bristled at the thought of foreign intervention in their own sphere of influence, the Western Hemisphere. After the war the United States moved to make the Monroe Doctrine multilateral. Under the Act of Chapultepec (1945) all American states except Argentina agreed that an attack on one would be taken as an attack on all. The Treaty of Rio de Janeiro (1947), with Argentina now included, repeated the principle and imposed an obligation on all to aid any fellow American state attacked, whether from outside the hemisphere or by another American state.

If international conditions set the stage for the Cold War, the actions of political leaders and thinkers set events in motion. President Truman, in following the advice Senator Vandenberg gave during the crisis in Greece and Turkey, may have scared hell out of the American people all too well. The loyalty program, following hot on the heels of the Truman Doctrine, may have spurred on the anti-Communist hysteria of the times. George Kennan's policy of containment itself proved hard to contain, its author later confessed, in part because he failed at the outset to spell out its limits explicitly. "Repeatedly," Kennan wrote in his *Memoirs*, ". . . I expressed in talks and lectures the view that there were only five regions of the world—the United States, the United Kingdom, the Rhine valley with adjacent industrial areas, the Soviet Union, and Japan—where the sinews of military strength could be produced in quantity; I pointed out that only one of these was under Communist control; and I defined the main task of containment, accordingly, as one of seeing to it that none of the remaining ones fell under its control."

The years after World War II were unlike any other postwar years in American history. Having taken on global burdens, the nation had become, if not exactly a "garrison state," at least a country committed for the first time to a major and permanent National Military Establishment, along with the attendant National Security Council, Central Intelligence Agency, and by presidential directive in 1952, the enormous National Security Agency, entrusted with extensive monitoring of media and communications for foreign intelligence. The new policy initiatives of the Truman years had led the country to abandon its long-standing aversion to peacetime alliances not only in the NATO pact but in the agreements with Japan, the Philippines, and the other American states. It was a far cry from the world of 1796, when George Washington in his Farewell Address warned his countrymen against "those overgrown military establishments which . . . are inauspicious to liberty" and advised his country "to steer clear of permanent alliances with any portion of the foreign world."

FURTHER READING

The Cold War, like Reconstruction, is an area of American history still hotly debated by scholars. Traditional interpretations by Herbert Feis in *From Trust to Terror: The Onset of the Cold War, 1945–1950* (1970), and John L. Gaddis in *The United States and the Origins of the Cold War, 1941–1947* (1972),° can be balanced with the revisionists Walter LaFeber in *America, Russia, and the Cold War, 1945–1980* (1981),° and Gabriel Kolko in *The Limits of Power: The World and United States Foreign Policy, 1945–1954* (1972). Two more encompassing works, which also balance the two sides of argument, are the traditional John L. Gaddis's *Strategies of Containment: A Critical Appraisal of Postwar American National Security Policy* (1982) and the more revisionist Norman A. Graebner's *The Age of Global Power: The United States since 1938* (1979).

°These books are available in paperback editions.

Other scholars concentrate on more specific events in the buildup of international tensions. Lynn Etheridge Davis's *The Cold War Begins: Soviet-American Conflict over Eastern Europe* (1974), George C. Herring, Jr.'s *Aid to Russia, 1941–1946* (1973), Thomas G. Paterson's *Soviet-American Confrontation* (1973), and Bruce Kuklick's *American Policy and the Division of Germany* (1972) deal with initial tensions at the close of the war. Herbert Feis's *Between War and Peace: The Potsdam Conference* (1960) examines Truman's attitude. How tensions widened to other areas of the world is shown in Bruce R. Kuniholm's *The Origins of the Cold War in the Near East: Great Power Conflict and Diplomacy in Iran, Turkey, and Greece* (1980). For the foundations of the Truman Doctrine, consult Lawrence S. Wittner's *American Intervention in Greece, 1943–49* (1982), and William Roger Louis's *Imperialism at Bay: The United States and the Decolonization of the British Empire* (1978). For the Marshall Plan, two helpful books are Hadley Arkes's *Bureaucracy, the Marshall Plan, and the National Interest* (1974) and Robert H. Ferrell's *George C. Marshall* (1966). For subsequent tensions and policy, see W. Phillips Davison's *The Berlin Blockade* (1958) and Robert E. Osgood's *NATO* (1962). Also helpful on defensive arrangements in Europe is John Bayliss's *Anglo-American Defence Relations, 1939–1980: The Special Relationship* (1981). For the Truman administration's reliance on the atomic bomb monopoly, see Joseph I. Lieberman's *The Scorpion and the Tarantula: The Struggle to Control Atomic Weapons, 1945–1949* (1970), Alexander L. George and Richard Smoke's *Deterrence and American Foreign Policy: Theory and Practice* (1975), Michael Mandelbaum's *The Nuclear Question: The United States and Nuclear Weapons, 1946–1976* (1979), and Daniel Yergin's *Shattered Peace: The Origins of the Cold War and the National Security State* (1977).°

A solid study of the career bureaucrats who helped shape policy is Lloyd C. Gardner's *Architects of Illusion: Men and Ideas in American Foreign Policy, 1941–1949* (1970). Those who opposed such policies are the subject of Thomas G. Paterson's *Cold War Critics: Alternatives to American Foreign Policy in the Truman Years* (1972) and Robert J. Maddox's *The New Left and the Origins of the Cold War* (1973).

Two favorable biographies of Truman are Margaret Truman's *Harry S. Truman* (1973) and Merle Miller's *Plain Speaking: An Oral Biography of Harry S. Truman* (1974).° Other scholars view Truman through his activities as president; they include Robert J. Donovan's *Conflict and Crisis: The Presidency of Truman, 1945–1948* (1977),° Bert Cochran's *Truman and the Crisis Presidency* (1973), and Alonzo L. Hamby's *Beyond the New Deal: Harry S. Truman and American Liberalism* (1973).

The domestic policies of the Fair Deal receive analysis in William C. Berman's *The Politics of Civil Rights in the Truman Administration* (1970), Richard O. Davis's *Housing Reform during the Truman Administration* (1966), Richard M. Dafiumes's *Desegregation of the United States Armed Forces* (1969), Maeva Marcus's *Truman and the Steel Seizure* (1977), and R. Alton Lee's *Truman and Taft-Hartley* (1967). Other scholars concentrate on the difficulties Truman had with the conservatives in Congress, including Charles D. Hadley's *Transformations of the American Party System: Political Coalitions from the New Deal to the 1970s* (1978), Ronald Radosh's *Prophets on the Right: Profiles of Conservative Critics of American Globalism* (1975), and Susan Hartmann's *Truman and the Eightieth Congress* (1971). For the fabled election of 1948, see Richard N. Smith's *Thomas E. Dewey and His Times* (1982), Norman D. Markowitz's *The Rise and Fall of the People's Century: Henry A. Wallace and American Liberalism, 1941–1948* (1974), Allen Yarnell's *Democrats and Progressives: The 1948 Election as a Test of Postwar Liberalism* (1974), and Samuel Lubell's *The Future of American Politics* (1952).

For an introduction to the tensions in Asia, see Akira Iriye's *The Cold War in Asia* (1974). More specific to China are Ely J. Kahn, Jr.'s *The China Hands: America's Foreign Service Officers and What Befell Them* (1975), Kenneth E. Shewmaker's *Americans and the Chinese Communists, 1927–1945* (1971), and Tang Tsou's *America's Failure in China, 1941–1950* (1971). For the Korean conflict, see Bruce Cumming's *The Origins of the Korean War: Liberation and the Emergence of Separate Regimes, 1945–1947* (1980), Joseph C. Goulden's *Korea: The Untold Story of the War* (1982), and David Rees's *Korea: The Limited War* (1964). The high command perspective is shown in Robert Smith's *MacArthur in Korea: The Naked Emperor* (1982), William Manchester's *American Caesar: Douglas MacArthur, 1880–1960* (1978),° John W. Spanier's *The Truman-MacArthur Controversy* (1965), and Trumball Higgins's *Korea and the Fall of MacArthur* (1960).

The anti-Communist syndrome which helped produce McCarthy is surveyed in David Carter's *The Great Fear: The Anti-Communist Purge under Truman and Eisenhower* (1978).° Other works on the topic include Athan Theoharis's *Seeds of Repression: Harry S. Truman and the Origins of McCarthyism* (1971), Richard Freeland's *The Truman Doctrine and the Origins of McCarthyism* (1972), Alan Harper's *The Politics of Loyalty: The White House and the Communist Issue, 1946–1952* (1968), and Mary S. McAuliffe's *Crisis on the Left: Cold War Politics and American Liberals, 1947–1954* (1978). Richard Freeland's *Men against McCarthy* (1976), Edwin R. Bagley's *Joe McCarthy and the Press* (1981),° and Thomas C. Reeves's *The Life and Times of Joe McCarthy* (1982)° cover McCarthy himself. For the Rosenberg trial, consult Walter and Miriam Schneir's *Invitation to an Inquest* (1972). Allen Weinstein's *Perjury! The Hiss-Chambers Conflict* (1978)° covers that subject well.

For the rise of the intelligence network, see Thomas F. Troy's *Donovan and the CIA: A History of the Establishment of the Central Intelligence Agency* (1981) and Anthony C. Brown's *The Last Hero: Wild Bill Donovan* (1982).

32

CONFLICT AND DEADLOCK:
THE 1950s

"TIME FOR A CHANGE"

By 1952 the Truman administration had piled up a heavy burden of political liabilities. Its bold stand in Korea had brought a bloody stalemate abroad, renewed wage and price controls at home, reckless charges of subversion and disloyalty, and the exposure of corrupt lobbyists and influence peddlers who rigged favors in Washington. The disclosure of "the Mink Dynasty" and the "five percenters" led Truman to fire nearly 250 employees of the Bureau of Internal Revenue and, among others, an assistant attorney-general in charge of the Justice Department's Tax Division. But doubts lingered that Truman, protégé of the Kansas City Pendergast machine, would ever finish the housecleaning. There were two Trumans, the newscaster Elmer Davis had said: "The White House Truman does all the big things right, and the courthouse Truman does all the little things wrong." But by 1952 few things, big or little, seemed to be going right. The country had bogged down in "Plunder at home, blunder abroad."

EISENHOWER'S POLITICAL RISE It was, in another maxim of the day, "time for a change," and South Dakota's Sen. Karl Mundt had a simple formula for Republican victory: $K_1 C_2$—Korea, communism, and corruption. The GOP (Grand Old Party, or Republican party) field quickly narrowed to two men, Sen. Robert A. Taft and Gen. Dwight D. Eisenhower, with General MacArthur alert for a deadlock. The party wheelhorses turned instinctively to Taft, "Mr. Republican," long a faithful party worker. Taft had become the foremost spokesman for domestic conservatism and for a foreign policy which his enemies branded isolationist. A man of stubborn integrity, he did not usually trim his sails to the prevailing winds. He had openly opposed the war-crimes trials, for instance, arguing that they were *ex post facto* and a dangerous precedent. His conservatism left room for federal aid to education and public housing, and his foreign policy, a "unilateralist" one, favored an active American role in opposing communism but opposed "entangling alliances" such as NATO. He joined the "Asia Firsters" in stressing the strategic importance of the Pacific area, but warned against the dangers of a land war on the Asian mainland. In Korea, he felt, the time had come to go all out for victory or to withdraw completely.

But Taft inspired little enthusiasm beyond the party regulars. He projected an image of little glamor, and as a leader used to taking controversial stands, he had made enemies. The eastern, internationalist wing of the party turned instinctively to Eisenhower, then the NATO commander. As a war hero he had the glamor that Taft lacked, and his captivating and unpretentious manner inspired support. His leadership had been tested in the fires of war, but as a professional soldier he had escaped the scars of political combat. He stood, therefore, outside and above the vulgar arena of public life, although his political instincts and skills were sharpened during his successful army career.

Eisenhower nevertheless seemed genuinely immune to the presidential bug until Sen. Henry Cabot Lodge, Jr., and others appealed to his sense of duty: only he could stop Taft and the isolationists. In January 1952 the general affirmed that he was a Re-

Dwight D. Eisenhower (right) and Richard M. Nixon (third from right), the Republican standard-bearers for 1952. [United Press International]

publican and in the following months permitted his name to be entered in party primaries. In June he left his NATO post and joined the battle in person. An outpouring of public enthusiasm began to overwhelm Republican party regulars. Bumper stickers across the land announced simply, "I like Ike." The closely divided convention resolved itself into a series of contests between rival delegations which the younger Taft could not control. Eisenhower won the nomination on the first ballot. He balanced the ticket by choosing as his running mate a youthful Californian, the thirty-nine-year-old Sen. Richard M. Nixon, who had built a career on opposition to "subversives" and gained his greatest notoriety as the member of the House Un-American Activities Committee most eager in the pursuit of Alger Hiss.

THE 1952 ELECTION   The Twenty-second Amendment, ratified in 1951, in a belated thrust at Roosevelt forbade any president to seek a third term. The amendment exempted the incumbent, but weary of the war, harassed by charges of subversion and corruption in government, his popularity declining, Truman chose to withdraw and his exit threw the Democratic race wide open. An early lead was mustered by Tennessee's Estes Kefauver, who had chaired a nationally televised investigation of organized crime. Sporting a coonskin cap, the symbol of his campaign, Kefauver worked the streets and shook every hand in reach. But his primary victories failed to move Democratic party regulars. Truman preferred Gov. Adlai E. Stevenson of Illinois but, rebuffed by the governor's insistent refusal, threw his support to Vice-President Alben W. Barkley. Just before the convention, however, a group of "certain self-appointed political labor leaders" told Barkley he was too old (at seventy-five) and asked him to withdraw. When he did, Truman threw his support again to Governor Stevenson, who aroused the delegates with an eloquent speech welcoming them to Chicago. On the third ballot the convention drafted Stevenson, who then chose Sen. John J. Sparkman of Alabama as his running mate.

The campaign matched two of the most magnetic personalities ever pitted in a presidential contest. Both men attracted new followings among people previously apathetic to politics, but the race was uneven from the start. Eisenhower, though a political novice, was a world figure who had been in the public eye for a decade. Stevenson, the politician, was hardly known outside of Illinois and never able to escape the burden of Truman's liabilities. The genial general, who had led the crusade against Hitler, now opened a domestic crusade to clean up "the mess in Washington." To this he added a promise, late in the campaign, that as president-elect he would go to Korea to secure "an early and honorable" peace. The Democrats' charge that he was grandstanding had little impact in the face of his long military experience. Stevenson's forte was a lofty eloquence spiced with a quick wit, but his resolve to "talk sense" and "tell the truth to the American people" came across as just a bit too aloof, a shade too intellectual. The Republicans hastened to cast him in the role of an "egghead," a latter-day Hamlet, in contrast to Eisenhower, the man of the people, the man of decision and action.

The war hero triumphed in a landslide of 33.9 million votes to Stevenson's 27.3 million, and 442 electoral votes to Stevenson's 89. The election marked a turning point in Republican fortunes in the South: for the first time since the heyday of the Whigs the South was moving toward a two-party system. Stevenson carried only eight southern states plus West Virginia; Eisenhower picked up five states in the outer South: Florida, Oklahoma, Tennessee, Texas, and Virginia. In the former Confederacy the Republican ticket garnered 48.9 percent of the votes. The "nonpolitical" Eisenhower had made it respectable, even fashionable, to vote Republican in the South. Elsewhere, too, the general made inroads in the New Deal coalition, attracting supporters among the ethnic and religious minorities in the major cities.

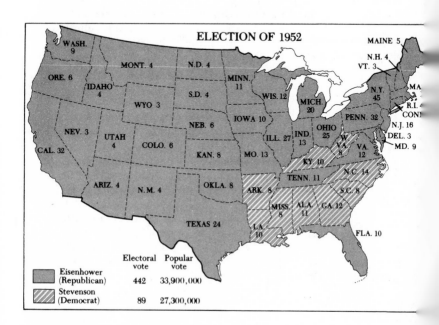

ELECTION OF 1952

	Electoral vote	Popular vote
Eisenhower (Republican)	442	33,900,000
Stevenson (Democrat)	89	27,300,000

The voters, it turned out, liked Ike better than they liked his party. Democrats retained most of the governorships, lost control of the House by only eight votes, and broke even in the Senate, where only the vote of the vice-president ensured Republican control. The congressional elections two years later would weaken the Republican grip on Congress, and Eisenhower would have to work with a Democratic Congress until he left office.

IKE Born in Dennison, Texas, on October 14, 1890, Dwight David Eisenhower grew up in Abilene, Kansas, near the geographical center of the country and Harry Truman's hometown of Independence, Missouri. Young Eisenhower's first memory of presidential politics was a torchlight parade in 1896, but after graduating from West Point he went on to spend nearly his entire adult life in the military service. He spent World War I stateside as a tank instructor, and then worked his way through the ranks. He served as staff officer to General MacArthur in Washington and the Philippines. After Pearl Harbor, Gen. George C. Marshall made Brigadier-General Eisenhower his chief of operations. Later, as a major-general, he took command of American forces in the European theater and directed the invasion of North Africa in November 1942. In 1944 he assumed the post of supreme commander of allied forces in preparation for the invasion of the continent. After the war, by then a five-star general of the armies, he became chief of staff and supreme commander of NATO forces, with a brief interlude in between as president of Columbia University.

Eisenhower's inauguration brought a change in style to the White House. The contrast in character between the feisty Truman and the avuncular Ike was reinforced by a contrast in philosophy and approach to the presidency. Eisenhower's military experience developed in him an instinct for methodical staff work. He met with the cabinet and the National Security Council nearly every week, and relied heavily on them as consultative bodies. Under the direction of his chief assistant, former New Hampshire Gov. Sherman Adams, the flow of routine paperwork reached the Oval Office digested into single-page summaries. "I count the day lost," Adams said, "when I have not found some new way of lightening the President's load."

Such procedures, it seemed, tended to isolate the president from conflicting viewpoints and to reduce the policy choices available to him. The public image of Ike confirmed that view, but it endeared him all the more to the people as a man who rose above politics. He was unpretentious, an ardent golfer, a common man who read little but western novels, uninformed on the currents of intellectual and artistic life, and given to copybook maxims: "Everybody ought to be happy every day. Play hard, have fun doing it, and despise wickedness." George Kennan said: "He was the nation's number one Boy Scout."

But those who were closer to him have presented another side to the man. When provoked he could release a massive temper and scalding profanity. While Ike talked with genuine feeling about such traditional virtues as duty, honesty, and thrift, he was not above a calculated dissimulation. The scrambled syntax in which he answered reporters' questions was sometimes deliberate evasion. Eisenhower deliberately toned down eloquent passages which speech writers tried to smuggle into his public utterances, although he had written florid speeches for General MacArthur. One recent student of Eisenhower's techniques has spoken of a "hidden-hand presidency" in which Ike deliberately cultivated an image of passivity to hide his active involvement in policy decisions.

"DYNAMIC CONSERVATISM" AT HOME   Like Ulysses Grant, however, Eisenhower betrayed a weakness for men with money. His cabinet, a column in the *New Republic* quipped, consisted of "eight millionaires and a plumber." The plumber, Secretary of Labor Martin Durkin, was gone in eight months, charging that the administration had reneged on a promise to change the Taft-Hartley Act. Charles E. Wilson, president of General Motors, became secretary of defense and two auto distributors, Douglas McKay and Arthur Summerfield, became secretary of the interior and postmaster-general respectively. The New Dealers, Adlai Stevenson wryly remarked, "have all left Washington to make way for the car dealers."

Unaccustomed to the glare of Washington publicity, several cabinet members succumbed to foot-in-mouth disease. It was perhaps innocent enough for Charles E. Wilson to say at his confirmation hearings, "I thought what was good for our country was good for General Motors, and vice versa," except that it was readily translated into: "What is good for General Motors is good for the country." Douglas McKay put it more baldly: "We're here in the saddle as an Administration representing business and industry." Treasury Secretary George Humphrey, head of Mark Hanna's old coal and oil firm in Cleveland, put Andrew Mellon's picture on the wall, and replied when asked if he had read Hemingway's *The Old Man and the Sea:* "Why would anybody be interested in some old man who was a failure and never amounted to anything anyway?"

Eisenhower called his program "dynamic conservatism," which meant being "conservative when it comes to money and liberal when it comes to human beings." Stevenson conjectured: "I assume what it means is that you will strongly recommend the building of a great many schools to accommodate the needs of our children, but not provide the money." Budget cutting was a high priority for the new administration, which set out after both domestic programs and national defense. Eisenhower warned repeatedly against the dangers of "creeping socialism," "huge bureaucracies," and budget deficits. But though Eisenhower chipped away at New Deal programs, his presidency in the end served rather to legitimate the New Deal.

In 1953 Eisenhower won quick congressional approval for turning over to the coastal states the oil-rich "tidelands" which the Supreme Court had awarded to the federal government. Eisenhower also abolished the Reconstruction Finance Corporation, ended wage and price controls, and reduced farm price subsidies. Eisenhower also moved the government away from the Roosevelt-Truman commitment to public power. In fact, had Ike had his way the government would have sold the TVA. The Republican Congress rejected a proposal in 1953 to build a new TVA steam plant to supply the power needs of Memphis, Tennessee, and thereby release power to serve the AEC's atomic weapons plant at Paducah, Kentucky. Opposed to any further expansion of TVA, the administration instead got behind a plan of the Dixon-Yates utility syndicate to build a private plant. Controversy over the proposal dragged out for two years until investigations revealed that the government consultant who recommended the plant was vice-president of an investment firm handling Dixon-Yates securities.

The embarrassed administration then seized upon an alternative, a municipal powerplant with which the city of Memphis promised to supply the need. Another protracted struggle over public power ended differently when the Idaho Power Company won a license to build three small dams on the Snake River in place of a gigantic federal dam proposed for Hell's Canyon. Still another step away from public power came with the Atomic Energy Act of 1954, which opened the door for construction of private nuclear powerplants under AEC license and safeguards.

In fiscal policy the administration found its passion for budget cutting encumbered by unyielding facts. Its first budget had already been prepared by Truman's men, providing for expenditures of $80 billion and a deficit of $9.9 billion, which Eisenhower's heroic efforts reduced by only $4.4 billion. In 1954 Treasury Secretary George Humphrey formulated tax reductions which resembled Andrew Mellon's programs of the 1920s in providing benefits mainly to corporations and individuals in the upper brackets. The new budget slashed expenditures by $6.5 billion, nearly 10 percent, and Humphrey joined with the Federal Reserve Board in tightening credit and raising interest rates to avert inflation. But the business slump which followed reduced government revenues, making it harder to balance the budget. After that experience Eisenhower's fiscal and monetary policies became less doctrinaire and more flexible. The government accepted easier credit and deficits as necessary "countercyclical" methods. The Keynesian Age, if not yet acknowledged, endured.

In some ways, moreover, the administration not only maintained the New Deal but extended its reach, especially after 1954 when it had the help of Democratic Congresses. Amendments to the Social Security Act in 1954 and 1956 brought coverage to millions in categories formerly excluded: professional people, domestic and clerical workers, farm workers, and members of the armed forces. In 1959 the program's benefits went up 7 percent. The federal minimum wage rose in 1955 from 75¢ to $1 an hour. Federal expenditures for public health rose steadily in the Eisenhower years and the president went so far as to endorse federal participation in health insurance, but Congress twice refused to act. Low-income housing continued to be built, although on the much-reduced scale of some 35,000 units annually.

Some farm-related programs were expanded during the Eisenhower years. The Rural Electrification Administration announced on its twenty-fifth birthday in 1960 that 97 percent of American farms had electricity. The Farmers Home Administration and a Rural Development Program continued the program of loans to support farm ownership and improvements, although on a much smaller scale than the New Deal's Farm Security Administration. Cordell Hull's program of reciprocal trade agreements was regularly renewed. Under the Agricultural Trade Development and Assistance Act of 1954 the government undertook on a large scale to finance the export of surplus farm products in exchange for foreign currencies, an idea much like the McNary-Haugen scheme of the 1920s. Surpluses were exported also as gifts to needy nations and to provide milk for schoolchildren. By an amendment to the act in 1959, surpluses became available to the needy by issuing food stamps redeemable at grocery stores.

Despite Eisenhower's general disapproval of public power

programs, he continued to support public works for which he saw a legitimate need. Indeed two such programs left major monuments to his presidency: the St. Lawrence Seaway and the Interstate Highways. The St. Lawrence Seaway, designed to open the Great Lakes to ocean-going ships by means of locks and dredging, had languished in Congress since the time of President Hoover because of opposition by eastern business and railroad interests afraid of the competition. In 1954 Eisenhower finally broke the opposition by pointing to Canadian determination to go ahead anyway and to the growing need of American steel producers for Laurentian ore as the Mesabi deposits gave out. Congress then approved joint participation with the Canadians, and five years later the seaway was open. The Federal Aid Highway Act of 1956 authorized the federal government to put up 90 percent of the cost of building 42,500 miles of limited-access interstate highways to serve the needs of commerce and defense, as well as private convenience. The states put up the remaining 10 percent. It was only afterward that people realized that the huge national commitment to the automobile might have come at the expense of America's railroad system, already in a state of advanced decay.

CONCLUDING AN ARMISTICE   America's new position in the postwar world, however, continued to absorb Eisenhower's attention. The most pressing problem when he entered office was the continuing, painful deadlock in the Korean peace talks. The main stumbling block at Panmunjom was the insistence of North Korea and Red China that all prisoners be returned regardless of their wishes. To break the deadlock, Eisenhower resolved upon a bold stand. In mid-May 1953 he stepped up aerial bombardment of North Korea, then had Secretary of State Dulles convey to Peking through the Indian government a secret threat to remove all limits on weapons and targets. It was a thinly veiled warning of atomic warfare against Red forces, perhaps even against China itself. Whether for that reason or others, negotiations then moved quickly toward an armistice along the established battle line just above the Thirty-eighth Parallel, and toward a complicated arrangement for prisoner exchange which allowed captives to accept or refuse repatriation.

On July 26, 1953, President Eisenhower announced the conclusion of the armistice. But most of the Korean peninsula was devastated. Whether or not Eisenhower had pulled a masterful bluff in getting the armistice has never become clear; no one knows whether or not he actually would have forced the issue with atomic weapons. Perhaps the more decisive factors in bringing about a settlement were the size of Chinese Communist losses, which even they found unacceptable, and the new spirit of uncertainty and caution felt by Russian Communists after the death of Josef Stalin on March 5, 1953—six weeks after Ike's inauguration.

CONCLUDING A WITCH-HUNT   The Korean armistice helped to end another dismal episode: the meteoric career of Sen. Joseph R. McCarthy, which had flourished amid the anxieties of wartime. Eventually the logic of McCarthy's tactics led to his self-destruction, but not before he had left still more personal careers and reputations in ruins. The Republicans thought their victory in 1952 would curb his recklessness, and Senator Taft sought to deflect him into the chairmanship of the Permanent Investigation Subcommittee of the Senate Committee on Government Operations, but merely provided him a platform and staff resources. McCarthy's new sensations overshadowed those of the regular subversive-hunting committees of the House and Senate.

When Eisenhower nominated Charles E. Bohlen, a career diplomat, as ambassador to Russia, McCarthy and other Senate militants attacked Bohlen for association with the Yalta "betrayal." Not only had Bohlen been Roosevelt's interpreter there, he had even defended the Yalta agreements before a Senate committee. The intervention of Senator Taft brought Senate approval of the nomination, but thirteen members persisted in voting against Bohlen. McCarthy then began to fill the headlines with gossip and innuendoes about the State Department's Voice of America. During the summer of 1953 he sent two youthful assistants, Roy M. Cohn and G. David Schine, on a junket to Europe to purge the libraries of the International Information Agency. "Subversive works," such as the writings of Emerson and Thoreau, were removed from shelves and in some cases burned. Dulles ordered American information centers abroad to exclude the works of "any Communists, fellow travellers, et cetera."

McCarthy finally overreached himself when he tried to peddle the absurdity that the United States Army itself was "soft" on communism. The cases in point, it seemed, were a "pink" dentist at Fort Monmouth, New Jersey, since given an honorable discharge, and the army's refusal to give special treatment to a draftee, G. David Schine, McCarthy's former assistant, who was being held "hostage." A confusing tangle of charges and countercharges led to televised hearings by McCarthy's subcommittee, with Sen. Karl Mundt temporarily in the chair. From April

The Army-McCarthy hearings of 1954 marked the end of the senator's influence. [Copyright 1954 by Herblock in the Washington Post]

22 to June 17, 1954, the Army-McCarthy hearings displayed McCarthy at his capricious worst, bullying witnesses, dragging out lengthy irrelevancies, repeatedly calling "point of order." He became the perfect foil for the army's gentle but unflappable counsel, Joseph Welch of Boston, whose rapier wit repeatedly drew blood. When a witness used the word "pixie," McCarthy demanded a definition and Welch sweetly explained that a pixie was "a kind of fairy." But when McCarthy tried to smear one of Welch's young associates, the counsel went into a cold rage: "Until this moment, Senator, I think I never really gauged your cruelty or your recklessness. . . . Have you no sense of decency, sir, at long last?" When the audience burst into applause, the confused senator was reduced to whispering, "What did I do?"

Apparently he never found out, but at that point the house he had thrown together began to crash around his ears. He descended into new depths of scurrility, now directed at his own colleagues, calling Ralph Flanders of Vermont "senile" and Robert C. Hendrickson of New Jersey "a living miracle . . . the only man who has lived so long with neither brains nor guts." On December 2, 1954, the Senate voted 67 to 22 to "condemn" McCarthy for contempt of the Senate. Samuel J. Ervin, Jr., of North Carolina, a newly appointed senator, accused him of "disorderly conduct by flyblowing . . . a strong Anglo-Saxon word, but a very expressive one." McCarthy was finished, and increasingly took to alcohol. Three years later, at the age of forty-eight, he was dead.

The witch-hunt was over. McCarthyism, Ike joked, had become McCarthywasm, though not for those whose reputations and careers had been wrecked. To the end Eisenhower kept his resolve not to "get down in the gutter with that guy" and sully the dignity of the presidency, but he did work resolutely against McCarthy behind the scenes. Eisenhower shared, nevertheless, the deeply held conviction of many citizens that espionage posed a real danger to national security. He denied clemency to Julius and Ethel Rosenberg, convicted of transmitting atomic secrets to the Russians, on the grounds that they "may have condemned to death tens of millions of innocent people." They went to the electric chair at Sing-Sing Prison on June 19, 1953.

INTERNAL SECURITY   Even earlier, Eisenhower stiffened the government security program which Truman had set up six years before. Executive Order 10450, dated April 27, 1953, broadened the basis for firing government workers by replacing Truman's criterion of "disloyalty" with the new category of "security risk." Under the new edict federal workers lost their jobs because of dubious associations or personal habits that might make them careless or vulnerable to blackmail. In December 1953 the AEC removed the security clearance of the physicist J. Robert Oppenheimer, the "father of the atomic bomb," on the grounds that he had expressed qualms about the hydrogen bomb in 1949–1950 and had associated with Communists or former Communists in the past. Lacking evidence of any disloyalty or betrayal, the AEC nevertheless branded him a "security risk" because of "fundamental defects in his character."

The Supreme Court, however, modified some of the more extreme expressions of the Red Scare. In September 1953 Chief Justice Frederick M. Vinson died and Eisenhower chose former Gov. Earl Warren of California to take his place, a decision the president later pronounced the "biggest damnfool mistake I ever made." Warren, who had seemed safely conservative while active in politics, proved to have a social conscience and a streak of libertarianism which Eisenhower's next appointee, William I. Brennan, Jr., shared. The "Warren Court" (1953–1969), under the chief justice's influence, became an important agency of social and political change on through the 1960s. In connection with security programs and loyalty requirements, the Court veered back in the direction of traditional individual rights. In *Yates v. United States* (1957) an opinion by Justice John Marshall Harlan narrowly construed the Smith Act of 1940 to apply to those advocating revolutionary action, not those merely teaching revolutionary doctrine in the abstract. This, plus other decisions setting rigid standards for evidence, rendered the Smith

Act a dead letter. In *Pennsylvania v. Nelson* (1956) the Court banned state prosecution for subversion against the United States since Congress had preempted that field. Much later, in *Albertson v. Subversive Activities Control Board* (1965), the Warren Court held that the McCarran Act's requirement that Communist party leaders register with the board violated the Fifth Amendment guarantee against self-incrimination. This left the board little to do until it was abolished in 1973.

DULLES AND FOREIGN POLICY The Eisenhower administration promised new departures in foreign policy under the direction of Secretary of State John Foster Dulles. Grandson of one former secretary of state and nephew of another, Dulles had pursued a lifetime career as an international lawyer and sometime diplomat. At the age of nineteen he had been secretary to the Chinese delegation at the 1907 peace conference at The Hague; in 1919 he had assisted the American delegates at the Versailles Conference. As counselor to the Truman State Department he had, among other things, negotiated the Japanese peace treaty of 1951. Son of a minister and himself an active Presbyterian layman, Dulles, in the words of British Ambassador Sir Oliver Franks, resembled those old zealots of the wars of religion who "saw the world as an arena in which the forces of good and evil were continuously at war."

The foreign policy planks of the 1952 Republican platform, which Dulles wrote, showed both the moralist and the tactician at work. The policy of containment was needlessly defensive, Dulles thought. This conviction meshed nicely with the conventional wisdom of the right wing that Yalta was perhaps a betrayal, at best a blunder. The 1952 platform, therefore, promised to "repudiate all commitments . . . such as those of Yalta which aid Communist enslavement" and to end "the negative, futile and immoral policy of 'containment' which abandons countless human beings to a despotism and godless terrorism. . . ." A new policy of liberation, the platform promised, "will inevitably set up strains and stresses within the captive world which will make the rulers impotent to continue in their monstrous ways and mark the beginning of the end."

The policy came perilously close to proclaiming a holy war, but Dulles took care to explain that he did not intend forcible liberation. Soon it became apparent that it was less a policy than a web of rhetoric to catch ethnic voters whose homelands had fallen captive. The Republican party's new Ethnic Origins Division made the most of it. Eisenhower in his inaugural address promised to "unleash" Chiang Kai-shek—that is, cancel the Seventh Fleet's orders to prevent his invading the Chinese mainland. The fleet's more realistic mission of protecting Taiwan continued, however.

When it came to repudiating Yalta, the administration drew back. Ike was conscious of his own vulnerability as the commander who had implemented the agreement and who had stopped American forces short of Berlin and Prague. The administration's Captive Peoples Resolution merely rejected any misuse of the Yalta agreements, "which have been perverted to bring about the subjugation of free peoples." The real betrayal, in short, had been Russian violation of the Yalta accords. Even that resolution died in congressional committee. That the liberation rhetoric rang false became more evident in June 1953 when workers in East Germany rebelled against working conditions and food shortages. When Russian tanks rolled over the demonstrators, the administration did nothing except to deplore the situation. For three years more Dulles was able to maintain the belief that his rhetoric was undermining the Communist hold on eastern Europe—until suppression of the 1956 uprising in Hungary underscored the danger of stirring futile hopes among captive peoples.

COVERT ACTIONS   Insofar as interventions occurred, they were covert operations by the Central Intelligence Agency in countries outside the Soviet sphere. Under Eisenhower, Allen Dulles, brother of the secretary of state, rose from second in command to chief of the CIA. A veteran of the wartime Office of Strategic Services, he had already had a hand in beefing up the CIA's capacity for cloak-and-dagger operations. In two cases early in the Eisenhower years this capability was actually used to overthrow governments believed hostile to American interests: in Iran (1953) and in Guatemala (1954).

In Iran, Premier Mohammed Mossadegh, a seventy-year-old nationalist, whipped up popular feeling against British control of Iranian oil production and then expropriated the foreign properties. In thus challenging Western interests he had the support of the Tudeh, Iran's Communist party, and left the impression that he either had gone over to their side or would become their dupe. In these circumstances, Allen Dulles sent a crack agent, Kermit Roosevelt (Theodore Roosevelt's grandson), along with Col. H. Norman Schwartzkopf, who had helped the shah of Iran, Mohammed Reza Pahlavi, to organize his secret police. Armed chiefly with about a million dollars, they stirred up street demonstrations against Mossadegh which, reinforced by soldiers loyal to the shah, toppled the premier, sent him to jail, and brought the young shah back from exile in Rome. A new premier made an arrangement under which the British and Americans each got 40 percent of Iran's oil production, the Dutch 14 percent, and the French 6 percent.

In Guatemala, Jacobo Arbenz Guzman had become president in an election in which he had Communist backing. While the administration lacked evidence that Arbenz was a Communist, Ambassador John Peurifoy said "he talked like a Communist, he thought like a Communist, and he acted like a Communist, and if he is not one, he will do until one comes along." Critics of the intervention contended that Arbenz's chief sin was that he had expropriated 225,000 acres of United Fruit Company land. He had also secured weapons from East Germany with which to arm a peasant militia. With Eisenhower's consent the CIA chose one Col. Carlos Castillo Armas to stage a coup from a base in Honduras. The operation, however, was mainly a war of nerves, with rumors spread by clandestine radio stations and token raids on Guatemala City run by surplus planes from World War II. Arbenz panicked, resigned, and fled the country. Defenders of the action were those who agreed with the conclusion of a committee commissioned to investigate the CIA in 1955: "It is now clear that we are facing an implacable enemy whose avowed objective is world domination by whatever means and at whatever cost. There are no rules in such a game. Hitherto acceptable norms of conduct do not apply."

BRINKSMANSHIP   Actually, Dulles made no significant departure from the strategy of containment created under Acheson and Truman. Instead he institutionalized containment in the rigid mold of his Cold War rhetoric and extended it into the military strategy of deterrence. He betrayed a fatal affinity for colorful phrases which left him, according to Arthur Larsen, "perpetually poised between a cliché and an indiscretion." To his lexicon of "liberation" and "roll back," Dulles added two major new contributions while in office: "massive retaliation" and "going to the brink."

"Massive retaliation" is actually a shorthand version of Dulles's phrase "massive retaliatory power," a description of the "New Look" in military strategy, an effort to get, in the slogan soon current, "more bang for the buck" or "more rubble for the ruble." Budgetary considerations lay at the root of military plans, for Eisenhower and his cabinet shared the fear that in the effort to build a superior war power the country could spend itself into bankruptcy. During 1953 new members of the Joint Chiefs of Staff, headed by Adm. Arthur W. Radford, set to work on planning a new military posture. The heart of their New Look was the assumption that nuclear weapons could be used in limited-war situations, allowing reductions in conventional forces and thus budgetary savings. Dulles, who announced the policy on January 12, 1954, explained that savings would come "by placing more reliance on deterrent power, and less dependence on local defensive power." No longer could an enemy "pick his time and place and method of warfare." American responses would be "by means and at places of our choosing." No longer would "the Communists nibble us to death all over the world in little wars," Vice-President Nixon explained in March 1954.

By this time both the United States and Russia had exploded hydrogen bombs. With the new policy of deterrence, what Winston Churchill called a "balance of terror" had replaced the old "balance of power." The threat of nuclear holocaust was terrifying, but the notion that the United States would risk such a disaster in response to local wars had little credibility.

Dulles's policy of "brinksmanship" depended for its strategic effect on those very fears of nuclear disaster. Dulles argued in 1956 that in following a tough policy of confrontation with communism, one sometimes had to "go to the brink" of war: "The ability to get to the verge without getting into war is the necessary art. If you cannot master it, you inevitably get into war. . . . We walked to the brink and we looked it in the face. We took strong action." The first occasion on which a firm stand had

"Don't Be Afraid—I Can Always Pull You Back"

Secretary of State Dulles pushes a reluctant America to the brink of war. [Herblock's Special for Today (New York: Simon & Schuster, 1958)]

halted further aggression had been America's threat in 1953 to break the Korean stalemate by removing restraints from the armed forces. The second had come in 1954, when aircraft carriers moved into the South China Sea "both to deter any Red Chinese attack against Indochina and to provide weapons for instant retaliation. . . ."

INDOCHINA: THE BACKGROUND TO WAR   Dulles's reference to Indochina was an oversimplification: it neglected the complexity of the situation there, which presented a special if not unique case of the nationalism which swept the old colonial world of Asia and Africa after World War II, damaging both the power and prestige of the colonial powers. By the early 1950s most of British Asia was independent or on the way: India, Pakistan, Ceylon (later Sri Lanka), Burma, and the Malay States (later the Federation of Malaysia). The Dutch and French, however, were less ready than the British to give up their colonies and thus created a dilemma for American policy-makers. Americans sympathized with colonial nationalists who sometimes invoked the example of 1776, but Americans also wanted Dutch and French help against communism. The Truman administration felt obliged to answer their pleas for aid. Both the Dutch and the French were obliged to reconquer areas which had passed from Japanese occupation into the hands of local patriots. In the Dutch East Indies the Japanese had created a puppet Indonesian Republic which emerged from World War II virtually independent. The Dutch effort to regain control met resistance which exploded into open warfare.

Eventually, American pressure persuaded the Dutch to accept self-government under a Dutch-Indonesian Union in 1949, but that lasted only until 1954 when the Republic of Indonesia became independent. In April 1955 the Bandung Conference in Indonesia, attended by delegates from twenty-nine independent countries of Asia and Africa, signaled the emergence of a "Third World" of underdeveloped countries, unaligned with either the United States or the Soviet bloc. Among other actions the conference condemned "colonialism in all its manifestations," a statement which implicitly condemned both the USSR and the West.

French Indochina, created in the nineteenth century out of the old kingdoms of Cambodia, Laos, and Vietnam, offered a variation on Third World nationalism. During World War II Japanese control of the area had required their support of pro-Vichy French civil servants and opposition to the local nationalists. Chief among the latter were the Vietminh (Vietnamese League for Independence), who fell under the influence of Communists

Ho Chi Minh. [Warder Collection]

led by Ho Chi Minh. At the end of the war this group controlled part of northern Vietnam, and on September 2, 1945, Ho Chi Minh proclaimed a Democratic Republic of Vietnam, with its capital in Hanoi.

Ho's declaration borrowed clearly from Thomas Jefferson, opening with the words "We hold these truths to be self-evident. That all men are created equal." American officers were on the reviewing stand in Hanoi and American planes flew over the celebration. Ho had received secret American help against the Japanese during the war, but bids for further aid after the war went unanswered. Vietnam took low priority in American diplomatic concerns at the time.

In March 1946 the French government, preoccupied with domestic politics, recognized Ho's new government as a "free state" within the French union. Before the year was out, however, Ho's forces came into conflict with French efforts to establish another regime in the southern provinces, and this clash soon expanded into the First Indochina War. In June 1949, having set up former native kings as puppets in Laos and Cambodia, the French installed Bao Dai of an old Vietnamese ruling family as emperor of Vietnam. The victory of the Chinese Communists later in 1949 was followed by Red China's diplomatic recognition of the Vietminh government in Hanoi, and then the recognition of Bao Dai by the United States and Britain.

The Vietminh movement thereafter became more completely dominated by Ho Chi Minh and his Communist associates, and more dependent on Russia and Red China for help. In 1950, with the outbreak of fighting in Korea, the struggle in Vietnam took on more and more the appearance of a battleground in the Cold War. When the Korean War ended, American aid to the French in Vietnam, begun by the Truman administration, continued. By the end of 1953 the Eisenhower administration was paying about two-thirds of the cost of the French effort, or about $1 billion annually. By 1954 the United States found itself at the edge of the "brink" to which Dulles later referred. A major French force had been sent to Dien Bien Phu, near the Laos border, in the hope of luring Vietminh guerrillas into a set battle and grinding them up with superior firepower. The French instead found themselves trapped by a superior force which threatened to overrun their stronghold.

In March 1954 the French government requested an American air strike to relieve the pressure. The request had been encouraged by Adm. Arthur W. Radford, chief of staff, who argued for raids by B-29s from the Philippines covered by carrier-based fighters. The forceful chief of staff won the support of Dulles and Vice-President Nixon. Army Gen. Matthew B. Ridgway, however, disagreed. Effective action, he feared, would require American ground forces, which were not up to the assignment. Eisenhower himself seemed to endorse forceful action when he advanced his "domino theory" to a news conference on April 7, 1954: "You have a row of dominoes set up, you knock over the first one, and what will happen to the last one is the certainty that it will go over very quickly." He was nevertheless playing a cautious game. When congressional leaders expressed reservations, he took a stand against American action unless the British lent support. When they refused, he backed away from unilateral action.

THE GENEVA ACCORDS AND U.S. POLICY On May 7, 1954, the massive attacks loosed by Vietminh Gen. Vo Nguyen Giap finally overwhelmed the last French resistance at Dien Bien Phu. It was the very eve of the day an international conference at Geneva took up the question of Indochina. Six weeks later, as French forces continued to meet defeats in the Red River Delta, a new French government under Premier Pierre Mendès-France promised to get an early settlement. On July 20 representatives of France, Britain, Russia, the People's Republic of China, and the Vietminh reached agreement on the Geneva Accords, and the next day produced their Final Declaration which proposed to neutralize Laos and Cambodia and divided Vietnam at the Seventeenth Parallel. The Vietminh would take power in the north and the French would remain south of the line until elections in

1956 should reunify Vietnam. American and South Vietnamese representatives refused either to join in the accord or to sign the Final Declaration, with the result that Russia and China backed away from their earlier hints that they would guarantee the settlement. In the end, nobody at all signed the Declaration and participants confined themselves to unilateral statements in which they endorsed or dissociated themselves from particular parts of the Geneva Accords.

The American response was an effort to set up mutual defense arrangements for Southeast Asia. On September 8, 1954, at a meeting in Manila, the United States joined seven other countries in an agreement that Dulles wanted known as the Manila Defense Accord (MANDAC), but which the press quickly labeled as the Southeast Asia Treaty Organization (SEATO). The impression that it paralleled NATO was false, for the Manila Accord was neither a common defense organization like NATO nor was it primarily Asian. The signers agreed that in case of attack on one, the others would act according to their "constitutional practices," and in case of threats or subversion they would "consult immediately." The members included only three Asian countries—the Philippines, Thailand, and Pakistan—together with Britain, France, Australia, New Zealand, and the United States. India and Indonesia, the two most populous countries in the region, refused to join. A special protocol added to the treaty extended coverage to Indochina. The treaty reflected what Dulles's critics called "pactomania," which by the end of the Eisenhower administration contracted the United States to defend forty-three other countries.

Eisenhower announced that though the United States "had not itself been party to or bound by the decision taken at the [Geneva] Conference," any renewal of Communist aggression "would be reviewed by us as a matter of grave concern." In Vietnam, when Ho Chi Minh took over the north, those who wished to leave for South Vietnam did so with American aid. Power in the south gravitated to a new premier imposed on Emperor Bao Dai by the French at American urging: Ngo Dinh Diem, who had opposed both the French and the Vietminh, took office during the Geneva talks. Before that he had been in exile at a Catholic seminary in New Jersey. In October 1954 Eisenhower offered to assist Diem "in developing and maintaining a strong, viable state, capable of resisting attempted subversion or aggression through military means." In return the United States expected "needed reforms." American aid was forthcoming in the form of CIA and military cadres charged with training Diem's armed forces and police.

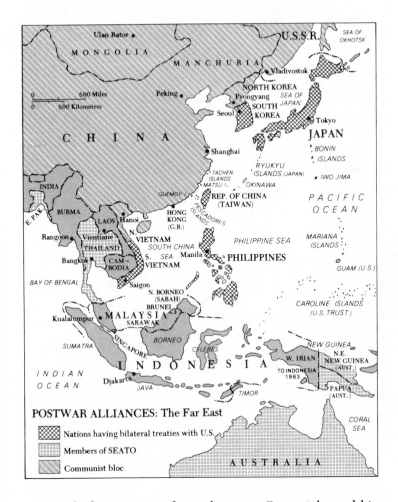

POSTWAR ALLIANCES: The Far East

- ⊠ Nations having bilateral treaties with U.S.
- ▦ Members of SEATO
- ▨ Communist bloc

Instead of instituting reforms, however, Diem tightened his grip on the country, suppressing opposition on both right and left, offering little or no land distribution, and permitting widespread corruption. In 1956 he refused to join in the elections to reunify Vietnam, and after French withdrawal from the country, ousted Bao Dai and installed himself as president. His efforts to eliminate all opposition played into the hands of the Communists, who found recruits and fellow travelers among the discontented. By 1957 guerrilla forces known as the Vietcong had begun attacks on the government, and in 1960 the resistance emerged as the National Liberation Front. As guerrilla warfare gradually disrupted the country, the Eisenhower administration was helpless to do anything but "sink or swim with Ngo Dinh Diem."

QUEMOY AND MATSU   Having backed away from the "brink" in Vietnam, Eisenhower and Dulles soon found themselves approaching another. Just before the Manila conference in September 1954, Red Chinese artillery began shelling the Quemoy islands at the entrance to Amoy harbor, and soon afterward brought under fire the nearby Matsu and Tachen groups, all of which were held by Chiang Kai-shek's Nationalists. On his way back from Manila Dulles stopped in Taipei and worked out a mutual defense treaty which bound the United States to defend Taiwan and the nearby Pescadores Islands, and which bound Taiwan to undertake offensive action only with American consent. The treaty omitted mention of the offshore islands, and the mainland Chinese continued their pressure, occupying one of the Tachens. In January 1955 the president secured in Congress a resolution giving him full power to go to the defense of Taiwan and the Pescadores, and also authorizing him to secure and protect "such related positions of that area now in friendly hands" in order to defend Taiwan. Congress's endorsement was overwhelming—the resolution drew only three negative votes in each house—for so sweeping a grant of power.

The Red Chinese kept up their activity nonetheless, and under pressure from the American government the Nationalists evacuated the Tachens as indefensible. But Quemoy and Matsu became symbols of the will to protect Taiwan, and were perhaps strategically useful too. In any case Adm. Robert B. Carney, chief of naval operations, "leaked" word to newsmen that the administration was considering a plan "to destroy Red China's military potential and thus end its expansionist tendencies." Soon afterward the Chinese backed away from the brink. At the Bandung Conference in April, with diplomatic encouragement from other Asian nations, Premier Chou En-lai said Red China was ready to discuss the Formosa Strait issue directly with the United States. In May 1955 representatives of the two governments began meetings in Geneva, and the guns fell silent.

A THAW IN THE COLD WAR   The quiet in the Formosa Strait was but one signal of a "thaw" in the Cold War. Europe remained the chief focus of American foreign policy, and there friendly gestures came from the Soviet government and the Communist party secretary Nikita Khrushchev, who had come out on top in the post-Stalin power struggles. While American and Chinese officials were discussing Quemoy and Matsu, the Soviets agreed to the Austrian State Treaty, ending the four-power occupation of that little country and restoring its independence as a neutral but

Western-oriented state. At Geneva, during July 18–23, 1955, President Eisenhower, British Prime Minister Anthony Eden, and Premiers Edgar Fauré of France and Nikolai Bulganin of the Soviet Union held the first summit conference since the one at Potsdam ten years before, but unlike the Potsdam meeting this one was strictly a cosmetic affair. The leaders displayed cheerful grins and conveyed a mood of affability that had newsmen writing about the amicable "spirit of Geneva." But they decided nothing of substance on any of the major issues they discussed.

The high point of the conference came on July 21, when Eisenhower set forth what came to be called his "Open Skies" proposal, a prelude to disarmament by which Russia and the United States would give each other "a complete blueprint of four military establishments from beginning to end," and would each open its skies to the other for aerial surveillance. Khrushchev, who was present at the meeting, told the president privately that it was "a very transparent espionage device." It would give Americans information they did not already have while providing the Russians little they did not already know. In consequence the conference did nothing except to lay the groundwork for cultural and diplomatic exchanges. The conference left behind a vague aura of peace, but it also made clear the arrival of a thermonuclear stalemate.

An H-Bomb hideaway. The Geneva Conference marked a thaw in the Cold War, but the continuing threat of nuclear war caused many Americans to invest in underground fallout shelters such as the Kidde Kokoon, designed to protect "a family for three to five days after an H bomb blast." [United Press International]

"The Affluent Society"

THE CONSUMER ECONOMY   The warm afterglow of Geneva made the prospect of nuclear conflict seem remote. With the guns silent in Vietnam and the Formosa Strait, the world enjoyed its first season of peace in nearly two decades, while a flourishing economy ushered the United States into what the economist John Kenneth Galbraith soon called the "affluent society." The consumer culture which had emerged in the 1920s now resumed the growth stunted by depression and war. Pent-up demand and wartime savings triggered the postwar prosperity, which was maintained by Cold War outlays and increased consumer buying. Advertising and credit spurred the process, and credit cards, used at least since the 1930s, proliferated with advances in plastics and computers.

The electronic computer, the first of which was built in 1945, went on the market in the 1950s. But at this time consumers were more interested in new products such as television, transistorized FM radios, electric floor polishers, electric can openers, electric pencil sharpeners, antibiotics, and automatic car transmissions. Consumers enjoyed easy access to these goods in the new drive-in shopping malls spreading in the suburbs. Government expenditures for the St. Lawrence Seaway, the interstate highways, new rocketry, and the space program created new boom towns. The increased demand for housing called forth arrays of homogenized houses, typified by the sprawling Lévittowns in Pennsylvania and Long Island, or by Daly City, California, where the snuggeries perched along the hillsides inspired a

Dr. Jonas Salk. Salk's polio vaccine, developed in the mid-1950s, proved effective in preventing infection by the crippling viral disease. [March of Dimes, Birth Defects Foundation]

popular song, "Little Boxes": "And they're all made out of ticky-tacky and they all look just the same."

At the same time relaxed trade restrictions encouraged Americans to enjoy a variety of exotic foreign products and fashions. The reciprocal trade agreements started by Cordell Hull in 1934 were expanded into a multilateral policy under the General Agreement on Tariffs and Trade signed at Geneva in1947. By 1960 the average level of American duties was down to about 12 percent from above 50 percent in 1930. The flow of American funds abroad made the dollar the chief medium of international exchange.

The United States now had by far the most productive economy in the world. In 1955, with about 6 percent of the world's population, the nation produced nearly half the world's goods. The median family income rose from $3,083 in 1949 to $5,657 in 1959, a rise, when corrected for inflation, still of some 48 percent. Inflation, measured at a low 1.6 percent annually from 1948 to 1963, was kept in check by efforts to hold the line on governmental expenditures. These efforts contributed to recessions in 1949, 1953–1954, 1957–1958, and 1960–1961. Despite the visible rise in wealth, the American economy grew more slowly from 1948 to 1960 than most other major world economies: its growth rate was 2.9 percent compared to 8.7 percent for Japan, 7.2 percent for Germany, 5.8 percent for Italy, 4.2 percent for France, and 2.7 percent for Great Britain. But America had started from a much higher plateau after the war, and the 1960s would bring a renewed spurt of economic growth.

STIRRINGS IN CIVIL RIGHTS   If the Eisenhower presidency seems an interlude of relative tranquility between two decades of domestic and foreign strife it should be remembered that those years saw the onset of a revolution in race relations which historians have come to call the Second Reconstruction. Eisenhower entered office committed to civil rights in principle, and did push the issue in areas of federal authority. During his first three years public services in Washington, D.C., were desegregated, as were navy yards and veterans hospitals. Beyond that, however, two aspects of the president's philosophy inhibited vigorous action: his preference for state or local action, and his doubt that law could be effective in such matters. "I don't believe you can change the hearts of men with laws or decisions," he said. For the time, then, leadership in the civil rights field came from the judiciary more than from the executive or legislative branch of the government.

Segregation began to be tested in the courts by the NAACP in the late 1930s. [Library of Congress]

In the 1930s the NAACP had resolved to test the "separate but equal" doctrine which had upheld racial segregation since the *Plessy* decision in 1896. Charles H. Houston, dean of the Howard University Law School, laid the plans and his former student, Thurgood Marshall, served as chief NAACP lawyer. They decided to begin with the expensive field of postgraduate study. At the time no southern or border state provided such study for blacks, although some offered grants for them to go out of state. In the case of Lloyd L. Gaines (1938) the Supreme Court ruled that such a grant failed to provide the equal protection of the laws required under the Fourteenth Amendment. Missouri hastily improvised a separate law school, but before Gaines's lawyers could resolve the issue, he mysteriously vanished. In *Ada Lois Sipuel v. Board of Regents* (1948) the court found a black woman entitled to attend the University of Oklahoma Law School in the absence of a separate facility, and in *Sweatt v. Painter* (1950) ruled that a separate law school in Texas failed to measure up because of intangible factors, such as its isolation from most of the future lawyers with whom its graduates would interact.

THE *BROWN* DECISION   By that time challenges to segregation in the public schools were rising through the appellate courts. Five such cases, from Kansas, Delaware, South Carolina, Virginia, and the District of Columbia—usually cited by reference to the first, *Brown v. Board of Education of Topeka, Kansas*—came to the Supreme Court for joint argument in 1952. Chief Justice Earl Warren wrote the opinion, handed down on May 17, 1954, in which a unanimous Court declared that "in the field of public education the doctrine of 'separate but equal' has no place." In support of its opinion the Court cited current sociological and psychological findings presented by the eminent Kenneth Clark, a black psychologist. It might well have cited historical evidence that Jim Crow facilities had been seldom equal and often not available to blacks at all. A year later, after further argument, the Court directed "a prompt and reasonable start toward full compliance"; the process should move "with all deliberate speed."

The white South's first response was relatively calm, deceptively so as it happened. Eisenhower refused to take any part in leading white southerners toward compliance. Privately he remarked: "I am convinced that the Supreme Court decision *set back* progress in the South *at least fifteen years.* The fellow who tries to tell me you can do these things by *force* is just plain *nuts.*" While token integration began as early as 1954 in the border states, hostility mounted in the Deep South and Virginia, led by the newly formed Citizens' Councils and similar groups. Before the end of 1955, moderate sentiment in the South gave way to reaction. Virginia's Sen. Harry F. Byrd supplied a rallying cry: "Massive Resistance." State legislatures passed pupil assignment laws and adopted other dodges, all futile, to interpose their power between the courts and the schools. In March 1956, 101 southern members of Congress lent their names to a "Southern Manifesto" which denounced the Court's decision as "a clear abuse of judicial power." At the end of 1956, in six southern states, not a single black child attended school with whites. In several of the others the degree of desegregation was minuscule.

THE MONTGOMERY BUS BOYCOTT   At the end of 1955 the drive for civil rights took a new turn in Montgomery, Alabama, "the cradle of the Confederacy." There, on December 1, 1955, Mrs. Rosa Parks was arrested for refusing to give up her seat on a city bus to a white man. The next night black community leaders met in the Dexter Avenue Baptist Church to organize a massive bus boycott under the Montgomery Improvement Association.

In Dexter Avenue's twenty-six-year-old pastor, Martin Luther King, Jr., the movement found a charismatic leader who spoke eloquently in cadences familiar to the Bible Belt. He brought the movement a message of nonviolent, passive resistance compounded from the Gospels, the writings of Thoreau, and the example of Mahatma Gandhi in India. "We must use the weapon of love," he told his people. "We must realize so many people are taught to hate us that they are not totally responsible for their hate." To his antagonists he said: "We will soon wear you down by our capacity to suffer, and in winning our freedom we will so appeal to your heart and conscience that we will win you in the process."

The bus boycott achieved a remarkable solidarity. Blacks in Montgomery formed car pools, hitchhiked, or simply walked. But the white town fathers, who were not so quickly worn down, held out against the boycott and against the pleas of a bus company tired of losing money. The boycotters finally won through the federal courts a case they had initiated against bus segregation, and on December 20, 1956, the Supreme Court let stand without review an opinion of a lower court that "the separate but equal doctrine can no longer be safely followed as a correct statement of the law." The next day King and other blacks boarded the buses, but they still had a long way to travel before Jim Crow could be laid finally to rest. Trying to keep alive the spirit of the bus boycott, King and a group of associates in 1957 organized the Southern Christian Leadership Conference (SCLC).

Despite Eisenhower's reluctance to take the lead in desegregating schools, he had no problem with supporting the right to vote. In 1956, hoping to exploit divisions between northern and southern Democrats and to reclaim some of the black vote for Republicans, Eisenhower proposed legislation which became the Civil Rights Act of 1957. The first civil rights law passed since Reconstruction, it finally got through the Senate, after a year's delay, with the help of Majority Leader Lyndon B. Johnson, who won southern acceptance by watering the act. Still, it established for a period of two years the Civil Rights Commission, which was later extended indefinitely, and a new Civil Rights Division in the Justice Department, which could seek injunctions to prevent interference with the right to vote. The SCLC promptly announced a campaign to register 2 million black voters. The Civil Rights Act of 1960 provided for federal court referees to register blacks where a court found a "pattern and practice" of discrimination, and also made it a federal crime to interfere with any court order or to cross state lines to destroy any building.

LITTLE ROCK   There had been sporadic violence in resistance to civil rights efforts, but a few weeks after the 1957 act passed, the governor of a state for the first time stood in outright defiance of the law. Arkansas Gov. Orval Faubus called out the National Guard to prevent nine black students from entering Little Rock's Central High School under federal court order. A conference between the president and the governor proved fruitless, but on court order Faubus withdrew the Guard. When the students tried to enter the school, a hysterical mob outside forced their removal for their own safety. At that point Eisenhower, who had said two months before that he could not "imagine any set of circumstances that would ever induce me to send federal troops,"

Federal troops at Little Rock High School. [Burt Glinn, Magnum Photos]

ordered a thousand paratroopers to Little Rock to protect the students, and placed the National Guard on federal service. The soldiers stayed through the school year.

The following year Faubus peremptorily closed the high schools of Little Rock, and court proceedings dragged on into 1959 before the schools could be reopened. The year 1959 proved an important turning point, for in that year massive resistance in Virginia collapsed when both state and federal courts struck down state laws which had cut off funds from integrated schools. Thereafter, massive resistance for the most part was confined to the Deep South where five states, from South Carolina west through Louisiana, still held out against even token integration.

A LANDSLIDE FOR IKE   When President Eisenhower suffered a "moderately severe" coronary seizure during a Colorado vacation in September 1955, some journalists felt that he could not have chosen a more opportune time: there was no immediate crisis on the horizon. He recovered quickly and was getting back in harness within a month. In February 1956, after his doctor pronounced him recovered, the president announced his decision to run again. A serious operation for ileitis, an inflammation of the intestine, in June 1956 did not change his plans. In August the Republican convention renominated him by acclamation and, despite a quixotic effort by Harold Stassen to dump Nixon, again named him as the vice-presidential candidate. The party platform endorsed Eisenhower's "modern Republicanism."

The Democrats turned again to Stevenson, who had campaigned vigorously in the primaries against Sen. Estes Kefauver. After Stevenson freed the convention to name its own candidate for vice-president, the delegates chose Kefauver by a narrow margin over young Sen. John F. Kennedy. The platform evaded the civil rights issue and otherwise stuck to Democratic staples: less "favoritism" to big business, repeal of the Taft-Hartley Act, parity for farmers, tax relief for those in low-income brackets.

Neither candidate generated much excitement during the campaign. The Democrats did what they could with the issue of the president's health, but centered their fire on the heir apparent, Richard Nixon, a "man of many masks." Stevenson aroused little enthusiasm for two controversial proposals: to drop conscription and rely on an all-volunteer army, and to ban H-bomb tests by international agreement. Both involved military questions which put Stevenson at a disadvantage by pitting his judgment against that of a successful general.

During the last week of the campaign the season of world peace was broken by shooting wars along the Suez Canal and in the streets of Budapest. The two crises made it possible for Stevenson to declare the administration's foreign policy "bankrupt." Most voters, however, seemed to reason that the crises spelled a poor time to switch horses, and they handed Eisenhower a landslide victory. He lost one border state, Missouri, but in carrying Louisiana became the first Republican to win a Deep South state since Reconstruction; nationally, he carried all but seven states. The decision was unmistakably clear: he won more than 35.6 million popular votes to a little over 26 million for Stevenson, 457 electoral votes to the Democrat's 73.

A Season of Troubles

CRISIS IN THE MIDDLE EAST   The twin crises in the Suez and Hungary were unrelated but occurred almost as if placed in malicious juxtaposition by some evil force. The attack on Egypt by Britain, France, and Israel disrupted the Western alliance and damaged any claim to moral outrage at Russian actions in Hungary. For the Soviets, the Suez War afforded both a smokescreen for the subjugation of Hungary and a chance to enlarge their influence in the Middle East, an increasingly important source of oil.

After 1953 the Eisenhower-Dulles policy in the region departed from the Truman-Acheson focus on Israel and distanced itself from British-French economic interests in order to cultivate Arab friendship. To forestall Russian penetration, Dulles in 1955 completed his line of alliances across the "northern tier" of the Middle East. Under American sponsorship Britain joined the Moslem states of Turkey, Iraq, Iran, and Pakistan in the Middle East Treaty Organization (METO), or Baghdad Pact, as the treaty

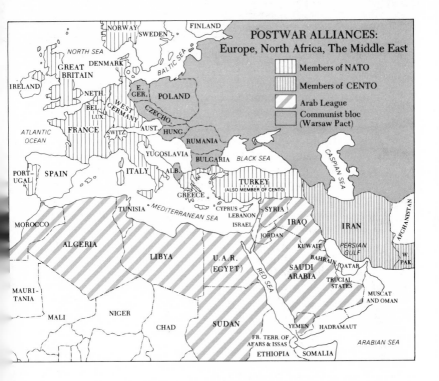

was commonly called. By linking the easternmost NATO state (Turkey) to the westernmost SEATO state (Pakistan), METO had a certain superficial logic, but after Iraq, the only Arab member, withdrew in 1959 it became clear that the whole thing had been moribund from the start. Below the northern tier, moreover, the Arab states remained aloof from the organization. These were the states of the Arab League (Egypt, Jordan, Syria, Lebanon, and Saudi Arabia), which had warred on Israel in 1948–1949 and remained committed to its destruction.

The most fateful developments in the region turned on the rise of Egyptian Gen. Gamal Abdel Nasser, leader of the army officers who overthrew King Farouk in 1952. The bone of contention was the Suez Canal, which had opened in 1869 as a joint French-Egyptian venture. But in 1882 the British government had acquired the largest block of stock and from the next year on British forces were posted there to protect the British Empire's "lifeline" to India and other colonies. When Nasser's new regime pressed for the withdrawal of British forces from the canal zone, Eisenhower and Dulles supported its demand, and in 1954 an Anglo-Egyptian treaty provided for British withdrawal within twenty months. Nasser, like other leaders of the Third World, remained unaligned in the Cold War and sought to play both sides off against each other. In 1955 Nasser made a deal for Czech armaments in return for Egyptian cotton. The United States, meanwhile, courted Egyptian support by offering the prospect of American assistance in building a great hydroelectric plant at Aswan on the Nile River.

From the outset the administration's proposal was opposed by Jewish constituencies concerned with Egyptian threats to Israel, and by southern congressmen who feared the competition from Egyptian cotton produced by irrigation at Aswan. When Nasser then increased trade with the Soviet bloc and recognized Red China, Dulles abruptly canceled the loan offer in July 1956. The outcome was far from a triumph of American diplomacy. The chief victims, it turned out, were Anglo-French interests in the Suez. Unable to retaliate against the United States, Nasser nationalized the Suez Canal Company and earmarked its revenues for the Aswan project, thereby enhancing his prestige in the Arab world. The British and French, directly challenged and faced with loss of control of the crucial Suez Canal, reacted strongly. Fruitless negotiations dragged out through the summer, and finally, on October 29, Israeli forces invaded the Gaza Strip and the Sinai peninsula. The Israelis invaded ostensibly to root out Arab guerrillas, but actually to synchronize with the British and French, who began bombing Egyptian air bases and on November 3 occupied Port Said. Their actions, the British and French claimed, were meant to protect the canal against the opposing belligerents.

The Suez War put the United States in a quandary. Either the administration could support its Western allies and see the troublesome Nasser crushed, or it could stand on the United Nations

The Twentieth Century Dilemma. *The Suez crisis forced America into a difficult choice.[Long in the Minneapolis Tribune]*

Charter and champion Arab nationalism against imperialistic aggression. The latter course was adopted, with the unusual result that Russia sided with the United States' position. Once the threat of American embargoes had forced Anglo-French-Israeli capitulation, the Russians capitalized on the situation by threatening to use missiles against the Western aggressors. This belated bravado won for Russia some of the credit in the Arab world for what the United States had done.

REPRESSION IN HUNGARY   All the while, Khrushchev was engaged in the subjugation of Hungary, a sharp reversal to the campaign of "de-Stalinization" he had launched in his "secret" speech on the crimes of the Stalin era, delivered at the Communist Party Congress in February 1956. Khrushchev joined this confession of Communist tyranny with hints of relaxed policies and suggestions that different countries might take "separate roads to socialism." In the satellite countries this put Stalinist leaders on the defensive and emboldened the more independent national leaders. In June riots in the Polish city of Poznan led to the rise of Wladyslaw Gomulka, a Polish nationalist, to leadership of the Polish Communist party. Gomulka managed to win a greater degree of independence by avoiding an open break with the Russians.

In Hungary, however, a similar movement got out of hand. On October 23 fighting broke out in Budapest, followed by the installation of Imre Nagy, a moderate Communist, as head of the government. Again the Russians seemed content to let "de-Stalinization" follow its course, and on October 28 they withdrew their forces from Budapest. But Nagy's announcement three days later that Hungary would withdraw from the Warsaw Pact brought Russian tanks back into Budapest. They installed a more compliant leader, Janos Kadar, and hauled Nagy off to Moscow, where a firing squad executed him in 1958. It was a tragic dénouement to a movement that, at the outset, promised the sort of moderation which might have vindicated Kennan's policy of "containment," if not Dulles's notion of "liberation."

LEGISLATIVE STUMBLING   In the euphoria of his landslide victory on November 6, Eisenhower said on election night: "I think that modern Republicanism has now proved itself. And America has approved of modern Republicanism." He later defined this as "the political philosophy that recognizes clearly the responsibility of the Federal Government to take the lead in making certain that the productivity of our great economic machine is distributed so that no one will suffer disaster, privation, through no fault of his own." Eisenhower Republicans, it seemed clear, had assimilated the New Deal as an accomplished fact. But decisive as was the vote for Eisenhower, the winner's coattails failed to swing a congressional majority for his own party in either house, the first time this had happened since the election of Zachary Taylor.

A season of troubles followed Eisenhower's smashing victory. It began with the "great budget battle" of 1957. In January the president sent up to Capitol Hill a $71.8-billion budget for fiscal 1958, up $3 billion from the previous year, the biggest peacetime budget ever. The size of the budget, which increased foreign aid, military spending, and allocations for atomic energy, housing, public works, and education, startled and alarmed even the president, who had little time to cut it back. Eisenhower sent the bill to Congress, still hopeful that continued prosperity and high revenues would supply a surplus.

On the day the budget went to Congress, January 16, 1957, Secretary of the Treasury George Humphrey told reporters "there are a lot of places in this budget that can be cut," and suggested that if government could not reduce the "terrific" tax burden "you will have a depression that will curl your hair." Eisenhower claimed to share Humphrey's desire to reduce the budget, but the spectacle of a treasury secretary challenging the budget on the day it went to Congress conveyed an impression of divided purpose and conflict in the administration. Both Democrats and Old Guard Republicans declared an open season on the administration's budget requests, and in the end they hacked out about $4 billion, including heavy cuts in foreign aid, the United States Information Agency, and the Defense Department. By the time the battle was over in August, an economic slump had set in and tax revenues dropped. In spite of the cuts, the administration projected a $500-million deficit.

SPUTNIK On October 4, 1957, came the Soviet launching of the first man-made satellite, called *sputnik*, an acronym for the Russian phrase "fellow traveler of earth." Sputnik I weighed 194 pounds, but less than a month later the Soviets launched a capsule of 1,120 pounds, and it carried a dog wired up for monitoring. Americans, until then complacent about their technical primacy, suddenly discovered an apparent "missile gap." If the Russians were so advanced in rocketry, then perhaps they could hit American cities just as Nazi rockets had hit London in 1945. All along Eisenhower knew that the "gap" was more illusory than real, but could not reveal that high-altitude American U-2 spy planes were gathering this information. Even so, American missile development was in a state of disarray, with a tangle of

By the Rocket's Red Glare. *The Soviet success in space shocked Americans. [Poinier in the Detroit News]*

agencies and committees engaged in waste and duplication. To the embarrassment of the administration, Sen. Lyndon B. Johnson's Preparedness Subcommittee of the Armed Services Committee laid out the facts about all this. The launching of Explorer I, the first American satellite, on January 31, 1958, did not quiet the outcry.

Russia's success with Sputnik launched efforts in America to enlarge defense spending, to offer NATO allies intermediate-range ballistic missiles (IRBMs) pending development of long-range intercontinental ballistic missiles (ICBMs), to set up a new agency to coordinate space efforts, and to establish a crash program in science education. The "sputnik syndrome," compounded by a sharp recession through the winter of 1957–1958, loosened the purse strings of economy-minded congressmen, who added to the new budget more than Eisenhower wanted for both defense and domestic programs. During 1958 Britain, Italy, and Turkey accepted American Thor and Jupiter missiles on their territory. In July 1958 Congress created the National Aeronautics and Space Agency (NASA) to coordinate research and development in the field. Before the end of the year NASA had a program to put a manned craft in orbit, but the first manned flight, by Commander Alan B. Shepard, Jr., did not take place until May 5, 1961. Finally, in September 1958 Congress enacted the National Defense Education Act, which authorized federal grants especially for training in mathematics, science, and modern languages, as well as for student loans and fellowships.

CORRUPT PRACTICES During the first two years of Eisenhower's second term, public confidence in his performance, as registered by opinion polls, dropped sharply from 79 percent to 49 percent. Emotional issues such as civil rights and defense policy had compounded his troubles. The president's image was further tarnished when congressional investigations revealed that the administration, which had promised to clean up "the mess in Washington," was itself touched by scandals, one of which involved Sherman Adams, the White House "chief of staff." Adams, it seemed, had done little more than open some doors at the Securities and Exchange Commission and the Federal Trade Commission with introductions for Boston industrialist Bernard Goldfine, but he had taken gifts of a fur coat and an Oriental rug from Goldfine. In September 1958 the president reluctantly accepted Adams's resignation. Republicans also faced the growing opposition of farmers, angry with cuts in price supports, and labor, angry because many Republicans had made "right-to-work" (or open-shop) laws a campaign issue in 1958. The Democrats came out of the midterm elections with nearly two-to-one majorities in Congress: 282 to 154 in the House, 64 to 34 in the Senate.

Eisenhower would be the first president to face three successive Congresses controlled by the opposition party. One consequence was that the president could manage few new departures in domestic policy. The most important legislation of the last two years in the Eisenhower presidency were the Landrum-Griffin Labor-Management Act of 1959, the Civil Rights Act of 1960, and the admission of the first states not contiguous to the continental forty-eight. Alaska became the forty-ninth state on January 3, 1959, and Hawaii the fiftieth on August 21, 1959.

The Landrum-Griffin Act of September 14, 1959, aimed at controlling union corruption, was actually a compromise between the views of its House sponsors and the somewhat less stringent views of Sen. John F. Kennedy and some of his colleagues. It reflected, nevertheless, popular feeling against racketeering and monopolistic practices in unions, especially the Teamsters, which had been revealed by an extensive Senate probe directed by John L. McClellan of Arkansas. The act safeguarded democratic procedures, penalized the misuse of union funds and coercion of members, and excluded from office persons convicted of certain crimes. The act also strengthened restrictions on secondary boycotts and blackmail picketing. Most of its provisions were directed against unfair union practices, but the act also monitored employer payments to union officers or labor-management consultants.

FESTERING PROBLEMS ABROAD   Once the Suez and Hungary crises faded from the front pages, Eisenhower enjoyed eighteen months of smooth sailing in foreign affairs. A brief flurry occurred in May 1958 over hostile demonstrations in Peru and Venezuela against Vice-President Nixon, who was on a goodwill tour of eight Latin American countries. Then in July 1958 the Middle East flared up again. By this time the president had secured from Congress authority for what came to be called the Eisenhower Doctrine, which promised to extend economic and military aid to Middle East nations, and to use armed forces if necessary to assist any such nation against armed aggression from any Communist country.

President Nasser of Egypt meanwhile had emerged from the Suez crisis with heightened prestige, and in February 1958 created the United Arab Republic (UAR) by merger (a short-lived one) with Syria. Then on July 14 a leftist coup in Iraq, supposedly inspired by Nasser and the Russians, threw out the pro-Western government and killed King Faisal, the crown prince, and the premier. In Lebanon, already unsettled by internal conflict, President Camille Chamoun appealed to the United States for support against a similar fate. Eisenhower immediately ordered 5,000 marines into Lebanon on July 15, where they limited themselves to the capital, Beirut, and its airfield. He proposed to go no farther because, he said later, if the government could not hold out with such protection, "I felt we were backing up a government with so little popular support that we probably should not be there." British forces meanwhile went into Jordan at the request of King Hussein. Once the situation stabilized, and the Lebanese factions reached a compromise, American forces (up to 15,000 at one point) withdrew in October.

East Asia heated up again when, on August 23, 1958, Red China renewed its bombardment of the Nationalists on Quemoy and Matsu. In September the American Seventh Fleet began to escort Nationalist convoys, but stopped short of entering Chinese territorial waters. To abandon the islands, President Eisenhower said, would amount to a "Western Pacific 'Munich.'" But on October 1 he suggested that a cease-fire would provide "an opportunity to negotiate in good faith." Red China ordered such a cease-fire on October 6, and on October 25, which happened to be the day the last American forces left Lebanon, said that it would reserve the right to bombard the islands on alternate days. With that strange stipulation the worst of the crisis passed, but the problem continued to fester.

The problem of Berlin festered too; Premier Khrushchev called it a bone in his throat. West Berlin provided a "showplace" of Western democracy and prosperity, a listening post for Western intelligence, and a funnel through which news and propaganda from the West penetrated what Winston Churchill called "the iron curtain." Although East Germany had sealed its western frontiers, refugees could still pass from East to West

Berlin. On November 10, 1958, at a Soviet-Polish friendship rally in Moscow, Khrushchev threatened to transfer Soviet obligations in the occupation to East Germany. After the deadline he set, May 27, 1959, Western occupation authorities would have to deal with the East German government, in effect recognizing it, or face the possibility of another blockade.

But Eisenhower refused to budge from his position on Berlin. At the same time he refused to engage in saber-rattling or even to cancel existing plans to reduce the size of the army. As Stephen Ambrose, an Eisenhower biographer, wrote: "He thought the greatest danger in the Berlin crisis was that the Russians would frighten the United States into an arms race that would bankrupt the country." Khrushchev, it turned out, was no more eager for confrontation than Eisenhower. In talks with British Prime Minister Harold Macmillan, he suggested that the main thing was to begin discussions of the Berlin issue, and not the May 27 deadline. Macmillan in turn won Eisenhower's consent to a meeting of the Big Four foreign ministers.

There was little hope of resolving different views on Berlin and German reunification, but the talks distracted attention from Khrushchev's deadline of May 27: it passed almost unnoticed. In September, after the Big Four talks had adjourned, Premier Khrushchev paid a visit to the United States, going to New York, Washington, Los Angeles, San Francisco, and Iowa, and dropping in on Eisenhower at Camp David. In talks there Khrushchev endorsed "peaceful coexistence," and Eisenhower admitted that the Berlin situation was "abnormal." They agreed that the time was ripe for a summit meeting in the spring.

THE U-2 SUMMIT   The summit meeting, however, blew up in Eisenhower's face. On May 1, 1960, near Sverdlovsk, east of the Urals, a Soviet rocket brought down an American U-2 spy plane. Such planes had been flying missions over Russia for three and a half years. Khrushchev played up the news for domestic consumption to keep in good standing with Soviet "hard-liners." He set out to entrap Eisenhower and succeeded, by announcing first only that the plane had been shot down. When the State Department insisted that there had been no attempt to violate Soviet airspace, Khrushchev then announced that the Soviets had pilot Francis Gary Powers, "alive and kicking," and his pictures of military installations. On May 11 Eisenhower finally took personal responsibility—an unprecedented action for a head of state—and justified the action on grounds of national security. "No one wants another Pearl Harbor," he said. In Paris, five days later, Khrushchev withdrew an invitation for Eisenhower to visit the USSR and called on the president to repudiate the U-2 flights and "pass severe judgment on those responsible." When Eisenhower refused, Khrushchev left the meeting.

Eisenhower's frustration in Paris was magnified by several foreign-policy setbacks he encountered as his term drew to a close. Another came a month afterward when he set out in June on a tour to Formosa, the Philippines, and Japan. Japan had just agreed to a new military treaty which extended the American right to station armed forces in Japan indefinitely, subject to renunciation on one-year's notice. Although the treaty removed all remnants of Japan's status as an occupied country, neutralists and pacifists—together with a small number of Communists—argued that the treaty would draw Japan into the Cold War. Others complained that the treaty did not return the Ryukyu and Bonin Islands to Japanese administration. Massive anti-American riots and demonstrations reached such a level that on June 16 Premier Nobusuke Kishi notified Eisenhower in Manila that the Japanese government could not guarantee his safety. He had no choice but to fly back home. Premier Kishi then resigned.

CASTRO'S CUBA But the greatest thorn in Eisenhower's side was the Cuban regime of Fidel Castro, which came to power on January 1, 1959, after three years of guerrilla warfare against the dictator Fulgencio Batista. In their struggle against Batista, Castro's forces had the support of many Americans who hoped for a new day of democratic government in Cuba. When American television picked up trials and executions conducted by the victorious Castro, such hopes were dashed. Staged like a Roman holiday before crowds of howling spectators, the trials vented anger against Batista's officials and police, but offered little in the

Cuban Premier Fidel Castro. [Magnum Photos]

way of legal procedure or proof. Castro, moreover, planned a social revolution and opposed the widespread foreign control of the Cuban economy. When he began programs of land reform and nationalization of foreign-owned property, relations worsened. Some observers believed, however, that by rejecting Castro's requests for loans and other help the American government lost a chance to influence the direction of the revolution, and by acting on the assumption that Communists already had the upper hand in his movement the administration may have ensured that fact.

Castro, on the other hand, showed little reluctance to accept the Communist embrace. In February 1960 he entered a trade agreement to swap Cuban sugar for Soviet oil and machinery. In July, after Cuba had seized three British-American oil refineries which refused to process Soviet oil, Eisenhower cut sharply the quota for Cuban sugar imports. Premier Khrushchev in response warned that any military intervention in Cuba would encounter Russian rockets. In October 1960 the United States suspended imports of Cuban sugar and embargoed most shipments to Cuba. One of Eisenhower's last acts as president was to suspend diplomatic relations with Cuba on January 3, 1961. In the hope of creating "some kind of non-dictatorial 'third force,' neither Castroite nor Batistiano," as Eisenhower put it, the president authorized the CIA to begin training a force of Cuban refugees (some of them former Castro stalwarts) for a new revolution. But the final decision on its use would rest with the next president, John F. Kennedy.

ASSESSING THE EISENHOWER YEARS

The Eisenhower years have not drawn much acclaim from journalists and historians. One journalist called Ike's administration "the time of the great postponement," during which the president "lived off the accumulated wisdom, the accumulated prestige, and the accumulated military strength of his predecessors" and left domestic and foreign policies "about where he found them in 1953." Yet even these critics granted that Eisenhower had succeeded in ending the war in Korea and settling the dust raised by McCarthy. But if he had failed to end the Cold War and in fact had institutionalized it as a global confrontation, he sensed the limits of American power and kept its application to low-risk situations. If he took few initiatives in addressing the social problems that would erupt in the 1960s, he left the major innovations of the New Deal in place and thereby legitimized them. If he tolerated unemployment of as much as 7 percent at times, he kept inflation to an average rate of 1.6 percent during his terms. His farewell address to the American people, delivered on radio and television three days before he left office, showed his remarkable foresight in his own area of special expertise, the military.

Like Washington, Eisenhower couched his wisdom largely in the form of warnings: that America's "leadership and prestige depend, not merely upon our unmatched material strength, but on how we use our power in the interests of world peace and human betterment"; that the temptation to find easy answers should take into account "the need to maintain balance in and among national problems"; and above all that Americans "must avoid the impulse to live only for today, plundering, for our own ease and convenience, the precious resources of tomorrow."

As a soldier, Eisenhower highlighted perhaps better than anyone else could have the dangers of a military establishment in a time of peace. "This conjunction of an immense military establishment and a large arms industry is new in the American experience," he said. "In the councils of government we must guard against the acquisition of unwarranted influence, whether sought or unsought, by the military-industrial complex. The potential for the disastrous rise of misplaced power exists and will persist." With the new importance of technology, "a government contract becomes virtually a substitute for intellectual curiosity" in directing university research. This new circumstance created the dual danger "of domination of the nation's scholars by Federal employment," and the shaping of policy by "a scientific-technological elite."

His great disappointment as he lay down his responsibilities, Eisenhower said, was his inability to affirm "that a lasting peace is in sight," only that "war has been avoided." But he prayed "that, in the goodness of time, all peoples will come to live together in a peace guaranteed by the binding force of mutual respect and love."

FURTHER READING

Two scholars admirably document the political and cultural trends of the 1950s—William E. Leuchtenberg in *A Troubled Feast: American Society since 1945* (1979)° and Godfrey Hodgson in *America in Our Time: From World War II to Nixon, What Happened and Why* (1976).°

Scholarship on Eisenhower is extensive. The best overview of the

°These books are available in paperback editions.

period is Charles A. Alexander's *Holding the Line: The Eisenhower Era, 1951–1961* (1975). Other studies include Herbert S. Parmet's *Eisenhower and the American Crusade* (1972), Peter Lyon's *Eisenhower: Portrait of a Hero* (1974), James L. Sundquist's *Politics and Policy: The Eisenhower, Kennedy, and Johnson Years* (1968), Arthur Larsen's *Eisenhower: The Person Nobody Knew* (1968), and Blanche Wiesen's *The Declassified Eisenhower: A Divided Legacy* (1981). For the manner in which Eisenhower conducted foreign policy, see in particular Robert A. Divine's *Eisenhower and the Cold War* (1981) and Richard A. Aliano's *American Defense Policy from Eisenhower to Kennedy* (1975).

The conservatism of the 1950s is documented best in studies of Congress and its members. A good start is James T. Patterson's *Mr. Republican: A Biography of Robert A. Taft* (1975). Also helpful are Gary W. Reichard's *The Reaffirmation of Republicanism: Eisenhower and the Eighty-third Congress* (1975) and George B. Nash's *The Conservative Intellectual Movement in America: Since 1945* (1976).° How the liberals fared in the 1950s is included in John Bartlow Martin's *The Life of Adlai E. Stevenson* (2 vols.; 1976–1977), which is also the best work on Eisenhower's two-time opponent. Also see Joseph B. Gorman's *Kefauver: A Political Biography* (1971).

Among the numerous titles on the Cold War listed in Chapter 31, several cover the Eisenhower years, including John L. Gaddis's *Strategies of Containment: A Critical Appraisal of Postwar American National Security Policy* (1982) and Norman A. Graebner's *The Age of Global Power: The United States since 1938* (1979). The role played by the secretary of state is analyzed in Townsend Hoopes's *The Devil and John Foster Dulles* (1973) and Louis Gerson's *John Foster Dulles* (1973).

Specific Eisenhower decisions also have received scrutiny. Chester Cooper's *The Lion's Last Roar: Suez, 1956* (1978), and Hugh Thomas's *Suez* (1967) cover Eisenhower's handling of the crisis. For the buildup of American involvement in Indochina, consult James P. Harrison's *The Endless War: Fifty Years of Struggle in Vietnam* (1982), Melvin Gurov's *The First Vietnamese Crisis* (1967), and George C. Herring's *America's Longest War: The United States and Vietnam, 1950–1975* (1979).° For negotiations on use of the atomic bomb, see Robert A. Divine's *Blowing in the Wind: The Nuclear Test Ban Debate, 1954–1960* (1978). How the Eisenhower Doctrine came to be implemented is traced in Stephen Ambrose's *Rise to Globalism: American Foreign Policy, 1938–1980* (1981).° For intelligence activities during the Eisenhower administration, consult Harry Rositzke's *The CIA's Secret Operations: Espionage, Counterespionage, and Covert Action* (1977) and Richard H. Immerman's *The Central Intelligence Agency in Guatemala* (1982).

Two introductions to the impact wrought by the Warren Supreme Court during the 1950s are Alexander Bickel's *The Supreme Court and the Idea of Progress* (1970)° and Paul Murphy's *The Constitution in Crisis Times* (1972).° Also helpful are Archibald Cox's *The Warren Court: Constitutional Decision as an Instrument of Reform* (1968)° and Phillip B. Kurland's *Politics, the Constitution, and the Warren Court* (1970). Biographical studies of the chief justice include John D. Weaver's *Warren* (1967), Leo Katcher's *Earl Warren* (1967), and G. Edward White's *Earl Warren: A Public Life* (1982). A masterful study of the important Warren Court decision on school desegregation is Richard Kluger's *Simple Justice: The History of Brown v. Board of Education and Black America's Struggle for Equality* (1975).°

A good follow-up to the Kluger work is Benjamin Muse's *Ten Years of Prelude: The Story of Integration since the Supreme Court's 1954 Decision* (1964). Other surveys of the era include John Hope Franklin's *From Slavery to Freedom: A History of Negro Americans* (1974),° Charles F. Kellogg's *NAACP* (1967), and Harvard Sitkoff's *A New Deal for Blacks: The Emergence of Civil Rights as a National Issue* (1978). For the story from Montgomery, see David L. Lewis's *King: A Critical Biography* (1970)° and Stephen B. Oates's *Let the Trumpet Sound: The Life of Martin Luther King, Jr.* (1982).° William H. Chafe's *Civilities and Civil Rights: Greensboro, North Carolina, and the Black Struggle for Freedom* (1980)° examines how one community dragged its feet on the Brown implementation order. J. B. Martin's *The Deep South Says Never* (1957) and Anthony Lewis's *Portrait of a Decade: The Second American Revolution* (1964) look at massive resistance on a regional level.

In addition to the surveys by Leuchtenberg and Hodgson cited above, other scholars have examined 1950s culture and society. John Kenneth Galbraith's *The Affluent Society* (1958)° and *The New Industrial State* (1971)° are studies of the influence exerted by corporate managers in shaping American policies and values. How the corporate ethic was itself shaped by overseas conditions is treated in Mira Wilkin's *The Maturing of Multinational Enterprise: American Business Abroad from 1914 to 1970* (1974). For religion, consult W. L. Miller's *Piety along the Potomac: Notes on Politics and Morals in the Fifties* (1964). For the suburban society, the best case study is Zane L. Miller's *Suburb: Neighborhood and Community in Forest Park, Ohio, 1935–1976* (1981). Bruce Cook's *The Beat Generation* (1971) examines the roots of the youth rebellion which surfaced after 1960. Views of women in the 1950s can be found in Carl N. Degler's *At Odds: Women and the Family in America from the Revolution to the Present* (1980)° and Sheila M. Rothman's *Woman's Proper Place: A History of Changing Ideas and Practices, 1870 to the Present* (1978).

33

INTO THE MAELSTROM:
THE SIXTIES

Eisenhower's misgiving about the military-industrial complex sounded a warning that countered the complacency and buoyant optimism of the 1950s. By the end of that decade a chorus of voices was deploring the triumph of materialistic values that arrived with what John Kenneth Galbraith had labeled "the affluent society." If we are so rich, social critics wondered, why do we feel so poor? "With the supermarket as our temple and the singing commercial as our litany," asked Adlai Stevenson, "are we likely to fire the world with an irresistible vision of America's exalted purposes and inspiring way of life?"

Eisenhower greeted these lamentations in the traditional way: he named a presidential commission to study the matter. *Goals for Americans: A Report of the President's Commission on National Goals* (1960) appeared just as Eisenhower was leaving office. The commission saw no need to worry. The gross national product had more than doubled since the end of the war and there was no reason to doubt its continued growth. If government investment in education kept pace with the economy, one could expect a new cadre of professionals—doctors, economists, social workers—to solve the problems that came with prosperity. The only real danger came from abroad, in the form of Communist aggression and subversion. The report contrasted the Communist ideal of the state with the American ideal of the individual. How a nation of 180 million individuals could achieve a sense of collective purpose while still pursuing their unbridled self-interest was, appropriately, a matter best left to the individuals themselves.

But the members of the commission were better historians than prophets. As the complacent 1950s yielded to another decade, few if any people foresaw the collapse of consensus, the hopes dashed, the ironic turns of fortune ahead. An alert prophet might have found a sign in an unlikely quarter—the Woolworth lunch counter in Greensboro, North Carolina, where just one month into the 1960s, on February 1, four black freshmen from a nearby college sat down and asked for coffee. It took them nearly six months to get service, but by then they had set in motion the completion of a Second Reconstruction and had introduced two salient styles of the 1960s: civil disobedience and the youth rebellion, two protean phenomena that would assume many different shapes before the decade ended.

DEMOGRAPHIC AND ECONOMIC TRENDS

"A NEW GENERATION" John Fitzgerald Kennedy's election to the presidency in 1960 was symbolic in several ways. Most obviously, Kennedy was young and visibly vigorous, at forty-three the youngest person ever elected president. Eisenhower at seventy was then the oldest man ever to occupy the White House. When Kennedy told the inaugural crowd that "the torch has been passed to a new generation of Americans," he was on the mark in both a political and a demographic sense.

The much-mentioned "generation gap" that came to popular attention in the 1960s had a solid foundation in population statistics. Between 1945 and 1960 America's total population increased by almost 40 million. In the 1950s alone the population went up by 28 million, an 18.5 percent increase that was the largest since the peak years of immigration in the first decade of the twentieth century. Much of America's social history since the 1940s has been the story of the "baby boom" generation and its progress through life. The population explosion created a massive demand for family housing in the 1950s and thereby spurred the remarkable growth of suburbs, and the highways and cars required for transport to them. By the 1960s the population explosion had generated a demand for new high schools and colleges, a rise in auto accidents and "juvenile delinquency," and toward the end of the decade, a glutted job market and a high rate of unemployment among people in their teens and twenties. The youth culture that attracted so much attention in the 1960s was not the figment of some Madison Avenue imagination, although advertisers responded quickly to the rapidly growing youth "market." America's population was dominated by a generation that was accustomed to affluence, nurtured on the homogenizing effects of television, unexposed to depression or major wartime dislocations, aware of the Cold War primarily as a battle of words and gestures without immediate consequences for them, and secure in the belief that nuclear annihilation was a remote and unreal possibility.

Meanwhile the older generation fell roughly into two groups. Americans aged fifty or over, who had been born well before the depression, constituted a disproportionately large group, reflecting the relatively high birth rates of the 1910s. This group created a demand for retirement condominiums in Florida and Arizona, more geriatric wards and medical facilities, and legislation to benefit "senior citizens." Another large age cohort born in the 1920s was reaching age forty. The generation born during the depression, however, was somewhat smaller, reflecting the decline in births during that time of economic distress. Mostly in their thirties during the 1960s, this group, because of their small numbers, experienced less competition for executive and professional jobs. Born and raised with memories of the Great Depression and World War II, and finding in the 1960s easy access to prosperity and enhanced status, this group had few reasons to complain about the justice of "the system." As the products of the postwar "baby boom" passed through high school and college, it was this older generation, so different in size and experience, that held the lucrative jobs which younger Americans coveted. Here was one powerful reason for the rallying cry of the young: "Never trust anyone over thirty."

The "baby boom" of the postwar decades made a mockery of most earlier predictions about the ultimate size of the United States' population. Earlier forecasters had tended to expect a leveling-off at about 150 million in 1970. Instead the population reached 205 million that year and was still growing. A dramatic slowing of the upward trend occurred during the 1960s when, despite an increase of 24 million people, the percentage increase was only 13.3, the lowest in American history except for the depression. In fact the birth rate in 1968 reached the lowest level ever recorded in America, 17.5 births per 1000 population. The rate rose slightly above that the next two years, then fell even lower on through the 1970s.

As the average size of families declined, so did the demand for new housing, appliances, and durable goods. Reliable and handy contraceptives, especially "the pill," allowed prospective parents to opt for a second car or a better home rather than another child, and permitted working wives to choose a career over extended childrearing. The dip in the birth rate also made the notion of "zero population growth," a goal of liberal reformers from the mid-1960s on, seem within reach by the middle of the next century.

CITIES AND SUBURBS   Almost the entire population increase of the 1950s and 1960s (97 percent) was an urban phenomenon. The flight from the farm accelerated in the postwar years: 20 million Americans left the land for the city between 1940 and 1970. The old America of small towns and family farms, Norman Rockwell's vision of picket fences and cracker-barrel conversations in the general store, became more quaintly nostalgic with each passing year. In 1870 about three-fourths of the American people were classified as rural residents; exactly one century later the residential patterns had reversed themselves and three-fourths of the population lived in towns and cities. Much of the urban population growth occurred in the South, the Southwest, and the West, in an arc that stretched from the Carolinas down through Texas and into California, diverse states that by the 1970s were being lumped together into the "Sunbelt." The surging cities of the old Spanish borderlands included Atlanta, Miami, Dallas, Houston, San Antonio, Phoenix, and Los Angeles. But the Northeast remained the most densely populated area; by the early 1960s, 20 percent of the total population lived in the land corridor that stretched from Boston to Norfolk, Virginia.

While more concentrated in cities, Americans were simultaneously spreading out within metropolitan areas. In 1950 the Census Bureau redefined the term "urban" to include suburbs as well as central cities. In fact the real postwar population growth was suburban rather than urban. In the 1960s eight of the ten largest cities in the United States actually lost population, yet all of the metropolitan areas surrounding these cities (except for one, Pittsburgh) grew in size. By 1970 more Americans lived in suburbs (76 million) than central cities (64 million). The most striking example of urban sprawl occurred in southern California, where Los Angeles became a centerless collection of freeways and fast-food restaurants that spread from Santa Barbara to the Mexican border, over 200 miles to the south. At the other end of the continent, Manhattan actually lost population in the 1960s and sections of the Bronx became rat-infested wastelands that resembled the bombed-out cities of Europe after World War II.

Sheer statistics cannot convey the magnitude of the social problems that the new urban demography had created by the 1960s. The suburbs had become rings of affluence around cores of poverty. In such suburbs as Darien, Connecticut, Shaker

Herblock's cartoon Vicious Circle *captures the plight of the cities in the 1960s and 1970s. [Herblock in the* Washington Post*, March 23, 1969]*

Heights, Ohio, and Kenilworth, Illinois, mothers drove children to new schools and shopping malls in wood-paneled station wagons. Meanwhile in the center cities of New York, Cleveland, and Chicago, trash piled up on the sidewalks and "white flight" left black and Puerto Rican youth mired in what the anthropologist Oscar Lewis called "the culture of poverty." In 1965, when a massive power failure in the Northeast plunged New York City into darkness for one evening, some observers took it as evidence that Gotham was dead and beyond any hope of recovery. But nine months later, hospitals reported a flood of new births, thereby demonstrating that the darkness had inspired fresh feats of human communication and adaptation. Such signs of hope, however, were but minor incidents in the larger pattern of urban segregation. America's urban geography had become a series of concentric circles, with the central cities bull's-eyes of festering racial and economic problems.

THE POSTWAR ECONOMY   The dominant theme in the story of the American economy during the postwar years was growth, unprecedented rates of sustained growth that produced a cornucopia of goods and services and the highest standard of living ever experienced by so many people in the history of the planet. The gross national product went from a low of $58 billion in 1932 to

$211.9 billion in 1945. This growth was primarily a result of wartime mobilization, but in the next twenty-five years the growth continued without the stimulus of all-out war, nearly doubling by 1960 to $503.7 billion and reaching the verge of $1 trillion by 1970. Between 1932 to 1970 America's per capita income rose almost tenfold, from $401 to $3,945. By 1970 the gap between living standards in the United States and the rest of the world had become a chasm: with 6 percent of the world's population, Americans produced and consumed two-thirds of the world's goods.

Some older Americans who remembered the Great Depression warned that the upward cycle that began in 1897 had come to disaster in 1929. Perhaps, they warned, the economic growth from 1945 to 1970 would end the same way. But the federal government now assumed the responsibility for managing or "fine-tuning" the economy during times of potential recession or depression. The timely manipulation of fiscal and monetary policies to stimulate economic growth in sluggish phases had proven successful on several occasions in the late 1940s and throughout the 1950s. And when President John Kennedy increased government spending and cut taxes in 1963, the "Eisenhower recession" ended and the economy took off on a growth spurt that lasted through the 1960s. Secretary of Labor W. Willard Wirtz later called it "the ultimate triumph of the spirit of John Maynard Keynes over the stubborn shade of Adam Smith."

But the incredible wealth generated by the postwar expansion was not filtering evenly throughout the society. True, the unrelenting growth of the economy improved the material well-being of all sectors of the society. This was what Kennedy meant when he observed that "a rising tide raises all boats." Nevertheless, in 1960 the top 5 percent of the population received about 20 percent of the wealth while the bottom 20 percent received only 5 percent. The American social structure was less like a pyramid than a diamond. The great mass of citizens, about half the population, were members of that amorphous American entity called "the middle class," which was the chief beneficiary of the postwar boom. In 1947 only 8.9 percent of American families had an annual income of $10,000 or more. By 1968, even after allowing for inflation, 36.9 percent were in that category. By 1970 there were five times as many Americans in college as in 1940; about four times as many Americans owned cars.

A major cause of the Great Depression had been a distribution of income so unbalanced in favor of the wealthy that levels of consumption were inadequate to keep the economy moving. The apparently insatiable appetite of middle-class Americans who came of age in the 1950s and 1960s virtually guaranteed that underconsumption would not afflict the economy. Moreover, income had become more evenly spread during and immediately after World War II. But between 1950 and 1970 the distribution of income changed hardly at all. During that time the people at the bottom of American society had their standard of living raised relative to the rest of the world, but their position relative to the middle class did not improve at all: the bottom 20 percent of the population continued to claim only 5 percent of the wealth throughout the administrations of Eisenhower, Kennedy, and Johnson. In 1968 an estimated 25 million Americans still lived below the "poverty line," even though another 14 million had moved above the line since Kennedy's election. Pockets of poverty, often in the central cities and in such rural areas as Appalachia, persisted despite national prosperity. And the increasingly gaudy affluence of middle-class life—"two cars in the garage, a television in each room, a kitchen full of modern appliances and a mind empty of inspiration" was how one cynic put it—presented poor Americans with a vision of the good life that kept receding into the middle distance.

THE NEW FRONTIER

KENNEDY VS. NIXON   The presidential election of 1960 pitted two candidates who seemed to symbolize the unadventurous politics of the 1950s. Neither Richard M. Nixon nor John F. Kennedy seemed an embodiment of national purpose. Though better known than Kennedy because of his eight years as vice-president, famous for his debate with Soviet Premier Nikita Khrushchev in the exhibit of an American kitchen in Moscow, Nixon had also developed the reputation of a cunning chameleon, the "Tricky Dick" who concealed his duplicity behind a series of masks. "Nixon doesn't know who he is," Kennedy told an aide, "and so each time he makes a speech he has to decide which Nixon he is, and that will be very exhausting."

Kennedy himself seemed equally calculating. Despite an abundance of assets, including a record of heroism in the Pacific, an attractive young wife, a Harvard education, a large and rich family, and an engaging wit, Kennedy's record in the Senate was undistinguished. Author of a Pulitzer Prize–winning study of political leaders who "made the tough decisions" entitled *Profiles in Courage* (1956), Kennedy, said the Washington pundits, had shown more profile than courage during the McCarthy years and had a weak record on civil rights. Eric Sevareid, a television commentator who covered the campaign, likened both candidates to the kind of banal young men he remembered prancing about fraternity rows in college "thinking the proper thoughts, cultivating the proper people. I always sensed that they would end up running the big companies in town," said Sevareid, "but I'm damned if I ever thought one of them would end up running the country."

During his campaign for the Democratic nomination Kennedy had shown that he had the energy to match his ambition. As the first Catholic to run for the presidency since Al Smith, Kennedy realized that he had to dispel the impression that his religion was a major political liability. "If the nomination ever goes into a back room," he told a friend, "my name will never emerge." By the time of the Los Angeles convention in August he had traveled over 65,000 miles, visited 25 states, and made over 350 speeches. Hubert Humphrey, the liberal senator from Minnesota, was knocked out of the race in the West Virginia primary. Stuart Symington, the early favorite, conceded that Kennedy had shown "just a little more courage, stamina, wisdom and character than the rest of us." In his acceptance speech Kennedy found the rhetoric that would stamp the rest of his campaign and his presidency: "We stand today on the edge of a New Frontier—the frontier of unknown opportunities and perils—a frontier of unfulfilled hopes and threats."

Two events shaped the campaign that fall. First, in a speech before the Houston Ministerial Association on September 12, Kennedy confronted the question of his Catholicism directly. In America, he told the Protestant clergy, "the separation of church and state is absolute" and "no Catholic prelate would tell the President—should he be a Catholic—how to act and no Protestant minister should tell his parishioners for whom to vote." The religious question thereafter drew little public attention; Kennedy had neutralized it. Second, Nixon violated one of the cardinal rules of politics when he agreed to debate his less known opponent on television. In the first of four debates a national audience of 70 million saw Nixon, still weak from a recent illness, looking haggard and uneasy before the camera. Kennedy, on the other hand, displayed a poise that made him seem equal, if not superior, in his fitness for the office. Kennedy immediately shot up in the polls and was never headed. Reporters discovered that he had "charisma" and noted the bobby-soxers who greeted his arrival at campaign stops with what Theodore White called "the ups and downs of a thoroughly sexy oscillation." In the words of a bemused southern senator, Kennedy combined "the best qualities of Elvis Presley and Franklin D. Roosevelt."

The fourth debate, October 21, 1960. Kennedy's forthrightness impressed viewers and voters. [United Press International]

When the votes were counted Kennedy and his running-mate, Lyndon B. Johnson of Texas, had won the closest presidential election since 1888. Kennedy's winning margin was only 118,574 votes out of the 68 million cast. His wide margin in the electoral vote, 303 to 219, belied the paper-thin margin in several key states, especially Illinois, where Mayor Richard Daley's Democratic machine appeared to have lived up to its legendary campaign motto: "In Chicago we tell our people to vote early and to vote often." Nixon had in fact carried more states than Kennedy, sweeping most of the West, and holding four of the six southern states Eisenhower had carried in 1956. Kennedy's majority was built out of victories in southern New England, the populous Middle Atlantic states, and key states in the South where black voters had provided the crucial margin of victory.

THE NEW ADMINISTRATION   Kennedy's cabinet appointments put an accent on youth and "Eastern Establishment" figures. Adlai Stevenson was favored by liberal democrats for secretary of state, but Kennedy chose Dean Rusk, a career diplomat who then headed the Rockefeller Foundation. Stevenson got the relatively minor post of ambassador to the United Nations. Robert S. McNamara, one of the "whiz kids" who had reorganized the Ford Motor Company with his "systems analysis" techniques, was asked to bring his managerial magic to bear on the Department of Defense. C. Douglas Dillon, a banker and a Republican, was made secretary of the treasury in an effort to assure conservative businessmen. When critics attacked the appointment of Kennedy's thirty-five-year-old brother Robert as attorney-general, the president quipped, "I don't see what's wrong with giving Bobby a little experience before he goes into law practice."

McGeorge Bundy, whom Kennedy called "the second smartest man I know," was made special assistant for national security affairs, lending additional credence to the impression that foreign policy would remain under tight White House control. John Kenneth Galbraith recommended Walter Heller, an outspoken advocate of Keynesian policies, as chairman of the Council of Economic Advisors. Theodore Sorenson, the former campaign head, became special counsel and chief speechwriter. House Speaker Rayburn expressed to Lyndon Johnson a wry "wish just one of them had run for sheriff once."

The inaugural ceremonies set the tone of elegance and youthful vigor that would come to be called the "Kennedy style." The bracing and glittering atmosphere of snow-clad Washington seemed to symbolize fresh promise. After Robert Frost paid tribute to the administration in verse, Kennedy dazzled listeners with epigrammatic eloquence that recalled the speeches of Lincoln and Jefferson. "Let the word go forth from this time and place," he proclaimed, "Let every nation know, whether it wishes us well or ill, that we shall pay any price, bear any burden, meet any hardship, support any friend, oppose any foe, to assure the survival and success of liberty. And so, my fellow Americans:

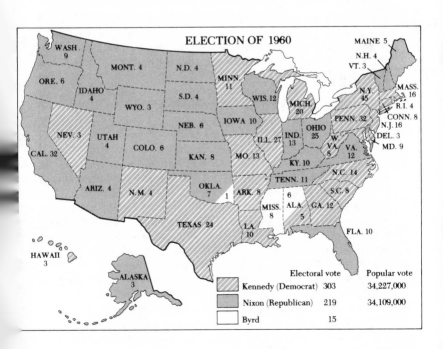

ELECTION OF 1960

	Electoral vote	Popular vote
Kennedy (Democrat)	303	34,227,000
Nixon (Republican)	219	34,109,000
Byrd	15	

Kennedy and wife Jacqueline at the inauguration, January 20, 1961. [Paul Schutzer, Life magazine, © 1961 Time Inc.]

ask not what your country can do for you—ask what you can do for your country." Spines tingled at the time; Kennedy, the journalist I. F. Stone wrote, was the first of all the presidents to be a Prince Charming. But years later, especially after the disastrous involvement in Vietnam, the speech would appear less a vibrant new message than a call to arms reminiscent of the anti-Communist tirades of John Foster Dulles.

THE KENNEDY RECORD Historical evaluation of Kennedy's brief presidency, like reaction to his inaugural address, has oscillated widely in the past two decades between mindless celebration and bitter denunciation; it is only now beginning to settle into a more balanced assessment. It is clear, for example, that Kennedy's domestic record was mixed. Despite a few dramatic gestures of support toward civil rights leaders, he never grasped the significance of the most widespread reform movement of the decade. The Congress, although overwhelmingly Democratic, remained in the grip of a conservative coalition that blocked Kennedy's effort to increase federal aid to education, provide health insurance for the aged, and create a new Department of Urban Affairs to address the problems of the central cities. The Senate killed his initiatives in behalf of unemployed youth, migrant workers, and mass transit. When in January 1963 Kennedy finally came around to the advice of his Keynesian advisors and submitted a drastic tax cut of $13.6 billion, Congress blocked that as well. Four days before his death the *Congressional Quarterly* calculated that Kennedy had won acceptance for only one-third of his legislative program.

Administration proposals, nevertheless, did win some notable victories in Congress. Those involving defense and foreign policy generally won favor; indeed defense appropriations exceeded administration requests. On foreign aid there were some cuts, but Congress readily approved the proposals for a Development Loan Fund to help underdeveloped countries, broad "Alliance for Progress" programs to help Latin America, membership in the Organization for Economic Cooperation and Development (OECD) in which Canada and eighteen western European countries collaborated on improving world trade and helping underdeveloped nations, and the celebrated Peace Corps, created in March 1961 to supply volunteers for educational and technical services abroad. Kennedy's biggest legislative accomplishment in any field probably was the Trade Expansion Act of 1962, which after the "Kennedy Round" of negotiations in 1964–1967 eventually led to tariff cuts averaging 35 percent between the United States and the European Common Market.

In the field of domestic social legislation the administration did score a few legislative victories, most of them during this first year, 1961. They included a new Housing Act which afforded nearly $5 billion for urban renewal over four years, a raise in the minimum wage from $1 to $1.25 and its extension to more than 3 million additional workers, the Area Redevelopment Act of May 1961 which provided nearly $400 million in loans and grants to "distressed areas," an increase in Social Security benefits, and additional funds for sewage treatment plants. Kennedy also won support for an accelerated program to reach the moon before the end of the decade. Upon hearing that Kennedy wanted to beat the Russians there, Eisenhower shook his head: "Anybody who would spend $40 billion on a race to the moon for national prestige is nuts."

FOREIGN FRONTIERS

EARLY SETBACKS   Kennedy's record in foreign affairs was also mixed, though more spectacularly so. He had made the existence of a "missile gap" a major part of his campaign. Upon taking office he discovered that there was no "missile gap"—the United States was far ahead of the Soviets in nuclear weaponry—but that there was an ongoing training exercise under the supervision of the CIA designed to prepare 1500 anti-Castro Cubans for an invasion of their homeland. The Joint Chiefs of Staff assured Kennedy that the plan was feasible; diplomatic advisors assured him that the invasion would inspire indigenous uprisings against Castro. In retrospect, it is clear that the scheme, poorly planned and poorly executed, had about as much chance of succeeding as John Brown's raid on Harper's Ferry a little over a century earlier. When the invasion force landed at the Bay of Pigs in Cuba on April 19, 1961, it was subdued in three days and 1,200 men were captured. Cyrus Sulzberger, the New York *Times* columnist, lamented that the United States "looked like fools to our friends, rascals to our enemies, and incompetents to the rest." It was hardly an auspicious way for the new president to demonstrate his mastery of foreign policy. "Victory has a thousand fathers," Kennedy said sadly, "but defeat is an orphan."

Two months after the Bay of Pigs debacle Kennedy met Russian Premier Khrushchev in Vienna, Austria. It was a tense confrontation during which Khrushchev threatend to limit Western access to Berlin, the divided city located deep within East Germany. Kennedy was shaken by the aggressive Soviet stand, but returned home determined to demonstrate American resolve. He called up reserve and national guard units and asked Congress for another $3.2 billion in defense funds. The Soviets responded by throwing up the Berlin Wall, begun with barbed wire on August 13, eventually solidified into a cinder-block barrier which cut off movement between East and West Berlin. Although no shooting incident triggered an accidental war, the Berlin Wall plugged the most accessible escape hatch for East Germans, showed Soviet willingness to challenge American resolve in Europe, and became another intractable barrier to the opening of new frontiers.

THE MISSILE CRISIS   A year later Khrushchev posed another challenge, this time not on the exposed periphery of American power but near its heart, ninety miles off the coast of Florida. Kennedy's unwillingness to commit the forces necessary to overthrow Castro and his acquiescence in the Berlin Wall seemed to signify a failure of will, and the Russians apparently reasoned that they could install missiles in Cuba with relative impunity. While such missiles would hardly alter the military balance, they would come from a direction not covered by radar systems and arrive too quickly for warning. More important to Kennedy's eyes was the psychological effect of American acquiescence to a Soviet presence on its doorstep. This might weaken the credibility of the American deterrent for Europeans and demoralize anti-Castro elements in Latin America. At the same time the installation of missiles served Khrushchev's purpose of demonstrating his toughness to both Chinese and Russian critics of his earlier advocacy of peaceful coexistence. But he misjudged the American response.

On October 14, 1962, American intelligence discovered from

photographs made on high-altitude U-2 flights that Russian missile sites were under construction in Cuba. From the beginning the administration was determined that they had to go; the only question was how. In a series of secret meetings the Executive Committee of the National Security Council narrowed the options down to a choice between a "surgical" air strike and a blockade of Cuba. The decision went for a blockade, which was carefully disguised by the euphemism "quarantine," since a blockade was technically an act of war. It offered the advantage of forcing the Soviets to shoot first, if it came to that, and leaving open the further options of stronger action. Monday, October 22, began one of the most anxious weeks in world history. On that day the president announced to members of Congress and then to the public the discovery of the missile sites in Cuba; he also announced the quarantine.

Tensions grew as Khrushchev blustered that Kennedy had pushed mankind "to the abyss of a world missile-nuclear war." Soviet ships, he declared, would ignore the quarantine. But on Wednesday, October 24, five Soviet ships, presumably with missiles aboard, stopped short of the quarantine line. Two days later an agent of the Russian embassy privately approached John Scali, a television newscaster, with a proposal for an agreement: Russia would withdraw the missiles in return for a public pledge by the United States not to invade Cuba. Secretary of State Rusk sent back word that the administration was interested, but told Scali: "Remember, when you report this, that eyeball to eyeball, they blinked first." The same evening Kennedy received two mes-

Russian missiles under construction at San Cristobal, Cuba, October 23, 1962. [U.S. Air Force]

sages from Khrushchev, the first repeating the offer reported by Scali, the second demanding removal of American missiles from Turkey. The two messages probably reflected divided counsels in the Kremlin. Ironically, Kennedy had already ordered removal of the outmoded missiles in Turkey, but he refused now to act under the gun. Instead he followed Robert Kennedy's suggestion that he respond favorably to the first letter and ignore the second. On Sunday, October 28, Khrushchev agreed to remove the missiles and added a conciliatory invitation: "We should like to continue the exchange of views on the prohibition of atomic and thermonuclear weapons, general disarmament, and other problems relating to the relaxation of international tension."

In the aftermath, the level of tension between the United States and Russia was quickly lowered. Kennedy, aware that Khrushchev had problems with his own hawks in the Kremlin, cautioned his associates against any gloating over the favorable settlement and began to explore in correspondence the opening provided by the premier's invitation. Several symbolic steps were taken to relax tensions: an agreement to sell Russia surplus wheat, the installation of a "hot line" between Washington and Moscow to provide instant contact between the heads of government, and the removal of obsolete missiles from Turkey, Italy, and Britain. On June 10, 1963, the president announced in a speech at American University that discussions with the Soviets would soon begin, and called upon the nation to reexamine its attitude toward peace, the Soviet Union, and the Cold War. In Moscow, Averell Harriman negotiated a treaty with Russian and British representatives to stop nuclear testing in the atmosphere. The treaty, ratified in September 1963, did not provide for on-site inspection nor did it ban underground testing, which continued, but it promised to end the dangerous pollution of the atmosphere with radioactivity. The treaty was an important symbolic and substantive move toward détente. As Kennedy put it: "A journey of a thousand miles begins with one step." Unfortunately it was a small step, and one that not everybody chose to take. Neither France nor China, which now had atomic capabilities, agreed to go along.

KENNEDY AND VIETNAM   In Southeast Asia events were moving toward what would become within a decade the greatest American foreign policy debacle of the century. During John Kennedy's "thousand days" in office the turmoil of Indochina never preoccupied the public mind for any extended period, but it dominated international diplomatic debates from the time the administration entered office. The landlocked kingdom of Laos, along with Cambodia, had been declared neutral in the Geneva Accords of 1954, but had fallen into a complex struggle for power between the Communist Pathet Lao and the Royal Laotian Army. There matters stood when Eisenhower left office and told Kennedy: "You might have to go in there and fight it out." Adm. Arleigh Burke, chairman of the Joint Chiefs of Staff, argued in favor of a stand against the Pathet Lao, even at the cost of direct intervention. After a lengthy consideration of alternatives, Washington decided to favor a neutralist coalition which would preclude American military involvement in Laos, yet prevent a Pathet Lao victory. The Soviets, who were extending aid to the Pathet Lao, indicated a readiness to negotiate, and in May talks began in Geneva with the veteran diplomat Averell Harriman leading the American delegation. After more than a year of tangled negotiations the three factions in Laos agreed to a neutral coalition. American and Russian aid to the opposing parties was supposed to end, but both countries kept up covert operations, while North Vietnam kept open the Ho Chi Minh trail through eastern Laos, over which it supplied its Vietcong allies in South Vietnam.

There things kept getting worse under the leadership of Premier Ngo Dinh Diem, despite encouraging reports from Gen. Paul Harkins, the military commander of American "advisors" in South Vietnam. At the time the problem was less the scattered guerrilla attacks than Diem's failure to deliver social and economic reforms and his inability to rally popular support. His repressive tactics, directed not only against Communists but also against Buddhists and other critics, played into the hands of his enemies. In 1961 White House assistant Walt Rostow and Gen. Maxwell Taylor became the first in a long train of presidential emissaries to South Vietnam's capital, Saigon. Focusing on the military situation, they proposed a major increase in the American military presence. Kennedy refused, but continud to dispatch more "advisors" in the hope of stabilizing the situation: when he took office there had been 2,000; by the end of 1963 there were 16,000, none of whom had been committed to battle.

By 1963 sharply divergent reports were coming in from the country. Military advisors, their eyes on the inflated "kill ratios" reported by the Army of the Republic of Vietnam (ARVN), drew optimistic conclusions of progress. Political reporters like David Halberstam of the New York *Times,* watching the reactions of the Vietnamese people, foresaw continued deterioration without the promised political and economic reforms. By mid-year growing Buddhist demonstrations made the discontent more plainly visible. The spectacle of Buddhist monks immolating themselves in protest brought from Diem's sister-in-law only sarcasm about "barbecued monks." By the fall of 1963 the administration had decided that Diem was a lost cause. When dissident generals proposed a coup d'état, American ambassador Henry Cabot Lodge assured them that Washington would not stand in the way. On November 1 they seized the government and murdered Diem, though without American approval. But the generals provided no more stability than earlier regimes, as successive coups set the country spinning from one military leader to the other.

KENNEDY'S ASSASSINATION   Kennedy seemed to be facing up to the intractability of the situation in Vietnam by the fall of 1963. In September he declared of the South Vietnamese: "In the final analysis it's their war. They're the ones who have to win it or lose it. We can help them as advisors but they have to win it." And the following month he had McNamara and Taylor announce the administration's intention to withdraw United States' forces from South Vietnam by the end of 1965. What Kennedy would have done has remained a matter of endless controversy among historians, endless because it is unanswerable and unanswerable because on November 22, 1963, while visiting Dallas, he was shot in the neck and head by Lee Harvey Oswald, whose motives remain unknown, and died almost immediately. Kennedy's death, then the murder of Oswald by Jack Ruby, a Dallas nightclub owner, were shown over and over again on televison, the medium that had so helped Kennedy's rise to the presidency and that now captured his death and the moving funeral at Arlington Cemetery, thereby assuring his enshrinement in the public imagination as a martyred leader. Shortly afterward Jacquelyn Kennedy reminisced for a reporter. At night they would play records, and the song he loved most came from a current Broadway hit *Camelot*, based on the legends of King Arthur: "'Don't let it be forgot, that once there was a spot, for one brief shining moment, that was known as Camelot'—and it will never be that way again." A Gallup poll in 1976 showed that a majority of Americans regarded Kennedy as the greatest of all American presidents.

LYNDON JOHNSON AND THE GREAT SOCIETY

Lyndon Johnson took the oath as president of the United States on board the plane that took John Kennedy's body back to Washington. At age fifty-five he had spent twenty-six years on the Washington scene and had served nearly a decade as Demo-

Kennedy's vice-president, Lyndon B. Johnson, takes the presidential oath as Air Force One *returns from Dallas with Jacqueline Kennedy (right), the presidential party, and the body of the assassinated president. [Wide World Photos]*

cratic leader in the Senate, where he had displayed the greatest gift for compromise since Henry Clay. Johnson brought to the White House a change of style as sharp as that which had come with Kennedy. The first southern president since Woodrow Wilson, he harbored always, like another southern president, Andrew Johnson, a sense of being the perpetual "outsider" despite his long experience with power. And indeed he was so regarded by "insiders" who, charmed by Kennedy's Boston Irish accent, could never warm to the man who, a probably fictional lady in Texas was supposed to have said, spoke without an accent.

Those who viewed Johnson as a stereotypical southern conservative reckoned without his long-standing admiration for Franklin Roosevelt, the depth of his concern for humble people, and his commitment to the cause of civil rights. "By political background, by temperament, by personal preference," wrote the journalist Philip Geyelin, Johnson was "the riverboat man. He was brawny and rough and skilled beyond measure in the full use of tricky tides and currents, in his knowledge of the hidden shoals. He was a swashbuckling master of the political midstreams—but only in the crowded, well-traveled and familiar inland waterways of domestic politics." In foreign affairs he was, like Wilson, a novice.

POLITICS AND POLICY Quite naturally, domestic politics became his first priority. Johnson exploited the national grief after the assassination by declaring that Kennedy's cabinet and advisors would stay on and that his legislative program, stymied in several congressional committees, would be passed. Given to ceaseless work, fourteen hours or more a day, Johnson loved the kind of political infighting and legislative detail that Kennedy loathed. "Not a sparrow falls," reported one aide, "that he doesn't know about." Recalcitrant congressmen and senators were brought to the White House for what became famous as "the Johnson Treatment." The columnists Rowland Evans, Jr., and Robert D. Novak described the experience: "He moved in close, his face a scant millimeter from his target, his eyes widening and narrowing, his eyebrows rising and falling. From his pockets poured clippings, memos, statistics. Mimicry, humor, and the genius of analogy made the Treatment an almost hypnotic experience and rendered the target stunned and helpless." The logjam in the Congress that had blocked Kennedy's program broke under Johnson's forceful leadership and a torrent of legislation poured through. Virtually the entire agenda of twentieth-century liberalism would be enacted.

Before the year 1963 was out Congress finished action on the pending foreign aid bill and a plan to sell wheat to the Soviet Union. But America's commitment to foreign aid pointed up its own people's needs. In January 1964 the Council of Economic Advisors reported that 9.3 million American families, about 20 percent of the population, was below the "poverty line" of $3,000 per year for a family of four. "Unfortunately, many Americans live on the outskirts of hope," Johnson told the Congress in his first State of the Union message on January 8, 1964, "some because of their poverty and some because of their color, and all too many because of both." At the top of his agenda he put the stalled measures for tax reduction and civil rights, then added to his "must" list a bold new idea which bore the LBJ brand: "This Administration today, here and now, declares unconditional war on poverty in America." The particulars were to come later, the product of an administration task force already at work before Johnson took office.

To get the tax cut, Johnson emphasized fiscal responsibility. Advisors told him that a budget of $108 billion could be defended, but the budget had never before exceeded $100 billion, and Johnson pressed to keep it below that level, dramatizing his determination by the gesture of turning off unneeded lights in the White House. The budget submitted in January was a surprisingly low 97.9 billion, a figure which reduced the projected deficit by one-half. With congressional conservatives like Sen. Harry F. Byrd mollified, the tax reduction of more than $10 billion passed in February, and the increasing purchasing power thus generated started one of the longest sustained booms in American history.

The administration's task force on poverty had its Economic Opportunity Bill ready to submit in March. The bill was an omnibus measure that incorporated a wide range of programs: a Job Corps for youths aged sixteen to twenty-one, job-training programs, work-study projects for students, grants to farmers and rural business, loans to those willing to hire the hard-core unemployed, the Volunteers in Service to America (VISTA, a "domestic Peace Corps"), and the Community Action Program, which would provide "maximum feasible participation" of the poor in directing programs designed for their benefit. Speaking at Ann Arbor, Michigan, in May 1964, Johnson called for a "Great Society" resting on "abundance and liberty for all. The Great Society demands an end to poverty and racial injustice, to which we are fully committed in our time." It was liberalism triumphant.

THE 1964 ELECTION   In the Republican party, on the other hand, a new frenzy of activity was developing on the right. For years the conviction had grown within the party that it had fallen into the hands of an eastern establishment that had given in to the same internationalism and big-government policies as liberal Democrats. Ever since 1940, so the theory went, the party had nominated "me-too" candidates who merely promised to run more efficiently the programs that Democrats promoted. Offer the voters "a choice, no an echo," they reasoned, and a conservative majority would assert itself. Left leaderless by the death of Robert Taft in 1953, the Republican Right began to drift toward varieties of dogmatic conservatism, ranging from a kind of "aristocratic" intellectual "new conservatism" which found voice in the *National Review,* edited by William F. Buckley, Jr., to the John Birch Society, founded by Robert Welch, a New England candy manufacturer given to accusing such distinguished citizens as Eisenhower, Dulles, Chief Justice Warren, and Gen. George Marshall of supporting a Communist conspiracy.

By 1960 Arizona's Sen. Barry Goldwater had begun to emerge as the leader of the Republican Right. In his book *The Conscience of a Conservative* (1960), Goldwater proposed abolition of the income tax, sale of the TVA, and a drastic overhaul of Social Security. Almost from the time of Kennedy's victory in 1960 a movement to draft Goldwater got under way, mobilizing right-wing activists to capture party caucuses and contest primaries. In 1964 they took an early lead before party regulars knew what was happening. Goldwater's chief opponent, Nelson Rockefeller, then governor of New York, stigmatized by a recent divorce and remarriage, never caught up. Goldwater swept the all-important California primary and his forces controlled the Republican convention when it gathered in Los Angeles. Johnson, the incumbent, was conceded the Democratic nomination from the start, and after rebuffing a move to make Robert F. Kennedy his running mate, chose Hubert H. Humphrey of Minnesota, a prominent liberal senator who had led the civil rights forces of the 1948 convention, and a man whose reputation far outshone that of his Republican counterpart, William E. Miller, an obscure congressman from upstate New York.

By the end of the campaign Goldwater had achieved a position of splendid isolation on the far right of the political spectrum. He had an unusual gift for frightening voters. Accusing the administration of waging a "no-win" war in Vietnam, he urged wholesale bombing of North Vietnam and left the impression of being trigger-happy. In Tennessee he urged the sale of TVA; in St. Petersburg, Florida, a major retirement community, he questioned Social Security. He had voted against both the nuclear test ban and the Civil Rights Act, the latter on constitutional principle. Although that principle was not segregation, he was not without reason identified with the segregationist forces. During the campaign Sen. J. Strom Thurmond, the greatest Dixiecrat (conservative southern Democrat) of them all, announced his conversion to the "Goldwater Republican Party."

Johnson appealed to the great consensus that spanned most of the political spectrum. He responded to Goldwater's bellicose rhetoric on Vietnam with a pledge that won great applause at the time and much comment later: "We are not about to send American boys nine or ten thousand miles from home to do what Asian boys ought to be doing for themselves"—a statement reminiscent of the assurance which Johnson's idol, Franklin Roosevelt, voiced regarding the European war in 1940. Much of the campaign could be summed up in the Goldwater slogan "In your heart you know he's right," and the Democratic riposte "In your heart you know he might."

The result was a landslide. Johnson polled 61 percent of the total votes; Goldwater carried only Arizona and five states in the Deep South, where race remained the salient issue. Vermont went Democratic for the first time ever in a presidential election. Johnson won the electoral vote by a whopping 482 to 52. In the Senate the Democrats increased their majority by two (68 to 32) and in the House by thirty-seven (295 to 140). The columnist

Walter Lippman noted: "The returns prove the falsity of the claim . . . that there is a great, silent majority of 'conservative' Republicans who will emerge as the Republican party turns its back on 'me-tooism' and offers them a 'choice.' The Johnson majority is indisputable proof that the votes are in the center." Even so, LBJ was aware that a mandate such as he had received could quickly erode. He told aides, "every day I'm in office, I'm going to lose votes. I'm going to alienate somebody. . . . We've got to get this legislation fast. You've got to get it during my honeymoon."

LANDMARK LEGISLATION   A flood of Great Society legislation poured through the Eighty-ninth Congress at a pace unseen since Franklin Roosevelt's Hundred Days. Priority went to health insurance and aid to education, proposals that had languished since President Truman advanced them in 1945. For twenty years the proposal for a comprehensive plan of medical insurance had been stalled by the American Medical Association. But now that Johnson had the votes, the AMA joined Republicans in boarding the bandwagon for a bill serving those over age sixty-five. The AMA proposed, in addition to hospital insurance, a program for payment of doctor bills and drug costs with the government footing half the premium. The act that finally emerged went well beyond the original program. Rep. Wilbur Mills's Ways and Means Committee not only incorporated the new proposal into the Medicare program for the aged, but added another program, dubbed Medicaid, for federal grants to states that would help cover medical payments for the indigent. President Johnson signed the bill on July 30 in Independence, Missouri, with eighty-one-year-old Harry Truman looking on.

Five days after he submitted his Medicare program, Johnson sent to Congress his proposal for $1.5 billion in federal aid to elementary and secondary education. Such proposals had been ignored since the 1940s, blocked alternately by issues of segregation or separation of church and state. The first had been laid to rest, legally at least, by the Civil Rights Act of 1964. Now Oregon's Sen. Wayne Morse and Secretary of Health, Education and Welfare Wilbur Cohen devised a means of extending aid to "poverty-impacted" school districts regardless of their public or parochial character. This measure Johnson signed in the dilapidated one-room schoolhouse he had first attended, with his first-grade teacher looking on.

The momentum generated by the progress of these measures had already begun to carry others along, and the momentum continued through the following year. Before the Eighty-ninth Congress adjourned, it had established a record in the passage of landmark legislation unequaled since the time of the New Deal. Altogether the tide of Great Society legislation had carried 435 bills through the Congress. Among them was the Appalachian Regional Development Act of 1966, which provided $1.1 billion for programs in remote mountain coves. The Housing and Urban Development Act of 1965 provided aid for construction of 240,000 units of housing and $2.9 billion for urban renewal. Funds for rent supplements for low-income families followed in 1966, and in that year a new Department of Housing and Urban Development appeared, headed by Robert C. Weaver, the first black cabinet member. Johnson had, in the words of one Washington reporter, "brought to harvest a generation's backlog of ideas and social legislation."

FROM CIVIL RIGHTS TO BLACK POWER

THE CIVIL RIGHTS MOVEMENT   Part of the harvest was the legislation which provided the legal capstone to the Second Reconstruction. But an explanation of the civil rights movement that focused on the corridors of Congress would be something like an explanation of a hurricane that focused on the Weather Bureau. Federal legislation, and the presidential leadership provided by both Kennedy and Johnson, lagged behind the grass-roots reform movement that had begun in the South when Rosa Parks refused to move to the rear of the bus in 1955, triggering the Montgomery, Alabama, bus boycott which catapulted Martin Luther King into prominence. King's philosophy of "militant nonviolence" inspired thousands to challenge Jim Crow practices with direct action. At the same time lawsuits to desegregate the schools had activated thousands of parents and young people. The momentum built up to the first genuine mass movement in the history of black Americans when the four black students sat down and demanded service at Woolworth's lunch counter in Greensboro, North Carolina, on February 1, 1960. Within a week the "sit-in" movement had spread to six more towns in the state, and within a month to towns in six more states. In April 1960 the student participants, black and white, formed the Student Nonviolent Coordinating Committee (SNCC), which worked with King's Southern Christian Leadership Conference (SCLC) to spread the movement. The "sit-ins" at restaurants became "kneel-ins" at churches and "wade-ins" at pools, and everywhere the protestors refused to retaliate, even when struck with clubs or burned with lighted cigarettes. The editor of the conservative Richmond *News Leader* conceded admiration for their courage:

> Here were the colored students, in coats, white shirts, ties, and one of them was reading Goethe, and one was taking notes from a biology text. And here, on the sidewalk, outside, was a gang of white boys come to heckle, a ragtail rabble, slack-jawed, black-jacketed, grinning fit to kill, and some of them, God save the mark, were waving the proud and honored flag of the Southern States in the last war fought by gentlemen.

In May of 1961 the Congress of Racial Equality (CORE) sent a group of black and white "freedom riders" on buses to test both a Supreme Court decision, *Morgan v. Virginia* (1946), which had prohibited discrimination against interstate travelers, and an order of the Interstate Commerce Commission which had banned segregation on buses and trains and in terminals since 1955. First in Anniston, Alabama, and then in Birmingham and Montgomery mobs assaulted the travelers and burned one of the buses.

Then in 1962 Gov. Ross Barnett of Mississippi defied a court order and refused to allow James H. Meredith to enroll at the University of Mississippi. Federal marshalls entered the campus to enforce the law. They lined up around Lyceum Hall, the administration building, only to be assaulted by a mob which grew more violent as night fell. Ironically, the protesters were urged on by Edwin Walker, a retired general who had commanded the federal troops at Little Rock's Central High in 1957. Once again federal troops had to break up a mob, but only after two deaths and many injuries. Meredith was registered at "Ole Miss" the next morning.

In April of 1963 King launched a series of nonviolent demonstrations in Birmingham, where Police Commissioner Eugene "Bull" Connor proved the perfect foil for King's tactics. Connor used attack dogs, tear gas, electric cattle prods, and fire hoses on the protesters while millions of outraged Americans watched the confrontation on television. Martin Luther King, who was arrested and jailed during the demonstrations, wrote his "Letter from the Birmingham Jail," a defense of his nonviolent strategy that became a classic of the civil rights movement. That fall Gov. George Wallace stood in the doorway of a building at the University of Alabama to block the enrollment of several black students but stepped aside in the face of the National Guard. That night President Kennedy spoke eloquently of the moral issue facing the nation: "If an American, because his skin is black, cannot enjoy the full and free life which all of us want, then who among us would be content to have the color of his skin changed and stand in his place? Who among us would be content with the counsels of patience and delay?" Later the same night NAACP official Medgar Evers was shot to death as he returned home in Jackson, Mississippi.

The high point of the phase of the civil rights movement that had begun with the Montgomery bus boycott, a movement with integration as its goal and nonviolent confrontation as its strategy,was reached on August 28, 1963, when over 200,000 blacks and whites marched down the Mall in Washington, D.C., toward the Lincoln Memorial singing "We Shall Overcome." The March on Washington was the largest civil rights demonstration in American history. Standing in front of Lincoln's statue, King delivered one of the memorable public speeches of the century: "Even though we face the difficulties of today and tomorrow, I still have a dream. It is a dream chiefly rooted in the American dream . . . one day . . . the sons of former slaves and the sons of former slave-owners will be able to sit together at the table of brotherhood." That the time had not yet arrived, however, became clear a little over two weeks later when a bomb exploded in a Birmingham church killing four black girls who had arrived early for Sunday school.

The widespread demonstrations across the South became a series of local defeats that eventually inspired a national triumph. The intransigence and violence that civil rights workers encountered won converts to their cause all across the country. President Kennedy endorsed a pending omnibus civil rights bill

Martin Luther King, Jr. (second from right), and other prominent civil rights leaders at the head of the March on Washington for Jobs and Freedom, August 28, 1963. [National Archives]

during the Birmingham demonstrations. After Kennedy's death President Johnson, who had maneuvered through the Senate the Civil Rights Acts of 1957 and 1960, called for passage of the pending bill as a memorial to the fallen leader. With bipartisan support he weakened the grip of the House Rules Committee and finally broke the Senate filibuster which was mounted by a diminishing band of bitter-enders. "Nothing," said Republican Senate leader Everett Dirksen, quoting the French writer Victor Hugo, "is so powerful as an idea whose time has come." On July 2 Johnson signed the Civil Rights Act of 1964, the most far-reaching civil rights measure ever enacted by the Congress. The act outlawed discrimination in hotels, restaurants, and other public accommodations. It required that literacy tests for voting be administered in writing, and defined as literate anybody who had finished the sixth grade. The attorney-general could now bring suits for school desegregation, relieving parents of a painful necessity. Federally assisted programs and private employers alike were required to eliminate discrimination. An Equal Employment Opportunity Commission (the old Fair Employment Practices Committee reborn) administered a ban on job discrimination by race, religion, national origin, or sex.

Early in 1965 King announced a drive to register the 3 million blacks in the South who had not registered to vote. In Selma, Alabama, the focus at the outset, he found in Sheriff Jim Clark a foil as perfect as Birmingham's police chief. On March 7 civil rights protesters began a march to Montgomery, only to be met and violently dispersed by state troopers and a mounted posse at the Edmund Pettus Bridge across the Alabama River. A federal judge, Frank M. Johnson, Jr., agreed to allow the march, and President Johnson provided protection with National Guardsmen and army military police. By March 25, when the demonstrators reached Montgomery, some 35,000 people were with them, and King addressed them from the steps of the state capitol. That night snipers shot and killed a white woman from Detroit who was driving a marcher home. Several days before the march President Johnson went before Congress with a moving plea which reached its climax when he slowly intoned the words of the movement hymn: "And we shall overcome." The resulting Voting Rights Act of 1965, passed to ensure all the right to vote, rejected the old case-by-case procedures and authorized the attorney-general to dispatch federal examiners to register voters. In states or counties where fewer than half the adults had voted in 1964, the act suspended literacy tests and other devices commonly used to defraud citizens of the vote. By the end of the year some 250,000 blacks were newly registered.

"BLACK POWER" A new phase in the civil rights movement began on August 11, 1965, less than a week after the passage of the Voting Rights Act. The Watts area of Los Angeles exploded in a frenzy of black riots and looting. When the uprising ended, there were thirty-four dead, almost 4,000 rioters in jail, and property damage exceeding $35 million. Liberal commentators were both stunned and surprised, since the riots occurred in the wake of the greatest legislative victories for black Americans since the first Reconstruction. Moreover, Watts was not an outrageous slum. The national Urban League in fact had rated Los Angeles as the most prosperous and desirable city for black urban residents in the United States. But events did not stand still to await white liberal comprehension. Chicago and Cleveland, along with forty other American cities, had racial riots in the summer of 1966. The following summer Newark and Detroit burst into flames. Detroit provided the most graphic example of urban violence, as tanks rolled through the streets and soldiers from the 101st Airborne used machine guns to deal with snipers in the tenements. *Pravda,* the official Soviet newspaper, ran the story with accompanying pictures of the carnage on its front page. Firemen who tried to put out the flames in several of the urban riots were showered by bricks and bottles thrown by the very people whose houses were burning.

In retrospect, it was predictable that the civil rights movement would focus on the plight of urban blacks. By the middle 1960s about 70 percent of the black population lived in metropolitan areas, most of them in central-city ghettos that had been bypassed by the postwar prosperity. And again it seems clear, in retrospect, that the nonviolent tactics which had worked in the rural South would not work in the northern cities, where the

Detroit's black ghetto exploded in rioting on Sunday, July 23, 1967. [Wide World Photos]

problems were de facto segregation resulting from residential patterns, not de jure segregation amenable to changes in law, and where white ethnic groups did not have the cultural heritage which southern whites shared with blacks. "It may be," wrote a contributor to *Esquire*, "that looting, rioting and burning . . . are really nothing more than radical forms of urban renewal, a response not only to the frustrations of the ghetto but to the collapse of all ordinary modes of change, as if a body despairing of the indifference of doctors sought to rip a cancer out of itself." A special Commission on Civil Disorders headed by Gov. Otto Kerner of Illinois noted that, unlike earlier race riots, the urban upheavals of the middle 1960s were initiated by blacks themselves; earlier riots had been started by whites, which had then provoked black counterattacks. Now blacks visited violence and destruction on themselves in an effort to destroy what they could not stomach and what civil rights legislation seemed unable to change.

By 1966 "Black Power" had become the new rallying cry. Radical members of SNCC had become estranged from Martin Luther King's theories of militant nonviolence. As King became the center of attention from the white media, SNCC members began to refer to him cynically as "de Lawd." When Stokely Carmichael, a twenty-five-year-old graduate of Howard University, became head of SNCC in May 1966, the separatist philosophy of black power became official and whites were ousted from the organization. "We reject an American dream defined by white people and must work to construct an American reality defined by Afro-Americans," said a SNCC position paper. H. Rap Brown, who succeeded Carmichael as head of SNCC in 1967, even urged blacks to "get you some guns" and "kill the honkies." Meanwhile Carmichael had moved on to the Black Panther party, a self-professed group of urban revolutionaries founded in Oakland, California, in 1966 and headed by Huey P. Newton and Eldridge Cleaver. Under their leadership the Black Panthers echoed the separatist demands of Marcus Garvey, terrified the public by wearing bandeleros and carrying rifles, but eventually fragmented in spasms of violence.

Perhaps the most articulate spokesman for black power was one of the earliest, Malcolm X (formerly Malcolm Little, with the "X" denoting his lost African surname). Malcolm had risen from a ghetto childhood of narcotics and crime to become the chief disciple of Elijah Muhammad, the Black Muslim prophet who rejected Christianity as "the religion of white devils." "Yes, I'm an extremist," Malcolm acknowledged in 1964. "The black race in the United States is in extremely bad shape. You show me a black man who isn't an extremist and I'll show you one who needs psychiatric attention." By 1964 Malcolm had broken with Elijah Muhammad and founded his own organization, which was committed to the establishment of alliances between the blacks of the United States and the nonwhite peoples of the world. But just after the publication of his *Autobiography* in 1965, Malcolm was gunned down in the Audubon Ballroom in Harlem by Black Muslim assassins. With him went the most effective voice for urban black militancy since Marcus Garvey.

Black power was a slogan more than a philosophy. The conclusion of the Kerner Commission on Civil Disorders was harsh but accurate: "Black Power rhetoric and ideology actually expresses a lack of power. . . . Powerless to make any fundamental changes in the life of the masses . . . many advocates of Black Power have retreated into an unreal world, where they see an outnumbered and poverty-stricken minority organizing itself independently of whites and creating sufficient power to force white Americans to grant its demands." But if Lyndon Johnson's Great Society encountered harsh realities in American cities, it was running into even harsher realities in the Vietnamese countryside.

The Tragedy of Vietnam

DIMENSIONS OF A WAR   At the time of President Kennedy's death there were 16,000 American troops in Vietnam. Johnson inherited a commitment to prevent a Communist takeover in South Vietnam along with a reluctance to assume the military burden for fighting the war. One president after another did just enough to stall off the prospect of being charged with having "lost" Vietnam. Such an outcry, Johnson feared, would undermine his influence and endanger his Great Society programs in Congress. Therefore he found himself drawn inexorably deeper into intervention in Asia. During the presidential campaign of 1964 Johnson had opposed the use of American combat troops and had privately described Vietnam as "a raggedy-ass fourth-rate country" not worthy of American blood and treasure. Nevertheless, by the end of 1965 there were 184,000 American troops in Vietnam; in 1966 the troop level reached 385,000; and by 1969, the height of the American presence, 542,000. By the time the last American troops left in March 1973, 51,000 Americans had died in combat and another 270,000 had been wounded. The war had cost the American taxpayers $150 billion, generated economic dislocations that destroyed many

Great Society programs, produced 570,000 draft offenders and 563,000 less-than-honorable discharges from the service, toppled Johnson's administration, and divided the country as no event in American history had since the Civil War.

ESCALATION The official sanction for "escalation"—a Defense Department term coined in the Vietnam era—was the Tonkin Gulf Resolution, voted by Congress on August 7, 1964. Johnson told a national television audience that two American destroyers, the U.S.S. *Maddox* and *C. Turner Joy*, had been attacked by North Vietnamese vessels on August 2 and 4 in the Gulf of Tonkin off the coast of North Vietnam. Although Johnson described the attack as unprovoked, in truth the destroyers had been monitoring South Vietnamese attacks against two North Vietnamese islands—attacks planned by American advisors. The Tonkin Gulf Resolution authorized the president to "take all necessary measures to repel any armed attack against the forces of the United States and to prevent further aggression." Only Sen. Wayne Morse of Oregon and Sen. Ernest Gruening of Alaska voted against the resolution, which Johnson thereafter interpreted as equivalent to a congressional declaration of war.

Soon after Johnson's landslide victory over Goldwater in 1964, the crucial decisions that shaped American policy in Vietnam for the next four years were made. On February 5 Vietcong guerrillas killed 8 and wounded 126 Americans at Pleiku. Further attacks on Americans later that week led Johnson to order operation "Rolling Thunder," the first sustained bombings of North Vietnam, which were intended to stop the flow of soldiers and supplies into the south. Six months later a task force headed by Adam Yarmolinsky, a former Pentagon planner in the Kennedy years, conducted an extensive study of the bombing's effects on the supplies pouring down the "Ho Chi Minh Trail" from North Vietnam through Laos. Yarmolinsky concluded that there was "no way" to stop the traffic.

In March 1965 the new American army commander in Vietnam, Gen. William C. Westmoreland, requested and got the first installment of combat troops, who waded ashore at Da Nang. By the summer American troops were engaged in "search and destroy" operations, thus ending the fiction that American soldiers were only "advisors." And as combat operations increased, so did the mounting list of American casualties, announced each week on the nightly news along with the "body count" of alleged Viet Cong dead. "Westy's War," although fought with helicopter gunships, chemical defoliants, and napalm, became like the trench warfare of World War I—a war of attrition.

THE CONTEXT FOR POLICY   Johnson's decision to "Americanize" the war, so ill-starred in retrospect, was consistent with the foreign policy principles pursued by all American presidents after World War II. The version of the containment theory articulated in the Truman Doctrine, endorsed by Eisenhower and Dulles throughout the 1950s, and reaffirmed by Kennedy, pledged United States opposition to the advance of communism anywhere in the world. "Why are we in Vietnam?" Johnson asked rhetorically at Johns Hopkins University in 1965. "We are there because we have a promise to keep. . . . To leave Vietnam to its fate would shake the confidence of all these people in the value of American commitment." Secretary of State Dean Rusk repeated this rationale before countless congressional committees, warning that Thailand, Burma, and the rest of Southeast Asia would fall to communism if American forces withdrew. American military intervention in Vietnam was not an aberration, but a logical culmination of the assumptions widely shared by the foreign policy establishment and leaders of both political parties since the early days of the Cold War.

If Vietnam was not an aberration, *The Pentagon Papers* subsequently made clear that the United States did not "stumble into a quagmire." Undersecretary of State George Ball consistently warned of disaster: "Once on the tiger's back we cannot be sure of picking the place to dismount." Or as Maxwell Taylor, ambassador to South Vietnam during the crucial 1964–1965 period, put it: "Once we brought troops in, it was the nose of the camel." It was also clear to Johnson and his advisors from the start that American military involvement could not reach levels that would provoke the Chinese or Soviets into direct intervention. And this meant, in effect, that military victory in any traditional sense of the term was never possible. "It was startling to me to find out," said the new secretary of defense Clark Clifford in 1968, "that we had no military plan to end the war." The goal of the United States was not to win the war, but to prevent the North Vietnamese and Viet Cong from winning. This meant that America would have to maintain a military presence as long as the enemy retained the will to fight.

As it turned out, American support for the war eroded faster than the will of the North Vietnamese leaders to tolerate casualties. Opposition to the war on college campuses began in 1965 with "teach-ins" at the University of Michigan. And in January 1966 Sen. J. William Fulbright of Arkansas, chairman of the Senate Foreign Relations Committee, began congressional investigations into American policy. George Kennan, the founding father of the containment doctrine, told Fulbright's committee that the doctrine was appropriate for Europe, but not Southeast Asia. Gen. James Gavin testified that Westmoreland's military strategy had no chance of achieving victory. By 1967 opposition to the war had become so pronounced that antiwar demonstrations in New York and at the Pentagon attracted massive support. Nightly television accounts of the fighting—Vietnam was the first war to receive extended television coverage—stripped the war of any nobility and made official optimism appear fatuous. By May 1967 even Secretary of Defense McNamara was wavering: "The picture of the world's greatest superpower killing or injuring 1000 noncombatants a week, while trying to pound a tiny backward nation into submission on an issue whose merits are hotly disputed, is not a pretty one."

VIETNAM, 1966

□ Major U.S. bases

0   200 Miles

0   200 Kilometers

THE TURNING POINT   On January 31, 1968, the first day of the Vietnamese New Year (Tet), the Viet Cong defied a holiday truce to launch assaults on American and South Vietnamese forces throughout South Vietnam. The city of Hue fell to the Communists and Viet Cong units temporarily occupied the grounds of the American embassy in Saigon. General Westmoreland proclaimed the Tet offensive a major defeat for the Viet Cong, and most students of military strategy later agreed with him. But while Viet Cong casualties were enormous, the impact of the events on the American public were more telling. *Time* and *Newsweek* soon ran antiwar editorials urging American withdrawal. Walter Cronkite, the dean of American television journalists, confided to his viewers that he no longer believed the war was winnable. "If I've lost Walter," Johnson was reported to say, "then it's over. I've lost Mr. Average Citizen." Polls showed that Johnson's popularity declined to 35 percent, lower than any president since Truman's darkest days.

Johnson was increasingly isolated. Clark Clifford, the new secretary of defense, reported to Johnson that a task force of prominent soldiers and civilians saw no prospect for a military victory. Even Dean Acheson, the preeminent cold warrior, believed that the cause was hopeless. Robert Kennedy was reportedly considering a run for the presidency in order to challenge Johnson's Vietnam policy. And Sen. Eugene McCarthy of Minnesota had already made the decision to oppose Johnson in the primaries. With antiwar students rallying to his candidacy, McCarthy polled 42 percent of the vote to Johnson's 48 percent in New Hampshire's March primary. It was a remarkable showing for a little-known senator, even though Johnson was a write-in candidate. Each presidential primary now promised to become a referendum on Johnson's Vietnam policy. In Wisconsin, scene of the next primary, Johnson's political advisors forecast a humiliating defeat: "We sent a man [to campaign for Johnson] and all we've heard from him since is a few faint beeps, like the last radio signals from the Bay of Pigs."

Despite Johnson's troubles in the conduct of foreign policy, he remained a master at reading the political omens. On March 31 he went on national television to announce a limited halt to the bombing of North Vietnam and fresh initiatives for a negotiated cease-fire. Then he added a dramatic postscript: "I have concluded that I should not permit the Presidency to become involved in the partisan divisions that are developing in this political year. Accordingly, I shall not seek, and I will not accept, the nomination of my party for another term as your President."

Although American troops would remain in Vietnam for five more years and the casualties would continue, the quest for military victory had ended. Now the question was how the most powerful nation in the world could extricate itself from Vietnam with a minimum of damage to its prestige.

SIXTIES CRESCENDO

A TRAUMATIC YEAR   History seemed to move at a fearful pace throughout the 1960s, but 1968 was a year of extreme turbulence even for that decade. On April 4, only four days after Johnson's announced withdrawal, Martin Luther King was gunned down while standing on the balcony of his motel in Memphis, Tennessee. The assassin, James Earl Ray, had expressed hostility toward blacks, but debate still continues over whether he was a pawn in an organized conspiracy. King's death set off an outpouring of grief among whites and blacks. It also set off riots in over sixty American cities, with the most serious occurring in Chicago and Washington, D.C. Two months later, on June 6, Robert Kennedy was shot in the head by a young Palestinian, Sirhan Sirhan, who resented Kennedy's strong support of Israel. Kennedy's death occurred at the end of the day on which he had convincingly defeated Eugene McCarthy in the California primary, thereby assuming leadership of the antiwar forces in the race for the Democratic nomination for president. David Halberstam thought back to the assassinations of John Kennedy and Malcolm X, then the violent end of King, the most influential black leader of the twentieth century, and then Robert Kennedy,

America's violent underside became all too apparent in the 1960s. [Cartoon by Franklin— Daily Mirror, London]

"ALWAYS THERE IS A BLACK SPOT IN OUR SUNSHINE— IT IS THE SHADOW OF OURSELVES."—CARLYLE the heir to leadership of the Kennedy clan. "We could make a calendar of the decade," Halberstam wrote, "by marking where we were at the hours of those violent deaths."

Although the Democratic nomination was now a foregone conclusion—Hubert Humphrey was virtually assured of winning as the candidate most acceptable to regular Democrats—the forces converging on Chicago in August possessed energies that had been seething and simering throughout the decade. Bizarre activists like Jerry Rubin, the "Yippie" leader who threatened to put LSD into Chicago's water supply, were but the extreme fringe of a movement of alienated Americans, most of them young, that resembled a religious crusade more than a political movement. In the last two years of the decade, first at the Democratic convention in Chicago and then at the Woodstock Festival in upstate New York in August 1969, what soon became known as "the counterculture" expressed itself in varieties of protest, public singing, drug use, and sexual experimentation.

THE COUNTERCULTURE   The explicitly political strain of the counterculture had its origins on college campuses and in the civil rights movement. In 1962 the Students for a Democratic Society (SDS) was organized in Michigan and issued the Port Huron Statement: "We are the people of this generation, bred in at least moderate comfort, housed in universities, looking uncomfortably to the world we inherit." In 1964 students at the University of California at Berkeley initiated the Free Speech Movement, a protest in behalf of student rights that quickly escalated into a more general criticism of the modern university, the impersonal character of bureaucracy, and as it spread to colleges throughout the country, a hostility to all established institutions. Disaffected and radical students flowed into the antiwar movement but focused their anger most frequently on the institutions closest to them, the colleges and universities. The eventful spring of 1968 witnessed the disruption of Columbia University until police forcibly ejected student protesters who had seized the offices of campus officials. Harvard and Cornell were afflicted with similar disruptions within the next two years. The New Left, as it came to be called, was a predominantly white, middle-class movement, populated by idealistic young Americans who had developed a sense of themselves as a discrete generation in rebellion against authorities of all kinds. Campus parietals, government policies in Vietnam, the draft, and parental restrictions on dress and hair length all provoked their censure.

Drugs and rock music were more important than political ideology to the "hippies," the direct descendants of the "beatniks" of the 1950s and the flaming youth of the 1920s who drank gin, bobbed their hair, and danced the Charleston. "Tune in, turn on, drop out" became a slogan popularized by Timothy Leary, a Harvard professor turned high priest of the drug culture. Hallucinogenic drugs were necessary to strip away what Theodore Roszak, the friendly chronicler of the counterculture, called "the myth of objective consciousness" and "the scientific world view with its entrenched commitment to an egocentric and cerebral mode of consciousness." Rock concerts that featured Janis Joplin or Jimi Hendrix became "happenings" in which the youth culture flaunted its freedom. By the end of the 1960s *Rolling Stone* magazine warned that pretensions of artistic purity ignored the commercial corruption of heroes like Hendrix and Bob Dylan, and groups like the Beatles: "The difference between a rock star and a robber baron is six inches of hair." As the Democratic convention convened in Chicago, disc jockeys debated whether the Beatles' song "Revolution I" was counterrevolutionary ("But if you go carrying a picture of Chairman Mao, you ain't gonna make it with anyone anyhow"). Many disc jockeys preferred the new tune by the Rolling Stones that began "The time is right for fighting in the streets."

CHICAGO AND MIAMI   While Democratic delegates gathered inside the convention hall at Chicago, 24,000 police and National Guardsmen and a small army of television reporters stood watch over an eclectic gathering of protesters herded together miles away in a public park. The counterculture was represented by antiwar groups carrying signs supporting the Viet Cong and by

The violence at the 1968 Democratic National Convention in Chicago seared the nation. [R. Malloch, Magnum Photos]

the Yippies, who staged a "Festival of Life" intended to contrast with "Lyndon and Hubert's celebration of death." Mayor Richard Daley, who had given "shoot-to-kill" orders to police during the April riots protesting King's assassination, warned that he would not tolerate disruptions. But riots broke out in front of the Conrad Hilton Hotel and were televised nationwide. As police tear gas and billy clubs struck demonstrators, others took up the chant "The whole world is watching."

The liberal tradition represented by the Democratic party was clearly in disarray, a fact that gave heart to the Republicans who gathered in Miami to nominate Richard Nixon. Only six years earlier, after he had lost the California gubernatorial race, Nixon had told reporters, "You won't have Nixon to kick around anymore, because, gentlemen, this is my last press conference." But by 1968 he had become a preeminent spokesman for all the values the counterculture was against. Russell Baker of the New York *Times* said the Miami convention had been "planned in advance by six bores and a sadist." And Norman Mailer, who covered both conventions to gather material for a book on American politics, likened the convention in Miami to a Rotarian gathering in a cemetery. But Nixon and the Republicans were offering a vision of stability and order that a majority of Americans—soon to be called "the silent majority"—wanted desperately.

George Wallace, the governor of Alabama who had made his reputation as a defender of segregation, became a third candidate in the campaign on the American Independent party ticket. Wallace moderated his position on the race issue, but appealed even more candidly than Nixon to the fears generated by protesters, the welfare system, and the growth of the federal government. Although never a possible winner, Wallace's candidacy did pose the possibility of denying Humphrey or Nixon an electoral majority and thereby throwing the choice into the House of Representatives, which would have provided an appropriate climax to a chaotic year.

NIXON AGAIN   It did not happen that way. Nixon enjoyed an enormous lead in the polls, which narrowed as the election approached. Wallace's campaign was hurt by his running mate, retired Air Force Gen. Curtis LeMay, who favored expanding the war in Vietnam and spoke approvingly of using nuclear weapons. (It was reported that LeMay was the model for the deranged general in the film *Doctor Strangelove*.) In October, Humphrey announced that he would stop bombing North Vietnam "as an acceptable risk for peace." Eugene McCarthy, who

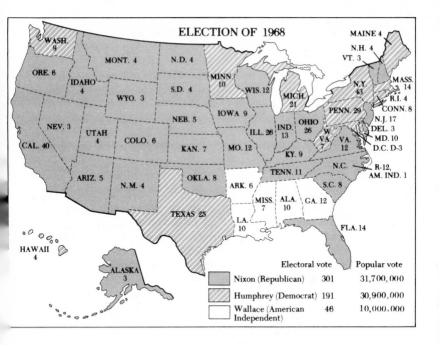

ELECTION OF 1968

	Electoral vote	Popular vote
Nixon (Republican)	301	31,700,000
Humphrey (Democrat)	191	30,900,000
Wallace (American Independent)	46	10,000,000

had been strangely silent and had even spent some time cloistered in a Benedictine monastery, eventually came out in support of Humphrey. "I believe the Vice-President is a man who can be relied on to tell the difference between the pale horse of death and the white horse of victory," said McCarthy. "I am not sure Nixon can make that distinction."

Nixon and Gov. Spiro Agnew of Maryland, his running mate, eked out a narrow victory by about 800,000 votes, a margin of about one percentage point. The electoral vote was more decisive, 301 to 191. Wallace won 10 million votes, 13.5 percent of the total, for the best showing by a third-party candidate since Robert La Follette in 1924. All of Wallace's 46 electoral votes were from the Deep South. Nixon swept all but four of the states west of the Mississippi. Humphrey's support came almost exclusively from the Northeast.

And so at the end of a turbulent year near the end of a traumatic decade, power passed peacefully to a president who was associated with the complacency of the 1950s. A nation that had seemed on the verge of consuming itself in spasms of violence looked to Richard Nixon to provide what he had promised in the campaign: "peace with honor" in Vietnam and a middle ground on which a majority of Americans, silent or otherwise, could come together.

FURTHER READING

A number of scholars have chronicled the events of the 1960s, often with analysis based on their personal experiences from the decade. Among the most popular of these works is William L. O'Neill's *Coming Apart: An Informal History of America in the 1960s* (1971).° More concise is William Leuchtenberg's *A Troubled Feast: American Society since 1945* (1979),° which depicts well how the events of the 1950s led into the conflicts of the 1960s. Godfrey Hodgson's *America in Our Time: From World War II to Nixon, What Happened and Why* (1976),° is detailed and probes the underlying forces which led to discontent. Other overviews include Morris Dickstein's *Gates of Eden: American Culture in the Sixties* (1977),° Ronald Berman's *America in the Sixties* (1968),° and Jim F. Heath's *Decade of Disillusion: The Kennedy-Johnson Years* (1975).

For the context of the Camelot years, consult first James L. Sundquist's *Politics and Policy: The Eisenhower, Kennedy, and Johnson Years* (1968).° Herbert Parmet traces the influence of Kennedy in two volumes, *Jack: The Struggle of John Fitzgerald Kennedy* (1980) and *JFK: The Presidency of John Fitzgerald Kennedy* (1983). Favorable memoirs from White House staffers include Arthur S. Schlesinger, Jr.'s *A Thousand Days: John F. Kennedy in the White House* (1965)° and Theodore C. Sorenson's *Kennedy* (1965). A former New Frontiersman, Roger Hilsman offers an argument about Kennedy's effectiveness in *To Move a Nation: The Politics of Policy in the Administration of John F. Kennedy* (1967).° Less favorable assessments come from Henry Fairlie's *The Kennedy Promise* (1973) and Bruce Miroff's *Pragmatic Illusions: The Presidential Politics of John F. Kennedy* (1976). For details of the assassination, see William Manchester's *The Death of the President* (1967).° Anthony Summer's *Conspiracy* (1980)° reviews best the many theories about the death of Kennedy, including the evidence provided in the official Warren Report.

There are fewer works about Kennedy's successor, but many are solidly detailed. Lyndon Johnson's own *The Vantage Point: Perspectives on the Presidency, 1963–1969* (1971),° can be balanced with Doris Kearns's *Lyndon Johnson and the American Dream* (1976).° Also helpful is Merle Miller's *Lyndon: An Oral Biography* (1980).° Tom Wicker's *JFK and LBJ: The Influence of Personality upon Politics* (1968)° examines Johnson's effective control of Congress. Eric Goldman's *The Tragedy of Lyndon Johnson* (1969)° is critical of Johnson's Vietnamese escalation. Ronnie Dugger's *The Politician: The Life and Times of Lyndon Johnson* (1982) depicts in detail Johnson's early career, as does the first volume of Robert Caro's biography, *The Years of Lyndon Johnson* (1982).°

Among the works which interpret the policy of the liberals are W. W. Rostow's *The Diffusion of Power, 1957–1972* (1972), and Robert Lekachman's *The Age of Keynes* (1966).° Also helpful is the memoir of a

°These books are available in paperback editions.

leading Keynesian, John Kenneth Galbraith, *A Life in Our Times* (1981). For liberal social programs, consult the assessment of the Great Society by Sar Levitan and Robert Taggart, *The Promise of Greatness* (1976).° Very helpful for background on the formation of this policy is James T. Patterson's *America's Struggle against Poverty, 1900–1980* (1981). The polemical literature of the period is also helpful; see Daniel Moynihan's *Maximum Feasible Misunderstanding: Community Action in the War on Poverty* (1970)° and Kenneth Davies's *The Paradox of Poverty in America* (1969). For the way social policy affected cities, see Mark I. Gelfand's *A Nation of Cities* (1975) and Sam Bass Warner's *The Urban Wilderness* (1972).°

For the foreign policy of the liberals, see Louise Fitzsimmon's *The Kennedy Doctrine* (1972) and Richard Walton's *Cold War and Counter-revolution: The Foreign Policy of John F. Kennedy* (1972).° To learn more about Kennedy's problems in Cuba, see Haynes Johnson's *The Bay of Pigs* (1964). Herbert S. Dinerstein analyzes the Soviet perspective in *The Making of a Missile Crisis* (1976). For the Alliance of Progress, see Jerome Levinson and Juan de Onis's *The Alliance That Lost Its Way* (1970). Jerome Slater's *Intervention and Negotiation* (1970) depicts Johnson's use of military force in Santo Domingo. Also helpful on foreign policy are Warren Cohen's *Dean Rusk* (1980) and Leonard Silk and Mark Silk's *The American Establishment* (1980).

The establishment's policy in Vietnam has received voluminous treatment from all political perspectives. Three of the most popular negative accounts of the struggle are Chester L. Cooper's *The Lost Crusade* (1970), Frances Fitzgerald's *Fire in the Lake: The Vietnamese and the Americans in Vietnam* (1972),° and David Halberstam's *The Best and the Brightest* (1972).° Subsequent surveys of American involvement include Paul Kattenberg's *The Vietnam Trauma in American Foreign Policy, 1945–1980* (1980), and James Pinckeney Harrison's *The Endless War: Fifty Years of Struggle in Vietnam* (1982). Works which see American policy in a favorable light include Norman Podhoretz's *Why We Were in Vietnam* (1982), Guenter Lewy's *America in Vietnam* (1978),° and Leslie Gelb and Richard Bett's *The Irony of Vietnam: The System Worked* (1979).° The life of the common soldier is depicted in Peter Goldman and Tony Fuller's *Charlie Company: What Vietnam Did to Us* (1983) and Robert Pison's *The End of the Line: The Siege of Khe Sanh* (1982).

For an overview of the antiwar movement spawned by the Vietnam War, see Todd Gitlin's *The Whole World Is Watching* (1981). Other works on anti-war protest include Kirkpatrick Sales's *SDS* (1973),° Theodore Roszak's *The Making of the Counterculture* (1969),° Irwin Unger's *The Movement* (1974),° Lawrence Lader's *Power on the Left* (1979), and Thomas Powers's *The War at Home* (1974). Richard Flack's *Youth and Social Change* (1971) and William Strauss's *Change and Circumstance* (1978) are particularly detailed about opposition to compulsory military service.

Many scholars have dealt with various aspects of the civil rights movement and race relations of the 1960s. A recent introduction to the period is Sar A. Levitan, William B. Johnson, and Robert Taggart's *Still a Dream: The Changing Status of Blacks since 1960* (1975).° Studies of the national politics of civil rights include Carl Brauer's *John F. Kennedy and the Second Reconstruction* (1977)° and Lee Rainwater and William L. Yancey's *The Moynihan Report and the Politics of Controversy* (1967). Two biographies of Martin Luther King, Jr., are helpful: Stephen B. Oates's *Let the Trumpet Sound* (1982)° and David Lewis's *King: A Critical Biography* (1970).° David J. Garrow has two specialized studies of King, *Protest at Selma* (1978)° and *The FBI and Martin Luther King, Jr.: From "Solo" to Memphis* (1981).° King is also enlightening in his own book *Why We Can't Wait* (1964).° Other personalities in the civil rights movement are studied in Charles F. Kellogg's *NAACP* (1967), August Meier and Elliott Rudwick's *CORE* (1973),° and Howard Zinn's *SNCC: The New Abolitionists* (1964). For legal turns the civil rights movement took during the 1960s, see J. Harvie Wilkinson's *From Brown to Bakke: The Supreme Court and School Integration, 1954–1978* (1978). William Chafe's *From Civilities to Civil Rights: Greensboro, North Carolina, and the Black Struggle for Freedom* (1980)° details the original sit-ins.

For race relations subsequent to the Civil Rights Act, consult Theodore Draper's *The Discovery of Black Nationalism* (1970). Important books by blacks during the period include Alex Haley (ed.), *The Autobiography of Malcolm X* (1965),° Eldridge Cleaver's *Soul on Ice* (1967),° George Jackson's *Soledad Brother* (1970),° and Stokely Carmichael and Charles Hamilton's *Black Power* (1967).° Also valuable is Archie Epp's *Malcolm X and the American Negro Revolution* (1969). For background on the urban riots, see Robert Fogelson's *Violence as Protest* (1971) and Joe R. Feagin and Harlin Hahn's *Ghetto Revolts* (1973). Claude Brown's *Manchild in the Promised Land* (1975)° explores the world of ghetto life.

For the tumultuous events of the 1968 campaign, start with Theodore H. White's *The Making of the President, 1968* (1969).° Less favorable to Nixon is Joe McGinnis's *The Selling of the President* (1969).° For the McCarthy movement, see Norman Ben Stavis's *We Were the Campaign* (1969). Arthur S. Schlesinger, Jr.'s *Robert Kennedy and His Times* (1978)° and Marshall Frady's *Wallace* (1976)° report the campaign from the viewpoint of other candidates.

34

THE 1970s AND BEYOND: THE SEARCH FOR STABILITY

The sixties was a state of mind as well as a discrete decade. For some Americans the 1960s ended with the assassinations of Martin Luther King and Robert Kennedy in 1968. For others the end came in 1973, when they inched their cars into gas stations and discovered that scarcity had replaced abundance at the fuel pump. For many Americans, however, the Vietnam War was the dominant event of the decade. Until the war was ended and all American troops had returned home, the nation found it difficult to achieve the equilibrium and moderation that the new president had promised. In his State of the Union message of 1970, President Nixon called on Americans to pursue "the lift of a driving dream," a memorable phrase that reporters asked him to define. "Well, before we can get the lift of a driving dream," Nixon explained, "we have to get rid of the nightmares we inherited. One of the nightmares is a war without end."

NIXON AND VIETNAM

GRADUAL WITHDRAWAL   During the campaign of 1968 Nixon had claimed to have a secret plan that would bring "peace with honor" in Vietnam. After the election Clark Clifford, the former secretary of defense, went to Henry Kissinger, the professor of international relations at Harvard who had been tapped to serve as Nixon's special assistant for national security affairs, and suggested that "within ninety days of taking office, Mr. Nixon could announce that he was starting the withdrawal of American troops and would continue to withdraw them until they were all gone." Clifford's advice was similar to the suggestion put forward by Sen. George Aiken of Vermont that "we declare victory and leave." But neither Nixon nor Kissinger found such advice acceptable. Kissinger insisted that the war in Indochina was a mere "sideshow" of considerably less significance than American interests in Europe and the Middle East, but American withdrawal from Vietnam was agonizingly slow nonetheless. Like several preceding administrations, the Nixon administration, even while withdrawing American forces, held to a policy that it was contrary to the national interest to let the North Vietnamese dominate Indochina. When a settlement was finally reached in 1973, another 20,000 Americans had died, the morale of the American army was shattered, millions of additional Asians were killed or wounded, and fighting in fact continued in Southeast Asia. In the end, Nixon's policy gained nothing he could not have accomplished in 1969.

The new Vietnam policy of the Nixon administration moved along three separate fronts. First, American negotiators in Paris insisted on the withdrawal of Communist forces from South Vietnam and the preservation of the American-supported regime of President Nguyen Van Thieu. The North Vietnamese and Viet Cong negotiators insisted on the retention of a military presence in the south and the reunification of the Vietnamese people under a government dominated by the Communists. There was no common ground on which to come together. It required months before the parties could even agree on the shape of the table around which they would meet.

Second, Nixon sought to undercut domestic unrest over the war. He reduced the number of American troops in Vietnam, justifying the reduction as the natural result of "Vietnamization"— the equipping and training of the South Vietnamese to assume the burden of ground combat in place of Americans. From a peak of 540,000 in 1969, American combat troops were withdrawn at a gradual and steady pace that matched almost precisely the pace of the American buildup from 1965 to 1969. By 1973 only 50,000 American troops remained in Vietnam. Nixon also established a lottery system that clarified the likelihood of being drafted—only those with low lottery numbers would have to go —and in 1973 he did away with the draft altogether by creating an all-volunteer army. Nixon was more successful in achieving the goal of reducing antiwar activity than at forcing concessions from the North Vietnamese in Paris.

Third, while reducing the number of American combat troops, Nixon and Kissinger actually expanded the air war in an effort to persuade the enemy to come to terms. On March 18, 1969, American planes began "Operation Menu," a fourteen-month-long bombing of Communist sanctuaries in Cambodia. Congress did not learn of these secret raids until 1970, although the total tonnage of bombs dropped was four times that dropped on Japan during World War II. Then on April 30, 1970, Nixon went on television to announce what he called an "incursion" into Cambodia by United States troops to "clean out" Communist staging areas. The head of Cambodia's government for two decades, Prince Norodom Sihanouk, had previously objected to such raids into his country, but Sihanouk had been replaced in a coup by Gen. Lon Nol earlier in the spring, clearing the way for the American invasion. Finally, on December 18, 1972, the president ordered the saturation bombing of Hanoi and Haiphong, the two largest cities in North Vietnam. These so-called Christmas bombings by B-52s, and the simultaneous mining of North Vietnamese harbors, aroused worldwide protest. "Civilized man will be horrified," read a New York *Times* editorial. Captured American pilots—fifteen of the giant B-52s were shot down—were paraded before television cameras to express regret at the civilian deaths and carnage, which the Pentagon described as the unfortunate consequence of North Vietnamese decisions to place military targets, such as airfields and munitions depots, in the middle of highly populated areas.

DIVISIONS AT HOME   The effect of America's gradual withdrawal on the morale and reputation of the American military was devastating. Beginning in 1969, when it became clear that military victory was no longer the goal, whole combat units refused to obey orders to fight. "No one wants to be the last grunt to die in this lousy war," said one soldier. In May 1969 the newspaper *GI Says* offered a bounty of $10,000 for the murder of the officer who ordered the assault on "Hamburger Hill," where 476 American soldiers had died to capture a position which was abandoned the following day. Between 1969 and 1971 there were 730 reported "fragging" incidents, efforts to kill or injure officers, usually with fragmentation grenades. Even the old marching chants became cynical, as troops shouted, "If I die in a combat zone, box me up and ship me home," while keeping cadence. Drugs became a major problem. In 1971 four times as many American troops were hospitalized for drug abuse as for combat-related wounds. "In Vietnam," wrote Col. Robert

The face of a "nightmare war," south of the demilitarized zone, Vietnam. [Larry Burrows, Life magazine, © Time Inc.]

Heinl, Jr., the army "is numbly extricating itself from a nightmare war . . . foisted on them by bright civilians who are now back on campus writing books about the folly of it all."

And back on the homefront the public learned of previously suppressed events in Vietnam that caused even the staunchest supporters of the war to wince. Late in 1969 the story of the My Lai massacre broke in the press and plunged the country into two years of exposure to the gruesome tale of Lt. William Calley, who ordered the murder of over 200 civilians in My Lai village in March 1968. Twenty-five army officers were charged with complicity in the massacre and subsequent cover-up, but only Calley was convicted; Nixon eventually granted him parole.

Perhaps the loudest public outcry against Nixon's Indochina policy occurred in the wake of the Cambodian "incursion." Nixon's television speech of April 30, 1970, sounded the tocsin: "we will not be defeated. . . . If, when the chips are down, the world's most powerful nation . . . acts like a pitiful, helpless giant, the forces of totalitarianism and anarchy will threaten free nations and free institutions throughout the world." Campuses across the country exploded in what William J. McGill, the president of Columbia University, called "the most disastrous month of May in the history of American higher education." Hundreds of colleges and universities closed down. At Kent State University the Ohio National Guard was called in to quell rioting in which the campus Reserve Officer Training Corps (ROTC) building was burned. The young guardsmen panicked and opened fire on the demonstrators, killing four bystanders. Eleven days later, on May 15, Mississippi highway patrolmen riddled a dormitory at Jackson State College with bullets, killing two black students.

Although an official investigation of the Kent State episode condemned the "casual and indiscriminate shooting," polls indicated that the American public supported the actions by the National Guard; students had "got what they were asking for." In New York City, antiwar demonstrators who gathered to protest the deaths at Kent State and the invasion of Cambodia were attacked by "hard-hat" construction workers, who forced the student protesters to disperse and then marched on City Hall to raise the flag that had been lowered to half-staff in mourning for the Kent State victims.

The following year, in June 1971, the New York *Times* began publishing excerpts from a secret Defense Department study commissioned by Robert McNamara before his departure from government. The so-called *Pentagon Papers*, leaked to the press by a former Defense Department official, Daniel Ellsberg, confirmed what many critics of the war had long suspected: as in the case of American naval aid to Britain in 1941, Congress and the people had not received the full story on the Gulf of Tonkin incident of 1964; and as in 1940–1941, contingency plans for American entry into the war were being drawn up while Johnson was promising the American people that combat troops would never be sent to Vietnam. Moreover there was no plan for bringing the war to an end so long as the North Vietnamese persisted. The Nixon administration attempted to block publication of the *Pentagon Papers*, arguing that they endangered national security and that their publication would prolong the war. By a vote of 6 to 3 the Supreme Court ruled against the government. Newspapers throughout the country began publication the next day.

The Vietnam War caused vehement divisions between "hawks" and "doves," old and young, even parents and children. [Conrad in the Los Angeles Times]

"Son . . . !" "Dad . . . !"

Conrad in The Los Angeles Times

WAR WITHOUT END   The mounting social divisions at home and
the approach of the 1972 presidential elections combined to
produce a shift in the American negotiating position in Paris. In
the summer of 1972 Henry Kissinger began meeting privately
with Le Duc Tho, the North Vietnamese negotiator, and
dropped his insistence on the removal of all North Vietnamese
troops from the south before the withdrawal of American troops.
On October 26, only a week before the American presidential
election, Kissinger announced: "Peace is at hand." But the Thieu
regime in South Vietnam objected to the plan for a cease-fire,
fearful that the presence of North Vietnamese troops in the south
virtually guaranteed an eventual Communist victory. The talks
broke off on December 16 and the next day the B-52 raids on
Hanoi and Haiphong began. The "Christmas bombings" stopped
on December 30, and the resumption of talks in Paris soon followed. On January 27, 1973, the United States signed an
"agreement on ending the war and restoring peace in Vietnam."
While Nixon and Kissinger both claimed that the bombing had
brought North Vietnam to its senses, in truth the North Vietnamese never altered their basic stance; they kept troops in the south
and remained committed to the reunification of Vietnam under
one government. What had changed since the previous fall was
the willingness of the South Vietnamese to accept these terms,
albeit reluctantly, on the basis of Nixon's promise that the United
States would respond "with full force" to any violation of the
agreement.

On March 29, 1973, the last American combat troops left
Vietnam. And on that same day the last of several hundred American prisoners-of-war, most of them downed pilots, were released from Hanoi. Within a period of months the cease-fire in
Vietnam ended, however, the war between north and south resumed, and the military superiority of the Communist forces
soon became evident. In Cambodia and Laos, where fighting had
been more sporadic, Communist victory also seemed inevitable.
In March 1975 the North Vietnamese launched a full-scale offensive against the south, which appealed to Washington for assistance. Congress refused. The much-mentioned "peace with
honor" had proven to be, in the words of one CIA official, only a
"decent interval"—enough time for the United States to extricate itself from Vietnam before the collapse of the South Vietnamese government. On April 30 Americans watched on
television as North Vietnamese tanks rolled into Saigon, soon to
be named Ho Chi Minh City, and helicopters lifted the officials in
the American embassy to ships waiting offshore. In those last des-

As Saigon falls to the North Vietnamese, mobs scale the 14-foot wall of the U.S. Embassy to reach helicopters for evacuation, May 1, 1975. [World Photos]

perate moments, crying South Vietnamese hung on the landing gear of the helicopters as they took off; a sign in the embassy courtyard read "Turn off the light at the end of the tunnel when you leave."

The longest and most controversial war in American history was over, leaving in its wake a bitter legacy that was a mirror-image of the goals that the United States had cited as justifications for involvement ten years earlier. The war fought to prevent the "domino effect" in Asia had left Communists in control of Vietnam, Laos, and Cambodia, and threatening in Thailand. The war described as a noble crusade in behalf of democratic ideals instead suggested that democracy was not easily transferrable to Third World regions that lacked any historical experience with liberal values and representative government. The war designed to serve as a showcase for American military power instead eroded respect for the military so thoroughly that many young Americans came to regard military service as corrupting and ignoble. The war fought to show the world that the United States was united in its convictions, divided Americans more drastically than any event since the Civil War, and prompted European nations to doubt American reliability and revolutionary leaders in the Third World to mock American pretensions.

Little wonder that the dominant reaction to the war's end was the urge to "put Vietnam behind us," in President Gerald Ford's phrase, and forget. Although subsequent debates over American foreign policy in the Middle East, Africa, and Latin America frequently involved recourse to "the lessons of Vietnam," the phrase was used by different factions for diametrically opposed purposes, ranging from refusal to commit American troops and resources in El Salvador to an insistence on massive military commitments unfettered by any diplomatic restrictions that might preclude outright victory. "In the end, then," wrote Leslie H. Gelb, a longtime student of American policy on the Vietnam era, "there was no end at all."

NIXON AND MIDDLE AMERICA

Richard Nixon had been elected in 1968 as the representative of "Middle America," the champion of those middle-class citizens fed up with the politics and promises of the 1960s. The Nixon cabinet and White House staff reflected their values. The chief figures were John Mitchell, the gruff attorney-general who had made his fortune as a municipal bond lawyer in Nixon's old firm; H. R. Haldeman and John Ehrlichman, advisers on domestic policy whose major experience before their association with the Nixon campaign had been in advertising; William Rogers, the secretary of state, an oldtime Nixon friend whose control over foreign policy was quickly preempted by Henry Kissinger; and Melvin Laird, the secretary of defense, who also found his influence undercut by Kissinger's access to the White House. Robert Finch, the secretary of health, education and welfare, and Walter Hickle, the secretary of the interior, demonstrated instincts for independence that soon led to their resignations. The cabinet was all white, all male, all Republican. "There are no blooded patricians in the lot," said *Time* magazine, "just strivers who have acted out the middle-class dream."

DOMESTIC AFFAIRS   If a balanced assessment of the Kennedy foreign policy is only now becoming possible, a detached evaluation of the domestic record of the Nixon administration remains out of reach, in part because the Watergate scandal affixed a stigma on Nixon's administration that colors all judgments, in part because the major legislative achievements happened largely in spite of rather than because of Nixon's efforts. Nixon was the first new president since 1849 to confront a Congress in which both houses were under the control of the opposition party. It therefore followed that he focused his energies on foreign policy, where presidential initiatives were less encumbered and where he, in tandem with Kissinger, achieved several stunning breakthroughs. The domestic front became a holding action in which Nixon, like Eisenhower before him, found it difficult to stop the march of liberal programs.

Despite the efforts of the Nixon administration, the civil rights legislation enacted during the Johnson years continued to take

In July 1969, a program begun by Kennedy reached its goal: putting a man on the moon. [NASA]

effect. "There are those who want instant integration and those who want segregation forever," said Nixon in September of 1969. "I believe we need to have a middle course between these extremes." In practice this "middle course" took the shape of a concerted effort in 1970 to block congressional renewal of the Voting Rights Act and to delay implementation of court orders requiring the desegregation of school districts in Mississippi. "For the first time since Woodrow Wilson," said the head of the NAACP, "we have a national administration that can be rightly characterized as anti-Negro." Sixty-five lawyers in the Justice Department signed a letter of protest against the administration's stance and Robert Finch eventually resigned from the cabinet in protest. Congress then extended the Voting Rights Act over Nixon's veto. The Supreme Court, in the first decision made under the new Chief Justice Warren Burger—a Nixon appointee—ordered the integration of the Mississippi schools. In *Alexander v. Holmes County Board of Education* (1969) a unanimous Court ordered a quick end to segregation. Fifteen years after the original school desegregation cases, the standard of "all deliberate speed" no longer applied. During Nixon's first term more schools were desegregated than in all the Kennedy-Johnson years combined.

Nixon's attempts to block desegregation efforts in urban areas also failed. The Burger Court ruled unanimously in *Swann v. Charlotte-Mecklenburg Board of Education* (1971) that cities must bus students out of their neighborhoods if this was necessary to achieve integration. As it happened, one little-noticed result was that the change caused shorter bus trips, on average, for

Charlotte-Mecklenburg students. Protest over desegregation now began to manifest itself more in the North than in the South as white families in Boston, Denver, and other cities denounced the destruction of "the neighborhood school"; and angry parents in Pontiac, Michigan, fire-bombed school buses. Sensing the anxieties that white parents felt about the busing issue, Nixon asked Congress to impose a moratorium on all busing orders by the federal courts. The House of Representatives, equally attuned to voter outrage at busing, went along. But in the Senate, Walter Mondale of Minnesota and Jacob Javits of New York led a filibuster that blocked the president's antibusing bill. Busing opponents won a limited victory when the Supreme Court ruled, in *Milliken v. Bradley* (1974), that desegregation plans in Detroit requiring the transfer of students from the inner city to the suburbs were unconstitutional. This landmark decision, along with the *Bakke v. Board of Regents of California* (1978) decision which restricted the use of quotas to achieve racial balance, marked the transition of desegregation from an issue of simple justice to a more tangled thicket of conflicting group and individual rights.

The shift of the Supreme Court toward a more moderate posture was a clear Nixon legacy, although even here the president got only part of what he wanted. The Warren Court had become a bastion of liberal values and a visible symbol of all that the "silent majority" loved to hate. Not only had its civil rights decisions disrupted traditional social patterns in the North as well as the South, but its stand on civil liberties had offended the sensibilities of almost all the groups that voted for Nixon. In *Engel v. Vitale* (1962) the Court had ruled that a school prayer adopted by the New York State Board of Regents violated the constitutional prohibition against an established religion. In *Baker v. Carr* (1962) the Court had ordered the Tennessee state legislature to apportion representation in accord with the "one man, one vote" principle. In *Gideon v. Wainwright* (1963) the Court required that every felony defendant be provided a lawyer regardless of the defendant's ability to pay. And in *Miranda v. Arizona* (1966) the Court had confirmed the obligation of police to inform arrested suspects of their rights. This litany of liberal decisions had made the Warren Court a prime target for mostly middle-class Americans who resented what they regarded as the federal government's excessive protection of the "undeserving."

Fate and the aging of the justices on the Warren Court gave Nixon the chance to make four new appointments. His first,

Warren Burger, caused no uproar. But Nixon's next two nominations generated opposition in the Senate. Clement F. Haynsworth, a federal appeals court judge from South Carolina, had the support of the American Bar Association but drew fire from civil rights groups and labor unions for his conservative record. There was no question of Haynsworth's integrity, but the Senate rejected him when it learned that he had heard a case involving a subsidiary of a corporation in which he owned a small amount of stock. The nomination of G. Harold Carswell, a judge of the Florida appeals court, created even more opposition. Carswell had not only been an out-and-out defender of white supremacy, but he was acknowledged by all parties to be singularly lacking in distinction. By a vote of 51 to 45 the Senate rejected Carswell. Nixon, who was accused by several senators of tarnishing the image of the Court in order to pursue his "Southern Strategy" for reelection, condemned the Senate rejection as "an act of regional discrimination." But he took care thereafter to nominate jurists of stature for the Supreme Court: Harry Blackmun, a compatriot of Burger's from Minnesota; Lewis F. Powell, Jr., a respected conservative judge from Virginia; and William Rehnquist, an articulate, conservative lawyer in the Justice Department. None encountered serious opposition in the Senate. And none, save perhaps Rehnquist, would consistently support Nixon's interpretation of the Constitution.

Nixon had also promised to "get tough on crime," a promise difficult to fulfill because criminal statutes were local and state concerns. In July 1969, however, he proposed a crime bill for the District of Columbia designed to clarify his administration's tough stance and thereby assume symbolic leadership as "the nation's number one cop." The bill empowered judges to jail suspects for sixty days before trial ("preventive detention") and allowed policemen to break into houses without a warrant ("no knock"). Sen. Samuel J. Ervin, Jr., of North Carolina called it "A bill to repeal the fourth, fifth, sixth and eighth amendments to the Constitution." Afraid of appearing "soft" on crime, Congress passed the bill, but its influence on state and local laws proved negligible.

The single most innovative piece of domestic legislation proposed by the administration was the Family Assistance Plan, a proposal to overhaul the welfare system and cut out several layers of the bureaucracy created by Great Society programs. Daniel Patrick Moynihan, head of the Council on Urban Affairs, drafted the plan, which called for direct grants of $1,600 to poor families: in short, a guaranteed income floor. The idea had support among a wide range of experts, including some conservatives, but the plan's constituency had little political clout. The Family Assistance Plan went down to defeat in the Congress, in part because Nixon had insisted that it was "workfare and not welfare." In truth the plan was unadulterated welfare—a guaranteed income—but liberals in Congress, befuddled by Nixon's characterization of the plan, or miffed that it did not go far enough, joined with conservatives in an unusual alliance to kill the bill.

Nixon invented several names for his domestic program. At one point it was called the "New Federalism," which would "start resources and power flowing back from Washington to the people." To that end he proposed, and got from Congress in 1972, a five-year revenue-sharing plan which would distribute $30 billion of federal revenues to the states for use as they saw fit. At another point Nixon called for a "New American Revolution" to revive traditional values. These catch-phrases never caught on, as had the "New Frontier" or the "Great Society," because Nixon's domestic program was essentially defensive and negative.

In the fall of 1969 Nixon sent Vice-President Spiro Agnew on a national speaking tour to stigmatize the opposition. Agnew and a clutch of White House speechwriters described war protesters as "anarchists and ideological eunuchs," the liberal news media as "an effete corps of impudent snobs" and "nattering nabobs of negativism." It was time, said Agnew, "to rip away the rhetoric and divide on authentic lines. . . . When the president said 'bring us together,' he meant the functioning, contributing portions of the American citizenry." But while Agnew turned phrases, the Democratic Congress moved forward with new legislation: the right of eighteen-year-olds to vote in national elections (1970), extended to all elections by the Twenty-sixth Amendment (1971); an increase in Social Security benefits and food-stamp funding; passage of the Occupational Safety and Health Act (1970), the Clean Air Act (1970), new acts to control water pollution (1970 and 1972), and the Federal Election Campaign Act (1972).

ECONOMIC MALAISE   The economy proved even less responsive to conservative rhetoric than the Democratic Congress. The inflation rate began to rise in 1967, when it was at 3 percent. By 1973 it was at 9 percent; a year later it was at 12 percent, and it remained in double digits for most of the 1970s. The Dow-Jones average of major industrial stocks, at 985 a month after Nixon's election, fell to 631 on May 26, 1970, its steepest decline in over thirty years. In 1970 real gross national product (adjusted for inflation) declined for the first time since 1958, and the following year American imports exceeded exports for the first time since 1893. Meanwhile unemployment, at a low of 3.3 percent when Nixon took office, climbed to 6 percent by the end of 1970 and threatened to keep rising. Somehow the American economy was undergoing a recession and inflation at the same time. Economists coined the term "stagflation" to describe the syndrome which defied the orthodox laws of economics.

The economic malaise had at least three deep-rooted causes. First, the Johnson administration had attempted to pay for both the Great Society and the war in Vietnam without a major tax increase, generating huge federal deficits, a major expansion of the money supply, and the inevitable price inflation. Second, and more important, by the late 1960s American goods faced stiff competition in international markets from West Germany, Japan, and other emerging industrial powers. No longer was American technological superiority unquestioned. Third, the American economy had depended heavily on cheap sources of energy; no nation was more dependent on the automobile and the automobile industry, and no nation was more careless in its use of fossil fuels in factories and homes. Just as domestic petroleum reserves began to dwindle and dependence on foreign sources increased, the Organization of Petroleum Exporting Countries (OPEC) combined to use their oil as a political and economic weapon. In 1973 when the United States sent massive aid to Israel after a devastating Syrian-Egyptian attack on Yom Kippur, the holiest day in the Jewish calendar, OPEC announced in October that it would not sell oil to nations supporting Israel and that it was raising its prices by 400 percent. Motorists faced long lines at gas stations, schools and offices closed down, factories cut production, and the inflation rate took off as if fueled by all the oil not being delivered to the United States.

Stagflation posed a new set of economic problems, but Nixon responded erratically and ineffectively with the old remedies. First, he tried to reduce the federal deficit by raising taxes and cutting the budget. When the Democratic Congress refused to cooperate with this approach, he followed the advice of Milton Friedman, the conservative economist at the University of Chicago, and encouraged the Federal Reserve Board to reduce the money supply by raising interest rates. The stock market immediately collapsed and the economy plunged into the "Nixon recession."

In 1969, when asked about wage and price controls, Nixon had been unequivocal: "Controls. Oh, my God, no! I was a lawyer for the OPA [Office of Price Administration] during the war and I know all about controls. . . . We'll never go to controls." But on August 15, 1971, he reversed himself, probably under the influence of John Connally, the aggressive new secretary of the treasury. He froze all wages and prices for ninety days and announced that the United States would no longer convert dollars into gold for foreign banks. This ended an era that had begun with the international agreement reached at Bretton Woods, New Hampshire, in 1944. The United States had made the dollar convertible to gold at $35 an ounce, thereby setting a firm standard by which other currencies were measured. Now the dollar, its link to gold cut, drifted lower on world currency exchanges. After ninety days Nixon established mandatory guidelines for subsequent wage and price increases under the supervision of a federal agency. Still the economy floundered. When administration economists kept predicting an imminent upturn, journalists recalled General Westmoreland's predictions of victory in Vietnam. By 1973 the wage and price guidelines were made voluntary, and therefore almost entirely ineffective.

Nixon Triumphant

CHINA If the ailments of the economy proved more than Nixon could remedy, in foreign policy his administration managed to diagnose and treat American relations with the major powers of the Communist world—China and the Soviet Union—and to shift fundamentally the pattern of the Cold War. In July 1971 Henry Kissinger made a secret trip to Peking° to explore the possibility of American recognition of China. Since 1949, when Mao Tse-tung's revolutionary movement overturned the government of Chiang Kai-shek, the United States had refused to recognize Communist China, preferring to regard the exiled regime on Taiwan as the legitimate government of China. In one simple but stunning stroke, Nixon and Kissinger ended two decades of diplomatic isolation for the People's Republic of China and drove a wedge between the two chief bastions of communism in the world.

° The traditional spellings are used here. After Mao's death the Chinese government adopted the "Pinyin" transliterations that are used today: Peking = Beijing; Mao Tse-tung = Mao Zedong; and Chou En-lai = Zhou Enlai.

President Nixon and the chairman of the Chinese Communist party, Mao Tse-tung, February 22, 1972. [United Press International]

In February 1972 Americans watched on television as their president visited famous Chinese landmarks, which had been invisible to the West for over two decades, and drank toasts with Premier Chou En-lai and Mao Tse-tung. The United States and China agreed to scientific and cultural exchanges, steps toward the resumption of trade, and the eventual reunification of Taiwan with the mainland. A year after the Nixon visit, "liaison offices" were established in Washington and Peking that served as unofficial embassies, and in 1979 diplomatic recognition was formalized. Richard Nixon, the former anti-Communist crusader who had condemned the State Department for "losing" China in 1949, accomplished a diplomatic feat his more liberal predecessors could not.

DÉTENTE   In truth, China welcomed the breakthrough in relations with the United States because its rivalry with the Soviet Union, with which it shared a long border, had become more bitter than its rivalry with the West. The Soviet leaders, troubled by the Sino-American agreements, were also anxious for an easing of tensions now that they had, as the result of a huge arms buildup following the Cuban missile crisis, achieved virtual parity with the United States in nuclear weapons. Once again the president surprised the world, by announcing that he would visit Moscow in May 1972 for discussions with Leonid Brezhnev, the Soviet premier. The high theater of the China visit was repeated in Moscow, with toasts and elegant dinners between world leaders who had previously regarded one another as incarnations of evil.

What became known as "détente" with the Soviets offered the

promise of a more orderly and restrained competition between the two superpowers. Nixon and Brezhnev signed agreements reached at the Strategic Arms Limitation Talks (SALT) which negotiators had been working on since 1969 in Helsinki and Vienna. The SALT agreement did not end the arms race, but it did set limits to the number of intercontinental ballistic missiles (ICBMs) and sharp limits to the construction of antiballistic missile systems (ABMs). In effect the Soviets were allowed to retain a greater number of missiles with greater destructive power while the United States retained a lead in the total number of warheads. No limitations were placed on new weapons systems, though each side agreed to work toward a permanent freeze on all nuclear weapons. The Moscow summit also produced new trade agreements, including an arrangement whereby the United States sold almost one-quarter of its wheat crop to the Soviets at a favorable price. American farmers rejoiced, since the wheat deal assured them a high price for their crop, but domestic critics grumbled that the deal would raise food prices in the United States and rescue the Russians from troublesome economic problems.

SHUTTLE DIPLOMACY   The Nixon-Kissinger initiatives in the Middle East were less dramatic and conclusive than the China or Russia agreements, but did show that America recognized Arab power in the region and its own dependence on the oil from Islamic states fundamentally opposed to Israel. After the Six-Day War of 1967, in which Israeli forces routed the armies of Egypt, Syria, and Jordan, Israel seized territory from all three Arab nations. Moreover the Palestinian refugees, many of them homeless since the creation of Israel in 1948, were made much more numerous by the Israeli victory in 1967. When Israel recovered from the initial shock of the surprise Yom Kippur War of 1973, Kissinger negotiated a cease-fire and exerted pressure to prevent Israel from seizing additional Arab territory. American reliance on Arab oil led to closer ties with Egypt and its president, Anwar el-Sadat, and more restrained support for Israel. Kissinger, whose "shuttle diplomacy" among the capitals of the Middle East won acclaim from all sides, failed to find a comprehensive formula for peace in the troubled region and ignored altogether the Palestinian problem, but did lay groundwork for the subsequent accord between Israel and Egypt in 1977.

THE 1972 ELECTION   Nixon's foreign policy achievements allowed him to stage the campaign of 1972 as a triumphal procession. At the Republican convention Nixon's nomination was a foregone conclusion. Film stars who symbolized the certitudes of an earlier era—John Wayne, Jimmy Stewart, Glenn Ford—delivered patriotic endorsements. The main threat to Nixon's re-election came from George Wallace, who had the potential as a third-party candidate to deprive the Republicans of conservative votes and thereby throw the election to the Democrats or the Democratic-controlled Congress. But on May 15, 1972, Wallace was shot and left permanently paralyzed below the waist by Arthur Bremer, a white midwesterner anxious to achieve a grisly brand of notoriety. Wallace was forced to withdraw from the campaign.

Meanwhile the Democrats were further ensuring Nixon's victory by nominating Sen. George S. McGovern of South Dakota, a crusading liberal who embodied antiwar and social welfare values associated with the turbulence of the 1960s. At the Democratic convention in Chicago McGovern's nomination was made easier by party reforms which increased the representation of women, blacks, and minorities, but which alienated the party regulars. Mayor Richard Daley of Chicago was actually ousted from the convention, and the AFL-CIO refused to endorse the Democratic candidate. McGovern also suffered from his handling of the crisis that developed when it was revealed that his running mate, Sen. Thomas Eagleton of Missouri, had undergone shock treatments for emotional disturbances. McGovern first announced complete support for Eagleton, then bowed to critics and dropped him in favor of Sargent Shriver, leaving an impression of vacillation and indecisiveness.

The campaign was an exercise in futility for McGovern, while Nixon made only a few formal political trips and cast himself in the role of "global peacekeeper." Nixon won the greatest victory of any Republican presidential candidate in history, winning 521 electoral votes to only 21 for McGovern. The popular vote was equally decisive: 45.9 million to 28.4 million, a margin of 60.8 percent that was second only to Johnson's victory over Goldwater in 1964. During the course of the campaign McGovern complained about the "dirty tricks" of the Nixon administration, most especially the curious incident in which a group of burglars was caught red-handed breaking into the Democratic National Committee headquarters in the Watergate apartment complex in Washington. McGovern's accusations seemed shrill and biased at the time, the lamentations of an obvious loser. Nixon and his staff made plans for "four more years" as the investigation of the fateful Watergate break-in proceeded apace.

WATERGATE

Under the relentless prodding of Judge John J. Sirica, one of the burglars began to tell the full story of the Nixon administration's complicity in the Watergate episode. James W. McCord, a former CIA agent and security chief for the Committee to Re-elect the President (CREEP), was the first in a long line of informers and penitents in a melodrama which unfolded over the next two years and which mixed the special qualities of soap opera and Machiavellian intrigue. It ended in the first resignation of a president in American history, the conviction and imprisonment of twenty-five officials of the Nixon administration, including four cabinet members, and the most serious constitutional crisis since the impeachment trial of Andrew Johnson.

UNCOVERING THE COVER-UP The trail of evidence pursued first by Judge Sirica, then a grand jury, then a Senate investigation committee headed by Sen. Samuel J. Ervin, Jr., of North Carolina, led directly to the White House. Sen. Howard Baker of Tennessee, a member of the Ervin Committee, put the crucial questions succinctly: "What did the President know and when did he know it?" There was never any evidence that Nixon ordered the break-in or that he was aware of plans to burglarize the Democratic National Committee. What the evidence did show conclusively was that from the start Nixon was personally involved in the cover-up of the incident, that he used his presidential powers to discredit and block the investigation, and most alarming, that the Watergate burglary was merely one small part of a larger pattern of corruption and criminality sanctioned by the Nixon White House.

The White House had become committed to illegal tactics in May 1970 when the New York *Times* broke the story of the secret bombings in Cambodia. Nixon had ordered illegal telephone taps on several newsmen and government employees suspected of leaking the story. The covert activity against the press and critics of Nixon's Vietnam policies increased in 1971 during the crisis generated by the publication of the *Pentagon Papers*, when a team of burglars under the direction of White House adviser John Ehrlichman had broken into a psychiatrist's office in an effort to obtain damaging information on Daniel Ellsberg. By the spring of 1972 Ehrlichman commanded a team of "dirty tricksters" who performed various acts of sabotage against prospective Democratic candidates for the presidency, including falsely accusing Hubert Humphrey and Sen. Henry Jackson of sexual improprieties, forging press releases, setting off stink-bombs, and associating the opposition candidates with racist remarks. By the time of the Watergate break-in, the money to finance such "pranks" was being illegally collected through the Committee to Re-elect the President and placed under the control of the White House staff.

The cover-up unraveled further in April 1973 when L. Patrick Gray, acting director of the FBI, resigned after confessing that he had confiscated and destroyed several incriminating documents. On April 30 Ehrlichman and Haldeman resigned, together with Attorney-General Richard Kleindienst. Then the Ervin Committee heard John Dean, whom Nixon had dismissed as counsel to the president, testify that there had been a cover-up and that Nixon had approved it. In another "bombshell" disclosure Alexander Butterfield, a White House aide, told the committee that Nixon had installed a taping system in the White House—many of the conversations about Watergate had been recorded.

A year-long battle for the "Nixon tapes" began. The Harvard law professor Archibald Cox, who had been appointed by Nixon as special prosecutor to handle the Watergate case, took the president to court in October 1973 in order to obtain the tapes. Nixon, pleading "executive privilege," refused to release the tapes and ordered Cox fired. In what became known as the "Saturday Night Massacre," Attorney-General Elliot Richardson and Deputy Attorney-General William Ruckelshaus resigned rather than execute the order. Cox's replacement as special prosecutor, Leon Jaworski, proved no more pliable than Cox, and also took the president to court. On July 24, 1974, the Supreme Court voted unanimously that the president must surrender the tapes. A few days later the House Judiciary Committee voted to recommend three articles of impeachment: obstruction of justice through the payment of "hush money" to witnesses and the witholding of evidence; using federal agencies to deprive citi-

Sen. Sam Ervin, chairman of the Senate Watergate Committee, swears in the ex-White House Counsel John Dean, whose testimony linked President Nixon to the cover-up. [United Press International]

Having resigned his office, Richard Nixon waves farewell outside the White House, August 9, 1974. [Wide World Photos]

zens of their constitutional rights; and defiance of Congress by withholding the tapes. But before the House of Representatives could meet to vote on impeachment, Nixon handed over the complete set of White House tapes. On August 9, 1974, fully aware that the evidence on the tapes implicated him in the cover-up, he resigned from office, the only president ever to do so.

EFFECTS OF WATERGATE   Nixon was not succeeded by Spiro Agnew because Agnew himself had been forced to resign in October 1973 when it became known that he had accepted bribes from contractors before and during his term as vice-president. The vice-president at the time of Nixon's resignation was Gerald Ford, the former minority leader in the House whom Nixon had appointed, with the approval of Congress, under provisions of the Twenty-fifth Amendment, which had been ratified in 1964 in the wake of President Kennedy's assassination. Ford insisted that he had no intention of pardoning Nixon, who was still liable for criminal prosecution. "I do not think the public would stand for it," said Ford. But a month after Nixon's resignation the new president explained that a pardon was necessary to end the national obsession with the Watergate scandals.

Many concluded that Nixon and Ford had made a deal, though there was no evidence to confirm the speculation. President Ford testified personally to a congressional committee: "There was no deal, period." But Watergate spawned a wave of cynicism. In the spring of 1974 polls showed that a majority of Americans believed that Nixon was lying about his complicity, but that four out of five judged him as no more guilty of wrongdoing than his presidential predecessors. The Watergate scandals and Nixon's resignation seemed to justify the most distrustful appraisals of American leaders and political institutions; little wonder that less than half the eligible electorate would vote in the next presidential election. Apart from Nixon's illegal action, the language used in the White House and made public in the tapes stripped away the veils of mystery surrounding national leaders and left even the die-hard defenders of presidential authority shocked at the crudity and duplicity of Nixon and his subordinates. If there was a silver lining in this dark cloud, it was the vigor and resiliency of the institutions that had brought a president down—the press, Congress, the courts, and an aroused public opinion.

Although many observers attributed Watergate to the idiosyncracies of one man, Richard Nixon, claiming that his entire political career revealed a quest for hidden enemies, Congress responded to the revelations of Watergate with several pieces of legislation designed to curb executive power in the future. The War Powers Act (1973) required the president to consult with Congress before sending American troops into combat abroad and to withdraw troops after sixty days unless Congress specifically approved their stay. In an effort to correct abuses of campaign funds, Congress enacted legislation in 1974 that set new ceilings on contributions and expenditures. And in reaction to the Nixon claim of "executive privilege," Congress strengthened the Freedom of Information Act to preclude the government from denying access to official documents "arbitrarily or capriciously."

REFORM SEVENTIES STYLE

While a president was being toppled, while Henry Kissinger was shuttling from the Paris peace talks to the Mideast, and while the nation was doing its best to forget the war in Vietnam, several social movements were gliding through the America of the 1970s with a life and momentum of their own. Women, Hispanics, and American Indians rode the waves created in the 1960s toward fresh goals. And the protection of the environment emerged as the prototypical reform movement in post-1960s America, demanding limitations rather than liberation and calling for a fatalistic acceptance of difficult economic and environmental "trade-offs."

THE WOMEN'S MOVEMENT   The movement for women's rights had roots in the rebellious sixties, and even deeper roots in the suffrage movements of the nineteenth century. But in the 1970s women achieved significant political and economic gains, overshadowing those of other minority groups which had occupied center stage in the 1960s but then suffered "benign neglect" in the Nixon years. This was in keeping with a century-old pattern in which women's rights blossomed during the latter stages of liberal reform movements: the Seneca Falls movement during the abolitionist crusade against slavery; the suffrage movement during the progressive era; and now the modern feminist movement in the wake of the civil rights and antiwar protests of the 1960s.

Betty Friedan's *The Feminine Mystique* (1963) launched the new phase of female protest. Friedan called attention to the fact that women had actually lost ground during the years after World War II, when "Rosie the Riveter" allegedly went home from the wartime assembly line and settled down before the television set in suburbia to watch "Queen for a Day" and care for the kids. In Friedan's view, the American middle-class home had become "a comfortable concentration camp" where women suffocated in an atmosphere of mindless consumption and affluent banality. The major rallying cry for the National Organization for Women (NOW), founded in 1966 by Friedan and soon regarded as the NAACP of the women's movement, became Title VII of the Civil Rights Act of 1964, which forbade discrimination in the workplace on the basis of sex. This title had been added to the original legislation by Rep. Howard Smith of Virginia, who had presumed that such a provision would make the bill so absurd as to kill it in Congress. NOW spearheaded efforts to end job discrimination, to legalize abortion, and to obtain federal and state support for child-care centers.

Statistical evidence confirmed that such bread-and-butter reforms spoke to a national need: in 1963 the average woman wage-earner made only 63¢ for every $1 a man earned; in the 1950s women comprised a smaller portion of the college population than they had in the 1920s. By the early 1970s Congress and the Supreme Court began to respond to pressure from women's groups committed to the cause of sexual equality. Under Title IX of the Educational Amendments Act of 1972, colleges were required to institute programs of "affirmative action" to ensure equal opportunity for women. In the same year Congress overwhelmingly approved the Equal Rights Amendment, which had been bottled up in a House committee for almost half a century, and the Supreme Court, in *Roe v. Wade*, struck down state laws forbidding abortions during the first three months of pregnancy. Meanwhile the educational bastions of male segregation, including Yale and Princeton, led a new movement for coeducation that swept the country. "If the 1960s belonged to blacks," said one feminist, "the next ten years are ours."

By the end of the decade divisions within the women's movement between moderate and radical feminists, as well as the movement's failure to broaden its appeal much beyond the confines of the middle class, caused reform efforts to stagnate. The Equal Rights Amendment, which had once seemed a straightforward assertion of equal opportunity ("Equality of rights under the law shall not be denied or abridged by the United States or by any State on account of sex") and assured of ratification, was stymied in several state legislatures. Despite a congressional extension of the normal time allowed for ratification, by 1982 it died several states short of passage. And the very success of NOW's efforts to change abortion laws generated a powerful reaction, especially among Catholics and fundamentalist Protestants, who mounted a "right to life" crusade of enormous power.

But the successes of the women's movement seemed likely to endure despite setbacks and long after the militant rhetoric had evaporated. For in fact women were not just another minority group pursuing the traditional path of liberal reform. They were a majority: they constituted 51 percent of the population. Their political power, only partially mobilized in the 1970s, had enormous potential for achieving social change. Moreover, their growing presence in the labor force assured women of a greater share of economic and political influence. In the year of the bicentennial, over half the married women in America and nine of ten women college graduates were employed outside the home, a development that one economist called "the single most outstanding phenomenon of this century." Many career women did not regard themselves as feminists; they took jobs because they and their families needed the money to survive or to achieve higher levels of material comfort. But regardless of their motives, traditional sex roles and childrearing practices were being changed to accommodate the two-career family. Indeed the two-career family had replaced the established pattern of male breadwinner and female housekeeper as the new American norm. "The classic differences between masculinity and femininity are disappearing," observed one sociologist, "as both sexes in the adult generation take on the same roles in the labor market." This quiet revolution continued apace into the 1980s.

HISPANICS   In the 1970s Hispanics also emerged as a new and powerful force that politicians could no longer ignore. In the 1960s the chief focus of attention was Cesar Chavez, who almost single-handedly founded the United Farm Workers (UFW) in California, then launched a series of strikes for an increase in the wages and benefits of migrant workers. By 1970 the UFW had won recognition from California's grape growers and national visibility for the plight of Hispanic farm laborers through well-publicized boycotts of table grapes and lettuce. By the middle 1970s the UFW was challenged less by the growers than by competition from the Teamsters Union, which attempted to muscle the UFW aside.

But the chief strength of the Hispanic movement lay less in the duplication of civil rights strategies than in the sheer growth of the Hispanic population. In 1960 Hispanics had numbered slightly more than 3 million; by 1970 they had increased to 9 million, and by 1980 they numbered 20 million, making them the largest minority in America after blacks. The most numerous among them were Mexican-Americans, or Chicanos, who were concentrated in California and the Southwest. Next came the Puerto Rican population, most of whom lived in New York City and the Connecticut Valley. Finally there were the Cubans, many refugees from Castro's regime, who were concentrated in southern Florida.

Although affluent Hispanics became influential in Miami and Los Angeles, the vast bulk of the Hispanic population were poor, deprived, and often isolated from the mainstream of American life by the language barrier. Bilingualism—the belief that Hispanics were entitled to schooling in Spanish as well as English—divided the Hispanic community between those who wished to cultivate their heritage and those who feared that failure to adopt English as their primary language would block their social advance. By 1980, however, aspiring presidential candidates were openly courting the Hispanic vote, promising support for urban renewal projects in New York and amnesty programs for illegal immigrants in Texas, and delivering rousing anti-Castro speeches in Miami. The voting power of Hispanics and their concentration in states with key electoral votes had helped give the Hispanic point of view political clout.

NATIVE AMERICANS   In addition to women and Hispanics, American Indians—some of whom preferred to call themselves Native Americans—emerged as a new political force in the 1970s. The Indian population grew in the 1960s, but remained tiny by national standards, totaling about 800,000 in 1970. Two conditions conspired to make Indian rights a priority: first, white Americans felt a deep and centuries-old sense of guilt for the destructive policies of their ancestors toward a people who had, after all, been here first; second, the plight of the Indian minority was more desperate than that of any other minority group in the country. Indian unemployment was ten times the national rate, their life expectancy was twenty years lower than the national average, and the suicide rate was a whopping one hundred times higher than the rate for whites. If blacks had extracted a deserved promise of compensation for past injustices from whites in the 1960s, Indians felt that they had an even more compelling claim on white consciences in the 1970s.

At first the Indian militants copied the tactics of civil rights and black power activists. In 1968 the American Indian Movement (AIM) was founded. The leaders of AIM occupied Alcatraz Island in San Francisco Bay in 1969, claiming the site "by right of discovery." And in 1972 an Indian "sit-in" at the Bureau of Indian Affairs in Washington attracted national attention to their cause. But the most celebrated protest occurred at Wounded Knee, South Dakota, in January 1973. It dramatized the impoverished conditions of Indians living on the reservations near Wounded Knee, which also happened to be the site of the infamous massacre of Sioux Indians by federal troops in 1890.

Soon Indian protesters discovered a more effective tactic than direct action and "sit-ins." They went into the federal courts armed with copies of the treaties signed by nineteenth-century American government officials and demanded that the violations of these treaties become the basis for restitution. In Alaska, Maine, and Massachusetts they won significant settlements that provided legal recognition of their tribal rights and financial compensation at levels that upgraded the standard of living on several reservations.

THE ENVIRONMENTAL MOVEMENT   The sudden emergence of widespread support for environmental protection in the early 1970s was a product of many Americans' recognition that there were limits to growth. The realization that cities and industrial development were damaging the physical environment and altering the earth's ecology was not new: Rachel Carson's *Silent Spring* (1962) had sounded the warning years earlier. But in Nixon's first term Congress took concerted action, passing several acts to protect and clean up the environment, and blocking support for development of the supersonic transport (SST) plane on grounds that its sonic boom would disrupt the atmosphere. The administration at the same time created by executive order the Environmental Protection Agency, a consolidation of existing agencies,

An Earth Day demonstration dramatizing the dangers of air pollution, April 1972. [Wide World Photos]

to oversee federal guidelines for air pollution, toxic wastes, and water quality.

The energy crisis that struck home after the Arab oil boycott and the OPEC price increase heightened the public awareness that natural resources were not infinitely expendable. "Although it's positively un-American to think so," said one sociologist, "the environmental movement and energy shortage have forced us all to accept a sense of our limits, to lower our expectations, to seek prosperity through conservation rather than growth." Historians, always interested in precedents, recalled Frederick Jackson Turner's observation that the disappearance of the frontier in the 1890s marked a new epoch in American history by ending the geographic expansion over the continent. Richard Nixon had "promised to bring us together," noted one critic of the new mood, "but he didn't tell us that we would be gathering around diminished energy supplies, a no-growth economy and a reduced sense of national power."

Although the environmental movement cut across class, racial, and ethnic lines by appealing to the collective interests of all Americans in clean air and water, it simultaneously aggravated the competition between regional vested interests. In Texas, where the oil lobby resented controls on gas prices and speed limits, bumper stickers read: "Drive fast, freeze a Yankee." In Tennessee, where a federal dam project was halted because it threatened the snail darter—a species of fish—with extinction, local developers took out ads asking residents to "tell the government that the size of your wallet is more important than some two-inch-long minnow."

As stagflation persisted into the middle and late 1970s, corporate criticism that environmental regulations were cutting into jobs and profit margins began to sound more persuasive, especially when the staggering cost of cleaning up accumulated toxic wastes became known. "Why worry about the long run," said one unemployed steelworker in 1976, "when you're out of work right now." Faith in the ability of the federal government to monitor environmental safeguards dissipated in the wake of the crisis at the nuclear power plant at Three Mile Island, Pennsylvania, in March 1979, when a combination of faulty equipment and inadequate safety provisions caused the radioactive core of the plant to overheat, threatening a large portion of the northeastern United States with radiation poisoning. Exposure of corrupt practices within the EPA during the Reagan administration also hurt the environmental cause. Polls showed that protection of the environment remained a high priority among a majority of Americans, but that few were willing to suffer a cutback in their standard of living to achieve that goal. "It was," bemoaned one journalist, "as if passengers knew they were boarding the *Titanic*, but preferred to jostle with one another for first class accommodations so they might enjoy as much of the voyage as possible."

DRIFTING: FORD AND CARTER

During Nixon's last year in office the Watergate crisis so dominated the Washington scene that the major domestic and foreign problems received little executive attention. Henry Kissinger assumed virtually complete control over the management of foreign policy, watching helplessly as the South Vietnamese forces began to crumble before North Vietnamese attacks, attempting with limited success to establish a framework for peace in the Middle East, and supporting the CIA role in overthrowing Salvador Allende, the popularly elected Marxist president of Chile who was subsequently murdered and replaced by Gen. Augusto Pinochet, a military dictator supposedly friendly to the United States. The persistent combination of inflation and recession and the mounting energy crisis received little attention.

THE FORD YEARS Gerald Ford inherited these simmering problems. An amiable and eminently honest man, Ford enjoyed widespread popular support for only a short time. His pardon of Nixon on September 8, 1974, generated a storm of criticism. And as president he soon took on the posture he had developed as a conservative minority leader in the House: nay-saying leader of the opposition who simply did not believe that the federal government should exercise much power over domestic affairs. In

President Gerald Ford, a week after taking office. [United Press International]

his fifteen months as president Ford vetoed thirty-nine bills, thereby outstripping Herbert Hoover's veto record in less than half the time. By resisting congressional pressure to reduce taxes and increase federal spending, he succeeded in plummeting the economy into the deepest recession since the Great Depression. Unemployment jumped to 9 percent in 1975 and the federal deficit hit a record $60 billion the next year. When New York City announced that it was near bankruptcy, unable to meet its payrolls and bond payments, Ford vowed "to veto any bill that has as its purpose a federal bailout of New York City." But he relented after the Senate and House banking committees guaranteed the loan; New York was, at least temporarily, saved from insolvency. Ford rejected wage and price controls to curb inflation, preferring voluntary restraints which he tried to bolster by passing out "WIN" buttons, symbolizing his campaign to "Whip Inflation Now." The WIN buttons instead became a national joke and a popular symbol of Ford's ineffectiveness in the fight against stagflation.

In foreign policy, Ford retained Henry Kissinger as secretary of state and attempted to pursue Nixon's goals of stability in the Middle East, rapprochement with China, and détente with the Soviet Union. Late in 1974 Ford met with Leonid Brezhnev at Vladivostok in Siberia and accepted the framework for another arms-control agreement that was to serve as the basis for SALT II. Meanwhile Kissinger's tireless shuttling between Cairo and Tel Aviv produced an agreement: Israel promised to return to Egypt most of the Sinai territory captured in the 1967 war, and the two nations agreed to rely on negotiations rather than force to settle future disagreements. These limited but significant achievements should have enhanced Ford's image, but they were drowned in the sea of criticism and carping that followed the collapse of South Vietnam in May 1975.

Not only had a decade of American effort in Vietnam proven futile, but the Khmer Rouge, the Cambodian Communist movement, had also won a resounding victory, plunging that country into a fanatical bloodbath. And the Arab oil cartel was threatening another boycott while other Third World nations denounced the United States as a depraved and declining imperialistic power. Daniel Patrick Moynihan, the new American ambassador to the United Nations, attempted to answer these shrill accusations with his own unique blend of Irish passion and patriotic stridency, but succeeded in further antagonizing American relations with the developing countries. Ford also lost his patience, sending in the Marines to rescue the crew of the American merchant ship *Mayaguez*, which had been captured by the Cambodian Communists in May 1975. This vigorous move won popular acclaim until it was disclosed that the Cambodians had already agreed to release the captured Americans; the marines killed in the operation had died needlessly.

THE 1976 ELECTION   The Democrats could hardly wait for the 1976 election. Ford managed to beat off a powerful challenge for the nomination from the right wing of the Republican party, who rallied behind the former California governor and Hollywood actor, Ronald Reagan. Since even the Republicans were divided over Ford's leadership, and since Ford's failure to solve the economic and energy problems was beyond dispute, the Democratic nominee seemed a shoo-in for the presidency. "We could run an aardvark this year," said one Democratic leader, "and win."

His party chose an obscure former naval officer turned peanut farmer who had served one term as governor of Georgia. Jimmy Carter campaigned harder than any of the other Democratic hopefuls; he capitalized on the post-Watergate cynicism by promising "I will never tell a lie to the American people" and citing his inexperience in the byways of Washington politics as an asset. With the help of a skilled Atlanta advertising executive, Gerald Rafshoon, and by dint of full-time campaigning for over a year, the Georgian outdistanced his better known rivals and sewed up the nomination before the convention. Facing the prospect of the first president from the Deep South since 1849, and the first ever born and bred in that particular briar patch, the media suffered a surfeit of "southern fried chic." Reporters marveled at a Baptist candidate who claimed to be "born-again," and began to speculate that Carter's native region harbored some

Georgia's Jimmy Carter campaigned full-time for a year before winning the Democratic nomination. [Library of Congress]

forgotten virtues down home, after all. Sen. Sam Ervin's performance at the Watergate hearings had prepared the way.

To the surprise of many pundits Carter drew together the New Deal coalition of southern whites, blacks, urban labor, and ethnic groups to win 41 million votes to Ford's 39 million, and a narrow electoral majority of 297 to 241. Polls showed that the Carter victory was attributable to a heavy turnout of blacks in the South, where Carter swept every state but Virginia. Carter also benefited from the appeal of Walter F. Mondale, his liberal running mate and a favorite among blue-collar workers and the urban poor. He lost most of the trans-Mississippi West, but no other Democratic candidate had made much headway there since Harry Truman in 1948. The big story of the election was the low voter turnout. "Neither Ford nor Carter won as many votes as Mr. Nobody," said one reporter, commenting on the fact that almost half the eligible voters, alienated by Watergate and the lackluster candidates, chose to sit out the election.

CARTER'S TERM   During the televised debates between the presidential candidates in 1976, Jimmy Carter had chided Ford by saying, "Anything you don't like about Washington, I suggest you blame on him." Once in office, Carter suffered the fate of all American presidents since Kennedy: after an initial honeymoon, during which Carter displayed folksy charms by walking down Pennsylvania Avenue after his inauguration rather than riding, and wearing cardigan sweaters during televised "fireside chats," his popularity and political effectiveness waned. Soon *Newsweek* was referring to the "corn bread-and-cardigan atmospherics" and television journalists were noting that, during one "fireside chat," the fire actually went out. The truth was that, like Ford before him, Carter faced an almost insurmountable set of domestic and international problems. He was expected to cure the economic recession and inflation at a time when all industrial economies were shaken by a shortage of energy and confidence. He was expected to reassert America's global power at a time of waning respect for America's international authority. And he was expected to do this, as well as buoy the national spirit, through a set of political institutions in which many Americans had lost faith. In short, Carter was predestined to fail at an impossible task.

During the first two years of his term Carter enjoyed several successes, most reflecting the values of moderate liberalism. His administration included more blacks and women than ever before in history; his appointment of Andrew Young, a former follower and protégé of Martin Luther King, as ambassador to the United Nations attracted the most attention. He created a federal task force to study the problem of Vietnam-era draft evaders and eventually offered amnesty to the thousands of young Americans who had fled the country rather than serve in Vietnam. He reformed the civil service and created new cabinet-level Departments of Energy and Education. And he pushed several significant environmental bills through Congress, including a bill to establish controls over strip mining, a "superfund" of $1.6 billion to clean up chemical waste sites, and a proposal to protect over 100 million acres of Alaskan land from development.

Carter's political predicament began to become clear in the debate over energy policy. Borrowing a phrase from William James, the president declared that solving the energy problem was "the moral equivalent of war" and presented the Congress with what he called "a comprehensive energy program" that would assure victory. Carter, like Hoover, served at a time of diminishing resources, and like that other engineer-businessman, had a distaste for "stroking" congressmen or wheeling and dealing to get legislation through. The energy bill passed in August 1978 was a gutted version of the original, reflecting the power of both conservative and liberal special-interest lobbies. One Carter aide said that the energy bill looked like it had been "nibbled to death by ducks."

Carter also urged the coupling of deregulation of the oil industry, which would increase prices and encourage domestic oil discovery, with a "windfall profits tax" on the oil companies, whose profits would skyrocket as a result of deregulation. Liberal congressmen resented deregulation because it meant higher prices for consumers. Conservatives opposed the windfall profits tax. The result was a bill that made no one happy. With party discipline in the Congress in a shambles and each special-interest group clamoring for its own program, the White House was forced to create what one Carter aide described as a "roll-your-own majority" for each presidential proposal. And Carter, unlike Wilson, FDR, and LBJ, was ill-equipped at maneuvering his proposals around congressional obstacles.

In the summer of 1979, when renewed violence in the Middle East produced a second fuel shortage, motorists were forced to wait in long lines again for limited supplies of gas that they regarded as excessively expensive. Opinion polls showed Carter with an approval rating of 26 percent, lower than Nixon during the worst moments of the Watergate crisis. Carter called his advisors to an extraordinary retreat at Camp David, Maryland, and emerged ten days later proclaiming a "crisis of confidence" and a need for "a rebirth of the American spirit." He also called for a "new and positive energy program." But motorists in the gas lines traded jokes about Carter's "born-again energy theology" and Congress only partially funded the major feature of his new plan—a federal agency to encourage development of synthetic fuels.

Several of Carter's early foreign policy initiatives also got caught in political crossfires. Soon after his inauguration Carter vowed that "the soul of our foreign policy" should be the defense of human rights abroad. But the human rights campaign came under attack from several sides: those who feared it sacrificed a detached appraisal of national interest for high-level moralizing, and those who pointed to the administration's inconsistency in applying the standard. But foreign policy always turns on multiple considerations, and the Carter policy was a reaffirmation of American ideals which heartened prisoners of conscience around the world.

Similarly, Carter's successful negotiation of treaties to turn over control of the Panama Canal to the government of Panama came under intense attack. Republican Ronald Reagan claimed that the Canal Zone was sovereign American soil purchased "fair and square" in Theodore Roosevelt's administration. (In the congressional debate one senator quipped, "We stole it fair and square, so why can't we keep it?") Carter argued that recognition of the limitations on American influence in Latin America, and the deep resentment toward American colonialism in Panama, left the United States with no other choice. The Senate ratified the treaties by a paper-thin margin (68 to 32, two votes more than the required two-thirds), but conservatives lambasted

Carter for surrendering American authority in a strategically critical part of the world. Finally, Carter completed the restoration of diplomatic relations with China, a process that had begun under Nixon. But because the Sino-American agreement of December 1978 required the United States to sever diplomatic relations with Taiwan, conservative critics condemned the agreement as a "sell-out" of the Taiwanese and another instance of American international withdrawal from past commitments.

ACHIEVEMENT AND FAILURE The crowning achievement of the Carter foreign policy, which even his most devoted critics applauded, was the arrangement of a peace agreement between Israel and Egypt. In November 1977 President Anwar el-Sadat flew to Tel Aviv at the invitation of Israeli Prime Minister Menachem Begin. Sadat's bold act, and his accompanying announcement that Egypt was now willing to recognize the legitimacy of the Israeli state, opened up diplomatic opportunities that Carter and Secretary of State Cyrus Vance quickly pursued. In September 1978 Carter invited Sadat and Begin to the presidential retreat at Camp David for two weeks of difficult negotiations. The first part of the eventual agreement called for Israel to return all land in the Sinai in exchange for Egyptian recognition of Israel's sovereignty. This agreement was successfully implemented in April 1982 when the last Israeli settler vacated the Sinai. But the second part of the agreement, calling for Israeli willingness to negotiate with Sadat to resolve the Palestinian refugee dilemma, began to unravel soon after the Camp David summit. By the time Begin and Sadat returned to Washington on March 26, 1979, to sign the formal treaty, Begin had already made clear his refusal to block new Israeli settlements on the West Bank of the Jordan River, which Sadat had regarded as a prospective homeland for the Palestinians, and most of the Arab nations had condemned Sadat as a traitor to their Islamic cause. Still, Carter and Vance were responsible for a dramatic display of high-level diplomacy that, whatever its limitations, made an all-out war between Israel and the Arab world less likely in the foreseeable future.

Carter's crowning failure, which even his most avid supporters acknowledged, was his management of the economy. In effect he inherited a bad situation and left it worse. Carter employed the same economic policies as Nixon and Ford to fight stagflation, but he reversed the order of the federal "cure," preferring to fight unemployment first with a tax cut and increased public spending. Unemployment declined slightly, from 8 to 7 percent in 1977, but inflation soared; at 5 percent when he took office, it reached 10 percent in 1978 and kept going. During one month in 1980 it measured an annual rate of no less than 18 percent. Like previous presidents, Carter then reversed himself to fight the other side of the economic malaise. By midterm he was delaying tax reductions and vetoing government spending programs that he had proposed in his first year. The result, however, was the worst of both possible worlds—a deepened recession with unemployment at 7.5 percent in 1980, mortgage rates at 15 percent, and interest rates at an all-time high of 20 percent; and a runaway inflation averaging between 12 and 13 percent. It was as if a seriously ill patient had been wheeled from one physician to another, receiving from each medication that worsened the original ailment, and then was told there was nothing else that medical science could do.

The conclusion of the SALT II treaty with the Soviets put Carter's leadership to the test just as the mounting economic problems made him the subject of biting editorial cartoons nationwide. Like SALT I, the new agreement did not do much to slow down the nuclear arms race. It placed a ceiling of 2,250 bombers and missiles on each side and set limits on the number of warheads and new weapons systems. In order to quell his conservative critics, who charged that SALT II would give the Soviets a decided advantage in the number and destructive power of land-based missiles, Carter announced that the United States would build a new missile system, called the MX, that would be housed in a vast maze of underground tunnels connected by railroad, creating a sort of "nuclear shell game" that would prevent Soviet planners from knowing where to strike. Liberal critics called the MX plan "a combination of Disneyworld and Armageddon" and criticized the SALT II agreement as "a step sideways rather than backwards in the arms race." Conservatives questioned the whole idea of détente, arguing that the Soviets would never have signed the agreement if it did not guarantee them nuclear superiority. Whether or not the SALT II treaty would pass the Senate became an open question.

The question became moot in December 1979 when the Soviet army invaded Afghanistan in order to rescue the faltering Communist government there, which was being challenged by Muslim rebels. Carter immediately shelved SALT II, suspended shipments of grain to the Soviet Union, and began a campaign for an international boycott of the 1980 Olympics, which were to be held that summer in Moscow. Zbigniew Brzezinski, Carter's hard-line national security advisor, won out over Cyrus Vance in the behind-the-scenes shuffling for influence and persuaded the president that the Soviet invasion of Afghanistan was only the first step in a Soviet scheme to dominate the oil-rich Persian Gulf. Calling the Soviet invasion "the gravest threat to world peace since World War II," Carter proclaimed that the United States would oppose by force any further Soviet advances in the Middle East. Military experts claimed that the United States lacked the forces and capability to block a Soviet move into the region, but Carter was determined to assert American power, even if, as one congressman put it, "the act of fighting for the oil would undoubtedly destroy all the oil fields, if not lead to thermonuclear war."

IRAN   Then came the Iranian crisis, a year-long cascade of unwelcome events that epitomized the reduced stature of the United States in the world. The crisis began with the fall of the shah of Iran in January 1979. The revolutionaries who toppled the shah rallied around Ayatollah Ruhollah Khomeini, a Muslim religious leader who symbolized the Islamic values the shah had tried to replace with Western ways and whose hatred of the United States dated back to the CIA-sponsored overthrow of Iran's Mossadegh government in 1953. Nor did it help the American image that SAVAK, the shah's ruthless secret police force, was also trained by the CIA. Late in October the exiled shah was allowed to enter the United States in order to undergo treatment for lymphatic cancer. A few days later, on November 4, 1979, a

The year-long Iranian hostage crisis damaged America's prestige and President Carter's chances for reelection. [United Press International]

frenzied mob stormed the American embassy in Teheran and seized the diplomats and staff inside. Khomeini endorsed the mob action and demanded the return of the shah along with all his wealth in exchange for the release of the fifty-three American hostages. In the meantime the Iranian militants staged daily demonstrations for the benefit of worldwide news and television coverage in which the American flag and effigies of the American president were burned and otherwise desecrated.

Carter's range of options was limited. He appealed to the United Nations, protesting what was a clear violation of diplomatic immunity and international law. But Khomeini scoffed at U.N. requests for the release of hostages. Carter then froze all Iranian assets in the United States and appealed to American allies for a trade embargo of Iran. The trade restrictions were only partially effective—even America's most loyal European allies did not want to lose their access to Iranian oil—so Carter authorized a rescue attempt by American commandos in April 1980. Secretary of State Vance resigned in protest against the rescue attempt, and against Carter's sharp turn toward a more hawkish foreign policy. The commando raid was aborted because of helicopter failures, and ended with eight fatalities when another helicopter collided with a transport plane in the desert. Nightly television coverage of the taunting Iranian rebels generated widespread popular craving for action, cries of "Let's nuke the whole damn Iranian country" from frustrated Americans, and a near obsession with the falling fortunes of the United States and the fate of the hostages. The end came after 444 days of captivity when Carter, in his last act as president, released several billion dollars of Iranian assets to ransom the kidnapped hostages. A plane carrying them left Teheran for Algiers moments after Ronald Reagan finished his inaugural address. Carter then flew to Wiesbaden, West Germany, as the new president's envoy to greet the released hostages at an American base.

THE REAGAN RESTORATION

Ronald Reagan had initially appeared as an even more improbable presidential possibility than Jimmy Carter had four years earlier. A small-town midwestern boy who had gone west in the 1930s in search of fame and fortune, Reagan had found both in Hollywood. Though never a major film star, he became president of the Screen Actors Guild and a disciple of New Deal politics. The rhetoric of FDR stayed with him, but in the 1950s, as he toured the small towns and byways of middle America as a representative of General Electric, whose weekly television program he hosted, Reagan's political values changed. In 1964 he delivered a rousing speech on behalf of Barry Goldwater at the Republican convention. But Goldwater's crushing defeat seemed to show that such uncompromising conservatism as Reagan had come to embrace had no prospect of achieving a national following. During two terms as governor of California Reagan combined his fervid commitment to conservative principles with pragmatic skills as a performer and a political realist capable of compromise. Nevertheless, by the middle 1970s Reagan's brand of conservatism still appeared too extreme for a national audience and his "back-to-basics" speeches regularly provoked barbed jokes from journalists: "Ronald Reagan wants to take us back to the fifties," wrote an Associated Press reporter, "back to the 1950's in foreign policy and back to the 1850's in economic and domestic policy."

THE MOVE TO REAGAN   By the late 1970s, on the eve of the presidential election, Reagan had become the beneficiary of two developments that made his conservative vision of America much more than a harmless flirtation with nostalgia. First, the Census of 1980 revealed that the American population (226,505,000) was getting older and was moving in large numbers from the Northeast to the "Sunbelt" states of the South and West. This dual development—a 24 percent increase in the population classified as "elderly" and the steady transfer of political and economic power to regions of the country where hostility to "big government" was a powerful force—meant that demographic forces were carrying the United States toward Reagan's position.

Second, in the 1970s the country experienced a major revival of evangelical religion not unlike the Great Awakenings of the eighteenth and early nineteenth centuries. No longer a local or provincial phenomenon that could be dismissed as "a bunch of Bible thumping lunatics down in the hill country of Tennessee who talk directly with God and play with snakes," Christian evangelicals now owned their own television and radio stations and operated their own schools and universities. A survey in 1977 revealed that more than 70 million Americans described themselves as "born-again" Christians who had "a direct personal relationship with Jesus." The Rev. Jerry Falwell's "Moral Majority" expressed the political sentiments of countless other evangelical groups: free enterprise should remain free, big government should be made little, abortion should be outlawed as murder, the scientific version of evolution should be replaced in schoolbooks by the biblical story of creation, and Soviet expan-

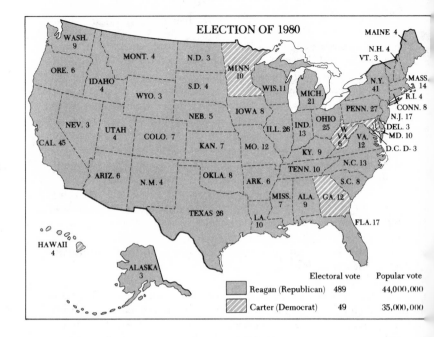

ELECTION OF 1980

State	Electoral vote
WASH.	9
ORE.	6
MONT.	4
IDAHO	4
N.D.	3
MINN.	10
WIS.	11
MICH.	21
MAINE	4
N.H.	4
VT.	3
N.Y.	41
MASS.	14
R.I.	4
CONN.	8
S.D.	4
WYO.	3
IOWA	8
OHIO	25
PENN.	27
N.J.	17
NEB.	5
ILL.	26
IND.	13
NEV.	3
UTAH	4
COLO.	7
KAN.	7
MO.	12
KY.	9
W. VA.	6
VA.	12
DEL.	3
MD.	10
D.C.	D-3
CAL.	45
ARIZ.	6
N.M.	4
OKLA.	8
ARK.	6
TENN.	10
N.C.	13
S.C.	8
MISS.	7
ALA.	9
GA.	12
TEXAS	26
LA.	10
FLA.	17
HAWAII	4
ALASKA	3

	Electoral vote	Popular vote
Reagan (Republican)	489	44,000,000
Carter (Democrat)	49	35,000,000

sion should be opposed as a form of pagan totalitarianism. "You show me one of them liberal 'secular humanists,' " said one evangelical minister, "and I'll show you a fellow on his way to hell." The religious zeal and financial resources of the religious right made them at once formidable and effective opponents of liberal political candidates and programs. As defenders of traditional and local values—prayer in schools, families in which women stayed home to care for children, tough criminal laws—the religious right rallied to Reagan, opposing even the "born-again" Jimmy Carter.

And by 1980 Reagan also benefited from the deep popular disenchantment with the president, whose campaign was burdened by the frustrations of the Iranian hostage crisis, a desperately sick economy, and the party divisions created by Sen. Edward M. Kennedy's luckless quest for the Democratic nomination. On election day Reagan swept to a decisive victory, with 489 electoral votes to 49 for Carter, who carried only six states. The popular vote was equally lopsided: 44 million (51 percent) to 35 million (41 percent), with 7 percent going to John Anderson, an independent Republican who had bolted the party after Reagan's nomination. Reagan had won almost everywhere, in an election with the lowest voter turnout in the twentieth century. He had pulled enough Republican candidates along on his coattails to provide his administration with a Republican majority in the Senate and a House of Representatives that, though still Democratic, was sufficiently conservative to support White House initiatives during his first two years.

EARLY ASSESSMENTS The jury is still out on the achievements of Reagan's presidency. Not enough time has passed since he took office to permit judgments that qualify as history in any meaningful sense of the term. It is possible to conclude with confidence that Ronald Reagan brought to Washington the most conservative philosophy since Calvin Coolidge, whom he admired, that he brought skills as a public speaker and experienced television performer which served him well in presenting his views to the American people, and that, unlike the three previous presidents, he refused to compromise his basic outlook on what ailed the economy or what America's role in the world should be. Drift and equivocation were replaced with confident leadership that even some liberal critics admired. "Reagan is probably taking us down the wrong road," said a New York *Times* columnist, "but he's doing it with the style and grace and 'don't-look-back' bravado that the job requires."

Reagan's economic proposals were pure full-strength conservative medicine for the decade-long stagflation. His "supply-side" economics, soon dubbed "Reaganomics," presumed that the economic problems were a result of government intrusions into the marketplace and excessive taxes on workers and business. So Reagan proposed a three-year rate reduction in personal and corporate income taxes. Since reduced revenues required

President Ronald Reagan, "the great communicator." [United Press International]

reduced federal expenditures, Reagan and David Stockman, his tough-minded budget director, proposed reductions in welfare, education, and other social services to the amount of $40 billion. Despite loud protests from liberal groups and congressmen, the entire Reagan economic package was passed by the summer of 1981. "Reaganomics" was based on the assumption that the tax cuts to consumers and corporations would stimulate a general economic revival and that prospective deficits would be made up with tax revenue collected in the wake of the recovery. "Reaganomics" in fact resembled the "Mellonomics" of Coolidge's secretary of the treasury in that it emphasized tax cuts to the rich on the assumption that their investments would stimulate the economy.

By the summer of 1983 a major economic recovery was under way, but its duration and the long-term implications of "Reaganomics" were clouded in controversy. The chief culprit was the huge budget deficit of approximately $200 billion, which in part was inherited from Reagan predecessors, in part resulted from Reagan's massive spending on arms and defense, and in part reflected the tardiness of the recovery. A liberal economist likened the American economy under Reagan's management to "a dying man who has stumbled out of the desert and receives a canteen of water, but meanwhile the arrow buried into his back [the deficit] is ignored."

In foreign policy, Reagan believed that Americans had over-learned the lessons of Vietnam and had forgotten the lessons of Munich. He embarked on a major buildup of nuclear and conventional weapons to close the gap that he claimed had developed between Soviet and American military forces, recovering the rhetoric of John Foster Dulles and the Kennedy inaugural address to describe American resolve in the face of "Communist aggression anywhere in the world." Ironically, Reagan's rhetoric was so apocalyptic that it contributed to a sudden and massive upsurge in the protest against nuclear weapons, which focused on a "freeze" on all nuclear weapons development and a declaration of "no first use" in Europe, where the NATO forces relied on tactical nuclear weapons to deter a Soviet invasion.

Détente deteriorated even further under Reagan's tough talk about "Communist imperialism" and in the face of the imposition of martial law in Soviet-controlled Poland in the winter of 1981. The crack-down came after Polish workers, united under the banner of an independent union called Solidarity, challenged the Communist monopoly of power. As in Hungary in 1956 and Czechoslovakia in 1968, there was little the United States could do except register protest and impose economic sanctions against the Communist government of Poland. Even Reagan accepted, albeit reluctantly, the limitations on American policy in central and eastern Europe.

Central America became the region in which Reagan detected the most serious Communist threat and into which he projected the most bellicose version of American resolve. Indeed Central America became to the Reagan administration in the early 1980s what Cuba had become to Kennedy in the early 1960s or Vietnam had become to Johnson in the mid-1960s. The tiny nation of El Salvador, caught up in a brutal struggle between Communist-supported revolutionaries and a repressive government, received American commitments of economic and military assistance. Reagan stopped short of sending American troops, but did increase the number of military advisors to the Salvadoran government. When Jimmy Carter had been confronted with a similar development in Nicaragua in 1979, he had concluded that the leftist takeover was inevitable and had not attempted to save the corrupt Somoza regime, even though Cuban-sponsored Communists were part of the revolutionary group. Critics of Reagan's policy in El Salvador argued that American involvement assured that the revolutionary forces would emerge as the victorious representatives of Salvadoran nationalism. Supporters countered by warning that American failure to act would allow for a repeat of Communist victories in Nicaragua and that Honduras, Guatemala, and then all of Central America would eventually enter the Communist camp.

Under Ronald Reagan the United States moved toward the year in which George Orwell's novel *1984* had foreseen worldwide dictatorship. America's mood most resembled the complacent hedonism of the 1950s. Russell Baker, writing in the New York *Times,* described "the hunt for the ideal restaurant, the perfect head of lettuce, the totally satisfying human relationship" as the current "equivalents of the Eisenhower age's passion for bigger tail fins, dryer martinis, darker steak houses and cozier evenings with the family." The world had changed a great deal since the 1950s, of course, and America was also a more complex and troubled society in which the bitter memories of Vietnam, assassinations, Watergate, and stagflation lingered like bad dreams. For the moment, however, the nation seemed eager to dispell these recent memories and recover the faith of the 1950s. Almost five centuries after Europeans had discovered the North American continent, over two centuries after American colonists had broken free from England, over a century after the sectional crisis had been resolved in civil war, the American people were pausing, wary of the future, looking back.

FURTHER READING

A good start for the events of the Nixon years is the former president's memoirs, *RN: The Memoirs of Richard Nixon* (1978).° Studies of Nixon at the time of his resurgence to power include Garry Wills's *Nixon Agonistes* (1970)° and Paul Hoffman's *The New Nixon* (1970). Fawn Brodie's *Richard Nixon* (1980)° is a critical work based on post-Watergate analysis. James David Barber's *The Presidential Character* (1972)° insightfully compares Nixon to his predecessors in the White House.

No one survey captures all the details of the Watergate scandal. The works of the two *Washington Post* reporters involved, Robert Woodward and Carl Bernstein, recount their role in the events; follow *All the President's Men* (1974)° with *The Final Days* (1976).° Arthur S. Schlesinger, Jr.'s *The Imperial Presidency* (1973)° looks for the scandal's cause in the growing power given the president to conduct foreign affairs. Other views of Watergate can be found in Theodore H. White's *Breach of Faith* (1975),° Jonathan Schell's *The Time of Illusion* (1976),° and Anthony Lukas's *Nightmare* (1976). For the impact of Watergate on the office of the presidency, see T. E. Cronin's *The State of the Presidency* (1975).

For the way the Republicans handled affairs abroad, consult Tad Szulc's *The Illusion of Power: Foreign Policy in the Nixon Years* (1978). Secretary of State Henry Kissinger recounts his role in policy formation in *The White House Years* (1978). Less favorable reports of the Kissinger role appear in David Landau's *Kissinger: The Uses of Power* (1972) and Seymour M. Hersh's *The Price of Power: Kissinger in the Nixon White House* (1983). Also helpful is Lloyd C. Gardner's *The Great Nixon Turnaround* (1975), for background on Nixon's relations with Russia and China.

The loss of Vietnam and the end of American involvement are traced in A. E. Goodman's *The Lost Peace: America's Search for a Negotiated Settlement of the Vietnam War* (1978) and Gareth Porter's *A Peace Denied: The United States, Vietnam and the Paris Agreement* (1975). William Showcross's *Sideshow: Kissinger, Nixon, and the Destruction of Cambodia* (1978)° deals with the broadening of the war, while Larry Berman's *Planning a Tragedy: The Americanization of the War in Vietnam* (1982)° and Leslie Gelb and Richard Betts's *The Irony of Vietnam: The System Worked* (1979)° assess the final impact of American involvement.

For the domestic side of the Nixon years, see R. P. Nathan (ed.), *Monitoring Revenue Sharing* (1975) and Daniel P. Moynihan's *The Politics of a Guaranteed Income: The Nixon Administration and the Family Assistance Plan* (1973).° Also helpful is Otis L. Graham, Jr.'s *Toward a Planned Society: From Roosevelt to Nixon* (1976).

For other views of politics during the 1970s, consult Henry S. Parmet's *The Democrats: The Years after FDR* (1976),° particularly for the McGovern campaign of 1972. Gerald Ford's memoir, *A Time to Heal:*

°These books are available in paperback editions.

The Autobiography of Gerald R. Ford (1979), is illuminating on the post-Watergate years.

The dimension of ethnic politics which figured in the early 1970s is explored in Edgar Litt's *Beyond Pluralism: Ethnic Politics in America* (1970) and Peter Schrag's *The Decline of the WASP* (1971). Ronald Taylor's *Chavez and the Farm Workers* (1975) discusses the ethnic politics of the Southwest. The plight of Indians is traced in Vine De Loria, Jr.'s *Behind the Trail of Broken Treaties* (1974). The feminist movement is depicted in William Chafe's *The American Woman: Her Changing Social, Economic, and Political Roles, 1920–1970* (1972),° and Jo Freeman's *The Politics of Women's Liberation* (1975).

To examine the rise of Jimmy Carter, consult Betty Glad's *Jimmy Carter: In Search of the Great White House* (1980) and Victor Lasky's *Jimmy Carter: The Man and the Myth* (1979). A work critical of the Carter administration is Haynes Johnson's *In the Absence of Power: Governing America 1980.* Zbigniew Brzezinski's *Power and Principle: Memories of the National Security Advisor, 1977–1981* (1983), gives insight to the Carter approach to foreign policy. Background on how the Middle East came to dominate much of American policy is found in Richard Stookey's *America and the Arab States* (1975) and William B. Quandt's *Decade of Decision: American Policy toward the Arab-Israeli Conflict, 1967–1976* (1977).° What followed in the Camp David Accords is handled best by Jimmy Carter in *Keeping Faith: The Memoirs of a President* (1982). Background on the SALT controversy is provided in Harold B. Moulton's *From Superiority to Parity: The United States and the Strategic Arms Race, 1961–1972* (1973).

Many recent books deal with various aspects of contemporary American culture. Zane L. Miller's *Suburb* (1981) and William Kornblum's *Blue-Collar Country* (1974) examine different elements of modern American society. Landon Y. Jones's *Great Expectations: America and the Baby Boom Generation* (1980)° explores how childraising affects current attitudes. Christopher Lasch's *The Culture of Narcissism: American Life in an Age of Diminishing Expectations* (1979)° criticizes the materialist element of modern culture. David Halberstam's *The Powers That Be* (1979)° investigates the influence and operation of mass media. The environmental crisis is treated in William Ophuls's *Ecology and the Politics of Scarcity* (1979) and Thomas R. Dunlop's *DDT: Scientists, Citizens, and Public Policy* (1981). The rise of the computer is traced in Kent C. Redmond's *Project Whirlwind: The History of a Pioneer Computer* (1980) and Geoffrey D. Austrian's *Hermann Hollerith: Forgotten Giant of Information Processing* (1982).

Peter Steinfel's *The Neoconservatives* (1979) heralded the election of conservatives in 1980. Lou Cannon's *Reagan* (1983) is one of the better studies of the president. Robert B. Reich's *The Next American Frontier* (1981)° examines the nation's recent industrial crisis.

APPENDIX

THE DECLARATION OF INDEPENDENCE

WHEN IN THE COURSE OF HUMAN EVENTS, it becomes necessary for one people to dissolve the political bands which have connected them with another, and to assume the Powers of the earth, the separate and equal station to which the Laws of Nature and of Nature's God entitle them, a decent respect to the opinions of mankind requires that they should declare the causes which impel them to the separation.

We hold these truths to be self-evident, that all men are created equal, that they are endowed by their Creator with certain unalienable rights, that among these are Life, Liberty, and the pursuit of Happiness. That to secure these rights, Governments are instituted among Men, deriving their just powers from the consent of the governed. That whenever any Form of Government becomes destructive of these ends, it is the Right of the People to alter or to abolish it, and to institute new Government, laying its foundation on such principles and organizing its powers in such form, as to them shall seem most likely to effect their Safety and Happiness. Prudence, indeed, will dictate that Governments long established should not be changed for light and transient causes; and accordingly all experience hath shown, that mankind are more disposed to suffer, while evils are sufferable, than to right themselves by abolishing the forms to which they are accustomed. But when a long train of abuses and usurpations, pursuing invariably the same Object evinces a design to reduce them under absolute Despotism, it is their right, it is their duty, to throw off such Government, and to provide new Guards for their future security.—Such has been the patient sufferance of these Colonies; and such is now the necessity which constrains them to alter their former Systems of Government. The history of the present King of Great Britain is a history of repeated injuries and usurpations, all having in direct object the establishment of an absolute Tyranny over these States. To prove this, let Facts be submitted to a candid world.

He has refused his Assent to Laws, the most wholesome and necessary for the public good.

He has forbidden his Governors to pass Laws of immediate and pressing importance, unless suspended in their operation till his Assent should be obtained; and when so suspended, he has utterly neglected to attend to them.

He has refused to pass other Laws for the accommodation of large districts of people, unless those people would relinquish the right of Representation in the Legislature, a right inestimable to them and formidable to tyrants only.

He has called together legislative bodies at places unusual, uncomfortable, and distant from the depository of their public Records, for the sole purpose of fatiguing them into compliance with his measures.

He has dissolved Representative Houses repeatedly, for opposing with manly firmness his invasions on the rights of the people.

He has refused for a long time, after such dissolutions, to cause others to be elected; whereby the Legislative powers, incapable of Annihilation, have returned to the People at large for their exercise; the State remaining in the mean time exposed to all dangers of invasion from without, and convulsions within.

He has endeavoured to prevent the population of these States; for that purpose obstructing the Laws of Naturalization of Foreigners; refusing to pass others to encourage their migrations hither, and raising the conditions of new Appropriations of Lands.

He has obstructed the Administration of Justice, by refusing his Assent to Laws for establishing Judiciary powers.

He has made Judges dependent on his Will alone, for the tenure of their offices, and the amount and payment of their salaries.

He has erected a multitude of New Offices, and sent hither swarms of Officers to harass our People, and eat out their substance.

He has kept among us, in times of peace, Standing Armies without the Consent of our legislature.

He has affected to render the Military independent of and superior to the Civil Power.

He has combined with others to subject us to a jurisdiction foreign to our constitution, and unacknowledged by our laws; giving his Assent to their Acts of pretended Legislation:

For quartering large bodies of armed troops among us:

For protecting them, by a mock Trial, from Punishment for any Murders which they should commit on the Inhabitants of these States:

For cutting off our Trade with all parts of the world:

For imposing taxes on us without our Consent:

For depriving us of many cases, of the benefits of Trial by jury:

For transporting us beyond Seas to be tried for pretended offences:

For abolishing the free System of English Laws in a neighbouring Province, establishing therein an Arbitrary government, and enlarging its Boundaries so as to render it at once an example and fit instrument for introducing the same absolute rule into these Colonies:

For taking away our Charters, abolishing our most valuable Laws, and altering fundamentally the Forms of our Governments:

For suspending our own Legislatures, and declaring themselves invested with Power to legislate for us in all cases whatsoever.

He has abdicated Government here, by declaring us out of his Protection and waging War against us.

He has plundered our seas, ravaged our Coasts, burnt our towns, and destroyed the lives of our people.

He is at this time transporting large armies of foreign mercenaries to compleat the works of death, desolation, and tyranny, already begun with circumstances of Cruelty & perfidy scarcely paralleled in the most barbarous ages, and totally unworthy the Head of a civilized nation.

He has constrained our fellow Citizens taken Captive on the high Seas to bear Arms against their Country, to become the executioners of their friends and Brethren, or to fall themselves by their Hands.

He has excited domestic insurrections amongst us, and has endeavoured to bring on the inhabitants of our frontiers, the merciless Indian Savages, whose known rule of warfare, is an undistinguished destruction of all ages, sexes, and conditions.

In every stage of these Oppressions We have Petitioned for Redress in the most humble terms: Our repeated Petitions have been answered only by repeated injury. A Prince, whose character is thus marked by every act which may define a Tyrant, is unfit to be the ruler of a free people.

Nor have We been wanting in attention to our British brethren. We have warned them from time to time of attempts by their legislature to extend an unwarrantable jurisdiction over us. We have reminded them of the circumstances of our emigration and settlement here. We have appealed to their native justice and magnanimity, and we have conjured them by the ties of our common kindred to disavow these usurpations, which, would inevitably interrupt our connections and correspondence. They too must have been deaf to the voice of justice and of consanguinity. We must, therefore, acquiesce in the necessity, which denounces our Separation, and hold them, as we hold the rest of mankind, Enemies in War, in Peace Friends.

WE, THEREFORE, the Representatives of the UNITED STATES OF AMERICA, in General Congress, Assembled, appealing to the Supreme Judge of the world for the rectitude of our intentions, do, in the Name, and by Authority of the good People of these Colonies, solemnly publish and declare, That these United Colonies are, and of Right ought to be FREE AND INDEPENDENT STATES; that they are Absolved from all Allegiance to the British Crown, and that all political connection between them and the State of Great Britain, is and ought to be totally dissolved; and that as Free and Independent States, they have full Power to levy War, conclude Peace, contract Alliances, establish Commerce, and to do all other Acts and Things which Independent States may of right do. And for the support of this Declaration, with a firm reliance on the Protection of Divine Providence, we mutually pledge to each other our Lives, our Fortunes, and our sacred Honor.

The foregoing Declaration was, by order of Congress, engrossed, and signed by the following members:

John Hancock

NEW HAMPSHIRE
Josiah Bartlett
William Whipple
Matthew Thornton

MASSACHUSETTS BAY
Samuel Adams
John Adams
Robert Treat Paine
Elbridge Gerry

RHODE ISLAND
Stephen Hopkins
William Ellery

CONNECTICUT
Roger Sherman
Samuel Huntington
William Williams
Oliver Wolcott

NEW YORK
William Floyd
Philip Livingston
Francis Lewis
Lewis Morris

NEW JERSEY
Richard Stockton
John Witherspoon
Francis Hopkinson
John Hart
Abraham Clark

PENNSYLVANIA
Robert Morris
Benjamin Rush
Benjamin Franklin
John Morton
George Clymer
James Smith
George Taylor
James Wilson
George Ross

DELAWARE
Caesar Rodney
George Read
Thomas M'Kean

MARYLAND
Samuel Chase
William Paca
Thomas Stone
Charles Carroll,
of Carrollton

VIRGINIA
George Wythe
Richard Henry Lee
Thomas Jefferson
Benjamin Harrison
Thomas Nelson, Jr.
Francis Lightfoot Lee
Carter Braxton

NORTH CAROLINA
William Hooper
Joseph Hewes
John Penn

SOUTH CAROLINA
Edward Rutledge
Thomas Heyward, Jr.
Thomas Lynch, Jr.
Arthur Middleton

GEORGIA
Button Gwinnett
Lyman Hall
George Walton

Resolved, That copies of the Declaration be sent to the several assemblies, conventions, and committees, or councils of safety, and to the several commanding officers of the continental troops; that it be proclaimed in each of the United States, at the head of the army.

ARTICLES OF CONFEDERATION

To ALL TO WHOM these Presents shall come, we the undersigned Delegates of the States affixed to our Names send greeting.

Whereas the Delegates of the United States of America in Congress assembled did on the fifteenth day of November in the Year of our Lord One Thousand Seven Hundred and Seventy-seven, and in the Second Year of the Independence of America agree to certain articles of Confederation and perpetual Union between the States of Newhampshire, Massachusetts-bay, Rhodeisland and Providence Plantations, Connecticut, New York, New Jersey, Pennsylvania, Delaware, Maryland, Virginia, North-Carolina, South-Carolina and Georgia in the Words following, viz.

"Articles of Confederation and perpetual Union between the States of Newhampshire, Massachusetts-bay, Rhodeisland and Providence Plantations, Connecticut, New-York, New-Jersey, Pennsylvania, Delaware, Maryland, Virginia, North-Carolina, South-Carolina and Georgia.

ARTICLE I. The stile of this confederacy shall be "The United States of America."

ARTICLE II. Each State retains its sovereignty, freedom and independence, and every power, jurisdiction and right, which is not by this confederation expressly delegated to the United States, in Congress assembled.

ARTICLE III. The said States hereby severally enter into a firm league of friendship with each other, for their common defense, the security of their liberties, and their mutual and general welfare, binding themselves to assist each other, against all force offered to, or attacks made upon them, or any of them, on account of religion, sovereignty, trade or any other pretence whatever.

ARTICLE IV. The better to secure and perpetuate mutual friendship and intercourse among the people of the different States in this Union, the free inhabitants of each of these States, paupers, vagabonds and fugitives from justice excepted, shall be entitled to all privileges and immunities of free citizens in the several States; and the people of each State shall have free ingress and regress to and from any other State, and shall enjoy therein all the privileges of trade and commerce, subject to the same duties, impositions and restrictions as the inhabitants thereof respectively, provided that such restrictions shall not extend so far as to prevent the removal of property imported into any State, to any other State of which the owner is an inhabitant; provided also that no imposition, duties or restriction shall be laid by any State, on the property of the United States, or either of them.

If any person guilty of, or charged with treason, felony, or other high misdemeanor in any State, shall flee from justice, and be found in any of the United States, he shall upon demand of the Governor or Executive power, of the State from which he fled, be delivered up and removed to the State having jurisdiction of his offence.

Full faith and credit shall be given in each of these States to the records, acts and judicial proceedings of the courts and magistrates of every other State.

ARTICLE V. For the more convenient management of the general interests of the United States, delegates shall be annually appointed in such manner as the legislature of each State shall direct, to meet in Congress on the first Monday in November, in every year, with a power reserved to each State, to recall its delegates, or any of them, at any time within the year, and to send others in their stead, for the remainder of the year.

No State shall be represented in Congress by less than two, nor by more than seven members; and no person shall be capable of being a delegate for more than three years in any term of six years; nor shall any person, being a delegate, be capable of holding any office under the United States, for which he, or another for his benefit receives any salary, fees or emolument of any kind.

Each State shall maintain its own delegates in a meeting of the States, and while they act as members of the committee of the States.

In determining questions in the United States, in Congress assembled, each State shall have one vote.

Freedom of speech and debate in Congress shall not be impeached or questioned in any court, or place out of Congress, and the members of Congress shall be protected in their persons from arrests and imprisonments, during the time of their going to and from, and attendance on Congress, except for treason, felony, or breach of the peace.

ARTICLE VI. No State without the consent of the United States in Congress assembled, shall send any embassy to, or receive any embassy from, or enter into any conference, agreement, alliance or treaty with any king, prince or state; nor shall any person holding any office of profit or trust under the United States, or any of them, accept of any present, emolument, office or title of any kind whatever from any king, prince or foreign state; nor shall the United States in Congress assembled, or any of them, grant any title of nobility.

No two or more States shall enter into any treaty, confederation or alliance whatever between them, without the consent of the United States in Congress assembled, specifying accurately the purposes for which the same is to be entered into, and how long it shall continue.

No State shall lay any imposts or duties, which may interfere with any stipulations in treaties, entered into by the United States in Congress assembled, with any king, prince or state, in pursuance of any treaties already proposed by Congress, to the courts of France and Spain.

No vessels of war shall be kept up in time of peace by any State, except such number only, as shall be deemed necessary by the United States in Congress assembled, for the defence of such State, or its trade; nor shall any body of forces be kept up by any State, in time of peace, except such number only, as in the judgment of the United States, in Congress assembled, shall be deemed requisite to garrison the forts necessary for the defense of such State; but every State shall always keep up a well regulated and disciplined militia, sufficiently armed and accoutred, and shall provide and constantly have ready for use, in public stores, a due number of field pieces and tents, and a proper quantity of arms, ammunition and camp equipage.

No State shall engage in any war without the consent of the United States in Congress assembled, unless such State be actually invaded by enemies, or shall have received certain advice of a resolution being formed by some nation of Indians to invade such State, and the danger is so imminent as not to admit of a delay, till the United States in Congress assembled can be consulted: nor shall any State grant commissions to any ships or vessels of war, nor letters of marque or reprisal, except it be after a declaration of war by the United States in Congress assembled, and then only against the kingdom or state and the subjects thereof, against which war has been so declared, and under such regulations as shall be established by the United States in Congress assembled, unless such State be infested by pirates, in which case vessels of war may be fitted out for that occasion, and kept so long as the danger shall continue, or until the United States in Congress assembled shall determine otherwise.

ARTICLE VII. When land-forces are raised by any State of the common defence, all officers of or under the rank of colonel, shall be appointed by the Legislature of each State respectively by whom such forces shall be raised, or in such manner as such State shall direct, and all vacancies shall be filled up by the State which first made the appointment.

ARTICLE VIII. All charges of war, and all other expenses that shall be incurred for the common defense or general welfare, and allowed by the United States in Congress assembled, shall be defrayed out of a common treasury, which shall be supplied by the several States, in proportion to the value of all land within each State, granted to or surveyed for any person, as such land and the buildings and improvements thereon shall be estimated according to such mode as the United States in Congress assembled, shall from time to time direct and appoint.

The taxes for paying that proportion shall be laid and levied by the authority and direction of the Legislatures of the several States within the time agreed upon by the United States in Congress assembled.

ARTICLE IX. The United States in Congress assembled, shall have the sole and exclusive right and power of determining on peace and war, except in the cases mentioned in the sixth article—of sending and receiving ambassadors—entering into treaties and alliances, provided that no treaty of commerce shall be made whereby the legislative power of the respective States shall be restrained from imposing such imposts and duties on foreigners, as their own people are subjected to, or from prohibiting the exportation or importation of and species of goods or commodities whatsoever—of establishing rules for deciding in all cases, what captures on land or water shall be legal, and in what manner prizes taken by land or naval forces in the service of the United States shall be divided or appropriated—of granting letters of marque and reprisal in times of peace—appointing courts for the trial of piracies and felonies committed on the high seas and establishing courts for receiving and determining finally appeals in all cases of captures, provided that no member of Congress shall be appointed a judge of any of the said courts.

The United States in Congress assembled shall also be the last resort on appeal in all disputes and differences now subsisting or that hereafter may arise between two or more States concerning boundary, jurisdiction or any other cause whatever; which authority shall always be exercised in the manner following. Whenever the legislative or executive authority or lawful agent of any State in controversy with another shall present a petition to Congress, stating the matter in question and praying for a hearing, notice thereof shall be given by order of Congress to the legislative or executive authority of the other State in controversy, and a day assigned for the appearance of the parties by their lawful agents, who shall then be directed to appoint by joint consent, commissioners or judges to constitute a court for hearing and determining the matter in question: but if they cannot agree, Congress shall name three persons out of each of the United States, and from the list of such persons each party shall alternately strike out one, the petitioners beginning, until the number shall be reduced to thirteen; and from that number not less than seven, nor more than nine names as Congress shall direct, shall in the presence of Congress be drawn out by lot, and the persons whose names shall be so drawn or any five of them, shall be commissioners or judges, to hear and finally determine the controversy, so always as a major part of the judges who shall hear the cause shall agree in the determination: and if either party shall neglect to attend at the day appointed, without reasons, which Congress shall judge sufficient, or being present shall refuse to strike, the Congress shall proceed to nominate three persons out of each State, and the Secretary of Congress shall strike in behalf of such party absent or refusing; and the judgment and sentence of the court to be appointed, in the manner before prescribed, shall be final and conclusive; and if any of the parties shall refuse to submit to the authority of such court, or to appear or defend their claim or cause, the court shall nevertheless proceed to pronounce sentence, or judgment, which shall in like manner be final and decisive, the judgment or sentence and other procedings being in either case transmitted to Congress, and lodged among the acts of Congress for the security of the parties concerned: provided that every commissioner, before he sits in judgment, shall take an oath to be administered by one of the judges of the supreme or superior court of the State where the cause shall be tried, "well and truly to hear and determine the matter in question, according to the best of his judgment, without favour, affection or hope of reward:" provided also that no State shall be deprived of territory for the benefit of the United States.

All controversies concerning the private right of soil claimed under different grants of two or more States, whose jurisdiction as they may respect such lands, and the states which passed such grants are adjusted, the said grants or either of them being at the same time claimed to have originated antecedent to such settlement of jurisdiction, shall on the petition of either party to the Congress of the United States, be finally determined as near as may be in the same manner as is before prescribed for deciding disputes respecting territorial jurisdiction between different States.

The United States in Congress assembled shall also have the sole and exclusive right and power of regulating the alloy and value of coin struck by their own authority, or by that of the respective States—fixing the standard of weights and measures throughout the United States—regulating the trade and managing all affairs with the Indians, not members of any of the States, provided that the legislative right of any State within its own limits be not infringed or violated—establishing and regulating post-offices from one State to another, throughout all of the United States, and exacting such postage on the papers passing thro' the same as may be requisite to defray the expenses of the said office—appointing all officers of the land forces, in the service of the United States, excepting regimental officers—appointing all the officers of the naval forces, and commissioning all officers whatever in the service of the United States —making rules for the government and regulation of the said land and naval forces, and directing their operations.

The United States in Congress assembled shall have authority to appoint a committee, to sit in the recess of Congress, to be denominated "a Committee of the States," and to consist of one delegate from each State; and to appoint such other committees and civil officers as may be necessary for managing the general affairs of the United States under their direction—to appoint one of their number to preside, provided that no person be allowed to serve in the office of president more than one year in any term of three years; to ascertain the necessary sums of money to be raised for the service of the United States, and to appropriate and apply the same for defraying the public expenses—to borrow money, or emit bills on the credit of the United States, transmitting every half year to the respective States an account of the sums of money so borrowed or emitted,—to build and equip a navy—to agree upon the number of land forces, and to make requisitions from each State for its quota, in proportion to the number of white inhabitants in such State; which requisition shall be binding, and thereupon the Legislature of each State shall appoint the regimental officers, raise the men and cloath, arm and equip them in a soldier like manner, at the expense of the United States; and the officers and men so cloathed, armed and equipped shall march to the place appointed, and within the time agreed on by the United States in Congress assembled: but if the United States in Congress assembled shall, on consideration of circumstances judge proper that any State should not raise men, or should raise a smaller number of men than the quota thereof, such extra number shall be raised, officered, cloathed, armed and equipped in the same manner as the quota of such State, unless the legislature of such State shall judge that such extra number cannot be safely spared out of the same, in which case they shall raise officer, cloath, arm and equip as many of such extra number as they judge can be safely spared. And the officers and men so cloathed, armed and equipped, shall march to the place appointed, and within the time agreed on by the United States in Congress assembled.

The United States in Congress assembled shall never engage in a war, nor grant letters of marque and reprisal in time of peace, nor enter into any treaties or alliances, nor coin money, nor regulate the value thereof, nor ascertain the sums and expenses necessary for the defence and welfare of the United States, or any of them, nor emit bills, nor borrow money on the credit of the United States, nor appropriate money, nor agree upon the number of vessels to be built or purchased, or the number of land or sea forces to be raised, nor appoint a commander in chief of the army or navy, unless nine States assent to the same: nor shall a question on any other point, except for adjourning from day to day be determined, unless by the votes of a majority of the United States in Congress assembled.

The Congress of the United States shall have power to adjourn to any time within the year, and to any place within the United States, so that no period of adjournment be for a longer duration than the space of six months, and shall publish the journal of their proceedings monthly, except such parts thereof relating to treaties, alliances or military operations, as in their judgment require secrecy; and the yeas and nays of the delegates of each State on any question shall be entered on the Journal, when it is desired by any delegate; and the delegates of a State, or any of them, at his or their request shall be furnished with a transcript of the said journal, except such parts as are above excepted, to lay before the Legislatures of the several States.

ARTICLE X. The committee of the States, or any nine of them, shall be authorized to execute, in the recess of Congress, such of the powers of Congress as the United States in Congress assembled, by the consent of nine States, shall from time to time think expedient to vest them with; provided that no power be delegated to the said committee, for the exercise of which, by the articles of confederation, the voice of nine States in the Congress of the United States assembled is requisite.

ARTICLE XI. Canada acceding to this confederation, and joining in the measures of the United States, shall be admitted into, and entitled to all the advantages of this Union: but no other colony shall be admitted into the same, unless such admission be agreed to by nine States.

ARTICLE XII. All bills of credit emitted, monies borrowed and debts contracted by, or under the authority of Congress, before the assembling of the United States, in pursuance of the present confederation, shall be deemed and considered as a charge against the United States, for payment and satisfaction whereof the said United States, and the public faith are hereby solemnly pledged.

ARTICLE XIII. Every State shall abide by the determinations of the United States in Congress assembled, on all questions which by this confederation are submitted to them. And the articles of this confederation shall be inviolably observed by every State, and the Union shall be perpetual; nor shall any alteration at any time hereafter be made in any of them; unless such alteration be agreed to in a Congress of the United States, and be afterwards confirmed by the Legislatures of every State.

And whereas it has pleased the Great Governor of the world to incline the hearts of the Legislatures we respectively represent in Congress, to approve of, and to authorize us to ratify the said articles of confederation and perpetual union. Know ye that we the undersigned delegates, by virtue of the power and authority to us given for that purpose, do by these presents, in the name and in behalf of our respective constituents, fully and entirely ratify and confirm each and every of the said articles of confederation and perpetual union, and all and singular the matters and things therein contained: and we do further solemnly plight and engage the faith of our respective constituents, that they shall abide by the determinations of the United States in Congress assembled, on all questions, which by the said confederation are submitted to them. And that the articles thereof shall be inviolably observed by the States we respectively represent, and that the Union shall be perpetual.

In witness thereof we have hereunto set our hands in Congress. Done at Philadelphia in the State of Pennsylvania the ninth day of July in the year of our Lord one thousand seven hundred and seventy-eight, and in the third year of the independence of America.

THE CONSTITUTION OF
THE UNITED STATES

WE THE PEOPLE OF THE UNITED STATES, in order to form a more perfect Union, establish Justice, insure domestic Tranquility, provide for the common defence, promote the general Welfare, and secure the Blessings of Liberty to ourselves and our Posterity, do ordain and establish this Constitution for the United States of America.

ARTICLE. I.

Section. 1. All legislative Powers herein granted shall be vested in a Congress of the United States, which shall consist of a Senate and House of Representatives.

Section. 2. The House of Representatives shall be composed of Members chosen every second Year by the People of the several States, and the Electors in each State shall have the Qualifications requisite for Electors of the most numerous Branch of the State Legislature.

No Person shall be a Representative who shall not have attained to the Age of twenty five Years, and been seven Years a Citizen of the United States, and who shall not, when elected, be an Inhabitant of that State in which he shall be chosen.

Representatives and direct Taxes shall be apportioned among the several States which may be included within this Union, according to their respective Numbers, which shall be determined by adding to the whole Number of free Persons, including those bound to Service for a Term of Years, and excluding Indians not taxed, three fifths of all other Persons. The actual Enumeration shall be made within three Years after the first Meeting of the Congress of the United States, and within every subsequent Term of ten Years, in such Manner as they shall by Law direct. The Number of Representatives shall not exceed one for every thirty Thousand, but each State shall have at Least one Representative; and until such enumeration shall be made, the State of New Hampshire shall be entitled to chuse three, Massachusetts eight, Rhode-Island and Providence Plantations one, Connecticut five, New-York six, New Jersey four, Pennsylvania eight, Delaware one, Maryland six, Virginia ten, North Carolina five, South Carolina five, and Georgia three.

When vacancies happen in the Representation from any state, the Executive Authority thereof shall issue Writs of Election to fill such Vacancies.

The House of Representatives shall chuse their Speaker and other Officers; and shall have the sole Power of Impeachment.

Section. 3. The Senate of the United States shall be composed of two Senators from each State, chosen by the legislature thereof, for six Years; and each Senator shall have one Vote.

Immediately after they shall be assembled in Consequence of the first Election, they shall be divided as equally as may be into three Classes. The Seats of the Senators of the first Class shall be vacated at the Expiration of the second Year, of the second Class at the Expiration of the fourth Year, and of the third Class at the Expiration of the sixth Year, so that one third maybe chosen every second Year; and if Vacancies happen by Resignation, or otherwise, during the Recess of the Legislature of any State, the Executive thereof may make temporary Appointments until the next Meeting of the Legislature, which shall then fill such Vacancies.

No Person shall be a Senator who shall not have attained to the Age of thirty Years, and been nine Years a Citizen of the United States, and who shall not, when elected, be an Inhabitant of that State for which he shall be chosen.

The Vice President of the United States shall be President of the Senate, but shall have no Vote, unless they be equally divided.

The Senate shall chuse their other Officers, and also a President pro tempore, in the Absence of the Vice President, or when he shall exercise the Office of President of the United States.

The Senate shall have the sole Power to try all Impeachments. When sitting for that Purpose, they shall be on Oath or Affirmation. When the President of the United States is tried, the Chief Justice shall preside: And no Person shall be convicted without the Concurrence of two thirds of the Members present.

Judgment in Cases of Impeachment shall not extend further than to removal from Office, and disqualification to hold and enjoy any Office of honor, Trust or Profit under the United States: but the Party convicted shall nevertheless be liable and subject to Indictment, Trial, Judgment and Punishment, according to Law.

Section. 4. The Times, Places and Manner of holding Elections for Senators and Representatives, shall be prescribed in each State by the Legislature thereof, but the Congress may at any time by Law make or alter such Regulations, except as to the Places of chusing Senators.

The Congress shall assemble at least once in every Year, and such Meeting shall be on the first Monday in December, unless they shall by Law appoint a different Day.

Section. 5. Each House shall be the Judge of the Elections, Returns and Qualifications of its own Members, and a Majority of each shall constitute a Quorum to do Business; but a smaller Number may adjourn from day to day, and may be authorized to compel the Attendance of absent Members, in such Manner, and under such Penalties as each House may provide.

Each House may determine the Rules of its Proceedings, punish its Members for disorderly Behaviour, and, with the Concurrence of two thirds, expel a Member.

Each House shall keep a Journal of its Proceedings, and from time to time publish the same, excepting such Parts as may in their Judgment require Secrecy; and the Yeas and Nays of the Members of either House on any question shall, at the Desire of one fifth of those Present, be entered on the Journal.

Neither House, during the Session of Congress, shall, without the Consent of the other, adjourn for more than three days, nor to any other Place than that in which the two Houses shall be sitting.

Section. 6. The Senators and Representatives shall receive a Compensation for their Services, to be ascertained by Law, and paid out of the Treasury of the United States. They shall in all Cases, except Treason, Felony and Breach of the Peace, be privileged from Arrest during their Attendance at the Session of their respective Houses, and in going to and returning from the same; and for any Speech or Debate in either House, they shall not be questioned in any other Place.

No Senator or Representative shall, during the Time for which he was elected, be appointed to any civil Office under the Authority of the United States, which shall have been created, or the Emoluments whereof shall have been encreased during such time; and no Person holding any Office under the United States, shall be a Member of either House during his Continuance in Office.

Section. 7. All Bills for raising Revenue shall originate in the House of Representatives; but the Senate may propose or concur with Amendments as on other Bills.

Every Bill which shall have passed the House of Representatives and the Senate shall, before it become a Law, be presented to the President of the United States; If he approve he shall sign it, but if not he shall return it, with his Objections to that House in which it shall have originated, who shall enter the Objections at large on their Journal, and proceed to reconsider it. If after such Reconsideration two thirds of that House shall agree to pass the Bill, it shall be sent, together with the Objections, to the other House, by which it shall likewise be reconsidered, and if approved by two thirds of that House, it shall become a Law. But in all such Cases the Votes of both Houses shall be determined by yeas and Nays, and the Names of the Persons voting for and against the Bill shall be entered on the Journal of each House respectively. If any Bill shall not be returned by the President within ten Days (Sundays excepted) after it shall have been presented to him, the Same shall be a Law, in like Manner as if he had signed it, unless the Congress by their Adjournment prevent its Return, in which Case it shall not be a Law.

Every Order, Resolution, or Vote to which the Concurrence of the

Senate and House of Representatives may be necessary (except on a question of Adjournment) shall be presented to the President of the United States; and before the Same shall take Effect, shall be approved by him, or being disapproved by him, shall be repassed by two thirds of the Senate and House of Representatives, according to the Rules and Limitations prescribed in the Case of a Bill.

Section. 8. The congress shall have Power To lay and collect Taxes, Duties, Imposts and Excises, to pay the Debts and provide for the common Defence and general Welfare of the United States; but all Duties, Imposts and Excises shall be uniform throughout the United States.

To borrow Money on the credit of the United States;

To regulate Commerce with foreign Nations, and among the several States, and with the Indian Tribes;

To establish an uniform Rule of Naturalization, and uniform Laws on the subject of Bankruptcies throughout the United States;

To coin Money, regulate the Value thereof, and of foreign Coin, and fix the Standard of Weights and Measures;

To provide for the Punishment of counterfeiting the Securities and current Coin of the United States;

To establish Post Offices and Post Roads;

To promote the Progress of Science and useful Arts, by securing for limited Times to Authors and Inventors the exclusive Right to their respective Writings and Discoveries;

To constitute Tribunals inferior to the supreme Court;

To define and punish Piracies and Felonies committed on the high Seas, and Offences against the Law of Nations;

To declare War, grant Letters of Marque and Reprisal, and make Rules concerning Captures on land and Water;

To raise and support Armies, but no Appropriation of Money to that Use shall be for a longer Term than two Years;

To provide and maintain a Navy;

To make Rules for the Government and Regulation of the land and naval Forces;

To provide for calling forth the Militia to execute the Laws of the Union, suppress Insurrections and repel Invasions;

To provide for organizing, arming, and disciplining, the Militia, and for governing such Part of them as may be employed in the Service of the United States, reserving to the States respectively, the Appointment of the Officers, and the Authority of training the Militia according to the discipline prescribed by Congress;

To exercise exclusive Legislation in all Cases whatsoever, over such District (not exceeding ten Miles square) as may, by Cession of particular States, and the Acceptance of Congress, become the Seat of the Government of the United States, and to exercise like Authority over all Places purchased by the Consent of the Legislature of the State in which the Same shall be, for the Erection of Forts, Magazines, Arsenals, dock-Yards, and other needful Buildings;—And

To make all Laws which shall be necessary and proper for carrying into Execution the foregoing Powers, and all other Powers vested by this Constitution in the Government of the United States, or in any Department or Officer thereof.

Section. 9. The Migration or Importation of such Persons as any of the States now existing shall think proper to admit, shall not be prohibited by the Congress prior to the Year one thousand eight hundred and eight, but a Tax or duty may be imposed on such Importation, not exceeding ten dollars for each Person.

The Privilege of the Writ of Habeas Corpus shall not be suspended, unless when in Cases of Rebellion or Invasion the public Safety may require it.

No Bill of Attainder or ex post facto Law shall be passed.

No Capitation, or other direct, Tax shall be laid, unless in Proportion to the Census or Enumeration herein before directed to be taken.

No Tax or Duty shall be laid on Articles exported from any State.

No Preference shall be given by any Regulation of Commerce or Revenue to the Ports of one State over those of another: nor shall Vessels bound to, or from, one State, be obliged to enter, clear, or pay Duties in another.

No Money shall be drawn from the Treasury, but in Consequence of Appropriations made by Law, and a regular Statement and Account of the Receipts and Expenditures of all public Money shall be published from time to time.

No Title of Nobility shall be granted by the United States: And no Person holding any Office of Profit or trust under them, shall, without the Consent of the Congress, accept of any present, Emolument, Office, or Title, of any kind whatever, from any King, prince, or foreign State.

Section. 10. No State shall enter into any Treaty, Alliance, or Confederation; grant Letters of Marque and Reprisal; coin Money; emit Bills of Credit; make any Thing but gold and silver Coin a Tender in Payment of Debts; pass any Bill of Attainder, ex post facto Law, or Law impairing the Obligation of Contracts, or grant any Title of Nobility.

No State shall, without the Consent of the Congress, lay any Imposts or Duties on Imports or Exports, except what may be absolutely necessary for executing it's inspection Laws: and the net Produce of all Duties and Imposts, laid by any State on Imports or Exports, shall be for the Use of the Treasury of the United States; and all such Laws shall be subject to the Revision and Controul of the Congress.

No State shall, without the Consent of Congress, lay any Duty of Tonnage, keep Troops, or Ships of War in time of Peace, enter into any Agreement or Compact with another State, or with a foreign Power, or engage in War, unless actually invaded, or in such immiment Danger as will not admit of delay.

ARTICLE. II.

Section. 1. The executive Power shall be vested in a President of the United States of America. He shall hold his Office during the term of four

Years, and, together with the Vice President, chosen for the same Term, be elected, as follows.

Each State shall appoint, in such Manner as the Legislature thereof may direct, a Number of Electors, equal to the whole Number of Senators and Representatives to which the State may be entitled in the Congress: but no Senator or Representative, or Person holding an Office of Trust or Profit under the United States, shall be appointed an Elector.

The Electors shall meet in their respective States, and vote by Ballot for two Persons, of whom one at least shall not be an Inhabitant of the same State with themselves. And they shall make a List of all the Persons voted for, and of the Number of Votes for each; which List they shall sign and certify, and transmit sealed to the Seat of the Government of the United States, directed to the President of the Senate. The President of the Senate shall, in the Presence of the Senate and House of Representatives, open all the Certificates, and the Votes shall then be counted. The Person having the greatest Number of Votes shall be the President, if such Number be a Majority of the whole Number of Electors appointed; and if there be more than one who have such Majority, and have an equal Number of Votes, then the House of Representatives shall immediately chuse by Ballot one of them for President; and if no Person have a Majority, then from the five highest on the List the said House shall in like Manner chuse the President. But in chusing the President, the Votes shall be taken by States, the Representation from each State having one Vote; A quorum for this Purpose shall consist of a Member or Members from two thirds of the States, and a Majority of all the States shall be necessary to a Choice. In every Case, after the Choice of the President, the Person having the greatest Number of Votes of the Electors shall be the Vice President. But if there should remain two or more who have equal Votes, the Senate shall chuse from them by Ballot the Vice President.

The Congress may determine the Time of chusing the Electors, and the Day on which they shall give their Votes; which Day shall be the same throughout the United States.

No Person except a natural born Citizen, or a Citizen of the United States, at the time of the Adoption of this Constitution, shall be eligible to the Office of President, neither shall any Person be eligible to that Office who shall not have attained to the Age of thirty five Years, and been fourteen Years a Resident within the United States.

In Case of the Removal of the President from office, or of his Death, Resignation, or Inability to discharge the Powers and Duties of the said Office, the Same shall devolve on the Vice President, and the Congress may by Law provide for the Case of Removal, Death, Resignation or Inability, both of the President and Vice President, declaring what Officer shall then act as President, and such Officer shall act accordingly, until the Disability be removed, or a President shall be elected.

The President shall, at stated Times, receive for his Services, a Compensation, which shall neither be encreased or diminished during the Period for which he shall have been elected, and he shall not receive within that Period any other Emolument from the United States, or any of them.

Before he enters on the Execution of his Office, he shall take the following Oath or Affirmation:—"I do solemnly swear (or affirm) that I will faithfully execute the Office of President of the United States, and will to the best of my Ability, preserve, protect and defend the Constitution of the United States."

Section. 2. The President shall be Commander in Chief of the Army and Navy of the United States, and of the Militia of the several States, when called into the actual Service of the United States; he may require the Opinion, in writing, of the principal Officer in each of the executive Departments, upon any Subject relating to the Duties of their respective Offices, and he shall have Power to grant Reprieves and Pardons for Offences against the United States, except in Cases of Impeachment.

He shall have Power, by and with the Advice and Consent of the Senate, to make Treaties, provided two thirds of the Senators present concur; and he shall nominate, and by and with the Advice and Consent of the Senate, shall appoint Ambassadors, other public Ministers and Consuls, Judges of the supreme Court, and all other Officers of the United States, whose Appointments are not herein otherwise provided for, and which shall be established by Law; but the Congress may by Law vest the Appointment of such inferior Officers, as they think proper, in the President alone, in the Courts of Law, or in the Heads of Departments.

The President shall have Power to fill up all Vacancies that may happen during the Recess of the Senate, by granting Commissions which shall expire at the End of their next Session.

Section. 3. He shall from time to time give to the Congress Information of the State of the Union, and recommend to their Consideration such Measures as he shall judge necessary and expedient; he may, on extraordinary Occasions, convene both Houses, or either of them, and in Case of Disagreement between them, with Respect to the Time of Adjournment, he may adjourn them to such Time as he shall think proper; he shall receive Ambassadors and other public Ministers; he shall take Care that the Laws be faithfully executed, and shall Commission all the Officers of the United States.

Section. 4. The President, Vice President and all civil Officers of the United States, shall be removed from Office on Impeachment for, and Conviction of, Treason, Bribery, or other high Crimes and Misdemeanors.

ARTICLE. III.

Section. 1. The judicial Power of the United States, shall be vested in one supreme Court, and in such inferior Courts as the Congress may from time to time ordain and establish. The Judges, both of the supreme and inferior Courts, shall hold their Offices during good Behavior, and shall, at stated Times, receive for their Services, a Compensation, which shall not be diminished during their Continuance in Office.

Section. 2. The judicial Power shall extend to all Cases, in Law and Equity, arising under this Constitution, the Laws of the United States, and Treaties made, or which shall be made, under their Authority;—to all Cases affecting Ambassadors, other public Ministers and Consuls;—to all Cases of admiralty and maritime Jurisdiction;—to Controversies to which the United States shall be a Party;—to Controversies between two or more States;—between a State and Citizens of another State;—between Citizens of different States;—between Citizens of the same State claiming Lands under Grants of different States, and between a State, or the Citizens thereof, and foreign States, Citizens or Subjects.

In all cases affecting Ambassadors, other public Ministers and Consuls, and those in which a State shall be Party, the supreme Court shall have original Jurisdiction. In all the other Cases before mentioned, the supreme Court shall have appellate Jurisdiction, both as to Law and Fact, with such Exceptions, and under such Regulations as the Congress shall make.

The Trial of all Crimes, except in Cases of Impeachment, shall be by Jury; and such Trial shall be held in the State where the said Crimes shall have been committed; but when not committed within any State, the Trial shall be at such Place or Places as the Congress may by Law have directed.

Section. 3. Treason against the United States, shall consist only in levying War against them, or in adhering to their Enemies, giving them Aid and Comfort. No Person shall be convicted of Treason unless on the Testimony of two Witnesses to the same overt Act, or on Confession in open Court.

The Congress shall have Power to declare the Punishment of Treason, but no Attainder of Treason shall work Corruption of Blood, or Forfeiture except during the Life of the Person attainted.

ARTICLE. IV.

Section. 1. Full Faith and Credit shall be given in each State to the public Acts, Records, and judicial Proceedings of every other State. And the Congress may by general Laws prescribe the Manner in which such Acts, Records and Proceedings shall be proved, and the Effect thereof.

Section. 2. The Citizens of each State shall be entitled to all Privileges and Immunities of Citizens in the several States.

A Person charged in any State with Treason, Felony, or other Crime, who shall flee from Justice, and be found in another State, shall on Demand of the executive Authority of the State from which he fled, be delivered up, to be removed to the State having Jurisdiction of the Crime.

No Person held to Service or Labour in one State, under the Laws thereof, escaping into another, shall, in Consequence of any Law or Regulation therein, be discharged from such Service or Labour, but shall be delivered up on Claim of the Party to whom such Service or Labour may be due.

Section. 3. New States may be admitted by the Congress into this Union; but no new State shall be formed or erected within the Jurisdiction of any other State; nor any State be formed by the Junction of two or more States, or Parts of States, without the consent of the Legislatures of the States concerned as well as of the Congress.

The Congress shall have Power to dispose of and make all needful Rules and Regulations respecting the Territory or other Property belonging to the United States; and nothing in this Constitution shall be so construed as to Prejudice any Claims of the United States, or of any particular States.

Section. 4. The United States shall guarantee to every State in this Union a Republican Form of Government, and shall protect each of them against Invasion; and on Application of the Legislature, or of the Executive (when the Legislature cannot be convened) against domestic Violence.

Article. V.

The Congress, whenever two thirds of both Houses shall deem it necessary, shall propose Amendments to this Constitution, or, on the Application of the Legislatures of two thirds of the several States shall call a Convention for proposing Amendments, which, in either Case, shall be valid to all Intents and Purposes, as Part of this Constitution, when ratified by the Legislatures of three fourths of the several States, or by Conventions in three fourths thereof, as the one or the other Mode of Ratification may be proposed by the Congress; Provided that no Amendment which may be made prior to the Year One thousand eight hundred and eight shall in any Manner affect the first and fourth Clauses in the Ninth Section of the first Article; and that no State, without its Consent, shall be deprived of it's equal Suffrage in the Senate.

Article. VI.

All Debts contracted and Engagements entered into, before the Adoption of this Constitution, shall be as valid against the United States under this Constitution, as under the Confederation.

This Constitution, and the Laws of the United States which shall be made in Pursuance thereof; and all Treaties made, or which shall be made, under the Authority of the United States, shall be the supreme Law of the Land; and the Judges in every State shall be bound thereby, any Thing in the Constitution or Laws of any State to the Contrary notwithstanding.

The Senators and Representatives before mentioned, and the Members of the several State Legislatures, and all executive and judicial Officers, both of the United States and of the several States, shall be bound by Oath or Affirmation, to support this Constitution; but no religious Test shall ever be required as a Qualification to any Office or public Trust under the United States.

Article. VII.

The Ratification of the Conventions of nine States, shall be sufficient for the Establishment of this Constitution between the States so ratifying the Same.

Done in Convention by the Unanimous Consent of the States present the Seventeenth Day of September in the Year of our Lord one thousand seven hundred and Eighty seven and of the Independence of the United States of America the Twelfth. In witness thereof We have hereunto subscribed our Names,

G°: WASHINGTON—Presidᵗ
and deputy from Virginia

New Hampshire { John Langdon
Nicholas Gilman

Massachusetts { Nathaniel Gorham
Rufus King

Connecticut { Wᵐ Samˡ Johnson
Roger Sherman

New York   Alexander Hamilton

New Jersey { Wil: Livingston
David A. Brearley.
Wᵐ Paterson.
Jona: Dayton

Pennsylvania { B. Franklin
Thomas Mifflin
Robᵗ Morris
Geo. Clymer
Thoˢ. FitzSimons
Jared Ingersoll
James Wilson
Gouv Morris

Delaware { Geo: Read
Gunning Bedford jun
John Dickinson
Richard Bassett
Jaco: Broom

Maryland { James McHenry
Dan of Sᵗ Thoˢ
Jenifer
Danˡ Carroll

Virginia { John Blair—
James Madison Jr.

North Carolina { Wᵐ. Blount
Richᵈ Dobbs Spaight.
Hu Williamson

South Carolina { J. Rutledge
Charles Cotesworth Pinckney
Charles Pinckney
Pierce Butler.

Georgia { William Few
Abr Baldwin

AMENDMENTS TO THE CONSTITUTION

Articles in addition to, and Amendment of the Constitution of the United States of America, proposed by Congress, and ratified by the Legislatures of the several States, pursuant to the fifth Article of the original Constitution.

AMENDMENT I.

Congress shall make no law respecting an establishment of religion, or prohibiting the free exercise thereof; or abridging the freedom of speech, or of the press; or the right of the people peaceably to assemble, and to petitition the Government for a redress of grievances.

AMENDMENT II.

A well regulated Militia, being necessary to the security of a free State, the right of the people to keep and bear Arms, shall not be infringed.

AMENDMENT III.

No Soldier shall, in time of peace be quartered in any house, without the consent of the Owner, nor in time of war, but in a manner to be prescribed by law.

AMENDMENT IV.

The right of the people to be secure in their persons, houses, papers, and effects, against unreasonable searches and seizures, shall not be violated, and no Warrants shall issue, but upon probable cause, supported by Oath or affirmation, and particularly describing the place to be searched, and the persons or things to be seized.

AMENDMENT V.

No person shall be held to answer for a capital, or otherwise infamous crime, unless on a presentment or indictment of a Grand Jury, except in cases arising in the land or naval forces, or in the Militia, when in actual service in time of War or public danger; nor shall any person be subject for the same offence to be twice put in jeopardy of life or limb; nor shall be compelled in any criminal case to be a witness against himself, nor be deprived of life, liberty, or property, without due process of law; nor shall private property be taken for public use, without just compensation.

AMENDMENT VI.

In all criminal prosecutions, the accused shall enjoy the right to a speedy and public trial, by an impartial jury of the State and district wherein the crime shall have been committed, which district shall have been previously ascertained by law, and to be informed of the nature and cause of the accusation; to be confronted with the witnesses against him; to have compulsory process for obtaining witnesses in his favor, and to have the Assistance of Counsel for his defence.

Amendment VII.

In Suits at common law, where the value in controversy shall exceed twenty dollars, the right of trial by jury shall be preserved, and no fact tried by a jury, shall be otherwise re-examined in any Court of the United States, than according to the rules of the common law.

Amendment VIII.

Excessive bail shall not be required, nor excessive fines imposed, nor cruel and unusual punishments inflicted.

Amendment IX.

The enumeration in the Constitution, of certain rights, shall not be construed to deny or disparage others retained by the people.

Amendment X.

The powers not delegated to the United States by the Constitution, nor prohibited by it to the States, are reserved to the States respectively, or to the people. [The first ten amendments went into effect December 15, 1791.]

Amendment XI.

The Judicial power of the United States shall not be construed to extend to any suit in law or equity, commenced or prosecuted against one of the United States by Citizens of another State, or by Citizens or Subjects of any Foreign State. [January 8, 1798.]

Amendment XII.

The Electors shall meet in their respective states, and vote by ballot for President and Vice-President, one of whom, at least, shall not be an inhabitant of the same state with themselves; they shall name in their ballots the person voted for as President, and in distinct ballots the person voted for as Vice-President, and they shall make distinct lists of all persons voted for as President, and of all persons voted for as Vice-President, and of the number of votes for each, which lists they shall sign and certify, and transmit sealed to the seat of the government of the United States, directed to the President of the Senate;—The President of the Senate shall, in the presence of the Senate and House of Representatives, open all the certificates and the votes shall then be counted;—The person having the greatest number of votes for President, shall be the President, if such number be a majority of the whole number of Electors appointed; and if no person have such majority, then from the persons having the highest numbers not exceeding three on the list of those voted for as President, the House of Representatives shall choose immediately, by ballot, the President. But in choosing the President, the votes shall be taken by states, the representation from each state having one vote; a quorum for this purpose shall consist of a member or members from two-thirds of the states, and a majority of all the states shall be necessary to a choice. And if the House of Representatives shall not choose a President whenever the right of choice shall devolve upon them, before the fourth day of March next following, then the Vice-President shall act as President, as in the case of the death or other constitutional disability of the President.—The person having the greatest number of votes as Vice-President, shall be the Vice-President, if such number be a majority of the whole number of Electors appointed, and if no person have a majority, then from the two highest numbers on the list, the Senate shall choose the Vice-President; a quorum for the purpose shall consist of two-thirds of the whole number of Senators, and a majority of the whole number shall be necessary to a choice. But no person constitutionally ineligible to the office of President shall be eligible to that of Vice-President of the United States. [September 25, 1804.]

Amendment XIII.

Section 1. Neither slavery nor involuntary servitude, except as a punishment for crime whereof the party shall have been duly convicted, shall exist within the United States, or any place subject to their jurisdiction.

Section 2. Congress shall have power to enforce this article by appropriate legislation. [December 18, 1865.]

Amendment XIV.

Section 1. All persons born or naturalized in the United States, and subject to the jurisdiction thereof, are citizens of the United States and of the State wherein they reside. No State shall make or enforce any law which shall abridge the privileges or immunities of citizens of the United States; nor shall any State deprive any person of life, liberty, or property, without due process of law; nor deny to any person within its jurisdiction the equal protection of the laws.

Section 2. Representatives shall be apportioned among the several States according to their respective numbers, counting the whole number of persons in each State, excluding Indians not taxed. But when the right to vote at any election for the choice of electors for President and Vice President of the United States, Representatives in Congress, the Executive and Judicial officers of a State, or the members of the Legislature thereof, is denied to any of the male inhabitants of such State, being twenty-one years of age, and citizens of the United States, or in any way abridged, except for participation in rebellion, or other crime, the basis of representation therein shall be reduced in the proportion which the number of such male citizens shall bear to the whole number of male citizens twenty-one years of age in such State.

Section 3. No person shall be a Senator or Representative in Congress, or elector of President and Vice President, or hold any office, civil or military, under the United States, or under any State, who, having previously taken an oath, as a member of Congress, or as an officer of the United States, or as a member of any State legislature, or as an executive or judicial officer of any State, to support the Constitution of the United States, shall have engaged in insurrection or rebellion against the same, or given aid or comfort to the enemies thereof. But Congress may by a vote of two-thirds of each House, remove such disability.

Section 4. The validity of the public debt of the United States, authorized by law, including debts incurred for payment of pensions and bounties for services in suppressing insurrection or rebellion, shall not be questioned. But neither the United States nor any State shall assume or pay any debt or obligation incurred in aid of insurrection or rebellion against the United States, or any claim for the loss or emancipation of any slave; but all such debts, obligations and claims shall be held illegal and void.

Section 5. The Congress shall have power to enforce, by appropriate legislation, the provisions of this article. [July 28, 1868.]

AMENDMENT XV.

Section 1. The right of citizens of the United States to vote shall not be denied or abridged by the United States or by any State on account of race, color, or previous condition of servitude—

Section 2. The Congress shall have power to enforce this article by appropriate legislation.—[March 30, 1870.]

AMENDMENT XVI.

The Congress shall have power to lay and collect taxes on incomes, from whatever source derived, without apportionment among the several States, and without regard to any census or enumeration. [February 25, 1913.]

Amendment XVII.

The Senate of the United States shall be composed of two senators from each State, elected by the people thereof, for six years; and each Senator shall have one vote. The electors in each State shall have the qualifications requisite for electors of the most numerous branch of the State legislature.

When vacancies happen in the representation of any State in the Senate, the executive authority of such State shall issue writs of election to fill such vacancies: *Provided,* That the legislature of any State may empower the executive thereof to make temporary appointments until the people fill the vacancies by election as the legislature may direct.

This amendment shall not be so construed as to affect the election or term of any senator chosen before it becomes valid as part of the Constitution. [May 31, 1913.]

Amendment XVIII.

After one year from the ratification of this article, the manufacture, sale, or transportation of intoxicating liquors within, the importation thereof into, or the exportation thereof from the United States and all territory subject to the jurisdiction thereof for beverage purposes is hereby prohibited.

The Congress and the several States shall have concurrent power to enforce this article by appropriate legislation.

This article shall be inoperative unless it shall have been ratified as an amendment to the Constitution by the legislatures of the several States, as provided in the Constitution, within seven years from the date of the submission thereof to the States by Congress. [January 29, 1919.]

Amendment XIX.

The right of citizens of the United States to vote shall not be denied or abridged by the United States or by any State on account of sex.

The Congress shall have power by appropriate legislation to enforce the provisions of this article. [August 26, 1920.]

Amendment XX.

Section 1. The terms of the President and Vice-President shall end at noon on the twentieth day of January, and the terms of Senators and Representatives at noon on the third day of January, of the years in which such terms would have ended if this article had not been ratified; and the terms of their successors shall then begin.

Section 2. The Congress shall assemble at least once in every year, and such meeting shall begin at noon on the third day of January, unless they shall by law appoint a different day.

Section 3. If, at the time fixed for the beginning of the term of the President, the President-elect shall have died, the Vice-President-elect shall become President. If a President shall not have been chosen before the time fixed for the beginning of his term, or if the President-elect shall have failed to qualify, then the Vice-President-elect shall act as President until a President shall have qualified; and the Congress may by law provide for the case wherein neither a President-elect nor a Vice-President-elect shall have qualified, declaring who shall then act as President, or the manner in which one who is to act shall be selected, and such person shall act accordingly until a President or Vice-President shall have qualified.

Section 4. The Congress may by law provide for the case of the death of any of the persons from whom the House of Representatives may choose a President whenever the right of choice shall have devolved upon them, and for the case of the death of any of the persons from whom the Senate may choose a Vice-President whenever the right of choice shall have devolved upon them.

Section 5. Sections 1 and 2 shall take effect on the 15th day of October following the ratification of this article.

Section 6. This article shall be inoperative unless it shall have been ratified as an amendment to the Constitution by the legislatures of three-fourths of the several States within seven years from the date of its submission. [February 6, 1933.]

Amendment XXI.

Section 1. The eighteenth article of amendment to the Constitution of the United States is hereby repealed.

Section 2. The transportation or importation into any State, Territory or possession of the United States for delivery or use therein of intoxicating liquors, in violation of the laws thereof, is hereby prohibited.

Section 3. This article shall be inoperative unless it shall have been ratified as an amendment to the Constitution by convention in the several States, as provided in the Constitution, within seven years from the date of the submission thereof to the States by the Congress. [December 5, 1933.]

Amendment XXII.

Section 1. No person shall be elected to the office of the President more than twice, and no person who has held the office of President, or acted as President, for more than two years of a term to which some other person was elected President shall be elected to the office of the President more than once. But this Article shall not apply to any person holding the office of President when this Article was proposed by the Congress, and shall not prevent any person who may be holding the office of President, or acting as President, during the term within which this Article becomes operative from holding the office of President or acting as President during the remainder of such term.

Section 2. This article shall be inoperative unless it shall have been ratified as an amendment to the Constitution by the legislatures of three-fourths of the several states within seven years from the date of its submission to the States by the Congress. [February 27, 1951.]

AMENDMENT XXIII.

Section 1. The District constituting the seat of government of the United States shall appoint in such manner as the Congress may direct:

A number of electors of President and Vice-President equal to the whole number of Senators and Representatives in Congress to which the District would be entitled if it were a State, but in no event more than the least populous State; they shall be in addition to those appointed by the States, but they shall be considered, for the purposes of the election of President and Vice-President, to be electors appointed by a State; and they shall meet in the District and perform such duties as provided by the twelfth article of amendment.

Section 2. The Congress shall have the power to enforce this article by appropriate legislation. [March 29, 1961.]

AMENDMENT XXIV.

Section 1. The right of citizens of the United States to vote in any primary or other election for President or Vice President, for electors for President or Vice President, or for Senator or Representative in Congress, shall not be denied or abridged by the United States or any State by reason of failure to pay any poll tax or other tax.

Section 2. The Congress shall have power to enforce this article by appropriate legislation. [January 23, 1964.]

AMENDMENT XXV.

Section 1. In case of the removal of the President from office or of his death or resignation, the Vice President shall become President.

Section 2. Whenever there is a vacancy in the office of Vice President, the President shall nominate a Vice President who shall take office upon confirmation by a majority vote of both Houses of Congress.

Section 3. Whenever the President transmits to the President pro tempore of the Senate and the Speaker of the House of Representatives his written declaration that he is unable to discharge the powers and duties of his office, and until he transmits to them a written declaration to the contrary, such powers and duties shall be discharged by the Vice President as Acting President.

Section 4. Whenever the Vice President and a majority of either the principal officers of the executive departments or of such other body as Congress may by law provide, transmit to the President pro tempore of the Senate and the Speaker of the House of Representatives their written declaration that the President is unable to discharge the powers and duties of his office, the Vice President shall immediately assume the powers and duties of the office as Acting President.

Thereafter, when the President transmits to the President pro tempore of the Senate and the Speaker of the House of Representatives his written declaration that no inability exists, he shall resume the powers and duties of his office unless the Vice President and a majority of either the principal officers of the executive departments or of such other body as Congress may by law provide, transmit within four days to the President pro tempore of the Senate and the Speaker of the House of Representatives their written declaration that the President is unable to discharge the powers and duties of his office. Thereupon Congress shall decide the issue, assembling within forty-eight hours for that purpose if not in session. If the Congress, within twenty-one days after receipt of the latter written declaration, or, if Congress is not in session, within twenty-one days after Congress is required to assemble, determines by two-thirds vote of both Houses that the President is unable to discharge the powers and duties of his office, the Vice President shall continue to discharge the same as Acting President; otherwise, the President shall resume the powers and duties of his office. [February 10, 1967.]

Amendment XXVI.

Section 1. The right of citizens of the United States, who are eighteen years of age or older, to vote shall not be denied or abridged by the United States or by any State on account of age.

Section 2. The Congress shall have power to enforce this article by appropriate legislation [June 30, 1971.]

PRESIDENTIAL ELECTIONS

Year	Number of States	Candidates	Parties	Popular Vote	% of Popular Vote	Electoral Vote	% Voter Participation
1789	11	**GEORGE WASHINGTON**	No party designations			69	
		John Adams				34	
		Other candidates				35	
1792	15	**GEORGE WASHINGTON**	No party designations			132	
		John Adams				77	
		George Clinton				50	
		Other candidates				5	
1796	16	**JOHN ADAMS**	Federalist			71	
		Thomas Jefferson	Democratic-Republican			68	
		Thomas Pinckney	Federalist			59	
		Aaron Burr	Democratic-Republican			30	
		Other candidates				48	
1800	16	**THOMAS JEFFERSON**	Democratic-Republican			73	
		Aaron Burr	Democratic-Republican			73	
		John Adams	Federalist			65	
		Charles C. Pinckney	Federalist			64	
		John Jay	Federalist			1	

Year	Number of States	Candidates	Parties	Popular Vote	% of Popular Vote	Electoral Vote	% Voter Participation
1804	17	**THOMAS JEFFERSON**	Democratic-Republican			162	
		Charles C. Pinckney	Federalist			14	
1808	17	**JAMES MADISON**	Democratic-Republican			122	
		Charles C. Pinckney	Federalist			47	
		George Clinton	Democratic-Republican			6	
1812	18	**JAMES MADISON**	Democratic-Republican			128	
		DeWitt Clinton	Federalist			89	
1816	19	**JAMES MONROE**	Democratic-Republican			183	
		Rufus King	Federalist			34	
1820	24	**JAMES MONROE**	Democratic-Republican			231	
		John Quincy Adams	Independent			1	
1824	24	**JOHN QUINCY ADAMS**	Democratic-Republican	108,740	30.5	84	26.9
		Andrew Jackson	Democratic-Republican	153,544	43.1	99	
		Henry Clay	Democratic-Republican	47,136	13.2	37	
		William H. Crawford	Democratic-Republican	46,618	13.1	41	

Year	Number of States	Candidates	Parties	Popular Vote	% of Popular Vote	Electoral Vote	% Voter Participation
1828	24	**ANDREW JACKSON**	Democratic	647,286	56.0	178	57.6
		John Quincy Adams	National Republican	508,064	44.0	83	
1832	24	**ANDREW JACKSON**	Democratic	688,242	54.5	219	55.4
		Henry Clay	National Republican	473,462	37.5	49	
		William Wirt	Anti-Masonic } Democratic	101,051	8.0	7	
		John Floyd				11	
1836	26	**MARTIN VAN BUREN**	Democratic	765,483	50.9	170	57.8
		William H. Harrison	Whig			73	
		Hugh L. White	Whig	739,795	49.1	26	
		Daniel Webster	Whig			14	
		W. P. Mangum	Whig			11	
1840	26	**WILLIAM H. HARRISON**	Whig	1,274,624	53.1	234	80.2
		Martin Van Buren	Democratic	1,127,781	46.9	60	
1844	26	**JAMES K. POLK**	Democratic	1,338,464	49.6	170	78.9
		Henry Clay	Whig	1,300,097	48.1	105	
		James G. Birney	Liberty	62,300	2.3		
1848	30	**ZACHARY TAYLOR**	Whig	1,360,967	47.4	163	72.7
		Lewis Cass	Democratic	1,222,342	42.5	127	
		Martin Van Buren	Free Soil	291,263	10.1		

Year	Number of States	Candidates	Parties	Popular Vote	% of Popular Vote	Electoral Vote	% Voter Participation
1852	31	**FRANKLIN PIERCE** Winfield Scott John P. Hale	Democratic Whig Free Soil	1,601,117 1,385,453 155,825	50.9 44.1 5.0	254 42	69.6
1856	31	**JAMES BUCHANAN** John C. Frémont Millard Fillmore	Democratic Republican American	1,832,955 1,339,932 871,731	45.3 33.1 21.6	174 114 8	78.9
1860	33	**ABRAHAM LINCOLN** Stephen A. Douglas John C. Breckinridge John Bell	Republican Democratic Democratic Constitutional Union	1,865,593 1,382,713 848,356 592,906	39.8 29.5 18.1 12.6	180 12 72 39	81.2
1864	36	**ABRAHAM LINCOLN** George B. McClellan	Republican Democratic	2,206,938 1,803,787	55.0 45.0	212 21	73.8
1868	37	**ULYSSES S. GRANT** Horatio Seymour	Republican Democratic	3,013,421 2,706,829	52.7 47.3	214 80	78.1
1872	37	**ULYSSES S. GRANT** Horace Greeley	Republican Democratic	3,596,745 2,843,446	55.6 43.9	286	71.3
1876	38	**RUTHERFORD B. HAYES** Samuel J. Tilden	Republican Democratic	4,036,572 4,284,020	48.0 51.0	185 184	81.8
1880	38	**JAMES A. GARFIELD** Winfield S. Hancock James B. Weaver	Republican Democratic Greenback-Labor	4,453,295 4,414,082 308,578	48.5 48.1 3.4	214 155	79.4

Year	Number of States	Candidates	Parties	Popular Vote	% of Popular Vote	Electoral Vote	% Voter Participation
1884	38	**GROVER CLEVELAND**	Democratic	4,879,507	48.5	219	77.5
		James G. Blaine	Republican	4,850,293	48.2	182	
		Benjamin F. Butler	Greenback-Labor	175,370	1.8		
		John P. St. John	Prohibition	150,369	1.5		
1888	38	**BENJAMIN HARRISON**	Republican	5,477,129	47.9	233	79.3
		Grover Cleveland	Democratic	5,537,857	48.6	168	
		Clinton B. Fisk	Prohibition	249,506	2.2		
		Anson J. Streeter	Union Labor	146,935	1.3		
1892	44	**GROVER CLEVELAND**	Democratic	5,555,426	46.1	277	74.7
		Benjamin Harrison	Republican	5,182,690	43.0	145	
		James B. Weaver	People's	1,029,846	8.5	22	
		John Bidwell	Prohibition	264,133	2.2		
1896	45	**WILLIAM McKINLEY**	Republican	7,102,246	51.1	271	79.3
		William J. Bryan	Democratic	6,492,559	47.7	176	
1900	45	**WILLIAM McKINLEY**	Republican	7,218,491	51.7	292	73.2
		William J. Bryan	Democratic; Populist	6,356,734	45.5	155	
		John C. Wooley	Prohibition	208,914	1.5		

Year	States	Candidates	Parties	Popular Vote	%	Electoral Vote	% Participation
1904	45	**THEODORE ROOSEVELT**	Republican	7,628,461	57.4	336	65.2
		Alton B. Parker	Democratic	5,084,223	37.6	140	
		Eugene V. Debs	Socialist	402,283	3.0		
		Silas C. Swallow	Prohibition	258,536	1.9		
1908	46	**WILLIAM H. TAFT**	Republican	7,675,320	51.6	321	65.4
		William J. Bryan	Democratic	6,412,294	43.1	162	
		Eugene V. Debs	Socialist	420,793	2.8		
		Eugene W. Chafin	Prohibition	253,840	1.7		
1912	48	**WOODROW WILSON**	Democratic	6,296,547	41.9	435	58.8
		Theodore Roosevelt	Progressive	4,118,571	27.4	88	
		William H. Taft	Republican	3,486,720	23.2	8	
		Eugene V. Debs	Socialist	900,672	6.0		
		Eugene W. Chafin	Prohibition	206,275	1.4		
1916	48	**WOODROW WILSON**	Democratic	9,127,695	49.4	277	61.6
		Charles E. Hughes	Republican	8,533,507	46.2	254	
		A. L. Benson	Socialist	585,113	3.2		
		J. Frank Hanly	Prohibition	220,506	1.2		
1920	48	**WARREN G. HARDING**	Republican	16,143,407	60.4	404	49.2
		James M. Cox	Democratic	9,130,328	34.2	127	
		Eugene V. Debs	Socialist	919,799	3.4		
		P. P. Christensen	Farmer-Labor	265,411	1.0		
1924	48	**CALVIN COOLIDGE**	Republican	15,718,211	54.0	382	48.9
		John W. Davis	Democratic	8,385,283	28.8	136	
		Robert M. La Follette	Progressive	4,831,289	16.6	13	

Year	Number of States	Candidates	Parties	Popular Vote	% of Popular Vote	Electoral Vote	% Voter Participation
1928	48	**HERBERT C. HOOVER**	Republican	21,391,993	58.2	444	56.9
		Alfred E. Smith	Democratic	15,016,169	40.9	87	
1932	48	**FRANKLIN D. ROOSEVELT**	Democratic	22,809,638	57.4	472	56.9
		Herbert C. Hoover	Republican	15,758,901	39.7	59	
		Norman Thomas	Socialist	881,951	2.2		
1936	48	**FRANKLIN D. ROOSEVELT**	Democratic	27,752,869	60.8	523	61.0
		Alfred M. Landon	Republican	16,674,665	36.5	8	
		William Lemke	Union	882,479	1.9		
1940	48	**FRANKLIN D. ROOSEVELT**	Democratic	27,307,819	54.8	449	62.5
		Wendell L. Willkie	Republican	22,321,018	44.8	82	
1944	48	**FRANKLIN D. ROOSEVELT**	Democratic	25,606,585	53.5	432	55.9
		Thomas E. Dewey	Republican	22,014,745	46.0	99	
1948	48	**HARRY S TRUMAN**	Democratic	24,179,345	49.6	303	53.0
		Thomas E. Dewey	Republican	21,991,291	45.1	189	
		J. Strom Thurmond	States' Rights	1,176,125	2.4	39	
		Henry A. Wallace	Progressive	1,157,326	2.4		
1952	48	**DWIGHT EISENHOWER**	Republican	33,936,234	55.1	442	63.3
		Adlai E. Stevenson	Democratic	27,314,992	44.4	89	

Year	States	Candidates	Parties	Popular Vote	% of Popular Vote	Electoral Vote	% Voter Participation
1956	48	**DWIGHT D. EISENHOWER** Adlai E. Stevenson	Republican Democratic	35,590,472 26,022,752	57.6 42.1	457 73	60.6
1960	50	**JOHN F. KENNEDY** Richard M. Nixon	Democratic Republican	34,226,731 34,108,157	49.7 49.5	303 219	64.0
1964	50	**LYNDON B. JOHNSON** Barry M. Goldwater	Democratic Republican	43,129,566 27,178,188	61.1 38.5	486 52	61.7
1968	50	**RICHARD M. NIXON** Hubert H. Humphrey George C. Wallace	Republican Democratic American Independent	31,785,480 31,275,166 9,906,473	43.4 42.7 13.5	301 191 46	60.6
1972	50	**RICHARD M. NIXON** George S. McGovern John G. Schmitz	Republican Democratic American	47,169,911 29,170,383 1,099,482	60.7 37.5 1.4	520 17	55.5
1976	50	**JIMMY CARTER** Gerald R. Ford	Democratic Republican	40,830,763 39,147,793	50.1 48.0	297 240	54.3
1980	50	**RONALD REAGAN** Jimmy Carter John B. Anderson Ed Clark	Republican Democratic Independent Libertarian	43,901,812 35,483,820 5,719,722 921,188	50.7 41.0 6.6 1.1	489 49 0 0	53.0

Candidates receiving less than 1 percent of the popular vote have been omitted. Thus the percentage of popular vote given for any election year may not total 100 percent.
Before the passage of the Twelfth Amendment in 1804, the Electoral College voted for two presidential candidates; the runner-up became vice president.

ADMISSION OF STATES

Order of Admission	State	Date of Admission
1	Delaware	December 7, 1787
2	Pennsylvania	December 12, 1787
3	New Jersey	December 18, 1787
4	Georgia	January 2, 1788
5	Connecticut	January 9, 1788
6	Massachusetts	February 7, 1788
7	Maryland	April 28, 1788
8	South Carolina	May 23, 1788
9	New Hampshire	June 21, 1788
10	Virginia	June 25, 1788
11	New York	July 26, 1788
12	North Carolina	November 21, 1789
13	Rhode Island	May 29, 1790
14	Vermont	March 4, 1791
15	Kentucky	June 1, 1792
16	Tennessee	June 1, 1796
17	Ohio	March 1, 1803
18	Louisiana	April 30, 1812
19	Indiana	December 11, 1816
20	Mississippi	December 10, 1817
21	Illinois	December 3, 1818
22	Alabama	December 14, 1819
23	Maine	March 15, 1820
24	Missouri	August 10, 1821
25	Arkansas	June 15, 1836
26	Michigan	January 26, 1837
27	Florida	March 3, 1845
28	Texas	December 29, 1845
29	Iowa	December 28, 1846
30	Wisconsin	May 29, 1848
31	California	September 9, 1850
32	Minnesota	May 11, 1858
33	Oregon	February 14, 1859
34	Kansas	January 29, 1861
35	West Virginia	June 30, 1863
36	Nevada	October 31, 1864
37	Nebraska	March 1, 1867
38	Colorado	August 1, 1876
39	North Dakota	November 2, 1889
40	South Dakota	November 2, 1889
41	Montana	November 8, 1889
42	Washington	November 11, 1889
43	Idaho	July 3, 1890
44	Wyoming	July 10, 1890
45	Utah	January 4, 1896
46	Oklahoma	November 16, 1907
47	New Mexico	January 6, 1912
48	Arizona	February 14, 1912
49	Alaska	January 3, 1959
50	Hawaii	August 21, 1959

POPULATION OF THE UNITED STATES

Year	Number of States	Population	Percent Increase	Population per Square Mile
1790	13	3,929,214		4.5
1800	16	5,308,483	35.1	6.1
1810	17	7,239,881	36.4	4.3
1820	23	9,638,453	33.1	5.5
1830	24	12,866,020	33.5	7.4
1840	26	17,069,453	32.7	9.8
1850	31	23,191,876	35.9	7.9
1860	33	31,443,321	35.6	10.6
1870	37	39,818,449	26.6	13.4
1880	38	50,155,783	26.0	16.9
1890	44	62,947,714	25.5	21.2
1900	45	75,994,575	20.7	25.6
1910	46	91,972,266	21.0	31.0
1920	48	105,710,620	14.9	35.6
1930	48	122,775,046	16.1	41.2
1940	48	131,669,275	7.2	44.2
1950	48	150,697,361	14.5	50.7
1960	50	179,323,175	19.0	50.6
1970	50	203,235,298	13.3	57.5
1980	50	226,504,825	11.4	64.0

PRESIDENTS, VICE-PRESIDENTS,
AND SECRETARIES OF STATE

President	Vice-President	Secretary of State
1. George Washington, Federalist 1789	John Adams, Federalist 1789	T. Jefferson 1789 E. Randolph 1794 T. Pickering 1795
2. John Adams, Federalist 1797	Thomas Jefferson, Dem.-Rep. 1797	T. Pickering 1797 John Marshall 1800
3. Thomas Jefferson, Dem.-Rep. 1801	Aaron Burr, Dem.-Rep. 1801 George Clinton, Dem.-Rep. 1805	James Madison 1801
4. James Madison, Dem.-Rep. 1809	George Clinton, Dem.-Rep. 1809 Elbridge Gerry, Dem.-Rep. 1813	Robert Smith 1809 James Monroe 1811
5. James Monroe, Dem.-Rep.-1817	D. D. Tompkins, Dem.-Rep. 1817	J. Q. Adams 1817
6. John Quincy Adams, Dem.-Rep. 1825	John C. Calhoun, Dem.-Rep. 1825	Henry Clay 1825
7. Andrew Jackson, Democratic 1829	John C. Calhoun, Democratic 1829 Martin Van Buren, Democratic 1833	M. Van Buren 1829 E. Livingston 1831 Louis McLane 1833 John Forsyth 1834
8. Martin Van Buren, Democratic 1837	Richard M. Johnson, Democratic 1837	John Forsyth 1837
9. William H. Harrison, Whig 1841	John Tyler, Whig 1841	Daniel Webster 1841

President	Vice-President	Secretary of State
10. John Tyler, Whig and Democratic 1841		Daniel Webster 1841 Hugh S. Legare 1843 Abel P. Upshur 1843 John C. Calhoun 1844
11. James K. Polk, Democratic 1845	George M. Dallas, Democratic 1845	James Buchanan 1845
12. Zachary Taylor, Whig 1849	Millard Fillmore, Whig 1848	John M. Clayton 1849
13. Millard Fillmore, Whig 1850		Daniel Webster 1850 Edward Everett 1852
14. Franklin Pierce, Democratic 1853	William R. D. King, Democratic 1853	W. L. Marcy 1853
15. James Buchanan, Democratic 1857	John C. Breckinridge, Democratic 1857	Lewis Cass 1857 J. S. Black 1860
16. Abraham Lincoln, Republican 1861	Hannibal Hamlin, Republican 1861 Andrew Johnson, Unionist 1865	W. H. Seward 1861
17. Andrew Johnson, Unionist 1865		W. H. Seward 1865
18. Ulysses S. Grant, Republican 1869	Schuyler Colfax, Republican 1869 Henry Wilson, Republican 1873	E. B. Washburne 1869 H. Fish 1869
19. Rutherford B. Hayes, Republican 1877	William A. Wheeler, Republican 1877	W. M. Evarts 1877

President	Vice-President	Secretary of State
20. James A Garfield, Republican 1881	Chester A. Arthur, Republican 1881	J. G. Blaine 1881
21. Chester A. Arthur, Republican 1881		F. T. Frelinghuysen 1881
22. Grover Cleveland, Democratic 1885	T. A. Hendricks, Democratic 1885	T. F. Bayard 1885
23. Benjamin Harrison, Republican 1889	Levi P. Morton, Republican 1889	J. G. Blaine 1889 J. W. Foster 1892
24. Grover Cleveland, Democratic 1893	Adlai E. Stevenson, Democratic 1893	W. Q. Gresham 1893 R. Olney 1895
25. William McKinley, Republican 1897	Garret A. Hobart, Republican 1897 Theodore Roosevelt, Republican 1901	J. Sherman 1897 W. R. Day 1897 J. Hay 1898
26. Theodore Roosevelt, Republican 1901	Chas. W. Fairbanks, Republican 1905	J. Hay 1901 E. Root 1905 R. Bacon 1909
27. William H. Taft, Republican 1909	James S. Sherman, Republican 1909	P. C. Knox 1909
28. Woodrow Wilson, Democratic 1913	Thomas R. Marshall, Democratic 1913	W. J. Bryan 1913 R. Lansing 1915 B. Colby 1920
29. Warren G. Harding, Republican 1921	Calvin Coolidge, Republican 1921	C. E. Hughes 1921
30. Calvin Coolidge, Republican 1923	Charles G. Dawes, Republican 1925	C. E. Hughes 1923 F. B. Kellogg 1925

President	Vice-President	Secretary of State
31. Herbert Hoover, Republican 1929	Charles Curtis, Republican 1929	H. L. Stimson 1929
32. Franklin D. Roosevelt, Democratic 1933	John Nance Garner, Democratic 1933 Henry A. Wallace, Democratic 1941 Harry S Truman, Democratic 1945	C. Hull 1933 E. R. Stettinius, Jr. 1944
33. Harry S Truman, Democratic 1945	Alben W. Barkley, Democratic 1949	J. F. Byrnes 1945 G. C. Marshall 1947 D. G. Acheson 1949
34. Dwight D. Eisenhower, Republican 1953	Richard M. Nixon, Republican 1953	J. F. Dulles 1953 C. A. Herter 1959
35. John F. Kennedy, Democratic 1961	Lyndon B. Johnson, Democratic 1961	D. Rusk 1961
36. Lyndon B. Johnson, Democratic 1963	Hubert H. Humphrey, Democratic 1965	D. Rusk 1963
37. Richard M. Nixon, Republican 1969	Spiro T. Agnew, Republican 1969 Gerald R. Ford, Republican 1973	W. P. Rogers 1969 H. A. Kissinger 1973
38. Gerald R. Ford, Republican 1974	Nelson Rockefeller, Republican 1974	H. A. Kissinger 1974
39. Jimmy Carter, Democratic 1977	Walter Mondale, Democratic 1977	C. Vance 1977 E. Muskie 1980
40. Ronald Reagan, Republican 1981	George Bush, Republican 1981	A. Haig 1981 G. Schultz 1982

INDEX